LATIN AMERICA
AND THE CARIBBEAN

A HANDBOOK

HANDBOOKS TO THE MODERN WORLD

AFRICA, edited by Colin Legum
ASIA, edited by Guy Wint
WESTERN EUROPE, edited by John Calmann

LATIN AMERICA
AND THE CARIBBEAN

A Handbook

Edited by
CLAUDIO VÉLIZ

FREDERICK A. PRAEGER, *Publishers*
New York · Washington

BOOKS THAT MATTER

Published in the United States of America in 1968
by Frederick A. Praeger, Inc., Publishers
111 Fourth Avenue, New York, N.Y. 10003

7224

Library of Congress Catalog Card Number: 68-14143

Printed in Great Britain

CONTRIBUTORS

Richard N. Adams

Carlos Alberto

Gregorio Amunátegui

Alan Angell

Solon Barraclough

Jorge Barría

Jaime Bellalta

Robin Blackburn

Dirk Bornhorst

Alec. S. Bright

John C. G. Brooks

Peter Calvo

Leopoldo Castedo

Stephen Clissold

Kenneth P. Cocks

J. M. Cohen

Maryse Condé

Gordon Connell-Smith

Luiz Heitor Corrêa de Azevedo

Peter Coy

Frank Dauster

Christopher Eckenstein

Gerald Elliot

Ulrich Fanger

John Halcro Ferguson

Jean Franco

Alberto Fuentes Mohr

Celso Furtado

Ezequiel Gallo

Alberto González

Teresa Hayter

Ernest Hecht

Colin Henfrey

June M. Henfrey

Alistair Hennessy

Fernando Henriques

Felipe Herrera

Harry Hoetink

Hugh Holley

Ronald Houghton

David Howarth

David Huelin

James C. Hunt

Alain Joxe

Emanuel de Kadt

Jorge Katz

Joseph A. Lauwerys

David Lehmann

Kevin J. Lyonette

Alejandro D. Marroquín

Jean Meyriat

Carmen A. Miró

Guillermo Morón

Peter Nehemkis

Peter R. Odell

Franklin D. Parker

Fred Parkinson

Andrew Pearse

Daniel Pécaut

George Pendle

Fredrick B. Pike

Rev. Renato Poblete Barth, SJ

David Preston

Herman van Renselaar

John Rettie

Colin Rickards

Continued overleaf

CONTENTS

PART ONE: THE COUNTRIES OF SOUTH AND CENTRAL AMERICA AND THE CARIBBEAN*

SOUTH AMERICA

*The country-by-country Basic Information is compiled by Kenneth Cocks.

ix

A*

PART FOUR: THE LATIN AMERICAN
SOCIAL BACKGROUND

THE PEOPLE

xiii

PLATES

PAINTING AND SCULPTURE   BETWEEN PAGES

PLATE 1 Diego Rivera *Zapata* . . . . . . 808 AND 809

PLATE 2 David Alfaro Siqueiros *Nuestra imagen actual;*
Rufino Tamayo *Hombre a la puerta* . . . . .

PLATE 3 Antonio Berni *La mujer del sweater rojo;* Emilio
Pettoruti *Autorretrato;* Fernando Botero *El hombre de las
barbas*

PLATE 4 Cándido Portinari: Fresco in Church of St Francis,
Pampulha; Osvaldo Guayasamín *Cansancio* (detail) .

PLATE 5 Wilfredo Lam *Figura;* Joaquín Torres García
Uruguay . . . .

PLATE 6 Alejandro Obregón *Toro y condor;* Roberto Matta
Le même si . . . .

PLATE 7 Bruno Giorgi: Bronze; Lily Garáfulic *Signo I* .

PLATE 8 Edgar Negret *Aparato mágico;* Alicia Peñalba
Absente . . . .

MAPS

A NOTE ON THE MAPS

ALL the maps included in this book have been specially designed and drawn for the purpose. The aim has been to provide maps which would add to the understanding of a country, area or topic rather than merely indicate the relative locations of cities and railways, rivers and mountains, etc. Thus, there is no set pattern for the maps on particular countries. Some countries are mapped individually; others, where facts of relief, climate or patterns of human occupancy and development indicate its appropriateness, in groups —as, for example, in the case of the three Andean republics of Bolivia, Ecuador and Peru, whose human and physical geography has many aspects in common. The phenomena shown on each of the country maps were selected to bring out and clarify analysis made in the accompanying article and/or to illustrate other significant themes of the geography of the area concerned. Thus, in the case of Brazil, the whole country, with its projected nation-wide highway network, is shown only on a very small scale whilst most of the available space is devoted to a more detailed treatment of the economically important, highly populated coastal area. For Paraguay, attention is devoted to its territorial changes and its geo-political position as an inland state. On the other hand, for Puerto Rico, whose 'Operation Bootstrap', implemented within the framework of a favourable tax and tariff position vis-à-vis the United States, has brought rapid industrial development, the maps show the attempts to distribute this economic growth sector around the island. In such ways it is intended and hoped that the maps will make a positive contribution to the readers' understanding of Latin America.

I should like to acknowledge my debt to Mrs Sheila Weston, the carto-grapher, for all the maps except one. Her experience and expertise as a cartographer have enabled her to produce a series of attractive and well-designed maps.

Peter R. Odell
Senior Lecturer in Geography,
London School of Economics

FOREWORD

IT is impossible to edit a volume such as this single-handed and equally impossible to list all the persons and institutions who have given their valuable assistance to the Editor. However, not to name my wife, Paula, who convinced me of the worth of the enterprise and gave encouragement and advice throughout its lengthy preparation would be unforgivable. Equally important is to express my sincere gratitude to Miss Daphne Kirkpatrick, untiring pioneer of Latin American studies in Britain who for many years thought that a book like this one ought to be prepared and who was only prevented from undertaking the task herself by other responsibilities, notably those involved in her work with the Society for Latin American Studies.

Mrs Monica Pidgeon, Editor of *Architectural Design*, gave invaluable advice on the organisation of the section on architecture; Mr Kenneth Cocks, of the Economic Intelligence Department of the Bank of London and South America Ltd, London, prepared the Basic Information material; Dr Peter Odell, Senior Lecturer in Geography at the London School of Economics and Political Science, was responsible, together with Mrs Sheila Weston, for the maps, which were specially drawn for this volume; Mr Stephen Clissold, Mr David Huelin, Manager of the Economic Intelligence Department of the Bank of London and South America Ltd, London, and Dr Alistair Hennessy, Reader in History at Warwick University, were at all times ready to assist the Editor not only with their advice and expert counsel, but also with their excellent contributions.

My greatest debt however is to Mr Antony Wood who in his capacity as house editor to the publisher not only offered sound advice at every stage of the preparation of the book but generously gave much more than was his due after I had to leave England in 1966. Had it not been for his unsparing dedication and the interest he took in the subject it is difficult to imagine how this volume would have been completed.

C.V.

AN HISTORICAL INTRODUCTION

CLAUDIO VÉLIZ

MUCH of what Europe and the United States have hopefully and sometimes arrogantly expected from Latin America in recent decades reflects what North Atlantic orthodoxy considers principal stages in its own historical development. This, of course, should not surprise; there is an understandable tendency to universalise personal or collective experience and make whatever has been enjoyed, suffered or endured into a necessary ingredient of the recipe for general advancement passed on to posterity or to lesser contemporaries. This is certainly true of the optimistic expectations that have been nurtured in the United States about the growth of social or liberal democracy, or the coming of the industrial revolution to Latin America.

In the 19th and early 20th centuries, similar expectations—always well-meaning and worth supporting—were founded on a sympathetic understanding of European history; they represented a forward projection of successful European experiences planned by Latin Americans who, having scanned the world's political and social horizons, thought they had discovered what was best and devoted themselves to transplanting it to Latin American soil—mostly with limited success.

In our times the initiative for similar enterprises has been assumed by the United States, moved by complex motives nevertheless dominated by the need to ensure political support in a region which she traditionally regards as within her direct sphere of influence. These efforts have been intensified since the success of the Cuban Revolution yet, in spite of the considerable resources invested and although a reasonable endorsement for United States policies has been secured at critical times, the grand design to modernise Latin America according to formulae based on other nations' experiences has not been realised. There have been many changes and perhaps some progress but the specific improvements hopefully planned for have not come about.

The early fate of the Alliance for Progress is the most interesting example of this failure; in the six years since the launching of this scheme which made the reception of financial assistance from the United States conditional on the implementation of certain reforms and democratic practices there have been twelve right-wing military coups in eight countries which have yet to bring about the needed reforms. All these countries continue to receive aid from the United States and reciprocate by extending to their northern neighbour the required measure of political support.

The purpose of this historical introduction is to suggest that a valid explanation for these persistent failures may be found in an understanding of Latin America's political and cultural traditions; and further, that the solution to this problem can only be found inside Latin America and that the only version of modernity which can possibly take root in the region is one created and defined by Latin Americans.

Three fundamental elements in the making of Western European tradition —which in this sense also includes countries such as Canada, the United States and Australia—are absent from the collective experience of Latin America; these are feudalism, nonconformity and the industrial revolution. In addition to many other considerations, Latin America also differs qualitatively in having an important pre-industrial urban civilisation with characteristics which appear to be relatively immune to the frontal impact of the capital-intensive industrialisation which has come to the region within the last few decades.[1]

'FEUDALISM'

Columbus discovered the New World in 1492, the same year of the taking of Granada by the Catholic monarchs and the consolidation of their rule over Spain. Latin America entered modern history during the following century, that is, three hundred years after feudalism had ceased to be a vital factor in European affairs.

The institutions which the Spanish conquerors and colonists took across the Atlantic were not those of the Iberian feudal tradition—such as it was— but those of the Renaissance, as seen from Madrid, the self-conscious capital city of one of the strongest monarchies in Europe. At the risk of digressing slightly, it must be pointed out that a generation before Henry VIII challenged the Pope from London, Ferdinand, the reins of power firmly in his hands after the difficulties which followed the death of Isabella, managed in 1508 to secure from Pope Julius II the concession granted in perpetuity to the crown of Castile for organising ecclesiastical affairs, establishing churches and nominating sees and livings in all the territories overseas which it then possessed or which it might acquire in the future. This remarkable privilege was embodied in the bull *Universalis ecclesiae regimini* which was also the legal foundation for the royal *patronato* which was to prove such a source of difficulties between the Vatican and the republican governments of the 19th century. Amongst many other implications, this bull of 1508 gave the Spanish monarchy absolute temporal power and *de facto* though not strictly *de jure* control of the Church over the richest and most formidable empire of the time.

To challenge such a strong central power was no mean feat and what Iberian warlords had failed to do after centuries of struggle against the Moors, the conquerors of Spanish America, themselves warlords of an expanding frontier, also failed to do in spite of the apparent protection of distance and isolation. There was enough vitality in Madrid to give life to the fist at the end of the longest administrative arm in Christendom; Governor Diego Colon's lesser stirrings prompted the crown to establish an *audiencia* and a royal treasury in Hispaniola to keep him under control. More serious attempts to behave with greater independence than the

---

[1] It is evidently impossible to establish valid generalisations for the whole of Latin America and the Caribbean and no such attempt is made here. However, the most important exception —that offered by Brazil—is abundantly described and analysed in this book, especially in the articles by Prof. Celso Furtado and Emanuel de Kadt. It is worth noting that a significant difference between Spanish and Portuguese America is that the latter never attained the degree of political and administrative centralisation typical of the former during the colonial period.

crown was willing to tolerate were—justly or unjustly—punished with ferocity, as the decapitation of Balboa and Pizarro or the garrotting of old Diego de Almagro and the obscure deaths of many others abundantly proved.

In Spanish America there never developed the almost autonomous regional loci of political power typical of European feudalism. There was certainly exploitation and the treatment of the native inhabitants was often cruel, but oppression and discrimination are not defining characteristics of feudalism; they were common many centuries before the coming of feudal institutions to Europe and they have not entirely disappeared today. On the other hand, the existence of strong regional sites of political power, able to check and at times override the central power of the monarchy, is a defining characteristic of feudalism and this certainly did not occur in the Spanish dominions in the Indies.

The Western European phenomenon of the transfer of power from an aristocratic, feudal periphery to a central monarchy is absent from Spanish America where even the most authoritarian local colonial governor, captain-general or viceroy was only using—or misusing—a power delegated directly to him from Madrid and whose legitimacy was absolutely dependent on the continued and explicit support of the metropolis. This power could and often was invalidated with the stroke of a pen by the Council of the Indies in Madrid and then the local tyrant of yesterday would become a commoner, subject moreover to the dreaded Juicio de Residencia in Spain, in which he had to give a detailed account—often under questioning by sceptical bureaucrats—of every aspect of his administration.

This strong centralist tradition was transferred to Latin America not only as an attitude and an institutional habit but also through the complex bureaucratic structure which from the earliest decades of colonial government was established in the new territories. At first almost every man to cross to the Indies was a soldier; later on they were joined by a handful of priests; a generation later both these were outnumbered by crown officials, administrators, lawyers, accountants and the like; all members of a rapidly expanding and emphatically urban bureaucracy.

In the Latin American cultural and historical experience there is therefore no continued tradition of extra-legal and accepted political challenge of the centre by the periphery; no traditional use of instruments of conciliation which could possibly result in the institutionalisation of a system of compromise. On the other hand, there did develop during the three centuries of colonial life—which are, of course, the centuries of Spain's imperial status—a tradition of responsible central administration with a strong imprint of paternalism; this resulted in turn in the creation of a vast bureaucratic mechanism with a formidable respect for legality, a voracious appetite for antecedents and information which were invariably and carefully filed away (and are still found in the enormous Archivo de Indias, a veritable gold-mine for historians), and a generalised tendency to be as meticulous and all-embracing as possible.

The republican uprisings of the first decade of the 19th century represent the only and definitive exception to what has been suggested above. In the years following 1810 peripheral political entities successfully challenged the metropolis and proclaimed their independence. However, they did this in the first instance in the name of the king and against the French invaders and at this early stage their assumption of power was an act of support for the monarchy. Later the character of the response changed drastically and each colonial centre went through a settlers' revolt similar in some ways to that led by Mr Ian Smith in Southern Rhodesia. The revolution, therefore, even when completely successful, did not represent an absolute break with the colonial past; excepting a small number of higher officials of Spanish nationality, the bureaucratic establishment of the republic was practically the same as that of the last years of the colonial period; the creole upper classes certainly did not change in composition while the attitudes, habits, legal and administrative institutions of the colonial period also remained largely unaltered well into the 19th and sometimes into the 20th century.

The successful rebellions of 1810 therefore marked, rather than the beginning of a neo-feudal era, a massive transfer of central power from Madrid to each republican capital, together with the colonial bureaucratic tradition with its hierarchical tendencies and a punctillious regard for the form, if not the content, of legality.

NONCONFORMITY

A second important aspect of Western European—in this case, perhaps, principally English—tradition lacking in Latin America is non-conformity; not merely the Reformation, but the populist, doctrinal challenge from within which characterised the religious revival coincident with the beginnings of the industrial revolution. In the Hispanic historical experience the alternative to the Catholicism of the central political power has invariably been anti-clericalism; in England the alternatives have been various but among them the most interesting and typical was non-conformity. Moreover, in England this challenge found its most receptive supporters among the industrial masses and even today the strongholds of Methodism are in the North-East, Wales, the Midlands and Cornwall, where miners and industrial workers first followed Wesley in the 18th century.

Just as in political affairs there have been no peripheral sites of power, in religion the Catholic Church has not lost its privileged, unchallenged doctrinal position; when political revolutionary movements have for one reason or another clashed with ecclesiastical authority, these confrontations have always been outside the field of religious doctrine. Even the strongest and most persistent attack on Roman Catholicism—that of the second half of the 19th century, the result of complex causes but with a great degree of affinity with the French Radical tradition—predictably turned into a wave of violent anti-clericalism; priests were shot and churches burned down, but the religious authority of the Church, based on doctrine, was never challenged. The reformists who followed Juarez in Mexico or supported the radicals in Chile were not interested in presenting their contemporaries with a religious alternative; on the contrary, the choice was very clearly one of Catholicism versus agnosticism, atheism or any other kind of irreligiosity. Whenever the radical onslaught resulted in a formal separation of church and state, victory was proclaimed but the Catholic Church remained as the sole religious institution in the land however much its temporal power had been curtailed.

THE INDUSTRIAL REVOLUTION

The industrialisation of Latin America has neither been the result of the exertions of an industrial bourgeoisie nor has it resulted in the formation of a vast industrial proletariat; it can also be said that it has not been 'revolutionary' in that it has not brought about the substantial social, political and cultural changes associated with the 19th-century phenomenon. Latin America has been by-passed by the industrial revolution.

In England and much of Western Europe the formation of industrial capital and the more vigorous economic activities associated with the rise of industry were the marginal result of a way of life; a part of a complex cultural whole which included attitudes towards art and literature, education, architecture and even public and private morality. The group or class identified with these attitudes—the industrial bourgeoisie—presented a challenge to tradition which was generally triumphant and perhaps attained its fulfilment in the heyday of Victorian England. A great cultural and social distance was covered between the times of the Prince Regent and those of the Prince Consort; none of the Latin American industrialising groups has been able or particularly concerned to emulate this feat. Far from adopting an anti-traditionalist or anti-aristocratic stance, the Latin American groups associated with the rise of industry who have acquired wealth from this process have tended to join the established social groups reinforcing their social standing and lending their own vitality and resourcefulness to the perpetuation of the existing social structure. The result of three decades of intensive industrialisation has not been a frontal attack on tradition but rather the institutionalisation of social climbing.

This has been partly caused by the accidental nature of industrialisation, due more to the artificial conditions brought about by the second world war than to any coalition of factors associated with the rise of a reformist, forward-looking, capitalist, 'roundhead' and generally modernising group of traders, industrialists and entrepreneurs. Social prestige has remained in the hands of the established traditional groups and the new rich who have risen to social heights have done so by accepting the traditional rules of the game rather than by imposing theirs.

Further, the evident progress of industrial technology in the last century has at least resulted in the widespread adoption of labour-saving devices at all stages of industrialisation. This means that the technology used in Latin America is by definition—as it has been incorporated mostly within the last thirty years—capital- rather than labour-intensive. This factor, added to a non-expansionist, monopolist industrial structure, working for limited markets and dependent on state support, has in turn resulted in the formation of a small and relatively well-paid group of industrial workers, mostly skilled, who aspire to middle-class status and who cannot in any way be considered an industrial proletariat of the classical type.

In England and much of Western Europe, a direct correlation can be established between the rise of industry and the growth of cities; in fact, the modern city is made up significantly of industrial workers, industrial managers and their staff. This is not so in Latin America where the large urban centres precede the coming of industry by many generations. In the region there exists a pre-industrial urban civilisation with roots which go back to the early days of the Conquest and the attitudes and habits of the Spaniards. Today Latin America has relatively more urban inhabitants in cities of 100,000 or more than Europe without in any way approaching Europe's degree of industrialisation. This pre-industrial urbanisation has led many observers to believe that those inhabitants of Latin American cities who are neither paupers, industrial workers, recently arrived peasants or plutocrats constitute a middle class similar to the one which developed in England and Europe during the 19th century. This is an interesting mistake which—like others outlined here—results from the uncritical application of

European models of growth to a Latin American situation which, save for the fact of industrialisation, is essentially different.

Before the first world war, when industrial development was almost insignificant, Buenos Aires, Santiago, Mexico City and Rio de Janeiro were already large cities, holding a remarkably high proportion of their respective countries' population. The people who lived in these cities were mostly engaged in service occupations as bureaucrats, professionals, white-collar employees, small tradesmen, artisans and the like. The coming of industry has decimated the ranks of the self-employed artisans and craftsmen but has enlarged those of the white-collar workers of all types; the present increase in the numbers of people employed in service occupations is only a continuation of a process that has been going on for well over a century. These bureaucrats, professionals, white-collar employees, domestic and service workers are not the Latin American equivalent of the rising English middle class of 1832; they are directly or indirectly associated to or dependent either on the central state or the traditional social structure, have no or very few industrial commitments, and their political activities are directed at securing greater participation in the existing social organisation rather than at demolishing it and replacing it for another.

But perhaps most important of all, the rise of industry in Latin America has not been accomplished against, or in spite of, the policies, attitudes or preferences of the central state; there has not been a confrontation between an industrialising bourgeoisie and a traditional state. Far from it; industrialisation has depended directly on state intervention and success for the entrepreneur is often more dependent on good relations with a governing party than on technical or business efficiency. The state channels credit, allocates tenders, assumes the risk in the greater industrial schemes, and generally decides where and to what extent the infrastructural conditions for industry will be developed. Also the state can handle foreign exchange regulations in ways which recall the dexterous use of patronage in the halcyon days of the Spanish imperial tradition.

There was a time when these conditions did not apply as clearly as they do today. During much of the 19th century and the first decades of the 20th, many Latin American countries derived the bulk of their wealth from the almost unrestricted export of a few primary commodities. The state exacted very moderate duties which amply sufficed to cover the limited expenditure of governments bent—typically—on being more liberal and free-trading than their European counterparts. The collapse of these conditions after the 1929 crisis and the second world war led to the rapid rise of an import-substitution industry which generally restored to the central governments their decisive role in economic life. It can be said that the deterioration of the export economy has forced a return to the cultural and political mainstream of Latin America with the state in its traditional dominating position.

THE TREND TOWARDS GREATER CENTRALISM

The absence of feudalism, non-conformity and the industrial revolution from the collective experience of Latin America largely accounts for the dominant role which centralism plays in contemporary life. In the perspective of history, the years when the political and cultural institutions of pluralistic liberalism were in general acceptance are few indeed and their acceptance at the time can be ranked with the adoption of French styles in architecture, English public schools as models for education and German uniforms for the armed forces; liberalism was imported at a good price by ruling classes which had more than enough wealth to afford it. The revulsion, violent or not, against the inadequacy of such foreign models has invariably resulted in the reconstruction of a political structure in which the state has a dominant role; the Mexican Revolution led to what is virtually a one-party system in which the central government and the Partido Revolucionario Institucional dominate, albeit with moderation, all aspects of national life. Both the Cuban and the Bolivian revolutions led to one-party systems and it would take a considerable degree of fascination with the outer formalities of liberal democracy to maintain that the rest of Latin America is not moving towards systems of greater central control.

Latin America stands now on the frontier of ideology; none of those systems based on the European experience of the industrial revolution—including classical radicalism, socialism, liberalism, communism and the like—seems to apply to a situation which excludes the social and political concomitants of industrialisation. Yet industry grows apace and new forms of social organisation and economic aspirations are emerging which demand at least a reasonable scheme for future action. So far, the traditional urban—non-industrial—middle class has shown itself remarkably sterile in producing viable alternatives, while to hope that the peasantry or the socially conformist groups of industrial workers will play the role which the industrial bourgeoisie played in Western Europe seems illusory. The military, also of middle-class origins and reflecting middle-class aspirations, have proved embarrassingly unable to initiate modernising reforms, let alone to create new and viable social and political arrangements. In such a situation, perhaps displaying a greater pragmatic capacity than is generally acknowledged, Latin America has gradually returned to her own essential traditions of centralism. This is neither good nor bad but a fact of contemporary Latin American life which may very well afford the most realistic indication of things to come.

PART ONE

THE COUNTRIES OF SOUTH AND CENTRAL AMERICA AND THE CARIBBEAN

SOUTH AMERICA

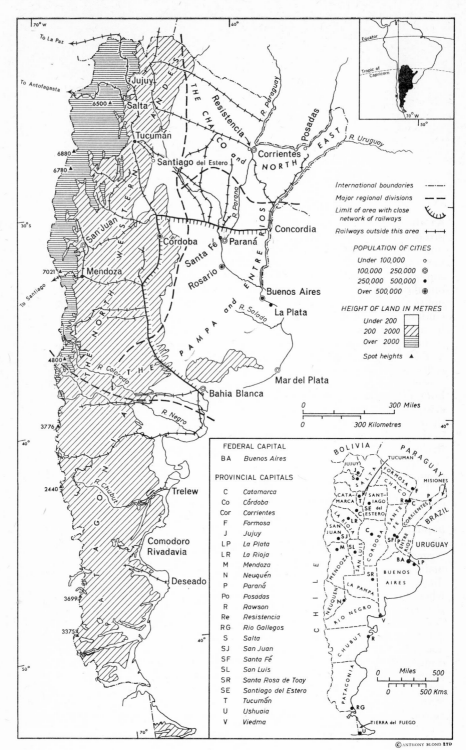

ARGENTINA

4

ARGENTINA

JAMES C. HUNT

At the time of the 1930 economic depression Argentina, by the tests of prosperity, economic development, constitutional government, administration and education, was amongst the world's most advanced countries. On a per capita basis the Argentine and Australian economies were broadly similar. Since then, while Australia has forged ahead, Argentina has had unbalanced development with slow growth, and a chequered and sterile political history. Of the nine regimes that have ruled, four—up to and including that of General Onganía—have been essentially military, four broadly representative and constitutional, and one only formally constitutional. Of the fourteen presidents, nine have been generals and five civilians. This perplexing alternation, souring the life of the nation, has reflected the alienation of large sectors of society in both middle and working classes, and tensions within them whose roots lie deep in Argentine history, but especially in the period of most rapid advance, 1880–1914. The economic crisis of 1930 exposed these tensions. To contain them the military have made their successive entries into politics so that, with the rise of organised labour in the mid–1940s as a centralised political instrument under General Perón, the institutions of representative democracy have become unable to effect economic and social change. Nationalism has offered the only common ground between Argentina's distinct authoritarian and liberal traditions.

The most Latin country in Latin America, neighbouring Uruguay excepted, Argentina's population of nearly 23 million (mid-1966 estimate) is almost entirely of European stock. Yet a hundred years ago, when the population was less than a tenth of what it now is, only a fifth was white, of Spanish origin, while three-quarters were Indian and mestizo, and the rest Negro and mulatto. The transformation came partly through wars, but mainly through immigration from Europe. The Negro elements suffered in the front line during the sanguinary war of the Triple Alliance (1865–70), when Argentina fought alongside Uruguay and Brazil to thwart the expansionary ambitions of the Paraguayan dictator, Francisco Solano López, while the Indians were decimated as a result of General Julio A. Roca's campaigns against them culminating in the 'Conquest of the Desert' (1879) and now number perhaps 100,000. In the three decades to 1914 net immigration was well over 2 million, so earning for these years the name 'the alluvial period'. By 1914 30 per cent of the population was foreign-born; in 1960 it was still nearly 13 per cent (double the proportion in the United States). Although half the migrants were Italian and one-sixth northern European, Spanish culture has been preserved in Argentina by its well established system of schooling and nationalist teaching. In 1960 Argentina boasted the lowest illiteracy rates in Latin America—under 9 per cent amongst the population of 14 years of age or over.

Italian influence, however, is to be detected in the Argentine accent and in family names as well as in the course of politics, especially after the 1930 crisis. No 'white Argentina' policy has ever been proclaimed, but there are no Asian communities as in some neighbouring countries, and by the second world war immigration laws were being applied restrictively as the Jews found; even so the Jewish community of some 450,000 is the largest in Latin America. In the past fifty years population growth has slowed markedly and since the 1947 census has been shown to be appreciably less than the Latin American average. Within the country, nevertheless, an accelerating movement from rural to urban areas has occurred. As early as 1910 urban population, in communities of over 2,000, exceeded rural and by 1965 it was 72 per cent of the total, with a heavy concentration in Greater Buenos Aires, and Rosario and Córdoba vying for second place. During the last twenty years there has been an appreciable rural replenishment of almost 800,000 through immigration from Paraguay, Chile and Bolivia. In turn Argentina has suffered an emigration of trained persons, over 11,200 going to the United States in 1951–63.

HISTORY

The colonial epoch

The Spaniards first approached Argentina from the Atlantic, searching for an eastern route to the Andean silver-bearing regions, and it was from Upper Peru and Chile that they first effectively settled Argentina, founding towns, most of them now provincial capitals, in the north-western Andean piedmont in the second half of the 16th century. In a distinct and slightly later phase Buenos Aires (1580) and centres along the Paraná river were established from Asunción, 1,000 miles upstream from the sea. The polarity between these two groups of settlements has influenced Argentine history up to modern times.

For two centuries the entire region was part of the Viceroyalty of Peru until in 1776 the Viceroyalty of the River Plate was created at Buenos Aires. The trade of the region, initially of small consequence to the crown, was strictly regulated, if with decreasing effectiveness, along the overland route to Lima, from there to join the convoys running between the Caribbean and Spain. Although slow and costly, this route was much safer than that over the South Atlantic through Buenos Aires. To prevent smuggling through Buenos Aires to and from Potosí and Santiago de Chile, a customs barrier was erected at Córdoba (1618), then moved north to Salta and Jujuy (1676) in recognition of Buenos Aires' control over the interior market. Another relaxation was the *asiento*, or right, England won under the Treaty of Utrecht (1714) for one ship a year to call at Buenos Aires. The creation of the Viceroyalty of the River Plate—consisting of the regions that are now Argentina, Paraguay, Uruguay and much of Bolivia—accentuated the re-orientation of Spanish trade with South America. By then illegal trade through Buenos Aires exceeded that through legitimate channels, so conditioning an attitude to authority which has persisted. Silver bullion exports from Potosí were legalised. Trade licences with seven Spanish ports besides Cadiz and Seville were granted. In a decade exports of hides from Buenos Aires increased by over five times and royal revenues on trade by ten times. Security played as large a part as trade and administrative considerations in setting up the new viceroyalty. The Portuguese had encroached west of the Line of Tordesillas down to the north bank of the River Plate, which changed hands several times in the 18th century before being finally secured for Spain by the first viceroy.

The Viceroyalty at Buenos Aires lasted thirty-four years; Spain had neither the resources nor the ability to maintain the imperial compact. The centralised and exclusive structure began to crack more or less simultaneously throughout Spanish America; undermined by the contagion of ideas from the Enlightenment and United States independence and weakened by the absolutist Spanish reaction to the French Revolution, it broke with the Bonapartist usurpation of the Spanish throne. In Buenos Aires, moreover, creoles (*criollos*, locally born Spaniards) resented the influx of peninsular officials to staff the viceregal administration. Merchants and farmers wanted the right to trade openly with England and other countries besides Spain. As it was, only a quarter of imports into Buenos Aires were of Spanish origin and the vulnerability of its trade was shown when British blockades reduced it in the Napoleonic wars. The two British invasions of 1806 and 1807 served at once to advance the cause of free trade, which was temporarily opened up, and more especially to engender self-confidence in the creoles; for on both occasions the Spanish viceroy fled and the British were repulsed by local levies. When news reached Buenos Aires of the French overthrow of the Spanish government, representing the captive Ferdinand VII, the creoles there successfully demanded the convening of a *cabildo abierto* or open council on 25 May 1810, declared that in the absence of the sovereign the people had the right to legislate for themselves and deposed the viceroy.

Independence—creole disunity

The creoles took seventy years painfully to unite as a nation. When Spanish rule collapsed so did legality, leaving a scatter of informal local loyalties over a wide area. The River Plate was soon cleared of Spaniards; only in Upper Peru, later to become independent as Bolivia, were the patriots defeated, while the main campaigns by the Argentine Liberator, General José de San Martín, were fought in Chile and Peru. However, the doctrine of residual sovereignty of the people used against the Spanish was turned against the liberal *criollos porteños* (i.e. of Buenos Aires), intellectuals like Mariano Moreno, who headed the nine-man junta of 25 May, when they tried to annex to the government of Buenos Aires the entire area of the former viceroyalty. Dr Francia went to the logical extreme of refusing to recognise the junta and made Paraguay an isolated independent state. Similar sentiments existed in Uruguay, which eventually acquired its separate buffer status as a result of wars between the Argentine Confederation and Brazil between the 1820s and '40s. The formal proclamation of Argentine independence at the Congress of Tucumán on 9 July 1816, delayed partly to avoid antagonising the British government, failed to heal the rift between the two chief contending factions, which became known as unitarians and federalists.

Some unitarians, despairing at anarchy, espoused the cause of monarchy. But most unitarians were doctrinaire liberals whose reforms, affecting entailed estates, the powers of the Church, Indian serfdom, Negro slavery (eventually abolished in the 1850s) and representative institutions, were deeply offensive to the widely held conservative notions of the interior. Attempts to implement the constitutions of 1819 and 1826, drawn up on unitarian lines with firm central government in Buenos Aires, were forcibly frustrated by federalists there no less than elsewhere. Rule by local caudillos became the norm, the most notorious being Facundo Quiroga of La Rioja province whose slogan was 'Religion or Death'. Buenos Aires went the same way; its caudillo, Juan Manuel de Rosas, collaborated with the others, outwitted and outlived them, besides coming to terms with the marauding Indians. With a commanding influence among the gauchos, the independent rural horsemen, himself a wealthy farmer and owner of the *saladero* (meat-salting) monopoly, and with the support of the Church, Rosas backed his mask of federalism by a harsh absolutism which at last united the country (1835–52). To internal order he added external distraction through his attempts to annex Uruguay and cajole Paraguay. After Britain and France ceased their muddled intervention to thwart him, the cost of his foreign adventures—financed through Buenos Aires control on foreign commerce, of the littoral provinces especially—compounded by resentment at his intolerable personalism led to his overthrow at the battle of Monte Caseros in 1852 at the hands of dissident federalists under General Justo José Urquiza, governor of Entre Ríos province.

Neither then did Urquiza enforce his victory on Buenos Aires, nor later when his failure to press his advantage after initial success in the 1859–61 civil war led to his eventual defeat by General Bartolomé Mitre. Caudillo though Urquiza was, and distrusted by most porteño intellectuals, he nevertheless began the opening of the littoral and made possible the liberal, federal constitution of 1853 which, with amendments and an interval (1949–56) while a Peronist adaptation applied, has remained in force ever since.

The long rivalry between *porteños* and the interior was not resolved until 1880 when the city of Buenos Aires was forcibly detached from the province and made the federal capital. A confusion of personality and legalistic issues apart, the differences stemming from colonial days were economic. Buenos Aires kept the customs and excise revenues of the port and virtual monopoly on foreign trade, so obliging the interior to levy retrograde interprovincial duties. Buenos Aires' recalcitrance, as much as the unitarian-federalist discord, had in 1827 led the most enlightened Porteño unitarian leader, Bernardino Rivadavia, to resign when he failed to nationalise the revenues. So did the narrow interest of supposedly enlightened Buenos Aires help perpetuate the struggle between 'civilisation and barbarism', between—in effect—the educated townsman and the caudillos with their rude gaucho hordes, as Domingo Faustino Sarmiento characterised the condition of Argentina in his famous book *Life in the Argentine Republic in the Days of the Tyrants*, which he published in 1845 in Santiago, Chile during his exile there.

Nationhood, expansion and the oligarchy

Argentina was transformed into the leading country of Latin America during the last quarter of the 19th century and the period up to the first world war. The rapid growth in population by immigration—second only to that of the United States but relatively more intense—and even faster economic development both resulted from technological changes in shipping, railway and port construction, and meat canning and freezing, heavily financed by foreign capital; British investments, the main capital source, rose some ten times to £291 million between 1880 and 1910. The advances arose from the open-door social and economic principles of the 1853 constitution, the modernising presidencies of Mitre (1861–8) and Sarmiento (1868–74), the full extension of the Argentine Republic (the term won acceptance under Mitre) to its present frontiers, and comparatively orderly constitutional government maintained by systematic electoral fraud. The landed creole oligarchy, liberal in economic policies, made rich by them, secular regarding education, European in culture, politically and socially conservative, held political power until electoral reforms enabled Hipólito Irigoyen, the Radical leader, to win the presidency in 1916.

In any event the flood of immigrants would have raised major problems; they were aggravated by the exclusion of immigrants from national politics and the scarcity of land for ownership. By 1880 most usable public land in the Province of Buenos Aires was distributed in large plots at virtually token prices. The great expansion in grain cultivation, stock raising and exports of foodstuffs so inflated land values that new immigrants, mostly peasants and labourers, could at best become tenant farmers, for the law gave no fixity of tenure. Half the migrants came seasonally, for the harvests; many gravitated to the towns, attracted by the building boom of Buenos Aires especially. In the words of Domingo Sarmiento, Buenos Aires was at this period full of rootless 'strangers', a 'city without citizens'. Easy naturalisation laws did not bestow political rights and Argentines were not made until the second generation.

The oligarchy nearly lost control in the 1890 political and financial crises. President Juárez Celman was forced to resign in favour of the capable vice-president, Dr Carlos Pellegrini, a nephew of John Bright, following an abortive revolt by the newly founded Unión Cívica Radical. Shortly afterwards, only the intervention of the Bank of England prevented loss of confidence in Argentine securities from bankrupting Baring Brothers, who had marketed Argentine bonds since the first large foreign loan of 1824. The crucial factor precipitating the 1890 crisis, which brought immigration and foreign capital to a halt after a decade of accelerating inflow, was the bad harvest of the previous year. Excessive optimism, waste, misjudgments and financial scandals also played a part. The chief causes, however, lay in slack credit policies and severe inflation favouring rural interests at the expense of urban dwellers. Owing to the disorganised system of indirect taxes, the government was denied the revenue to meet its obligations. These were especially heavy as the bulk of foreign loans and investments carried fixed interest charges even before any real return was produced. Economically, the crisis carried the seed of its own recovery once the many incomplete railways became operational and good harvests in the 1890s made for rising exports. Politically, the restoration of foreign confidence through refinancing settlements effectively undermined the country's federal structure as the national government assumed responsibility for provincial indebtedness. By a political manoeuvre, moreover, Pellegrini frustrated the pressure of the emerging Porteño middle classes for a voice in public affairs, though—with Mitre—he was later amongst the first to see the need for reform. Even so, not until 1912 did fear of mounting anarchy among the working classes enable President Roque Sáenz Peña to secure the passage of the electoral reform law which bears his name; the proportion of adult males voting in the next elections more than trebled.

The Radical interlude

Electoral reform amply confirmed the expectations of the liberals who had espoused it, as much to avert drastic social change as on account of patriotic justice. The Radicals took over in 1916, but once in power scarcely departed from the established polity and so little prepared the nation to take the strain of the 1930 economic depression as to be overthrown themselves in that year. The democratic principles they stood for, if not always observed, suffered irreparably.

9

Irigoyen, the new president, had fashioned Radicalism as a cause, somewhat in his own messianic if scarcely charismatic image, having entrenched his command over the party during its two decades of bitter opposition at the cost of several splinterings. The leader of one of these, the Socialist Party, charged Irigoyen with having been too preoccupied with winning power to know how to use it. Certainly he steadfastly refused to enunciate a programme and saw the Radicals' function as to make reparation for past injustices as much in virtue of holding power as of anything done with it. Convinced as he was of this doctrine, it also made a virtue of necessity. Although he achieved his first term as president by a large popular vote under the new compulsory balloting, he had a majority of only one in the electoral college. Similarly, the concentration of Radical support in a few areas meant that the party suffered under the incomplete list system, which allocated two-thirds of the seats in the Federal and provincial legislatures to the majority party and the remainder to the leading minority party. For practical political reasons, Irigoyen consequently exercised the right of Federal intervention in the provincial governments more often than any of his predecessors, bar the first under the 1853 constitution, which remained Federal in form only. Another obstacle to policy-making was that the Radical Party was neither middle class nor proletarian. Irigoyen's apt description was 'a conjunction of forces', so that his pronouncements were often more leftist than his acts. His personalism, however, provoked a rift with his successor, Marcelo Alvear, under whose 'anti-personalist' leadership (1922–8) the Radicals became identified with conservative interests. When in 1928 Irigoyen won a decisive popular mandate for his second term, he was too senile to confront the emerging economic crisis.

Nationalism, still somewhat incohate, was the unifying quality of the Radical administrations. Outstanding was the neutral posture adopted in the first world war, partly for economic self-interest, partly in reaction to the United States. This provided the precedent for Argentine foreign policy during the second world war. Paradoxically, the stimulus the war gave to domestic industry was—in the interests of consumers—deliberately not reinforced by tariff protection afterwards, for it was in the hands of foreign-born entrepreneurs; alone excepted was the sugar industry belonging to old Argentine families. However, beyond setting up a state oil entity, Yacimientos Petrolíferos Fiscales (YPF), and refusing private firms any new oil concessions, no steps were taken against foreign enterprises, despite the rising nationalist criticism of them. A peripheral land reform was the only enactment against the hated oligarchy; piecemeal labour reforms were offset by rigorous suppression of strikes, most ruthlessly during the 'Tragic Week' of 1919 when fear of bolshevism was at its height. Workers' movements switched from internationalism and anarchism to organised nationalist trade unionism, but remained apart from the Radical Party and still do so.

The 1930 crisis and the infamous decade

General José Uriburu's coup of September 1930, bloodless though it was, marked Argentina's sharpest turn from democracy since independence with parallels to that a century before. The upheaval in government caused by the economic crisis was not itself special, but it demonstrated the country's imbalances. Exposure brought no regeneration, only a choice between a fascist solution and pragmatic placebos. A fascist state, with a corporativist structure replacing party political institutions, was Uriburu's explicit objective; yet after only fourteen months he handed over to General Agustín

Justo, who had been elected with the backing of a coalition (Concordancia) of the conservatives (National Democrats), the Anti-Personalist Radicals and Independent Socialists, which was to govern the country until 1943. Both Uriburu and Justo had been associated with the Anti-Personalist Radicals, but while the latter was, until his death just before the 1943 coup, to play a role in office and out similar to that of General Roca in the 1880s and 1890s, the former had become thoroughly disillusioned by the corruption of the party system and influenced by the ideas of Primo de Rivera and Charles Maurras which were in line with the hierarchic and authoritarian strand in Argentine history. But Uriburu's commitment to observe the constitution, his failure to organise a political force to support him (a lesson not lost on Captain Juan Domingo Perón, one of his collaborators), his ill-health and his determination to prevent the return of the Personalist Radicals whose popular appeal soon recovered—all led him to acquiesce in an electoral manipulation only less fraudulent than that which was to follow in 1937. He was not the only one who trimmed to save appearances. Many upright democrats supported the Concordancia in the mistaken hope of moderating fascist and military influences. Fascist societies, secret and overt, flowered. The concept of the redemptive role of the military gained ground, at variance though it was with the military tradition stemming from San Martín.

The contradictions of limited democracy were reflected in policy. The first was the Roca-Runciman Agreement of 1933 designed to safeguard the market for Argentine produce in Britain which was threatened by the institution of Imperial Preference. Nationalist opinion, perhaps unrealistic but undoubtedly forcible, was that the terms intensified economic dependence on Britain just when Argentina should have ceased being part of Britain's 'informal empire'. Next, the foundations of a directed economy were laid, notably through protection for domestic industry and the establishment of four agricultural development and marketing boards. The Central Bank was set up; exchange control and income tax were introduced. But there was a striking neglect of social measures despite the hastened growth of the urban proletariat. Another neglected social group was the emerging middle-class manufacturer born in Argentina, distinct from the established professional and commercial middle class; much more nationalist, antiforeign enterprise and free trade, and readier to collaborate with labour forces in populist policies.

Perón's rise and fall

Manoeuvrings for the approaching presidential elections precipitated the military coup of June 1943. Nearly three years then elapsed before the elections took place, during which appearances disguised the reality of the power struggle. A short-lived attachment to the constitution, democratic ideals and the Allied war cause was succeeded by right-wing Roman Catholic nationalism with a pro-Axis tendency and an industrialisation programme which won much business backing. Meanwhile military intervention in most sectors had given charge of the new Department of Labour to Colonel Perón, the key member of the Grupo de Oficiales Unidos (GOU), the clique of, significantly, mostly young officers who engineered the coup. Combining that post with one at the Ministry of War until becoming vice president, Perón activated the masses politically as they never had been before by a mixture of coercion, cajolery and long overdue reforms in social security and trade union rights. Through the brilliant propaganda and welfare work of Eva Duarte, later his wife, the movement was indelibly stamped with their two personalities. The new force was tested and proved in October 1945; fear of it provoked a group of the military to detain Perón and then to release him. That assured Perón's victory at the polls in February 1946 by a 56 per cent majority. He shed his military rank 'to revive the almost forgotten civilian tradition' and resumed it afterwards as a general. The Roman Catholic hierarchy and several leftist parties, including a faction of Radicals, gave support against a weak coalition of the Radical, Socialist, Progressive Democratic and Communist parties with the backing of the Conservatives. The United States State Department's issue of the *Blue Book on Argentina* about Perón's pro-Axis record served only to confirm his championship of Argentine sovereignty.

Perón defies conventional definition. Authoritarian by training, he was undeniably totalitarian in his police methods and control of the press, other media and education. After the death of Eva in the same year as the severe 1952 drought, his political skill faltered and he became harsher. Yet he maintained the pretence of democracy even in the farcical 1951 elections and after. His institutional changes were aimed less at creating Uriburu's corporate state so much as a strongly centralised one. The 1949 constitution was designed to reinforce his political power, by permitting his reelection and extending the franchise to women. Nor was his regime strictly fascist, for to the 'Cross and Sword' he added the pillar of organised labour. Yet he made no frontal assault on the established social order. *Justicialismo* was the doctrine he shaped to give coherence to his policies of nationalism, social justice and economic independence. A theory of conflict derived from Hegel and Marx, it sought the equilibrium, the Third Position, between the forces of materialism and idealism, and of individualism and collectivism. Justicialismo well depicted the contradictions in Argentine society, and compounded them. As a guide to action, its weakness was that the equilibria it posited were predicated on unresolved and irresolvable conflicts without any sanction of consent. In practice it degenerated into a theory of expediency.

In external affairs, the Third Position anticipated that of the uncommitted nations without projecting Argentina to the forefront of the world stage; in Latin America it failed to reestablish Argentine hegemony over the territories of the former viceroyalty. At home, initially propitious conditions made possible a massive redistribution of incomes. 'Economic independence' was achieved by spending two-thirds of the wartime accumulated foreign exchange reserves of $1·5 billion on repaying foreign debt and purchasing foreign utilities, chiefly the British and French railways. When the terms of trade deteriorated and export earnings declined, Perón had to alter many of his policies. Drastic import cuts, the gradual reversal of discrimination against agriculture, where bad harvests made incentives ineffectual, and credit restrictions halted industrial expansion while accentuating inflation. Urban wage-earners became disaffected, despite some economic improvement after 1953, and were cool towards his appeals to link wages to productivity. He was, therefore, especially sensitive when the Church began to encroach in the domain of labour. His sharp retaliation, however, was a major cause of the uprising against him. Another was his attempt to relieve the country of rising petroleum imports by concluding a contract for exploration and development in Argentina by a United States concern. This seemed a betrayal of his own nationalism. Here were enough ingredients for a revolt; but it took two risings—led by the navy—in June and September 1955 to remove him. After three days fighting following the second rising, he fled the country.

Alternations of military and civilian rule

For eleven years after Perón's overthrow, attempts were made to revert to constitutional democracy without him or his followers regaining power: twice, after periods of military rule or dominance, by repressing Peronism and denying it electoral recognition; and twice, during the alternations of civilian rule, by trying and failing to defeat Peronism in fair electoral combat. In one guise or another, Peronism consistently commanded the loyalty of about a third of the electorate. No other single party regularly captured more; the Radicals, potentially stronger, foundered on successive personality and tactical disputes.

In the first military interregnum, conciliation of Peronism quickly gave way to severity. Perón was humiliated, his party outlawed, his supporters purged from public life and the armed forces, and much of his institutional structure dismantled. Hopes that Peronism would disintegrate were wrecked by the wage restraint for urban workers which accompanied the partial economic liberalisation and measures favouring agriculture. Peronist strength was decisive in the February 1958 elections. The victor, Dr Arturo Frondizi, leader of the breakaway Unión Cívica Radical Intransigente (UCRI), owed his success—nearly 43 per cent of the poll—over the main Radicals, Unión Cívica Radical del Pueblo (UCRP), to a pact with Perón. General Pedro Aramburu (provisional president 1955–8) had held power long enough to cause the Peronists, by his conservative policies, to regroup as a more strictly labour movement than before, but not long enough to overcome the rigidities in the economy. Frondizi, one of the most brilliant presidents since Rivadavia, recognised and grappled vigorously with both problems. His consequent political gyrations, inconsistencies and reversals of policy, however, cost him support on all sides. When, in fulfilment of his bargain with Perón, Peronists were allowed to stand in the March 1962 elections and triumphed, the military arrested him. The Peronist Justicialista party, with nearly 30 per cent of the vote, had won in ten provinces, including Buenos Aires, plus appreciable representation in Congress. The UCRI came second with just under 25 per cent. These results confirmed the distrust of Frondizi felt all along by the military and intensified by his soft line on Castro at the previous OAS meeting which decided on Cuba's expulsion from the inter-American system.

The deposition of Frondizi, after twenty-three minor uprisings against him, had tragic consequences. His economic stabilisation and development programme, under the auspices of the IMF, depended on foreign finance to moderate its austere monetary and fiscal disciplines; public and private capital and credits, mainly from the United States, had come in amounts not experienced for over thirty years, $827 million net in 1960–1, the bulk going into the petroleum, chemicals, steel, engineering and motor industries. The expansion was not yet pervasive when, by destroying confidence, the coup halted it. But the tight money policies were intensified, and the economy plunged into depression with grave social results, besides discrediting the IMF and exacerbating sentiments against foreign capital. A succession of manoeuvres, involving fighting, between the hard-line (*colorado*, red) group in the army, backed by the navy, and the legalist (*azul*, blue) group supported by the air force, which eventually got the upper hand, produced an incipient civil war. To preserve the principle of civilian rule, Frondizi's legal successor, Dr José María Guido, took office. The mockery of democracy this implied was saved by his crucial role in holding fresh general elections in July 1963. Proportional representation, however, replaced the Sáenz Peña law. Again

13

Peronist parties were proscribed, while Frondizi was kept under arrest. In the confused electoral fray, the Peronist coalition front, headed by a conservative, collapsed but local neo-Peronists took over 4 per cent of the poll, blank Peronist votes accounting for over 18 per cent. The UCRI had 15 per cent and, to the general surprise, the UCRP gained a plurality with 24 per cent.

The new president, Dr Arturo Umberto Illia, a physician from Córdoba province and a stranger on the national scene, was the first from the interior this century. He astutely tried to pacify and 'heal the nation's wounds' and to convert the UCRP into the majority party. These inconsistent objectives made for indecisive government and his summary dismissal by the military after only two-and-a-half years of his six-year term. As the beneficiary of investments in the Frondizi era and of abundant harvests, he pursued an expansionist if increasingly inflationary economic policy. To permit this, ties with the IMF were loosened, but despite tighter exchange control the peso was devalued seven times. The sharp reduction in unemployment, however, did not secure labour peace, and mounting waves of strikes battered economic order. On constitutional grounds Illia annulled Frondizi's petroleum service contracts with thirteen private, mostly foreign, concerns; nationalism cost dear in compensation payments and strain to the trade balance when self-sufficiency in output could not be maintained. On the other hand, nationalist pride was hurt by the weakness of foreign policy, while the abstention from support for the United States in the Dominican crisis angered the zealously anti-communist military.

These muddles might have counted for less had Illia's political strategy worked. As a necessary condition of pacification, the Peronists were allowed to contend the March 1965 congressional elections. Their Unión Popular led with nearly 31 per cent of the 9·3 million votes. The UCRP polled 28·5 per cent against just over 19 per cent in the analogous circumstances of 1962 and slightly better than in 1958 when it had attracted votes in protest against the Frondizi-Perón pact. This time the official UCRI secured only 4·4 per cent though the Movimiento de Integración y Desarrollo, yet another Frondizi break-away, obtained 6·3 per cent. The conservative alliance, Federación Nacional de Partidos de Centro, had 5·4 per cent, about the same as at the previous two polls. Many minor parties, including the Socialists and Christian Democrats, accounted for the remainder of the vote. These results still left the UCRP the largest party in the Chamber of Deputies with 70 seats against 52 held by the Peronist parties out of a total of 192. Rather than form an anti-Peronist coalition, Illia chose vainly to exploit the growing tensions between orthodox and neo-Peronists, but misjudged their character. After seven provincial by-elections, in all but one of which the Peronists held the lead, it seemed evident that the UCRP could not hope to advance sufficiently on its own to win the March 1967 elections for the renewal of the other half of the Chamber of Deputies and many key provincial governorships.

Military intervention to avert Peronist control of Congress became inevitable. To end the uncertainty pending the elections, Illia was dismissed on 28 June 1966. Recognising the impossibility of winning power democratically, Perón and Peronists also actively favoured the coup; to promote a coup, the 'Peronist without Perón' movement, which under Timoteo Augusto Vandor dominated a majority of trade unions, had deliberately fomented unrest. A more remarkable portent was the readiness of some intellectuals, dismayed by Argentina's long stagnation, to drop their democratic attachments in favour of 'populism' in an alliance with labour and the armed forces. A leader of the necessary stature, General Juan Carlos Onganía, was called out from retirement to become president. A stern disciplinarian, staunch Catholic and formerly of the *azul* faction in the army, he had served as its commander-in-chief for three years until he fell out with Illia the previous November. Unlike other military regimes, Onganía's took power for an explicitly indefinite period, up to ten years being spoken of. Drastic institutional overhaul was decreed by a Revolutionary Statute with precedence over the constitution where the two conflicted; to ensure this, the Supreme Court was reconstituted. The selection of the president, now vested with legislative powers, and of a civilian executive was assumed by the commanders-in-chief of the armed forces acting jointly. Socio-economic advisory councils were to be set up by the president. Congress was dissolved, political parties abolished and provincial governments brought under direct central control. Significantly, the trade unions were unmolested, on the understanding they kept out of politics. The Church, however, discreetly repulsed the regime's overtures. Within weeks the state universities were proceeded against and their system of 'co-government', instituted by Irigoyen in 1918 giving the students a strong say in administration, was dismantled. The outcry against the violence provoked, and against signs of anti-semitism and press censorship, caused the regime to recoil from further extremism.

ECONOMY[1]

Essay at a 'Great Transformation'

The 'authentic authority' the Onganía regime sought to restore had for objective the 'transformation and modernisation of society through the incorporation of science and technology in national life.' Although many of the conditions for the achievement of these aims already existed, it remained a pious hope until the beginning of 1967 when a cabinet reshuffle placed the economic direction under the charge of Dr Krieger Vasena. He applied both monetarist and structuralist techniques across a broad front to begin eliminating inflation, which had been running at over 30 per cent a year, and breaking the bottlenecks which had kept to just over 1 per cent the average annual economic growth per head in 1950–66.

Rationalisation of the public sector, whose large payroll reflected the absence of any unemployment benefit system in Argentina, was set in train to redeploy labour to the private sector and to attempt the balancing of the budget, the main cause of successive governments' deficits having been the heavy losses of the railways. With the adoption also of a firm prices and incomes policy, conflict inevitably resulted with the trade unions, over which however the authorities gained the upper hand.

A swingeing devaluation of 40 per cent and freeing of the exchange market was designed to resolve the foreign payments problem, fiscal measures being taken to moderate the immediate inflationary impact. To double exports was the target set. As it was, exports—still largely agricultural—had averaged over a third more in 1963–6 than in the late 1950s. The reinstatement of priorities for agriculture over the previous decade had gradually proved effective, despite their inflationary consequences, often contrary external demand trends and climatic vagaries. While farming had become more intensive, the scope for further improvement was illustrated by the

[1] See also 'The Industrialisation of Argentina,' p. 597.

extent to which yields and stock-carrying capacity still fell short of comparable international standards.

In the promotion of manufacturing industry[1], now accounting for over
a third of GNP, efficiency criteria were placed foremost, monopoly practices
attacked, and the doctrine of import-substitution moderated; for instance,
tariff protection was cut by nearly half to an average of 62 per cent ad
valorem. The emphasis on making industry more competitive in export
markets, no less than domestically, was related to a more constructive
approach towards Latin American economic integration. Another major
decision was that to reopen the country to foreign oil companies through
the offer of exploitation concessions.

Endorsement of the programme was shown in business and financial
quarters by the repatriation of much flight capital, and refinancing of the
substantial short-term external debt, and the grant of long-term loans.
On the Onganía regime's capacity for confirming these optimistic expectations of sustained success in its 'great transformation' of the economy rests
its one justification for staunching Argentine democracy.

BIBLIOGRAPHY

Alexander, Robert J. *Labour Relations in Argentina, Brazil and Chile*, McGraw-Hill, London
and New York, 1962.
Blanksten, George I. *Perón's Argentina*, Russell and Russell, New York; Cambridge Univ.
Press, London, 1953.
Eshag, Eprime and Thorp, Rosemary. 'Economic and Social Consequences of Orthodox
Economic Policies in Argentina in Postwar Years', *Bulletin of the Oxford Univ. Institute of
Statistics*, XXVII, 1, Oxford, February 1965.
Ferns, H. S. *Britain and Argentina in the Nineteenth Century*, Oxford Univ. Press, New York,
1960.
Finer, S. E. 'The Argentine Trouble—Between Sword and State', *Encounter*: 'Rediscovering
Latin America', September 1965.
Ford, A. G. *The Gold Standard 1880–1914: Britain and Argentina*, Oxford Univ. Press, London
and New York, 1962.
Pendle, George. *Argentina*, Oxford Univ. Press for Royal Institute of International Affairs,
London and New York, 3rd ed. 1963.
Ramis, Peter. 'Background to the 1965 Argentine Elections', *The World Today*, XXI, 5,
London, May 1965.
Romero, José Luis. *A History of Argentine Political Thought*, Stanford Univ. Press, Stanford,
Calif.; Oxford Univ. Press, London, 1963.
Scobie, James R. *Argentina: A City and a Nation*, Oxford Univ. Press, London and New York,
1964.
Silvert, Kalman H. *The Conflict Society: Reaction and Revolution in Latin America*, Hauser Press,
New Orleans, 1961.
Whitaker, Arthur P. *Argentina*, Prentice-Hall, Englewood Cliffs, NJ and London, 1964.

BASIC INFORMATION

CLIMATE

	Bahia Blanca	Buenos Aires	Mendoza	Santa Cruz
Lat./long.	39° S, 62° W	34° 30' S 58° 30' W	33° S, 62° W	50° S, 62° W
Altitude	95 ft/29 m.	89 ft/27 m.	2,625 ft/ 800 m.	39 ft/12 m.
Mean temp. of hottest month	24°C/75°F (Jan.)	24°C/74°F (Jan.)	24°C/75°F (Jan.)	15°C/59°F (Jan.)

[1] See also 'The Industrialisation of Argentina,' p. 599.

CLIMATE—*continued*

	Bahia Blanca	Buenos Aires	Mendoza	Santa Cruz
Mean temp. of coolest month	9°C/48°F (June)	9°C/49°F (June)	8°C/47°F (July)	1°C/35°F (July)
Absolute max.	109°F/43°C	104°F/40°C	109°F/43°C	94°F/34°C
Absolute min.	18°F/−8°C	22°F/−6°C	15°F/−9°C	1°F/−17°C
Relative humidity at midday of hottest and coolest months	41%/64%	61%/78%	42%/48%	41%/61%
Wettest months	2·5 in./ 64 mm. (March)	4·3 in./ 109 mm. (March)	1·2 in./ 31 mm. (Feb.)	0·7 in./ 18 mm. (Dec.)
Driest months	0·9 in./ 23 mm. (June)	2·2 in./ 56 mm. (July)	0·2 in./ 5 mm. (July)	0·3 in./ 8 mm. (Feb./March, Sept./Oct.)
Annual av. rainfall	20·6 in./ 523 mm.	37 in./ 950 mm.	7·5 in./ 191 mm.	5·3 in./ 135 mm.

POPULATION

TOTAL (*million*): 1960 (census, adjusted) 20·7; mid-1966: 22·7; 1980 (ECLA projection) 27·6.

DENSITY, mid-1965: 8 persons per sq. km.

CRUDE RATES (*per 000*), 1965: birth 22·5, death 8·2, infant mortality 60·7.

GROWTH RATES (%): 1947–60: 1·8; 1960–5: 1·6.

DISTRIBUTION (% *of total pop.*): Ethnic, mainly white (largely of Spanish or Italian origin): 90. Foreign-born, 1947: 15·3; 1960: 12·8. Language: Spanish. Religion: Roman Catholic, 94; Protestant, 2; Jewish, about 1·5. Urban (*centres 2,000 inhab. or over*), ECLA data, 1950: 64·2; 1960: 67·6; 1980: 71·7. Largest cities (*000 inhab.*), 1960: Buenos Aires 6,763 (FC 2,967 and Greater BA 3,796), latest estimate 7,000; Rosario 672; Córdoba 589; La Plata 330.

CONSTITUTIONAL SYSTEM (*up to June 1966*)

CONSTITUTION: Proclaimed May 1853; finally adopted Oct. 1860; modified 1866 and 1898. New constitution introduced March 1949 (Perón president 4 June 1946 to 22 Sep. 1955). 1853 constitution reinstated with modifications 1957. Rigid: amended by two-thirds majority of special constituent assembly. (Modified by Charter of the Revolution, 29 June 1966).

SYSTEM: Federal Republic. Federal Capital, 22 provincial governments and one national territory (Tierra del Fuego). Separate executive, legislature and judiciary. Provinces retain all powers not specifically delegated to Federal government.

EXECUTIVE: Power vested in president, who is commander-in-chief of armed forces. President and vice-president elected by popular vote (by electoral colleges); 6-year term, no immediate reelection. Vice-president presides over Senate.

LEGISLATURE: Bi-cameral, National Congress of Senate and Chamber of Deputies. *Senate:* 46 members, 2 from each province (elected by provincial legislatures) and 2 from Federal Capital (by electoral college) for 9 years, one-third retiring every 3 years. *Deputies:* 192 seats, elected by proportional representation (d'Hont system) for 4 years, one-half retiring every 2 years. *Suffrage:* Universal, compulsory voting for adults over 18 years. Registered voters, end-1965: men 6·2 m., women 6·1 m. *Elections:* Presidential, July 1963: Dr Arturo Illia with 270 votes in electoral college of 476 votes. Chamber of Deputies, one-half, March 1965, seats held: Unión Cívica Radical del Pueblo (UCRP) 70, Unión Popular 36, Partido Justicialista 16. Latter 2 parties later formed Peronista bloc.

RECENT EVENTS: President Illia deposed 28 June 1966. General Carlos Onganía installed as president by the armed forces. Congress and all political parties dissolved, and Supreme Court judges and provincial governors dismissed. President endowed with legislative powers exercised by Congress.

DEFENCE

DEFENCE BUDGET: 1965: 46,300 m. pesos; 1·4 per cent of GDP.
ARMED FORCES: National service: between 20–45 years of age; 1 year in army or air force, or 2 years in navy. Strength: army 80,000; navy 34,000; air force 250 pilots; total 114,000 plus 250,000 trained reserve.

INTERNATIONAL RELATIONS

Member of the UN and many of its international specialised agencies, including: IBRD and affiliates, IMF, FAO, ICAO, IMCO, ILO, ITU, UNDP, UNESCO, UPU, WHO and WMO; IAEA; provisionally acceded to GATT, UNCTAD representative. Also member of OAS, Alliance for Progress, ECLA, IDB and LAFTA.

ECONOMY

PRODUCTION

AGRICULTURE (000 tons)	1948–53[1]	63/64	64/65	65/66[2]
Cereals:	9,994	17,647	20,121	.
Wheat	5,175	8,940	11,260	5,400
Maize	2,509	5,350	5,140	7,040
Barley	656	1,020	826	404
Sugar (cane)	638	1,055	1,200	900
Grapes	1,657	2,370	2,290	2,635
Linseed (flax)	513	771	815	570
Cotton (lint)	118	99	138	105

[1] Average 1948/9—1952/3.   [2] Provisional.

LAND USE, 1960 (%): Arable 7, permanent pasture 43, forested 36, urban and other 14.
OTHER AGRICULTURAL DATA: Agricultural holdings, 1960 (census): number 0·47 m.; area 175 m. hectares. Tractors in use (000s), 1960: 111. Fertiliser consumption (000 tons), 1965/66: 36·6.
LIVESTOCK: Numbers (m. head), mid-1965: cattle 46·7; sheep 48·3; pigs 3·6. Products (000 tons), 1964: meat 2,345; beef and veal 2,056. 1965: wool 180·1.
FISH: Landed (000 tons), 1965: total 205·2, merluza (hake) 76·6, hawkfish 30·1, anchovy 16·6.
MINING, 1965: (000 tons), iron ore 43; zinc 30; lead 26; manganese 13; sulphur 28. Fuels: coal 382; (m. cubic metres) crude petroleum 15·6; natural gas 4,260.
MANUFACTURING, 1965: (000 tons) pig-iron 664; steel ingots 1,348; cement 3,300; wheat flour 2,260; (m. litres) wine 2,120; beer 249. Liquid fuels (m. cubic metres): diesel oil 1·26; fuel oil 8·39; motor spirit 4·29. Motor vehicles (000 units), cars 141·1, comm. vehicles (incl. chassis) 54·8.
CONSTRUCTION: (000 sq. m. floor area), 1965: building permits approved 11,900; completed 4,900.

ENERGY

CONSUMPTION (tons coal equiv.), 1964: total 27·4; per head 1·24.
ELECTRICITY, 1965: generated (kwh) 14,700 m.; installed capacity (kw) 5·1 m.

GOVERNMENT EXPENDITURE

DISTRIBUTION (% of total), 1967: defence 17, education 17, social services 10, economic development 23.

GROSS PRODUCT

GDP (*ooo m. pesos*): at current market prices, 1964: 2,363; 1965: 3,257; at 1960 market prices, 1964: 1,052; 1965: 1,133; 1966: 1,120. Per head (*US$*), UN estimate, 1964: 612.

DISTRIBUTION (%), 1964: agriculture 19; manufacturing 33; trade 14; transport 7.

GROWTH RATES (%), 1950–60: total 3·1; per head 1·2; 1960–5: total −0·1, per head −1·7.

EXTERNAL TRADE (*US$m.*):	1955	1960	1964	1965	1966
EXPORTS (f.o.b.)	929	1,079	1,410	1,493	1,593
Cereals and linseed	321	324	500	576	544
Wheat	246	143	242	373	.
Maize	23	124	168	154	.
Meat	206	219	329	329	397
Wool	124	145	129	112	128
Hides	66	70	58	50	83
IMPORTS (c. & f.)	1,173	1,249	1,077	1,199	1,124
TRADE BALANCE	−244	−170	+333	+295	+469

DIRECTION OF TRADE (%)

	Exports			Imports		
	1955	1960	1965	1955	1960	1965
LAFTA	(20·5)	15·0	15·5	(16·4)	8·5	21·3
USA	12·7	8·4	6·2	13·2	26·2	22·8
EEC	23·9	38·8	40·4	22·6	27·9	22·8
UK	21·7	20·5	10·3	6·5	9·1	6·0

FINANCE

EXCHANGE RATE (*pesos/US$*): Free market, end-year 1960: 83; 1965: 188; 1966: 247; end-Mar. 1967: 350.

BALANCE OF PAYMENTS (*US$m.*): Goods and services (net), 1960: −198; 1964: +34; 1965: +195.

COST OF LIVING (*Dec. 1958 = 100*), December, 1960: 226; 1965: 737; 1966: 958.

INDUSTRIAL WAGES (*pesos*): Nominal average per hour, 1966: craftsmen 117, labourers 94.

TREASURY ACCOUNTS (*ooo m. pesos*), 1966: Revenue = expenditure 560, incl. credits 123; public debt servicing 36; financing deficits of state enterprises: operating 67 (railways 54), investment 31 (railways 23).

EMPLOYMENT

ECONOMICALLY ACTIVE (%), 1960: of total pop. 38 (men 59, women 17); of pop. 14 years and over 53·5. In manufacturing 25, services 20, agriculture 19.

TRANSPORT AND COMMUNICATIONS

RAILWAYS: Traffic, 1965: 12,828 m. pass.-km.; 14,028 m. net ton-km. Length of track 44,100 km.

MOTOR VEHICLES: In use (*ooo*), 1964: pass. cars 725; comm. vehicles 530. Road system, 1963: 45,953 km.

SHIPPING: Merchant fleet (*ooo g.r. tons*), 1965: 1,289 (incl. tankers 544). International sea-borne shipping (*m. tons*), 1965: goods loaded 15·2; goods unloaded 11·1. Main ports: Buenos Aires; Rosario; San Nicolás; Quequén (Necochea); Bahía Blanca; La Plata.

AIR: Scheduled services, 1965: total 1,128 m. pass.-km.; 13·8 m. cargo ton-km. International: 535 m. pass.-km.; 8·4 m. cargo ton-km. Main airports: Buenos Aires: Ezeiza (international), Aeroparque; Córdoba; Comodoro Rivadavia; Mendoza.

TELEPHONES: No. in use, 1964: 1·74 m.

SOCIAL WELFARE

SYSTEM: Social insurance benefits and services provided mainly by trade unions and corresponding institutes; financed by employees' and employers' contributions. For pensions, contributions based on remuneration: employees 9–12%, employers 3–16%. Employment legislation covers working hours; holidays; payment of wages, overtime and annual bonus; employers' liability for compensation for accidents, dismissal and death indemnities.

HEALTH: 670 persons per physician; 170 persons per hospital bed.

NUTRITION: Net food supply (*per head, per day*), 1962: 2,660 calories; protein 77 g.

EDUCATION

ILLITERACY RATE (%), 1960 (census sample): 14 years and over, 8·6.

COMPULSORY: 7 years (between 6 and 14 years of age). Pupils in primary and secondary schools as % of pop. aged 5 to 19, 1959: 48.

SCHOOLS, 1963: Pre-school and primary: no. 20,250; pupils 3·1 m.; teachers 133,300. Secondary: no. 832; p. 164,300; t. 27,100. Technical: no. 1,804; students 36,500; t. 49,300. Teacher-training: no. 633; st. 159,500; t. 17,600. Higher (including universities, faculties): no. 361; st. 216,900; t. 13,600.

UNIVERSITIES (mainly 1963/4 data):

State: Buenos Aires 75,000 students, academic staff 913 (172 full-time). National universities: Córdoba 17,500 st., a.s. 276 (85 f.-t.); Tucumán 7,320 st., a.s. 997 (941 f.-t.); La Plata 47,160 st., a.s. 497; Litoral, Santa Fe 20,000 st., a.s. 800; Nordeste, Corrientes 7,040 st., a.s. 763 (26 f.-t.); Cuyo, Mendoza 13,830 st., a.s. 547 (123 f.-t.); Sur, Bahia Blanca 5,800 st., a.s. 300; La Pampa, Santa Rosa 575 st. Others: Tecnológica, Buenos Aires; Provincia de Buenos Aires, Mar del Plata; universities being established in Entre Ríos and La Rioja.

Private: Buenos Aires: Pontificia Universidad Católica Argentina, Santa María 2,400 st., a.s. 391; Salvador 3,190 st., a.s. 465 (33 f.-t.); Instituto Tecnológico 213 st., a.s. 110 p.-t.; U. Católica de Córdoba 1,260 st., a.s. 360 (357 f.-t.); U.C. de Santa Fe 720 st.; U.C. de Cuyo, San Juan; U.C. de Mar del Plata; U. Privada 'Juan Agustín Maza', Mendoza; U. de Mendoza del Instituto Cuyano de Educación Integral; U. de Patagonia, 'San Juan Bosco', Comodoro Rivadavia.

MASS MEDIA

BROADCASTING: No. of receivers in use, end-1964: TV 1·5 m.; radio 6·2 m. Stations: TV 16; radio 90.

CINEMAS: No., 1964: 1,679. Attendance, 1960: total 145 m.; per head 7·2.

NEWSPRINT: Consumption, 1964: total 177,000 tons; per head 8·0 kg.

NEWSPAPERS: Daily, 1964: 232. Estimated circulation, 1959: 3·2 m.; copies per 000 of pop., 155. Principal dailies in Buenos Aires (*circulation, 000s*): *La Prensa* 258, *La Nación* 238, *Clarín* 343, *El Mundo* 192, *Buenos Aires Herald* 15, *La Razón* (evening) 472.

BOOKS: Titles published, 1964: 3,319.

BOLIVIA

ALISTAIR HENNESSY

THE richest possession of the Spanish crown at the height of its greatness, Bolivia—or Upper Peru as it was then known—is today one of the poorest countries in Latin America. In 1952 Bolivia began the first fundamental social and political revolution since that of Mexico some forty years before. Subsequent years have not measured up to the bright promise of the early days: the economy has lagged and the military coup of November 1964 marked the failure to find a political solution. But against this must be set the social gains of bringing the Indians into the national life and the beginning of the slow process of opening up the vast and potentially rich tropical eastern areas. Few Latin American governments have had to struggle against such intractable geographic, climatic and cultural problems or a history so dogged by failure, barbarism and incompetence.

Bolivia, the fifth largest of the South American countries, has the lowest population density and one of the slowest rates of population growth. The population of the country, twice the size of Spain, is not only barely half that of London but is unevenly distributed and characterised by racial diversity. Approximately 70 per cent are of Indian stock, either Aymara- or Quechua-speaking. The highest density is on the Altiplano, the bleak Andean uplands, which although comprising only 15 per cent of Bolivia's area accounts for 60 per cent of the population and 43 per cent of the cultivated area as well as being the centre of the mining industry. Here Aymara and Quechua Indians grow root crops on *minifundia* which since 1952 have replaced the large estates. In the centre are the semi-tropical valleys of the Yungas near La Paz and the high valleys round Cochabamba and Sucre, comprising 25 per cent of the land area and 40 per cent of the cultivated ground. The vast Oriente, 60 per cent of the country and 11 per cent of the cultivated area, consists of savannah in the south and jungles to the north through which drain tributaries of the Amazon.

Until recently, these three areas had very little communication with each other; only in 1954 was a metalled road completed between Cochabamba and Santa Cruz. Communications, therefore, remain a key problem in Bolivia's development. The two Amazonian departments of Pando and Beni, comprising some 20 per cent of the country's area, are inhabited by only 5 per cent of the population and these could only be reached by a dangerous river journey of many weeks before the coming of the weekly flight from La Paz.

During the pre-colonial period the centre of gravity of the area was in the Altiplano centring on the impressive and still unexplained ruins of Tiahuanaco, lying a few miles south of Lake Titicaca. Broadly speaking, what is now Bolivia was the ancient Kollasuyo, one of the four territorial quarters of the Inca Tawantinsuyu. The cultural pull which in pre-colonial days had been to the west was strengthened during the colonial period by the discovery of silver in the Altiplano. Thus the eastern areas, thinly colonised from the La Plata region, remained a backwater where, until the mid-18th century, the Jesuit missionaries exercised undisputed sway in the *reducciones* (self-contained Indian communities). Recently colonisation of this area by Indians from the Altiplano as well as by scattered groups of Japanese, Italian and Okinawan settlers has begun.

But if Bolivia's present area is impressive in its vastness (412,800 square miles), it is a fraction of its extent at the time of independence (904,952 square miles). The difference is explained by losses to its neighbours—to Chile, including its Pacific sea-board in the War of the Pacific (1879–83),[1] Acre to Brazil in 1903, and further areas to Argentina, Peru and Paraguay. These losses, leaving Bolivia completely landlocked, have left an abiding sense of resentment against the country's 19th-century rulers and a feeling of injustice that surrounding countries, in particular Chile, have not made territorial amends. Bolivia's political incapacity in the 19th century and the dominance of illiterate *cholo* (mestizo) caudillos bred a sense of hopelessness which was reflected in the writings of her greatest historians, Alcides Arguedas and Gabriel René Moreno, who believed that the cholo incorporating the 'worst features of both races' was the source of the country's troubles.

History

The colonial period

In 1545, thirteen years after Pizarro's conquest of Peru, prospectors discovered the great silver mountain at Potosí. With the labour of captive and imported Indians it soon became the richest city in the western world. The flood of silver, rising to a climax in the late 16th century, became the basis of Spanish power in Europe. Potosí was the Klondike of the age, attracting adventurers from all over the continent, until by 1600 with a population of over 120,000 it was the largest city in the Americas. A century and a half later, when the mines were exhausted, silver production declined to a trickle and Potosí yielded its silver supremacy to Guanajuato in Mexico. By 1800 the population was barely 10,000, inhabiting a ghost town where huge baroque churches and ornamental palaces were the only reminders of the once richest city of the Spanish empire. Not until the late 19th-century tin boom could outsiders be attracted back to the rarefied air of its 15,000 feet.

Under the empire, Upper Peru was part of the viceroyalty of Lima, but in 1559 Philip II created, within the viceroyalty, the *audiencia*[2] of Charcas based on Chuquisaca. By the end of the 16th century the most important towns of western Bolivia had been founded, and economic wealth and geographical isolation gave the Audiencia a strong sense of regional unity. When in 1776 the Bourbon reforms created the new viceroyalty of La Plata, based on Buenos Aires, the Audiencia lost some of its far-flung powers. Economic links with Buenos Aires were tenuous but during the emancipation period many of the patriot leaders there were graduates of Chuquisaca university.

Although La Paz was the seat of one of the earliest independence movements against Spain, Upper Peru had to wait until 1825 to gain its independence. The inability of Argentinian armies to make headway against the Spaniards on the Altiplano resulted in years of confused guerrilla warfare

---

[1] See 'Chile', p. 61.
[2] A judicial council which also had administrative responsibilities.

and it was not until the Colombian General Sucre had defeated the Spaniards at Ayacucho in 1824 that Spanish power in Upper Peru was finally broken.

Independence: the age of the caudillos, 1825-80

The first Assembly, meeting under the presidency of General Sucre in 1825, declared Upper Peru an independent state with the title of Bolivia. Simón Bolívar, who himself visited the country in 1825, drew up the first constitution and became its first president. Eclectic in origin and complex in form, the constitution reflected Bolívar's belief in the need for a strong life-presidency. It also showed the complete divorce between theory and practice. Bolivia was to experience strong presidential government, but unchecked by the complicated balancing machinery of Bolívar's impracticable masterpiece. Its jettisoning in 1831 was the first of Bolivia's fifteen constitutional turnovers.

On Bolívar's withdrawal Sucre (after whom Chuquisaca was re-named when it became the legal capital) accepted the presidency on condition he relinquished it after two years. Sucre provided a model of probity and austerity, the example of which was completely lost on his presidential successors. He was succeeded in 1828 by Santa Cruz, an able mestizo general, whose administrative ability, reflected in the codification of laws and educational projects, was nullified by his ambition to restore the old viceroyalty of Peru. He did create a Peruvian-Bolivian Confederation in 1836 which, sensible in theory, in practice challenged the prevailing balance of power and led to war with Chile and Argentina. Santa Cruz was defeated; the Confederation broke up in 1839 and Bolivia had to face an attempt by Peru to establish her domination by force. For the first and last time a Bolivian army was victorious and General José Ballivián, the 'victor of Ingavi', became a national hero and the next president. Ballivián was the last of the early caudillos who, though ruling despotically, did so with some idea of the nation's welfare in mind.

Between 1825 and the end of the War of the Pacific in 1883 there were only two civilian presidents (Linares, 1857–61 and Frías, 1872–4), those after Ballivián being tatterdemalion generals whose bloody coups and *de facto* power was confirmed by rigged elections in which rarely more than 10,000 ever voted. The name of Mariano Melgarejo, an illegitimate mestizo who began his career in the army as a pack-boy at the age of nine, was to become a byword for the barbarous caudillo. His six-year rule (1864–71) was a national disaster. Both the War of the Pacific (1879–83) and the conflict with Brazil over the Amazonian jungle area of Acre have their origins in Melgarejo's reckless granting of concessions for his own immediate financial gain. He also despoiled the Indians of their communal lands, title to which had been promised by Bolívar; in 1868 these were sold on the open market (barely a quarter of this money finding its way into the treasury) or granted to followers, thus creating a new oligarchy of upstart favourites.

The War of the Pacific gave the death-blow to this old-style *caudillismo*. The bizarre Colorados regiment of President Daza gave a splash of barbaric splendour to La Paz military parades, but was unused to the blistering heat of the Atacama desert: the camaraderie of the brothel and the barracks was no substitute for the discipline needed to withstand Chile's well-trained army. The war finally exposed the generals' incompetence.

The constitutional period, 1880–1932

The formation of the first genuine parties in Bolivian politics dates from the debates over whether to withdraw from the war or not. But this issue

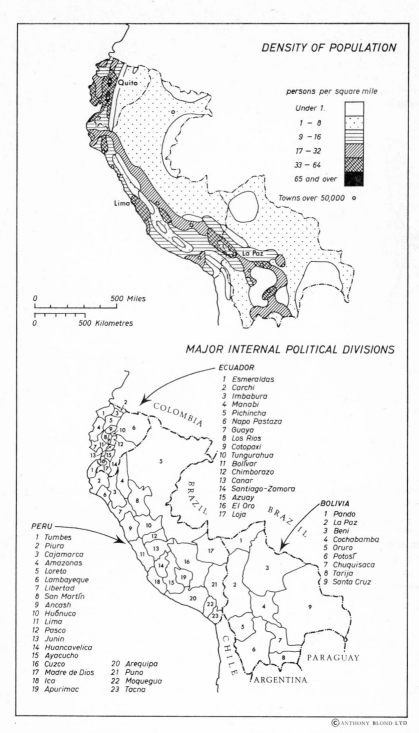

DENSITY OF POPULATION

persons per square mile

Under 1.
1 – 8
9 – 16
17 – 32
33 – 64
65 and over

Towns over 50,000   o

Quito

Lima

La Paz

| 0 | | 500 Miles |
| 0 | | 500 Kilometres |

MAJOR INTERNAL POLITICAL DIVISIONS

ECUADOR

1 Esmeraldas
2 Carchi
3 Imbabura
4 Manabi
5 Pichincha
6 Napo Pastaza
7 Guaya
8 Los Rios
9 Cotopaxi
10 Tungurahua
11 Bolívar
12 Chimborazo
13 Canar
14 Santiago-Zamora
15 Azuay
16 El Oro
17 Loja

COLOMBIA

BRAZIL

BRAZIL

BOLIVIA

1 Pando
2 La Paz
3 Beni
4 Cochabamba
5 Oruro
6 Potosí
7 Chuquisaca
8 Tarija
9 Santa Cruz

PERU

1 Tumbes
2 Piura
3 Cajamarca
4 Amazonas
5 Loreto
6 Lambayeque
7 Libertad
8 San Martín
9 Ancash
10 Huánuco
11 Lima
12 Pasco
13 Junin
14 Huancavelica
15 Ayacucho
16 Cuzco   20 Arequipa
17 Madre de Dios 21 Puno
18 Ica   22 Moquegua
19 Apurimac   23 Tacna

CHILE

PARAGUAY

ARGENTINA

BOLIVIA, ECUADOR AND PERU: POPULATION AND POLITICAL DIVISIONS

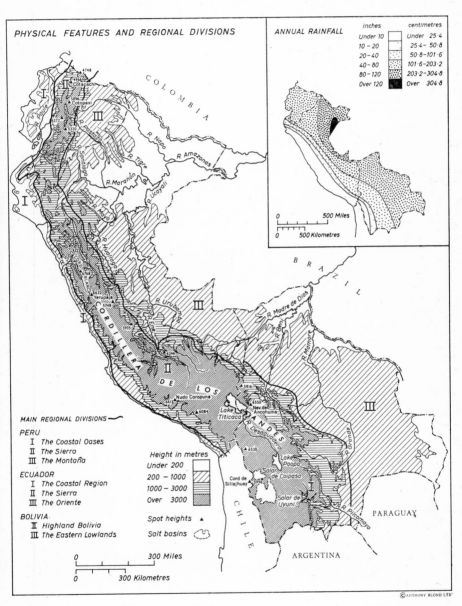

PHYSICAL FEATURES AND REGIONAL DIVISIONS

ANNUAL RAINFALL

inches	centimetres
Under 10	Under 25·4
10 – 20	25·4 – 50·8
20 – 40	50·8 – 101·6
40 – 80	101·6 – 203·2
80 – 120	203·2 – 304·8
Over 120	Over 304·8

MAIN REGIONAL DIVISIONS

PERU
 I   The Coastal Oases
 II The Sierra
 III The Montaña

ECUADOR
 I   The Coastal Region
 II The Sierra
 III The Oriente

BOLIVIA
 II Highland Bolivia
 III The Eastern Lowlands

Height in metres
 Under 200
 200 – 1000
 1000 – 3000
 Over 3000

Spot heights ▲
Salt basins

BOLIVIA, ECUADOR AND PERU : RELIEF, RAINFALL AND REGIONS

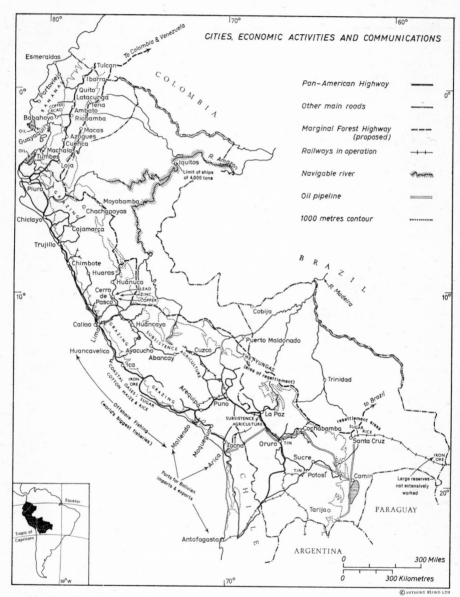

BOLIVIA, ECUADOR AND PERU : CITIES, ECONOMIC ACTIVITIES AND COMMUNICATIONS

soon widened under the influence of imported positivist ideas which questioned the whole basis of the Bolivian state. Conservatives and Liberals now divided over issues of religious freedom, separation of church and state, lay education and civil matrimony. Nevertheless, the differences between the two should not be exaggerated. The methods of political control did not vary; the franchise remained limited by a property qualification; Indians and cholos were still outside the political nation and most Indians were outside the economic nation as well. Politics continued to be linked to the spoils of office and from this standpoint at least the pattern had not much changed. Until the early 1930s politics was played out within the framework of the 1880 constitution which provided a remarkable stability in comparison with the early years of the republic. Personalism still existed but was contained within the framework of the party system.

Civilian politicians pushed generals into the background. Between 1880 and the end of the Chaco War, there were only three soldier-presidents (Campero, 1880–4, Pando, 1899–1904 and Montes, 1904–9 and 1913–17), but these were party candidates, not old-style caudillos. The political function of the army (which in common with others at the end of the century began to be modernised and professionalised) was reduced to providing the machinery, by means of the provisional junta, for fixing the changeover between parties which the parties themselves were unable to operate. Thus it was a provisional military junta which brought to an end each party's dominance—the Conservatives' by the Federal Revolution in 1898, the Liberals' by the 1920 coup and the Republicans' by that of 1930.

The gradual recovery of silver mining since the mid-1850s underlay the new civilian predominance. Thus the age of Conservative rule from 1880 to 1898 is known as the 'Silver Age', and the representative figures of the new self-made mining bourgeoisie were Presidents Pacheco (1884–8) and Arce (1888–92). In opposition, the Liberals were constantly frustrated by the Conservatives 'working' the elections but Liberal success in the municipal elections of 1897 and a conflict between the government and the municipal council in La Paz brought to a head the crisis over the failure of the parties to rotate. By exploiting regional differences, which had always been a factor in Bolivian politics, the Liberals with army and some mass support overthrew the Conservatives in the Federal Revolution of 1898.

Rising tin prices made the Liberal era, the age of tin, one of marked economic expansion. From 1,000 tons p.a. in 1890, production rose to 15,000 tons by 1905. By this date, Simón Patiño (to become the greatest of Latin American entrepreneurs) was the most important figure in the tin industry and was to be the king-maker of Bolivian politics until his death in 1947, although because of his mestizo blood he was never accepted by the old-established families.

In 1915 the Republican party was founded by Daniel Salamanca and Bautista Saavedra, drawing its support from disgruntled Liberals hit by the administrative purges necessitated by the economic effects of the European war. Ex-Conservatives joined the new party, seeing an opportunity to enjoy the spoils of office again. When the army made a coup in 1920 in favour of the Republicans, the Liberals had become a closed oligarchy with no popular support. The Republicans, however, soon split into two factions, one under the new president Saavedra; the other, the 'Genuine Republicans', under Salamanca. As the latter drew support from their ex-Liberal opponents Saavedra was forced to base his support more on the urban cholos. The area of politics was gradually widening and new radical ideas imported from Europe began to take root, as in the work of writers like Franz Tamayo. As in 1920, so again in 1930 it was the army which forced the party change-over, bringing the Genuine Republicans under Salamanca into power.

The Chaco War and proto-revolution, 1932–52

Salamanca is one of the most controversial figures in modern Bolivian politics. He soon broke with his Liberal allies and then, in the trough of the Great Depression, declared war against Paraguay against the advice of the General Staff.[1] The disasters of the war swept away the old Bolivia; the rigid caste system was eroded as Indians, conscripted to fight in the tropical lowlands, became conscious for the first time of the 'nation'. On demobilisation, many refused to return to their former servitude and drifted to the towns where they became politicised 'cholos', providing the mass base for new revolutionary parties and for a militant trade unionism.

At first, the key leaders of the new radicalism were two young officers, Colonels David Toro and Germán Busch. Busch's refusal to use the army to suppress a general strike caused the overthrow of Tejada Sorzano's government in May 1936 and ushered in a ten-year period in which the military played a crucial political role and provided six out of nine presidents up to 1952. Toro's difficulties in trying to run in harness with Saavedra caused Busch to stage a coup in June 1936 and for the next three years, until his suicide in August 1939, he ruled as a 'military socialist' without the support of organised political parties. During these years trade unions were organised, a Ministry of Labour established, the Indians' tribute of *ponguaje* abolished, the Standard Oil Company was nationalised and replaced by the Yacimientos Petrolíferos Fiscales Bolivianos (YPFB). An attempt was also made to control the tin interests which still exercised a powerful influence behind the scenes, but the failure to do this was a factor leading to Busch's suicide (or, as some suspect, murder).

After Busch's death there was a conservative reaction under Generals Carlos Quintanilla and Enrique Peñaranda until a coup by Major Gualberto Villarroel in December 1943 brought in another radical regime. Villarroel was largely a front-man for the Movimiento Nacionalista Revolucionario (MNR). This party had been formed in 1941 by Paz Estenssoro and a group of radical middle-class intellectuals, most of whom were Chaco War veterans. Recognising that the army was the crucial political force they came to a working alliance with a group of neo-fascist officers. During their office in the Villarroel regime (1943–July 1946) the MNR built up a following among the tin miners whose leader, Juan Lechín, now joined the party. However, the MNR's strength was still insufficient to prevent it from being overthrown when a popular outburst against Villarroel strung him up on a lamp post outside the presidential palace. For the next six years, the *sexenio*, when most of the MNR leaders were in exile, the old Liberal and Republican parties revived, first under Dr. Enrique Hertzog (1947–9) and then Mamerto Urriolagoytia (1949–51). In the 1951 presidential elections Paz and Hernán Siles, running for president and vice-president, received more votes than their divided rivals but instead of the choice being submitted to Congress, power was handed over to a military junta. Eleven months later, in April 1952, a rising in La Paz and other cities overthrew the government and brought the MNR into power with overwhelming support.

[1] See 'Paraguay', p. 104.

The Revolution, 1952–64

The fighting was short and bitter. In La Paz MNR activists were assisted by groups of miners whilst a decisive factor was the defection of the *carabineros*, the militarised police. Hernán Siles, son of an earlier president, led the revolt as Paz himself was still in Buenos Aires. After the rising's success Paz returned to take over the presidency. At first, support for the revolution was widespread among the middle classes whose discontent stemmed from the inflationary spiral of the late 1940s, but the main impetus behind reform came from the revivified labour movement and especially from the miners, whose part in the rising enabled them to use the newly formed Confederación de Obreros Bolivianos (COB) to secure the right of nomination to four ministerial posts. From the beginning, therefore, the revolution was based on an alliance between the nationalist middle classes under Paz and organised labour under the miners' leader Lechín.

The first year was marked by a series of far-reaching reforms which destroyed the whole structure of the old regime in which 70 per cent of landed property was owned by 5 per cent of the population and three tin companies dominated economic and political life. Universal adult suffrage turned the Indians (now called *campesinos*) from social pariahs into potential citizens. The major tin producers (controlling 70 per cent of the tin exports and 80 per cent of Bolivia's foreign exchange) were nationalised. The miners' participation in management was recognised by the setting up of the *controles obreros*, where miners had the power to veto all but technical decisions.

The dissolution of the army broke the basis of the old power structure. The most far-reaching reform, however, affected the peasants. The army's dissolution had removed the traditional protectors of the large landowners and the last restraint on the peasant revolution. Initially, the MNR's contacts among the peasantry were minimal—the party was largely urban-oriented. But independently of the MNR, peasants were becoming politically conscious, particularly in the Cochabamba area where from the mid-1930s they had been drawn into the market economy. The return of Chaco War veterans sharpened this new political consciousness and led to the formation of peasant syndicates. The success of the rising in La Paz was therefore a signal for assaults on landowners, most of whom were driven away or killed. This popular rural outburst compelled the government to give top priority to agrarian reform, which was hastily promulgated on 2 August 1953, the basis being to break up the large estates and to give land to those who worked it.

The political consequences of the rural revolution modified the original revolutionary equation. Increasingly the peasants, organised into a network of syndicates, became the mass basis of MNR support. Already by 1953 the army had been reconstituted as a counterweight to the miners' militias who still retained their arms.[1] Now the peasants were similarly organised into a militia to be used, as in the 1963 miners' disturbances, as an additional counterweight.

The political importance of the peasants increased, both during the 1952–6 period of Paz's presidency when hyper-inflation began to erode some of the MNR's middle-class support and also during the price stabilisation period of Siles' presidency between 1956 and 1960. As many peasants were still outside the money economy and hence comparatively unaffected

---

[1] Entry into the officer corps was made selective and MNR cells were established to ensure the army's loyalty—with what success may be judged from the 1964 coup.

by price fluctuations, the MNR could keep their loyalty whilst those who had been drawn into the money economy benefited from the rising demand for domestic agricultural products.

The economic difficulties of the 1950s caused by the initial drop in agricultural production after agrarian reform, by the drop in the demand for tin and by widespread government spending had political consequences. The image of the MNR was tarnished by the corruption of some of its officials who benefited from the black market and there began a slow drift of MNR middle-class supporters to the opposition parties, particularly the Falange Socialista Boliviana (FSB), the most vocal right-wing group.

The opposition

The FSB had been founded in 1946 as a right-wing nationalist party with distinct fascist tendencies. Its following was limited to some army officers and the urban middle class, disoriented by inflation and resentful of exclusion from the spoils of office. Its consistent opposition to the governments of the *sexenio* made it the MNR's main contender for power in 1952 but its weakness lay in the putschist mentality of its leader Unzaga de la Vega, under whose inspiration five abortive revolts were staged between 1953 and 1959. In the last and most serious of these in La Paz, Unzaga was killed. Since then, the party has modified its tactics and at its 1963 Congress under its new leader, the Santa Cruz lawyer Mario Gutiérrez, it renounced its fascist past.

The Partido Social Cristiano (PSC), founded in 1956, attracted those repelled by the MNR's strong-arm methods and corruption and by Unzaga's mystique of violence. In 1964 the PSC reregistered as the Christian Democrats —much to the chagrin of the FSB who considered themselves the traditional defenders of Catholic values.

On the left, the opposition has always been in disarray. The earliest of these splinter groups was the Partido Izquierdista Revolucionario (PIR) founded in 1940 as a non-Communist, national Marxist party. Its founder, Ricardo Anaya, a Cochabamba university professor, is still the party's leader. Some Piristas were absorbed into the MNR, others broke away to join the PCB, the Bolivian Communist Party which had been founded in 1949 (although there had been some isolated 'Communist' groups since the 1920s).

More important than either of these parties has been the Trotskyist Partido Obrero Revolucionario (POR), founded in exile during the Chaco War. Although rent by internal divisions it has and still does enjoy wide support among the tin miners, particularly at the important Catavi-Siglo XX mines.

The MNR

None of these groups has been able to challenge the MNR because of the latter's control of elections and the difficulties of breaking its hold on the peasant syndicates. The most important and significant developments in the opposition have occurred within the MNR itself. Although there has always been a hard core, the MNR was a collection of diverse interests and not a monolithic party. Its ideology was eclectic, drawing on Peruvian *Aprismo*, the Mexican Revolution and *Peronismo*, whilst much of its language has been Marxist and the presuppositions of many of its miner supporters have been Trotskyist. But the MNR failed to mould these disparate groups into a strong governmental party on the Mexican PRI pattern where inner contradictions can be resolved within the party.

The first overt breach occurred during the late 1950s when Guevara Arze, an old-time MNR supporter, who had been passed over for the presidency in 1956, began to organise a group to challenge Paz's candidacy for a second term in 1960. As Minister of Government from 1958 he was in a strong position to place his men in key local government posts where the elections could be influenced. The main mass support for his party, the Movimiento Nacionalista Revolucionario Auténtico (MNRA), came from peasants in the Cochabamba valleys—which helped to make it the leading opposition party in the 1960 elections. In the 1962 elections, however, the MNRA dropped to third place, unable to compete against government pressure.

Guevara's defection marked the beginning of the fragmentation of the MNR, although on the surface it looked at first as if intra-party conflicts were being kept inside the party. In 1960, for example, Lechín formed the Left Sector within the MNR—to strengthen the miners' position but more specifically to further his own presidential ambitions for 1964. The next year Aníbal Aguilar formed the Socialist Sector—ostensibly to block Lechín's candidature but also to give a greater say to growing Santa Cruz interests. His key position in the ministry of labour enabled him to whittle away Lechín's support in the unions. These sectors were not of the Mexican PRI type—that is they did not primarily represent specific-interest groups organised horizontally but were vertical sectors cutting across social and economic divisions and were, in fact, little more than electoral machines built to contest the 1964 elections. In addition there was the FUN (Frente Unidad Nacional), who backed Paz for yet another term.

Paz's determination to stand for a third term in 1964 and his increasing equation of the revolution with his own continuance in office brought the final confrontation between him and vice-president Lechín. The Left Sector, partly emboldened by the Cuban Revolution, stepped up its attacks on Paz's method of government and his dependence on US aid. The Tri-angular Plan of 1961 to reorganise the mines with the aid of US, BID and West German funds ($37 million over three years) crystallised the miners' resentment. The price of this financial support was the disciplining of the miners and the reduction of the power of the *controles obreros* which to the miners was a major conquest of the revolution.

Paz's re-election in May 1964 was only achieved at the high cost of packing the MNR convention, driving Lechín out of the party and forcing him to set up his own party, the Partido Revolucionario Izquierdista Nacional (PRIN) and by capitulating to the ambition of General René Barrientos whom Paz was forced to accept as his new vice-president. Barrientos's rise to power marks the return of the armed forces to active politics. With his peasant background, knowledge of Quechua (rare among Bolivian politicians), and his success in pacifying the Cliza Valley, he was a popular figure, especially in the Cochabamba area. When, therefore, Paz's un-popularity sparked off riots in the major cities and the mining centres in October 1964, Barrientos was able to lead the revolt against the discredited MNR and to drive Paz into exile and to set up a military junta. The MNR collapsed with remarkable ease because its urban base had been narrowed by its failure to exercise patronage in favour of even its own supporters and because the peasants' militia could be effective only so long as the army provided the transport.

In spite of its initial popularity and its claim to be restoring the Revolution which had been 'diverted from its original aims' the junta soon declined in popularity, assailed by the left for its tough handling of the miners and by civilian politicians for the tardy return to constitutionalism. Paz's fall was followed by a mushrooming of twenty or so small factions, each trying to capitalise on the junta's failure to fulfil its early promises. The military under the interim president, General Ovando, the army's commander-in-chief, did not withdraw from politics but continued to hold cabinet posts including the key mining ministry. The situation in the nationalised mines deteriorated and nationalist feeling was affronted by concessions to foreign companies.

At the presidential and congressional elections held in July 1966 Barrientos was elected president; supported by the opposition group Comunidad Democrática Cristiana, ex-Chaco war veteran General Bernardino Bilbao gained 14 per cent of the votes. During his first year's presidency Barrientos had to face strong political opposition, especially from the miners. Early in 1967 some of the nationalised mines were occupied by the army after resistance. This was accompanied by the outbreak of guerrilla activity in the isolated jungle region of the south-east, although it is unclear if there was any precise relation between the two. The capture of Régis Debray, the French ideologist of guerrilla warfare, followed by the killing of Ché Guevara and the Bolivian guerrilla leader Coco Peredo in October by a US-trained anti-guerrilla force were severe blows to the movement.

ECONOMY

Before the Revolution

Bolivia's economic history has been that of its mining industry. When production began to decline in the 17th century the importance of Upper Peru declined as well. During the 18th century it became an economic backwater —important only as a communications link between Salta in Argentina and Lower Peru. At independence, mines owned by Spaniards became the property of the state but despite efforts to revive the mining industry it was difficult to attract foreign capital away from more profitable investments elsewhere in the newly opened continent. Agriculture which had been stimulated by the presence of the mines languished until it became largely subsistence agriculture and until the 1960s Bolivia remained a net importer of foodstuffs. In addition to these economic disadvantages Bolivia's outlet to the sea at Antofagasta, isolated by a desert hinterland, was not conducive to trade—hence the economic motivation behind Santa Cruz's Peruvian-Bolivian Confederation of 1836–9. The valuable nitrate deposits of the Atacama desert might have become a source of wealth but Melgarejo's reckless granting of concessions to foreigners and the Chilean occupation of the area after the War of the Pacific precluded this.

Early governments had been unable to stimulate economic growth, partly because they were defrauded of their major source of revenue from customs by widespread smuggling, encouraged by high tariffs and long exposed land frontiers. Bonanzas failed to materialise, as when synthetics ruined the market for both cocaine and quinine. Amazonian rubber had its brief moment of glory but prospectors' conflicts involved Bolivia in a confrontation with Brazil which resulted in the loss of Acre in 1903. Oil, which has still to fulfil the promise expected of it, was also a contributory cause of conflict with Paraguay over the Chaco in the 1930s. It is only within the last few years in fact that a diversified economy has come within the bounds of possibility with the gradual development of the potentially rich Oriente and even now, for practical purposes, Bolivians are still dominated by the 'tin fixation' which has replaced that of silver.

The first signs of a reviving mining prosperity came with the foundation in 1856 of the Huanchaca Company and for a few decades silver again dominated the Bolivian economy. But when prices dropped and the demand for tin rose towards the end of the 19th century attention was turned to the metal which had previously been spurned as spoilage from the silver mines. When the railway from Antofagasta reached Oruro in the 1890s it became the centre of the newly burgeoning industry. In 1900, Simón Patiño discovered the La Salvadora mine which, within ten years, with the help of English capital, was producing 10 per cent of the world's tin. One result of the tin boom was to distort the communications structure as railways were built to link the mines with the coast whilst the rest of the country was ignored. Another result was that tin dominated politics. In practice this meant Patiño, whose mines accounted for 55 per cent of Bolivia's total production. The political implications are clear when it is remembered that from 1931 the major tin-producing states (represented on the International Tin Council of which Patiño was chairman) agreed to government-sponsored restriction to bolster world prices, thus leading to the rivalry of the 1930s and 1940s between Patiño and the Aramayos and Hochschilds (who produced 15 per cent and 10 per cent of Bolivia's total production respectively) for influence over the government in order to receive preferential treatment.

The mines

When the revolutionary government nationalised the three great tin companies in October 1952 it struck at an industry which controlled 70 per cent of the country's mineral exports and earned 80 per cent of its foreign exchange. The smaller mines were untouched although the State Mining Bank was given the monopoly over purchase and sale of their production, which in contrast to the state mines increased three-fold over the next 10 years (from 3,800 tons in 1950 to 8,400 tons in 1962—roughly a third of the state mines' production). Economically, however, nationalisation was a mixed blessing. Not only did it coincide with the end of the Korean war boom but the new state mining corporation (COMIBOL) inherited the problems of an industry in technical decline. Patiño, long before his death in 1947, had started to diversify his interests, recognising that as a high-cost producer Bolivia could not hold its own with the placer deposits of Africa and Asia. Few of the profits therefore had been reinvested in equipment or in exploration of new seams to offset the declining tin content of existing ones. Expert technicians left just when they were most required, nor could antiquated universities fill the gap—only 210 engineers of *all* kinds were graduated between 1953 and 1962.[1] The tin boom had also inflated the labour force, which for political purposes could not be reduced. Operating costs therefore mounted. COMIBOL's pay roll increased by a third at the same time as productivity per worker dropped. Tin production fell from 32,472 tons in 1952 to 17,690 tons in 1965. In 1966 tin accounted for 70 per cent of the country's foreign earnings.

The government argued that the rehabilitation of the mines depended on being able to attract foreign capital and technical assistance. But as this was dependent on discipline being restored in the mines, the problem was ultimately political. The miners themselves argued that reorganisation was at their expense—the proposal, for example, to resettle redundant miners in agricultural land in Oriente ignored the very great cultural adjustment

---

[1] The Instituto Tecnológico Boliviano was set up in 1962 to remedy this. After the 1964 coup it was incorporated into the University of San Andrés in La Paz.

involved and the solidarity of closed mining communities. Their criticisms were directed against COMIBOL for its bureaucratic incompetence and its overstaffing to provide jobs for MNR supporters. But both miners and extreme nationalists see the solution to the mining problem in the establishment of a tin smelter on Bolivian soil. At present, ores rarely have over 2 per cent tin content. Concentration plants can bring this up to 25 per cent but the final process needs specialised tin smelters. Since the post-war closing down of the Texas City smelter the greater part of Bolivia's tin is smelted at either Williams, Harvey at Bootle or Capper Pass at Hull. Thus a specialised smelter in Bolivia would not only cut out the high freight charges but would put the seal on the nation's economic emancipation, especially as it is felt that the industry is still under the control of Patiño Consolidated Company who in addition to receiving compensation for expropriated properties controls Williams, Harvey.

Agriculture

As late as the mid-1950s, and in spite of Bolivia's immense agricultural potential, food imports, paid for by tin exports, only fulfilled 40 per cent of its food needs. Production dropped in the early years of agrarian reform as considerations of productivity were subordinated to political and social needs. At first there was insufficient awareness of the need for technical advisory services and of the difficulties of cultural readjustment. Furthermore, agriculture, as with all fields of the Bolivian economy, has been severely handicapped by the shortage of trained Bolivian experts—between 1952 and 1962 only 71 agronomists and 14 vets were graduated.

The Agrarian Reform Law of 1953 recognised six types of tenure: homesites, small family-worked properties, medium property requiring hired labour, large cattle farms, collective and cooperative lands, and communal property. By 1963, about 238,000 titles had been granted, about 75 per cent of which were concentrated in the Altiplano. An immediate result of reform was the creation of inefficient and unproductive minifundia, but with the possibilities of social mobility some movement from overpopulated areas to the tropical lowlands is now taking place. Much of this is voluntary; some is government-sponsored, as with the settlement of conscript soldiers and miners, which does not seem to have been a success.

The recovery of agricultural production which promises to make Bolivia self-sufficient in foodstuffs and a limited exporter of tropical products is a result of increases in the Santa Cruz region (especially rice, corn, sugar and wheat) and the newly opened areas of the semi-tropical Yungas valleys. On the Altiplano, agriculture remains backward and often Indian communities are resistant to attempts to foster collectivist or cooperative solutions.

Industry

Although Bolivia has great hydroelectric potential, industrial development has so far been hampered by power shortages as well as by the lack of iron and limited markets. During the 1950s light industry experienced a boom under the stimulus of favourable exchange regulations. However, the inauguration of a monetary stabilisation policy in 1956 at the insistence of the IMF, as a means to curb the runaway inflation, led to a serious contraction and the manufacturing share of GDP dropped from 14 per cent to 6 per cent. Industrial employment dropped from 25,000 to 15,000 and many marginal firms collapsed. The gradual industrial recovery from 1961 onwards may be attributed to the expansion of food-processing plants (reflecting the recovery of agriculture) and the building materials industry, particularly cement, in response to an increasing public works programme.

Petroleum

Since the nationalisation of the Standard Oil Company in 1937 and its replacement by the YPFB (see page 28 above) the high hopes placed on oil production have been slow to materialise, although there was a rapid rise in production in the mid-1950s. In anticipation of the country's becoming a major oil exporter, pipe lines were laid from the oil-fields in south-east Bolivia to Arica on the Pacific, to Yacuiba in Argentina and to Corumba in Brazil. Shortage of working capital, partly due to the defaulting of other state agencies on their debts, has put a brake on production. A new Petroleum Code in 1956 allowed foreign oil companies to prospect and start operations and as a result some fourteen have done so. The ten-year plan envisages an increase in production from 8,000 barrels per day in 1962 to 50,000 in 1971.

Foreign aid

Both the left- and right-wing nationalists accused the MNR government of bolstering its position with US funds. Without the large injection of US aid it is doubtful, in fact, if the MNR regime would have survived as long as it did. Between 1946 and 1957 the United States contributed $118 million in foreign aid, a large proportion of which went on budgetary support of the government. Until 1961, US aid was designed to shore up a tottering economy, but with the Alliance for Progress a more directed effort was made to plan for sustained growth based on the 1962–71 plan. Much of the new aid, which rose to $60 million in 1963, has gone into infrastructure development, particularly communications. A high proportion of Bolivia's defence budget, which is one of the lowest in Latin America, is provided by US military aid. Without this it is unlikely that the armed forces would have been in a position to have overthrown the MNR in 1964.

Investment and development

Comparative political and labour peace and the stability of the peso encouraged foreign investment in 1966. The giant Bank of America planned to become the second US bank in La Paz. Domestic investment was stimulated by an expanded corporation network benefiting smaller businesses and industries; taxes were expected to be eliminated on inter-provincial movement of goods. A large-scale colonisation programme was planned to begin in 1967 in 10 million acres of government 'virgin lands'.

BIBLIOGRAPHY

Alexander, R. J. *The Bolivian National Revolution*, Rutgers Univ. Press, New Brunswick, 1958.
Arnade, C. W. *The Emergence of the Republic of Bolivia*, Florida Univ. Press, Gainesville, 1957. 'The Historiography of Colonial and Modern Bolivia', *Hispanic American Historical Review*, Baltimore, August 1962. 'Bolivia's Social Revolution 1952–9', *Journal of Inter-American Studies*, Coral Gables, Florida, July 1959.
Finot, Enrique. *Nueva Historia de Bolivia*, La Paz, 1964.
Hanke, Lewis Ulysses. *The Imperial City of Potosi*, Martinus Nijhoff, The Hague, 1956.
Heath, D. B. 'Land Reform in Bolivia', *Inter-American Economic Affairs*, XII, 4, Washington, DC, 1958–9.
Osborne, Harold. *Bolivia: a Land Divided*, Oxford Univ. Press for Royal Institute of International Affairs, London and New York, 3rd ed. 1964. *Indians of the Andes*, Routledge and Kegan Paul, London; Harvard Univ. Press, Cambridge, Mass., 1952.
Zondag, C. H. *The Bolivian Economy*, 1952–65, Frederick A. Praeger, New York; Pall Mall Press, London, 1966.

BASIC INFORMATION
CLIMATE
La Paz

Lat./long.	10° 30′ S, 68° W	Relative humidity	
Altitude	12,001 ft/3,659 m.	at midday of hot-	n.a.
Mean temp. of hottest month	13°C/54°F (Nov.)	test and coolest months	
Mean temp. of coolest month	9°C/48°F (July)	Wettest month	4·5 in./114 mm. (Jan.)
Absolute max.	80°F/26°C	Driest month	0·3 in./8 mm. (June)
Absolute min.	26°F/−4°C	Annual av. rainfall	22·6 in./564 mm.

POPULATION

TOTAL (*million*): 1950 (census, adjusted): 3·02; mid-1966: 3·75; other estimates, 1965: 4·33; 1980 (ECLA projection): 6·00.

DENSITY, mid-1965: 3-4 persons per sq. km. Regional: Altiplano and valleys 8, E. plains 1.

CRUDE RATES (*per 000*), 1959–61 (ECLA data): birth 43–5, death 21–3; infant mortality (1966) 98.

GROWTH RATES (% *p.a.*), 1945–65: 1·3; 1960–5: 1·4.

DISTRIBUTION (% *of total pop.*): ethnic, 1950: Amerindian 63; mixed or white 37. Foreign-born, 1950: 1·3. Language, 1950: Spanish 36; Amerindian 64 (mainly Aymará or Quechua). Religion: mainly Roman Catholic; Protestant, 1962: about 1·2. Urban (*centres 2,000 inhab. or over*), ECLA data, 1950: 25·8; 1960: 29·9; 1980 (proj.): 41·9. Largest cities (*000 inhab.*), 1962: La Paz 353 (1965: 361), Cochabamba 92, Oruro 87, Santa Cruz 73, Potosí 55, Sucre (legal capital) 54.

CONSTITUTIONAL SYSTEM

CONSTITUTION: First 1826; modified 1880, 1938, 1945, amended 1947 and 1952. New constitutions 1961 and 1967.

SYSTEM: Unitary republic, comprising 9 departments (divided into provinces and cantons; municipal councils in large towns) and 3 *delegaciones*. Separate executive, legislature and judiciary.

EXECUTIVE: Power vested in president and ministers of state. President is elected by popular vote for a 4-year term (1961 constitution provided for reelection for second 4-year term).

LEGISLATURE: Bi-cameral, National Congress of Senate and Chamber of Deputies. *Senate:* 3 from each department; elected directly by simple majority for 6 years, one-third retiring every 2 years. *Chamber:* 4 from each department, one additional for each 100,000 inhabitants or fraction over 50,000; elected by proportional vote and double quotient system, for 4 years, one-half retiring every 2 years. *Suffrage:* Universal compulsory voting for adults over 21 years of age, or 18 if married. Registered voters, March 1966: estimated at about 1 m. *Elections:* July 1966: Presidential, General René Barrientos Ortuño (*president*) and Luis Adolfo Siles Salinas (*vice-president*), candidates of FRB. Seats held:

Party	% votes	Senate	Chamber of Deputies
Frente de la Revolución Boliviana (FRB)	60	18	82
Comunidad Democrática Cristiana (CDC)	14	8	19
Movimiento Revolucionario Pazestenssorista (MRP)	5	1	1
Other parties or blank votes	21	—	—
Total	100	27	102

JUDICIARY: Supreme Court (at Sucre), 10 judges elected by Chamber of Deputies for renewable 6-year term; district courts, judges elected by the Senate; other local courts.

DEFENCE

DEFENCE BUDGET: 1965: 150 m. pesos; 2·1 % of GDP.
ARMED FORCES: Military service: between 19 and 49 years of age; men aged 19–21, up to 2 years in army. Strength: army 10,000, air force 1,800; total 12,000 plus trained reserve.

INTERNATIONAL RELATIONS

Member of the UN and many of its international specialised agencies, including: IBRD and affiliates, IMF, FAO, ICAO, ILO, ITU, UNDP, UNESCO, UPU, WHO and WMO; IAEA; UNCTAD representative; also a member of various regional organisations, including: UN ECLA, OAS, Alliance for Progress, IDB and LAFTA.

ECONOMY

PRODUCTION

AGRICULTURE (ooo tons)	1960	1963	1964	1965	AGRICULTURE (ooo tons)	1960	1963	1964	1965
Wheat	68	55	58	42	Sugar cane	308	823	936	933
Maize	248	260	261	239	Potatoes	580	622	622	650
Barley	59	60	62	65	Coffee	1·5	1·7	2·1	3·2
Rice	28	30	28	29	Cotton	0·7	1·1	1·3	1·4

LAND, 1950 (%): Arable 3, permanent pasture 10, forested 43, other 44.
OTHER AGRICULTURAL DATA: Tractors in use (ooos), 1957: 20. Fertiliser consumption (ooo tons), 1965/66: 1·5.
LIVESTOCK: Numbers (m. head), 1964/65: cattle 2·75; 1963/64: sheep 5·55, pigs 0·60. Products (ooo tons), 1962: beef and veal 17, pork 1.
FISH LANDED (ooo tons), 1964: total 1·4.
MINING, 1965: Metal content of ores exported (ooo tons): tin 24·2, antimony 8·8, lead 17·5, zinc 13·7, copper 4·7, wolfram 1·1; sulphur (exports) 10; (tons) silver 128·0, gold 2·64. Fuels (m. cubic metres): crude petroleum 0·55; natural gas, 1964: 4,145.
MANUFACTURING, 1964: (ooo tons) Tin (primary, exports) 3·7, cement 65, sugar 100, wheat flour 14; (m. litres) beer 26·4. Liquid fuels (ooo cubic metres): diesel oil 84, fuel oil 130, motor spirit 188.

ENERGY

CONSUMPTION (tons coal equiv.), 1964: Total 0·63 m., per head 0·17.
ELECTRICITY, 1965: Generated (kwh) 554 m.; installed capacity (kw) 173,500.

GOVERNMENT EXPENDITURE

DISTRIBUTION (% of total), 1965: Defence 17, education 25, social services 8.

EXTERNAL TRADE (US$m.)	1955	1960	1964	1965	1966
EXPORTS (c.i.f.)	99	66	112	129	148
Tin	57	43	81	93	93
Silver	5	5	6	5	7
Lead	6	5	5	6	6
Zinc	6	1	3	4	5
Antimony	—	1	6	6	.
EXPORTS (f.o.b.)	76	51	93	110	126
IMPORTS (c.i.f.)	81	69	97	126	131
TRADE BALANCE	−5	−18	−4	−17	−4

DIRECTION OF TRADE (%)

	Exports			Imports		
	1955	*1960*	*1965*	*1955*	*1960*	*1965*
LAFTA	(4·3)	12·1	2·7	(18·2)	14·3	11·0
USA	59·6	23·3	42·6	31·2	43·3	43·7
EEC	4·3	4·9	8·1	15·6	21·8	18·6
UK	32·3	54·3	44·6	6·1	5·2	5·3

GROSS PRODUCT

GDP (*ooo m. pesos*): At current market prices, 1964: 6·51; 1965: 7·23; at 1963 market prices, 1964: 6·06; 1965: 6·39. Per head (US$), UN estimate, 1964: 144. DISTRIBUTION (%), 1965: Agriculture and livestock 28, mining and petroleum 12, manufacturing 12, trade and finance 13.
GROWTH RATES (%), 1952–60: total −0·7, per head −2·7; 1960–4: total 4·9, per head 3·4.

FINANCE

EXCHANGE RATE (*per US$*): Official selling, end-year, 1960: 11,885 bolivianos; 1964: 11·88 pesos; 1966: 11·88 pesos.
BALANCE OF PAYMENTS (*US$ m.*): Goods and services (net), 1960: −31; 1964: −24; 1965: −40; 1966: −35.
COST OF LIVING (*Dec. 1958 = 100*), La Paz, December, 1960: 122; 1964: 147; 1965: 154; 1966; 168.
INDUSTRIAL WAGES: Average monthly (*pesos*), 1964: petroleum (YPFB) 1,045, mining (COMIBOL) 850.
PUBLIC SECTOR ACCOUNTS (*m. pesos*), 1966: Revenue 2,529, expenditure 2,928, deficit 399.

EMPLOYMENT

ECONOMICALLY ACTIVE (%), 1950: Total pop. 50 (men 59, women 42), pop. 15 years and over 75. In agriculture 71, manufacturing 9, services 5. Labour force, 1965: agriculture 49, mining and petroleum 3, industry 6, construction 6.
UNEMPLOYMENT (%), 1965: 17.

TRANSPORT AND COMMUNICATIONS

RAILWAYS: Traffic, 1957: 236 m. pass.-km., 300 m. net ton-km. Length of track, 1964: 3,580 km.
MOTOR VEHICLES: In use, 1963: pass. cars 14,500, comm. vehicles 26,600. Road system 24,300 km., paved 615 km.
AIR: Scheduled services, 1964: total 49·8 m. pass.-km., 3·6 m. cargo ton-km. International: 16·1 m. pass.-km., 0·58 m. cargo ton-km. Main airports: La Paz (El Alto, international), Cochabamba, Santa Cruz.
TELEPHONES: No. in use, 1964: 20,000.

SOCIAL WELFARE

SYSTEM: Social insurance funds and benefits are administered principally by the national social security fund; there are also several trade union funds. Financed by employees' and employers' contributions. Under the national fund, contributions based on remuneration: employees 7·5%, employers 28%; contributions to other funds vary. Employment legislation covers working hours; holidays; payment of wages, overtime and annual bonuses; dismissal and death indemnities.
HEALTH: 1963: 3,700 persons per physician; 1960: 580 persons per hospital bed.
NUTRITION: Net food supply (*per head per day*), 1961–3: 1,830 calories; protein 47 g.

EDUCATION

ILLITERACY RATE (%), 1950: 15 years and over, 69.
COMPULSORY: 7 years (between 7 and 14 years of age). Pupils in primary and secondary schools as % of pop. aged 5 to 19, 1963: 50.
SCHOOLS, 1964: pre-school and primary: no. 7,000, pupils 0·6 m., teachers 16,000. Secondary: no. 261, p. 71,400, t. 3,200. Technical: no. 46, students 6,700, teaching staff 680. Teacher-training: no. 15, st. 4,900, t. s. 120. Higher (including universities, faculties), 1962: no. 10, st. 7,600.
UNIVERSITIES (mainly 1963/64 data): San Andrés, La Paz: students 4,392, academic staff 669 (58 full-time). San Simón, Cochabamba: st. 1,772, a.s. 274 (27 f.t.). San Francisco Xavier de Chuquisaca, Sucre: st. 1,300, a.s. 200. Tomás Frias, Potosí: st. 1,200, a.s. 140. Juan Misael Saracho, Tarija: st. 761, a.s. 150 (12 f.t.). Gabriel René Moreno, Santa Cruz de la Sierra: st. 500. Técnica de Oruro: st. 500. Technical institutes in La Paz: I.T. Boliviano and Esc. I de la Nación Pedro Domingo Murillo.

MASS MEDIA

BROADCASTING: No. of receivers in use, 1964: radio 500,000. Transmitters: radio 43. Television service planned.
CINEMAS: No., 1964: 210. Attendance, 1964: total 3·2 m.; per head 0·9.
NEWSPRINT: Consumption (printing paper), 1962: total 3,600 tons; per head 1·0 kg.
NEWSPAPERS: Daily, 1961: 6. Estimated circulation 92,000, copies per 000 of population 26. Principal dailies in La Paz (*circulation, ooos*): *El Diario* 36, *La Nación* 20, *Última Hora* (evening) 20.

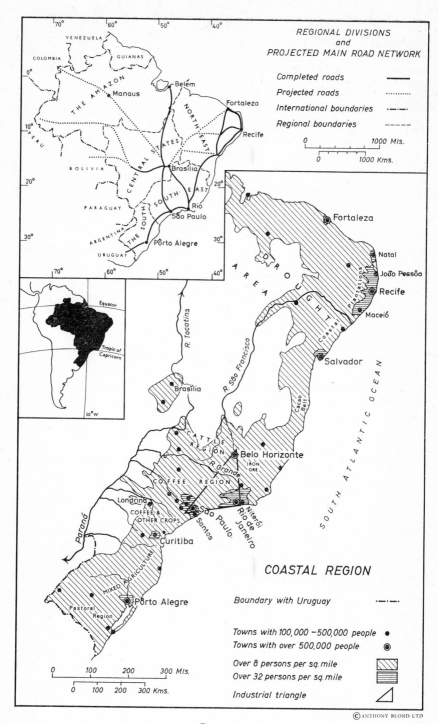

BRAZIL

BRAZIL

EMANUEL DE KADT

THE COLONIAL PERIOD

THE early history of Brazil as a colony of Portugal was dominated not by the Crown or by the Church, not by soldiers, generals or bishops, but by the sugar-cane planter in the fertile coastal lands of Brazil's north-east. Despite the fact that already in 1548 Portugal had dispatched the first governor-general to Bahia, in most of the country real political power rested in the hands of the patriarchal landowners, who had little sympathy for interfering royal officials—or, for that matter, for emissaries from the ecclesiastical authorities.

Sugar-cane had early on become the lynch-pin of the Brazilian economy. Cultivated on large plantations which required a substantial labour force, it had posed a serious problem to the colonists: their vision of life overseas had hardly included direct involvement in degrading manual labour. But the Brazilian Indians, instantly regarded as God-sent labourers, were much less settled peoples than those of Latin America's western and northern highlands: they consistently tried to avoid being captured and pressed into work, and when caught proved singularly unadaptable to hard plantation labour. Brazil's labour needs had to be met from elsewhere—from Africa. In 1550 the first African slaves were brought to Brazil. They came to constitute a most important element of the country's population.

The Indians, on the other hand, all but disappeared. They were driven into the interior, and felled by unfamiliar European diseases. The only people to take an interest in them were the Jesuits. They founded mission villages in the centre and north of the country into which they concentrated the indigenous population. The Indians were given a rudimentary education, instructed, of course, in the Catholic faith, and set to work at agriculture and simple crafts under the strict guidance of the Jesuits. Though they were treated as children, never capable of growing up, the paternalistic regime did give them relative security. But their villages, over which the Jesuits exercised complete authority until shortly before they were expelled in 1759 by Portugal's enlightened but despotic prime minister Pombal, were from an early time threatened by bands of roaming frontiersmen, the so-called Bandeirantes.

The Bandeirantes were descendants of Portuguese who had settled in São Vicente, near present-day Santos. They were less prosperous and more adventurous than the landowners of the north-east, and rather than settle and till the land they went on long expeditions in search of Indians, land and gold. Tough, courageous, a law unto themselves, they opened up vast areas of the country. They gave Brazil depth and provided a dynamic

41

balancing element to the settled and outward-looking plantation-owners in the narrow coastal strip. Pitched battles between these adventurers and Indian villages armed in self-defence by their Jesuit masters had occurred well before the latter had fallen out of grace with the government. Not seldom the result had been the capture of hundreds of conveniently assembled Indians. It is hardly surprising that after the expulsion of the Fathers the story of the Indian settlements rapidly drew to a close.

The Portuguese crown never developed the tight kind of control over Brazil which its Spanish counterpart set up in Hispanic America. The sheer size of the land militated against that from the beginning; the smallness of Portugal and its weakness after the 16th century was another important factor. Moreover, the only consistently pursued purpose of the Portuguese authorities in Brazil was mercantilist: the colony was to produce (and import) goods which would yield high income through taxation on commerce—how these goods were produced or what the social relations were under which the population lived was of little concern to the rulers in Lisbon. While they built up a strict and rigid monopoly on trade, later even developing a system of regular transatlantic convoys to prevent smuggling, they left the plantation-owners in their far-flung domains to fend for themselves and work out their own salvation.

The slaves who were set to work on the plantations were mercilessly exploited. Yet there is some evidence to suggest that slavery in Brazil was a little less savage than that in North America or the Caribbean. The Portuguese, themselves ruled for many years by the Moors, were more accustomed to dark-skinned people, and the men mixed freely with the more attractive of the African women. The offspring of these unions were generally taken into the *casa grande* (the residence of the landowner and his family) and raised together with the master's legitimate children. Manumission became relatively frequent, and as time went by there were increasing numbers of free Negroes. African religious cults were allowed to flourish after a token conversion of the slaves by the plantation chaplain—a man more dependent on the landowner than on his bishop. While the master's power over his estate and its inhabitants was almost unlimited, he used it patriarchally and not merely arbitrarily: he behaved like a father whose authority was not to be questioned rather than as a despot whose force could not be challenged. Thus the basis was laid for two features still prominent in modern Brazil: the prevalence of paternalism and dependence relations on the one hand, and on the other what Gilberto Freyre has so proudly called Brazil's racial democracy (though, as other Brazilian scholars have lately pointed out, the second legacy of slavery is a rigid class system in which darker skin and lower class do, as a rule, go together).

In the 1690's gold was found by a group of Bandeirantes in Minas Gerais, and about thirty years later diamonds were added to the list of Brazil's exportable goods. These events brought a major shift of the country's centre of gravity. Sugar-cane seemed suddenly a dull unpromising business, and landowners moved in strength with their households and slaves to the gold and diamond area. Soon the government found that trade no longer went through the north-eastern ports of Olinda and Bahia; custom house and government offices were moved to Rio de Janeiro, which became the centre of the colony's centralised administration in 1763. New cities sprang up close to the most thriving mining centres. When the mining cycle was over by about 1800 they had become near-deserted, but still today they stand preserved as national monuments of great beauty, where the restrained exterior architecture of the baroque churches hides restless and often ostentatious interiors.

But little of the wealth from the mines found productive use in Brazil itself, although some small-scale industry—textiles and metal, mainly—did develop in the latter part of the century in spite of Portugal's restrictions. The money flowed to Lisbon, where it was spent on keeping one of Europe's most pompous courts, eventually finding its way to England, where it helped to build the foundations for the Industrial Revolution. The increasingly harsh exactions of the gold-tax gatherers led in 1789 to a conspiracy against Portugal by a small group of men under Tiradentes. It was discovered, Tiradentes was executed and the matter had no further consequence, apart from providing Brazil with one of her national heroes.

By the end of the 18th century mining revenues had declined sharply, cotton and sugar were planted again, and Portugal's trading monopoly had disappeared in all but name. British influence was growing in the colony, and when Napoleon's forces invaded the metropolis in 1807 the weak armies of D. João, king of Portugal, were in no position to put up effective resistance. The British supplied a fleet which took on board the royal family and thousands of court officials, dependants and hangers-on. They were landed early in 1808 in Brazil. Rio de Janeiro now became the capital of the Portuguese Empire, an empire much in debt to the British in the background. Immediately all tariffs, which had kept trade down to a minimum and had protected what little industry existed in Brazil, were abolished. They were replaced by a small duty which, for some fifty years, would allow British goods a virtual monopoly on the Brazilian market.

After staying in Brazil for fourteen years D. João sailed for Lisbon in 1821, leaving his son Pedro behind to look after things on his behalf. He is reputed to have told the young man upon his departure that he would do better to lead a movement for independence, should it arise, than to fight it. So it happened. Recalled in 1822 by a mistrustful Portuguese parliament, ostensibly in order to complete his education, D. Pedro refused to go. On 7 September, on the banks of the Ipiranga river, he dramatically cried out 'Independence or death', and by the end of the year he had been crowned Emperor of Brazil. The transition to independence had been made peacefully and easily, providing continuity with the past and a form of government whose legitimacy had a much stronger foundation than the tenuous political formulae upon which the successor-states to the Spanish Empire were built.

THE EMPIRE

Pedro I, having shown some early sympathies towards the liberal ideas fashionable in Lisbon at the time, quickly showed himself a ruler determined to have things his own way. In 1823 he rejected a draft constitution too liberal for his liking; he disbanded the Constituent Assembly and named a Council of State of trusted men who produced a document more to his taste. It was promulgated in 1824 and remained the country's charter till the end of the Empire in 1889. Perhaps its most important feature was the *poder moderador*—the moderating or regulating power—accorded to the emperor. It gave him the right to nominate senators for life, the right to convoke parliament and veto its acts, and the right to dissolve it at will and call new elections for the Chamber of Deputies. This instrument made the emperor into the supreme arbiter of the country's politics. Pedro I behaved more and more like a potentate; his early popularity faded completely. In 1831, after abdicating in favour of his five-year old son Pedro II, he was persuaded to sail for Lisbon.

It is almost a miracle that Brazil did not fly apart during the ten years when successive regents ruled the country on behalf of the young emperor. The central government was weak, and hardly a year went by when its tiny armed forces were not called upon to put down a secessionist movement somewhere in the country. A respected central authority was lacking—as it had been in the former Spanish colonies. Herring has suggested that the Empire could easily have dissolved into three autonomous states: a sugar-growing country in the north-east, a mining nation in the centre and a cattle-raising people in the south. The gravity of the situation was understood by those in charge of the country. In 1840, when Pedro was not yet fifteen years old, he was declared of age and made to assume full powers himself.

For ten years the young emperor had been given the best education which could be provided in Brazil, and Pedro never lost his taste for science and philosophy. He was an enlightened man, more at ease throughout his life with scholars or poets than with diplomats or politicians, never really a serious intellectual, but as an amateur immensely interested and open-minded. He was the incarnation of the *poder moderador*, balancing the various factions and oligarchies. While he was willing to hail reform and improvement, he was never quite willing to push for change which, though necessary, would disturb the delicate balance he was so bent on preserving.

At least eleven times during his rule (1831–89) he used his power ·to dissolve parliament and call for new elections, convinced that the government of the party in power had lost the support of public opinion. But public opinion was extremely limited; politics reflected the local oligarchies in the provinces—sugar-planters, miners, and later coffee-planters—and the opinions of the small electorate made up of landowners and of some few thousand lawyers, physicians, engineers, priests, officials and businessmen. Even by the end of the Empire the total electorate probably numbered not much more than 150,000, around 1 per cent of the total population.

For the first twenty years of the rule of Pedro II the issue of the slave trade was never far from the centre of the political scene. Brazil's economy, once again centred on sugar (and cotton), was based on slavery, but the British, having prohibited the import of slaves into the West Indies, were determined to prevent it elsewhere too. As a gesture towards their British protectors, the Brazilians had in 1831 passed a bill prohibiting international trafficking, but nobody took any notice. For the next twenty years imports of Africans increased: by 1849 they were up to over 50,000 a year. It took drastic measures on the part of Britain (her cruisers went as far as capturing slave ships anchored in Brazilian harbours) to persuade Brazil in 1850 to adopt stringent measures. The flow ceased, at last, in 1852.

Perhaps the most important effect of ending the slave trade was the impact on Brazil's economic structure. Capital so far invested in human stock came onto the market in search of profitable employment. This led to a rise in economic activity and a surge of small-scale industry accompanied by considerable inflationary pressure during the years immediately following 1850. Contributing to this situation was the fact that protective tariffs had been raised in the previous decade and were again put up in 1860, and a further stimulus to industry was provided by the war against Paraguay (1865–70).[1] In the last analysis, however, industrial development in the

[1]See 'Paraguay', p. 104.

19th century was stunted by the smallness of the internal market. So money flowed on an increasing scale to the coffee plantations near Rio de Janeiro and São Paulo, where attempts at overcoming the labour shortage led at first to the unsuccessful use of slave and free labour side by side. Soon, however, the south turned against slavery altogether: they had become convinced that slaves made inefficient producers and non-existent consumers.

Almost forty years were to pass between the end of the slave trade and the final abolition of slavery. The half-way mark was reached late in 1871, when freedom was granted to all children born to women still in slavery. Significantly the master of the child's mother was made the legal guardian of the child and thus the effective owner of his labour till he came of age. Fourteen years later all slaves over sixty were freed. Finally, on 13 May 1888, while the emperor was in Europe for his health, the regent princess Isabel signed the decree abolishing slavery. Pedro was relieved when he received the news.

And yet for many years he had allowed successive governments influenced by the slave-owning planters to fight a rearguard action against abolition under the guise of slow but progressive legislation. When he finally gave up trying to 'moderate' an intractable conflict, a procedure which had lost him many friends and convinced the south that their interests did not lie with a highly centralised political structure, the traditional landowners (who had received no compensation) turned against him too. This sealed the fate of the Empire. On 15 November 1889 a group of military under Deodoro da Fonseca proclaimed the Republic and sent Pedro and his family into exile to Europe.

The Republic

In the years leading to the proclamation of the Republic a curious and somewhat controversial role had been played by a small group of men influenced by the positivist doctrines of Auguste Comte. Comte held that non-rational aspects of social organisation could be fully overcome and believed in the possibility of ruling society through 'positive science'. From the middle of the century onwards the professional schools in Rio de Janeiro, the polytechnic and the military academy, had been providing scientifically oriented courses some of which were frankly positivist. Education in these establishments contrasted sharply with the traditional style of learning pursued particularly in the country's various law schools, attended mainly by the sons of the landed upper class. A free education was available to all who wanted to take up a military career, and many sons of modest urban families made use of this opportunity. Benjamin Constant, an ardent positivist and declared Republican, influenced many at the military academy.

A small group, the most fanatical positivists, were faithful to the curious mixture of philosophy and religion which Comte had concocted in his older days. They had a passing influence during the first few months of the Republic; their most lasting contributions are the design for Brazil's flag, and its motto, Order and Progress. Like Comte they had dictatorial inclinations—perhaps more relevant to the Brazil of the pupils than the France of the master—and saw in the moralisation of politics and of existing social relations the cure to all evils. Ultimately, however, it was those only partly touched by positivist doctrines who contributed most to the advance of their country: the doctors, engineers, and military men who conquered disease, built roads or protected the Indians from extinction.

Straddling Empire and Republic was the first wave of immigrants. Slavery was on its last legs and hands were badly needed both on the newly opened coffee plantations and on the lands being colonised in the extreme south of Brazil. They came predominantly from Portugal, where it was increasingly hard to make a living, from Italy, following the political turmoil of 1870 and its aftermath, from Spain, Germany and later Japan. In the last decade of the century more than 100,000 people entered Brazil each year. The Italians settled mainly in and around São Paulo, where their influence is still thoroughly felt. The Portuguese went everywhere, seeking the big cities, finding employment often in commerce and working their way to small-scale independence. Germans went to the extreme south of Brazil. They remained very much a group unto themselves—as did the Japanese—speaking their own language, setting up schools and newspapers, and looking to the Fatherland for inspiration. It took special legislation towards the end of the 1930s under the Vargas dictatorship to create the conditions for their almost forcible assimilation into the mainstream of Brazilian life and culture. Ethnically, however, both groups continue to be largely separate—especially the Japanese.

The men who had been active at the top of politics under Pedro II were back where they had been formerly once conditions in the Republic had settled down, and locally the oligarchies did not change. But the centralism of the Empire was replaced by a federal structure which gave wide powers to the old provinces, now called states. This resulted in the domination of national politics by the two states most powerful in manpower and resources: São Paulo and Minas Gerais. Their state militias were veritable armies; the policies they pushed through the Federal Congress expressed the interests of their own élites, particularly those of the coffee-planters, and São Paulo and Minas supplied Brazil's civilian presidents for alternating terms of office until 1930.

The army, having been instrumental in undoing the Empire, emerged as a power to be reckoned with on the political scene. In fact the military took over the imperial moderating power, without, however, their role being clearly defined. The armed forces have been mentioned in the various constitutions as guardians of the country's political integrity, but the when and how of their possible intervention has nowhere been spelled out. At crucial moments of Brazil's 20th-century history men in top military posts have stepped in to prevent or safeguard certain political developments, sometimes supporting forces for change, at other times backing up the status quo. As a rule the armed forces have closely watched the swing of the political pendulum, intervening whenever in their opinion it was going too far. Obviously this position tends *ipso facto* to conservatism. But despite that fact they have not, on the whole, prevented gradual changes in the distribution of social and political power, nor did they make more than temporary excursions into the political arena before April 1964.

It was young army officers who provided the first open expression of the growing discontent with the functioning of the Republic. In July 1922 they sparked off a revolt against the Federal government. The whole affair, known as the Tenentes' (Lieutenants') Revolt, was on a small scale and easily repressed—but the rumblings continued throughout the following years. They erupted again in 1924, when São Paulo was held for almost a month by revolutionaries.

The old Republic was to continue harried but intact until 1930. Then the world slump finally bankrupted the economic policies of the Minas-São

Paulo axis. Since industrial expansion started in the first world war an embryonic awareness of common interests was to be found among the budding industrial bourgeoisie. The growing cities had thrown up a bureaucratic, professional and commercial middle class, while in the army the ranks of junior officers had been increasing. A measure of prosperity had come to the south of Brazil, especially to Rio Grande do Sul, though poverty and marginality continued to plague the states of the north-east. All these groups had good reasons to be thoroughly dissatisfied with the way in which the central government danced to the tunes of the dominant people in the two dominant states. When in 1930 the pseudo-democratic elections once again resulted in the victory of a representative of the old guard, the defeated candidate Getulio Vargas, ex-governor of Rio Grande do Sul, supported by the armed forces and hailed by a large section of the politically articulate population, marched on Rio and took over the country's government.

Vargas and Getulismo

It did not take the new president very long to curtail the powers of the states and thoroughly increase those of the central government. He removed state officials and replaced them by his own men, made a start with cutting the state militias down to size, and removed tariff barriers internal to the country. In 1934 a Constituent Assembly promulgated a new constitution. But although Vargas had pledged his government to a new economic policy which no longer kept Brazil mortgaged to coffee interests, he soon found out that coffee was too important for the economy to be simply disregarded. The buying up of excess stocks with Federal money continued, though now—as opposed to pre-depression days—the financing had to be done with internally created credit rather than with loans obtained abroad. Widespread unemployment in the coffee sector was avoided, and profits continued to be made. As the international economic outlook was so uncertain investment found its way to the more promising sectors producing for the home market. They were all the more attractive since large-scale import of consumer goods had become impossible: earnings of foreign currency had almost dried up after commodity prices had plunged to previously unknown depths.

Vargas, whose rule had been broadly speaking constitutional until he proclaimed the Estado Nôvo (New State) at the end of 1937, had been under attack both from the right and from the left. Urban growth and industrialisation had led to the development of an urban proletariat, a fraction of which formed a nucleus of class-conscious members of the working class. The Communist Party was small but had to be reckoned with: in November 1935 it instigated a well-planned barracks revolt which, once repressed, strengthened Vargas' hand. From the other end of the political spectrum Plínio Salgado's Integralistas pressed Vargas to move in the direction of a more explicitly fascist corporative state. Vargas was interested in being dictator, but not really inclined to formal fascism. After the declaration of the Estado Nôvo Plínio soon lost his hopes and illusions, and in May 1938 the Integralistas staged their own abortive little coup.

Vargas' putsch in 1937 had forestalled a not improbable victory at the polls, planned for early in 1938, of the traditional political machines which controlled the vast majority of Brazil's rural and small-town voters. His own concern was much more with the urban middle class, with industrialists, white-collar workers, the military and the growing working class. Under his regime the government bureaucracy expanded enormously, creating jobs for thousands of people who became dependent for their living on the government's largesse. While the second world war further stimulated Brazil's industrial development in a spontaneous and unplanned manner, Vargas gave it a directed boost by initiating in 1941 work on the nationally-owned steel plant at Volta Redonda. As for the working class, it was given a wide-ranging system of social security and, in 1943, perhaps the most advanced labour code in the world. Unfortunately its implementation has left much to be desired.

Vargas, a man who wanted to break the hold of Brazil's traditional élites on the country, took a leaf out of their book by introducing into his New State on a massive scale techniques of paternalism and the creation of bonds of dependency which had long been the dominant features of social relations in the interior. He gave the urban middle class bureaucratic employment. He gave the workers rights, social security and a trade union system directed by the ministry of labour, after prohibiting the functioning of the already existing autonomous workers' organisations. He also used the government apparatus, which he controlled by means of a chain of personal loyalties down to the municipal level, to bind people to him in gratitude for favours dispensed.

Brazil had joined the Allies in August 1942. As the war waged in the name of democracy was drawing to its conclusion, Getúlio had plans for the perpetuation of himself in power under a somewhat democratised regime. But his manoeuvres could not save him: the army intervened in October 1945 and called for his resignation. He was allowed, however, to organise his forces and participate in the elections. Two parties were formed to tap the Getulista vote; the Brazilian Labour Party, PBT, and the Social Democratic Party, PSD. The former aimed at the urban working class; the latter was a monster of incompatibility which united support for Getúlio among the middle class and bourgeoisie in the cities with the machines built up by Vargas among the traditional politicians of the interior. PTB and PSD launched General Dutra for the presidency. He easily defeated Brigadier Gomes of the UDN, the National Democratic Union—an anti-Getulista coalition of urban middle-class voters and political bosses from the interior who had been 'out' during the rule of Getúlio. Vargas himself was elected for different constituencies to the Chamber of Deputies as well as to the Senate; he chose to sit as senator from his own state of Rio Grande do Sul.

Dutra's five years of government are characterised more than anything else by economic mismanagement. Brazil's foreign currency reserves, swollen during the war, almost completely disappeared in a gay spree of indiscriminate spending. Early in 1948 the brakes were slammed on, and the country entered a period of ever more complicated import and exchange controls, which did little to alleviate the basic economic problems.[1] Nevertheless, when elections came around late in 1950 the personal magic of Vargas still worked with the masses: he was elected for a five-year term to start at the beginning of 1951.

Vargas' second government was a disappointment. Contradictory opinions of this period hold either that Vargas, now an old man harking back to the past, surrounded himself with incapable corrupt politicians—or that Vargas, with a remarkable clear-sightedness, unsuccessfully attempted to bring about an alliance of bourgeoisie, middle class and working class in

---

[1] See 'The Industrialisation of Brazil' (p. 610).

order to break the stranglehold of the oligarchies in the states. According to the latter interpretation, the army, expressing once again the will of the middle class, gradually increased the pressure on a president too interested in the masses. Both versions have the same dénouement. In August 1954 an assassination attempt on Carlos Lacerda, a prominent violently anti-Vargas journalist, appeared to be inspired by people in Vargas' immediate entourage. The leaders of the armed forces called for his resignation. Vargas, however, preferred suicide. A typewritten, unsigned 'political' testament, in which he accused international financial and economic groups of standing in the way of the Brazil he dreamt of, has left echoes which are still heard, even though its authenticity has been questioned. Vice-President Café Filho took over. Congressional elections were held in October 1954 and presidential elections a year later. Once again the Getulista ticket was victorious: Juscelino Kubitschek of the PSD was elected to the presidency, with Vargas' ex-minister of labour João Goulart of the PTB as vice-president. The result much displeased the army leaders. A great deal of plotting went on between October and December 1955 which aimed at forestalling the installation of the elected candidates. Finally General Lott, a defender of legality and a man who was loth to see the armed forces become permanently involved in politics, carried out a preventive coup which ensured that the government was constitutionally passed on to Kubitschek.

Kubitschek's presidency was a mixed blessing for the country. He built Brasília, the exciting new capital on the central plateau. He spent government money on an unprecedented scale, accelerating an hitherto fairly mild inflation into a wave which yearly added on average one quarter to the cost of living during his presidency and two-thirds during the four following years. But also under him the growth rate of Brazil's GNP reached an impressive 3 per cent a year per head. He spread a sense of purpose through the land which made Brazil into one of the most exciting countries of the continent. At the same time he allowed lots of people to make lots of money out of the enthusiasm in ways which frequently could hardly pass even Brazil's relatively mild tests of acceptable public conduct.

The five years of Kubitschek's presidency were years of glory for Brazil's industrial bourgeoisie, who almost came to believe in their destiny as a nationalistic force. They were the years of the first serious efforts at economic planning, the years of the successful Basic Targets Plan, formulated to re-adjust to each other the different sectors of the economy which had grown haphazardly in past years. But they were also years during which the existing imbalances between the industrialised south and the rest of the country were allowed to grow further. Kubitschek was not keen on confronting the traditional oligarchies in the interior, and he hoped that time and the operation of economic forces would by themselves effect the changes needed. It was during Kubitschek's term of office that some prelates of Brazil's Roman Catholic Church began to speak out with greater insistence against these imbalances and against the human misery and injustice that went with them. Especially the bishops in Brazil's neglected north-east (where per capita income was less than one-third of that in the south) began to steer the Church into active intervention in the region's social and economic problems, and also began to bring pressure to bear upon the government to take a more active interest in them.

The negative side of Kubitschek's term of office—the inflation, light-hearted optimism, the corruption—was obvious enough. After Jânio Quadros had campaigned in 1960 on the promise of cleaning out the stables

49

and providing decent, incorrupt government, he was elected with the biggest plurality in Brazilian electoral history. Quadros was somewhat of a political enigma. From out of nowhere he had risen to prominence in São Paulo. Without support from the traditional party machines he had become first mayor of the city, then governor of the state. During his presidential campaign he once more ran independently, though he was supported by the anti-Getulista parties. He stood for all things to all people; once in office he combined orthodox economic policies with progressive social ideas and an independent line in foreign policy. He spurned the hallowed methods of political patronage, and though he shook the civil service into giving of its best he soon turned hundreds of important people into his enemies. By August 1961, a mere seven months after taking office, he was being warned by the 'moderating' army to change his line and his methods. Suddenly, in one of the most curious episodes of recent Brazilian political history, he resigned—perhaps in the hope of returning with his hand strengthened by a great popular manifestation in his favour. There was, however, no chance of his return: the people were stupefied, and the army moved fast.

João Goulart of the PTB, who had been elected vice-president against Quadros' own running-mate, was a man even less palatable to the armed forces and their civilian allies than the former president himself. After a tense period of manoeuvring he was allowed to assume the presidency, but not until his powers had been drastically cut by the interposition of a prime minister between himself and Congress. The following sixteen months saw an almost complete paralysis of the country's federal administration; the period was spent in proving to the country that parliamentarianism was unworkable. Goulart regained full presidential authority in January 1963, after a conclusive plebiscite had relegated the office of prime minister to a place in the country's textbooks on constitutional law.

By that time Goulart had been convinced that the country needed both large-scale economic planning and a serious attack on the hitherto neglected problems of the countryside—not least in order to ensure a rise in agricultural productivity, ever lagging behind the increase in population which by then was running at over 3 per cent a year. Celso Furtado, who had been directing the development agency for the north-east, SUDENE, was made minister of planning, but within less than six months his cabinet post was little more than nominal, By the end of 1963 he was back full-time at SUDENE. The reshuffling of his ministry got Goulart nowhere. He was faced—as Quadros had been before him—with a Congress hostile to his ideas, dominated by legislators who expressed the interests of the most conservative forces in society. On the other hand the clamour in the country for radical policies was growing, and Goulart, a power-seeker with a demogogic streak, barked more radically than he might have been expected to bite.

The strength of left-wing sentiments was on the increase, particularly among intellectuals and students. Few of these were full-blooded Marxists, and even among the members of the illegal Brazilian Communist Party there were many who would have cut a poor figure in a more disciplined body. But the left did make concerted efforts to capture the greatest possible number of important elective or appointive posts, in government agencies and ministries as well as in voluntary organisations such as the rural trade union movement.

In partial opposition to the various groups on the left young Catholic militants, encouraged by the encyclicals of John XXIII and by the progressive stance of the Vatican Council, elaborated a radical Christian viewpoint of their own, which found expression especially in the youth movements of Catholic Action. Later this viewpoint spilled over into Ação Popular (AP), whose socialistic humanism was perhaps the most radical—without on all points being the best elaborated—ideology on the Brazilian scene.

The country was obviously in ferment. Since 1962 the working conditions of agricultural labourers had been governed by the Rural Workers' Statute, which extended the main provisions of the country's social legislation to the countryside. In some states governments had come to power which were willing to stand up for the implementation of those laws, and even negotiate with the militant Peasant Leagues—notably in the case of Pernambuco, where Miguel Arrais was elected governor late in 1962. Goulart, in deadlock with Congress, was desperate to keep the initiative in his own hands, to prevent popularity and power from shifting increasingly to such men as Arrais or his own even more left-wing brother-in-law Leonel Brizola. From early in 1964 he increasingly appealed directly to the masses, over the head of Congress. His manoeuvres were causing the most serious misgivings among those less radically inclined, from the industrialists who had been forging closer links with foreign companies, through the middle class and the army, to the dominant landowning groups in Brazil's less developed states. Late in March hundreds of thousands of women took to the streets of São Paulo and Belo Horizonte in near-hysterical anti-Goulart marches 'of the family, with God, for Liberty'. By 1 April it was all over: an army coup, supported by the governors of the powerful states of Minas, São Paulo and Guanabara (the city of Rio), deposed Goulart, exposed the myth of the well-organised and dangerous left, and disposed of the ex-president and hundreds of others by depriving them of their political rights and forcing many of them into exile.

Developments since 1964

This time the intervention of the armed forces was not, as it had been at other recent occasions, a passing affair. The presidency was bestowed upon Marshal Castelo Branco, an hitherto politically uninvolved and well-respected officer, who had participated in the Brazilian expeditionary force in Italy during the second world war and had later been identified with the Superior War College. The guiding ideas of the 'Revolucão' became to fight subversion, corruption and inflation, tasks which masked profound differences between the various anti-Goulart groups. Roberto Campos, ex-ambassador to Washington, was called upon to implement an orthodox deflationary programme which would set the country's financial house in order and restore Brazil's credit-worthiness with institutions such as the World Bank. His drastic measures affected the lowest paid half of the population much more severely than those with greater means and wider opportunities for escaping the impact of the squeeze. But they cut down inflation, which had been a little under 80 per cent during the last full year of Goulart's government, to about half that figure two years later, though for 1966 it was still well over 40 per cent. Simultaneously income-tax collection was rationalised, and perhaps for the first time ever did Brazilians (and especially salaried people in the middle-income brackets) pay taxes rather than evade them.

But Campos' economic policies have had serious side-effects. They have, for instance, led to a systematic neglect of education, despite the fact that at all levels it is in desperate need of attention. Approximately half the adult population is illiterate; the proportion is almost three quarters in the north-east. Secondary education is geared almost exclusively to university entrance. As for the universities (a few of excellent quality, most with abysmally low standards), they are hardly able to raise the proportion of graduates in engineering, agronomy, veterinary science or economics in relation to the traditional prestige-giving qualifications in medicine, dentistry or law (in 1961 law students accounted for 24 per cent of the total).

The civil-military government has been placing its hopes on the gradual success of its economic policies, on its capacity to ensure for Brazil a growing share in the material wealth of the international economic system of which the United States is the lynch-pin. Virtually its only remaining supporters late in 1966 were to be found among Brazil's great industrial enterprises, mostly engaged in basic and heavy industry, many of which have direct or indirect links with foreign companies. These links have made them impervious to the credit restrictions which heavily hit the fully national, mainly small and medium-sized firms. The latter were also more vulnerable as a result of the greater consumer-orientation of their production—and, it must be said, because of their frequently less efficient methods.

The coup of April 1964 was motivated primarily by the spectre of the masses unleashed. All activity which had contributed to that possibility was denounced as subversion—no doubt with good reason from the point of view of those interested in preserving the status quo. Soon after the coup it became apparent that among its supporters, quite apart from groups with differing economic interests, were men of different political inclinations. There were those who wished to build safeguards for the country's constitutional order, keep the swing of the pendulum within 'reasonable' limits, and return to normality as soon as possible. There were others more disposed to use the Revolucão's power to make a clean sweep. Among these there were groups of middle-rank army officers, many of them involved in ad hoc military inquiries into past subversive activities, who had vague Nasserite inclinations and looked for inspiration to Carlos Lacerda, by then governor of Guanabara, and one of the civilian leaders of the Revolucão. Castelo Branco steered a middle course between the various factions for about eighteen months; then, in November 1965, he enlarged the government's executive powers by decree and disbanded the existing political parties, which were replaced by a government party, ARENA (Aliança Renovadora Nacional), and an opposition grouping, MDB (Movimento Democrático Brasileiro). With this he drove Lacerda into violent opposition.

In October 1966 the deputies and senators of the government party (the opposition did not participate) confirmed Marshal Artur da Costa e Silva as presidential successor. In the final months of his term of office President Castelo Branco virtually forced Congress to pass a new constitution which enshrined many of the modifications brought by the successive Institutional Acts since April 1964. The shift in the balance of power which had occurred since that time, away from the states and the legislature towards the Federal executive, was confirmed in the new charter. Direct presidential elections, which had probably been the most genuine expression of the 'popular will' in Brazil, were—significantly—abolished.

Marshal Costa e Silva took over the presidency on 15 March 1967. His accession, though apparently presaging a shift in immediate policies to a greater concern with the urban masses and a more nationalistic economic line, seemed to herald the basic continuity of the political and social systems which had been underpinned by the Revolução.

BIBLIOGRAPHY

Azevedo, Thales. *Social Change in Brazil*, Univ. of Florida Press, Gainesville, Fla., 1963.

Boxer, C. R. *Race Relations in the Portuguese Colonial Empire, 1415–1825*, Oxford Univ. Press, London and New York, 1963.

Costa, João Cruz. *A History of Ideas in Brazil*, Univ. of California Press, Berkeley, Calif. and London, 1964.

Cunha, Euclydes da. *Rebellion in the Backlands*, Univ. of Chicago Press, Chicago, Ill., 1964.

Dell, Edmund. *Brazil: The Dilemma of Reform*, Fabian Society, London, 1964.

Freyre, Gilberto. *New World in the Tropics*, Vintage Books, New York, 1963.

Furtado, Celso. *Development and Underdevelopment*, Univ. of California Press, Berkeley, Calif., 1964; Cambridge Univ. Press, London, 1965. *Economic Growth of Brazil*, Univ. of California Press, Berkeley, Calif., 1963.

Havighurst, Robert J. and Moreira, J. Roberto. *Society and Education in Brazil*, Univ. of Pittsburgh Press, Pittsburgh, Pa., 1965.

Herring, Hubert. *A History of Latin America*, Jonathan Cape, London, 1961; Alfred A. Knopf, New York, 1963.

Horowitz, Irving L. *Revolution in Brazil*, E. P. Dutton, New York, 1964.

de Kadt, Emanuel. 'Religion, the Church, and Social Change in Brazil', *The Politics of Conformity in Latin America*, ed. Claudio Véliz, Oxford Univ. Press, London and New York, 1967.

Leeds, Anthony. 'Brazilian Careers and Social Structure: An Evolutionary Model and Case History', *American Anthropologist*, LXVI, 6, Part I, Washington, DC, 1964.

Robock, Stefan H. *Brazil's Developing Northeast: A Study of Regional Planning and Foreign Aid*, Brookings Institution, Washington, DC; Faber, London, 1963.

Smith, T. Lynn. *Brazil, People and Institutions*, Louisiana State Univ. Press, Baton Rouge, La., 2nd ed. 1963.

Wagley, Charles. *An Introduction to Brazil*, Columbia Univ. Press, New York and London, 1963.

BASIC INFORMATION

CLIMATE

	Corumba	Manaus	Paraná	Recife	Rio de Janeiro
Lat./long.	19°S/ 57° 30′ W	3°S/60°W	12° 30′S/ 48°W	8°S/35°W	23°S/43°W
Altitude	381 ft./ 116 m.	144 ft./ 44 m.	853 ft./ 260 m.	97 ft./30 m.	201 ft./ 61 m.
Mean temp. of hottest month	29°C/84°F (Nov.)	29°C/84°F (Oct.)	25°C/76°F (Oct.)	27°C/81°F (Jan./Feb.)	26°C/79°F (Feb.)
Mean temp. of coolest month	23°C/73°F (June)	27°C/81°F (Apl.)	21°C/70°F (July)	24°C/76°F (July)	21°C/69°F (July)
Absolute max.	41°C/ 106°F	39°C/ 101°F	40°C/ 105°F	35°C/ 94°F	39°C/ 102°F
Absolute min.	1°C/33°F	18°C/64°F	3°C/37°F	18°C/64°F	10°C/50°F
Relative humidity of hottest and coolest months	57%/66%	59%/73%	53%/51%	68%/75%	71%/68%
Wettest months	7·3 in./ 185 mm. (Jan.)	10·3 in./ 262 mm. (March)	12·2 in./ 310 mm. (Dec.)	10·9 in./ 277 mm. (June)	5·4 in./ 137 mm. (Dec.)
Driest months	0·3 in./ 8 mm. (July)	1·5 in./ 38 mm. (Aug.)	0·1 in./ 2 mm. (June)	0·5 in./ 13 mm. (Oct./Nov.)	1·6 in./ 41 mm. (July)
Annual av. rainfall	48·5 in./ 1,232 mm.	71·3 in./ 1,811 mm.	62·3 in./ 1,582 mm.	63·4 in./ 1,610 mm.	42·6 in./ 1,082 mm.

POPULATION

TOTAL (*million*): 1960 (census) 71·0, excluding jungle population estimated at 0·15 in 1956; 1966 (mid-year): 83·9; 1980 (ECLA projection): 123·6.
DENSITY, mid-1965: 10 persons per sq. km. Regional, 1960: South 31, East 20, North-East 16, Central-West 2, North less than 1.
CRUDE RATES (*per 000*), 1959–61 (ECLA data): birth 40–43; death 11–13; infant mortality (1940–50) 170.
GROWTH RATES (% *p.a.*): 1945–65: 2·9; 1960–65: 3·1.
DISTRIBUTION (% *of total pop.*): Ethnic, 1950: white 62, mixed 26, Negro 11. Foreign-born, 1950: 2·3. Language, 1950: Portuguese 98, German 1, Spanish and others less than 1. Religion, 1950: Roman Catholic 93, Protestant 3. Urban (*centres 2,000 inhab. or over*), ECLA data, 1950: 30·8; 1960: 40·3; 1980 (projection): 54. Largest cities (*000 inhab.*), 1960: São Paulo 3,825, Rio de Janeiro 3,307, Recife 797, Belo Horizonte 693, Salvador (Bahia) 656, Pôrto Alegre 641, Fortaleza 515, Belém 402, Brasília (Federal District) 142.

CONSTITUTIONAL SYSTEM

CONSTITUTION: First Republican constitution 1891, amended 1926. New constitutions 1934 and September 1946. Amended January 1967 to incorporate many legislative provisions of the Institutional Acts by the Castelo Branco government. Purpose of amendments: to strengthen the executive power and the Union at the expense of the legislative power and the states.
SYSTEM: Federal Republic. Union of Federal District (Brasília), 22 states and four federal territories. Separate executive, legislature and judiciary. States governed by own constitutions and laws. The states retain all powers not withheld by Federal constitution. Municipal autonomy in local tax and public service matters.
EXECUTIVE: Power vested in president, as specified in the 1946 constitution, which provided for election of president and vice-president by popular vote for a five-year term. Under 1967 reform, provision for indirect election of president by an electoral college comprising members of Congress and delegates of state legislatures.
LEGISLATURE (1964 constitution): Bi-cameral, National Congress of Senate and Chamber of Deputies. *Senate*: 3 members from each state and 3 from Federal Capital, elected by majority vote for 8 years, one-third or two-thirds retiring alternately every 4 years. *Deputies*: Elected by proportional representation (1 for each 150,000 inhabitants up to 20 deputies, then 1 for each 250,000 inhabitants; 1 deputy for each territory and minimum of 7 for each state and for Federal District) for 4 years. *Suffrage*: Compulsory voting for men and employed women, 18–65 years of age; optional for unemployed women and persons over 65; illiterates and servicemen excluded. Registered voters, 1962: 18·6 m. *Elections*: Presidential, October 1960: Jânio Quadros with 5·6 m. votes (45%) of 12·6 m. votes cast. João Goulart reelected vice-president with 4·5 m. votes (36%). Quadros resigned August 1961. Succeeded by Goulart, who was deposed March 1964. General Castelo Branco elected president at joint meeting of Senate and Chamber of Deputies, April 1964. Marshal Artur da Costa e Silva elected president by Congress in October 1966 and Pedro Aleixo elected vice-president; they took office on 15 March 1967. Congressional, October 1962, seats held: Chamber of Deputies (404)—Partido Social Democrático (PSD) 122, Partido Trabalhista Brasileiro (PTB) 97, União Democrática Nacional (UDN) 96, Partido Social Progressista (PSP) 23, Partido Democrático Cristão 18, others 48. Senate (66)—PSD 23, PTB 18, UDN 17, others 8. Membership of Congress and relative strength of political parties subsequently altered. In 1965 number of parties reduced to two: the pro-government Aliança Renovadora Nacional (ARENA) and the opposition Movimento Democrático Brasileiro (MDB). The government increased its majorities in November 1966 elections: of 23 senators elected, ARENA 18 and MDB 5; in Chamber of Deputies, ARENA 276 seats and MDB 133.
JUDICIARY: Judicial power exercised by Federal Supreme Court; Federal Court of Appeals; military, electoral and labour judges and courts. Federal Supreme Court

of Justice is at Brasília, and is composed of 11 (to be increased to 16) or more Federal justices appointed by president with approval of Senate. Federal courts in each state and territory. In the states justice is administered by state courts.

DEFENCE

DEFENCE BUDGET: 1965: 872,262 m. cruzeiros; 3·0% of GDP.
ARMED FORCES: National service: between 21–45 years of age; 1 year in army, 8 in reserve and 14 in a supplementary reserve. Strength (000): army 200, navy 43, air force 30; total about 275.

INTERNATIONAL RELATIONS

Member of the UN and many of its international specialised agencies, including: IBRD and affiliates, IMF, FAO, ICAO, IMCO, ILO, ITU, UNDP, UNESCO, UPU, WHO and WMO; IAEA; GATT; UNCTAD representative. Also member of OAS, Alliance for Progress, ECLA, IDB and LAFTA.

ECONOMY

PRODUCTION
LAND, 1960 (%): Arable 2, permanent pasture 13, forested 61, other 24.
OTHER AGRICULTURAL DATA: Agricultural holdings, 1960 (census); number 3·35 m., area 265 m. hectares. Tractors in use (000s), 1960: 63·5. Fertiliser consumption (000 tons), 1963: 252·5.

AGRICULTURE (000 tons)	1948–53[1]	63/64	64/65	65/66
Coffee	973	1,692	600	2,220
Cotton (fibre)[2]	395	652	590	662
Cacao[2]	124	143	154	178
Beans, dry	1,256	1,951	2,290	1,513
Rice	3,025	6,345	7,580	5,072
Maize	5,916	9,408	12,912	10,369
Sugar cane[3]	1,649	3,333	3,827	4,800
Mandioca (Cassava)	12,466	22,249	24,356	24,993
Bananas	2,207	6,262	6,764	6,970
Oranges and tangerines	1,320	2,223	2,485	.
Sisal[2]	44	199	229	242
Tobacco[2]	113	207	210	248

[1] Average 1948/9 − 1952/3.　[2] Calender years 1948/52, 1963, 1964, 1965.　[3] Raw value.

LIVESTOCK: Nos. (m. head), 1965: cattle 91, pigs 63, sheep 22. Products (000 tons), 1964: meat 2,065 (beef and veal 1,437, pork 578); cattle hides 181; wool (greasy) 28·1.
FISH: Landed (000 tons), 1964: total 331; sardines 47·5, corvina 31·2, shrimps 27·2.
MINING, 1964 (000 tons): metallic content of ores: iron 11,541 (1960: 6,355), copper 3, lead 17, manganese 594, chrome 16, nickel 1·04, tin 1·22; (tons) gold (mined) 4·4, silver 9·5, tungsten 190, zirconium 516, beryllium 576, titanium (rutile) 326. Other important minerals include (000 tons): bauxite 132, asbestos 133, phosphate 278, magnesite 94, graphite 4·7, mica 1·5, quartz crystal 0·8, diamonds (350,000 metric carats). Fuels (m. tons): coal (incl. waste) 2·9; (m. cubic metres) crude petroleum 5·3, natural gas 532.
MANUFACTURING, 1964 (000 tons): pig iron 2,487, steel ingots 3,089, finished steel 2,385, plates and sheets 1,055, tin plate 145, aluminium 27, lead 13, tin 2, copper 2, cement 5,171, pulp for paper etc. 570, newsprint 119, tobacco 210, sugar 3,425; (m. litres) wine 178, beer 661; (m. cubic metres) diesel oil 3·7, fuel oil 6·2, motor spirit 5·60; (000 units) motor vehicles: cars 111, commercial vehicles 73. Merchant vessels launched 42,000 g.r. tons (1960: nil).

CONSTRUCTION (*ooo sq. metres floor area*), 1965: building permits issued in state capitals 8,494, São Paulo 4,517.

ENERGY

CONSUMPTION (*tons coal equiv.*), 1964: total 28·7 m., per head 0·36.
ELECTRICITY, 1965: generated (*kwh.*) 31,600 m., installed capacity (*kw*) 7·41 m.

GOVERNMENT EXPENDITURE

DISTRIBUTION (% *of total*): Federal govt., 1965: defence 23, education and health 14; states and Federal District, 1964: education 15, health 7.

GROSS PRODUCT

GDP (*ooo m. cruzeiros*): at current market prices, 1964: 18,867; 1965: 31,034; at 1949 market prices, 1964: 441; 1965: 468. Per head (*US$*), UN estimate, 1963: 156.
DISTRIBUTION (%), 1960: agriculture 28; mining, manufacturing and construction 26; trade 12; transport and communications 8.
GROWTH RATES (%), 1950–60: total 5·8, per head 2·7; 1960–63: total 4·7, per head 1·5.

EXTERNAL TRADE (*US$ m.*)	1955	1960	1964	1965	1966
EXPORTS (f.o.b.)	1,423	1,269	1,430	1,595	1,741
Coffee	844	713	760	707	777
Cotton	131	46	108	96	111
Iron ore	30	54	80	103	101
Sugar (cane)	47	58	33	57	80
Pinewood	58	43	46	53	56
Cacao	91	69	35	28	51
IMPORTS (c.i.f.)	1,306	1,462	1,263	1,096	1,496
TRADE BALANCE	+117	−193	+167	+499	+245

DIRECTION OF TRADE (%)

	Exports			Imports		
	1955	1960	1965	1955	1960	1965
LAFTA	(10·2)	7·0	12·3	(14·9)	7·4	17·3
USA	42·3	44·4	31·3	23·6	30·3	29·7
EEC	18·5	19·6	25·8	20·5	20·1	17·0
UK	4·2	5·1	3·9	1·4	3·5	2·8

FINANCE

EXCHANGE RATE (*cruzeiros/US$*): Free market, end-year, 1960: 205; 1964: 1,850; 1965: 2,220; Feb. 1967: 2,715 = 2·715 new cruzeiros.
BALANCE OF PAYMENTS (*US$m.*): Goods and services (net), 1960: −521; 1964: +39; 1965: +198.
COST OF LIVING (*Dec. 1958 = 100*), São Paulo, December 1960: 189; 1965: 2,060; 1966: 3,010.
INDUSTRIAL WAGES: Average earnings per month (*cruzeiros*), 1965 (sample): 104,000; in industry, in São Paulo 108,000.
TREASURY ACCOUNTS (*ooo m. cruzeiros*), 1965; Revenue 3,140, expenditure 3,728; deficit 588, financed by Central Bank 265, treasury bills 323.

EMPLOYMENT

ECONOMICALLY ACTIVE (%), 1960 (sample): Total pop. 32 (men 53, women 12). In agriculture and fishing 52, manufacturing 9, trade 7, transport and communications 5.

TRANSPORT AND COMMUNICATIONS

RAILWAYS: Traffic, 1964: 17,004 m. passenger-km., 18,411 m. net ton-km. Length of track: 35,349 km.
MOTOR VEHICLES: In use (*ooo*), 1964: passenger cars 906, commercial vehicles 898.
National road system, 1964: 548,510 km.

SHIPPING: Merchant fleet (*ooo g.r. tons*), 1965: 1,253. International sea-borne shipping (*million tons*), 1965: goods loaded 19·7, goods unloaded 16·6. Main ports: Santos, Rio de Janeiro, Vitória, Salvador (Bahia) São Sebastião, Recife, Paranaguá and Rio Grande.
AIR: Scheduled services, 1965: Total, 2,778 m. pass.-km., 85·2 m. cargo ton-km. International, 991 m. pass.-km., 33·6 m. cargo ton-km. Main airports: São Paulo, Rio de Janeiro (GB); Santos Dumont and Galeão; Recife; Brasília; Pôrto Alegre and Belém.
TELEPHONES: No. in use, 1964: 1·26 m.

SOCIAL WELFARE

SYSTEM: Social insurance benefits and services provided mainly by trade unions and corresponding institutes; financed by employees' and employers' contributions up to a maximum of 10 times highest minimum wage: employees 9% and employers 12% plus. Employment legislation covers working hours; holidays; payment of wages, overtime and annual bonus; employers' liability for compensation for accidents, dismissal and death indemnities. Unemployment assistance programme has been introduced. Labour code under review.
HEALTH: 3,600 persons per physician, 360 persons per hospital bed.
NUTRITION: Net food supply (*per head per day*), 1962: 2,920 calories; protein: 69 g.

EDUCATION

ILLITERACY RATE (%), 1950: 10 years and over, 51.
COMPULSORY: 4 years (between 7 and 11 years of age). School enrolment ratios (%), 1st and 2nd levels, 1963: 43, adjusted 58.
SCHOOLS, 1963: Primary: no. 109,000, pupils 8·9 m., teachers 0·29 m. Secondary: no. 4,607, p. 1·25 m., t. 74,500. Technical: no. 2,117, st. 0·32 m., t. 27,500. Teacher-training: no. 1,615, st. 148,600, t. 18,500. Higher (including universities, faculties): no. 1,227, st. 124,200; t. 28,900.

UNIVERSITIES (mainly 1963/64 data):
Official: 24, including: Universidade da Bahia, Salvador 6,000 students, academic staff 550; Brasil, Rio de Janeiro, GB 8,250 st., a.s. 1,410; Brasília 872 st., a.s. 154 (133 f.-t.); Ceará, Fortaleza 4,851 st., a.s. 558 (63 f.-t.); Juiz de Fora 1,312 st., a.s. 234; Minas Gerais, Belo Horizonte 3,600 st., a.s. 820; Pará, Belém 1,400 st., a.s. 300; Paraná, Curitiba 6,234 st. +38,635 external st., a.s. 649; Recife 4,603 st.; Rio Grande do Sul, Pôrto Alegre 4,300 st., a.s. 1,050; Santa Maria, RG do S 2,073 st., a.s. 241 (17 f.-t.); São Paulo 11,147 st., a.s. 2,012.
Catholic: Universidade Católica de Bahia, Salvador; U.C. de Campinas, SP, 2,105 students, academic staff 307 part-time; U. de Goiás, Goiânia 1,082 st., a.s. 133 (20 f.-t.); U.C. de Minas Gerais, Belo Horizonte 320 st., a.s. 80; Pontifícia U.C. de Paraná, Curitiba 1,250 st., a.s. 200; U.C. de Pelotas 1,500 st., a.s. 200; U.C. de Pernambuco, Recife 950 st., a.s. 50; P.U.C. de Rio Grande do Sul, Pôrto Alegre 2,965 st.. a.s. 376 (10 f.-t.); P.U.C. de Rio Janeiro, GB 3,512 st., a.s. 405; P.U.C. de São Paulo 3,670 st., a.s. 540.

MASS MEDIA

BROADCASTING: No. of receivers in use, end-1964: TV 2·2 m.; radio 7·5 m. Stations: TV 32, radio 924 transmitters.
CINEMAS: No., 1963: 3,260. Attendance, 1963: total 314 m., per head 4·1.
NEWSPRINT: Consumption, 1963: total 199,100 tons, per head 2·6 kg.
NEWSPAPERS: Daily, 1963: 255. Circulation 4·2 m.; copies per ooo of population, 54. Principal dailies (*circulation, ooos*), Rio de Janeiro: *A Noticia* 80 (Sunday 160), *Diário de Noticias* 80 (s. 150), *Correio da Manha* 60, *Diário Carioca* 60, *Jornal do Brasil* 54 (s. 128), *O Globo* (evening) 197, *Brazil Herald* 15 (s. 18). São Paulo: *O Estado de São Paulo* 150 (s. 200), *A Gazeta* 100 (Monday 120). Pôrto Alegre: *Correio do Povo* 60, *Diário de Notícias* 40, Santos: *A Tribuna* 48.
BOOKS: Titles published, 1963: 5,133.

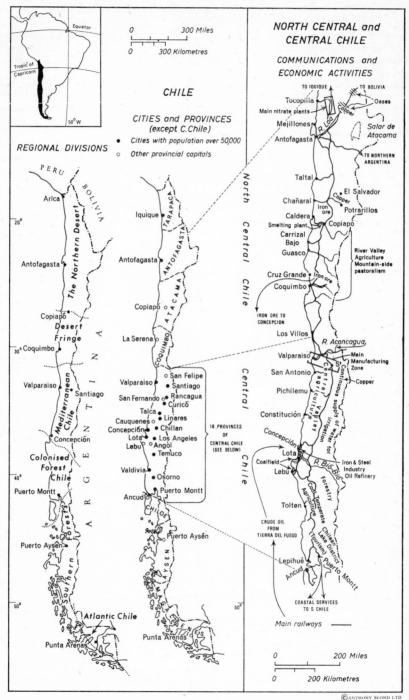

CHILE. The provinces of Central Chile are: Aconcagua (capital San Felipe), Valparaíso, Santiago, O'Higgins (Rancagua), Colchagua (San Fernando), Curicó, Talca, Maule (Cauquenes), Linares, Nuble (Chillan), Concepción, Bío-Bío (Los Angeles), Arauco (Lebu), Malleco (Angol), Cautín (Temuco), Valdivia, Osorno, Llanquihue (Puerto Montt). The name of the provincial capital is given in brackets except where it is the same as the name of the province

CHILE

FREDRICK B. PIKE

HISTORY

From independence to 1938

CHILEANS had to obtain their independence twice from the Spaniards. Once they did it on their own, in the period between 1810 and 1814. But royalist forces from Peru swept down upon the land and reimposed colonial rule. José de San Martín's patriot army, trained in Mendoza on the eastern side of the Andes, then made a remarkable crossing of the mountains and with the assistance of Chilean freedom fighters in 1817 routed the Spaniards. By 1820 San Martín had gone on to liberate Peru and the Chileans were left to work out their own political destiny under the initial leadership of one of their heroes of the independence movement, Bernardo O'Higgins.

Chile at this time faced many of the same problems that brought chaos and civil war to sister republics. One group of intellectuals and statesmen, made up of both civilians and military officers, desired to preserve conservative traditions. They stressed authority, social hierarchy and discipline, and argued the need for presidential supremacy, centralism, close church-state collaboration, and government supervision of the economy. On the other hand liberals stressed individual liberty and the need for social openness, and advanced the causes of parliamentary supremacy, federalism, anticlericalism and the unregulated market economy. O'Higgins sought to achieve a compromise between conservatives and liberals, failed to satisfy either, and was forced into exile in 1823.

Seven years of chaos ensued until conservative forces under the military officer Joaquín Prieto and the civilian businessman Diego Portales crushed their opponents in 1830 and ushered in the period of the 'Autocratic Republic.' Although killed in 1837, Portales was the great architect and guiding genius of the Autocratic Republic. Conservative because of pragmatic rather than doctrinaire reasons, he avoided fanaticism and established a tradition of political moderation.

In addition to the wisdom of some of their statesmen, Chileans were aided in their quest for stability by geographic and ethnic factors. Because the still unconquered Araucanian Indians controlled much of the region south of Concepción, and would continue to do so until 1883, and because the uninviting desert lay to the north of Coquimbo, the Chilean population was concentrated in a central valley region extending from north to south between the Andes and a range of coastal mountains. The central valley made up about one-third both of Chile's overall length of 2,600 miles and of its 286,396 square miles of territory. Communications in this all-important region presented comparatively few problems. Moreover, the Chilean population was relatively homogeneous despite a significant minority of Basque origin. The Araucanian Indians were not numerous and Chile has never been faced with the difficulties arising from a huge and unassimilated Indian mass. As of the 1830s the Indians represented only a military rather than a social problem and as of 1960 they constituted virtually no problem at all; in that year there were only about 200,000 Indians in all Chile.

During the period of the Autocratic Republic economic development went hand in hand with political stability. A relatively poor and neglected part of the Spanish colonial empire with virtually no utilised resources except its fertile central valley lands, Chile began in the 1830s to reveal its vast mineral wealth to a number of intrepid prospectors. First there were impressive silver strikes followed by discovery of coal deposits. Then, in the 1870s the nitrates of the northern desert region began to produce immense wealth for the Republic. Already by 1864 approximately 70 per cent of Chile's exports by value consisted of mine products, while by 1881 the figure had risen to over 78 per cent. Mining helped trigger a general process of economic expansion. New banks were formed rapidly and between 1845 and 1860 the volume of commerce tripled. A great boon to trade was the completion in 1863 of the railroad connecting Santiago, the capital city in the middle of the central vally, to Valparaíso, the country's main port. The mid-19th century also witnessed the beginnings of scientific livestock-raising in the south. Wine production became increasingly important and by 1865 there were twenty-six breweries in the country, some of them owned by the German immigrants who in the late 1850s had begun to settle in considerable numbers in the Puerto Mont-Puerto Varas region of southern central Chile.

Rapid economic expansion produced a veritable social revolution in Chile. Rather than remaining static and closed, the traditional landed aristocracy opened its ranks willingly and almost eagerly to men of new wealth. By the latter part of the 19th century the aristocracy was studded with new Chilean as well as English, Scottish, French and German names. In May 1883 Valparaíso's leading daily *El Mercurio* noted that of the fifty-nine personal fortunes in Chile of over one million pesos only twenty-four were of colonial origin while the remainder belonged to coal, nitrate, copper and silver interests, or to merchants and bankers, all of whom had begun their march toward fortune in the post-independence period. The striking degree to which a colonial aristocracy absorbed men of new wealth whose operations were largely urban-centred contributed to Chile's political stability by preventing the development of rural-city conflicts.

By the late 1840s a new generation of liberal intellectuals and statesmen had arisen. Under the leadership of Francisco Bilbao, Santiago Arcos and many others, they demanded extension of the suffrage, decentralisation, curtailment of presidential powers, and suppression of the church's temporal influence. These issues, and most particularly that of the church, led to the emergence by the end of the 1850s of two of Chile's political parties of major historical importance. The Liberal Party asserted that the individual could develop his inherent virtue only through democracy and that democracy could never be introduced so long as the church excercised the power to control the political decisions of the faithful. On the other hand, the avowedly confessional and somewhat ultramontanist Conservative Party declared that the weakening of church influence would lead to the general dissolution of society. Reasons of expediency actually led Liberals and Conservatives to cooperate throughout the 1860s. By the mid-1870s, however, the Liberal-Conservative fusion had been dissolved. Liberals at this time found new allies in the Radical Party which had elected its first deputies to Congress in 1864, and the Conservative Party ceased for many years to wield appreciable power.

Between 1865 and 1885 the Chilean republic was considerably liberalised. Political practices and even the constitution itself, framed in 1833 under the Portales influence, were modified to provide for a system in which ministers were largely responsible to Congress. Suffrage was expanded by reduction of property requirements and the church was deprived of its control over cemeteries and the civil register and, more significantly, of much of its influence in education. The anticlerical programme was spearheaded by the Radical Party which regarded its fundamental purpose to be the ending of church intervention in the temporal order.

Chilean stability had become sufficiently well established to survive the reemergence of the Conservative-Liberal dispute. Changes that were produced elsewhere in Latin America only through bloodshed and civil war were introduced by peaceful and constitutional means in Chile, even though a few zealous churchmen occasionally resorted to mass excommunication of political foes. By 1879 the country was still characterised by political order, which in turn contributed to the essentially uninterrupted process of economic development. These factors were basically responsible for Chile's victory in the War of the Pacific (1879–83) over the combined forces of Peru and Bolivia.

Politically disorganised and unable to proceed with consistency toward economic development, Peru and Bolivia had not adequately developed their considerable coastal nitrate resources. Enterprising Chilean entrepreneurs had become active in the nitrate industries of the two sister republics and from this situation arose economic disputes which led to the eruption of armed hostilities. Gaining control of the seas by 1880, Chile crushed its two adversaries and by 1883 had expanded its frontiers far to the north, acquiring vast new nitrate resources and depriving Bolivia of its coastal region and Peru of a considerable portion of its southern coastal desert area. Not until 1929, when it was agreed that Chile would retain Arica and that Tacna, occupied since the war by Chilean forces, would revert to Peru, was a definitive boundary agreement reached between the two countries.

The military challenge from abroad overcome, Chile in 1891 temporarily succumbed to internal difficulties and for the first time since 1830 engaged in a brief civil war. Elected to the presidency in 1886, handsome, slender, dynamic José Manuel Balmaceda decided that his country, despite its military victory and acquisition of imposing new resources, was slipping into a period of inertia. Centralised economic planning was necessary, Balmaceda felt, so that government revenue deriving from export taxes on nitrates would be invested in special development projects rather than used to defray ordinary costs of administration. To meet the ordinary costs of government, Balmaceda proposed a new series of imposts on business firms and individuals. He also urged steps to prevent foreign, especially British, interests from acquiring complete control over Chilean nitrates. Satisfied that only a strong president could institute changes of the magnitude he had in mind, Balmaceda became arbitrary in his actions and attempted to curtail the powers of Congress. Many of his ideas were sound but, with the advent of the vogue of positivism, laissez-faire economic practices were championed with more rabid enthusiasm than ever before and Balmaceda's designs for government planning were denounced in most circles. Led by naval officers, forces which believed in a parliamentary political system and an unregulated market economy precipitated a civil war and drove the president from power in September 1891.

Chile's period of parliamentary government, during which presidents were distinguished primarily by their inactivity, endured from 1892 to 1920. During those years the country's leadership narrowly averted a war with Argentina over boundary disputes, reaching an often strained and uneasy accord with the neighbour republic in 1902, and witnessed with satisfaction the expansion of mining and industrial activities as well as the completion in 1909 of the trans-Andean railroad between Valparaíso and Buenos Aires. However, this was in general an era of apathy on the part of the ruling classes whose attitude was best summarised by Ramón Barros Luco, president from 1910 to 1915, when he observed: 'There are two kinds of problems, those which have no solution and those which solve themselves'.

New problems which appeared in the early 20th century did not solve themselves. Labour unrest became commonplace and strikes, some of them violently suppressed, increased in frequency. In 1910 Alejandro Venegas, a school-teacher, published under a pseudonym *Sinceridad*, an eloquent and indignant commentary on the country's mounting social problems. Predictably, the book was largely ignored.

One basic cause of Chile's social problems was a rural to urban demographic shift. Between 1892 and 1920 the country's population rose only from 3·3 to 3·8 million. Yet the urban population, a mere 27 per cent of the total in 1875, was over 43 per cent in 1907. From 1885 to 1895 the number of inhabitants in Santiago increased by over 30 per cent and by 1907 had mounted an additional 22 per cent. Population growth in Antofagasta, Iquique, Concepción, and Valparaíso tended to be even more striking. In the course of the population shift the old paternalism and sense of *noblesse oblige* that had frequently characterised *patrón-inquilino* (master-serf) relations broke down and urban labouring forces became subject to an intense form of exploitation. The economic dislocations of the first world war, during which Chile joined with Argentina in maintaining a neutrality that was actually pro-German, vastly exacerbated the situation.

In the 1920 presidential campaign Arturo Alessandri Palma was the candidate of the Liberal Alliance, a political grouping made up of parties, including the Liberals and Radicals as well as the nearly defunct Democrats, that had important support among the growing middle sectors of society. Waging a new type of campaign Alessandri appealed to the lower classes, extending glittering promises of social reform. Apparently his goal was to substitute a system of government-administered paternalism for the old structure of private paternalism that was ceasing to function. Elected by a narrow margin over Luis Barros Borgoño, candidate of the National Union whose main strength came from the Conservatives, Alessandri was at first unable to win congressional approval for any of his mild and moderate reform measures. Following a brief period of military intervention during which he was exiled, Alessandri was recalled in 1925 and presided over the adoption of a new constitution.

The 1925 constitution replaced one which, with amendments, had been in effect since 1833. In addition to reestablishing presidential rule, the new constitution provided for church-state separation, despite the passionate opposition of the clergy and the Conservative Party, and introduced an impressive body of social and labour laws.

After a brief interlude of political confusion a military man, Carlos Ibáñez del Campo, seized the presidency in 1927, ushering in a four-year period of mild dictatorship that witnessed many positive accomplishments and establishment of the institutions through which Chile would be governed for the ensuing quarter-century. The increasing rate of United States economic penetration which had been apparent during Alessandri's administration continued under Ibáñez. Amounting to some $200 million in 1920, United States direct investment had more than doubled by 1929. Between 1925 and 1929 foreign capital, with United States dollars accounting for 60 per cent of the whole, represented an average of 36 per cent of total annual investments in Chile. When the world-wide depression struck in 1929 and Chile lost its markets and ready access to foreign investment and loan capital, catastrophic results ensued. The value of exports declined by over 80 per cent in three years and the economic crisis led to the overthrow of Ibáñez in 1931 and to a brief period of political instability. Presidential elections in December 1932 in which Arturo Alessandri was chosen for a second term heralded Chile's return to constitutional order.

During the 1920s first Alessandri and then Ibáñez had failed to produce an adequate system of government paternalism. Although foreign capital had contributed to prosperity in some sectors, the trickle-down to the needy had been negligible and neither president seemed willing to inaugurate tax programmes aimed at capturing adequate amounts of internal capital to finance expensive social programmes. In their unwillingness to introduce basic tax revisions Alessandri and Ibáñez reflected the sentiments of the large middle groups which supported them. Because the aristocracy was continuing to open its ranks to new members, Chile's expanding middle groups still hoped for and occasionally achieved, as in the 19th century, a rise to upper-class status. Middle groups, by and large, therefore, remained the effective guardians of the privileged élite.

In the second Alessandri administration (1932–8) the most notable political development was the accord reached between Conservatives and Liberals. Long sharing similar beliefs about the socio-economic structure and agreed that the established order had to be maintained intact, Conservatives and Liberals had differed mainly over the church-state issue. When Conservatives saw that the separation proclaimed in 1925 did not lead to persecution of the church but instead seemed to benefit it, they saw no reason to continue their dispute with the Liberals and joined with them in backing the Alessandri regime.

Happily accepting Conservative–Liberal support, Alessandri and his finance minister, Gustavo Ross, devoted themselves to economic recovery rather than reform, upholding what seems to be the historical rule that Latin American republics do not initiate basic social transformations in times of particularly acute economic crises. With the intense debates raging among Fascists, Communists, Marxian Socialists and proponents of classical economics, the president could probably not have won, even had he conscientiously sought it, concerted support for any ideological approach to reform. Apparently on the threshold of significant change in 1920, Chile remained fundamentally unaltered as of 1938.

From 1938 to 1958

For the 1938 presidential elections a Popular Front was formed by the Radical, Socialist and Communist parties. Owing largely to last-minute support from the Fascists, the Popular Front candidate Pedro Aguirre Cerda, a member of the Radical Party, triumphed over Gustavo Ross and his Conservative–Liberal partisans. Although the Socialists soon ceased to collaborate in the government and Aguirre Cerda died in 1941, the Front initiated three years of the most energetic administration that Chile had yet enjoyed in the 20th century. A development corporation (Corporación de Fomento or CORFO) was founded to provide government stimulus to industry, extensive housing and school building programmes were undertaken, and all the while labour union membership soared as real wages for the working classes advanced.

By 1942 the Radical Party was showing signs of division and a strong centre-right group was no longer willing to cooperate either with Socialists or Communists. This group advanced the candidacy of Juan Antonio Ríos in 1942 and helped assure victory for him in the presidential elections, thus initiating ten years of Radical ascendency. Ríos died in 1945, after having slowly led Chile into a pro-Allied position in the second world war, and was succeeded the following year by another Radical leader, pleasure-loving Gabriel González Videla. The ten years of Radical rule were notable primarily for mounting inflation, with wages beginning to lag behind cost of living increases, for suspension of various social projects begun by the Popular Front, and for proliferation of the bureaucracy: between 1940 and 1955 the bureaucracy increased by 60 per cent (from 72,000 members to 116,000) while the country's entire active population expanded by 23·5 per cent. Disgruntled voters in 1952 endorsed a man whose symbol was a broom and who promised to do away with the waste and inefficiency of the previous ten years of government. This was Carlos Ibáñez, the dictator of the 1927–31 period. With his candidacy officially supported only by two minor parties, Ibáñez was elected by one of the largest majorities in the nation's history.

As constitutional president Ibáñez displayed little of the energy that had characterised his dictatorial rule. Flirting briefly with Peronism, he ultimately rejected any notion of attempting to introduce extensive changes and reforms. He filled his time largely with political manoeuvring and dealing with a never-ending series of cabinet crises. In all, he appointed 135 different ministers ranging from far right to far left. Although new legislation encouraged additional foreign investment in the copper industry, the economy continued to lag.

When the 1958 presidential elections took place a vast segment of the electorate expressed discontent with the preceding sixteen years of governmental inertia by voting for Salvador Allende, candidate of a Communist-Socialist alliance, the Frente de Acción Popular (FRAP). Allende failed by only some 35,000 votes (he received 352,915) to defeat Liberal Jorge Alessandri Rodríguez (who won 387,297 votes), son of Arturo Alessandri and candidate of the Conservative and Liberal parties. The Christian Democratic candidate, Eduardo Frei Montalva, received 255,168 votes, while the Radical Party standard-bearer Luis Bossay drew 190,832.

The rise of the Christian Democratic Party

The most significant aspect of the 1958 elections was the strength shown by two new political groups. One of these, the FRAP, had been organised only in 1956. It united various Marxian socialist groups, whose principal leaders included Allende and Raúl Ampuero, with the Chilean Communist Party which, suppressed by the González Videla administration but allowed to function under a different name, was relegalised by Ibáñez at the end of his term. Under the leadership of such men as Elías Lafertte, 'the grand old man of Chilean communism,' Carlos Contreras Labarca, a one-time leader of the Chilean University Students who joined the Party in 1931 and served from then until 1947 as its secretary-general, and Luis Corvalán, the principal political strategist during the late 1950s and early 1960s, the Communist Party had come to enjoy a respected position among Chilean intellectuals. Together with various socialist groups it had also succeeded in giving a strong Marxian orientation to the organised labour movement.

Basically, the FRAP has been an uneasy alliance, in part because Chile's Marxian Socialists are strongly nationalistic and suspicious of internationally controlled movements. Traditionally, moreover, the Socialists have advocated immediate social revolution while the Communists, since 1935, have been committed to gradualism in the belief that the times are not propitious for drastic change. The FRAP was weakened in the early- and mid-1960s by the cleavage between Peking and Moscow oriented Communists. After a considerable struggle the Moscow group managed to retain supremacy in the Party as well as the decision-making majority over Marxian Socialist members.

The other new political group that made a strong showing in the 1958 elections was the Christian Democratic Party (PDC). The PDC originated in 1937 as the Falange Nacional, the guiding spirit coming from such youthful leaders as Eduardo Frei, Bernardo Leighton, and Manuel Garreton Walker, all of them former Conservatives. At first the Party attracted virtually no popular support. In 1957, however, the Falange, which had become more outspoken in attacking social and economic ills and demanding basic reform, changed its name to the Christian Democratic Party and began to establish the smoothly-functioning and comprehensive organisational system that helped towards its impressive showing in 1958.

Chile's Christian Democrats regard social pluralism and political democracy as essential goals. They also accept religious pluralism as an established fact of national existence and maintain that theirs is not a confessional party—a necessary position in view of the continuing strength of Chilean anticlericalism and the rapidly increasing Protestant population. Advocating what they term the 'Communitarian Society,' Christian Democrats assert that capitalism as practised in the United States is opposed to natural-law morality, being concerned with the profit of the few rather than the common good. Strongly opposed to the materialistic godlessness of communism, Christian Democrats stress the need for an economically integrated Latin America to assume a third position between capitalism and communism. In advocating a united Latin America as the means of escaping the overweaning influence and intervention of powerful foreign countries, Christian Democrats hearken back to a long-recurring theme in Chilean diplomatic history.

Taking office at a time of obviously widespread discontent, Jorge Alessandri, an efficient administrator of impeccable integrity but lacking personal magnetism, sought to bring about certain modifications within the established order. Although not markedly daring, Alessandri's ideas were often too advanced for the Conservative–Liberal–Radical alliance called the Democratic Front on which the president depended for congressional support. By this time the Radicals had distinctly moved from the position to the left of centre that they had occasionally occupied in the 1930s and early 1940s and had taken up a new one that was considerably to the right of centre. A mild land reform bill submitted by Alessandri was rendered virtually meaningless through numerous amendments before gaining the approval in 1962 of the Democratic Front congressional majority. Furthermore, Alessandri was unsuccessful in fulfilling his major purpose, the curtailing of inflation. Between January 1959 and September 1962 the cost of living rose 61 per cent; in 1964 alone it increased approximately 40 per cent. The escudo was devalued several times and foreign exchange reserves plummeted alarmingly.

As the 1964 elections approached Conservative and Liberal leaders failed to persuade the still popular Alessandri, whose good intentions and contributions to housing programmes were widely recognised, to support a constitutional amendment permitting immediate reelection. They concluded then that the charismatic Christian Democratic candidate Frei offered the only hope for defeating the rather stolid Allende, standard-bearer once again of the FRAP. Although the Democratic Front at first advanced the candidacy of the Radical Julio Durán, most of its members swung their support to Frei. Between 1958 and 1964 the number of registered voters had increased from 1,750,000 to nearly 3 million in an estimated total population (1964) of 8·3 million—illiterates and military personnel have always been disenfranchised. With 2·5 million of those registered actually voting Frei received 56 per cent of the votes, Allende 39 per cent and Durán just under 5 per cent.

The elections revealed a sharp decline in traditional rightist parties. Chilean politics had become polarised between one party urging sweeping change and indeed a social revolution in freedom and with a Christian basis, and another calling for a Marxian-inspired redistribution of wealth and implying that a certain element of authoritarian direction might be necessary at least in the initial stage of the class revolution. This polarisation became even more discernible in March 1965 when congressional elections resulted in an absolute majority for Christian Democrats in the Chamber of Deputies and also increased the strength of the FRAP.

The Chilean sociologist Eduardo Hamuy has theorised that by the 1960s the middle class had grown so dramatically, coming to represent perhaps 1·5 million persons, that its members could no longer hope for accommodation within the aristocracy. Abandoning their traditional tendency to identify with the aristocracy which they had once hoped to join, middle sectors decided to unite with the lower classes in a new political alignment that would hopefully be mutually advantageous. The middle class, speculates Hamuy, therefore supported the Christian Democrats.

In the 1964 campaign Christian Democrats met the middle class more than half way. Moderating some of the promises that had been extended to the masses in the 1957–63 period, Party leaders began to stress productivity rather than redistribution and opportunity rather than equality in an obvious appeal to public and private managerial and technical personnel. Chile's middle class, however, is too fragmented and heterogeneous to have accounted alone for the Christian Democratic victory.

Women of all social classes played an important role in Frei's triumph, giving him 63 per cent of their votes compared to 32 per cent for Allende. Probably they were influenced by the advanced position adopted in the early 1960s by the Catholic Church. This position has been ably championed by Raúl Silva Henríquez, the progressive cardinal-archbishop of Santiago, and succinctly explained in a 1962 joint pastoral letter of the Chilean hierarchy (*El deber social y político en la hora presente*) stressing the need for rapid attainment of social justice based on Christian norms. In the two cities of Santiago and Valparaíso, which together account for 40 per cent of the country's votes and which employ 30 per cent of the active population in industry, Frei received majority endorsement from the working classes, male and female. In addition he won the backing of large landowners, middle-class farmers, businessmen and clerks of provincial towns, and better-paid mining workers of the northern copper area, although FRAP candidate Allende carried the copper zone. The elections revealed that while Communist-Socialist strength was decreasing somewhat in the large cities, where the FRAP apparently suffered because of its continuing approval of the Cuban revolution with which middle sectors were disillusioned, it was mounting among rural workers and peasants.

ECONOMY

The division of the Chilean electorate between two parties both of which urge major structural changes must be traced to the fact that since the second world war the country has been stagnant and complacent at the top, abused and impatient at the bottom.

Stagnation at the top is suggested by statistics which show that manufacturing production (employing about 20 per cent of the active population) increased only 22 per cent between 1955 and 1959 while the population rose 16 per cent. Chile underwent sufficient industrialisation between the two world wars to become a moderately developed rather than an underdeveloped country, but by the late 1940s had entered a period of economic deterioration. Factors contributing to the present situation include, in addition to ineffective anti-inflation programmes, a tax structure that calls upon wealthy groups to pay only some 15 per cent of their income in taxes and an overall investment rate in productive enterprise during the 1950s that averaged merely 11 per cent of GNP.

The agrarian sector of the economy (employing about 30 per cent of the active labour force) also showed signs of deterioration during the early and middle 1960s. Per capita food production declined, in part because the 1·5 per cent of the landowners who owned 70 per cent of the usable terrain had no interest in expanding productivity. As a result Chile by 1965 spent one-fifth of its approximately $500 million import expenditure on food.

Between 1940 and 1954 there occurred a regressive redistribution of income carried out at the expense of the lower-income groups, and between 1950 and 1960 an absolute decline in wages took place. Numerous other statistics point to the existence of a culture of poverty. The top 5 per cent of Chile's higher-income groups enjoys a mean annual income twenty-two times greater than the average income of labourers. As of the early 1960s, 50 per cent of working-class children did not finish the third grade and 27 per cent finished only one year of school. The illiteracy rate, moreover, has remained constant at between 20 and 25 per cent during the past thirty years. The infant mortality rate, owing largely to malnutrition, is one of the highest in the world and clinical tests conducted in 1960 indicated that the average height of the population was declining due to undernourishment.

The demographic shift which began before the turn of the century has continued and by 1965 the population was over 65 per cent urban. Santiago alone boasted, or complained of, a population of two million. Along with urbanisation have come problems in services, transportation, food supply and housing. Some 30 per cent of urban inhabitants live in slum housing areas. A high proportion of those who occupy the slums (*callampas*— 'mushrooms') is made up of families which have migrated to cities since the second world war. However serious their plight they tend to regard city life as an improvement over conditions of virtual serfdom in the rural regions which they have fled. Thus they have shown patience and in 1964 supported the less extreme of Chile's two reform parties. Many sociologists wonder if a second generation growing up in the slums will manifest comparable resignation. In the past, however, authorities have underestimated the inward strength of the masses and their capacity for suffering. Whether fatalistic or realistic, the Chilean masses may continue to be disinclined to take to the barricades in demanding an immediate Utopia, provided they are given a sense of being treated fairly within the framework of the currently limited potentials of their country.

While Chile needs to expand productivity significantly in order to generate the capital with which to finance improvement of the infrastructure and the undertaking of social projects, there is also the urgent need to give to the ignored masses a sense of belonging to and participating in society. Opposed both by the FRAP on the left and by a wide assortment of frightened but still intransigent rightists, and handicapped in some quarters by a programme of action stressing production rather than the redistribution of wealth called for by pristine party ideology, the Christian Democratic administration in the first half of its six-year tenure was able to do little to prove to the neglected one-third or more of the population that the government had their interests primarily at heart. The Frei administration succeeded in launching a programme of land redistribution aimed at relieving social tensions; but the question remained unanswered as to whether a majority of the middle sectors was meaningfully concerned about the lower classes.

Whatever the ultimate outcome, events in the present-day Chile attest that political stability, constitutional order, relative democracy, a friendly climate for foreign investment, individual liberties and freedom of expression often surpassing in scope what is found in the United States, and an active, productive, intellectual and cultural life among society's élite can coexist with mass misery and economic and social stagnation, at least in the short term.

BIBLIOGRAPHY

Burr, Robert N. *By Reason or Force: Chile and the Balancing of Power in South America, 1830–1905*, Univ. of California Press, Berkeley, Calif., 1965.

Butland, Gilbert J. *Chile: An Outline of its Geography, Economics and Politics*, Oxford Univ. Press, London and New York, 3rd ed. 1956.

Cope, Orville G. 'The 1964 Presidential Election in Chile: The Politics of Change and Access', *Inter-American Economic Affairs*, XIX, 4, Washington, DC, spring 1966.

Daugherty, Charles H. (ed.) *Chile: Election Factbook*, Institute for the Comparative Study of Political Systems, Washington, DC, 1963.

D'Antonio, William V. and Pike, Frederick B. (eds.) *Religion, Revolution and Reform: New Forces for Change in Latin America*, Frederick A. Praeger, New York and Washington, 1964.

Gil, Federico. *The Political System of Chile*, Houghton Mifflin, Boston, Mass., 1966.

Halperin, Ernst. *Nationalism and Communism in Chile*, MIT Press, Cambridge, Mass., 1965.

Hirschman, A. O. *Journeys Toward Progress*, Twentieth Century Fund, New York, 1963.

Johnson, John J. *Political Change in Latin America*, Stanford Univ. Press, Stanford, Calif., 1958.

McBridge, G. M. *Chile: Land and Society*, American Geographical Society, New York, 1936.

BASIC INFORMATION

CLIMATE

	Antofagasta	Punta Arenas	Santiago	Valdivia
Lat./long.	24° S, 70° W	53° S, 71° W	33° 30′ S, 71° W	40° S, 73° W
Altitude	308 ft/94 m.	26 ft/8 m.	1,706 ft/ 520 m.	16 ft/5 m.
Mean temp. of hottest month	20°C/69°F (Jan.)	11°C/52°F (Jan.)	20°C/69°F (Jan.)	17°C/63°F (Jan.)
Mean temp. of coolest month	14°C/57°F (Aug.)	2°C/35°F (July)	9°C/48°F (June)	8°C/46°F (July)
Absolute max.	85°F/30°C	86°F/30°C	99°F/37°C	97°F/36°C
Absolute min.	41°F/5°C	11°F/−12°C	24°F/−5°C	24°F/−5°C
Relative humidity at midday of hottest and coolest months	71%/73%	68%/79%	38%/64%	64%/89%
Wettest months	0·2 in./5 mm. (July)	1·6 in./41 mm. (June)	3·3 in./84 mm. (June)	17·7 in./ 450 mm. (June)
Driest months	0 (Dec.–Mar.)	0·7 in./ 18 mm. (Nov.)	0·1 in./ 2·5 mm. (Jan./Feb.)	2·6 in./ 66 mm. (Jan.)
Annual av. rainfall	0·5 in./ 13 mm.	14·4 in./ 366 mm.	14·1 in./ 358 mm.	102·4 in./ 2,601 mm.

POPULATION

TOTAL (*million*): 1960 (census): 7·74 (adjusted for underestimation); 1965 (mid-year): 8·57; 1980 (ECLA projection): 12·9.
DENSITY, mid-1965: 12 persons per sq. km.
CRUDE RATES (*per 000*), 1965: birth 32, death 10·7; 1964: infant mortality 114·2.
GROWTH RATE (% *p.a.*), 1945–65: 2·2.
DISTRIBUTION (% *of total pop.*): Ethnic, mainly mixed racial origin: estimated 65 mixed, 30 white, 5 Amerindian; indigenous: Araucanians, Changos, Fuegians. Foreign-born, 1960: 1·4. Language, Spanish. Religion, 1960 (sample): Christian 95 (1952: Roman Catholic 90, Protestant 4). Urban (*centres 2,000 inhab. or over*), ECLA data, 1950: 54·8; 1960: 63·7; 1980 (projection): 75. Largest cities (*000 inhab.*), 1960: Santiago 1,169, plus suburbs 1,907 (Greater Santiago, March 1966: 2,475); Valparaíso 253; Concepción 148; Viña del Mar 115; Antofagasta 88; Talcahuano 84.

CONSTITUTIONAL SYSTEM

CONSTITUTION: First 1818. Main constitution 1833. New constitution 18th September 1925; amended 1943, 1957 and 1959. Amendments may be made by majority vote at joint session of Congress or by plebiscite.
SYSTEM: Unitary Republic. Centralised system of administrative areas, comprising 25 provinces (headed by an *intendente* with a provincial assembly), divided into departments (administered by governors) which are sub-divided into sub-delegations and districts. Cities have municipal councils headed by mayors.
EXECUTIVE: Power vested in president, who is commander-in-chief of armed forces. President elected by direct popular vote for 6-year term; no immediate reelection. Normally no vice-president, except when president dies, is incapacitated or is abroad.

President's powers, although extensive, are restricted by Congress; presidential veto may be overridden by two-thirds vote of a majority of members of Congress.

LEGISLATURE: Bi-cameral, National Congress of Senate and Chamber of Deputies. *Senate:* 45 members, 5 from each of 9 provincial groups elected (by popular vote) for 8 years, one-half retiring every 4 years. *Deputies:* 147 seats, elected (by popular vote by departments based on population, using proportional representation system) for 4 years. *Suffrage:* Universal, voting for literate adults of 21 years of age or over. Registered voters, September 1964: 2·9 m. *Elections:* Presidential, September 1964 (000 votes): Frei Montalva 1,418, Allende Gossens 982, Durán Neumann 125. Congressional, March 1965: seats held:

Party	Senate	Chamber of Deputies
Christian Democrat	13	82
Radical	10	20
Communist	3	18
Socialist	7	15
Liberal	5	6
Others	7	6
Total	45	147

In June 1966 the Conservative and Liberal parties combined with the Acción Nacional and some independents to form the National Party (Partido Nacional). JUDICIARY: Single judicial system headed by Supreme Court of 13 members, appointed for life by the president, from list submitted by the Court. Has right to declare laws unconstitutional. Ten appellate courts in principal cities. Courts of first instance in each departmental capital.

DEFENCE

DEFENCE BUDGET: 1965: 371·5 m. escudos; 1·8 per cent of GDP.
ARMED FORCES: National service: between 20–45 years of age; 1 year in army. Strength: army 21,500, navy 15,000, air force 8,000; total 44,500 plus 300,000 trained reserve.

INTERNATIONAL RELATIONS

Member of the UN and many of its international specialised agencies, including: IBRD and affiliates, IMF, FAO, ICAO, ILO, ITU, UNDP, UNESCO, UPU, WHO and WMO; IAEA, GATT, UNCTAD representative; also a member of ECLA, OAS, Alliance for Progress, IDB and LAFTA.

ECONOMY

PRODUCTION

AGRICULTURE (000 tons)	1948–53[1]	63/64	64/65	65/66
Wheat	910	1,319	1,276	1,167
Maize	70	206	221	246
Barley	83	138	138	141
Oats	83	133	116	123
Rice	76	86	89	83
Potatoes	467	763	736	705
Dry Beans	71	100	74	93
Lentils	14	21	14	11
Dry peas	17	8	9	7
Beet sugar	—	108	108	104

[1] Average 1948/9–1952/3.

LAND (%), 1955: Arable 4, permanent pasture 14, forested 28, other 54.
OTHER AGRICULTURAL DATA: Agricultural holdings, 1965 (census): number 0·26 m.,
area 28·7 m. hectares. Tractors in use (ooos), end-1963: 16·5. Fertiliser consumption
(ooo tons), 1964: 123.
LIVESTOCK: No. (m. head), 1964/65: cattle 3·12, sheep 6·46, pigs 1·07. Products
(ooo tons), 1965: meat 177, beef and veal 133, wool (greasy) 23.
FISH: Landed (ooo tons), 1965: total 708·5, anchoveta 438·5 (1964: 934), hake 106·0.
MINING, 1965: (ooo tons) Copper 605, iron ore 8,089, manganese 7; (tons) molybdenum
3,725, zinc 1,200, mercury 13, gold 1·96, silver 91·9; (ooo tons) nitrate 1,158, iodine
2·28, sulphur 37, coal 1,658; (m. cubic metres) crude petroleum 2·02, natural gas
1,781 (1964).
MANUFACTURING, 1965: (ooo tons) Copper bars 568, refined 289; pig iron 309, steel
ingots 474, cement 1,186, paper 139, newsprint 77 (1964), fish meal 81 (1964: 166),
wheat flour 737; (m. litres) wine 695, beer 165; (ooo cubic metres) diesel oil 464, fuel
oil 599, motor spirit 999.
CONSTRUCTION (ooo sq. metres, floor area), 1965: building permits issued for private
projects 1,502; public construction started 1,819.

ENERGY
CONSUMPTION (tons coal equiv.), 1964: total 9·16 m., per head 1·08.
ELECTRICITY, 1965: generated (kwh) 6,250 m.; installed capacity (kw) 1·52 m.

GOVERNMENT EXPENDITURE
DISTRIBUTION (% of total), 1965: defence 10, education 12, social services 8.

GROSS PRODUCT
GDP (ooo m. escudos): at current market prices, 1964: 15·1; 1965: 20·8; at 196?
market prices, 1964: 6·21; 1965: 6·58. Per head (US$), UN estimate, 1964: 456.
DISTRIBUTION (%), 1964: agriculture 10, mining 7, manufacturing 19, trade 21,
transport and communications 9.
GROWTH RATES (%) 1950–60: total 3·6, per head 1·2; 1960–4: total 3·5, per head 1·0.

EXTERNAL TRADE (US$m.)	1955	1960	1963	1964	1965
EXPORTS (f.o.b.)	472	488	540	624	685
Copper	322	344	372	399	481
Iron ore	6	35	57	70	78
Nitrate	56	26	30	30	30
IMPORTS (c.i.f.)	376	526	558	607	604
TRADE BALANCE	+96	−38	−17	+16	+81

DIRECTION OF TRADE (%)

	Exports			Imports		
	1955	1960	1965	1955	1960	1965
LAFTA	(12·2)	6·2	7·7	(22·1)	16·4	20·1
USA	42·3	37·1	31·0	43·1	47·8	39·3
EEC	22·7	30·5	32·1	17·3	18·6	18·1
UK	16·8	17·7	11·2	5·6	7·1	6·4

FINANCE
EXCHANGE RATE (escudos/US$): Free market, end-year, 1960: 1·05; 1965: 4·22;
1966: 5·00.
BALANCE OF PAYMENTS (US$m.): Goods and services (net), 1960: −177; 1964:
−145; 1965: −52.
COST OF LIVING (Dec. 1958=100), Santiago, December 1960: 141; 1965: 498;
1966: 583.
INDUSTRIAL WAGES: Monthly earnings in manufacturing, April 1964: 152 escudos.

TREASURY ACCOUNTS (m. escudos), 1965: Revenue 3,254, expenditure 3,981, deficit 727. Expenditure: current 2,604, capital 1,145, amortisation 232. Financing of deficit: internal loans 182, external loans 461, other 84.

EMPLOYMENT

ECONOMICALLY ACTIVE (%), 1960: of total pop. 32 (men 51, women 14); of pop. 12 years and over: 67. In agriculture and fishing 28, services and utilities 24, manufacturing 18, trade 10, mining 4.

UNEMPLOYMENT, Greater Santiago, March 1966 (sample): 40,000 (4·7 per cent).

TRANSPORT AND COMMUNICATIONS

RAILWAYS: Traffic (main railways), 1965: 2,412 m. pass.-km.; 2,616 m. net ton-km. Length of track, 1963: total 8,640 km., state railways 8,310 km.

MOTOR VEHICLES: In use (ooo), 1964: pass. cars 89, comm. vehicles 99. National road system, 1963: 45,270 km.

SHIPPING: Merchant fleet (ooo g.r. tons), 1965: 296. International sea-borne shipping (million tons), 1965: goods loaded 12·8, goods unloaded 1·5. Main ports: Valparaíso, Arica, Iquique, Tocopilla, Antofagasta, Chañaral, Coquimbo, San Antonio, Talcahuano, Punta Arenas.

AIR: Scheduled services, 1965: Total 511 m. pass.-km., 25·6 m. cargo ton-km. International, 1964: 143 m. pass.-km., 2·8 m. cargo ton-km. Main airports: Santiago; Cerrillos (international), replaced by Pudahuel; Arica; Iquique; Antofagasta; Concepción; Puerto Montt; Punta Arenas.

TELEPHONES: No. in use, 1964: 250,000.

SOCIAL WELFARE

SYSTEM: Social insurance benefits and services provided by three main organisations: (1) Servicio de Seguro Social (covering all wage earners), (2) Caja de Previsión de Empleados Particulares (private employees), and (3) Caja Nacional de Empleados Públicos y Periodistas (civil servants and newspaper employees; financed by employees' and employers' contributions). Contributions based on remuneration: (1) wage earners 5%, employers 14·5%, government 5·5%; (2) employees 12% (not exceeding 6 times minimum salary), employers 18%; (3) civil servants 16%, govt depts 6·5%. Employment legislation covers working hours; holidays; payment of wages, overtime, annual bonus and participation in profits; employers' liability for compensation for accidents, dismissal and death indemnities.

HEALTH, 1960: 1,800 persons per physician, 185 persons per hospital bed.

NUTRITION; Net food supply (per head per day), 1962: 2,370 calories; protein 80 g.

EDUCATION

ILLITERACY RATE (%), 1960: 15 years and over, 16.

COMPULSORY: 7 years (between 7 and 15 years of age). Pupils in primary and secondary schools as % of pop. aged 5 to 19, 1963: 78.

SCHOOLS, 1963: Primary: no. 4,830; pupils 1·3 m. Secondary: no. 535; p. 0·19 m. Technical (public): no. 184; st. 0·13 m. Teacher-training: no. 17; st. 7,260. Universities: no. 8; st. 59,000; teaching staff 8,500.

UNIVERSITIES (mainly 1963/64 data):

State: Universidad de Chile, Santiago, 34,000 students, academic staff 4,800. Private (but state-aided): Pont. U. Católica de Chile, Santiago 7,000 st., a.s. 1,000; U. de Concepción 3,900 st., a.s. 838 (346 full-time); U. C. de Valparaíso 2,850 st., a.s. 600; U. Austral de Chile, Valdivia 650 st., a.s. 130 (70 f.-t.); U. del Norte, Antofagasta 670 st., a.s. 142 (28 f.-t.); U. Técnica del Estado, Santiago 9,500 st., a.s. 864 (114 f.-t.); U. T. Federico Santa María, Valparaíso 365 st., a.s. 94 (50 f.-t.).

MASS MEDIA

BROADCASTING: No. of receivers in use, end 1964: TV 60,000; 1962: radio 1·5 m.
Stations: TV 3, radio 119.
CINEMAS: No., 1963: 395. Attendance, 1963: total 56 m., per head 6·8.
NEWSPRINT: Consumption, 1963: total 35,500 tons, per head 4·3 kg.
NEWSPAPERS: Daily, 1964: 46. Estimated circulation (43 dailies) 1·0 m., copies per
000 of population 118. Principal dailies (*circulation, 000*): Santiago: *El Mercurio* 130
(Sunday 150), *La Nación* 100, *La Tercera* 85, *El Diario Ilustrado* 55 (S 64), *Las Últimas
Noticias* 50 (Sat. 65); Valparaíso: *El Mercurio* 45, *La Unión* 28 (S 40), *La Estrella* 20;
Concepción: *El Sur* 42, *La Patria* 26, *Crónica* 20; Antofagasta: *El Mercurio* 25.
BOOKS: Titles published, 1964: 1,577.

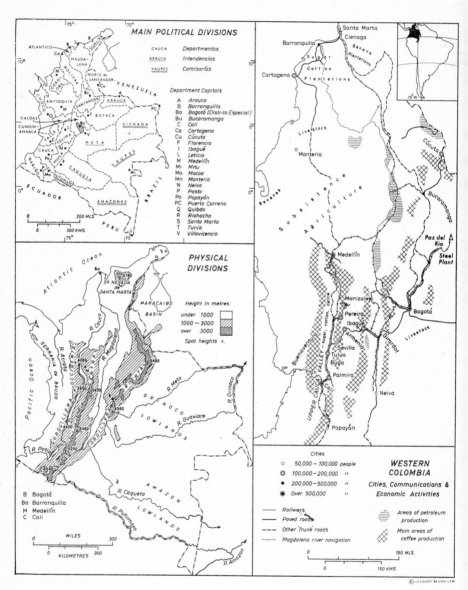

MAIN POLITICAL DIVISIONS

CAUCA   Departmentos
ARAUCA   Intendencias
VAUPES   Comisarías

Department Capitals

A   Arauca
B   Barranquilla
Bo   Bogotá (Distrito Especial)
Bu   Bucaramanga
C   Cali
Ca   Cartagena
Cu   Cúcuta
F   Florencia
I   Ibagué
L   Leticia
M   Medellín
Mi   Mitu
Mo   Mocoa
Mn   Monteria
N   Neiva
P   Pasto
Po   Popayán
PC   Puerto Carreno
Q   Quibdo
R   Riohacha
S   Santa Marta
T   Tunja
V   Villavicencio

300 MLS.
0
0   300 KMS.

PHYSICAL DIVISIONS

Height in metres
under 1000
1000 – 3000
over 3000
Spot heights ×

B   Bogotá
Ba   Barranquilla
M   Medellín
C   Cali

MILES
0   300
0   300
KILOMETRES

WESTERN COLOMBIA
Cities, Communications & Economic Activities

Cities
○   50,000 – 100,000 people
◎   100,000 – 200,000 ″
●   200,000 – 500,000 ″
●   Over 500,000 ″

——— Railways
——— Paved roads
--- Other Trunk roads
········ Magdalena river navigation

Areas of petroleum production
Main areas of coffee production

© ANTHONY BLOND LTD

COLOMBIA

COLOMBIA

KEVIN J. LYONETTE

HISTORY

The colonial period

BEFORE the Spanish Conquest there seems to have been little development of integrated societies in what is now Colombia. After the establishment of Santa Marta and Cartagena, Gonzalo Jiménez de Quesada advanced south, subduing or subverting the rival Indian tribes of whom the Chibchas were the most important. Eventually the Chibchas were subdued and in 1538 Quesada founded Bogotá which became the capital of the Spanish colony of New Granada, comprising what is now Colombia and part of northern Ecuador. About the same time, Sebastian Benalcazar, one of Pizarro's captains, conquered the Cauca Valley in the west. Contrary to Spanish expectations New Granada did not yield vast amounts of treasure. Bogotá itself, physically almost isolated from the rest of the country, evolved a tradition of conservation of Spanish culture and academic distinction which led to its being known as the 'Athens of South America'.

New Granada followed much the same pattern as the other colonies of South America. The administration of the region was in the hands of the *audiencias*, judicial, advisory and executive bodies appointed by the Spanish monarch to help and, on occasions, check the viceroy. The colonies were legally personal possessions of the Spanish king and the majority of public posts were filled by Spaniards nominated by him. Trade was strictly regulated between Spain and the colonies and, naturally enough, contraband trade soon appeared while Santa Marta and Cartagena were often subject to raids by French and British pirates. The Spanish colonisers brought peace and order which independent Colombia has hardly known. They laid the bases of the economy, organised agricultural production and established a legal system. At the same time the Catholic Church, mostly through Jesuit missions, carried out the work of conversion of the indigenous population and their pioneer spirit greatly contributed to the extension and consolidation of Spanish control in the interior of the region. Both because of its close relationship to the colonial political and administrative officers and because of the large land-grants made to it by the Spanish monarch, the Catholic Church assumed a social and political role in New Granada which was to be of great importance in independent Colombia. Indeed, the 'Church question' has not been fully solved even now.

Towards the end of the 18th century there occurred several embryonic independence movements in New Granada. The best known is the revolt of the *comuneros* (small landholders) in the north in 1781. This uprising was probably the result of a new tax imposed upon them, but small independence movements were forming at this time under the influence of French liberalism and the successful North American revolution. In 1794 Antonio Nariño published a Spanish translation of the French Declaration of the Rights of Man, and other books and pamphlets dealing with the new political ideas were circulated. Small groups of intellectuals formed to discuss the new theories and despite the harsh treatment given to such organisations by the Spanish administration their ideas and influence spread in New Granada in much the same way as the Enlightenment came to other parts of South America.

Following the ousting of the Bourbons in Spain by Napoleon in 1808 Bogotá maintained its loyalty to Ferdinand VII but proclaimed its dissatisfaction with Spanish rule and in 1810 the regional junta finally broke with the Spanish regency. Other regional councils followed but there was little sense of direction and even less cooperation between the various provinces. Simón Bolívar on behalf of the central government attempted to win over those provinces which refused to accept central authority but was unable to complete the task before General Pablo Murillo with a Spanish army invaded the territory, laid siege to Cartagena and occupied Bogotá in May 1816. A reign of terror and vicious repression of the rebel movements followed. The first confused and indecisive independence movement had failed.

Independence: the 19th century

By 1818 Bolívar had a small army and navy at Angostura in Venezuela. With the help of José Antonio Paez and Francisco de Paula Santander and several hundred professional soldiers, mainly from Britain, he began the campaign which in August 1819 culminated in the defeat of the Royalists at Boyacá and secured New Granada's independence.

In December 1819 the Republic of 'Gran Colombia' was proclaimed, comprising what is now Venezuela, Ecuador and Colombia; Bolívar was president. For some time Bolívar's dream of a centralised republic was realised but separatist movements led by Santander in Bogotá and Paez in Venezuela began the process of disruption and by 1830, with the secession of Ecuador, Gran Colombia was in ruins and Bolívar had resigned his presidency. In 1831 the Provinces of Boyacá, Cauca, Cundinamarca, Magdalena and Panamá were reconstituted as the 'Republic of New Granada' with the same boundaries as the colonial Viceroyalty.

In this period there appeared the division between Centralists, in favour of strong centralised government, and Federalists, who supported the idea of an inorganic federation of autonomous provinces. Along with the problem of the Catholic Church this division dominated 19th-century politics in Colombia. Santander, a Federalist, was president from 1833 to 1837. He provided firm administration, established legal and financial systems and instituted a programme of educational development. He limited the influence of the Church, especially in education, thus aggravating the split between the Federalist, anti-clerical Liberals and the Centralist, Church-supporting Conservatives. His successors continued the process.

However, as President Tomás Mosquera came to the end of his term in 1849, the antagonism between Conservatives and Liberals and the influence of the French Revolution of 1848 produced a climate of tension and unrest. The Conservative Party split and a Liberal, General José Hilario López, was elected president. The next thirty years were chaotic and violent. The Liberals proclaimed freedom of the press and religion, abolition of slavery and in the constitution of 1853 disestablished the Church. The Conservatives seized power in 1854 and surprisingly adopted a federalist policy which culminated in 1858 in the conversion of the Republic into the Granadan Confederation of States. The political pendulum swung violently; elections were continuous, bloody and hardly ever orderly or honest. Mosquera, now turned Liberal, seized power in 1861 and carried out measures including the dissolution of religious orders, confiscation of Church property and the subjection of clerics to the legal scrutiny of the state. The constitution of 1863 incorporated these reforms with federalism and the nation changed its name to the United States of Colombia.

Chaos continued until Rafael Nuñez, an ex-diplomat and the leader of the Independent Liberal Party, was elected president in 1879. His main plea was for tolerance and cooperation. With Conservative support he was elected president again in 1883 and appealed to the radical Liberals to join in a moderate policy of stability and progress. The Liberals, however, refused and civil strife began in 1884; this has continued at intervals up to the present day. By the end of 1885 Nuñez had joined with the Conservatives and in 1886 a new constitution was promulgated. It included centralisation of government, restoration of Church privileges, compensation for confiscated Church property, renewal of Church control of education and limitation of the freedom of the press. These measures were confirmed by the 1887 concordat between the Nuñez government and the papacy.

Until his death in 1894 Nuñez continued to exert great political influence and the recurring Liberal revolts were successfully quelled. In 1899 the Liberals staged their most powerful revolt which turned into a civil war, now known as 'The War of the Thousand Days'. When the Liberals were finally defeated in 1902, 100,000 men had died and extensive damage had been done to the economy. Moreover, the political problems of the Republic remained unsolved.

The 20th century

Work on the construction of a canal across the Isthmus of Panama—then Colombian territory—began in 1878 but the company went bankrupt and work was halted until 1903. In that same year a treaty was signed between the United States and Colombia granting the former a 99-year lease of a ten-mile wide strip of land across the Isthmus. Ratification was delayed by the Colombian Senate and on 3 November 1903, with assurances of United States support, Panama seceded from Colombia. Two weeks later the United States signed a treaty with Panama guaranteeing perpetual use of the strip of land across the Isthmus.[1] Relations between Colombia and the United States remained hostile until in 1921 the Colombian Senate ratified the 1914 agreement providing for United States compensation of $25 million to be paid. Anti-Americanism on this score still persists in Colombia and in 1963 served as a convenient rallying-cry for anti-American demonstrations in Colombia during the riots in the Canal Zone.

In 1904 General Rafael Reyes became president. Much impressed by the strong rule and pro-Americanism of Porfirio Díaz in Mexico, Reyes followed suit. Congress was dissolved, deputies imprisoned and a puppet National Assembly established. In 1906 a law was passed despite the supremacy of the Conservatives providing for Liberal minority representation in Congress and cabinet. Reyes governed firmly, initiated public works

[1] See 'Panama', p. 230.

projects and tried to attract foreign capital, especially American, by signing a reconciliation treaty with the United States. Congress baulked at this and Reyes was eventually forced to retire in 1909. A Constituent Assembly in 1910 reformed the constitution, limited the presidential term, established popular elections and guaranteed minority Liberal representation. The Conservatives regained control in 1914 and retained it until after 1930.

In the early part of the present century three factors influenced Colombian affairs. During the war the world coffee market declined, creating inflation and resulting in the concentration of national financial and economic control in the hands of the rich families. This control was increased in the 1920s by the policies of external borrowing and foreign capital investment, since the agencies for such external finance were controlled by the rich families of Colombia. The net result of this policy of 'prosperity by debt' was to make the rich richer without helping the poor.

On the other hand the influence of socialism and the Russian Revolution was being felt and strikes and social disturbances occurred. Financial reform was undertaken by President Pedro Ospina (1922–6) but little social benefit accrued to the majority of the people and the large borrowing programme coupled with the upsurge in the world market following the end of the world war increased inflationary pressures.

President Miguel Abadía Méndez (1926–30) began large public works programmes, especially in transportation. The labour force was drawn from the rural areas, thus producing a decrease in agricultural production and a rise in the cost of living. Despite high wages and the $280 million United States investment in Colombia between 1922 and 1930, the internal consumer market decreased, rapid urbanisation created new and urgent problems and the average real wage of the worker actually decreased in the same period of time.

Isolation and regionalism had begun to diminish since 1920 with the introduction of a national press, a national broadcasting system and a network of air communications. Political activity increased and in 1930 the Liberal revival began. Due to internal divisions in the Conservative Party, a moderate Liberal, Enrique Olaya Herrera, was elected president in that year. His coalition government was hard hit by the depression. World markets dwindled, domestic markets almost disappeared and credit dried up. The financial oligarchy strengthened its position by servicing the public debt. Olaya Herrera attempted, although without much success, to alleviate the worst effects of the depression. By 1934 the Liberals with an increased following elected Alfonso López as president. López amended the 1886 constitution, reduced the power of the Church, passed laws encouraging trade unions and proclaimed the social function of property, the duty of the state to provide public assistance and the right of the state to expropriate land and even nationalise private businesses in the interests of equity. López also initiated tax and land reform programmes.

In the 1938 elections the radical Liberals of López were beaten by the moderate group led by Eduardo Santos. The pace of reform was slowed down in the hope of achieving a rapprochement with the Conservatives, now led by Laureano Gómez, a fiercely Roman Catholic, pro-Axis admirer of Franco and 'Hispanidad'. In 1942 López with the backing of the radical Liberals became president once more. Gómez' opposition increased and López was opposed by a Liberal Congress while the economic situation worsened with increasing inflation. Gómez exploited the split in the Liberals and waged a campaign of personal abuse against López who, following his capture in 1944 by army officers in an abortive coup, emerged discredited and resigned in 1945. Alberto Lleras Camargo served out the term until 1946 when Gómez by exploiting the split between moderate and radical Liberals (led by Jorge Eliecer Gaitán) achieved the election of the Conservative Mariano Ospina Pérez. Gómez became foreign minister in the new government.

Opposition concentrated itself behind Gaitán, whose eloquence and honesty evoked great popular support. Political rivalry increased and Ospina Pérez declared a state of siege. In April 1948, during the holding of the Ninth Inter-American Conference in Bogotá, Gaitán was assassinated. Riots followed in which the mob, allegedly encouraged by Communists, burned the capital, looted shops and private houses and ransacked churches. The violence spread despite Ospina Pérez' attempts to control it and a virtual civil war between Liberals and Conservatives ensued. Villages were burned by rival factions, provinces split among themselves, rivalries appeared in the armed forces and the police and with the return of Gómez from Spain in 1949 and his election as president in that year the violence grew worse. Repressive measures were increased, mass killings took place, bands of guerrillas took to the mountains to continue the fight and, as a result of Gómez' attitudes, the situation assumed religious overtones which the Catholic Church did little to dispel. During this time the economic position of Colombia improved abroad but owing to the internal situation little domestic benefit accrued to the majority of the Colombian people.

In 1953 after anti-Gómez factions had appeared even in the Conservative Party, the armed forces under General Gustavo Rojas Pinilla assumed power. Rojas Pinilla succeeded in establishing relative peace and order and initiated reforms covering tax, banking, import restrictions and encouragement of nationalised industries in aviation and oil. Development programmes previously undertaken in the Cauca Valley and in the eastern plains, as well as steel production planned at Paz del Rio, were further stimulated and a new quasi-Peronist trade union organisation, the Confederación Nacional de Trabajadores (CNT) was set up to overcome the influence of the Confederación de Trabajadores Colombianos (CTC), established in 1934 under López, and the Unión de Trabajadores Colombianos (UTC), Church-directed and established under Gómez. For a while Rojas Pinilla enjoyed popular support and his political movement, the quasi-Peronist Movement of National Action or 'Third Force', was created in 1955. The renewal of political activity and the increasing opposition to Rojas on the part of the oligarchy, the press and the traditional political parties opened old wounds and, although Rojas Pinilla dissolved his new party, violence broke out once more in 1955–6. In May 1957, following increasing corruption and authoritarianism, Rojas Pinilla was exiled by the united forces of the Liberals and Conservatives.

In July 1957 Lleras Camargo and Gómez met at Sitges in Spain and issued a pact recommending bipartisan government in the interest of national peace. The Pact of Sitges was ratified and the period of experiment was extended to sixteen years. Elections eventually took place and in August 1958 Lleras Camargo became president.

The National Front
The corruption of Rojas Pinilla's regime was largely eradicated and the economic situation seemed more hopeful, but the world market price of coffee soon declined, the cost of living was high, inflation threatened, the

79

rate of investment was low and political parties had yet to solve their problems of internal division and violent rivalry.

A plebiscite held in December 1957 established a bipartisan National Front government and equality of party representation in the cabinet and in departmental and municipal councils. Roman Catholicism was recognised as the national religion, a non-political civil service was to be established and at least 10 per cent of the national budget was to be spent on education.

In his first year Lleras Camargo reduced violence and began a programme of economic stabilisation. The return to Colombia of Rojas Pinilla in October 1958, albeit to stand trial for misappropriation of funds, heightened the political temperature while the task of maintaining the National Front government was not helped by policies such as increased taxation, wage control, government intervention in industry and import restrictions which were necessary to stabilise Colombia's position abroad and to bring about national domestic development.

With the approach of the 1960 Congressional elections which were to decide the relative influence of political groups in the presidential candidacy for 1962, party activity increased and factions appeared within each party. The Conservatives split into two groups led by Laureano Gómez on the one hand and Alzate Avendaño with Mariano Ospina Pérez on the other. The majority of Liberals supported Lleras Camargo but there appeared splinter groups led by Alfonso López Michelsen and by Luís Emiro Valencia and his wife, Gloria, the daughter of the assassinated Gaitán. In the elections a 50 per cent abstention was recorded, the Gómez group was soundly beaten and the López Michelsen faction gained 20 per cent of the Liberal vote.

By 1962 Lleras Camargo by his policies of austerity and planned development had put Colombia's economy in a fairly strong position. Coffee, Colombia's main source of export revenue, had been helped by the 1959 International Coffee Agreement. Cotton was being exported, internal credit was available and foreign loans had been successfully negotiated. Oil was producing foreign exchange dividends, land reform had been initiated and transport and communication networks had been developed. On the other hand, labour disputes and unrest were increasing and signs of real political progress were few. Despite the decrease in rural violence and the partial solution of the Church question, it was in the midst of party factions on both sides that the Conservative, Guillermo León Valencia, was elected president in 1962. The bipartisan National Front government agreement barely survived.

The years 1962–6 saw greater political divisions accompanied by renewed inflationary pressures and an insufficiently strong world market price for coffee. Guerrilla activity was renewed, now stimulated by Castroist and extreme left-wing elements, and the attempts of the Alliance for Progress to help Colombia stabilise herself proved relatively unavailing.[1] Despite much opposition the Valencia government proposed austerity economic measures, including devaluation. The effects were felt severely by wage-earners and by the small concerns considered basic to industrial diversification. Political divisions intensified both within and outside the National Front government, and were further increased on the left by the influence of the Cuban Revolution. The Movement of Liberal Recuperation under López Michelsen split, the extremists combining in support of violent revolution and using guerrilla activity to create social and political chaos.

---

[1] See 'The Alliance for Progress', p. 568.

The ineffectiveness of the economic and social measures taken by the Valencia government, the deadlock between a Conservative president and a divided Congress meant that little progress was made. Communist infiltration and direction of guerrilla groups added a new factor to the tendency to violence. The Alliance for Progress attempted to relieve some of Colombia's social and economic problems but despite the dollars made available, owing mainly to the political situation the Alliance failed in large part to bring about the economic and social changes urgently needed.

In 1962–3, under the titular leadership of Rojas Pinilla, there appeared the National Popular Alliance (ANAPO) which attempted to unite itself with left-wing dissident groups. The movement, populist but with personalist elements, in 1964 and 1966 gained a sizeable Congressional representation. However, ANAPO and MRL failed to agree on a joint opposition presidential candidate in 1966 and on 1 May Carlos Lleras Restrepo, the Liberal National Front candidate, was elected president. In Congress, however, the National Front did not achieve the two-thirds majority necessary for major legislation.

Political divisions and the traditional tendency to violence reduce the comparative success of the bipartisan experiment in politics. Violence, whether led by communists, increased by lawless elements or simply the effect of social unrest, is still apparent. National integration is hampered also by bureaucracy and lack of technical expertise. Economic progress seems disjointed, income and land-tenure is still unequally distributed and whatever reform has taken place since 1948 does not appear to have been of great benefit even to the urban mass of the people. The illiteracy rate remains high and measures such as land reform and rural community development are needed to stem the flow of population to the cities and raise the living standard of almost 35 per cent of the population above subsistence level. In 1966, as in 1962, the new political experiment survived but the continuing existence of fundamental national problems made its future uncertain.

ECONOMY

Colombia's economy has long been excessively dependent on the export of coffee. Coffee revenue has at times accounted for 80 per cent of foreign exchange and still predominates. Fluctuations in the world market price of coffee, therefore, have a fundamental effect on the Colombian economy. At the time of the Korean War during Gómez's presidency, the price of coffee was high and so despite the violence and political upheavals there was a certain prosperity. Prices have fluctuated since and although international coffee agreements guaranteeing price support through export production quotas have helped, there remains a basic need for diversification of exports and development of national industries.

In basic agriculture, production is insufficient and development limited. In coffee especially, rationalisation of production is limited by the fact that too much underproduction takes place on *minifundios* which are not economically viable. On the other hand almost feudal land tenure systems hold back production and productivity increase and make it extremely difficult to bring the workers in such areas above subsistence level. The National Colombian Institute of Land Reform (INCORA) has made some progress on these problems, however.

Rice and cotton are also exported and gold production creates export revenue. Fruit production, previously controlled by the United Fruit

Company but now undertaken by individual farmers with technical, transportation and marketing assistance from United Fruit, has begun again to figure in export lists. Oil, under the control of Ecopétrol and foreign companies, in 1964 produced foreign capital investment of $35 million, while the development of the petrochemical industry helps national diversification. Industrial diversification has been a constant policy but apart from exceptions like textile industries has had limited success principally because of lack of dependable development resources, lack of qualified workers and a lack of effective overall planning. The situation has been relieved to some extent by the emergence of industrial centres such as Medellín and Cali with strong groups of entrepreneurs and skilled workers.

Colombia has suffered not only from monocultural weaknesses but from a recurring cycle of inflation, necessitating foreign investment and loans, and national austerity programmes which for political reasons or bad management have been relatively ineffective. Wages and costs have risen, foreign debts have had to be reserviced and the balance of payments has been in chronic deficit because of unstable coffee prices and high public spending, except for 1959 when Lleras Camargo, with a capable and determined team of advisers, achieved a surplus.

The necessity for foreign investment and loans has been constant. In 1962 the Alliance for Progress approved the 10-year Colombian development plan calling for $200 million per year of foreign investment alone. In that year the Alliance provided $76 million while the International Monetary Fund, the Agency for International Development and European banks also contributed. Despite this and because of political obstacles, lack of qualified personnel, low world coffee prices and a recurring balance-of-payments problem, Colombia was forced to devalue the peso in 1962. In 1963 the Alliance for Progress provided $127 million but there was a short-fall on the targets of the ten-year plan.

1964–5 was a year of relative price stability and export diversification, but large government spending and a $90 million balance-of-payments deficit offset most of the advantages. Exports, however, rose to $508 million including new items such as cement, timber and frozen meat. On the other hand, Colombia's trade with the countries of the Latin American Free Trade Area (which she joined in 1961) showed a constant deficit amounting in 1964 to over $20 million. Contraband increased these problems and the foreign exchange and domestic investment situation was worsened by the outflow of Colombian money.

The year 1965 began with a partial devaluation, austerity measures including higher income tax, luxury taxes, cuts in public spending and new customs tariffs along with severe import restrictions even upon goods from LAFTA countries. These measures might have helped appreciably but the delay by Congress in approving the policies sapped confidence at home and abroad and 1965 saw a net outflow of foreign exchange. Once more foreign loans were negotiated but Colombia still needs a diversification of exports, a controlled industrial development and rationalisation of agricultural production. Current obstacles are increasing unemployment, the persistently high cost of living, recurrent inflation and high public spending. Rural violence appeared again in 1964–6, adding to the difficulties.

The basic obstacles to economic reform and progress in Colombia remain political and unless the political situation is solved it is likely that Colombia will continue without economic reform and subject to a recurring and ever more severe inflationary cycle.

Violencia

Violencia implies the large-scale guerrilla and bandit political activity, especially in rural areas, which has been a constant factor in Colombian life since at least 1948. Violence has some tradition in Colombia as in many Latin American countries. The civil war at the end of the 19th century accounted for some 100,000 men. In the post-1948 violence, according to some estimates, 200,000 people died before the Pact of Sitges was signed.

Pressure for social reform grew during the 1930s and some reforms were undertaken by Alfonso López but met with the determined opposition of the paternalist-minded élite including the Church. López's reforms were diluted by Santos while López himself in his second term did little to consolidate them. The reform pressures of a mass of people with a sense of personal rights and independence concentrated upon Gaitán who by his eloquence, sincerity and forcefulness provided an almost charismatic leadership for such a social mass movement. It is almost certain that Gaitán would have been elected president and in his election lay the chance for revolution. With the murder of Gaitán the movement for reform was left without direction, with an increased sense of frustration which seems to have turned itself into a desire for revenge. Revenge took various forms of violence: personal violence, complete destruction of social structures and political revenge on the Conservatives who were blamed for Gaitán's death. The political repression undertaken by Ospina Pérez and increased by Gómez served only to exacerbate the situation. Little was done to solve the problem by undertaking genuine social reform and even under Rojas Pinilla during whose term violence decreased the hopes of the revolutionary mass were not fulfilled. The Pact of Sitges once more raised hopes of a solution but since 1958 the opposition of various political interest-groups has effectively blocked genuine reform and measures taken to control violence, though well-intentioned and accompanied by rural development projects, have understandably appeared as repression to certain sections of the population. Violence has also spread to the cities and the universities.

Obviously such a leaderless but strong movement has at times and in varying degrees received support and direction from Castro and communist groups in accord with 'Che' Guevara's advice on how to wage guerrilla wars and the communist policy of encouraging 'wars of national liberation'. Moreover, there is evidence to support the view that the traditional parties have at least in the past not only proved ineffective in eradicating violence but have at times utilised it to conserve their own political power.

The problem is compounded by the appearance of second-generation participants in the violence. Such people have increased the element of sheer banditry and lawlessness even to the extent of setting up 'independent republics' within Colombia. Regionalism, difficult terrain and a lack of transport and communications facilities have helped to prolong the situation. Neither the traditional parties nor the National Front has as yet fully accepted the need to break with the social criteria and paternalistic values of the past and to undertake the reforms, especially educational, which are urgent. Without such reforms, violence may well continue and become even more institutionalised, with the explosive potential of the situation attracting extremist agitation and direction.

BIBLIOGRAPHY

Fals Borda, Orlando. *Peasant Society in the Colombian Andes*, Univ. of Florida Press, Gainesville, Fla., 1957. 'Violence and the Break-up of Tradition in Colombia', *Obstacles to Change in Latin America*, ed. Claudio Véliz, Oxford Univ. Press, London and New York, 1965.

Fluharty, V. *Dance of the Millions: Military Rule and the Social Revolution in Colombia*, Univ. of Pittsburgh Press, Pittsburgh, Pa., 1957.

Galbraith, W. O. *Colombia: A General Survey*, Oxford Univ. Press for Royal Institute of International Affairs, London and New York, 1953.

Hobsbawm, Eric J. 'The Revolutionary Situation in Colombia', *The World Today*, London, June 1963.

Holt, P. M. *Colombia: Today and Tomorrow*, Frederick A. Praeger, New York, 1964; Pall Mall Press, London, 1965.

Martz, John D. *Colombia: A Contemporary Political Survey*, Univ. of North Carolina Press, Chapel Hill, NC, 1962.

Romoli, K. *Colombia: Gateway to South America*, Doubleday, New York, 1941.

BASIC INFORMATION

CLIMATE

	Andagoya	*Bogotá*
Lat./long.	5° S, 77° W	4° 30′ N, 74° W
Altitude	197 ft/60 m.	8,678 ft/2,646 m.
Mean temp. of hottest month	28°C/82°F (Jan.)	15°C/59°F (Apr.)
Mean temp. of coolest month	27°C/81°F (Nov./Dec.)	14°C/58°F (Dec./Jan.)
Absolute max.	97°F/36°C	75°F/24°C
Absolute min.	62°F/16°C	40°F/5°C
Relative humidity at midday of hottest and coolest months	n.a.	57%/51%
Wettest months	25·8 in./655 mm. (June)	6·3 in./160 mm. (Oct.)
Driest months	19·5 in./495 mm. (Dec./Mar.)	2·0 in./50 mm. (July)
Annual av. rainfall	281·1 in./7,159 mm.	41·7 in./1,059 mm.

POPULATION

TOTAL (*million*): 1964 (census) 17·5; mid-1965: 18·1; 1980 (ECLA projection): 27·7. DENSITY, mid-1965: 16 persons per sq. km.
CRUDE RATES (*per 000*), 1965: birth 36·7, death 9·9, infant mortality 82·4.
GROWTH RATES (% *p.a.*): 1945–65, 2·9; 1960–5, 3·2.
DISTRIBUTION (% *of total pop.*): Ethnic: mixed 65, white 25, Negro 5, Amerindian 5. Foreign-born, 1950: 0·4. Language, Spanish. Religion: Mainly Roman Catholic; Protestant about 1. Urban (*centres 2,000 inhab. or over*), ECLA data, 1950: 36·4. 1960: 46·1; 1980 (projection): 62·1. 1964 (*census—centres of 1,500 inhab. or over*): 53. Largest cities (*000 inhab.*), 1964: Bogotá (Special District) 1,697, Medellín 773, Cali 638, Barranquilla 498, Cartagena 242, Bucaramanga 230, Manizales 222.

CONSTITUTIONAL SYSTEM

CONSTITUTION: Promulgated in 1886. Subsequently amended; major changes in 1936 and 1945; amended 1957, 1959, 1960, 1967.
SYSTEM: Unitary republic, comprising 21 departments (divided into municipalities); Special District of Bogotá; 3 *intendencias;* 5 *comisarías*. Separate executive, legislature

and judiciary. Council of State, elected by Congress, with representatives in each department, advises the government on administrative matters, for which it is the supreme tribunal.

EXECUTIVE: Power vested in president and his cabinet. He is elected by popular vote for 4-year term, no immediate reelection. Under a constitutional amendment the office of president alternates every 4 years, until 1974, between Conservative and Liberal parties. These two traditional parties share equally in the cabinet and in all representative bodies. A presidential designate is elected by Congress every 2 years. President can declare a 'state of siege' and constitutionally govern by decree.

LEGISLATURE: Bi-cameral, National Congress of Senate and Chamber of Representatives. Legislation normally requires two-thirds majority in both chambers; simple majority for economic subjects. President can issue decrees under his 'state-of-siege' powers. Constitutional reforms require approval by each chamber in two different years. *Senate:* one senator for every 190,000 citizens (or fraction over 95,000), elected by popular vote for 4-year term; minimum of 3 for each department. *Representatives:* one representative for every 90,000 citizens (or fraction over 45,000), elected by popular vote for 2-year term; minimum of 3 for each department. *Suffrage:* universal voting for adults over 21 years of age. Registered voters: about 7·1 m. eligible at 1966 elections. *Elections:* Presidential, May 1966: Liberal candidate of National Transformation Front, Dr Carlos Lleras Restrepo 1·88 m. votes (72%): Alianza Nacional Popular (ANAPO) candidate, Dr José Jaramillo Giraldo 0·74 m. votes (28%). Composition of Congress after Congressional elections, March 1966:

Party	Votes (000)	Representatives	Senate
National Transformation Front:	1,639	111	67
Liberals	1,118	71	46
Unionista Conservatives	522	40	21
Opposition:	1,204	79	39
Alianza Nacional Popular	519	36	18
Movimiento Revolucionario Liberal	352	20	7
Alvarista Conservatives	334	23	14
Total seats		190	106

JUDICIARY: Appointments based on equal party representation. Supreme Court of 20 magistrates: 6 Civil, 6 Labour and 8 Penal; originally elected by Congress for 5-year term from lists submitted by president, later life tenure of office with compulsory retirement at age of 70. The Court rules on constitutionality of decrees issued under 'state-of-siege' powers. Superior tribunals and courts in each judicial district; circuit courts, minor courts, local criminal, police and municipal courts. Council of State represented on superior tribunals and courts, and controls administrative tribunals in departmental capitals.

DEFENCE

DEFENCE BUDGET, 1965: 1,083 m. pesos; 1·8 per cent of GDP.

ARMED FORCES: National service, between 18–30 (30–45 in Reserve) years of age, for 1 year. Strength: army 12,000–15,000; navy 7,800; total 20,000–23,000, plus 500,000 trained reserve (including Territorial Army).

INTERNATIONAL RELATIONS

Member of the UN and many of its international specialised agencies, including: IBRD and affiliates, IMF, FAO, ICAO, ILO, ITU, UNDP, UNESCO, UPU, WHO and WMO; IAEA, UNCTAD representative; also a member of various regional organisations, including: UN ECLA, OAS, Alliance for Progress, IDB and LAFTA.

ECONOMY

PRODUCTION

AGRICULTURE (000 tons)	1948–53[1]	63/4	64/5	65/6
Coffee	359	492	456	480
Bananas	354	573	895	965
Cotton	10	73	69	65
Sesame	7	35	49	72
Sugar (cane)[2]	171	426	513	677
Wheat	124	160	126	106
Maize	733	782	1,150	972
Barley	50	118	74	65
Rice	248	550	547	673
Potatoes	506	780	885	816

[1] Average 1948/9–1952/3.   [2] Raw value.

LAND, 1960 (%): Arable 4, permanent pasture 13, forested 61, urban and other 22.
OTHER AGRICULTURAL DATA: Agricultural holdings, 1960 (census): no. 1·21 m.;
area 27.3 m. hectares. Tractors in use (000s), 1960: 23·5. Fertiliser consumption
(000 tons), 1965/6: 182.
LIVESTOCK: No. (m. head), Dec. 1965: cattle 15·0, pigs 1·8. March 1964: sheep 1·5.
Products (000 tons), 1964: beef and veal 399, pork 46.
FISH: Landed (000 tons), 1964: total 53·3, characin 17·8.
MINING, 1965: (000 tons) iron ore 370, sulphur 12, salt 331; (tons) gold 9·5, silver 3·3.
Other important minerals: platinum and emeralds (world's main source). Fuels:
(m. tons) coal 3·1; (m. cubic metres) crude petroleum 11·6, natural gas 917.
MANUFACTURING, 1965: (000 tons) pig iron 193, steel ingots 241, cement 2,053. Liquid
fuels (000 cubic metres): gas and diesel oil 703, fuel oil 1,596, motor spirit 1,911. Wood
(cubic metres, sawn), 1964: 0·99 m. Motor vehicles (000 units, assembled), 1963: cars
2·7, commercial vehicles 0·8.
CONSTRUCTION: (000 sq. metres floor area), 1965: building permits approved 3,864.

ENERGY

CONSUMPTION (tons coal equiv.), 1964: total 8·64 m ; per head 0·49.
ELECTRICITY (public supply), 1965: generated (kwh) 4.952 m.; total installed capacity
(kw) 1·64 m.

GOVERNMENT EXPENDITURE

DISTRIBUTION (% of total), 1967: defence 15, police 9, education 17, health 4, public
works 9.

GROSS PRODUCT

GDP (000 m. pesos): at current market prices, 1964: 52·7; 1965: 58·8; at 1958 market
prices, 1964: 27·8; 1965: 28·7. Per head (US$), UN estimate, 1963: 268.
DISTRIBUTION (%), 1963: agriculture 31, manufacturing 19, trade 12, transport 8.
GROWTH RATES (%), 1950–60: total 4·5, per head 2·3; 1960–3: total 4·4, per head
2·1.

EXTERNAL TRADE (US$m.)	1955	1960	1964	1965	1966
EXPORTS (f.o.b.)[1]	580	466	546	537	507
Coffee	484	334	394	344	328
Petroleum	62	80	75	88	71
Bananas	17	14	12	19	20
Gold	13	15	13	11	10
IMPORTS (c.i.f.)	669	519	586	454	674
TRADE BALANCE	−90	−53	−40	+83	−167

[1] Excluding gold. Unrecorded exports have been estimated at US$ 30 m. a year.

DIRECTION OF TRADE (%)

	Exports			Imports		
	1955	1960	1965	1955	1960	1965
LAFTA	(0·5)	1·1	3·0	(1·8)	1·2	8·4
USA	73·8	64·1	46·1	62·9	57·3	47·8
EEC	12·3	19·1	21·0	17·6	19·1	17·1
UK	0·9	4·6	3·9	4·3	6·1	4·9

FINANCE

EXCHANGE RATE (*pesos/US$*), Free market, end-1960: 7·23. Capital market, end-1966: 16·30; 1965: 18·29; 1966: −283.
BALANCE OF PAYMENTS (*US$m.*): Goods and services (net), 1960: −85; 1964: −137; 1965: −14.
COST OF LIVING (*Dec. 1958=100*), December 1960: 112; 1965: 213; 1966: 243.
INDUSTRIAL WAGES: Average hourly earnings in manufacturing, 1965: 3·65 pesos.
TREASURY ACCOUNTS (*m. pesos*), 1964: revenue 5,097, expenditure 4,706; end-1964: fiscal surplus 26. 1965: revenue 5,826, expenditure 5,844; end-1965: fiscal deficit 418.

EMPLOYMENT

ECONOMICALLY ACTIVE (%), 1951: of total pop. 33 (men 55, women 12); of pop. 15 years and over: 56. In agriculture 54, services 16, manufacturing 12.
MANUFACTURING: Employment (*1958=100*), 1965: 113. Hours of work, 1965: 50 hours per week.

TRANSPORT AND COMMUNICATIONS

RAILWAYS: Traffic, 1965: 513 m. pass.-km.; 890 m. net ton-km. Length of track, 1965: 3,435 km.
MOTOR VEHICLES: In use (*000*), 1964: pass. cars 119·4; comm. vehicles 105·3. National road system, 1964: 41,400 km.
SHIPPING: Merchant fleet (*000 g.r. tons*), 1965: 160. International sea-borne shipping (*million tons*), 1965: goods loaded 7·0, goods unloaded 1·1. Main ports: Buenaventura, Barranquilla, Cartagena, Santa Marta, Tumaco and Turbo.
AIR: Scheduled services, 1965: total 1,301 m. pass.-km., 55·7 m. cargo ton-km. International 388 m. pass.-km., 16·3 m. cargo ton-km. Main airports: Bogotá, Eldorado (international); Medellín; Cali; Barranquilla; Bucaramanga; Cartagena; Cúcuta; Pereira.
TELEPHONES: No. in use, 1964: 410,000.

SOCIAL WELFARE

SYSTEM: Social security benefits and services are organised by Instituto Colombiano de Seguros Sociales. Employees of large firms receive numerous supplementary benefits and payments, including retirement pensions and group life insurance, provided by employers and related mainly to the size of the firm's capital. Employment legislation covers labour contracts; working hours; holidays; payment of wages, overtime and half-yearly bonuses; employers' liability for compensation for accidents, dismissal and death indemnities.
HEALTH, 1963: 2,000 persons per physician, 320 persons per hospital bed.
NUTRITION: Net food supply (*per head per day*), 1963: total 2,130 calories, protein 49 g.

EDUCATION

ILLITERACY RATE (%), mid-1964: 15 years and over, 38.
COMPULSORY: 5 years (between 7 and 11 years of age). Pupils in primary and secondary schools as % of pop. aged 5 to 19, 1963: 60.

SCHOOLS, 1963: Pre-school and primary: no. 23,800, pupils 2·14 m., teachers 57,800. Secondary: no. 1,180, p. 0·2 m., t. 15,600. Technical: no. 850, st. 92,000, t. s. 8,000. Teacher-training: no. 335, st. 47,700, t. s. 4,200. Higher (including universities, faculties): no. 250, st. 33,700, t. s. 6,000.

UNIVERSITIES (mainly 1963/4 data):
State: Universidad Nacional de Colombia, Bogotá 5,000 students, academic staff 195 (full-time); other colleges at Manizales, Medellín and Palmira (total st., including Bogotá, 1965: 9,300). U. Pedagógica Nacional Femenina, Bogotá. U. Distrital Francisco José de Caldas, Bogotá 750 st., a.s. 105. U. del Atlántico, Barranquilla 1,366 st., a.s. 128 (25 f.-t.). U. Industrial de Santander, Bucaramanga 1,250 st., a.s. 50. U. del Valle, Cali 1,348 st., a.s. 284 (201 f.-t.). U. de Cartagena 1,013 st., a.s. 196 (54 f.-t.). U. del Tolima, Ibagué 596 st., a.s. 83 (59 f.-t.). U. de Caldas, Manizales 954 st., a.s. 216 (94 f.-t.). U. de Antioquía, Medellín 4,000 st., a.s. 160. U. de Nariño, Pasto (Nariño) 1,557 st., a.s. 82 (48 f.-t.). U. Tecnológica de Pereira 392 st., a.s. 34 (26 f.-t.). U. del Cauca, Popayán 1,600 st., a.s. 140. U. P. y T. de Colombia, Tunja 2,737 st., a.s. 60.
Private (partly state-aided): Universidad de América, Bogotá. U. de Bogotá 'Jorge Tadeo Lozano', Bogotá 2,020 st., a.s. 170 (10 f.-t.). U. Externado de Colombia, Bogotá 500 st., a.s. 6. U. de la Gran Colombia, Bogotá 2,960 st. Pont. U. Javeriana, Bogotá 5,750 st., a.s. 518 (48 f.-t.). U. Libre de Colombia, Bogotá 2,040 st., a.s. 250. U. de Los Andes, Bogotá 918 st., a.s. 162 (91 f.-t.). Colegio Mayor de Nuestra Señora del Rosario, Bogotá 200 st. U. Libre Seccional del Atlántico, Barranquilla. U. Santiago de Cali 100 st. U. P. Bolivariana, Medellín 5,030 st., a.s. 400 (168 f.-t.). U. de Medellín, Medellín 476 st., a.s. 77 (8 f.-t.).

MASS MEDIA

BROADCASTING: No. of receivers in use, end-1964: TV 0·35 m.; 1962: radio 3 m. Transmitters: TV 14, radio 220.
CINEMAS: No., 1963: 790. Attendance, 1963: total 66 m., per head 4·4.
NEWSPRINT: Consumption, 1963: total 39,600 tons, per head 2·6 kg.
NEWSPAPERS: Daily, 1963: 26. Estimated circulation 0·8 m., copies per 000 of population 52. Principal dailies (*circulation, ooos*): Bogotá: *El Tiempo* 176 (Sunday 350), *El Espectador* 171 (S. 182), *La Paz* 70, *La República* 60, *El Siglo* 55. Barranquilla: *Diario de Colombia* 75, *Diario del Caribe* 25. Cali: *El País* 78. Medellín: *El Colombiano* 66.

ECUADOR

DAVID PRESTON

ECUADOR is the smallest of the Andean republics, the effectively occupied territory being little larger than the area of Britain. The rural areas in the mountains are inhabited largely by Indians; only in the province of Carchi in the extreme north and the southern half of Loja in the far south are the rural people mestizos. On the coast the pure Indian element has been absorbed into an ethnically mixed population which differs from the mestizos of the Andes by having a more pronounced Negroid element. In the northern part of the coastlands a pure Negro element becomes noticeable along the coast and two small groups of indigenous Indians, the Cayapa and the Colorado, are found in isolated inland areas.

HISTORY

The Inca and colonial periods

Although incorporated in the Inca Empire, Ecuador lay on the periphery of the main American civilisations. The cultures that developed here were by no means primitive; the mountain chiefdoms that the Incas overcame were well organised, and some had constructed large settlements and had a material culture not much inferior in some respects to that of the Incas. Early Spanish explorers, touching on the west coast of Ecuador in 1526, likewise found large settlements. The importance of the Incas, conquering Ecuador with some difficulty in the last quarter of the 15th century, lay in their creation of the necessary infrastructure for imperial government. This included a regional organisation of power centred upon the Inca himself in Cuzco and a national road system which stimulated production for the support of the administrators and satisfied imperial needs. Inca roads, although largely abandoned, can be traced throughout Ecuador, but only one major Inca structure remains—the fortress Ingapirca in Cañar province.

Ecuador claims as its first national figure Atahualpa, the son of the Inca Huayna Capac, reputedly the result of the union of the Inca with the daughter of a major Ecuadorian tribal chief. Huayna Capac had died before the arrival of the Spanish, leaving the kingdom to Huascar, one of his sons by his principal sister-wife. Atahualpa successfully rebelled against his brother but the Spanish, arriving under Pizarro in 1532, captured him and later treacherously murdered him. Sebastián de Belalcázar, a subordinate of Pizarro, entered Quito in 1534.

The colonial period saw far greater social and economic change than the Incas had caused less than a century previously. New crops and livestock were introduced and new towns built, although often on old sites. Today many Ecuadorian towns and even some villages have churches and other old buildings dating from the 16th century. The various religious orders played an important part in the establishment of the Spanish Empire in Ecuador; native craftsmen were trained to reproduce the styles of the Old World but often introduced their own modifications. Indigenous artists, trained by Roman Catholic priests, portrayed Christian subjects with pagan fervour. No major developments could take place in Ecuador because it remained at the periphery of the divisions of the empire, governed at different times from Lima and Bogotá. Thus the development of Ecuadorian agriculture and such minor industries as were permitted by the crown was stifled by Lima or Bogotá, since these cities naturally represented the interests of Peruvian or Colombian producers to the detriment of potential competitors. In this way the vines of Pimampiro, in northern Ecuador, were ordered to be destroyed lest their grapes produce wine to compete with that produced by the estates of the inhabitants of Lima.

The Republic of the Equator

The herald of the Republican period in Ecuador was Eugenio de Santa Cruz y Espejo. Of humble origin, Espejo was one of the first Ecuadorians to propagate the new and European ideas then spreading to the New World. In the early 1790s until his death in prison in 1795, he advocated emancipation from Spain, republican government and the disestablishment of the church. It was not until 1822 however that Spanish rule was ended by the forces of Simón Bolívar, coming from the north. The decisive battle of Pichincha (1822) took place outside Quito and Venezuelan Antonio José Sucre was the victorious commander, later, however, to be murdered. The first president was another Venezuelan general, Juan José Flores, who ruled as a virtual military dictator with little pretence at liberalism. The ideals of the French Revolution, partly the cause of the Latin American independence movements, were laid aside and the Spanish land-owning and power-monopolising aristocracy was replaced by a creole Ecuadorian oligarchy. The political unit that first came into being was the Confederation of Gran Colombia, which included the territories of what are now Venezuela, Colombia and Ecuador. Founded on the inspiration of Bolívar, the ideologist of liberation movements in northern South America, the Confederation had little unity of interest; Venezuela seceded in 1830 and later in the same year Ecuador did likewise, becoming the Republic of the Equator—Ecuador—although many felt that the Republic of Quito would have been a more logical name.

The thirty years following independence produced little save political chaos and stagnation. In 1852 slavery was abolished but there were few legally enslaved who could benefit from this: those enslaved by custom, many of the rural Indians, had no redress. The first figure of note in this period was Gabriel García Moreno (president in 1861–5 and 1869–75). He sought to bring order to the chaotic country. He was a devout Roman Catholic and a convinced conservative. He embarked upon a public works programme, building roads, schools and public buildings, and he was responsible for the commencement of the Quito–Guayaquil railway. He increased the power of the church and sought to remedy some of Ecuador's ills by bringing Roman Catholicism into everyday life. His ideas were contrary to the growing liberal feeling in the country and he was assassinated in 1875.

With slow economic progress and social change the difference in political feelings and social climate between the conservative mountains and the progressive coast became more apparent. The feudal nature of Andean society had been but little modified by the growth of its towns and of the mestizo sector of the population. On the other hand the coastlands, centred upon Guayaquil, depended more for their livelihood on international trade and were more in touch with international affairs. Furthermore, the agricultural lands of the coast were not under huge estates as were those of the highlands, and a unique small landowner class came into being on the coast. It was naturally from the lowlands that the first important liberal leader emerged. Eloy Alfaro (president in 1897–1901 and 1906–11) was the first popular Ecuadorian political figure—García Moreno had attracted little mass support. Alfaro's people's army defeated the government forces in a brief civil war and he assumed power in 1896. Under Alfaro, state and church were separated, education was secularised and civil liberties were guaranteed. However, he made little effort to combat the land problem or to remedy national economic problems. In 1912, accused of authoritarianism, he was deposed and barbarously murdered by an angry mob.

Under the nominally liberal rule of Leonidas Plaza (president in 1901–4 and 1912–16) little progress was made. Following the end of Plaza's second term of office in 1916, Ecuador entered upon a phase of economic expansion, stimulated in part by the disruption of trade caused by the 1914–18 war which encouraged home industries and the growth of urban centres. The small oilfield west of Guayaquil was developed largely with British capital at this time. The Guayaquil Commercial and Industrial Bank, too, developed rapidly in association with rising agricultural exports, in particular cacao. It was able to dominate the economic life of the coast and influenced political activity. It was capitalist industrialists and the few large coastal landowners who benefited most of all from economic expansion and the position of the workers did not improve materially. The Andean region had, for once, little influence upon the political life of the country. Workers' revolts such as that in Guayaquil of November 1922 were suppressed with brutality. Finally the Army, composed of Andeans, rebelled and in July 1925 attempted to bring the situation under control by military action. The Central Bank was set up at Quito and given a monopoly of the issue of banknotes, in part to counteract the commercial dominance of the coast.

The most important and tragic date in recent Ecuadorian history was July 1941, when Peru invaded the south-western province of El Oro ignoring offers of mediation, pressing her claim to part of Ecuador's Amazon lowlands. The highly-trained and well-equipped Peruvian force easily defeated the small Ecuadorian army and Ecuador was prevailed upon by the United States and others to cede the disputed area to Peru by the Protocol of Rio de Janeiro in January 1942. The disputed area that was lost was over 180,000 square kilometres, equivalent to the area of Scotland and England together. Thus Ecuador lost a major part of her eastern lowlands, was deprived of an outlet on the Amazon and a sharp blow was dealt to national pride.

Recent political developments

The ensuing years were politically unsettled and there was no long period of stability or marked growth. Ecuadorian politics have long been dominated by charismatic individuals, often without a firm set of political beliefs, who once in power have failed to achieve even their most limited objectives. The catalogue of presidents and military juntas since 1925 is long and little coherent pattern can be traced. One figure, however, stands out who has held the presidency on four separate occasions over a span of thirty years— José María Velasco Ibarra. Velasco was president in 1933–5, 1944–7,

1952–6 and 1960–1. On only one of those occasions, in 1952, did he stay in office for the full presidential term of four years. He has at different times attracted the support of fascists and Marxists, liberals and conservatives, but despite the immense and geographically widespread popular appeal of his personality, fostered in barnstorming electoral campaigns throughout the country, his policies have never had long-term goals and excessive spending and resultant depletion of the treasury's resources marked his one full term, 1952–6. The major change in the political scene in 1960 brought about by Velasco was the rejection of the Protocol of Rio de Janeiro and the renewal of the cold war with Peru over the lost Amazon territories, accompanied by the slogan '*Ecuador, país amazónico!*'. Despite having been ousted from the presidency and being accused by his successors in 1957 and 1961 of undermining the economy, his grass-roots appeal far surpasses that of any contemporary Ecuadorian politician.

Two other presidents since 1945 have had sufficient effect upon the national political scene to be worthy of special mention. Galo Plaza, son of former President Leonidas Plaza, brought a brief period of peace without progress to Ecuador between 1948 and 1952. Having been educated in the United States his good personal relations with this country enabled him to bring numerous technicians to Ecuador to advise on the ways in which social and economic change might be induced. The concrete achievements of this programme were few, however, and the electorate, accustomed to rash promises and fiery oratory, was unimpressed by mere stability. Plaza was appropriately succeeded by Velasco. Appointed UN mediator in Cyprus by U Thant in 1964, he may have gained sufficient prestige to be a force to be reckoned with in future elections.

The leader of the minority Christian Socialist Party, Camilo Ponce Enríquez, was elected president by a small majority in 1956. His period in office, like that of Plaza, was noted largely for its tranquillity and the fact that no major reforms were attempted. He was, however, able to hold together a cabinet including liberals and conservatives and he was regarded as a strong contender for the presidency in 1964. The fourth period of Velasquismo in 1960 following Ponce's term ended in a minor revolution caused, among other things, by unpopular taxes. Velasco was replaced by Carlos Julio Arosemena, then vice-president, who came to power with the aid of the military. Arosemena was not a success and his oscillations between the right and the left of the political spectrum, together with the frequency with which he appeared in public drunk, caused any support that he might have had to vanish. He was replaced on 11 July 1963 by a military quadrumvirate comprising General Marcos Gándara Enríquez, General Cabrera Sevilla, Colonel Guillermo Freile Posso (dismissed on 29 June 1965 for urging a return to constitutionalism), and Rear-Admiral Ramón Castro Jijón. This group, despite their fundamentally undemocratic nature, hoped to bring order, honesty and professionalism into the national government— commodities rarely apparent in Ecuadorian politics. They made some modifications in the taxation system and in 1964 passed a weak Agrarian Reform Law.

As the rule of the junta continued, disillusionment grew, some people in important positions resigned and emigrated to the United States and pressure for a return to constitutional government grew as economic chaos set in. Finally, after pleas from ex-presidents Plaza and Ponce, on 29 March 1966 the junta was replaced by the economist Clemente Yerovi Indaburu who was intended to preside over the transitional period during which elections for the National Assembly could be held. He declared a general amnesty under which the Communist Party became legal once more. The elections of 16 October 1966 were fair but inconclusive and on 16 November 1966 the newly-elected Assembly nominated Otto Arosemena Gomez (nephew of ex-president Carlos Julio Arosemena) as interim president. Although formerly a non-party centre-leftist Arosemena has been subject to strong pressures from the right. In late 1967 a new constitution was approved with only minor changes from the previous constitution, such as allowing equal legal rights for natural and legitimate sons. Presidential elections are likely in mid-1968; present trends suggest the fifth coming of Velasco Ibarra, if he is allowed to be a candidate.

Political parties

The personalities previously mentioned are the most important elements of the Ecuadorian political scene. Traditional parties are without a unified approach to national problems and their importance is closely associated with individuals whose appearance on the political scene may be momentary. The legal training common to many Ecuadorian politicians is associated with a love of theory and a dislike of reality. Finally, since the electorate comprises little more than 15 per cent of the population, the political parties represent the views of only a minority of the populace.

The Liberal Radical Party under Pedro José Arteta nominally supports agrarian reform, believes in a social security system and advocates religious tolerance, but when in power believes primarily in maintaining its position and disregards stated objectives. The Conservative Party, with strong rural support and the powerful force of the church behind it, was the first to propose land reform in 1962 and seems to represent the more progressive factions in the church. It is led by Gonzalo Cordero Crespo. The Velasquista Party, the well organised populist party of Velasco Ibarra, is oriented to his own peculiar political beliefs and prepared for his fifth coming. The Christian Socialist Party, led by Ponce Enríquez, is the Ecuadorian arm of the Christian Democratic movement, founded in 1951 to unite 'those who were desirous of wrenching the banner of social justice from the Marxists who had usurped it'.

None of the other parties has much impact upon the current political scene. The Socialist Party is weak and the Communist Party outlawed although allegedly Communist-inspired guerilla activity is reported sporadically from isolated parts of the country, including the lowland Santo Domingo area west of Quito.

ECONOMY

The financial stability that has obtained in Ecuador for the past decade has been advantageous for existing industries but despite the moderate level of economic growth the benefits of national progress have remained confined to the urban population and a minority of rural dwellers in the coastlands.

The Andes remain the most backward area of the country with dense rural population and little land available for settlement. A series of dry years in the early sixties further aggravated rural poverty. The high density of rural population in areas of freeholdings and the associated large, feudally-organised estates inhibit the development of both modern commercial agriculture and an efficient system of intensive agriculture appropriate to large estates and smallholdings respectively. The resolutely self-sufficient nature of

Andean peasant agriculture has been little changed by US aid and only slightly modified in small areas as a result of work by government agencies and the United Nations Andean Action programme. A few large estates have developed efficient systems of commercial agriculture based most frequently on the rearing of cattle for milk and beef.

By contrast the form of agriculture on the coastlands has, in many areas, long been based upon the production of a marketable surplus and a small-scale commercial agriculture prevails in all areas where goods can be transported to market; the rural population owns its own land and there is abundant land available for settlement. A characteristic of the agriculture of the coastlands has been for producers to concentrate on the production of one main export crop. Cacao was the leading crop produced for export until the early thirties when diseases brought a sharp fall in production. For a time, particularly during the second world war, rice was an important export commodity but by 1951 bananas had increased their share of exports and in 1952 Ecuador was the world's leading banana exporter. Exports increased from 23.7 million stems in 1955 to 41.4 million stems in 1964. Ecuador accounts for a quarter of world banana trade and exports more than the combined exports of the other major exporters, Honduras and Costa Rica. By contrast with Central American banana plantations, which are very large and owned by US fruit monopolies, in Ecuador where banana growers are organised by the National Banana Board (Dirección Nacional del Banano) holdings average about 137 acres (1960-1), and producers on even a small scale are assisted and encouraged to improve the quality of their fruit.

Like those of many other small Latin American countries, Ecuadorian industries are hampered by small markets and lack of enterprise. Moreover, industry's share of total national production fell from 16 per cent in 1950 to 15.4 per cent in 1962. The mass of rural workers flooding the cities provides a reservoir of cheap, unskilled labour that could be used in labour-intensive industries. Economic stability has created a favourable climate for investment but the size of the country and its political problems have discouraged more significant flow of foreign investment other than as direct aid from the United States and various international organisations.

The industries of greatest importance are food processing and textiles, together accounting for 54 per cent of industrial production by value in 1960. Food processing plants are widely dispersed, there being, for example, a tuna cannery in Manta, but the largest concentrations are in Guayaquil and Quito. The main textile factories are likewise near the major cities and in the northern Andes around Otavalo.

Urbanisation

While the agricultural sector of the economy provides the country with foreign exchange and occupies over half the national labour force (56.5 per cent in 1962) the most important population shift is towards the towns. Between 1950 and 1962 the proportion of the population in urban areas rose from 28.5 to 35.3 per cent and in that time Guayaquil almost doubled its population. The character of the towns in the mountains and on the coast is very different. In the mountains almost all the towns are of 16th- or 17th-century colonial origin and have grid-pattern streets and small, single-storey houses—except near the centre—with brown tiled roofs and white-washed walls. Only in Quito are many large modern buildings to be found. Industrial development is noticeable only in Quito and to the south in

Cuenca; in other towns industrial establishments, though numerous, are so small as not to be noticeable. Urban sprawl is most noticeable in Quito, although most towns have some shanty-town development on their periphery.

By contrast all the coastal towns have the appearance of having been constructed recently and in a hurry. Only Guayaquil looks like a modern city. The population of coastal Ecuador increased by 50 per cent between 1950 and 1962 compared with a 35-per-cent increase in the Andes. This is the result of a rapid increase in the size of many towns, Quevedo, for example, having quintupled in size and Machala having trebled in the period 1950–62. Much of the increase has been through immigration; the newcomers are often rural folk with a peasant standard of living and have settled in a rash of shanties on the edges of all the coastal towns. In the towns, many of whose houses are small, split-cane walled and corrugated iron roofed, the large number of small industrial establishments is striking. Many are newly established and Guayaquil has attracted the largest number by virtue of being the only major commercial centre in western Ecuador.

Current changes

Although industrial growth from its present narrow base is to be expected, the changes most likely to occur that will affect export earnings are in agriculture. Least change is foreseeable in Andean agriculture, where traditional methods of farming and the archaic landholding system are major obstacles to development. The modernisation of existing farming practices on many large estates offers considerable hope for improved yields but only a minority of owners, particularly those between Cayambe and Latacunga, have developed their estates into efficient economic units. Recent attempts to improve the quality of highland sheep by the introduction of the Corriedale and other high-quality strains, as well as the growing production of pyrethrum (used in the manufacture of insecticides), may increase the productivity of high-altitude areas. New ideas and crops are most eagerly accepted by the richer, large-scale farmers, but the effects of new ideas upon peasant agriculture are slight.

The improvement of peasant farming in the Andes is a difficult problem capable of solution only over a long period. The existence of a landless group of rural folk in an area of high-population densities can only be solved by land reform and large-scale, peasant-oriented colonisation projects, neither of which seems imminent. Improvement of existing agricultural practices and the maximisation of yields from the area presently cultivated can only be achieved by intensive agricultural extension work but this is hampered by a lack of qualified people to do such work. The agrarian reform instituted in 1964 had, by September 1966, distributed titles to 15,959 farmers for 172,811 acres but the emphasis has been on distributing formerly unoccupied land for colonisation and breaking up the state-owned estates. It has become illegal not to pay farm workers (as was common under the *huasipungo* system), but the reforms have not fundamentally changed the agrarian structure in the face of strong and articulate opposition.

The greatest potential for agricultural development of maximum benefit to the nation as a whole lies in the western lowlands. The inherent danger of overdependence upon one crop for a majority of export earnings was illustrated in 1965 and 1966 by a sharp fall in banana exports associated in part with the cessation of exports to Japan, which had been an important buyer of Ecuadorian fruit for several years while Taiwan plantations recovered from devastation by disease. A fall in demand for Ecuadorian fruit has also been linked with increased Central American production and a drop in banana prices from US$9 per 100 lbs. in 1957 to $5·71 in 1963 has further reduced banana earnings. The proposal to develop a Franco-Ecuadorian banana fleet to decrease dependence upon foreign shippers indicates a useful method of strengthening the banana industry. Traditional crops such as cacao, coffee and sugar are all increasing in importance as export crops and new crops such as the African oil palm offer possibilities for the supply of internal markets.

The most rapid development in agriculture has been witnessed along the line of new roads in both the coastlands and on the Andean margin of the eastern lowlands. In many cases in the western lowlands farmers have cleared land and left their first crops to rot awaiting the arrival of the road for their produce to be taken to port. The solitary new railway, completed in 1957, to the tiny port of San Lorenzo on the north-west coast was intended to stimulate development in the humid northern lowlands, but it has been a failure. High freight rates and inadequate port facilities have prevented agricultural produce being shipped to markets. The area around Santo Domingo, west of Quito, has grown rapidly and roads from there to Quevedo and Esmeraldas have aided the spread of bananas in the area. A new road under construction in 1966 from Babahoyo to Quevedo is likely to open up another potentially fertile area to commercial agriculture. The opening up of the Oriente to the east is being carried out slowly with the construction of roads to Zamora, in Loja province, and east of Ambato in the forest north of Puyo towards Tena. The latter road has stimulated settlement and facilitated the sale of the various fruit crops of the area, in particular *naranjilla* (Solanum quitoense), destined for Quito markets. In 1966 a major colonisation project in the central eastern lowland province of Morona-Santiago was announced.

The rate of change that occurs in Ecuador is directly proportional to the efficiency with which successive governments stimulate progress. Since for the majority of people in the Andean region progress means a diminution in the authority of the politically powerful landowners, it may not be expected to come rapidly save in a revolutionary situation. In the eastern and western lowlands improved communications stimulate colonisation and prosperity for new settlers, and it is in these areas that change can be introduced most easily and productively.

BIBLIOGRAPHY

Blomberg, Rolf (ed.) *Ecuador: Andean Mosaic*, Gerber, Stockholm, 1952.

Casagrande, J. B. *et al.* 'Colonization as a Research Frontier: the Ecuadorian Case', *Process and Pattern in Culture*, ed. R. A. Manners, Aldine Press, Chicago, 1964.

Collier, John Jr. and Buitrón, Anibal. *The Awakening Valley*, Univ. of Chicago Press, Chicago, 1949.

Icaza, Jorge. *Huasipungo*, Dennis Dobson, London, 1962. *Villagers*, Southern Illinois Univ. Press, Carbondale, Ill., 1964.

Linke, Lilo. *Ecuador. Country of Contrasts*, Oxford Univ. Press, London and New York, 3rd ed. 1960.

Miller, E. V. 'Agricultural Ecuador', *Geographical Review*, Vol. 49, New York, April 1959.

BASIC INFORMATION

CLIMATE

	Guayaquil	Quito
Lat./long.	2° S, 80° W	0°S, 78° 30′ W
Altitude	20 ft/6 m.	9,446 ft/2,880 m.
Mean temp. of hottest month	27°C/80°F (Mar./Apr.)	15°C/59°F (Sep.)
Mean temp. of coolest month	24°C/76°F (July/Aug.)	14°C/58°F (June/July)
Absolute max.	98°F/36°C	86°F/30°C
Absolute min.	57°F/14°C	32°F/0°C
Relative humidity at midday of hottest and coolest months	n.a.	44%/51%
Wettest months	10·9 in./277 mm. (Mar.)	6·9 in./175 mm. (Apr.)
Driest months	0 (Aug.)	0·8 in./20 mm. (July)
Annual av. rainfall	38·8 in./986 mm.	43·9 in./1,115 mm.

POPULATION

TOTAL (*million*): 1962 (census) 4·48, excluding nomadic Indians; end-Oct. 1966: 5·39; 1980 (ECLA projection): 8·08.

DENSITY, 1965: 19 persons per sq. km.

CRUDE RATES (*per 000*), 1965: birth 44·0, death 11·7, infant mortality 93·0.

GROWTH RATES (% *p.a.*) 1945–65: 3·1; 1960–5: 3·3.

DISTRIBUTION (% *of total pop.*): Ethnic, 1942: mixed 41, Amerindian 39, white 10, Negro 5. Languages: Spanish and Quechua, also Jíbaro. Religion: Mainly Roman Catholic. Urban (*centres 2,000 inhab. or over*), ECLA data, 1950: 27·5; 1960: 33·0; 1980 (proj.): 44·2. Largest cities (*000 inhab.*), 1962: Guayaquil 506, Quito (capital) 348, Cuenca 60, Ambato 52, Riobamba 41.

CONSTITUTIONAL SYSTEM (*based on 1946 constitution*)

CONSTITUTION: First 1830; main constitution 1906; revised 1929, 1938, 1945; latest 1946: codified 1955, amended 1960, suspended 1963, fully reinstated 1966. New constitution to be promulgated.

SYSTEM: Unitary republic, comprising 20 provinces (including the Galápagos Islands) and 97 cantons. Separate executive, legislature and judiciary.

EXECUTIVE: Power vested in president, elected by popular vote for a 4-year term; no reelection within four years of end of term.

LEGISLATURE: Bi-cameral, National Congress of Senate and Chamber of Deputies. *Senate:* 2 members from each province and 1 from the Galápagos Islands, elected by direct popular vote; and 12 functional senators; 4-year term, and may be reelected indefinitely. *Deputies:* 1 deputy for each 5,000 inhabitants in each province, with an additional deputy if there is an excess of 25,000; minimum of 2 deputies for each province (except Galápagos Islands); 2-year term and may be reelected indefinitely. *Suffrage:* Universal, compulsory (for men, optional for women) voting for literate citizens over 18 years of age. *Elections:* Presidential, June 1960: Dr José María Velasco Ibarra (Movimiento Nacional Velasquista) 373,585 votes, Plaza Lasso (Lib.) 175,076, Dr Cordero Crespo (Cons.) 172,690. Pres. Velasco resigned Nov. 1961; succeeded by Dr Carlos Julio Arosemena Monroy. Composition of Congress (June 1960):

Party group	Senate	Deputies
Independents	18	32
Conservatives	8	17
Anti-Communist Front	4	17
Others	5	6

RECENT EVENTS: Pres. Arosemena Monroy deposed July 1963 by coup; military Junta, headed by Rear Adml. Ramón Castro Jijón, set up. Junta deposed March 1966, Clemente Yerovi Indaburu chosen Interim President. Elections (of deputies) for Constituent Assembly October 1966: Movimiento Social Cristiano (headed by ex-Pres. Camilo Ponce Enríquez) 36 seats, Liberal party 22. Constituent Assembly elected Dr Otto Arosemena Gómez Interim Constitutional President (Dr Ponce having withdrawn); term extended by C.A. until September 1968.

JUDICIARY: Supreme Court (at Quito), of 15 justices (elected for 6 years) and 2 fiscals. 11 superior courts and many lower courts.

DEFENCE

DEFENCE BUDGET: 1965: 406 m. sucres; 2·0 per cent of GDP.

ARMED FORCES: Military service: between 18–20 years of age, 1 year in army. Strength: army 10–20,000, navy 4–7,000, air force up to 5,000; total 15–30,000.

INTERNATIONAL RELATIONS

Member of the UN and many of its international specialised agencies, including: IBRD and affiliates, IMF, FAO, ICAO, IMCO, ILO, ITU, UNDP, UNESCO, UPU, WHO and WMO; IAEA; UNCTAD representative; also a member of various regional organisations, including: UN ECLA, OAS, Alliance for Progress, IDB and LAFTA.

ECONOMY

PRODUCTION

AGRICULTURE (*ooo tons*)	1948–53[1]	63/4	64/5	65/6[2]
Bananas	450	2,098	3,300	3,300
Coffee	20	43	56	60
Cacao	27	34	50	38
Rice (paddy)	127	191	167	157
Wheat	24	67	63	61
Maize	79	192	129	191
Barley	57	130	81	93
Sugar	55	149	183	177
Manioc	22	209	189	254
Cotton seed	4	6	9	12

[1] Average 1948/9–1952/3.   [2] Provisional.

LAND, 1961 (%): Arable 11, permanent pasture 8, forested 55, urban and other 26.

OTHER AGRICULTURAL DATA: Agricultural holdings, 1954 (census): no. 344,234; area 6·0 m. hectares. Tractors in use (*ooos*), 1964: 1·7. Fertiliser consumption (*ooo tons*), 1965/6: 15·3.

LIVESTOCK: Nos (*m. head*), 1964/5: cattle 1·73, sheep 1·93, pigs 1·54. Products (*ooo tons*), 1964: meat 72, beef and veal 43, wool 12.

FISH: Landed (*ooo tons*), 1965: total 53·5; skipjack (bonito) 14·8, shrimps 5·7.

MINING: 1964: (*tons*) copper ore 200, lead ore 200, silver 3·6, gold 0·55, salt 26,400. 1965: (*ooo cubic metres*) crude petroleum 452, natural gas 200.

MANUFACTURING, 1965: (*ooo tons*) cement 325, wheat flour 101; (*m. litres*) beer 39·6. Liquid fuels, 1964: (*ooo cubic metres*) diesel oil 138, fuel oil 204, motor spirit 178.

ENERGY

CONSUMPTION (*tons, coal equiv.*), 1964: total 0·95 m., per head 0·195.

ELECTRICITY, 1965: generated (*kwh*) 590 m., installed capacity (*kw*) 0·19 m.

GOVERNMENT EXPENDITURE

DISTRIBUTION (% *of total*), 1965: defence 15, education 17, social services 11.

GROSS PRODUCT

GDP (*ooo m. sucres*): At current market prices, 1964: 19·4; 1965: 20·8; at 1960 market prices, 1964: 16·8; 1965: 17·4. Per head (*US$*), UN estimate, 1964: 194.
DISTRIBUTION (%), 1964: agriculture 36, manufacturing 17, trade 12.
GROWTH RATES (%), 1950–60: total 4·9, per head 1·8; 1960–4: total 4·0, per head 0·8.

EXTERNAL TRADE (*US$ m.*)	*1955*	*1960*	*1963*	*1964*	*1965*
EXPORTS (f.o.b.)[1]	115	149	151	162	175
Bananas	62	90	85	98	95
Coffee	23	22	18	21	36
Cacao	19	21	20	16	21
IMPORTS (c.i.f.)	114	114	129	169	171
TRADE BALANCE	—	+35	+22	−7	+4

[1] Adjusted.

DIRECTION OF TRADE (%)

	Exports[1]				*Imports*	
	1955	*1960*	*1965*	*1955*[2]	*1960*	*1965*
LAFTA	(9·6)	5·0	8·1	(7·0)	3·5	5·2
USA	61·2	62·3	58·7	52·4	48·3	41·5
EEC	17·6	23·1	27·9	23·3	28·3	20·0
UK	0·9	0·8	0·3	6·2	5·7	5·2

[1] Unadjusted data.   [2] Through port of Guayaquil only.

FINANCE

EXCHANGE RATE (*Sucres/US$*): Free market, end-year, 1960: 17·50; 1964: 18·52; 1965: 18·52; 1966: 20·48.
BALANCE OF PAYMENTS (*US$ m.*): Goods and services (net) 1960: −20; 1964: −30; 1965: −31.
COST OF LIVING (*Dec. 1958=100*), Quito, December, 1960: 104; 1964: 120; 1965: 127; 1966: 131.
INDUSTRIAL WAGES: Average earnings per hour, 1964: 3·18 sucres.
TREASURY ACCOUNTS (*m. sucres*), 1965: Revenue 2,524, expenditure 3,154, deficit 630.

EMPLOYMENT

ECONOMICALLY ACTIVE (%), 1962: Of total (excl. Indian jungle pop.) 32 (men 54, women 11). In agriculture 56, manufacturing 15, services 13, commerce 7.

TRANSPORT AND COMMUNICATIONS

RAILWAYS: Traffic, 1965: 52 m. pass.-km.; 97 m. net ton-km. Length of track 1,152 km.
MOTOR VEHICLES: In use (*ooo*), 1965: pass. cars 17·5, comm. vehicles 22·0. Roads 16,700 km., paved 1,480 km.
SHIPPING: Merchant fleet (*ooo g.r. tons*), 1965: 43. International sea-borne shipping (*m. tons*), 1965: goods loaded 1·2, goods unloaded 0·7. Main port: Guayaquil; others: Puerto Bolívar, Manta, San Lorenzo, Bahía de Caráquez, Esmeraldas.
AIR: Scheduled services, 1964: Total 64 m. pass.-km., 1·05 m. cargo ton-km. International 36·9 m. pass.-km., 0·30 m. cargo ton-km. Main airports: Quito, Mariscal Sucre (int.); Guayaquil, Simón Bolívar (int.).
TELEPHONES: No. in use, 1964: 43,400.

SOCIAL WELFARE

SYSTEM: Social insurance benefits and services administered by Instituto Nacional de Previsión through the Cajas de Pensiones and del Seguro. Financed by employees' and employers' contributions based on remuneration: employees 5%; employers 6%, also a month's wages to reserve funds and 5% net profits for workers' benefits.

Employment legislation covers working hours; holidays; payment of wages, overtime and reserve fund; sickness; employers' liability for compensation for accidents, dismissal and death indemnities.

HEALTH: 4,000 persons per physician, 520 persons (in Quito) per hospital bed.

NUTRITION: Net food supply (*per head per day*), 1963: 1,826 calories; protein 48 g.

EDUCATION

ILLITERACY RATE (%), 1962 (census sample): 15 years and over, 33.

COMPULSORY: 6 years (between 6 and 14 years of age). Pupils in primary and secondary (including night) schools as a % of pop. aged 5 to 19, 1963: 57. High drop-out rate.

SCHOOLS, 1963: Pre-school and primary: no. 6,180, pupils 0·17 m., teachers 19,000. Secondary: no. 239, p. 54,200, t. 5,450. Technical: no. 135, st. 31,200, t. s. 2,060. Teacher-training: no. 33, st. 10,600, t. s. 670. Higher (incl. universities, faculties): no. 15, st. 12,030, t. s. 1,525.

UNIVERSITIES (mainly 1963/4 data):

Autonomous, but state aided: Central del Ecuador, Quito 4,770 students, academic staff 527 (5 full-time). Pont. U. Cat. del Ecuador, Quito 1,990 st., a.s. 150. Esc. Politécnica Nacional, Quito 800 st., a.s. 64. Guayaquil 4,000 st.; a.s. 456. Santiago de Guayaquil. Esc. Sup. Politécnica del Litoral 364 st.; a.s. 40 (10 f.-t.). Cuenca 1,260 st., a.s. 128 (6 f.-t.). Loja 510 st., a.s. 67 (63 f.-t.). Técnica de Manabí, Portoviejo 140 st., a.s. 35.

MASS MEDIA

BROADCASTING: No. of receivers in use, 1966: TV 20,000, radio 0·65 m. Stations: TV 2, radio 195.

CINEMAS: No., 1961: 122. Attendance, 1952: total 8·3 m., per head 2·4.

NEWSPRINT: Consumption, 1962: total 7,600 tons, per head 1·7 kg.

NEWSPAPERS: Daily, 1962: 27. Estimated circulation (18 dailies) 0·24 m., copies per 000 of population 52. Principal dailies (*circulation, ooos*) in Guayaquil: *El Universo* 69 (S. 77), *El Telégrafo* 28 (S. 34), *La Prensa* 10. Quito: *El Comercio* 48, *Últimas Noticias* 32.

PARAGUAY

GEORGE PENDLE

PARAGUAY lies in the middle of South America, about 1,000 miles by river—through Argentine territory—from the Atlantic Ocean, and blocked by the jungles of Bolivia and the Andean *cordillera* from access to the Pacific. Throughout Paraguay's history the course of events has been determined, to an extraordinary degree, by geographical circumstances. Remote, land-locked, subject to political, military and economic pressure from surrounding powers, the Paraguayan nation has preserved a racial homogeneity—that of the indigenous Guaraníes, with a relatively small Spanish admixture—unparalleled in South America. While Spanish is the official language, the mass of the population still prefer to speak their melodious Guaraní.

Paraguay is cut into two quite different parts by the great River Paraguay. On the eastern side of the river lies the Arcadia to which Voltaire—who, of course, never went to South America—sent his Candide. This is a rolling, fertile, red-earthed country of pastures and cultivated fields (mandioca and maize), dotted with palm-trees; a blue haze hangs over cone-shaped hills that rise, here and there, above dense woodlands. The country people live in small *ranchos* made of stakes and sticks plastered with mud and with floors of beaten earth. Paraguay's chief towns are situated in this eastern part of the republic, and the capital, Asunción—with its pleasant suburbs, white-washed houses, red-tiled roofs, flowering shrubs and trees—is on the eastern bank of the river.

The other side of the river is another world. The Chaco, a flat land of about 95,400 square miles, is half as large again as eastern Paraguay. It is a brackish prairie covered mainly with rough grass and scrub trees. After heavy rainstorms the Chaco's riverside regions are flooded, and herds of cattle may be drowned; when the waters subside and the swamps dry up, the animals are in danger of dying from thirst. Upstream the trees are taller, among them the *quebracho*, the source of tannin. Only about 50,000 of Paraguay's 1,800,000 inhabitants live in the Chaco.

HISTORY

The colonial era

The history of Paraguay begins in the first half of the 16th century, when Charles V sent an expedition from Spain to the Río de la Plata with instructions to build forts as a defence against possible infiltration by the Portuguese and to undertake the hopeless task of opening a route from the Atlantic Ocean to the silver mines of Peru. In 1537 a few members of this expedition, having journeyed 1,000 miles up the rivers, and needing to repair their boats,

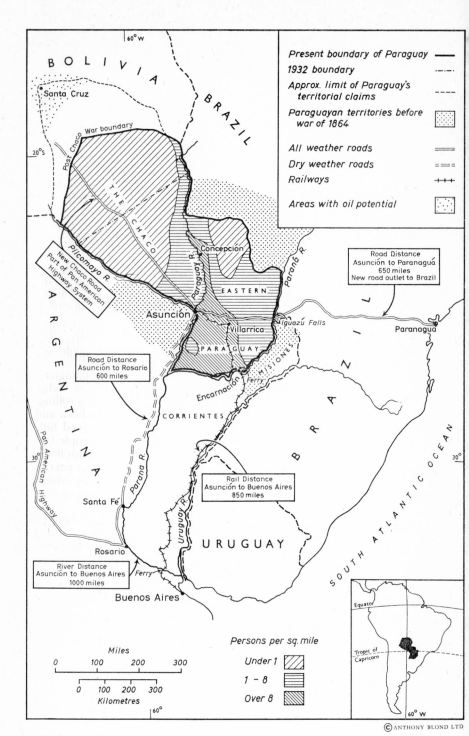

Paraguay

took them into a small bay on the eastern bank of the Río Paraguay, where they erected a fort on a headland overlooking the water, and baptised the place 'Nuestra Señora de la Asunción'. Asunción became Spain's head-quarters for the whole Plata region and remained so until Buenos Aires superseded it at the beginning of the 17th century. Thereafter Spanish interest in Paraguay declined; Madrid found that by the time its instructions had been taken up the rivers into the interior of the continent, they had lost their force and had little effect.

Meanwhile the Catholic Church was at work, especially the Jesuits, who established themselves in the fertile districts of the Upper Paraná, marshalling their Guaraní converts into mission towns, methodically organising the communities, teaching useful crafts, employing the people in looking after the cattle that had been brought from Spain (and which had multiplied exceedingly), cultivating cotton and tobacco, and harvesting *yerba mate* ('Paraguay tea'), which was their most valuable export.

Although the Jesuits were in Paraguay for 200 years, they exercised no permanent influence. When the authorities in Madrid, alarmed at the power and wealth of the Order, decreed their banishment from the Spanish dominions in 1767, the Guaraníes began to abandon the mission towns, returning to their former unorganised way of life; within a few years the Jesuit churches and communal dwellings were in ruins and overgrown by tropical vegetation.

The Paraguayans declared their independence from Spain in 1811, after they had defeated and driven down-river a military force that had been sent by the Buenos Aires government to take the country over as a province of the Río de la Plata.

Francia and López

During the 19th century the actions of Paraguay's rulers were profoundly affected by their country's position on the map, the basic problem being to decide whether Paraguay would benefit more by affirming her isolation or by trying to break out from it. Personal ambitions, of course, played an important part.

Dr José Gaspar Rodriguez Francia (1766–1840) became head of state in 1814; he was appointed dictator for life, with the title of El Supremo, in 1816, and supreme he remained until his death. Having studied theology and law in Argentina at the University of Córdoba, Francia was a man of unusual learning for the Paraguay of that time; but like his contemporaries in government, he looked upon summary imprisonment and execution as normal methods of dealing with those who were suspected of plotting against authority, and employed the army and a host of spies to round up suspects.

With the collapse of Spain's power, European prospectors and speculators poured into the Spanish American territories. Fearing intrigue on behalf of foreign interests, Francia stopped all personal and commercial traffic with the outside world; foreigners who had already reached Asunción were expelled and forbidden to return—among them two Scotsmen, the Parish Robertson brothers, who later wrote their best-selling memoirs *Letters on Paraguay* (London, 1838–9).

Francia was a disinterested patriot, a man of complete honesty and utterly incorruptible. Under his dictatorship Paraguay was spared the anarchy which developed in most of the other countries newly emancipated from Spain. The Supremo's isolationist policy ruined Paraguay's external trade, but it kept the country independent and self-reliant. The Paraguayan people held him in awe. His interest in mathematics and astronomy convinced them that he must be a magician; they fled in horror when he began to survey the streets of Asunción with a theodolite; it is said that for years after his death they dreaded that he might return.

Following Francia's death an attempt was made by his successor, Carlos Antonio López, to reverse the policy of the 'closed door' by negotiating a commercial treaty with the neighbouring Argentine province of Corrientes, but as Corrientes was then in rebellion against Buenos Aires, this angered the Argentine ruler Rosas, who retaliated by imposing a blockade on Paraguay's river traffic, thus closing the door from the outside.

Francisco Solano López, who succeeded his father Carlos Antonio in 1862, led Paraguay into the most tragic of wars. Conceited and arrogant but extraordinarily resourceful, López was determined that his great neighbours, Brazil and Argentina, should acknowledge Paraguay as having equal status with themselves, and when the Brazilians overran the down-river country of Uruguay he chose to treat this as a threat to his own right to come and go in the Río de la Plata. He then committed a fatal error—instead of wooing Brazil's natural rival, Argentina, he sent an army across Argentine territory in an attempt to force the Brazilians to evacuate Uruguay. The immediate result of this expedition was the formation in 1865 of a formidable alliance: Brazil, taking Uruguay with her, was joined by Argentina in a solemn pact to destroy the Paraguayan dictator. Once again Paraguay was cut off.

The so-called War of the Triple Alliance dragged on until 1870; year by year López, accompanied by his Irish mistress, Eliza Lynch, was forced further and further into the heart of his country; there, defiant and alone, he was finally trapped by the Brazilians and killed. His last words are supposed to have been 'Muero con mi patria'—which was almost literally true, for Paraguay was exhausted, and most of her men were dead.

The Chaco War and its aftermath

By 1932 the nation had recovered; the losses in population had been made up, foreign capital had helped to develop the cattle and tannin industries, and the army was reorganised. Yet social progress, such as it was, was now destined to be interrupted by another war whose origins lay mainly in geography.

Paraguay's western neighbour, Bolivia, had been deprived of her Pacific seaboard by Chile in the 1880s and dreamed of securing an alternative outlet across the Chaco to the River Paraguay and the Atlantic. But Paraguay, like Bolivia, considered that she had an historical right to the Chaco—where, incidentally, oil deposits were now known to exist. Both nations staked their claim by setting up armed outposts in that inhospitable and almost uninhabited region.

One can only guess at the part that the international oil companies may have played in the conflict between the two countries. On the one hand the Standard Oil Company of New Jersey, who already had oil concessions in Bolivia, were accused of encouraging the Bolivians to press onwards into the Chaco; on the other hand Royal Dutch Shell were said to be encouraging Paraguay, backed by Anglo-Argentine wealth.

The Chaco War began officially in 1932. The Bolivian conscripts greatly outnumbered the Paraguayans, but they were mostly Indians, brought down from the bleak Andean altitudes to fight in the unaccustomed heat of the lowland plain. The Paraguayans were acquainted with the terrain; the Paraguayan commander, Colonel Estigarribia, outwitted the Bolivians by sending his men in small groups or singly behind their lines to cut communications and seize supplies. The Paraguayans advanced steadily towards the Andes. In 1935, after heavy casualties on both sides, Bolivia agreed to an armistice and ceded to Paraguay most of the vast area that Estigarribia's troops had conquered.

It was understandable that the young officers returning to Asunción in the late 1930s after routing the Bolivians should be impatient of the old politicians and aspire to reorganise the country on efficient, i.e. totalitarian lines. Paraguay had acquired a democratic, parliamentary constitution in 1870, after which date two political parties had come into existence: the Colorados (Conservatives) and the Liberals. Neither party paid much attention to the constitution, but around the turn of the century a generation of political intellectuals—Cecilio Báez, Manuel Gondra, Eusebio Ayala and several more—introduced liberal ideas. They governed until the Chaco War, after which they were overthrown and replaced by the military and the Colorados.

Morínigo and Stroessner

From 1940 Paraguay has been dominated by two men, General Higinio Morínigo, who ruled until 1947, and General Alfredo Stroessner, who became president in 1954.

Morínigo was fortunate in that, during his period of office, Paraguay's geographical position worked to his advantage. During the second world war the United States, suspicious of Argentina's pro-Axis sympathies and wishing to have a strategic base on the borders of that country, supplied lend-lease goods to Paraguay, financed the building of roads, and gave technical assistance for the development of agriculture and health services; Brazil, Argentina's traditional rival, offered loans, and went out of her way to win Paraguayan friendship; and there was an increased foreign demand for the local products—tinned meat, hides, cotton, petit grain and tannin. Morínigo extracted every possible benefit from this state of affairs, taking care to maintain his cordial relations with the Argentine military hierarchy.

While developing Paraguay's connections with foreign countries, Morínigo drastically restricted individual liberties at home. Morínigo's argument in justification of dictatorship was the usual one, that strong personal rule alone could maintain order. It is true that when, at the end of the second world war, Morínigo considered it prudent to make a show of democracy and allowed the exiles to return, there was chaos.

Civil war broke out in 1947. While the fighting lasted, Morínigo had the general support of the Colorado Party, but when in the following year the rebels were defeated, the Colorados split into two factions, those who supported him and those who did not. Later in 1948 a group of military officers, to prevent Morínigo from seizing power again, forced him to leave the country. First one civilian Colorado then another occupied the presidency and attempted to restore unity in the party and order in the country, but the disunity and the disorder continued.

In 1954 the commander-in-chief of the armed forces, General Alfredo Stroessner, intervened in the fruitless quarrels of the Colorado politicians and, as official Colorado candidate, was duly elected president, there being no other candidate. He resumed where Morínigo had left off. He imposed martial law, arrested political opponents and routed the bands of Liberal

E

guerillas that invaded the Paraná region from Argentina; by the end of 1961 he was so firmly in power that he felt able to rule more tolerantly, and he released political prisoners and allowed greater freedom to the two small opposition newspapers *Tribuna* and *Enano*. At the 1963 elections a *renovación* faction of the Liberal Party (bitterly repudiated by the Liberals in exile) was, for the sake of democratic appearances, permitted, or persuaded, to play the role of an opposition party. The Renovacionistas were, of course, defeated at the polls, but they were rewarded with a minority (one-third) of the seats in Congress, and their presidential candidate, Gavilán, was sent to London as ambassador. At elections for a Constituent Assembly in May 1967 the main body of the old Liberal Party, returning from exile, participated. They secured 28 seats in the Assembly, second to the Colorados with 80.

ECONOMY

Stroessner maintained order for so long that Paraguay became, though naturally on a small scale, one of Latin America's economically most reliable countries. Deficit financing was kept down, loans were repaid according to schedule, the currency (from 1960) remained stable, and there was little inflation. Foreign financial agencies were encouraged, and the benefits that they brought were considerable.

Stroessner inherited his predecessors' dual problem: to protect Paraguay from outside pressure and yet to deal with the outside world. The great weakness of Paraguay's external communications was always that virtually all transport, river or railway, went through Argentina; even today a word from Buenos Aires can close the door. But Stroessner developed other—if slight— lines of communication. The airport at Asunción has been enlarged to receive jet aircraft from anywhere; a road crosses the river Paraná by a new international bridge and joins the Brazilian highway leading to the Atlantic coast at Paranaguá, where Brazil has granted free port facilities. Another pioneering road has been driven across the Chaco to the Bolivian border. In 1967 Paraguay secured concessions from Chile which may result in the port of Antofagasta becoming a main trading centre for the land-locked nation.

In eastern Paraguay a programme of land distribution is closely connected with that of road construction. Many thousands of acres that the roads have opened up have been distributed to landless families, and schools and hospitals have been built. US financial and technical aid has played a large part in pushing Paraguay forward into the 20th century.

Paraguay generally has a favourable balance of trade. Principal exports are meat products (to the USA and UK), wood from the forests (to Argentina), oilseeds, quebracho extract, tobacco, coffee, essential oils, and *yerba mate*. Chief imports are machinery and vehicles (from the USA, Western Germany and UK), wheat (USA and Argentina), fuels and lubricants (Argentina and Netherlands Antilles).

No one knows how many Paraguayans have left the country for Argentina, Brazil and Uruguay. Perhaps as many as 600,000 now live abroad, not only political refugees but also labourers attracted away by higher wages, and students, writers and musicians seeking the wider culture of neighbouring lands. The leading Paraguayan novelist of today, Augusto Roa Bastos, has lived for many years in Buenos Aires, producing nostalgic stories of his homeland. There are signs, however, that this wastage of talent is now being reduced, and that, as the country becomes more prosperous, some families are returning home.

BIBLIOGRAPHY

Cunninghame Graham, R. B. *A Vanished Arcadia*, Heinemann, London, 1901. *Portrait of a Dictator*, Heinemann, London, 1933.

Land of Lace and Legend, La Colmena, Asunción, 2nd ed. 1960.

Meyer, Gordon. *The River and the People*, Methuen, London; International Publications Service, New York, 1965.

Pendle, George. *Paraguay and Uruguay* (*Lands and Peoples* series), A. and C. Black, London; Macmillan, New York, 1959. *Paraguay: A Riverside Nation*, Oxford Univ. Press for Royal Institute of International Affairs, London and New York, 3rd ed. 1966.

Raine, Philip. *Paraguay*, Scarecrow Press, New Brunswick, NJ, 1956.

Reh, Emma. *Paraguayan Rural Life*, Institute of Inter-American Affairs, Washington, DC, 1946.

Service, Elman R. and Helen S. *Tobatí: Paraguayan Town*, Univ. of Chicago Press, Chicago, Ill. and London, 1954.

Warren, Harris Gaylord. *Paraguay: An Informal History*, Univ. of Oklahoma Press, Norman, Okla., 1949.

BASIC INFORMATION

CLIMATE

Asunción

Lat./long.	25° S, 57° 30′ W	Relative humidity	56%/61%
Altitude	456 ft/139 m.	at midday of	
Mean temp. of hottest month	28°C/83°F (Jan.)	hottest and coolest months	
Mean temp. of coolest month	17°C/63°F (June)	Wettest month	6·2 in./157 mm. (Dec.)
Absolute max.	110°F/44°C	Driest month	1·5 in./38 mm. (Aug.)
Absolute min.	29°F/−2°C		
		Annual av. rainfall	51·8 in./1,316 mm.

POPULATION

TOTAL (*million*): 1962 (census) 1·82, excluding adjustments for Indian tribes and underenumeration; mid-1966: 2·09; 1980 (ECLA projection): 3·07.

DENSITY, mid-1965: 5 persons per sq. km.

CRUDE RATES (*per 000*), 1959–61 (ECLA data): birth 42–45, death 14–17; 1962 (incomplete data) infant mortality 45·5.

GROWTH RATES (% *p.a.*): 1945–65, 2·5; 1960–5, 3·0.

DISTRIBUTION (% *of total population*): Ethnic: mixed 74, white 21, Amerindian 3, Negro 1. Foreign-born, 1950: 3·5. Languages: Spanish and Guaraní. Religion: mainly Roman Catholic. Urban (*centres 2,000 inhab. or over*), ECLA data, 1950: 28·1; 1960: 28·7; 1980 (projection): 30·0. Largest cities (*000 inhab.*), 1962: Asunción 261, capital districts 289; urban areas: Encarnación 19, Concepción 18, Villarrica 16.

CONSTITUTIONAL SYSTEM (*based on 1940 constitution*)

CONSTITUTION: First 1816; main 1870; next 1940. Constituent Assembly elected May 1967 to draft new constitution.

SYSTEM: Unitary Republic, comprising capital (Asunción) and eastern and western regions (divided into 13 and 3 departments respectively). Departments governed by Ministry of Interior delegate, appointed by president. Elected municipal councils.

EXECUTIVE: Power vested in president who is elected by direct suffrage for 5-year term; may be reelected; commander-in-chief of the armed forces. He appoints ministers of state (the cabinet) and members of Supreme Court and other officials, and may dismiss councillors of state. He may declare a state of siege in an emergency; he has right to issue decree-laws during a parliamentary recess and to veto bills passed by the Chamber of Deputies. Assisted by Council of State composed of the ministers of state and 9 councillors representing the National University, the church, industry, agriculture, banking and the armed forces.

LEGISLATURE: Uni-cameral, National Congress of Chamber of Representatives. *Representatives:* One for every 25,000 inhabitants; elected by proportional representation and complete list systems for 5 years. *Suffrage:* Universal voting (compulsory for men) for adults over 18 years of age. Registered voters for Constituent Assembly, May 1967: 670,010. *Elections:* Presidential, 11 July 1954: General Alfredo Stroessner. Reelected 1958 by plebiscite (only candidate), and in 1963 elections, with 556,872 of 638,070 votes cast. Chamber of Representatives, February 1963, 60 seats: Colorado Party 40 and Liberal Renovación 20. Constituent Assembly elections, May 1967: Colorados 80 delegates, Liberal Radicals 28, Liberals 8, Febreristas 3.

JUDICIARY: Supreme Court of 3 members (may be increased to 5), appointed for 5-year term by president with Council of State approval; Tribunal of Public Accounts and courts of first instance appointed by president with Supreme Court approval.

DEFENCE

DEFENCE BUDGET: 1965: 959 m. guaranies; 1·7 per cent of GDP.

ARMED FORCES: National service: between 18–20 years of age, 2 years in army; between 20–45 in reserves. Strength: army 9,600, navy 2,000, air force 200; total 12,000 plus conscripts and trained reserve.

INTERNATIONAL RELATIONS

Member of the UN and many of its international specialised agencies, including: IBRD and affiliates, IMF, FAO, ICAO, ILO, ITU, UNESCO, UPU, WHO and WMO; IAEA; UNCTAD representative. Also member of OAS, Alliance for Progress, ECLA, IDB and LAFTA.

ECONOMY

PRODUCTION

AGRICULTURE (*ooo tons*)	*1949–53*[1]	*1963*	*1964*	*1965*
Wheat	1	5	7	8
Maize	116	120	206	210
Rice	17	16	20	22
Mandioca	903	1,000	1,449	1,512
Sugarcane	357	700	964	992
Cotton (lint)	14	13	12	14
Tobacco	8	25	9	17
Potatoes (sweet)	74	74	86	100

[1] Average.

LAND, 1964 (%): Arable 2, permanent pasture (mainly rough grazing) 24, forested 51, urban and other 23.

OTHER AGRICULTURAL DATA: Agricultural holdings, 1961 (census): no. 160,777; area 17·5 m. hectares. Tractors in use, 1956: 531. Fertiliser consumption (*ooo tons*), 1965/6: 1·6.

LIVESTOCK: No. (*m. head*), 1964/5: cattle 5·8; 1963/4: sheep 0·42. Products (*ooo tons*), 1964: meat 80, preserved meat 14·3, hides 17·3.

MANUFACTURING, 1965: (*ooo tons*) cement 29, tannin 30, wheat flour 55, sugar 35; (*m. litres*) beer 7·8.

ENERGY

CONSUMPTION (*tons coal equiv.*), 1964: total 0·21 m, per head 0·11.

ELECTRICITY, 1965: generated (*kwh*) 136 m., installed capacity (*kw*) 50,000.

GOVERNMENT EXPENDITURE
DISTRIBUTION (% of total), 1965: defence 18, education 14, health 4.

GROSS PRODUCT
GDP (ooo m. guaranies): at current market prices, 1964: 51·3; 1965: 55·8; at 1962
market prices, 1964: 48·0; 1965: 50·8. Per head (US$), UN estimate, 1963: 126.
DISTRIBUTION (%), 1963: agriculture 37, manufacturing 16, trade (incl. banking,
insurance, etc.) 22.
GROWTH RATES (%), 1950–60: total 2·7, per head 0·3; 1960–3: total 3·5, per head 1·0.

EXTERNAL TRADE (US$m.)	1955	1960	1964	1965	1966
EXPORTS (f.o.b.)	35	27	50	57	49
Meat products	2	7	15	19	14
Timber	13	5	7	10	11
Quebracho extract	6	3	4	3	3
IMPORTS (c.i.f.)	32	38	40	52	58
TRADE BALANCE	+3	−11	+10	+6	−9

DIRECTION OF TRADE (%)

	Exports			Imports		
	1955	1960	1965	1955	1960	1965
LAFTA	(48·4)	33·0	29·6	(45·5)	25·2	20·7
(Argentina	45·6	28·5	25·7	43·4	25·0	20·2)
USA	18·2	26·8	25·3	13·8	25·2	21·7
EEC	13·4	15·9	13·9	14·1	16·6	24·5
UK	9·4	10·6	10·1	6·9	7·6	7·0

FINANCE
EXCHANGE RATE (guaranies/US$), official selling, end-year, 1960: 126; 1966: 126.
BALANCE OF PAYMENTS (US$ m.): Goods and services (net), 1960: −13; 1964: −11;
1965: −9; 1966: −17.
COST OF LIVING (1964=100), Asunción, December 1965: 106; 1966: 107·4.
WAGES: Minimum per day, Asunción, 1964: 234 guaranies.
TREASURY ACCOUNTS (m. guaranies), 1965: Revenue 5,882, expenditure 5,898, deficit 15.

EMPLOYMENT
ECONOMICALLY ACTIVE (%), 1962 (sample): Of total (excl. Indian jungle) pop. 34
(men 53, women 15). In agriculture 52, services 17, manufacturing 15, commerce 7.

TRANSPORT AND COMMUNICATIONS
RAILWAYS: Traffic, 1963: 38 m. pass.-km., 18 m. net ton-km. Length of track
1,147 km.
MOTOR VEHICLES: In use (ooo), 1965: pass. cars 12·7, comm. vehicles 5·5. Road
system, 1965: 12,500 km., paved 1,000 km.
SHIPPING: Merchant fleet (ooo g.r. tons), 1965: 19. Main river ports: Asunción,
Concepción, Encarnación, Bahía Negra.
AIR: Scheduled services, 1964: Total 40,000 pass. departures, cargo arrival 445 tons.
International: 34,000 pass. departures. Main airports: Asunción (international),
Concepción, Encarnación.
TELEPHONES: No. in use, 1964: 13,600.

SOCIAL WELFARE
SYSTEM: Social insurance benefits and services provided by the Instituto de Previsión
Social. Financed by employees' and employers' contributions based on remuneration:
employees 6%, employers 13½%, the state 1½%. Benefits cover accidents or death at

work, but not unemployment. Separate pension funds for railway and bank employees and civil servants (11% contribution by latter). Employment legislation covers working hours; holidays; payment of wages, overtime and annual bonus; dismissal indemnities.

HEALTH: 1,700 persons per physician, 430 persons per hospital bed.

NUTRITION: Net food supply (*per head per day*), 1962: 2,580 calories, protein 66 g.

EDUCATION

ILLITERACY RATE (%), 1962: 15 years and over 26.

COMPULSORY: 6 years (between 6 and 12 years of age). Enrolment ratios (%), 1st and 2nd levels, 1963: 52, adjusted 65.

SCHOOLS, 1962: Pre-school and primary: no. 2,386, pupils 0·33 m., teachers 11,300. Secondary: no. 146, p. 17,100, t. 2,260. Technical: no. 23, st. 4,240, t. 490. Teacher-training: no. 38, st. 8,100, t. 910. Higher (universities): no. 2, 5,400 st., t. 880.

UNIVERSITIES: Nacional de Asunción; 3,500 students; academic staff 500. Católica 'Nuestra Señora de la Asunción', Asunción: 1,900 st., a.s. 380.

MASS MEDIA

BROADCASTING: No. of receivers in use, 1966: TV 1,000, radio 0·16 m. Stations: TV 1, radio 15.

CINEMAS: No., 1963: 37. Seating capacity 25,000.

NEWSPRINT: Consumption, 1964: total 1,400 tons, per head 0·7 kg.

NEWSPAPERS: Daily: 9. Estimated circulation (5 dailies): 90,000; copies per 000 pop., 45. Principal dailies in Asunción (*circulation, 000*): *La Tribuna* 30 (Sunday 40), *El País* 20, *La Tarde* (evening) 10, *Informaciones* 3.

PERU

FREDRICK B. PIKE

HISTORY

From independence to 1919

BECAUSE of its imposing mineral wealth and the presence of a large and generally docile Indian population, during much of the colonial period Peru was the principal focus of Spanish attention in South America. The swollen Spanish bureaucracy and powerful military establishment deterred Peruvians from acting effectively to achieve their independence, although there were abortive uprisings in the 1780–1814 period. Then in 1820 José de San Martín landed at the head of a formidable army that had sailed from already-liberated Chile. The following year in Lima he proclaimed Peru's independence. The final task of crushing the remaining Spanish armies was left to the great liberator of the north, Simón Bolívar, and his Ecuadorean–Venezuelan–Colombian troops.

By late 1826 Bolívar had departed from an increasingly hostile Lima and returned to Bogotá, Colombia. Left to rule themselves, Peruvians faced enormous problems. Geographically, their vast country of 514,000 square miles presented grave obstacles to political administration, being divided into at least four distinct and isolated regions: the coast with its capital city of Lima and the rich agricultural estates whose owners would become the major social and political power in the republic; the sierra where the Indian population lived; the largely uninhabited *montaña* or eastern slopes of the Andes; and the equally sparsely settled *selva*, the tropical, jungle, eastern lowland area.

Ethnic divisions were even greater than those resulting from geography. The coastal population, largely white, Negro and mulatto, looked with contempt upon the Indian and mestizo inhabitants of the sierra, and was in turn regarded with hostility and apprehensiveness by the *serranos*. The situation was complicated by the fact that the Aymara Indians of highland southern Peru neither understood the language nor the temperament of the Quechua Indians of the more central area. In general the Indians, whose total number was estimated in 1797 to be nearly 700,000 out of a population of just over a million, did not speak or understand Spanish.

Through the generations Peruvians have been torn by agonising doubts as to whether their national identity lay with the Indian and his civilisation or with the European and his way of life. *Indigenistas* have unilaterally exalted the racial virtue and the culture of the Indian while *hispanistas* have exclusively extolled the ethnic superiority and tangible accomplishments of the Europeans. Not until the 1940s did signs appear that a majority of Peruvian intellectuals were beginning to agree that genuine 'Peruvianness' rested upon *mestizaje,* the biological mixing of Indians and Europeans and the blending of their ways of life.

Between 1826 and 1845 a number of military caudillos, some of them self-seeking opportunists, others enlightened and patriotic, vied for political control. At the same time civilian idealists, especially lawyers and priests, debated whether the country should be governed according to liberal or conservative precepts. Especially dear to the hearts of Peruvian liberals was the cause of federalism. Some of them advocated federalism because of ideological convictions. Probably a larger number merely had local interests in mind and wished to avoid a situation in which their freedom to rule or to misrule could be limited by a Lima bureaucracy. In particular the proud populace of Arequipa, Peru's second largest city nestling in the southern approaches to the Andes, embraced federalism and struggled with consistency and zeal against the centralising schemes of conservative Lima politicians.

In addition to intense ideological debates, Peruvians confronted a chronic dispute with neighbouring Bolivia. In colonial times the richest silver-producing locale of the Viceroyalty of Peru and referred to as Upper Peru, Bolivia had in 1825 been declared an independent republic in accordance with the wishes of some of its inhabitants and with the approval of Bolívar. One of its early political leaders, Andrés Santa Cruz, sought several times to reunite Bolivia and Peru in a decentralised political structure under his control. Supported by a strong Bolivian army, by certain Peruvian liberals and especially by important Arequipa leaders who saw in decentralisation the means of escaping Lima's dominance, Santa Cruz succeeded in establishing a Confederation between 1835 and 1839. Alarmed that the balance of power in southern South America seemed to be upset by the Peru–Bolivia union, Chile sent a powerful force which, joined by many Peruvians, especially of conservative persuasions, defeated Santa Cruz and dissolved the Confederation.

In 1845, following six years of strife and instability, Ramón Castilla came to power and initiated a seventeen-year period of progress and sound government. The most talented of the 19th-century caudillos and referred to in Peru as the Liberator because in 1854 he freed the Negro slaves and abolished Indian tribute, Castilla began his first presidential term at a time when prosperity was returning to Peru. Guano (bird droppings), lying thick along the coast and offshore islands and not utilised since the Spanish conquest, had come into world-wide demand as a high-grade fertiliser. The sale of guano, especially to England and France, touched off an era of economic advance and although Castilla did not use the resulting revenue in any carefully planned manner to develop a self-sustaining economy he did insist upon administering government funds honestly.

The greatest accomplishment of Castilla, a pragmatic statesman who was indifferent to the idealists, was to effect a compromise between conservatives and liberals. This he achieved by separating the purely political issues involved in the old dispute from the religiously tinged ones. To the conservatives he gave essentially the desired type of political organisation, one in which a strong executive presided over a centralist administrative structure. To the liberals he awarded certain anticlerical enactments: the state ended its collection of tithes, private ecclesiastical courts were abolished, and the church was deprived of its monopolistic control over education as the government took steps to establish a public system. Although conservatives and liberals occasionally grumbled and resumed their traditional feud, Castilla's compromise, incorporated into a new constitution in 1860, two years before the end of his second and last term, basically served its purpose. The conservative–liberal debate seldom again led to sustained conflict and when major political parties appeared somewhat later they were concerned largely with different issues.

When the brilliant and well-born Manuel Pardo helped found the Civilista Party in 1871, its official programme included certain provisions that a few sensitive churchmen condemned as anticlerical. Economics, however, was the main interest of Pardo and the Civilistas in general. Pardo insisted that the wealth of a nation did not depend upon its resources so much as upon the habits and character of its people. He urged an educational programme that would stress practical knowledge and instil productive, capitalist virtues in the populace. He also asserted that guano wealth and the increasingly important nitrate revenue should be invested by the government in special development projects so that when these two resources had been exhausted Peru would be left with permanent benefits.

Shortly after the appearance of *civilismo* as a political movement, Nicolás de Piérola founded the Democratic Party. A former treasury minister for the José Balta administration (1868–72), Piérola had helped Yankee promoter Henry Meiggs undertake ambitious railroad-building projects intended to connect coastal Peru with its Andean mineral heartland. Although he had studied for the priesthood and was proclerical, Piérola like Pardo turned his main attention and that of his party to economics. He argued that the wealth of a country depended more upon its providentially bestowed resources than upon the character of its people. Peru, he optimistically asserted, possessed limitless resources and there was no need to alter the educational structure to inculcate new values in the populace. Instead, Peru's resources could be used as collateral for securing foreign loans which would make possible sustained and painless economic development while allowing the country's educated classes to engage in gentlemanly rather than business pursuits.

When Pardo was elected to the presidency in 1872 the disputes between Civilistas and Democrats intensified. In 1878, two years after completion of his presidential term which had been marred by a partial economic collapse occasioned by the world-wide recession of 1873, Manuel Pardo was assassinated. Outraged Civilistas without justification accused Piérola, in temporary exile, of master-minding the crime and briefly imprisoned his wife.

Meantime Peru faced a threat from abroad. Certain Chilean capitalists who had become active in Peruvian nitrates were incensed when Pardo in 1875 nationalised part of the industry. Although realising that the situation was dangerous Pardo, unable because of the depression and also temperamentally unwilling to spend on military preparedness programmes, had relied on treaties with sister republics to protect Peru. In 1873 his administration had signed an offensive-defensive treaty with Bolivia. When Chile declared war on Bolivia in 1879 owing to a dispute over Chilean nitrate operations on Bolivian soil, the Santiago government immediately demanded to know whether Peru would honour its 1873 treaty. The administration of Mariano Ignacio Prado in Lima reluctantly decided to abide by the treaty and thus Peru was involved in the War of the Pacific. Following a series of military disasters and a prolonged occupation of Lima, Peru signed a peace treaty with Chile in 1883.

A number of factors contributed to Peru's defeat in the War of the Pacific which resulted in the permanent loss of the nitrate-rich southern coastal area, including the important town of Arica. Perhaps the most important cause of Peru's weak military showing was the Civilista-Democratic dissension which continued unabated even as the war against Chile was being waged. For twelve years after the war came to an end Civilistas and Democrats continued to find it impossible to cooperate and Andrés A. Cáceres, the only military leader who had consistently been successful against the Chileans, dominated politics through the largely military Constitutional Party which he had founded. In 1895 Civilistas and Democrats finally resolved their differences and launched a revolution which overthrew Cáceres and brought Piérola to the presidency for a four-year term.

Wiser and more mature than when he had first appeared on the political scene, Piérola proved to be one of his country's ablest presidents. Spending wisely the revenue produced by the silver boom that began late in the 1880s in the central highlands, he balanced the budget and administered funds with honesty and efficiency, undertook important public works projects, founded a ministry of development to engage in economic planning and provide stimulus to business, and encouraged labour organisation. In his approach to economics Piérola came to accept the views first advanced by Pardo. He took steps to expand public education and to change its curriculum so as to stress technical knowledge and productive virtues. He also introduced a comprehensive tax programme so that income from mineral resources could be invested in special development projects.

Piérola and his successors benefited enormously from the support of a new group of intellectuals, including Joaquín Capelo, Javier Prado, José Matías Manzanilla and Manuel Vicente Villarán, who were concerned not only with material progress but with socio-economic reform along the coast and with uplifting the Indians of the sierra. Especially under José Pardo, son of Manuel and president from 1904 to 1908 and again from 1915 to 1919, economic progress continued and many of the vast sugar and cotton estates were modernised and transformed into models of efficient operation. In addition, important labour and social legislation was passed. Although little of a practical nature was accomplished to aid the Indian, it was significant that a majority of respected intellectuals spoke out strongly against all notions of racial inferiority, thus challenging long-held prejudices, and recognised that Peru could never emerge as a modern republic until the men of the sierra had been assimilated.

From 1919 to 1956

In 1919 the presidential elections were won by the maverick Civilista Augusto B. Leguía who had served as chief executive from 1908 to 1912. Rather than govern with a congress in which there was a hostile majority, Leguía seized the presidency by force shortly before he was to be inaugurated, disbanded congress, and prepared elections for a constituent congress in such a way as virtually to preclude the possibility of success for opponents. In this manner he initiated an eleven-year period of dictatorial rule known as the 'Oncenio'.

Although Leguía was undoubtedly animated by many good intentions, although a number of his public works projects aided the country, and although he helped strengthen a new urban middle group as a countervailing force against a traditional oligarchy, his lengthy administration was often characterised by hypocrisy. Leguía, for example, posed as a champion of the Indians and initially appointed a commission to protect the natives. But when the sierra landowners protested, Leguía sent the original members of the commission into exile and then dispatched the armed forces to protect the landlords against a series of Indian invasions.

While the Oncenio seemed to stimulate considerable material progress, prosperity was more apparent than real and was based upon foreign investments and loans rather than upon internal capitalisation. During Leguía's rule United States private investment came to surpass that of Great Britain. W. R. Grace and Company continued its expansion in both the agrarian and industrial sectors of the economy and by 1925 the United States-controlled Cerro de Pasco Corporation, a giant in the extractive industry of central highland Peru, was conservatively estimated to have made an investment of over $50 million. Also, the International Petroleum Company, a Standard Oil of New Jersey subsidiary, came into possession of the rich oilfields in the Talara region of the northern coast and began the operations that would lead it by 1959 to handle 98 per cent of all crude oil refined in Peru. Between 1919 and 1928, moreover, Peru's foreign debt rose from approximately $10 million to $100 million. Nearly all foreign loans were obtained from international banking firms in the United States.

During the Oncenio Marxian socialism became an important intellectual force in Peru. Leguía allowed its spokesmen, among them the brilliant and idealistic José Carlos Mariátegui and Luis E. Valcárcel, to operate with relative impunity, largely because they made little attempt to woo but instead bitterly assailed the one group that was most important to the dictator, the urban middle sectors. Moreover, Leguía was confident that because of the lack of political awareness on the part of the Indian masses there was little imminent danger in the Marxian call for a proletariat uprising. Marxian Socialists and Communists identified their cause with *indigenismo*, praising the 'communistic' practices of the descendants of the Incas, proclaiming that the Indians must by violence take over the coast and impose upon it their higher civilisation, and implying frequently that Indians were racially superior to other Peruvians.

In 1924 a group of Peruvian intellectuals in exile, headed by Víctor Raúl Haya de la Torre, founded the Alianza Popular Revolucionaria Americana (APRA), which advanced an *indigenista* line and stressed the need for a violent revolution which would be followed by a period of authoritarian government. Although it was strongly influenced by Marxism and preached the destruction of capitalism and the elimination of foreign investment which was equated with imperialism, the members of APRA ('Apristas') glorified the middle sectors and appealed to them to lead the social revolution. Thus the APRA seemed a more immediate threat to Leguía than the conventional Marxists who reviled the petit-bourgeoisie, and he kept its leaders in exile or in jail.

Through the heavy-handed methods by which he maintained political stability Leguía applied the *coup de grâce* to already moribund political parties. The Civilista, Democratic and Constitutional parties never played important roles in Peruvian politics following the Oncenio. Largely because of their own freely-chosen policies, moreover, Marxian Socialist and Communist groups were destined to remain insignificant in the post-Leguía period. Leaders of these movements had associated their causes with indigenismo. And in coastal Peru, which has always been the country's power centre, there exists among most of the inhabitants a deep-seated, abiding dislike of the Indians and of the culture of the sierra. The identification between Marxian movements and indigenismo established during the 1920s is a fundamental factor in explaining why Marxian Socialist and Communist parties have never been powerful in Peru.

Despite the persecution directed against it, the APRA was the only political group that emerged at the end of the Oncenio as a formidable power. Although the Apristas had at times advanced an indigenista line, they had not done so with convincing militancy and their major appeal had been made to the middle sectors of the coast.

When the world depression commenced in 1929 Peru's prosperity collapsed overnight. Resulting discontent led to a popularly supported military uprising in Arequipa under the command of Luis M. Sánchez Cerro which toppled Leguía. Aprista leaders returned from exile and began to win a significant following among the middle sectors who, in the throes of a bleak depression, had become disillusioned with capitalism and were ready to seek totally new alternatives. The anti-Aprista Sánchez Cerro, however, a dark-skinned mestizo, was idolised by the masses and reluctantly accepted by the oligarchy as a man capable of preventing a violent social revolution.

A brief period of rule by a junta came to an end with the presidential elections of 1931 in which Haya de la Torre and the APRA opposed Sánchez Cerro and the recently formed Unión Revolucionaria. Sánchez Cerro, following an energetic campaign in which he visited some of the most remote parts of Peru, convincingly defeated his Aprista opponent in relatively free and honest elections. Immediately charging electoral fraud, Haya de la Torre called his followers into open insurrection, and for the next sixteen months Peru was in a state of near civil war.

In 1933 Sánchez Cerro was assassinated by an Aprista fanatic and General Oscar R. Benavides was installed in the presidency. Although Benavides cancelled the results of the 1936 presidential elections when an Aprista-backed candidate won and remained in power himself until 1939, he relaxed somewhat the repressive measures directed against the APRA, spurned the advice of many friends from conservative Catholic circles that he inaugurate a fascist-type dictatorship, and directed his country to a remarkable economic recovery.

The less than free and democratic elections of 1939 were won by the official candidate Manuel Prado, member of a wealthy Lima banking family and a descendant of Mariano Ignacio Prado, president at the start of the War of the Pacific. A shrewd manipulator of men rather than a statesman, Prado gained unearned popularity because of the high prices commanded by Peruvian commodities at the time of the second world war, throughout which he assumed a staunchly pro-Allied stance, and because of a boundary dispute[1] that led to a striking military victory over Ecuador that aroused frenzied national enthusiasm. A subsequent 1942 treaty, guaranteed by the United States, Argentina, Brazil and Chile, awarded Peru a considerable amount of land claimed by Ecuador and has served to nourish continuing Ecuadorean hostility against its southern neighbour.

During Prado's term *Aprismo* began to undergo a change. With prosperity returning and with the middle sectors losing their revolutionary zeal, the APRA's high command suddenly advocated accommodation with the established order. Believing that it would now be possible to cooperate with the Apristas, Prado and Benavides successfully solicited their support for the candidate they had determined to advance in the 1945 elections, José Luis Bustamante y Rivero, a diplomat and educator of middle-class origins from Arequipa. Elected by a wide majority, Bustamante set out to introduce a series of significant social and economic reforms, hoping to gain the collaboration of the APRA in this endeavour. This proved to be impossible, principally

[1] See 'Territorial Disputes', p. 405.

because one group of top-level APRA leaders had ceased to be vitally interested even in mild reform and was principally concerned with acquiring absolute political power, while another group of young militants, loyal to the movement's pristine ideology, sought a massive social upheaval rather than piecemeal reform. Unable to gain the cooperation of either group of Apristas, Bustamante watched with apparent helplessness as the country was plagued by economic dislocations following the second world war, by labour disputes, and by APRA-inspired violence. Claiming that the president was incapable of dealing with the country's problems, the military arose in Arequipa in a revolution headed by General Manuel A. Odría and forced Bustamante into exile.

Odría presided over an eight-year period of dictatorial rule (1948–56), known as the Ochenio. Toward the outset of his rule the Korean War drove prices of Peruvian exports sharply upward and the country for a time savoured a prosperity eclipsing even that of late second world war days. The rate of new foreign investment increased at a dizzy rate, nearly doubling between 1948 and 1956. The 140 per cent increase in industrial productivity between 1950 and 1955 was due in large part to foreign investment.

Shortly after the Korean War prices for Peruvian exports plummeted and, with government corruption becoming increasingly evident, the economy declined alarmingly. Resorting to printing-press money, the Odría administration set off an inflationary process and in 1956 the cost of living was 93 per cent higher than it had been in 1948. Under these unpromising circumstances, and with labour discontent rising because of a fall in real wages, Odría's military dictatorship came to an end in 1956 when Manuel Prado won carefully supervised presidential elections and was inaugurated for a second six-year term.

Economic Crisis and New Political Responses, 1956–66

By the early 1960s the middle class, accounting for probably over 15 per cent of the population, had come to hold the balance of political power in Peru. A continuing rural-to-urban shift had contributed to this development. In the years between 1940 and 1961 more than 15 per cent of the rural population had moved to cities. A census conducted in 1961 revealed that urban inhabitants had come to make up almost 48 per cent of Peru's population of nearly 11 million.

Once in the cities many of the new arrivals in a short time succeeded in entering at least the lower middle-class strata. The rapid expansion of industry vastly facilitated their entry. By 1963 industry was producing nearly 20 per cent of GNP, employing some 18 per cent of the active population and paying an estimated average of two dollars a day to workers. Industrial output seemed about to outstrip in value that of agriculture which, employing over 50 per cent of the active labour force, accounted for 20 per cent of GNP. A new fish meal industry was by 1964 a $150 million concern and challenging Japan for leadership in world production of the commodity[1]. Gains in certain sectors of mining were also spectacular. By 1962, with its annual production having climbed to 167,000 tons, Peru was the world's sixth largest producer of copper; by the same year it had become the fifth largest producer of lead and zinc. The technically advanced coastal estates continued to produce bumper crops of Peru's main exports, sugar and cotton, and also

---

[1] See 'The Fishing Industry of Peru' (p. 646).

contributed to the rise to middle-class status of wage-earning rural labourers, many of whom enjoyed sufficient economic security to put their children through secondary schools and even universities. Higher education had, in fact, by the early 1960s definitely ceased to be the exclusive privilege of the aristocracy. In 1940, 3,383 students were enrolled in Peru's seven universities. In 1964 some 48,000 students attended the country's thirty universities and many of them came from backgrounds of considerable poverty.

Still, all was not promising for Peru's mushrooming middle class. In many ways economic opportunities were not keeping pace with the increase in population which since the second world war has averaged close to 3 per cent per year. As of 1963 the Peruvian economy was supplying only some 10,000 new job opportunities per year, while most economists agreed that within ten years, if the country was to avoid staggering unemployment problems and economic stagnation, the number of annual new employment openings would have to rise to at least 100,000. Moreover, notwithstanding the remarkable expansion of higher-education facilities, Peru's universities admitted only 14 per cent of applicants in 1964 because of lack of space and inadequate preparation of secondary students.

Numerous other economic-social difficulties confronted not only the middle class but also the masses. One million children above the age of five as of 1965 had never had even primary education and the overall national illiteracy rate was approximately 40 per cent. There was an increasing tendency toward drunkenness and excessive reliance on mastication of the coca leaf among sierra Indians, whose only source of genuine nourishment was in many instances the potato. Problems attendant upon land, its use and division, had assumed staggering proportions by the early 1960s, resulting in annual decreases in per capita food production. Only some 1·5 per cent of Peru's territory was under cultivation. This meant that agriculturally utilised land came to only half an acre per capita, an amount deemed woefully inadequate to furnish Peruvians with a satisfactory diet.

While distribution was probably not the major land problem, it was serious. On the coast the prevalence of minifundia was an impediment to efficient farming, with some 40,000 landholders owning estates of less than 25 acres, while 27,000 claimed plots of less than 5 acres. In contrast, 181 proprietors held estates of more than 1,250 acres each. In the sierra there were nearly 33,000 landowners. Over 27,000 of them held farms of 75 acres or less. Within this category more than a third, or nearly 10,000 proprietors, held property of 5 acres or less. Many labourers, known as *yanaconas*, were virtual serfs, being given the right to use tiny plots of land, often no more than a furrow or two, in exchange for contributing a specified number of days of labour throughout the year to the estate-owner. On the other hand, the 1,233 sierra landowners each of whom held property of more than 2,500 acres controlled nearly 80 per cent of the land under cultivation or used for pasture. In the 1960s the right-wing Peruvian press attributed Indian invasions of sierra estates to communist agitation. The truth is that since 1680 the inequitable patterns of property distribution have touched off sporadic Indian attempts to reclaim land.

As the 1962 presidential elections approached Peruvians were presented with a choice among three candidates. General Odría had already convinced most serious observers that he was not interested in an energetic quest for solutions to the basic problems of the land. Haya de la Torre had come to be the representative primarily of a small group of the higher middle class whose members had already found a place of security in their country's economic and social life. In the 1962 campaign Haya spoke as if there were no reason for grave apprehension among the electorate. He called for patience and maintained that Peru's economic and social problems were not especially pressing. The only candidate who urged reform and basic structural change was the architect, Fernando Belaúnde Terry, whose Acción Popular party (AP), founded only in 1956, had already become a major political force.

In the past even the progressive elements of the coastal population had been frightened by the indigenista overtones of most genuine reform movements. And Belaúnde, who personally travelled during his campaign to the most isolated Andean communities, sounded much like a socialist indigenista when in the sierra. Unstintingly praising Inca traditions, including those of communal landownership and labour, Belaúnde called upon the members of native communities to advance themselves through the energetic use of the same methods employed by their distant ancestors. He sought to instil among the Indians as the mystique of progress a pride in the achievements of their pre-conquest predecessors.

Unlike the socialist indigenistas who had so alarmed coastal Peruvians since the 1920s, Belaúnde did not call upon the Indians to spread their way of life, by force if necessary, throughout the land. He did not suggest that Indian-style socialism would contribute to bringing about the required prodigies of economic expansion in the industrial, commercial and mining enterprises of the coast or in its scientifically managed and technologically advanced privately owned farms, although he did stress the need for greater overall economic planning. Belaúnde envisioned a genuinely pluralistic country in which the coast could advance with its Westernised, capitalist traditions modified but not eradicated, while the sierra progressed through its at least semi-socialistic Inca customs.

Although some sociologists and anthropologists maintain that Peru's present-day Indians are more individualistic than socialistic and that therefore the AP's programme for the sierra is not soundly conceived, the fact remains that Belaúnde devised an approach to reform which did not intimidate coastal elements while arousing the interest and hopes of the more politically aware Indians. The AP has won the enthusiastic backing of a large proportion of the expanding coastal middle class as well as of the urban masses, and even gained the support of some members of the coastal aristocracy. By gaining at the same time the following of many Indian communities, even though most of their members are illiterate and therefore disenfranchised, it has helped to fashion a political bridge between coast and sierra.

Official returns of the 1962 elections awarded to APRA candidate Haya de la Torre 557,000 votes, to the AP leader Belaúnde 544,000, and to Odría, supported by the Unión Nacional Odriista (UNO), 520,000. As none of the candidates had received a third of the votes congress, according to constitutional provisions, would be called upon to select one of them. Quickly the APRA's leaders agreed to support their one-time implacable foe Odría on condition that upon becoming president he would guarantee that all Aprista congressmen and senators, chosen at the same time that the presidential elections had been held, would be seated. Many Peruvians were shocked by the pact between Haya de la Torre and Odría, who had earlier declared the Aprista leader morally unworthy of citizenship. At this point the military, claiming Aprista fraud in the elections, a charge later substantiated to a considerable degree, intervened to nullify the elections and established a junta which ruled the country for one year. New elections were held in 1963 which pitted the same three contestants of the previous year against each other. This time Belaúnde, picking up additional support from the Christian Democratic Party that had been founded in 1956, won more than the required one-third of the votes and was installed in presidential office in July.

Belaúnde was handicapped in implementing his reform programme by the hostile congressional majority made up of Apristas and Odriistas who continued to honour the pact of 1962. In spite of this the president was able in 1964 to gain approval of a land reform law, considerably weaker than the legislation orginally proposed, which afforded protection to the efficient coastal estates but pledged redistribution of sierra land so as to benefit Indian communities. Belaúnde also called the first municipal elections to be held since 1919, and began to send government missions to the approximately 5,000 Indian communities of the sierra to encourage their inhabitants to undertake community development programmes involving the building of roads, clinics and schools. In addition he helped initiate a programme known as 'Cooperación Popular' under the auspices of which thousands of volunteers, including many university students who had already acquired considerable technological knowledge, dedicated their skills to helping Indian communities take the first steps toward modernisation.

In his reform programmes Belaúnde benefited from the support of the armed forces which showed a new concern with national revitalisation and became active in a number of projects concerned with road building, community development and related endeavours. With the issue of a joint pastoral letter in 1958 urging a social justice crusade, the Roman Catholic hierarchy of Peru also assumed a new and progressive position. This has aided Belaúnde in a land where the populace still inclines to be devout, in spite of its increasing defiance of church proscriptions against birth control.

With one project which he deemed to be of particular importance, the building of a *carretera marginal de la selva* (marginal highway of the *selva*), Belaúnde was able to make little initial progress. Construction of this highway, which would run along the eastern slopes of the Andes and encourage colonisation programmes and also link Peru, Ecuador and Bolivia, was obstructed in part by the inability of the Belaúnde government to gain substantial financial support from the United States. The Lyndon B. Johnson administration was worried by Belaúnde's allegedly unfriendly attitude toward the highly privileged position of the International Petroleum Company.

In spite of difficulties, as his administration reached the half-way point (1966) Belaúnde could point to fiscal stability with the sol holding steady at an exchange rate of 27 to the dollar even though the domestic cost of living increased 16 per cent in 1965. The president could also claim a record of sustained economic growth which saw GNP rising at an annual rate of over 7 per cent (it dipped to 5 per cent in 1965) and an average of some 600 new industrial plants being established every year. Increase in Japanese and Australian trade and investment was notable, and such United States firms as General Motors and Ford opened large assembly plants in 1965. One troublesome aspect of the economy was that smaller manufacturing concerns, which add about $3,000 million each year to Peru's GNP, were importing ever greater amounts of foreign parts and primary materials and adding to a balance of payments problem occasioned primarily by the decline of sugar and cotton prices on the world market. Many Peruvians, moreover, continued to be concerned about their country's economic dependence on the United States. By 1964 total United States investment in Peru had climbed to approximately $450 million and about 35–40 per cent of the country's GNP came from the activities of foreign enterprises, mainly United States-controlled.

As of mid-1966 it was apparent that if he had done nothing more, Belaúnde had at least bought time for Peru. Increasingly politically conscious and informed of events throughout the land by means of the transistor radios which they keep always with them, the Peruvian Indians, comprising some 40 per cent of the population, were at last able to see indications that an administration was concerned with their interests. It remains to be seen whether the policies of the AP will prepare the way for the peaceful accomplishment of what so far has been brought about in the Indian republics of Latin America only by revolutionary violence: that is, the mass-scale incorporation of the natives into meaningful participation in the national life.

BIBLIOGRAPHY

Baudin, Louis. *Daily Life in Peru under the Last Incas*, Allen and Unwin, London, 1961; Macmillan, New York, 1962.
Ford, Thomas R. *Man and Land in Peru*, Univ. of Florida Press, Gainesville, Fla., 1955.
Kantor, Harry. *The Ideology and Programme of the Peruvian Aprista Movement*, Univ. of California Press, Berkeley, Calif., 1953.
Mason, J. Alden. *The Ancient Civilisations of Peru*, Penguin Books, London, 1957.
Owens, R. J. *Peru*, Oxford Univ. Press for Royal Institute of International Affairs, London and New York, 1963.
Payne, James L. *Labor and Politics in Peru. The System of Political Bargaining*, Yale Univ. Press, New Haven, Conn. and London, 1965.
Pike, F. B. *The Modern History of Peru*, Weidenfeld and Nicolson, London; Frederick A. Praeger, New York, 1967.
Prescott, W. H. *History of the Conquest of Peru*, Everyman's Library, Dent, London, 2 vols, 1957 (originally published 1847).

BASIC INFORMATION

CLIMATE

	Cuzco	*Lima*
Lat./long.	13° 30′ S, 72° W	12° S, 77° W
Altitude	10,581 ft/3,226 m.	394 ft/120 m.
Mean temp. of hottest month	15°C/58°F (Nov.)	24°C/72°F (Feb.)
Mean temp. of coolest month	10°C/50°F (July)	16°C/61°F (Aug.)
Absolute max.	84°F/29°C	93°F/34°C
Absolute min.	16°F/−9°C	49°F/10°C
Relative humidity at midday of hottest and coolest months	26%/23%	66%/78%
Wettest months	6·4 in./163 mm. (Jan.)	0·3 in./7·6 mm. (Aug./Sept.)
Driest months	0·2 in./5 mm. (June/July)	0·1 in./2 mm. (Feb.– Apr. and Dec.)
Annual av. rainfall	32·0 in./813 mm.	1·6 in./41 mm.

POPULATION

TOTAL (*million*): 1961 (census): 9·91, adjusted 10·42; mid-1966: 12·01, excluding Indian jungle pop.; 1980 (ECLA projection) 18·53.
DENSITY, mid-1965: 9 persons per sq. km. Regional densities: Coast 15, Sierra 16 East 1.
CRUDE RATES (*per ooo*), 1966: birth 28·5, death 8·4, infant mortality 66·5. ECLA estimates, 1959–61: birth 43–45, death 14–15.
GROWTH RATES (% *p.a.*): 1945–65: 2·1; 1960–5: 3·1.
DISTRIBUTION (% *of total pop.*): Ethnic, 1940: mixed 53, Amerindian 46. Foreign-born, 1940: 1·2. Languages: Spanish, Aymará and Quechua. Religion: mainly Roman Catholic. Urban (*centres 2,ooo inhab. or over*), ECLA data, 1950: 31·3; 1960: 38·9; 1980 (proj.): 52·8. Largest cities (*ooo inhab.*), 1961: Lima, urban area 1,436, Province 1,632; Callao 156; Arequipa 135; Trujillo 100.

CONSTITUTIONAL SYSTEM

CONSTITUTION: First 1823; main 1860; latest 1933, frequently amended.
SYSTEM: Unitary republic, comprising 23 departments (divided into 141 provinces and subdivided into districts) and the 'constitutional province' of Callao. Separate executive, legislature and judiciary.
EXECUTIVE: Power vested in president and his Council of Ministers (cabinet headed by chairman or prime minister appointed by the president). Ministerial resignation follows congressional censure. President and 2 vice-presidents elected by direct suffrage; 6-year presidential term and no immediate reelection.
LEGISLATURE: Bi-cameral, National Congress of Senate and Chamber of Deputies. *Senate:* 45 members, 1 from each electoral district; elected by direct popular vote for 6 year term. *Deputies:* 140 seats, 1 from each electoral district; elected by direct suffrage for 6 years. *Suffrage:* Universal, compulsory voting for literate adults between 21 and 60 years of age. Registered voters, Nov. 1966, municipal elections: men 1·46 m., women 0·86 m. *Elections:* Presidential, June 1963: Fernando Belaúnde Terry (Acción Popular) 708,931 votes, Haya de la Torre 623,532. Congressional, June 1963, seats held:

Party	Senate	Deputies
Alianza Popular Revolucionaria Americana	18	58
Acción Popular-Demócrata Cristiano	20	50
Unión Nacional Odriísta	7	27
Independents	—	5
	45	140

JUDICIARY: Supreme Court, at Lima, of 11 judges nominated by the executive and approved by Congress. Superior courts in certain departments and courts of first instance in provinces.

DEFENCE

DEFENCE BUDGET: 1965: 3,000 m. soles; 2·6% of GDP.
ARMED FORCES: Military service: between 20–25 years of age; 2 years in army. Strength: army 43,000, navy 7,000, total 50,000.

INTERNATIONAL RELATIONS

Member of the UN and many of its international specialised agencies, including: IBRD and affiliates, IMF, FAO, ICAO, ILO, ITU, UNDP, UNESCO, UPU, WHO and WMO; IAEA; GATT, UNCTAD representative. Also member of: OAS, Alliance for Progress, ECLA, IDB and LAFTA.

ECONOMY

PRODUCTION

AGRICULTURE (ooo tons)	1948–52[1]	1963	1964	1965
Cotton (lint)	75	146	141	131
Cottonseed	121	245	241	215
Sugar (raw value)	87	807	770	755
Coffee	6	49	53	52
Rice (paddy)	191	217	341	284
Maize	276	362	380	530
Barley	208	207	210	184
Wheat	146	150	150	143

[1] Average.

LAND (%), 1962: Arable 1, permanent pasture 14, forested 55, urban and other 30.
OTHER AGRICULTURAL DATA: Agricultural holdings, 1961 (census): no. 0·88 m., area 18·6 m. hectares. Tractors in use (ooos), 1962: 7·4. Fertiliser consumption (ooo tons), 1962/3: 113·1.
LIVESTOCK: Nos. (m. head), 1964/5: cattle 3·6, sheep 14·5, pigs 2·0. Products (ooo tons), 1961: meat 160, beef and veal 78. 1965: wool (sheep and alpaca) 15·6.
FISH: Landed (ooo tons), 1965: total 7,462, anchoveta 7,242 (1964: 8,863).
MINING, 1965: (ooo tons), metal content of ores: iron 3,895, copper 177, lead 147, zinc 259; salt 124; (tons) gold 3·0, silver 1,097, tin 37, tungsten 546, antimony 529, molybdenum 1,317, bismuth 755, cadmium 247, mercury 98, selenium 9. Fuels: coal 150; (m. cubic metres) crude petroleum 3·7, natural gas 1,660.
MANUFACTURING, 1965; (ooo tons) pig iron 20, steel ingots 81, copper 196, cement 1,022, fishmeal 1,282, wheat flour 431; (m. litres) beer 173. Liquid fuels (ooo cubic metres) 1963: diesel oil 859, fuel oil 383, motor spirit 819. Motor vehicles (ooo units assembled), 1965: 3·0; 1966: 13·2.
CONSTRUCTION: (ooo sq. metres floor area), 1963: building permits approved (Lima District) 160.

ENERGY

CONSUMPTION (tons coal equiv.), 1964: Total 6·81 m., per head 0·60.
ELECTRICITY, 1965: Generated (kwh) 3,813 m., installed capacity (kw) 1·18 m.

GOVERNMENT EXPENDITURE

DISTRIBUTION (% of total), 1967: Defence 17, education 24, health 6; development and public works 13.

GROSS PRODUCT

GNP (ooo m. soles): At current market prices, 1964: 95·5; 1965: 114·7; at 1963 market prices, 1964: 84·9; 1965: 88·5. Per head (US$), UN estimate, 1964: 240.
DISTRIBUTION (%), 1965: Agriculture 17, manufacturing 19, trade 18, mining 6, construction 6.
GROWTH RATES (%), 1950–60: 4·9, per head 2·4; 1960–5: 6·6, per head 3·0.

EXTERNAL TRADE (US$m.)	1955	1960	1964	1965	1966
EXPORTS (f.o.b.)	268	430	666	667	764[1]
Fish and products	13	50	166	187	207
(Fishmeal	13	39	143	143	182)
Copper	29	95	103	121	186
Cotton	68	73	91	87	85
Iron	8	33	39	47	53
Sugar and derivatives	37	48	64	38	46
Silver	16	24	45	39	41
IMPORTS (c.i.f.)	300	373	571	719	817
TRADE BALANCE	−31	+58	+95	−52	−54

[1] Adjustments for unregistered exports and undervaluation of copper increase total to 791.

DIRECTION OF TRADE (%)

	Exports			Imports		
	1955	*1960*	*1965*	*1955*	*1960*	*1965*
LAFTA	(18·6)	7·8	8·1	(8·0)	7·4	11·1
USA	36·0	36·1	33·7	50·0	44·1	39·8
EEC	20·5	30·8	32·1	18·2	22·5	20·3
UK	10·2	7·8	5·8	8·9	6·8	5·2

FINANCE

EXCHANGE RATE (*soles/US$*): Single market, end-year 1960: 26·76; 1964: 26·82; 1966: 26·82.
BALANCE OF PAYMENTS (*US$*): Goods and services (net), 1960: +2; 1964: +7; 1965: −166; 1966: −190.
COST OF LIVING (*Dec. 1958=100*), Lima and Callao, December 1960: 120; 1964: 164; 1965: 190; 1966: 206.
INDUSTRIAL WAGES: Earnings in manufacturing per hour, 1964: 9·40 soles.
GOVERNMENT ACCOUNTS (*m. soles*), 1966: Revenue 19,470, expenditure 23,854, deficit 4,384, adjusted deficit 5,660.

EMPLOYMENT

ECONOMICALLY ACTIVE (%), 1961: of enumerated pop. 32 (men 50, women 14). In agriculture 50, manufacturing 13, services 10, trade 9.
UNEMPLOYMENT (%), 1965: 3·7; high underemployment in agriculture.

TRANSPORT AND COMMUNICATIONS

RAILWAYS: Traffic, 1965: 263 m. pass.-km., 593 m. net ton-km. Length of track 3,300 km.
MOTOR VEHICLES: In use (*000*), 1965: pass. cars 117, comm. vehicles 92. National road system: 41,500 km., paved 4,950.
SHIPPING: Merchant fleet (*000 g.r. tons*), 1966: 192. International sea-borne shipping (*million tons*), 1965: goods loaded 10·8, goods unloaded 2·6. Main ports: Callao, Chimbote; other ports: Talara, Paita, Salaverry, Puerto Chicama, Huacho, Supe, Matarani, Ilo, Pisco; river ports: Iquitos, Pucallpa.
AIR: Scheduled services, 1964: total 425 m. pass.-km., 9 m. cargo ton-km. International 324 m. pass.-km., 3·4 m. cargo ton-km. Main international airports: Lima (Jorge Chávez), Talara, Iquitos. National airports at most large towns.
TELEPHONES: No. in use, 1964: 132,400.

SOCIAL WELFARE

SYSTEM: Social security benefits and services provided by: *a*) Caja Nacional de Seguro Social Obrero (for workers) and *b*) Seguro Social del Empleado (for white collar and government employees). No general unemployment insurance or family allowances. Financed by contributions based on remuneration: employees: *a*) 5% on part wages, *b*) 3·5%–4%; employers: *a*) 8%, *b*) 5%–6%; government: *a*) 2%, *b*) ½%. Employers pay additional cont. if capital or gross income over specified level. Employment legislation covers working hours; holidays; payment of wages, overtime and annual bonus; employers' liability for retirement pensions, sickness, compensation for accidents, dismissal and death indemnities and life assurance. Benefits cost employers additional 50% or more of wages and salaries paid.
HEALTH: 2,200 persons per physician, 490 persons per hospital bed.
NUTRITION: Net food supply (*per head per day*), 1962: 2,360 calories, protein 59 g.

EDUCATION

ILLITERACY RATE (%), 1961 (census sample): 17 years and over, 40.
COMPULSORY: 6 years (between 6 and 16 years of age). School enrolment ratios (%), 1st and 2nd levels, 1964: 50, adjusted 68.
SCHOOLS, 1964: Pre-school and primary: no. 17,280, pupils 1·92 m., teachers 53,600.
SECONDARY: no. 777, p. 260,700, t. 16,100. Technical: no. 343, st. 64,800, t. 6,650.
Higher (1963): st. 46,500.
UNIVERSITIES: *National:* Lima: San Marcos: 15,000 students, academic staff 1,640; Amazonia Peruana: 452 st., a.s. 29. Ingeniería: 5,500 st. San Agustín, Arequipa: 6,050 st., a.s. 320. San Antonio Abad del Cuzco: 13,000 st., a.s. 242. Central del Peru, Huancayo: 2,924 st., a.s. 144. San Cristóbal de Huamanga, Ayacucho: 930 st., a.s. 87. San Luis Gonzaga, Ica: 4,000 st., a.s. 392. Lambayeque. Técnica del Altiplano (in formation), Puno: 130 st., a.s. 35. Tingo María. 'La Libertad, Trujillo': 6,000 st., a.s. 340. *Others:* Lima: Pontificia Católica del Perú: 5,000 st., a.s. 580; del Pacífico: 416 st., a.s. 51; Particular de Lima; Agraria: 1,630 st., a.s. 350; Peruana de Ciencias Médicas y Biológicas: 410 st.; 'Julio C. Tellò'; 'San Martín de Porres'; Peruana Cayetano Heredia: 470 st., a.s. 356. Particular de Santa María, Arequipa. Técnica de Cajamarca. Técnica de Piura. Particular 'Gran Chimu', Trujillo.

MASS MEDIA

BROADCASTING: No. of receivers in use, 1965: TV 0·18 m., radio 2 m. Transmitters: TV 22, radio 100.
CINEMAS: No., 1961: 399. Attendance, 1958: total 67 m., per head 6·6.
NEWSPRINT: Consumption, 1962: total 26,000 tons, per head 2·2 kg.
NEWSPAPERS: Daily, 1959: 53. Estimated circulation 0·5 m., copies per 000 of population, 47. Principal dailies in Lima (*circulation, 000s*): *El Comercio* 90, *La Prensa* 85 (Sunday 124), *La Crónica* 74 (S. 111), *Correo* 50, *La Tribuna* 26, *El Peruano* 10, *Última Hora* (evening) 114.
BOOKS: Titles published, 1964: 946.

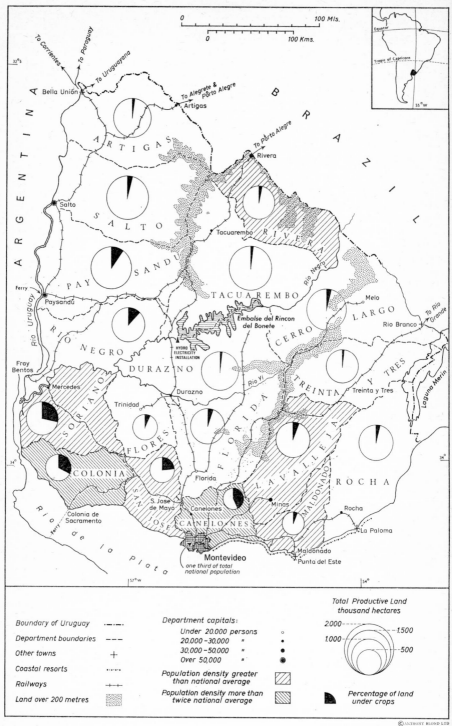

URUGUAY

126

URUGUAY

GEORGE PENDLE

SOUTH AMERICA's smallest republic occupies the north-eastern corner of the Río de la Plata, that wide estuary through which the silt-laden waters from the rivers of the interior of the continent flow into the Atlantic Ocean. This pleasant country, with its sandy beaches, grassy hills, wooded valleys, streams and broad pasturelands, is a buffer state separating two great nations, Brazil and Argentina.

Uruguay's three million inhabitants (nearly half of whom live in the south-eastern corner around Montevideo), almost wholly of European stock (predominantly, but not exclusively, Spanish and Italian), gladly accept the fact that theirs is a small land. The Uruguayan essayist Carlos Maggi has written, with the disparaging humour that is typical of his compatriots: 'Here is a country whose people do not aspire to greatness, or to anything absolute, but who desire that things shall be kept in good, human proportion and that human values shall be treated with proper respect. Such a people does not build empires or alter the course of history. Here nothing is rigorous. Everything is improvised, haphazard, and rather ineffectual. In the end, everything is settled by conversation, and never completely.' Yet the Uruguayans are patriotic, in an affectionate way. Maggi remarked: 'We recognise the greatness of our country when we make a little journey by bicycle.'

HISTORY

The colonial era

During most of the long period of Spanish rule in South America, the Spaniards paid little attention to the so-called 'oriental' side of the Plata estuary[1], because it was so inaccessible from their main base (in Peru), and no deposits of precious minerals were to be found there; but the cattle that a far-sighted governor of La Plata, Hernando Arias (popularly known as Hernandarias) put ashore at the beginning of the 17th century multiplied prolifically, attracting gauchos of the province of Buenos Aires, who crossed the river to lasso them and collect their hides. These gauchos were nomads, with no desire to own land; gradually, however, to facilitate the trade in hides, merchants from Buenos Aires settled on the Uruguayan side of the river, employed their own herders, and spread inland, so that by the end of the 17th century, although Spain had not officially claimed the territory of Uruguay, a vast area was in fact being exploited by Spanish colonials.

In 1680 a Portuguese expedition arrived in the estuary to set up an encampment on the site of the modern town of Colonia, immediately opposite

---

[1] The Spanish-speaking inhabitants at Buenos Aires referred to this bank of the estuary as 'oriental', or eastern, and the country's official title today is still 'República Oriental del Uruguay.'

Buenos Aires. The Spanish authorities at Buenos Aires were thus obliged to take action to protect their control of the waterway and its trade; their men crossed the river and defeated the intruders. This was the beginning of the long struggle between Portugal and Spain, followed by the rivalry of their Brazilian and Argentine heirs, for possession of Uruguay. In 1726 the Spaniards built a fortress at the point where the town of Montevideo later grew up. The Spanish military commander at Montevideo was always subordinate to Buenos Aires, which, as the years passed, was increasingly resented by the Montevideans, who, although they remained loyal to the Spanish throne, had no loyalty for the city on the other side of the river. The link with Buenos Aires was broken when British forces invaded the Plata in 1806.[1]

In 1806–7, while awaiting reinforcements from Britain for a second attack on Buenos Aires, British troops landed on the Uruguayan coast, moved against the Spanish garrison at Montevideo, captured the town, and occupied it for seven months, during which period hundreds of British ships lay in the harbour. In addition to men-of-war and military transports, scores of merchant vessels had arrived, laden with British manufactures. Into Montevideo, besides 4,000 British soldiers, there swarmed 2,000 British traders, eager to sell their cargoes of textiles, ironware, furniture, saddles, etc. The local people had never known such activity and prosperity, and after the British (having been defeated at Buenos Aires for the second time) were compelled to evacuate the Plata, the brief experience of free trade was not forgotten.

The former relationship between Montevideo and Buenos Aires was never completely restored. In 1810 the citizens of Buenos Aires deposed the Spanish viceroy in that city, and a new era began. It was an era of warfare and confusion.

The struggle for independence

In 1811 the ruling junta at Buenos Aires launched an attack on Spain's garrison at Montevideo; the Spanish governor appealed to the Portuguese to come from Brazil to help him; and when the Portuguese swarmed into the country, the Uruguayan hero José Gervasio Artigas led thousands of his compatriots away from the scene in a great retreat to the west. This extraordinary exodus is the epic event in Uruguayan history—wild horsemen, cartloads of women and children, Indians from the former Jesuit missions, with pack-mules and cattle, joined in a two months' trek to the River Uruguay, crossed the river, set up an encampment on the other side, and remained there for over a year.

From his remote, makeshift headquarters Artigas quarrelled with Buenos Aires, who refused to recognise his claim for Uruguay's autonomy. The Spanish commander at Montevideo then surrendered the town to the attacking Argentine forces, but they were soon expelled by the inhabitants. The Portuguese invaded again, and in 1820 Artigas was driven to seek asylum in Paraguay, where he resided until his death. Although defeated in battle, he had stimulated among his people a sense of nationality that was to survive all the ravages and disasters that were still in store.

After the downfall of Artigas, Uruguay was formally annexed by Brazil as a province. The repercussions were widespread. The British government had long foreseen that if either Brazil or Buenos Aires seized Uruguay, this would lead to hostilities between the two, with the consequent disruption of

[1] See the chapter on Argentina, p. 7.

Britain's valuable commerce with the Plata ports. Those forebodings were now fulfilled, and George Canning, as Foreign Secretary, quickly took diplomatic action to reopen the estuary. In 1828, largely as a result of British mediation, Brazil and Buenos Aires signed a treaty recognising Uruguay as an independent republic.

This outcome marked neither the beginning of internal peace nor the end of foreign intervention. During the ensuing civil wars General Rivera was supported by Brazil, while his rival General Oribe was backed by Buenos Aires. The troops of each side wore distinguishing colours: Rivera's men adopted red, and the Colorado Party of present-day Uruguayan politics are his heirs[1]; Oribe's followers wore white, and were the ancestors of the modern Blancos. The principles of the two parties have never been clearly defined, but traditionally the Colorados profess to represent liberalism and progress, while the Blancos are supposed to have the approval of the conservative, rural and clerical members of the population.

The creation of the welfare state

Because of constant disorder, the development of Uruguay's economy was retarded. The construction of railways was begun, but progressed slowly, as British investors lacked confidence. The interior of the republic was almost totally neglected. The production of wool was profitable, but a long time passed before landowners felt inclined to invest in the improvement of their estates.

Then at the end of the 19th century a statesman appeared on the scene who, by sheer force of personality, transformed South America's most chaotic nation into the most orderly and democratic of all. This was José Batlle[2] y Ordóñez, a Colorado who for a number of years had been publishing in his own newspaper, *El Día*, his diagnosis of Uruguay's troubles and the remedies that he proposed for them. Batlle became president of the republic in 1903; he crushed a revolution in the following year and then devoted himself energetically and disinterestedly to putting into effect his plans for reorganising the nation. His chief reforms, which were worked out not only under his own administrations (1903–7 and 1911–15) but also under those of Williman (1907–11) and Viera (1915–19), were very far in advance of anything attempted in South America up to that time; they can be divided into four categories:

1. Justice for the under-privileged. Batlle demanded an eight-hour working day, holidays for workers, compensation for discharged workers and old-age pensions.

2. State-ownership. Batlle believed that the state was competent to own and manage the public services and basic industries. On his recommendation, the state acquired the monopoly of such services as electricity and telephones, and today it manufactures cement and alcohol, and refines all petroleum imported into the country. (Uruguay has no oil-wells.) The British-owned railways were bought by the state at the end of the second world war.

3. Reduction of the power of the Roman Catholic Church. On Batlle's advice, religious instruction in the national schools was discontinued, marriage in church was declared no longer compulsory, and divorce was made legal. In practice, these 'anti-clerical' measures were carried out in a

---

[1] It was while fighting in defence of Montevideo against the Argentine dictator Rosas that Garibaldi and his legionaries wore the red shirts that they subsequently made famous in Italy.

[2] Pronounced '*Bah*-jay'.

very tolerant manner, and when the church was finally disestablished, it was allowed to retain its property. Uruguay remains a Catholic country, but the Uruguayans are not a religious people.

4. Reduction in the powers of the president of the republic. Batlle was convinced that the revolutions which had plagued the nation for so long were the consequence of the excessive powers allowed the president. He therefore proposed that the office of president should be abolished and that executive power should be invested in a National Council, somewhat on the Swiss model. This reform (so much at variance with the Latin American tradition of *personalismo*) was not fully carried out until 1952, in which year the *colegiado*, or 'collegiate' system, came into being, headed by a nine-member council consisting of six members from the party that received the largest number of votes at general elections and three from the second party.

Batlle had changed the national temper: there were no more revolutions, Uruguay continued to be the orderly democracy that he planned. Even when the opposition party, the Blancos, at last won the elections in 1958, they could not immediately do away with the *colegiado* (which they had always ridiculed as an ineffective method of government), so enduring was the influence of the great Colorado leader, although by then he had been dead for thirty years.

After the 1952 constitutional reform there was, however, a general slowing down of governmental processes. Government by a council in which the opposition were represented was in principle enlightened, but in practice it frequently happened that the nine members were unable to agree among themselves on important points of policy. In 1966 there was a growing demand, among Blancos and Colorados alike, for a return to presidential government, and this was restored by plebiscite in November.

Economy

Many Uruguayans have long felt that welfare legislation has become too expensive for this basically two-product country. In periods when the world prices of wool and meat are high—as during the second world war, and the brief Korean War boom—the whole economy prospers; but when prices are in decline, the state has difficulty not only in financing the social benefits, such as pensions, for which the laws provide, but even in paying the wages of public employees (let alone meeting their demands for increases). The situation was aggravated by the governmental indecision under the *colegiado* system.

Uruguay's economy is still too dependent on the products of her pampa— wool, beef and veal, hides and skins, the principal customers for which are usually Britain, the United States, the Netherlands and Western Germany. The chief imports are raw materials (sugar, cotton, etc.), vehicles, machinery and petroleum; the principal suppliers are the United States, the Arab countries (petroleum), Western Germany and Brazil. The tourist trade is an important source of foreign currency. The purchasers and builders of chalets on the fashionable Atlantic coast, and most of Uruguay's tourists —of whom there are some 200,000 in a normal year—are Argentinians.

Despite stringent import restrictions, in recent years Uruguay has had an unfavourable balance of trade both with the world in general and with her fellow members in the Latin American Free Trade Association (LAFTA). The Bank of London and South America has published the following comment which is a fair summing-up of the condition of this welfare state in the mid-1960s: 'Uruguayan production costs tend to be higher than those of neighbouring countries partly because of the exaggerated cost of labour in relation to productivity, and partly because of the small scale, even by Latin American standards, of Uruguay's industries. Greater emphasis has been placed by the business community on protection from competitive imports than on attempts to enter neighbouring markets. A certain passive and rather unadventurous mentality has become characteristic of Uruguayan society; there is a tendency to blame the Government for all commercial failures and to demand the Government's support for all ventures.'[1]

BIBLIOGRAPHY

Fitzgibbon, Russell H. *Uruguay: Portrait of a Democracy*, Rutgers Univ. Press, New Brunswick, NJ, 1954; Allen and Unwin, London, 1956.

Hanson, Simon G. *Utopia in Uruguay: Chapters in the Economic History of Uruguay*, Oxford Univ. Press, New York, 1938.

Hudson, W. H. *The Purple Land* (a partly autobiographical novel first published in 1885), Duckworth, London, 1904.

Maggi, Carlos. *El Uruguay y su gente*, Montevideo, 1963.

Martínez Lamas, Julio. *Riqueza y Pobreza del Uruguay*, Atlántida, Montevideo, 2nd ed. 1946.

Pendle, George. *Uruguay*, Oxford Univ. Press for Royal Institute of International Affairs, London and New York, 3rd ed. 1965.

Street, John. *Artigas and the Emancipation of Uruguay*, Oxford Univ. Press, London and New York, 1959.

Vanger, Milton I. *José Batlle y Ordóñez of Uruguay, the Creator of his Times, 1902–1907*, Harvard Univ. Press, Cambridge, Mass., 1963.

Zum Felde, Alberto. *Proceso intelectual del Uruguay*, Claridad, Montevideo, 1941. *Evolución histórica del Uruguay*, Máximo García, Montevideo, 3rd ed. 1945.

BASIC INFORMATION

CLIMATE

Montevideo

Lat./long.	35° S, 56° W	Relative humidity	
Altitude	72 ft/22 m.	at midday of	53%/69%
Mean temp. of hottest month	23°C/73°F (Jan.)	hottest and coolest months	
Mean temp. of coolest month	10°C/50°F (June)	Wettest months	3·9 in./99 mm. (Mar./Apr.)
Absolute max.	109°F/43°C	Driest months	2·6 in./66 mm. (Oct./Feb.)
Absolute min.	25°F/−4°C		
		Annual av. rainfall	37·4 in./950 mm.

POPULATION

TOTAL (*million*): 1963 (census): 2·59, adjusted 2·66; mid-1966: 2·75; 1980 (ECLA projection): 3·13.

DENSITY, mid-1965: 15 persons per sq. km.

CRUDE RATES (*per 000*), 1962: birth 25·1, death 8·7, infant mortality (1960) 47·4.

GROWTH RATES (% *p.a.*): 1945–65: 0·9; 1960–5: 1·4.

[1] *Quarterly Review*, London, January 1966.

DISTRIBUTION (% of total pop.): Ethnic: white 90, mixed 10. Foreign-born, 1963 (sample) 6·4. Language, Spanish. Religion: mainly Roman Catholic; not state supported. Urban (centres 2,000 inhab. or over), ECLA data, 1950: 79·0; 1960: 81·5; 1980 (proj.): 85·3. Largest cities (000 inhab.), 1964: Montevideo 1,204, Paysandú, 60, Salto 60, Rivera 40.

CONSTITUTIONAL SYSTEM

CONSTITUTION: First 1830; 1918—collegiate system of government; 1934—individual presidency, amended 1942; 1951—National Council of Government; 1967—presidential system reintroduced after plebiscite at November 1966 elections.
SYSTEM: Unitary republic, composed of 19 departments. Separate executive, legislature and judiciary. Departmental governments comprise chief executive (intendente) and a board of 31 members.
EXECUTIVE: Power vested in president (in vice-president when pres. vacancy) and council of 11 ministers. President and vice-president elected by simple majority under simultaneous double vote system, at the same time as candidates for the General Assembly; 5-year term and no immediate reelection. Vice-president presides over General Assembly and is chairman of the Senate. Government has power to require both chambers to vote on urgent matters within 45-day period, failing which bills become law without alterations.
LEGISLATURE: Bi-cameral, General Assembly of Senate and Chamber of Representatives. Senate: 30 members elected by direct popular vote, in a single electoral district, by integral proportional representation, for 5 years. Representatives: 99 members elected directly by popular vote under proportional representation system, for 5 years. At least two representatives for each department. Suffrage: Universal, compulsory voting for citizens over 18 years of age. Registered voters, 1966: 1·66 m.
Elections: Presidential, November 1966: General Oscar Daniel Gestido 262,000 votes, Jorge Batlle 216,000; both candidates of Colorado Party groups. Vice-president, Jorge Pacheco Areco. General Assembly, composition after provisional results:

Party	Votes (000)	Senate	Representatives
Colorado	608	17[1]	50
Nacional (Blanco)	497	13	41
Frente Izquierda de Liberación (FIDEL)	70	1	5
Others	57	—	3
	1,232	31[1]	99

[1] Including vice-president as chairman.

JUDICIARY: Supreme Court of 5 members, appointed by two-thirds vote of General Assembly for 10 years; no reelection within 5 years. Supreme Court appoints lawyer judges and justices of the peace.

DEFENCE

DEFENCE BUDGET, 1964: 370 m. pesos, 0·9% of GDP.
ARMED FORCES: Army is composed of volunteers between 18–45 years of age on one- or two-year service contracts; compulsory annual military training of citizens. Strength: army 9,000, navy 1,900, total 11,000, plus 100,000 trained reserve.

INTERNATIONAL RELATIONS

Member of the UN and many of its international specialised agencies, including: IBRD, IMF, FAO, ICAO, ILO, ITU, UNDP, UNESCO, UPU, WHO and WMO, IAEA, GATT, UNCTAD representative. Also member of: OAS, Alliance for Progress, ECLA, IDB and LAFTA.

ECONOMY

PRODUCTION

AGRICULTURE (ooo tons)	1948–53[1]	63/4	64/5	65/6
Cereals	739	451	927	961
Wheat	469	237	646	547
Barley	23	18	40	28
Oats	44	56	86	97
Maize	156	91	63	180
Rice	44	47	90	107
Linseed (flax)	106	62	71	38
Sunflowerseed	84	63	39	100
Beet sugar (raw)	6	39	41	57

[1] Average 1948/9–1952/3.

LAND (%), 1961: Arable 12, permanent pasture 74, forested 3, urban and other 11.
OTHER AGRICULTURAL DATA: Agricultural holdings, 1961 (census): no. 86,928, area 17·0 m. hectares. Tractors in use (ooos), 1961: 24·7. Fertiliser consumption (ooo tons), 1965/6: 32·5.
LIVESTOCK: Nos. (m. head), May 1965: cattle 8·1, sheep 21·9. Products (ooo tons), 1965: beef 336, wool (greasy) 83.
FISH: Landed (ooo tons), 1965: total 15·8, hake 7·6.
MANUFACTURING, 1965: (ooo tons) Cement 425, wheat flour 231; (m. litres) wine 125 (1962), beer 64·6. Liquid fuels (ooo cubic metres), 1963: diesel oil 82, fuel oil 657, motor spirit 368.
CONSTRUCTION: (ooo sq. metres floor area), 1961: Building permits issued, Montevideo: 2,735.

ENERGY

CONSUMPTION (tons coal equiv.), 1964: Total 2·23 m., per head 0·83.
ELECTRICITY, Public supply, 1965: Generated (kwh) 1,850 m., installed capacity (kw) 0·45 m.

GOVERNMENT EXPENDITURE

DISTRIBUTION (% of total), 1964: Defence 9, education 17, health 8.

GROSS PRODUCT

GDP (ooo m. pesos): At current market prices, 1963: 22·5; 1964: 33·3; at 1961 market prices, 1963: 16·8; 1964: 17·4; 1965: 17·6. Per head (US$), UN estimate, 1963: 558.
DISTRIBUTION (%), 1964: Agriculture 15, manufacturing and mining 23, trade 15, transport and communications 9, government and services 21.
GROWTH RATES (%), 1955–60: −0·1, per head −1·2; 1960–4: 0·2, per head −1·0.

EXTERNAL TRADE (US$m.)	1955	1960	1964	1965	1966
EXPORTS (f.o.b.)	183	129	179	191	186
Wool	106	67	68	90	86
Meat	7	31	74	61	45
Hides	15	15	17	15	17
Wheat	38	—	—	5	7
Linseed oil	5	5	2	3	3
IMPORTS (c.i.f.)	229	218	198	151	164
TRADE BALANCE	−45	−88	−19	+41	+22

DIRECTION OF TRADE (%)

	Exports			Imports		
	1955	*1960*	*1965*	*1955*	*1960*	*1965*
LAFTA	(17·1)	2·6	8·2	(20·8)	12·0	21·3
USA	8·9	15·3	16·8	19·3	26·8	13·6
EEC	38·7	36·6	33·2	23·2	17·4	24·6
UK	13·6	23·7	16·1	10·9	7·8	10·0

FINANCE

EXCHANGE RATE (*pesos*/*US$*): Free market, end-year 1960: 11·03; 1964: 24·35; 1965: 69·20; 1966: 76·50; 1967 (early August) 95–100.
BALANCE OF PAYMENTS (*US$ m.*): Goods and services (net), 1960: −75; 1964: −8; 1965: +69; 1966: +36.
COST OF LIVING (*Dec. 1958=100*), Montevideo, December, 1960: 202; 1964: 483; 1965: 908; 1966: 1,360.
GOVERNMENT ACCOUNTS (*m. pesos*), 1965: Revenue 5,452, expenditure 8,087, deficit 2,635. Estimated deficit, 1966: 16,900, comprising adjusted deficit from 1965 6,300; railway and public works board 1,200, municipal debts 1,400, 1966 estimated deficit 8,000.

EMPLOYMENT

ECONOMICALLY ACTIVE (%), 1963 (sample): of total pop. 39 (men 59, women 20). In services 27, manufacturing 21, agriculture 18, commerce 13, construction 5.
UNEMPLOYMENT (%), 1963: 12·8.

TRANSPORT AND COMMUNICATIONS

RAILWAYS: Traffic, 1965: 560 m. pass.-km., 434 m. net ton-km. Length of track 3,100 km.
MOTOR VEHICLES: In use (*000*), 1965: pass. cars 114, comm. vehicles 99. Nationa road system: 48,935 km., paved 2,736 km.
SHIPPING: Merchant fleet (*000 g.r. tons*), 1965: 153 (tankers 65). Main port: Montevideo; river ports: Nueva Palmira, Fray Bentos, Paysandú, Salto.
AIR: Scheduled services, 1965: Total 87 m. pass.-km., 0·58 m. cargo ton-km. International, 1964: 57 m. pass.-km., 0·43 m. cargo ton-km. Main airport: Montevideo: Carrasco (international).
TELEPHONES: No. in use, 1965: 190,000.

SOCIAL WELFARE

SYSTEM: Social insurance benefits and services provided mainly by Caja de Jubilaciones y Pensiones de la Industria y Comercio and other retirement and pension funds; finance largely by employees' and employers' contributions. For pensions and unemployment insurance (Industry and Commerce Fund), contributions based on remuneration: employees, from 12 to 21 per cent (related to wages); employers about 19 per cent. Contributions to other funds vary. Employment legislation covers working hours; holidays; payment of wages, overtime and annual bonus; employers' liability for compensation for accidents, dismissal and death indemnities.
HEALTH: 1,100 persons per physician, 200 persons per government hospital bed.
NUTRITION: Net food supply (*per head per day*), 1961: 2,970 calories, protein 94 g.

EDUCATION

ILLITERACY RATE (%), 1963 (census sample): 15 years and over, 10.
COMPULSORY: 6 years (between 8 and 14 years of age). School enrolment ratios (%), 1st and 2nd levels, 1963: 57, adjusted 71.

Schools, 1962: Primary: no. 2,174; pupils 0·32 m., teachers 10,400. Secondary: no. 177, p. 76,000. Teacher-training: no. 24, st. 3,350, t. 710. Higher: st. 14,900.
Universities (Montevideo, state), 1965: U. de la República: 16,500 st., academic staff 2,230. U. del Trabajo del Uruguay.

MASS MEDIA

Broadcasting: No. of receivers in use, end-1964: TV 0·18 m., radio 1·0 m. Transmitters: TV 5, radio 97.
Cinemas: No., 1963: 386. Attendance, 1963: total 17 m., per head 6·5.
Newsprint: Consumption, 1964: total 27,500 tons, per head 10·3 kg.
Newspapers: Daily, 1963: 35. Estimated circulation 0·8 m., copies per 000 of population 314. Principal dailies in Montevideo (*circulation, ooos*): *El País* 115, *El Día* 80 (Sunday 120), *El Debate* 65, *La Mañana* 37, *El Diario* (evening) 170.
Books: Titles published, 1964: 194.

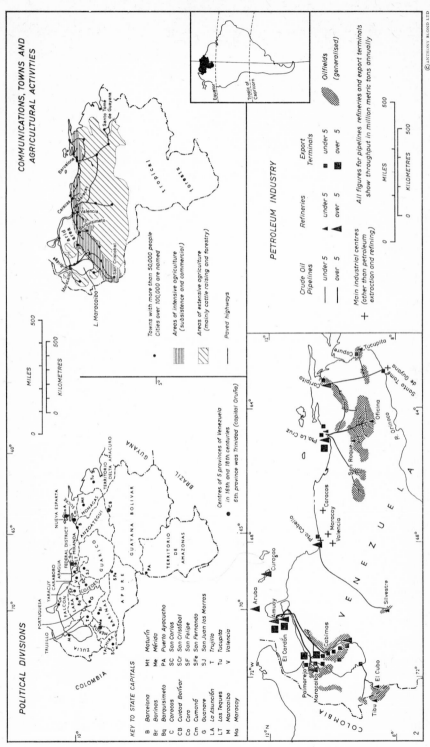

POLITICAL DIVISIONS

COMMUNICATIONS, TOWNS AND
AGRICULTURAL ACTIVITIES

KEY TO STATE CAPITALS

B	Barcelona	Mt	Maturín
Br	Barinas	Me	Mérida
Bq	Barquisimeto	PA	Puerto Ayacucho
C	Caracas	SC	San Carlos
CB	Ciudad Bolívar	SCr	San Cristóbal
Co	Coro	SF	San Felipe
Cm	Cumaná	SFe	San Fernando
G	Guanare	SJ	San Juan los Morros
LA	La Asunción	T	Trujillo
LT	Los Teques	Tu	Tucupita
M	Maracaibo	V	Valencia
Ma	Maracay		

Towns with more than 50,000 people
Cities over 100,000 are named

Areas of intensive agriculture
(subsistence and commercial)

Areas of extensive agriculture
(mainly cattle raising and forestry)

Paved highways

Centres of 5 provinces of Venezuela
in 16th and 18th centuries
6th province was Trinidad (capital Oruña)

PETROLEUM INDUSTRY

Crude Oil
Pipelines
—— under 5
══ over 5

Refineries
▲ under 5
▲ over 5

Export
Terminals
■ under 5
■ over 5

Oilfields
(generalised)

+ Main industrial centres
(other than petroleum
extraction and refining)

All figures for pipelines refineries and export terminals
show throughput in million metric tons annually

VENEZUELA

© ANTHONY BLOND LTD

VENEZUELA

GUILLERMO MORÓN

HISTORY

Ethnic history

VENEZUELA as a nation rests on traditions that go back over 450 years. Venezuelan history properly begins in the 16th century, though the territory was discovered in 1498 by Christopher Columbus on his third voyage. In the course of the country's centuries of history a national character has evolved, rooted in an established culture. Venezuela is among those Latin American countries most evidently based on Spanish structures—political, social, cultural and linguistic—and fundamentally uninfluenced by its indigenous peoples.

When the Spanish pioneers arrived, the aboriginal communities in the territory remained at a relatively unadvanced stage of cultural development. For this reason, and because of a low density of population, they soon disintegrated and were liquidated or absorbed by the new arrivals. In the 16th century the Spanish settlers brought about a radical transformation in the human landscape of Venezuela. There has never been an indigenous or predominantly indigenous majority or potential majority in the population, as in Mexico; no purely indigenous communities have survived to be a problem to the state, as in Guatemala. Miscegenation was common throughout the 16th and 17th centuries, and the Spanish element was preponderant. The Indian heritage of the Venezuelan people is purely biological, particularly noticeable in some individuals and in certain small towns or villages, but it does not characterise the population as a whole. The Negro element is even less significant; the Negroes originally brought as slaves to the Spanish provinces that are now Venezuela are a small minority, concentrated mainly in the northern part of the country along the so-called Windward Coast.

By the 18th century, the fusion and integration of all the races was universal. In Venezuela racial tension has always been non-existent; a complete absence of discrimination on account of colour is a characteristic feature of the national history and culture. General miscegenation has formed a situation of basic racial equality.

The three phases of Venezuelan history

Three distinct phases may be distinguished in Venezuelan history—the era of administrative fragmentation, that of territorial unification and that of Venezuela as a sovereign nation.

The era of administrative fragmentation occupied the 16th, 17th and part of the 18th centuries. Each of six separate Provinces was a politically and administratively autonomous entity, in the charge of a Governor and Captain

F

General appointed by the king of Spain. Before making any such appointment, the king would normally consult the Council of the Indies, an advisory
body competent in matters relating to the Overseas Provinces, as the
Spanish possessions in America were called. At the same time, the Council
would consider the demands of the settlers themselves, which would reach
it by way of the Reales Audiencias, judicial bodies established in the principal
centres of America. The political and military affairs of each Venezuelan
Province were the responsibility of its Governor and Captain General,
but the judiciary was dependent on the Real Audiencia of Santo Domingo
or that of Bogotá.

The six Provinces which were to constitute present-day Venezuela were
the following: Venezuela, with its capital in Caracas; Mérida, with its
capital in the city of that name: Nueva Andalucía with its capital in Cumaná;
Guayana with its capital in Angostura, now Ciudad Bolívar; Margarita
with its capital in La Asunción; and Trinidad with its capital in Port-of-Spain,
formerly called Oruña. All these, with the exception of Trinidad, which
became a British colony at the end of the 18th century, are now part of
Venezuela.

Towards the end of the 18th century there was a tendency away from
administrative autonomy, and a more centralised government was established
in Caracas. The various stages towards administrative unification may be
summed up as follows. In 1776 an Intendancy of the Royal Exchequer was
established in Caracas, with jurisdiction over the six Provinces. In 1777
the Governor of Caracas, in his capacity as Captain General, was given
military authority over the six Provinces. The Real Audiencia of Caracas,
with legal jurisdiction over the six Provinces, was created in 1786. The
geographical boundaries of this high court's legal competence were to
serve as a basis for the territorial claims of Venezuela when political
independence from Spain came about in 1811. In 1792 came the creation of
the Real Consulado of Caracas, a kind of chamber of commerce that
regulated trade in all the Provinces. At the time of Venezuela's declaration
of independence in 1811, the Provinces had already reached a stage of
territorial and to some extent administrative unity. Political authority,
however, vested in the Governors, was still confined to each Province.

Francisco de Miranda

Francisco de Miranda (1750–1816) was the guiding force behind not only
Venezuelan independence but the Hispanic American revolution which
gave birth to all the new republics. A merchant's son born in Caracas, he
served with the Spanish and revolutionary French armies (becoming a
field-marshal in the latter) and travelled in the United States and Europe
full of curiosity about national ideas, customs and politics. He organised
conspirators' cells in Paris and London, where future Spanish American
independence leaders such as Bernardo O'Higgins were trained. In 1790 he
submitted to Pitt a plan for the independence of Spanish America—for an
'Inca Empire' consisting of most of the Spanish-speaking area, an idea later
replaced by a plan for a Colombian republic which influenced Bolívar in his
scheme for a Greater Colombia. In 1806 Miranda led two unsuccessful
revolutionary expeditions to Venezuela. At Coro on the second of these he
made a proclamation in which he spoke of Spanish America 'recovering'
her lost independence—a reflection of the current theory that all peoples were
originally free. This and other of Miranda's ideas found expression in the
Venezuelan independence constitution of 1811.

The republic

In 1811 a rebellion broke out in Caracas, led by the ruling class composed mainly of landowners, merchants and members of the university. The aim of the rebellion was to disavow the terms of the Spanish king's forced abdication in Bayonne and to reaffirm Venezuela's allegiance to Spain. But the rebellion soon grew into a revolution, and in 1811 a congress convened to proclaim independence of Spain and the creation of a sovereign Venezuela. From this moment on and until 1821 the whole country was involved in a struggle against Spain and the Spanish forces sent across the Atlantic to quell the rebellion. The rebel forces were led by Simón Bolívar (1783–1830), who laid the foundations for a modern state and was the creator not only of Venezuela but also of Colombia, Bolivia and Ecuador, and the liberator of Peru. His thoughts and deeds are at the roots of the nation, which did not adopt the name of Venezuela until 1830.

After 1830 the republican form of government in Venezuela ranged from centralism to federalism until the presidential system finally imposed itself. To this day no less than twenty-three constitutions have succeeded each other, and more than thirty-five revolutions, including the Federal War (1859–63). Only sixteen presidents have served a full term of office; fifteen have been overthrown by force. Since the turn of the century there have been three military dictatorships (that of General Cipriano Castro, 1899–1908; Juan Vicente Gómez, 1908–35; General Marcos Pérez Jiménez, 1952–8) and a party dictatorship following the October revolution of 1945, based on the support of the Acción Democrática party, which lasted until 1948. The state has managed nonetheless to survive, adapt itself and establish democratic rule.

According to the constitution of 1961, 'the Republic of Venezuela is a federation of states'. The federal territory consists of twenty States, one District, two Territories and a number of Dependencies that are, in fact, islands. In practice, the authority of the various members of this federation is extremely limited, while the central government is very powerful.

At the present time Venezuela is a country with a profoundly messianic temperament with egalitarian sentiments at the very roots of its history, a democracy with an elected government and universal suffrage. Economic inequality only serves to intensify the feeling of personal and social equality. There is no exclusive ruling class, nor have there ever been any traditionally all-powerful sectors to impose their special structure on political democracy; money is the only instrument of class-distinction.

Recent political developments

General Juan Vicente Gómez, a dictator of peasant extraction, died in 1935 after ruling for twenty-seven years. His successor, former war and naval minister General Eleazar López Contreras, was constitutionally elected for the period 1936–43. He governed in accordance with the law, permitted political parties to function and carried out the progressive reforms which were to propel the country into the modern world. He may therefore be considered the founder of Venezuela's contemporary political democracy. His policies were based, roughly speaking, on the following principles: the creation of a nationalistic ideology centred on the veneration of Venezuela's liberator, Simón Bolívar, thus preventing other ideologies of foreign origin, particularly fascism and communism, from gaining ground; non-violent transition from a dictatorial form of government, which had become an accepted tradition over the years, to a democratic form of government that would have the support of all moderate sectors of the population; freedom of the press and of association, as well as the maintenance of all political and civil rights and obligations; and lawful procedure in all spheres of public life, that is to say, constitutional government.

General López Contreras abandoned the presidency in 1941, on account of changes in the constitution which shortened the presidential period by two years. In the subsequent elections the victor was yet another military figure, General Isaías Medina Angarita. He had been minister of war in the previous administration, and as head of state he rapidly became very popular and even a symbol of honest and efficient government. Under his leadership the economic situation showed a marked improvement and he was able to implement a number of basic reforms: a new Civil Code (1942), new legislation affecting oil companies (1943), new tax legislation (1942), a reform of the constitution (1945) and a new agrarian law (1945).

In the normal course of events the popular government of General Medina would have stayed in power until 1946, but he was toppled by a coup in October 1945 led by a group of young army officers in close collaboration with the Acción Democrática party (AD). The self-appointed revolutionary junta included two army officers, four members of the AD and one independent. Its president was Rómulo Betancourt, undisputed leader of the AD from its beginnings in 1941 to the present day. Other members of the junta were Dr Luis Beltrán Prieto Figueroa, Dr Raúl Leoni and Dr Gonzalo Barrios. All three were among the founders of the AD; in 1964 Leoni was elected president of the Republic, Barrios becoming minister of the interior, a position equivalent to prime minister, and Prieto Figueroa chairman of Congress and of the AD.

The new regime was quick to deal with those whom it felt to be untrustworthy. Two former presidents, Medina and López Centreras, and a number of their collaborators were brought to trial before a specially appointed tribunal on charges of having abused their official positions for personal gain. They were found guilty and denied normal rights of appeal. Both ex-presidents were expelled from the country, along with Dr Arturo Uslar Pietri—a former cabinet minister and key figure in the Medina administration—and many other politicians. A newly elected Constituent Assembly met for the first time in December 1946 and approved a new constitution in 1947. The subsequent presidential elections took place in an atmosphere of tension.

Four political groups participated in the 1947 elections: the ruling AD, whose candidate got 872,000 votes; the conservative Social Christian Party (COPEI) which obtained 267,000 votes under the leadership of Dr Rafael Caldera; the Democratic and Republican Union Party (URD), whose candidate withdrew; and the Communist Party (CVP), whose candidate, Dr Gustavo Machado, polled 37,000 votes. The AD's candidate, Rómulo Gallegos, Venezuela's most distinguished novelist, obtained an overwhelming majority and became the new president in February 1948.

Only a few months later, however, in November 1948, the same officers who had overthrown Medina in 1945 staged yet another coup. Once again Venezuela was ruled by a military junta. Now it was the turn of the AD's leaders to go into exile. The new junta remained in power until 1952, though its first president, Colonel Carlos Delgado Chalbaud, was murdered in November 1950 and replaced by a civilian, Dr German Suárez Flamerich. In the general elections held in November 1952 the result was a landslide victory for the URD, led by Jóvito Villalba, a veteran of twenty-five years in opposition. In the election of 1947, his party had participated in the campaign but finally withdrawn its candidate. This time it benefited from the fact that both the AD and the CVP had been outlawed. Its only rivals, the COPEI, obtained few votes. The military regime refused to accept the result of the elections, and in December Colonel Marcos Pérez Jiménez seized power on behalf of the armed forces.

The period of dictatorship under Pérez Jiménez produced some solid achievements and increasing prosperity, but also a great deal of corruption and police terror. The leaders of the political parties, particularly the AD, CP and URD, were ruthlessly persecuted, while the men close to the president enriched themselves by all manner of illicit means. The president himself, who went to the United States after his downfall and was extradited in 1964, was imprisoned pending trial on charges of corruption.

The dictatorship came to an end in January 1958 as a result of a military rebellion supported by strikes and popular demonstrations. At first a military junta was appointed, but it soon gave way to a junta of civilians, and in 1959 a presidential election was won by Rómulo Betancourt with 49 per cent of the vote. Since he did not obtain an absolute majority, he was obliged to form a coalition government with the COPEI.

It is established in Venezuela's constitution that the president may not stand for re-election at the end of his term of office. Accordingly, in the election of 1964, the successful candidate of the AD was Dr Raúl Leoni, though his share of the vote dropped to 33 per cent. He too was forced to form a coalition government with the URD and a new party that appeared on the political scene at the time of the 1964 elections, the Democratic National Front (FND) under the leadership of Arturo Uslar Pietri, a one-time active supporter of the Medina regime and greatly respected both as a politician and as a writer.

POLITICAL PARTIES

It will here be convenient to analyse the political parties that have dominated Venezuelan public life since 1936.

Acción Democrática (AD)

The party was legally recognised under its present name in 1941; it had been active clandestinely since 1937 under the name of National Democratic Party (PDN). By 1945 it had some 20,000 members. In the three years following the coup which brought the party to power, its membership increased to about 700,000. It was outlawed as a result of another military coup in October 1948, but continued to be active underground. It re-emerged into the open in January 1958 and at present it has some 900,000 members.

Many of the AD's founders were active in the Communist parties of the Caribbean from 1928 to 1931, especially in Costa Rica. On 22 March 1931 they signed the so-called Plan of Barranquilla, an analysis of the political situation in Latin America, and particularly in Venezuela. They pledged themselves to the struggle against military dictatorship, the protection of the working classes against capitalist exploitation, a revision of all agreements made by the state and concessions to local and foreign capitalists, and state control of all monopolies in the sector of public utilities. After 1937 the Communists affiliated to the International broke with the PDN which was becoming increasingly nationalistic (the AD after 1941 maintained this line).

In 1960 the younger leaders of the party broke away and formed a new group called the Movement of the Revolutionary Left (MIR). Basically this split was due to the fact that the traditional leaders did not apply in government those socialist principles which the party had proclaimed since its foundation. In 1961 a further split occurred. The splinter group is called the Nationalist Revolutionary Party (PRN) and is led by a former presidential candidate, Dr Raúl Ramos Giménez. The main body of the AD, the AD Vieja Guardia, continues to be led by veterans such as Rómulo Betancourt, Gonzalo Barrios, Raúl Leoni and prominent members of the trade unions.

It is one of the fundamental theories of the AD that the state should intervene as moderator in all aspects of public life. With regard to oil legislation, it is opposed to granting concessions. On an international level, it stands firmly within the Western Alliance. Betancourt, now living abroad, has become a Latin American leader and more than a purely Venezuelan politician.

Democratic and Republican Union Party (URD)

This party was formed in 1946 in opposition to the government of Rómulo Gallegos. When the latter was overthrown in November 1948, the party continued to grow and it even won the elections for the Constituent Assembly in November 1952. With the establishment of the Pérez Jiménez dictatorship, the party went underground. It was reorganised in 1958 and participated in Betancourt's coalition government. In 1960 it went into opposition. At present it is once again part of a coalition government with the AD. It is led by its founder, Dr Jóvito Villalba. Though Dr Villalba has great prestige, his leadership was contested by the late Dr Aliro Ugarte Pelayo, a distinguished lawyer and writer and a skilful politician who made his mark as a member of the government of Medina Angarita (1941–5).

The programme of the URD does not differ very considerably from that of the AD. Its principal aims are to carry out a 'democratic revolution', to place Venezuela's enormous resources at the disposal of private enterprise in an effort to industrialise the country, and to implement an agrarian reform based on cooperative and community organisation. The party is also committed to reform of the executive that would reduce the personal aspect of the presidential system to a policy of greater autonomy at the municipal level, to reform of public administration and to judicial reform. With regard to Venezuela's oil resources, it stands for changes in the system of concessions, greater technical control over the activities of oil companies, nationalisation of natural gas, greater support for the OPEP (Organización de Países Exportadores de Petróleo) and a general review of costs. It is also in favour of regulating foreign investments in order to lessen the dangers inherent in 'powerful foreign nuclei that might infringe on the sovereignty of the nation'.

Social Christian Party (COPEI)

This party was founded in 1946 under the name Committee for Independent Political and Electoral Organisation (the abbreviation of which is still used to denote the party) with the intention of putting up a candidate in the next elections. Its candidate, Dr Rafael Caldera, obtained a significant number of votes in 1947 and was represented in Congress by sixteen deputies and six senators. After the coup of November 1948 and until 1958, the COPEI was in opposition. When Betancourt became president in 1958 the party joined the coalition government.

The programme of this party is based on the social doctrines of the Roman Catholic Church. It has become rather more radical in recent years and is particularly active among young people. Its leaders are Dr Rafael Caldera and Luis Herrera Campins, the well-known journalist and lawyer.

Communist Party

The Communist Party was first organised clandestinely in 1931 as a section of the Third International. In 1943 it appeared on the political scene under the name Venezuelan Popular Union (UPV). In 1945 it emerged openly, since the constitutional reform of that year had eliminated the paragraph making a Communist Party illegal. It was outlawed in May 1950 and remained illegal until 1958; in 1962 it was again prohibited. Many of its leaders have been imprisoned or forced to leave the country, since they are held responsible for the activities of terrorists in the cities and guerrilla groups in the countryside throughout the last few years. This violence has lowered the prestige of the Communist Party considerably, although there are many Communist students in schools and universities.

The leader of the Communist Party, Jesús Faría, is the most outstanding leader of the working class that Venezuela has known. When the party was outlawed he was imprisoned and expelled to Moscow. He is now among the most important Communist leaders of Latin America.

National Democratic Front

This group was founded in 1964 by Arturo Uslar Pietri. His closest collaborators are Pedro Segnini La Cruz and Ramón Escovar Salem, ministers of agriculture and justice respectively in Leoni's coalition government.

ECONOMY

In Venezuela there is a wide gap between rich and poor, and although the state has huge resources much of the population is poor. According to the budget, public expenditure in 1966 amounted to 7,852 million bolivars (US$1,745 million); yet the average income of a peasant family is approximately Bs800 a year; it is evident that while the state is very rich, the poor are very poor. Reforms are gradually being implemented to correct this imbalance in the socio-economic situation. An official body known as CORDIPLAN now carries out the technical studies essential to an effective national plan. The government has invested heavily, in some cases jointly with foreign companies, in the mineral- and HEP-rich state of Guayana (Bolivar), where a new petro-chemical industry (synthetic fibres, fertilisers and plastics) has been started in addition to steel and aluminium manufacturing. The giant Angostura bridge over the Orinoco, completed in January 1967, is a major factor in the opening up of this hitherto isolated south-eastern province.

The system of differential currency exchange untrammelled by restrictions, a feature of Venezuelan economic policy since about 1943, has been modified. A large deficit in the balance of payments due to an excessive outflow of foreign currency led to the introduction of controls in November 1960, and two rates of exchange were established: the free rate was set at Bs4·54 to the US dollar, while the controlled rate was set at Bs3·35 to the dollar. This arrangement was substituted in 1964 by yet another system with the following characteristics: the 'oil dollar' was set at Bs4·40; the rate of exchange for the general public was set at Bs4·50 to the dollar; that for the government and the banks was set at Bs4·485 to the dollar. Moreover, a differential rate was established in connection with coffee and cocoa exports and a special rate in connection with certain imports. An agreement was signed recently to make the bolivar an international currency; in 1966 it was one of Latin America's hardest currencies and the country's foreign exchange reserves remained high.

Steps have been taken to effect an agrarian reform. Venezuela had to rely mainly on her agricultural resources until the discovery of oil, and the pervading structure was one of semi-feudal latifundia. An attempt was made at agrarian reform by the regime of General Medina, but the first land reform was not passed until 1960. In accordance with this law, land was to be given to all the 300,000 peasant families. By 1964, 1,670,000 hectares had been distributed to 66,000 families in over 700 settlements at a total cost of Bs485 million. But the results of this change in the social structure of rural areas are still very relative. The system is something of a hybrid: it has stopped short of a socialist reform and is not quite a capitalist reform. Parallel to this state initiative private agriculture has increased production of tobacco, maize, sesame and other products so that 80 per cent of agricultural production is now sufficient to cover the country's requirements.

In the period 1930–58 Venezuela did not incur any debts abroad, but in 1959 loans were contracted through various inter-American organisations and US banks in order to finance public works and balance the budget. In 1966 Bs218 million of the national budget was covered by foreign loans. In 1965 Venezuela requested admission to the Latin American Free Trade Association and membership became effective in 1966.

Throughout the last twenty years, Venezuela has tried to industrialise in an effort to substitute imports by local products. High import tariffs and low income taxes have helped in the establishment of industries with Venezuelan and foreign capital. The main burden of taxation has fallen on oil revenues and on salaried and wage-earning employees.

Oil constitutes the backbone of Venezuela's economy, with a current daily production of 3,500,000 drums. It accounts for 90 per cent of the country's foreign currency, 70 per cent of national income and 30 per cent of GNP. Oil has provided the country's basic wealth for the last fifty years and is expected to continue to do so for some time to come. The policy of negotiating with foreign oil companies and granting concessions for exploitation was abandoned in 1958, and no other formula was adopted until in October 1966 the government approved a new service scheme increasing the state's share in profits; the Venezuela Petroleum Corporation (CVP) was to join with the companies in developing new reserves and play an increased part in all phases of business. This scheme, however, was still not ratified by Congress as at August 1967. The US Import Control Program hit Venezuelan crude exports in 1966, exports to East Coast refineries dropping to their lowest level in a decade. Venezuelan feeling was particularly injured because Venezuela has consistently been among the largest buyers of US goods (in 1965 larger than Brazil, Argentina and Uruguay combined).

BIBLIOGRAPHY

Hasbrouck, Alfred. *Foreign Legionaries in the Liberation of Spanish South America*, Columbia Univ. Press, New York, 1928.

Hussey, Roland D. *The Caracas Company 1728–1784*, Harvard Univ. Press, Cambridge, Mass., 1934.

Lieuwen, Edwin. *Petroleum in Venezuela: A History*, California Univ. Press, Calif., 1954.
Venezuela, Oxford Univ. Press for Royal Institute of International Affairs, London and New York, 1961.
Masur, Gerhard. *Simon Bolivar*, Univ. of New Mexico Press, Albuquerque, 1948.
Morón, Guillermo. *A History of Venezuela*, Allen and Unwin, London, 1964.
Robertson, W. S. *The Life of Miranda*, Univ. of North Carolina Press, Chapel Hill, N.C., 1933.
Thend, J. B. *Bolivar and the Indepenuence of Spanish America*, London, 1946.

BASIC INFORMATION

CLIMATE

	Caracas	Maracaibo	Santa Elena
Lat./long.	10° 30′ N, 67° W	10° 30′ N, 71° 30′ W	4° 30′ N, 61° W
Altitude	3,418 ft/ 1,042 m.	20 ft/6 m.	2,816 ft/ 859 m.
Mean temp. of hottest month	21°C/71°F (May)	30°C/85°F (Aug./Sept.)	24°C/76°F (Mar.)
Mean temp. of coolest month	19°C/66°F (Jan.)	27°C/82°F (Jan./Feb.)	23°C/73°F (Dec./Jan.)
Absolute max.	91°F/33°C	102°F/39°C	95°F/35°C
Absolute min.	45°F/7°C	66°F/19°C	53°F/11°C
Relative humidity at midday of hottest and coolest months	n.a.	69%/72%	57%/62%
Wettest months	4·3 in./109 mm. (July/Aug./ Oct.)	5·9 in./ 50 mm. (Oct.)	9·9 in./251 mm. (June)
Driest months	0·4 in./10 mm. (Feb.)	0·1 in./2 mm. (Feb.)	2·0 in./50 mm. (Jan.)
Annual av. rainfall	32·8 in./ 833 mm.	22·7 in./ 577 mm.	64·1 in./ 1,628 mm.

POPULATION

TOTAL (*million*): 1961 (census): 7·52, adjusted for underenumeration, nearly 8 million; end-1966: 9·19; 1980 (ECLA projection) 14·83.
DENSITY, mid-1965: 10 persons per sq. km.
CRUDE RATES (*per 000*), 1965: birth 43·5, death 7·0, infant mortality 45·9. ECLA estimates, 1959–61: birth 47–50, death 9–12.
GROWTH RATES (% *p.a.*): 1945–65: 3·6; 1960–5: 3·4.
DISTRIBUTION (% *of total pop.*): Ethnic: mixed 65, white 20, Negro 8, Amerindian 7. Foreign-born, 1950: 4·1; 1961: 6·2. Language, Spanish. Religion: mainly Roman Catholic. Urban (*centres 2,000 inhab. or over*), ECLA data, 1950: 48·7; 1960: 62·9; 1980 (proj.): 74·4. Largest cities (*000 inhab.*), 1964: Caracas (metrop. area) 1,589, Maracaibo 503, Barquisimeto 227, Valencia 184, Macaray 154.

CONSTITUTIONAL SYSTEM

CONSTITUTION: First (Gran Colombia) 1811, Venezuela 1830. Major changes in 1858, 1864, 1872, 1936, 1947, 1953; latest 1961.
SYSTEM: Federal Republic composed of 20 states (divided into 156 districts), Federal District (2 departments), 2 federal territories (7 departments), and federal dependencies (72 Caribbean islands). Separate executive, legislature and judiciary. States have elected legislatures, and are theoretically autonomous, except in judicial matters, but are financially dependent on federal government.

145

EXECUTIVE: Power is vested in president, who is elected by direct vote for five years; no reelection. He is commander-in-chief of the armed forces; he appoints ministers, who form council of ministers, and governors of the Federal District and the territories; he can declare state of emergency.

LEGISLATURE: Bi-cameral, National Congress of Senate and Chamber of Deputies. *Senate:* Two senators from each state and the Federal District, elected by direct vote for five years. Additional senators for minority representation, also life members (elected ex-presidents). *Deputies:* One deputy for every 50,000 inhabitants and at least two from each state and one for each territory, elected by direct vote, with proportional representation of minorities, for 5 years. *Suffrage:* Universal, compulsory voting for adults over 18 years of age. Registered voters, Sept. 1963: 3·5 m. *Elections:* Presidential, December 1963 (*ooo votes*): Dr Raúl Leoni (Acción Democrática—Gobierno) 957·7, elected; Dr Rafael Caldera (Social Cristiano—COPEI) 588·4; total 2,918·9. Composition of Congress after 1963 elections:

Party	Votes (ooo)	Senate	Deputies
Acción Democrática—Gobierno (AD)	936	23	65
Social Cristiano—COPEI	596	9	40
Unión Republicana Democrática (URD)	497	7	29
Independiente Pro-Frente Nacional[1]	382	5	22
Fuerza Democrática Popular	274	4	16
Others	176	2	7
TOTAL	2,862	50	179

[1] Renamed Frente Nacional Democrático (FND). In 1966 the FND and 8 deputies of the URD left the government coalition.

JUDICIARY: Supreme Court, composed of divisions with at least 5 judges elected by Congress for 9-year terms, one-third being renewed every 3 years; courts of ordinary jurisdiction: superior tribunals, courts of first instance, district and municipal courts; courts of special jurisdiction.

DEFENCE

DEFENCE BUDGET: 1964: 636 m. bolivares, 1·8% of GDP.

ARMED FORCES: National service: at 18 years of age; 2 years in army, air force or navy. Strength: army 18,000, navy and marines 5,700, air force 3,500, total 27,200 plus national guard of about 10,000.

INTERNATIONAL RELATIONS

Member of the UN and many of its international specialised agencies, including: IBRD and IFC, IMF, FAO, ICAO, ILO, ITU, UNDP, UNESCO, UPU, WHO and WMO; IAEA; UNCTAD representative. Also a member of OAS, Alliance for Progress, ECLA, IDB and LAFTA.

ECONOMY

PRODUCTION

AGRICULTURE (ooo tons)	1948–53[1]	63/4	64/5	65/6
Maize	303	430	475	521
Rice (paddy)	41	131	166	200
Coffee	44	61	56	54
Cacao	16	21	22	22
Sugar	60	315	361	401
Bananas	950	1,456	1,203	1,230
Beans (dry)	47	38	40	42

[1] Average 1948/9—1952/3.

LAND, 1961 (%): Arable 3, permanent pasture 18, forested 21, other 58.
OTHER AGRICULTURAL DATA: Agricultural holdings, 1961 (census): no. 0·32 m.,
area 26·2 m. hectares. Tractors in use (ooos), 1964: 14·2. Fertiliser consumption
(ooo tons), 1965/6: 47.
LIVESTOCK: Numbers (ooo head), 1965/6: cattle 6,700, sheep 77. Products (ooo tons),
1965: meat 194, beef and veal 162.
FISH: Landed (ooo tons), 1965: total 119·3, sardines 43·8.
MINING, 1965: Iron ore 10·9 m. tons, gold 0·74 tons, diamonds 91,000 metric carats.
Fuels: coal 31,300 tons; (m. cubic metres) crude petroleum 201·5, natural gas 40,846
(used as fuel, etc. 6,448).
MANUFACTURING, 1965: (ooo tons), pig iron 324 (1964), steel ingots 625, cement
2,109, salt (marine) 172, wheat flour 302; (m. litres) beer 278. Liquid fuels (m. cubic
metres): diesel oil 11·7, fuel oil 40·9, motor spirit 8·3. Motor vehicles (ooo units),
cars 41·3, commercial vehicles 15·4.
CONSTRUCTION: (ooo sq. metres floor area), 1965: building permits issued 3,085.

ENERGY
CONSUMPTION (tons coal equiv.), 1964: total 25·3 m., per head 3·00.
ELECTRICITY, 1965: Generated (kwh) 8,245 m., installed capacity (kw) 2·11 m.

GOVERNMENT EXPENDITURE
DISTRIBUTION (% of total), 1966: Defence 10, education 12, health and social assistance
14, public works 21.

GROSS PRODUCT
GDP (ooo m. bolivares): At current market prices, 1964: 35·7; 1965: 38·1; at 1957
market prices, 1964: 32·1; 1965: 33·8. Per head (US$), UN estimate, 1964: 792.
DISTRIBUTION (%), 1965: Agriculture 7, petroleum and gas 28, manufacturing 13,
trade 14, services 15.
GROWTH RATES (%), 1950-9: Total 8·3, per head 4·1; 1960-5: total 5·0, per head 1·5.

EXTERNAL TRADE (US$ m.)	1955	1960	1964	1965	1966
EXPORTS (f.o.b.)	1,873	2,432	2,703	2,744	2,713
Petroleum and derivatives	1,761	2,149	2,344	2,283	.
Iron ore	49	158	108	123	.
IMPORTS (c.i.f.)	1,058	1,188	1,269	1,453	1,331
TRADE BALANCE	+815	+1,244	+1,434	+1,291	+1,382

DIRECTION OF TRADE (%)

	Exports			Imports		
	1955	1960	1965	1955	1960	1965
LAFTA	(2·1)	7·8	5·4	(0·7)	1·4	2·5
USA	38·0	38·1	34·7	59·6	51·7	50·6
EEC	5·8	5·4	6·5	19·6	22·8	20·5
UK	3·9	7·9	7·4	7·4	6·0	5·8

FINANCE
EXCHANGE RATE (bolivares/US$): Comm. banks, end-year 1960: 3·35; 1964: 4·50;
1966: 4·50.
BALANCE OF PAYMENTS (US$ m.): Goods and services (net), 1960: +482; 1964: +283;
1965: +81; 1966: +39.
COST OF LIVING (Dec. 1958=100), Caracas, December 1960: 106; 1964: 104; 1965:
109; 1966: 109.
TREASURY ACCOUNTS (m. bolivares), 1966: Revenue 7,951, expenditure 7,922, surplus
29. Reserves, end-1966: 702.

EMPLOYMENT

ECONOMICALLY ACTIVE (%), 1961 (sample): Of total (excluding Indian jungle) pop. 32; men 51, women 12. In agriculture 32, manufacturing 12, services 24, commerce 13.

UNEMPLOYMENT (%), 1966: 8·1 (of labour force of 2·93 m.).

TRANSPORT AND COMMUNICATIONS

RAILWAYS: Traffic, 1964: 37 m. pass.-km.; 26 m. net ton-km. Length of track 770 km.

MOTOR VEHICLES: In use (ooo), 1965: pass. cars 352, comm. vehicles 146. Road system, 1963: 48,200 km., paved 13,220.

SHIPPING: Merchant fleet (ooo g.r. tons), 1965: 313. International sea-borne shipping (m. tons), 1965: goods loaded 188, goods unloaded 3. Main ports: La Guaira, Puerto Cabello, Maracaibo, Puerto Ordaz.

AIR: Scheduled services, 1965: Total 659 m. pass.-km., 51 m. cargo ton-km. International, 1964: 305 m. pass.-km., 37 m. cargo ton-km. Main airports: Caracas: Maiquetía (international); Maracaibo: Grano de Oro.

TELEPHONES: No in use, 1964: 260,000.

SOCIAL WELFARE

SYSTEM: Social insurance benefits and services provided mainly by Seguro Social Obligatorio; benefits related to part of monthly income. Financed by employees' and employers' contributions based on remuneration: employees 4%; employers from 7% to 9%. Contributors to other insurance schemes vary. Employment legislation covers working hours; holidays; payment of wages, overtime and profit sharing; employers' liability for compensation for accidents, dismissal and death indemnities.

HEALTH: 1,300 persons per physician, 300 persons per hospital bed.

NUTRITION: Net food supply (per head per day), 1962: 2,340 calories, protein 61 g.

EDUCATION

ILLITERACY RATE (%), 1961 (census sample): 15 years and over, 34.

COMPULSORY: 6 years (between 7 and 14 years of age). School enrolment ratios (%), 1st and 2nd levels, 1963: 61, adjusted 83.

SCHOOLS, 1964/5: Pre-school and primary: no. 10,840, pupils 1·42 m., teachers 41,470. Secondary: no. 539, p. 0·17 m., t. 8,340. Technical: no. 232, st. 82,100, t. 4,190. Teacher-training: no. 117, st. 17,340, t. 1,750. Higher: no. 10, st. 41,500, t. 4,200.

UNIVERSITIES: State (autonomous): U. Central de Venezuela, Caracas 24,000 students, academic staff 2,400 (700 full-time); U. del Zulia, Maracaibo 5,000 st., a.s. 550 (150 f.-t.); U. de Los Andes, Mérida 4,200 st., a.s. 450; U. de Oriente, Cumaná (Sucre) 2,000 st., a.s. 460; U. de Carabobo, Valencia 2,300 st., a.s. 420. Private: U. Católica Andrés Bello, Caracas 3,700 st., a.s. 290; U. Santa María Caracas 1,500 st., a.s. 120.

MASS MEDIA

BROADCASTING: No. of receivers in use, end-1964: TV 0·59 m., radio 2·4 m. Transmitters: TV 18, radio 79.

CINEMAS: No. 1959: 744. Attendance, 1959: total 60 m., per head 8·4.

NEWSPRINT: Consumption, 1964: total 38,100 tons, per head 4·5 kg.

NEWSPAPERS: Daily, 1963: 27. Estimated circulation (17 dailies) 0·63 m., copies per ooo of population 78. Principal dailies (circulation, ooos), Caracas: El Universal 92, El Mundo 86, El Nacional 75, La Esfera 36, Daily Journal 15 (Sunday 17), Últimas Noticias (evening) 85. Maracaibo: Panorama 62.

BOOKS: Titles published, 1963: 743.

MEXICO AND CENTRAL AMERICA

MEXICO

RAFAEL SEGOVIA

HISTORY

The colonial period

IN 1518,. when the Spaniards embarked on the conquest of the territory that would later be called New Spain, they found a number of peoples whose cultural levels ranged from the very advanced development of the Aztecs, Mixtecs and others to the half-civilised state of the Chichimecs. The rivalries between these peoples facilitated the conquest of the central region cf Mexico. The old Aztec capital was made the base for the conquest, oolonisation and evangelisation of Mexico, a process which lasted until 1722, when Nayarit in the north-west was subjugated.

Immediately after the Conquest, the Spaniards imposed a form of government imported from Europe. The personal rule of Hernán Cortés gave way to the *audiencias*—judicial bodies with certain legislative functions —and in 1535 the first viceroy arrived. The viceroys were to be closely supervised by the Council of the Indies in Seville, the supreme legislative and judicial organ for the colonies. A complex juridical and administrative system was evolved on the basis of special legislation known as the Laws of the Indies, which was not always respected.

The structural basis of colonial society was the system of land-tenure: some Indians retained possession of the land on an individual basis, in contrast to the pre-Conquest tradition of communal ownership; a limited number of lands were still held communally, and supplied the needs of the Indian villages. The *mercedes* or royal grants of land made to the Conquistadors and colonists were, in part at least, the origin of the system of large estates which was to last until the Revolution of 1910. The colonists were determined to tie the Indians to their lands by any means: the semi-enslaved labour force which resulted was principally employed in the mines.

From the very beginning, two parallel societies existed: the Indians, deprived of their political, economic and cultural heritage but retaining their traditional system of values; and the Europeans, who played a dominating role in the ownership of land and mines, in trade, administration and ecclesiastical affairs. A rigid caste system tended to establish an ever-increasing difference between the Spaniards and the creoles (persons born in New Spain of Spanish descent); these differences were magnified by discrimination in employment and the colonial system. For three centuries, however, the efforts of the viceregal and ecclesiastical authorities kept the richest of Spain's colonies isolated from the rest of the world. The extra-ordinary growth of the silver mines during the 18th century served to palliate the discontent of the creoles.

From independence to the Revolution

The discontent of the creoles, undefined but with a real basis, crystallised and found expression with the disappearance of the Spanish monarchy as a result of Napoleon's invasion of Spain in 1808. In 1810 the first insurrection took place under creole leadership and supported by vast masses of Indians. The insurrection had much of the spontaneous character of a peasants' revolt, which made it difficult for the leaders to manoeuvre. In 1811 an army made up of Spaniards and creoles, small in numbers but well-disciplined, suppressed the rebellion in the areas where it had broken out with the greatest violence. The war of independence continued in semi-clandestine form, open conflict breaking out with the campaigns of Morelos and Guerrero and dying down again after the former's capture and execution in 1815. In 1821 the most powerful elements among the creoles opted for independence in order to avoid having to apply in Mexico the liberal constitution of Cadiz, which had been reestablished in Spain after the insurrection of Riego.

The first problems that the newly independent Mexico had to face were political: liberalism versus conservatism, federalism versus centralism, religious freedom versus unity of church and state. These controversies divided the creole élite, but in no way affected the existing social structure inherited from the colonial period. Among other decisive factors, the system of ownership of land remained fundamentally unchanged. The economy certainly suffered upheavals, e.g. the slump in the mining industry during the war of independence, a sharp decline in production being accompanied by dislocation of the administrative system. Lack of ready money obliged

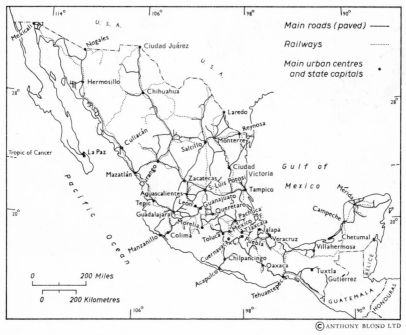

© ANTHONY BLOND LTD

MEXICO: MAIN CITIES AND COMMUNICATIONS

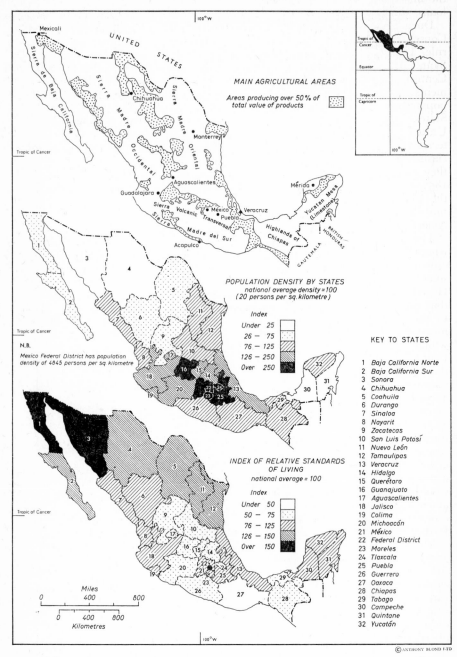

MAIN AGRICULTURAL AREAS

Areas producing over 50% of
total value of products

POPULATION DENSITY BY STATES
national average density = 100
(20 persons per sq. kilometre)

Index
Under 25
26 — 75
76 — 125
126 — 250
Over 250

N.B.
Mexico Federal District has population
density of 4845 persons per sq kilometre

KEY TO STATES

1 Baja California Norte
2 Baja California Sur
3 Sonora
4 Chihuahua
5 Coahuila
6 Durango
7 Sinaloa
8 Nayarit
9 Zacatecas
10 San Luis Potosí
11 Nuevo León
12 Tamaulipas
13 Veracruz
14 Hidalgo
15 Querétaro
16 Guanajuato
17 Aguascalientes
18 Jalisco
19 Colima
20 Michoacán
21 México
22 Federal District
23 Moreles
24 Tlaxcala
25 Puebla
26 Guerrero
27 Oaxaca
28 Chiapas
29 Tabago
30 Campeche
31 Quintane
32 Yucatán

INDEX OF RELATIVE STANDARDS
OF LIVING
national average = 100

Index
Under 50
50 — 75
76 — 125
126 — 150
Over 150

Miles
0   400   800

0   400   800
Kilometres

© ANTHONY BLOND LTD

MEXICO: MAIN AGRICULTURAL AREAS, POPULATION AND STANDARD OF LIVING

the first independent governments to have recourse to British and French loans, which were to lead to claims, threats and interventions.

During the first thirty years of independence Mexico was ruled by Conservative governments, with brief interludes of Liberal or Federalist rule. The outstanding figure of this period was General Antonio López de Santa Anna, who fought on different occasions under Federalist and Centralist colours, but always supported strong and authoritarian governments: he was a perfect example of the demagogue who succeeds in retaining popularity, since he survived politically even after the war with the United States (1846–8)—contesting sovereignty over Texas, annexed by the United States in 1845—which resulted in the loss of over half of Mexico's territory. The Liberal forces gradually increased in strength until they clashed with the Conservatives in civil war (1858–61); from this conflict they emerged victorious, and put into effect the Liberal constitution of 1857 and other legislation designed to terminate the special privileges of the Church and the army. The Liberal victory drove the Conservatives into the arms of Napoleon III, who wished to establish a Latin empire in America in opposition to the United States.

The imperialist designs of Napoleon III and Maximilian of Austria (to whom, at the former's instigation, the Mexican Conservatives offered the crown), mark the end of Conservatism as an ideological force in Mexico, since from that time on Liberalism would be identified with nationalism. However, in the early stages of French intervention, it seemed probable that the Conservatives would win a decisive and enduring victory, owing to the military superiority of the French, the liberal and conciliatory measures passed by Maximilian, the financial insolvency of the country which only French loans could prevent, and above all, the fact that the United States was preoccupied with its own civil war. Juárez, president of the Republic, and the Liberal forces were penned up in a tiny corner of the national territory, and only their will-power enabled them to carry on the apparently futile struggle to maintain Republican legality. The increasing menace of Prussia in Europe, and the pressures exercised by the United States, which were becoming more overt every day, led to the evacuation of the French troops; this transformed Maximilian into a mere puppet of the extreme Conservative elements, who fought desperately against a Republican army which, with the financial support of the United States, eventually captured, tried and shot the emperor (1867). From then on, governments would inevitably be based on an ideology of uncompromising nationalism, above all because the United States, again a united country and developing economically at a rapid rate, was on the threshold of a gigantic expansion. Its pressures and interventions were to become increasingly flagrant.

Mexico was ruined by thirteen years of war, and its foreign debt totalled 454 million pesos, a large part of which represented debts contracted by the Empire and therefore disowned. The mobilisation of the population caused by the conflict and the dislocation of a governmental structure that was anyway extremely fragile opened the door to Caudillo rule and regionalistic tendencies. The Juárez government had to face this situation with diminished resources, and it took scrupulous care to respect formal civil liberties, while its parliamentary position was increasingly weakened by the dissensions within the Liberal forces. The undefeated Conservative forces were to take advantage of this situation, as was the Church, which felt itself to have been despoiled by the Reform Laws, by which ecclesiastical property had been taken over in order to increase the circulation of wealth.

A struggle between various Liberal factions, both within and outside the framework of the constitution, resulted in the triumph of General Porfirio Díaz, who maitained himself in power from 1876 until 1910.

The thirty-four year personal rule of Porfirio Díaz achieved the re-organisation of the political and administrative system: ideological controversies faded into the background, and the positivist philosophy which inspired the governing clique made the slogan of the regime that of Comte: Order and Progress. Foreign capital in vast quantities came to Mexico (in 1911 US investments alone totalled $1,100 million), and was channelled into the most productive sectors—mines and to a certain extent land—and into an economic sector complementary to those two spheres, railways. The enforcement of the Reform Laws, which abolished the communal land ownership system of the Indians and assigned common land to individuals who applied for titles, led to the growth of excessively large estates. By 1910 over 97 per cent of the peasants were landless and living in a state of peonage. Although the *hacienda* or large estate would seem to have been the most rational form of agricultural production, Mexico's social problem became progressively worse. The army was reduced in size, and became better disciplined and professionalised; the Federal administrative system with its accompanying political machinery was hesitantly extended to cover the whole country, leaving untouched the prerogatives of those *caciques* it could not eliminate or absorb into the apparatus of government. For the first time since independence the Mexican government was based on the consensus of almost all ruling sectors, and had the support of all politically active groups. Thirty-four years of personal rule, however, caused a gradual erosion of this base.

The Revolution

Porfirio Díaz's last attempt to secure his own reelection in 1910 provoked an armed insurrection which, after minor conflicts that took place far from the capital, led to the victory of the revolutionaries. At this stage no fundamental change took place. Francisco Madero, who led the Revolution initially, was a scion of one of the most powerful landowning families in northern Mexico; he attempted to introduce changes in the political structure of the country without dealing with the basic problem, that of land reform. With the Federal army inherited from the Díaz regime he fought against Emiliano Zapata, who was fighting in the south of Mexico under the slogan 'Land and Liberty'. The half-hearted reforms of Madero, and his inability to deal with the growing unrest which preceded a revolution more radical than the previous one, provoked a coalition of Porfirista Conservatives supported by the army and enjoying the enthusiastic collaboration of Henry Lane Wilson, US ambassador. The resulting coup and assassination of Madero, followed by the assumption of the presidency by General Huerta in 1913, sparked off the real revolution. Venustiano Carranza, formerly a state governor under the Díaz regime, considered himself the inheritor of republican legality, and the more progressive states of the Republic—those of the north—gave him their support. Pancho Villa and Emiliano Zapata joined forces with the 'Constitutionalists', and the United States, on the slightest of pretexts, occupied Veracruz and Tampico in 1914, thus preventing the dispatch of German arms to the Huerta government.

Carranza represented the last attempt to prevent the political revolution from developing into a social revolution. Assuming power in 1914, he continued to fight against the radical elements such as Zapata (assassinated in 1919) and Villa, whose troops, defeated in the field by General Álvaro Obregón, fell back on guerrilla warfare. Before this last development he was obliged to seek the support of the workers' forces organised around the House of the World Worker, founded during his presidency, and also to promulgate the first agrarian reform laws in order to assuage momentarily the land-hunger of the revolutionary peasants. As a sort of appendix to this period, the constitution of 1917 was promulgated; based on that of 1857, it included radical articles on the Church and clergy (No. 130) and workers' rights (No. 123), with the paradoxical result that a very advanced system of labour legislation was in force before there existed a real working class to take advantage of it. The most important article was No. 27, concerning the ownership of land, which established the rights of the nation over the ownership of the subsoil; this followed an old Hispanic juridical tradition and provided the legal basis for the recuperation of the nation's oil resources. The nationalistic policy of Porfirio Díaz—with its emphasis on the establishment of a central authority capable of giving an impulse to modernisation—was completed during this phase of the Revolution when the government took steps to establish control over economic policy or, at least, to create a legislative system which would permit it to do so in the near future. Impelled by the prevailing situation and persuaded by Carranza himself, the architects of the 1917 constitution gave increased powers to the president of the Republic, including the right to abolish the legislative and executive powers of the states; this was a direct consequence, according to Carranza, of direct suffrage for male citizens (universal suffrage was not to come until the granting of the vote to women in the Federal elections of 1952).

Finally, the Revolution gave impetus to another modernising trend in that it began the incorporation of the masses into the nation's political life. It also attempted to prevent the perpetuation in power of political figures and encourage their mobility by prohibiting the reelection of the president. But all this was to be achieved only after a long period of insurrections and violence.

Sonora rule

Although the Revolution established, as a cardinal principle, that the president could not be reelected, attempts were made to overcome this obstacle by 'imposing' a successor; it is therefore possible to speak of a Sonora 'dynasty', since almost all the presidents between 1920 and 1934 came from that state. The first president to attempt to impose his successor on the electorate was Carranza himself; this led to a revolt by several generals and Carranza's assassination in 1920. The rule of the Sonorenses was a period of reconstruction and reorganisation, punctuated by crises and outbreaks of violence. All these questions were overshadowed by the greatest problem of the period, that of Mexico's relations with the United States.

The United States withheld diplomatic recognition from the government of Álvaro Obregón until he resolved the conflict arising from Article 27 of the constitution, which the oil companies held to be confiscatory. By the terms of the Bucareli Agreement, the Mexican government agreed not to apply the terms of the article retroactively. Obregón was able, however, to distribute 2,800,000 acres of land to smallholders in such a way that the reform measures did not dislocate production. The labour movement grew apace, and the biggest—virtually the only—labour organisation had

1,200,000 affiliated members by 1924. Obregón's transference of power to his most loyal general, Plutarco Elías Calles, was fraught with the usual danger—the dissatisfaction of a considerable sector of the army. The first schism appeared within the 'great revolutionary family' when a former minister of commerce led an armed insurrection; but this incident only served to prove a principle that has since remained inviolate in Mexico, namely that once a decision has been taken within the governing élite it is completely accepted by all the 'revolutionary family'; all those (and there have been many) refusing to accept such decisions have been defeated.

The revolutionary left reached the apogee of its power under Calles. Luis Morales, leader of the Mexican Workers' Regional Confederation (CROM), claimed to have 2,250,000 paid-up members. This figure, although almost certainly exaggerated, is an indication of the strength of the labour movement. It is worth noting that the state was not yet a big employer of labour, and this partly explains the industrial unrest of the early years of Calles's presidency. Economic nationalism was also an overriding theme during this period, a trend which led to another confrontation with the United States, when the oil companies (which enjoyed the support of the United States irrespective of their nationality) refused to accept the cancellation of the concessions in perpetuity and their replacement by fifty-year concessions. Like Obregón, Calles was unable to withstand the pressure of the United States, and had recourse to a subterfuge to avoid applying the law. The measures he took to modernise and integrate the country led to conflicts with caciques and local political machines, the expansion of the Federal bureaucracy, and the complete professionalisation of the revolutionary army (achieved with the help of an exceptional general, Joaquín Amaro). The process of recovery of financial solvency was given impetus by the establishment of a central bank in 1925.

All these efforts to achieve more rapid economic development almost pale into insignificance compared with the struggle between Calles and the Catholic Church. This led to a widespread insurrection in the western part of Mexico, where similar insurrections, and for the same reasons, had taken place in the 19th century. Violent conflict between the Federal army and the rebels—known as *cristeros*—went on from 1926 to 1929. The government's intolerance in the religious sphere, however, did not extend to its other activities: in 1928 there was a radical change in its policy with regard to workers and peasants. It declared that the agrarian reform had been completed, condemned strikes and took the side of the employers; it made every effort to encourage production, and appealed for foreign capital to aid development.

When Calles finished his term of office, Obregón was again elected president. This was a serious mistake, for one of the golden rules of the Revolution had been broken by one of its leaders. There was unrest among the generals, and some of them led insurrections, which were ruthlessly suppressed by the army itself. This did not save Obregón from assassination (in 1928); this event was followed by a period of Callista government, although Calles was no longer president, but held the title of Supreme Leader of the Revolution. Calles' political instincts urged him to create, in 1929, the great National Revolutionary Party (PNR), the fundamental aim of which was to provide a national political framework for the interests of the Revolution, which would constitute a nation-wide electoral machinery and end forever parish-pump politics. The mediocre presidents of this period were mere puppets—the Supreme Leader pulled all the strings.

Lázaro Cárdenas

Calles' political and economic policies suffered a radical change during the presidency of Lázaro Cárdenas (1934–40), who, after accepting a post in a government imposed by the Supreme Leader, permitted and even encouraged working-class agitation, and eventually broke openly with the power behind the throne, sending Calles into exile in 1935. The army remained loyal to the new president: General Amaro handed over command to General Cedillo, a known Cardenista, without there being the slightest attempt at insurrection. The authority of Cárdenas was soon firmly established, both because of his great personal popularity among the workers and peasants and because of the purge of Callistas (14 out of 28 state governors were replaced for one reason or another); his honesty in the conduct of public affairs contrasted with the shady 'politicking' of the followers of Calles. He had to wait four years before setting about the reform of the PNR, but from the first moment he was able to nominate to the presidency of it a man he fully trusted.

The reforms of Cárdenas were more social than leftist; in other words, there is no discernible ideological basis, even an ostensible one, for his measures. Cárdenas was concerned only with the most evident problems of the moment: the misery of the peasants who, despite the Revolution, were still the victims of the system of large estates, and of the urban working class, the victims of the Depression and of exploitation by Mexican and foreign employers, and dominated by the Callista labour unions. In order to initiate the reforms, Cárdenas relied on the support of these two sectors. In 1936 the Mexican Workers' Confederation (CTM) was founded. Its first leader, Vicente Lombardo Toledano, was a convinced Marxist, but was obliged to accept both Stalinists and Trotskyists in the new labour organisation, and also to accept assistance from the state, owing both to rivalry between unions and his own weakness, which impeded the struggle to achieve wage increases and modest social welfare benefits.

Agrarian reform was the greatest achievement of Cárdenas and his followers. In six years he liquidated the system of large estates: 45 million acres were distribuuted in the form of *ejidos* (communal lands owned by groups of peasants) in the teeth of innumerable problems—lack of irrigation, capital, and even the most elementary agricultural skills. But the cause of most Latin American revolutions was eliminated. The reform measures not only affected the ownership of land but organised rural communities on the basis of a gigantic system, the National Peasant Confederation (CNC), which was to become part of the reorganised Revolutionary Party and constitute the strongest political element in the regime after the president himself. In 1937 the PNR was reorganised as the Party of the Mexican Revolution (reformed in 1946 as the present Institutional Revolutionary Party or PRI), and in the same year another great labour organisation was created, this time for employees in state enterprises; this, together with the workers 'and peasants' confederations, became one of the decisive factors in the new political set-up.

Though Cárdenas was an innovator, in many respects he followed the broad lines of revolutionary policy, including economic nationalism. An industrial conflict between the oil companies and their workers, apparently insoluble, culminated in the expropriation of the companies. Cárdenas's policy reached a climax in 1938; his popularity was at its height, and he was portrayed in the national and foreign press as the incarnation of the extreme left. However, his dislike of pure and uncompromising ideology led him to achieve a definite solution of the religious conflict, to refuse to form a popular front—as some of his followers were urging—and to permit the existence, for the first time since the beginning of the Sonora dynasty, of an opposition party. His unconditional support for Ethiopia and Republican Spain, and his open antipathy towards tyranny—he declined to reestablish diplomatic relations with the Soviet Union, which had been broken off by Calles—did not prevent him from, for example, finding a market for Mexican oil in Germany and Italy when the United States, Britain and France organised a world-wide boycott of the Mexican product in retaliation for the expropriation of their companies. While it would have been difficult, if it had not been for Roosevelt and the Good Neighbour Policy, for Cárdenas to have put his programme fully into effect, Mexico's ensuing political stability would hardly have been possible without Cárdenas' organisational achievements based on solid popular support.

From Ávila Camacho to Díaz Ordaz

Cárdenas himself probably realised that his policy could not continue unchanged after he left the presidency, and that the country needed a breathing-space. His successor, General Ávila Camacho, represented a general swing to the right, even though he personally remained loyal to Cardenista principles. The second world war was the most decisive political event of this period. Relations with the United States became more cordial than they had been since independence, because the United States needed certain Mexican products and, in addition, the ideological differences which might have separated the two countries were attenuated in the face of the common enemy (Mexico entered the war in May 1942). These events led Ávila Camacho to suppress the remains of the 'radical' and 'revolutionary' ideology and proclaim a policy of 'national unity' which would permit the industrial development of the country: he took the precaution of promulgating a law concerning the ownership of industry, according to which 51 per cent of the shareholding of certain key industries was to be in the hands of Mexican citizens. This law was, however, rarely enforced in practice.

During the presidency of Miguel Alemán (1946–52), the boom economy inherited from his predecessor led to a more marked swing to the right. The oil industry strike which broke out at the beginning of this period was quickly suppressed, and the reform of Article 27 of the constitution gave rise to manifold abuses connected with land ownership, of which the members of the president's immediate entourage were the chief beneficiaries. The increase in exports due to the Korean War temporarily mollified a movement of popular discontent which became overt when Alemán tried to secure his own reelection. The opposition was vociferous, and crystallised round the figure of Lázaro Cárdenas: the PRI was on the point of suffering a schism when Alemán, renouncing his original plans, decided to seek a solution by imposing a candidate of proven loyalty to himself. A compromise between the Alemanista and Cardenista factions resulted in the election of Adolfo Ruiz Cortines, who was more of an administrative than a political figure. The new president faced many difficulties, including the opposition of powerful pressure groups (e.g. chambers of commerce and industry, and employers' organisations), and trade unions whose leaders could not repress the popular unrest provoked by the constant increase in the cost of living—aggravated by a 30 per cent devaluation—and corruption among the union leaders themselves. Ruiz Cortines tried to placate public opinion by dismissing various governors appointed by the previous administration. The policy of dynamic growth, industrialisation and national prestige associated with the previous six years gave way to a policy of wait-and-see, saving and austerity. For six years (1952–8) Mexico dedicated her efforts to recovering from a bout of uncontrolled investment and speculative fever.

The presidency of Adolfo López Mateos (1958–64) marked another attempt to give a leftwards turn to Mexico's policies: the new president declared that his government would be extreme left-wing. The vociferous protests of the financial and managerial groups in answer to this obliged him to modify this statement and say: 'My government will be extreme left-wing within the limits of the constitution.' The real cause of this modification was threefold: the diplomatic pressure exercised by the United States on Mexico as a consequence of Mexico's independent line with regard to Castro's Cuba; the working-class agitation resulting from the action of extreme left-wing groups (Communists and Trotskyists); and the policy of saving and enforced capitalisation that had been pursued for some years. The original intentions of the López Mateos government were frustrated and it was obliged to return to a policy of centrism and, to a certain extent, of *immobilisme*. President Gustavo Díaz Ordaz appears to have returned to the careful, austere and authoritarian policy of Ruiz Cortines; he has resisted increasingly strong pressures from both right and left, both of which elements appear to be becoming dissatisfied with the institutional framework provided by the Mexican political system. This raises the whole question of whether this political system, which has been in many respects a model for the political development of the countries of the Third World, possesses the intrinsic qualities necessary to resolve the growing tensions and to harmonise the conflicting interests within a country going through a stage which, at least in some important sectors, is no longer characterised by underdevelopment. Be that as it may, the comparative stability of the Mexican political system is certainly worth noting.

THE PARTIES

There did not exist, in 19th-century Mexico, any political organisation corresponding to a party in the accepted sense of the word. The political activity of the élite groups was channelled through the masonic lodges, clubs and the offices of the caciques; there were half-hearted attempts to establish proper electoral machinery, but this was hampered by the system of indirect suffrage. During the government of Porfirio Díaz parties were organised that corresponded to the so-called 'cadre parties', most of them supporting the president; these, together with the opposition or 'anti-reelectionist' parties, disappeared in the 1910 Revolution. During the presidencies of Obregón and Calles there arose a number of political organisations which flourished under the wing of the revolutionary leaders and perished with their deaths: e.g. the Constitutionalist Liberal Party, founded in 1916, which first supported Venustiano Carranza and later Álavro Obregón; the National Cooperative Party; the Labour Party; and the National Agrarian Party. None of these survived the death of Obregón. Only the Communist Party (founded in 1919) maintains a precarious existence to this day. All the parties of this period possessed pronounced regional characteristics which seriously reduced their effectiveness.

The assassination of Obregón in 1928 decided Calles to form a party which could, if need be, unite the diffused and sometimes conflicting interests of the revolutionaries and provide a basis of agreement. The foundation of the National Revolutionary Party was an event of fundamental importance in the history of Mexico—its consequences still remain. The PNR possessed, from the very beginning, sufficient flexibility to absorb both the local political groups and the nascent workers' and peasants' organisations. The first reform (in 1932) abolished the Federal form of organisation and established a new one based on the hierarchy of conventions (municipal, state and national); this was a first step towards the centralisation of the administrative machinery, which was actually achieved in 1937 with the reforming of the PNR as the Party of the Mexican Revolution, in which the most important corporate interests in the country were represented. This sectoral division was preserved when the new party was abolished in its turn in 1946 to make way for the present Institutional Revolutionary Party (PRI).

The electoral law of 1954 gave official recognition to other political parties, in fact it decreed that their existence was necessary before Federal elections could be held; provision was also made for independent candidates. This law was a reflection of the desire of the Federal government for national integration; a minimum of 75,000 signatures was needed for a party to be recognised as 'national', and those signatures had to come from a minimum number of states. Only the PRI and the National Action Party (PAN)—right of centre—can claim to be national parties. However, the Federal government was interested not only in mobilising public opinion but also in affording opportunities for interests outside the PRI to be represented. For this reason, recognition as 'national' parties was accorded to the Popular Socialist Party, led by Vicente Lombardo Toledano, which is to the left of the PRI and to the right of the Communist Party, and to the Authentic Party of the Mexican Revolution, composed of veterans of the Revolution. There is a large number of smaller parties. The personalist nature of many of these is evident, especially in the case of parties founded to support a particular candidate in the presidential elections in opposition to the official party, as happened in 1939 and 1957; such parties disintegrated immediately after the candidate concerned had conceded defeat. In the 1964 elections only the PAN, besides the PRI, put forward a presidential candidate.

Economy

The economic system of Mexico is mixed, i.e. the state acts as entrepreneur in some sectors (petroleum, electric energy, petrochemicals), and plays a part in the regulation of the economy, making investments in certain sectors where private enterprise is unable or unwilling to fulfil this task. Public investment has not increased as fast as private. Despite increasing coordination of these two sectors and a rate of development which has not been evenly sustained but has been consistently fairly high, Mexico is still a developing country in the sense that per capita income is only US $400.

The primary-producing sector (agriculture, stock-raising, forestry and fishing) is subject to more serious problems than industry and commerce—it contributes only 17·6 per cent of GNP, whereas over half the population derives its livelihood from it. Its annual growth during the period 1950–5 was 4·5 per cent—enough to achieve national self-sufficiency on the basis of modern agricultural techniques employed in extensive irrigated areas, thus making it possible to end the importation of basic food products (maize, wheat, beans) and leave a surplus for export. Agriculture also provides the coffee, cotton, sugar, fruit and vegetables, etc. which together with cattle and fish comprise two-thirds of total exports.

From 1936 onwards there have been attempts, through agrarian reform, to solve the human problems of the rural sector, especially by distributing land to the peasants in the form of *ejidos*. These lands represent 37 per cent of the registered land in the country. Both ejidos and smallholdings, owing to population growth, have shown a pronounced tendency to split into uneconomically small sub-holdings; the absolute growth of the rural population has today created a situation in which over 2 million peasants have a statutory right to share in an ejido. Areas recently brought under cultivation or affected by the agrarian reform measures could at best accommodate only 40 per cent of these; therefore there is a need for 1,200,000 new jobs.

Improvement of living conditions and per capita income in the rural sector will be a factor contributing to the maintenance of the rate of growth of Mexican industry. Industrial development will have to absorb the labour that is surplus to the requirements of the rural sector, meet internal demand and diminish the country's dependence on imported goods, and even export manufactured products. The rate of growth of the industrial sector has been greater (6 per cent per annum) than that of agriculture, and between 1950 and 1965 manufacturing industry grew at a rate of 7·6 per cent per year, oil production by 7·2 per cent and electrical energy by 9·5 per cent. Mining, on the other hand, has been going through a period of stagnation, whereas previously it was one of the most important sectors of the economy. 1965 and 1966 saw the rise of an automobile industry, and cars and lorries are now assembled from parts 60 per cent of which are manufactured in the country. Another source of employment has been the development of services (public administration, banking and finance, commerce and the tourist trade); this sector has been growing at a rate of 6 per cent per year. In spite of all this there is still underemployment; it has been estimated that it will be necessary to create 400,000 new jobs every year for people entering the labour market (including agriculture).

Mexico's exports, which are relatively diversified, reached in 1965 the record figure of US $1,146 million; to this must be added the net income from the tourist trade—$350 million. However, this was not sufficient to avoid a deficit in the same year, imports totalling $1,560 million. About $250 million are paid for the servicing of foreign private capital and international loans; however, the rate of growth of exports is considerably higher than that of imports, and four-fifths of the latter consist of capital goods. The fact that two-thirds of Mexico's foreign trade takes place with the United States creates problems which lie outside the field of economics.

BIBLIOGRAPHY

Brandenburg, Frank R. *The Making of Modern Mexico*, Prentice Hall, Englewood Cliffs, NJ, 1964.

Cline, Howard F. *Mexico, From Revolution to Evolution 1940–1960*, Oxford Univ. Press, London and New York, 1962. *The United States and Mexico*, Harvard Univ. Press, Cambridge, Mass., 1953; Oxford Univ. Press, London, 1963.

Coe, Michael D. *Mexico*, Thames and Hudson, London; Frederick A. Praeger, New York, 1962.

Cosío Villegas, Daniel. *American Extreme*, Texas Univ. Press, Austin, Texas, 1965.

Gibson, Charles. *The Aztecs under Spanish Rule*, Oxford Univ. Press, London; Stanford Univ. Press, Stanford, Calif., 1964.

González Casanova, Pablo. *La democracia en México*, Era, Mexico, 1965.
Hutton, Graham. *Mexican Images*, Faber and Faber, London, 1963.
Mexico, Mexican National Foreign Trade Bank, Mexico City, annual.
Nicholson, Irene. *The X in Mexico: Growth within Tradition*, Faber and Faber, London, 1965; Doubleday, New York, 1966.
Parkes, Henry B. *A History of Mexico*, Houghton Mifflin, Boston, Mass., 1960; Eyre and Spottiswoode, London, 1962.
Paz, Octavio. *The Labyrinth of Solitude: Life and Thought in Mexico*, Evergreen Books, London; Grove Press, New York, 1961.
Peterson, F. *Ancient Mexico*, Allen and Unwin, London; Capricorn Books, New York, 1959.
Simpson, Lesley Byrd. *Many Mexicos*, Univ. of California Press, Berkeley, Calif., 1959.
Tannenbaum, Frank. *Mexico: The Struggle for Peace and Bread*, Alfred A. Knopf, New York, 1956.
Vernon, Raymond. *The Dilemma of Mexico's Development*, Harvard Univ. Press, Cambridge, Mass., 1963.

BASIC INFORMATION

CLIMATE

	La Paz	Mexico City	Monterrey	Salina Cruz
Lat./long.	24° N, 110° W	19° 30′ N, 99° W	26° N, 100° W	16° N, 95° W
Altitude	43 ft/13 m.	7,575 ft/ 2,308 m.	1,732 ft/ 527 m.	184 ft/56 m.
Mean temp. of hottest month	30°C/85°F (July)	19°C/66°F (May)	28°C/82°F (Aug.)	29°C/85°F (May)
Mean temp. of coolest month	18°C/64°F (Jan.)	12°C/54°F (Jan.)	14°C/58°F (Dec.)	26°C/79°F (Dec.–Feb.)
Absolute max.	108°F/42°C	90°F/32°C	107°F/42°C	98°F/37°C
Absolute min.	35°F/2°C	27°F/–3°C	25°F/–4°C	62°F/17°C
Relative humidity at midday of hottest and coolest months	67%/78%	29%/34%	57%/55%	64%/60%
Wettest months	1·4 in./ 36 mm. (Sept.)	6·7 in./ 170 mm. (July)	5·2 in./ 132 mm. (Sept.)	11·7 in./ 297 mm. (Sept.)
Driest months	0 (Mar.–May)	0·2 in./5 mm. (Feb.)	0·6 in./15 mm. (Jan.)	0·1 in./2 mm. (Mar./Apr.)
Annual av. rainfall	5·7 in./ 145 mm.	29·4 in./ 747 mm.	22·8 in./ 579 mm.	40·4 in./ 1,026 mm.

POPULATION

TOTAL (*million*): 1960 (census adjusted), nearly 36·0; mid-1966: 44·1; 1980 (ECLA projection): 72·4.

DENSITY, mid-1965: 21 persons per sq. km.

CRUDE RATES (*per 000*), 1965: Birth 44·2, death 9·5, infant mortality 60·7.

GROWTH RATES (% *p.a.*): 1945–65, 3·0; 1960–5, 3·2.

DISTRIBUTION (% *of total pop.*): Ethnic: Mixed 55, Amerindian 30, white 15. Foreign-born, 1950: 0·4; 1960: 0·6. Languages, 1964: Spanish 89, bilingual Spanish/Indian dialects 6, monolingual Indian 4. Religion, 1950: Roman Catholic 98, Protestant 1. Urban (*centres 2,000 inhab. or over*), ECLA data, 1950: 46·1; 1960: 54·8; 1980 (projection): 70·7. Largest cities (*000 inhab.*), 1960: Mexico City 2,832 (1966: 3,290), Guadalajara 737, Monterrey 597, Puebla 289, Ciudad de Juárez 262, León 210.

CONSTITUTIONAL SYSTEM

Constitution: First 1824; 1857; main and latest 1917, frequent additions and alterations.
System: Federal Republic of 29 states, the Federal District (Mexico City) and two territories. Separate executive, legislature and judiciary. States have own constitution and elect, by popular vote, a governor for a 6-year term and a Chamber of Deputies for a 3-year term.
Executive: Power vested in the president, who is elected by popular vote for a 6-year term; no reelection.
Legislature: Bi-cameral, General Congress of Senate and Chamber of Deputies. *Senate:* 60 members, 2 from each state and 2 from Federal District, elected by direct popular vote for 6-year term. *Deputies:* 1 deputy (and 1 alternate) for every 200,000 inhabitants or fraction over 100,000 with a minimum of 2 deputies for each state and 1 for each territory; elected by direct popular vote for 3-year term. A national political party obtaining 2½% of the total vote has the right to have 5 'party' deputies from among its candidates, plus one more, up to a maximum of 20, for each additional ½% of the vote. *Suffrage:* Universal voting for citizens over 21 years of age, 18 if married. Registered voters, July 1967: about 15 m. *Elections:* Presidential, July 1964: Gustavo Díaz Ordaz, Partido Revolucionario Institucional (PRI), 8·4 m. out of 9·4 m. votes. Chamber of Deputies, July 1967: PRI (87% of vote) 177 seats, Partido de Acción Nacional (PAN) (8% of vote) 16 seats. Partido Popular Socialista (PPS) (3% of vote) 6 seats. Senate, July 1964: PRI 60 seats.
Judiciary: Supreme Court of 21 judges appointed, by the president with the approval of the Senate, for life; assize courts; and district courts.

DEFENCE

Defence budget, 1965: 1,910 m. pesos, 0·8% of GDP.
Armed forces: National service: at 18 years of age; 1 year in army or marines. Strength: army 51,000, navy 11,000, air force 5,000; total 67,000 plus trained reserve.

INTERNATIONAL RELATIONS

Member of the UN and many of its international specialised agencies, including: IBRD and affiliates, IMF, FAO, ICAO, IMCO, ILO, ITU, UNDP, UNESCO, UPU, WHO and WMO; IAEA; UNCTAD representative. Also member of: OAS, Alliance for Progress, ECLA, IDB and LAFTA.

ECONOMY

PRODUCTION
AGRICULTURE

(*000 tons*)	1948–53[1]	63/64	64/65	65/66[2]		1948–53[1]	63/64	64/65	65/66[2]
Cotton	222	486	550	577	Wheat	534	1,703	2,144	2,088
Cottonseed	384	857	969	1,017	Maize	3,090	6,424	8,454	8,865
Coffee	63	142	145	178	Barley	160	186	171	173
Sugar (cane)	733	1,932	2,071	2,102	Sorghum	—	402	483	650
Bananas	252	376	421	426	Rice (paddy)	173	296	274	333
Sesame seed	80	170	172	180	Beans, dry	235	816	891	945
Tobacco[3]	35	69	68	69	Henequen[3]	104	158	160	161

[1] Average 1948/9–1952/3.   [2] Provisional.
[3] Calendar years 1948–52 (av.), 1963, 1964, 1965.

Land (%), 1960: Arable 12, permanent pasture 40, forested 22, other 26.
Other agricultural data: Agricultural holdings, 1960 (census): no. 1·37 m., area 169·1 m. hectares. Tractors in use (*ooos*), 1957: 39. Fertiliser consumption (*ooo tons*), 1965/66: 192.
Livestock: Nos (*m. head*), 1965: cattle 33·1, sheep 6·4, pigs 13·8. Products (*ooo tons*), 1962: meat 544 (beef and veal 390); 1963: cattle hides 56·8; 1965: wool (greasy) 7·8.

Fish: Landed (*ooo tons*), 1965: total 256, shrimp 59, pilchards and anchovy 30, oysters 30.

Mining, 1965: (*ooo tons*) metal content of ores: iron 1,593, zinc 225, lead 170, copper 69, manganese 59, white arsenic 10·7, tin 0·4, sulphur 1,581; (*tons*) gold 6·7, silver 1,254, mercury 662, antimony 3,424, molybdenum 77, bismuth 484, cadmium 712, selenium 6. Fuels: coal 1,533; (*m. cubic metres*) crude petroleum 21·2, natural gas 14,000.

Manufacturing, 1965: (*ooo tons*) pig iron 1,159, steel ingots 2,455, tinplate 116, copper (electrolytic) 46, cement 4,200, man-made fibres 35, newsprint 24, sugar 1,893, wheat flour (1964) 1,190; (*m. litres*) beer 1,098; (*ooo units*) motor vehicles: cars 67, commercial vehicles 29. 1964: (*ooo cubic metres*) diesel oil 3,157, fuel oil 6,360, motor spirit 5,326.

Construction (*ooo sq. metres floor area*), 1965: buildings completed in Federal District 2,806.

ENERGY

Consumption (*tons coal equiv.*), 1964: total 40·8 m., per head 1·03.
Electricity, 1965: Generated (*kwh*) 17,256 m., installed capacity (*kw*) 5·31 m.

GOVERNMENT EXPENDITURE

Distribution (% *of total*), 1965: Defence 11, education 24, social services 16.

GROSS PRODUCT

GDP (*ooo m. pesos*): At current market prices, 1964: 228; 1965: 246; at 1950 market prices, 1965: 99·6; 1966: 106·6. Per head (*US$*), UN estimate, 1964: 428.
Distribution (%), 1965: Agriculture 17, petroleum 3, manufacturing 25, trade 26.
Growth rates (%), 1950–60: 6·1, per head 2·9; 1960–5: 6·2, per head 3·0.

External trade (*US$m.*)	*1955*	*1960*	*1964*	*1965*	*1966*[1]
Exports (f.o.b.)[2]	785	763	1,054	1,146	1,228
Cotton	230	158	170	212	222
Coffee	104	72	95	73	84
Sugar	10	53	77	60	57
Shrimp	16	34	54	43	53
Zinc	28	30	43	43	44
Petroleum and derivatives	51	14	30	40	40
Sulphur	5	28	38	34	35

[1] Provisional. [2] Including revaluation.

	1955	*1960*	*1964*	*1965*	*1966*
Imports (c.i.f.)	884	1,186	1,493	1,560	1,605
Trade balance	−99	−423	−439	−414	−377

Direction of Trade (%)

	Exports			Imports		
	1955	*1960*	*1965*	*1955*	*1960*	*1965*
LAFTA	(0·8)	0·7	3·2	(0·2)	0·3	1·9
CACM	(1·6)	1·3	1·3	(0·0)	0·0	0·0
USA	74·4	59·6	54·9	79·3	72·2	65·8
EEC	8·0	7·6	4·8	8·4	11·7	15·9
UK	4·5	1·6	0·7	2·3	4·9	3·4

FINANCE

Exchange rate (*pesos/US$*): Free Market, end-year, 1960: 12·49; 1966: 12·49.
Balance of payments (*US$ m.*): Goods and services (net), 1960: −319; 1964: −408; 1965: −364; 1966: −344.
Cost of living (*Dec. 1958=100*), Mexico City, December 1960: 108; 1964: 111; 1965: 116; 1966: 121.

INDUSTRIAL WAGES: Earnings in manufacturing per month, 1966: 1,379 pesos.
GOVERNMENT ACCOUNTS (*ooo m. pesos*), 1964: Revenue 29·0, expenditure 28·3, balance 0·7.

EMPLOYMENT

ECONOMICALLY ACTIVE (%), 1960: Of total pop. 32 (men 53, women 12). In agriculture 54, manufacturing 14, services 14, trade 10.

TRANSPORT AND COMMUNICATIONS

RAILWAYS: Traffic, 1965: 3,869 m. pass.-km.; 18,332 m. net ton-km. Length of track, 1964: 23,620 km.
MOTOR VEHICLES: In use (*ooo*), 1965: pass. cars 771, comm. vehicles 419. National road system, 1964: 57,500 km., paved 34,500.
SHIPPING: Merchant fleet (*ooo g.r. tons*), 1966: 306 (tankers 216). International sea-borne shipping (*m. tons*), 1965: goods loaded 9·22, goods unloaded 1·43. Main ports: Gulf: Veracruz, Tampico, Progreso, Coatzacoalcos (free zone). Pacific: Santa Rosalía, Ensenada, Manzanillo, Guaymas, Mazatlán, Acapulco, Salina Cruz (free zone).
AIR: Scheduled services, 1965: Total 1,826 m. pass-km., 30·5 m. cargo ton-km. International: 1,146 m. pass.-km., 7·8 m. cargo ton-km. Main airports: Mexico City, Acapulco, Chihuahua, Guadalajara, Hermosillo, Mazatlán, Mexicali, Monterrey, Tampico, Tapachula and Tijuana.
TELEPHONES: No. in use, 1965: 0·82 m.

SOCIAL WELFARE

SYSTEM: Social insurance benefits and services administered by the Instituto Mexicano de Seguro Social (IMSS); separate systems for civil servants and the armed forces. Total contributions received by the IMSS from employees, employers and the state amount to about 16·5% of aggregate wages. Scales of employers' contributions to cover industrial accidents vary according to remuneration and to the risk insured; other social insurance contributions are: employee $3\frac{3}{4}$%, employer $7\frac{1}{2}$%, the government 4%. Employment legislation covers working hours; holidays; payment of wages, overtime and profit sharing; employers' liability for compensation for accidents, dismissal and death indemnities.
HEALTH: 1,800 persons per physician, 590 persons per hospital bed.
NUTRITION: Net food supply (*per head per day*), 1962: 2,640 calories, protein 73 g.

EDUCATION

ILLITERACY RATE (%), 1960 (census): 15 years and over, 35.
COMPULSORY: 6 years (between 6 and 12 years of age). School enrolment ratios (%), 1st and 2nd levels, 1963: 50, adjusted 68.
SCHOOLS, 1965: Pre-school and primary: no. 41,500, pupils 7·25 m., teachers 0·16 m. Secondary and technical: no. 3,785, st. 0·85 m. Teacher-training: no. 212, st. 63,600, t. 6,800. Higher: st. 133,400, t. 17,200.
UNIVERSITIES (43): Principal: Mexico City: Nacional Autónoma de México 80,000 students, academic staff 7,200; Instituto Politécnico Nacional 27,000 st., a.s. 2,900; Iberoamericana (private) 3,300 st., a.s. 600. Guadalajara: U. de G. 15,200 st., a.s. 1,130; Autónoma de G. (private) 4,100 st., a.s. 500. Monterrey: U. de Nuevo León 13,200 st., a.s. 1,000. There are state or state-aided universities in all the states and several other private universities. Colegio de México was given university status in 1962.

MASS MEDIA

BROADCASTING: No. of receivers in use, end-1965: TV 1·8 m., radio 8·24 m. Stations: TV 37; 1964: radio 495.
CINEMAS: No., 1965: 1,555. Attendance: total 347 m., per head 8·5.

NEWSPRINT: Consumption, 1965: total 115,700 tons, per head 2·8 kg.
NEWSPAPERS: Daily, 1965: 220. Estimated circulation 4·76 m., copies per 000 of
pop. 116. Principal dailies in Mexico City (*circ. 000*): *Excelsior* 128, *La Prensa* 110,
Novedades 97, *El Universal* 74, *La Afición* 74, *El Nacional* 50, *The News* 20; evening:
Últimas Noticias de Excelsior 115, *Diario de la Tarde* 95.

BRITISH HONDURAS

CLYDE SANGER

HISTORY

THE people of British Honduras display a variety of racial origins remarkable in so scant a population: a premier whose ancestry is partly Welsh and partly Maya Indian; Negro taxi-drivers with Irish names like McSweany; Spanish and Chinese, and German Mennonites; a customs officer who is also a prize-winning poet with a Punjab name. People have drifted into the country from numerous parts of the globe.

The Maya Indians came first, bringing their remarkable civilisation from its centre in El Petén, in what is now Guatemala, to the modest highlands in the west of the country. Around 1640, seven centuries after the end of the Mayan civilisation, with its achievements in astronomy and mathematics, the first British settlement was established by a Scottish buccaneer, Peter Wallace. One tradition traces the name of Belize City to a corruption of his name, others give it a lengthier history. What is more certain is that neither before the British buccaneers came, nor during the next two centuries when the territory was several times evacuated, did the Spanish ever try to establish a permanent settlement along this stretch of coast. The buccaneers were attracted by the concealed anchorages whence they could sail out to attack Spanish shipping; they stayed because of the steadier gains offered by the forests of logwood which provided a dye then in great demand in Europe.

A treaty after the Seven Years War ended in 1763 affirmed Spanish sovereignty over the coast, but in 1783 the Spanish gave in return formal permission to the Baymen to cut logwood between the present Mexican border and the Belize river, and three years later extended the concession southwards, including mahogany. After the defeat of a Spanish attack in 1798 there were no further challenges against the British settlement; but Spanish sovereignty was recognised into the 1840s, long after Mexico and Guatemala had declared their independence. The Anglo-Guatemalan treaty of 1859 defined the country's present boundaries; the treaty was welcomed by Guatemalans who were worried by American freebooters heading south in the trail of the California gold-rush, and saw in the treaty the promise of British friendship and protection. Britain for its part was keen to clear up any possibility of dispute with the United States over the 1850 Bulwer-Clayton treaty, under which both countries pledged themselves to refrain from any further settlement in Central America, and the 1859 treaty carefully made clear that the border had existed before the 1850 negotiations with the United States.

In the continuing dispute with Guatemala, which claims the entire territory, the British have lately used this point to reinforce their argument that the 1859 treaty involved no cession of territory by Guatemala, but only a recognition of existing boundaries.[1]

Ethnic structure

By the time that the territory formally became a British colony in 1862, the population was remarkably mixed. In addition to the inland Mayans and the British settlers, Negro slaves had been brought in to work in the forests. Their conditions were never so oppressive as on the island plantations, and after emancipation in 1833 they had stayed on as forest workers willingly enough. In the south was a settlement of Carib Indians, who had been deported from the Windward Islands and who mingled with Africans to become the ethnologically unique Black Caribs; in the north were thousands of Spanish and mixed-blood refugees from uprisings in Mexico. The latter communities have increased so that today one-third of the population is primarily Spanish-speaking. The latest arrivals are some 3,000 Mennonites, religious communities with Russian origins who moved down from Mexico in 1958, refrain from politics and put their energies into farming.

The present premier, George Price, proclaims an 'open door' immigration policy (understandably, since British Honduras is twice the size of Jamaica, but with only 6 per cent of that island's population). Although the inflow is not large, there has recently been a noticeable increase of West Indians taking up middle-rank commercial jobs. A few years ago one might have predicted problems between the main linguistic groups, but the situation has been quietly resolved. It is a definite advantage for a civil servant to have a command of Spanish, which may assure him swifter promotion.

Administration

Administration in the early colonial period was carried out somewhat informally through public meetings and by magistrates. Britain appointed Superintendents (usually military officers) from 1786, but they left the thrice-yearly Meetings a free hand to pass regulations, vote funds and petition Britain. Initially magistrates had executive as well as judicial power, but had to stand for reelection every year. Free Negroes were included as full members of the Meetings, although in later years a property qualification kept numbers down. Not until 1840 were British laws enforced, and then in 1854 the Public Meeting voted (under pressure from Britain) to replace itself with a 21-man Legislative Assembly (18 elective), and only residents earning more than £100 a year could qualify as voters. In 1871 the Legislative Assembly itself was abolished in favour of Crown Colony government, a move by Britain to prevent the domination of the non-white majority by a handful of settlers.

The Governor-in-Council ran British Honduras with a council of his officials plus nominated non-officials, until 1936 when five out of 12 councillors were non-officials chosen by an electorate comprising less than 8 per cent of the adult population. The Governor, meanwhile, had been given reserve powers in a 1932 revision of the constitution: so there was no alarm among officials at this development by which elected members entered the Council. Under a new constitution in 1954 a Legislative Assembly was set up in which the nine elected members outnumbered the three officials and three nominated non-officials; and adult suffrage was introduced. The next year four of the elected members were given portfolios on the

---

[1] See 'Guatemala', p. 197 and 'Territorial Disputes', p. 407.

Governor's Executive Council, but the Governor controlled a majority on the Executive Council through his nominees. Self-government came in 1963, with all 18 seats in the Assembly filled by adult suffrage and an eight-man Senate. Until independence the Governor (and behind him Britain's Colonial Secretary) retains the final word on foreign affairs and defence, but daily policy is controlled by the seven-man cabinet; the Senate has only small powers of reservation.

The political scene from 1949

Politics began in earnest only in December 1949, when the Governor used his reserved powers to devalue the BH dollar in line with the devalued pound. Since this raised the cost of US imports and jeopardised economic links with the United States, a group of men allied to the General Workers Union saw the issue in clear colonialist terms, and there was early talk in the party they formed—the Peoples United Party (PUP)—of secession from the British Empire and association with the United States. From the outset George Price was prominent in the PUP, and came through a series of quarrels with close colleagues with little damage. Within a few months of the PUP's being deeply split over allegations of peculation from union funds in mid-1956, the group led by Price and the accused union leader Nicholas Pollard won all nine elective seats in the Legislative Assembly; they did this by concentrating argument on the importance of keeping clear of a West Indian Federation for fear of possible domination by Jamaica. Price's alternative was to look to some association with the Central American republics, an association he left undefined. (The presidents of all the Central American republics except Guatemala have stated their intention of supporting an independent 'Belize'.)

When, as the Assembly's Member for Natural Resources, Price went to London for financial talks in November 1957, he was indiscreet enough to introduce his colleagues to the Guatemalan ambassador there, who reportedly argued that Britain was bound to leave British Honduras to fend for itself soon, and Price and his colleagues should anticipate this by forming an association with Guatemala immediately, in which Guatemala would handle foreign affairs and would finance development. The Guatemalan spokesman is also said to have threatened that Guatemala would break trade relations if these proposals were not accepted. When the British Colonial Secretary was told by his shocked colleagues that Price had said this protection was a good weapon in case the financial talks showed signs of failing, he broke off the talks. Governor Sir Colin Thornley dismissed Price from the Executive Council and explained in a radio broadcast that he could only conclude 'Mr Price was prepared in certain eventualities to see you, the people of British Honduras, handed over to the Guatemalan Republic lock, stock and barrel'.

Price survived even this blow, although Pollard left him. He became First Minister after winning the Assembly elections in 1961, and Premier and Minister of Finance in January 1964 with self-government. In March 1965 his PUP won 16 seats in the House of Representatives with nearly 58 per cent of the votes cast, while the National Independence Party (NIP) led by Philip Goldson (a journalist-politician who split from the PUP in 1956) won two seats with just over 39 per cent of the votes. The NIP's main plank is still that Price intends to hand the country over to Guatemala after independence (expected by the end of 1968), and its leaders declare his 1960 affirmation of desire to remain in the Commonwealth to be merely expedient talk. They quarrel with his intention of calling the country Belize and the flying of a blue-and-white flag in the capital, both of which they claim as showing Guatemalan influence; they further maintain that his refusal to raise a defence force—British Honduras has a military tradition, having contributed a battalion to the Allies in the second world war—is evidence of his plan to hand over to Guatemala. Understandably, the NIP leaders call for further general elections before independence, and are unhappy about the abolition of proportional representation in local Council elections which resulted in the PUP winning all nine seats in the Belize City Council of December 1965 (the NIP had previously held four).

ECONOMY

Britain has provided nearly all development funds for the country. Several years ago a British Treasury survey suggested planned immigration of 7,000 a year as an attempted solution to the serious problem of underpopulation, to make new services fully worthwhile and development steady; a British MP, Dame Joan Vickers, even produced the idea of bringing over thousands of Chinese from Hong Kong. Price's 'open door' immigration policy is not likely to be allowed by his government to open as wide as that. Apart from the question of prohibitive resettlement costs, the influx of a number of Chinese could cause problems of racial feeling, which is at present remarkably quiescent considering that the population is nearly equally divided between coloured people of a Caribbean-African background and people of Spanish and Indian origin. Although up to 20 per cent of British Honduras' exports (mainly pine lumber to Jamaica) and 10 per cent of its imports (mainly Trinidad oil) has recently been with the West Indies, there is a reluctance to encourage large immigration from that direction. This antipathy became apparent with an early inflow of Jamaicans as railway-builders and banana-workers, and although in the last few years there has been a noticeable increase of Jamaicans in the upper rungs of commerce, people who call themselves Belizeans are not keen to see Jamaicans arrive in large numbers to take over the better jobs. This attitude may curb potential development.

The development of agriculture is the government's greatest concern. Until 1959 mahogany, pine, cedar and other forest products were of greater value than all agricultural output. Then agriculture, spurred by the citrus developments around Stann Creek, moved ahead, and in 1963 Tate and Lyle came to the Mexican border country with a promise of ultimately investing £8 million in sugar estates.[1] The Tate and Lyle venture set off a rush of land speculation by American real-estate men, and in January 1966 the Minister of Natural Resources, Alexander Hunter, introduced a Rural Land Utilisation Tax bill, proposing a tax of up to $BH3 (15s sterling) an acre on undeveloped land. He explained that 40 per cent (3,500 square miles) of the country is held in large estates, and only about 3 per cent of the country is yet cultivated. The proposal particularly alarmed the country's biggest landowner, Belize Estate and Produce Company, which has been reducing its holdings but until recently owned one-third of the land and used it mainly for the exploitation of mahogany. The mahogany trade,

[1] Appropriately the first verse of the poem by S. A. Haynes, *Land of the Gods*, already chosen as the national anthem after independence, ends thus:
'By the might of truth and the grace of God
No longer shall we be hewers of wood'.

which had its peak in the railway-coach boom of the late 19th century, is in decline, and the Company is unclear about ways of land redevelopment. Hunter, who next to Price provides the most invigorating influence in a quietly unambitious people, insists that the land use tax will not be punitive, but is aimed at discouraging speculators and encouraging genuine development. There is high hope of opening up the Belize river valley to beef production, and an earlier Colonial Development Corporation setback with livestock is discounted.

Meanwhile rice production is rising steadily and British Honduras should be self-sufficient in this product by 1968. Cigar tobacco production in Cayo district is a recent venture. Hopes of minerals centre on Shell and Gulf's exploration for oil near the Turneffe Islands. The fishing industry is being studied by a UN marine biologist, and while crayfish are at present the most important product, anchovies in large schools are a new possibility (a similar discovery brought great benefit to Peru). With the world's second largest barrier reef, with marlin, snapper and sailfish in those waters, with sandy keys to sail out to, and with Mayan ruins and a variety of wild animals (including jaguar and wild pig) in the hills and jungles, the possibilities for enterprising tourists are immense. The tourist industry is at present virtually undeveloped (there is only one good, 35-room hotel in Belize City).

Belize City, almost totally destroyed in 1931 and damaged again by 'Hurricane Hattie' in 1961, will not much longer keep its village-like atmosphere, with main street being the quiet river with sailboats moored near the market and all traffic having to cross by a narrow swing-bridge. Already Canada has given money for a modern bridge upstream, and by 1970 the first stage of establishing a new capital 51 miles inland near Roaring Creek should have been finished.

Britain has provided £4·1 million for the new capital, although by 1967 British Honduras was able to finance its recurrent budget whose expenditure totalled £2·9 million. Britain almost entirely financed the £1,750,000 capital budget. The 1964–70 development plan proposed expenditure of £11 million, the largest four items being: roads; agriculture, industry and tourism; housing; and education. With a per capita income of more than £80 as at 1963 and the aim of having 6,500 children in secondary schools by 1970, standards are high for Central America and the Caribbean. Price announced in January 1966 wide measures to tackle the trade gap problem by taxing luxury imports (perfumes, alcohol and large cars) and protecting local industry (notably tobacco), so raising an extra £200,000 revenue. But there will be a continuing dependence on British support, and the British proportion of trade is greatly increasing as sugar and citrus become more important exports while logs and lumber, of which the United States used to take the biggest part, become less so. Trade with the Central American republics is still almost negligible, and there could be little reason for an independent Belize to join their common market in this situation unless as a political gesture.

BIBLIOGRAPHY

Downie, Jack. *An Economic Policy for British Honduras*, Belize, 1959.
Humphreys, R. A. *The Diplomatic History of British Honduras 1638–1901*, Oxford Univ. Press for Royal Institute of International Affairs, London and New York, 1961.
Taylor, D. M. *The Black Carib of British Honduras*, Wenner–Gren, New York, 1951.

Waddell, D. A. G. *British Honduras*, Oxford Univ. Press for Royal Institute of International Affairs, London and New York, 1961.
Central Office of Information, London. *British Honduras: The Guatemalan Claim*, June 1960.
Information Department, Belize City. *The Premier Speaks* (nine speeches 1962–4). *The Premier Challenges Graduates* (six speeches during 1964). *The 1966 Budget* (December 1965). *Rural Land Utilisation Tax* (January 1966 speech by A. A. Hunter).

BASIC INFORMATION

CLIMATE

Belize

Lat./long.	17° 30′ N, 88° W	Relative humidity	87%/89%
Altitude	17 ft/5 m.	at midday of	
Mean temp. of hottest month	28°C/82°F (Aug.)	hottest and coolest months	
Mean temp. of coolest month	23°C/74°F (Jan.)	Wettest month	12·0 in./305 mm. (Oct.)
Absolute max.	97°F/36°C	Driest month	1·5 in./38 mm.
Absolute min.	49°F/10°C		(Mar.)
		Annual av. rainfall	74·4 in./1,890 mm.

POPULATION

TOTAL (*000*), 1960 (census): 90; mid-1966: 109; 1980 (ECLA projection): 173. DENSITY, mid-1965: 5 persons per sq. km.
CRUDE RATES (*per 000*), 1964: Birth 44·4, death 7·1, infant mortality 54·1.
GROWTH RATES (% *p.a.*), 1945–65: 3·0; 1960–5: 3·1.
DISTRIBUTION (% *of total pop.*): Ethnic, 1960: Amerindian Carib. 42, African 33, European 4, Asian 3. Foreign-born, 1960: 8·4. Languages (spoken), 1960: English 51, bilingual English/Spanish 20, Spanish 10; also Creole and Maya dialects. Religion, 1960: Christian 94 (1946: Roman Catholic 59, Protestant 40); Jewish 1·2. Urban (legally established towns) 1960: 54. Largest city (*000 inhab.*): Belize City, 1960: 18; 1966: 38.

CONSTITUTIONAL SYSTEM

CONSTITUTION: 1862 Colony, under Governor of Jamaica until separated 1884. Constitutional reforms 1954, 1960 and 1963 leading to internal self-government 1964.
SYSTEM: Parliament comprising the Queen, represented by the Governor, and National Assembly. Governor is C-in-C, retaining reserved powers for defence, external affairs, internal security and certain other powers relating to finance and public officers' service.
CABINET: Collectively responsible to the Assembly. Prime minister is chairman.
LEGISLATURE: Bi-cameral, National Assembly of Senate and House of Representatives. *Senate:* 8 members appointed by the Governor: 5 selected by prime minister, 2 by leader of the opposition and 1 by the Governor. *Representatives:* 18 members, representing single-member constituencies, elected for 4 years. *Suffrage:* Universal voting for adults over 21 years of age. Registered voters, end-February 1965: 38,000, of whom nearly 70% voted. *Elections:* House of Representatives, March 1965: People's United Party (G. C. Price) 16, National Independence Party (P. S. W. Goldson) 2. JUDICIARY: Supreme Court, and courts of summary jurisdiction in 6 districts.

ECONOMY

PRODUCTION

AGRICULTURE (000 tons)	Av. 1948–52	1964	1965	1966[1]	1967[1]
Sugar (cane)	2	34	36	44	76
Rice (paddy)	2	2	3	.	.

[1] Provisional.

LAND (%), 1964: Arable 1, permanent pasture 1, forested 46, other 52.
OTHER AGRICULTURAL DATA: Agricultural holdings: area 1·3 m. hectares; ownership: crown lands 1·27 m. ha., private 1·03 m. ha. (0·39 m. by one company). Tractors in use, 1964: 402. Fertiliser consumption (000 tons), 1965/66: 0·5.
LIVESTOCK: Nos (000 head), 1961: Cattle 22·1, sheep 1·3, pigs 13·5.
FISH: Landed (000 tons), 1958: total 0·9.
MANUFACTURING, 1965: (000 cu. metres, sawn) wood 32 (1963: 41).
CONSTRUCTION: (000 sq. metres floor area), 1963: No. of building permits issued, 490.

ENERGY

CONSUMPTION (tons coal equiv.), 1965: Total 0·04 m., per head 0·4.
ELECTRICITY (public supply), 1964: Generated (kwh) 11 m., installed capacity (kw) 4,700.

GOVERNMENT EXPENDITURE

DISTRIBUTION (% of total), 1966: Education 19, health 8, public works 11.

GROSS PRODUCT

GDP (US$): Per head, estimate, 1961: 340.

EXTERNAL TRADE (US$ m.)	1955	1960	1963	1964	1965
EXPORTS (f.o.b.)	6	8	13	13	12
Sugar, raw	0	1	4	4	3
Orange juice and concentrates	—	—	2	3	.
Wood	2	3	2	2	.
IMPORTS (c.i.f.)	10	13	19	24	24
TRADE BALANCE	−4	−5	−6	−10	−12

DIRECTION OF TRADE (%)

	Exports			Imports		
	1955	1960	1965	1955	1960	1965
CACM	(—)	—	1·7	(—)	0·4	0·6
LAFTA	(11·9)	7·7	8·3	(0·7)	1·4	1·6
Jamaica	15·7	17·3	5·0	1·4	1·9	5·8
USA and Canada	29·8	13·4	41·7	37·4	41·5	41·6
EEC	1·8	1·6	0·8	8·2	7·9	7·0
UK	25·3	53·7	40·8	35·1	32·3	32·5

FINANCE

EXCHANGE RATE (BH$/US$): Par value 1·429. BH$4 = £1.
COST OF LIVING (1958=100), Belize, December 1960: 101; 1964: 106; 1965: 108; 1966: 111.
BUDGET ACCOUNTS (BH$ m.), 1965: Revenue 9·3, expenditure 14·1, deficit 0·3.

EMPLOYMENT

ECONOMICALLY ACTIVE (%), 1960: Total pop. 30 (men 50, women 11). In agriculture 39, services 20, manufacturing 14, trade 8, construction 7.

TRANSPORT AND COMMUNICATIONS

MOTOR VEHICLES: In use (*ooo*), 1965: cars 1·4; comm. vehicles 1·2. Road system: 1,200 km.

SHIPPING: International sea-borne shipping (*ooo tons*), 1965: Goods loaded 76, goods unloaded 76. Main ports: Belize, Stann Creek, Corozal.

AIR: International: Passenger movement, 1964: 17,600. Main airport: Belize City (international and municipal).

TELEPHONES: No. of subscribers, 1965: 1,000.

SOCIAL WELFARE

HEALTH: 3,550 persons per physician; 230 persons per hospital bed.

EDUCATION

ILLITERACY RATE (%), 1960: 15 years and over 13.

COMPULSORY: 8 years (between 6 and 14 years of age). School enrolment ratios (%), 1st and 2nd levels, 1963: 86, adjusted 92.

SCHOOLS, 1964: Primary: no. 160, pupils 26,500, teachers 940. Secondary: no. 16, p. 2,100, t. 160. Technical: no. 1, st. 180, t. 10. Teacher-training (1966): no. 1, st. 160. Higher: no. 2, st. 60; t. 10.

MASS MEDIA

BROADCASTING: No. of radio licences issued, 1965: 6,300. Transmitters: radio 2. TV service planned.

CINEMAS: No., 1965: 10. Seating capacity 5,000.

NEWSPRINT: Consumption, 1960: total 54 tons, per head 0·6 kg.

NEWSPAPERS: Daily, 1964: 2. Estimated circulation 6,000, copies per ooo of population 58. Principal dailies in Belize (*circ. ooo*): *Belize Times* 3 (Sunday 4), *Billboard* 2.

COSTA RICA

ULRICH FANGER

HISTORY

COSTA RICA was discovered by Columbus on his fourth voyage to the New World. He landed in 1502 near the Indian village of Cariari on the Caribbean coast, the location of the later Port Limón. Columbus is said to have given this part of the coast the name of Costa Rica ('lush coast'), a name much later applied to the entire country. At the time of discovery the country's tribal groups lived in widely scattered small villages. None had set up urban settlements or formed larger ceremonial centres, as were common among the Meso-American peoples of Mexico and Guatemala.

Colonial history

The Spanish colonisation of Costa Rica began relatively late, when the colonial settlements of Panama, Santo Domingo, Nueva Granada, Mexico, Caracas, Lima and Santiago had already been founded. The extension of Spanish power over Costa Rica during 40 years from Gil Gonzalez de Avila's expedition in 1522 took the form of brutal incursions decimating the Indian population. Once Costa Rica, under the name of Gobernación de Nueva Cartago, formed part of the Captaincy-General of Guatemala, a second phase of the conquest began, and settlers were brought into the province. Cartago was founded in 1563 as the first major Spanish settlement.

The centre of gravity of the colony was the Central High Plateau, an area with agricultural potential where an extremely small Indian population offered no prolonged resistance. Most of the population lived here, and here also the government was installed. During the 17th and the first half of the 18th century the small colony nearly bled itself white in a series of hapless efforts to conquer the mountainous hinterland and to subdue the fierce woodland Indian tribes. Moreover, British Caribbean and Zambo-Mosquito pirates for two centuries plagued the cocoa plantations in the Caribbean lowlands, disastrously retarding Costa Rica's economic development. The country was robbed of the benefits which it was beginning to derive from the sale of cocoa to European markets, and above all to England. Cocoa was the only cash crop known at the time and constituted the only potential source of income by trade for the colony, which lacked other resources.

The lack of trade relations, however, together with an absence of private fortunes, had the effect that no one group could rise to economic dominance. This fact also produced a movement of internal migration in contrast to the tendency towards urban concentration in most other Spanish colonies. The small farmers in Costa Rica withdrew more and more from the larger towns and settled on isolated and fairly self-sufficient small properties. This led to the development of a rural democracy and a land-tenure system of smallholdings which prevailed throughout the colonial period. The fact that Costa Rica never produced a 'hacienda society' of absentee landowners contributed to the development of a climate of social justice without much internal tension. Peasant immigration mainly from Galicia and other parts of northern Spain made for a homogeneous society.

The republican period

Independence from Spain was achieved in 1821, when Costa Rica, with only 60,000 inhabitants, joined with the other seven provinces of Central America to form the loose political association known as the United Provinces of Central America, whose internal conflicts led to its disbandment in 1838. Full national sovereignty was not established until 1848. The period between 1838 and 1902, beginning with the unconstitutional reign of Braulio Carrillo (1838–42) and ending with the autocratic rule of Rafael Yglesias (1894–1902), was largely one of dictatorships succeeding one another through coups. During this period Costa Rica had to defend the annexation of the border province of Guanacaste against a Nicaraguan invading force in 1836, and Costa Rican armies took a decisive part in the war of 1853–7 which led to the defeat of the North-American adventurer William Walker and his troops in Nicaragua. Some economic progress was achieved during these years, enhanced by mounting exports of coffee, which had been introduced in 1808, and by the establishment of vast banana plantations on the Atlantic coast after 1878. The Northern Railway concession was granted in 1871, and work on this difficult run was completed in 1890. The Pacific railroad to Port Puntarenas was not finished until 1909.

Under the administrations of Ascensión Esquivel (1902–6), Cleto González Víquez (1906–10) and Ricardo Jiménez Oreamuno (1910–14), the constitutionality of the political regime in Costa Rica was consolidated. Since 1902 the political life of the country has been relatively stable and has shown a progressive trend towards genuinely democratic standards. In contrast to political developments in most neighbouring countries, there have been only two interruptions to the regular succession of presidents in Costa Rica since the turn of the century.

On 23 January 1917 General Federico Tinoco Granados, war minister under the presidency of Alfredo González Flores (1914–17) toppled the constitutional regime and set up a dictatorial system in which the military faction was hand-in-glove with the recently emerged coffee oligarchy. The outrageous nepotism under Tinoco came to be known as *tinoquismo*. A popular uprising in August 1918 forced Tinoco to abdicate and leave the country. As a consequence of this episode the military was systematically relegated from power under the following liberal presidents, a development that led in 1944 to a constitutional amendment prohibiting the formation of a regular army or of para-military groups, and thus eliminating from the political scene a traditional source of extra-constitutional interference in government.

Another revolutionary upheaval which had the most profound effect on subsequent political developments came in early 1948, as a consequence of the administrations of Dr Rafael Calderón Guardia (1940–4) and of his chosen successor, Teodoro Picado Michalsky (1944–8). Calderón Guardia, leader and *jefe máximo* of his highly personalistic Partido Republicano Nacional (PRN), had first attracted attention through his activities as a medical doctor among the poorer classes of San José. His progressive platform caught the attention of reform-minded intellectuals, and his

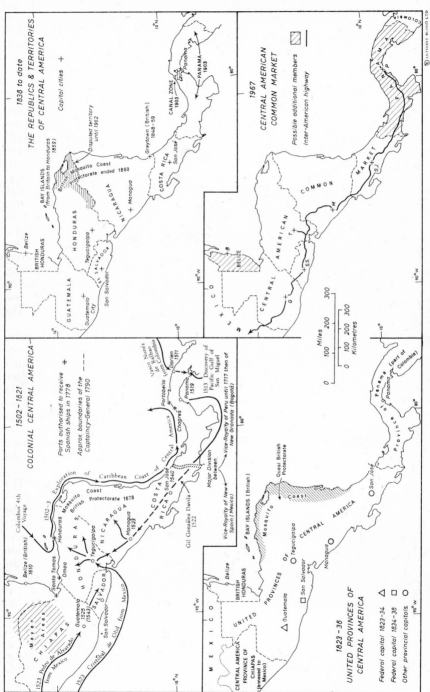

CENTRAL AMERICA: HISTORICAL DEVELOPMENT

G*

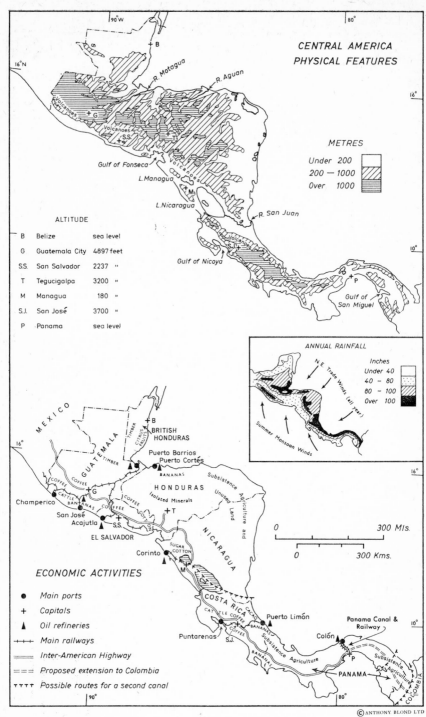

CENTRAL AMERICA
PHYSICAL FEATURES

METRES

Under 200
200 — 1000
Over 1000

ALTITUDE

B   Belize   sea level
G   Guatemala City   4897 feet
S.S.   San Salvador   2237 "
T   Tegucigalpa   3200 "
M   Managua   180   "
S.J.   San José   3700 "
P   Panama   sea level

ANNUAL RAINFALL

Inches
Under 40
40 – 80
80 – 100
Over 100

ECONOMIC ACTIVITIES

● Main ports
+ Capitals
▲ Oil refineries
+++ Main railways
=== Inter-American Highway
=== Proposed extension to Colombia
ΤΤΤΤ Possible routes for a second canal

© ANTHONY BLOND LTD

CENTRAL AMERICA : PHYSICAL FEATURES AND ECONOMIC ACTIVITIES

178

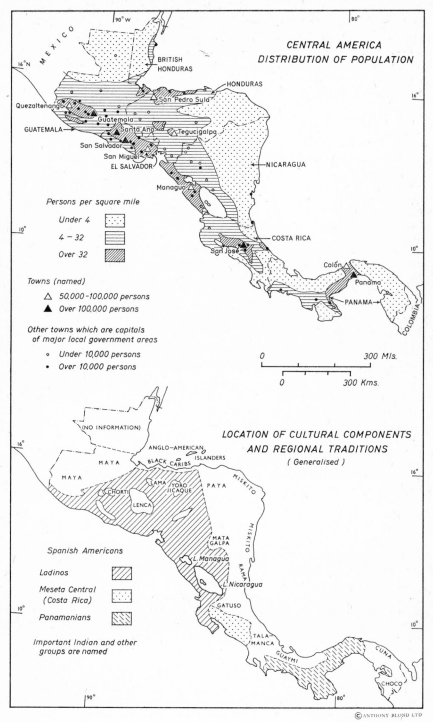

CENTRAL AMERICA
DISTRIBUTION OF POPULATION

Persons per square mile

Under 4

4 – 32

Over 32

Towns (named)

△ 50,000–100,000 persons

▲ Over 100,000 persons

Other towns which are capitals
of major local government areas

○ Under 10,000 persons

• Over 10,000 persons

LOCATION OF CULTURAL COMPONENTS
AND REGIONAL TRADITIONS
(Generalised)

Spanish Americans

Ladinos

Meseta Central
(Costa Rica)

Panamanians

Important Indian and other
groups are named

© ANTHONY BLOND LTD

CENTRAL AMERICA: POPULATION AND CULTURAL GROUPINGS

magnetic personality secured him electoral victory by an enormous margin. However, his progressive social reforms, including the addition of a set of 'Social Guarantees' to the constitution and the passing of a Labour Code (which has remained in effect), cost him the support of the powerful conservative interests of the country. On the other hand, his regime was marked by corruption, inefficiency and excessive government spending, all of which brought about an erosion of popular confidence in the regime. To secure a victory for his PRN in the 1944 elections Calderón Guardia was forced to enter into a close alliance with the Communist Party of Costa Rica (Vanguardia Popular) under Rafael Mora. During the Picado administration, Vanguardia Popular steadily accumulated its influence and power. By 1948 the number of Communist deputies had grown to seven; the Communist-lining labour organisation CNTCR enjoyed the full support of the government against the Christian-Democratic trade union Rerum Novarum; and several key positions in the Ministry of Labour were now held by Communists. As a consequence, political unrest reached a climax during the election campaign of 1947-8. The presidency was contested between Calderón Guardia and Otilio Ulate, leader of the Partido Unión Nacional (PUN), formed in 1946. Ulate, who had the support of all three opposition parties, won in the fairly free and orderly elections of 8 February 1948. The administration of the holdover president, Picado, who was surprised and displeased by Ulate's popular victory, induced Congress, where PRN and Vanguardia Popular controlled a majority of votes, to annul the election on 28 February.

Civil war and subsequent political developments

Civil war broke out as groups of civilians took to the hills to join an armed revolt headed by José Figueres Ferrer, founder of the Partido Social Demócrata (PSD), a well-known politician and agriculturist who had been forced into exile under Calderón Guardia. In a brief but bloody war the considerably larger forces of the administration were defeated, and Calderón Guardia and Picado fled to Nicaragua. One of the three vice-presidents, Santos León Herrera, was placed in charge of the government. On 28 April 1948 Figueres and his civilian troops entered San José, and on 8 May he became head of a provisional 'Junta Revolucionaria'. Elections for a Constitutional Assembly were held on 8 December 1948; of the 45 elected members of the Assembly, 34 were supporters of Ulate. The Assembly drafted the new constitution of 1949, under which a National Legislative Assembly and two vice-presidents were elected by popular vote. The Constitutional Assembly had previously confirmed Ulate's election as president of the republic.

Neither the junta administration, nor the following governments of Ulate (1949–54) and Figueres (1954–8), elected in February 1954, committed the error of dismantling the basic structure of Calderón Guardia's social reforms. Under the influence of the Figueres party (now Partido Liberación Nacional or PLN), several important reforms were introduced. As early as 1948 the commercial banks were expropriated by the government, and with the help of a public bond issue a nationalised banking system was created, complemented in 1950 by a separate, government-owned Central Bank. Other important economic and social functions, as nationalised insurance, social security and the exploitation of water-power resources, were vested in a group of legally unique autonomous and semi-autonomous public corporations.

The PUN administration under President Mario Echandi (1958–62) was marked by a high degree of inefficiency due in part to many government proposals being blocked in the Legislative Assembly, where the opposition PLN still retained the majority, in part to the presidential veto voiding legislative proposals introduced by the opposition. This stalemate was overcome under the administration of Francisco Orlich Bolmarcich (1962–6) of Liberación Nacional. Important new legislation included a land-reform project and the formation of a National Institute of Land and Colonisation (ITCO) which is opening new areas of settlement to cooperative colonisation.

The political system and parties

Under the 1949 constitution Costa Rica enjoys the most clearly defined system of division of powers in all the Central American republics. Legislative power is vested in the one-chamber Legislative Assembly. Its 57 deputies, each representing an electorate of 8,000 inhabitants, are elected for four years and are not reeligible for the next term. Executive authority is in the hands of the president of the republic, elected also for a four-year term by popular direct vote; he cannot be reelected for the next term.

The highest body of judicial power is the Tribunal Supremo de Elecciones. Elections for municipal offices, for deputies of the National Assembly and for the presidency are held every four years in February; all three ballots are thrown in one voting procedure. Costa Rican elections appear to have become increasingly honest and free. Largely owing to the fact that the majority of Costa Rican voters are, along personalistic patterns, more or less permanently grouped in one of the two major and similarly-sized political followings, leaving only a narrow portion of not permanently affiliated voters to act as a decisive margin, there tends to be a swing to the opposite party with each election. Continuism in office had been constitutionally barred since the middle of the 19th century. Largely owing to this fact and to the absence of military pressure groups, Costa Rica has contrasted favourably with the political instability and frequent military coups of other Central American republics. Since the 1944 constitution banned military organisations the country has maintained only a small National Guard corps.

Apart from a few major groupings, the party spectrum has been subject to constant and ephemeral fluctuations. The major party is Partido Liberación Nacional (PLN), founded by José Figueres after the 1948 revolution. This party is one of the classic examples of the democratic left in Latin America, and the only one in Costa Rica with a well-organised party structure, including a youth federation and a political academy.

In 1965 three opposition parties formed an electoral coalition, Unificación Nacional, whose candidate, José Joaquín Trejos Fernandez, was elected president of the republic in 1966. Unificación Nacional has been called 'the coalition of the ex-presidents', as its three component parts are the small and ultra-conservative Partido Republicano of ex-President Rafael Calderón Guardia, a highly personalistic party and second largest political grouping in the country, and the liberal-conservative Partido Unión Republicana Auténtica, a small splinter group under former President (1958–62) Mario Echandi.

The government coalition, Unificación Nacional, is an amalgam of conservative and left elements. As this alliance won a 51 per cent majority of the popular vote in the 1966 presidential election but was short of a majority in the Legislative Assembly the coalition depends for parliamentary vote-calls on the support of the third party represented in parliament, the small personalistic Unión Cívico Revolucionaria, with rightist tendencies, under former security minister Frank Marshall Jiménez.

Costa Rica is the only country in the western hemisphere where all officially recognised parties enjoy the privilege of being kept on the government payroll; all parties may recover the costs of their election campaigns from the newly elected government.

There are a number of non-official parties outside parliament, the most important being the Communist-lining Alianza Popular Socialista (APS) under Manuel Mora and Marcial Aguilúz Orellana. The APS was illegalised in 1965 shortly after having been officially inscribed. This implies only that the party lost its official status, and cannot participate in elections; it does not preclude other party activities. This leftist party has its major strongholds among the banana workers at the United Fruit Company plantations on the Southern Pacific coast.

ECONOMY

Although Costa Rica is the most advanced socially and politically of the five isthmian republics, her economic situation is far from satisfactory. The country is still largely dependent on agriculture, and industrialisation is only beginning to make significant impact. Costa Rica is lacking in most of the basic natural resources. No commercially exploitable oil has yet been found; there are no coal deposits, and deposits of iron and non-ferrous metals are insignificant and have not been exploited.

The country was the first in Central America to introduce coffee and bananas to build a cash crop basis for export purposes. The economy has been increasingly dependent on this product for the last century. Costa Rican hard-bean coffee obtains high prices, and most of the crop goes to the United States and Germany. Bananas have been controlled since 1899 by the United Fruit Company (UFCO). Panama disease led the UFCO to abandon all plantations on the Caribbean side between 1935 and 1940. The old banana lands were partly turned over to cocoa or abacá (manila hemp) cultivation, but the disappearance of the banana plantations brought about a relapse to a near-subsistence level economy for many former plantation workers who in addition were affected by the breakdown in world-market prices for cocoa. Nearly all banana plantations in Costa Rica are now located along the southern part of the Pacific littoral, but attempts are being made to rehabilitate the lost plantations by flood-fallowing and the development of a new type of plantain resistant to the disease.

Of the total value of exports, coffee accounts for about 53 per cent, bananas for 28 per cent, and cocoa for 4 per cent. All banana exports, and most of the cocoa exports, go to the United States and Canada. Other export products include, in order of importance, live cattle and beef, abacá and sugar. Main trade partners are the United States, the Federal Republic of Germany, Britain, Canada and Japan. The role played by these countries in both export and import trade is shown in the table on the next page.

The external trade balance has generally been negative since 1958. From 1958 to 1961 the price of coffee declined severely and caused lower export earnings, budgetary difficulties, and diminished foreign exchange reserves. Since 1962 exports and imports have risen equally, so that the trade deficit has continued, reaching in 1963 US $62·3 million. Under the 1962–6

EXTERNAL TRADE, 1963

(Per cent of total Costa Rican trade)

	Imports from Costa Rica	Exports to Costa Rica
United States	55·5	47·0
Germany	21·5	10·8
Britain	0·8	5·4
Canada	0·6	2·9
Japan	—	6·9

government of Francisco Orlich Bolmarcich, a programme of additional taxes, increased tariffs, new bond issues and reduced public expenditure was drawn up. The monetary unit, the colón, was devalued to 6·625 colones to the US dollar, or 18·55 to the pound sterling. Budgetary deficits, and deficits in the balance of trade and of payments, have continued to grow. Despite stand-by credits, granted by the IMF during the Irazú volcanic crisis, and loans from the IDB, the Costa Rican government was forced, in January 1967, to resort to a system of import controls, coupled with multiple exchange rates and a rationing of foreign exchange. This appears to have had the effect of a de facto devaluation of the colon. GNP per head in 1963 was US $373, one of the highest rates in Latin America. The cost of living is fairly high when compared with some Latin American countries, e.g. Mexico or Colombia, but it is lowest among the five Central American republics.

Though taxation is better developed than in the neighbouring countries, it still accounts for a mere 10·2 per cent of GNP, 42 per cent of it collected in the form of direct and 58 per cent in the form of indirect taxes. Production of alcohol, banking and insurance are government monopolies, Costa Rica being the only country outside the Socialist bloc to have nationalised all private banks. Further social legislation has provided for the establishment of a Social Security Office (CSS), a national Institute for Urbanisation (INVU) and a nationalised Electric Power Institute (ICE) that operates alongside the older, foreign-owned Compañía Nacional de Fuerza y Luz. A series of hydroelectric power plants is in operation or under construction, and Costa Rica is prominent among Latin American countries as to per capita output and consumption of electric power.

In 1965, 51 per cent of the labour force was still engaged in agriculture. As nearly 80 per cent of potentially arable land is already under cultivation, the fast-growing (over 4 per cent p.a.) population will necessarily have to turn to intensive industrialisation. The vast forested regions of the country are still hardly exploited. Some caoba and mahogany wood in the Atlantic lowlands is felled for domestic construction work and the production of furniture, but there is virtually no export of these precious woods. Only 11 per cent of the labour force is employed in manufacturing (as against 28 in services and trade). Of 6,000 establishments operating in manufacture, mining and agricultural services, only 80 employ more than 50 persons.

Under the Central American Common Market Agreement intra-regional tariffs and other trade barriers have largely been removed, and Costa Rica has been in a position to substantially improve her intra-regional trade balance. Changes to be expected as a consequence of the Central American Common Market may lead to favourable economic development for Costa Rica.

BIBLIOGRAPHY

Biesanz, John. *Costa Rican Life*, Colombia Univ. Press, New York, 1945.
Busey, James. 'Foundations of Political Contrast: Costa Rica and Nicaragua', *Western Political Quarterly*, XI, 3, Institute of Government, Univ. of Utah, Salt Lake City, September 1958.
Goldkind, Victor. 'Cultural Contrasts in Rural and Urban Settlement Types in Costa Rica', *Rural Sociology*, 26, Maddison, Wis., December 1961.
Hayes, Joe C. and Wiltbank, Milford J. *A Study of the Agrarian Problem in Costa Rica*, International Development Services, New York, 1960.
Hill, George W. 'The Agrarian Reform in Costa Rica', *Land Economics*, XL, 1, Madison, Wis., February 1964.
Jones, Chester Lloyd. *Costa Rica and Civilisation in the Caribbean*, Univ. of Wisconsin Press, Madison, Wis., 1941.
Loomis, Charles and Powell, Reed M. *Class Status in Rural Costa Rica: A Peasant Community Compared with a Hacienda Community*, Pan American Union, Washington, DC, 1951.
May, Stacy and Lasso, Galo Plaza. *United Fruit Company in Latin America*, National Planning Association, Washington, DC, 1958.
Nunley, Robert E. *The Distribution of Population in Costa Rica*, National Research Council, Washington, DC, 1960.
Wagner, Philip L. *Nicoya (Costa Rica): A Cultural Geography*, Univ. of California Press, Berkeley, Calif., 1958.
Watt, Stewart. *Keith and Costa Rica*, Univ. of New Mexico Press, Albuquerque, NM, 1941.

BASIC INFORMATION

CLIMATE

San José

Lat./long.	10° N, 84° W	Relative humidity	70%/63%
Altitude	3,760 ft/1,146 m.	at midday of	
Mean temp. of hottest month	22°C/71°F (May)	hottest and coolest months	
Mean temp. of coolest month	19°C/67°F (Dec./Jan.)	Wettest month	12·0 in./305 mm. (Sept.)
Absolute max.	92°F/33°C	Driest month	0·2 in./5 mm. (Feb.)
Absolute min.	49°F/10°C	Annual av. rainfall	70·8 in./1,798 mm.

POPULATION

TOTAL (*million*): 1963 (census) 1·34; Oct. 1966: 1·50; 1980 (ECLA projection): 2·49.
DENSITY, mid-1965: 28 persons per sq. km.
CRUDE RATES (*per 000*), 1965: birth 40·5, death 8·1, infant mortality 75·1.
GROWTH RATES (% *p.a.*): 1945–65: 3·7; 1960–5: 4·1.
DISTRIBUTION (% *of total pop.*): Ethnic: white 80, mixed 20. Foreign-born, 1950: 5·0; 1963: 2·8. Language: Spanish. Religion: mainly Roman Catholic. Urban (*centres 2,000 inhab. or over*), ECLA data, 1950: 29·9; 1960: 31·3; 1980 (proj.): 43·0. Largest cities (*000 inhab.*), 1965: San José 181, Alajuela 26, Puntarenas 21, Heredia 21, Limón 21, Cartago 20.

CONSTITUTIONAL SYSTEM

CONSTITUTION: First 1825; main 1871, many amendments; latest 1949, frequent amendments.
SYSTEM: Unitary republic, composed of 7 provinces (divided into cantons). Separate executive, legislature and judiciary.

EXECUTIVE: Power vested in president, elected with 2 vice-presidents by popular vote for 4-year term; no immediate reelection. He appoints government ministers.
LEGISLATURE: Uni-cameral, Legislative Assembly: 57 deputies (number related to population at each census) elected by proportional representation for 4 years. *Suffrage:* Universal, compulsory voting for citizens over 20 years of age. Registered voters, Feb. 1966: 550,000. *Elections,* Feb. 1966: Presidential, Dr José Joaquín Trejos Fernández, Unificación Nacional, 222,810 votes, elected; Daniel Oduber Quirós, Liberación Nacional, 218,590 votes. Legislative Assembly: Liberación Nacional 29 seats, Unificación Nacional 26, Unión Cívico-Revolucionaria 2.
JUDICIARY: Supreme Court, of 17 judges appointed by Legislative Assembly for 8-year term, with 4 appeal courts and Court of Cassation; provincial lower courts and local justices.

DEFENCE

ARMED FORCES: No compulsory military service; army disbanded.

INTERNATIONAL RELATIONS

Member of the UN and many of its international specialised agencies, including: IBRD and affiliates, IMF, FAO, ICAO, ILO, ITU, UNDP, UNESCO, UPU, WHO and WMO; UNCTAD representative. Also member of: OAS, Alliance for Progress, ECLA, IDB, ODECA, BCIE and CACM.

ECONOMY

PRODUCTION

AGRICULTURE (*ooo tons*)	*1948/9–52/3*[1]	*63/4*	*64/5*	*65/6*
Coffee	23	62	47	60
Bananas	434	437	486	567
Sugar (raw value)	27	112	102	104
Cacao	5	10	11	8

[1] Average 1948/9–1952/3.

LAND, 1963 (%): Arable 12, permanent pasture 18, forested 16, urban and other 53.
OTHER AGRICULTURAL DATA: Agricultural holdings, 1955 (census): 47,286; area 1·85 m. hectares. Tractors in use (*ooos*), 1963: 4·45. Fertiliser consumption (*ooo tons*), 1965/6: 68.
LIVESTOCK: Nos. (*ooo head*), 1964/5: cattle 1,143, pigs 87.
FISH: Landed (*ooo tons*), 1964: total 2·9.
MANUFACTURING, 1964: (*ooo tons*) cement 33, wheat flour 4; (*m. litres*) beer 9. Wood (*ooo cubic metres, sawn*), 1963: 290.
CONSTRUCTION: (*ooo sq. metres floor area*), 1964: building permits approved 393.

ENERGY

CONSUMPTION (*tons coal equiv.*), 1964: total 0·37 m., per head 0·27.
ELECTRICITY, 1965: Generated (*kwh*) 640 m.; installed capacity (*kw*) 157,000.

GOVERNMENT EXPENDITURE

DISTRIBUTION (% *of total*), 1967: Education 24, health 3.

GROSS PRODUCT

GDP (*ooo m. colones*): At current market prices, 1964: 3·70; 1965: 4·00; 1966 (est.) 4·28. Per head (*US$*), UN estimate, 1964: 270.
DISTRIBUTION (%), 1963: agriculture 32, manufacturing 14, trade 9.
GROWTH RATES (%), 1960–5: 6·0, per head 1·9.

External trade (US$ m.)	1955	1960	1964	1965	1966
Exports (f.o.b.)	81	86	114	112	139
Coffee	37	45	48	47	53
Bananas	33	20	28	28	33
Cacao	6	6	4	2	3
Meat and livestock	1	5	8	5	.
Imports (c.i.f.)	87	110	139	178	179
Trade balance	−7	−24	−25	−66	−40

Direction of trade (%)

	Exports			Imports		
	1955	1960	1965	1955	1960	1965
CACM	(1·3)	2·7	16·4	(0·8)	3·4	8·2
LAFTA	(2·3)	1·0	1·8	(2·5)	2·0	3·6
USA	54·8	54·8	50·4	59·5	47·0	39·9
EEC	32·9	33·3	22·6	16·3	21·3	19·6
UK	0·9	0·8	0·4	6·9	5·8	4·7

Finance

Exchange rate (colones/US$): end-year, 1960: for imports, 5·67–6·65; 1966: 6·65.
Balance of payments (US$ m.): Goods and services (net), 1960: −20; 1964: −29; 1965: −73; 1966: −50.
Cost of living (Dec. 1958=100), San José, December, 1960: 103; 1964: 113; 1965: 112; 1966: 114.
Industrial wages: Earnings in manufacturing, per month (colones), 1963: 351. (1957=100) 1963: 183; 1965: 256.
Government accounts (m. colones), 1965: Revenue 570·6, expenditure 569·4, surplus 1·2; after adjustments, deficit 117·0 (financing, external credit 63·8). Treasury deficit 49·2.

Employment

Economically active (%), 1963: of total pop. 30 (men 50, women 10); agriculture 49, services 17, manufacturing 12, trade 10.

TRANSPORT AND COMMUNICATIONS

Railways: Traffic, F. del Norte, 1963: 21 m. pass.-km; 44 m. net ton-km. Length of track: 1,100 km.
Motor vehicles: In use (000), 1965: pass. cars 24, comm. vehicles 16. Road system 19,000 km., paved 1,100 km.
Shipping: Merchant fleet (000 g.r. tons), 1958: 510; 1960: 92. International seaborne shipping (m. tons), 1965: goods loaded 0·5, goods unloaded 0·7. Main ports: Puerto Limón, Puntarenas, Golfito and Quepos.
Air: Main airports: San José: El Coco (international), Sabana.
Telephones: No. in use, 1964: 21,560.

SOCIAL WELFARE

System: Social insurance benefits and services administered by Caja Costarricense de Seguro Social, which fixes contribution quotas payable by employees and employers; the State also contributes. Employment legislation covers working hours; holidays; wages, overtime and annual bonus; employers' liability for compensation for accidents, dismissal and death indemnities; compulsory insurance for occupational risks.
Health: 2,600 persons per physician, 220 persons per hospital bed.
Nutrition: Net food supply (per head per day), 1962: 2,430 calories; protein 54 g.

EDUCATION

ILLITERACY RATE (%), 1963 (census sample): 15 years and over: 16.
COMPULSORY: 6 years (between 7 and 14 years of age). School enrolment ratios (%),
1st and 2nd levels, 1963: 61, adjusted 84.
SCHOOLS, 1965: Pre-school and primary: no. 200, pupils 0·28 m. teachers 10,000.
Secondary: no. 85, p. 41,000, t. 2,000. Technical: no. 35, st. 7,000, t. 400. Teacher-
training: no. 1, st. 2,400, t. 24. Higher: no. 5, st. 8,600, t. 500.
UNIVERSITY: U. de Costa Rica, San José: 5,300 st., t. 430.

MASS MEDIA

BROADCASTING: Receivers in use, end-1964: TV 35,000, radio 123,000. Stations:
TV 4, radio 48.
CINEMAS: No., 1960: 136.
NEWSPRINT: Consumption, 1963: total 4,600 tons, per head 3·4 kg.
NEWSPAPERS: Daily, 1964: 6. Estimated circulation (5 dailies) 0·11 m.; copies per 000
of population, 77. Principal dailies in San José (*circulation, 000*): *La Nación* 43,
La República 16, *Diario de Costa Rica* 12, *The Daily Press* 1; evening: *La Prensa Libre* 14,
La Hora 13.
BOOKS: Titles published, 1963: 13.

EL SALVADOR

ALEJANDRO D. MARROQUÍN

HISTORY

EL SALVADOR is the smallest country in Latin America, its approximate area being 7,720 square miles. It forms a narrow strip along the coast of the Pacific in the centre of the Central American isthmus; its coastline is 200 miles long and its maximum breadth 62 miles. From the earliest times this area, owing to its geographical position and climate, was a favourite route for migratory movements originating in the north of the American continent. The earliest culture of which there is any evidence, the Archaic or pre-Maya, appears to have lasted until the third century AD, when tribes related to the Mayas invaded the region and annihilated or absorbed its inhabitants. The next invaders, in the 10th century, were the Pipils who coexisted peacefully with the Mayas with considerable mutual cultural influence. The Pipils came to constitute the majority of the indigenous population at the time of the Spanish Conquest. The name of their capital, Cuscatlán, is still sometimes used as that of the country.

The colonial period

The Spaniards occupied Cuscatlán in 1524, taking three years to subdue the Pipils. The town of San Salvador (founded in 1525) and neighbouring Sonsonate developed as separate provinces subject to the Audiencia of Guatemala. San Salvador thrived on stock-raising, general agriculture and the manufacture of indigo; the port of Acajutla in the western part of the territory became important in the export trade of cacao. In 1786 San Salvador was raised to the status of an intendancy, still subordinate to the Spanish government in Guatemala. Both Sonsonate and San Salvador had by this time a large mestizo population, while the larger Indian villages had become progressively hispanicised. Interbreeding between the Spanish and indigenous population took place to such an extent that by the end of the colonial period the population of El Salvador was predominantly mestizo.

San Salvador played an active role in the Central American independence movement. A rising was attempted in San Salvador in 1811, led by the priest José Matías Delgado (later San Salvador's first bishop) and his nephew Manuel José Arce. When in 1821 Guatemala declared independence from Spain San Salvador, after seeking absolute independence, remained within the Central American Confederation. Arce was federal president from 1825 to 1829 and the federal capital was transferred to San Salvador in 1834.

The republican period

El Salvador emerged as a sovereign and independent republic in 1841 upon the break-up of the Central American Confederation. Although mestizos, creoles (i.e. persons of Spanish descent born in America) and Indians had fought side by side in the war of independence, it was the creoles who reaped the benefit after independence, retaining their already considerable economic power through ownership of the big coffee estates—coffee soon became vital to the country's economy—and acquiring political power in addition. This situation remained virtually unchanged until 1931. For several decades after independence one coup followed another and 'liberals' and 'conservatives', two rival bands of powerful creoles hardly differing in ideology, struggled for power.

In contrast to the restrictionist policy followed during the colonial period, republican governments, influenced by laissez-faire liberalism, gave over key sectors of the national economy to foreign investment. The country soon experienced the pressures of economic imperialism, which worked in alliance with the creole oligarchy. Predominantly British and United States capital controlled commerce, railways and banking.

While in the last years of the 19th and the first three decades of the present century the political situation became more peaceful and presidential succession more regular than in the early post-independence period, social problems grew increasingly intractable. The contrast between rich and poor was extreme and agricultural workers lived at subsistence level. In 1931, in the wake of the world-wide economic depression, a communist-led armed insurrection by peasants took place. Successful for a time in the western part of the country, it was repressed with great brutality by General Maximiliano Hernández Martínez, who seized presidential power in the same year, ousting the candidate chosen by Congress. Martínez exercised dictatorial powers for the next thirteen years. The victories of the democratic powers in the second world war encouraged a revulsion against the dictatorship which culminated in a sit-down strike and the fall of the dictatorship in May 1944. A political system was then established which—although coups alternated with elections—was more orientated towards political, social and economic reforms.

In 1950 Major Oscar Osorio was elected president and remained in office for a full term of six years. Some economic progress took place during this period, including the development of cotton industry. The lot of the rural masses however remained unimproved. In the field of foreign affairs El Salvador played a prominent part in the movement for Central American economic union. The Charter of San Salvador, providing for regular high-level meetings between the Central American republics on economic and cultural unity, was written in the city in 1951. José Guillermo Trabanino of El Salvador became the first secretary-general of the Organization of Central American States.

Osorio's Partido Revolucionario de Unificación Democrática (PRUD) dominated the country's political life until 1960, when a bloodless leftist coup led by Col. César Yánez Urías overthrew the government of his successor, José María Lemus, dissolved a Congress consisting almost entirely of PRUD members and set up a six-man junta. The new junta was itself overthrown by another military group which organised elections for a National Assembly in which the Partido de Conciliación Nacional (PCN), created by the army, won all seats. In April 1962 Col. Julio Adalberto Rivera was elected president unopposed for a term of five years, a new constitution adopted by the Assembly early in 1962 making it illegal for the president to succeed himself in office. Free elections were held for a new legislative Assembly in 1964; while opposition groups gained seats for the first time in several years, the PCN retained its strong majority, as it did in the next biennial Assembly elections in 1966.

Political instability

The five coups d'état which have taken place in El Salvador since May 1944 have resulted in as many quasi-dictatorial regimes. There appears to be no escape from the classic Latin American antithesis of stable and oppressive regimes on the one hand, unstable and democratic governments on the other. Furthermore El Salvador clearly lies within the sphere of influence of the United States and since the Cold War has suffered considerably from pressures in favour of regimes supposedly more energetically anti-communist than others.

The social structure underlies many of El Salvador's political problems. There is a close correlation between ethnic and social categories (the upper class, small but influential, is predominantly white, while the middle and lower classes are mestizo and Indian). Class-consciousness is not however fully developed in any social group and political divisions rarely follow hard-and-fast class lines. Foreigners constitute an important group within the upper class, and their control over importing and exporting activities gives them an increasing influence in the economic life of the country.

The army is now no longer the tame servant of the feudal oligarchy, but has developed a remarkable degree of political consciousness and a comparatively progressive outlook; it has the potential, in conjunction with popular forces, to achieve real progress for the country as a whole. The historic Liberal and Conservative parties have vanished without trace. Today there is an illegal Communist Party and a recently formed Christian Democrat Party. These are the only parties with a definite ideology, the others being merely personal followings of particular political figures. The Communist Party enjoys little popular support, and expends much of its energy in academic theorising; it sides with Moscow in the Sino–Soviet dispute.

The glaring contrasts between rich and poor and the abysmally low standard of living of the rural population (one-third of which lives at subsistence level) have given rise to pronounced social tensions. The increased support for radical solutions has been to a great extent canalised by the Christian Democrat Party, whose programme is based on Roman Catholic social doctrines, and which contemplates, among other measures, thoroughgoing agrarian reform. Despite its recent origin, this party has achieved some spectacular electoral successes. It has so far failed, however, to produce a leader with strong popular appeal.

Before the March 1967 presidential elections there was widespread popular feeling that, after being ruled by generals since 1931, the country should have a civilian president. The feudal oligarchy, while generally favouring military rule, was aware that some recent military governments have not been so subservient to their interests as they could have wished. In the event, the PCN's candidate, Col. Sánchez Hernández, was elected. It is, perhaps, the peasant, with his strong attachment to tradition and imperviousness to transitory innovations, who points the way to a solution to El Salvador's present political instability.

ECONOMY

The economy of El Salvador presents so heterogeneous a picture that it is hardly possible to speak of a national economy. There are, rather, three coexisting systems. The few remaining purely Indian regions preserve the relics of communal ownership of the land; barter trade is prevalent and there has been little technical advance since pre-Conquest times. This sector comprises about 10 per cent of the total economy. The second sector (comprising some 35 per cent of the economy) is the feudal or semi-feudal system, based on the *latifundio* or large estate. Its products are destined primarily for internal consumption. The third and most rapidly growing sector is that of nascent capitalism, which accounts for 55 per cent of the economy; its development affects, to a greater or lesser degree, the entire economy.

The absence of iron, coal and any source of energy other than hydro-electric in El Salvador has prevented the rise of heavy industry. The economic progress of the country is inevitably orientated towards secondary industry, particularly the production of chemicals directly connected with agriculture. There is a marked concentration on the production of goods for export, and a consequent dependence on the fluctuations of prices in foreign markets; other sectors of the economy tend to be neglected. There is excessive pro-duction of luxury goods for the home market, where patterns of consumption tend to reflect those of more developed countries, even though the corres-ponding industrial techniques are lacking. The entire economy is highly dependent on outside factors, including steadily increasing foreign capital investment.

The exceptional fertility of the soil has determined the central position of agriculture in the economy. Virtually all arable land in El Salvador is already under cultivation, but in most cases lack of capital and rudimentary techniques results in very low yield. Only where there is authentically capitalist exploitation of the land, e.g. to produce coffee or cotton for the foreign market, can it be said that the land is being worked with maximum efficiency. The archaic and inequitable system of land tenure results in the concentration of a great area of land in the hands of a few owners. It has been estimated that over 90 per cent of the peasants are landless, and are obliged to pay rent for the land they work or take employment as day-labourers.

The project for a Central American Common Market holds out some hopes for an improvement in the economic situation. It must be recognised, however, that little progress has been made towards effective integration, since no attempt has been made to restrict competitive production in the countries concerned, nor to carry out substantial reforms in the agrarian structure. In the period 1950–62 El Salvador's exports to the other Central American countries increased by 5 per cent, whereas imports from those countries increased by 8 per cent; El Salvador is becoming increasingly dependent on imports for her supply of cereals.

DEMOGRAPHIC PROBLEMS

The population explosion is perhaps the most urgent problem facing El Salvador, which already has the greatest density of population on the mainland of America, exceeded only by Jamaica, Haiti and Puerto Rico. If the present rate of increase is maintained, the population will double over the next 25 years.

The population is still predominantly rural. Some of the consequences of this are low levels of literacy and health, a slow increase in productivity, technical backwardness and the prevalence of a conservative mentality.

Ethnically, the population may be roughly classified as 10 per cent white, 85 per cent mestizo and 5 per cent Indian. The Negro population is numerically insignificant. The fact that El Salvador is the most mestizo country in Latin America has both advantages and drawbacks. On the one hand, the people are receptive to foreign cultural influences; on the other, the absence of a firmly based national consciousness makes successful assimilation of such influences difficult. The low level of literacy will make it necessary to divert an increasing proportion of the government's expenditure towards the expansion of educational facilities, particularly in rural areas.

BIBLIOGRAPHY

Adams, Richard N. *Cultural Surveys of Panama—Nicaragua—Guatemala—El Salvador—Honduras*, Pan American Sanitary Bureau, Washington, DC, 1957.
El Salvador, Pan American Union, Washington, DC, 1960.
Osborne, Lilly de Jongh. *Four Keys to El Salvador*, Funk and Wagnalls, New York, 1956.
Parker, Franklin D. *The Central American Republics*, Oxford Univ. Press for Royal Institute of International Affairs, London and New York, 1964.
Raynolds, D. R. *Rapid Development in Small Economies—The Example of El Salvador*, Pall Mall Press, London; Frederick A. Praeger, New York, 1967.

BASIC INFORMATION

CLIMATE

San Salvador

Lat./long.	14° N, 89° W	Relative humidity	
Altitude	2,238 ft/682 m.	at midday of	50%/45%
Mean temp. of hottest month	26°C/79°F (Apr.)	hottest and coolest months	
Mean temp. of coolest month	24°C/75°F (Nov./Jan.)	Wettest month	12·9 in./328 mm. (June)
Absolute max.	105°F/40°C	Driest month	0·2 in./5 mm. (Feb.)
Absolute min.	45°F/7°C	Annual av. rainfall	70·0 in./1,778 mm.

POPULATION

TOTAL (*million*): 1961 (census) 2·51; mid-1966: 3·04. Projections: ECLA, 1980: 4·73; official, 1981: 4·74–5·00.
DENSITY, mid-1965: 137 persons per sq. km.
CRUDE RATES (*per 000*), 1966: birth 45·2, death 9·9, infant mortality 61·4.
GROWTH RATES (% *p.a.*): 1945–65: 2·6; 1960–5: 3·6.
DISTRIBUTION (% *of total pop.*) Ethnic, 1940: mixed 75, Amerindian 20, white 5. Foreign-born, 1950: 1·0; 1961: 0·6. Language: Spanish. Religion: mainly Roman Catholic. Urban (*centres 2,000 inhab. or over*), ECLA data, 1950: 27·6; 1960: 29·0, 1980 (proj.) 36·1. Largest cities (*000 inhab.*), 1961: San Salvador 256 (1965: 305); Santa Ana 121, San Miguel 83.

CONSTITUTIONAL SYSTEM

CONSTITUTION: First 1824; main 1886; latest 1962. Provision is made in the 1962 constitution for the reestablishment of the Central American Republic, without approval by a constituent assembly but subject to certain safeguards.

SYSTEM: Unitary republic, composed of 14 departments (divided into municipalities). Separate executive, legislature and judiciary.
EXECUTIVE: Power is vested in the president, who appoints ministers and under-secretaries of state. He is elected by direct popular vote for 5-year term; no immediate reelection. Election of the president and vice-president not held simultaneously with that of deputies. President is commander-in-chief of the armed forces.
LEGISLATURE: Unicameral, Legislative Assembly. Legislative Assembly: 52 deputies for electoral districts based on population; elected by direct popular vote for 2 years; they may be reelected. *Suffrage:* Universal, voting for adults over 18 years of age.
Elections: Presidential, March 1967: Col. Fidel Sánchez Hernández, Conciliación Nacional, 267,447 votes, elected; Dr Abraham Rodríguez 106,358 votes. Legislative Assembly, March 1966: Conciliación Nacional 31 deputies, Demócrata Cristiano 15, Acción Renovadora 4, others 2.
JUDICIARY: Supreme Court (of 10 judges) and chambers of second instance (2 judges) elected by Legislative Assembly; courts of first instance, judges appointed by Supreme Court; and justices of the peace in all towns. Judges elected for 3-year term and may be reelected for life after third successive term.

DEFENCE

DEFENCE BUDGET: 1966: 25·7 m. colones; 1·2% of GDP.
ARMED FORCES: Strength: army 4,500; total about 5,000 plus national guard.

INTERNATIONAL RELATIONS

Member of the UN and many of its international specialised agencies, including: IBRD and affiliates, IMF, FAO, ICAO, ILO, ITU, UNDP, UNESCO, UPU, WHO and WMO; IAEA; UNCTAD representative. Also member of OAS, Alliance for Progress, ECLA, IDB, ODECA, BCIE and CACM.

ECONOMY

PRODUCTION

AGRICULTURE (*ooo tons*)	1948–53[1]	63/64	64/65	65/66[2]
Coffee	75	115	125	108
Cotton	8	75	90	.
Maize	191	207	192	193
Rice	26	21	36	38
Sugar (raw value)	28	71	112	128

[1] Average 1948/9—1952/3.   [2] Provisional.

LAND, 1962 (%): Arable 23, permanent pasture 28, forested 24, other 25.
OTHER AGRICULTURAL DATA: Agricultural holdings, 1961 (census): No., 224,290; area 1·56 m. hectares. Tractors in use (*ooos*), 1956: 1·2. Fertiliser consumption (*ooo tons*), 1965/6: 58.
LIVESTOCK: No. (*ooo head*), 1964/5: cattle 921, pigs 322.
FISH: Landed (*ooo tons*), 1965: total 8·5.
MANUFACTURING, 1965: (*ooo tons*), cement 81, wheat flour 38; (*m. litres*) beer 13.
CONSTRUCTION: (*ooo sq. metres floor area*), 1965: Building permits approved 161.

ENERGY

CONSUMPTION (*tons coal equiv.*), 1964: total 0·50 m., per head 0·18.
ELECTRICITY, 1965: Generated (*kwh*) 410 m.; installed capacity (*kw*) 0·15 m.

GOVERNMENT EXPENDITURE

DISTRIBUTION (% *of total*), 1966: Defence 9, education 21, health 11, public works 12.

GROSS PRODUCT

GDP (*ooo m. colones*): At current market prices, 1964: 1·88; 1965: 2·01; 1966: 2·14. Per head (*US$*), UN estimate, 1963: 178.
DISTRIBUTION (%), 1965: Agriculture 29, manufacturing 18, trade 24.
GROWTH RATES (%), 1960–5: 6·6, per head 3·3.

EXTERNAL TRADE (*US$ m.*)	1955	1960	1964	1965	1966
EXPORTS (f.o.b.)	107	117	178	189	192
Coffee	92	81	93	96	91
Cotton	9	16	37	38	24
Cotton goods	.	2	6	7	9
IMPORTS (c.i.f.)	92	122	191	201	220
TRADE BALANCE	+15	−6	−13	−12	−27

DIRECTION OF TRADE (%)

	Exports			Imports		
	1955	1960	1965	1955	1960	1965
CACM	(3·8)	10·5	24·0	(7·5)	11·0	21·2
LAFTA	(0·2)	0·1	—	(1·2)	1·6	1·5
USA	64·3	35·1	24·9	57·0	43·0	31·3
EEC	22·5	38·3	28·0	18·7	24·6	19·1
UK	1·9	0·5	0·3	3·5	4·0	4·1

FINANCE

EXCHANGE RATES (*colones/US$*): Par value, end-year, 1960: 2·50; 1966: 2·50.
BALANCE OF PAYMENTS (*US$ m.*): Goods and services (net), 1960: −72; 1964: −80; 1965: −62; 1966:−121.
COST OF LIVING (*Dec. 1958=100*): San Salvador, December, 1960: 99; 1964: 101; 1965: 101; 1966: 99.
INDUSTRIAL WAGES: Earnings in manufacturing, per hour, 1965: 0·73 colones.
TREASURY ACCOUNTS (*m. colones*), 1965: Revenue 242·0 (incl. credits 17·4), expenditure 248·2 (incl. payments pending), deficit 6·2.

EMPLOYMENT

ECONOMICALLY ACTIVE (%), 1961: total pop. 32 (men 54, women 11). In agriculture 60, manufacturing 13, services 13, and commerce 6.
UNEMPLOYMENT (%), 1961: 5·3; under-employment high.

TRANSPORT AND COMMUNICATIONS

RAILWAYS: Length of narrow gauge track, 620 km.
MOTOR VEHICLES: In use (*ooo*), 1964: pass. cars 26·4, comm. vehicles 4·6. Road system: 8,526 km., paved 1,056.
SHIPPING: International sea-borne shipping, 1965: goods loaded 0·49, goods unloaded 0·90. Main ports: Acajutla, La Libertad, La Unión.
AIR: Main airport: San Salvador: Ilopango (international).
TELEPHONES: No. in use, 1966: 46,000.

SOCIAL WELFARE

SYSTEM: Social insurance benefits and services administered by the Instituto Salvadoreño del Seguro Social. Financed by employees', employers' and state contributions, amounting in aggregate to about 10% of employees' wages. Employment legislation covers working hours; holidays; payment of wages, overtime and annual bonus; employers' liability for compensation for accidents, dismissal and death indemnities.
HEALTH: 4,700 persons per physician, 480 persons per hospital bed.
NUTRITION: Net food supply (*per head per day*), 1962: 2,120 calories, protein 58 g.

EDUCATION

ILLITERACY RATE (*per cent*), 1961 (census sample): 10 years and over, 52.
COMPULSORY: 6 years between 7 and 14 years of age. School enrolment ratios (%),
1st and 2nd levels, 1963: 40, adjusted 54.
SCHOOLS, 1963: Pre-school and primary: no. 2,620, pupils 0·38 m., teachers 10,000.
Secondary: no. 268, p. 27,600. Technical: no. 117, st. 8,200. Teacher-training:
no. 54, st. 7,000, t. 565. Higher: no. 3, st. 3,500, t. 540.
UNIVERSITY (autonomous): U. de El Salvador, San Salvador: 3,400 st., 516 t.
(138 full-time).

MASS MEDIA

BROADCASTING: No. of receivers in use, end-1964: TV 27,000, radio 0·40 m. Stations:
TV 2, radio 36.
CINEMAS: No., 1960: 55. Attendance, 1960: total 15·1, per head 5·8.
NEWSPRINT: Consumption, 1964: total 7,800 tons, per head 2·8 kg.
NEWSPAPERS: Daily, 1963: 15. Estimated circulation 0·13 m., copies per 000 of pop.
47. Principal dailies in San Salvador (*circ. ooos*): *El Diario de Hoy* 65 (Sunday 82),
La Prensa Gráfica 54 (S. 84), *El Mundo;* evening: *Diario Latino* 17.
BOOKS: Titles published, 1963: 75.

GUATEMALA

ALBERTO FUENTES MOHR

History

IN the tropical lowlands in northern Guatemala, a region now almost unpopulated, the Maya civilisation flourished in its classic form from the 4th to the 9th centuries AD. After the Spanish conquest of Guatemala in 1524, a feudal system was founded which pervaded Guatemalan life for centuries afterwards. The mobilisation of unpaid labour permitted the development of what was known as the Captaincy-General of the Kingdom of Guatemala, which included not only present-day Guatemala but also El Salvador, Honduras, Nicaragua and Costa Rica—a colony with a rigidly organised economy which produced cocoa, indigo, leather, gold and silver.

At the end of the 18th century the Spaniards and their descendants were a small minority among a population overwhelmingly indigenous. Yet it was these descendants, many of them of mixed blood, who were to play the most important role in the immediate future of the country. In spite of being a fairly well educated and politically conscious group they did not enjoy the economic and social privileges held by the peninsular Spaniards. This situation made them particularly receptive to liberal ideas and it was this group which led the country to its independence and provided political leadership during the next half century.

Independence and civil war

Movements in favour of severing ties with Spain took place from 1811 onwards. The Captaincy-General of Guatemala proclaimed its independence on 15 September 1821, as a result of the defeat of the Spanish armies in Mexico. Conservative reaction was prompt to follow. In Mexico, General Agustín de Iturbide, whose abandonment of the Spanish camp with a large army had tipped the scales in favour of independence, had proclaimed himself head of a conservative empire which the Central American provinces were led to join while a Mexican army marched southwards. But the improvised emperor was soon dethroned, and in July 1823 a Central American constituent assembly confirmed the independence of the former kingdom of Guatemala under the name of United Central American Provinces.

The constituent assembly, which abolished slavery and introduced a number of reforms into the old colonial order, was under strong liberal influence; and so were the state and federal governments. But soon the federal executive, frustrated in its attempts to establish its authority, fell under conservative influence. Meanwhile, the provinces, inebriated with their newly acquired autonomy, were reluctant to accept a central authority and fell prey to disorders and rivalries which had been kept dormant by Spanish power.

Under these circumstances, in 1826 civil war became inevitable. It opposed, on the one hand, a federal executive increasingly under the influence of the conservative party and increasingly identified with the interests of the Guatemalan aristocracy, and on the other, an alliance of provincial forces under the leadership of the liberal party headed by the Honduran General Francisco Morazán.

By 1829, after a series of victories over the conservative forces, General Morazán reorganised the Federal Republic under a liberal administration. But in spite of Morazán's efforts to organise a modern state and ensure Central American unity, the country remained in a state of turmoil. The anarchic fiscal administration did not provide the means to sustain the government and lack of adequate communications made it difficult to control local uprisings. By 1839 the Federation had been dissolved and in 1840 Morazán went into exile after being routed by the Guatemalan chieftain Rafael Carrera. In 1842 Morazán made an attempt to re-establish the Federation after seizing the government of the state of Costa Rica, but local forces overcame him and he was captured and summarily executed. Thus ended a period of Central American history. From then onwards, and in spite of many successive attempts to re-establish the Federation, the republics of Guatemala, El Salvador, Honduras, Nicaragua and Costa Rica took separate courses.

The conservative years

Rafael Carrera, at the time of his victory over Morazán, was in his early twenties. An illiterate mestizo, audacious, cruel and of keen intelligence, he began his career at the head of a peasant rebellion against the established order and the new liberal legislation. The rebellion fed on the resentment of the ignorant and exploited rural population against the privileged urban classes; fanned by the church and ably channelled by conservative leaders, however, it had the paradoxical result of reverting Guatemala to the colonial order. From 1838 until his death in 1865 Carrera was the arbiter of Guatemalan public life. His chosen successor, General Cerna, held the presidency until the liberal revolution in 1871.

During the three decades of conservative rule colonial laws and customs were re-established. The church regained all its privileges. Under a strong authoritarian government Guatemala knew a period of peace which allowed it to be organised as an independent state. Although contacts with the outside world were as few as possible, Carrera was compelled in 1859 to sign a treaty with Britain recognising the latter's sovereignty over the portion of territory now known as British Honduras. In exchange, the British Government undertook to aid Guatemala with fifty thousand pounds for the construction of a road from the interior to the Atlantic coast. Britain's failure to honour this commitment is the basis of Guatemala's claim that the treaty is null and void and that consequently the territory which it calls Belize should return under its sovereignty.

The liberal revolution of 1871 and the 'liberal' regimes

Under the conservative regime the economy of the country—apart from the subsistence agriculture practised by the Indian masses—continued to be based on a few export products. The main one was the dye produced with cochineal, which in the 1860s declined precipitously in price as the result of the discovery and industrial production in Europe of artificial dyes. As other exports carried relatively little weight, a serious economic crisis affected

Guatemala. Cultivation of coffee—considered by some the export crop of the future—found many obstacles in the established order. Among these were concentration of lands and capital in the hands of the church, lack of credit, absence of transport facilities, lack of a labour market, and, in general, obsolete legislation on economic matters compounded by static governmental attitudes.

It was under these conditions that in 1871 the conservative regime was overthrown by a liberal revolution headed by an old respected liberal, Miguel García Granados, and the impetuous young Justo Rufino Barrios. Soon Barrios emerged as the main figure of the movement and instituted a 'liberal dictatorship'. Among the first measures taken by the revolutionary government were the separation of church and state and the outright confiscation of all clergy-held properties. Next, the government undertook to change the system of land tenure and to further the cultivation of coffee by distributing former church and crown lands among the favourites of the new regime. Foreign trade developed rapidly, based on coffee exports. Together with the distribution of land, the government gave great impulse to banking, sea ports were developed, and railways and telegraphic lines began to appear. In the fields of legislation and public administration a thoroughgoing reform took place. Education, taken away from the hands of the church, became more democratic and a responsibility of the state.

Barrios's larger aim was the reunification of Central America. Having failed to bring into his scheme three of the other Central American governments, he characteristically proceeded in 1885 to decree unilaterally the union of the five states which had belonged to the former Federation. Unconcerned by the displeasure of the United States and Mexican governments, he crossed the border into El Salvador at the head of his army. He was killed by an enemy bullet and the Guatemalan government gave up the attempt to unify Central America by force.

The liberal regime inaugurated in 1871 disrupted the relative peace which the rural population had come to enjoy. In the first place, the new agrarian legislation, with its emphasis on the registration of land titles, often meant the individual appropriation of lands cultivated by Indian communities or by peasants who had no such titles. Secondly, the scarcity of labour for the cultivation and harvesting of coffee resulted in the resurrection of the system of colonial levies.

After Barrios's death a succession of governments, most of them headed by generals of the army, competed with one another to preserve the interests of the new dominating class of coffee-growers, which were gradually merged with those of the older conservative aristocracy. Only in one respect did these governments maintain a liberal tradition—in their compliance with the laws separating church and state. Otherwise, even while keeping the trappings of a constitutional and representative democracy, they were dictatorships ranging from the mild to the utterly repressive. Most presidents acquired power by means of their control of the army and were dispossessed of it only through assassination, natural death, a coup d'état or popular explosions. While their legal term of office was six years, 're-elections' were frequent.

An important feature of the so-called liberal regimes was their over-generous attitude towards foreign investment, mainly of United States origin. This resulted in the establishment of monopolies in the fields of railway transportation and harbour facilities, the production and exportation of bananas, and power generation and distribution. The concessions which gave rise to these monopolies reflect, on the one hand, the appearance of the

United States as the paramount power in the Caribbean, and on the other, the need felt by dictatorial governments to be in Washington's good graces at a time when dollar diplomacy and the 'big stick' policy were proclaimed and enforced by military intervention in several Latin American countries. Indeed, many of the concessions granted coincide with political crises, plans for 're-election', or the seeking of recognition after a coup d'état.

The furtherance and protection of United States interests led to increasing intervention by Washington in Guatemala's affairs. By 1931 the United States minister was powerful enough to play a decisive role in the rise to power of General Jorge Ubico, the strong man who governed Guatemala during the next fourteen years.

The 1944 revolution and its aftermath

Ubico came to power when the country suffered a severe economic depression brought about by a decline in the price of coffee in the world market. His austere economic policies aggravated the crisis. Credit was restricted; salaries were lowered or frozen; public expenditure was kept at a low level and the public debt was paid off. These policies would not have been possible but for a harsh dictatorship with fascist overtones.

The regime's fascist tendencies, however, were concealed at the outbreak of the second world war. When the United States joined the conflict Guatemala followed suit, declaring war on the Axis powers, and the dictator was forced to render lip-service to the cause of democracy. The impact of the second world war on Guatemalan life was considerable. Allied propaganda became widespread. Public opinion enthusiastically supported the democratic cause and *sotto voce* comparisons began to be made between the ideals proclaimed in the Atlantic Charter and the state of affairs in Guatemala.

Meanwhile new factors were acting upon the country's economy. Coffee exports were limited by the war and Guatemala, unlike larger Latin American countries, was not as yet producing some of the manufactured goods which could not be imported. On the other hand, the United States government undertook the construction of an air base and of a strategic highway, and the scarcity of imported goods and the higher wages paid by the foreign contractors resulted in an inflationary pressure. Most wages, however, had not been adjusted for years, and it was increasingly hard for the middle class to support the burden of forced saving imposed by Ubico during fourteen years. Moreover, a sector of the upper class eager to engage in the industrial development made possible by the scarcity of imported goods was also made restive by the lack of credit and economic expansion under Ubico.

By the middle of 1944 both the economic and ideological factors which were to lead to the overthrow of the dictatorship existed among the urban population. Students at the national university, most of them of middle-class origin, began to voice their grievances. The repression exerted by the government resulted in the spreading of discontent and street demonstrations took place in Guatemala City which were fired upon unmercifully by the army and the police. The population's answer was a general strike, and Ubico chose then to surrender power to a military triumvirate which later elected among themselves General Federico Ponce as provisional president. With minor changes, Ponce's government was only a continuation of Ubico's, and it was soon obvious that the provisional regime aimed at perpetuating itself in power even while going through the formality of elections. Yet the government was unable to prevent the organisation of opposition parties where university students and teachers played a leading role. Soon hundreds of young leaders were touring the country, spreading their revolutionary ideas in provincial cities and rural areas, while demands for higher wages and improved working conditions led to the organisation of labour and peasant unions.

When several opposition parties chose as their presidential candidate Dr Juan José Arévalo—a relatively unknown university lecturer who had lived for many years in exile in Argentina—it was soon evident that he embodied the need for a change felt by the great majority of the population. Dissatisfaction with the repressive regime spread to a group of young army officers who on 20 October 1944 secured control of an army base from which arms were freely distributed to students and workers who routed government troops in the capital, while in the provinces scattered rebellions also took place.

With Ubico, Ponce and all the other army generals sent into exile, a junta of two young officers and a civilian was formed which held elections for legislative and constituent assemblies. These assemblies, formed mainly of representatives of the parties supporting Arévalo, were to define the ideological tendencies of the 1944 revolution. In essence, the revolution was a social democratic movement imbued with the type of nationalism common in several underdeveloped countries in the post-war period. The constitution put into force in 1945 diminished the powers of the executive branch of government and rendered the ministers responsible to congress; it forbade the re-election of the president; it established the army as a professional body not responsible to the president alone; it furthered the independence of the judiciary; and it sought to guarantee free elections and to avoid government interference in the electoral process. On the other hand, the state was given a definite responsibility in the fields of economic development, education and social security.

Arévalo's victory at the presidential elections held under the new constitution was overwhelming. Thus the revolution had not only succeeded in overthrowing the last of the 'liberal' governments and in creating a revolutionary consciousness among a large segment of the population; it had also established a new institutional framework and elected a government in accordance with the rules of constitutional democracy.

Arévalo's presidential term of office lasted from 1945 to 1951. Helped by an improvement in coffee prices his government furthered economic expansion with an emphasis on the redistribution of wealth through pro-labour legislation, the organisation of a social security system and greater educational facilities. Politically, Arévalo's aim was to acquaint the population with the workings of constitutional democracy, and in spite of many attempted coups d'état he was able to govern without the repression which up to 1944 was a Guatemalan tradition. Relations with the United States, however, tended to deteriorate, not only because the government exerted pressure against the United Fruit Company and other US firms which often found themselves in labour conflicts, but also because of Washington's increasing concern about Arévalo's refusal to repress Communist or pro-Communist elements active in the labour movement. At the height of the cold war this was regarded with suspicion by the State Department.

When at the end of his term in 1951 Arévalo surrendered power to his elected successor, Colonel Jacobo Arbenz, relations with the United States reached their lowest ebb. While Washington was taking an increasingly uncompromising attitude towards the Guatemalan government, Arbenz was depending more than Arévalo on left-wing forces, including the newly organised Communist Party. But in spite of the verbal radicalism adopted by his government and the conspicuousness of Communist leaders, the programme under which Arbenz was elected, and which he began to put into force, was not a Communist one. Its aim was to set the basis for a more rapid and independent economic development through four main projects: first, the construction of a road from the interior to the Atlantic coast, which would compete with the railway monopoly; secondly, the development of a port on the Atlantic, which would also compete with the harbour owned by the railway company; thirdly, the building of a large hydroelectric plant near the capital city, which would lessen dependence on the power monopoly; and fourthly, an agrarian reform expropriating uncultivated lands over and above a basic exemption of 222 acres, with payments to the owners to be made in bonds redeemable in twenty years, and with provisions to allot the property thus acquired to landless peasants who would acquire their individual plots in usufruct.

In June 1954, two years after the agrarian reform law had been enacted, some 1,500,000 acres had been expropriated, including uncultivated lands belonging to the United Fruit Company. Together with 500,000 acres of national lands these had been allotted to about 100,000 peasants either in individual plots or through cooperatives. Besides, about twelve million dollars' worth of credit had been granted to the new property owners. These measures were undoubtedly bringing into the political arena the traditionally isolated rural population which, slowly awakening, was beginning to lose its passivity. But this was a cause for concern even for segments of the urban population which had originally supported the revolution. Moreover, the administration of the agrarian reform was not free of arbitrary and corrupt practices, so that while gaining support in the rural areas, the government lost it in the capital and other cities.

Meanwhile, the United States decision to change the course of affairs in Guatemala had become evident. At the Inter-American Conference in Caracas in March 1954, Secretary of State Dulles obtained a majority vote for a resolution condemning the 'domination or control of the political institutions of any American State by the International Communist movement', which was clearly aimed at Guatemala. In the meantime, the Central Intelligence Agency became engaged in activities tending to subvert the army, and it patronised a counterrevolutionary force made up of Guatemalan exiles and foreign elements which was organised in Honduras and Nicaragua under the command of Carlos Castillo Armas, a colonel who had previously fled Guatemala after taking part in an attempted revolt. When this force invaded Guatemala in June 1954, the government appealed to the Security Council of the United Nations, but ineffectively. In spite of world-wide publicity and strong popular reaction in most Latin American countries against United States intervention, the position of the Arbenz government became untenable. Pressure from the US embassy led the chief military leaders to seek a compromise with Castillo Armas, Arbenz resigned the presidency and took asylum in the Mexican embassy, and in spite of attempted armed resistance by some of the peasants favoured by the agrarian reform, Castillo Armas became head of state with the enthusiastic support of the clergy, the upper class and a sizeable segment of the middle class. Subsequently political repression became acute and the lands expropriated under the agrarian reform were given back to their original owners. Massive US aid to the Castillo Armas regime led to larger public and private investment, but for the great majority of the population the maintenance of a

H

defective land tenure system and the outlawing of labour and peasant organisations meant that their incomes were kept at subsistence or very low levels.

In 1957 Castillo Armas was assassinated. Facing street riots and a growing opposition, his heirs were compelled to surrender power to General Miguel Ydígoras Fuentes, who had been elected to the presidency by a combination of forces which stretched from conservatives to revolutionaries. Ydígoras, while following a conservative line, put an end to the political repression experienced under Castillo Armas, but the government's record was not helped by an economic recession from 1957 to 1961. With presidential elections due in 1963 it appeared that the revolutionary opposition might be successful in re-electing former president Juan José Arévalo. This was a cause for concern for several military leaders, who blamed Ydígoras for taking too bland an attitude towards the revolutionary groups. Favoured by Ydígoras' loss of popularity, therefore, in March 1963 the army ousted him from the presidency and decided to keep power for three years before allowing a return to constitutional normalcy.

Political parties

Whereas before 1944 political activities were traditionally limited to a relatively small urban sector, the attempt made after the revolution to bring about a transformation of the basic economic and social structure mobilised a larger segment of public opinion. The traditional liberal and conservative parties disappeared with the 1944 revolution and new political groups came into existence. The Revolutionary Party (PR)—an organisation with tendencies similar to Venezuela's Acción Democrática or Peru's APRA—appears as the main heir to the 1944 movement even though its purge of left-wing elements and the existence of more radical groups do not make it the only representative of the revolution. The National Liberation Movement (MLN), a right-wing party founded by Castillo Armas, is the main advocate of aggressive anti-communism even though other right-wing parties, generally more moderate, are sometimes organised as short-lived entities. Finally, it appears as if the Christian Democratic Party, trying to follow the Chilean pattern, might also become an important movement, while the Communist Party (Partido Guatemalteco del Trabajo—PGT) remains active as a clandestine group.

Before holding elections in March 1966 the military government patronised a new party—the Party of Democratic Institutions (PID)—which was expected to win at the polls through official favour. Reflecting the population's increased political consciousness, however, a relatively heavy ballot resulted in the victory of the PR's presidential candidate, Julio César Mendez Montenegro, former dean of the National University's law faculty. The PR also won more than half the seats in Congress and over fifty per cent of the local governments.

The defeat by the PR of both the candidates of the military government and of the MLN was due in part to the fact that other left-wing movements, including the Christian Democrats, were not allowed to present candidates; but in any case the electoral results reveal a widely held conviction that somehow the 1944 revolution is bound to proceed on its course.

It is also significant that in spite of strong resistance from some sectors of the military government, Mendez Montenegro was allowed to inaugurate his administration in July 1966. Since then, armed action from Communist-led guerrillas which became active under the military regime, as well as right-wing terrorism, have provoked political difficulties which have been compounded by an economic recession caused by conditions in the coffee market. Yet, by the end of 1967 the government seemed to have strengthened its position and most Guatemalans agreed that its survival was essential to achieve the peaceful change which is required for the country's development.

ECONOMY

From 1950 to 1965 the Guatemalan economy showed a relatively slow rate of growth. While population increased at a rate of over 3 per cent p.a., the GNP averaged an annual growth of 5 per cent. There is evidence that the unequal distribution of wealth has become more pronounced. While in 1950 the average per capita income of subsistence farmers and agricultural wage-earners—including about sixty-five per cent of the population—was in the neighbourhood of $87, at present it is estimated at some $83. On the other hand, about 7 per cent of the population enjoys an average per capita income of around $2,200 as against an average of $1,750 in 1950.

Both the slow growth of the economy and the uneven distribution of wealth are largely the result of the very few changes that have taken place in the systems of land tenure and agricultural production. About 70 per cent of all lands in private hands are held by only 2 per cent of all existing properties, with an average area of 875 acres, while 88 per cent of all properties, with an average area of a little more than 4 acres, extend over only 14 per cent of privately held lands. These small properties, moreover, are generally found in the highland districts, where soil fertility is poor. Another obstacle to economic development is the fact that a large segment of the population of Indian origin has not been fully integrated, socially or economically, into the life of the country. Nearly half the Republic's inhabitants could be classed in this segment.

The Guatemalan economy continues to be dependent on the exportation of a few commodities. With 187 million US dollars' worth of exports in 1965, coffee constitutes 45 per cent of the total, the remainder being mainly cotton, meat, sugar, bananas and essential oils. The country has, therefore, been subject to periodical crises resulting from falls in the price of coffee in the world market. Apart from the effects of these fluctuations on private investment, the dependence of fiscal revenues on import and export duties has meant that public expenditure has a tendency to rise and fall together with foreign trade. Thus after a period of increasing exports which reached its peak in 1954 a sharp fall of coffee prices brought a period of recession from 1957 to 1961 which was accompanied by a decline in public investment. The lack of tax reforms and a mounting public debt, both internal and external, has meant that in the years following 1961 repayments have absorbed a large proportion of public savings, thus leaving very little for investment.

Together with a serious fiscal crisis, the country confronts an increasing pressure on its balance of payments. The failure to curb imports, together with an expansion of credit while exports fail to keep pace with imports, has resulted in a situation in which the balance of payments is kept afloat by means of short-term indebtedness, both private and public.

In the field of recent development, long-term US nickel and steel investments have been started in the Lake Izabel area, and in 1966 US concerns began to consider reactivation of old silver, zinc and lead mines. Oil exploration is due to begin on the Pacific side where communications are good, but the sizeable natural gas deposits discovered in the Peten area near the British Honduras border remain unexploited owing to bad communications.

The immediate difficulties with which the Guatemalan economy is faced cannot be attributed, as in the case of other Latin American countries, to the problems of growth. It would rather seem that these difficulties are the result of lack of development, and that the solutions to long-term stagnation and the immediate fiscal and balance-of-payments difficulties, as well as a more decisive and profitable participation in the Central American Common Market, will require Guatemala to undertake structural reforms in fields such as taxation, land tenure and agricultural production.

BIBLIOGRAPHY

Bancroft, Hubert Howe. *History of Central America*, The History Co. Publishers, San Francisco, 1886–87.
Burgess, Paul. *Justo Rufino Barrios*, Dorrance, Philadelphia, 1926.
Curtis, Wilgus A. *South American Dictators during the First Century of Independence*, George Washington Univ. Press, Washington, 1937.
Gage, Thomas. *Travels in the New World*, ed. J. Eric S. Thompson, Univ. of Oklahoma Press, Norman, 1958.
Galich, Manuel. *Por Qué Lucha Guatemala*, Elmer Editor, Buenos Aires, 1956.
Jones, Chester Lloyd. *Guatemala, Past and Present*, Univ. of Minnesota Press, Minneapolis, 1940.
Morley, Sylvanus Griswold. *The Ancient Maya*, Stanford Univ. Press, Stanford, Calif., 1960.
Munro, Dana G. *The Five Republics of Central America: Their Political and Economic Development and Their Relations with the United States*, Oxford Univ. Press, New York, 1918. *The United States and the Caribbean Area*, Boston World Peace Foundation, Boston, 1934.
Recinos, Adrian. 'Centenary of Justo Rufino Barrios, 1835–1885', *Bulletin of the Pan American Union*, Vol. 69, New York.
Recinos, Adrian and Vuh, Popol. *The Sacred Book of the Ancient Quiché Maya*, Univ. of Oklahoma Press, Norman, 1950.
Stephens, John L. *Incidents of Travel in Central America, Chiapas and Yucatan*, Rutgers Univ. Press, New Brunswick, 1949.
Toriello, Guillermo. *La Batalla de Guatemala. Cuadernos Americanos*, 39, Mexico, 1955.

BASIC INFORMATION

CLIMATE

Guatemala City

Lat./long.	14° 30′ N, 90° 30′ W	Relative humidity at midday of hottest and coolest months	55%/69%
Altitude	4,855 ft/1,479 m.		
Mean temp. of hottest month	22°C/72°F (May)	Wettest month	10·8 in./274 mm. (June)
Mean temp. of coolest month	17°C/63°F (Jan.)	Driest month	0·1 in./2 mm. (Feb.)
Absolute max.	90°F/32°C		
Absolute min.	41°F/5°C	Annual av. rainfall	51·8 in./1,316 mm.

POPULATION

TOTAL (*million*): 1964 (census) 4·28, adjusted 4·44; end-1966: 4·65; 1980 (ECLA projection): 6·94.
DENSITY, mid-1965: 41 persons per sq. km.
CRUDE RATES (*per 000*), 1965: birth 43·5, death 16·8, infant mortality 94·6.
GROWTH RATES (% *p.a.*): 1945–60: 2·9; 1960–5: 3·3.

DISTRIBUTION (% *of total pop.*): Ethnic, 1950: Amerindian 54, mixed 46. Foreign-born, 1950: 1·1. Languages, 1950: Spanish, many Maya-Quiche dialects and Mexican Pipil and Nahuatl. Religion, 1950: Roman Catholic 97, Protestant 3. Urban (*centres 2,000 inhab. or over*), ECLA data, 1950: 24·0; 1960: 29·9; 1980 (*proj.*): 41·6. Largest cities (*000 inhab.*), 1964: Guatemala City 573, Quezaltenango 45, Escuintla 25, Puerto Barrios 22.

CONSTITUTIONAL SYSTEM

CONSTITUTION: First, as Republic, 1851; main 1879; next 1945, replaced 1954; 1956, replaced 1963 by Fundamental Charter of Government; latest 1965, effective May 1966. Article 266 of 1965 constitution provides for amendments relating to Central American union and to the incorporation of Belize.

SYSTEM: Unitary republic, composed of 22 departments (divided into municipalities) and the Central District (Guatemala City and environs). Separate executive, legislature and judiciary.

EXECUTIVE: Power vested in president, who is elected by absolute majority of votes for 4-year term; no immediate reelection. Congress elects president if no absolute majority at general election. He appoints ministers of state and departmental governors. Council of State of 15 members, composed of the vice-president and representatives of Congress, Supreme Court, professions, municipalities, urban and rural workers, and industrial sectors, acts as a consultative body.

LEGISLATURE: Uni-cameral Congress. *Congress:* Two deputies (and one alternate) for each electoral district and an additional deputy for each 100,000 inhabitants or fraction over 50,000 when pop. exceeds 200,000; elected by popular vote for 4-year term, and may be reelected once only, after lapse of one term. *Suffrage:* Universal, compulsory voting for literate adults over 18 years of age; optional for illiterates. *Elections*, March 1966: presidential (*000 votes*): Julio César Méndez Montenegro 201, Juan de Dios Aguilar de León 146, Miguel Ángel Ponciano 110. No absolute majority; Dr Méndez elected president by Congress, by 35 votes to 19. Congressional: Partido Revolucionario 30 seats, Institucional Democrático 20, Movimiento de Liberación Nacional 5.

JUDICIARY: Supreme Court (of at least 7 judges) and courts of appeal (9 civil and 2 labour); judges elected by Congress for 4-year term and may be reelected. Supreme Court appoints judges of courts of first instance and lower courts.

DEFENCE

DEFENCE BUDGET: 1964: 11 m. quetzales, 0·8% of GDP.
ARMED FORCES: Military service: between 18–50 years of age; 2 years in army. Strength: army about 7,000; total about 8,000 plus trained reserve.

INTERNATIONAL RELATIONS

Member of the UN and many of its international specialised agencies, including: IBRD and affiliates, IMF, FAO, ICAO, ILO, ITU, UNDP, UNESCO, UPU, WHO and WMO; IAEA; UNCTAD representative. Also a member of OAS, Alliance for Progress, ECLA, IDB, BCIE, ODECA and CACM.

ECONOMY

PRODUCTION

AGRICULTURE (*000 tons*)	*1948–53*[1]	*63/64*	*64/65*	*65/66*[2]
Coffee	58	105	98	120
Cotton (lint)	2	65	72	87
Bananas	191	154	124	90
Sugar (cane)	31	144	132	159
Maize	460	589	643	678

[1] Average 1948/9—1952/3.   [2] Provisional.

LAND (%), 1950: Arable 14, permanent pasture 5, forested 44, other 37.
OTHER AGRICULTURAL DATA: Agricultural holdings, 1950 (census): No. 348,687, area 3·72 m. hectares. Fertiliser consumption (*ooo tons*), 1965/6: 14·5.
LIVESTOCK: Nos. (*m. head*), 1964/5: cattle 1·55, sheep 0·77, pigs 0·43.
FISH: Landed (*ooo tons*), 1965: total 3·7.
MINING, 1963: (*ooo tons*) Iron ore 6, zinc 1·2, lead 0·7; (*tons*) silver 2·0. Other minerals include antimony, mercury, nickel, sulphur and uranium.
MANUFACTURING, 1965: (*ooo tons*) Cement 231, wheat flour 60; (*m. litres*) beer 23. Wood (*cu. metres, sawn*), 1963: 97,000.
CONSTRUCTION (*ooo sq. metres floor area*), 1965: Guatemala City: building permits approved 424, buildings completed 153.

ENERGY

CONSUMPTION (*tons coal equiv.*) 1964: Total 0·75 m., per head 0·175.
ELECTRICITY, 1965: Generated (*kwh*) 480 m., installed capacity (*kw*) 102,600.

GOVERNMENT EXPENDITURE

DISTRIBUTION (% *of total*), 1967: Defence 9, education 6, health and social assistance 8, communications and public works 22.

GROSS PRODUCT

GDP (*ooo m. quetzales*): at current market prices, 1964: 1·33; 1965: 1·43; at 1958 market prices, 1964: 1·34; 1965: 1·44. Per head (*US$*), UN estimate, 1964: 295.
DISTRIBUTION (%), 1964: Agriculture 28, manufacturing 14, trade 29.
GROWTH RATES (%), 1950–60: 3·8, per head 0·8; 1960–4: 6·1, per head 2·8.

EXTERNAL TRADE (*US$ m.*)	*1955*	*1960*	*1963*	*1964*	*1965*	*1966*
EXPORTS (f.o.b.)	107	117	154	167	187	228
Coffee	76	79	78	72	92	.
Cotton	5	6	25	32	34	.
Bananas	17	17	12	10	4	.
IMPORTS (c.i.f.)	107	138	171	202	229	207
TRADE BALANCE	+1	−21	−17	−35	−42	+20

DIRECTION OF TRADE (%)

	Exports			Imports		
	1955	*1960*	*1965*	*1955*	*1960*	*1965*
CACM	(1·7)	4·3	19·2	(1·4)	4·9	13·7
LAFTA	(0·1)	0·2	—	(5·6)	1·4	1·9
USA	74·1	55·6	36·7	65·1	48·9	42·2
EEC	15·7	28·2	22·6	11·4	21·0	17·8
UK	0·6	0·7	0·9	3·7	4·1	4·6

FINANCE

EXCHANGE RATE (*quetzales/US$*): Par value, end-year, 1960: 1·00; 1966: 1·00.
BALANCE OF PAYMENTS (*US$ m.*): Goods and services (net), 1960: −26; 1964: −49; 1965: −57.
COST OF LIVING (*Dec. 1958=100*), Guatemala City, December, 1960: 97; 1964: 99; 1965: 98; 1966: 101.
INDUSTRIAL WAGES: Earnings in manufacturing, 1965: Guatemala City, 0·37 quetzales; minima: 0·17–0·25 quetzales.
TREASURY ACCOUNTS (*m. quetzales*), 1965: Revenue 122·6, expenditure 128·5, deficit 6.

EMPLOYMENT

ECONOMICALLY ACTIVE (%), 1964 (census sample): 31 (men 54, women 8). In agriculture 65, manufacturing 12, services 12 and trade 6.

TRANSPORT AND COMMUNICATIONS

RAILWAYS: Traffic, 1963: 207 m. net ton-km. Length of track 1,150 km.
MOTOR VEHICLES: In use (ooo), 1964: pass. cars 28, comm. vehicles 15. Road system 12,200 km., paved 1,500.
SHIPPING: Merchant fleet (ooo g.r. tons), 1966: 3·6. International sea-borne shipping (ooo tons), 1962: goods loaded 308, goods unloaded 750. Main ports: Puerto Barrios, Matías de Gálvez, San José and Champerico.
AIR: Scheduled services, 1964: Total 34 m. pass.-km., 2·9 m. cargo ton-km. International: 21 m. pass.-km., 2·4 m. cargo ton-km. Main airport: Guatemala City: La Aurora (international).
TELEPHONES: No. in use, 1964: 23,400.

SOCIAL WELFARE

SYSTEM: Social insurance benefits and services administered by the Instituto Guatemalteco de Seguridad Social. Financed by contributions based on remuneration: employees 1–2%, employers 3–5%, the state 1·5–2·5%. Employment legislation covers working hours; holidays; payment of wages, overtime and annual bonus; employers' liability for compensation for accidents, dismissal and death indemnities.
HEALTH: 3,600 persons per physician, 420 persons per hospital bed.
NUTRITION: Net food supply (per head per day), 1962: 2,160 calories, protein 58 g.

EDUCATION

ILLITERACY RATE (%), 1950: 15 years and over, 70; 1964: 62.
COMPULSORY: 6 years (between 7 and 14 years of age). School enrolment ratios (%), 1st and 2nd levels, 1963: 28, adjusted 38.
SCHOOLS, 1963: Pre-school and primary: no. 4,300, pupils 0·40 m, teachers 12,100. Secondary: no. 211, p. 30,300, t. 3,870. Technical: no. 50, st. 4,460, t. 855. Teacher-training: no. 89, st. 5,100, t. 1,080. Higher (universities): no. 2, st. 6,870, t. 514.
UNIVERSITIES: Guatemala City: U. de San Carlos de Guatemala (autonomous but largely financed by state): 6,340 st., t. 450. U. Rafael Landívar (private): 530 st., t. 64.

MASS MEDIA

BROADCASTING: No. of receivers in use, 1965: TV 55,000; 1961: radio 0·21 m. Stations: TV 3, radio 84.
CINEMAS: No., 1962: 115. Attendance, 1962: total 9·7 m., per head 2·4.
NEWSPRINT: Consumption, 1964: total 4,600 tons, per head 1·1 kg.
NEWSPAPERS: Daily, 1962: 8. Estimated circulation 0·13 m., copies per ooo of population 31. Principal dailies in Guatemala City (circ. ooo): Prensa Libre 40, El Imparcial 34, Impacto 22; evening: Diario de Centro América 12, La Hora 12.
BOOKS: Titles published, 1963: 90.

HONDURAS

FRANKLIN D. PARKER

HONDURAS is the middle of the five states of Central America, both in geography and population. Guatemala and El Salvador, each of which has a larger population than Honduras, lie to the north-west. Nicaragua and Costa Rica, each with a smaller population, lie to the south-east. All five were once united under Spanish rule, and remained so for a few years after the Spanish hold on their great isthmus was relinquished. Since their separation, Honduras has often been considered the most impoverished and least developed of them all. Yet 20th-century Honduras, plagued as she has been with a host of problems, has not been so backward politically as two of her immediate neighbours; and very recently she has moved both economically and culturally toward a livelier participation in the affairs of the hemisphere of which she lies so near the heart.

HISTORY

The people of Honduras, who numbered two million in 1963, are a mixture of Indian, Negro and Spanish, with the Indian element predominant. The eleven Indian languages known to have been spoken in the region before it was discovered by Columbus were of seven linguistic stocks, testimony of the extent to which this was a meeting ground of cultures from both north and south. The earliest Indian group now recognised were the Maya who inhabited Copán and made it a centre of astronomical study and arithmetical knowledge second to none in the entire world of the first Christian millennium; many Chortí Maya inhabit the area near Copán today. The most extensive Indian group of the 16th century were the Lenca, whose historical ties remain undefined but whose culturally distinct descendants form nearly half the population of three of the Honduran *departamentos* facing El Salvador. The latest Indian language to arrive was that of the Black Caribs, a group with part-African ancestry who came from the Antilles in the late 18th century and form a separate element on the north coast. Two other tiny linguistic enclaves persist, the Jicaque and the Paya in the north-east, but the great mass of Hondurans today, regardless of the extent of Indian ancestry, speak Spanish.

Spaniards and Negroes first came to Honduras to live in 1524. The Spaniards were interested in farming the land and exploiting the scattered findings of gold and silver. As time went by, a number of Africans, probably greater than that of the Spaniards, came to serve as labourers. Within sixty years the Spaniards founded Trujillo, San Pedro Sula, Gracias, Comayagua, Choluteca, San Jorge de Olancho (a gold-mining site no longer on the map), and Tegucigalpa (originally a producer of silver).

Gracias was for a short time (1544–9) the seat of the Spanish administration (*audiencia*) ruling the entire isthmus. When the isthmian capital was moved to Santiago de Guatemala, however, Honduras became a relatively neglected land, with only her two local capitals (Comayagua and Tegucigalpa) of any real importance in Spanish life. The population became mixed until it was about nine-tenths homogeneous, but reached less than 200 thousand in numbers by the time of independence in 1821. English-speaking Negroes and whites came into Honduras with the acquisition of the Bay Islands in 1859, and since then there has been an influx of English-speaking Negroes from the West Indies settling along the north coast.

Honduras was the scene of much turbulence during the first half-century of freedom from Spain. Native sons played an active role in the Central American federation of 1821–39, José Cecilio del Valle writing the declaration of independence and Francisco Morazán serving two terms (1830–9) as president. Federal interventions stunted the growth of local self-reliance, however, and after 1837 civil strife became incessant as unionists and anti-unionists fought all over the isthmus. Honduras had no real chance to catch her breath even under the rule of the anti-unionist *caudillos* Francisco Ferrera (1841–7), Santos Guardiola (1856–62) and José María Medina (1863–72). The only bright period during all this time was the rule of Juan Lindo (1847–52), the creator of Tegucigalpa's university. A contract signed in 1853 for an interoceanic railway might have done a great deal to develop the country, but unfortunately the railroad has never been built.

A new era began with the presidencies of Marco Aurelio Soto (1876–83) and Luis Bográn (1883–91). Law codes replaced the caprice of individuals as the will of the state, which was governed after 1880 from Tegucigalpa. The first cart roads were built, money was stabilised, banks were formed, and foreign investment made welcome in mining. Science was introduced in the university, secular primary schools were established, and the national library and archives organised. Such a renaissance in the life of Honduras was bound to produce some demand for democracy in government. Those who opposed Bográn for his second term chose the theme of democracy as their platform in founding the Liberal Party. Lawyer Policarpo Bonilla, chief among this group when the party was organised in 1890–1, became president for 1893–9 by means of revolution.

The years from 1891 to 1923 were a time when most presidential candidates considered themselves Liberals, but when few elections were carried out in the manner prescribed by liberalism. The growth of the banana industry on the north coast and the greatly increased interest of the United States in isthmian affairs changed the setting for the political conflicts (as the fruit companies or the United States favoured one side or the other), but not their nature. The idea of a new party to work for a national consensus to stop the perennial strife occurred to more than one group. When the originally popular president Francisco Bertrand (1911–12, 1913–15, 1916–19) attempted to choose his own successor, he was opposed by such a party led by the journalist Paulino Valladares and the soldier Tiburcio Carías Andino. In 1923 this group chose to name itself the National Party.

Under her ninth constitution (1924–36) Honduras for a time enjoyed free elections in which the contenders each four years were the Nationalists and a reorganised party of Liberals. The peaceful alternation of parties in power (marred only by one brief conflict in 1932) seemed to indicate a greater political maturity than achieved at that time by any other state on the isthmus. Honduras became during these same years the world's foremost producer of bananas, her first big source of revenue. Tiburcio Carías Andino broke the political pattern in 1936 by continuing himself in power without holding elections. During Carías' entire 16 years in the presidency (1933–49), despite the new revenues there was very little development of the nation apart from the banana coast. Juan Manuel Gálvez (1949–54), Carías' choice as successor, finally brought in new ideas (the first paved roads, an income tax and a central bank, for instance) which by this time were already familiar to Honduras' neighbours.

Gálvez did what he could in 1954 to return to the practice of fair elections. His own Nationalist party split over the desire of Carías to return to office, the minority of dissidents organising the National Reformist movement. This gave the advantage to Ramón Villeda Morales, the physician who became the candidate of the Liberals and for the first time (by taking a pro-labour stand in a great north-coast strike) gave this party an orientation clearly to the left of the Nationalists. Villeda won a plurality of the popular vote, but was blocked from the presidency when the Nationalists and Reformists refused to provide a quorum in Congress for his or anyone else's election. In this impasse, Vice-President Julio Lozano Díaz constitutionally assumed power, but then set about organising his own party which somehow won every seat in the 1956 elections for a new constitutional convention.

Lozano was evicted two weeks after his elections by a three-man military junta. New and fair elections were held in September 1957, seating thirty-six Liberals, eighteen Nationalists, and four Reformists in a convention which wrote Honduras' eleventh constitution. Ramón Villeda Morales was chosen by this body as president, to serve until December 1963. The new constitution gave the unicameral Congress (elected like the president for a six-year period) an important role, both in choosing the nation's judiciary and in making final executive decisions should a contest of wills arise between the president and the chief of the armed forces. The strange provision that the chief of the armed forces should have the right to dispute a president's orders (the dispute then to be taken to Congress) was an acknowledgement of the role the military had played in ridding the nation of Lozano.

President Villeda Morales came near serving out his term. During his not-quite-six years in office, the pulse of the whole nation quickened. Schools were built on a scale never before envisioned; public health programmes were much strengthened; a social security system was introduced; a radical labour code gave real dignity to employees and their labour unions. A fifty-four-year-old boundary dispute with Nicaragua was settled peacefully and entirely in accord with Honduras' contentions. Yet though Villeda's regime was energetic, it was not extreme in most respects. Armed insurrections by one Armando Velásquez Cerrato were of course put down, but harsh criticism of the regime from both left and right was allowed to continue. A civil guard directly responsible to the president was created in 1959, but an army major was chosen to head it. An agrarian reform programme was adopted in 1962, but Villeda promised that it would be implemented or modified in such fashion as to meet objections of the fruit companies. As a final gesture, Villeda in 1963 invited the Organization of American States to observe the elections for the following term.

The elections were scheduled for 13 October. Modesto Rodas Alvarado, candidate of the Liberals, stated openly that as president he would seek amendment of the constitution to eliminate the privileged position of the chief of the armed forces. Rodas was considered by outsiders the contender likely to win, though his opponent Ramón Ernesto Cruz was the candidate of a reunited National Party. Neither Rodas nor Cruz stood a chance, however, when Colonel Oswaldo López Arellano, chief of the armed forces, on 3 October simply deposed President Villeda Morales and called off the voting.

López Arellano now made himself provisional president while the nation once again went through the paces of choosing a constitutional convention. Shortly before the elections for the latter gathering, held early in 1965, the Nationalists announced that if they should win a majority they would keep López Arellano in the presidency. The announced results were thirty-five seats for the Nationalists and twenty-nine for the Liberals (later thirty-seven to twenty-seven when two Liberals refused to serve). Honduras' twelfth constitution took effect on 6 June 1965, when López was inaugurated for a six-year term. A month and a half later, Tiburcio Carías Castillo, son of the leader whose sixteen-year rule lay but sixteen years in the background, became foreign minister of the new government.

ECONOMY

Despite the political problems, the first sixteen years after the step-down of the older Tiburcio Carías saw a considerable change in the face of Honduras. Some of the change can be shown by statistics, though these contain distressing as well as hopeful aspects. The remainder is a change in spirit, based partly upon the solid groundwork laid by Juan Manuel Gálvez and Ramón Villeda Morales and partly upon the new horizons of the 'sixties.

The GNP of Honduras advanced from 384 million lempiras or $192 million in 1948 to $427 million in 1963. (The rate of exchange, 2 lempiras = $1, has been constant.) The country's exports increased from $55 million in 1948 to $84 million in 1963. If Honduras' population had not increased during this period, these figures would seem quite significant. But on a per capita basis, the national income from 1948 to 1963 increased only from $152 to $211, while the nation's exports actually lost slight ground, from $44 to $41. Even the rise in per capita income disappears when a forty-per-cent inflation in retail prices during this period is also taken into account. When it is remembered that because of the very unequal distribution of wealth the great majority of Hondurans have incomes much lower than the average the picture seems bleak indeed.

A brighter side to the statistics can be found through an analysis of components. From 1948 to 1963 the proceeds from manufacturing increased from seven to thirteen per cent of the Honduran national product, and trade increased from ten to thirteen per cent, while agriculture decreased from fifty-three to forty-two per cent. From the 1950 census to that of 1961, the percentage of economically active persons engaged in agricultural pursuits dropped from eighty-three to sixty-seven, while the percentage employed in manufacturing enterprises rose from six to eight, that in trade from one-and-a-half to five, and that in service occupations from four-and-a-half to twelve. These figures contain more than one indication of a move from a subsistence to a developing economy. Nearly two-thirds of those performing service occupations in 1961, for instance, were family domestic servants. Their great increase in number seems best explained by the presumption of an increase in the number of families financially able to hire them. This in turn suggests, regardless of the size of the servants' earnings, that there already exists the beginning of a wider distribution of wealth, a factor of great significance.

An analysis of exports develops this side of the picture further. Bananas constituted sixty-one per cent of Honduras' sales to the outside world in 1953 but only forty per cent ten years later. Coffee, the second most valuable item on the list, stood close to seventeen per cent at both ends of this time span. Lumber exports (mostly worked pine), on the other hand, nearly doubled during this period. Lead and zinc were added to silver as significant mineral commodities. A market was found in El Salvador for Honduran corn and beans, while nearly twice as many live hogs and cattle were delivered to El Salvador and Guatemala respectively, and fresh beef in sizeable quantities was for the first time carried from Honduras to the United States. Add to this a new interest in the cultivation of cotton for Italy, Japan and West Germany, and one sees the beginnings of a genuine economic diversification. If the trend in this direction continues, such emergencies as the ruination of six million acres of pine forest by ravages of pine beetle in 1962–4 need never approach the proportions of a national catastrophe.

Developments in the decade of the Alliance for Progress (as originally conceived, ten years beginning in 1961) have brought additional promise. One major factor is Honduras' participation since 1962 in the Central American Common Market, with the very exciting possibilities this raises. It is true that in the first few years Honduras benefited less from the association than any of her partners. But such is the case only because she was the least equipped to take advantage of the new conditions. With electric power available from Lake Yojoa since 1963 and the near-completion of four cross-country highways, it seems that Honduras will soon be in a position to earn her full share of the surging intra-regional commerce. In September 1966 she gained the Common Market's permission to give more fiscal incentives to investors than other Common Market members.

A second major reason for new hope in the 'sixties is the decision of banana companies owned in the United States to invest new money in Honduras. The United Fruit Company, operating from Puerto Cortés and Tela, had been hesitant for some time concerning this shore, where floods, blow-downs, labour strife and plant disease had seriously affected its operations. Since 1963, however, it has joined its competitor the Standard Fruit Company (whose port is La Ceiba) in the production of new varieties of disease-resistant bananas, in the use of boxes in place of bags for shipping the fruit, and in the development of other tropical agricultural interests. With her other sources of revenue continuing, Honduras exported nearly fifty per cent more bananas in 1965 than in 1964. This new stimulus to activity on the north coast is certain to help San Pedro Sula continue the phenomenal progress which in 1964 made it the fastest growing city in Central America.

Every year but one since 1960 (the exception is the year of the forceful overthrow of the government) both Honduras' GNP and her total value of exports have grown far faster than her population. The chief lag in the years 1963–5 was the slowness of the government (not foreign or national business-men) to invest available funds. If this handicap is overcome (and the 1965–9 National Plan of Economic and Social Development devised in late 1965 suggests strongly that it will be), the first decade of the Alliance for Progress will be a good one for a large number of Hondurans.

THE OLD AND THE NEW

In other ways than in business, Honduras is moving ahead. Her annual death rate, with better medical care available, was cut back from twelve per thousand in 1955 to ten in 1963. Her percentage of children of primary-school age who were attending school moved up from forty in 1957 to fifty-two in 1963. Illiteracy among persons over ten years of age dropped from sixty-five per cent in 1950 to fifty-three per cent in 1961. In 1963 there were nearly three times the number of trucks, over five times as many automobiles, and nearly thirty times as many buses as in 1950. But it should not be forgotten that in 1961, with three-quarters of the population still living in rural areas, ninety-one per cent of rural homes were without piped water (inside or outside the residence) and ninety-eight per cent without electricity, while the elsewhere ubiquitous sewing machine and radio had reached only eleven and eight per cent of rural homes respectively. A part of Honduras' charm for the visitor lies, of course, precisely in the fact that it is so easy to escape from radio and television to her vast expanses of solitude, and that, for example, while nearly one-half of rural homes are lighted by kerosene lamps a roughly equal number make the *ocote* or pine torch serve that purpose.

The speed at which Honduras moves towards full statehood in a renewed Central American union, and a role in the modern world, will in part depend on her intellectual and artistic leadership. Honduras' university, growing in quality as well as enrolment, has recently adopted a general studies requirement which should do much to encourage individual responsibility toward the nation. The careers of recent Honduran writers indicate that even before this innovation such a quality was not missing.

Rafael Heliodoro Valle, poet-historian-essayist whose home was in Mexico at his death in 1959, exalted Honduras through his own literary efforts (see *La rosa intemporal*, an anthology of his poetry, for example) and through his appreciation of the achievements of his countrymen (in such studies as *El periodismo en Honduras* and the posthumous *Historia de las ideas contemporáneas en Centro-América*). Other Hondurans away from home—Arturo Mejía Nieto with his stories *Zapatos viejos* and Argentina Díaz Lozano with her novel *Peregrinaje*—had earlier shown their devotion to the life they had known in childhood. Eliseo Pérez Cadalso in his short stories *Achiote de la comarca* shows that one who prefers to stay in Honduras can comprehend its living very well and that many nuances of that living are well worth preserving.

BIBLIOGRAPHY

Carr, Archie F. *High Jungles and Low*, Univ. of Florida Press, Gainesville, 1963.

Chamberlain, Robert S. *The Conquest and Colonization of Honduras, 1502–1550*, Carnegie Institution, Washington, 1953.

Checchi, Vincent and others. *Honduras: A Problem in Economic Development*, Twentieth Century Fund, New York, 1959.

Karnes, Thomas L. *The Failure of Union: Central America, 1824–1960*, Univ. of North Carolina Press, Chapel Hill, 1961.

Lester, Mary. *A Lady's Ride across Spanish Honduras*, William Blackwood and Sons, Edinburgh, 1884; facsimile ed., Univ. of Florida Press, Gainseville, 1964.

Marinas Otero, Luis. *Honduras*, Ediciones Cultura Hispanica, Madrid, 1963.

Parker, Franklin D. *The Central American Republics*, Oxford Univ. Press for Royal Institute of International Affairs, London and New York, 1964.

Stokes, William S. *Honduras: An Area Study in Government*, Univ. of Wisconsin Press, Madison, 1950. 'Honduras: Dilemma of Development', *Current History*, Vol. 42, Philadelphia, February 1962. 'Honduras: Problems and Prospects', *Current History*, Vol. 50, Philadelphia, January 1966.

Von Hagen, V. Wolfgang. *Jungle in the Clouds*, Duell, Sloan and Pearce, New York, 1940.

'Agrarian Reform Law in Honduras', *International Labour Review*, Vol. 87, Washington, June 1963.

BASIC INFORMATION

CLIMATE

Tegucigalpa

Lat./long.	14° N, 87° W	Relative humidity	
Altitude	3,018 ft/920 m.	at midday of	n.a.
Mean temp. of	25°C/78°F (May)	hottest and	
hottest month		coolest months	
Mean temp. of	20°C/68°F (Jan.)	Wettest month	21·3 in./541 mm.
coolest month			(June)
Absolute max.	98°F/37°C	Driest month	0·3 in./8 mm.
Absolute min.	45°F/7°C		(Feb.)
		Annual av. rainfall	63·8 in./1,621 mm.

POPULATION

TOTAL (*million*): 1961 (census, adjusted): 1·99; mid-1966: 2·36; 1980 (ECLA projection): 3·88.

DENSITY, mid-1965: 20 persons per sq. km.

CRUDE RATES (*per 000*), 1965: Birth 43·7, death 8·6 (ECLA estimates, 1959–61: birth 47–50, death 15–17), infant mortality 41·2.

GROWTH RATES (% *p.a.*): 1945–65: 3·0; 1960–5: 3·3.

DISTRIBUTION (% *of total pop.*): Ethnic, 1945: Mixed 86, Amerindian 10, Negro 2, white 2. Foreign-born, 1961: 2·4. Languages: mainly Spanish but some Amerindian and English. Religion, 1945: Roman Catholic 98, Protestant 2. Urban (*centres 2,000 inhab. or over*), ECLA data, 1950: 17·3; 1960: 22·2; 1980 (projection): 35·2. Largest cities (*000 inhab.*), 1965: Tegucigalpa 168, San Pedro Sula 85, La Ceiba 25.

CONSTITUTIONAL SYSTEM

CONSTITUTION: First 1825; 1894 main; next 1924 and 1936; new constitutions 1957 and 1965.

SYSTEM: Unitary republic, composed of 18 departments (divided into municipalities). Separate executive, legislature and judiciary.

EXECUTIVE: Power vested in president (in his absence, in one of three elected designates), who is elected by popular vote for 6–year term; no reelection. Presides over Council of Ministers and exercises office of chief of the armed forces. Congress elects commander-in-chief of the armed forces.

LEGISLATURE: Uni-cameral, Congress of Deputies. *Deputies:* One deputy (and one alternate) for each 30,000, or fraction over 15,000, inhabitants, elected by popular vote for 6 years. *Suffrage:* Universal, compulsory voting for adults over 18 years of age. *Elections:* Presidential, March 1965: Gen. Osvaldo López Arellano, who headed the government since the coup of October 1963, elected president by Constituent Assembly. Congress, Feb. 1965, for Constituent Assembly (which became the Congress in June 1965): Partido Nacional 328, 412 votes and 35 seats, Partido Liberal 276,808 votes and 29 seats.

JUDICIARY: Supreme Court of 7 judges elected for 6-year term by Congress, 6 appeal courts, departmental and lower courts.

DEFENCE

DEFENCE BUDGET: 1965: 11·4 m. lempiras, 1·1% of GDP.

ARMED FORCES: National service between 18–55 years of age; 8 months in army. Strength: army 2,500.

INTERNATIONAL RELATIONS

Member of the UN and many of its international specialised agencies including: IBRD and affiliates, IMF, FAO, ICAO, IMCO, ILO, ITU, UNESCO, UPU, WHO and WMO; IAEA; UNCTAD representative. Also member of OAS, Alliance for Progress, ECLA, IDB, BCIE, ODECA and CACM.

ECONOMY

PRODUCTION

AGRICULTURE (*ooo tons*)	*1948–53*[1]	*63/64*	*64/65*	*65/66*[2]
Bananas	813	885	917	1,180
Coffee	13	29	29	35
Maize	205	302	352	414
Sorghum	48	59	62	47
Rice	18	22	22	27
Sugar (cane)	5	29	30	37

[1] Average1948/9—1952/3.   [2] Provisional.

LAND (%), 1963: Arable 7, permanent pasture 30, forested 27, other 35.
OTHER AGRICULTURAL DATA: Agricultural holdings, 1952 (census): no. 156,135, area 2·51 m. hectares. Tractors in use, 1964: 340. Fertiliser consumption (*ooo tons*), 1965/6: 10.
LIVESTOCK: Nos. (*m. head*), 1964/5: cattle 1·67, pigs 0·85. Products (*ooo tons*), 1964: meat 19, (beef and veal 16).
MINING, 1964: (*tons*) zinc (US imports) 5,600, lead 5,400, gold 0·10, silver (exports) 100.
MANUFACTURING, 1965: (*ooo tons*) Cement 94, wheat flour 13; (*m. litres*) beer 19. Wood (*cubic metres, sawn*), 1962: 0·47 m.

ENERGY

CONSUMPTION (*tons coal equiv.*), 1964: Total 0·34 m., per head 0·16.
ELECTRICITY, 1965: Generated (*kwh*) 150 m., installed capacity (*kw*) 69,600.

GOVERNMENT EXPENDITURE

DISTRIBUTION (% *of total*), 1966: Defence and public security 9, education 21, health and welfare 8, communications and public works 21.

GROSS PRODUCT

GDP (*m. lempiras*): At current market prices, 1964: 932; 1965: 1,028; at 1948 market prices, 1964: 661; 1965: 710. Per head (*US$*), UN estimate, 1963: 195.
DISTRIBUTION (%), 1963: Agriculture 45, manufacturing 13, trade 15.
GROWTH RATES (%), 1950–60: 3·5, per head 0·5; 1960–3: 4·0, per head 0·7.

EXTERNAL TRADE (*US$ m.*)	*1955*	*1960*	*1963*	*1964*	*1965*	*1966*[1]
EXPORTS (f.o.b.)	51	63	83	95	127	145
Bananas	24	29	33	34	53	72
Coffee	11	12	14	17	22	20
Wood	5	8	9	11	10	11
Silver	3	2	4	3	4	3
IMPORTS (c.i.f.)	54	72	95	102	122	149
TRADE BALANCE	−3	−9	+12	−7	+5	−4

[1] Provisional.

DIRECTION OF TRADE (%)

	Exports			Imports		
	1955	*1960*	*1965*	*1955*	*1960*	*1965*
CACM	(9·8)	13·2	16·6	(4·1)	7·2	20·8
USA	69·0	56·3	58·3	66·1	55·4	46·8
EEC	9·6	12·6	15·2	10·7	12·4	11·0
UK	0·6	1·7	0·5	2·6	3·7	3·1

FINANCE

EXCHANGE RATE (*lempiras/US$*): Par value, end-year, 1960: 2·00; 1966: 2·00.
BALANCE OF PAYMENTS (*US$ m.*): Goods and services (net), 1960: +6; 1964: − 30; 1965: − 19; 1966: −37.
COST OF LIVING (*Dec. 1958=100*), Tegucigalpa, December, 1960: 100; 1964: 111; 1965: 115; 1966: 119.
INDUSTRIAL WAGES: Earnings in manufacturing, per month, 1960: 84·4 lempiras.
TREASURY ACCOUNTS (*m. lempiras*), 1966: Revenue 121·7, expenditure 122·7, deficit 1·1.

EMPLOYMENT

ECONOMICALLY ACTIVE (%), 1961 : Of total pop. 30 (men 53, women 8). In agriculture 67, services 12, manufacturing 8.

TRANSPORT AND COMMUNICATIONS

RAILWAYS: Length of track 1,100 km.
MOTOR VEHICLES: In use (*ooo*), 1965: pass. cars 9·0, comm. vehicles 7·5. Road system 3,640 km., paved 400.
SHIPPING: Merchant fleet (*ooo g.r. tons*), 1966: 70. International sea-borne shipping (*m. tons*), 1964: goods loaded 0·61, goods unloaded 0·33. Main ports: Puerto Cortés, La Ceiba, Tela, Ampala (Pacific coast).
AIR: Scheduled services, 1965: Total: 58·5 m. pass.-km., 5·9 m. cargo ton-km. International: 44·2 m. pass.-km., 4·8 m. cargo ton-km. Main airports: Tegucigalpa and San Pedro Sula (both international).
TELEPHONES: No. in use, 1965: 8,850.

SOCIAL WELFARE

SYSTEM: Social insurance benefits and services administered by Instituto Hondureño de Seguridad Social. Financed by contributions based on insurable remuneration: employees 2·5%, employers 5% and the state 2·5%. Employment legislation covers working hours; holidays; payment of wages and overtime; employers' liability for compensation for accidents, dismissal and death indemnities.
HEALTH: 8,900 persons per physician, 540 persons per hospital bed.
NUTRITION: Net food supply (*per head per day*), 1962: 2,070 calories, protein 53 g.

EDUCATION

ILLITERACY RATE (%), 1961 (census): 15 years and over, 55.
COMPULSORY: 6 years (between 7 and 15 years of age). School enrolment ratios (%), 1st and 2nd levels, 1963: 36, adjusted 49.
SCHOOLS, 1964: Pre-school and primary: No. 3,820, pupils 0·27 m., teachers 9,400. Secondary, technical, and teacher-training: no. 93, st. 21,200, t. 2,080. Higher: no. 6, st. 2,240.
UNIVERSITY (1963/4): U. Nacional Autónoma de Honduras, Tegucigalpa (with departments in Comayagüela and San Pedro Sula): 1,700 st., academic staff 188 (170 full-time).

MASS MEDIA

BROADCASTING: No. of receivers in use, end-1965: TV 8,000, radio 135,000. Stations: TV 3; 1963: radio 51.
CINEMAS: No., 1963: 40, seating capacity 36,000,
NEWSPRINT: Consumption, 1963: total 1,400 tons, per head 0·7 kg.
NEWSPAPERS: Daily, 1964: 7. Estimated circulation (4 dailies) 41,000, copies per 000 of pop. 19. Principal dailies in Tegucigalpa (*circ. ooo*): *El Día* 14, *El Cronista* 12, *El Pueblo* 7, *El Nacional;* San Pedro Sula: *Correo del Norte* 7.
BOOKS: Titles published, 1962: 189.

NICARAGUA

FRANKLIN D. PARKER

NICARAGUA is the largest of the Central American states in area, but next to the smallest in population. Her geographical situation is such that men have long pondered the ease with which her area of low terrain might be sliced to connect the waters of two oceans. Costa Rica to the south-east and Honduras to the north-west are more completely obstructed by mountains. Other differences between Nicaragua and her neighbours on either side are that both neighbours have developed some experience of democracy in governmental affairs in the 20th century and some real taste for egalitarian living. Nicaragua has remained by contrast a land in both political and economic thraldom to one family and its close friends, the great majority of her people enjoying only a small fraction of the benefit which might be expected from newly developing economic trends.

HISTORY

The one-and-a-half million persons living in Nicaragua in 1963 were nearly all descended from the Indian tribes which inhabited the area before Columbus, with mixed elements of African and Spanish heritage. Fourteen Indian languages of five quite unrelated stocks were spoken in the region before the advent of Europeans. Ten of the languages were spoken in central and eastern zones where the culture was generally orientated toward the south and less highly developed. Six of these languages persist to modern times, Rama and four others collectively called Sumo having but a few hundred users each, and Tauira on the east coast being spoken by several thousand Miskitos of a part-African part-Indian background. The other four languages, of three distinct origins (their attachments all in the continent to the north), were spoken along the Nicaraguan Pacific coast where far more people lived and where the level of existence was more sophisticated. Here is the region where most Nicaraguans live today also, though these four languages and most of the customs that went with them are now forgotten.

The western zone of Nicaragua was first traversed by Spaniards proceeding from Panama in 1522. Two years later another expedition, led by Francisco Hernández de Córdoba, founded the cities of Granada and León. Other Nicaraguan centres which had reached a population of 10,000 by 1963— Managua, Masaya, Chinandega, Matagalpa, Estelí and Diriamba—were all built around or very near Indian pueblos under Spanish domination. For 300 years León served as the colonial capital of the province, subject to higher authority in Guatemala City. Through the use of both Indian and imported Negro labour, the Spaniards of that time managed quite a good living, owning estates on which were raised cattle, a variety of subsistence crops, and cacao for the export market. Realejo, the colonial port on the Pacific, not only sent out cacao to Peru and Europe, but built ships to carry on the trade.

The two-thirds of Nicaragua which slants toward the Caribbean received scant attention from the Spaniards, apart from the River San Juan which was used for commerce. Negroes escaping from servitude, as well as French, British and Dutch buccaneers, found refuge here and contributed to the prevailing miscegenation. British interest in the region grew in the 18th century to the point where British armed forces attempted to enter Spanish-held territory at the River San Juan in 1780; but in 1786 Great Britain agreed to evacuate her subjects from all the so-called Mosquito Coast.

At the time of independence from the Spanish regime (celebrated as 1821, but not really effective in this province until 1823), Nicaragua held about 180,000 people, the great majority living on the western side, of mixed ancestry and speaking Spanish. Administratively, in matters both secular and religious, her capital León then enjoyed real distinction in the Central American realm, only Guatemala City having greater prestige. But disgraces of the immediate pre-independence period (1811–21) and of the decades of the Central American Federation (1823–38) placed severe impediments in the way of Nicaraguan progress for some time to come. Sharp feeling arose when a rebellion of both León and Granada against the governing intendant ended with León's sanction of the use of Guatemalan force against Granada. The feud which began at this time continued into independence, with Granada differing from León at nearly every turn. Because of internecine conflict, Nicaragua was the last of the states in the Federation to write a constitution (1826). Her first chief of state was executed (1828) and her third was murdered while in office (1837). Secession from the union in 1838 brought a constitution providing for a 'supreme director' of the state to serve a two-year term, but with only an occasional respite the confusion and the widespread lawlessness and slaughter continued.

In the course of these calamities, most of the leading families of León came to consider themselves 'Liberals', while those of Granada were called 'Conservatives'. The Liberal stance included pro-federation and anti-clerical sentiment, and the Conservative position the opposite, though the real conflicts devolved almost entirely around personalities. Other cities besides these two became involved in constantly shifting alliances, even Managua, chosen as a compromise capital in 1852. Looking outside the isthmus for assistance, the Liberal Party of León in 1854 invited a band of adventurers from the United States to fight at their side. William Walker arrived as leader of the band in 1855, took Granada from the Liberals, and then continued as he saw fit to deal with both Conservatives and Liberals discomfited by his presence, until he became, briefly, president of the part of the country he held in 1856, and was finally (by joint effort of the isthmian nations) evicted in 1857. Walker wished to develop Nicaragua's already established importance as a major transisthmian route for passengers between the United States east coast and California. A railroad across Panama completed in 1855, however, sharply diminished the interest in the Nicaraguan passage.

Tomás Martínez, the leading anti-Walker general of the Conservatives, now ruled (1857–67) a much quieter land. The state assumed its present geographical proportions when the British in 1860 relinquished a protectorate they had established over the Miskitos during the confusion. Five men from Granada succeeded Martínez as president, each serving out a four-year term, as well as a sixth who died in office. Nicaragua had time to recover from her wounds during this period, and began such projects as the building of the present 250-mile government-owned railway system. But progress was slow, the country having no real economic foundation, and the leadership showing little zeal for the tasks at hand. Matters hardly improved when the Granada circle was broken in 1889 and José Santos Zelaya ruled as a Liberal from 1893 to 1909. Through his interferences with neighbouring nations, Zelaya incurred the wrath of the United States government, much interested in the Caribbean area since the turn of the century, and thereby brought about his own downfall and a first United States intervention.

Conservative Adolfo Díaz, who may fairly be described as the United States choice for the position, ruled as president of Nicaragua from 1911 to 1917. Conservative Emiliano Chamorro Vargas served next (1917–21) under the same auspices. The latter had helped to arrange a treaty, ratified in 1916, whereby the United States was given the right to build the Nicaraguan transisthmian canal if ever one was built. When the small number of United States marines who had backed these regimes were withdrawn in 1925, new fighting arose, resulting in the reimposition of Díaz (1926–9) and the return of United States forces (1927–33). The earlier intervention had coincided with the holding of the Nicaraguan railway, central bank, and customs stations by New York financial interests. This second intervention had no such overtones, and was actually the occasion for two fair presidential elections won by Liberals (José María Moncada, 1929–33; Juan Bautista Sacasa, 1933–6). Yet the opposition role now played by the dissident general and guerrilla warrior Augusto César Sandino attracted hemispheric attention, and served much to heighten the *yanqui* reputation for meddling. In 1934, after making peace with his own government, Sandino was murdered by members of the National Guard, created a few years earlier under United States tutelage.

As Nicaragua moved into a new era, the National Guard took the position of prominence formerly held by either Liberals or Conservatives. Its head, Anastasio Somoza García, announced in 1935 his determination to have the presidency, though two constitutional provisions stood in his way. These he resolved in 1936 by forcing his uncle, President Sacasa, out of office and then temporarily resigning his military command just long enough to be elected; his nomination came from factions of both old parties. Taking office on the first day of 1937, Somoza next arranged a new constitution which extended his term to 1 May 1947. At that time he permitted his former rival, Leonardo Argüello, to succeed him, only to change his mind within the month as Argüello showed signs of independence. A more reliable friend, another uncle, Víctor Manuel Román y Reyes, then acted as president for nearly three years (1947–50) until he died, after which Somoza García resumed the position. Another new constitution (Nicaragua's eleventh) then granted dictator 'Tacho', as he was called, one more term to run for six years from 1 May 1951. Under the provisions of this charter, Somoza was ineligible to succeed himself. The clauses prohibiting this were repealed in 1955, and the following year after Somoza had accepted another nomination, he was shot dead.

Anastasio ('Tacho') Somoza García had two sons to succeed him. The younger, Anastasio ('Tachito') Somoza Debayle, inherited the headship of the National Guard and has retained that position. The older, Luis Somoza Debayle, became president first to fill out his father's term and then to hold office six more years (1957–63) after an election. Luis Somoza's party was called the Nationalist Liberal. Opposition elements from both old parties—the Independent Liberals and the Traditionalist Conservatives —refused to run candidates in the 1957 elections, though a weak group denominated the 'Nicaraguan Conservatives' did participate and win seats guaranteed to the minority in the bicameral Congress.

President Luis Somoza early announced that he would not campaign for a second full term. The constitution was duly rewritten to forbid again either his own or his brother's election. This did not of course prevent the choice of a faithful friend to carry on the cause; the Somozas found one in René Schick Gutiérrez. While the Independent Liberals, the Traditionalist Conservatives, and a number of new minor parties called for international supervision of the 1963 elections to ensure fairness, the Nationalist Liberals and Nicaraguan Conservatives made their preparations by limiting the new president, before his election, to a four-year term. There was no international supervision, the real opposition abstained as in 1957, and Schick easily defeated the Nicaraguan Conservatives. The winning Nationalist Liberal (and National Guard) candidate for the presidency in 1967, as expected, was 43-year-old Anastasio Somoza Debayle.

Economy

The long Somoza regime, arbitrary and unfair to its opponents as it has been, has not passed without some redeeming features. Chief among these is the fact that the Nicaraguan economy has taken on substantial proportions for the first time since independence from Spain. For the greater part, until the 1960s this meant only that a small class of persons favoured by the government were able to rebuild for themselves the type of comfortable existence known by the owners of the estates in colonial days. But with the influence of a variety of social legislation, and of the Central American Common Market and the Alliance for Progress, a better life for the Nicaraguan labourer now seems in sight.

The progress of the Nicaraguan economy as a whole has been in a series of distinct stages. During their first hundred years of independence, Nicaraguans paid little attention to the cultivation of coffee and bananas exported by neighbours on either side. An attempt to build an east-coast banana industry about Puerto Cabezas, begun in the 1920s, failed because of plant disease in the 1930s. Some mining of gold (which has remained quite steady in volume for a quarter-century) supplied one item to ship abroad as the banana trade subsided; but in 1940 (the fourth year of the Somoza regime) the total exports of the country were only $9,600,000, or about $12 per head of population. Five years later, at the end of the second world war, the annual per capita figure had grown only to $15.

Then the great changes began. From 1945 to 1950, exports per capita more than doubled in value to $33, as great fields were planted to coffee, much interest was shown in the raising of sesame, and markets developed for Nicaraguan lumber. The 1950s were the decade of cotton (whose value along with that of cottonseed constituted 42 per cent of the outgoing trade in 1963), as a virtual agricultural revolution (cotton vying for space with corn and beans) swept over five warm departments from Chinandega to Granada. Coffee continued to sell (16 per cent of the total in 1963) and live cattle, sugar and rice became minor exports. By 1959 the per capita figure for exports had risen to $53. The 1960s saw a new surge ahead. By

1963, with Japan and West Germany buying sizable quantities of cotton, with coffee being shipped to the United States and West Europe, with new large interests selling beef and sugar, and with the continuing factors of sesame and lumber, a new development in the mining of copper, and even experimental plantings of west coast bananas, Nicaragua exported $106,800,000 worth of merchandise and gold in one year, or $69 per head.

Of all Nicaragua's five isthmian neighbours, only Costa Rica did better with outgoing trade in 1963, and even here there was less than $2 per capita difference. In ten years (1953–63) Nicaragua's annual GDP had also increased from $264,000,000 to $449,000,000, or $226 to $292 per capita, a change of some significance when it is remembered that Nicaraguan prices like her foreign exchange (7 córdobas = $1) remained almost constant during this period. But with all the brightness of these statistics by comparison with those of a few years preceding, it should be remembered that Nicaragua is really only beginning to emerge from an economy of most meagre subsistence, and in doing so is developing in a manner prescribed largely by her own leadership, which until the 1960s put complete emphasis upon the planting of new exportable crops on land which had long known cultivation, with meagre attention to the resources of the remainder of the country or to the needs of the labouring man whose welfare would count much toward the sustenance of a developing economy.

Manufacturing activity did not keep pace with the new volume of farming, representing only 14 per cent of the national income in 1963, while trade stood at 20 per cent and agriculture 35 per cent. Between the censuses of 1950 and 1963, while the proportion of economically active persons employed in agriculture dropped from two-thirds to three-fifths, the percentage engaged in trade increased from 4·6 to 7·4, that in service occupations from 10·6 to 14·2, and that in manufacturing from 11·4 only to 11·7. A National Development Institute (INFONAC) created in 1953 has now developed plans for new industrial life made possible by the completion of a new power source on the River Tuma (1965) and Nicaragua's entrance into the Central American Common Market (1961). The efforts of INFONAC and other planning agencies (both domestic and international), especially as expressed through the National Plan of Economic and Social Development for 1965–9, seem indeed to be designed to cure most of Nicaragua's business disorders of the past. Even the plight of the labourer is to be given some attention.

In 1960 the average wage for the factory worker in Nicaragua was 22·1 US cents per hour, the lowest on the isthmus, while such food staples as corn and beans retailed at prices little lower than those in the United States. Mining wages were even lower, while no one had undertaken a study of the condition of the toiler on the average Nicaraguan farm. In 1963 as in 1952 (when agricultural censuses were taken), about one-and-a-half per cent of farm proprietors owned two-fifths of the cultivated land—the large estates on which the great cotton crop has been grown. In 1952 it was estimated by an international study team that about 25 per cent of all Nicaraguan income came to the richest one per cent of her population. If this ratio changes during the 1960s, some contribution to that effect may have been made by an income tax (passed in 1952, strengthened in 1962), a social security system (created in 1956), an institute for agrarian reform (organised in 1964), and perhaps a new trade union movement begun in 1962 outside the Somoza patronage.

GENERAL PROSPECTS

Further advances can be measured. The annual death rate in Nicaragua dropped from 95 per 10,000 in 1958 to 72 in 1964. With new schools being provided, absolute illiteracy was cut from 63 per cent in 1950 to 49 per cent in 1963; a new programme begun in 1964 was designed to carry this progress faster. Nicaragua's national university, situated chiefly at León (where degrees began to be conferred in 1812), is being modernised through a new emphasis on science and a general education programme. A Roman Catholic university began functioning in Managua in 1961. Western Nicaragua, with the completion of two paved highways connecting the major cities and the modern port of Corinto, is becoming acquainted with the sight of motorised traffic. Nicaragua has since 1953 had its own merchant marine for overseas shipping. Even the 165-mile Rama road, which (through its connections with seagoing commerce on the River Escondido emptying at Bluefields) is expected to provide good access from the developing west of Nicaragua to the still drowsy east, was virtually complete in 1967 after almost a quarter-century of construction.

Well blessed in most years with both sunshine and rain, with a plenitude of arable space into which to expand, with recreational possibilities to appeal to every interest but the alpine, Nicaragua has all that is needed in the way of geography to attract visitors and to keep her own people contented at home. And certainly many Nicaraguans are happy. Isolated communities of individuals in the eastern river valleys live the simple life of Moravian converts and worry little about politics. Thousands of western youth (over half Nicaragua's population is less than twenty years of age) daily linger in the baseball lots (each small village has one), unconcerned with the thought that their sport derives from the recreational preferences of a one-time occupation force. Many city and farm inhabitants do the best they can to live with what they have, believing that such is their lot in life and that their rulers really are doing the best possible for them. But a country in which struggles may explode with chairs, guns and knives in the very Chamber of Deputies (July 1962); in which leading citizens have been subjected time after time to imprisonment and torture; or in which 20,000 persons visit the funeral of an eighteen-year-old killed by government guards while in detention (September 1960) shows clear signs of basic discontent and tragedy.

The tragedy, one too easily argues, is the Somoza family dictatorship. Such is the theme of books by Nicaraguan writers like *Cárcel criolla* (1955) by the novelist Hernán Robleto and *Estirpe sangrienta* (1959) by the opposition newspaper director Pedro Joaquín Chamorro Cardenal. A much more comprehensive approach was taken by Salvador Mendieta, who before his death in 1958 brought to willing readers in the entire Central American isthmus a sense of their own responsibility for their own plight. The stark realism of *La enfermedad de Centro-América*, three volumes of essays from his pen, contrasts sharply with the escapist *modernista* trend set in poetry by Nicaragua's famed Rubén Darío, only twelve years Mendieta's senior.

The tragedy is really that until the 1960s Nicaragua has had to choose between intervention, dictatorship or anarchy, there being no other alternative. The Traditionalist Conservatives, considered the most effective opposition to the Somozas as late as 1967, had until this decade little to offer an oppressed people except the same conditions under a different leadership, that of the aged figure of Emiliano Chamorro Vargas, president during the first world war. A younger faction in this party shows some signs of developing the social consciousness needed by the persons who will some day fill the leadership vacuum, as do a number of other budding groups in labour and politics. Until that development comes to fruition, the best hope of the Nicaraguan people is that they live on an isthmus and in a hemisphere where life is improving, and that their own fortune is not likely to lag very far behind.

BIBLIOGRAPHY

Adams, Richard N. *Cultural Surveys of Panama–Nicaragua–Guatemala–El Salvador–Honduras*, Pan American Sanitary Bureau, Washington, 1957.

Alvarez Lejarza, Emilio. *Las constituciones de Nicaragua*, Ediciones Cultura Hispánica, Madrid, 1958.

Dozier, Craig L. *Indigenous Tropical Agriculture in Central America*, National Academy of Sciences, Washington, 1958.

Gallegos, Paco. *Nicaragua: Tierra de maravillas*, Editorial San José, Managua, 1964. Well illustrated and partly written in English.

Goldwert, Marvin. *The Constabulary in the Dominican Republic and Nicaragua*, Univ. of Florida Press, Gainesville, 1962.

International Bank for Reconstruction and Development. *The Economic Development of Nicaragua*. (Johns Hopkins Press, Baltimore, 1953.)

Kleiner, Karol C. and Kidney, Juliet F. 'Labor Law and Practice in Nicaragua', US Dept. of Labor, Bureau of Labor Statistics *Report* No. 265, Washington, January 1964.

Martz, John D. *Central America: The Crisis and the Challenge*, Univ. of North Carolina Press, Chapel Hill, 1959.

Parker, Franklin D. *The Central American Republics*, Oxford Univ. Press for Royal Institute of International Affairs, London and New York, 1964.

Sever, Bruce B. 'Basic Data on the Economy of Nicaragua', US Dept. of Commerce *Overseas Business Reports*, No. 65–42, Washington, June 1965.

Tweedy, Maureen. *This Is Nicaragua*, East Anglian Magazine, Ipswich, 1953.

Winters, Donald H. 'The Agricultural Economy of Nicaragua', *Journal of Inter-American Studies*, Coral Gables, Florida, Vol. 6, October 1964.

BASIC INFORMATION

CLIMATE

	Managua	Puerto Cabezas
Lat./long.	12° N, 86° W	14° N, 83° 30' W
Altitude	184 ft/56 m.	43 ft/13 m.
Mean temp. of hottest month	28°C/82°F (May)	27°C/81°F (Apr./May/Sept.)
Mean temp. of coolest month	26°C/79°F (Jan.)	25°C/77°F (Jan.)
Absolute max.	n.a.	n.a.
Absolute min.	n.a.	n.a.
Relative humidity at midday of hottest and coolest months	n.a.	n.a.
Wettest months	12·0 in./306 mm. (Oct.)	18·8 in./478 mm. (July)
Driest months	0·1 in./2 mm. (Jan.)	1·5 in./38 mm. (Mar.)
Annual av. rainfall	47·5 in./1,207 mm.	123·0 in./3,124 mm.

POPULATION

TOTAL (*million*): 1963 (census) 1·54; end-1965: 1·69; 1980 (ECLA projection): 2·94. DENSITY, mid-1965: 12 persons per sq. km.

CRUDE RATES (*per 000*), 1965: birth 43·1, death 7·3 (ECLA estimates, 1959–61: birth 46–50, death 14–16); infant mortality 51·6.

GROWTH RATES (% *p.a.*): 1945–65, 3·0; 1960–5, 3·2.

DISTRIBUTION (% *of total pop.*): Ethnic, 1955: Mixed 68, white 15, Negro 9, Amerindian 5. Foreign-born, 1963: 0·7. Languages, 1950: Spanish 96, Amerindian 2

(Sumo and Miskito), English 1. Religion, 1950: Roman Catholic 96, Protestant 4 1962:3). Urban (*centres 2,000 inhab. or over*), ECLA data, 1950: 28·0; 1960: 34·0; 1980 (projection): 45·7. Largest cities (*000 inhab.*), 1963 (census): Managua (National District) 235, León 45, Granada 29, Masaya 23, Chinandega 22.

CONSTITUTIONAL SYSTEM

CONSTITUTION: First 1826; 1838 as separate state; 1858 as republic; next 1893; several between 1905 and 1948; main and latest 1950 (amended in 1955, 1959 and 1962). Article 6 of 1950 constitution provides for treaties for Central American union; the defence of an inter-oceanic canal; and the use of part of the national territory for continental defence.
SYSTEM: Unitary republic, composed of 16 departments (divided into 123 municipalities) and one territory. The Department of Managua includes the National District. Separate executive, legislature and judiciary.
EXECUTIVE: Power vested in the president, who is elected (with 3 vice-presidents) by popular vote for a 4-year term; no immediate re-election. He appoints ministers of state, who form the Council of Ministers, and commands the armed forces.
LEGISLATURE: Bi-cameral, National Congress of Senate and Chamber of Deputies. System of electoral quotient applies with minority representation up to one-third of total membership of each chamber. *Senate*: 16 elected senators, 1 from each department, elected directly in single national electoral district, for 4-year term. Presidential candidate who was second in the voting and all elected ex-presidents are members of Senate. *Deputies*: 1 deputy (and 1 alternate) for every 30,000 inhabitants or fraction exceeding 15,000 in each of 4 regional electoral districts, elected by direct vote for 4-year term. *Suffrage*: Universal voting for citizens over 21 years of age (over 18 if literate). *Elections*, February 1967: Presidential: General Anastasio Somoza Debayle (Partido Liberal Nacionalista) elected. Congress: (*000 votes*) Partido Liberal Nacionalista (PLN) 480, P. Conservador de Nicaragua (PC de N) 157, P. Conservador Nicaragüense 15. Senate (elected) PLN 11, Opposition 5. Deputies: PLN 34, Opposition 17.
JUDICIARY: Supreme Court of 7 judges (five of whom form a tribunal) elected by Congress for life or until 75 years of age, with initial provision for 3 magistrates from minority party lists of candidates; five Courts of Appeal; Superior Labour Tribunal; district courts in departmental capital cities and local courts in municipalities.

DEFENCE

DEFENCE BUDGET: 1965: 62·5 m. córdobas; 1·6% of GNP.
ARMED FORCES: Strength: National Guard 5,500 plus trained reserve of about 4,000.

INTERNATIONAL RELATIONS

Member of the UN and many of its international specialised agencies, including: IBRD and affiliates, IMF, FAO, ICAO, ILO, ITU, UNDP, UNESCO, UPU, WHO and WMO; IAEA, GATT, UNCTAD representative. Also member of: OAS, Alliance for Progress, ECLA, IDB, BCIE, ODECA and CACM.

ECONOMY

PRODUCTION

AGRICULTURE (*000 tons*)	*1948–53*[1]	*63/64*	*64/65*	*65/66*[2]
Cotton (lint)	8	94	125	111
Cottonseed	16	159	207	189
Coffee	20	30	31	33
Sugar (cane)	27	104	100	105
Maize	95	142	142	140
Rice	23	29	30	35
Sorghum	36	42	47	.

[1] Average 1948/9–1952/3.　　　　[2] Provisional.

LAND (%), 1960: Arable 13, forested 46, other 41.
OTHER AGRICULTURAL DATA: Agricultural holdings, 1963 (census): no., 102,201;
area, 3·82 m. hectares. Tractors in use (ooos), 1955: 2·4. Fertiliser consumption
(ooo tons), 1965/66: 16.
LIVESTOCK: Nos. (m. head), 1964/65: cattle 1·52.
MINING, 1964: (tons) copper 9,200, gold 6·3, silver 10, salt 17.
MANUFACTURING, 1964: (ooo tons) cement 66; (m. litres) beer 10.3. Wood (cubic
metres, sawn), 0·14 m. Liquid fuels (ooo tons): fuel oils 112, motor spirit 79.
CONSTRUCTION (ooo sq. metres floor area), 1962: Building permits approved (Managua)
102.

ENERGY

CONSUMPTION (tons coal equiv.), 1964: total 0·37 m., per head 0·23.
ELECTRICITY, 1965: Generated (kwh) 311 m., installed capacity (kw) 134,400.

GOVERNMENT EXPENDITURE

DISTRIBUTION (% of total), 1966: Defence 11, education 15, health 8, development
and public works 28.

GROSS PRODUCT

GDP (ooo m. córdobas): At current market prices, 1964: 3·64; 1965: 4·10; at 1958
market prices, 1965: 3·65, 1966: 3·79. Per head (US$), UN estimate, 1964: 229.
DISTRIBUTION (%), 1964: Agriculture 36, manufacturing 14, trade 20.
GROWTH RATES (%), 1952–60: 3·7, per head 0·7; 1960–5: 8·3, per head 4·6.

EXTERNAL TRADE (US$m.)	1955	1960	1964	1965	1966
EXPORTS (f.o.b.)[1]	72	56	118	144	138
Cotton	31	15	51	66	57
Coffee	28	19	21	26	22
Meat	0	3	7	6	10
Cottonseed	3	2	7	9	8
Sugar	1	3	6	5	2
Copper	—	2	5	5	.
Gold	8	7	7	6	5
IMPORTS (c.i.f.)	70	72	136	161	182
TRADE BALANCE	+2	−16	−18	−17	−45

[1] Excluding gold.

DIRECTION OF TRADE (%)

	Exports			Imports		
	1955	1960	1965	1955	1960	1965
CACM	(1·4)	4·0	8·3	(2·2)	3·8	13·3
LAFTA	(1·6)	—	0·1	(1·9)	1·5	2·2
USA	37·9	44·8	25·2	65·2	52·6	47·1
EEC	35·1	25·4	20·5	11·4	14·1	15·3
UK	6·1	4·1	3·0	3·3	4·2	3·9

FINANCE

EXCHANGE RATE (córdobas/US$): Official selling, end-year, 1960: 7·05; 1966: 7·05.
BALANCE OF PAYMENTS (US$ m.): Goods and services (net), 1960: −11; 1964: −15;
1965: −29; 1966: −61.
COST OF LIVING (Dec. 1958=100), Managua, December 1960: 100; 1964: 103;
1965: 107; 1966: 112.
INDUSTRIAL WAGES: Earnings in manufacturing per week, 1965: 135 córdobas.
TREASURY ACCOUNTS (m. córdobas), 1965: Revenue 448·3, expenditure 430·7.

EMPLOYMENT

ECONOMICALLY ACTIVE (%), 1963: Of total pop. 31 (men 50, women 12), In agriculture 60, services 14, manufacturing 12.

TRANSPORT AND COMMUNICATIONS

RAILWAYS: Traffic, 1965: 51 m. pass.-km., 13 m. net ton-km. Length of track, 1962: 403 km.
MOTOR VEHICLES: In use (*ooo*), 1965: pass. cars 13·0, comm. vehicles 5·0. Road system 6,600 km., paved 870.
SHIPPING: Merchant fleet (*ooo g.r. tons*), 1965: 14 (vessels over 1,000 tons). International sea-borne shipping (*m. tons*), 1964: goods loaded 0·35, goods unloaded 0·23. Main ports: Corinto, San Juan del Sur, Puerto Somoza, El Bluff (Bluefields) and Puerto Cabezas.
AIR: Scheduled services, 1965: Total 33·5 m. pass.-km., 0·7 m. cargo ton-km. International: 26·8 m. pass.-km., 0·3 m. cargo ton-km. Main airports: Managua: Las Mercedes (International); Puerto Cabezas.
TELEPHONES: No. in use, 1965: 12,320.

SOCIAL WELFARE

SYSTEM: Social insurance benefits and services administered by Instituto Nacional de Seguridad Social; covers Managua and León. Financed by contributions based on remuneration: employees 3%, employers 7½%, state 3%. Employment legislation covers working hours; holidays; payment of wages, overtime and annual bonuses; employers' liability for compensation for accidents, dismissal and death indemnities.
HEALTH: 2,700 persons per physician, 440 persons per hospital bed.

EDUCATION

ILLITERACY RATE (%), 1963 (census): 15 years and over, 50.
COMPULSORY: 6 years (between 7 and 14 years of age). School enrolment ratios (%), 1st and 2nd levels, 1963: 36, adjusted 49. Schools 1964: Primary: no. 2,200, pupils 0·2 m., teachers 5,450. Secondary: no. 76, p. 15,800, t. 1,050. Technical: no. 19, st. 2,800, t. 200. Teacher-training: no. 27, st. 4,760, t. 360. Higher: no. 6, st. 2,770, t. 400.
UNIVERSITIES, 1965/66: U. Nacional de Nicaragua, León (autonomous, state-aided): 2·240 st., academic staff 300 (74 full-time). U. Centroamericana (Sección de Nicaragua), Managua (R. Catholic): 730 st., a.s. 67.

MASS MEDIA

BROADCASTING: No. of receivers in use, end-1965: TV 16,000, radio 0·15 m. Stations: TV 2; 1961: radio 63.
CINEMAS: No., 1963: 104. Attendance: total 7·5 m., per head 4·9.
NEWSPRINT: Consumption, 1964: total 2,700 tons, per head 1.7 kg.
NEWSPAPERS: Daily, 1965: 6. Estimated circulation (5 dailies) 81,000; copies per 000 of pop. 49. Principal dailies (*circ. ooo*), Managua: *La Prensa* 30, *La Prensa Gráfica* 20, *Novedades* 18, *La Noticia* 10, *La Nación* 5; León: *El Centroamericano* 4.

PANAMA

DAVID HOWARTH

HISTORY

The colonial era

THE chief importance of Panama lies in its narrowness: all its history stems from the fact that the isthmus offers the easiest route from Atlantic to Pacific. The Republic of Panama was founded in 1903, but the history of the isthmus goes back to Columbus. The Spanish conquest of the isthmus began in 1507 under Vasco Nuñez de Balboa. Balboa, alone among the Conquistadors, came to terms of mutual trust with the Indians, and with their help in 1509 he marched across the isthmus and discovered the Pacific. But his position as leader had not had the sanction of the king of Spain, and in 1514 the king appointed a governor named Pedrarias, who had Balboa executed and massacred his Indian allies. In 1519 Pedrarias founded Panama on the Pacific shore. This city may claim to be the oldest on the continent.

Within ten years of Balboa's discovery, the Spaniards were talking of cutting a canal to join the oceans; but after the discovery of the riches of Peru the kings of Spain became obsessed with the problems of keeping rivals out of the Pacific, rather than letting them in. For three hundred years, therefore, the only permitted crossing of the isthmus was a muddy track through the jungle between Panama City and the Caribbean fortresses of Nombre de Dios and Portobello.

The isthmus was often the scene of strife. In 1572 Francis Drake marched through the jungle, attacked the mule trains carrying treasure on the trail and seized £50,000 in gold and silver. Portobello was captured many times by British forces. In the 17th century the isthmus was often assaulted by the buccaneers, and in 1670 Henry Morgan with twelve hundred followers crossed it and sacked the city of Panama. In 1698 Scotland tried to found a colony on the isthmus which would provide a crossing open to the trade of all nations; but the enterprise was badly organised and soon succumbed to disease and Spanish opposition.

It was not until the end of the Spanish Empire early in the 19th century, that the old idea of a canal became a political possibility. From 1820 to 1850 many explorers, engineers and cranks claimed to have found good routes for canals and obtained concessions to build them from the government of New Granada[1], to which the isthmus then belonged. But none of them had any conception of the practical difficulties of carrying out such a huge engineering work in a tropical jungle. New urgency was given to the problem of a crossing by the Californian Gold Rush of 1849. Thousands of prospectors—the 'forty-niners'—flocked across the isthmus on their way to

[1] See 'Colombia', p. 76.

California; but the only route was still the Spanish trail, and the Rio Chagres which it crossed in the heart of the jungle. Many died on the way from yellow fever and malaria—the mosquito-born diseases of the isthmus which had always plagued the Spanish settlers. Under the impetus of this rush, American financiers built a railroad from Panama City to a point on the Caribbean side where they founded the town of Colón. This, in the 1850s, was the first successor to the 16th-century trail.

Canal prospectors were still busy, and one of them, a Frenchman named Lucien Napoleon Bonaparte Wyse, made the important discovery that the American railroad company had only obtained from the New Granada government a concession to build a railroad: nobody owned a concession to build a canal on the railroad route. After surveying the route from the train he obtained a concession in Bogotá and then went home to France, where he sold the concession to Ferdinand de Lesseps, builder of the Suez Canal. The enterprise was begun with hardly any preparation. De Lesseps never considered any other route, or made any serious survey. The Panama Canal, indeed, only stands where it does today because the railroad was there before it and gave easy access to the route; and the railroad was only there because the Spanish trail had been there since the 16th century.

De Lesseps' plan was defeated by rain, mud and fever. Between 16 and 22,000 men are believed to have died in the attempt. A lock canal would have needed much less excavation; but he refused, until it was too late, to give up his idea of a sea-level canal—a second Suez. By 1889 all the available funds in France had been used, and the company floated for the building of the canal went bankrupt in a scandal which shook the nation. For the next fifteen years the work was abandoned, except for sufficient desultory digging to keep the concession in force.

By the turn of the century it had become clear that the only body with the resources to finish the job was the government of the United States. The United States had always preferred the idea of a canal through the Lake of Nicaragua; but lobbyists set to work, on behalf of the French company, to persuade Congress to change its mind and to buy the Company's assets and its concession. The two leading lobbyists were a New York lawyer, William Nelson Cromwell, who was retained by the Company, and a Frenchman named Philip Bunau-Varilla, who had once been de Lesseps' chief engineer. These two men worked independently and were seldom on speaking terms; but they succeeded in swinging the vote in Congress, and in 1902 President Roosevelt was authorised, by a small majority, to buy out the Company and make a treaty with Colombia (as New Granada was then called) for the building of the Canal. If the Company's titles could not be proved, or if a satisfactory treaty could not be made with Colombia, he was authorised to build a canal in Nicaragua.

The Revolution

From the end of the Spanish Empire till the year 1903, the history of Panama had simply been that of an outlying province of New Granada or Colombia—a province resentful of neglect by its distant government, and often on the verge of revolution. Its history since then has arisen directly from the extraordinary provisions of the Hay-Bunau-Varilla Treaty, concluded between the United States and a revolutionary government of Panama which had existed for only a fortnight. To understand the present politics of the isthmus, and its recent past, one must first understand how this treaty came to be drafted.

With the authority of Congress, President Roosevelt's Secretary of State, John Hay, negotiated and signed a treaty with Colombia. It authorised the French company to sell out to the United States, and granted the United States administrative control, for a hundred years, of a strip of land six miles wide along the route of the canal. Sovereignty over the strip remained Colombia's. For control of the land, the United States was to pay $10 million in gold, plus a quarter of a million annually beginning nine years after the date of the Treaty. The United States also agreed to buy the French company's assets for $40 million.

The treaty was ratified by the United States Senate, but the Colombian Senate procrastinated, probably in the hope that the French company's concession would be allowed to expire and its 40 million dollars' worth of property would revert to Colombia. These tactics exasperated Roosevelt, and he sent Colombia a series of threatening telegrams, without effect. Also exasperated were the leading inhabitants of Panama, who saw the canal as a promise of future prosperity. They threatened revolution unless the Treaty were quickly ratified, but the Colombian Senate had adjourned and nothing was done. Here was in fact a golden opportunity for anyone in Panama with revolutionary tendencies, for if they could declare independence and quickly conclude the Treaty with the United States, they could expect to receive the $10 million—enough to set a revolution on its feet.

In November 1903, a revolutionary clique in Panama sent an emissary, Dr Manuel Amador, to New York to find out what help a revolution might expect from the United States, and particularly to ask for a loan to buy armed ships to defend the Panamanians against the Colombian navy. He first visited Cromwell, but Cromwell saw the dangers of involving the French company in a revolution which might be a failure. But then he met Bunau-Varilla, who offered to go to Washington to sound opinion there.

By a treaty already half a century old, Colombia had guaranteed that the crossing of the isthmus would always be open to citizens of the United States, and the United States had guaranteed Colombia's sovereignty over Panama. In the past, when disturbances had threatened to interrupt the crossing, the United States had often sent naval forces to keep the peace. Bunau-Varilla guessed they would do so again if revolution threatened. By treaty these forces should have been on the side of Colombia. But Bunau-Varilla made a further guess: that the president was so angry with Colombia that the navy would at least be neutral. On this basis, he returned to New York and assured Dr Amador that the revolutionaries would have no need of ships: within forty-eight hours of the proclamation of a new republic, the US navy would be there to protect it. He also promised personally to lend $100,000 to the revolution, on condition that the new government appointed him its minister in Washington.

Bunau-Varilla's motives were neither political nor mercenary. He was a fanatically patriotic Frenchman, and after the scandal of de Lesseps' downfall he had determined to devote his life to proving that France—and he himself as an engineer—had been right to choose the Panama route for the canal, rather than Nicaragua or any other. To this obsession he now added another: to achieve the personal honour of signing the Treaty himself as the representative of Panama.

Soon after Dr Amador returned to Panama, the conspirators heard that Colombian troops were assembling to sail towards Colón. In a coded telegram they requested Bunau-Varilla to make good his assurance of US navy protection—which they mistakenly believed had been given to him by the US government. Bunau-Varilla had read in the New York papers that the US cruiser *Nashville* had just left Jamaica under sealed orders. With a further guess he telegraphed that help was on its way; and on this hollow assurance the revolution was declared. But his guess was right. The *Nashville* steamed into Colón a few hours before the Colombian troopship. The revolutionaries took it for granted she had come at their request. The Colombian troops were unable to cross the isthmus to Panama because the American officials of the railroad, which belonged to the French company, had sent all their trains across to the Pacific side. On the following day the *Nashville*'s commander received orders to maintain free transit of the isthmus and to prevent the landing of any armed force. By borrowing from the local banks on the promise of Bunau-Varilla's loan, the revolutionaries were able to buy off the Colombian forces already in Panama, and the revolution was over. Two days later President Roosevelt gave de facto recognition to the new government.

Bunau-Varilla hastened to present his credentials to the president as ambassador of Panama, and on the same day he told Secretary Hay that he wanted to conclude the Canal treaty at once. Two days later, Hay sent him a copy of the Colombian Treaty, only altered to apply to the new Republic. But Hay told him that some senators had suggested the $10 million ought to be divided between Panama and Colombia. Bunau-Varilla also heard that delegates were on their way from Panama to discuss the Treaty. He therefore decided, solely in order to have the honour of signing the Treaty himself, that he would change it and make it so favourable to the United States that Hay and his advisors would accept it before the Panamanian delegation arrived. Without consulting the government he was claiming to represent, he altered the draft which Hay had sent him, so that it gave the United States, instead of administrative control for a hundred years, sovereign rights in perpetuity over the Canal Zone. The ruse was successful. Hay and his colleagues were astonished by such unasked generosity, but they believed Bunau-Varilla was acting on instructions from Panama, and saw no reason to refuse the offer. The Treaty was signed a few hours before the representatives from Panama arrived in Washington. Bunau-Varilla was able to bully the Panamanian government into ratifying it, because the members of the government, new to the job, had very little idea of the value of the rights they were giving away, and because they desperately needed the $10 million. Thus both parties to the Treaty were deceived through a Frenchman's distorted patriotism and personal vanity.

Ever since, the political situation of Panama has been bedevilled by the contradictory terms of the Treaty. Clause 2, which Bunau-Varilla borrowed from the earlier Colombian Treaty, gave the United States merely the use, occupation and control of the Canal Zone 'for the construction, maintenance, operation, sanitation and protection' of the Canal. But Clause 3, which he wrote himself without consulting anybody, gave the United States all the rights, power and authority in the Canal Zone 'which it would possess if it were sovereign of the territory', to the exclusion of any such rights for Panama. Nominally, Panama remained the sovereign power; but what was sovereignty without any sovereign rights? Panama has ever since insisted, on the basis of Clause 2, that the United States has no right to do anything in the Zone that is not necessary for the running of the Canal. But the United States, on Clause 3, has insisted broadly speaking that it can do anything it likes, and that anything it agrees not to do is a concession to Panama.

Panamanians have learnt to live with the innumerable practical difficulties arising from the Treaty, but emotional difficulties have steadily increased. Bunau-Varilla's whim had given the United States something foreign to its traditions: a colony. Moreover, it was a colony which divided an otherwise sovereign state into two separate parts, and a colony vastly and enviably richer than the surrounding country. The Americans, who completed the canal in 1914, regarded it as a source of national pride and also as an essential part of their national defence. They were reluctant to surrender any degree of authority over it, and those of them who live in the Zone developed a typically colonial mentality, and were inclined to treat Panamanians with undisguised contempt. For example, US employees in the Zone were paid in gold, and immigrant workers and Panamanians in silver, a practice which led to a caste system of 'Gold Men' and 'Silver Men', Americans and non-Americans.

The Canal Zone

The Canal, and the United States presence in the Zone, dominate the political and economic life of Panama. Three agencies of the United States government operate in the Canal Zone: the Zone government, the Panama Canal Company and the armed forces. The Governor, who is in charge of the administration, is also ex-officio a director and president of the Company. The Company is required by law to recover all costs of operation, maintenance and depreciation of the Canal. It also pays interest to the US Treasury on the net direct investment of the US government, and reimburses the Treasury for the annuity payments to the Republic under the Treaty, and for the net cost of operating the Zone government. Thus the whole Canal enterprise is sustained by the dues paid by the shipping which uses the Canal.

Politically, the American presence has had a stabilising influence, insofar as defence of the Republic is the responsibility of the United States, and the Republic, having no army (only an armed National Guard), is therefore spared the risk of military coups. But under this strong protection, democratic practises are open to abuse. Panamanian governments have mostly been short-lived, and have often been accused of corruption; elections have been suspect, and anti-American feeling has been invoked to win party support. It is often said that the whole power and wealth of the Republic are in the hands of fifty families, and although this may be a figure of speech it does reflect the wide gap between the rich and powerful, who are mainly of Spanish descent, and the extremely poor majority, who are mixtures in every degree of Spanish, Negro and Indian.

Republican politics

Since 1903 there have been, as at autumn 1967, 47 presidents of whom only three have completed their term of office. The presidency has been dominated by the Arias family since 1931. In 1940 Dr Arnulfo Arias began a regime of fascism, which ended in a bloodless revolt in September 1941. The new president, Ricardo Adolfo de la Guardia, revoked the Arias constitution and created a National Assembly with 53 representatives. Eight years later, however, Arias, with the help of Roberto Chiari, millionaire owner of Panama's biggest sugar factory, and police chief José Remón, regained the presidency by intrigue and restored the 1940 fascist constitution. He was again removed by popular revolt two years later, Remón turning against him and becoming president himself in an election (May 1952) in which Arias initially stood. Remón managed to establish some economic stability and stifle general corruption—not, however, his own. He was assassinated—the only Panamanian president to meet this fate—in January 1955. The next president, Ernesto de la Guardia, put down a revolt in 1959 by Roberto Arias, nephew of Arnulfo, and completed his term of office in 1960, when opposition candidate Roberto Chiari won the presidential election in a disputed result.

The 1903 Canal Treaty had been modified several times and the annual payment to Panama increased, but Chiari, urged by general popular dissatisfaction, pressed President Kennedy for Panamanian sovereignty over the Canal Zone and a larger share in the proceeds. Anti-American feeling reached a climax in the riots of January 1964. President Kennedy had agreed that the United States and Panamanian flags should be flown side by side at certain points in the Canal Zone, but the children of an American high school, with the encouragement of their parents, defied the president's order and flew the US flag alone. Panamanian students entered the Zone to protest, and the argument suddenly blew up into an adult battle in which eighteen Panamanians were killed.

This outburst led the Americans to recognise that their occupation of the Canal Zone was morally hard to justify. Within a year the US government agreed at last to discuss an entirely new treaty, and in September 1965 President Johnson announced that the new treaty would effectively recognise Panama's sovereignty over the Zone, and would integrate the Zone politically, socially and economically with the rest of the Republic. Panama would share with the United States the management of the Canal, and its benefits. The Treaty would also provide for the building of a new sea-level canal, possibly excavated by nuclear explosives, to replace the present lock canal which is becoming too small for modern traffic. US-Panamanian talks began in June 1966, but the drafting of the Treaty proved a long-drawn-out process, and it was still unsigned in the autumn of 1967.

The political situation in the Republic was complicated in October 1966 when the opposition Panamenista party, led by Arnulfo Arias, claimed that the 1964 presidential election won by Marco A. Robles had been fraudulent, and refused to recognise the Robles regime. Earlier in the year there had been serious and bloody anti-government student riots over a leftist student's death, for which the students held the government responsible.

Economy

Economically, the Zone adds about $90 million a year to the income of the Republic: $39 million in wages, the rest in purchases of Panamanian products by US government agencies and residents of the Zone. To this is added the annual payment provided by the Treaty, which in 1967 ran at nearly $2 million a year. The Canal has another less direct influence on the economy and the development of the country. The US defence commitment for the past sixty years has made Panama seem safe and attractive for private US investment, and huge tracts of country have been cleared and planted by US companies. The largest of these is the United Fruit Company, and the main product is bananas. Coffee is also produced in Panama.

US aid commitments to Panama under the Alliance for Progress have been heavy in recent years. A newer source of funds from all parts of the world has been won by the government's introduction of tax-free deposits and numbered bank accounts.

Economic developments have all taken place to the west of the Canal Zone. To the east of it, the isthmus has changed very little since Balboa crossed it. It is still covered by primeval jungle, as far as the frontier of Colombia and beyond. There is no road in this wild country: it is the only gap in the Pan-American Highway, which otherwise extends the length of north and south America. In this jungle, and on the Caribbean coast, Indians still live aloof from the modern world. But it is there that the first peaceful use may be made of nuclear explosives, when the time comes, as it soon must, to build a new canal.

BIBLIOGRAPHY

Adams, Richard N. *Cultural Surveys of Panama—Nicaragua—Guatemala—El Salvador—Honduras*, Pan American Sanitary Bureau, Washington, 1957.

Biesanz, John and Biesanz, Mavis. *The People of Panama*, Oxford Univ. Press, London; Columbia Univ. Press, New York, 1955.

'Coming out of the Twilight' (article on the Panama Canal and the new US-Panama Treaty), *The Economist*, CCXVII, 6383, London, 25 December 1965.

Dubois, J. *Danger over Panama*, Bobbs-Merrill, New York, 1964.

Joint Tax Program OAS/IDB. *Fiscal Survey of Panama*, Oxford Univ. Press, London; Johns Hopkins Univ. Press, Baltimore, Md, 1964.

Keeler, Clyde E. *Land of the Moon Children: The Primitive San Blas Culture in Flux*, Univ. of Georgia Press, Athens, Ga., 1956.

Larsen, Henry and Larsen, May. *The Forests of Panama*, Harrap, London, 1964.

Panama, Pan American Union, Washington, DC, 1964.

BASIC INFORMATION[1]

CLIMATE

Cristóbal

Lat./long.	9° N, 80° W	Relative humidity	
Altitude	35 ft/10 m.	at midday of	82%/88%
Mean temp. of hottest month	28°C/82°F (May)	hottest and coolest months	
Mean temp. of coolest month	26°C/80°F (Nov.)	Wettest month	22·3 in./566 mm. (Nov.)
Absolute max.	95°F/35°C	Driest months	1·5 in./38 mm. (Feb./Mar.)
Absolute min.	66°F/19°C		
		Annual av. rainfall	130·3 in./ 3,310 mm.

POPULATION

TOTAL (*ooo*): 1960 (census) 1,076 (CZ 42); mid-1966: 1,287 (CZ 56, US citizens 39); 1980, ECLA projection: 1,930.

DENSITY, mid-1965: 16 (CZ 38) persons per sq. km.

CRUDE RATES (*per ooo*), 1965: birth 39·1 (CZ 12·8), death 7·1 (ECLA data 9–13) (CZ 2·9), infant mortality 44·7 (CZ 20·3).

GROWTH RATES (% *p.a.*): 1945–65: 2·9; 1960–5: 3·2.

DISTRIBUTION (% *of total pop.*): Ethnic, 1940: mixed 65, Negro 15, white 10, Amerindian 10 (CZ, 1950: white 61). Foreign-born, 1950: 6·1; 1960: 4·2. Languages, 1950: Spanish 92, English 8 (CZ: mainly English). Religion, 1956: Roman Catholic 95, Protestant 5. Urban (*centres 2,ooo inhab. or over*), ECLA data, 1950: 35·4; 1960: 42·4; 1980 (proj.) 53·5. Largest cities (*ooo inhab.*), 1960: Panama City 273 (1964: 319), Colón 60, David 23.

[1] Data relates mainly to the Republic; that on the Canal Zone is indicated by the prefix CZ.

J

CONSTITUTIONAL SYSTEM

CONSTITUTION: First, 1904; next 1941; latest 1946, amended 1956, 1959 and 1963. *Canal Zone:* 1903 Treaty permitted the United States to build and operate the Canal and to have sovereignty over and occupy the Canal Zone. In return the United States pays an annual annuity, which was increased in 1936 and 1955. New treaty being negotiated.

SYSTEM: Unitary republic, composed of 9 provinces (divided into partly autonomous municipalities) and the Intendencia de San Blas. Separate executive, legislature and judiciary.

EXECUTIVE: Power vested in the president and his cabinet. He is elected, with two vice-presidents, by direct popular vote for a 4-year term; no re-election within two succeeding terms. (CZ: Canal Zone Government headed by a governor who is also president of the Canal Zone Company).

LEGISLATURE: Uni-cameral National Assembly. *National Assembly:* 1 deputy (and 2 alternates) for electoral districts of 25,000 inhabitants plus an additional deputy for a remainder of not less than 15,000; a province with less than 25,000 (e.g. Darién) elects 1 deputy; they are elected by direct popular vote for a 4-year term. Representation is to be increased when total pop. exceeds 1·5 m. *Suffrage:* Universal voting for citizens over 21 years of age. Total votes, May 1966: 305,225. *Elections,* May 1964: Presidential (*000 votes*), Marco A. Robles, Partido Liberal (130); Arnulfo Arias Madrid, P. Panameñista (120). National Assembly: P. Liberal 13 seats, P. Panameñista 11, Coalición Patriótica Nacional 3, P. Republicano 3, Tercer P. Nacionalista 3, others, including independents, 9; total 42.

JUDICIARY: Supreme Court of 9 judges appointed by the president with cabinet consent and approval of the National Assembly, one every 2 years for 18 years; 4 superior courts (2 in Panama City); circuit courts (6 in Panama City).

DEFENCE

ARMED FORCES: The Republic has none, but can be mobilised in an emergency. (CZ: US Caribbean Command, HQ at Quarry Heights).

INTERNATIONAL RELATIONS

Member of the UN and many of its international specialised agencies, including: IBRD and affiliates, IMF, FAO, ICAO, IMCO, ILO, ITU, UNDP, UNESCO, UPU and WHO; IAEA; UNCTAD representative. Also member of OAS, Alliance for Progress, ECLA and IDB.

ECONOMY

PRODUCTION

AGRICULTURE (*000 tons*)	1948–53[1]	63/64	64/65	65/66[2]
Bananas	346	493	.	.
Sugar (cane)	16	51	50	54
Coffee	2·9	4·5	4·4	4·4
Maize	61	77	83	86
Rice	84	111	128	156

[1] Average 1948/9–1952/3. [2] Provisional.

LAND (%), 1961: Arable 7, permanent pasture 11, forested 70, other 12.

OTHER AGRICULTURAL DATA: Agricultural holdings, 1961 (census): no. 95,505, area 1·81 m. hectares. Tractors in use, 1961: 347. Fertiliser consumption (*000 tons*), 1965/66: 8.

LIVESTOCK: Nos. (*m. head*), 1964/65: cattle 0·84, pigs 0·20. Products (*000 tons*), 1962: meat 30 (beef and veal 26).

FISH: Landed (*000 tons*), 1964: total 25·6.

MINING: (*ooo tons*) Manganese (exports to United States), 1961: 1·01; salt, 1964: 11·0.
MANUFACTURING, 1964: (*ooo tons*) cement 125; (*cubic metres, sawn*) wood (1963): 31,000; (*m. litres*) beer 27·4; (*ooo cubic metres*) liquid fuels: diesel and fuel oils 719, motor spirit 325, manufactured gas 19,000.
CONSTRUCTION (*ooo sq. metres floor area*), 1965: Private building permits issued (Panama City) 190.

ENERGY

CONSUMPTION (*tons coal equiv.*), 1964: total 1·07 m., per head 0·91.
ELECTRICITY, 1964: Generated (*kwh*) 390 m., installed capacity (*kw*) 193,900.

GOVERNMENT EXPENDITURE

DISTRIBUTION (% *of total*), 1967: Education 26, social services 14, public works 8.

GROSS PRODUCT

GDP (*m. balboas*): At current market prices, 1964: 583; 1965: 646; at 1960 factor cost, 1964: 526; 1965: 572. Per head (*US$*), UN estimate, 1964: 483.
DISTRIBUTION (%), 1964: Agriculture 23, manufacturing 16, trade 10.
GROWTH RATES (%), 1950–60: 4·5, per head 1·7; 1960–5: total 8·0, per head 4·7.

EXTERNAL TRADE (*US$ m.*)	*1955*	*1960*	*1964*	*1965*	*1966*
EXPORTS (f.o.b.)	36	27	70	79	89
Bananas	26	18	29	40	45
Petroleum (refined)	—	—	25	23	26
Shrimp	3	5	7	8	9
IMPORTS (f.o.b.)	75	109	165	190	215
TRADE BALANCE (f.o.b.)	−39	−81	−96	−110	−125

DIRECTION OF TRADE (%)

	Exports			Imports		
	1955[1]	*1960*[1]	*1965*	*1955*	*1960*	*1965*
LAFTA	(6·5)	—	0·3	(1·6)	1·7	1·4
Venezuela	0·5	0·5	0·3	0·1	0·1	19·6
CACM	(2·3)	—	1·3	(1·5)	0·4	0·8
USA and Canada	86·6	96·9	72·5	62·0	53·1	43·0
Canal Zone	—	—	8·8	9·0	9·4	0·8
EEC	1·9	1·5	6·5	9·2	11·7	8·8
UK	0·5	—	4·2	4·5	4·1	3·2

[1] % based on unadjusted data.

FINANCE

EXCHANGE RATE (*balboa/US$*): Par value, end-year, 1960: 1·00; 1966: 1·00.
BALANCE OF PAYMENTS (*US$ m.*): Goods and services (net), 1960: −32; 1964: −16; 1965: −30 (transactions with CZ +93). Direct financial benefits from the Canal, 1965: 103·2 m.; plus 1·93 m. in rent paid by USA.
COST OF LIVING (*1962=100*), Panama City, Oct.–Dec. 1965: 103; 1966: 104.
INDUSTRIAL WAGES: Earnings in manufacturing, per week, 1964: 22·40 balboas.
TREASURY ACCOUNTS (*m. balboas*), 1965: Revenue 89, expenditure 92; deficit 3.

EMPLOYMENT

ECONOMICALLY ACTIVE (%), 1964: Of total pop. 30 (1960: men 51, women 15). In agriculture 46, manufacturing 8, services 20, trade 10; working in CZ 6.
UNEMPLOYMENT (%), 1964: Urban areas 10; underemployment high in rural areas.

TRANSPORT AND COMMUNICATIONS

RAILWAYS: Length of track, 1964: 577 km.
MOTOR VEHICLES: In use (*ooo*), 1964: pass. cars 24·7, comm. vehicles 12·1. Road system: 6,242 km., paved 1,135.
SHIPPING: Merchant fleet (*ooo g.r. tons*), 1966: 4,543 (tankers 2,522). Main ports: Panamá, Colón, Bocas del Toro, Puerto Armuelles. Canal ports: Balboa and Cristóbal.
AIR: Scheduled services, 1964: Total 62·8 m. pass.-km., 2·4 m. cargo ton-km. International: 52·5 m. pass.-km., 2·2 m. cargo ton-km. Main airports: Panama City: Tocumen (international) and Marcos A. Gelabert; Puerto Armuelles: David.
TELEPHONES: No. in use, 1965: 46,450.

SOCIAL WELFARE

SYSTEM: Social insurance benefits and services administered by the Caja de Seguridad Social. Financed by contributions based on remuneration: employees and employers 4% each. Employment legislation covers working hours; holidays; payment of wages, overtime and annual bonus; employers' liability for compensation for accidents, dismissal and death indemnities.
HEALTH: 2,300 (CZ 530) persons per physician; 280 (CZ 50) persons per hospital bed.
NUTRITION: Net food supply (*per head per day*), 1960/62: 2,310 calories; protein 58 g.

EDUCATION

ILLITERACY RATE (%), 1960 (census): 15 years and over, 23.
COMPULSORY: 6 years (between 7 and 15 years of age). School enrolment ratios (%), 1st and 2nd levels, 1963: 56; adjusted 70.
SCHOOLS, 1964: Pre-school and primary: no. 1,600, pupils 0·2 m., teachers 6,600. Secondary: no. 58, p. 33,000, t. 1,720. Technical: no. 104, st. 16,800, t. 740. Teacher-training: no. 1, st. 1,350, t. 56. Higher: no. 3, st. 6,300, t. 320.
UNIVERSITIES: U. de Panamá, Panama City (autonomous): 6,700 st., academic staff 284. U. 'Santa María La Antigua', Panama City (R. Catholic).

MASS MEDIA

BROADCASTING: No. of receivers in use, end-1965: TV 70,000, radio 0.5 m. Transmitters: TV 8 (3 stations), radio 84.
CINEMAS: No., 1960: 62. Seating capacity: 52,000.
NEWSPRINT: Consumption, 1965: total 3,500 tons, per head 2·8 kg.
NEWSPAPERS: Daily, 1965: 10. Estimated circulation (8 dailies) 101,000, copies per ooo of pop. 81. Principal dailies, Panama City (*circ. ooo*): *La Hora* 22, *La Estrella de Panamá* 16 (Sunday 22), *Star and Herald* 10; evening: *El Panamá-América* 18, *The Panama American* 13.

THE CARIBBEAN

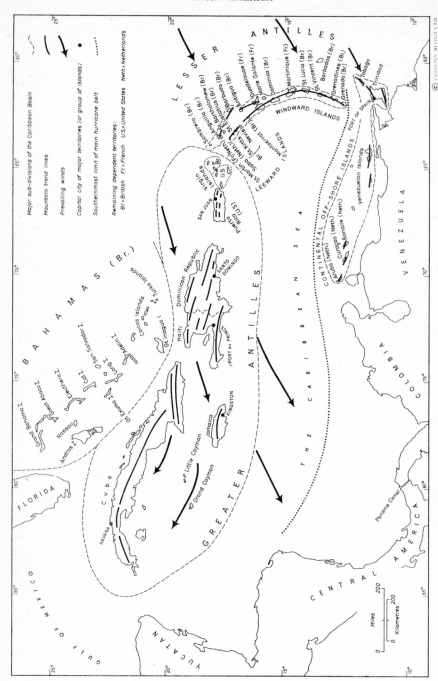

THE CARIBBEAN : GENERAL CHARACTERISTICS

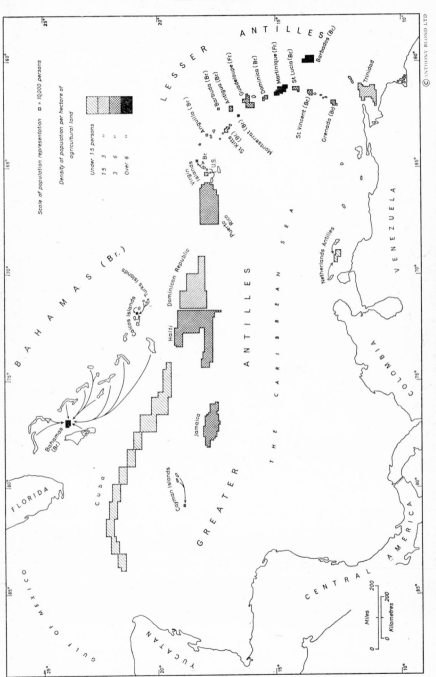

THE POPULATION OF THE CARIBBEAN: ITS DISTRIBUTION AND ITS PRESSURE ON LAND RESOURCES

Countries and territories are shown diagrammatically in their correct locations but country shapes are built up of a number of squares each of which represents a population of 10,000

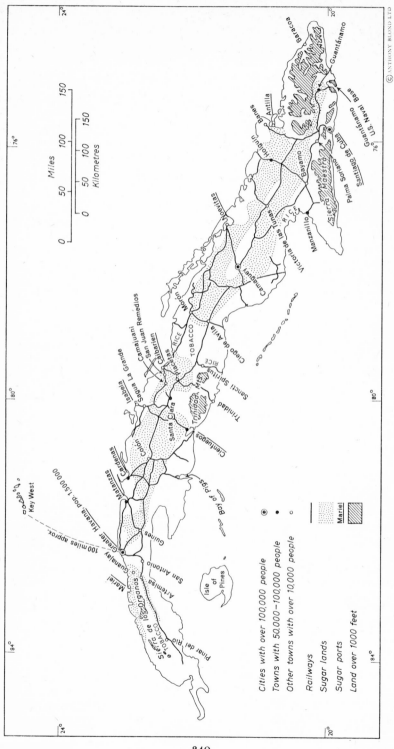

CUBA

Miles

0   50   100   150
Kilometres
0   50   100   150

Cities with over 100,000 people
Towns with 50,000–100,000 people
Other towns with over 10,000 people
Railways
Sugar lands
Sugar ports
Land over 1000 feet

Mariel

© ANTHONY BLOND LTD

CUBA

JOHN HALCRO FERGUSON

CUBA is much the largest of the Caribbean islands, bigger than each of the Netherlands, Belgium, Denmark and Austria. Her population of nearly 8 million is relatively homogeneous. Apart from a few small minority groups such as Jews and Chinese, Cubans are almost exclusively of Spanish or African descent, or a mixture of the two, Spaniards being the larger group. Though the high proportion of Spanish-descended Cubans, as compared to Mexicans, Central Americans and South Americans of 'pure' Spanish race, is undoubtedly due to Cuba having remained a Spanish colony until the beginning of this century, there has also been an unusually high rate of immigration from Spain since 1901, which received a further boost after the Spanish Civil War. A number of these immigrants, particularly those in the retail trade in which Spaniards were strongly represented, returned home after the 1959 revolution, but the proportion was not markedly higher than that of established Cubans in similar occupations who went into exile, and it is interesting that Spain, despite the political orientation of its regime, is one of the Western countries with which the communist government of Cuba maintains the closest diplomatic, commercial and cultural relations.

Much information about Cuba that reaches the outside world is unreliable. Leaving aside such official Cuban organs as *Granma*, which, though published in three languages by the Central Committee of the Cuban Communist Party, reaches a comparatively small overseas readership, the Committees for Fair Play for Cuba and similar bodies paint such a rosy picture of Cuban conditions that they invite scepticism if not outright disbelief. The same can be said of the over-enthusiastic reports of distinguished foreign intellectuals. On the other side, the Cuban exile groups in Miami put out a stream of 'information' about Cuba which is no more reliable than that purveyed by most exile organisations. The daily output of the Agencia de Informaciones Periodísticas (AIP) in Miami has a limited circulation, but it includes the major US news agencies, which tend to give undue credence to such sources in the absence of reliable news from within Cuba, the more particularly since US public opinion is conditioned to believe the worst of post-revolutionary Cuba.

HISTORY

The colonial period

When Spain's mainland colonies asserted their independence, all the Caribbean islands—with the exception of Hispaniola—remained under colonial rule. Cuba, along with Puerto Rico and the Philippines, remained as one of the scattered remnants of Spain's vast, 300-year-old empire.

J*

Slavery, as in the other European colonies, remained in force, and was only abolished gradually and patchily in the last part of the 19th century, long after its abolition in the British Empire and effectively two decades later than in the United States.

Such actions as the unsuccessful insurrection by Negro slaves in 1812 tended to retard rather than advance independence. With the horrific example of near-by Haiti, where the slaves had massacred the French, a threatened slave revolt was more likely to reconcile the colonists to the authoritarian but reassuring presence of the metropolitan power. The first time the red, white and blue flag of Cuba with its lone white star was flown was in a bid not for independence but for annexation by the United States. In 1848 the Venezuelan Narciso López landed in Cuba with a small band of followers—as Fidel Castro was to do in 1956, but with the difference that most of López' 'partisans' were North Americans. A few years earlier, in an even more bizarre attempt to enlist US support, a group of wealthy Cubans in New York had tried to hire a North American general, William J. Worth, to lead an invasion of the island—a plan which was not, however, acceptable to the US government of the time.

Naïve and ludicrous though these attempts may now seem, they were symptomatic of an ambivalent attitude towards the United States (and indeed towards Spain) which persists to this day. Although even the most angry Cuban exile in Miami would not dare to suggest a US occupation of his country, there is a strong undercurrent of identification with North America even among Cubans in Cuba, where officials still rely for much news on *The New York Times* (several days late). But even in 1848 things were not as simple as that. Apart from the pro-US annexationists and those who clung to Spain for fear of finding something worse (both predominantly upper-class groups), there were the *autonomistas* and the *independentistas*, mostly intellectuals, who wanted Cuba for the Cubans. None of these currents of opinion had much effect on the Negro slaves and poor whites, in whose descendants' name over a century later Fidel Castro was to raise the standard of revolt.

In the years following 1848 a more favourable economic situation and more liberal Spanish policy reduced the tension, and the setting up of a Junta de Información in 1866, with the avowed intention of framing a new colonial policy, won most of the dissidents over to a moderate policy of *reformismo*. However, the projected reforms promised too little, too late. On 10 October 1868 Carlos Manuel de Céspedes called on his countrymen to rise and fight for their freedom, an appeal which came to be known as the Grito de Yara (the Cry of Yara), on the analogy of the Grito de Dolores which had launched Mexico on its fight against Spain in 1810. Cuba's first war of independence had begun.

But Spain, now relieved of her huge imperial responsibilities from Texas to Cape Horn, proved a tougher nut to crack than the Cubans had foreseen, even though this time the revolutionaries comprised a broad spectrum of the island's population, from landowners to intellectuals to newly-freed Negro slaves. After ten years' fighting, in 1878, they agreed to sign the Pact of Zanjón, in exchange for Spanish promises to initiate reforms. Many, however, remained unconvinced of the worth of these promises and a hard core fought on, inspired by José Martí, today revered as Cuba's national hero. Though he was to die in battle, Martí was basically an intellectual, a man of words as much as action, and in the prose or verse of El Apóstol, as he is known, Cubans can find a quote to suit almost any circumstance.

Martí was killed in 1895, but his memory and reputation are undimmed, and neither Fidel Castro nor his 'old guard' communist allies have dreamed of lessening them. While Fidel is honoured in ephemeral photographs and heroic posters, solid busts and statues of Martí are to be found in almost all public places, and his more pithy sayings are engraved in suitable surroundings—one, in a newspaper office foyer, reads: 'Revolutions need wings; governments need feet.'

It could be said that Martí, though he failed in his immediate political aims, gave Cuba for the first time a feeling of genuine national identity and a philosophy she could aspire to live by. Though, despite the brave promise of 1959, this philosophy has not yet been put into practice, Martí's teaching and example are still officially as well as privately accepted as an inviolable part of Cuban tradition and belief.

The Yanqui years

When renewed fighting broke out in Cuba in 1895, US interest in the conflict was limited to a desire that it be stopped as an impediment to trade. The US president, Grover Cleveland, told the Spaniards he was willing to help them pacify the island; his successor, William McKinley, elected in 1896, while considerably less friendly towards the Spaniards, also thought that the war should be stopped: '[It] injuriously affects the normal functions of business, and tends to delay the conditions of prosperity to which this country is entitled.'

This observation reflected the growing economic involvement of the United States in Cuba, where North American interests were moving in as apprehensive Spanish sugar-growers sold out. Its tone also foreshadows the Big Stick policy of President Theodore Roosevelt (1901–08) who succeeded McKinley after the latter's assassination. The US attitude to Cuba was to a great extent dictated by her interest in the Philippines, which Theodore Roosevelt saw it as the United States' 'manifest destiny' to annex.

On 15 February 1898 the US battleship Maine blew up in Havana harbour, with the alleged but disputed loss of 264 lives. The cause of the explosion is equally disputed. The Spaniards maintain it was the work of the Cubans. Some Cubans insist that the North Americans blew the Maine up themselves as a pretext for intervention. The United States found the Spaniards to blame. On 11 April McKinley asked Congress to sanction the despatch of armed forces 'to secure a full and final termination of the hostilities between the Government of Spain and the people of Cuba', thus in effect starting the Spanish-American War and putting into play not only Cuba but Puerto Rico and the Philippines. But it is significant that while the emphasis had shifted from President Cleveland's offer of help to the Spaniards to a stress on 'the people of Cuba', the US government did not see fit to recognise the authority of the rebel Cuban regime, an indication that Washington regarded the Cubans less as allies than as a pretext for a war with Spain which would increase US power and influence in both the Atlantic and the Pacific.

When the war ended with US victory in 1901, Cuba was not annexed outright like Puerto Rico and the Philippines, but allowed to become independent under a republican constitution. In fact, however, this was little more than a façade, since the country was still occupied by US forces, and the so-called Platt Amendment to the new constitution, passed under US pressure, permitted such forces to intervene in Cuba at any time 'in the interests of the Cuban people' as adjudged by the president of the

United States. At the same time the amendment permitted the United States to build and occupy a base in Guantánamo Bay on the south-east coast of Cuba, for which rent would be paid but which would otherwise remain in perpetuity under US sovereignty. Cuba thus started her independent life not only considerably indebted to another power for her 'liberation'—a potentially humiliating factor which did not apply to any other Latin American nation until Panama was split from Colombia two years later—but she was also left mistress of her own affairs only in so far as her policies suited the United States.

The conditions of occupation of the Guantánamo base (which continued to apply when President Franklin Roosevelt abrogated the rest of the Platt Amendment in 1934 as part of the Good Neighbour Policy) remained a thorn in the flesh of nationalistic or merely patriotic Cubans, in the same way as Panamanians resent the US lease 'in perpetuity' of the Panama Canal. Add to this the ultimate powerlessness of Cuban governments, and the increasing hold on the national economy of US interests in alliance with get-rich-quick Cuban businessmen, and it is understandable that honest and patriotic Cubans tended to eschew a career in politics, leaving this to less scrupulous compatriots. At the same time the absence of a creole upper class, such as had grown up elsewhere in Latin America, while it prevented the perpetuation of a semi-feudal system, also meant that there was no group with inherited wealth and a tradition of authority and public service which could at least temporarily succeed the departed Spanish authorities. As a result the country came to be ruled by a succession of ambitious but inexperienced *políticos* whose main interest in power was the lining of their own pockets. The rule of these men produced a situation so chaotic (and not only in the judgment of the president of the United States) that the country was twice occupied by US Marines under the Platt Amendment and from 1906 to 1908 came under direct US military rule.

Gerardo Machado

This state of affairs led almost inevitably to dictatorship, since 'democracy' had become a bitter joke. In 1925 Gerardo Machado was 'elected' president, and two years later nominated a constitutional convention which repealed the clause in the constitution preventing a president from succeeding himself. He was 'reelected' in 1928. When the Wall Street slump hit Cuba the following year (with added effect because of Cuba's virtual integration with the US economy), Machado reacted by cutting civil service salaries and increasing the size of the armed forces as a precaution against public unrest. After protests by members of the Radical opposition (who were charged with sedition and deported) and riots by students, a tame Congress suspended all constitutional guarantees.

After an unsuccessful revolt in 1931, Machado was finally ousted in 1933, less because his opponents were more powerful than because they now had US support. In May that year the new US president, Franklin D. Roosevelt, sent Sumner Welles as mediator to try to restore order in an increasingly turbulent Cuba—a notable change from his predecessors' tendency to send the Marines. Welles interceded for arrested opposition leaders; Machado agreed to make concessions, then changed his mind. A bus strike in Havana snowballed into a spontaneous general strike against the regime. Senior officers turned against Machado, fearing US armed intervention. Ironically, if traditionally, Machado took refuge in the United States.

But Machado's fall was not to mean the end of dictatorship. Apart from the discredit into which democracy had fallen, there was little likelihood of its resuscitation in a country where politics was the preserve of Havana, and in Havana of the same *políticos* who had so mismanaged affairs before. The immediate aftermath of Machado's flight was a period of total chaos, and on 4 September a soldier stepped in to restore order.

Fulgencio Batista

This was no traditional coup by ambitious officers. It was an NCOs' revolt, masterminded by the mulatto Sergeant Fulgencio Batista, a man of humble origins who had become a senior sergeant-clerk with wide access to confidential communications. At first Batista restricted his role to keeping order and left the civilians—which meant for the moment the students—to run the country. After a comic interlude of student government under Dr Ramón Grau San Martín and an equally ineffective administration under Carlos Mendieta, Batista, who had been quietly building up his authority, virtually assumed power in December 1935.

At first he ruled through handpicked presidents, regularising the position in 1936 with the engineered election of Miguel Gómez. But Batista craved popular support and personal election, and to this end initiated pro-labour legislation and legalised the Communist Party, which was powerful in some trades unions and could bring him useful electoral support. In 1939 comparatively free elections were held for a constituent assembly to draw up a new constitution. This document, known as the 1940 Constitution, was the one whose implementation was the ostensible *raison d'être* of Fidel Castro's later struggle against Batista. It enshrined human and civil rights, inviolability of domicile and correspondence, independence of the judiciary, and freedom of assembly and of the press. It abolished the death penalty and declared that public officials should be appointed on merit and not be subject to removal by the executive. It provided for a minimum wage, compulsory social insurance, a 44-hour week, holidays with pay and the right to strike. It proposed a complete reorganisation of Cuba's inadequate public educational system.

In 1940 Batista, heading a coalition including the Communists, was elected president under the terms of this constitution. Batista's candidate was surprisingly defeated in honest elections in 1944 by Dr Grau San Martín, now head of the middle-class, liberal Auténtico Party. After a traditionally corrupt administration under the Auténtico Carlos Prío Socarrás (1948–52), Batista decided to run again for president. But when public opinion polls showed him running third to the candidates of the Auténtico and Ortodoxo parties (the latter a new idealistic party opposing the Socarrás corruption, and of which Fidel Castro was an early member), Batista seized power by a bloodless coup. The stage was set for Fidel Castro's landing from the *Granma* in Oriente Province in 1956.

Fidel Castro's early years

Like many revolutionary leaders, Fidel Castro Ruz came from a well-to-do background, his father being an employee of the US-owned United Fruit Company. Fidel was educated at Jesuit schools at Santiago de Cuba, the capital of his native Oriente Province, and Havana, and in 1945 entered the law faculty of Havana University. Here he immediately became involved in Cuba's turbulent politics, in 1948 attending an anti-colonialist congress in Bogotá, Colombia and being marginally involved in the 'Bogotazo', the violent and destructive wave of riots which followed the assassination of the left-wing Colombian politician Jorge Eliecer Gaitán, leaving much of the city in ruins and causing the red flag to be hoisted briefly in one or two Colombian provincial capitals. This, and the fact that the Colombian Communist Party attempted to gain control of the popular uprising, has been linked—without evidence—with Castro's fortuitous presence to date his connection with communism back to this period.

As a practising lawyer Castro tended to concentrate on unremunerative cases with a sociological angle, and much of his time was taken up with politics. He was among the 'young lions' of the Ortodoxo Party, with whom he planned and carried out the doomed attack on the Moncada Barracks in Santiago de Cuba, which took place on 26 July 1953 and later gave its name to the 26 de Julio movement. The 165 attackers, from all walks of life, had no fixed ideological adherence, and their protest was explicitly aimed at Batista's flouting of the 1940 constitution. Forty-five of them were killed and the remaining 120 were brought to trial. The archbishop of Santiago, Monsignor Enrique Pérez Serantes, had earlier spoken up for Castro, almost certainly saving his life, and Fidel himself spoke for more than five hours in his own defence, ending up 'Condemn me! No matter! History will absolve me!'

He was sentenced to 15 years imprisonment on the Isle of Pines, where he found his younger brother Raúl who had been sentenced before him, and proceeded to give revolutionary lectures to the other prisoners—for which he was placed in solitary confinement. In 1955 he was released under a general amnesty. Forbidden by the government to put his views on radio and TV, he and his brother proceeded to Mexico, a traditional haven for revolutionaries, where they teamed up with a small band of plotters, among them the Argentine Dr Ernesto ('Ché') Guevara, already a dedicated fighter for international revolution. Here, at a secret camp near Popocatépetl, the insurrectionary movement 26 de Julio was born.

The 26 de Julio and the Revolution

On 25 November 1956 Castro and 81 companions set out from Mexico to invade Cuba in the tiny yacht *Granma*. On 2 December they reached the coast of Oriente, but the vessel was overloaded and could not make the shore, the immediate hinterland proved to be a swamp, and Batista's army and air force had been forewarned, so that 70 of Castro's force were almost immediately cut down. Twelve lived to find their way into the rugged Sierra Maestra.

Here Castro set up a *comandancia*, and by winning local support managed to make his hide-out secure from Batista's forces and began to draw adherents to his side. The movement snowballed, bound together less by a coherent programme than by detestation of Batista and admiration for the bearded young leader. At this time the Cuban Communist Party wanted no part of this amateur movement, though individual Communists joined Castro in the Sierra Maestra, and when supporters of the 26 de Julio called a general strike in Havana and other cities in April 1958, the Communists opposed it.

When the *barbudos*, or bearded ones, as Castro's men had come to be called, entered Havana in triumph in January 1959, it was with promises of a restoration of the 1940 constitution, elections for Congress, and all the trappings of a 'bourgeois' democracy. The first governmental appointments, such as that of Judge Manuel Urrutia as president-designate, were also calculated to calm the possible apprehensions of the middle classes—or at any rate those of them who were not implicated in the enormities of the

Batista regime. The 1956 manifesto of the 26 de Julio movement seemed to bear out this interpretation. It had called for democracy as understood by Jefferson and Lincoln, nationalism in the sense of economic independence, and social justice as applying to individual human rights and involving agrarian reform. The first programme issued after the start of the guerrilla war had stressed freedom for political and military prisoners, freedom of speech and the press, again agrarian reform, and—for the first time—industrialisation.

But things did not go quite this way. On 12 January 1959 the new regime summarily tried and shot 71 Batista supporters accused of crimes against humanity, of which many were certainly guilty, and the shootings—not always of provedly guilty men—continued for several months, causing genuine indignation in the United States which was exploited by reactionary groups and served to widen a growing split between Cuba and the United States which a goodwill visit by Castro in April did little to disguise, even though Raúl Castro, already tagged as a 'communist' (a charge he rather tortuously denied), was widely blamed for the executions.

However, when the first Agrarian Reform Law was enacted in May 1959, landowners and other opponents were allowed time on radio and TV to oppose it. But it was hard to know who was in charge. On 25 July the moderate President Urrutia was replaced by Dr Osvaldo Dorticós, at the time regarded as a Castro puppet but later recognised as a communist fellow-traveller or even Party member. His appointment was seen by foreign observers as a move by Fidel Castro towards the official Communist Party led by 'professionals' like Blas Roca, and a victory within the 26 de Julio for the views of the international revolutionary Guevara and young Raúl, whose attitude had always been harder and more bitter than that of his euphoric elder brother.

The Bay of Pigs Invasion

Within Cuba attention was distracted from these developments by rumours of US-backed counter-revolutionary landings and acts of sabotage, and by pompous and condescending lectures from the US government. Meanwhile Blas Roca and Juan Marinello of the Cuban Communist Party, after so long looking askance at Castro's amateurism, saw their chance to identify the Party with Cuban patriotism—no doubt with a green light from the Soviet Union, to whom the value of a strategic and ideological base in the western hemisphere must have been evident. Now Cuba proceeded rapidly towards becoming an authoritarian state with communist sympathies. On 13 April 1960 a US meat firm was virtually expropriated. Soon afterwards a cultural agreement was signed with Jugoslavia; relations with the Soviet Union, broken off by Batista in 1952, were resumed; the conservative and Catholic Havana daily *Diario de la Marina*, the principal source of foreign news, was closed—the beginning of a series of closures and mergers culminating in 1966 with the amalgamation of the two more important of Havana's three remaining dailies under the name *Granma*.

In June US–Cuban relations worsened. US aid came to an end, the US oil companies were ousted, and Washington filed an indictment with the OAS accusing Cuba of causing tension in the Caribbean by 'lies and slander'. In July the United States banned sugar imports, whereupon Khrushchev pledged the Soviet Union to take up the cancelled 700,000 tons, and as a reprisal for the US action Cuba expropriated the remaining major US assets, including the Cuban Telephone Company. By August it had become public knowledge that Cuban counter-revolutionaries were training near Miami and probably in Nicaragua and Guatemala, a threat which could be linked to a statement by the US admiral in charge of the Guantánamo base: 'We are going to stay here . . . This land is leased in perpetuity.' On 1 September the Workers' Militia, a cross between a home guard and a territorial army to which all able-bodied Cubans are under strong pressure to belong, took over what was left of US property in Cuba. At a public meeting Castro literally tore up the bilateral military aid treaty with the United States, recognised the People's Republic of China, and asked the assembled crowd if they would accept Soviet aid if Cuba were invaded: 'Sí! Sí!' they shouted back.

The Bay of Pigs or Playa Jirón invasion on 16 April 1961 was one of the most bungled offensives in military history. A Cuban exile brigade trained by US 'advisers' in Nicaragua came ashore in an area of dangerous reefs and was spotted almost immediately by a Cuban army jeep, the resulting exchange of fire destroying the element of surprise. The US air cover expected by the invaders was not forthcoming, and the plans made by the US 'advisers' proved impracticable. Most important of all, Washington's intelligence reports had greatly underestimated the strength and efficiency of the Cuban defence and even more misjudged the temper of the people. Castro's government quickly rounded up known critics and opponents of the regime, and the rest, whatever their reservations about Castro, were not prepared to support an armed invasion by men whose eventual aims were unclear.

In a rousing official communiqué, ending with the revolutionary slogan 'Fatherland or Death! We shall win!' the government called on the people to rally to the fight, and they did. In four days it was over, and the victory gave an enormous fillip to the regime; government and people were alike convinced that this was but the first US attempt to crush the revolution, so that the country must remain perpetually on guard. The government tightened its hold even more strongly. At the same time the US embargo on trade with Cuba, dating from 1960 and reinforced by naval and air surveillance, also aligned people behind the government, which described the operation as a blockade. (This technically it is not, since the United States does not interfere with shipping by owners who do not trade with the United States). All shortages and difficulties could thus be blamed on the US 'blockade'. The gringo threat could also be used to distract attention from the tensions within the revolutionary movement. The alignment with the Communist bloc had been viewed with some alarm not only by ordinary Cubans but by the former *barbudos* of the 26 de Julio, who for both patriotic and personal reasons resented the increasing influence of the old Communist Party. Yet if the revolution were to survive, a marriage of convenience between idealism and a minimum of efficiency was inevitable.

The Missile Crisis and the formation of the Cuban Communist Party

In the autumn of 1962 came another diversion from outside. US reconnaissance planes, part of the routine force which continually overflies Cuba, discovered secret Soviet missile sites on the island. Whatever the extent of the Cuban government's detailed knowledge of these (or the reasons for its acquiescence in their construction), the population at large was taken by surprise by the revelation. Upon the terrifying US–Soviet confrontation of October 1962 the Soviet Union backed down. In Cuba the 'missile crisis' had two major results. In the long term it revealed Castro to the rest of

Latin America as being basically dependent on an outside power, thus limiting his appeal as a continental revolutionary leader (and possibly paving the way for the departure of 'Ché' Guevara, the theoretician of the revolution). In the short term it caused a coolness between Cuba and the Soviet Union.

But this coolness could not prevent the inevitable fusion of the two domestic revolutionary groups. Already in the aftermath of the Bay of Pigs the 26 de Julio, the Popular Socialist (i.e. Communist) Party, and the Havana-based Revolutionary Directorate, up till then loosely allied in the Integrated Revolutionary Organisation (ORI), had been uneasily merged in the United Party of the Socialist Revolution (PURS). The members of the new party had to satisfy criteria laid down in five points: (1) They must accept the Party programme as formulated in two 'Declarations of Havana'; (2) accept Party discipline; (3) prove they had a clean record and had not taken part in the 'bogus' elections of 1958; (4) set a good example in daily life and work; (5) contribute to Party funds. But the PURS was still an insufficiently monolithic body, and internal squabbles were bitter, with Castro listening first to one faction and then another. Amiable but incapable 26 de Julio men were quietly eased out, but some Communist heads also metaphorically rolled—notably that of Aníbal Escalante, veteran member of the Politburo and National Committee of the Popular Socialist Party, who left the country. Another Communist demotion (though not regarded as such by some) was that of Carlos Rafael Rodriguez, head of the powerful Institute of Agrarian Reform (INRA) who was transferred to another post.

On 3 October 1965 Fidel Castro announced the formation of the Communist Party of Cuba, a monolithic body with a structure based on that of the Communist Party of the Soviet Union. Castro himself, who as well as prime minister had been first secretary of the PURS, retained the same position in the new party. A notable absentee at the time of this announcement, and on public occasions for several months before, was Guevara, about whose whereabouts public speculation was growing. To quieten this speculation Castro read out in public an undated letter purportedly from Guevara, stating his intention to leave Cuba and further revolution elsewhere. The genuineness of this document has been widely doubted, but both the succinct style (very different from Castro's) and the gesture are Guevaran. Despite his 26 de Julio rank and his acceptance of Cuban nationality he had never ceased to be an internationalist, and there is evidence that he had become increasingly irritated by the internal squabbles of post-revolutionary Cuba. At the same time he must have felt frustrated at Castro's necessary acceptance of at least some of the cautious Soviet line in foreign policy, when his whole instinct and ideology was closer to the Chinese world-revolutionary thesis.

Castro's later explanations that Guevara was 'continuing his revolutionary vocation elsewhere' are borne out by internal evidence in a supplement (April 1967) of *Tricontinental*, organ of the Organisation of Asian, African and Latin American Solidarity (OSPAAL) set up by left-wing groups, parties and governments in Havana in January 1966.[1] The author, who, linguistic analysis suggests, may be Guevara, deals with world problems from Vietnam to the Congo, including many Latin American, and their proposed solutions fit in well with those espoused by the Organisation of Latin American Solidarity (OLAS), founded at the same time as OSPAAL.

[1] See 'The Sino–Soviet Dispute and Revolutionary Movements', p. 463.

The supplement ends: 'Our very action is a battle-cry against imperialism, and a battle-hymn for the people's unity against the great enemy of mankind: the United States of America. Wherever death may surprise us, let it be welcome, provided that this, our battle cry, may have reached some receptive ear and another hand may be extended to wield our weapons . . . '

Such a call holds embarrassment for Castro, torn between his commitments to guerrilla movements throughout Latin America and his economic dependence upon a Soviet Union which has begun to do business with the governments of the countries in which the guerrillas are operating. But he may be able to override such apparent contradictions, though the clash at the OLAS Conference of August 1967 between supporters and opponents of 'armed struggle throughout Latin America' suggested trouble ahead. In September 1965 he made the unprecedented offer that all Cubans who wished to do so, and were willing to leave behind them all but a change of clothes and a few necessary possessions, could leave the country. Though teenagers and other categories of people were excluded from the offer, thousands of Cubans left by air for Spain and the United States. This strange offer has been variously interpreted as a means of getting rid of possible fifth columnists and the unenthusiastic, of embarrassing the United States which might not want these unsought immigrants, of exporting surplus population from rationed Cuba, of proving that given this *carte blanche* opportunity most Cubans would remain, as most of them, whatever their reasons, did.

Economy

Cuba is far from economically self-sufficient. This was underlined shortly after the Tricontinental Conference, during which there was a violent clash between the Soviet and Chinese delegates. The Cuban organisers did their best to minimise the matter, and many of them, like Guevara, must have sympathised with the Chinese position. But within weeks of the meeting Castro exploded in public fury against the Chinese, causing an almost complete rupture between the two countries, not because of ideology but because the Chinese had not delivered a stipulated quantity of rice, which along with yucca and *frijoles* (red beans), forms a staple article of Cuban diet. In recent years rice and other basic commodities have been in short supply. In general, imports have to be paid for by exports of agricultural produce at the expense of home consumption. The $35 million purchase of French heavy road-building equipment in June 1966, for example, is being paid for at $7 million p.a. in coffee, which is rationed in Cuba.

Although nobody is starving (as Miami reports tend to claim) and distribution is certainly more equitable than before the revolution, the overall quantity of food available is less, a situation exacerbated by the inefficiency of the rationing system. Fresh milk was still unavailable in 1967 except for all children under seven and adults over 65 in medical need of it. Many shortages are due to defective transport, so that, for instance, in 1964, when Cuba had the largest tomato harvest on record, little of it reached Havana and the supplies that did were for the most part already rotten. The transport shortage is due to the fact that most vehicles in Cuba are pre-1959 and 'made in USA', so that they cannot be replaced or supplied with spares except by 'cannibalisation', while the socialist countries are in a poor position to fill the vacuum; this explains why the British Leyland buses imported in 1964–5 were greeted with such rapture. In September 1966 minister Carlos Rafael Rodriguez reported that Cuban factories were operating at only half capacity because of lack of spare parts and raw materials. In addition there is an acknowledged serious lack of technicians and an alarming rate of industrial depreciation. Peasant productivity is very low, peasants preferring to work their own small plots rather than state farms and to sell on the black market rather than to state purchasing agencies.

After the revolution a large share of the blame must be laid at the door of the Cubans themselves for their failure to make use of the natural resources they have. Before independence sugar easily supported the economy, and there was little need to grow or manufacture anything else as only a small section of the population demanded much above subsistence. Cuba was long the world's largest sugar producer. Further, the nature of sugar cultivation divided people into two basic classes, the rich who owned the land and the poor who worked it (as Castro expensively discovered, small-holdings are uneconomic and impracticable). This alone was enough to blunt a sense of Cuban national identity until the end of the 19th century.

The social division became accentuated as the old Spanish families pulled out or, with increasing mechanisation, confined themselves to cultivation and sold their unprocessed crops to large sugar factories or *ingenios*, which even before independence increasingly tended to be US-owned. Many of the large sugar companies owning the ingenios found it more profitable to buy out the landowners and operate the land as an adjunct to the factory, so that all contact was lost between *peones* and distant employers, whose only object was to supply their markets and get the highest possible return on their capital. This situation distorted the whole development of Cuba. Railways were built not to link cities or provide a public service but to take the sugar from the fields to the ingenio and from there to the nearest port. Provincial cities languished while Havana swelled with the newly rich and those dependent on them, who formed a sort of rootless middle class whose descendants have left in large numbers for Miami.

After independence the United States agreed with Cuba a sugar quota which not only committed her to buying a guaranteed percentage of Cuban sugar but also fixed a tariff above the world price, thus binding Cuba more closely to the US economy. In 1920 a temporary drop in sugar prices meant that most of the remaining small Cuban-owned ingenios passed into the hands of US banks.

Between the two world wars Cuba developed a second major industry, tourism, which reinforced the US connection. Increasing affluence brought thousands of North American tourists to Havana, only 90 miles from Miami. Chicago gangsters opened casinos in Havana. After 1945 the boom increased. Hotels multiplied everywhere, for North Americans only: in 1958 the Havana Riviera was built for gamblers who saw nothing of Cuba but the airport and the hotel gaming-tables and fruit machines. Cuba earned millions of dollars —and lost her self-respect.

This self-respect was one of the things Castro meant to restore by his revolution. At the same time he wanted to free his country from economic dependence on sugar and tourism. To this end he set up three economic planning organisations with interlocking and often overlapping functions. The old sugar-estates were converted into cooperatives and collectives, and early but inexpert efforts were made at diversification. The first notable effect of these was a sharp fall in sugar production, causing sharp criticism from the Soviet Union, which in effect told the Cubans to stick to doing what they knew best (one of the many causes of dissension among Cuban leaders). With the aid of 'voluntary' labour from the cities at harvest time, and increased mechanisation where this is possible (Soviet machines cannot tackle hilly terrain), the Cubans claim that sugar production has now climbed back beyond the highest pre-revolutionary figures.

This, they claim, has been done without prejudice to the development of other crops. The cattle industry is being rejuvenated and poultry farming developed. The revolutionary government started with far too industrial ambitious aims, trying to build an industrialised nation on the Western European pattern without the mineral resources to sustain it. In many cases infant industries, processing imported raw materials, could not compete in price with finished articles from overseas, and in the light of this other projected industries were abandoned. Now the Cubans have begun to cut their coat according to their cloth, and are concentrating on such practical products as chemicals and canned foods. One new factory involving both industry and agriculture is a huge fertiliser plant being erected by a British firm.

In 1963 Cuba accepted the communist principal of international division of labour, and Castro postponed industrialisation to concentrate once more on sugar; in 1966 sugar represented 85 per cent of Cuba's exports, most of it being traded with the Soviet bloc which continues heavily to subsidise Cuba (in 1966 at over 10 per cent of Cuba's GNP according to some estimates—i.e. at twice the amount envisaged in the 1966 trade agreement between the two countries).

Despite many initial mistakes there are signs that Cuba is beginning to find her economic feet. Her standard of living is still well above the Latin American average—a statement better confirmed by observation than by statistics, which for instance quote the peso at the official rate of par with the US dollar rather than its real exchange value of about five cents (as at mid-1967) and according to which GNP in 1966 was close to that of 1957 with population increased by an estimated one-fifth.

But one galling economic truth remains. Cuba remains tied to a major overseas economy: she has merely exchanged US economic domination for that of the Soviet Union. This explains the eagerness of the Cuban government to trade with Western Europe, as she indeed does, notably with Britain, France and Spain. It also explains the irritation of the United States and the outright anger of the Miami exiles at the countries which break the US embargo (now subscribed to by all western hemisphere countries except Canada and Mexico, the only two to retain diplomatic relations with Havana). Economically, as politically, Cuba's situation is neither so rosy as her supporters claim nor so disastrous as her detractors insist.

BIBLIOGRAPHY

Draper, Theodore. *Castro's Revolution: Myths and Realities*, Thames and Hudson, London; Frederick A. Praeger, New York, 1962. *Castroism: Theory and Practice*, Pall Mall Press, London; Frederick A. Praeger, New York, 1965.

Ferguson, J. Halcro. *The Revolutions of Latin America*, Thames and Hudson, London, 1963.

Goldenberg, Boris. *The Cuban Revolution and Latin America*, George Allen and Unwin, London; Frederick A. Praeger, New York, 1965.

González, Manuel Pedro. *José Martí*, Univ. of North Carolina Press, Chapel Hill, NC, 1953; Centro de Estudios Martianos, Havana, 1961.

Huberman, Leo and Sweezy, Paul M. *Cuba: Anatomy of a Revolution*, Monthly Review Press, New York, 2nd ed. 1961.

Perkins, Dexter. *The United States and the Caribbean*, Oxford Univ. Press, London, 1947.

Sheer, Robert and Zeitlin, Maurice. *Cuba, an American Tragedy*, Grove Press, New York, 1963;
Penguin, London, 1964.
Weyl, Nathaniel. *Red Star Over Cuba*, Devin-Adair, New York, 1960.
Williams, William Appleman. *The United States, Cuba and Castro*, Monthly Review Press,
New York, 1962.
Wright Mills, C. *Listen, Yankee*, Ballantyne Books, New York, 1960; issued as *Castro's Cuba*,
Secker and Warburg, London, 1961.

BASIC INFORMATION

CLIMATE

Havana

Lat./long.	23° N, 82° W	Relative humidity	
Altitude	80 ft/24 m.	at midday of	62%/64%
Mean temp. of	28°C/82°F	hottest and	
hottest month	(July/Aug.)	coolest months	
Mean temp. of	22°C/72°F	Wettest month	6·8 in./173 mm.
coolest month	(Jan./Feb.)		(Oct.)
Absolute max.	96°F/35°C	Driest months	1·8 in./46 mm.
Absolute min.	50°F/10°C		(Feb./Mar.)
		Annual av. rainfall	48·2 in./1,224 mm.

POPULATION

TOTAL (*million*): 1953 (census): 5·83; mid-1966: 7·83; 1980 (ECLA projection): 10.
DENSITY, mid-1965: 67 persons per sq. km.
CRUDE RATES (*per 000*), 1965: birth 34·6, death 6·5, infant mortality 37·7.
GROWTH RATES (% p.a.): 1945–65: 2·2; 1960–5: 2·3.
DISTRIBUTION (% *of total pop.*): Ethnic, 1953: white 73, mixed 14, Negro 12. Foreign-
born, 1953: 2·6. Language, Spanish. Religion: mainly Roman Catholic; Protestant
(1962) 3·7. Urban (*centres 2,000 inhab. or over*), ECLA data, 1950: 50·0; 1960: 56·1;
1980 (projection): 65·2. Largest cities (*000 inhab.*), mid-1964: Havana 941, Mariano
(1960) 230, Santiago de Cuba 231, Camagüey 153, Guantánamo 122, Santa Clara
121.

CONSTITUTIONAL SYSTEM

CONSTITUTION: First 1901; main 1940, suspended 1952–5 and in 1959, reestablished
1959; being replaced by a socialist constitution.
SYSTEM: Unitary republic of 6 provinces divided into 44 regions and 550 municipalities. Separation of powers, under 1940 constitution, modified by transfer of
legislative power to Council of Ministers.
EXECUTIVE: Power vested in cabinet, headed by prime minister and first secretary of
the Communist Party, appointed by the president. Prime minister is chief of the
armed forces. *Elections:* Presidential, Dr Osvaldo Dorticós Torrado elected by
cabinet. Prime minister and first secretary (or secretary-general) of the Communist
Party, Dr Fidel Castro Ruz. No Congressional elections.
JUDICIARY: Supreme Court of 15 judges elected by Council of Ministers; courts of
appeal in each province and lower courts in provincial judicial districts and municipalities; Revolutionary summary tribunals.

DEFENCE

ARMED FORCES: National service: men between 17 and 45 years of age, 3 years in
army; women between 17 and 35 may volunteer for 2 years. Strength (*000*): army 90,
navy 6, air force 20; total 116, plus armed militia 250.

INTERNATIONAL RELATIONS

Member of the United Nations (UN) and some of its international specialised agencies, including: FAO, ICAO, ILO, ITU, UNDP, UNESCO, UPU, WHO and WMO; IAEA; GATT, UNCTAD representative; ECLA.

ECONOMY

PRODUCTION

AGRICULTURE (*ooo tons*)	*1948–53*[1]	*63/64*	*64/65*	*65/66*[2]	*66/67*[2]
Sugar (cane)	5,786	4,398	6,051	4,455	6,100
Tobacco[3]	34	48	59	43	.
Rice	106	193	160	.	.
Maize	224	140	125	.	.
Coffee	31	29	36	28	.

[1] Average 1948/9–1952/3.   [2] Provisional.
[3] Calendar years 1948–52 (av.), 1963, 1964, 1965.

LAND (%), 1946: Arable 17, permanent pasture 34, forested 11, other 37.
OTHER AGRICULTURAL DATA: Agricultural holdings, 1952 (census): no. 100,965, area 77,904 hectares. Tractors in use (*ooos*), 1963: 18. Fertiliser consumption (*ooo tons*), 1965/66: 240.
LIVESTOCK: Nos (*ooo head*), 1964: cattle 3,400, sheep 50, pigs 470.
FISH: Landed (*ooo tons*), 1965: total 40·3.
MINING, 1964: (*ooo tons*), iron ore 5, manganese 33, copper 6, nickel 18, chrome (1963) 18, salt 80; (*tons*) silver (1960) 4, cobalt (1963) 174; (*ooo cubic metres*) crude petroleum 16.
MANUFACTURING, 1964: (*ooo tons*) cement 805, newsprint 5, motor spirit 938; (*ooo cu. metres, sawn*) wood (1963) 140; (*m. litres*) beer 104.

ENERGY

CONSUMPTION (*tons coal equiv.*), 1965: Total 7·25 m., per head 0·95.
ELECTRICITY, 1965: Generated (*kwh*) 3,700 m., installed capacity (kw) 1 m.

GOVERNMENT EXPENDITURE

DISTRIBUTION (% *of total*), 1965: Defence 8, education and social services 27.

GROSS PRODUCT

Net material product, i.e. excluding 'non-productive' services (*m. pesos*): At current market prices, 1964: 3,922; 1965: 4,038. Per head (*US$*), UN estimate, 1958: 302.
DISTRIBUTION (%), ECLA data, 1963: Agriculture (incl. sugar cane 6) 21, manufacturing (incl. sugar ind. 3) 32, trade 32, transport and communications 7, construction 6.
GROWTH RATES (%), ECLA data, 1961–3: 9 (sugar −17·6, trade +31·8).

EXTERNAL TRADE (*US$m.*)	*1955*	*1960*	*1963*	*1964*	*1965*
EXPORTS (f.o.b.)	611	618	544	714	686
Sugar	473	468	472	627	591
Tobacco and mfrs.	43	63	21	29	33
Nickel ore and concentrates	14	2	33	22	15
Copper ore and conc.	13	4	2	5	7
IMPORTS (c.i.f.)	633	638	867	1,015	865
TRADE BALANCE	−22	−20	−323	−301	−179

DIRECTION OF TRADE (%)

	Exports			Imports		
	1955	1960	1965	1955	1960	1965
LAFTA	(1·3)	1·1	—	(2·0)	0·6	0·4
CACM	(0·1)	0·0	—	(0·3)	0·3	—
USA	67·5	56·7	—	73·6	47·4	—
EEC	5·9	6·4	1·5	7·4	10·0	2·1
UK	1·2	3·2	1·8	2·3	4·4	5·9
Sino-Soviet area	6·6	18·7	77·3	0·2	16·5	75·4
USSR	6·1	16·7	47·0	0·0	13·8	49·3

FINANCE

EXCHANGE RATE (*Peso/US$*): Basic rate, end-year, 1960: 1·00; 1966: 1·00.
BUDGET ACCOUNTS (*m. pesos*), 1965: Revenue=expenditure: 2,535.

EMPLOYMENT

ECONOMICALLY ACTIVE (%), 1953: Of total pop. 34 (men 58, women 9). In agriculture 41, services 20, manufacturing 17, trade 12.
EMPLOYMENT (%): ECLA data, 1963: Of total pop. 31; in agriculture 40, industry and construction 19, other 41.
UNEMPLOYMENT, 1957: About 16% of labour force; reduced by about one-half by 1963.

TRANSPORT AND COMMUNICATIONS

RAILWAYS: Traffic, 1956: 278 m. pass.-km., 1,008 m. net ton-km. Length of track, 1957: 4,784 km.
MOTOR VEHICLES: In use (*ooo*), 1965: cars 162, comm. vehicles 104. Road system, 1960: 15,650 km., paved 7,700.
SHIPPING: Merchant fleet (*ooo g.r. tons*), 1966: 238. Main ports: Havana and Santiago de Cuba.
AIR: Scheduled services, 1965: Total 281 m. pass.-km., 5·1 m. cargo ton-km. International: 116 m. pass.-km., 3·1 m. cargo ton-km. Main airports: Havana: José Marti (international); Camagüey, Santiago de Cuba, Santa Clara.
TELEPHONES: No. in use, 1965: 231,000.

SOCIAL WELFARE

SYSTEM: Principles embodied in 1940 constitution. Welfare services, particularly for health, greatly expanded under state system in recent years. Employment legislation based mainly on 1940 constitution and subsequent modifications covered working hours; holidays; payment of wages and overtime; compensation for accidents, dismissal and death.
HEALTH: 1,200 persons per physician, 170 persons per hospital bed.

EDUCATION

ILLITERACY RATE (%), 1953 (census sample): 15 years and over, 22.
COMPULSORY: 6 years (between 6 and 14 years of age). School enrolment ratios (%), 1st and 2nd levels, 1963: 59, adjusted 64.
SCHOOLS, 1964: Pre-school and primary: no. 14,000, pupils 1·3 m., teachers 38,500. Secondary: no. 338, p. 135,700, t. 8,400. Technical: no. 134, st. 53,350, t. 3,200. Teacher-training: no. 15, st. 27,000, t. 1,260. Higher (1965): no. 3, st. 27,300, t. 2,800.
UNIVERSITIES: *State:* U. de la Habana, Havana: 19,000 students, academic staff 2,100; U. de Oriente, Santiago de Cuba: 4,300 st., a.s. 350; U. Central de las Villas, Santa Clara: 4,000 st., a.s. 340.

MASS MEDIA

BROADCASTING: No. of receivers in use: TV 0·55 m., radio 1·35 m. Transmitters, 1963: TV 25; 1961: radio 142.

CINEMAS: No., 1961: 489. Attendance: total 49·9 m., per head 7·2.

NEWSPRINT: Consumption, 1964: total 30,700 tons, per head 4·2 kg.

NEWSPAPERS: Daily, 1961: 10. Estimated circulation 0·6 m., copies per 000 of population 88. Principal dailies in Havana (*circ., 000*): *Granma* 360, *El Mundo* 145, *Juventud;* evening *La Tarde.*

BOOKS: Titles published, 1963: 509.

THE DOMINICAN REPUBLIC

RICHARD SOUTHERN

HISTORY

Before independence

THE Dominican Republic occupies the eastern two-thirds of the Caribbean island of Hispaniola, which it shares with Haiti, where a larger population is confined to the least fertile part of the island. Santo Domingo, the capital, was the first permanent European settlement in the New World, and its magnificent colonial architecture is the sole relic of the country's brief period of prosperity and importance in the early 16th century. With the discovery of the fabulous wealth of Mexico and Peru, the more mundane opportunities offered by the rich soil of Hispaniola lost their attraction, and there followed a steady decline that lasted for the remainder of the colonial period. The annihilation of the Arawak and Taino Indians and the emigration of many of the original Spanish settlers left the territory almost depopulated.

Meanwhile Haiti became, under French rule, one of the richest colonies in the world. In 1801, under Toussaint Louverture, the Haitians invaded the Spanish part of the island and occupied it until 1809, after which the territory again became a Spanish colony. In 1821 the lawyer José Núñez de Cáceres led a successful insurrection to proclaim the Dominican Republic. Within nine weeks the Haitians reimposed their rule, but this time the occupation lasted for twenty-three years and was characterised by a severity the Dominicans never forgot.

1844–1930

In 1844 Dominican liberals, led by the noble and idealistic Juan Pablo Duarte, expelled the Haitians from Dominican soil; but Duarte and his followers had no opportunity of governing their liberated country. They were unceremoniously turned out of office by the first of a series of power-hungry strong men who were to mismanage the country's affairs, line their own pockets, and leave almost insoluble problems for their successors.

The principal *caudillos* of the ensuing two decades, Pedro Santana and Buenaventura Báez, were alike in their inability to rule except by exercising a merciless and corrupt despotism. In 1861 the Dominican Republic even became a Spanish colony again. The arrogance and ineptitude displayed by Spanish bureaucrats, soldiers and clergy soon inflamed popular discontent, and Spanish rule came to an end three years later, followed by virtual civil war as each successive ruler further increased the Dominican Republic's indebtedness by obtaining foreign loans on ruinous terms and neglecting to spend the proceeds on the development of the country. In 1876 an attempt was made to arrest the drift under the idealistic President Ulises

257

HISPANIOLA: DOMINICAN REPUBLIC AND HAITI

Main urban centres
Other important towns (all less than 30,000 pop.)
Frontier (Garrison) towns in Dominican Republic
Main areas of sugar cultivation
Dominican Republic agricultural colonies (N.B. Note concentration on Haitian frontier)

Height of land in feet
Under 1000
1000 – 2000
2000 – 5000
Over 5000

50 Miles
50 Kilometres

N.B. Haitian urban centres shown (all over 5000 pop.) account for only 7% of country's population.

Haiti only – areas with a density of rural population exceeding 250 per square mile

DOMINICAN REPUBLIC

HAITI

Cordillera Septentrional
Cordillera Central
Sierra de Ocoa
Valle de Río Yaque del Norte
Cibao
Plain of Seibo
Very Sparsely Populated
R.Yuna
R.Yaque del Sur

Puerto Plata
Monte Cristi
Santiago pop. 90,000
Moca
La Vega
San Francisco de Macorís
Samaná
Seibo
San Pedro de Macorís
Santo Domingo pop. 360,000
Azua
Barahona
Enriquillo
Comendador
Banica
Dajabón
Pedernales

CACAO
COFFEE

Cap Haïtien
Port de Paix
Gonaïves
St. Marc
Port au Prince pop. 150,000
Pétionville
Petit Goâve
Jacmel
Jérémie
Les Cayes
Massif du Nord
Plateau Central
Vallée de l'Artibonite
Massif de la Selle
Massif de la Hotte
COFFEE

C ANTHONY BLOND LTD

258

Espaillat, who was however unable to initiate the necessary reforms. He died in 1878, his good intentions drowned in another wave of insurrections and public disorder.

During the last two decades of the 19th century the Dominicans endured the dictatorship of Ulises Heureaux ('Lilís'). This general, a Negro of Haitian origin, climbed to power from his position as minister of the interior. Once in office, he established absolute personal rule with the full apparatus of a vindictive police-state. In this, as in his sordid private life, he was a forerunner of Trujillo, and his reign helped to pave the way for the predicament in which the Dominican Republic was to find herself three decades later. The country's external finances were still in a parlous state, and Heureaux bought time by raising yet more loans from foreign bankers and, in security for them, mortgaging the Dominican Republic's unpredictable future revenues: an utterly disastrous policy which was to lead, in the long run, to the sacrifice of the nation's precarious sovereignty.

In a crescendo of terror and extortion Heureaux was assassinated in 1899. Chaos followed the event. In the ensuing period of instability and misrule the presidency of the able and progressive Ramón Cáceres (1906–11) stands out as an exception; but it was too late to reverse the trend. Cáceres, who had been the assassin of Heureaux, was himself murdered in 1911, and the Dominican Republic steadily drifted towards total anarchy.

By the terms of an agreement signed in 1905 the United States government had established a lien on the Dominican Republic's customs revenues, and now, in the era of the Big Stick policy, edged closer and closer towards outright intervention. In 1916 the Marines invaded the country and a military government was established. Eight years of Marine rule brought some material advance; order and financial stability were established. Yet most Dominicans bitterly resented the occupation, and there was widespread guerrilla resistance. The United States authorities, in their turn, organised a National Constabulary, but could find Dominican recruits for this force only among criminals and gangsters. One such recruit was Rafael Trujillo, who was to rise to command of the force and later bring the entire country under his despotic control.

The Trujillo era

No progress was made, despite sincere efforts of both Dominicans and Americans, towards the establishment of strong and viable civic institutions which would ensure the Dominican Republic a healthy political life by the time the Marines withdrew in 1924. Six years of confusion followed, and effective constitutional government was never reestablished. The 1929 crisis threatened to wipe out the economic gains of the previous years. Trujillo stepped into the vacuum. He came to power in 1930 after a bloody coup and rigged elections, and instituted an absolute personal despotism that has few parallels in modern history. After a hurricane had destroyed the capital he eventually rebuilt the city as the showpiece of the country's new prosperity and renamed it after himself, Ciudad Trujillo.

He faced the problem of national indebtedness, which had plagued his predecessors, with an energy and efficiency for which even his enemies have given him credit, and which naturally delighted foreign bankers. The principal method he employed was a vast increase in indirect taxation. Within a decade (by the agreement signed by Trujillo and Cordell Hull on 24 September 1940) the humiliating customs convention was ended, and by 1947 the last of the foreign debt had been paid off. Trujillo achieved this by encouraging production and capital investment and diversifying the still predominantly agricultural economy. The country made considerable economic progress during this period, even though a large proportion of profits swelled the Trujillo family fortune, and the mass of the peasantry remained virtually outside the money economy altogether. Especially significant were the achievements in the field of public works, which offered excellent opportunities for graft and impressed foreign visitors. After three decades of absolute rule Trujillo was one of the richest men in the world.

The Trujillo regime had no political or ideological content whatever: the doctrine of *Trujillismo* was mere word-spinning. Far from being ostensibly based on a totalitarian theory, the regime scrupulously preserved the external forms of democratic institutions and legal procedures. There was a constitution providing for separation of powers and other traditional safeguards, and an all-embracing bill of rights. But the apparatus of repression was systematic and ruthless, and pervaded every aspect of Dominican life. It was completely effective in stifling all opposition within the country, and even Trujillo's critics abroad were not safe from his agents. The Spanish writer, Jesus de Galindez, who published a devastating exposure of the regime, was kidnapped in broad daylight in New York, taken by air to the Dominican Republic and there tortured and murdered.

Trujillo's foreign policy was cynically opportunistic; he flirted with Hitler in the 1930s, bestowed fulsome praise on Stalin after the Allied victory, and proclaimed himself the champion of anti-communism in the Americas when the Cold War was at its height. He played skilfully on the Dominicans' traditional (and often well-founded) fear of Haiti, which had become something of a national neurosis: this became the pretext for the creation and preservation of overwhelmingly strong armed forces. The old National Constabulary was transformed into a modern, well-equipped army, and a navy and air force were added. These forces were to constitute both a threat to the country's Caribbean neighbours and an instrument of internal repression. The creation of a powerful military caste was not the least among Trujillo's disastrous legacies to his successors.

In 1960 Trujillo unwisely embarked on a policy of flagrant intervention in the internal affairs of Venezuela. His agents were implicated in a plot to assassinate President Betancourt, who arraigned him before the Organisation of American States as a threat to the peace of the hemisphere. This time Trujillo had overstepped the mark. This was the era of the first flush of optimism over the Alliance for Progress, and it was evident that United States support for his regime was incompatible with the principles underlying the Alliance. The United States belatedly reversed its policy and supported the Latin American countries in a series of increasingly severe diplomatic and economic sanctions against the Dominican Republic. An embargo on oil shipments to the country was fully effective as far as the Americas were concerned; had it been total, it would probably have brought the Dominican economy to a standstill in a matter of weeks. As it was, oil shipments from Western Europe gave the regime a valuable breathing-space. During this period a large proportion of the funds accumulated by Trujillo's underlings in three decades of graft and extortion were transferred abroad. This compounded the economic difficulties to be faced by any government that succeeded the Trujillo regime.

Trujillo was assassinated by conspirators on 30 May 1961; within the next few days all but two of them were killed by the police. They had not represented any coherent political force, let alone a movement of democratic opposition; they had been simply disaffected followers of Trujillo attempting a 'palace revolution'. The Trujillo regime survived its creator: it was too strongly built a structure to collapse overnight, and the vested interests involved were too powerful to abdicate without a fight. Joaquín Balaguer, the titular president, found himself holding the reins of power, supported by the Trujillo family and the military caste that controlled the apparatus of repression.

The Balaguer and Bosch regimes

Trujillo left behind him a total vacuum. Whereas it was impossible to imagine any 'strong man' powerful enough to step into his shoes and take over the regime, it was almost as difficult to prophesy the nature and leadership of any movement destined to change the existing political, economic and social structure. Virtually all dedicated Dominicans were tainted by collaboration with the Trujillo regime; a man's political enemies would, of course, put the broadest possible interpretation on this term. The position of the exiles was even more difficult. So effective had been Trujillo's control over the media that their very names were unknown to most Dominicans; they were, moreover, open to the charge of cowardice in 'sunning themselves on foreign beaches' during the Trujillo era, and abandoning their countrymen to the rigours of persecution.

The post-Trujillo era has therefore been a period of pronounced political instability. In addition to the Republic's internal difficulties, relations with Haiti have deteriorated, border incidents being frequent; diplomatic relations were severed in May 1963.

The first active opposition to the Balaguer regime came from the National Civic Union (NCU), which pressed for the dismantling of the police-state and the establishment of constitutional democracy; its leaders were mostly business and professional men, and its chief spokesman was Dr Viriato Fiallo. In the circumstances surrounding its origin, when any display of opposition was extremely dangerous, its members acted with great courage and were largely responsible for the liberalisation of the nation's political life. It must be remembered that the regime was also under pressure from the team of observers sent by the Organisation of American States. In essence, however, the NCU advocated a cautious and conservative liberalism; it was a movement led by the upper middle-class, and had little enthusiasm for the social and economic reforms that were long overdue. The NCU, therefore, came to constitute the right as soon as normal political dialogue was reestablished. Paradoxically, in the earlier stages, its position as a 'non-political patriotic movement' that appeared certain to assume power made it vulnerable to infiltration by the Communists, and it had some difficulty in ridding itself of these elements.

In the 1962 elections the left was chiefly represented by the Dominican Revolutionary Party (PRD) led by Juan Bosch, an intellectual who had spent many years in exile. This party was democratic and mildly socialist; it emphasised the need for thorough agrarian reform. It was never pro-communist, although its opponents denounced Bosch as a second Castro. It carried out a 'grass-roots' campaign that stirred the Dominican peasants out of their torpor and into political consciousness, and gained their over-whelming support. There were three communist, or crypto-communist, factions: the official and pro-Soviet Popular Socialist Party; the pro-Chinese Dominican Popular Movement; and the vaguely Castroist '14th of June' Movement. All these groups boycotted the elections and bitterly denounced

Bosch as a stooge of US imperialism. They were not strong numerically, and expended much of their energy on internecine quarrels. The PRD gained an absolute majority of the vote in an orderly election, and Bosch had a clear mandate.

This experiment in democratic government, as so many previously, was short-lived. Bosch's plans for agrarian reform and redistributive taxation ran counter to vested interests, and the precarious economic situation of the country (aggravated by a fall in sugar production) necessitated the curtailment of imports and other unpopular 'austerity' measures. Bosch's very virtues proved a handicap, for his simon-pure liberalism and scrupulous respect for the letter and spirit of the constitution prevented his silencing either the Communists or the right-wing military caste; both, for widely differing reasons, were determined to make his task as difficult as possible.

For this Bosch must be held partly responsible. Of humble origin and entirely self-educated, he was excessively suspicious of the 'first families' that formed the upper and upper-middle classes, and assumed from the outset that they were determined to thwart him. He ignored the University of Santo Domingo whose students, though in many cases scions of the 'first families', were radical in outlook and even sympathetic to Castroism. Nor did he attempt a *rapprochement* with such sectors of the armed forces as might have given him at least passive support. Increasingly isolated, Bosch relied on the support of the peasants and urban workers. He failed to appreciate that three decades of psychological bludgeoning by Trujillo's propaganda machine had converted this class, if such it could be called, into a volatile and bewildered *Lumpenproletariat*. When Bosch was eventually ousted, the 'masses' did not lift a finger to help him, although they had voted him into power less than a year before.

Junta rule: December 1963—April 1965

There were abortive plots against Bosch in March, April, July and August 1963. The plot of 25 September 1963 was successful, and he was obliged to relinquish his office and leave the country. Those responsible for the coup accused Bosch of administrative inefficiency and leniency towards the Communists. What ensued was in fact a military junta but, following a trend discernible in other Latin American countries, this was camouflaged by a façade of civilian 'interim' government.

The United States government expressed its disapproval of the coup by breaking off diplomatic relations and suspending economic and military aid. But, disenchanted with Bosch, it became first a passive and eventually an active supporter of the new regime. This period saw the murder of President Kennedy and the development by the Johnson administration of what was euphemistically called a 'flexible' policy towards unconstitutional regimes in Latin America.

The junta remained in power from December 1963 until the outbreak of civil war in April 1965. Donald Reid Cabral, a businessman of Scottish descent, became the nominal leader of a government that was the pawn of the armed forces. The economic situation obliged the junta to continue the stabilisation and 'austerity' programme along much the same lines as Bosch; and, as had been the case with Bosch, increased taxation and controls provoked disaffection and unrest, mainly in the form of strikes and riots. There was a slight improvement in business confidence, and even a trickle of fresh foreign investment; in March 1964 the government invited tenders for the establishment of an oil refinery. Foreign indebtedness, however, rose from US $80 million in September 1963 to US $161 million in March 1965.

Civil war and US intervention

The junta, partly in an effort to improve its dubious reputation abroad, promised to hold 'free' elections, and these were scheduled for 15 September 1965; but the situation was to change completely before that date. On 24 April 1965 a 'constitutionalist' insurrection against the ruling junta broke out; its supporters included a section of the armed forces and demanded the return of Bosch and the reestablishment of legal government. The revolt was led by Col. Francisco Caamaño Deñó, and it appears certain that it would have been successful but for the disastrous intervention of the United States. It was well organised, enjoyed overwhelming support, and had the advantage of surprise. US intervention gave the right-wing militarists supporting the junta time to rally their forces, and the rebels were able to seize only the Old City of Santo Domingo (containing the principal banks and commercial offices and the port), where they entrenched themselves. Reid Cabral resigned, and the pro-junta forces were commanded by Gen. Elías Wessin y Wessin, and later by Gen. Antonio Imbert Barreras (one of the surviving assassins of Trujillo).

The Marines were sent into the Dominican Republic ostensibly to protect the lives of American residents, but their presence there signified *de facto* support for the junta. President Johnson, in a speech of 2 May 1965, attempted to justify his government's action by describing the insurrection as an initially democratic movement which had fallen under Communist control. This version of events conflicted sharply with the reports of US journalists, who saw no evidence to suggest that the Dominican Communists, still divided into warring factions, were capable of even attempting such a coup.

Considerable resentment was caused in Latin America by the arbitrary manner in which the United States had by-passed the OAS and the United Nations, and decided unilaterally to invade the territory of a sovereign nation on grounds that were, at best, questionable. The United States subsequently submitted the matter to the consideration of the OAS, requesting retrospective sanction for its action, obtaining it by a majority of one vote—that of the Dominican Republic (i.e. the nominee of the junta). The major countries of the region, excluding Brazil, voted against the United States. The occupation force in the Dominican Republic, which had established a precarious 'peace' by separating the contending parties, became at least nominally international by the addition of token contingents from Brazil and some Central American countries. OAS mediators in the Dominican Republic managed to effect a compromise between the Constitutionalists and the supporters of the junta; it was agreed to form a provisional government that would rule until free elections could be held. It was headed by Dr Héctor García Godoy, an 'apolitical' lawyer and diplomat who was, for the time being at least, acceptable to both factions.

The provisional government

The provisional government depended, in the last resort, on the backing of the OAS which had virtually created it. Dr García Godoy made skilful efforts to give his government a non-partisan character and avoid antagonising the extremists of right and left. But the centrifugal tendencies reasserted themselves, and by the end of the year the country was on the brink of another civil war. The Constitutionalists had been allowed to keep their weapons, and it was intended gradually to reintegrate them into the armed forces, but clashes between them and the former supporters of the junta became more frequent. The Inter-American Force was increasingly involved in the tasks of street patrolling and riot control, and both factions resented its presence. Yet it is doubtful if the provisional government would have survived its withdrawal for twenty-four hours.

On 4 January 1966 the provisional government faced its most serious crisis: the Constitutionalists formally withdrew their support from it, alleging that it had done nothing to prevent or punish terroristic attacks against former 'rebels'. Dr García Godoy in reply proposed a compromise solution: the 'exiling' to diplomatic posts abroad of the leaders of both factions, in order to achieve a calmer atmosphere and prepare the ground for free elections. This exercise in impartiality nearly triggered off another coup by outraged army officers, but Dr García Godoy held his ground, supported by the OAS, the United States and the church. Eventually the Constitutionalist officers accepted the proposal. The former junta supporters, however, failed to keep their side of the bargain, and none of them left the country except the former Secretary of the Armed Forces, Commodore Francisco Rivera Caminero, who went to the United States in February. Widespread public indignation at this breach of faith led to another wave of unrest, culminating in a seven-day general strike called by the PRD; its success testified to the strong numerical support which that movement still enjoyed in the country.

The elections of 1 June 1966

The PRD claimed, with some justification, that the government's failure to 'exile' the right-wing officers seriously prejudiced the chances of the next presidential election being held in an atmosphere free from intimidation. Juan Bosch was, however, eventually persuaded to accept nomination as PRD candidate. The other candidates were Rafael Bonnelly, a conservative respected as an efficient administrator (he had headed an interim government before the 1962 elections), and Joaquín Balaguer, who had staged a remarkable comeback after being thoroughly discredited as a puppet of Trujillo. The presence of the OAS force, in full support of the provisional government, enabled elections to be held as scheduled on 1 June.

Balaguer won a surprising and decisive victory. Various reasons were alleged for the failure of Bosch and his PRD to repeat their triumph of 1962. Bosch himself, owing to threats against his life, was confined to his house under police protection during a large part of the campaign and thus prevented from campaigning properly; moreover, his political enemies found it easy to label him as a 'coward' because of his failure to return to the country when the insurrection broke out in April 1965. Above all, the votes of the women and the extreme right (for the latter soon realised that Bonnelly stood little chance) were thrown behind Balaguer.

However this may be, Balaguer's margin of victory was sufficiently clear for him to claim a mandate for the right-of-centre policy of his Reformista Party. This programme (like those of his opponents) envisaged the speedy withdrawal of the Inter-American Force: this was completed by mid-September. As many had feared, there was renewed violence and terrorism, but these were sporadic and uncoordinated, and in June 1967 Balaguer was still President, although his position was precarious and he ruled virtually by permission of the armed forces. The greatest sufferers from the reprisals and counter-reprisals were the now disorganised supporters of the PRD (Bosch had resigned the leadership and left the country in October 1966); perhaps the only real beneficiaries were the increasingly active Communists, vociferously supported by Peking. US financial support enabled Balaguer to achieve some success in halting the deterioration in the economy, and there were signs that the Church was belatedly paying attention to the country's social problems.

ECONOMY

The Dominican economy suffers from two chronic ills. The first is the enormous burden of the armed forces, which often absorb over half the annual budget. The second is the country's excessive dependence on sugar, exports of which account for around 60 per cent of foreign exchange earnings: the economy is thus vulnerable to the effects of shortfalls in production or a decline in the world price. Similar considerations apply to the less important export crops such as coffee and cacao.

Most sugar is grown near the capital in an area stretching eastwards and inland. This constitutes 22 per cent of the total cropland (which in turn represents 14 per cent of the total area of the country. The Dominican Republic has had its full share of the problems inseparable from a large-scale sugar industry (i.e. it requires a large seasonal labour force, it encourages monoculture and necessitates large-scale land fertilisation). The sugar industry is now almost entirely owned and managed by the government following the confiscation of the enormous Trujillo properties (it is estimated that the 'Benefactor' and his family owned over half the cultivable land in the country).

Mineral resources are limited, the most successful mining operation to date being the bauxite mine in Cabo Rojo (production reached 1·3 million tons in 1960). Here the Dominican Republic faces direct competition from Jamaica. There is a wide variety of light industry (footwear, chemicals, etc.), also the legacy of the Trujillos, the concerns being owned by the dictator and his family and artificially protected from competition. This sector, now owned by the government, caters almost exclusively for the still exiguous home market. The tourist trade, which is of course dependent on peace and political stability, has great potential. The Dominican Republic boasts some of the finest and most varied scenery in the world, including beaches and a rugged and mountainous interior.

To the endemic problems described above there have been added a host of others caused by the events of the past few years. Fresh foreign investment has virtually ceased as the political upheavals have progressively eroded business confidence. The civil war of April–September 1965 is estimated to have cost over US $250 million, i.e. 30 per cent of the estimated GNP for 1965 (most of this sum, however, represents the loss caused by the paralysis of the economy; the physical damage to installations and plants was comparatively small). At the beginning of 1966 it was apparent to most observers that the economy could be saved from collapse only by massive injections of foreign aid. Average income per head was about US $200 per annum, the majority of the population was living at subsistence level, and probably half the total labour force was unemployed. Industry and commerce were almost at a standstill. Few expected the three goals of diversifying the economy, trimming the armed forces' share of the budget and attracting foreign investment to be achieved in the near future. The necessary economic measures could not be taken while political instability continued; and, conversely, there was little likelihood of a viable and healthy political life developing while the economic situation was so desperate. There seemed to be no escape from this vicious circle.

SOCIAL STRUCTURE

Dominican society is still hierarchical in spirit, the landowning families enjoying considerable wealth and great social prestige, although some of their power, both in relative and absolute terms, was whittled away during the Trujillo era. This patrician class is of wholly European descent, while the poorest class is completely Negro; nevertheless social conflict is rarely expressed in racial terms.

Dominican social mores stem from the country's tragic history and from the need to assert the nation's Hispanic character in contrast to the Franco-African culture of Haiti, towards which most Dominicans feel hostility and apprehension. Dominicans are, therefore, almost aggressively 'European' and 'Spanish': even the Negro has a strong consciousness of his Dominican nationality, and does not feel anything in common with the Haitian. Internal communications were long so poor that there was little contact between one province and another. Strong regional characteristics have remained, and there are three regional accents.

The Dominican contribution to Latin American literature and thought has been considerable in relation to the size of the country and the enormous difficulties which Dominican intellectuals have so often had to face. The stifling of all forms of free expression during the Trujillo era is largely responsible for the present stagnation and absence of any definable sense of direction among Dominican intellectuals and among the population as a whole.

BIBLIOGRAPHY

Bosch, Juan. *The Unfinished Experiment: Democracy in the Dominican Republic*, Frederick A. Praeger, New York, 1965; Pall Mall Press, London, 1966.
Galindez, Jesús de. *La Era de Trujillo*, Editorial del Pacífico, Santiago, 1956.
Rodman, Selden. *Quisqueya: A History of the Dominican Republic*, Univ. of Washington Press, Seattle, 1964.
Welles, Sumner. *Naboth's Vineyard: The Dominican Republic 1844–1924*, 2 vols, Payson and Clarke, New York, 1928.

BASIC INFORMATION

CLIMATE

Santo Domingo

Lat./long.	18° 30′ N, 70° W	Relative humidity	
Altitude	57 ft/17 m.	at midday of	66%/64%
Mean temp. of hottest month	27°C/80°F (Aug.)	hottest and coolest month	
Mean temp. of coolest month	24°C/75°F (Jan.)	Wettest month	7·3 in./185 mm. (Sept.)
Absolute max.	90°F/32°C	Driest month	1·4 in./36 mm. (Feb.)
Absolute min.	64°F/18°C		
		Annual av. rainfall	55·8 in./1,417 mm.

POPULATION

TOTAL (*million*): 1960 (census) 3·05; mid-1966: 3·75; 1980 (ECLA projection): 6·17. DENSITY, mid-1965; 74 persons per sq. km. CRUDE RATES (*per 000*), 1963: Birth 32·6, death 6·5 (ECLA data, 1959–61: birth 48–50, death 15–17), infant mortality 81·3. GROWTH RATES (% *p.a.*) 1945–65: 3·3; 1960–5: 3·6. DISTRIBUTION (% *of total pop.*): Ethnic, 1950: mulatto 70, white 15, Negro 15. Foreign-born, 1950: 1·6; 1960: 1·4. Languages, 1950: Spanish 98, French 1, English nearly 1. Religion, 1950: Roman Catholic 98, Protestant 2. Urban (*centres 2,000 inhab. or over*), ECLA data, 1950: 21·5; 1960: 27·5; 1980 (projection): 39·6. Largest cities (*000 inhab.*), 1960: Santo Domingo 370 (National District, 1964: 529), Santiago de los Caballeros 86, San Francisco de Macorís 27.

CONSTITUTIONAL SYSTEM (*1962 constitution*)

CONSTITUTION: First 1844. US military occupation 1916–24. Tenth constitution 1947; 1961, provisional; 1962; 1963, abolished and replaced by that of 1962; new constitution promulgated November 1966. SYSTEM: Unitary republic, composed of 26 provinces and the National District. Separate executive, legislature and judiciary. EXECUTIVE: Power vested in president, elected (with a vice-president) by direct vote for 4-year term; no immediate reelection. LEGISLATURE: Bi-cameral, Congress of Senate and Chamber of Deputies. *Senate:* 1 senator (and 1 alternate) from each province and the National District, elected by direct vote for 4-year term. *Deputies:* 1 deputy (and 1 alternate) for every 50,000 inhabitants or fraction greater than 25,000; minimum of 2 deputies for each province, elected by direct vote for 4-year term. *Suffrage:* Universal voting for citizens over 18 years of age (earlier if married). *Elections,* June 1966: Presidential (*000 votes*): Joaquín Balaguer 754 (elected), Juan Bosch 518, Rafael Bonnelly 45. Composition of Congress: Senate—Partido Reformista (PR) 22 seats, P. Revolucionario Dominicano (PRD) 5; Deputies—PR 48, PRD 26. JUDICIARY: Supreme Court, of 10 judges, elected by the Senate; Courts of Appeal; courts of first instance; lower courts in each province and municipality.

DEFENCE

DEFENCE BUDGET: 1964: 38 m. pesos; 4·3 per cent of GDP. ARMED FORCES: Strength (*000*): Army 12, navy 4, air force 3, total 20.

INTERNATIONAL RELATIONS

Member of the UN and many of its international specialised agencies, including: IBRD and affiliates, IMF, FAO, ICAO, IMCO, ILO, ITU, UNESCO, UPU, WHO and WMO; IAEA; GATT, UNCTAD representative. Also member of: OAS, Alliance for Progress, ECLA and IDB.

ECONOMY

PRODUCTION

AGRICULTURE (*000 tons*)	1948–53[1]	63/64	64/65	65/66[2]	66/67[2]
Sugar (cane)[3]	539	825	583	692	793
Coffee	28	41	41	42	45
Cacao	30	45	33	30	.
Rice	65	145	137	150	146
Tobacco[3]	18	20	20	23	.
Bananas	377	447	.	.	.

[1] Average 1948/9–1952/3.　　　[2] Provisional.
[3] Calender years: 1948–52, 1964, 1965, 1966, 1967.

LAND (%), 1946: Arable 14, permanent pasture 12, forested 46, other 28.
OTHER AGRICULTURAL DATA: Agricultural holdings, 1960 (census): no. 450,335, area 2·64 m. hectares. Tractors in use, 1952: 500. Fertiliser consumption (*ooo tons*), 1965/66: 19·5.
LIVESTOCK: Nos (*ooo head*), 1960: cattle 1,002, sheep 70, pigs 1,170. Products (*ooo tons*), 1961: meat 29 (beef and veal 20).
FISH: Landed (*ooo tons*), 1965: total 4·1.
MINING (*ooo tons*), 1963: Iron ore 140; 1965: bauxite 914; 1964: salt 33.
MANUFACTURING, 1963: (*ooo tons*) Cement 229, wheat flour 44; (*ooo cu. metres, sawn*): wood (1962) 55; (*m. litres*) beer (1964) 30.

ENERGY

CONSUMPTION (*tons coal equiv.*), 1965: Total 0·70 m., per head 0·194.
ELECTRICITY, 1965: Generated (*kwh*) 640 m., installed capacity (*kw*), 1963: 0·12 m.

GOVERNMENT EXPENDITURE

DISTRIBUTION (% *of total*), 1966: Defence 16, education 16, social services 9, public works and communications 13.

GROSS PRODUCT

GDP (*m. pesos*): At current market prices, 1963: 992; 1964: 1,085; at 1962 market prices, 1963: 919; 1964: 977. Per head (*US$*), UN estimate, 1964: 206.
DISTRIBUTION (%), 1964: Agriculture 24, manufacturing 16, trade 18, government 12.
GROWTH RATES (%), 1950–60: 5·7, per head 2·1; 1960–4: 5·0 (1965: − 12), per head 2·0 (1965: − 15).

EXTERNAL TRADE (*US$ m.*)	*1955*	*1960*	*1964*	*1965*	*1966*
EXPORTS (f.o.b.)	115	174	179	123	137
Sugar	45	89	93	62	77
Coffee	28	23	31	21	21
Cacao	24	21	16	7	11
Tobacco	5	7	15	9	7
Bauxite	—	8	9	12	10
Bananas and plantains	2	11	5	3	1
IMPORTS (f.o.b.)	98	87	192	92	160
IMPORTS (c.i.f.)	114	100	221	106	184
TRADE BALANCE	+1	+74	−42	+17	−47

DIRECTION OF TRADE (%)

	Exports			Imports		
	1955	*1960*	*1965*	*1955*	*1960*	*1965*
LAFTA	(0·1)	—	—	(1·5)	—	—
CACM	(0·2)	—	—	(—)	—	—
USA	55·3	61·9	82·5	65·6	52·8	54·0
EEC	10·8	11·9	8·0	10·6	15·8	16·2
UK	21·3	12·4	0·6	3·0	4·9	2·8

FINANCE

EXCHANGE RATE (*Peso/US$*): Par value, end-year, 1960: 1·00; 1966: 1·00.
BALANCE OF PAYMENTS (*US$ m.*): Goods and services (net), 1960: +46; 1964: −80; 1965: −36; 1966: −76.
COST OF LIVING (*Dec. 1958=100*), Santo Domingo, December 1960: 97; 1964: 116; 1965: 113; 1966: 122.
INDUSTRIAL WAGES: Earnings in manufacturing, per month, 1963: 63 pesos.
TREASURY ACCOUNTS (*m. pesos*), 1966: Revenue 163, expenditure 194, deficit 31.

EMPLOYMENT

ECONOMICALLY ACTIVE (%), 1960: Of total pop. 27 (men 48, women 6). In agriculture 61, services 11, manufacturing 8, trade 7.

TRANSPORT AND COMMUNICATIONS

RAILWAYS: Length of track: 1,265 km.
MOTOR VEHICLES: In use (ooo), 1965: cars 29·2, comm. vehicles 12·3. Road system, 1962: 9,325 km., paved 4,250.
SHIPPING: Merchant fleet (ooo g.r. tons), 1966: 7·6. International sea-borne shipping (m. tons), 1964: goods loaded 2·23, goods unloaded 1·07. Main ports: Santo Domingo, Puerto Plata, San Pedro de Macorís, Manzanillo.
AIR: Scheduled services, 1964: Total 11·7 m. pass.-km., 0·4 m. cargo ton-km. International: 7·2 m. pass.-km., 0·3 m. cargo ton-km. Main airports: Santo Domingo: Punta Caucedo (international); Cabo Rojo.
TELEPHONES: No. in use, 1965: 31,300.

SOCIAL WELFARE

SYSTEM: Social insurance benefits and services administered by the Instituto Dominicano de Seguros Sociales; separate system for civil servants. Financed by employees' and employers' contributions based on remuneration: employees 4%, employers 7%, and state contributions. Employment legislation covers working hours; holidays; payment of wages; overtime and annual bonus; compensation for accidents, dismissal and death indemnities.
HEALTH: 1,600 persons per physician, 440 persons per hospital bed.
NUTRITION: Net food supply (per head per day), 1959: 2,080 calories, protein 49 g.

EDUCATION

ILLITERACY RATE (%), 1960 (census): 15 years and over, 36.
COMPULSORY: 6 years (between 7 and 14 years of age). School enrolment ratios (%), 1st and 2nd levels, 1962: 48, adjusted 65.
SCHOOLS, 1962: Primary: no. 4,820, pupils 0·48, teachers 9,300. Secondary: no. 352, p. 40,400, t. 1,820. Technical: no. 190, st. 25,300, t. 730. Teacher-training: no. 5, st. 350, t. 43. Higher (1965): no. 2, st. 5,600, t. 425.
UNIVERSITIES: U. de Santo Domingo, Santo Domingo: 5,000 st., a.s. 385. U. Católica Madre y Maestra, Santiago de los Caballeros: 600 st., a.s. 40. U. Nacional Pedro Henriquez Ureña (private), established 1966.

MASS MEDIA

BROADCASTING: No. of receivers in use, TV 50,000, radio 150,000. Transmitters: TV 4, radio 68.
CINEMAS: No., 1961: 96. Attendance: total 5·3 m., per head 1·7.
NEWSPRINT: Consumption, 1964: total 3,800 tons, per head 1·1 kg.
NEWSPAPERS: Daily, 1965: 7. Estimated circulation (4 dailies) 98,000, copies per ooo of population 27. Principal dailies in Santo Domingo (circ., ooos): El Caribe 50, Listín Diario 35; evening El Nacional, Prensa Libre. Santiago de los Caballeros: La Información 13.
BOOKS: Titles published, 1963: 71.

THE FRENCH ANTILLES AND FRENCH GUIANA

JUNE M. HENFREY

HISTORY

Settlement and colonisation

THE Caribbean islands of Martinique and Guadeloupe (with its small dependencies) and the South American mainland territory of French Guiana are all that now remains of the once considerable French empire in the New World. This empire was never a stable one. Colonial expansion and the increased commercial activity to which it gave rise created intense rivalry between the European powers, which often flared into open war, and the chequered history of France's presence in the New World mirrors her performance in these wars, particularly those of the 18th century.

The portion of the South American mainland that lies between the Amazon and Orinoco rivers was early identified with the Eldorado of travellers' tales and explorers' dreams. Official French attempts at settlement lagged behind the Dutch and the British. During the 17th century, however, several French companies, with government encouragement, made attempts at organised settlement. Most of these attempts failed miserably, and by 1715 effective occupation was still limited to a very small area round the island of Cayenne, which was administered as a dependency of the French Windward Islands. By this time former French ambitions for a vast empire on the mainland of South America had played themselves out, and the colony remained virtually forgotten until 1763 when it unexpectedly found itself once more the centre of attention.

Unlike most of French America, the poor, undeveloped colony of Cayenne had not been captured by the British during the Seven Years' War. When the Peace of Paris considerably reduced France's territorial dominions in the New World, French eyes began to turn to Cayenne as the base from which French colonial fortunes could be rebuilt. It was envisaged that the territory would supply France's Caribbean islands with essential products like timber, salted meat and fish and other foodstuffs. Colonists were attracted from all over France and even from Germany, but disaster soon struck in the form of famine, disease and Indian attacks. The French subsequently learned from the experience of the Dutch in neighbouring Surinam. A measure of success was achieved so that by the 1770s and '80s the colony, though small, was relatively stable. However, it has always remained sparsely populated and neglected, a poor relation of the more important islands of Martinique and Guadeloupe.

The islands of Martinique and Guadeloupe were settled in 1635. Situated in the fertile chain of the Lesser Antilles, they soon prospered. Sugar, introduced into the Caribbean by the Dutch, began to be grown in the

French islands some time before 1650, and by 1715, when France had lost most of her other possessions in the Lesser Antilles, Martinique and Guadeloupe had assumed a position of supreme importance in the French colonial empire. During the 18th century, in spite of their continued value to the French economy, they were temporarily eclipsed by the far richer island of Saint-Domingue, but reverted to their dominant position once Saint-Domingue had become the independent country of Haiti.

Both islands were captured by the British during the Seven Years' War and returned by the terms of the Peace of Paris in 1763. Between 1763 and 1789 their prosperity was at its zenith. Their output of sugar soared. They had long been trading illicitly with the British colonies in North America, and after 1776 they openly took over from the British West Indies the lucrative trade with the newly independent United States. This period of growth and prosperity was brought to an abrupt conclusion by the French Revolution.

1789–1848

Since they were created as purely commercial concerns, the French American colonies were at first administered by the trading companies which had founded them under government monopolies. Between 1674 and the Revolution the crown assumed direct control of the colonies, which were governed by a system of dual administration. The supreme command of the Caribbean territories and Guiana was entrusted to a lieutenant-general under whom stood the military governors of the several territories, whose rule was in practice absolute. Consequently the French colonies never achieved the degree of local autonomy which evolved in the British colonies through the mechanism of elected assemblies.

Creole society began to assert itself in Martinique and Guadeloupe in the 18th century despite the undisputed Frenchness of the islands; it had become prosperous, self-confident and proud. It is not without significance that the populations of Martinique and Guadeloupe were only too eager to surrender to the British during the Seven Years' War in order to safeguard their own economic interests. So too, the denial of genuine political responsibilities to the colonists helped to advance the forces of disunity and rebellion set loose in the colonies by the events of 1789.

The influence of the Revolution on France's American colonies was chiefly connected with the single fact of slavery. The lifeblood of the islands' economy was sugar produced on plantations worked by large numbers of Negro slaves. Guiana too depended on slave labour. Thus, broadly speaking, creole society consisted of a small group of white landowners surrounded by masses of slaves who, throughout the period of slavery, were constantly on the verge of revolt. There also existed two smaller but potentially equally significant groups: the *petits blancs*, mostly small proprietors, retail traders and craftsmen, jealous of the rich planters but seeing slavery as the only safeguard of the social and political privileges which they as whites enjoyed; and the free coloured, many of them educated and articulate but smarting under severe legal and political disabilities. When the Revolution came the white population eagerly seized the opportunity which it afforded for their direct participation in the national government of France; but they were loth to see the extension of its principles to the slave societies of the colonies. For their part, the free coloured and the slaves clamoured for the full application of the principles of liberty, equality and fraternity which would guarantee them the rights of free citizens.

After 1789 the planters, represented in the new National Assembly, used their influence to throttle and delay all attempts to abolish slavery. The revolutionary fervour of the 1830s in France, however, gave new impetus to those groups who advocated the establishment of free societies in the colonies. The free coloured were the first to benefit from the new wave of liberalism; in 1831 they were given the rights of full citizens. Between 1830 and 1848 the manumission of slaves was also greatly encouraged, and slavery was finally abolished in 1848.

1848–1946: the period of colonial decline

The passing of power to new social groups and the legally guaranteed freedom of the slaves created a new situation in the colonies. In each case the ex-slaves left the plantations in droves and converged on the capital cities, creating a dual problem: the economy was severely hit and a huge, largely unemployed urban proletariat developed. The French government sought to ease this situation by creating an autocratic system of administration by decree which lasted from 1852 to 1870.

The labour shortage on the plantations had to be met somehow. The effects of abolition were most keenly felt in Guiana where agriculture almost came to a standstill. The solution attempted there was drastic and served to blacken the reputation of the territory still further. A penal colony was established whose inhabitants, it was hoped, would usefully serve their sentences by contributing to the development of the country. This hope was never fulfilled and the presence of this colony, only recently abolished, has been a serious psychological obstacle to the progress and well-being of Guiana. In Martinique and Guadeloupe the old system of indenture was reintroduced. By 1887 large numbers of Indians and Africans and a few hundred Chinese had been brought to the islands. Today these groups have largely merged with the rest of the population.

A more liberal form of government was set up as the economic situation eased. Trial by jury was introduced and the colonists elected their own municipal officials on a fairly wide franchise. But social and economic conditions grew steadily worse and the colonies entered a period of slow decline which lasted unbroken until 1946. Their excessive dependence on France produced a state of famine when France was twice crippled by war. By 1946 they were badly in need of a thorough-going scheme of reconstruction and reorganisation.

Departmental status and assimilation

In 1946 Martinique, Guadeloupe and Guiana were declared departments of metropolitan France, with the same rights and privileges as other departments. In theory the colonies had been granted this status in 1871, but the law of 1946 proposed to make it a working reality. Under this law, which is still in effect, the three territories send elected deputies to the French National Assembly, whose laws have automatic effect in the territories. This policy of 'assimilation' runs counter to the trends which have dominated thinking and policy in most colonial and ex-colonial countries during the post-war period, but it has some historical logic. Tight control throughout the period of their existence has created a quality of Frenchness in France's American territories which is unparalleled by the British legacy in the English-speaking Caribbean. The law of 1946 met, in fact, with general approval when first proposed.

Even its most hostile critics admit that assimilation has brought tangible benefits in the form of better educational and health facilities, improved communications and social services. But it is also abundantly clear that such measures merely scratch the surface of the economic and social problems which confront the territories.

Immediately after the war Communist parties appeared in the territories. Branches of the Communist Party of France, they draw their members mostly from the coloured professional and intellectual classes. In 1956 the leader of the Communist Party of Martinique, the poet Aimé Césaire. (mayor of Fort de France since 1950) resigned from the Communist Party and formed the Progressive Party of Martinique (PPM). Because of his immense personal prestige, this independent party of the left has tended to eclipse the Communist Party in recent elections. In Guadeloupe the Communist Party has recently been losing ground to parties of the centre and the right, which are themselves branches of metropolitan parties· The left continues to be vocal in all three territories in its demands for independence.

The French authorities have not been slow to react. Since 1960 the Prefects of these overseas departments have been given the power to expel or suspend any government employee who is suspected of favouring independence. Against these decisions there is no appeal. The supporters of independence are still, however, in a minority. Majority attitudes to France are at best highly favourable, at worst no more than ambivalent. When President de Gaulle visited the three territories in 1964 he was given an enthusiastic reception in spite of the efforts of the pro-independence groups to turn the occasion to their advantage. What is significant is that many of those who welcomed him so warmly to Martinique had cast their votes for the pro-independence PPM only a few weeks before in the local elections. The long centuries of close contact with France have done their work.

ECONOMY

The colonial legacy

The present economic position of France's American territories is to be seen against the colonial background. Colonies were founded as commercial enterprises to be operated strictly for the benefit of the mother country, and to provide where possible those products which the mother country was incapable of producing. Any notion that the colonies could or should develop viable, independent economies was alien to the spirit of the times; colonies could trade only with the mother country and only in metropolitan ships. With very little modification this is the system which France has applied to her American colonies up to the present time.

The other economic factor of overwhelming importance in the history of the islands, though not of Guiana, is sugar. Once it had been demonstrated that the crop could be successfully grown in the region, territory after territory was given over to it. By the middle of the 17th century it was already well on the way to becoming a monoculture in Martinique and Guadeloupe. The Caribbean's past history and its present economic reality both hinge on this fact. Sugar created a plantation society and culture out of which have developed the unique racial, social and cultural patterns which exist in the islands today. It was and remains a rich man's crop, requiring considerable capital expenditure and depending on the existence of a large, well-disciplined work-force. This last fact provided the economic justification for slavery. It is estimated that by the beginning of the 18th century

Martinique alone had 21,000 Negro slaves, and in Guadeloupe they also formed a majority of the population.

During the 18th century Martinique and Guadeloupe thrived on sugar and the slave trade. The period from 1789 and 1848, however, inaugurated the general decline in prosperity which has continued almost unchecked to the present day. From the first hint of the abolition of slavery the economic system, whose stability was based on slavery, started to disintegrate. Moreover, the dangers of monoculture were amply exemplified by the appearance of beet sugar on the European market. The islands' economies continued to decline, despite a slight boost provided by the demand for rum in Europe during the Crimean War and again during the first world war.

Martinique and Guadeloupe

Today the economic and social structure of the islands remains much as it has been throughout their history. Sugar is the basis of the economy, although recently the production of bananas has been encouraged, particularly in Guadeloupe, where they seem likely to eclipse sugar as the principal product. In Martinique an overwhelming proportion of the arable land is still owned by the descendants of the white planters of colonial times and the mass of the population is still employed by the wealthy few on the plantations. In Guadeloupe the land and the production of sugar is under the control of large French-owned companies. To a certain extent the recent emphasis on bananas has helped the small local proprietor, but in exporting his crop he is at the mercy of a single huge French company, the Compagnie Générale Transatlantique (CGT). This company has an effective monopoly on all freight between France and the islands and charges rates in excess of those of other companies operating in the Caribbean.

The islands have remained primary producers. Few industries of any significance have developed but both islands possess a number of rum refineries and minor enterprises, manufacturing products like aluminium, venetian blinds, canned fruit, cement and biscuits, either for export or for the local market. The islands import a high percentage of their foodstuffs, chiefly from France. There is chronic unemployment and underemployment, since sugar demands an intensive labour force for only half the year. A tourist industry is rapidly developing, especially in Martinique, which is particularly popular with French Canadians.

Guiana

The bulk of Guiana's population—of mixed European, Negro and Asiatic origin—still lives almost entirely on the coastal strip. The interior is given over to a number of small, indigenous Indian tribes and to an even smaller number of Bush Negroes, the descendants of runaway slaves who entered the country over the border from Surinam.

Guiana has never suffered the disadvantages of a monoculture as have Martinique and Guadeloupe, but its economic problems are even more acute. A large territory, it is still underpopulated and much of the interior is wholly undeveloped and even unexplored. It produces small quantities of sugar and rum, but its most important product is gold, though this has declined in recent years. In addition it exports forest products such as timber and rosewood essence. Recently an attempt has been made at stockraising on the interior savannahs; a ready market for meat exists in the Caribbean territories. But a genuine economy remains to be developed. Like the other Guianas, the territory is believed to have mineral resources capable of commercial development; the truth of this theory is, however, still to be tested. Its forest products have certainly never been competently exploited or marketed.

THE FUTURE

Feelings of loyalty to France are strong in the French Antilles and Guiana, but the groups favouring some form of local independence include some of the most articulate and best-informed sections of the population: the coloured middle class of intellectuals and professionals. In the post-war period the feeling has been growing in the Caribbean as a whole that the economic future of the region lies in some form of cooperation. However, it seems self-evident that the French territories will be unable to participate in such a regional grouping while remaining in political union with France.

BIBLIOGRAPHY

Guérin, D. *The West Indies and Their Future*, Dennis Dobson, London; Hillary House, New York, 1961.

Hanotaux, G. and Martineau, A. (eds.) *Histoire des colonies françaises*, I, Société de l'Historie Nationale, Librairie Plon, Paris, 1929.

Leiris, M. *Contacts de civilisation en Martinique et en Guadeloupe*, UNESCO, Paris, 1956.

Parry, J. H. and Sherlock, P. M. *A Short History of the West Indies*, St Martin's Press, New York, 1956; Macmillan, London, 2nd ed. 1965.

Pouquet, J. *Les Antilles Françaises* (*Que sais-je*, No. 516), Presses Universitaires de France, Paris, 1952.

Revert, E. *Les Antilles*, Armand Colin, Paris, 1954. *La France d'Amérique*, Collections Terres Lointaines, Paris, 1949.

Rodway, J. *Guiana, British, Dutch, French*, T. Fisher Unwin, London, 1922.

Roberts, S. H. *A History of French Colonial Policy, 1870–1925*, F. Cass, London, 1963.

Roberts, W. A. *The French in the West Indies*, Bobbs-Merrill, New York, 1942.

Saintoyant, J. *La colonisation française pendant la Révolution*, La Renaissance du Livre, Paris, 1930.

BASIC INFORMATION[1]

CLIMATE

Fort-de-France
(*Martinique*)

Lat./long.	14° 30' N, 61° W	Relative humidity	79%/77%
Altitude	13 ft/4 m.	at midday of	
Mean temp. of hottest month	27°C/81°F (Sept.)	hottest and coolest months	
Mean temp. of coolest month	24°C/76°F (Jan.)	Wettest month	10·3 in./262 mm. (Aug.)
Absolute max.	96°F/36°C	Driest month	2·9 in./74 mm.
Absolute min.	56°F/13°C		(Mar.)
		Annual av. rainfall	80·2 in./2,037 mm.

[1] G—Guadeloupe (comprising Guadeloupe, Grande Terre, and dependencies Marie-Galante, La Désirade, Les Saintes, Petite-Terre, St Barthélémy and French St Martin); M—Martinique; FG—French Guiana (including territory of Inini).

POPULATION

TOTAL (*ooo*): 1961 (census): G 283, M 291, FG 34; mid-1966; G 319, M 327, FG (1965) 36; 1980 (ECLA projections): G 445, M 463, FG 53.
DENSITY: Persons per sq. km., mid-1965: G 178, M 291, FG less than 1.
CRUDE RATES (*per ooo*), 1965: Birth: G 33·2, M 32·7, FG 34·7; death (partial data): G 7·6, M 7·8, FG 11·1; infant mortality, 1964: G 36·6, M 36·5, FG 40·0 (1965).
GROWTH RATES (% *p.a.*), 1958–65: G 2·9, M 2·7, EG 2·4.
DISTRIBUTION (% *of total pop.*): Ethnic: mixed, mainly of Negro, European (French) and Asian (Indian, Chinese and Indo-Chinese) origin. Languages: French and Creole patois. Religion: mainly Roman Catholic but some Protestant sects. Largest cities (*ooo inhab.*), 1961: G Pointe-à-Pitre 28, Basse-Terre (the capital) 14; M Fort-de-France 85; FG Cayenne 18.

CONSTITUTIONAL SYSTEMS

CONSTITUTION: Overseas Departments of France, 1946.
SYSTEM: Departmental administration with prefect, representing the French government, an elected general council and elected municipal councils. Represented in French National Assembly by deputies (G and M 3 each and FG 1) and in the Senate by senators (G and M 2 each and FG 1). Also represented in French Economic and Social Council.
LEGISLATURE: General Council of members (G and M 36 each and FG 15) elected under universal adult suffrage for 6 years, one-half retiring every 3 years.

ECONOMY

PRODUCTION
AGRICULTURE (*ooo tons*)

	Guadeloupe		Martinique		Fr. Guiana	
	1948–53[1]	*65/66*[2]	*1948–52*[1]	*65/66*[2]	*1948–52*[1]	*63/64*
Sugar (cane), raw	73	167	40	53	·	·
Bananas	84	165	75	220	—	2
Cassava	13	4	3	3[3]	10	18
Sweet potatoes, yams	32	20	52	50[3]	4	9[3]
Pineapples	—	0·3	4	21[4]	—	—

[1] Average 1948/49–52/53.   [2] Provisional.   [3] 1962.   [4] 1964/65.

LAND (%), 1964 (FG 1963): Arable G 29, M 29, FG 0; permanent pasture G 9, M 18, FG 1; forested G 33, M 25, FG 95; other G 29, M 28, FG 4.
OTHER AGRICULTURAL DATA: Tractors in use, 1964: G 778; 1962: M 266. Fertiliser consumption (*ooo tons*), 1965: G 23, M 15.
LIVESTOCK: Nos (*ooo head*), 1965/66 (FG 1964): cattle G 70, M 37, FG 3; sheep G 3, M 25, G 1; pigs G 30, M 30, FG 6; goats G 24, M 10.
FISH: Landed (*ooo tons*), 1964: FG 2·0; 1963: G 3·2, M 2·5.
MINING (*tons*), 1963: FG gold (exports) 0·18; bauxite.
MANUFACTURING, 1965: (*m. litres*) rum (pure alcohol) G 13·1, M 10·7; (*cu. metres, sawn*) wood FG 8.

ENERGY
CONSUMPTION (*tons coal equiv.*), 1965: G 0·10 m., M 0·12 m., FG 0·02 m.; per head G 0·32, M 0·37, FG 0·44.
ELECTRICITY (public supply), 1965: Generated (*kwh*) G 46·3 m., M 45 m., FG 10·5 m.; installed capacity (*kw*) G 14,600, M 15,800, FG 5,800.

EXTERNAL TRADE (US$ m.)	Guadeloupe		Martinique		Fr. Guiana	
	1960	1965	1960	1965	1962	1963
EXPORTS (f.o.b.)	35	38	32	43	0·6[1]	0·7[1]
Bananas and plantains	12	11	13	18	.	.
Sugar	19	22	10	10	.	.
Rum	2	2	4	4	0·1	0·1
Timber	.	.	.	.	0·2	0·2
IMPORTS (c.i.f.)	48	85	47	91	10·6	11·3
TRADE BALANCE	−13	−47	−15	−48	−10·0	−10·6

[1] Including gold 0.2 and 0.1.

DIRECTION OF TRADE (%)

	Exports					
	Guadeloupe		Martinique		Fr. Guiana	
	1960	1965	1960	1965	1960	1965
USA and Canada	0·9	15·4	—	1·6	16·7	72·4
EEC	92·8	81·2	98·0	94·9	50·0	24·1
France	92·8	79·6	98·0	88·5	33·3	24·1
UK	—	—	—	—	—	—

	Imports					
USA and Canada	2·7	7·5	—	7·5	11·6	10·9
EEC	83·1	80·0	95·7	78·8	79·7	74·6
France	78·1	73·1	92·2	71·3	73·9	70·6
UK	0·8	1·1	—	1·2	1·4	1·5

FINANCE

EXCHANGE RATE (Francs/US$): Par value 493·70; from Jan. 1963: 4·937.

EMPLOYMENT

ECONOMICALLY ACTIVE (%), 1961: Of total pop. G 40, M 32, FG 31 (men: G 51, M 41, FG 40; women G 31, M 24, FG 23). In agriculture M 39, public utility services M 24, manufacturing M 12, and trade M 9.
UNEMPLOYMENT (%), 1966: No., G 2,200; seasonal unemployment high.

TRANSPORT AND COMMUNICATIONS

MOTOR VEHICLES: In use (ooo), 1965: cars G 16·6, M 18·1, FG 2·4; comm. vehicles G 9·6, M 9·7, FG 1·6. Road systems (km.): G 1,880, M 1,330, FG 550.
SHIPPING: International shipping (ooo tons), 1965: goods loaded G 308, M 294, FG 30; goods unloaded G 392, M 399, FG 68. Main ports: G Pointe-à-Pitre, M Fort-de-France, FG Cayenne.
AIR: Main international airports: G Pointe-à-Pitre (Raizet), M Fort-de-France (Lamentin), FG Cayenne (Rochambeau).
TELEPHONES: No. in use, 1965: G 7,000, M 11,000, FG 1,500.

SOCIAL WELFARE

HEALTH: No. of persons per physician: G 2,400, M 2,400, FG 1,500; no. of persons per hospital bed; G 160, M 100, FG 60.

EDUCATION

ILLITERACY RATE (%), 1961 (census): 15 years and over: M 15, FG 28, G (1954) 35.
COMPULSORY: G and M 8 years (between 6 and 14 years of age). Enrolment ratios (%), 1st and 2nd levels, 1963: G 79, M 86, FG 73 (incl. pre-school); adjusted G 99, M over 100, FG 91.

Schools, 1964: Primary: no. G 430, M 228, FG 47; students (*ooo*) G 64, M 66, FG 8; teachers G 1,690, M 2,200, FG 215. Secondary: no. G 51, M 49, FG 2; students (*ooo*) G 14, M 21, FG 1·3; teachers G 540, M 725, FG 30. Teacher training: no. G 1, M 1; students G 125, M 330; teachers G 10, M 15. Higher: L'Institut Henri Vizioz in Point-à-Pitre, G (210 st.) and in Fort-de-France, M (540 st.), both attached to University of Bordeaux.

MASS MEDIA

Broadcasting: No. of receivers in use (*ooo*), 1965: radio: G 10, M 55, FG 7; TV: G 1, M 1. Stations: radio: G 1, M 1, FG 1; TV: G 1, M 1.

Cinemas: No., G 20 (1954), M 37 (1965), FG 6 (1960). Attendance, G 0·6 m. (1953) M 2·15 m. (1965), FG 0·4 m. (1960); per head, G 2·5 (1953), M 6·9 (1965), FG 12·9 (1960).

Newsprint: Consumption per head (*kg.*): G 0·7, M 0·8, FG 0·3.

Newspapers: Daily, 1965: G—*Le Nouvelliste* (circ. 3,000) M—*L'Information* (3,000), FG—*La Presse de Guyane* (1,500); copies per 000 of pop. G 9, M 9, FG 42.

GUYANA

COLIN HENFREY

HISTORY

Dutch settlement: trade and plantation (1580–1796)

DURING the period of European expansion in the New World, the balance of power in the Caribbean relegated the minor colonial powers in the area, the British, Dutch and French, to the crumbs of territory that fell from the Spanish and Portuguese tables. One of these, physically large but economically unattractive, was the area known to the Caribs as Guyana, 'the land of many waters'. Stretching east from the Orinoco towards Pernambuco and south from the muddy coastlands through an undefined extent of forest, rivers and savanna, it was the Cinderella of the region. The magnets of the New World were gold, Indians, the prospects of land and a wealth of romantic fables. In the case of Guyana, however, the gold was simply a dream of Raleigh's; the Indians, though numerous, were protected, unlike their island neighbours, by the depth of the tropical forest and their lack of a centralised social structure, like those of Mexico and Peru, which could be taken over by colonial rulers. Even the land was unpromising: much of the narrow coastal strip, broken by vast estuaries and sealed off by mangrove swamps, was below sea level, while the interior consisted mainly of uncultivated forest. Only the fables were there in profusion, from glittering crystal mountains to tribes of headless Indians; and after the greatest of them, that of El Dorado, had ended in Raleigh's disgrace, the British, the first to explore the region, abandoned it for the next two centuries.

Meanwhile the Dutch made substantial headway with the area between the Rivers Orinoco and Corentyne that was later to become British Guiana. By the end of the century the Dutch were trading extensively with the widely scattered and firmly established Amerindians for dyes, hemp and tobacco. After the formation of the Dutch West India Company in 1621, permanent settlements were founded around the River Essequibo, based on a fort named Kyk-over-al. For the next hundred years this fort was the centre of a steady expansion, backed by the powerful Dutch alliance of commerce and state in the West India Company and the States-General which had granted its charter.

Private tobacco and sugar plantations followed the trading posts, spreading into the neighbouring regions of Demerara and Berbice. These soon created a Caribbean rather than Latin American system of the small European plantocracy, vastly outnumbered by its slaves, which was to be the backbone of Guianese development. The high-point of this period was the remarkable rule (1742–72) of Laurens Storm van Gravesande as Commandeur of Essequibo. Owing mainly to soil exhaustion, the focus of settlement moved down to the coastal area. The three separate regions of Demerara, Essequibo

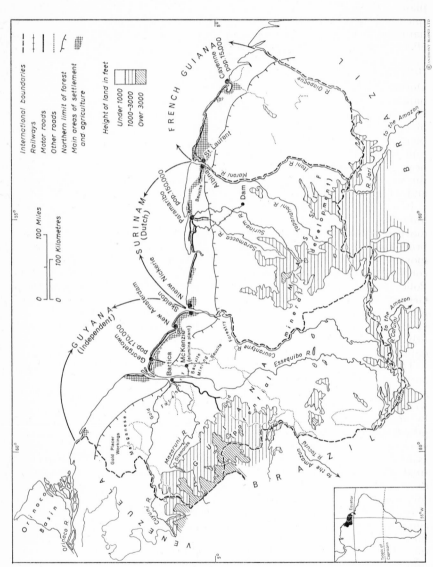

and Berbice were increasingly closely knit, with the emphasis shifting toward Demerara, the site of the future capital. The Amerindians were carefully cultivated, since they held the balance of power between the planters and their slaves. The Company was now importing five thousand Africans a year; revolts were frequent and cruelly suppressed and the Dutch and British planters flourished, often acquiring immense wealth and living in regal splendour. The 18th century, despite the—happily short-lived—oppressive nature of its society, was a period of stability and expansion which saw the effective conception of the future Guyana.

British Guiana: growth of a heterogeneous colonial society (1796–1947)
During the fifteen years after the Anglo-Dutch war of 1781, Guiana changed hands several times. The capital was moved to Stabroek, at the mouth of the Demerara, and renamed Georgetown when the British took effective control in 1796. The planters' loyalties were simply transferred to the new government and the three regions were combined into a single colony. Its constitution was based on a 'Court of Policy' consisting of nominated members heavily influenced by the planters. Georgetown flourished as an outpost of the Victorian world and the centre of gradual development as roads, bridges and schools were built around the coastal plantations.

By the turn of the century the slave population numbered close on one hundred thousand. But the planters were soon faced with the anti-slavery movement and the abolition of the slave trade in 1807 brought Guiana to the brink of radical social change. Education of slaves by the new missionary movements, together with parliamentary bills to regulate their working conditions, was fiercely opposed by the planters, backed by the Court of Policy. Their resistance culminated in a final slave revolt which threatened Georgetown itself and ended in savage suppression. But the tide had turned in the slaves' favour and in 1834 slavery was abolished. Most of the Africans moved away from the sugar estates to form the foundations of the future urban population. Many estates were abandoned and others were consolidated; a new source of labour had to be found.

The result was the indenture system. This drew mainly on southern India and also China, Malta and the West Indies, and provided immigrants with a passage to Guiana in return for seven years' unpaid labour. After this they were in theory free to return; but few had the means or the will to do so. By the time indenture was ended (1917) Guiana's three hundred thousand people formed a society as heterogeneous as any in the New World. The Indians were its largest group, numbering 126 thousand; the Africans were almost as many, whilst the Portuguese, Chinese, Amerindians and British formed small minorities. Despite their variegated backgrounds the Guianese early developed a central identity which is much more remarkable than their surviving distinctions. The roots of this process lay in two factors from which only the Amerindians and British were excepted. The immigrants were completely cut off from their countries of origin; and they all passed through the grist-mill of the sugar estates, which disinherited them and provided the elements of a uniform culture, especially for the Africans, who were subjected by their owners to calculated detribalisation to prevent uprisings.

Political instability was a further restraint on economic progress during the modern period. In a sense colonial status inhibited any real take-off, since it conflicted with the growth of a nationalism that would create an internalised economic momentum. But the picture is more complex than this: cause and effect are interwoven in the political-economic spiral of recent years. In a country where both political and economic status are still dependent, it is not surprising that the crises emerging from this spiral should have derived from external influences, mainly Anglo-American.

The rise of the People's Progressive Party (1947-61)

The constitutional stagnation preceding the modern period was a corollary of the economic situation of Guiana: permanent colonial status was the political bedfellow of foreign-controlled primary production. Only in 1927 did the new middle class gain an elective minority in a legislature still controlled by the governor's nominees. Twenty years later a new constitution allowed an elective majority which included the radical voice of Dr Cheddi Jagan, an Indian trained in the United States, who was the founder of the left-wing and nationalist People's Progressive Party (PPP). His deputy in the party was Mr Forbes Burnham, an African lawyer; together they pressed for independence and economic reform.

In the 1953 elections, based on universal suffrage, the PPP swept to victory with eighteen of the twenty-four seats in the lower House of Assembly, the effective organ of legislation, subject to the veto of the upper chamber controlled by the governor. The executive also included six PPP members, led by Jagan, who promptly initiated measures for the secularisation of schools, the strengthening of sugar-workers' unions and more direct taxes. When these bills were blocked by the conservative upper chamber, the PPP ministers encouraged popular discontent, including strikes and disturbances on the sugar estates, as a means of agitating for further reform of the constitution. But suddenly, without any warning, the existing one was suspended by the British governor. Troops were flown in 'to prevent communist subversion of the government', PPP leaders were detained and political meetings were banned. This was a panic decision by the British authorities and was subsequently white-washed by a McCarthy-like Colonial Office enquiry which pointed to school secularisation (previously suggested by a Colonial Office official) and literature such as Nehru's *Toward Freedom* as evidence of a communist plot. The truth was that Jagan and Burnham had refused to compromise in the way expected of colonial leaders to whom measured concessions are made.

The constitution remained suspended for a further four years. In terms of political awareness, the training of civil servants and the level of education, Guiana was ready for independence. The growth of the PPP had welded a complex social and ethnic structure into a tenuous whole which simply broke apart when deprived of responsibility and creative opportunities. The crisis came in 1955 when Burnham left the PPP on the grounds of Jagan's Marxism to form a more moderate party known as the People's National Congress (PNC). Their split, which was in fact over leadership rather than ideology, was confirmed by the next elections in 1957, when the PPP won nine seats in a new, single-chamber legislature, against the PNC's three. After a period of peaceful rule, internal self-government was granted under the new constitution of 1961, amounting to virtual self-rule, qualified by the governor's emergency powers and control of foreign policy.

Jagan's followers were mainly Indian, while Burnham's were African. But this was not exclusively true and reflected occupational differences rather than overt racial feelings; Jagan's reform programme was more agrarian than Burnham's, as well as being more radical. Meanwhile a new group had emerged, the United Force, led by a Portuguese businessman, Peter D'Aguiar, whose small, right-wing following was drawn mainly from business circles and the upper echelons of the public service. The positive side of their policy was to attract foreign investment by creating an atmosphere favourable to private enterprise: but their main aim was the downfall of the PPP.

Socio-political conflict and the economic crisis (1961-4)

In the 1961 elections the PPP regained power with nineteen seats in the House of Assembly: eleven went to the PNC and four to the UF. With Castro close by, Jagan's socialism was increasingly suspect, but he remained cautious, emphasising non-alignment and economic progress with aid from every possible source. In order to obtain it he promptly visited the United States, Britain and Western Europe; but he was clearly persona non grata with the State Department and it was mainly for this reason that he was refused effective aid by all the Western powers including Britain, with the only concrete offers coming from Poland, Czechoslovakia and Cuba. Subsequent events must be seen in the light of this calculated negative pressure from the West.

This lack of confidence lowered the government's prestige. Foreign investments dwindled and capital left the country; the government was soon faced with an economic crisis which forced it into a budget based on a capital gains and property tax and a compulsory savings bill for the higher-income brackets. The burden of these measures fell on big business and the middle class, most of which is centred on Georgetown and aligned with the UF. Meanwhile unemployment was mounting, while public service employees were restless owing to a wage restraint. When the budget was announced, the right-wing press, owned by D'Aguiar, launched a whirlwind attack denouncing Jagan for his Marxist, anti-working-class budget! When riots broke out in Georgetown in February 1962 both opposition leaders refused to appeal to the mob for order. The resulting damage stood at over £2 million.

The rational means of reunification after the riots would have been a renewal of the Jagan-Burnham coalition; but suspicion was deep on either side, fanned by the UF's dedication to bringing Jagan down. At the subsequent constitutional conference the PNC and the UF demanded proportional representation, the only way in which Jagan, with forty-three per cent of the vote, could possibly be removed; but the talks produced no agreement. In the following year a general strike ensued over the recognition of unions. Violence returned and its patterns were increasingly racial, while the strike itself was supported with $80 thousand a week from US sources. The US Secretary of State, Dean Rusk, advocated a constitutional suspension as a polite equivalent of the overthrow of the left-wing Guatemalan government in 1954. Deadlock had been reached and when it continued at the 1963 conference the Colonial Secretary imposed his own constitution. Independence was delayed indefinitely and new elections were to be held under proportional representation. This was a total concession to the UF, representing the right-wing sixteen per cent of the country's voters. Alternatives were ignored and there was no attempt to benefit from the examples of Surinam, with its multi-racial parties, or Trinidad. The implication was clear-cut. Independence could come only on terms acceptable to Britain and the United States.

The justification of this constitution was that it would reduce racial tension. But it was only after the West's rejection of Jagan and the rise of the UF that racialism had really existed in Guiana; and the prospect of proportional representation clearly increased it. In 1964 violence reached its peak, sparked off by a sugar-workers' strike which the PPP encouraged, probably as a means of delaying the impending elections. Dozens of people were murdered, hundreds were wounded and thousands had to leave communities where they proved ethnic minorities. The governor detained several PPP leaders, and racial alignments became a painful reality. This was a point of no return for Guianese unity. The opposition of the British to socialism made a reality of their fears, since it left Jagan with nowhere to turn but to the Communist bloc for support of his programme. By 1964 both Cuban-trained saboteurs and the US Central Intelligence Agency were playing their part in the violence. Altogether, the brief life of Guianese nationalism has been a pitiful illustration of the way in which a small and poor country can still be laid out and almost destroyed on the rack of the cold war.

Independence

New elections were scheduled for December 1964, under protest from Jagan, whose term of office was due to run for another nine months. The British governor announced in advance that he would not be obliged to ask the leading party to form a government unless it had an overall majority. This could be seen as a hint to Burnham that it might be profitable to seek support from the UF. The predictable election results made nonsense of the professed British aim of encouraging cross-racial voting and minor parties. Neither of the latter gained a seat and the count corresponded almost exactly to ethnic ratios. The PPP vote went up to forty-six per cent, reflecting the high Indian birth-rate, while the PNC had forty-and-a-half per cent and the UF twelve-and-a-half per cent. With a poll of ninety-six per cent in a total population of 640 thousand, this indicated that racial anxieties were now an exclusive political force. Jagan refused to resign and Burnham rejected a coalition offer from the PPP. The governor promptly asked Burnham to form a new government, which he accomplished through a coalition with the UF, with D'Aguiar as finance minister. Jagan was then removed by a constitutional amendment from Whitehall.

Emergency measures remained in force during most of 1965, but despite continuing sabotage there was no open violence, thanks mainly to the improvement of the economic situation. Substantial Anglo-American aid arrived, the stabiliser which Jagan had lacked, and unemployment dropped steadily. Burnham announced that a fair proportion of future development programmes would still be devoted to the agricultural, mainly Indian sector, and emphasised the need for aid, along with non-alignment and the concept of cooperation with other Caribbean territories. In the resulting lull, concrete plans went ahead at a pace which had been impossible under Jagan. Surveys in the interior revealed new mineral deposits, including copper, uranium and oil, trade and investment picked up, an agreement was made for a free trade area with Barbados and Antigua. Burnham accepted the proposals of the International Commission of Jurists for a greater intake of Indians into the public service and police and an Ombudsman to investigate racial complaints. Jagan, stymied, protested against the continued detention of PPP leaders, and boycotted the Commission's Enquiry, the new Legislative Assembly and the independence conference held in late 1965.

At this conference, 26 May 1966 was set as the date of independence under the existing government. The new sovereign state of Guyana, with a governor-general appointed by the Queen and a one-chamber legislature, would apply for Commonwealth membership and continue to hold elections under pro-portional representation. This hothouse solution, described even by Harold Wilson as 'a fiddled constitution', was fiercely contested by the PPP, which boycotted the celebrations when it came into effect. Its outcome remains an open book, as do the elections scheduled for 1968. There are several critical fac-tors. The primary one has always been the dependence of internal stability on Anglo-American aid, assured for as long as Burnham remains in power. In this sense circumstances have made him the only possible ruler of a Guyana which, for historical reasons, is inevitably subject to the indirect control of Britain and the United States. But Jagan and the PPP still command an immense influence which can only be excluded politically by the continued alliance of the UF and the PNC which, as right-wing and moderate socialist parties respectively, have little in common save for their opposition to Jagan. With the high Indian birth-rate the PPP may easily win the next election outright, if racial loyalties hold fast, as is now likely. On the other hand, the period of stability virtually assured by Burnham may win him Indian voters, most of whom are devoted to peaceful economic progress. Whatever the outcome, violence will always be close to the surface unless both present and future leaders recognise the cold war and racial conflict as the basis of Guyana's dilemma and accept the need to compromise accordingly.

ECONOMY

The interaction of economic and socio-political development is implicit in Guyanese history. The patterns described above are rooted in the plantation economy, which was represented in England by the powerful West India interest; until the modern, post-war period government in Guyana was little more than an extension of the sugar industry. The keynote of the economy is primary production controlled by overseas investors and dependent on precariously narrow overseas markets.

Sugar still represents nearly fifty per cent of Guyanese exports, though the industry itself has changed beyond recognition. Consolidations of the estates culminated in ownership by a London-based company who have holdings in everything from Georgetown's retail stores to Amerindian balata production, on which they hold a monopoly, giving the Amerindians a third of the price paid elsewhere. This company's present ambivalent position, combining a liberal image with a basically anachronistic role, fails to answer the funda-mental questions of how sugar, a traditional, essentially colonial product, is to be integrated with a modern economy which obviates Guyanese depend-ence on a single, fluctuating world market, and how the industry is to resolve the conflict between the interests of the Guyanese and those of overseas shareholders. Seemingly benevolent schemes like Commonwealth sugar preferences tend to disguise the fact that other industries such as rice may be more viable in terms of local conditions and markets, as well as being Guyanese-owned. The primary-producing countries formed by colonialism need intense reinvestment of profits as a means of increased production and rapid diversification. The expatriate company remains the historical barrier to this, unless it can convert itself into a virtual development body aiming at an eventual transfer to local ownership.

Rice production has increased dramatically in recent years, owing partly to the establishment of a rice marketing board which grades and buys all rice. Half the crop is consumed locally while the rest, comprising some four-teen per cent of the country's exports, goes mainly to the Caribbean, exclud-ing Cuba. A little copra is also exported and ground provisions are widely grown, mainly for home consumption. Manufactures are limited to a few small concerns, such as a brewery and soap factory, and will probably continue so unless Guyana participates in an economic federation with neighbouring territories, either Caribbean or continental.

There is a legend of wealth in the scarcely populated interior, descended with constant variations from Raleigh's dream of El Dorado, but there is little to confirm it. Bauxite, the second largest export at twenty-four per cent of the total, is mined at Mackenzie, up the River Demerara, by a Canadian-American firm. The past, especially the turn of the century, is studded with gold and diamond rushes, but attempts at commercial production have failed. The main source of cash employment for the Amerindian population is cutting timber, which also comprises a fraction of the export list and provides a favourite material for coastal buildings. The only predictable value of the interior lies in the timber and farming land which cannot be made viable without surface communications, virtually non-existent as yet and requiring enormous capital.

This wholesale lack of development is a normal colonial phenomenon; until the late 1940s Guyana was simply a sugar-mine for British investors and their tables. Apart from a few recent projects, including land reclamation for rice farmers, the infrastructure was ignored at the price of placatory gestures like housing and social services; Guyana is only now approaching the brink of economic take-off. Many of the more promising programmes failed for want of local experts who could relate economic theory to local circumstances, or of a central planning board to provide continuity and an internal impulse. It is only recently that these basic issues have been raised. Political independence at least gives the opportunity of steady economic expansion.

BIBLIOGRAPHY

Clements, Sir Cecil. *A Constitutional History of British Guiana*, Macmillan, London, 1937.

Gravesande, L. S. van. *The Rise of British Guiana*, 2 vols (Despatches, 1742–72), Hakluyt Society, London, 1911.

Henfrey, Colin V. P. *The Gentle People: A Journey amongst the Indian Tribes of Guiana*, Hutchinson, London, 1964.

Jagan, Cheddi B. *Bitter Sugar*, Georgetown, no date. *Forbidden Freedom*, Lawrence and Wishart, London, 1954. *The West on Trial: My Fight for Guyana's Freedom*, Michael Joseph, London 1966.

Nath, Dwarka. *A History of the Indians in British Guiana*, Nelson, London, 1950.

Pinckard, G. *Letters from Guiana, 1796–7*, Daily Chronicle, Georgetown, 1942.

Rodway, James. *History of British Guiana, 1688–1893*, 3 vols, Thomson, Georgetown, 1891–94.

Ruhomon, Peter. *Centenary History of the East Indians in British Guiana, 1838–1938*, Daily Chronicle, Georgetown, 1947.

Smith, Raymond T. *British Guiana*, Oxford Univ. Press, London and New York, 1962.

Swan, Michael. *British Guiana: the Land of Six Peoples*, HMSO, London, 1957. *The Marches of El Dorado*, Jonathan Cape, London, 1958.

Timehri: Journal of the Royal Agricultural and Commercial Society of British Guiana, Georgetown, 1882.

International Bank for Reconstruction and Development. *Economic Development of British Guiana*, Johns Hopkins Press, Baltimore, Md, 1953.

BASIC INFORMATION

CLIMATE

Georgetown

Lat./long.	7° N, 58° W	Relative humidity	69%/73%
Altitude	6 ft/2 m.	at midday of	
Mean temp. of	28°C/82°F	hottest and	
hottest month	(Sept./Oct.)	coolest months	
Mean temp. of	26°C/79°F	Wettest month	11·9 in./302 mm.
of coolest month	(Jan./Feb.)		(June)
Absolute max.	93°F/34°C	Driest month	3 in./76 mm.
Absolute min.	68°F/20°C		(Oct.)
		Annual average	88·7 in./2,253 mm.
		rainfall	

POPULATION

TOTAL (ooo): 1960 (census): 560; mid-1966: 662; 1980 (ECLA projection): 1,045. DENSITY, mid-1965: 3 persons per sq. km. CRUDE RATES (per ooo), 1966: Birth 39·9, death 8·1 (1951: 13·6), infant mortality 39·8. GROWTH RATES (% p.a.): 1945–65: 2.8. DISTRIBUTION (% of total pop.): Ethnic, 1965: Asian 51, African 31, mixed 12, Amerindian 5, European 1. Foreign-born, 1960: 2·6. Languages: Mainly English; some Hindi and Urdu, Creole, Amerindian dialects, and Spanish. Religion, 1960: Christian 57 (1946: Protestant 46, RC 12), Hindu 33, Moslem 9. Urban (Georgetown and New Amsterdam), 1960: 16. Largest cities (ooo inhab.), incl. surrounding urban areas, end-1965: Georgetown 168, Mackenzie 18, New Amsterdam 16.

CONSTITUTIONAL SYSTEM

CONSTITUTION: Created a colony 1831. Main constitutional reforms: 1891, 1928, 1943, 1953, 1956; internal self-government 1961; independent member of the Commonwealth 1966.
SYSTEM: Parliament comprising the Queen, represented by Governor-General, and National Assembly. Constitutional provision for presidential republic January 1969, if majority of Assembly approves.
CABINET: Collectively responsible to the Assembly. Comprises prime minister (appointed by Governor-General and member of Assembly having the support of the majority of its members) and other ministers. Ministers and secretaries appointed by the Governor-General with the advice of the prime minister; not more than 4 ministers may be non-elected members of the Assembly. Provision for appointment by the Governor-General of the leader of the opposition and an Ombudsman (for 4-year term).
LEGISLATURE: Uni-cameral parliament: National Assembly. Assembly: 53 members, elected by proportional representation for 4-year term, to be extended to 5 years. Suffrage: Universal voting for literate citizens (including those of the Commonwealth) over 21 years of age, who are domiciled or have been resident in Guyana for 1 year or more. Nearly 97% of registered electorate voted in 1964 elections. Elections: Assembly, December 1964: People's Progressive Party (Dr Jagan) 45·8% of votes and 24 seats; People's National Congress (L.F.S. Burnham) 40·5% and 22 seats; United Force (P.S. d'Aguiar) 12·4% and 7 seats. PNC and UF formed government coalition, with support of 3 PPP dissidents.
JUDICIARY: Supreme Court, comprising Court of Appeal and High Court, and courts of summary jurisdiction.

DEFENCE

DEFENCE BUDGET: 1966, incl. police: G$7·3 m., 2% of 1965 GDP.
ARMED FORCES: Strength: army 500.

INTERNATIONAL RELATIONS

New member of the UN and many of its international specialised agencies, including:
IBRD and affiliates, IMF, FAO, ILO, UNDP, UNESCO, UPU, WHO and WMO;
GATT, UNCTAD representative. Also a member of ECLA, CARIFTA and Sterling
Area.

ECONOMY

PRODUCTION

AGRICULTURE (ooo tons)	1948–53[1]	63/64	64/65	65/66[2]	66/67[2]
Sugar (cane)	218	263	314	294	351
Rice (paddy)	101	174	264	279	294

[1] Average 1948/49–1952/53.   [2] Provisional.

LAND (%), 1964: Arable 13, forested 77, other 10.
OTHER AGRICULTURAL DATA: Tractors in use (ooos), 1964: 4·0 (wheel only). Ferti-
liser consumption (ooo tons), 1965: 9·0.
LIVESTOCK: Nos (ooo head), 1965: Cattle 350, sheep 87, pigs 65. Products (ooo tons),
1965: Beef 3·9, pork 0·5.
FISH: Landed (ooo tons), 1965: total 12·0.
MINING, 1965: (ooo tons) Bauxite 2,873, alumina 279, manganese 65; (kg.) gold 65;
(ooo metric carats) diamonds 113 (industrial 68).
MANUFACTURING, 1965: (ooo cu. metres, sawn) Wood, 79; (m. litres) beer 4·9, rum 9·4
(pure alcohol).
CONSTRUCTION, 1963: No. of private urban dwellings completed in Georgetown,
1,876.

ENERGY

CONSUMPTION (tons coal equiv.), 1965: Total 0·52 m., per head 0·81.
ELECTRICITY, 1964: Generated (kwh) 212 m. (excl. sugar plantations), installed
capacity (kw) 98,100.

GOVERNMENT EXPENDITURE

DISTRIBUTION (% of total), 1965: Defence and police 11, education 17, health 10,
social services (incl. pensions) 9.

GROSS PRODUCT

GDP (G$ m.): At current market prices, 1964: 336; 1965: 360. Per head (US$),
UN estimate, 1964: 327.
DISTRIBUTION (%), 1965: Agriculture 25, mining 19, manufacturing 12, trade 12.
GROWTH RATES (%), current prices, 1952–60: 6·4, per head 3·4; 1960–5: 4·2, per
head 1·4.

FINANCE

EXCHANGE RATE (G$/US$): Par value 1·714.
COST OF LIVING (1958=100), Georgetown and N. Amsterdam, December 1960: 104;
1964: 111; 1965: 115; 1966: 116.
INDUSTRIAL WAGES: Earnings in sugar industry, per week, end-1963: skilled factory
employee £6·25.
BUDGET ACCOUNTS (G$ m.), 1967: Revenue 134; expenditure 129, surplus 5.

EXTERNAL TRADE

(US$ m.)	1955	1960	1963	1964	1965	1966
EXPORTS (f.o.b.)	53	74	102	95	97	109
Bauxite and conc.	14	17	30	33	39	45
Sugar, unrefined	24	34	43	31	26	.
Rice	7	9	12	13	13	.
Fish and preparations	—	1	2	3	3	.
Diamonds	1	3	2	3	3	.
Rum	2	2	2	2	3	.
Manganese	—	1	3	2	3	.
IMPORTS (c.i.f.)	55	86	69	87	104	118
TRADE BALANCE	−2	−12	+33	+8	−7	−9

DIRECTION OF TRADE (%)

	Exports			Imports		
	1955	1960	1965	1955	1960	1965
LAFTA	(0·2)	—	—	(0·4)	—	—
Trinidad	6·7	7·5	9·0	9·5	9·4	10·9
USA and Canada	44·3	41·2	41·5	19·2	30·3	32·6
EEC	1·9	3·0	5·1	10·1	8·7	9·9
UK	35·7	47·7	24·7	47·7	39·0	30·9

EMPLOYMENT

ECONOMICALLY ACTIVE (%), 1960: Of total pop. 31 (men 48, women 14). In agriculture 34, services 17, manufacturing 15.
UNEMPLOYMENT (%), 1960: Of economically active, 8.

TRANSPORT AND COMMUNICATIONS

RAILWAYS: Traffic, 1965: 75 m. passenger-km., 1 m. net ton-km. Length of track 150 km.
MOTOR VEHICLES: In use (000), 1965: cars 10·4, commercial vehicles 3·6. Road system: 1,800 km., paved 500 km.
SHIPPING: International sea-borne shipping (m. tons), 1965: goods loaded 2·68, goods unloaded 0·8. Main ports: Georgetown and New Amsterdam.
AIR: Main airports: Georgetown: Atkinson Field (International), Ruimveldt (for amphibian a/c.).
TELEPHONES: No. in use, 1965: 10,700.

SOCIAL WELFARE

SYSTEM: Social welfare services administered by ministries of home affairs and health. Sugar industry provides housing and health services for employees. Contributory social insurance schemes being developed.
HEALTH: 2,600 persons per physician, 190 persons per hospital bed.

EDUCATION

ILLITERACY RATE (%), 1946 (census): 15 years and over, 24.
COMPULSORY: 8 years (between 6 and 14 years of age). School enrolment ratios (%), 1st and 2nd levels, 1963: 71, adjusted 82.
SCHOOLS, 1964, Aided: primary: No. 380, pupils 0·15 m., teachers 4,600. Secondary: No. 31, p. 14,500, t. 500. Technical; No. 3, st. 1,600, t. 40. Higher: No. 2, st. 400, t. 144.
UNIVERSITY, 1965: U. of Guyana, Georgetown (state-aided): 330 students, academic staff 42 (27 full-time).

MASS MEDIA

BROADCASTING: No. of radio licences issued, 1963: 40,000. Stations: TV service planned; radio 2.

CINEMAS: No., 1963: 41. Attendance, total 4·4 m., per head 7·2.

NEWSPRINT: Consumption, 1962: total 1,400 tons, per head 2·3 kg.

NEWSPAPERS: Daily, 1964: 4. Estimated circulation 45,000, copies per 000 of population 72. Principal dailies in Georgetown (*circ. 000*): *Guyana Graphic* 22 (Sun. 36), *Daily Chronicle* 11 (S 21), *Mirror* 8 (S 25), *Sun* 3; *Evening Post* 8 (S 20).

HAITI

JOHN RETTIE

HISTORY

The colonial period

TWICE in less than 500 years, the population on the western part of Hispaniola has been completely eliminated and replaced by another, of a different race and culture. As a result, it is now a unique phenomenon in the Americas: a chunk of French Africa dumped unwillingly in the Caribbean, and forced to share a small island with a nation of predominantly Spanish culture with which it has little in common.

The island, about the size of Scotland, is the second largest of the Greater Antilles, and lies between Cuba and Puerto Rico. In 1492 Columbus named it 'Hispaniola'; but the Taïno Indians who already lived there called it 'Haïti', the mountainous land. The Spaniards soon wiped out the Indians, but in the 17th century lost the western third of the island to France. In 1697 Spain formally recognised this territory as the French colony of Saint-Domingue.

Thanks to the skill and industry of the new settlers, and to the labour of imported Negro slaves, Saint-Domingue earned fabulous wealth from sugar, coffee, indigo, cacao and spices exported to an eager European market. By 1789 the colony held 480,000 slaves, who suffered inhuman cruelties at the hands of some 30,000 whites. Most of the 25,000 mulattos were freedmen, but they were treated as social pariahs and deprived of many legal rights. They went into commerce, which they still dominate, and bought plantations in the south, where they behaved as harshly as the whites. Thus they became, and remain, the catalyst of violence and unrest.

The French Revolution inspired both Negroes and mulattos to revolt in 1791. After the imprisonment by the French of the great liberal-minded leader Toussaint Louverture, a former Negro slave, Negroes and mulattos, who had been bitterly divided, reunited under Toussaint's most brutal Negro lieutenant, Jean-Jacques Dessalines. The French were expelled. On 1 January 1804 Dessalines, having massacred all the whites, declared the first Negro nation of the Americas an independent republic. The flag of Haiti was red and blue—the French flag with the odious white torn from the centre by Dessalines himself.

The Republic

The new nation started badly. Dessalines was assassinated after he had crowned himself emperor. The country divided again between the north, under the Negro Henri Christophe, and the south, ruled by the popular mulatto President Alexandre Pétion. Despite his popularity Pétion, who died in 1818, set a bad precedent by repeatedly violating the constitution and introducing the noxious principle of life-presidency. After Christophe's suicide in 1820 Haiti was reunited under Pétion's successor, Jean-Pierre Boyer, another mulatto. Under Pétion and Boyer the great colonial estates were broken up, irrigation systems collapsed and agricultural techniques were forgotten. By 1843, when Boyer was overthrown, the peasants operated a mainly subsistence economy along African lines in abject poverty, ignorance and neglect.

Political power then passed to Negro army leaders, many of whom were illiterate, brutal and corrupt. But the mulattos, who remained a wealthy, educated élite, behaved little better. During the 19th century European powers were strongly challenged in the Caribbean by the United States. Haitian rulers resisted this new pressure much more firmly than their neighbours, the Dominicans. They preferred the French as creditors, and it was 1910 before US interests penetrated Haiti. By 1915 huge foreign debts and growing political anarchy had brought Haiti to the verge of collapse. On 27 July dozens of political prisoners were summarily executed when rebels launched yet another revolt. Next day crowds stormed the French legation, where President Guillaume Sam had taken refuge, and tore him limb from limb. US Marines promptly landed to restore order; they stayed for 19 years.

Haiti did gain some material advantage and administrative improvements from the occupation. The Marines disbanded the unruly army and trained a small, disciplined force which was supposed to be non-political. With excessive brutality they also disarmed and pacified the peasants, whose possession of weapons made them a fertile source of instability. The occupation restored to the mulatto élite (whom the United States favoured) the political power they had lost in 1843; the country's archaic social and political system was thus saved from collapse, but not reformed. But what had the most profound and damaging consequences was the bitter humiliation of being occupied by a foreign power—a white nation.

When Franklin Roosevelt withdrew the Marines in 1934, despotism, corruption and instability soon returned. Sténio Vincent, elected president in 1930 for six years, took control of the reformed army and immediately established a dictatorship. He was suspected of collusion with the Dominican dictator Trujillo in 1937, when thousands of Haitians living across the border were massacred. Vincent, who successfully prolonged his rule until 1941, selected as his successor another pro-American mulatto, Élie Lescot. But Negro resentment against oppressive mulatto rule was growing. In 1946, led by an alliance of liberals, nationalists, racists and Marxists, it exploded into revolution. Negro army officers, hastening back into politics, helped to depose the autocratic Lescot, but limited the revolution's scope; later that year they approved the election of Duvarsais Éstimé, a Negro school-teacher.

Under Éstimé, Haiti made its nearest approach to effective, democratic government. A programme of economic development and social reform was launched, and the status of the black man restored. Trade unions and political parties were free to develop, including the communist Parti Socialiste Populaire, the Social Christian Party and the Worker-Peasant Movement. The latter was founded by the belligerent Negro leader of the urban masses in Port-au-Prince, Daniel Fignolé; its secretary-general was a Negro doctor, François Duvalier, who also served as Secretary for Public Health and Labour. Éstimé's moderate regime was undermined both by political extremists and by the traditional habits of corruption which the new Negro élite adopted. In 1950, when he began preparing for his reelection by changing the constitution, the army deposed him.

The next President was General Paul Magloire, the central figure in the 1946 and 1950 army juntas, whose rule marked a return to military dictatorship. But at first the Korea War boom, the influx of foreign capital and an expanding tourist industry brought superficial prosperity—and with it, unparalleled corruption. Scandals, followed by the post-Korean fall in coffee prices, shook the regime; and when Magloire tried to prolong his rule in December 1956 he too was overthrown.

During the next nine months, strikes, riots and fighting between rival army factions broke five interim governments. Four main candidates were jockeying for power: Clément Jumelle who, as Magloire's finance minister, was too compromised; Daniel Fignolé, whose support was too narrowly based; Senator Louis Dejoie, a prominent mulatto land-owner, who organised effective strikes by traders and businessmen, but whose light skin proved a fatal handicap; and the winner, Dr Duvalier. A popular rural doctor, respected for fighting underground against Magloire's dictatorship, Duvalier skilfully manoeuvred his army supporters into control of the provisional military government which organised general elections on 22 September 1957. These he won easily, having previously eliminated all his opponents except Dejoie.

As a 'man of 1946', a doctor trained partly in the United States and an intellectual nationalist with a deep understanding of the Haitian peasant, Duvalier was expected to be a progressive reformer friendly to Washington. But his only detectable objective, or achievement, has been ruthless retention of power and silencing of all opposition. The army was purged and destroyed as an effective political and fighting force. Its power was transferred to a semi-secret civil militia resembling the undisciplined 19th century armies, officially entitled the 'Movement of National Renovation' but popularly called 'Tonton Macoutes' (literally 'Uncle Strawbag', a reference to scrounging folkloric bogeymen). Recruited from a rabble of loyal thugs, the militia practises arbitrary terror and extortion against rich and poor alike.

Duvalier engineered his unconstitutional reelection in April 1961, and in June 1964 had himself reelected president for life, with absolute powers, under a new constitution. To emphasise Haiti's links with Africa he changed the flag from red and blue to red and black. For his external security he made a secret agreement with Trujillo in December 1958. But Trujillo was assassinated in 1961, and two years later President Juan Bosch threatened to invade Haiti. The victory of Balaguer over Bosch in the 1966 Dominican elections brought great relief to Duvalier. Relations between the two governments improved quickly, and the activities of Haitian exiles in the eastern part of the island were restricted. Certain collaboration, for example between the two countries' political intelligence services, apparently exceeded Balaguer's wishes. But in any case, neither side has begun to face the permanent difficulty of coexisting within the same island. Duvalier's prestige gained most from his successful defiance of the United States. He encouraged the view that chaos and communism would follow his fall, permitted a little communist activity to exaggerate its threat, and hinted at seeking communist support abroad. The Eisenhower administration supplied lavish economic and military aid, much of which was diverted to underwriting Duvalier's tyranny. President Kennedy, however, was committed to fostering democracy under the Alliance for Progress, and relations soon deteriorated. At Punta del Este in January 1962 Haiti blackmailed the United States for more aid before casting her crucial vote for Cuba's exclusion from the OAS. After 1962, however, aid was suspended, and in May 1963 (the end of Duvalier's constitutional mandate) Kennedy unsuccessfully tried to overthrow his regime through intense economic, diplomatic and conspiratorial pressure. But while Kennedy could never bring himself to send in the Marines, President Johnson has demonstrated his willingness to use armed intervention in Santo Domingo 'to prevent a communist takeover'. After Duvalier goes, the same situation could arise in Haiti; if the United States then intervenes it would cause a direct racial confrontation which might have dire international consequences. Perhaps that, together with its concern for anti-communist stability, is why the Johnson administration in 1964 immediately established correct, if not cordial relations with Duvalier.

ECONOMY

The Government was probably not far wrong in estimating average per capita income in 1961 as US $58—the same as in 1954. This was the lowest figure in the Americas even then, and the economy has been declining since.

Haiti's two most urgent long-term problems are overpopulation and soil erosion. Most estimates put the 1965 population at nearly $4\frac{1}{2}$ million, increasing at an annual rate of $2\frac{1}{2}$–3 per cent. A total surface area of 10,714 square miles gives a population density of 420 per square mile. This pressure was formerly relieved by emigration to the Dominican Republic and, to a lesser extent, Cuba; but political obstacles now prevent it. Since 1804 many mountain slopes have been denuded of their rich soil by unchecked timber felling; while on the plains exceptionally primitive agricultural techniques have also caused rapid erosion. If it continues at the present rate there will be no cultivable land left by the end of this century, by which time the population would be 10 million at current growth rates.

With the collapse of the colonial agricultural system, sugar production for export ceased after independence. Coffee plantations were also abandoned, but such was the quality of the coffee produced, even from bushes growing wild, that France continued to buy large quantities. Today coffee earns about two-thirds of Haiti's foreign income. Sugar cultivation and more modern agricultural methods and irrigation systems were reintroduced on a limited scale during the US occupation, during which the Haitian economy became dependent on the United States. In 1919 the Haitian gourde[1] was fixed at 20 US cents, and it remains fully convertible at that rate; dollars are as acceptable in Port-au-Prince as gourdes. The United States buys half Haiti's exports and supplies two-thirds of her imports.

Industrial development has scarcely begun. Of an annual GNP of $200–$300 million, only $70 million is invested in the manufacturing sector, of which some two-thirds is foreign capital, mostly North American. This sector includes sisal, sugar, textiles, electric power, flour, cement, copper and bauxite mining. In 1954 a serious effort was made to raise agricultural productivity and lay the foundations of an industrial infrastructure. A

---

[1] The gourde was first introduced as a paper currency in the 1780s, when the colonial silver piastre became scarce owing to social and political unrest. After independence the gourde became accepted as the nation's sole currency. The choice of the word is obscure, but the fruit is believed to have been used as money in certain tropical countries in very ancient times. It may have been a derogatory reference to a worthless paper currency.

231-foot high dam, planned to irrigate 85,000 acres, was built in the central Artibonite Valley. But because of massive corruption, twice the estimated cost of $14 million (loaned by the Export-Import Bank) was spent in the first two years. The hydroelectric plant, which would have doubled the country's power output, was never installed, the irrigation system left incomplete, and the scheme finally abandoned in 1958. Tourism, which earned the country $8 million in 1956, brought in only $0·7 million in 1964, though the opening of a new jet airport brought some improvement after 1965. The external debt, less than $4 million in 1950, jumped to $40 million in 1956 and stood at $43·5 million in 1964. By then, foreign currency reserves were down to $0·7 million, and the gourde was saved from collapse only by regular IMF standby credits.

Budget revenue fell from an average $30 million in 1957–62 to about $20 million in 1964–5. Normally half this comes from import and export duties, and only 8 per cent from income tax (the peasant producer of coffee receives only 40 per cent of the export price). Of expenditure, about 60 per cent goes to the army, police and administration. About 13 per cent is allocated to education, though only 2 per cent to rural areas where it is really needed. Natural resources and rural development get a mere 7 per cent. The rural population, nearly 85 per cent of the total, produces roughly 90 per cent of the exports, but consumes only about 10 per cent of the imports. The hopelessness of the peasant's situation can be readily appreciated.

In the two decades after the second world war Haiti received nearly $100 million in US aid. In the period 1958–62, the United States covered Haiti's budget deficits by direct annual grants averaging $5–$6 million; in 1961 total US aid reached a record $13·5 million. It was disbursed largely under Haitian control, enabling Duvalier to retain an estimated $6–$10 million annually in a secret, 'non-fiscal' account for political and police purposes. The regime did not, as expected, collapse when US aid ceased, chiefly because most of the population lives outside the cash economy. Duvalier merely reduced public expenditure and squeezed the wealthy (but cowed) minority still harder through extortion by the 'Tonton Macoutes'. If this minority is squeezed dry, the regime may face a serious threat. But erosion and population pressure may combine to produce an explosion first.

SOCIAL STRUCTURE

One of the few cohesive elements in colonial society, for the slaves, was the arbitrary power of the whites. No satisfactory substitute for this power has been found since, though it is no longer wielded by whites. Thus social relationships are still tenuous and uncertain, a major cause of insecurity.

The peasant's apathy and fatalism arises from his inability to overcome the obstacles to his advancement. Of these, ignorance and under-nourishment are the most important, but the social structure also hinders him. In rural society, supreme local power belongs nominally to the *Chef de section*, the local army–police commander (army and police are identical in rural areas). But real power is now generally in the hands of the local 'Tonton Macoutes' commander who, like any secret police chief, is not publicly recognised. The peasant's finances are controlled by middlemen who help to ensure that he receives only a small proportion of his produce's value.

Political patronage is exercised through better-off peasants and other *notables* or *gros habitants*. These are relatively few, since the average peasant land-holding is less than three acres. The Roman Catholic priest and the *houngan*, the voodoo 'priest', compete hotly for influence that goes far beyond the spiritual. Lately, Duvalier's emphasis on Haiti's African nature has put the *houngans* far ahead. Within the family, a man may well not bother to contract a formal marriage (in any case, he probably cannot afford the fee), but he aspires to the social status acquired by becoming the head of a family, the 'Papa'. Duvalier's popular nickname 'Papa Doc' was intentionally created to raise his prestige.

As elsewhere in Latin America, many peasants have flocked to the towns as a way out of their hopeless situation. There they join the destitute unemployed, who already outnumber the lucky ones with jobs. The contrast between the misery of the shanty towns they live in and the affluence of the wealthy minority creates bitter and violent hostility between social classes. Most of the wealthy are mulattos, though in recent years Negroes have acquired riches, if not social equality. A small embryonic middle class, consisting of groups such as clerks and shopkeepers (mostly Negroes) is intensely nationalistic and resentful of mulatto racial prejudice.

CULTURE AND POLITICS

Haiti's official religion has been Roman Catholic since the Concordat with the Vatican in 1860 (since 1804 there had been no organised clergy), and the official language is French. But the popular language is Creole and the popular religion voodoo. Yet Christianity is inextricably mixed with voodoo, just as French forms a vital part of Creole. French priests, the majority, have generally supported the mulattos, and often displayed racial prejudice; Duvalier has therefore crippled their political power and social influence. He has been more lenient towards Haitian and Canadian priests who have shown greater tolerance of voodoo, and towards Protestant churches.

Voodoo is a synthesis of African ancestral beliefs based on the worship of a complex pantheon of West African tribal gods, Christian saints, and some curious figures from Haitian history. It also has a tradition of political significance dating from the colonial period; the first uprising in 1791 began at a voodoo ceremony. Voodoo worship thus has marked nationalist, racial and political aspects as well as those of spiritual devotion, entertainment and escapism. Duvalier has skilfully made voodoo one of his strongest weapons. During the mulatto regimes after the occupation he became one of Haiti's foremost experts on folklore and popular customs, and one of the leading intellectual opponents of attempts to replace everything Negro, popular and 'primitive' by sophisticated French (and later North American) 'civilised' values. Before 1957 this movement had positive results. Like the post-revolutionary reemphasis on Indian civilisations in Mexico, it restored to the most despised part of the population—in Haiti's case the black majority—a pride and concern in their origins and identity. It led to a revival of Creole and its initiation as a literary medium, and to a veritable outburst of painting.

But since he came to power Duvalier has accentuated all the most negative aspects of voodoo and other popular forms of expression. Superstitious ignorance, witchcraft, racial hatred and capricious violence are now Haiti's official values. Creative talents and intellectual thought have been suppressed; efforts to adapt the predominantly African part of Haiti's nature to the 20th century have been deliberately rejected. Many of the best artists and writers are in exile, while thousands of desperately needed experts are working in other lands. The people's good nature has not yet been exterminated; but spiritually, socially and politically, Duvalier has enmeshed the Haitians in the most destructive and primitive traits of their own character. As a result, many now accept his claim that 'God has given me power and only God can take it away.' Recovery, after he has gone, will be slow and difficult.

BIBLIOGRAPHY

Bellegarde, Dantès. *Histoire du peuple haïtien*, Paris, 1938 and Port-au-Prince, 1953. *La resistance haïtien*, Editions Beauchemin, Montreal, 1937.

Gates, William S. *Essays on Aspects of the Economic Development of Haiti*, Williamstown, Mass., 1959.

Guérin, Daniel. *The West Indies and their Future*, Dennis Dobson, London, 1961; Hillary House, New York.

Leyburn, James G. *The Haitian People*, Yale Univ. Press, New Haven and London, 1941.

Manigot, Leslie F. *Haiti of the Sixties: Object of International Concern*, Washington Center of Foreign Policy Research, 1964.

Métraux, Alfred. *Le Vaudou haïtien*, Gallimard, Paris, 1958.

Moral, Paul. *Le Paysan haïtien*, G. Maisonneuve et Larose, Paris, 1961.

Rodman, Selden. *Haiti: The Black Republic*, Devin-Adair, New York, 1954.

Desarrollo económico y social de Haití (Document 28, Haitian Government Report to OAS Economic and Social Council, Mexico, 30 September 1962).

United Nations. *Mission to Haiti* (UN Mission of Technical Assistance to Haiti), New York, 1949.

BASIC INFORMATION

CLIMATE

Port-au-Prince

Lat./long.	18° 30′ N, 72° W	Relative humidity	43%/44%
Altitude	121 ft/36 m.	at midday of	
Mean temp. of hottest month	29°C/84°F (July)	hottest and coolest months	
Mean temp. of coolest month	26°C/78°F (Jan.)	Wettest month	9·1 in./231 mm. (May)
Absolute max.	101°F/39°C	Driest months	1·3 in./33 mm.
Absolute min.	60°F/15°C		(Dec./Jan.)
		Annual av. rainfall	53·3 in./1,354 mm.

POPULATION

TOTAL (*million*), 1950: (census, adjusted) 3·35; mid-1966: 4·49; 1980 (ECLA projection): 6·91.

DENSITY, mid-1965: 168 persons per sq. km.

CRUDE RATES (*per 000*), 1959–61 (ECLA data): birth 45–50, death 20–25.

GROWTH RATES (% *p.a.*), 1945–65, 2·4; 1960–5: 2·3.

DISTRIBUTION (% *of total pop.*): Ethnic: Negro 95, mulatto 5. Foreign-born, 1950: 0·1. Languages: French and Creole. Religion: mainly Roman Catholic. Urban (*centres 2,000 inhab. or over*), ECLA data, 1950: 10·1; 1960: 12·4; 1980 (projection): 25·3. Largest cities (*000 inhab.*), 1950: Port-au-Prince 134, Cap-Haïtien 24, Gonaïves 14, Les Cayes 12, Jérémie 11.

CONSTITUTIONAL SYSTEM

CONSTITUTION: Many constitutions introduced between independence from France in 1801 and US military occupation 1915–34. New constitutions 1932, 1935, 1946, 1950 (19th); 1957, amended 1961; latest 1964.

SYSTEM: Unitary republic, composed of 9 departments, divided into districts and municipalities. Separate executive, legislature and judiciary.

EXECUTIVE: Power vested in president. Under 1950 constitution elected for 6-year term, with no immediate reelection; 1957 constitution made reelection possible. President appoints secretaries of state and public officials.

LEGISLATURE: Uni-cameral Legislative Chamber (bi-cameral up to April 1961). *Deputies:* 1957 constitution provided for 67 deputies elected for 6-year term, from April 1963. *Suffrage:* Universal voting for citizens over 21 years of age. *Elections:* Presidential, October 1957: Dr François Duvalier elected; reelected April 1961, only candidate; at same time 58 nominated deputies were elected to National Assembly which replaced bi-cameral Legislature. Dr Duvalier granted life presidency in 1964.

JUDICIARY: Supreme Court, courts of Appeal, courts of general jurisdiction, special courts, administrative courts, military courts. Judges appointed by the president. System of law is based on French (Roman) law.

DEFENCE

DEFENCE BUDGET, 1964/65: 37·3 m. gourdes; 1961/62: 1·8% of GDP.
ARMED FORCES: Strength: army 5,000, navy 300, air force 200; total 5,500, plus active reserve of 10,000.

INTERNATIONAL RELATIONS

Member of the UN and many of its international specialised agencies, including: IBRD and affiliates, IMF, FAO, ICAO, IMCO, ILO, ITU, UNESCO, UPU, WHO and WMO; IAEA; GATT, UNCTAD representative. Also a member of: OAS, Alliance for Progress, ECLA, IDB.

ECONOMY

PRODUCTION

AGRICULTURE (000 tons)	1948–53[1]	63/64	64/65	65/66[2]
Coffee	35	32	33	36
Sisal[3]	30	20	26	21
Sugar	53	62	65	59
Rice	32	32	40	.

[1] Average 1948/9–1952/3.　　　　　[2] Provisional.
[3] Calendar years: 1948–52 (av.), 1963, 1964, 1965.

LAND (%), 1950: Arable 13, permanent pasture 18, forested 25, other 43.
OTHER AGRICULTURAL DATA: Tractors in use, 1960: 244. Fertiliser consumption (000 tons), 1965/66: 1·9.
LIVESTOCK: Nos (000 head), 1959: cattle 670, sheep 52, pigs 1,136.
MINING, 1964: (000 tons) Bauxite 465, copper 6, salt 10; (tons) silver (recoverable) 2·9.
MANUFACTURING, 1964: (000 tons) Cement 56, wheat flour 46.

ENERGY

CONSUMPTION (tons coal equiv.), 1965: Total 0·15 m., per head 0·033.
ELECTRICITY, 1965: Generated (kwh), public supply, 110 m.; 1961: installed capacity (kw) 32,000.

GOVERNMENT EXPENDITURE

DISTRIBUTION (% of total), 1965: Defence 26, education 11, public health 12.

GROSS PRODUCT

GDP (m. gourdes): at current factor cost, 1960: 1,581; at 1955 factor cost (year to Sept.) 1962/63: 1,605; 1963/64: 1,623. Per head (US$), UN estimate, 1958: 85.

Distribution (%), 1965: Agriculture 43, manufacturing 14, government 7.
Growth rates (%), 1950–60: 1·9, per head −0·2; 1960–2: 2·7, per head 0·4; estimate, 1960–5: 1·0, per head −1·3.

External trade (US$ m.)	1955	1960	1963	1964	1965
Exports (f.o.b.)	36	33	41	40	36
Coffee	24	17	16	19	20
Sugar	2	4	5	3	3
Sisal	6	4	4	4	2
Others[1]	4	8	16	14	11
Imports (c.i.f.)	46	36	40	41	36
Trade balance	−10	−3	+1	−0	−0

[1] Others include bauxite (1965:4), essential oils, copper and cacao.

Direction of trade (%)

	Exports			Imports		
	1955	1960	1964	1955	1960	1964
LAFTA	(0·3)	—	—	(0·5)	—	—
CACM	—	—	—	(0·3)	—	—
USA	40·8	47·1	50·4	64·6	59·7	56·2
EEC	50·0	39·6	36·1	12·1	17·7	17·6
UK	2·5	0·8	0·3	3·8	6·2	4·3

Finance
Exchange rates (Gourde/US$): Par value, end-year, 1960: 5·00; 1966: 5·00.
Balance of payments (US$ m.): Goods and services (net), 1960: −39; 1964: −71; 1965: −113; 1966: −119.
Cost of living (Dec. 1958=100), Port-au-Prince, December 1960: 91; 1964: 115; 1965: 117; 1966: 131.
Budget accounts (m. gourdes), 1966/67: Revenue=expenditure 140·7.

Employment
Economically active (%), 1950: Of total pop. 56 (men 59, women 54). In agriculture 83, manufacturing 5, services 5.

TRANSPORT AND COMMUNICATIONS
Railways: Length of track: 254 km.
Motor vehicles: In use (000), 1965: cars 4·8, comm. vehicles 1·5. Road system, 1959: 3,257 km., paved 440.
Shipping: Merchant fleet (000 g.r. tons), 1965: 82. International sea-borne shipping (m. tons), 1964: goods loaded 3·65, goods unloaded 0·22. Main ports: Port-au-Prince, Cap-Haïtien, Les Cayes, Jacmel.
Air: Scheduled services, 1964: Total 1·5 m. pass.-km., 0·05 m. cargo ton-km. Main airports: Port-au-Prince: Mais Grate and Bowen Field (international); Chancerelles (domestic).
Telephones: No. in use, 1965: 4,400.

SOCIAL WELFARE
System: Social insurance benefits and services administered by the Institut d'Assurances Sociales d'Haïti (IDASH). Financed by employers' contributions, based on remuneration of employees, fixed by the IDASH. Employment legislation covers working hours; holidays; payment of wages and overtime; compensation for accidents, dismissal and death indemnities.
Health: 10,600 persons per physician, 1,800 persons per hospital bed

EDUCATION

ILLITERACY RATE (%), 1950 (census): 15 years and over, 89.
COMPULSORY: 6 years (between 7 and 14 years of age). School enrolment ratios (%), 1st (incl. pre-school) and 2nd levels, 1962: 20, adjusted 24.
SCHOOLS, 1964: Primary: no. 1,925, pupils 0·28 m., teachers 6,100. Secondary: no. 75, p. 19,000, t. 1,160. Technical: no. 26, st. 5,600, t. 360. Teacher-training: no. 4, st. 200, t. 46. Higher: no. 2, st. 1,700, t. 224.
UNIVERSITY (state): Université d'État d'Haïti, Port-au-Prince: 1,000 students, academic staff 150.

MASS MEDIA

BROADCASTING: No. of receivers in use, 1964: TV 4,000, radio 60,000. Transmitters: TV 1, radio 22.
CINEMAS: No., 1964: 21. Attendance: total 1·5 m., per head 0·3.
NEWSPRINT: Consumption, 1964: total 400 tons, per head 0·1 kg.
NEWSPAPERS: Daily, 1965: 6. Estimated circulation (4 dailies) 23,000, copies per 000 of pop. 5. Principal dailies in Port-au-Prince (*circ. ooos*): *Le Matin* 9, *Le Nouvelliste* 6, *Haïti-Journal* (French/English) 5, *Le Jour* 3.
BOOKS: Titles published, 1964: 39.

PUERTO RICO

JOHN RETTIE

HISTORY

The Spanish period

PUERTO RICO's claim to be part of 'Latin America' is based on a strictly literal interpretation of those words. The smallest and easternmost island of the Greater Antilles, it is unquestionably American; its language and culture are predominantly Spanish. But since Columbus discovered it in 1493, its people have never been independent, nor shown any clear desire to be so. Owned by Spain until 1898, Puerto Rico has since belonged to the United States, thus remaining outside the mainstream of Latin American political development.

Known by the native Arawak Indians as 'Borinquén', the island was christened by Columbus 'San Juan Bautista'. But a Spanish nobleman, Juan Ponce de León, who began colonising it in 1508, gave the name 'Puerto Rico' to the bay on the north coast where he founded the capital. That name stuck to the island, while the capital became known as 'San Juan'.

As elsewhere in the Caribbean, the Spaniards found little gold, and soon exterminated the Indians. Negro slaves imported from Africa to replace them were used to build fortifications against the fierce Carib Indians and, later, English, Dutch and French marauders. Guarding the gateway to the Caribbean, Puerto Rico protected the glittering flow of treasure that poured back to Spain from Mexico, and from South America across the isthmus of Panama. Politically, it was a neglected strategic bastion ruled by strict military governors for 300 years. Trade with other countries was prohibited, but the island was so poor that it could not afford to buy what it needed from Spain. In the 18th century it had a small share in the West Indies sugar boom, while its high quality coffee and tobacco also became popular in Spain. But unlike the rest of Latin America, Puerto Rico was barely influenced by the French and American Revolutions, and no significant movement for national independence developed. The maximum demand of even the most radical 19th-century politician was for greater internal self-government under Spain. This was finally achieved in 1897 by a new Charter of Autonomy. But it came too late; the following year the Spanish–American War broke out, and in July the United States, conscious of Puerto Rico's renewed strategic importance, occupied the island. It was formally ceded by Spain at the Treaty of Paris in December 1898.

US rule

For two years strict military rule returned to the island under its new Anglo-Saxon masters. But in 1900 President McKinley, without consulting the Puerto Ricans, signed the Foraker Act establishing civil government.

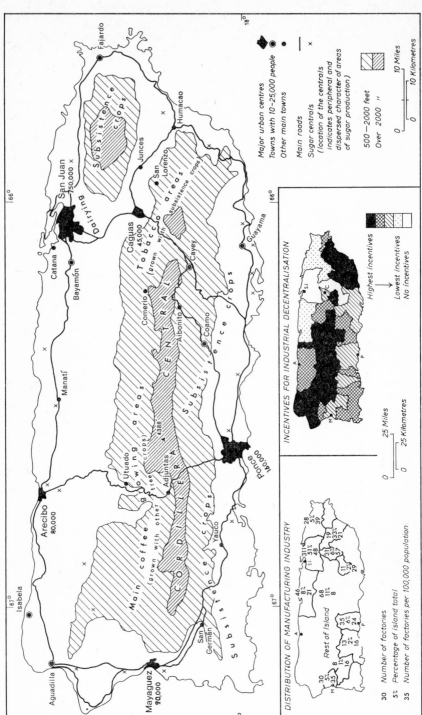

PUERTO RICO

Major urban centres ◆
Towns with 10–25,000 people ◉
Other main towns ●
Main roads —
Sugar centrals ×
(location of the centrals indicates peripheral and dispersed character of areas of sugar production)

500 – 2000 feet
Over 2000 "

0 10 Miles
0 10 Kilometres

© ANTHONY BLOND LTD

INCENTIVES FOR INDUSTRIAL DECENTRALISATION

Highest incentives ▨
Lowest incentives ▨
No incentives □

0 25 Miles
0 25 Kilometres

DISTRIBUTION OF MANUFACTURING INDUSTRY

30 Number of factories
5% Percentage of island total
35 Number of factories per 100,000 population

Rest of Island

San Juan 750,000
Fajardo
Humacao
Juncos
San Lorenzo
Caguas 45,000
Cayey
Guayama
Comerío
Aibonito
Coamo
Catano
Bayamón
Manatí
Arecibo 80,000
Isabela
Utuado
Adjuntas
Ponce 140,000
Yauco
San Germán
Aguadilla
Mayagüez 90,000

Dairying
Subsistence crops
Tobacco (grown with subsistence crops)
CENTRAL
CORDILLERA
▲4388
Main coffee growing areas (grown with other tree crops)
Subsistence crops

302

The island's inhabitants, designated 'citizens of Puerto Rico' (a state which did not even exist) but not of the United States, were granted no bill of rights. The governor, the Executive Council and the five Supreme Court judges were appointed by the President. Only the lower house of the legislature was popularly elected, but the governor, the president and the US Congress all retained veto rights over Puerto Rican legislation. The island was represented by a resident commissioner in Washington, where he sat in the House of Representatives but could not vote. The political clock had been put back to before 1897.

It was, indeed, a classic colonial situation. Many of the United States governors, officials and businessmen who poured into the island were at best ignorant of its affairs and language, and at worst opportunists and carpet-baggers. The '500-Acre Law' in the Foraker Act, designed to prevent companies buying up most of the arable land, was not enforced for 40 years. Puerto Rico thus became dominated by 'sugar baron' companies incorporated in the United States, and the island was virtually reduced to a one-crop economy. The gap between rich and poor widened, and until 1940 the poor were little better off than under Spanish rule.

But there were some compensations. Puerto Rico was exempted from Federal taxes and included within the US tariff structure, thus enjoying free trade with the mainland. Duties collected by Federal customs on foreign imports have, since 1900, been returned to the island government. Federal funds have financed the construction of houses, schools and hospitals, and the eradication of disease. The island's first university was established in 1903. In 1917 the US Congress passed the Jones Act, granting Puerto Ricans US citizenship (with full rights except that of voting in Federal elections) and creating an elected Senate. But the mainland appointees and vetoes remained. It was hardly surprising that the island's political status should have become the dominant issue, overshadowing all ideological and economic questions.

The policies of Muñoz Marín

The leading politician of the early years was Luis Muñoz Rivera, chief executive secretary in the abortive autonomous government of 1897. He became Puerto Rico's first resident commissioner in Washington; as a result, his son Luis Muñoz Marín, a fervent radical who was to dominate the island's affairs a generation later, grew up in the United States. Returning to Puerto Rico in 1926, Muñoz Marín joined the Liberal Party, which then favoured independence, and in 1932 was elected to the Senate. But the 1932 elections brought to power an incongruous coalition between the ultra-conservative Republican Party and the Socialists. At the time Puerto Rico, now closely tied to the US economy, was suffering severely from the Great Depression. Unrest grew, and relations with the United States deteriorated. In 1936 Nationalist Party extremists resorted to violence, assassinating the US-appointed police chief. Muñoz Marín, still a strong advocate of independence, refused to issue a public condemnation unconditionally. His outspoken radical leanings having made him unpopular with the Liberal Party's hierarchy, a hint from Washington in 1937 was enough to bring about his expulsion from the Party.

Until then, Washington's disfavour would have broken a Puerto Rican politician. But in 1938 Muñoz Marín formed a new political party, the Partido Popular Democrático (Popular Democratic Party or PPD). Campaigning among the *jíbaros* (mountain village peasants) on the traditional

Latin American revolutionary slogan 'Bread, Land and Liberty', he won a narrow victory at the general elections two years later. Still favouring independence, Muñoz Marín was becoming increasingly preoccupied with the island's desperate economic conditions.

Fortunately, President Roosevelt saw the need to welcome Muñoz Marín's victory, and in 1942 he appointed as governor the liberal reformist Dr Rexford Tugwell. Together Tugwell and Muñoz Marín laid the basis for future economic progress. The Foraker Act was enforced to limit to 500 acres the land held by corporations (though not by individuals), and much land was distributed. The government established public authorities to supply water and electric power, started agricultural diversification projects, and set up publicly owned manufacturing industries. The new regime created an atmosphere of such enthusiasm that in the 1944 elections the PPD vote jumped to 65 per cent of the total. But in Washington its programme caused such outraged protests about 'un-American socialism' that Tugwell had to resign in 1946. President Truman, however, was persuaded to appoint a Puerto Rican—the first in the island's history—as interim governor for two years. He was Jesús Piñero, resident commissioner in Washington. During his governorship, the US Congress approved the 1947 Act granting Puerto Ricans the right to elect their own governor. In 1948 Muñoz Marín, till then president of the Senate, was elected to the post with an overwhelming majority.

Now in control of his own government, Muñoz Marín switched from land reform and agricultural development to industrialisation. But the island's resources were far too small to create the necessary industrial base, especially in view of the rapid population growth. He saw that the only solution lay in tapping the vast capital resources and purchasing power of the United States. Steps were therefore taken to attract private industry from the mainland. State industries were sold to private enterprise, while United States and foreign manufacturers wishing to establish new industries in Puerto Rico were exempted from local taxes for ten years. (There were, of course, no Federal taxes.) Among the results of this programme, now world famous as 'Operation Bootstrap', has been the trebling of real per capita income between 1940 and 1965.

This new economic policy had far-reaching political effects. As early as 1946 Muñoz Marín had publicly abandoned independence as an immediate goal. This concept of autonomous status under the United States seemed increasingly attractive to him—though in 1948 he still emphasised that it should be transitory. But in 1950 he moved to set this arrangement on a more permanent basis. At the request of the island government, the US Congress passed Public Law 600 authorising Puerto Rico to call a constituent assembly—subject to public approval—to draft a new constitution. In a referendum held in June 1951 the island's electorate approved it by a large majority. The constitution drafted by the Constituent Assembly was adopted, again by a large majority, in a second referendum held in March 1952. It was then approved by the US Congress and promulgated by President Truman in July.

'Commonwealth' status

Under its terms, Puerto Rico was declared a 'Commonwealth' associated with the United States. But the word has a very different meaning from that of the British Commonwealth; Puerto Rico's designation in Spanish— *Estado Libre Asociado* (Free Associated State)—is much more accurate, though still ambiguous. Puerto Ricans were again declared to be US citizens, though still not entitled to vote in Federal elections (except if resident in one of the states of the Union), nor subject to Federal taxes. In all internal matters except those affecting national security, the territory is absolutely autonomous; the US Congress and president relinquished their veto powers over island legislation. Since this has to conform with Federal law, the US Supreme Court is now the only mainland body that can interfere with it. Puerto Rico's governor and congress, modelled on the American, are elected by universal suffrage, while the executive is responsible only to the governor, who also appoints the island's Supreme Court judges. The Federal government is responsible for defence and security, foreign relations, customs, immigration, postal services and currency.

The establishment of 'Commonwealth' status gave a great new impetus to economic development. By the 1956 elections—won, as in 1952, by the PPD with nearly two-thirds of the votes—the Party's official view was that the status issue was solved. But other groups thought differently. A section of the PPD, increasingly discontented with Muñoz Marín's abandonment of independence as a goal, broke away in 1946 to form the separate Partido Independentista Puertorriqueño (Puerto Rican Independence Party or PIP), but its success was limited. The extremist Nationalist Party once again turned to violence. In 1950 it staged an armed revolt and attempted to assassinate President Truman in Washington in protest against the plans for a new constitution. The revolt was quickly suppressed, but in 1954 four Nationalists in Washington opened fire on the House of Representatives from the visitors' gallery.

Though both these groups were numerically small, their existence has shown that a significant minority of the population is irrevocably opposed to a permanent union with the United States. At the same time, a much larger minority favours full statehood. This view is represented by the Partido Estadista Republicano (Republican Statehood Party or PER), affiliated since 1903 (though under different names) with the mainland Republican Party. The PER reflects two main currents of opinion: those who support union with the United States but consider that Puerto Rico has come of age, and that any status less than full statehood is degrading; and a conservative sector which feels its wealth and position will not be absolutely secure until full union with the United States is achieved. Although statehood would mean the end of Puerto Rico's privileged tax position, on which her economic prosperity still largely depends, the PER has increased its share of the poll from 13 per cent in 1952 to nearly 35 per cent in 1964. The only other active political group is the Christian Action Party (CAP), which entered the polls in 1960, winning 7 per cent of the vote in the wake of the Roman Catholic Church's objections to the government's birth control proposals. But the replacement of two US bishops by Puerto Ricans, the teachings of Pope John, and improved relations between Muñoz Marín and the Church reduced the CAP vote in 1964.

The PPD's 59 per cent of the vote in 1964 was achieved despite Muñoz Marín's refusal to stand for a fifth term. He nominated instead one of his closest administrative collaborators, Roberto Sánchez Vilella, who was duly elected governor while he himself 'retired' to the Senate. His declared aim was to establish the PPD on a strong institutional basis, rather than on a single dominant personality. The early prospects for this plan looked good. Sánchez Vilella proved an efficient and honest chief executive, while his aloof and austere character prevented him from dominating the political

L*

scene. But by announcing his wish to divorce his wife and marry a member of his staff, he put an end to his political career. The renewed leadership issue laid the party open to dangerously divisive rivalries. It will need all the skill of Muñoz Marín, now the elder statesman, to resolve it safely before the 1968 gubernatorial elections. But even if he succeeds, his plan for long-term political stability has received a serious setback.

The status issue soon returned to the centre of the political arena. The Cuban Revolution in 1959 challenged United States policies throughout the hemisphere. The United States replied with the Alliance for Progress, and tended to regard Muñoz Marín as one of the leaders of the 'democratic' counter-attack. While emphasising that Puerto Rico could not be a model for Latin America, the US administration often presented it as a 'showcase' for the Alliance. But Puerto Rico could afford neither afflictions nor advantages of nationalism; her progress depended fundamentally on her favoured economic position vis-à-vis the United States. Being outside the mainstream of Latin American political aspirations meant that the influence of even the most distinguished Puerto Rican in that region was limited. This was only slowly appreciated in the United States. At the same time, the status of Puerto Rico has several times been discussed in the United Nations Anti-Colonial Committee; she was deeply moved by the 1963 military coup against President Juan Bosch of the neighbouring Dominican Republic (a close friend of Muñoz Marín) and the subsequent unilateral US intervention.

These external events forced Puerto Ricans to reconsider their status. A joint US–Puerto Rican Commission was set up in 1964 'to study all factors bearing on the present and future relationship between the United States and Puerto Rico'. When it reported in August 1966, its chief recommendation was for a plebiscite to decide whether Puerto Ricans prefer statehood, independence or a continuation of the 'Commonwealth'. Opponents of the 1952 constitution pointed out that such a choice has never been presented to the island's electorate (and therefore declared the 1952 referendum invalid).

When the referendum was held in July 1967, just over 60 per cent of the votes were cast for the Commonwealth; thus the PPD retained its support. Although the PER officially boycotted the election, its presidential candidate, Luis Ferre, campaigned fiercely to lift the vote for statehood to 39 per cent; his supporters have therefore some grounds for saying the future belongs to them. The independence vote, down to 0.6 per cent, suffered badly from the PIP boycott, and looks like a declining force. Thus the Commonwealth still appears the only reasonably satisfying compromise. But the referendum showed that Puerto Ricans were not yet willing to opt for any final solution; it hardly justified Muñoz Marín's conclusion that the issue was definitely settled—as Washington had also devoutly hoped. For the foreseeable future, the island's status will almost certainly be central to all its affairs.

ECONOMY

Puerto Rico's basic economic problem has been that of poor natural resources and over-population. Only a relatively small part of its 3,435 square miles consists of high-productivity soils, and its mineral resources are few. The population rose from 1,869,000 in 1940 to 2,350,000 in 1960, and nearly 2,750,000 in 1966, representing a population density of almost

800 per square mile. Large-scale emigration to the United States took place between 1950 and 1960, but since 1964 Puerto Rico's prosperity has brought a net inflow of migrants, mainly returning emigrants, and the population is increasing rapidly again. In 1965 unemployment was about 11 per cent—more than double that of the mainland.

From the time the Puerto Rico Industrial Development Company (Fomento) was set up in 1942 (later reorganised as the Economic Development Administration) until 1962, more than 800 new industries were promoted or aided by the island government, and more than $670 million invested. By 1964 annual investment was running at the rate of $250 million a year, and average per capita income was almost $800, compared with $121 in 1940—a three-fold real income increase.

In 1940 Puerto Rico was a predominantly agricultural island; by 1965 manufacturing accounted for 57 per cent of the value of goods produced there. Clothing, textiles, petroleum and other manufactured products have now overtaken sugar, rum and molasses as the main exports to the United States. Other products include candy, cement, chemicals, cigars, electrical appliances, foods, furniture, leather goods, machinery, metals, paper products, pottery and china. The only important public industries are electric power and water supplies. But of private industry, only about a third belongs to Puerto Ricans. One of the biggest growth industries has been tourism; in 1965 receipts from over half a million tourists totalled more than $100 million for the first time, compared with $13·7 million in 1952. It is estimated that Puerto Ricans resident on the mainland remit over $60 million a year to the island, while over $300 million comes in Federal grants as aid for schools and hospitals, military pensions, surplus food and other welfare. The United States has also spent about $350 million on military bases on the island.

Apart from the advantages to industry conferred by the island's status, one of the greatest attractions to it has been the low-cost labour supply. But this advantage has diminished as US labour unions have tried to enforce Federal wage rates. Some Puerto Ricans, however, see a more serious threat to further industrialisation in the 'Kennedy Round' tariff cuts. Fears have been expressed that the lowering of US tariffs, especially on textiles and light industrial goods from the Far East, could threaten 30,000 Puerto Rican jobs.

Striking though its economic progress has been, Puerto Rico's average per capita income is still only half that of the poorest state in the Union, Mississippi. In 1959 Governor Muñoz Marín suggested that the island would only be ready for statehood when it had closed that gap. In this respect, Puerto Rico still has a long way to go.

BIBLIOGRAPHY

Anderson, Robert W. *Party Politics in Puerto Rico*, Stanford Univ. Press, Stanford, Calif., 1965.
Friedrich, Carl J. *Middle Road to Freedom*, Holt, Rinehart and Winston, New York, 1959.
Hanson, Earl Parker. *Puerto Rico: Ally for Progress*, Van Nostrand, Princeton, NJ, 1962.
   Transformation. The Story of Modern Puerto Rico, Simon and Schuster, New York, 1955.

Lewis, Gordon K. *Puerto Rico: Freedom and Power in the Caribbean*, Monthly Review Press, New York, 1963; Merlin Press, London, 1964.

Lewis, Oscar. *In the Life*, Random House, New York, 1966.

Marqués, René. *El puertorriqueño dócil*, Cuadernos Americanos, CXX, 1962.

Mathews, Thomas. *Puerto Rican Politics and the New Deal*, Univ. of Florida Press, Gainesville, Fla., 1960.

Morales Carrión, Arturo. *Puerto Rico and the Non-Hispanic Caribbean*, Univ. of Puerto Rico Press, San Juan, 1955.

Muñoz Amato, Pedro. *Congressional Conservatism and the Commonwealth Relationship*, Annals of the America Academy of Political and Social Science, CCLXXXV, 1955.

Muñoz Marín, Luis. *Del tiempo de Muñoz Rivera a nuestro tiempo: lo que ha mejorado y lo que no ha mejorado*, Editorial del Departamento de Instrucción Pública, San Juan, 1956.

Pagán, Bolívar. *Historia de los Partidos Políticos Puertorriqueños*, Librería Campos, San Juan, 1959.

Stead, William H. *Fomento: The Economic Development of Puerto Rico*, Public Pamphlet No. 103, National Planning Association, Washington, DC, 1958.

Tugwell, Rexford G. *The Stricken City*, Doubleday, New York, 1947.

Tumin, Melvin M. and Feldman, Arnold. *Social Class and Social Change in Puerto Rico*, Princeton Univ. Press, Princeton, NJ, 1961.

BASIC INFORMATION

CLIMATE

San Juan

Lat./long.	18° 30′ N, 66° W	Relative humidity	77%/76%
Altitude	82 ft/25 m.	at midday of	
Mean temp. of	27°C/80°F	hottest and	
hottest month	(Aug./Sept.)	coolest months	
Mean temp. of	24°C/75°F	Wettest months	6·3 in./160 mm.
coolest month	(Jan./Feb.)		(Aug./Nov.)
Absolute max.	94°F/35°C	Driest month	2·7 in./69 mm.
Absolute min.	62°F/16°C		(Feb.)
		Annual av. rainfall	60·8 in./1,544 mm.

POPULATION

TOTAL (*million*): 1960 (census): 2·35 (including armed forces); mid-1966: 2·67 (civilian 2·66); 1980 (ECLA projection): 3·12.

DENSITY, mid-1965: 296 persons per sq. km.

CRUDE RATES (*per 000*), 1966: Birth 28·3, death 5·9, infant mortality 42·0.

GROWTH RATES (% *p.a.*): 1958–64: 2·0.

DISTRIBUTION (% *of total pop.*): Ethnic, 1950: white 80, Negro 20. Languages, 1960: Spanish and English; bilingual 17. Religion: mainly Roman Catholic. Urban, 1960: 56. Largest cities (*000 inhab.*), 1965: San Juan 750, Ponce 158, Mayagüez 86, Arecibo 78.

CONSTITUTIONAL SYSTEM

CONSTITUTION: Territorial 1917, Commonwealth 1952.

SYSTEM: Commonwealth, Associated State of the USA, with internal self-government.

Defence and external affairs the responsibility of the US government. Represented in the US House of Representatives by non-voting Resident Commissioner (elected for 4-year term). Territory divided into 77 municipalities.

EXECUTIVE: Power vested in Governor, elected by direct vote for 4-year term. Governor advised by Council of Secretaries (cabinet), who are appointed by the Governor with the approval of the legislature.

LEGISLATURE: Bi-cameral Congress of Senate and House of Representatives. *Senate:* 32 members, 2 from each of 8 districts, 11 senators at large, and 5 additional senators for minority parties; elected by direct vote for 4-year term. *Representatives:* 64 members, 1 from each of 40 districts, 11 at large, and 13 for minority representation; elected for 4-year term. *Suffrage:* Universal voting for citizens over 21 years of age in Puerto Rican (but not US) elections; PR residents in US can vote there. *Elections,* November 1964: (*ooo votes*) Roberto Sánchez Vilella (Partido Popular Democrático) 487, Luis Ferrié (Partido Estadista Republicano) 284. Composition of Congress:

Party	Senate	Representatives
PPD	23	47
PER	9	17
TOTAL	32	64

JUDICIARY: Supreme Court, of 9 judges, and Court of First Instance. Superior Tribunal, District Tribunal and lower courts; all judges appointed by the Governor. US president appoints 2 US district judges to the US judiciary in PR. US law applies.

DEFENCE: US responsibility. Liability for national service in US armed forces.

ECONOMY

PRODUCTION

AGRICULTURE (*ooo tons*)	*1948–53*[1]	*63/64*	*64/65*	*65/66*[2]	*66/67*[2]
Sugar (cane)	1,157	898	814	792	700
Coffee	10	14	17	14	.
Bananas	209	119	107	118	.
Pineapples	30	59	60	80	74
Oranges, tangerines, etc.	29	40	34	36	.
Grapefruit	8	14	15	12	.
Tomatoes	8	21	21	18	.
Tobacco[3]	12	15	15	17	10

[1] Average 1948/9–52/3. [2] Provisional.
[3] Calendar years: 1948–52 (av.), 1963–66.

LAND (%), 1964: Arable 33, permanent pasture 35, forested 13, other 18.

OTHER AGRICULTURAL DATA: Agricultural holdings, 1960 (census): No. 45,792, area 0·66 m. hectares. Tractors in use (*ooos*), 1964: 4·42.

LIVESTOCK: Nos (*ooo head*), Jan. 1966: cattle 504, pigs 171. Products (*ooo tons*), 1963/64: meat 27 (beef and veal 16, pork 11).

FISH: Landed (*ooo tons*), 1965: total 5·0.

MANUFACTURING, 1965: (*ooo tons*) cement 1,240, refined sugar 250; (*m. litres*) beer 89; (*m. tons*) fuel oils 3·50, motor spirit 1·97.

CONSTRUCTION: 1966: No. of building permits issued 1,706.

ENERGY

CONSUMPTION (*tons coal equiv.*), 1965: 5·6 m., per head 2·13.

ELECTRICITY (public supply), 1965: Generated (*kwh*) 4,100 m., installed capacity (*kw*) 0·76 m.

GOVERNMENT EXPENDITURE

DISTRIBUTION (% *of total*), 1966: Education 5, health and social welfare 31.

GROSS PRODUCT

GDP (*US$ m.*): At current market prices, 1964/65: 2,815; 1965/66: 3,146; at 1963 market prices, 1964/65: 2,669; 1965/66: 2,978. Per head (*US$*), UN estimate, 1964: 963.
DISTRIBUTION (%), 1965/66: Manufacturing 23, trade 17, agriculture 7.
GROWTH RATES (%), 1950–60: 6·1, per head 5·4; 1960–5: 8·4, per head 6·1.

EXTERNAL TRADE (*US$ m.*)	1955	1960	1964	1965	1966
EXPORTS (f.o.b.)	382	604	936	1,006	1,135
(to USA)	(369)	(588)	(900)	(968)	(1,081)
IMPORTS (f.o.b.)	603	924	1,477	1,543	1,735
(from USA)	(549)	(771)	(1,234)	(1,275)	(1,420)
TRADE BALANCE	−221	−320	−541	−537	−600

FINANCE

BALANCE OF PAYMENTS (*US$ m.*): Goods and services (net), years ending June, 1960: −319; 1964: −549; 1965: −700; 1966: −685.
COST OF LIVING (*1958=100*), December, 1960: 106; 1964: 114; 1965: 118; 1966: 123.
INDUSTRIAL WAGES: Earnings in manufacturing, per hour, May 1967: US$1·40.
TREASURY ACCOUNTS (*US$ m.*), 1966: Revenue 757, expenditure 732, surplus 26.
ECONOMICALLY ACTIVE (%), 1966: Of total pop. 31 (1960: 25). In services 29 (24), manufacturing 19 (17), trade 17 (16), agriculture 17 (23).
UNEMPLOYMENT (%), June 1966: 10·8.

TRANSPORT AND COMMUNICATIONS

MOTOR VEHICLES: In use (*ooo*), 1965: cars 255, comm. vehicles 51. Road system, 1965: 7,200 km., state system 5,900 km.
SHIPPING: Main ports: San Juan, Ponce, Mayagüez.
AIR: Passenger movement through Isla Verde (main international airport), 1965: 2·8 m.
TELEPHONES: No. in use, 1965: 203,000.

SOCIAL WELFARE

SYSTEM: Some social insurance benefits and services provided under the US social service programme; own system for accident, disability, health and unemployment insurance.
HEALTH: 1,300 persons per physician, 200 persons per hospital bed.

EDUCATION

ILLITERACY RATE (%), 1960 (census): 15 years and over, 19.
COMPULSORY: 6 years (between 8 and 14 years of age). School enrolment ratios (%), 1st and 2nd levels, 1963: 77, adjusted 96.
SCHOOLS, 1964: Pre-school and primary: pupils 0·46 m., teachers 11,400. Secondary and technical: p. 0·22 m., t. 6,800. Higher (1964/5): no. 5, st. 37,000.
UNIVERSITIES (mainly 1964/5 data): U. de Puerto Rico, Río Piedras (nr San Juan): 25,000 students, academic staff 1,950. U. Católica de Puerto Rico, Ponce: 5,000 st., a.s. 230. Inter-American U. of Puerto Rico (U. Interamericana de Puerto Rico), San Germán: 5,600 st., a.s. 210.

MASS MEDIA

BROADCASTING: No. of receivers in use, end-1965: TV 0·4 m., radio 0·5 m. Stations: TV 14, radio 52.

CINEMAS: No., 1963: 106. Attendance: total 8·7 m., per head 3·4.

NEWSPRINT: Consumption, 1963/64: total 17,200 tons, per head 6·7 kg.

NEWSPAPERS: Daily, 1965: 4. Estimated circulation 0·17 m., copies per 000 of population 64. Principal dailies (*circ. 000*): San Juan: *El Mundo* 70 (Sat. 80–90), *El Imparcial* 50 (Thurs. 80–90), *San Juan Star* 30; Ponce: *El Dia* 16.

SURINAM AND THE NETHERLANDS ANTILLES

HERMAN VAN RENSELAAR and HARRY HOETINIK

SURINAM

HISTORY

Discovery and early history

THE 'wild coast of Guiana' was discovered by Alonso de Hojeda in 1499. During the 16th century groups of Spaniards roamed the country in quest of the riches of the legendary 'El Dorado'. At the beginning of the 17th century different groups of European settlers tried to colonise the country but were repeatedly expelled by the hostile autochthonous population (Amerindians of Carib and Arawak stock). In 1650 Lord Francis Willoughby of Parham succeeded in founding a permanent colony. The English planters, coming from Barbados, laid out a number of plantations along the main rivers and soon the colony flourished. In 1667, during the second Anglo-Dutch war, a Dutch fleet took Surinam—as the territory came to be called from the Indian name of the river on which it stands—from the English, and by the Treaty of Breda in the same year Surinam was ceded to the Netherlands. New colonists from the Netherlands replaced the English planters who gradually left the country. The extension of plantation agriculture made it necessary to bring in Negroes from West Africa in ever-increasing numbers. Plantation agriculture (sugar, coffee, cocoa and cotton) reached its peak around 1750. During the 19th century the colony's economy declined owing to a number of factors, among which the most important were the abolition of slavery, competition from beet sugar on the European market and the growing importance of plantation agriculture in the East Indies after the construction of the Suez Canal.

In 1863 slavery was abolished in Surinam. In order to replace slave labour the government recruited Chinese, Hindustani (from India) and Javanese workers under a system of indentured labour. A great many of them stayed on in the colony after their contracts expired, engaging either in retail trade or in smallholding, so that today the population of some 325,000 is diverse. Creoles[1] and Hindustani constitute the largest single elements, each numbering well over 100,000 inhabitants. There are significant minorities of Javanese and Bush Negroes, and smaller numbers of Amerindians, Chinese and Europeans. Over 80 per cent of the population is concentrated in the coastal belt, crowded into an occupied area of only about 2,000 out of the country's total area of over 55,000 square miles. Within this area 40 per cent of the population lives in the capital, Paramaribo.

[1] Here denoting people of Negro and mixed Negro-white descent, excluding Bush Negroes.

Self-government

After the second world war political parties were formed, mainly along lines of ethnic affiliation. The chief political parties are the National Party of Surinam (NPS), the Surinam Democratic Party (SDP), the United Hindustani Party (VHP), the Progressive Surinam People's Party (PSV), the Indonesian Peasants' Party (KTPI), the National Republic Party (PNR), the Independent Party for Nickerie (NOP), the Action Group (AG), the Farmers' Party (FP) and the Progressive National Party (PNP). The NPS, SDP, PSV, PNP and PNR draw their support mainly from the Creoles, the PSV containing most of the Roman Catholic voters and the PNR those who want to break entirely with the Netherlands. The VHP, AG and FP consist entirely of Hindustani and the KTPI of Javanese. The NOP is a small regional party in the Nickerie district, representing Creoles but dominated by Hindustani leaders.

In 1949 free and general elections were held. In 1954 Surinam, the Netherlands Antilles and the Netherlands were united by the Charter for the Kingdom of the Netherlands. Each country is entirely autonomous in the promotion of its internal affairs. The government of Surinam consists of a governor—representing the queen of the Netherlands—and a council of ministers. The ministers are responsible to the people's representatives in the States of Surinam, chosen by direct suffrage in free and secret elections held every four years. Twenty-seven of the 39 members of the States are chosen by candidature per constituency and the remaining seats are allocated among the parties in proportion to the results of national voting, each elector being entitled to vote for one political party for this purpose.

With the exception of the PNR political parties in Surinam represent no particular ideology or philosophy. The authority of most party leaders is based on their charismatic appeal for ethnic solidarity. Political tensions have arisen between Creoles and Hindustani over government positions of power. The Hindustani make up about 40 per cent of the country's population and their number is increasing at a faster rate than that of the Creoles, which promises their greater political influence in future. The 1967 elections brought a coalition government (NPS, AG, FP and SDP) under Johan Adolf Pengel. The PNR, led by Eddy Bruma, did not gain any significant support. This party strives for independence as an immediate political goal and believes in close cooperation among the three Guianas; Bruma is friendly with Cheddi Jagan. The growing nationalism stimulated by Bruma has forced Pengel to take a more independent stand toward the Charter of the Kingdom of the Netherlands. This has led to conflict with the VHP, which relies on the arbitrating influence of the Netherlands while the Hindustani are in a minority. The KTPI, led by Mr Sumita, is a withdrawn ethnic ingroup largely identified with the position of Indonesia; the rise of the Indonesian Republic was therefore of great importance to it and contacts with the Indonesian consul in Surinam have led to an active policy of cultural exchange and political indoctrination.

ECONOMY

Plantation agriculture is negligible. Most of those engaged in agriculture work on family-owned farms. Between the world wars an American and a Dutch company started to exploit the country's rich bauxite deposits. There is besides an important export trade in timber and wood products.

Although by far the greatest part of the people of working age is employed in agriculture, the gross value of mining products in 1957 was SF47 million as compared with SF21 million for agriculture, forestry and fishery. After the second world war the government devised several measures to encourage industrialisation. As elsewhere in the Caribbean, this was hindered by the restricted size of the home market and the geographic fragmentation of the main overseas markets. In 1954 the government embarked on a ten-year plan devised to improve the country's infrastructure by construction of roads, schools, hospitals, housing and airstrips in the interior for surveying new resources. Two-thirds of the necessary money was provided by the Netherlands, half as a gift, half as a loan. At Afobaka, south of Paramaribo, a dam has been built across the Surinam river for a hydro-electric scheme with an installed capacity of 150 megawatts; this is a joint venture by the government and the Suralco Bauxite Company. An aluminium smelter was opened in Paranam in 1965. Plans are being made for similar projects on other rivers. In 1962 Surinam became associated with the European Common Market, and received aid from the organisation's development fund for the Nickerie regional plan and the building of a number of schools.

H. van R.

THE NETHERLANDS ANTILLES

THE Netherlands Antilles consist of two groups of three small islands each: Curaçao, Aruba and Bonaire near the Venezuelan coast and the Dutch Leeward Islands composed of St Eustatius, Saba and the Dutch half of St Martin in the centre of the Caribbean island chain.[1] Curaçao and Aruba together have more than nine-tenths of the total population of 215,000.

HISTORY

Curaçao was discovered in 1499 by Alonso de Ojeda. Together with Aruba and Bonaire it was governed by the Spaniards under the jurisdiction of the Audiencia of Santo Domingo, until it was captured by the Dutch in 1634. The great part of the aboriginal population fled with the Spaniards. At about the same time St Eustatius, Saba and part of St Martin were taken into Dutch possession, Dutch rights being confirmed by the Treaty of Münster in 1648. The Dutch motives for the capture of the islands were strategic rather than economic: they were meant to serve as Caribbean footholds in the war against Spain. The Spaniards had called the islands 'islas inútiles' because of their scarcity of gold. The Dutch West India Company, under whose jurisdiction the islands fell till the end of the 18th century, failed in its efforts to make a real plantation colony of Curaçao: owing to the arid climate the cultivation of sugar and cotton did not prosper. The great economic importance achieved by the island in the 17th and 18th centuries was due to the slave trade and to commercial exchange, often of contraband. Slaves, bought in West Africa by the West India Company, were sold to the neighbouring Caribbean colonies; agricultural produce

[1] Curaçao, Aruba and Bonaire are termed by the Dutch the Dutch Leewards, and St Eustatius, Saba and Dutch St Martin the Dutch Windwards. For consistency with the classifications used in other parts of this book St Eustatius, Saba and Dutch St Martin are here termed the Dutch Leewards.

from the Spanish possessions was illegally imported and traded for European commercial products.

After the slave trade came to an end in the middle of the 18th century, wars and revolutions in the Caribbean area continued to bring profits to Curaçao merchants: the Seven Years War between France and Britain and also the United States War of Independence benefited the island, which functioned as a depot for weapons and food for France and the United States respectively. During Napoleon's occupation of Holland, the Netherlands Antilles were taken by the British, who governed the islands till Dutch sovereignty in Europe was restored.

Formation of the ethnic structure of the islands

Before the establishment of the oil industry in 1915, Curaçao's social structure was relatively simple. The dominant white group was divided into two segments—Sefardic Jews and Protestant whites of north-west European origin. The Jews, who had arrived as early as 1654, twenty years after the capture of the island by the Dutch from the Spaniards, had developed into an aristocracy of merchants and bankers, involved in economic and political activities throughout the Caribbean region and beyond. As in Aruba and Bonaire, the Protestant white group was divided into two 'estates'; the 'higher Protestants' were important government officials, army officers and owners of 'plantations' (colonial mansions with land on which only sorgum was grown and goats or sheep were kept), while the 'lower Protestants' were small merchants, artisans or owners of schooners. The 'higher Protestants' viewed themselves as representatives of Dutch civilisation, and Curaçao as an extension of the Netherlands. They married among themselves or with Dutch newcomers; they saw the Sefardic Jews essentially as 'foreigners', though little friction ever occurred between the two. The Jews were also endogamous, and until the 1870s maintained Portuguese as their synagogue language, while many of them spoke Spanish at home. The 'lower Protestants' were often forced, by lack of Dutch marriage partners, to contract marriages on the South American mainland, so that 'Latin' cultural traits were absorbed by this group. In the first decade of the present century the Curaçao whites numbered some 4,000, of whom about 1,000 were Jews.

The non-whites at this time numbered about 30,000. Since Curaçao had never been a real plantation colony, master-slave relations had been relatively mild and manumission of slaves, caused by poverty of the slave-owners, had been frequent. When in 1863 slavery was abolished, only a small proportion of the Negro population was affected by it. Within the coloured group, social gradation, based on physical traits, economic status and education, had taken place at an early stage, a lighter skin tending to correlate with a better economic and educational position. Of those coloureds who attained economic security and prestige before the industrialisation of the islands, most descended from extra-marital unions between Jewish merchants and Negro or coloured women; in general the Jewish fathers tended to protect their illegal offspring better than did their white Protestant counterparts.

Neither Jews nor Protestants had stimulated the conversion of non-whites to their religion; Christianising was left, at least in Curaçao, Aruba and Bonaire, to Roman Catholic missionaries, with the result that today the overwhelming majority of the population belongs to the Roman Catholic Church, the Dutch Protestant Church being limited to descendants of native whites. In the Dutch Leewards the Methodist Church, spreading from neighbouring British islands, also gained influence among the non-white population.

Three main cultural influences can be discerned in Curaçao, Aruba and Bonaire according to the provenance of the main population groups: from Africa, Latin America and the Netherlands. These influences have combined in the creation of a unique Creole language, Papiamentu (in the Leewards English Creole is spoken). Papiamentu is distinguished from other Caribbean Creole languages in that it is the vernacular of all native social strata—though Dutch is the official and school language. Originally, several 'higher Protestant' families in Curaçao spoke Dutch at home, but the mass immigration of foreigners after the establishment of the oil industry, and especially the increasing numbers of Dutch colonial officers since 1915, created a Curaçaoan in-group sentiment, which made these families also adopt Papiamentu as their common language. Improved economic and educational opportunities have considerably lessened the social gap between 'higher' and 'lower' Protestants. The Sefardic Jews have maintained their superior position in commerce in spite of competition from Syrians, Chinese, East European Jews and Dutch immigrants. The coloureds and Negroes have improved their economic condition during the oil boom, some entering government and the professions; they have not, however, so far produced economic entrepreneurs to rival the Sefardic Jews and the immigrants.

Self-government

Universal suffrage was introduced in 1949. In 1954, by the Charter for the Kingdom of the Netherlands, the Netherlands Antilles obtained political autonomy within the Kingdom of the Netherlands, with Surinam and the Netherlands as juridically equal partners. Defence and foreign affairs are the responsibility of the Kingdom government, in which the Antilles and Surinam are represented; all other matters are independently dealt with by each Kingdom partner.

The Netherlands Antilles have a federal structure in which each island or island area (the Leewards are grouped together) has its own local government with a high degree of internal autonomy. The country as a whole is governed by a parliament in Willemstad, Curaçao—the Staten, whose 22 seats are disproportionately divided among the islands (Curaçao 12, Aruba 8, Bonaire and the Leewards one each). A governor, appointed by the crown, occupies the same constitutional position as the queen in the Kingdom and acts as her representative. His political power is accordingly small. Each of the islands has its own party system. For the formation of the national government, these parties form coalitions in which the smaller islands' parties can sometimes gain disproportionate power.

Party programmes do not differ widely, party followings being based mainly on personal leadership and patronage; in some cases a political differentiation along ethnic or rural-urban lines can be observed. Given the geographic fragmentation of the Netherlands Antilles and the scant possibilities of economic independence, it is understandable that political aspirations towards complete independence and nationhood are not strongly represented among present political leaders. Growing economic dependence on the Netherlands reinforces the Netherlands Antilles' loyalty as a partner in the Kingdom.

ECONOMY

The population of Curaçao and Aruba has increased enormously in the past half-century (Curaçao from 33,000 in 1915 to 127,000 in 1960; Aruba from 10,000 in 1915 to 59,000 in 1960), while that of Bonaire and the Leewards has decreased. This situation was brought about by the building of oil refineries in Curaçao (1915) and Aruba (1924) by the Royal Dutch Shell and the Standard Oil Company respectively, which started to refine crude oil imported by tankers from Venezuela and Colombia, the Dutch islands being chosen for their political stability at the time and their good harbours. Before the establishment of these refineries the Netherlands Antilles were economically overpopulated. Their climate does not lend itself to agriculture and some of the growing population in the first decade of the present century emigrated to the neighbouring mainland and to the Greater Antilles.

After the establishment of the oil refineries migration took place from the other islands to Curaçao and Aruba. An economic boom began in Curaçao and Aruba, based not only on their refining activities but also on the establishment of several connected industries, the expansion of shipping and banking, and the growth of commerce and government services. Thousands of immigrants were attracted from the British West Indies, the Near East, India, South America (including Surinam) and the Netherlands. Amongst the non-indigenous 20 per cent of the Curaçao population in 1961 some 40 nationalities were represented. The end of the 1950s, however, saw a decrease in prosperity and a reverse migratory trend started. The 'streamlining' of refinery production, with the consequent decrease in oil company personnel, first sent many West Indians and other foreign unskilled or semi-skilled immigrants back home, while later workers of Dutch nationality were affected. Furthermore, in a situation of shrinking markets thousands of native Antilleans are yearly entering the productive age-groups and many of them can no longer be absorbed into the economy. In the mid-1960s unemployment in Curaçao was estimated at 14 per cent of the economically active population.

With financial assistance from the Netherlands a ten-year plan is being implemented by which it is hoped to attract industry and tourism. It is also hoped that the status of the Netherlands Antilles as an associate member of the European Common Market may improve the islands' economic position by attracting industries which might profit from the relatively low import duties in the commercial traffic from the Antilles to the ECM. It is not yet possible to foretell whether these projects will solve the long-range economic problems of the islands, which have their causes in the absence of agricultural or extractive resources of any importance (even fresh water has to be produced from the sea) and in an annual natural population increase of between 2 and 3 per cent.

H. H.

BIBLIOGRAPHY

Surinam

Dusseldorp, Dirk B. W. M. van. *Gesamtwirtschaftliche Agrarplanung in Surinam. Zeitschrift für ausländische Landswirtschaft*, Jahrgang 3, Heft 3, DLG-Verlag, Frankfurt-am-Main, 1964.
Lier, Rudolf A. M. van. *Samenleving in een grensgebied*, Martinus Nijhoff, Gravenhage, 1949.
Institute of Caribbean Studies, University of Puerto Rico. *Politics and Economics in the Caribbean. A Contemporary Analysis of the Dutch, French, and British Caribbean*, Special Study No. 3, San Juan, 1966.
Stichting Planbureau, Paramaribo. *Integraal Opbouwplan Suriname 1963–1972*, 1963.

Netherlands Antilles

Emmanuel, I. S. *Precious Stones of the Jews of Curacao: Curacao Jewry 1656–1957*, Bloch, New York, 1957.
Hoetink, H. *Het Patroon van de Oude Curacaose Samenleving* (with summary in English), De Wit N. V., Aruba, 2nd ed. 1966.
Keur, J. Y. and Keur, D. L. *Windward Children: A Study in Human Ecology of the Three Dutch Windward Islands in the Caribbean*, Assen, Van Gorcum City; Humanities Press, New York, 1960.
Department of Foreign Affairs, The Hague. *Surinam and the Netherlands Antilles: From Dependency to Partnership*, Staatsdrukkerij, The Hague, 1955.

BASIC INFORMATION

SURINAM

CLIMATE

Paramaribo

Lat./long.	6° N, 55° W	Relative humidity	
Altitude	12 ft/4 m.	at midday of	67%/74%
Mean temp. of	28°C/82°F	hottest and	
hottest month	(Sept./Oct.)	coolest months	
Mean temp. of	26°C/78°F (Feb.)	Wettest month	12·2 in./310 mm.
coolest month			(May)
Absolute max.	99°F/37°C	Driest month	3·0 in./76 mm.
Absolute min.	62°F/16°C		(Oct.)
		Annual av. rainfall	91·0 in./2,311 mm.

POPULATION

TOTAL (*ooo*): 1964 (census): 324, excluding tribal population (38 in 1962); mid-1965: 335; 1980 (ECLA projection): 567.
DENSITY, mid-1965: 2 persons per sq. km.
CRUDE RATES (*per ooo*), 1962: birth 43·0, death 7·5, infant mortality 40.
GROWTH RATES (% *p.a.*): 1945–64: 3·6; 1960–4: 4·7.
DISTRIBUTION (% *of total pop.*): Ethnic, 1962: Creoles 46, Hindus 34, Indonesians 15, Europeans 2. Languages: Dutch; also Surinamese and English, French and Spanish. Religion, 1964: Hindu 27, Roman Catholic 22, Protestant 22, Moslem 20. Largest cities (*ooo inhab.*), 1961: Paramaribo 123, Nieuw Nickerie 25.

CONSTITUTIONAL SYSTEM

CONSTITUTION: Based on the Charter for the Kingdom of the Netherlands, 1954. An associate member of the EEC.
SYSTEM: A part of the Kingdom of the Netherlands, with full internal autonomy. A minister-plenipotentiary represents Surinam in the Council of Ministers of the Kingdom. Divided into 8 districts.
EXECUTIVE: The sovereign of the Netherlands is head of government and is represented by a governor appointed by the sovereign. The governor is assisted by an advisory council of 6 members. The Ministerial Council, of 12 ministers, is responsible to the Legislative Council.
LEGISLATURE: Uni-cameral, Legislative Council of 39 members elected for 4 years. Universal adult suffrage. *Elections:* Legislative Council, March 1967: Nationale

Partij Suriname (17 seats), Verenigde Hindustaanse Partij (11), Acctie Groep Partij van de Landbouw (4), others (7).
JUDICIARY: Court of Justice, with 7 members appointed for life by the sovereign. Three cantonal courts.

ECONOMY

PRODUCTION

AGRICULTURE (ooo tons)	1948–52[1]	1962	1963	1964	1965
Rice (paddy)	54	79	75	88	90
Sugar (cane)	60	154	187	153	241
Coffee	0·4	0·3	0·4	0·4	0·4
Cacao	0·1	0·3	0·5	0·5	0·2
Bananas	6	4	5	3	16

[1] Average.

LAND (%), 1964: Arable 0·3, forested 76·2, other 23·5.
OTHER AGRICULTURAL DATA: Agricultural holdings, 1959 (census): no. 16,239, area 105,832 hectares. Tractors (wheel) in use, 1964: 650. Fertiliser consumption (ooo tons), 1965/6: 1·4.
LIVESTOCK: Nos. (ooo head), end-1964: cattle 43, sheep 4, pigs 8.
FISH: Landed (ooo tons), 1963: total 5.
MINING, 1965: Bauxite 4·4 m. tons, gold 195 kg.
MANUFACTURING, 1965: Sugar 19,000 tons, wood (sawn) 45,000 c. metres (plywood 18,000), gas (1963) 4 m. c. metres, rum 2·6 m. litres, beer 5·1 m. litres.

ENERGY

CONSUMPTION (tons coal equiv.), 1964: Total 0·29 m., per head 0·88.
ELECTRICITY, 1965: Generated (kwh) 244 m.; installed capacity (kw), Paramaribo, 1963: 39,100.

GOVERNMENT EXPENDITURE

DISTRIBUTION (% of total), 1966: education 19, health 11, public works and development 24.

GROSS PRODUCT

GDP (m. S guilders) at current market prices, 1963: 245; 1964: 268. Per head (US$), UN estimate, 1963: 359.
DISTRIBUTION (%), 1963: agriculture 12, manufacturing 18, other industry 29.

EXTERNAL TRADE (US$m.)	1955	1960	1963	1964	1965	1966
EXPORTS (f.o.b.)	27	44	46	48	59	87
Bauxite	21	35	35	39	43	·
Rice	2	3	3	2	3	·
Plywood	2	2	2	2	2	·
Alumina	—	—	—	—	3	·
IMPORTS (c.i.f.)	27	54	58	81	95	90
TRADE BALANCE	−1	−10	−12	−33	−36	−3

DIRECTION OF TRADE (%)

	Exports			Imports		
	1955	1960	1965	1955	1960	1965
USA	69·7	74·6	74·0	33·6	33·6	46·7
EEC	9·4	10·7	9·8	38·7	38·7	27·8
Netherlands	8·2	8·2	7·0	32·1	30·3	20·0
UK	—	0·4	—	6·6	7·9	5·8

FINANCE

EXCHANGE RATES (*Surinam guilders/US$*): Par value 1·886; official selling 1·90.
BALANCE OF PAYMENTS (*US$ m.*): Goods and services (net) 1960: 44; 1964: 95; 1965: 96.
COST OF LIVING (*1958=100*), Paramaribo, Sept.–Dec., 1960: 103; 1964: 110; 1965: 120; 1966: 125.
BUDGET ACCOUNTS (*m. S guilders*), 1965: Revenue 107·0, expenditure 117·3, deficit 10·3.

EMPLOYMENT

ECONOMICALLY ACTIVE (%), 1964: of total (excl. tribal) pop. 27 (men 42, women 13). In manufacturing 9, services 30, agriculture 25, mining 7, commerce 11.
UNEMPLOYMENT (%), 1964: 3·3.

TRANSPORT AND COMMUNICATIONS

RAILWAYS: Length of track 115 km.
MOTOR VEHICLES: In use (*000*), 1965: pass. cars 9·9, comm. vehicles 2·4. Road system, 1963: 1,260 km., paved 460 km.
SHIPPING: (*000 net reg. tons*), 1965: vessels entered 5,900. Main ports: Paramaribo, Nieuw Nickerie; river ports: Moengo, Paranam.
AIR: Passenger departures, 1965: total 15,550. Main airports: Paramaribo: Zanderij (international); Nieuw Nickerie, Moengo.
TELEPHONES: No. in use, 1964: 6,900.

SOCIAL WELFARE

SYSTEM: Social insurance benefits and services financed by equal contributions from employees and employers. Employment legislation covers working hours, holidays, payment of wages, overtime and accidents.
HEALTH, 1963: 2,400 persons per physician, 220 persons per hospital bed.
NUTRITION: Net food supply (*per head per day*), 1964: 2,310 calories, protein 51 g.

EDUCATION

ILLITERACY RATE (%), 1950 (est.): 10 years and over, 25–30.
COMPULSORY: 5 years (between 7 and 12 years of age). School enrolment ratios (%), 1st and 2nd levels, 1962: 71, adjusted 82.
SCHOOLS, 1962: Pre-school and primary: no. 335, pupils 77,600, teachers 2,200. Secondary: no. 21, p. 8,600, t. 440. Technical: no. 7, st. 1,100, t. 66. Teacher-training: no. 4, st. 1,270, t. 136. Higher: no. 3, st. 760, t. 87.
UNIVERSITIES: University to be established, with faculties of law, medicine and social sciences. Schools of law and medicine, Paramaribo: De Surinaamse Rechtschool and De Geneerskundige School (affiliated to Leyden University).

MASS MEDIA

BROADCASTING: No. of receivers in use, Jan. 1966: TV 8,000, radio 50,000. Stations: TV 1, radio 5.
CINEMAS: No. 1963: 7. Attendance, 1961: total 1·5 m., per head 4·6.
NEWSPRINT: Consumption, 1964: total 400 tons, per head 1·1 kg.
NEWSPAPERS: Daily, 1964: 5. Estimated circulation 20,000, copies per 000 of 60. Principal dailies in Paramaribo (*circulation, 000s*): De Ware Tijd 5, Nieuw Suriname 3·5, Suriname 3; evening: De West 6.

NETHERLANDS ANTILLES

CLIMATE

Willemstad (Curaçao)

Lat./long.	12° N, 69° W	Relative humidity	67%/67%
Altitude	75 ft/23 m.	at midday of	
Mean temp. of	29°C/84°F (Sept.)	hottest and	
hottest month		coolest months	
Mean temp. of	26°C/79°F	Wettest month	4·4 in./112 mm.
coolest month	(Feb./Mar.)		(Nov.)
Absolute max.	96°F/36°C	Driest months	0·8 in./20 mm.
Absolute min.	63°F/17°C		(Mar./May)
		Annual av. rainfall	22·9 in./582 mm.

POPULATION

TOTAL (*ooo*): 1960 (census) 189; mid-1966: 210 (1965: Curaçao 136, Aruba 59, Bonaire 7, Leewards 6); 1980 (ECLA projection): 260.
DENSITY, mid-1965: 216 persons per sq. km. (Leewards 66).
CRUDE RATES (*per ooo*), 1966: Birth 25·2, death 4·9, infant mortality 14·2.
GROWTH RATES (% *p.a.*), 1945–64: 2·4; 1958–64: 1·8 (A 1·7, B 1·4, C 1·9, L 2·8).
DISTRIBUTION (% *of total pop.*): Ethnic: mixed and European, many nationalities. Foreign-born, 1960: 11. Languages: Dutch, Creole 'Papiamento', and English (in L). Religion, 1960: Christian: A 95, C 91 (mainly Roman Catholic, some Dutch Protestants and Methodists); Jewish. Urban (Willemstad City), 1960: 32. Largest city (*ooo inhab.*), 1960: Curaçao: Willemstad 44.

CONSTITUTIONAL SYSTEM

CONSTITUTION: Based on the Charter for the Kingdom of the Netherlands, 1954. Associate member of EEC.
SYSTEM: A part of the Kingdom of the Netherlands, with full internal autonomy. A minister-plenipotentiary represents Netherlands Antilles in the Council of the Kingdom. Aruba, Bonaire, Curaçao and the Leewards are partly autonomous and each has an elected Council, an executive and a Lieut.-Governor.
EXECUTIVE: The sovereign of the Netherlands is head of the government and is represented by a Governor, appointed by the sovereign. The Governor is assisted by an advisory council of 10 members. A Council of ministers, of 7 members appointed by the Governor after consultation with the Advisory Council and legislature, with the prime minister as chairman, is responsible for internal affairs to the Staten (see below).
LEGISLATURE: Uni-cameral Legislative Assembly (Staten). *Staten:* 22 members (C 12, A 8, B 1, L 1), for 4 year-term. *Suffrage:* Universal voting for adults. *Elections:* Legislative Assembly, 1966: *Government:* Democratische Partij van Curaçao (Dr E. Jonckheer) 7, Partido Patriotico Arubano 4, Partido Democratico Bonairiano 1, Democratic Party of the Windwards 1. *Opposition:* Nationale Volkspartij (Curaçao) 4, Arubaanse Volkspartij 3, Curaçaose Onafhankelijke Partij 1, Unión Nacional Arubano 1.
JUDICIARY: Supreme Court in Curaçao, and courts of first instance. Netherlands law applies together with local legislation.

ECONOMY

PRODUCTION

AGRICULTURE: Negligible; most food is imported.
LAND (%), 1951: Arable 5, other 95.
OTHER AGRICULTURAL DATA: Tractors in use: 1952: 26. Fertiliser consumption (*ooo tons*), 1965/66: 5·0.

LIVESTOCK: Nos (*ooo head*): Cattle 6 (A 5), pigs 14 (C 10), sheep 20, goats 20 (C 15).
MINING, 1965: (*ooo tons*) phosphate rock (C 233).
MANUFACTURING, 1965: (*ooo tons*) fertiliser 39; (*m. tons*) exports of: fuel oils 26·36, paraffin 3·78, motor spirit 4·61, asphalt 0·82.
CONSTRUCTION, private, 1963: No. of buildings completed in Aruba and Curaçao, 1,012.

ENERGY

CONSUMPTION (*tons coal equiv.*), 1965: Total 4·0 m., per head (19).
ELECTRICITY, 1965: Generated (*kwh*) 1,080 m., installed capacity (*kw*) 0·26 m.

GROSS PRODUCT

GDP (*NA Guilder m.*): At current market prices, 1965: 447; 1966: 456; at 1958 market prices, 1965: 418; 1966: 420. Per head (*US\$*), estimate (at par value), 1966: 1,000.
GROWTH RATES (%), 1957–60: +0·8, per head −0·6; 1960–6: −0·9, per head −2·4.

EXTERNAL TRADE[1] (*US\$ m.*)	*1955*	*1960*	*1964*	*1965*	*1966*
EXPORTS (f.o.b.)	804	658	630	603	585[2]
Petroleum products	752	625	606	574	
Gas, diesel and fuel oils	437	335	340	303	
Motor spirit	197	168	138	141	
Fertilisers (crude + manuf'd.)	2	3	8	9	
Coffee	—	—	—	4	
IMPORTS (f.o.b.)	831	682	650	617	
IMPORTS (c.i.f.)[2]	996	824	784	746	745[2]
TRADE BALANCE	−192	−166	−154	−143	−160

[1] Data relate to Aruba, Bonaire and Curaçao only.   [2] IMF estimates.

DIRECTION OF TRADE (%)

	Exports			*Imports*		
	1955	*1960*	*1965*	*1955*	*1960*	*1965*
LAFTA	(17·9)	13·5	6·2	(3·8)	2·5	1·2
Venezuela	0·5	0·1	0·1	77·9	78·3	77·4
CACM	(2·1)	2·9	1·6	(0·1)	0·2	0·2
USA and Canada	30·4	40·0	49·2	7·8	9·3	11·0
EEC	9·6	7·8	9·2	4·3	4·5	4·1
Netherlands	3·8	3·5	4·0	3·6	3·2	2·6
UK	9·9	8·5	7·6	3·8	2·4	2·0

FINANCE

EXCHANGE RATE (*NA Guilders/US\$*): Par value 1·886, banks' selling rate 1·905.
BALANCE OF PAYMENTS (*US\$ m.*): Goods and services (net), 1960: + 16; 1964: +14; 1965: +18.
COST OF LIVING (*1958=100*), Curaçao, December 1960: 103; 1964: 106; 1965: 107; 1966: 108.
GOVT. ACCOUNTS (*NAG 000*), 1966: Central government—revenue 57,662, expenditure 57,600, surplus 62. 1964: Curaçao, rev. = expend. 53,320; Aruba, rev. 29,000, expend. 29,468.

EMPLOYMENT

ECONOMICALLY ACTIVE (%), 1960: Of total population 31 (men 47, women 16). In manufacturing 26 (oil refining: A 30, C 25), services 24, trade 14 and agriculture 2.

TRANSPORT AND COMMUNICATIONS

MOTOR VEHICLES: In use in Aruba and Curaçao (*ooo*), 1965: Cars 23·1, comm. vehicles 4·4. Road system, 1963: 970 km. (A 325, C 445, B 158).
SHIPPING: International sea-borne shipping (*m. tons*), 1962: Goods loaded 36·3, goods unloaded 48·0. Main ports: Curaçao: Willemstad; Aruba: Oranjestad; Bonaire: Kralendijk.
AIR: Main international airports: Curaçao: Dr Albert Plesman (Hato); Aruba: Prinses Beatrix.
TELEPHONES: No. in use, 1965: 21,300.

SOCIAL WELFARE

HEALTH: 1,450 persons per physician, 110 persons per hospital bed.

EDUCATION

SCHOOLS, 1964: Pre-school and primary: no. 200, pupils 50,000, teachers 1,320. Secondary: no. 34, p. 8,800, t. 340. Technical: no. 19, st. 3,100, t. 140.

MASS MEDIA

BROADCASTING: No. of receivers in use, end-1965: TV 25,000, radio 0·10 m. Stations: TV: Curaçao 1, Aruba 1; radio: Curaçao 4, Aruba 4, St Martin 1.
CINEMAS: No., 1964: 18. Attendance: total 1·0 m., per head 4·9.
NEWSPRINT: Consumption, 1965: total 300 tons, per head 1·4 kg.
NEWSPAPERS: Daily, 1964: 6. Estimated circulation 31,000, copies per ooo of population 151. Principal dailies (*circ. ooo*): Willemstad, Curaçao: *Beurs-en Nieuwsberichten* 8, *La Prensa* 7; evening: *Amigoe di Curaçao* 7. Oranjestad, Aruba: *Arubaanse Courant* 3, *Amigoe di Aruba* 3, *News* 3.

THE ENGLISH-SPEAKING WEST INDIES:
JAMAICA, TRINIDAD AND TOBAGO, BARBADOS, ASSOCIATED STATES, CROWN COLONIES

FERNANDO HENRIQUES and COLIN RICKARDS

HISTORY BEFORE INDEPENDENCE

THE earlier political history of the British Caribbean was dominated by the struggle for power by the major European maritime nations. Spain's original hegemony of the area was broken by the advent of the British, French and Dutch in the 17th century. Jamaica became a British possession in 1655. Trinidad passed from Spanish control to that of Britain in 1797. Barbados alone of the major territories has maintained an unbroken British connection since its settlement in 1624. Between 1625 and 1666 St Kitts enjoyed Franco–British ownership; apart from a brief French interlude in the 1780s the island has remained British since the era of the condominium. In the 17th and 18th centuries Grenada, St Vincent, St Lucia and Dominica all passed from France to Britain and back again, Britain emerging eventually as the controlling power. This shuttling of imperium can be regarded as a reflex of the development of the sugar trade.

SLAVERY AND THE FORMATION OF WEST INDIAN SOCIETY

Soon after the discovery of the West Indies in 1492 by Columbus the Spaniards introduced a form of quasi-slavery—the *encomienda* system—under which the colonist in the Indies was given the right to the labour of the Indian. The indigenous population was incapable of withstanding the rigours of slavery, and declined sharply in the first hundred years of Spanish dominion. The initial unsuccessful gold mining gave way to an agricultural economy and the problem of supplying a labour force. The Spaniards introduced sugar cane in the 16th century, and the large labour force necessary for sugar cultivation was met by the introduction of Negro slaves from Africa. The Negroes who were held in the slave 'factories' of the West African coast came mainly from an area bounded by the Gambia in the north and the Congo in the south. The linguistic and cultural diversity contained in this area is considerable, and had a significant effect on the developing societies of the Caribbean. Inability of one group to communicate with another assisted the slave-owner to produce docility in his stock. Again, the Negro in the British West Indies was forced to use English as his sole language; in the process his indigenous culture was largely destroyed.

The society into which the African came was entirely dependent upon the production of sugar. The unit of production was the estate. Society on the estate was essentially pyramidal in form. At the apex was the estate-owner and his family living in the Great House. Associated with him were the European 'book-keepers' who ran the estate. Separated from them by the immeasurable gulf of slavery were the workers. The slaves were not, however, an undifferentiated mass. The main labour force consisted of the majority of able-bodied men and women. A small number of the best male workers were selected as gang leaders or foremen. These were the aristocracy of the slaves, their occupation providing privileges denied to the rest. A further category comprised those known as domestic slaves who provided service in the Great House.

The rigid division between master and slave, between black and white, prevalent in the early period of slavery was soon modified. The European male utilised his position of authority to form sexual liaisons with slave women. Both the black concubine and her coloured offspring tended to occupy a privileged position in relation to the rest of the servile population. In time further modification was introduced by the growth of manumission. From the outset the slave had been able to purchase his freedom if the master agreed on the price, but few had been able to obtain their freedom in this manner. It was only the skilled slave, permitted by his master to work for money at his trade, who could purchase his freedom. But with the growth of sexual liaisons and their resultant progeny slave-owners began to manumit their offspring and their mistresses. Thus there developed a non-servile category in the society of freed coloured and black individuals.

The most popular form of manumission was by will on the death of the slave-owner. In many instances it was not only freedom that was granted, but property and slaves were bequeathed to the freedman. The practice grew to such proportions that governments in the Caribbean passed laws limiting the amount of property that it was permissible to dispose of in this way. It was clear that an unchecked development of this kind would have radically altered the nature of the slave society.

By the middle of the 18th century society in the British Caribbean had evolved a different type of pyramidal structure. The planter, and those Europeans associated with him, still dominated the scene. But now the category of the free and freed coloured and black was a significant group. Although not subject to a master such individuals were not possessed of the normal rights and privileges of the European. Many owned slaves and estates comparable to those of the whites. Nevertheless their position between whites and slaves remained anomalous. In manner, behaviour and custom they were often indistinguishable from their white counterparts but were fully aware of their equivocal status. On the one hand their condition was vastly superior to that of the slave, on the other they were the social and political inferiors of the dominant white group. Amongst the slaves at this period gradations and groupings according to occupation and colour had become firmly established.

The picture is thus of a highly stratified society in which the divisions and groupings are dependent upon colour and occupation. The white sector represented a microcosm of contemporary society in Europe at that time— the planter was the aristocratic landowner, and government officials, lawyers, doctors and merchants strove for social equality with him. The middle group comprised shopkeepers, highly skilled tradesmen, overseers of estates. Beneath them were the poor whites who obtained their living in any manner they could. But however lowly their occupation, however impoverished they were, all whites were the social superiors of the black and coloured population servile or free.

It is in this context that there developed the 'white bias' in Caribbean society, the tendency towards the adulation of that which is white or European, and the denigration of that which is African or black. This bias has profoundly affected the structure and functioning of contemporary society. The bias itself contains a contradiction. The African deprived of his indigenous culture was forced in the slave society to adopt the language of his masters. Presented with the daily example of European behaviour—a model for imitation—it was inevitable that imitation should take place. The political, social and economic control of society was in the hands of the European. Thus white connoted power, black servitude. Both the black and coloured freemen and freedmen gravitated towards the source of power. They became the medium through which English culture percolated through to the servile population. The paradox is inherent in the fact that the widespread cruelty of the slaveowner did not inhibit the growth of the 'white bias'.

The emancipation of the slaves in 1833-4 produced a series of important modifications in the structure of society in the British Caribbean. The free labour now available refused in many instances to continue to work on the estates. A system of apprenticeship had been designed to enable the transition from slavery to free labour to be achieved smoothly. It proved almost unworkable and had to be abandoned after a comparatively short time. Many individuals and families squatted on uncultivated estates or crown lands, and made their living as subsistence farmers. Others, in groups assisted by the nonconformist churches, purchased land from estate-owners, and in this way created settlements and villages. This was possible in colonies where there was a considerable amount of uncultivated, so-called ruinate, land, such as Trinidad, British Guiana and Jamaica. Such a development did not take place in the smaller islands, such as Barbados, St Kitts and Antigua, where little land of this description was available. It is interesting to note that in the latter areas, because the freed slaves were forced to remain upon the estates, almost up to the present time colour-class attitudes and behaviour were similar to those of the slave society.

As a result of this chronic labour shortage the governments of Trinidad, Jamaica and Guiana petitioned the imperial parliament for permission, and money, to import indentured labour from Africa and the far east. Accession to these requests was to have far-reaching effects for the West Indies. African immigration lasted for a period of some thirty years. All told, 36,000 individuals came from West Africa, 12,000 of whom after their indenture services returned home. It was quite different with East Indian immigration. Between 1838 and 1917 nearly 240,000 East Indians entered British Guiana as indentured labourers. Jamaica and Trinidad, in the period shortly after emancipation up to the first world war, received respectively 33,000 and 134,000 East Indians. Less than 5,000 Chinese arrived in Jamaica between 1860 and 1893; and 2,600 entered Trinidad in the period 1852–72. In this way the region's ethnic structure was established.

GOVERNMENTAL DEVELOPMENT

Crown Colony government

Throughout the British West Indies government, from the foundation of the different colonies, had been based on that of the settlements in New England—that is a governor appointed by the crown in association with a nominated Legislative Council, and an elected House of Assembly. It was a type of government which persisted until the late 19th century. The franchise was narrow in the extreme. St Kitts in 1855 possessed a population of 20,741. Of these only 166 were entitled to vote. The population of Jamaica in 1863 was 450,000. Of these 1,799 were registered electors.

The latter part of the century saw a number of constitutional changes throughout the islands. The most significant was in Jamaica where, as a result of the so-called rebellion during the governorship of Edward Eyre in 1865, the House of Assembly voted its own extinction. Under an Imperial Act of 1877 the new model of government consisted of a Legislative Council either in part nominated, or entirely nominated, together with an Executive Council presided over by the governor. The only colonies which managed to preserve the old form were the Bahamas, Barbados and Bermuda. The changes which resulted in what is known as Crown Colony government were induced very largely by the singular ineptitude and inefficiency of the governments in question. The Imperial Parliament could not stand aside and see the continued refusal of local governments to recognise the needs of the people. Crown Colony government persisted in the British Caribbean until the second world war.

Federation

Federation has always appealed to the constitution-makers of the British West Indies. The first experiment was made by Sir William Stapleton, governor of the Leeward Islands in 1674. Antigua, St Kitts, Monserrat and Nevis joined to send representatives to a General Assembly of the Leeward Islands. The experiment was not altogether a success—it lasted intermittently until 1798. While attempts to form a common legislature were a failure in both the Leewards and Windwards the colonies in both groups were federated, each under a single governor, but with each territory retaining its own government. The Acts of 1871 and 1885, by which this was accomplished, left the major centres of population Jamaica, Barbados, British Guiana and Trinidad outside any possible federation.

It was not until the present century that serious interest began to be expressed in the idea of a federation which included the whole of the British Caribbean. Both Lord Halifax in 1921–2, and the Royal Commission of 1939, while in favour of such a development found that the time was not yet come. The West Indian Conference held in Barbados in 1944 managed to persuade the British government that action should be taken. A further conference at Montego Bay in 1947 accepted the principle of a loose federation. At this stage only the Bahamas, British Honduras and British Guiana refused to cooperate. Nine years later, after numerous meetings and discussions with representatives of all the colonies the British parliament passed the British Caribbean Federation Act. In 1958 the new constitution came into being, and the first federal elections were held. Sir Grantley Adams became the first federal prime minister of a West Indies nation.

To understand why the Federation was so short-lived—its demise took place in 1962—it is necessary to review the political development of the area. There are practical difficulties: for example, geographical and historical separateness—Jamaica is a thousand miles from Trinidad. But there are also practical advantages—the creation of a single economic unit would benefit the whole area. Considerations such as these, however, did not really affect the issue, which appears to have been decided by the political ambitions of a number of leaders in the West Indies who capitalised on the inherent insularity of the peoples of the Caribbean.

In terms of population Jamaica and Trinidad dominate the British West Indies. Initially the smaller islands were fearful that this dominance would extend to the political sphere, and they would be exploited for the benefit of their larger neighbours. The latter regarded the small islands, with their inefficient economies, as liabilities. But there was not only economic liability to be considered. The deplorable social and economic conditions of the 1930s had touched off a series of riots, beginning with the St Kitts sugar strikes in 1935, which were followed by disturbances in the oil fields of Trinidad, and on the sugar estates in British Guiana and Jamaica in 1937–8. A Royal Commission was appointed in 1939 which recommended the setting up of the first agency in the world for aid to underdeveloped countries; the Colonial Development Corporation was set up in 1948. It also recommended that a new constitution based on universal adult suffrage should be granted to Jamaica. This constitution came into force in 1944. Thus by 1958 when the Federation was created Jamaica possessed the most advanced constitution in the British West Indies. Trinidad and Barbados were at a stage of development far superior to that of the small islands. These different stages of government undoubtedly had an effect on the dissensions which took place within the Federation.

Politicians had to take the decision as to whether they would attempt to lead Federal parties, or whether they would continue the leadership of their local parties. Sir Grantley Adams, the Barbadian premier, at the time opted for the larger field. Sir Alexander Bustamante, Norman Manley of Jamaica, and Eric Williams in Trinidad decided not to. It is possible that if either Trinidad or Jamaica had provided the premier of the Federation its extinction might have been averted. Manley was devoted to the idea of federation, and at that time he controlled the Jamaica government. Unfortunately he had agreed with Bustamante that the people of Jamaica should be offered the choice as to whether they should support the Federation or not. In the referendum held in September 1961 Bustamante, who had been campaigning actively against Federation, polled 251,935 votes (54 per cent) and Manley got 216,400 votes (46 per cent). Jamaica defected from the Federation, and won her own independence in August 1962. Trinidad very shortly followed Jamaica's example. With their going the grand conception of a British West Indian Federation collapsed.

Political parties

The political parties which functioned throughout this period, and are still functioning today, have their origin in the development of trade unionism in the area. They have no connection with the political twilight of Crown Colony government. They were born out of the riots of the 1930s, and have all been influenced by socialist thinking from moderate to extreme. All rely on the popular support of either the African or East Indian masses. With very few exceptions the European has been virtually excluded from political life—an operation which has been accomplished painlessly, unlike the case of some new African states. The pattern in the three major territories—Jamaica, Trinidad and Barbados—is strikingly similar.

Jamaica. In Jamaica unionism developed in response to the needs of the sugar workers. Bustamante in 1938 formed the Bustamante Industrial Trades Union. The same year Manley had created the Peoples National Party (PNP). The two leaders, who are cousins, worked together in these years. Bustamante went to prison in 1940 and was only released in 1942. Up to this time there had been no split between the leaders but in 1943 Bustamante founded the Jamaica Labour Party (JLP) as the political wing of his trade union. Manley in the same year created his Trades Union Council. It is from this time that real political rivalry developed between the two unions and the two parties. Both claim mass support, but the PNP has a traditional following amongst the intellectual middle classes and those in government service. Another section of the middle class—the business community—lends its support to Bustamante as they are frightened by the avowedly socialist doctrine of the PNP.

The ideological difference between the parties is reflected in their leadership. Manley is a lawyer and an intellectual—he was very friendly with Sir Stafford Cripps. He believes in a socialism of the left but has not allowed communism to influence him. Bustamante's politics are not based on a political philosophy but on the needs of the situation as he sees it. The JLP represents a kind of people's Toryism.

Trinidad. A Grenadan Negro, Uriah Butler, brought unionism to Trinidad in the 1930s. As a result of the riots in 1937–8 he attained great prominence, but was never able to form a successful political party. The constitution of 1945 was based on universal suffrage with a Legislative Council with nine elected seats. Prior to this in 1943 Dr David Pitt, now chairman of CARD, a prominent immigrant organisation in London, had founded the West Indian National Party (WINP), a loose federation of a number of small parties, study groups and unions. Albert Gomez, a Portuguese businessman, as a result of the elections of 1946, managed to secure an extremely powerful position. Butler's followers deserted him, and Gomez was in control. Federation in 1958 produced the Democratic Labour Party (DLP) headed by Bhadase Maraj, which represents the Indian community comprising over one-third of the total population and now (headed by Dr Rudranath Capildeo) provides the opposition to the present government.

Up to 1956 the Trinidadian political scene reflected an essentially fragmentary state—splinter parties forming and reforming—but in that year the brilliant historian-politician Dr Eric Williams, a protégé of Gomez, founded the People's National Movement (PNM). This was the first genuine, modern political party. In the following election the PNM gained 13 out of the 24 seats in the Legislative Council. Gomez lost his seat, Butler's Home Rule Party got 3, and the Trinidad Labour Party 2. Williams' PNM has maintained its popularity, and hold, upon government until the present time. The success of the PNM was undoubtedly due to its advent as a well organised body in a situation which was essentially chaotic. The contribution made by C. L. R. James, one of the pioneer West Indian politicians, was an important factor in this success. Williams' burning enthusiasm for everything which is Trinidadian has endeared him to the masses of the people.

Barbados. The planter-dominated island of Barbados managed to retain its limited franchise until the 1950s. In 1944 Sir Grantley Adams changed the name of his pioneer organisation, the Progressive League, to the Barbados Labour Party (BLP). It won 8 seats in the 24-seat House of Assembly in 1944. The West Indian National Congress Party (WINCP) of W.A. Crawford also won 8 seats in the same election. The planters' interests were represented by the Electors' Association. The BLP by 1951 had won over most of the supporters of the WINCP. Led by Sir Grantley it dominated Barbadian politics until 1961. Errol Barrow, now the prime minister of Barbados, broke away from the BLP in 1955 and helped to form the Democratic Labour Party (DLP). Both Barrow and Adams, unlike other major political leaders in the Caribbean, decided to enter Federal politics. Adams became

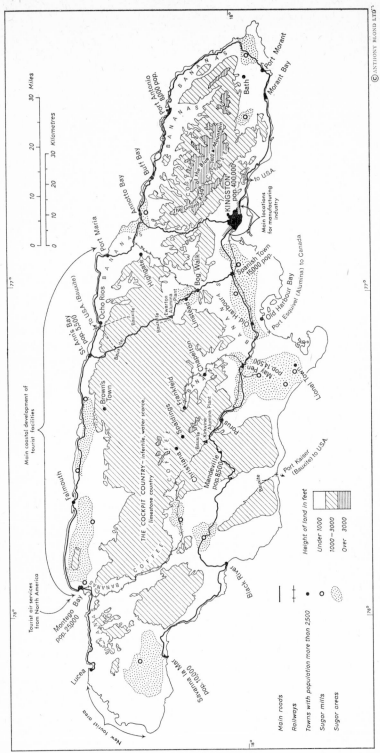

JAMAICA

Main roads
Railways
Towns with population more than 2500
Sugar mills
Sugar areas

Height of land in feet

Under 1000
1000 – 3000
Over 3000

New tourist area

Tourist air services
from North America

Montego Bay
pop. 25000

Lucea

Falmouth

Main coastal development of
tourist facilities

St Ann's Bay
pop. 5500

To U.S.A. (Bauxite)

Ocho Rios

Port Maria

Anotto Bay

Bluff Bay

Port Antonio
pop. 8000 pop.

B A N A N A S

Highgate

Bauxite

Everton
Bauxite   Alumina
Plant

B A N A N A

Brown's
Town

Bauxite

Bog Walk

Linstead

Charlton

C O F F E E

Spaldings   Frankfield

Christiana

Bauxite

Kirkvine
Alumina Plant

Mandeville
pop. 8500

Porus

B A N A N A

Spanish Town
pop. 15000 pop.

KINGSTON
pop. 400000

Gully

to U.S.A.

Main locations
for manufacturing
industry

Bath

Morant Bay

Port Morant

Old Harbour

Old Harbour Bay

Port Esquivel (Alumina) to Canada

Lionel Town

May Pen
pop. 14500

Bauxite

Port Kaiser
(Bauxite) to U.S.A.

Black River

Severina la Mar
pop. 10000

THE COCKPIT COUNTRY – infertile, water scarce,
limestone country

© ANTHONY BLOND LTD

330

the first and only Federal prime minister, but ceased to be a force on the Barbadian scene. Barrow failed to be elected to the Federal parliament but managed to return to the House of Assembly through a bye-election. In the elections of 1961 the DLP won 14 seats, the BLP 5, and the Barbados National Party (BNP) 4. The DLP was thus able to provide a government.

F.H.

STATEHOOD

JAMAICA

POLITICAL SITUATION

Having passed through Crown Colony status, the introduction of universal adult suffrage (1944), ministerial responsibility and internal self-government, Jamaica came to full independence as a Commonwealth member on 6 August 1962. Bustamante's JLP became the first government of the new nation, obtaining nearly 50 per cent of the votes and 26 seats in the independence elections to the PNP's nearly 49 per cent of the votes and 19 seats. Since universal adult suffrage Jamaica's governments had alternated between the JLP and the PNP; the two-party system patterned on Westminster was firmly entrenched in the island.

The most immediate problem facing the young nation was one of population explosion coupled with rising unemployment with thousands of school children each year coming onto the labour market. In the past the Jamaicans have been great migrants and this has not only eased the job situation in the island but has brought badly-needed money to Jamaica in the way of remittances sent home by nationals working abroad. Since the turn of the century the centres for migration have been successively the Panama Canal, Costa Rica for the banana plantations, Cuba for the sugar industry and latterly the United States for a variety of jobs in agriculture and industry. Most recently Jamaicans have migrated to Britain and have fitted into all walks of life. The 'exportation' of people has become traditional and Jamaican politicians say that the island needs to 'export' 16,000 people a year to keep pace with the rising generation seeking jobs. The June 1962 Commonwealth Immigration Act, coupled with tightened US immigration restrictions, presented the new nation with severe difficulties and every effort was made to attract suitable light industries to the island. The campaign was fairly successful, but even so, it is an uphill climb and Norman Manley has estimated that it takes some £2,000 of outside investment to provide only one job.

The aged and ailing Sir Alexander Bustamante named the widely respected finance minister Donald Sangster as acting prime minister in 1965 and for the next two years the island prospered under his leadership and vision. GNP rose along with per capita income and on 21 Feburary 1967 Donald Sangster led the JLP to victory in the first election after independence. In a legislature enlarged from 45 to 53 seats the JLP captured 33 to the PNP's 20. Donald Sangster died soon after the election and was succeeded by Hugh Shearer, an able trade unionist and politician who has been with Bustamante since 1941. As chairman of the Jamaica Delegation to the United Nations he established a reputation for putting his country's views eloquently and gained valuable experience in international affairs and statesmanship.

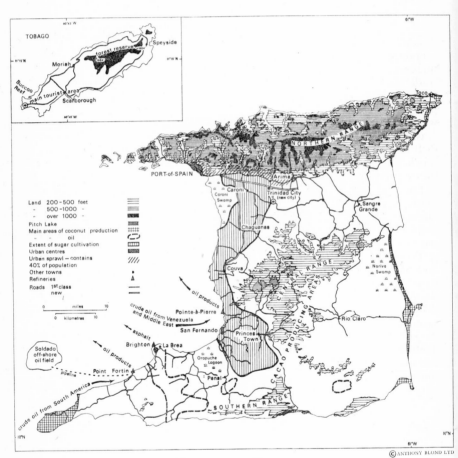

TRINIDAD AND TOBAGO

Government policy has been to live up to the national motto of 'Out of Many, One People' and to ensure that Jamaicans of all ethnic groups prosper without discrimination to race or religion. African and people of mixed descent predominate, with smaller numbers of Chinese, East Indians, European and Levantine people making up the rest of society. The last vestiges of racial discrimination have been eradicated, though hard-drawn class lines based on money and position still tend to divide the people, despite Jamaica's intense nationalism which has been of considerable help in uniting the small nation.

ECONOMY

Traditionally a sugar-producing country, and essentially an agricultural economy, Jamaica has suffered severe financial crisis in the past through fluctuating world prices and from hurricanes, although Commonwealth trade tariffs have at times considerably protected the economy. Under the Commonwealth Sugar Agreement Britain purchases at an annual negotiated price—as from the rest of the English-speaking Caribbean—which in 1962 was over twice the free market price. The government has embarked upon a crash programme to attract people back to the land following a considerable drift to the cities during the past decade and Jamaica's ability to produce as much as possible of her own food supply will be a key factor in the island's future progress.

Jamaica is the largest producer of bauxite, from which aluminium is made, in the world and American and Canadian firms have concessions to operate the industry. Workers are among the highest paid in the island and despite criticism that the company contracts were negotiated on too low a basis the bauxite industry brings much-needed prosperity to a substantial section of the island. Sugar still bulks large as an export crop and citrus and bananas are high on the list, despite the fact that they, like sugar, are more costly to produce in Jamaica and the West Indian islands in general than they are elsewhere. Over the past decade extensive steps have been taken to encourage the growth of a tourist industry and by progressive promotion Jamaica now ranks as one of the key resort areas for North America—particularly since Cuba is closed to tourists—as well as Britain. Tourism brings some £30 million annually to the island and the figure is still rising. Largest foreign-exchange earners in 1966 were (in order) bauxite, tourism and sugar. The average annual per capita income is US$430, one of the highest in the hemisphere and forty-fourth highest in the world.

TRINIDAD AND TOBAGO

POLITICAL SITUATION

After the break-up of the Federation of the West Indies following Jamaica's decision on independence, it was expected that some form of Eastern Caribbean Federation based on Trinidad and Tobago might be a possibility. However, Dr Eric Williams, the premier, decided that his country too should become independent in its own right and, accordingly, on 31 August 1962 Trinidad and Tobago became a fully independent member of the Commonwealth.

The PNM held 20 of the 30 seats in the island's House of Representatives, the remaining 10 being held by the DLP, led at that time by scientist-politician Dr Rudranath Capildeo. There have been fears that Trinidad, with its distinct Negro and East Indian populations, might find itself dividing politically along racial lines and in the past the politicians have been accused of stirring up racial feeling at election times for political ends. Even so, it is apparent that many voters choose their politicians regardless of racial origin, and Dr Williams has been successful in his campaign to get people to think of themselves as Trinidadians first, West Indians second and then—if at all—ethnically.

During the life of the first parliament after independence there were various splits in the DLP, the most serious being the breaking away of several members to form a Liberal Party. By late 1966 there were four parties on the scene: the PNM, DLP, the Liberal Party and the Workers' and Farmers' Party. Elections were held on 7 November 1966 with a House enlarged from 30 seats to 36. The PNM gained 24 of the seats and the DLP the remaining 12. The DLP claimed that the voting machines used in Trinidad (and the United States) can be manipulated.

Dr Williams' aim has been to reduce unemployment by the introduction of new industries and by the greater exploitation of existing ones. He launched a successful 'buy local' campaign aimed at persuading the public to buy Trinidad-produced goods in preference to imported ones and this theme has been copied by the other Caribbean islands. He has always been strongly in favour of a free trade area beginning with the English-speaking islands and ultimately becoming a Caribbean-wide trading bloc, but largely through personality clashes between Dr Williams and other island leaders this dream has not come about.

Recognising that Trinidad and Tobago's future depends on trade expanding along with population—now standing at over a million—Dr Williams has been more far-sighted than some of his neighbours and the young nation quickly established an office in Brussels to keep abreast of European Common Market moves when Britain was making her first attempt to join the Community. He also saw the country's geographical position as a potential springboard for South America and encouraged industries to establish themselves in Trinidad and Tobago with a view to extensive Latin American trading.

Membership of the Organization of American States seemed to offer possible trading potential, as well as giving access to various hemispheric financial development schemes, and after an exhaustive survey Dr Williams's government applied for membership and were accepted, the first English-speaking nation (except the United States) to be admitted, and the first Commonwealth one.

ECONOMY

Trinidad and Tobago's economy is heavily dependent on oil extraction and refining and several new oil-fields have been located in the last few years. In 1966 total petroleum products accounted for nearly 85 per cent of Trinidad's foreign-exchange earnings. The country's output increased 87 per cent in 1966 over 1965. Sugar is also a key industry in the southern part of Trinidad and along with it go by-products like rum and molasses. Citrus production and light industry (like clothing) also plays an important part in the islands' economy, as does the production of pitch for the roads of the world from the natural pitch lake discovered by Sir Walter Raleigh. Tourism is being encouraged by the government, aud Tobago, one of the loveliest islands in the West Indies, is being increasingly visited.

Annual per capita income is US$590, thirty-third highest in the world, higher than every African and Asian country and higher than all but two (Puerto Rico and Venezuela) in Latin America and the Caribbean.

BARBADOS

POLITICAL SITUATION

Barbados, roughly the size of the Isle of Wight and situated one hundred miles east of the Leeward and Windward Island chain, became independent on 30 November 1966 as a full member of the Commonwealth. The island's legislature is the second oldest outside Westminister (Bermuda's is older by a few years) and Barbados, often nicknamed 'Little England', is the most British of the West Indian territories. Its first settlers were English and the island, unlike its neighbours, was never captured by French, Dutch or Spanish fleets.

After Jamaica and Trinidad and Tobago withdrew from the Federation, Premier Barrow worked for an Eastern Caribbean Federation based on Barbados. When unity was seen not to be forthcoming, Barrow encouraged his party to think in terms of Barbados standing alone and the decision was finally taken. In the general election of 3 November 1966 the DLP secured 14 seats as in 1961, while the BLP under Adams took 8 and the BNP 2.

The island, with some 250,000 people packed into an area of only 166 square miles, has one of the highest population densities in the world and migration to the other islands, to the United States and to Britain has been high. Prime Minister Barrow and his colleagues have grappled with the problem of attracting outside industries to the island to provide work and keen interest has been shown in inter-regional trade. When Prime Minister Forbes Burnham of Guyana proposed a trading alliance the Barbados government were swift to accept, along with Premier Vere Bird of Antigua. This, in time, may become the nucleus of a trading bloc within the English-speaking Caribbean, ironic perhaps in that one of the rocks on which the Federation of the West Indies foundered was that of customs union.

ECONOMY

Sugar has traditionally been the main crop of Barbados—some 47,000 acres out of a total agricultural area of 66,880 acres—and accounts for 84 per cent of exports. It also employs nearly 20 per cent of the labour force. The manufacture of rum and molasses goes hand in hand with the sugar industry. Along with most other West Indian islands tourism has provided a boost for the economy and progressive promotion led to an expansion of the industry at an annual rate of 15 per cent in the period 1962–7. Light industry also plays its part, particularly in the extraction of oils and fats from coconuts, and oil seed and their conversion into margarine and shortening. The average annual per capita income is US$360, fifty-second highest in the world.

ASSOCIATED STATES

POLITICAL SITUATION

After Jamaica, Trinidad and Tobago and Barbados became independent, the British government, recognising that the islands remaining as colonies could never afford the cost of complete political independence, but neverthe-less demanded the right to control their own affairs, devised the system known as Associated Statehood with Britain. Under it Britain granted full internal control to the governments of the islands and undertook to continue to look after defence and foreign affairs. The scheme was not wholeheartedly approved of by the United Nations Committee of Twenty-Four on Colonial-ism and was also criticised from other quarters, but the leaders of six former units of the old federation accepted the Statehood principle at constitutional conferences held in London between January and June 1966 and all the territories became Associated States in 1967: Antigua, St Kitts–Nevis–Anguilla, Dominica, St Lucia, Grenada and St Vincent. Their Legislative Assemblies of various sizes are elected by universal adult suffrage.

ECONOMIES

The economies of the six States are all subject to fluctuating markets and efforts have been made to diversify crops. Antigua produces sugar and a small amount of sea island cotton as well as having a tourist industry. St Kitts–Nevis–Anguilla is heavily dependent on sugar (96 per cent of exports from St Kitts) but counts tourism to Nevis as a substantial money-earner, while Anguilla raises cattle and pigs as well as having a natural salt industry. (Charges that, for political spite, the central government in St Kitts had neglected Anguilla's development led to political crisis in June and July 1967 when the Anguillans broke away from the State and asked Britain to make them a State in their own right. They were ultimately persuaded to return to the three-island State of St Kitts–Nevis–Anguilla). The Windward Islands of Dominica, St Lucia, St Vincent and Grenada have all found a degree of prosperity in a new banana industry during the last decade, markets for traditional crops (like St Vincent's arrowroot, Dominica's citrus and Grenada's spices) having encountered strong competition from elsewhere. All six States look to the increasing tourist trade to help solve their financial difficulties.

CROWN COLONIES

POLITICAL SITUATION

The remaining English-speaking territories in the Caribbean are all under the Crown Colony system. They are Montserrat, the British Virgin Islands, the Cayman Islands and the Turks and Caicos Islands, plus the Bahamas which, strictly speaking, are not Caribbean islands. Montserrat is the only one of the ten units of the original Federation of the West Indies which is not now either independent or an Associated State with Britain. The island lacks both size and population to make even Associated Statehood a possi-bility. The Cayman Islands and the Turks and Caicos Islands were both dependencies of Jamaica for many years but when Jamaica attained independence in 1962 the two island groups opted to remain under British control.

ECONOMIES

Montserrat produces market garden produce like tomatoes for export and has begun to develop a tourist industry side by side with some successful schemes under which North Americans and others are buying small land plots and building retirement houses. Many of the population travel to Antigua to work in the sugar industry at crop time and others work in the United States Virgin Islands for part of the year. The British Virgin Islands are developing a tourist trade which has a great potential for careful exploitation and many of the islanders have already gained considerable experience in this industry by working part of the year in the hotels in the US Virgin Islands. A small cattle-raising industry has also been started with some success. The Cayman Islands are dependent upon the produce of the sea for exports and home consumption, and tourism has also brought some degree of prosperity to the islands. The Turks and Caicos Islands have so far resisted attempts by Britain to incorporate them with the Bahamas. Their traditional salt industry provides employment, as does the sea. Tourism here, too, has considerable potential.

C.R.

BIBLIOGRAPHY

Augelli, John P. 'The British Virgin Islands: A West Indian Anomaly', *Geographical Review*, LXIV, New York, 1956.

Augier, F. R., Gordon, S. C., Hall, D. G., and Reckford, M. *The Making of the West Indies*, Longmans, London, 1960; International Publications Service, New York, 5th ed. 1964.

Ayearst, Morley. *The British West Indies: The Search for Self-Government*, Allen and Unwin, London; New York Univ. Press, New York, 1960.

Beachey, R. W. *The British West Indies Sugar Industry in the Late 19th Century*, Blackwell, Oxford, 1957.

Bryans, Robin. *Trinidad and Tobago: Land of the Immortelle*, Faber and Faber, London, 1967.

Burns, Sir Alan Cuthbert. *History of the British West Indies*, Barnes and Noble, New York, 1965; Allen and Unwin, London, revised ed. 1966.

Henriques, Fernando. *Jamaica*, MacGibbon and Kee, London, 1957; London House and Maxwell, New York, 1964. *Family and Colour in Jamaica*, Eyre and Spottiswoode, London, 1953.

Lowenthal, David (ed.) *The West Indies Federation: Perspectives of a Nation*, Columbia Univ. Press, New York; Oxford Univ. Press, London, 1961.

Naipaul, V. S. *The Middle Passage*, André Deutsch, London, 1965.

Norris, Katrin. *Jamaica: The Search for an Identity*, Oxford Univ. Press, London and New York, 1962.

Pares, Richard and Sherlock, P.M. *A Short History of the West Indies*, Macmillan, London, 1956.

Rickards, Colin. *Caribbean Power*, Dennis Dobson, London, 1963.

Smith, M. G. *The Plural Society in the West Indies*, Univ. of California Press, Berkeley, Calif., 1965.

Starkey, Otis P. *The Economic Geography of Barbados: A Study of the Relationships between Environmental Variations and Economic Development*, Columbia Univ. Press, New York, 1939.

Williams, Eric Eustace. *History of the People of Trinidad and Tobago*, André Deutsch, London; Frederick A. Praeger, New York, 1964.

'Agricultural Marketing—A West Indies Problem', *West Indian Economist*, II, 6, December 1959.

'The Economics of Development in the West Indies', *West Indian Economist*, I, 11, May 1959.

West Indies and Caribbean Year Book, T. Skinner and Co., London; Iliffe, New York, annual.

M*

BASIC INFORMATION

JAMAICA

CLIMATE

Kingston

Lat./long.	18°N, 77°W	Relative humidity	70%/61%
Altitude	110 ft/34 m.	at midday of	
Mean temp. of	28°C/82°F	hottest and	
hottest month	(June–Aug.)	coolest months	
Mean temp. of	25°C/77°F	Wettest months	7·1 in./180 mm.
coolest month	(Jan./Feb.)		(Oct.)
Absolute max.	97°F/36°C	Driest month	0·6 in./15 mm.
Absolute min.	57°F/14°C		(Feb.)
		Annual av. rainfall	31·5 in./800 mm.

POPULATION

TOTAL (*million*): 1960 (census): 1·61; mid-1966: 1·84; 1980 (ECLA projection): 2·08.
DENSITY, mid-1965: 161 persons per sq. km.
CRUDE RATES (*per 000*), 1966: Birth 38·8, death 7·8, infant mortality (1965) 36·7.
GROWTH RATES (*per cent p.a.*): 1945–65, 1·7; 1960–5, 1·9.
DISTRIBUTION (% *of total pop.*): Racial origin, 1960: African 78, Afro-European 14, Afro-Asian 2, Asian 2, European 1. Foreign-born, 1960: 1·3. Languages: English; also an English dialect, Hindi, Chinese. Religion: Anglican 20, Baptist 19, Roman Catholic 7, other Christian 36. Urban, 1960: 30. Largest cities (*000 inhab.*), 1960: Kingston and St Andrew (Parishes) 419 (end 1965: 496), Kingston 377, Montego Bay 24, Spanish Town 15.

CONSTITUTIONAL SYSTEM

CONSTITUTION: Independent territory in the former Federation of the West Indies 1958; full internal self-government 1959; independent member of the Commonwealth 1962.
SYSTEM: Parliament consisting of the Queen, represented by the Governor-General, the Senate and the House of Representatives.
CABINET: Collectively responsible to Parliament. Comprises prime minister, appointed by Governor-General and normally the leader of the majority party in the House of Representatives; and not less than 11 ministers, of whom 2 to 3 are members of the Senate.
LEGISLATURE: Bi-cameral, Parliament of Senate and House of Representatives. *Senate:* 21 members appointed by Governor-General: 13 selected by prime minister and 8 by leader of the opposition. *Representatives:* 45 to 60 members, according to number of constituencies, elected for 5 years. *Suffrage:* Universal voting for adults over 21 years of age. *Elections:* House of Representatives, February 1967: Jamaica Labour Party 33 seats, People's National Party 20.
JUDICIARY: Supreme Court, Chief Justice and senior judges; Court of Appeal; magistrates' and minor courts.

INTERNATIONAL RELATIONS

Member of the UN and many of its international specialised agencies, including: IBRD and IFC, IMF, FAO, ICAO, ILO, ITU, UNDP, UNESCO, UPU, WHO and WMO; IAEA; GATT; UNCTAD representative. Also member of ECLA and the Sterling Area.

ECONOMY

PRODUCTION

AGRICULTURE (*ooo tons*)	*1948–53*[1]	*63/64*	*64/65*	*65/66*[2]	*66/67*[2]
Sugar (cane)	279	482	497	508	485
Oranges, tangerines, etc.	54	57	69	66	.
Grapefruit	20	31	30	34	.
Bananas	30	38	36	.	.

[1] Average 1948/9–1952/3. [2] Provisional.

LAND (%), 1964: Arable 21, permanent pasture 23, forested 19, other 36.
OTHER AGRICULTURAL DATA: Agricultural holdings, 1961/62 (census): no., 158,941, area, 0·69 m. hectares. Tractors in use (*ooos*), 1961: 1·56. Fertiliser consumption (*ooo tons*), 1965: 27.
LIVESTOCK: Nos (*m. head*), 1965: cattle 0·25, pigs 0·15; 1963: sheep 10. Products (*ooo tons*), 1964: meat 17 (beef and veal 12).
FISH: Landed (*ooo tons*), 1964: total 16.
MINING: 1965: (*ooo tons*) Bauxite 8,700, gypsum 209.
MANUFACTURING, 1965: (*ooo tons*) cement 316, fuel oils 943, motor spirit 193; (*m. litres*) beer 27, rum 10 (1964).
CONSTRUCTION (*ooo sq. metres floor area*), 1965: Permits issued for urban private building, Kingston and St Andrews: 118.

ENERGY

CONSUMPTION (*tons coal equiv.*), 1965: total 1·59, per head 0·9.
ELECTRICITY, 1965: Generated (*kwh*) 798 m.; 1963, installed capacity (*kw*) 186,000.

GOVERNMENT EXPENDITURE

DISTRIBUTION (% *of total*), 1965/66: Education 13: labour, health and social services 15; communications and public works 16.

GROSS PRODUCT

GDP (*J£ m.*): At current market prices, 1965: 327; 1966: 350; at 1960 market prices, 1964: 274; 1965: 295. Per head (*US$*), UN estimate, 1964: 528.
DISTRIBUTION (%), 1964: Trade 16, manufacturing 14, agriculture 13, constructions 11, mining 9.
GROWTH RATES (%), 1950–60: 8·9, per head 7·3; 1960–4: 4·0, per head 2.

EXTERNAL TRADE (*US$m.*)	*1955*	*1960*	*1964*	*1965*	*1966*
EXPORTS (f.o.b.)	93	184	218	214	225
Alumina	13	47	50	48	54
Bauxite	11	30	44	50	52
Sugar	32	38	57	48	49
Bananas	14	13	17	17	18
IMPORTS (c.i.f.)	128	217	289	289	321
TRADE BALANCE	−35	−33	−72	−74	−96

DIRECTION OF TRADE (%)

	Exports			Imports		
	1955	*1960*	*1965*	*1955*	*1960*	*1965*
Venezuela	—	0·1	0·0	—	0·7	7·5
USA and Canada	35·9	50·4	53·8	32·8	34·6	41·6
EEC	3·4	1·9	2·2	5·8	13·9	10·9
UK	50·0	31·4	27·2	40·3	34·5	24·1
Norway	5·6	9·9	7·0	0·2	0·4	0·4

FINANCE

EXCHANGE RATE (*US$/Jamaican pound*): Par value, end-year 1960: 2·80; 1966: 2·80.
BALANCE OF PAYMENTS (*US$ m.*): Goods and services (net), 1961: −9; 1964: −22;
1965: −17; 1966: −20.
COST OF LIVING (*Dec. 1958=100*), Kingston, December 1960: 110; 1964: 120;
1965: 123; 1966: 127.
INDUSTRIAL WAGES: Earnings in manufacturing, per week, 1964: J£7·0.
GOVT. ACCOUNTS (*J£ m.*), 1965: Revenue 58·2, expenditure 69·8; deficit 11·6.

EMPLOYMENT

ECONOMICALLY ACTIVE (%), 1960: Of total pop. 41 (men 52, women 30). In agriculture 36, services 20, manufacturing 14, trade 9, construction 8.

TRANSPORT AND COMMUNICATIONS

RAILWAYS: Traffic, 1965: 54 m. pass.-km., 117 m. net ton-km. Length of track
420 km.
MOTOR VEHICLES: In use (*ooo*), 1965: pass. cars 46, comm. vehicles 19. Road
system, 1966: 15,500 km.
SHIPPING: International (*m. tons*), 1965: goods loaded 10·0, goods unloaded 2·4.
Main ports: Kingston, Port Antonio, Port Esquivel, Port Morant, Savanna-la-Mar.
AIR: Passenger movement (Palisadoes and Montego Bay), 1965: 0·8 m. Freight
(*ooo tons*): inward 6·3, outward 3·0. Main international airports: Kingston: Palisa-
does; Montego Bay.
TELEPHONES: No. in use, 1965: 49,300.

SOCIAL WELFARE

SYSTEM: Comprehensive national insurance scheme covers the gainfully employed;
administered by Ministry of Labour and National Insurance. Financed by contributions to National Insurance Fund. Other welfare services undertaken by Ministries
of Development and Welfare and of Health.
HEALTH: 2,000 persons per physician, 235 persons per hospital bed.
NUTRITION: Net food supply (*per head per day*), 1958: 2,250 calories, protein 58 g.

EDUCATION

ILLITERACY RATE (%), 1960 (census): 15 years and over, 18.
COMPULSORY: 8 years (between 7 and 15 years of age). School enrolment ratios (%),
1st and 2nd levels, 1963: 37, adjusted 78.
SCHOOLS, 1963: Pre-school and primary: no. 1,170, pupils 0·34 m., teachers 5,400.
Secondary, 1961: no. 49, p. 23,200, t. 1,180. Technical: no. 10, st. 2,800, t. 120.
Teacher-training: no. 1, st. 270, t. 6. Higher (university), 1965: st. 3,000, t. 360.
UNIVERSITIES: HQ of the University of the West Indies, Mona, nr. Kingston;
College of Arts, Science and Technology, Kingston; School of Agriculture, Spanish
Town.

MASS MEDIA

BROADCASTING: No. of receivers in use, end-1965: TV 28,500, radio 0·35 m. Stations:
TV 1, radio 2 (12 transmitters).
CINEMAS: No., 1965: 56. Attendance: total 1·3 m., per head 0·7.
NEWSPRINT: Consumption, 1965: total 7,000 tons, per head 3·9 kg.
NEWSPAPERS: Daily, 1965: 2. Estimated circulation 0·12 m.; copies per ooo of
population, 69. Principal dailies in Kingston (*circ. ooo*): *Daily Gleaner* 65 (Sat. 71,
Sun. edition 74), *Star* (evening) 57.

TRINIDAD AND TOBAGO

CLIMATE

St Clair

Lat./long.	10° 30′ N, 61° 30′ W	Relative humidity	63%/66%
Altitude	67 ft/20 m.	at midday of	
Mean temp. of	27°C/81°F (May)	hottest and	
hottest month		coolest months	
Mean temp. of	26°C/78°F	Wettest month	9·7 in./246 mm.
coolest month	(Jan./Feb.)		(Aug.)
Absolute max.	101°F/38°C	Driest month	1·6 in./41 mm.
Absolute min.	52°F/11°C		(Feb.)
		Annual av. rainfall	64·2 in./1,631 mm.

POPULATION

TOTAL (*ooo*), 1960 (census): 828 (Tobago 33); mid-1966: 1,000; 1980 (ECLA projection): 1,450.
DENSITY, mid-1965: 190 persons per sq. km.
CRUDE RATES (*per ooo*), 1966: Birth 29·4, death 6·9, infant mortality (1964) 35·3.
GROWTH RATES (% *p.a.*) 1945–64, 2·9; 1960–4, 3·1.
DISTRIBUTION (% *of total pop.*): Ethnic, 1960: Negro 43, Asian 37, mixed 16, white 2. Foreign-born, 1960: 10. Language: English, some Spanish and Hindi. Religion, 1960: Roman Catholic 36, Protestant 34, Hindu 23, Moslem 6. Largest cities (*ooo inhab.*), 1960: Trinidad: Port-of-Spain 94, San Fernando 40, Arima 11; Tobago: Scarborough 2·5.

CONSTITUTIONAL SYSTEM

CONSTITUTION: Independent territory in the former Federation of the West Indies 1958; full internal self-government 1961; independent member of the Commonwealth 1962.
SYSTEM: Parliament of Trinidad and Tobago, comprising the Queen, represented by a Governor-General, a Senate and a House of Representatives.
CABINET: Collectively responsible to Parliament. Comprises prime minister, appointed by Governor-General and normally the leader of the majority party in the House of Representatives; the Attorney-General; and about 16 ministers. Not more than 2 ministers (apart from the Attorney-General) may be appointed from the Senate.
LEGISLATURE: Bi-cameral, Parliament of Senate and House of Representatives. *Senate:* 24 members, appointed by Governor-General: 13 selected by prime minister, 4 by leader of the opposition, 7 from economic, religious or social bodies, as advised by prime minister. *Representatives:* 36 members elected by single-member constituencies for 5 years. Not less than 2 constituencies in Tobago. *Suffrage:* Universal voting for adults over 21 years of age. *Elections:* Representatives, November 1966: People's National Movement 24 seats and Democratic Labour Party 12 seats.
JUDICIARY: High Court of Justice, Chief Justice and 10 judges; Court of Appeal, Chief Justice and appeal judges; High Courts; magistrates' courts.

INTERNATIONAL RELATIONS

Member of the UN and many of its international specialised agencies, including: IBRD, IMF, FAO, ICAO, IMCO, ILO, ITU, UNDP, UNESCO, UPU, WHO and WMO; GATT; UNCTAD representative. Also member of: OAS, IDB, ECLA and the Sterling Area.

ECONOMY

PRODUCTION

AGRICULTURE (ooo tons)	1948–53[1]	63/64	64/65	65/66[2]	66/67[2]
Sugar (cane)	151	233	257	215	203
Oranges, tangerines etc.	4	11	18	16	.
Grapefruit	15	22	36	29	.
Coffee	.	4·5	4·5	4·2	.
Cacao[3]	7·9	6·1	5·0	5·2	5·0

[1] Average 1948/9–1952/3. [2] Provisional.
[3] Calendar years 1948–52 (av. exports), 1963–6.

LAND (%), 1961: Arable 34, permanent pasture 1, forested 45, other 20.
OTHER AGRICULTURAL DATA: Agricultural holdings, 1946 (census): no. 30,511, area 168,000 hectares. Tractors in use, 1957: 350. Fertiliser consumption (ooo tons), 1965/66: 19·0.
LIVESTOCK: Animals slaughtered (ooo head), 1966: cattle 8·6, sheep and goats 4·1, pigs 22·3. Products (ooo tons), 1966: meat 2·9.
FISH: Landed (ooo tons), 1965: total 11·0, tunas, etc. 5·7.
MINING, 1965: (ooo tons) Natural asphalt 160. (m. cubic metres) crude petroleum 7·6, natural gas 1,174.
MANUFACTURING, 1965: (ooo tons) Cement 186, sugar 255, fuel oils 14,100, motor spirit 2,126; (m. litres) rum 6·1 (pure alcohol), beer 7·5.
CONSTRUCTION (ooo sq. metres floor area), 1965: New buildings approved 366.

ENERGY

CONSUMPTION (tons coal equiv.), 1965: Total 3·4 m., per head 3·48.
ELECTRICITY, 1965: Generated (kwh) 908 m., installed capacity (kw) 0·25 m.

GOVERNMENT EXPENDITURE

DISTRIBUTION (% of total), 1965: Defence 2, education 12, social services 11.

GROSS PRODUCT

GDP (TT$ m.): At current market prices, 1963: 1,105; 1964: 1,148. Per head (US$), UN estimate, 1964: 617.
DISTRIBUTION (%): Mining (incl. petroleum refining) 28, manufacturing 13, trade 13, agriculture 10.
GROWTH RATES (%), 1951–60: 8·5, per head 5·4.

EXTERNAL TRADE (US$m.)	1955	1960	1964	1965	1966
EXPORTS (f.o.b.)	166	287	405	403	426
Petroleum and products	124	229	335	329	338
Sugar	18	22	28	25	19
IMPORTS (c.i.f.)	172	294	426	471	457
TRADE BALANCE	−5	−7	−21	−68	−31

DIRECTION OF TRADE (%)

	Exports[1]			Imports		
	1955	1960	1965	1955	1960	1965
LAFTA	(6·9)	3·1	0·6	(1·5)	2·6	6·5
Venezuela	0·4	0·3	0·2	25·7	22·3	25·7
USA and Canada	9·1	24·6	36·7	18·3	19·3	22·0
EEC	2·3	10·8	14·9	5·1	7·1	3·1
UK	39·2	31·1	16·5	38·1	29·5	16·7
Sweden	2·8	2·5	6·1	0·3	0·2	0·2

[1] About 12% not classified by country.

FINANCE

EXCHANGE RATE (*US$/Trinidad and Tobago dollar*): Par value 1·714. TT$ 4·80 = £1.
BALANCE OF PAYMENTS (*US$ m.*): Goods and services (net), 1960: — 100; 1964: —86; 1965: — 137; 1966: —86.
COST OF LIVING (*1958=100*), December 1961: 106; 1964: 115; 1965: 118; 1966: 123.
INDUSTRIAL WAGES: Earnings in manufacturing, per week, 1964: TT$ 35.
TREASURY ACCOUNTS (*TT$ m.*), 1966: Revenue 233, expenditure 264, deficit 31.

EMPLOYMENT

ECONOMICALLY ACTIVE (%), 1960: Of total population 34 (men 50, women 18). In agriculture 20, services 24, manufacturing 15, trade 13, construction 11.

TRANSPORT AND COMMUNICATIONS

RAILWAYS: Traffic, 1964: 4·6 m. passengers, 7 m. net ton-km. Length of track 26 km.
MOTOR VEHICLES: In use (*ooo*), 1965: cars 55, commercial vehicles 16. Road system 4,000 km.
SHIPPING: International sea-borne shipping (*m. tons*), 1964: Goods loaded 11·1, goods unloaded 12·5. Main ports: Port-of-Spain, Scarborough (Tobago).
AIR: Scheduled services, 1965: Total 354 m. pass.-km., 3·1 m. cargo ton-km. International: 350 m. pass.-km., 3·1 m. cargo ton-km. Main airports: Port-of-Spain: Piarco (international), Crown Point (Tobago).
TELEPHONES: No. in use, 1965: 39,000.

SOCIAL WELFARE

SYSTEM: Social insurance benefits and services administered by Ministries of Health and Housing and of Community Development.
HEALTH: 2,550 persons per physician, 190 persons per hospital bed.

EDUCATION

ILLITERACY RATE (%), 1946 (census): 15 years and over 26.
COMPULSORY: 6 years (between 6 and 12 years of age). School enrolment ratios (%), 1st (excl. non-aided schools) and 2nd levels, 1963: 81, adjusted 87.
SCHOOLS, 1964: Primary: no. 591, pupils 0·21 m., teachers 6,200. Secondary: no. 102, p. 33,600, t. 1,000. Technical: no. 3, st. 1,000, t. 60. Higher (1965): st. 1,200, t. 120.
UNIVERSITY: Departments of U. of West Indies (Jamaica): College of Arts and Science, St Augustine, nr Kingston; Schools of Agriculture and Engineering; Institute of Education.

MASS MEDIA

BROADCASTING: No. of receivers in use, end-1965: TV 26,000, radio 0·17 m. Stations: TV 1, radio 4.
CINEMAS: No., 1964: 66. Attendance, 1959: total 6·7 m., per head 8·2.
NEWSPRINT: Consumption, 1964: total 4,500 tons, per head 4·6 kg.
NEWSPAPERS: Daily, 1965: 3. Estimated circulation 0·1 m., copies per ooo of population 102. Principal dailies in Port-of-Spain (*circ. ooo*): *Trinidad Guardian* 44 (Sunday 74), *Daily Mirror* 20, *Evening News* 33.

BARBADOS

CLIMATE

Bridgetown

Lat./long.	13° N, 54° 30′ W	Relative humidity	72%/66%
Altitude	181 ft/55 m.	at midday of	
Mean temp. of	27°C/80°F	hottest and	
hottest month	(June/Aug./Sept.)	coolest months	
Mean temp. of	25°C/76°F (Feb.)	Wettest month	8·1 in./206 mm.
coolest month			(Nov.)
Absolute max.	95°F/35°C	Driest month	1·1 in./28 mm.
Absolute min.	61°F/16°C		(Feb.)
		Annual av. rainfall	50·2 in./1,275 mm.

POPULATION

TOTAL (*ooo*): 1960 (census): 233; mid-1966: 245; 1980 (ECLA projection): 285. DENSITY, mid-1965: 568 persons per sq. km. CRUDE RATES (*per ooo*), 1966: Birth 25·2, death 8·2, infant mortality 49·3. GROWTH RATES (% *p.a.*): 1945–64, 1·4; 1960–4, 0·8. DISTRIBUTION (% *of total pop.*): Ethnic, 1960: Negro 89, mixed 6, white 4. Foreign-born, 1960: 4·1. Language, English. Religion, 1960: Christian 95 (Anglican 70, RC 2). Largest city (*ooo inhab.*), 1960: Bridgetown—City 11, urban area 94.

CONSTITUTIONAL SYSTEM

CONSTITUTION: Based on Charter of Barbados, 1652. Internal self-government 1961; joined former Federation of West Indies 1958; independent member of the Commonwealth 1962.
SYSTEM: Parliament comprising the Queen, represented by the Governor-General, the Senate and the House of Assembly.
CABINET: Collectively responsible to Parliament. Comprises prime minister (appointed by Governor-General and normally the leader of the majority party in the House of Assembly) and not less than 5 ministers (at present 9).
LEGISLATURE: Bi-cameral Parliament of Senate and House of Assembly. *Senate:* 21 members appointed by Governor-General: 12 selected by prime minister; 2 by leader of the opposition; 7 representing economic, religious, social or other interests, at Governor's discretion. *Assembly:* 24 members, 2 from each constituency, elected for 5 years. *Suffrage:* Universal voting for adults over 18 years of age. *Elections:* House of Assembly, November 1966: Democratic Labour Party 14, Barbados Labour Party 8, Barbados National Party 2.
JUDICIARY: Supreme Court, consisting of Court of Appeal and High Court, and magistrates' courts.

INTERNATIONAL RELATIONS

New member of the UN and is obtaining membership of its international specialised agencies. Previously an associate member of ITU, UNESCO, UPU and WMO. Also member of OAS, the Sterling Area and CARIFTA.

ECONOMY

PRODUCTION
AGRICULTURE (*ooo tons*): Sugar (incl. fancy molasses), av. 1948/49–52/53: 168; 1964/65: 199; 1965/66: 175; 1966/67: 211.
LAND (%), 1960: Arable 60, permanent pasture 9, other 30.

344

OTHER AGRICULTURAL DATA: Tractors in use, 1953: 239. Fertiliser consumption (*ooo tons*), 1965: 5·4.
LIVESTOCK: Nos (*ooo head*), 1964: Cattle 11, sheep 29, pigs 20.
FISH: Landed (*ooo tons*), 1964: total 3·6.
MINING, 1965 (*m. cubic metres*): Natural gas 3.
MANUFACTURING, 1965: (*ooo tons*) Fuel oils 31, motor spirit 7; (*m. litres, pure alcohol*) rum 5·3.

ENERGY

CONSUMPTION (*tons coal equiv.*), 1965: Total 0·22 m., per head 1·61.
ELECTRICITY, 1964/65: Generated (*kwh*) 66 m.; mid-1965: installed capacity (*kw*) 18,000.

GOVERNMENT EXPENDITURE

DISTRIBUTION (% *of total*), 1965/66: Education 23.

GROSS PRODUCT

GDP (*EC$ m.*): At current market prices, 1963: 167·2; 1964: 165·1. Per head (*US$*), UN estimate, 1964: 371.
DISTRIBUTION (%), 1964: Agriculture (incl. sugar milling) 26, trade 23, construction 10, manufacturing 9.
GROWTH RATES (%), at current prices, 1950–9: 7·4, per head 6·3; 1960–4: 5·1, per head 4·3.

EXTERNAL TRADE (*US$ m.*)	*1955*	*1960*	*1963*	*1964*	*1965*	*1966*
EXPORTS (f.o.b.)	23	24	41	35	38	40
Sugar, unrefined	15	16	24	18	19	.
Molasses	3	2	3	4	3	.
Rum	1	1	1	1	2	.
Reexports	2	3	9	9	10	.
IMPORTS (c.i.f.)	32	49	58	64	68	76
TRADE BALANCE	−10	−25	−17	−28	−30	−36

DIRECTION OF TRADE (%)

	Exports			Imports		
	1955	*1960*	*1965*	*1955*	*1960*	*1965*
LAFTA	(—)	—	—	(—)	—	1·8
Venezuela	—	—	—	—	1·2	7·3
Guyana	1·9	1·7	1·1	4·7	3·1	2·4
USA and Canada	42·1	14·2	18·1	24·0	23·6	30·0
EEC	0·7	—	1·6	6·4	10·4	8·1
UK	41·2	61·5	42·1	40·4	39·5	29·9

FINANCE

EXCHANGE RATE (*US$/Eastern Caribbean dollar*): Par value 1·714. EC$ 4·80 = £1.
BALANCE OF PAYMENTS (*US$ m.*): Goods and services (net), 1960: +1·0; 1961: +0·9.
COST OF LIVING (*1958=100*), December 1960: 104; 1964: 110; 1965: 114.
INDUSTRIAL WAGES: Earnings in manufacturing, per week, 1964: WI$ 28·15.
BUDGET ACCOUNTS (*EC$ m.*), 1966/67: Revenue 40·5, expenditure 42·0, current deficit 1·5, capital expenditure 16·3, loans 8·3, surplus balances 8·0.

EMPLOYMENT

ECONOMICALLY ACTIVE (%), 1960: Of total population 40 (men 51, women 31). In agriculture 24, services 22, trade 16, manufacturing 14, construction 10.

TRANSPORT AND COMMUNICATIONS

MOTOR VEHICLES: In use (*ooo*), 1965: Cars 10·5, comm. vehicles 3·2. Road system: 1,300 km., paved 1,150 km.
SHIPPING: Vessels entered (*ooo g.r. tons*), 1965: 3,580. Main port: Bridgetown.
AIR: Passenger movement, 1965: 0·2 m., freight 1,900 tons. Main airport: Bridgetown: Seawell (international).
TELEPHONES: No. in use, 1965: 15,500.

SOCIAL WELFARE

SYSTEM: Comprehensive social insurance system planned.
HEALTH: 2,600 persons per physician, 170 persons per hospital bed.

EDUCATION

ILLITERACY RATE (%), 1946; 15 years and over, 9.
COMPULSORY: To be introduced, between 5 and 14 years of age. School enrolment ratios (%), 1st and 2nd levels, 1962: 77, adjusted 82.
SCHOOLS (excluding private), 1964: Primary: no. 118, pupils 39,200, teachers 1,240. Secondary: no. 16, p. 15,400, t. 500. Higher: no. 2, st. 230, t.s. 45.
UNIVERSITIES: University of the West Indies in Barbados, Bridgetown (branches): College of Arts and Sciences and Erdiston College (Institute of Education).

MASS MEDIA

BROADCASTING: No. of receivers in use, end-1965: TV 6,200, radio 43,000. Stations: TV 1, radio 2 (1 wired net-work).
CINEMAS: No., 1963: 8. Attendance: total 1·6 m., per head 6·8.
NEWSPRINT: Consumption, 1965: Total 700 tons, per head 2·9 kg.
NEWSPAPERS: Daily, 1965: 2. Estimated circulation 27,000, copies per ooo of population 112. Principal dailies in Bridgetown (*circ. ooo*): *Advocate* 17 (Sunday 25), *Barbados Daily News* 9 (S. 11).

ASSOCIATED STATES[1]

POPULATION

POPULATION (*ooo*), 1960 (census): A 54, D 60, G 90, KNA 57, L 86, V 80; mid-1965 estimates: A 62, D 66, G 98, KNA 60, L 103, V 87.
DENSITY: Persons per sq. km., 1965: A 130, D 88, G 279, KNA 168, L 166, V 224.
CRUDE RATES (*per ooo*), 1965 (G 1966, V 1964): Birth: A 30·4, D 42·7, G 29·0, KNA 31·0, L 42·4, V 43·1; death: A 8·4, D 8·9, G 8·8, KNA 9·3, L 8·1, V 9·6; infant mortality: A 45·4, D 53·6, G 42·9, KNA 59·1, L 47·8, V 75·3.
GROWTH RATES (% *p.a.*), 1958–65: A 1·1, D 1·9, G 1·2, KNA 1·3, L 1·6, V 1·8.
DISTRIBUTION (% *of total pop.*): Ethnic, 1960: African A 92, D 66, G 53, KNA 89, L 69, V 70; mixed A 3, D 33, G 42, KNA 9, L 27, V 22; Asian (E. Indian) G 4, L 3, V 3; Amerindian Carib D 1, V 2; European A 1, G 1, KNA 1, L 1, V 2. Language: English and local French patois. Largest cities (*ooo inhab.*), 1960: A St John City 21·4, D Roseau 10·4, G St George's 7·3, K Basseterre 15·6, L Castries 4·4, V Kingstown 4·3.

[1] A—Antigua (including dependency Barbuda), D—Dominica, G—Grenada (including dependency Carriacou), KNA—St Christopher (St Kitts)–Nevis-Anguilla, L—St Lucia, V—St Vincent (including Grenadines dependencies).

CONSTITUTIONS: Members of West Indies Federation 1958–62; full internal self-government 1967 as West Indies Associated States. Association with UK is free and voluntary and may be terminated at any time. UK responsible for defence and external affairs, which are conducted through the British Government Representative in St Lucia. Antigua is a member of CARIFTA. D, G, L, V and Montserrat have established an Eastern Caribbean Common Market.

SYSTEMS: Parliament consisting of the Queen, represented by the Governor, and the legislatures.

CABINET: Collectively responsible to parliament, Governor required to act in accordance with advice of cabinet on internal matters. Consists of premier, who is appointed by the Governor and is member of and commands majority in the elected legislature; other ministers (A at least 1 senator, D up to 5 ministers, G member of either chamber), appointed on advice of premier; and the Attorney-General (ex-officio). Provision is made for appointment of parliamentary secretaries.

LEGISLATURES: Bi-cameral legislature of Senate and House of Representatives in A and G; uni-cameral House of Assembly in D, KNA, L and V (representatives). Term: 5 years. *Senates*: A—10 senators appointed by Governor, 7 on premier's advice and 3 after consultation with premier. G—9 senators appointed by Governor, 5 selected by premier, 2 by leader of the opposition and 2 on advice of premier after consulting other interests. L and V—constitutional provision for Senate, if Assembly approves. *Representatives*: Speaker and members elected in single-member constituencies (A not less than 10, G at present 10, V 9 to be increased to 13, 3 nominated) and Attorney-General. *Assemblies*: Speaker and members elected in single-member constituencies (at present D 11, KNA 10, L 10), 3 nominated members and the Attorney-General. *Suffrage*: Universal voting for adults. *Elections*: For former Legislative Councils, which are transitionally new legislatures: A (1960) Antigua Labour Party 10 seats; D (1961) Labour Party 10, United People's Party 1; G (1962) National Party 6, United Labour Party 4; KNA (1966) Labour Party 7, People's Action movement 2, United National Party 1; L (1964) United Workers' Party 8, Labour Party 2; V (1967) Labour Party 6, People's Political Party 3.

JUDICIARY: West Indies Associated States Supreme Court in Grenada, and puisne judges of that court in each of the Associated States.

ECONOMY

PRODUCTION

AGRICULTURE (*ooo tons*):

	Sugar cane, raw value		Bananas		Cacao	
	1948–53[1]	*66/67*	*1953*	*66*[2]	*1952/53*	*64/65*
Antigua	27	6	·	·	·	·
Dominica	·	·	14	49	0·1	0·2
Grenada	2	1	10	21	3·1	2·8
St Kitts—N—A	45	39	·	·	·	·
St Lucia	10	—	7	80	0·6	0·3
St Vincent	3	—	—	30	·	·

Other main export crops: cotton (A, G, KNA, V), citrus fruit (D), arrowroot starch (V).

[1] Average 1948/49–1952/53.　　　　[2] Exports.

LAND (%), 1964 (D 1963, KNA 1962): arable A 55, D 10, G 47, KNA 40, L 34, V 50; permanent pasture A 5, D 1, G 3, KNA 10, L 5, V 3; forested A 14, D 65, G 12, KNA 18, L 21, V 44; other A 27, D 24, G 38, KNA 33, L 41, V 3.

OTHER AGRICULTURAL DATA: Tractors in use, 1964: A 210, D 34; 1963: G 13, KNA 199, V 31; 1962: L 50. Fertiliser consumption (*ooo tons*), 1965/66: G 3·0, KNA 1·1, L 0·9, V 1·4.

LIVESTOCK (*ooo head*), 1963/64: Cattle A 7, D 6, G 10 (1955/56), L 11, V 7; pigs A 2 (1960/61), D 9, G 4 (1957/58), L 17, V 5; sheep A 5 (1960/61), D 4, KNA 7 (1955/56), L 8, V 5.

FISH: Total catch (*ooo tons*), 1965: A 0·8, D 0·4 (1958), G 0·1 (1962), KNA 0·5 (1958), L 0·4, V 0·5.

GOVERNMENT EXPENDITURE

DISTRIBUTION (% *of total*): Education A 9, D 34 (incl. health), G 13, KNA 11, L 19, V 20; health A 15, D (incl. in education), G 13, KNA 11, L 22, V 15; public works A 10, D 19, G 21, KNA 4, L 19, V 13.

GROSS PRODUCT

GDP, per head (*US$*), 1961: A 235, D 202, G 188, KNA 216, L 175, V 162.

EXTERNAL TRADE (*US$ m.*)

	Year	Total	Exports Raw sugar	Bananas	Others	Imports Total
Antigua[1]	1964	2·72	1·84	·	0·88	13·45
Dominica	1963	4·56	·	2·16	2·40[2]	6·99
Grenada	1965	6·34	·	1·33	5·02[3]	11·10
St Kitts—N—A	1964	5·61	5·18	·	0·43	7·85
St Lucia	1964	5·63	·	4·78	0·85	11·91
St Vincent	1964	3·77	·	1·97	1·80[4]	9·36

[1] Including Br. Virgin Is.   [2] Lime juice 0·42, essential oils 0·30, copra 0·30.
[3] Nutmegs 2·68, cacao 1·38.   [4] Arrowroot 1·00, nutmegs 0·12.

DIRECTION OF TRADE (%)

	Year	Exports UK	Canada	USA	Imports UK	Canada	USA
Antigua[1]	1964	74·0	·	·	26·2	12·5	27·7
Dominica	1963	85·1	·	1·8	20·5	13·2	7·1
Grenada	1965	40·4	14·2	21·2	30·8	11·5	9·7
St Kitts—N—A	1964	76·3	11·0	·	27·0	18·1	14·6
St Lucia	1964	84·9	·	·	32·2	12·7	11·5
St Vincent	1964	59·5	2·4	12·2	28·2	10·3	14·0

[1] Including Br. Virgin Is.

FINANCE

EXCHANGE RATE (*EC$/US$*): 1·714; linked with Sterling at *EC*$4·8=£1.
BUDGET ACCOUNTS (*EC$ m.*), 1966: A Revenue 11·67, expenditure 11·60; D (1965) rev. 8·17, expend. 8·45; G rev.=expend. 12·79, KNA rev. 11·12, expend. 11·65; L (1965) rev.=expend. 9·69; V rev.=expend. 9·29. In future, accounts will no longer be balanced by UK grants-in-aid.

EMPLOYMENT

ECONOMICALLY ACTIVE (%), 1960: Of total pop. A 34, D 39, G 31, KNA 35, L 36, V 31; men A 45, D 47, G 40, KNA 45, L 49, V 41; women A 23, D 32, G 23, KNA 26, L 25, V 23. In agriculture D 50, G 40, KNA 46, L 48, V 40; services D 14, G 17, KNA 18, L 13, V 15; manufacturing 10–11; trade 8–11; construction 8–11.

TRANSPORT AND COMMUNICATIONS

MOTOR VEHICLES: Registered (*ooo*), 1965: D 2·1, G 3·3, KNA 2·1; 1962: A 3·3, L 1·8, V 2·0. Road systems (*km.*): A 240, D 600, G 910, KNA 250, L 675, V 980 (650 all-weather).
SHIPPING: Main ports: A St John's, D Roseau and Portsmouth, G St George's, KNA Basseterre (K) and Charlestown (N), L Castries, V Kingstown.
AIR: Main airports: A Coolidge; D Melville Hall; G Pearls; KNA Golden Rock, Basseterre (K), Newcastle (N), Wall Blake (A); L Vigie and Beane Field; V Arnos Vale.
TELEPHONES: No. in use, 1965: A 1,200, D 830, G 1,325, KNA 550, L 1,035, V 550.

SOCIAL WELFARE

HEALTH: persons per physician: A 3,800, D 5,600, G 4,500, KNA 6,800, L 6,500, V 10,000; persons per hospital bed: A 140, D 220, G 160, KNA 300, L 210, V 220.

EDUCATION

ILLITERACY RATE (%): 15 years of age and over, 1960: A 11, KNA 12; 1946: D 41, G 24, L 48, V 24.

COMPULSORY: No. of years: A 9 (not enforced) between ages 5–14, KNA 8 (5–14), L 6 (6–12). Enrolment ratios (%), 1st and 2nd levels, 1963 (adjusted): A over 100, D 79, G 91, KNA over 100, L 78, V 95.

SCHOOLS, 1964 (A and D, 1963): Primary: no. A 50, D 51, G 56, KNA 44 (incl. combined primary and secondary), L 58, V 56; students A 11,100, D 15,400, G 28,000, KNA 16,300, L 23,400, V 24,600; teachers A 350, D 460, G 640, KNA 450, L 690, V 670. Secondary: no. A 47, D 4, G 9, KNA 5, L 3, V 9; students A 6,100, D 1,600, G 2,300, KNA 1,500, L 1,000, V 1,900; teachers A 120, D 80, G 100, KNA 70, L 60, V 110. Technical: no. D 3, KNA 2; students D 350, KNA 300; teachers D 16, KNA 4. Teacher training: no. G 1, L 1, V 4; students G 33, L 40, V 150; teachers G 13, L 7, V 8. Higher: no. A 1, students A 50, teachers A 3.

UNIVERSITY: U. of the West Indies, Jamaica.

MASS MEDIA

BROADCASTING: No. of receivers in use (ooo): radio A (1964) 3·8, G (1965) 7, L (1963) 1·5; TV A (1965) 1·5. Stations, radio: A 1, KNA 1, G 1 and sub-stations in D, L, and V; TV: L 1.

CINEMAS: G (1965), no. 6; attendance 150,000, per head 1·6. L (1961), no. 8; attendance 400,000, per head 4·6.

NEWSPAPERS: Daily, 1964: A 2, G (1965) 1, KNA 2. Circulation (ooo): A 1·3, G 1·2, KNA 1. Copies per ooo pop.: A 22, G 13, KNA 16. Principal newspapers: A—*Worker's Voice* (daily), *Antigua Star* (Wed. and Sat.); D—*Chronicle* (Wed. and Sat.), *Herald* (Sat.); G—*West Indian* (not Mon. or Fri.), *Torchlight* (Wed., Fri. and Sun.); KNA—*Daily Bulletin* (not Sun.), *Labour Spokesman* (not Sun.), *Democrat* (Sat.); L—*Voice of St Lucia* (Wed. and Sat.); V—*Vincentian* (Wed. and Sat.).

CROWN COLONIES [1]

POPULATION

POPULATION (ooo), 1960 (census): M 12·1, BVI 7·3, CI 7·6, TCI 5·7; mid-1965 estimates: M 14, BVI 9, CI 9, TCI 7.

DENSITY: persons per sq. km., 1965: M 143, BVI 59, CI 35, TCI 16.

CRUDE RATES (*per ooo*), 1965 (BVI 1964): Birth: M 27·4, BVI 26·5, CI 26·9, TCI 23·1; death: M 8·6, BVI 8·8, CI 7·0, TCI 10·4; infant mortality: M 54·8, BVI 66·7, CI (1961) 39·7, TCI 114·1.

GROWTH RATES (% *p.a.*), 1958–65: M 2·2, BVI 3·7, CI 1·6, TCI 2·2.

DISTRIBUTION (% *of total pop.*): Ethnic, 1960: African M 96, BVI 93, CI 17, TCI 94; mixed M 2, BVI 5, CI 63, TCI 4; European M 0·4, BVI 0·6, CI 18, TCI 1·4. Language: English and local dialects. Largest cities or towns (*ooo inhab.*), 1960: M Plymouth 1·9 (1965: 4·0), BVI Road Town 1·2, CI George Town 2·6, TCI Grand Turk 2·3.

[1] M—Montserrat, BVI—British Virgin Islands (groups Tortola, Virgin Gorda, Anegada, Jost van Dykes), CI—Cayman Islands (Grand Cayman, Cayman Brac, Little Cayman), TCI—Turks and Caicos Islands (Grand Turk and Salt Cay; S, E, N, W Caicos, Middle Caicos, Providenciales).

CONSTITUTIONAL SYSTEMS

CONSTITUTIONS: M member of the Federation of the West Indies, 1958–62; new colonial constitution 1960. BVI part of Colony of Leeward Islands until 1956, then separate colony administered by Governor of the Leeward Is. until Jan. 1960, when it became directly responsible to the Colonial Office; new constitution 1967. CI and TCI dependencies of Jamaica until 1959 constitution, under which Governor of Jamaica retained certain powers; separate colonies 1962. M is joining Eastern Caribbean Common Market established by West Indian Associated States.

SYSTEMS: Administrators (Governor of Bahamas became Governor of TCI in 1965), Executive Councils and Legislative Councils or Assemblies. Administrator appointed by the Queen by Commission. Executive Councils include the Administrator (as chairman), ex-officio members (Attorney-General and Financial Secretary), ministers (M and BVI), nominated members and elected members. Legislative Councils or Assemblies consist of the Administrator (as chairman), elected members (M and BVI 7, CI 12, TCI 9), nominated members (M and BVI 1, CI and TCI 2–3) and official members (2 to 3). Ministerial systems in M and BVI. *Suffrage:* Universal voting for adults. *Elections:* M (1966) Labour Party 4 seats, Workers' Progressive Party 2, Independent 1 (since joined Labour Party).

ECONOMY

PRODUCTION

AGRICULTURE: Main commodities: M cotton; M and BVI bananas, limes, sugar, vegetables; TCI sisal.

LAND (%), 1964: Arable M 38, BVI 13; permanent pasture BVI 27; forested M 25; BVI 7; other M 38, BVI 53.

LIVESTOCK (*ooo head*): Cattle M 5, sheep and goats M 6, pigs M 1·2.

FISH: Total catch (*ooo tons*), 1963: M 0·1, BVI 0·4.

EXTERNAL TRADE

DISTRIBUTION (*US$ooo*), 1965: M–exports: total 189, cotton (lint) 102, bananas 19; total imports 2,851. BVI–exports: total 99, livestock 69, fish 15; total imports 2,961. CI–exports: total 60, rope 25, turtles and shell 19; total imports 3,240. TCI (1964)–exports: total 132, crawfish 72, salt 35, sisal 8; total imports 842.

DIRECTION OF TRADE (%): M (1964)–exports: UK 65·5, Canada 4·7; imports: UK 35·7, USA 15·8, Canada 13·8. BVI (1965)–exports: US Territories 80·8; imports: US Territories 59·7, UK 21·6. CI–about two-thirds of trade is with USA. TCI (1964)–exports: Jamaica 17·7, other Commonwealth 3·7; imports: UK 11·0, other Commonwealth 26·9.

FINANCE

EXCHANGE RATES: M—EC$1·714/US$, linked with Sterling EC$4·8=£1; BVI— US$ in use; CI and TCI use £ sterling and £J.

BUDGET ACCOUNTS, 1965: M (*EC$ ooo*) revenue 3,057, expenditure 3,186; BVI (*US$ ooo*) rev. 1,194, expend. 1,987; CI (*£ooo*) rev. 333, expend. 289; TCI (*£ooo*) rev. 268, expend. 239.

EMPLOYMENT

ECONOMICALLY ACTIVE (%), 1960: Of total pop. M 36, BVI 27, CI 37, TCI 37; men: M 45, BVI 45, CI 56, TCI 47; women: M 28, BVI 10, CI 21, TCI 29.

TRANSPORT AND COMMUNICATIONS

MOTOR VEHICLES, 1965: M, BVI and CI about 500–600. Roads (*km.*): M 190, BVI 65, CI 100.

SHIPPING: Main ports: M Plymouth, BVI Road Town, CI George Town, TCI Grand Turk.

AIR: Main airports: M Blackburne, BVI Beef Island airfield (main airport at St Thomas, US VI), CI Owen Roberts, Grand Cayman, TCI GrandTurk.

SOCIAL WELFARE

HEALTH: persons per physician: M 4,300, BVI 3,800; persons per hospital bed: M 200, BVI 150, TCI 200.

EDUCATION

ILLITERACY RATE (%), 1960 (census): 15 years and over, M 20, BVI 7, CI 7, TCI 9.
COMPULSORY: M 5–14 years of age, BVI 7–14, CI, 7–14, TCI 7–14. Enrolment ratios (%), 1st and 2nd levels, 1963 (adjusted): M 74, BVI 93.
SCHOOLS, 1964: Primary: no. M 15, BVI 16, CI 17, TCI 13; students M 3,000, BVI 1,960, CI 1,460, TCI (incl. secondary) 1,500; teachers M 90, BVI (incl. secondary and technical) 88, CI 53. Secondary: no. M 1, BVI (incl. technical) 8, CI 3, TCI 1; students M 240, BVI (incl. tech.) 550, CI 430; teachers M 16.
UNIVERSITY: U. of the West Indies, Jamaica.

MASS MEDIA

BROADCASTING: Radio: M 2 stations, TV from Antigua; BVI 1 station.
NEWSPAPERS, weekly: M—*The Montserrat Mirror;* BVI–*The Island Sun;* CI–*Caymanian, Tradewinds.*

PART TWO

LATIN AMERICAN POLITICAL AFFAIRS

POLITICAL AFFAIRS WITHIN
THE CONTINENT

PARTY SYSTEMS IN LATIN AMERICA[1]

ALAN ANGELL

PARTIES AND DOCTRINES

THE notion of a party as a group united by a common ideal or doctrine is even less adequate an explanation of parties in Latin America than elsewhere. Doctrinal attachment is an aspect of party strategy, a tactic, useful and important in the battle for power, but not necessarily a guide to policies if power is attained, nor an explanation of what unites the party in opposition. This applies to so-called traditional parties and to modern reform parties where ideologies are used by the leaders to control and manipulate the masses. Latin American politicians pluck a European ideology from its context and use it to support already firm political convictions. Positivism, for example, though used in Latin American politics in the late 19th century as a basis for action, did not influence the Latin American situation ideologically.

This is not to say that Latin American parties do not adopt ideological postures and doctrinal positions. Indeed, given the intensity of party competition in some countries the adopted doctrine assumes the nature of a faith, or a rallying call for the faithful. But the party generals will reverse the policy aims if conditions demand it. In 1958 the Intransigent wing of the Argentine Radical Party (UCRI) campaigned on a very radical platform demanding a state-planned economy with nationalisation of electricity supply and petroleum, immediate and drastic agrarian reform, opposition to Roman Catholic and private universities, and an anti-imperialist foreign policy. In December 1960 the party convention dropped all these items and inserted instead respect for private property, cooperation between state and private education, and encouragement of foreign capital. Why the change? Partly because the UCRI won the 1958 elections and found their pledges impracticable, also because of army pressure, and because their assessment of electoral strategy indicated moderation.

The relative failure of socialist parties in Latin America offers some interesting insights. But one must note that simply because a party calls itself 'Labour' or 'Socialist', and even if it has connections with trade unions, this does not mean that it operates in a similar political context to the British Labour Party. For example, the post-war Brazilian Labour Party (PTB) 'was born as the heir of a corporative tradition; its leadership consists exclusively of landowners, industrialists and professional men, though some of them are self-made; its attitude to trade union organisation is still paternalistic; and it supported continued strict regulation of trade unions and the

[1] Reprinted in adapted form from the *Political Quarterly*, XXXVII, 3, London, July–September 1966.

prohibition of any legal organisation of trade unions which it feared might grow too strong for comfort'.[1]

Even where socialist and labour parties are not controlled in this way they are often too advanced and 'foreign' for the national level of social development. In Argentina before Perón 'socialism as an imported ideology that stressed rationality, internationalism and principle rather than romanticism, nationalism and personalities seemed somewhat un-Argentine to the lower class mind'[2]. Perón however, cared little for doctrinal consistency, stressing precisely those qualities of 'romanticism, nationalism and personalities' that did attract mass support.

Latin American communism, as Ernst Halperin notes (see bibliography), is remarkable for its lack of a revolutionary tradition. Even the relatively strong Chilean Communist Party has not one revolutionary rising to its credit, showing far more reluctance than the Socialist Party, or even centre and right parties, to employ violence as a political tactic. Apart from the 1935 uprising in Brazil, the communists have followed, sometimes even opposed, attempts at social revolution, but not led them. If the Soviet Union has an ally in Cuba, it is owing to its support of a radical, nationalist leader, Fidel Castro, not to the success of the Cuban Communist Party.

It is perhaps not so surprising that Latin American communism is weak. In many countries the communists are fiercely suppressed by the government. Their political intrigues with dictators like Batista, supporting him in return for control over trade unions, discredit them in the eyes of radical nationalists, who see these tactics as short-term political expediency indicating indifference to revolutionary objectives. Too often the tactics of Latin American communists have been those of international communism, even when this was unfavourable to their national strength. They had, for example, to jettison the advantages derived from alliances with social democratic parties in the Popular Front era, when the Cold War demanded opposition to all democratic groups. Indeed, their emphasis on internationalism, impersonal organisation and discipline has ill served them in a context where the political values of nationalism, personalism and individualism predominate. Their failure to provide either a revolutionary example or a theoretical critique appropriate to Latin America explains the impatience of the younger Castroist elements, who want to make the revolution now, not wait for the objective conditions to come about, and who want to proselytise amongst the peasantry not the urban trade unions. The caution of the traditional elements is understandable in the light of their fear that, even in the unlikely event of a successful communist coup, the Soviet Union would not want to repeat its massive commitment made in Cuba, whereas the United States would certainly repeat its opposition to this threat.

PARTIES AND SOCIETY

As European parties reflect the class cleavages of European society, so Latin American parties reflect the large number of competitive status groups that divide Latin American society. Party competition in Colombia, for example, is fierce and violent, but it is not the violence of 'class war' in the Marxist sense, for the conflict takes the form of a struggle between the

---

[1] E. Dell, *Brazil: The Dilemma of Reform*, Fabian Society, Research Pamphlets No. 241, London, 1964, p. 15.
[2] R. Potash, quoted in C. Wagley (ed.), *Social Science Research in Latin America*, New York, 1964, p. 107.

Liberal and Conservative parties, both of which are loose coalitions of personalist, regional and, less often, doctrinal groups. The parties group together influential people seeking an advantageous alliance in their struggle for political power. Parties are instruments for achieving success for individuals or small groups, not for collective advancement of a social class, because class consciousness of this sort does not exist in Colombian society. Social conflict is seen in individualistic or small group terms, the conflict of a society divided into a large number of status groups, and party conflict in Colombia reflects this sort of social division.

In the rural areas of the less developed countries of Latin America, and in Colombia, parts of Brazil and Ecuador, peasants may support a particular political party because it is the choice of their *patrón*, often the big landowner who controls land tenure. In this sense party identification is arbitrary; it is determined for the peasants, not by them. But it may take on a more active meaning, as a symbolic social ritual or myth, and party disputes may even be seen as the cause for hostility towards another village or group of peasants who have a different affiliation. Social grievances, that may have their root causes in such factors as the inequitable distribution of land or the arbitrariness of local administration, can be expressed in party terms, even though there is seemingly little rational motive in so doing. In Colombia, as M. Deas has pointed out: 'the mystery is the faithfulness and the fanaticism of the voters. From 1946 to 1953, the year when the army took over, they killed each other for the sake of party, frequently without hope of gain and with no encouragement. The Liberals went forth to the plains to fight, as they declared, for Francisco de Paula Santander (died 1840), for José Hilario López (president from 1849 to 1853) and for Rafael Uribe (assassinated 1914). They knew next to nothing about these men; they included no later figures and added no policy. Yet they cared a great deal'[1].

Urban politics in Latin America is heavily influenced by the fact that urbanisation on a large scale preceded industrialisation, leaving the role of many town dwellers ill-defined. Many are low paid workers in service occupations forming the swollen government bureaucracies, and the marginal lumpenproletariat, unemployed or underemployed, recently arrived from rural areas, existing in shanty towns surrounding the city. Only partially attached to society, their attachment to political life is sporadic and may become violent and extremist. Bringing with them rural values, the patrón relationship finds a new context. Perón succeeded in portraying himself as a larger-than-life patrón, making his appeal intelligible to people who could not understand the ideas of the intellectuals of the Socialist Party. The Chilean Christian Democrats reaped electoral benefits from making an appeal to the so-called *poblaciones marginales*, largely ignored by other left-wing parties concentrating on organised labour.

The small proportion of the Latin American working class engaged in industrial occupations often constitutes a labour aristocracy more concerned with maintaining its privileges than with radical social change. In Venezuela, for example, only 3 per cent of the labour force works in the major industry, petroleum. Trade unions in Latin America are rarely allowed to become independent political forces, for their activity and indeed the whole labour code is closely regulated by the government.

If extremist parties or groups take control of a trade union then government suppression of their control is easy, and predictable, and has a long history

---

[1] 'Politics and Violence', *Encounter*, XXV, 3, London, September 1965, p. 112.

going back to the suppression of anarchist and anarcho-syndicalist unions. But even if extremist groups do maintain control they face a political dilemma. Either they concentrate on benefits for their own members, in which case their broader political ends must be put aside; or else they work for their broader aims and face losing rank-and-file support, for, given the availability of cheap labour in Latin America, few workers will wish to lose their jobs for a long-term principle.

POPULIST PARTIES IN LATIN AMERICA

The so-called 'populist' parties of Latin America are sometimes seen as being multi-class, mass and reformist, in opposition to the 'traditional' parties, narrow-based, oligarchical and anti-reform. This contrast can be too sharply drawn. The Colombian party system, for example, is more competitive and draws on a wider section of the population (and pays at least lip service to reformist policies) than does the stereotype of the 'traditional' party system.

A compound of the many definitions of populism establishes the following features[1]. First, leadership comes from the upper and middle classes, though from groups with anti-status-quo motivations. The composition of this leadership varies considerably, and this can affect the nature of the movement. For example, it may include military elements, as did the Peronista movement in Argentina, and business elements, especially of 'newer' industries, again as in Argentina. Mostly, however, the alienated intellectual, the reforming student, provides a sort of déclassé leadership, as in the Castro movement before 1959, or the Movimiento Nacionalista Revolucionario of Bolivia, or Acción Democrática of Venezuela. These intellectuals find themselves in a position of what has been called 'status incongruence'; often lawyers in countries that have too many lawyers of low academic level, they feel hostile to a system that does not accord them a privileged position. And if they feel generally rejected within their own milieux, their radicalism is even more intense.

Secondly, populist parties have a popular mass base. These are Perón's *descamisados*, urban masses organised by him into trade unions, responsive to his demagogic nationalism, ready to support him in return for his recognition of their demands. The Bolivian tin miners' unions were a cohesive force in the Bolivian Revolution of 1952, and were easily mobilised for violence against their former masters. Rural areas can provide an agrarian setting for populist agitation as in the Mexican Revolution, or the peasant leagues of north-east Brazil.

Thirdly, populist parties lack precise doctrine but are held together by a set of basic social demands, or a state of collective enthusiasm, couched in terms of simple redistributive justice. Populism is in a sense an anti-ideological movement. It may employ the language of socialism, but it avoids ties with such international movements as socialism and communism, though it may try to use them. Populism is an ideology of revolt against the system, rather than a doctrine of government; a movement emphasising action for its own sake, difficult to fit into a left-right political spectrum.

Fourthly, populist parties are intensely nationalistic. The Mexican Revolution, for example, was seen as the last stage in a war of national liberation that started by expelling the Spaniards in the early 19th century,

---

[1] See T. di Tella, 'Populism and Reform in Latin America' in C. Véliz (ed.), *Obstacles to Change in Latin America*, London, 1965, and other essays in the same volume.

the French in the mid-19th century, and ended by driving out dictator Porfirio Díaz who, it was alleged, had sold the country to European and North American capitalists. Anti-American feeling is easily aroused and plays an important part in the nationalism of these movements, as in Cuba where there was a long tradition of anti-Americanism before Castro. The populist leaders portray the system they are trying to overthrow as anti-national, the exploitation of the nation by a privileged few, like the tin mine owners of Bolivia, and they portray themselves as nationalists who will return the country to the people.

Fifthly, a charismatic leader is important. Perón and his wife had a control over the masses of Argentina that cannot be explained in terms of organisation alone; populism in Brazil is linked to the figure of Getulio Vargas; the Peruvian Apra movement was controlled by the founder, Haya de la Torre. Populist demands are better expressed through a personal leader, for the masses, lacking practice in the complexity of political life, find identification with a movement facilitated through the medium of a leader, through the mediation of a patrón. And personalism has always been a strong feature of Latin American political life. Usually the leader's appeal is in terms of simple, almost irrational promises of immediate redistributive changes in favour of the masses.

It is instructive to compare Latin American with African populism, similar in being a movement of direct, extreme action against the 'system', that can be led to either right or left in its demand for radical action. But Latin American populism lacks the agrarian, cooperative emphasis of African populism; it does not, as does African populism, reject city-based capitalism and individualism in favour of the small rural community and cooperative. (There were similar anti-urban, anti-industrial, anti-centralisation, pro-village communitarianist tendencies in Russian populism and, indeed, in American populism.) It cannot be said of Latin American populism as of African that 'the populist is thus strongly communitarian; he is an enthusiast for local government, suspicious of the state and of all large-scale organisations'.[1]

Fascist movements in Eastern Europe also provide some interesting parallels. Eugen Weber writes of this region that 'where no left existed, the protest, the politicalisation of the unpoliticised, the cowed or ignorant, the resigned or indifferent—their nationalisation with all its revolutionary implications—all this was left to movements's like Codreanu's [Iron Legion in Rumania]'.[2] In Latin America too the left has been weak for a number of reasons. In Argentina, early anarchist and anarcho-syndicalist violence led to systematic repression of all extreme left movements, and in any case the appeal of movements like anarchism and socialism was mostly to European immigrants to Argentina rather than to the nationals. Thus the 'politicalisation of the unpoliticised' was left to populist movements.

But populism in Latin America, like fascism in Eastern Europe, is a movement of revolt, a movement of protest against the system. It faces considerable difficulties, therefore, when it *becomes* the system. In power, it is often the victim of its own success. It is possible to identify populist movements in opposition in Latin America; it is less easy to identify populist governments in power, or to recognise something distinctively populist about the way they govern. When a policy of simple redistribution no longer suffices because the

[1] P. Worsley, *The Third World*, London, 1965.
[2] 'The Men of the Archangel', *Journal of Contemporary History*, I, 1, London, January 1966, p. 124.

economy no longer has the resources, populist movements in power face the difficulties of *being* the system, of making governmental decisions that no longer distribute benefits but that demand sacrifices.

The wideness of the coalition of groups that form populist movements and the vagueness of their doctrine constitute two weaknesses of populism as a governing force, though in opposition they are its strength. A coalition of different groups held together in opposition is much more difficult to hold together when limited spoils and benefits have to be distributed. In Bolivia, with its meagre economic resources, the coalition of forces that formed the revolutionary populist movement disintegrated in power; it was not possible to satisfy the tin miners *and* the peasants *and* the students *and* the middle sector groups. Factional differences are reinforced by personal disputes and the government loses its populist characteristics. In Bolivia the overlap between group and personal conflict brought the system to the verge of chaos until the military stepped in; whilst in Argentina Perón could not permanently satisfy the workers *and* the military. Mexican populism reached stability by losing many of its populist characteristics. The constitution may still express populist aims, but political control is firmly in the hands of the party and government bureaucracies staffed by the new middle class. Sound capitalist development rather than populist redistribution of wealth characterises Mexican development. Castro in power found that his populist movement, the 26th of July Movement, and his populist ideas derived from the Cuban revolutionary José Martí, were less adequate as a theory of government than as a theory of revolt. Thus the 26th of July Movement was fused into a new Cuban communist party and Martí was exchanged for Marx.

Some populist leaders, for example Perón and Vargas, have remained in power for comparatively long periods, but only by shedding much of their reform programme. Perón, though he disturbed the large landowners, did not basically alter the economic structure of Argentina, whilst Vargas, who flirted lightly with fascism, Portuguese style, flirted even more lightly with reform. Under both men policies involving some redistribution of benefits in favour of the working class were introduced, but very much by grace of the state. The patrón distributed gifts to his people, and the people began to expect them regularly and to create trouble for later governments that were not so generous, but the patrón remained, as long as he could, firmly in control, with no desire to share political power.

PARTIES AND POLITICAL POWER

All political parties strive for power and the pursuit of power has consequences for their organisation and tactics. But the effect of this pursuit is particularly marked in Latin America. The intensity of party conflict, the modes of party behaviour that seem unusual to Western observers, the alliances made between parties that seem ideologically completely opposed, all seem to point to the particular importance of the pursuit of power in Latin American party politics.

Guillén Martínez writes:

Colombian parties originated after independence in the desire for power, for the domination of the central government which was the main employer, the supreme arbiter, the instrument of enrichment. Beneath the appearance of profound ideological differences these parties grouped together rival hordes of people of all conditions, from all social classes, from all professional groups, from all political and regional groups. What really united them was not a 'declaration of principle',

N

but the feeling and belief that this alignment in a political party gave them the strength to fight their rivals for the inexhaustible treasury that was the central government. The political programmes of the parties had, and have, little relationship with the real reason for their existence; the programmes served as conventional banners of identification in the battle, not even as permanent banners, but simply as the fleeting symbols of psychological cohesion.[1]

Party behaviour in Latin America is influenced in particular by the following aspects of political power.

First, in most countries political power means executive power and this means the power of the president. The whole governmental structure is highly centralised, leading up to the office of the presidency; if a group is excluded from this line of communication it is in the political wilderness. The power of legislatures has often been underestimated, it is true, but their power is largely negative. They may veto presidential decisions, as they did in Brazil, but this reaps few positive benefits. Anyhow presidents often enjoy wide decree-making powers and power under state of siege which is readily proclaimed if necessary.

Secondly, politics is thus basically a central activity, for relatively little can be decided at the local level. Genuine local government is rare in Latin America. Of course a group or person may enjoy considerable local influence, but in order to influence decisions this must be made meaningful at the national level by, for example, forming political alliances.

Thirdly, the scope of government power and influence is extensive. Many Latin American countries have enormously large bureaucracies and employ a high proportion of the working population. Furthermore, much business and industry is dependent on the government for finance, for import or export licences, for a certain tariff policy and so on. Thus executive power has wide control over social and economic structures.

Fourthly, power is seen in personal terms, not in impersonal institutionalised forms. This is especially true where Indians constitute a major proportion of the population. For them the president is the descendant of the viceroy; the person who by his power can mediate between them and local oppressors, between them and an incomprehensible and often harsh governmental machine. This is also true outside the Indian countries. Eduardo Frei, president of Chile, writes: 'A paternalistic structure has accustomed the people to expect aid from someone, salvation from somewhere; first from the patrón, then from the caudillo, now from the government . . . A very bad habit, a result of the present order is to expect change from a benefactor rather than a true promotion of the people. There emerges now a mystic hope that everything will be all right if the system is modified by the sole act of changing those in power, without giving real thought to the fact that what is really needed is a great effort toward change among all people in common. This phenomenon may be referred to as the psychology of distribution and not of creation'.[2] Paradoxically this 'psychology of distribution' has reached its highest point in Uruguay where there is no president but a nine-man executive council formed by both major parties. All groups and party factions in Uruguay have reached a *modus vivendi*, a common agreement to cooperate to distribute the spoils of government. The distinctive feature of this system is that parties share in the benefits of power

---

[1] *Raíz y futuro de la revolución*, Bogotá, 1963, p. 134.

[2] 'Paternalism, Pluralism and Christian Democratic Reform Movements' in V. D'Antonio and F. B. Pike, *Religion, Revolution and Reform*, London, 1964, p. 35.

and do not demand a monopoly of it, not that the aims of politicians are fundamentally different; i.e. parties have a 'psychology of distribution'.

STRATEGY, TACTICS AND ORGANISATION

In part because of this concentration of power, the modes of behaviour of Latin American parties have some unusual features.

The spectrum of possible party tactics is very wide, ranging from close cooperation to violent hostility. If moderate parties are out of power, their exclusion is often so complete that they take to extremist tactics to shorten the period in the wilderness. If this means military intervention in politics, it may be accepted as preferable to letting the other party remain in power. In the early days of Cuban independence politicians would even try to encourage the United States to invade in the hope that the outcome would favour them.

The intensity of party conflict explains the attempts to politicise non-party organisations. If the party can forge links with a trade union it has another power base that it may be able to use. Students often form party groups and student union elections are fought on party lines encouraged by the parties seeking to enlist supporters. Similarly peasant organisations may be another source of strength, even if this means having contacts with bandits. In Colombia, in a few regions some members of Congress could not be elected without the support of bandits who, in return, expect a certain amount of protection.

Any alliance is contemplated if this aids the party in the competition for power. In Peru, writes J. Payne, 'the desire to destroy the incumbent president is of paramount significance. The intensity with which this objective is pursued results not only in the use of violence . . . but also in the formation of seemingly incongruous alliances. For example, the Christian Democratic Party (in opposition in 1961) had a peasant affairs bureau which worked closely with members of the Trotskyite and rebel Apra parties who were attempting to foment a revolution through rural violence. That the Pope's sworn enemies should walk hand in hand with his disciples testifies to the overwhelming importance of the struggle against the executive in the eyes of the participants'.[1] Groups that are ideologically opposed frequently come into alliance, for groups that are similar in ideas and social basis are more obviously rivals.

The intense struggle for power and the lack of importance of doctrine help to explain the high degree of factionalism of many Latin American parties. Colombian and Uruguayan parties are little more than loose coalitions of different regional, personal and sometimes doctrinal groups that are frequently in competition within the party, rather than with the other party. The electoral system is partly responsible for the factionalism, both countries using a system of proportional representation with lists. But factionalism is further encouraged in both countries because nothing is lost by running another list, in terms of hurting the parties' chances. In Colombia, whatever the proportion of people who vote Conservative or Liberal, Congress and other elected assemblies are divided by law equally between the parties so that the only really effective choice is between the various lists within the parties. In Uruguay, irrespective of the number of competing lists within each party, all are added together to arrive at the overall party total which

---

[1] *Labor and Politics in Peru*, New Haven, 1965, p. 13.

decides which party takes the majority in the nine-man executive council. To talk of party membership or discipline in these circumstances is misleading. People may be members of particular groups within a party, and may be expelled from a group, but not from the party as such.

Factionalism is not characteristic of all Latin American parties. Where there has been a sustained attempt at organisation and discipline, and where there exists an undisputed leader, parties can be unified and united. The Apra party of Peru has built up what Payne calls 'exclusive, partisan communications patterns . . . . The Apristas have their own cafeteria and barber shop, their own medical assistance staff, soccer teams and party newspaper. In addition there are numerous functional groupings within the party: university students, workers, high school students, artists, lawyers and so on. Hence an Aprista may live within the party's world and never have his loyalty weakened by contradictory communications'.[1] There is even a separate organisation for children up to the age of 10 and another one for children from the ages 10 to 18. Secondly, the Apristas have their own leader and founder, Haya de la Torre, whose personal authority is of great importance in binding together the party, though there has been one split of Apristas dissatisfied with the increasing conservatism of the leadership. It is obviously much easier to maintain discipline and unity in a party that has an undisputed leader than in one where party authority is much looser and decentralised and where there is no common agreement on the power of an individual or body to embody the 'party'.

In conclusion, the structure and behaviour of Latin American parties cannot be understood by extrapolating from European experience, nor even from the experience of other countries of the 'Third World'. They must be looked at in terms of their own tradition, their own social structures, their own governmental system, their own internal system of organisation.

[1] *Op. cit.*

BIBLIOGRAPHY

Alexander, R. *Communism in Latin America*, Rutgers Univ. Press, New Brunswick, NJ, 1957.
   The Venezuelan Political Experiment, Rutgers Univ. Press, New Brunswick, NJ, 1964.
Frei, E. 'Paternalism, Pluralism and Christian Democratic Reform Movements', in d'Antonio,
   V. and Pike, F. B., *Religion, Revolution and Reform*, Burns and Oates, London; Frederick A.
   Praeger, New York, 1964.
Gil, F. *Genesis and Modernization of Political Parties in Chile*, Univ. of Florida Press, Gainesville,
   Fla., 1962.
Halperin, E. *Nationalism and Communism in Chile*, MIT Press, Cambridge, Mass., 1965.
Kantor, H. *The Ideology and Programme of the APRA Party*, Univ. of California Press, Berkeley,
   Calif., 1953.
McAlister, L. 'Social Structure and Social Change in New Spain', *Hispanic American Historical
   Review*, XLIII, 3, Durham, NC, August 1963.
Needler, M. (ed.) *Political Systems of Latin America*, Van Nostrand, Princeton, NJ and London,
   1964.
Payne, J. *Labor and Politics in Peru*, Yale Univ. Press, New Haven, Conn., 1965.
Pike, F. B. 'The Old and the New APRA in Peru', *Inter-American Economic Affairs*, XVIII,
   Washington, DC, autumn 1964.
Silvert, K. *Conflict Society: Reaction and Revolution in Latin America*, Hauser Press, New Orleans,
   La., 1961.
Snow, P. 'Argentine Radicalism', *Journal of Inter-American Studies*, V, 4, Coral Gables,
   Florida, October 1963.
Taylor, P. *Government and Politics of Uruguay*, Tulane Univ. Press, New Orleans, La., 1960.
Weber, E. 'The Men of the Archangel', *Journal of Contemporary History*, I, 1, London,
   January 1966.

THE MILITARY IN POLITICS

ALISTAIR HENNESSY

HISTORICAL BACKGROUND

THE Conquest of America by the Spaniards was a remarkable example of the triumph of superior military and technological skill over empires whose social organisations were geared to war. The Conquistadors were hardened military men with a crusading mentality who were reluctant to beat their swords into ploughshares. In the conflicts on the rough frontier societies of Upper Peru and New Spain some of the traits of later military attitudes may already be discerned—an exaggerated sense of honour, a feeling that the conflict of wills can only be resolved by appeal to arms and a belief in the inherent superiority of the man on horseback to the *letrado*.

In spite of its turbulent opening the Spanish Empire was not, however, a militarised society. There were no military roads resounding to the tramp of marching cohorts and unlike the Norman conquerors in England the Spaniards did not build castles over the country. During the great age of fortress-building in the 18th century the aim was to protect the exposed Caribbean against British depredations. Elsewhere the crumbling adobe of fortified haciendas on the Chichemeca frontier in northern Mexico or legends of Indian resistance against the invader on the Araucanian frontier of the far south is all that survives to remind us of the internal struggle against the indigenous peoples.

The 18th-century challenge from British power posed a manpower problem which the Spaniards could only meet by enlisting a colonial militia in which the creole élite could buy commissions and gain the prestige they were denied elsewhere. The crown's dependence on this militia for defence enabled creole aristocrats to secure juridical privileges, such as exemptions from civil courts. Thus already before independence can be found the germs of that sense of uniqueness as well as immunity from civil authority which only needed the successes of the liberating armies to be transformed into an active assertion of the superiority of the soldier over the civilian in the new states.

Many of the leaders of the liberating armies in the wars of independence were ex-militia officers like Bolívar, and the prestige acquired by their victories enabled them to step into the legitimacy vacuum created by the demise of royal power. In Brazil, where there was no such legitimacy vacuum nor a legacy of crippling war soldiers remained subordinate to the civil power until the 1870s, when in the aftermath of the Paraguayan war discontented soldiers began to intervene in politics until finally younger officers, mostly engineers nurtured on positivism, spearheaded the republican faction of the plantocracy-based Empire. The highly professionalised General San Martín recognised the dangers posed to the new states by ambitious soldiers, especially by new military leaders best symbolised by Páez, whose command of the wild mestizo horsemen of the Orinoco plains made him indispensable to Bolívar. The career of Páez, who eventually became president of Venezuela, shows how the army provided a channel of upward social mobility for the despised mestizo and also the importance of leadership qualities in a male-dominated society. The *macho* ('courage') complex together with the cult of *hombría* ('manliness'), crucial elements in hispanic culture, put a premium on strong leadership as well as on the ability to tame wild horses and master beautiful women, to excel with lance, *boleadoras*, *lazo* and dagger. These qualities, of course, tend to be admired in any frontier society, but in 19th-century Latin America the values of pastoral despotism all too frequently dominated the metropolises. In contrast to the United States, frontiers contracted rather than expanded and even in the viceregal capitals of Mexico, Lima and Buenos Aires during the Rosas period, there was no social group strong enough to challenge the dominance of rural-based caudillos. Residual admiration for the virile strong man still finds an echo in popular folk-lore, whether in Mexican *corridas* recalling Pancho Villa and Zapata or in the wistful urbanised *gauchismo* of Buenos Aires.

PROFESSIONALISATION

Towards the end of the 19th century the inter-American wars, in which the nascent middle class had an interest, exposed military inefficiency and the incompetence of the *caudillo* when faced with the simplest military manouevre, and gave an impetus to reform and professionalisation. Military academies were established and foreign military missions, staffed either by German or French officers, were introduced. As a consequence, a military career was closed to the illiterate cowboy whose ambitions or frustrations were turned into banditry or rural revolt, although some might come to terms with the changing social scene by becoming *caciques*, acting on behalf of town-based politicians. The army now became a safe career for cautious and unenterprising sons of provincial middle-class families or of lesser oligarchs who found that openings elsewhere were restricted. Although a military career became more exclusive in educational terms it still provided one of the best means of social mobility as, for example, in Argentina, where a large proportion of army officers were the sons of Italian and Spanish immigrants. Navies, in contrast, tended to be socially more exclusive, as in Brazil where naval officers were racially 'purer' than the army.

A decline in the number of military coups at the end of the 19th and early 20th century encouraged the view that professionalisation would weaken the tendency of soldiers to intervene in politics. Later experience showed that this was not the case. The professionalisation of the armed forces in Haiti, Nicaragua and the Dominican Republic during the United States occupation in the 1910s and 1920s inaugurated some of the bloodiest regimes in Latin American history. After 1930, the *annus mirabilis* for military coups, a new cycle of militarism began. Professionalisation thus changed the objectives and style but not the frequency of military intervention. Since 1930 there have been over a hundred violent changes of power in Latin America and during this period Mexico alone has suffered no military coup. Nor is there any sign to-day that military intervention is diminishing.

Whereas in the 19th century intervention may be partially explained by the low level of political culture in essentially stagnant rural societies, in the 20th it reflects crises in societies where modernisation has produced a disorientation of values, economic maladjustments, power vacuums and other symptoms of imbalance. The emergence of self-identifying middle classes does not necessarily guarantee civilian rule; there is no simple correlation between indices of development and military intervention. The military are as important in Argentina, by all criteria the highest developed Latin American country, as in Ecuador and Bolivia which are amongst the poorest. In fact, professionalisation has given the armed forces a homogeneity and an élite consciousness which they previously lacked and which has strengthened their position in relation to heterogeneous and divided middle groups.

MOTIVES FOR INTERVENTION

The motives behind intervention are as varied as the justifications given for them. A distinction must be made between soldiers acting in a personal capacity and the armed forces acting as an institution. In the 19th century caudillos seized power for personal gain, but with increasing professionalisation intervention has become formalised and it is now rare to find a general acting independently. If one does so, it is usually a sign of desperation not calculation. Of course, elements of personal gain play their part—salary increases have a way of following coups and often, as in the notorious case of the Dominican Republic, soldiers grant themselves privileges, such as customs exemptions. Where governments yield to military pressure grouping, direct intervention becomes unnecessary but soldiers may still have a political motive in intervening.

Although the military may believe in its patriotic mission to save the nation from the ravages of selfish or incompetent politicians, its attitude has more often been determined by group interests. Often these have a regional base, as with the cowboy caudillos of the Táchira clique who dominated Venezuela until the 1930s. In Ecuador, too, the army has traditionally represented the Sierra against the coast with commercial Guayaquil as the main focus of opposition during the periods of army-dominated politics at Quito. In Haiti the army was drawn from Negroes in contrast to the pre-Duvalier mulatto domination of government.

Professional grievances can also be a spur to political involvement. Promotion blockages used to be a constant source of friction, but the lowering of the retiring age has reduced this danger although it has led to the problem of the retired general with political ambition and influence. Lieutenant-colonel is a sensitive rank as only a limited number will be promoted to the highest posts. There is also, as throughout Latin American life, the conflict between generations, between older officers and younger more radical officers. This may take a political as distinct from a professional form, as in the case of the Brazilian *tenentes* of the 1920s who were the spearhead of radicalism. Interference with promotion procedures, as when political appointments bypass seniority, is still an incitement to political action although this now seems to be becoming less important than in the past.

There is no simple correlation between political attitudes and social origins. Assumptions that officer recruitment from low social strata will necessarily democratise the officer corps ignore the compulsive power of the military ethic. It is unusual for soldiers not to have a built-in scorn for civilians and it is rare for soldiers to refuse to shoot down their fellow citizens. It is rare also for NCOs and men to rebel against their officers, and when they do, it tends to make the officer corps close its ranks (this happened in

Brazil in 1964 after the sergeants' revolt in Brasilia and President Goulart's support for mutineers in Rio). The only successful coup of this sort was Batista's Sergeants' Revolt in Cuba in 1933.

In transitional societies the military must be viewed as one of many competing groups, acting as an autonomous estate rather than as the representative or defender of any civilian group. To label it as the arm of the oligarchy is an oversimplification. Undeniably some civilian groups do benefit from military takeovers, but soldiers intervene to defend their own group interests or what they conceive to be the 'national interest', not those of civilian groups they may well despise.

Civilian politicians are often accused of trafficking with the nation's well-being in order to further sectional interests. In an atmosphere of recurrent crises, ministerial instability or parliamentary corruption, soldiers may regard themselves as the guardians of the national interest, justifying intervention by a 'general will' political theory. Weaknesses in the political system may force a political role on the armed forces, as in Argentina where the failure to develop effective checks on the powers of the president together with the inability of congress and provincial governors to exercise real independent authority have contributed to the army assuming a self-appointed role of the balancing power. In Brazil too the army has long seen itself as the heir to the moderating power of the emperor.

The inability of civilian politicians to resolve crises may give the army little alternative to intervention as, for example, in Peru in July 1962 when a military junta took over after a deadlock in the presidential elections. Once in power it is not easy to withdraw: the delights of the palace make the boredom of the barracks more irksome. Withdrawal is also a sophisticated exercise which few military governments are able to pull off. The Peruvians succeeded, handing over to Belaúnde after new elections a year later (whether they would have done so had APRA won is a moot point); whereas in Ecuador the military junta which seized power in 1963 was forced out in 1966. Although juntas may announce their intention of holding elections and handing over to civilians, the way they exercise power tends to be self-defeating; restrictions are placed on political activity, which dooms the development of a genuine party system. Often the military takes the initiative in organising a civilian party as a 'national front' over which they hope to exercise veto power. The PCN (Partido de Conciliación Nacional) in El Salvador and the FRB (Frente de la Revolución Boliviana) are cases in point.

Soldiers may also claim they are more efficient than civilians. Standards of military education have risen and some military establishments, such as Peru's CAEM (Colegio de Altos Estudios Militares) or Brazil's War College, compare favourably with secular institutions. Officers are beginning to form an important branch of the technical intelligentsia—the more so because of the imbalance in civilian higher education between humanistic and scientific subjects. The increasing technical emphasis of officers' education not only makes dialogue with humanistically trained civilians difficult but encourages officers to regard themselves as the technocrats of social revolution which many of them see as necessary if only to stave off left-wing extremism.

Where violence is an integral part of the political system the army may become involved whether it wants to or not. In parts of Latin America violence has become institutionalised and does not carry with it any opprobrium. The level of violence varies from the ritualised mutilations of the Colombian *violencia*, reflecting a breakdown of social organisation and restraints, to street demonstrations which are deliberately used as a political tactic. The traditional leniency towards defeated rebels is a reflection of an attitude which regards violence virtually as an accepted norm.

The police are expected to cope with outbreaks of violence, but the division of authority between police forces, together with their inefficiency and corruption, often compels the military to intervene. Few countries can emulate Chile's efficient and ubiquitous *carabineros* whose public reputation had been enhanced by their social work and their role as frontier guards against Argentinian 'aggression'. Generally, police forces are underpaid, carry low social status, are ill-trained in riot drill and, being closely associated with the government in power, have to bear the brunt of its unpopularity. Police inefficacy is often a result of a government's deliberate refusal to unite the various police forces (as in Venezuela) for fear, perhaps, of praetorian pretensions or through pressure of soldiers who may fear the police being used as a counterbalance. Once soldiers become involved in restoring order they exact a price for incurring public odium, forcing a change of policy, exercising a veto power or, as in the case of the public disorders in Bolivia in 1964, overthrowing the government and taking over themselves.

Military intervention has often been justified in Latin American countries in terms of defending constitutional procedures (defence of which by the army is written into some constitutions) and of protecting civil rights. On occasions the army has acted with considerable popular support, as in the overthrow of Laureano Gómez in Colombia in 1953, of Perón in Argentina in 1955 and of Pérez Jiménez in Venezuela in 1958, and after a period of provisional military rule to prepare for elections it has withdrawn. In Argentina General Aramburu exercised power as trustee president for three years and in Venezuela, Admiral Larrazabal for one year. In the case of Rojas Pinilla, who overstepped his role of guardian in Colombia, loss of army and civilian support led to his being ousted in 1957. Brazil is the country where the army has taken its constitutional role most seriously, stemming from the prominent part which it played in overthrowing the Empire in 1889.

Soldiers may intervene to inaugurate change, not merely to restore the status quo. These movements tend to be neo-socialist, technocratic and authoritarian, forcing through reforms which may have been blocked by civilian dilatoriness. These groups are sometimes called *nasseristas*—although this describes a mood rather than a consciously thought-out philosophy. Latin America has not provided many examples of this type of intervention. Peronism, with its initial support by the radical officers of the GOU (Grupo de Oficiales Unidos), its populist base and neo-socialist policies, provides the closest parallel, although the army's role had latterly been challenged by organised labour. At present strong Nasserist elements, associated with CAEM, back President Belaúnde in Peru. El Salvador provides an example of a reform-minded junta carrying out a coup in 1961 against the extremes of right and left, but President Julio Rivera's precarious position showed the difficulties of this kind of regime exposed on the right to the golden handshake of the traditional oligarchy and on the left to violent extremist attacks. In this case the mass support of a genuine Nasserist movement has not emerged. The experiences of the Peruvian junta of 1962–3 and of the Ecuadorian junta between 1963 and 1966 show how reformers can be hampered by lack of technical expertise—hence the rationale behind an institution like CAEM's emphasis on contingency-planning.

CURBING THE MILITARY'S POWER

Most Latin American armed forces are now engaged on development projects such as road building, school construction, colonisation schemes, community development, etc. It is hoped that if the armed forces are employed constructively they will be anaesthetised politically. But this is as dubious an assumption as the earlier panacea of professionalisation. Civil-military friction can result when civil contracts are lost to the military, and the closer contact of the military with the local population and its understanding of the needs of rural dwellers may lead officers to act as their spokesmen, as to some extent happened under General Barrientos in Bolivia.

The Cuban Revolution and the threat of subversion by guerrilla activity (against which soldiers are deployed in Guatemala, Venezuela, Colombia and Peru) has given soldiers a military role which has removed one motive for intervention—boredom. It is difficult for an army to train indefinitely for an eventuality which never occurs. Counter-guerrilla theory also gives soldiers a civil role in helping to wean peasants away from guerrillas' blandishments by helping them in development projects. There is a danger, however, that as an élite corps counter-guerrilla units might develop praetorian ambitions like the French 'paras' in the Algerian war. There is also the danger that soldiers trained in counter-guerrilla work make good guerrillas—for example, Yon Sosa and Turcios, Guatemalan guerrilla leaders who were both trained in the United States counter-guerrilla schools in Panama.

It is rare, except in Central America, for old-style coups to be staged irrespective of popular feeling. Central to one theory of the military rising is the view that coups ought to be bloodless and for this public opinion must be tested carefully and only when it is favourable can a coup be risked (as seems to have been the case, for example, in Argentina in June 1966).

However, various measures are open to civilian governments to guard against military intervention. The army can be disbanded, but this presupposes defeat in war—as in the Costa Rican civil war of 1948 or as with the Bolivian and Cuban revolutions. In these cases the old professional armies were replaced by new revolutionary armies which created their own problems. In Cuba the early anarchical rebel army was gradually replaced by an efficient highly trained army in which the official party is strongly entrenched and which now constitutes one of the main foci of power. In Bolivia the army was reconstituted in 1953 to counterbalance the armed miners' militia, but in spite of efforts to apply a selective entry system to the officer corps and setting up party cells the MNR was unable to keep its loyalty.

In the absence of defeat in war governments must look to other means of control such as counterbalancing forces of militias or militarised police. However, this often provokes what it is designed to prevent. In Guatemala President Jacobo Arbenz's attempt to set up a militia (1950–3) was a factor in turning the army against him: in Argentina the army acted in September 1955 to forestall Perón creating a militia based on the trade unions. In Honduras Ramón Villeda Morales was overthrown in 1963 because the army feared he was going to use the National Guard as a party militia. Similarly, President Federico Chavez's attempt to militarise the police in Paraguay was a factor in bringing about the army coup of 1954.

Fomenting inter-service rivalry is another technique of countering the military. Inter-service rivalry is implicit in the structure of armed forces, but where they languish in occupational idleness this rivalry is exacerbated.

Armies resent the enormous budgetary allocations for expensive air forces and there may even be social friction between more generally conservative navies and the army. President Frondizi of Argentina, for example, fomented inter-service rivalries as a means of preventing united military action against him.

Generally speaking, navies and air forces tend to be less involved than armies in politics. This may be a consequence of their higher technical demands or a more conservative recruitment pattern and because they do not become embroiled to the same extent as the army in keeping public order; or, as with the Chilean navy, it may be felt that a refusal to be politically involved enhances the prestige of the service. Also, of course, navy and air forces' striking power is limited. The vulnerability of air-bases to ground attack is one reason why the aircraft-carrier issue has loomed so large in internal Brazilian and Argentine military politics. Marine corps, in the penumbra between naval and military control, tend to be especially sensitive politically and may spearhead revolts as they did at Puerto Cabello and Carupano in Venezuela. On a few occasions air forces have played a key role, for example in Ecuador (where the air force has been built up against Peru) in 1961 when it foiled an army coup to oust President Arosemena and, most notably, in Argentina where the air force was an important factor in the overthrow of Perón and in the complex politics of 1962–3.

More effective in controlling the military, because less compromising, are those administrative techniques which have been used with great success in Mexico. President Lázaro Cárdenas actually incorporated the military into the official party in the 1930s but this was soon replaced by more informal but effective techniques such as the rapid rotation of commands, appointment to non-military cabinet ranks, and seconding generals to party posts. Military service can in fact be a prelude to high party office. It is usual for the head of the PRI (Partido Revolucionario Institucional) to be an ex-general. In Brazil, where officers have for long been seconded to civilian posts, especially in state concerns, civilian life has become honeycombed by army officers who thus acquire a vested interest in perpetuating a particular form of government.

International Implications

Latin America's armed forces may seem to be little more than expensive prestige symbols, soaking up one-fifth of the continent's total annual budget, but there is little likelihood of their being reduced. The prime purpose of any army is the defence of national sovereignty and this, in spite of feelings of continental solidarity, is still a function which cannot be ignored. Inter-state conflicts remain a possibility so long as frontier disputes are unresolved. Although war seems a remote possibility a balance of power operates in the southern half of the continent with armament increases of one power being matched by its neighbour's.

An additional factor is the interest of the United States in the strengthening of Latin America's military forces, not against external aggression but against internal subversion. Hence United States lukewarmness towards purchases of prestige military hardware such as aircraft carriers for Brazil or Argentina and jet bombers for Ecuador. President Kennedy's warnings against predatory militarism went unheeded. Military budgets go on rising and intervention has continued. Arms provided by the United States for counter-subversion can equally well be used against the military's rivals.

In the 1920s and 1930s the military's scorn for parliamentary democracy was attributed to the influence of German and Italian military missions; the United States missions that have succeeded these have failed to produce democratic attitudes in the military.

The United States' short-lived policy of witholding or delaying recognition from unconstitutional regimes has failed to prevent coups, nor have threats to cut off economic aid had much success. Military regimes, as the Brazilian case showed, can degenerate into simple anti-communism, but this is not to say that they are the pawns of the State Department, as left-wing propaganda so readily assumes. In many ways and in a number of countries, the military is emerging as a coherent nationalist force. Ultimately, whatever its motives or aims, the military thinks itself indispensable to United States foreign policy. Until this is no longer true the risks of intervention must seem worth taking.

BIBLIOGRAPHY

Germani, G. and Silvert, K. H. 'Politics, Social Structure and Military Intervention in Latin America', *Archives européenes de sociologie*, II, 1, Paris, 1961.

Imaz, J. L. de. 'Las fuerzas armadas', *Los que mandan*, Editorial Universitaria, Buenos Aires, 2nd ed. 1965.

Johnson, J. J. *The Military and Society in Latin America*, Stanford Univ. Press, Stanford, Calif., 1964.

Johnson, J. J. (ed.) *The Role of the Military in Underdeveloped Countries*, Princeton Univ. Press, Princeton, NJ, 1962.

Lieuwen, E. *Arms and Politics in Latin America*, Frederick A. Praeger, New York, 1961; Pall Mall Press, London, 1963. *Generals versus Presidents*, Pall Mall Press, London; Frederick A. Praeger, New York, 1964.

MacAlister, Lyle. 'The Military', *Continuity and Change in Latin America*, ed. J. J. Johnson, Stanford Univ. Press, Stanford, Calif., 1965.

BACKGROUND TO MILITARY COUPS IN LATIN AMERICAN COUNTRIES

Country	Head of state removed since inauguration of Alliance for Progress	Nature of coup	Defence expenditure as % of national budget (1964)	US military aid 1950–64 ($ million)	Last military coup	Unconstitutional changes since 1930 (military coups in brackets)	Size of armed forces (1964)	Comments
Argentina	Arturo Frondizi (29/3/62)	Military coup installed Vice-Pres. Mario Guido; elections returned Illia on 12/10/63	15·6	13·6	1966	8 (5)	Army 85,000 (5,000 officers, 15,000 NCOs) Navy 33,000	Inter-service rivalry an important factor in military politics
	Arturo Illia (28/6/66)	Military coup installed General Juan Carlos Ongania as President. No announcement on elections						Gendarmerie under Ministry of Defence
Bolivia	Victor Paz Estenssoro (6/11/64)	Military coup forced Paz Estenssoro to flee. Vice-President General Rene Barrientos (air force) headed a military junta. Confirmed in power by elections in July 1966	10·6	10·9	1964	10 (9)	Army c. 30,000	Miners and peasants militia; also carabineros (militarised police). In theory these counter-balance each other. Failure of MNR celulas armadas to keep army's loyalty

BACKGROUND TO MILITARY COUPS IN LATIN AMERICAN COUNTRIES

Country	Head of state removed since inauguration of Alliance for Progress	Nature of coup	Defence expenditure as % of national budget (1964)	US military aid 1950–64 ($ million)	Last military coup	Unconstitutional changes since 1930 (military coups in brackets)	Size of armed forces (1964)	Comments
Brazil	João Goulart (1/4/64)	Forced out by military/civilian rising. Congress elected Marshal Humberto Castello Branco (9/4/64)	11·4	186·9	1964	5 (3)	Army c. 200,000 Navy 42,700 Air force 30,000	
Chile	—	—	11·0	74·3	1932	6 (2)	Army 21,500 Navy 13,900	Carabineros under Ministry of Interior
Colombia	—	—	15·3	55 3	1957	3 (1)	Army 60,000 Navy 7,800	Army deployed against rural bandits and guerrillas
Costa Rica	—	—	3·9	1·8	1948	2 (–)	Army abolished 1948; Civil Guard 1,200	
Cuba	—	—	n.a.	—	1952	8 (3)	c. 150,000	Communist party strongly entrenched in the armed forces

BACKGROUND TO MILITARY COUPS IN LATIN AMERICAN COUNTRIES

Country	Head of state removed since inauguration of Alliance for Progress	Nature of coup	Defence expenditure as % of national budget (1964)	US military aid 1950–64 ($ million)	Last military coup	Unconstitutional changes since 1930 (military coups in brackets)	Size of armed forces (1964)	Comments
Dominican Republic	Joaquín Balaguer (16/1/62)	Military seized power: Council of State organised under Dr Rafael Bonnelly at the end of Jan. '62 and governed till Juan Bosch inaugurated President in Feb. '63 after winning elections in Dec. '62	—	12·1	1965	5 (4)	Army 12,000 Navy 3,500	Air force controlled tanks—legacy of Trujillo
	Juan Bosch (25/9/63)	Military seized power and set up 3-man civilian junta under Donald Reid						
	Donald Reid (24/4/65)	Military revolt overthrew junta: succeeded by interregnum until provisional government headed by García Godoy (3/9/65)						
Ecuador	Carlos Julio Arosemena (11/7/63)	Military seized power: government by 5-man junta. Resigned under popular pressure on 29/3/66	10·7	29·6	1963	11 (8)	Army n.a. Navy 3,700	

375

BACKGROUND TO MILITARY COUPS IN LATIN AMERICAN COUNTRIES

Country	Head of state removed since inauguration of Alliance for Progress	Nature of coup	Defence expenditure as % of national budget (1964)	US military aid 1950–64 ($ million)	Last military coup	Unconstitutional changes since 1930 (military coups in brackets)	Size of armed forces (1964)	Comments
El Salvador	—	—	9·7	3·8	1961 (Jan.)	6 (5)	Army c. 2,500	Strong reformist wing in the army associated with President Rivera
Guatemala	Miguel Ydigoras Fuentes (30/3/63)	Overthrown by Defence Minister Col. Enrique Peralta who handed over after elections to Dr Julio Méndez Montenegro on 5/5/66	10·9	8·7	1963	8 (7)	Army c. 8,000	Army deployed against guerrillas
Haiti	—	—	n.a.	3·4	1957	7 (5)	La Force Armée d'Haiti c. 5,000 (directly under President) Army 1,100 Élite Presidential Guard 300	

BACKGROUND TO MILITARY COUPS IN LATIN AMERICAN COUNTRIES

Country	Head of state removed since inauguration of Alliance for Progress	Nature of coup	Defence expenditure as % of national budget (1964)	US military aid 1950–64 ($ million)	Last military coup	Unconstitutional changes since 1930 (military coups in brackets)	Size of armed forces (1964)	Comments
Honduras	Ramón Villeda Morales (3/10/63)	Overthrown by military. Election of Constituent Assembly on 16/2/65 confirmed Nationalists in power under Col. Osvaldo Lopez	—	3·6	—	3 (2)	Army 2,500	
Mexico	—	—	9·6	1·2	1924 (unsuccessful)	—	Army 51,000 Navy 6,200 Air force 5,000	Ex-generals commonly head of PRI
Nicaragua	—	—	15·4	6·6	—	3 (2)	National Guard 5,500	Somoza dynasty still an active political force
Panama	—	—	n.a.	n.a.	1955	5 (1)	National Police 3,500 (no army)	Site of US counter-guerrilla training school for Latin American officers
Paraguay	—	—	27·5	3·6	1954	7 (6)	n.a.	General Stroessner still in power supported by the military

BACKGROUND TO MILITARY COUPS IN LATIN AMERICAN COUNTRIES

Country	Head of state removed since inauguration of Alliance for Progress	Nature of coup	Defence expenditure as % of national budget (1964)	US military aid 1950–64 ($ million)	Last military coup	Unconstitutional changes since 1930 (military coups in brackets)	Size of armed forces (1964)	Comments
Peru	Manuel Prado (18/6/62)	Overthrown by military: junta rule for one year. Power handed over to Fernando Belaúnde after elections in June 1963	20·5	66·8	1962	5 (4)	Army 30,000 Navy 7,200 Police 18,000	Strong Nasserist influence in Colegio de Altos Estudios Militares. Some guerrilla activity
Uruguay	—	—	7·6	32·9	1933	1	n.a.	
Venezuela	—	—	10·7	3·7	1958	5 (3)	Army 15,000 Marines 2,500 Navy 3,200 National Guard under Defence Ministry 10,000	By the Betancourt Doctrine Venezuela refuses to recognise any government which has come to power by force

Note: Under the Alliance for Progress the United States paid for 6 per cent of Latin America's military expenditure in 1964, plus budgetary support under the economic aid section, but it is unknown what was used for military purposes. In 1964, 52 per cent of US military aid went in internal security; 24 per cent in naval defence; 15 per cent in civil action; 9 per cent in training.

Sources: *Inter American Economic Affairs*: 'US Dept of State Review of Illegal and Unscheduled Changes in Heads of State, 1930–65', XIX, 4, spring 1966; J. Fred Rippy, 'Latin America's post-war *Golpes de Estado*', XIX, 3, winter 1965; Simon G. Hanson, 'The Alliance for Progress, The Third Year: Military', XVIII, 4, winter 1964; *The Statesman's Year Book* 1965–6, London, 1965

STUDENTS IN POLITICS

ALISTAIR HENNESSY

STUDENTS AS A POLITICAL FORCE

SCARCELY a day passes without a student riot or demonstration somewhere in Latin America. Superficially, this turbulence may appear as irresponsible or misguided enthusiasm but in reality it is a complex phenomenon—the result of sharpening tensions in disturbed societies which compel students to turn to political action with a fervour compounded of opportunism, social malaise and genuine idealism.

Politicised students are a fact of life in underdeveloped countries. Lagging economies, social structures which are either too rigid or too fluid, restricted job opportunities, the caution and ineffectiveness of older generation politicians are factors which turn many students into political agitators. The academic inadequacies of many large Latin American universities where personal contacts with professors are rare and where syllabuses may appear irrelevant or out-of-date are additional frustrations. Often the absence of extra-curricular activities and poor sports facilities leave politics as the only prestigious student occupation.

In societies with high illiteracy rates students, as the recipients of higher education, have both high élite expectations and see themselves as the pace-makers of social change. Where alternative pressure groups, such as trade unions, are weak or concerned with purely sectional interests, students can have an important role to play, voicing the aspirations of the inarticulate and unorganised masses Where also there is only an attenuated form of parliamentary opposition, or perhaps no legal opposition at all, demonstrations by student organisations are often the only public expression of dissentient opinion.

Thus in Latin America student organisations have an established place in society and have become a political force which governments ignore at their peril. What is so striking about their political activities and marks them off from similar examples elsewhere are the built-in traditions which, since early in the century, have encouraged students to regard themselves as the shock troops of revolution. Student political organisations have been the nurseries of national politicians and parties such as Peru's APRA, Venezuela's Acción Democrática (AD), Cuba's 26th July Movement or Chile's Christian Democrats have had their origins in student groups. Although isolated examples of politicised students may be found in the 19th century—such as in the resistance to Venezuela's Gúzman Blanco in the 1880s—the crucial date which marks the beginning of a new self-conscious militant stage of their activity is 1918, when students at the Argentinian university of Córdoba instituted the University Reform movement.

379

THE UNIVERSITY REFORM MOVEMENT

By the beginning of the 20th century Latin American universities were badly in need of reform. Many had been founded during the colonial period but in spite of changes they still tended to be dominated by a colonial mentality. Their function was to prepare the sons of the wealthy for the élite professions of medicine and the law. The democratic element in university government—inherited from the medieval Bologna and Salamanca tradition, whereby a university was a corporation of professors, graduates and students—had lapsed and power had become concentrated in the hands of tight academic oligarchies. 'Up to now', in the words of the Córdoba manifesto, 'Universities have been the secular refuge of mediocrity, the salary of ignorance, the safe hospital for all intellectual invalids'.[1] However, it was only when the sons of an expanding middle class began to enter universities in greater numbers that the contrast between outworn institutions and the needs of society were brought into the open. It was in Argentina where the middle class had expanded most rapidly and at Córdoba, the oldest of Argentinian universities untouched by the winds of change, where the dichotomy was most marked.

In 1918 students at Córdoba formulated the principles on which the Reform movement was based. The two basic reforms were the recognition of the autonomy of the university with regard to its internal affairs and the principle of *co-gobierno* whereby students should have one third representation on faculty boards. This was held to be a valuable safeguard against the vested interests of professors. Thus students came to have a share in the academic decisions and elections to academic posts. Other principles included optional attendance at classes, free competition for chairs, freedom of instruction and the linking of universities to society by means of extension classes. Within two years the Radical government of Hipólito Irigoyen, representing the new middle classes, had passed a University Statute implementing and extending the reforms to other universities.

In a few years the Reform had swept through Latin America. In 1919 it was initiated at San Marcos University in Lima and at Montevideo, and in 1920 the Reform began in Chile. In 1921 the first International Students' Congress was held in Mexico City; in 1923 Havana joined the Reform; in 1928 Bolivia; in 1929 Paraguay. This remarkable expansion showed that the Reform struck a responsive chord among a frustrated student generation. Success was not due entirely to its university implications but also to the reformists' assertion of a new Latin American nationalism. They believed the first world war had destroyed Europe's claim to be the leader of world civilisation and thus they consciously rejected European models. The Reform movement was therefore one aspect of the new nationalistic surge of the 1920s which followed in the wake of the Mexican Revolution when *indigenismo* became an inspiration for intellectuals like Juan Carlos Mariátegui in Peru and Franz Tamayo in Bolivia. The continental scale of the new nationalism revived the Bolivarian ideal of a confederation of Latin American republics which would resist foreign encroachments. Anti-imperialism was built into reformist ideology: rejuvenated universities, producing a new generation of dedicated students, would be the means by which the continental ideals of the liberators would be made a reality.

[1] *University Reform in Latin America*, COSEC, Leiden, 1961, p. 8.

POLITICAL IMPLICATIONS OF THE REFORM

From the beginning of the Reform movement there was a division between those who wished to limit reform to university matters and those who argued that university problems could not be solved in a vacuum without reference to wider social and economic conditions. As a privileged group students had a duty towards society. At first this was expressed in extension classes— the *universidades populares* of González Prada in Lima or the José Martí schools in Havana, teaching workers to read and write; this 'social duty' soon broadened into political support as well—in Peru, for example, for the eight-hour movement. Thus student organisations came to be more than mere trade unions selfishly defending students' interest and developed into active political pressure groups.

Whereas in Argentina the Reform was largely a consequence of political change, elsewhere in countries lacking a dynamic middle-class party like the Radicals the situation was different. Where reform was successful the contrast between the 'democratic university republic' and an undemocratic national political system bred tensions between the two. In Peru this was especially true during the dictatorship of Augusto Leguía in the 1920s. In 1924 Victor Raúl Haya de la Torre, who had been president of the San Marcos student federation at the time of reform in 1919, founded the APRA party which until the 1960s drew much of its strength from the universities. Once in control of a university, Reformers could criticise governments from the inviolability of the campus. In the late 1920s, and even more so in the post-Depression years of the early 1930s, universities were often in open conflict with governments. In Cuba, where the Federación de Estudiantes Universitarios (FEU) waged a campaign against Machado, the university was closed down (1930–3). In Venezuela, where the Reform was inoperative until the 1940s, students of the 'Generation of 1928', including later Presidents Betancourt and Leoni, spearheaded the attack on the Gómez dictatorship.

A new cycle of military coups after 1930 brought students into the centre of politics. The Communists, for example, who at first had looked askance at the Reform as a bourgeois movement, began to see the importance of the university as an inviolable base and students as an untapped source for political activists; under their influence reformist ideology took on a general Marxist hue. Other parties too recognised the importance of having student affiliates. 'Professional students' now came to play an increasingly important part in university politics. Usually but not necessarily leftist and subsidised by parties, their career spanned several university generations, their function being to stage demonstrations, manage student elections and to recruit able students for active political careers. National parties now had an interest in student elections, fought on political rather than merely student issues. These elections were commonly regarded as being free from government pressure and hence a more genuine reflection of a party's real strength than the frequently rigged national elections.

ORGANISATION OF STUDENT GROUPS

The basic unit in Latin American universities is the Faculty, which enjoys a much greater independence than is usual in Britain. The annual election to the student faculty committees is the central political event of the year. These committees then elect members to the university student body which is thus a federation of faculty representatives. Students also elect representatives to the faculty boards and to other bodies such as Senate and Assembly (generally one-third representation—half in Bolivia and Honduras), keep a watching brief over students' interests and represent their views on such matters as syllabus alterations. Although faculty boards are primarily concerned with academic considerations, issues having political implications (such as rectorial elections) can bring together like-minded professors and students. Entrance and weeding-out examinations are particularly sensitive issues. Reformists have always regarded any attempt to introduce entrance examinations, over and above the ordinary matriculation requirements, as a reactionary class measure which penalises poorer students from inferior state secondary schools. Weeding-out exams are also resisted, as the main casualties from these are the ageing 'professional' students whose academic abilities may be very low.

The political colour of different faculties varies although law, economics, and philosophy and letters tend to be radical. Faculties with a high proportion of women, such as dentistry and education, tend to be conservative. It is difficult to generalise about medicine and engineering, but once these faculties are politicised the cohesion of their students can make them a very effective political force.

METHODS OF STUDENT ACTION

Strikes and demonstrations are the main way in which students try to exert their influence and impress their views on governments and the public. They tend to show most solidarity when acting against university authorities over academic matters or agitating for an increased budgetary allocation for the universities. Thus a communist-sponsored strike over an academic issue will probably receive more support than one called for a political purpose.

Students demonstrate to arouse sympathy for their own demands, to express solidarity with oppressed groups at home or abroad, to protest against injustices and with the express purpose of embarrassing the government. Students may spark off and lead demonstrations over local public grievances, such as the ubiquitous riots in response to increases in public transport fares (of which those of 1957 in Santiago and of 1958 in Mexico City are notable examples).

Anti-Americanism is a frequent motive behind demonstrations, particularly over issues like intervention in the Dominican Republic. In a sense students now constitute a new International—leaders are constantly going abroad to conferences and this has contributed to a growing sense of international solidarity—an added factor in making governments take student demonstrations seriously. Close relations have been cultivated with the communist-dominated International Union of Students, which has a lavish scholarship and financial aid programme. Equally, Catholic students are internationally oriented, not only in Latin America itself where the Organización Relacionadora de Movimientos Estudiantiles Universitarios (ORMEU) trains student leaders in Santiago but also in the close contacts between Latin American and European Christian Democrats. Because of the built-in anti-Americanism of the reformist tradition and of CIA activities contacts with United States organisations are often suspect.

Deliberate provocation of the police, as has happened at Caracas, to compel them to violate the university's autonomy is a frequently used tactic to rally popular opinion. These public demonstrations attract non-student support, which often makes them difficult to control. Opposition elements have an interest in raising the level of violence in order to provoke police brutality and so build up public indignation. If the army has to intervene it may exact a price and even replace the government. The movement to overthrow Paz Estenssoro in Bolivia in 1964 was sparked off by student riots which, by getting out of control, gave the army the justification to intervene. The effectiveness of these demonstrations is closely related to the siting of universities. Thus it is difficult to mount a demonstration in Mexico City from the university site on the outskirts whereas Lima and Santiago are more vulnerable, with universities strategically sited in the city centre. Until recently the metropolitan universities tended to be the most politicised, but there is now a marked tendency for provincial universities (which are often starved of money and talent) to become vocal centres of political agitation. In areas where there is a depressed peasantry and where students are recruited locally this can have important repercussions, as at Cuzco and Ayacucho in Peru.

EFFECTIVENESS OF STUDENT ACTION

In the more stable and traditional societies student influence tends to be minimal. Students may be vociferous but there is no substantial body of opinion waiting to be led or prepared to take up their cause. The most active students in Haiti and Paraguay, for example, are in exile and even in Honduras the ruling Nationalist Party is careful to make sure its sympathisers have control of the Student Federation.

Where a process of modernisation is beginning, as in El Salvador, the Dominican Republic, Ecuador or Peru, students are influential as social innovators and are often important in the formative phases of new parties, but this importance diminishes as the process of bureaucratisation and unionisation increases. Where, as in Panama, there is an absence of clearly defined parties students can be a very effective pressure group—as in the anti-US demonstrations over the Canal Zone issue.

In more complex societies like Venezuela and Colombia undergoing rapid industrialisation, with its attendant social dislocation, students are extremely vocal but as they are forced to compete with other organised interest groups such as trade unions their influence tends to be limited. In some countries, such as El Salvador and Bolivia, students may even be competing with strong reformist elements in the army. They can nevertheless still be influential in sparking off revolts, but where issues are not clear-cut or where public opinion fails to respond, their narrow social base makes it difficult for them to retain the initiative, which tends to pass to the military as in Cuba in 1934 or Bolivia in 1964. Although rapid industrialisation may cause acute social tensions and exacerbate inter-generational conflicts the opportunities afforded by an expanding economy drain off many students into new technical professions, often leaving academic laggards or those in overcrowded faculties as the most vocal political activists.

In those countries where institutional and political complexity has reached a high level, as in Mexico, Brazil or Argentina, students have been reduced to a comparatively unimportant interest group. In spite of the fact that Argentine students played a key role in overthrowing Perón they are now politically ineffectual in spite of their numbers (Buenos Aires has about 70,000) and the last big demonstration—in 1958—failed to prevent the legalisation of private Roman Catholic universities. In 1966 seven separate 'lines' could be identified in Buenos Aires University and within each of these there were a variety of different groupings. In Mexico both a booming economy and a highly organised official party have considerably reduced student influence, although poorly endowed provincial universities are still politically disturbed. The riots of April 1966 in which the rector, Dr Ignacio Chavez, was compelled to resign under student threats was partly a result of the rector's attempts to tighten academic standards and to whittle down an overexpanded law faculty. The political significance of what, even by Latin American standards, was a disgraceful situation lay in the refusal of the government to back the rector against the students' revolt—for what reason remains obscure.

PRESENT TRENDS

The most notable feature of student politics over the past ten years has been the decline of the democratic left. In Venezuela Acción Democrática has virtually no student following; the Peruvian APRA, once the most militant of all student groups, is a shadow of its former self, unable to hold its own in either San Marcos or even in Trujillo in the 'solid APRA north'. Elsewhere too the democratic left has had its following eroded by new militant Castroist groups. The importance of the Cuban Revolution as an influence on student political groupings cannot be emphasised too strongly. An authentic Latin American revolution, enhancing Latin America's importance in world politics, embarrassing the United States, it had a compulsive attraction for the younger nationalists, especially as the rapid rate of Cuban social (and particularly educational) change contrasted with societies elsewhere lacking a dynamic drive.

Students have always played an important part in Cuban history. Havana University was a focus of nationalist feeling against Spanish rule in the 1870s and from the foundation of the FEU in 1923 they were Machado's most bitter opponents. In 1933 they played a prominent part in Grau San Martín's government until it was overthrown by Batista's coup. In the 1950s they once again spearheaded the revolt against an unpopular dictatorship. Batista's overthrow seemed to confirm and justify the students' traditional conception of themselves as a revolutionary élite. A novel feature of the Cuban revolutionary movement of the 1950s was that students and radical intellectuals became guerrilla leaders whereas in the 1920s and 1930s they had been urban terrorists. So long as the educational system is unable to absorb or satisfy the expanding student population universities will be a fertile breeding ground for guerrilla activists. Revolutionary parties, failing to make much headway amongst industrial workers or the urban masses, see a depressed peasantry as the potential revolutionary force of the future with middle-class *déraciné* students as the shapers of the formless protest of rural revolt—as has happened in Venezuela, Peru and to a lesser extent in Central America and Colombia. However, the Sino-Soviet conflict, which has had wide repercussions among Latin American Communist parties over the question of revolutionary strategy, has affected the Communists' student affiliates as well.

In opposition to the Castroite groups which are ousting the declining democratic left throughout Latin America are the radical Christian Democrats. In Venezuela COPEI students are the main challengers of the communist left, whilst the Chilean Christian Democrats have dominated the universities since the late 1950s. Both had their origins in student groups formed in the mid-1930s and draw much of their inspiration from the French liberal Catholic tradition. Students play a similar role in the formative phase of the Christian Democrat parties as they did earlier with the democratic left.

It is comparatively easy to enlist students for an oppositional role but it is difficult for parties to carry their student affiliates with them in the transition to a ruling or established party. AD and APRA both failed to make the adjustment and now national Christian Democrat parties find they are being pushed harder than they might wish by their radical student groups.

Right-wing parties have made remarkably little impact among Latin American students. Conservatism is expressed by abstention from student politics—hence the attempt of recent government laws in Brazil and Ecuador to compel students to vote and thus whittle down the dominance of the left. Fascist groups (which had a strong influence among European students in the 1930s) have failed to get more than marginal support, as have the Mexican Sinarquistas (the peasant right-wing movement founded in the 1930s), the Chilean Nazis or the right-wing, anti-semitic Tacuara group in Argentina today. The mass populist parties of Perón and Vargas could rally little student support—in the end students played a crucial role in overthrowing Perón; and it was under Vargas that students in Brazil (who had previously been less politicised than in Spanish America) became politically conscious and a focus of opposition to the Vargas regime.

Conclusion

The reformist tradition has conditioned the attitude of Latin American students to politics. The view which sees them as a regenerating élite is rooted in the myth of the incorruptibility of youth. As Latin America's population gets younger—and already it is one of the youngest in the world—the importance of students will increase. An outworn university structure, reflecting values which have little relevance to development needs, has been and still is a major spur to political involvement. Although many universities are being reformed, academic reforms in a political university inevitably have political repercussions. The view that university reform is impossible without a full-scale social revolution still commands wide assent. Many students are convinced that universities need to become more not less politicised, arguing that without a political university as the guarantor of revolutionary change political reform at the national level will remain a chimera. Until this belief is exorcised by visible structural changes students will continue to play a role in politics which no government can afford to ignore.

BIBLIOGRAPHY

Del Mazo, G. *Estudiantes y gobierno universitario*, Libreria El Ateneo, Buenos Aires, 1955.
Hennessy, A. 'Students and National Politics', *The Politics of Conformity in Latin America*, ed. Claudio Véliz, Oxford Univ. Press, London and New York. 1967.
Lipset, S. M. (ed.) 'Student Politics', Special Number, *Comparative Education Review*, June 1966. Published in book form, Basic Books, New York, 1967.
Silvert, K. H. 'The University Student', *Continuity and Change in Latin America*, ed. J. J. Johnson, Stanford Univ. Press, Stanford, Calif., 1965.
University Reform in Latin America, COSEC, Leiden, 1961.

THE WORKING CLASS IN POLITICS

TORCUATO S. DI TELLA

THE strength of the working class varies considerably from country to country in Latin America. No generalisation is possible in a continent which includes such extremes of poverty and wealth as peasant Paraguay or Ecuador, industrial São Paulo or Monterrey, urban Buenos Aires or Santiago. Nor is it possible to attempt the easy explanation that it is the more developed parts of the area where the working class shows more strength. Miners in Bolivia demand more attention from the government and the military than the low degree of economic progress of the country would lead us to expect. Chilean trade unions exhibit an amount of political organisation above that of their wealthier counterparts in Argentina.

To understand the present situation of the working class in Latin America it is convenient to establish a typology of countries based on two criteria: the kind of physical or industrial concentration prevalent for most of the urban workers, and the possibilities of social mobility—that is, the chances a worker has of becoming a member of the middle class.

FORM OF CONCENTRATION OF THE WORKING POPULATION

At one extreme are small urban centres situated in a fundamentally rural country, where the working class is sparsely distributed over the whole area. In these small urban centres it is possible to find some skilled workers and craftsmen, with little trade union tradition, and somewhat larger numbers of unskilled labourers in the tertiary sector, equally difficult to organise. In a structure of this type, social conflicts are unlikely to result in a labour movement with an expression of its own, whether through trade unions or political parties. The main conflicts are likely to take place at another social level, as between sectors of the upper or the middle class (landowners v. industrial or commercial bourgeoisie, conservatives v. liberals, etc.). At the other extreme are large industrial urban concentrations with a working class organised in large unions and typically working in large factories. Under these conditions social mobility is high, especially through education, which tends to produce a high degree of social consensus and conflict legitimation. The conflicts between the organised working class and the mass of the middle and upper classes, though legitimised, assume a central role in this type of society.

What has been called the 'isolated mass' constitutes an intermediate situation. This exists where there are large concentrations of workers isolated from the main urban centres, where a homogeneous working class emerges around extractive or mining industries. Such workers are generally not highly skilled (though sometimes they may be highly paid in comparison with workers in the rest of the country), and have little contact with other social classes, since there are few middle-class individuals in isolated mining areas. Social mobility is low, and there is a common identification of the workers of the area against the 'rest of society', perceived as distant and hostile. The labour market is often unstable, and this has a particularly strong effect owing to the absence of alternative sources of employment in the area. Group or community solidarity fuses with union solidarity, giving rise to a pattern of sharp social antagonisms. In general the environment has little cult-ural diversification, on account of the absence of activities generally managed by middle-class individuals. The emotional charge that permeates the conflicts is particularly strong in such cases. The 'isolated mass' situation may obtain not only when there is actual physical, geographical isolation, but also when certain aspects of the work determine a marked social isolation notwithstanding physical proximity: for instance, meat-packing workers (even when in large cities) and longshoremen. The same is the case when the ethnic composition of the working class is markedly different from that of the economically highest groups.

If we attempt to classify the Latin American countries according to these criteria, we find that each of them presents diverse situations, classifiable in at least two of the categories stated above. The following rough categories may serve to distinguish one country from another.

Countries with large urban-industrial concentrations. Only Argentina, Brazil and Mexico may be included in this category, by virtue of the importance of their big cities in the determination of the nature of social relations in their whole urban sectors. This is not to say that social tensions are equal in all parts of the urban sector in each of these countries, nor that these large concentrations are characterised by a homogeneous situation. The classifica-tion is merely a simplifying one, whose usefulness must be tested by finding out whether it is correlated with other important social phenomena.

Countries without large urban-industrial concentrations, but with important 'isolated mass' situations. In this group we may include Bolivia (for the concen-trations of workers around the exploitation of tin), Peru (mining, sugar), Chile (copper, saltpetre, partly coal and meat-packing), Venezuela (petroleum), Cuba and the Dominican Republic (sugar).

Countries with a low degree of industrial concentration. This category includes Colombia, Ecuador, Uruguay, Paraguay, Haiti and the Central American countries. This category, being fundamentally residual, is perhaps more heterogeneous than the preceding ones. Some of these countries (e.g. Colombia) have a rapid rate of industrial expansion, though this represents only an incipient growth which, further, is distributed among several middle-sized cities instead of being concentrated in a single large city. Others (e.g. Uruguay) are highly urbanised, but have relatively little industry and are largely dependent upon rural production.

SOCIAL MOBILITY

Social mobility has, as is well known, a great influence in shaping working-class attitudes. It may be stated that in general social mobility tends to diminish the intensity of conflicts between the working class and the middle or upper classes. It tends to increase the degree of satisfaction with the existing social order. The size of the middle class as a percentage of the total population may be t.ken as a measure of social mobility in Latin American countries; *ceteris paribus*, this figure gives an idea of the possibilities of social ascent for the working class.

We may use for this purpose data compiled by Gino Germani[1]. Taking the percentage of total population formed by the urban and rural middle and upper strata, and using psychological and cultural criteria of the middle class, he forms a first category of countries which includes Argentina, Uruguay, Chile and Costa Rica. These are the typical 'middle-class countries' of Latin America. To differentiate the rest, characterised simply by the lesser importance of the middle class, we shall here consider the middle class percentage of the total urban population (countries having a small overall middle class may in more developed regions or in the urban sector of the population—which is a first approximate measurement of the 'developed sector'—have a high proportion of middle class): see Table 1.

TABLE 1

URBAN MIDDLE CLASS IN SELECTED COUNTRIES (c. 1950)

	Percentage urban middle class over total urban population		Percentage urban middle class over total urban population
Argentina	38	Chile	30
Mexico	37	Colombia	28
Cuba	36	Venezuela	27
Brazil	35	Ecuador	21
Costa Rica	31	Paraguay	27
		Bolivia	26

Source: G. Germani, *Política y sociedad en una época de transición*, Buenos Aires, 1962.

Thus when only the urban population is considered, Brazil, Mexico and Cuba are comparable to those countries with a large middle class mentioned above. Placing Brazil, Mexico and Cuba in an intermediate category, we have the following three categories:

Countries with a large middle class: Argentina, Chile, Uruguay, Costa Rica.
Countries with a large urban middle class: Brazil, Mexico, Cuba.
Countries with a small middle class: Venezuela, Colombia, Ecuador, Peru, Bolivia, Paraguay, the Central American countries (except Costa Rica), Haiti and the Dominican Republic.

STRUCTURAL CONTEXT OF THE WORKING CLASS IN LATIN AMERICA

To construct a typology of this type, we combine the first of the foregoing criteria—the form of concentration of the working class—with the second one—the possibilities of social mobility as measured by the percentage of middle class. We obtain the cross-classification shown in Table 2.

Passing from upper left to lower right we go in the direction of increasing development. Is it possible to establish any empirical correlations between this typology of 'structural contexts' of the working class and the union and political action of this class? The correlations that may be established will be only approximate, for several reasons. First, the number of cases is insufficient for establishing regularities, since for idiosyncratic or accidental reasons some countries may present anomalous phenomena. Secondly, the structural context only determines a field of forces favouring certain

[1] Germani, *Política y sociedad en una época de transición*, Buenos Aires, 1962.

TABLE 2

STRUCTURAL CONTEXT OF THE WORKING CLASS IN SELECTED COUNTRIES

	Countries with little urban or industrial concentration	*Countries with 'isolated mass' situations, but without large urban-industrial concentrations*	*Countries with large urban-industrial concentrations*
Countries with small middle class	Colombia, Ecuador, Paraguay, Central America (except Costa Rica), Haiti	Venezuela, Peru, Bolivia, Dominican Republic	—
Countries with large middle class in urban sector only	—	Cuba	Mexico, Brazil
Countries with large middle class	Uruguay, Costa Rica	Chile	Argentina

phenomena, not the specific occurrence of the latter. Thirdly, the action of the working class depends not only upon its own structural context, but also upon those of the other classes or élites, which may provide leadership for, or participate in, movements of which the working class is a part.

TYPES OF WORKING-CLASS ORGANISATION

We can make the following typology of Latin American countries according to the seven types of working-class organisation found (corresponding to the seven entries in Table 2).

Countries with little urban or industrial concentration and a small middle class

In Colombia, Ecuador, Paraguay, Central America (except Costa Rica) and Haiti unionism and the labour movement in general are weak. Political conflict tends to take the form of a contest between two traditional parties, generally conservative versus liberal, both handling electorates through 'bossism' (*caudillismo*) with little ideological coating and without marked charismatic features. In some cases, such as Colombia, several attempts to form movements of the 'popular nationalist' type (see under the next two headings) have typically failed.

Countries with 'isolated mass' situations, without large urban-industrial concentrations and with a small middle class

Venezuela, Peru, Bolivia and the Dominican Republic differ from the preceding countries in that they have important nuclei of working-class concentration, generally in isolated areas remote from the main urban centres. These concentrations, with a low rate of social mobility resulting from the small size of the middle class, constitute *foci* of class conflict. The working-class groups involved, however, have in general little tradition of voluntary association, little technical and educational qualification, and a way of life with many traditionalist and authoritarian elements with regard to family composition, socialisation patterns and mass-leader relations. For this reason these groups show a tendency towards sporadic and unstable action, and little ability for autonomous self-direction. This is why in these countries the labour movement finds typical expression within political structures of the type of 'popular nationalism'.

Popular nationalism is a coalition between recently mobilised masses and élites of various extractions. The formation of directing élites is important for any political movement, but especially in countries with this type of social structure, for in these cases the working-class mass has little capacity for forming its own independent associations, and therefore the élite concentrates in its hands a large part of the power (especially through charismatic leadership) and the demands for social improvement have a heavy emotional content. The formation of the popular nationalist movement, as well as its characteristics once it is formed, depend upon the social tensions existing at the level of the middle strata of society, and are therefore marginal to our present purpose. It may be mentioned, however, that such middle-class tensions perform a kind of catalytic function, for in their absence this type of working-class structural context may not result in an organised popular nationalist movement, but merely in a series of chaotic agitations.

In the countries mentioned popular nationalist movements (Aprismo in Peru, the Revolutionary Nationalist Movement in Bolivia, Acción Democrática in Venezuela and Juan Bosch's Dominican Revolutionary Party) have gained or share power, and others are in the process of formation— such as those which may emerge from the insurrectional agitation now taking place in Venezuela.

Countries with 'isolated mass' situations, without large urban-industrial concentrations, and with a large urban middle class

In Cuba also the conditions are present for the emergence of movements of the popular nationalist type. The comparatively large size of its urban middle class, however, introduces a difference, causing—*ceteris paribus*—popular nationalist movements to be more strictly centred on the rural sector. This may be a source of weakness, but also an incitement to look for new forms of struggle. The Castroist movement shows the general characteristics of popular nationalism, and the same may be said of the political structure supporting Batista at the time of his popularity. These two are very different versions of popular nationalism, but both involve strong charismatic elements in their power structure. As with the preceding category of countries, middle-class tensions provide the élites that link themselves with the working class to produce the popular nationalist movement. On the other hand, the case of Cuba is distinguished from the preceding by three elements: it is a considerably more urbanised country; university education is much more spread in relation to population; and its 'isolated mass', concentrated around the sugar mills, is a peculiar mixture of urban and rural workers with seasonal fluctuation, which helps to spread in the countryside certain behaviour patterns typical of industrialism.

Countries with little urban and industrial concentration but with a large middle class

In Uruguay and Costa Rica, which have a relatively high per capita income, the two components of the structural context that we are considering converge towards lessening the intensity of social conflict and hindering its expression in terms of class struggle. There arises a political pattern of polarisation into two typical multi-class parties, with little charismatic element, and a considerably advanced legitimation of their differences. In the two countries mentioned there has been a relatively peaceful alternation in power on the part of the two parties describable as centre-rightist and centre-leftist. This pattern differs from that seen in the first category above (Colombia, Ecuador, Paraguay, Central America, Haiti) in that the social distance between leaders and mass in political structures is shorter. On the other hand, labour unionism is more legitimised and functions as one more social pressure group with many 'contractualist'[1] features, and with ideological minorities exerting relatively little influence.

Countries with large urban-industrial concentrations and a large urban middle class

Mexico and Brazil are typical dual countries, with a highly developed 'central' region and a very underdeveloped hinterland functioning almost as an internal colony. The large reserve of cheap manpower in their rural sectors exerts a depressing influence upon industrial wages and the militancy of the urban workers. These are the two Latin American countries (apart from Puerto Rico, an obviously very special case) which have developed most rapidly in the last thirty years, as can be seen from Table 3.

TABLE 3.

INCREASE OF PER-CAPITA PRODUCT BETWEEN
1925–29 AND 1950–54 IN SELECTED COUNTRIES

Percentage ten-year increase

Argentina	9·1
Brazil	33·9
Chile	11·9
Cuba	0·2
Guatemala	−19·2 (negative)
Honduras	10·8
Mexico	33·0
Puerto Rico	30·4

Source: Bert Hoselitz, 'Economic Growth in Latin America', *Première conférence internationale d'histoire économique*, Stockholm, 1960, as reprinted in *Desarrollo económico*, II, 3, Buenos Aires, October–December 1962.

Brazil and Mexico seem to offer the conditions most favourable in Latin America for a dynamic capitalist development. The large size of the urban and 'central area' middle class gives stability to the system in its points of stress, generating currents of social mobility in the working class of industrial centres. The existence of a large reserve of rural manpower contributes to the emergence of a large internal market and weakens the unions without the need for severe repression by the political power—unlike the case of Argentina, with consequent institutional instability and lack of an atmosphere of security for business investment. The great numerical importance of the rural and in general the 'peripheral' area makes it possible to mount in it electoral machines controlled by the upper and middle strata; these classes thus gain allies in their conflicts with the urban working class, which has no such access to the rural sector. Finally, the rural sector does not accumulate

---

[1] See the definition given at the end of this chapter.

many social tensions, because there is no 'isolated mass' in important proportions, and because the dissatisfied members of the middle strata may easily emigrate to the central prosperous area, thus abandoning their potential role of protest movement leaders. According to this analysis the agitation of the Ligas Camponesas of Francisco Julião in north-east Brazil does not pose so great a threat to the status quo as would have been the case in Cuba.

All these factors contribute to the fact that in both Brazil and Mexico capitalism is very strongly established and operates a relatively modern and secure system of social control which includes the presence of integrative parties such as the Institutional Revolutionary Party (the governing party of Mexico) and its Brazilian counterpart, the coalition between the Social Democratic Party and the Labour Party (Partido Trabalhista). This coalition is an important part of the system of social control, especially when the populist coalition is in office; in many cases they have been organised by government action rather than on their own initiative. Though in any society a legitimised unionism performs certain important latent consensus-fostering functions, in cases such as those of Brazil and Mexico these functions are particularly marked and often take the form of a system characterised by union leaders with little connection with rank-and-file members and supported by government ministries or by governing political parties before the marked indifference of union members.

It should be noted that a country may pass from one category of our classification to another as a result of economic growth. Thus Brazil, particularly its central area, is approaching a situation similar to that of Argentina. The continued presence of its large rural sector, however, may be expected to delay considerably its adoption of Argentina's type of political and union system.

Countries with 'isolated mass' situations, without large urban-industrial concentrations and with a large middle class

Chile's type of structural context might produce a phenomenon of popular nationalism, the typical expression of the working class in an isolated mass situation in Latin America. However, there is a difference with respect to the previously considered cases of isolated mass—Venezuela, Peru, Bolivia, the Dominican Republic and Cuba. For the populations of these countries are mainly rural, whereas Chile is one of the most highly urbanised countries of Latin America. This high degree of urbanisation is virtually a correlative of the fact of having a large middle class, and both phenomena probably have a common underlying factor which might be termed a 'high degree of modernisation', including a high degree of urbanisation and a large middle class but not necessarily a high degree of industrialisation.

Chile's high degree of urbanisation is responsible for an intensification of communications, and thus the spread of behaviour and value patterns has originated in European centres, particularly cities, which function as positive reference groups in both the economic and cultural spheres. Furthermore, the ethnic composition of the Chilean population, which is similar to that of Argentina in this respect, makes for the rapid assimilation of European models, unlike the case of the other two large Latin American countries, Brazil and Mexico, where the tradition of semi-serfdom or slavery of the lower-class groups markedly depresses their aspirations, making them more immune to demonstration effects induced by material or cultural imports of

European or US origin. The lower classes of Mexico and Brazil do not 'have relatives' in Europe, while those of Argentina or Chile do, or believe they do.

Moreover, since the rural sector in Chile is small and relatively modernised (wine and wool production) and the merely subsistence rural economy is a much less important feature of the economic system of the country, the urban working class does not suffer the same depressing effects upon its standard of living and its militancy as in Brazil or Mexico.

All these factors contribute to make the expression of the working class in the Chilean structural context more autonomous than in the classic cases of popular nationalism, or in Brazil and Mexico with their rapid capitalist development. Its ideological orientation tends towards some form of socialism —which obtains in Chile through the electoral strength of the Marxist-oriented parties. The unions, on the other hand, have a long tradition of autonomy and struggle, and they have seldom been assisted by the state. The pattern of the labour leader-government official acting as intermediary between rank-and-file union members and the state or the governing parties does not obtain in Chile. On the contrary, its labour movement has a half-century-old tradition of militancy which is one of the most remarkable in Latin America.

Countries with large urban-industrial concentrations and a large middle class
This social structure is typical of a high degree of development. Argentina may be included in this category by comparison with the other Latin American countries. Moreover the Argentine situation has some similarity with that of the highly developed European countries, though with less industrialisation and more dependence upon external trade. This last element is important, for drastic changes in the situation of the economically dominant groups take place when there is an upheaval of the pattern of international trade, as was the case during the second world war.

In general, the structural context of the highly developed countries leads to the formation of a highly organised working class, with its own union and political expression, and consequent bipolarisation of the political spectrum. The bipolarisation is compatible, on the other hand, with a legitimation and moderation of class conflict, on account of the situation of relative prosperity and opportunities for individual social mobility. The specific forms of this political bipolarisation may vary according to the structural contexts of the other social classes. Three fundamental variants may be noted: the European model, with a political party composed and financed by workers; the United States model, with a political party concentrating the support of the working class but receiving also important support from other sections of society—with the consequence that class cleavage lines are less defined; and the Argentine Peronist model, consisting of the mass of the working class together with certain élites drawn from other social strata, resulting in a coalition of the popular nationalist type. The capacity of the working class to participate dynamically in the struggle for the distribution of the national income is fairly high in the last model. There is here an important difference with countries such as Brazil and Mexico: it is much more difficult to establish a system of adjudication and social control, for the social power, or at least the resistence or 'veto' power, is fairly widely distributed. This may easily result in a situation of 'social stalemate'.[1]

[1] A. Sturmthal, *La tragedia del movimiento obrero*, Mexico, 1945.

o

Of Argentina it might alternatively be said that the structural conditions of pluralism are fulfilled, but that the superstructural capacities required for the functioning of that complex system have not yet been developed. The unions have a long tradition in Argentina, which may be said to be the only country in Latin America to have passed from an élite unionism to a mass unionism. In the other Latin American countries unionism is either still at the stage of élite unionism (as in Chile) or was from the beginning a mass unionism (as in Brazil and Mexico) but under close government control. In Argentina, though the transition to mass unionism was favoured by the support of the Peronist government, the phenomenon tended to emerge autonomously, and took place *on the basis of already existing unions* with strong traditions of social and political activity which was not the case in Brazil or in Mexico. This accounts for the persistence of mass unionism in Argentina after the disappearance of the political power that favoured it.

CONCLUSION

In the analysis of unionism in the more developed countries of Latin America it is convenient, then, to use the following threefold classification: 'mature' élite unionism with socialist orientation—Chile; mass unionism with strong statist involvements, oriented towards what Alain Touraine has called 'legal reformism'—Brazil and Mexico; and mass unionism independent of the state and oriented towards 'contractualist reformism'—Argentina. 'Legal reformism' is the tendency to seek in the state the main means for settling labour conflicts and problems; 'contractualist reformism' is the attitude tending to rely rather on negotiations with business for solving those problems.[1]

[1] See Alain Touraine, 'Industrialisation et conscience ouvrière à São Paulo', *Sociologie du travail*, No. 4, Paris, 1961.

BIBLIOGRAPHY

Alexander, Robert J. *The Bolivian Nationalist Revolution*, Rutgers Univ. Press, New Brunswick, NJ, 1958.
Betancourt, Rómulo. *Política y petróleo*, Fondo de Cultura Económica, Mexico, 1956.
Burnett, Ben and Troncoso, Moisés Poblete. *The Rise of the Latin American Labour Movement*, College and Univ. Press, New Haven, Conn., 1962.
Edwards, Alberto. *La fronda aristocratica*, Editorial del Pacífico, Santiago, 1952.
Fluharty, Vernon. *Dance of the Millions: Military Rule and the Social Revolution in Colombia, 1930–56*, Univ. of Pittsburgh Press, Pittsburgh, Pa., 1957.
Germani, Gino. *Política y sociedad en una época de transición*, Paidós, Buenos Aires, 1962.
Kantor, Harry. *The Ideology and Programme of the Peruvian Aprista Movement*, Univ. of California Press, Berkeley, Calif., 1953.
Kerr, C. and Siegel, A. 'Interindustry Propensity to Strike', *Industrial Conflict*, ed. Kornhauser, Dubin and Ross, McGraw-Hill, London and New York, 1954.
Scott, Robert. *Mexican Government in Transition*, Univ. of Illinois Press, Urbana, Ill., 1959.
Seers, Dudley (ed.) *Cuba, the Economic and Social Revolution*, Oxford Univ. Press, London; Univ. of North Carolina Press, Chapel Hill, NC, 1964.
Sturmthal, A. *La tragedia del movimiento obrero*, Fondo de Cultura Económica, Mexico, 1945.
Taylor, Carl. *Rural Life in Argentina*, Univ. of Louisiana Press, Baton Rouge, La., 1948.
di Tella, T. *El sistema político argentino y la clase obrera*, EUDEBA, Buenos Aires, 1964.
di Tella, T., Germani, Gino and Graciarena, J. (eds.) *Argentina, sociedad de masas*, EUDEBA, Buenos Aires, 1965.
Touraine, Alain. 'Industrialisation et conscience ouvrière à São Paulo', *Sociologie du travail*, No. 4, Paris, 1961.

THE POLITICAL PROBLEMS OF LATIN AMERICAN INTEGRATION

GORDON CONNELL-SMITH

THE concept of a Latin American—or at least a Spanish American—nation is not new. It is associated with some of the great heroes of Spanish American independence, above all with Simón Bolívar. But the hopes of the Liberator and others were in vain, for independence brought fragmentation to Spain's empire in America, in ominous contrast with the subsequent expansion of the thirteen British colonies in North America to become the most powerful nation in the world. United States strength, alongside Latin American weakness, is the cardinal feature of international relations in the western hemisphere. If only in the light of this fact, it is not surprising that the idea of Latin American integration—or, as some would say, 'reintegration'—has never lacked advocates.

The story of efforts to give practical expression to this idea has been predominantly one of failure, both among the Latin American countries as a whole and in Central America, where attempts at integration in some form have been more persistent. Since the end of the second world war, however, more serious endeavours have been made to promote *economic* integration. The fruits of these endeavours, the establishment of the Latin American Free Trade Association (LAFTA) now including ten South American countries and Mexico, and the conclusion of the General Treaty of Central American Economic Integration, are described elsewhere in this volume. But—and this is especially true of LAFTA—these are only modest steps towards Latin American integration, which still remains little more than an aspiration. The path to its fulfilment is strewn with formidable political problems.

These problems fall into three categories: those relating to the internal organisation of the individual Latin American countries; those concerned with relations among the various republics; and those deriving from relations between Latin America and the United States. In the last category must be included problems arising from the existence and operation of the inter-American system: the international organisation embracing the United States and the Latin American countries, whose central institution, since its charter was adopted in 1948, has been the Organization of American States (OAS). There are significant links between these three groups of political problems.

PROBLEMS OF INTERNAL ORGANISATION

In the first place the idea of Latin American integration may be considered distinctly premature in the light of the internal organisation of most of the countries concerned. For, generally speaking, these have not yet completed

395

the process of national and social integration; they are still striving to create their national personalities in the face of regional and often racial differences, as well as tensions between social classes. Until a greater degree of unity has been achieved within the individual countries, Latin American civilian governments will lack sufficient authority to establish effective supra-national institutions of integration in the face of opposition from powerful domestic interest groups.

This would be so even if the Latin American governments, a large pro-portion of which are dominated by the military, possessed the will to bring about regional integration. There is little evidence that such is the case. Most of the leading advocates of Latin American integration in the period since the end of the second world war have been economists and other experts, not men holding high political office. An outstanding exception is President Eduardo Frei of Chile, who in January 1965 appealed to the other Latin American governments for a clear political commitment to a definite programme of integration and invited four distinguished economists to formulate specific proposals. Frei's motives and the response to his initiative will be considered presently. Meanwhile it should be noted that the Chilean president, whose election in 1964 could prove a breakthrough for the cause of economic and social advance within a democratic framework in Latin America, has yet to justify within Chile itself the high hopes placed in him.

RELATIONS BETWEEN LATIN AMERICAN COUNTRIES

Another problem is posed by the fact that, traditionally, relations among the Latin American countries have been neither intimate nor particularly friendly. Geography has imposed formidable obstacles to the development of a feeling of unity, while historical circumstances linked the Latin American countries more closely intellectually and economically to Europe than to one another. In the present century the power of the United States has made relations with it generally more important than those among the individual republics themselves. Even in the middle 1960s, when geographical obstacles have to a large extent been overcome, trade between Latin American countries, for example, still represents only some 10 per cent of their total overseas commerce.

At the same time, the development of closer cooperation between the Latin American countries has been hindered by rivalries among them. Their differing size and strength, ill-defined and frequently disputed frontiers, and the combination of internal strife and external ambition—these have all helped to foster discord. Rivalries and frontier disputes have persisted to the present day. For example, a long-standing territorial dispute between Ecuador and Peru has not only poisoned their relations with one another; it was a factor in the continued postponement of the Eleventh Inter-American Conference, which should have taken place at Quito in 1959. Again, Bolivia withdrew from the Council of the Organization of American States in 1962 and 1963 because this body failed to resolve its dispute with Chile over the waters of the River Lauca. The traditional rivalry between Argentina and Brazil is linked with the fundamental division of Latin America between the former Spanish and Portuguese empires.

Reference was made at the beginning of this chapter to the concept of a Latin American nation and to Latin American 'reintegration'. These concepts ignore the distinctive position of Brazil, which accounts for over one-third of Latin America's population, and whose policy towards integration, as the largest and most powerful of the twenty Republics, is crucial. Traditionally, Brazil has held aloof from efforts at closer cooperation initiated by Spanish American governments, and has been particularly friendly towards the United States within the wider, inter-American system. Although Brazil helped to form LAFTA and in the early 1960s followed a 'Latin American' rather than an 'inter-American' policy, the overthrow of President Goulart in April 1964 brought Brazil back to its traditional role of cooperation with the United States and away from a bid for the leadership of Latin America.

THE INFLUENCE OF THE UNITED STATES

The case of Brazil illustrates the significant influence their relations with the United States exert upon the individual Republics' relations with each other. Furthermore, the warm support given by the United States to the Brazilian government following the overthrow of President Goulart is a reminder of the influence, often decisive, which United States policy exercises upon determining the kind of governments that rule in Latin America. For these and other reasons stemming from its vast power, the attitude of the United States towards Latin American integration is of enormous significance. Obviously, with the support of the United States, prospects for integration would be greatly enhanced, while United States opposition, together with the problems of internal organisation in the individual Latin American countries and those arising from relations between them, would make Latin American integration well-nigh unattainable in the foreseeable future.

With the adoption of the Charter of Punta del Este establishing the Alliance for Progress in August 1961, the United States accepted the principle of Latin American economic integration as necessary to the economic and social development of the region. Yet the warmth of United States support must be questioned. In evaluating this, it is important to note that the initiative in fostering the economic integration of Latin America came from the United Nations, and specifically from the world body's Economic Commission for Latin America (ECLA). The United States did not favour the establishment of ECLA in 1948, and for a long time regarded its activities with suspicion. This suspicion was due partly to a feeling that ECLA was an intruder in the hemisphere, encouraging the Latin American countries to combine against the United States, and also to fears that the expansion of intra-regional trade would be detrimental to American economic interests. Like its proposal of the Alliance for Progress as a whole, United States support of economic integration seemed to stem more from a desire to prevent the spread of Castroism than from genuine conversion to Latin American ideas that it had opposed for so long.

It has been argued that Latin American integration is in the interests of the United States: that the latter's relations with an integrated Latin America would be more harmonious than the present delicate situation deriving from the great imbalance of power in the hemisphere. Moreover, such a Latin America would be less susceptible to communist influence. On the other hand, an integrated Latin America would almost certainly pursue an 'independent' policy rather than one supporting the United States to the extent that the individual countries have traditionally done; neither would it be as attractive to United States business interests. It is understandable that the United States, which has for so long benefited by possessing weak neighbours, should be a great deal less than enthusiastic in its support of developments which would strengthen them in relation to itself, and has tended to view Latin American integration as a challenge to the inter-American system.

For integration is not just a matter of increased trade and economic development, though this itself would work to redress the imbalance between the two parts of the hemisphere. It is also a matter of strengthening the countries of Latin America politically. The concept of integration has particular appeal for Latin Americans who believe that the interests of the region require the establishment of an effective Latin American grouping, and who reject the existing inter-American system as serving the interests of the United States rather than those of Latin America. President Frei has been a severe critic of the Organization of American States in its present form, and his initiative may be interpreted as a bid for the leadership of Latin Americans sharing his sentiments. United States intervention in Santo Domingo in April 1965, disregarding the humiliation this inflicted upon Latin Americans and the mockery it made of the OAS as an instrument of consultation, has strengthened this view.

THE INTER-AMERICAN SYSTEM

This leads to the important question of what effect the existence and operation of the inter-American system have had upon the prospects for Latin American integration. It must be remembered that the inter-American system is based upon Pan Americanism—the concept of a special relationship between the United States and Latin America—not a community of interests binding the Latin American countries together, this notwithstanding the sedulously cultivated myth that the inter-American system expresses the ideals of Simón Bolívar. The Pan American movement was promoted by the United States in the 1880s with the primary objective of securing Latin American support for its own national policy (embodied in the famous Monroe Doctrine) of excluding from the western hemisphere extra-continental influence inimical to United States interests. After the First International Conference of American States had been held in Washington (1889–90) an 'International Union of American Republics' was established, with a 'Commercial Bureau' (from which the Pan American Union developed) as its agency in the United States capital. The inter-American system thus launched was concerned with such matters as the peaceful settlement of disputes among its members and the furtherance of cooperation between them in numerous fields. Many conferences of a general and technical character were held. But achievements were very limited until the United States accepted the principle of 'non-intervention' and ceased sending marines into the territory of its small neighbours in the Central American-Caribbean region to protect what were conceived to be United States interests. In becoming the 'Good Neighbour', as Franklin Roosevelt described the new policy associated with his name, the United States made more fruitful relations with Latin America possible, above all during the second world war.

The post-war years saw the formalisation of the inter-American system with the conclusion of the Inter-American Treaty of Reciprocal Assistance at Rio de Janeiro in September 1947, and the adoption of the Charter of the Organization of American States at Bogotá in May 1948. But the post-war environment has not been favourable to the inter-American system. The new, extra-continental interests and commitments of the United States, inducing Latin American complaints of neglect in favour of other regions as well as fears of becoming involved in these commitments; the existence of the United Nations and the question of competence between the OAS and the world body; the Cold War in the western hemisphere and the threat of renewed United States intervention in meeting the new challenge from international communism; Latin American concern with economic and social development and dissatisfaction with the United States response to requests for large-scale governmental aid; the growth of neutralism south of the Rio Grande—these are but some of the factors which have subjected the inter-American system to new stresses during the post-war years and make its future prospects as an effective international organisation uncertain. They have underlined the essential divergence of interests between the United States and the Latin American countries, and their conflicting motives in operating the inter-American system. The United States looks to the OAS for endorsement of its policies; Latin Americans see it as an instrument to use, if possible, to persuade their powerful neighbour to modify its policies.

Clearly, the United States has found the inter-American system a useful instrument of its policy towards Latin America, and in influencing the latter's relations with extra-continental powers (and, in recent years, the United Nations). At the same time, the inter-American system has not been without value for the countries of Latin America. On occasion they have presented something like a united front on issues at inter-American con-ferences, enabling them to exert an influence upon United States policies which would probably not have been possible for individual countries through normal diplomatic exchanges. United States acceptance of the principle of non-intervention at the Seventh International Conference of American States (Montevideo, 1933) is perhaps the most notable instance when this occurred. More importantly, in the long term, the Latin American countries' participation in the inter-American system has gone some way to break down their comparative isolation from each other, providing them with a continuous form of multilateral diplomacy.

DISUNITY ON THE PROBLEM OF COMMUNISM

But in the 1960s—those very years in which more serious attempts have been made to bring about Latin American integration—the inter-American system has provoked disunity among the Latin American countries. This is due largely to the preoccupation of the Organization of American States with the problem of communism in the hemisphere, especially since the alignment of Castro's government in Cuba with the Soviet Union. The OAS has been dominated by the communist issue primarily because the United States has sought to use it as an instrument in combating communist penetration of the hemisphere. While some Latin American governments have unequivocally supported the United States on this, others have viewed its policy with considerable misgiving. Mexico has been the most consistent in refusing to endorse the United States position; the Central American dictatorships among its firmest adherents.

In January 1962 the American foreign ministers met at Punta del Este, in Uruguay (where the Alliance for Progress had been launched the previous August) to debate the application of severe measures against Castro. It was resolved that 'the present government of Cuba' should be excluded from the inter-American system, but the resolution was secured by the bare fourteen votes (a two-thirds majority) required. The six states that did not support this measure—Argentina, Bolivia, Brazil, Chile, Ecuador and Mexico—represented more than two-thirds of the population of Latin America, and included the most important countries of the region. Their stand, in the face of considerable United States pressure, was the most significant display of Latin American solidarity for many years. Some day it may be seen as even more significant in the evolution of a Latin American nation. But it did not last. President Frondizi of Argentina was overthrown by the military in March 1962, and President Goulart of Brazil two years later.

In fact, during the three years following the Punta del Este Meeting of Consultation of American Foreign Ministers, there were military coups also in Peru, Guatemala, Ecuador, the Dominican Republic, Honduras and Bolivia. Although the United States deprecated most of these coups, they had been encouraged by its policy of strengthening the military as an anti-communist force. The Johnson administration did not hide its satisfaction with the overthrow of President Goulart, which greatly reinforced the OAS as an anti-communist alliance. The trend towards military government in the region has undoubtedly meant a set-back to the cause of Latin American integration, for military leaders, generally speaking, do not support it. Moreover, the preoccupation of the OAS with the communist challenge has strengthened the powerful interest groups in many Latin American countries whose opposition has been a major factor deterring weak civilian governments from taking more far-reaching steps to make economic integration a reality.

By the autumn of 1964 the United States had managed to persuade all the Latin American governments except that of Mexico to sever diplomatic and trade relations with Cuba. But its intervention in Santo Domingo in the following spring once again divided the Latin American countries. Support for OAS action multilateralising United States intervention by the creation of an inter-American peace force was secured only by the bare two-thirds majority required; and even this included the vote of a Dominican delegation whose credentials were of very doubtful validity. Brazil was the United States' firmest supporter (providing the only sizeable contingent to the peace force and its nominal commander) and Argentina a more lukewarm one. The six countries that did not agree to legitimise the United States action were Chile, Ecuador, Mexico, Peru, Uruguay and Venezuela. The clear violation of the principle of non-intervention—the cornerstone of the inter-American system and the most solid achievement of the Latin American countries within it—highlighted the question of whether in a serious hemispheric crisis the OAS could ever be anything but a rubber stamp for endorsing United States policies, and whether the Latin American countries could now work through the inter-American system seriously to modify those policies. The case for Latin American integration was undoubtedly greatly strengthened by United States action in the Dominican crisis. Yet for the moment integration seemed to have been brought no nearer.

FUTURE PROSPECTS

In 1966 Latin American integration remained an aspiration. It is true that in Central America significant progress had been made towards establishing a common market. But the Latin American Free Trade Association, embracing the biggest countries of the region, while stimulating an increase of trade, had, in fact, enhanced the differences between the larger and the smaller members, for the former had so far been its chief beneficiaries. LAFTA had shown little signs of developing into an instrument of political integration. The response to President Frei's initiative confirmed this. Although the *Proposals for the Creation of the Latin American Common Market* drawn up by four distinguished Latin American economists supported Dr. Frei's call for a stronger central body for LAFTA, they emphasised the need for a more rapid expansion of intra-Latin American trade rather than accelerated progress towards integration. More importantly, a meeting of foreign ministers of the LAFTA countries held at Montevideo at the beginning of November 1965 rejected a Chilean proposal that a supranational central planning body should be established. Instead there would be an 'advisory group' of economic experts able to make recommendations to LAFTA'S executive committee or to the ministerial conference, but not to adopt any binding measures on its own. This could still prove an important step in the evolution of LAFTA; but it was a far cry from the act of political will for which President Frei had called.

Latin American integration must still be considered a remote prospect. Apart from economic factors—which present difficulties enough—the political obstacles appear to be at present insurmountable. For not only are the internal organisation of the individual Latin American countries and relations between them unfavourable, but these are both powerfully influenced by the United States, the consequences of whose policies (whatever her attitude towards Latin American integration in principle) are detrimental to its prospects. Thus until there are far-reaching changes in both the Americas, Latin American integration must remain an unfulfilled aspiration, the subject of increasing discussion as the case for it becomes more compelling, but inducing very little of the bold action which alone could make it a reality in the foreseeable future.

BIBLIOGRAPHY

Connell-Smith, Gordon. *The Inter-American System*, Oxford Univ. Press for Royal Institute of International Affairs, London and New York, 1966.

Dell, Sidney. *A Latin American Common Market?*, Oxford Univ. Press for Royal Institute of International Affairs, London and New York, 1966.

Herrera, Felipe. 'Disunity as an Obstacle to Progress', *Obstacles to Change in Latin America*, ed. Claudio Véliz, Oxford Univ. Press for Royal Institute of International Affairs, London and New York, 1965. 'Economic Integration and Political Reintegration', *Latin America: Evolution or Explosion?*, ed. Mildred Adams, Dodd, Mead, New York, 1963.

Karnes, Thomas L. *The Failure of Union: Central America, 1824–1960*, Univ. of North Carolina Press, Chapel Hill, NC, 1961.

O'Shaughnessy, Hugh. 'Central America: the Road from Poverty and Disunity', *The World Today*, XX, 7, London, July 1964.

Shonfield, Andrew. 'Latin American Integration: A New Phase?' *The World Today*, XXI, 11, London, November 1965.

Wionczek, Miguel S. 'Latin American Free Trade Association', *International Conciliation*, No. 551, New York, January 1965.

O*

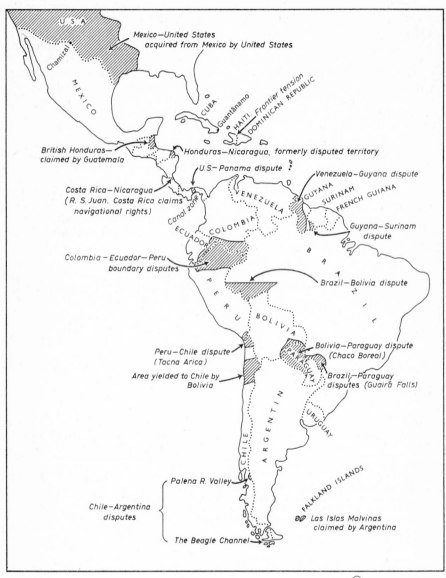

MAJOR TERRITORIAL CHANGES AND DISPUTES IN LATIN AMERICA AND
THE CARIBBEAN

TERRITORIAL DISPUTES

STEPHEN CLISSOLD AND ALISTAIR HENNESSY

THE HISTORICAL BACKGROUND

Most frontier disputes in Latin America are a legacy of the colonial period. The efforts of the early liberators to prevent the balkanisation of the Spanish Empire were frustrated by geographical intractability, sparseness of population and a particularist spirit which emphasised loyalty to regional areas rather than to Bolivarian confederal ideals.

The *uti possidetis* principle of 1810, whereby the boundaries of the new states should ordinarily coincide with those of the preceding Spanish administrative divisions, became the accepted basis for the new states. But as these boundaries were often based on faulty maps and inadequate cadastral surveys, or followed arbitrary lines across uncharted and unexplored territory, there was ample scope for dispute. Throughout the 19th century, therefore, the fiats of the Spanish crown were invoked to justify territorial claims, and colonial records were ransacked to provide precedents.

The frontier between Brazil and Spanish America was the first major bone of contention with precedents being sought as far back as the Treaty of Tordesillas (1494), and in the case of the Banda Oriental the dispute was solved only by the creation of Uruguay as a buffer state between Brazil and Argentina in 1828. This constituted the most striking failure in Brazilian diplomacy, which has otherwise been remarkably successful in increasing Brazilian territory at the expense of its Spanish-speaking neighbours.

A balance of power system was quick to develop and once larger units had been broken down (as, for example, in the case of the fragmentation of Gran Colombia or of the Central American federation) any attempt to reconstruct the larger units was resisted as a threat to the power balance, as with the repudiation by Chile and Argentina of the short-lived Peruvian-Bolivian Confederation of 1836–9.

Although there were frequent frontier disputes in the early years of independence these did not reach really serious proportions until the frontiers of settlement and exploration began to expand. The rubber boom at the end of the 19th century and the subsequent squabbles between rival prospectors led to the Brazilian-Bolivian dispute over Acre. Potentialities of an unexplored region or the discovery of new minerals often brought latent conflict into the open as between Bolivia, Peru and Chile over the nitrate deposits of the Atacama desert or between Bolivia and Paraguay over the supposed oil in the Chaco Boreal. Possibly the mineral-rich interior of Guyana was an additional factor behind the Venezuelan-British Guiana dispute. In a separate category but also a result of newly developing natural resources are the territorial waters disputes, the sharpest being the conflict between Brazil and France over lobster fishing off the Brazilian coast and the Peruvian, Ecuadorian and Chilean desire to extend the three-mile limit so as to benefit from the fishing bonanza.

Many frontiers crystallised along river lines, as in the case of the Putumayo between Colombia and Peru, the Paraguay and Paraná between Brazil, Paraguay and Argentina, the Uruguay between Argentina, Brazil and Uruguay, and the Pilcomayo between Paraguay and Argentina. But even such apparently easily definable frontiers can give rise to complex frontier disputes. These may arise out of a desire to harness a river's hydroelectric potential, or when navigable channels begin to silt up as happens in the Plata estuary, or when a river actually changes course as happened with the Rio Grande del Norte in 1864, thus causing the Chamizal dispute between the United States and Mexico which remained unsolved for a hundred years. Disputes have also arisen over the use of river waters for irrigation purposes. The use of the Lauca river, rising in Chile and flowing into Bolivia, is a constant source of friction between the two countries. The salinity of the Colorado river, which is caused by irrigation processes in the United States, and which is having an adverse effect on Mexican irrigated land, is a problem which has yet to be solved.

Hypersensitivity towards the smallest violation of territorial integrity makes a frontier dispute a highly inflammable issue which can easily be exploited by politicians for personal or party ends. Thus a faction in the Argentinian army seemed prepared to use the clash with Chile in 1965 as a means of embarrassing the already hard-pressed President Illia. Conversely, frontier disputes can spark off spontaneous riots, as with the popular Chilean reaction to the same incident. A frontier dispute is often the only opening available to an opposition party seeking to mobilise public opinion. Similarly, a party in power can revive its waning popularity by building up a frontier conflict. Any politician who agrees to an unacceptable settlement is immediately accused of trafficking with the national honour and is in danger of being overthrown, as was President Arroyo del Río in Ecuador for accepting the Rio Protocol.

BOLIVIA–CHILE

The origins of the bitter feelings between Bolivia and Chile are rooted in the formation of the Bolivian state when, in order to prevent Bolivia from being landlocked, she was given a portion of the old Captaincy-General of Chile. In the 1860s rich nitrate deposits were discovered in the region. A conflict over the exploitation of concessions led to the outbreak of war between the two countries in 1879 and Peru, linked by treaty to Bolivia, joined in. As a result of the war Bolivia lost her outlet to the Pacific and also the nitrate deposits. By the Treaty of Ancón, in return for her territorial and financial gains Chile allowed Bolivia transit rights and tax exemption on trade carried through Antofagasta. A Chilean-financed railway was built to export Bolivian minerals. Although Chileans claim that the treaty does not impede Bolivian trade, that any deficit is borne by the Chileans and that, by the *uti possidetis* principle, Chile is entitled to the area quite apart from the fact of conquest, the Bolivians regard their exclusion from the sea as a national disaster and the source of their economic troubles.

The Bolivians' determination to win back a footing on the Pacific accounts for the latest phase of the dispute with Chile centring on the River Lauca. This river rises in Chile but flows into Lake Coipasa in Bolivia. Under international law the two countries are co-owners and use of the river's waters must be by joint agreement. According to the Chileans (who claim the Bolivians were consulted), the Bolivians made no complaint about the Chilean decision to siphon off some half of the river's flow for irrigation purposes until 1961, by which time the work was almost completed. It may be that Bolivia indignation was in part the result of an MNR attempt to rally support for the 1962 elections, as this is one of the few issues on which Bolivians can agree, but more probably it sprang from a realisation that the Chileans' irrigation project would turn a hitherto barren desert into flourishing new settlements which would weaken Bolivia's irridentist claims. Diplomatic relations were broken off in 1961 and in that year Bolivia withdrew from the Organization of American States (OAS) because of its refusal to underwrite the Bolivian case. Bolivia returned to the OAS after Paz Estenssoro's fall in 1964.

ECUADOR–PERU

The frontier between these two countries has been in dispute since 1822. The disputed area originally consisted of the Comandancia General of Maynas, the Gobierno of Jaén and Guayaquil, and Tumbes, a sub-region of the Corregimiento of Piura, all part of the Viceroyalty of Peru. In the 18th century, however, Maynas was incorporated into the Viceroyalty of New Granada until it was reunited to Peru by royal warrant in 1802. In 1822 the Mosquera-Monteagudo Treaty agreed to settle the dispute between the newly liberated territories by mutual agreement. Guayaquil opted for Gran Colombia and Maynas became part of Peru. In 1826 Colombia objected to the incorporation of Maynas into Peru and declared war. By the peace of 1827 both parties agreed to abide by the old viceregal boundaries between Peru and New Granada. But the collapse of Gran Colombia in 1830 and the secession of Quito (which now became the independent Ecuador) prevented the ratification of this treaty. In 1832 Ecuador agreed to define her frontier with Peru but this was not implemented. Hostilities broke out in 1858; diplomatic relations were suspended but in 1887 Ecuador agreed to put the case to arbitration. On two occasions, between 1903 and 1910, and between 1936 and 1938, arbitration broke down. Border clashes in 1940–1 led to a state of war in which Ecuador was forced to admit Peruvian supremacy.

In 1942 the OAS passed the Rio Protocol which recognised Peru's *de facto* control of the upper Amazon basin, based on victory in the war and on a strong colonial title. Ecuador has since disputed the juridical basis of the Protocol but the Peruvians insist that it is valid, was freely ratified and is unalterable. Potentially this dispute may be the most serious in Latin America. The armed forces of both countries remain on the alert; military budgets are inflated and at every meeting of the OAS Ecuador has tried to get the verdict reversed in her favour. But the chances of the guarantor powers of the 1942 Protocol admitting the right of revision is unlikely as it would create a precedent for other countries with similar irredentist claims.

CHILE–ARGENTINA

Chile and Argentina share a frontier of some 2,900 miles of mountainous territory, largely unmapped and uninhabited in colonial times. As new sectors were settled and economic resources discovered, disputes over sovereignty arose. Argentina protested sharply when Chile took possession of the Magellan Straits and founded a settlement at Punta Arenas in the 1840s. Tension persisted until the conclusion of a treaty (1881) confirming

Chile in possession of the Straits and Argentina in that of eastern Patagonia. To the west, the frontier was declared to run along the ridge of the Cordillera along a line 'formed by the highest peaks that divided the waters.' It was discovered however that the line of the peaks did not everywhere coincide with the watershed. Disputes continued until, in 1898, Queen Victoria acceded to a request to arbitrate. Both parties accepted the arbitral opinion announced by King Edward VII in 1902 assigning the larger part of the disputed area to Chile, but the richer to Argentina.

A separate dispute over the Puna de Atacama was submitted to United States arbitration and resulted in an award (1899) giving most of the Puna to Argentina. Chilean dissatisfaction continued until 1902, when two pacts were signed pledging Chile and Argentina to limit their armaments and resort to arbitration in any future dispute.

The field of friction thereafter narrowed to two areas, the Beagle Channel and the Palena region. The former is a channel linking the Atlantic and the Pacific south of Tierra del Fuego. It was stipulated in 1902 that 'the islands south of the Beagle Channel should belong to Chile.' Argentina maintains that the islands at the easterly end of the Channel—Lennox, Picton and Nueva—which are generally accounted Chilean, should belong to her, since she regards the Channel as ending west of them. The disputed area, though remote, is of strategic importance and has been the scene of various naval incidents. The dispute may now be submitted for arbitration to the International Court at the Hague.

The dispute over the Palena region concerns some forty kilometres of frontier round the Palena river valley, the physical features of which were allegedly wrongly mapped at the time of the 1902 award. The presence of a numerous Chilean population on the Argentine side of the frontier has made the position more delicate. Border incidents involving loss of life led to a sharp deterioration in Argentine–Chilean relations in 1965. A request was made to Queen Elizabeth II to arbitrate, and an arbitral opinion was given in 1966 and accepted by both parties.

Though insubstantial in themselves, these frontier disputes tend to be exacerbated by nationalist fervour and mutual suspicion, and have proved a serious irritant in Chilean–Argentine relations.

VENEZUELA-GUYANA

Venezuela claims from Guyana (known until May 1966 as British Guiana) some 50,000 square miles of jungle—about two-thirds of the total area of the ex-colony—lying between the Essequibo river and the present Venezuelan-Guyanese frontier.

The dispute over 'Guyana Essequiba' goes back to the first half of the last century. Venezuela claimed the area as a former Spanish possession; Britain claimed it as ceded to her by the Netherlands under the Treaty of London (1814). The boundary was left undefined and the region largely unexplored until the survey carried out (1834–9) by Robert Schomburgk on behalf of the Royal Geographical Society.

Venezuela declined to accept the line recommended by Schomburgk, and the dispute continued until 1895 when, on Venezuelan insistence, President Cleveland forced Britain to submit the matter to arbitration. In 1897 Venezuela and Britain signed an arbitration treaty setting up a tribunal under the chairmanship of an impartial Russian jurist. In 1899 the tribunal announced its award, which was recognised by both parties as 'a full, perfect and final settlement.' Britain received the greater part of the disputed territory, but to Venezuela were assigned the Barima and Amacuro regions on the coast together with some 3,000 square miles of the interior, thus giving her dominion over the Orinoco which had been one of her chief aims. The demarcation of the boundary by a mixed commission was completed in 1905 and ratified by the Venezuelan Congress in 1907.

The dispute was generally regarded as closed until the posthumous publication in 1949 of a memorandum by Mallet Prevost, an American lawyer who had served as junior counsel on the tribunal, alleging that the award had been the result of a deal between the British judges and the Russian chairman. Claiming that Venezuela had formerly been unable to defend her rights, and probably influenced by the impending independence of British Guiana which threatened to prevent the area between the Essequibo and Orinoco rivers ever developing as one powerful economic unit, the Venezuelan government pressed Britain to reopen the question. The British and Guyanese representatives who examined the evidence could not however agree that it supported the Mallet Prevost allegations or invalidated the award. Following a meeting of the Venezuelan and British foreign ministers and the Guyanese prime minister in Geneva (February 1966) it was decided to set up a Venezuelan–Guyanese commission to attempt a settlement of the boundary question, and also to consider possibilities for economic cooperation, and that if the two sides failed to reach agreement within four years, recourse should be had to the United Nations' machinery for the settlement of disputes.

British Honduras

British Honduras (generally known as Belize in Latin America) has a population of mixed Negro, Mayan, Carib, European and East Indian extraction and the status of a self-governing British colony. Independence within the Commonwealth is the declared aim of the two major political parties.

The colony derives from a 17th-century settlement of buccaneers and log-cutters, whose presence—though not Britain's sovereignty—was recognised by Spain in the Treaty of Paris (1763) and subsequent treaties. Following a decisive victory (1798) over the Spaniards, the settlers claimed that the territory had become British by conquest. De facto British control increased as Spanish power declined, and in 1862 the settlement was formally declared a British colony.

The colony's existing boundaries were recognised by a treaty of 1859 between Britain and Guatemala who also reached agreement (article 7) 'for establishing the easiest communication . . . between the fittest place on the Atlantic coast near the settlement of Belize and the capital of Guatemala.' Since no such road has subsequently been built, Guatemala contends that the treaty is invalidated, and that she is entitled (as successor to Spain's Captaincy-General of Guatemala) to claim the whole territory, or alternatively that southern part of it between the rivers Sibun and Sarstoon which she had allegedly ceded in return for the promised road. The issue is complicated by Mexico's view that the disputed territory was formerly part of the Captaincy-General of Yucatán, and that she is entitled to the reversion of at least part of it should a change of sovereignty arise.

Controversy has continued intermittently between Britain and Guatemala, the latter breaking off diplomatic relations (July 1963) when Britain decided to grant the colony self-government by 1964. Subsequent tripartite talks foundered on the British Honduran delegates' misgivings that Guatemala's proposals for a 'federation' would be tantamount to absorption. British Honduras has a high per capita income for a developing country, and sees her future in some form of association with the Central American Common Market, providing her independence and the advantages stemming from the Commonwealth connection are not prejudiced.

THE FALKLAND ISLANDS

The Falkland Islands (known in Argentina as Las Islas Malvinas) comprise two large and some 200 small islands, with a total land area of about 4,700 square miles and a population of around 2,000, almost all of British descent and engaged in sheep-raising. Argentina claims sovereignty over the Falklands, and also over their dependencies, South Sandwich and the South Georgia group (annexed by Captain Cook in 1775), with a population of about 500 in the whaling season.

The history of the discovery and early occupation of the islands is complicated and obscure. The French appear to have been the first to establish themselves there (1764). The following year a British expedition, unaware of their presence, claimed possession of the islands for King George III. The French sold their rights to the Spaniards who in 1770 evicted the British. The latter, however, reestablished their settlement after negotiations with the Spaniards who agreed to a return of the *status quo*. The British withdrew their settlement for reasons of economy in 1774, and the Spaniards also withdrew theirs in 1811, but both countries maintained their claims. In 1828 a new settlement was established by Vernet, with authorisation from the government of Buenos Aires which regarded itself as inheriting Spain's claim to the islands. This claim was not however recognised by the United States who, alleging Argentine acts of piracy, sent a warship to destroy the settlement and declare the islands free of all government (1831). Two years later a small party of Argentine soldiers landed on the islands but was forced by a British expedition to reembark, apparently with the remnants of the Argentine settlement. Since then the islands have remained under continuous British occupation and administration.

Argentina claims the 'Islas Malvinas' chiefly on the grounds that (i) she has inherited Spain's previous titles to them; (ii) Vernet established and maintained an Argentine settlement between 1828 and 1833, when they had reverted to a status of *terra nullius;* (iii) they are hers by right of geographical proximity, since they are on the Continental Shelf; (iv) their present colonial status is anachronistic; (v) their economy has been neglected and would benefit from association with Argentina.

The Argentine claim has long been an irritant in Anglo-Argentine relations and was raised in the United Nations in 1964. Britain maintains that her legal and historical rights to the islands are sound and have been strengthened by the prescriptive title of long and uninterrupted occupation and administration, and that the overwhelming majority of the islanders would be opposed to a change of sovereignty. The British government has thus refused to negotiate on sovereignty, but has agreed to discussions with Argentina with a view to decreasing friction.

PANAMA–UNITED STATES

By the controversial Hay-Buneau-Varilla Treaty of 1903, the United States acquired from Panama 'in perpetuity, the use, occupation and control' of the Canal Zone, a strip of land extending for five miles on either side of the lock-type waterway linking the Atlantic and Pacific oceans. Despite the economic advantages reaped by Panama from the canal, the existence of this foreign enclave, with its population of 40,000 privileged 'Zonians', is keenly resented by Panamanian national opinion and has periodically given rise to anti-American riots. In September 1965 President Johnson announced that 'areas of agreement' had been reached with Panama in negotiations for a revision of the 1903 Treaty and also for the proposed construction of a second, sea-level canal. The basic problem is to reconcile Panama's demand for effective sovereignty, a larger share of the profits from the canal, and more say in its management with the requirements of United States defence and operational efficiency.

BRAZIL–PARAGUAY

The dispute between the two countries over the Guairá Falls (Sete Quedas) has recently been revived by the Paraguayans' assertion that in mid-1965 Brazilian troops moved into an undemarcated zone which a modern survey shows as part of Paraguay under the 1872 Treaty. Brazil refutes the Paraguayan claim that this treaty, which ended the war between the two countries, was imposed on a defeated nation and claims that the raising of the dispute is in violation of the treaties of 1872 and 1927. The reason for the dispute's revival may be due to growing recognition of the falls' immense hydroelectric potential which Brazil is in a better position than Paraguay to exploit.

GUYANA–SURINAM

The present frontier between these two countries, though never formalised, has long been accepted as formed by the Corentyne river. The source of the latter, Surinam has latterly claimed, is not the Coeroeni-Kutari, as hitherto assumed, but the New river, a tributary flowing in from the Guyanese side, which should entitle her to an extra triangular piece of territory (potentially rich in minerals) of some 6,000 square miles. The boundary at the mouth of the Corentyne also requires formal definition, since oil may be found in the continental shelf.

CENTRAL AMERICA

The Central American republics have been traditionally prone to frontier disputes, most of which are now settled or at least quiescent. There remain, however, underlying tensions stemming from fear of domination by more powerful neighbours (e.g. Guatemala by Mexico, which briefly absorbed all Central America in 1822, and the smaller Central American states by Guatemala, the strongest partner in the 1824–38 Federation), and from population pressure (e.g. 150–200,000 immigrants from El Salvador, which has 125 inhabitants per square kilometre, have moved into Honduras, which has only 17·4).

Frontier areas which are still sensitive include:

Costa Rica–Nicaragua. The frontier lies slightly to the south of the San Juan river which, though in Nicaraguan territory, is an important means of communication for Costa Rica, which claims navigational rights on it.

Honduras–Nicaragua. A wedge-shaped tract of territory, extending 150 miles along the Caribbean coast and some 175 miles inland, was assigned in 1960 to Honduras after reference to the Hague Court.

Costa Rica–Panama. The 196-mile boundary, over which the two countries went to war in 1921, was settled by treaty in 1944.

MEXICO–UNITED STATES

The Chamizal dispute (over an area of land between El Paso and Ciudad Juarez) was a constant source of irritation until its solution in 1963. The origin lay in the change of course of the Rio Grande river in 1864 which left some 600 acres of territory on the United States' side of the river. The Mexicans asserted that, in international law, a change in a river's course does not affect original ownership: the Americans countered with the 'law of slow change', arguing that erosion had removed the area from Mexico. In 1911 the United States' failure to accept the verdict of an arbitration court added a note of bitterness which was only removed when the area was returned to Mexico in 1963.

HAITI–DOMINICAN REPUBLIC

The Dominican Republic occupies 65 per cent and Haiti 35 per cent of the island of Hispaniola. The boundary was established by treaty in 1929 (the treaty was revised in 1936) and is not in dispute, though friction still arises over migration and water rights. Deeper causes of tension are Dominican memories of the 1822–44 Haitian occupation and fears of pressure from Haiti's dense, fast-growing population, and Haitian memories of Trujillo-instigated massacre of thousands of Haitian immigrant labourers in 1937, and exiles' anti-government activities from bases across the border.

CUBA–UNITED STATES

Guantánamo, at the eastern end of Cuba, is an important link in the chain of United States naval bases for the protection of the Panama Canal. By an agreement of 1903, modified by a treaty of 1934, Cuba leased the area round Guantánamo Bay for an unspecified period to the United States, which is authorised to exercise 'complete jurisdiction and control,' though Cuba retains 'ultimate sovereignty' over it. Cuban nationalist opinion resents the existence of this foreign enclave, and its recovery constitutes the fifth of the 'Five Points' announced by the Cuban government on 28 October 1962. Though the Cuban government attempted in 1964 to harass the base by cutting off its water supply and impeding the flow of Cuban labour, it has declared its intention of reclaiming the territory not by force but 'in the proper time and through proper political procedures' (President Dórticos, 2 November 1960).

ANTARCTICA

Antarctica is an area of complex overlapping territorial claims. These include Argentina's claim to the South Shetland and South Orkney Islands (formerly part of the Falkland Islands dependencies), and competing Argentine and Chilean claims on Graham Land, which now forms part of British Antarctic territory.

Fifteen states (including the seven which have territorial interests) have now acceded to the 1959 Antarctic Treaty which pledges them to 'freeze' their claims for thirty years in all territory south of 60° south, which is to be kept for peaceful purposes and scientific research.

BOLIVIA–BRAZIL

The Treaty of San Ildefonso (1777) between Spain and Portugal provided the basis for the Bolivian–Brazilian frontier. Following disputes, an attempt to rationalise the frontier was made in the 1867 treaty recognising the *uti possidetis* principle but the commissioners failed to agree. The dispute reached a climax when Brazilian rubber-gatherers refused to recognise Bolivian authorities in the disputed area. Brazil refused to recognise concessions granted by the Bolivians and war seemed imminent. Bolivia's clashes with the 'independent republic' of Acre set up in 1899 predisposed her to a settlement. By the 1903 Treaty of Petropolis Brazil undertook the pacification of the area and agreed to construct a railway along the rivers Mamore and Madeira, thus linking Bolivia with the Amazon.

After Bolivia's interest in Acre had been transferred to Brazil, relations between Brazil and Peru became strained but the frontier between the two countries was finally settled by treaty in 1909.

BOLIVIA–PERU

A confused area in the Amazonian jungle between the Madeira and Yavarí rivers was in dispute after independence. In 1902 a treaty of arbitration was signed by which the old Charcas area would go to Bolivia and that of the Viceroyalty of Peru would go to Peru. Argentina arbitrated and finally in 1909 Bolivia accepted the decision by which 22,000 square miles went to Bolivia and 33,000 square miles to Peru. The disputed zone was entirely unexplored and unoccupied. Such disputes as remain between the two countries result from minor infringements of frontier regulations by the Indians who span the frontier.

BOLIVIA–PARAGUAY

Bolivia's claim to the Chaco Boreal, a vast sparsely populated area of barren scrub, swamp and jungle, was based on the grounds that the Audiencia of Charcas had always had jurisdiction down to the west bank of the Paraguay river. Between 1879 and 1913 some five treaties were negotiated to determine the frontier but none was implemented. War had only just been avoided in 1898 by a revolution breaking out in Paraguay. The conflict came to a climax when Paraguay felt threatened by Bolivia's gradual advance into the disputed area, motivated by the desire to have an alternative outlet to the sea to that lost on the Pacific. The struggle over concessions between rival oil companies sharpened the latent hostility between the two countries. In 1927 fighting broke out between forts established in the disputed areas. Argentine conciliation failed to avert a major conflict, as did efforts of the Pan American Conference and League of Nations. In May 1933 Paraguay formally declared war and for the next two years a war of attrition was fought.[1] The final settlement, by which Bolivia lost 94,000 square miles, drew the frontier further west than the previous unratified treaties of 1879, 1887 and 1894.

[1] See 'Paraguay', p. 104.

PERU–CHILE

After Peru was defeated by Chile in the War of the Pacific[1] friction between the two countries centred on Tacna and Arica. The Treaty of Ancón left Chile with all the disputed territory, but provided for a plebiscite after ten years to decide its permanent status. Agreement could not be reached. Peru was angry that Chile had begun to colonise the area and in 1920 took the dispute to the League of Nations. Bolivia seized the opportunity to agitate for the return of her outlet to the sea but the League ruled that she had no right to intervene. In 1922, under the arbitration of the president of the United States, a commission to conduct a plebiscite was set up. The plebiscite proved impossible to carry out but in 1929 the dispute was settled by direct negotiation. Chile ceded Tacna to Peru and retained Arica, paying an indemnity and granting Peru special port facilities in Arica.

COLOMBIA–PERU

The Peruvian-Colombian Treaty of 1922 (ratified in 1928) fixed the frontier between the two countries along the Putumayo river, but gave Colombia a strip of territory from that river allowing her access to the Amazon at the small port of Leticia. In 1932 a band of armed Peruvian civilians seized Leticia, their coup being at first repudiated, then supported, by the Peruvian government. Hostilities broke out between Colombia and Peru in 1933. Colombia appealed to the League of Nations and eventually secured the withdrawal of Peruvian troops, the recognition of the 1922 Treaty, and the resumption of diplomatic relations.

[1] See 'Chile', p. 61.

BIBLIOGRAPHY

Bianchi, W. J. *Belize: The Controversy between Guatemala and Great Britain*, Las Americas Publishing House, New York, 1959.

Boxer, C. R. *Race Relations in the Portuguese Colonial Empire, 1415–1825*, Oxford Univ. Press, London and New York, 1963.

British Honduras: The Guatemalan Claim, Central Office of Information, London, 1962.

Burr, R. N. *By Reason or Force: Chile and the Balancing Power in South America, 1830–1905*, California Univ. Press, Berkeley, Calif., 1965.

Cawkell, M. B. R. *et al. The Falkland Islands*, Macmillan, London, 1960; St Martin's Press, New York, 1961.

Child, Clifton J. *The Venezuelan-British Guiana Boundary Arbitration of 1899*, American Journal of International Law, October 1950.

Christie, H. H. Hunter. *The Antarctic Problem*, Allen and Unwin, London, 1951.

Dubois, J. *Danger over Panama*, Bobbs–Merrill, New York, 1964.

Eyzaguirre, J. *Chile y Bolivia: esquema de un proceso diplomático*, Santiago, 1963.

Goebel, J. *The Struggle for the Falkland Islands*, Yale Univ. Press, New Haven, Conn., 1927.

Humphreys, R. A. *The Diplomatic History of British Honduras*, Oxford Univ. Press, London and New York, 1961.

Ireland, G. *Boundaries, Possessions and Conflicts in South America*, Harvard Univ. Press, Cambridge, Mass., 1938. *Boundaries, Possessions and Conflicts in Central and North America and the Caribbean*, Harvard Univ. Press, Cambridge, Mass., 1941.

Miller, H. G. *The Isthmian Highway*, Macmillan, New York, 1929.

Taubenfeld, H. J. *A Treaty for Antarctica*, Carnegie Endowment for International Peace, New York, 1961.

Waddell, D. A. G. 'Developments in the Belize Question, 1946–1960', *American Journal of International Law*, LV, 2, April 1961.

Wood, Bryce. *The United States and Latin American Wars, 1932–1942*, Columbia Univ. Press, New York, 1966.

Zook, D. H. *Zarumilla-Marañon: The Ecuadorian–Peruvian Dispute*, Twayne, New York, 1964.

Venezuelan Ministry of Foreign Affairs. *Los límites de Venezuela con la Guyana Británica*, Caracas, 1962.

FOREIGN RELATIONS

LATIN AMERICAN FOREIGN POLICIES

FRED PARKINSON

The International System of Nineteenth-Century Latin America (1820–80)

THOUGH some intra-state systems of communications in Latin America are well developed, there never existed a comprehensive system of intra-Latin American communications, because Latin America's centres of power were always virtually isolated. Whilst it is true that the Latin American oligarchies had fought together against their Iberian overlords and shared a common cultural heritage, the meagreness of Latin America's communications prevented them from developing any social, let alone political solidarity in the period following independence. Only the Brazilian empire retained a measure of unity which enabled the development of firmly based statehood (nationhood was still a long way off). In the remainder of Latin America the governing élites built state structures serving their own purpose. As the shafts of territorial sovereignty were sunk deeper into Latin American soil, so the prospects of supranational cohesion based on inter-oligarchic ties faded. Towards the end of the 19th century other classes began to be associated with the traditional oligarchies in political decision-making, but it was painfully clear that they too owed their first allegiance to the state, and they showed no inclination towards international solidarity on a Latin American scale. The international fragmentation of Latin America had come to stay.

The diplomatic problems which faced the new Latin American states were both thorny and unexpected. There was, for instance, the awkward question of delimiting frontiers, a problem which had never agitated Iberian colonial officials, to whom boundaries were a matter of administrative convenience lacking all political significance. However, to the Latin American successor states this question was often intimately bound up with their own security since the old colonial frontiers had become international frontiers.

There was also the question of the legitimacy of the new territories, many of which had fitted in neatly within the rigid hierarchical administrative system that suited the Iberian overlords, but found themselves out of place in this respect at the end of the wars of independence. There was a disruptive tendency on the part of some successor states to regard themselves as nuclei, not for the construction of a league of states of Latin America—as Bolívar would have preferred—but for the reconstitution of the various primary and secondary units of administration of the Spanish empire. The fragmentary nature of the Latin American system of communications had its counterpart in the formation of a disconnected balance of power, which produced two principal flashpoints of inter-state friction. On the Atlantic side there was the River Plate region, claiming the constant attention of Argentina, Brazil,

Uruguay and Paraguay, while on the Pacific seaboard there developed a nexus of international rivalries involving Chile, Peru, Ecuador and Colombia. In North America the presence of the United States was influential from the beginning. Conflict with Mexico over the Texan question was sharp and sustained, and only partially resolved by the war of 1846. Central America and the Caribbean region began to feel the proximity of the United States also.

THE GENESIS OF UNITED STATES HEGEMONY
(1880–1920)

As the economic expansion of the United States got under way it was matched by energetic action in the diplomatic, and eventually also in the military field. After 1890 the diplomatic pull of the United States was so powerful that it was felt in every corner of Latin America. In 1889–90 the United States took the lead in organising the International Union of American Republics (later known as the Pan American Union or PAU) which, centred on Washington, was from the beginning an instrument of United States foreign policy in relation to Latin America. This organisation was the forerunner of the Organisation of American States. Towards the turn of the century Britain conceded to the United States the sole rights of constructing the Panama Canal. Spain was forced out of the Caribbean during the war with the United States (1898). The Roosevelt Corollary to the Monroe Doctrine was proclaimed in 1904. United States hegemony on the American continent had become an established fact, and it looked as if the Latin American power blocs were being submerged in the Pan American system under the leadership of the United States.

Yet contrary to all expectations, this never happened. In the first place, though the United States had it in its power to dominate Latin America absolutely, it was powerfully deterred by the European conflict. In the second place, a countervailing centre of opposition had formed in the 'deep South' of America. Before 1861 the contrast between the strife-ridden Republic of Argentina and the serenely calm Empire of Brazil—Argentina's chief rival in the River Plate region—had been striking. For some decades after 1861, however, Argentina's political and economic progress was nearly as spectacular as that of the United States. Argentina's relative position of strength was enhanced when the Brazilian monarchy fell in 1889. When the International Union of American Republics was created in 1890, Argentina showed every intention of contesting the right of leadership which the United States had arrogated to itself.

That contest was an unequal one, and Argentine resistance would soon have ceased if other factors had remained equal. But this was not the case, and with the progressive involvement of the United States in the conflicts of Europe, Argentine diplomacy was able to exert an influence out of proportion to the size and resources of the country when compared with those at the command of the United States. Under the energetic leadership of President Irigoyen, Argentina remained adamantly neutral in the face of considerable diplomatic pressure on the part of the United States. Chile, Mexico and Colombia followed the Argentine example of neutrality in the first world war.[1] Brazil sided with the United States and took her place in Allied

---

[1] Brazil, Cuba, Costa Rica, Guatemala, Haiti, Nicaragua and Panama declared war against the Central Powers in 1917. Bolivia, Ecuador, Peru and Uruguay severed diplomatic relations.

councils at the Peace Conference in Paris in 1919. Argentine diplomacy suffered a reverse, while Brazil regained much of her former ascendancy in Latin America.

LATIN AMERICA'S REACTION (1920–36)

The first world war connected Latin America's international system—half-submerged though it had become in a developing Pan American system dominated by the United States—with the universal balance of power, with consequences fully appreciated only during the second half of the 20th century. Henceforth every major diplomatic event in the world was to have its repercussions through Latin America, and the Latin American balance of power was to function as a sub-system of a global diplomatic system.

The Latin American states did not follow the United States into isolation from Europe. Many of them saw in the League of Nations a political instrument capable of being turned to good account. Argentina regarded it as a potential counterweight to the Pan American Union, where the United States was holding sway. Most of these hopes were dashed. Though the League played a part in resolving the Chaco and Leticia conflicts between Bolivia and Paraguay on the one hand and Peru and Colombia on the other, this could not be accomplished without the diplomatic assistance of the United States, a non-member.

While the Latin American states occupied themselves with League of Nations affairs, the economic penetration of their continent by the United States continued with giant strides. Moreover, uncommitted to the fairly strict standards of the law of the Covenant of the League of Nations, the United States felt free to intervene at liberty, and on numerous occasions, in the domestic affairs of several Latin American states. So, far from being fruitful, Latin America's first organised foray into world affairs proved counter-productive.

A further setback was suffered in 1930 when the world economic crisis broke upon Latin America. Its political impact was equally forceful, and there was hardly a Latin American country that did not undergo a change of régime. As the economy of the United States itself was severely shaken, the copious flow of United States investments to Latin America came abruptly to a halt. For the first time in half a century the image of an all-powerful United States bestriding Latin America at will was blurred, producing in many of the newly arrived leaders of Latin America a fresh political mood leading to radical reappraisals of the very assumptions on which Latin American foreign policies had rested in the past.

Parallel, and largely unconnected with these developments, went steady Latin American counterpressure on the United States to revise the basic tenets of its policy towards Latin America. These demands were finally conceded at the Montevideo conference in 1933 and the Buenos Aires conference in 1936. By adopting the standard of the Good Neighbour, President Franklin D. Roosevelt committed the United States to observe the rule of non-intervention in its dealings with Latin America.[1]

---

[1] There was never much enthusiasm about the Good Neighbour policy in the United States, and a prominent diplomat observed that only a few members of the foreign service threw themselves energetically into its implementation. See L. Duggan, *The Americas*, 1949, p. 75.

HEMISPHERE DEFENCE (1936–45)

The sharpening of the European crisis may have been largely responsible for overcoming the last reservations of the United States regarding the Good Neighbour policy. For 1936 saw not only Nazi Germany triumphantly defying the Locarno powers over the reoccupation of the Rhineland and Fascist Italy victorious over Ethiopia; it also witnessed the outbreak of the Spanish Civil War, the first inkling in modern history of the opening of an era in which it would be difficult to draw a clear line between diplomacy and ideology. From now on, the United States was in many ways in greater need of the support of Latin America than at any time since the first world war.

In a number of Latin American states the Good Neighbour policy encouraged economic nationalism. In Bolivia the major United States oil companies were expropriated in March 1937, and Mexico followed suit exactly a year later, on a much larger scale.

Direct German diplomatic influence was certainly exerted, but began to be taken seriously only when German arms scored their first major successes in Western Europe in 1940. Admiral W. Canaris, chief of the Abwehr, the German military intelligence service, and retired Major-General W. Faupel, a former ambassador to Franco Spain (1936–7) and subsequently director of the Iberoamerikanisches Institut, Berlin, both showed a keen interest in Latin America, but were never able to communicate their enthusiasm to Hitler's entourage. President Oscar Benavides of Peru and President Germán Busch of Bolivia came closest to sympathising with Nazi Germany before 1939. German political as distinct from diplomatic penetration was never more than marginal.[1]

Unambiguous sympathies with the Soviet Union were felt only in Mexico, which from the outset developed staunch Republican sympathies in the Spanish Civil War, and in Chile, where the Frente Popular, a left-wing coalition, formed a government in 1938.

In 1936 the United States had proposed the extension of its own neutrality legislation to the entire western hemisphere, but its endeavour was thwarted by Argentina. It soon became evident that the latter, whose foreign policy was guided by Saavedra Lamas, now as in the past would prefer close relations with Europe to close relations with other American states, and would form the centre of opposition to any attempt by the Roosevelt administration to build a system of collective defence in the Americas. In 1937, for instance, Saavedra Lamas invoked the principle of the balance of power in South America in protesting to the United States against the lease of some destroyers to Brazil—proof enough that in Argentine eyes the 'coastal' balance of power had clear precedence over hemispheric defence.

Tentative collective measures were nevertheless taken in the field of hemispheric defence between 1938 and 1940 before the United States itself was plunged into war in December 1941. Now was the time for Latin American attitudes to be revealed. Impressed by the spectacular military successes of Germany in Europe, some Latin American statesmen had taken to wavering. President Vargas of Brazil, usually calm, unemotional and

---

[1] Gauleiter W. Bohle's Auslandsorganisation was active among Germans throughout Latin America, but was not influential and in some cases split; witness the simultaneous appearance in Argentina of the pro-Nazi *La Plata-Zeitung* and the anti-Nazi *Argentinisches Tageblatt*. The German civilian airline Lufthansa made its appearance in Latin American skies, but the Luftwaffe never followed suit.

coolly calculating when it came to foreign affairs, had his moments of doubt in 1941. President Arnulfo Arias of Panama, also in 1941, developed a marked distaste for military collaboration with the United States and began to sympathise with the Axis. Soon afterwards he was overthrown. In Argentina and Bolivia important sections among the military began to believe in an Axis victory, and to adjust their tactics.

In December 1941 the Caribbean and Central American group of states followed the United States into war immediately (Guatemala, El Salvador, Nicaragua, Honduras, Panama, Costa Rica, Haiti, Cuba and the Dominican Republic). The remaining Latin American countries showed varying degrees of reluctance, revealed at the Rio de Janeiro conference which was hastily summoned in January 1942.

Few of the governments of South America were spoiling for a fight with the Axis. Chile was only prevailed upon to break diplomatic relations with the Axis in January 1943, whilst Argentina followed a year later, in January 1944. Bolivia declared war in April 1943, a mere matter of days before President Peñaranda was overthrown by a national-revolutionary government based on an alliance between the military (some of them pro-German) and the pro-Nazi Movimiento Nacional Revolucionario. This government contained some outspokenly pro-Axis personalities, chief among them Víctor Paz Estenssoro, minister of finance. It was probably only owing to Bolivia's growing economic dependence—now that the United States was quickly succeeding in tightening its economic grip on the western hemisphere —that the government stayed in the war and that it agreed, in December 1943, to drop Paz Estenssoro from the cabinet.

Argentina nevertheless chose neutrality. The crucial factor determining her course was probably her great disappointment in having been refused United States arms deliveries sufficiently large to enable her to hold her own against Brazil, who, having declared war on the Axis in August 1942, was benefiting substantially from massive United States economic and military aid under Lend-Lease arrangements. In July 1943 a military *junta* seized power and soon its pro-Axis, though not necessarily pro-Nazi elements, came to the fore. When President Ramírez yielded to Allied pressure to the extent of breaking off relations with the Axis in January 1944, he was replaced by General Farrell, who was determined to make no further concessions.

Cordell Hull, President Roosevelt's Secretary of State, did well not to underestimate Argentina when he used all means at his disposal to isolate her. In March 1945, and as a condition of membership at the forthcoming founder meeting of the United Nations, Argentina at last grudgingly made the purely nominal gesture of declaring war on the Axis. Argentina's humiliation was complete when at the San Francisco conference of the United Nations in April 1945 she had to have her case for membership pleaded by the United States against stiff Soviet opposition. This did not put an end to Argentine suspicion of the United States, but it went a long way towards introducing elements of ambiguity into her subsequent foreign policy.

Since the advent of President Cárdenas, Mexico had been the most ideologically inclined country in Latin America where foreign policy was concerned. The war against the Axis, officially declared in May 1942, was looked upon as an ideological crusade. President Cárdenas himself never reestablished diplomatic relations with the Soviet Union, but his successor did.

Mexico played host to thousands of Spanish Republican refugees, and also to numerous German communist intellectuals. Alongside Brazil, she

418

actually contributed military contingents which took an active part in fighting overseas.

The feeling of historical kinship between the Mexican revolution and the Spanish Republic, which had led Mexico into espousing the Republican cause and pursuing a specifically anti-Fascist foreign policy, gradually yielded to a sentiment of Inter-American solidarity directly an amicable settlement of the oil dispute with the United States had been made. In March 1945 an Inter-American meeting was arranged under the acclamation of Mexico's statesmen in Chapultepec Castle in Mexico City to discuss measures for preserving the political cohesion of the western hemisphere beyond the end of the second world war. Ideology as a driving force in Mexican foreign policy was dead. To this day it has not been revived.

The Cold War: Bipolarity (1945–62)

The end of the second world war resulted in the creation of a bipolar world balance of power in which there was little chance for third countries to exert real influence. Latin America, until 1955 numerically well placed in the General Assembly of the United Nations, was a geographical backwater in the Cold War. The states of Asia, far more important strategically than Latin America, were the object of much attention, not all of it pleasant, from the two superpowers and their allies. Latin America was neglected. It was 'the continent that Harry Truman forgot'.

In a world situation such as this it was easy to assume that, in spite of the experiences of two world wars, it would after all be possible for Latin America to stay out of the Cold War, not by her own determined political efforts, but simply by keeping quiet. The Guatemalan crisis of 1954, and, infinitely more so, the Cuban crisis after 1959, shattered these illusions.

During the quiescent years of the post-war period the lively element in Latin American foreign policies was provided by Perón's Argentina. At home Perón advocated an ideological position of *justicialismo*[1] half-way between capitalism and communism; abroad he proposed the adoption of a 'third position' between the United States and the Soviet Union. In practice his foreign policy in the Cold War was ambiguous, relying far more on verbal pronouncement than on positive action.

More important than his attitudes in the Cold War were Perón's policies within the hemisphere. Carrying distinct hegemonic overtones, these were reminiscent of earlier Argentine ambitions on the South American continent. In their pursuit Perón employed two methods. He made use of ATLAS (Agrupación de trabajadores latinoamericanos sindicalistas), a Peronista-type trade union movement with branches throughout Latin America, as well as some specially appointed labour attachés in his Latin American embassies, in order to promote *justicialismo* and create a favourable political climate for his main diplomatic drive, which was economic rather than political, and directed towards the economic unification of Latin America under the aegis of Argentina.

Circumstances seemed to favour him. He concluded an impressive series of economic agreements with Chile, Bolivia, Ecuador, Nicaragua and Paraguay, and came very near signing some with Peru and Colombia also. For some time it seemed as if Latin America were going rapidly Peronista.

The success of Argentina's diplomatic offensive had, however, always depended on the economic strength of her own position, and when the

[1] See 'Argentina', p. 12.

country began to experience economic difficulties it petered out completely. What had started as an imaginative, energetic and hopeful attempt to regroup Latin America economically and, ultimately, politically, ended suddenly in an embarrassing anticlimax. Two years later the Perón régime was overthrown, and all its progress in foreign policy was undone.

Much of Perón's accumulated reserves of foreign exchange had been spent on arms purchases in an effort to draw level with Brazil. The latter was making headway in her programme of industrialisation, gradually leaving Argentina behind. Even in the field of foreign trade Argentina was outstripped by Brazil, making it unlikely that she would ever be in a position again to challenge Brazil on the east coast and, in the long run, perhaps even in the whole of South America.

Perón has been blamed for adopting policies which eventually led to Argentine inferiority *vis-à-vis* Brazil. But Brazilian ascendancy in Latin America springs from factors far more fundamental than the transient pursuit of certain policies. Brazil's own industrial expansion from 1890 onwards had to some extent matched that of Argentina. Perón's miscalculations merely hastened a development which was inevitable.

As Argentina's political fortunes sank to zero in 1955, Brazil's rise to diplomatic prominence was just beginning. President Getúlio Vargas' second term (1951–4) saw the veteran statesman preoccupied with domestic affairs—a preoccupation which, during that term, was not always entirely voluntary, as the President had to live increasingly under the shadow of potential military intervention. In June 1954, for instance, Brazil voted with the United States in the Security Council of the United Nations against a Guatemalan request to have a complaint placed on the agenda connected with its crisis which had come to a head in spring with the arrival of an armed shipment from Eastern Europe. It will probably always be a matter of speculation what Brazil's vote would have been if Vargas had been completely unrestrained at home. He committed suicide in August of the same year.

The ambitious drive towards top-speed industrialisation by President Kubitschek (1955–61) resulted in a severe balance of payments crisis. When the Brazilian president tried to resolve this with the aid of the International Monetary Fund in 1959, but was informed that aid must be made conditional on the abandonment of his unorthodox financial policies, Kubitschek refused to fall in with these conditions, and from this moment onwards his own attitude towards the United States began to cool, and Brazil began to chart a more self-reliant course in world affairs.

The Cold War itself affected Latin American foreign policies on three occasions. When the Korean War burst upon the world in 1950, it caused a bare ripple in Latin America. Only one country, Colombia, sent troops and signed the armistice agreement. A more immediate impact was made by the Guatemalan crisis in 1954. John Foster Dulles' attempts to isolate Guatemala and obtain from the Caracas meeting of the OAS, called in March 1954, a condemnation of 'international communism' caused resentment. Argentina and Mexico, for instance, abstained rather than vote for the United States-sponsored resolution.

The Cuban crisis was of an altogether different order. Towards the end of 1959 a marked estrangement developed between the United States and the Castro government in Cuba. In March 1960 this reached a point at which President Eisenhower authorised preparations for eventual action to overturn

Castro. In March 1960 also Cuba withdrew from the Rio Pact of 1947.[1] Diplomatic relations between Cuba and the Soviet Union, and later in the year also with China, were established. In July 1960 it was made evident that the Soviet Union was willing to give military support to the Cuban Revolution, though the precise extent of Soviet commitments was unknown. The volume of economic transactions between Cuba and the Soviet Union grew by leaps and bounds, and was soon supplemented by shipments of arms.

This development had gravely modifying effects on Latin American foreign policies. In Brazil, Presidents Vargas and Kubitschek had tried to balance a dynamic policy at home by a marked display of moderation abroad. President Jânio Quadros, on the other hand, beginning his presidential term in January 1961, pursued the opposite course. In place of the traditional Brazilian preoccupation with Argentina, now taking second place in South America, Quadros concentrated on asserting Brazil's independent role in world affairs. With some success he coordinated his policies with those of President Frondizi of Argentina. He also considered the reestablishment of diplomatic relations with Moscow and the establishment of relations with Peking. He had, however, gravely underestimated the extent of his opposition at home, and in August 1961 he suddenly resigned.

President Frondizi of Argentina (1958–62), like Quadros, foundered on the rock of the Cuban crisis in his foreign policy. Alongside Brazil, Mexico, Bolivia, Chile and Uruguay, he had refused to be manoeuvred by the United States into an uncompromising Cold War attitude towards Cuba. After he had proved less than cooperative towards the United States at the Punta del Este conference, convened in January 1962 to consider ways of excluding Cuba from the OAS, he was overthrown by the military in March of that year.

Mexico's post-war foreign policy was no longer dictated by ideological preferences. While resolutely anti-communist at home—and increasingly so—Mexico showed a certain indifference to communist fortunes abroad, proving critical of United States policies over the Guatemalan issue. However, she was clearly at pains to do nothing that could jeopardise her newly established *buena vecindad* with the United States. The Cuban Revolution brought a change of attitude; despite the distaste which President López Mateos and other highly placed Mexicans felt for the subsequent turn of political events in Cuba, Mexico regarded the policy of attrition which the United States practised towards Cuba from mid-1960 onwards as a reflection, by implication, on her own sovereignty.

Three other countries besides Brazil, Argentina and Mexico showed signs of disapproval of the way the United States was treating Cuba. In Chile, President Alessandri, who took office in 1958 after having been elected by an extremely narrow margin over the candidate of the left-wing coalition Frente de Acción Popular (FRAP), found that he had to take a resolute stand over Cuba if serious political complications at home were to be avoided. Bolivia's response over Cuba was similar to that of Chile. Nevertheless, the Bolivian administration chose a moment of intense diplomatic ferment engendered by the Cuban crisis to engage Chile in a dispute over the Lauca river.

The turmoil produced by the Cuban crisis in Latin America provided an excellent opportunity for Ecuador to raise once more her traditional dispute with neighbouring Peru over the Marañon area which had been awarded to

---

[1] See 'The Political Problems of Latin American Integration', p. 398.

the latter by the Rio Protocol in 1942. In September 1960 President Velasco Ibarra took the unprecedented step of carrying the dispute to the United Nations, by-passing the OAS in the process. Ecuador's attitude to the Cuban crisis, which was very similar to that of Chile and Bolivia, must therefore be seen against the backcloth of her dispute with Peru.

THE COLD WAR: GREAT POWER HEGEMONY AND THE 'THIRD WORLD'

What diplomatic influence the Latin American states possessed in world affairs before 1959 was exercised through their voting strength in the General Assembly of the United Nations. After 1955, when the Cold War showed definite signs of abating, and when 'parliamentary' methods of conducting international relations began to be more important, Latin American voting strength in the United Nations was all but swamped by a massive influx of new states, some from Europe and Asia, but most from Africa. Latin America got the worst of both worlds.

There were two Cold War developments which affected Latin America profoundly. One was the technological perfection of missiles which, for the first time in history, enabled the two superpowers to keep each other in military check in any part of the globe, making them more cautious in their mutual dealings than ever before. The other was the spectacular extension of what is loosely called the 'Third World'.[1]

The old bipolarity of world power had not disappeared, but its effectiveness was impaired. Many of these new trends were plainly beneficial to the Third World, but some were not; for there grew up an implicit, but for that matter no less effective consensus between the superpowers to respect each other's sphere of influence, and to regard regions situated outside those spheres as *res neutra*, as a result of which Latin America began to experience United States hegemony more severely than at any time since 1936.

In January 1961 diplomatic relations between the United States and Cuba were finally broken. In April of that year there followed the poorly conceived and badly executed attempt to topple the Castro government with the aid of a number of ill-assorted Cuban émigrés. In February 1962 the United States succeeded, after a great deal of arm-twisting and by the barest two-third majority consistent with the Charter of the OAS, in having the Cuban government 'excluded' from that organisation—a step which if anything served to strengthen Cuban resolve to engage the Soviet Union *à outrance* in the military defence of the island. In circumstances still shrouded in mystery a Cuban mission headed by Raúl Castro went to Moscow in the summer of 1962 to arrange for the dispatch of Soviet missiles and men to operate them. As these missiles were rapidly reaching the operational stage in October 1962—there were as yet no signs of any warheads—the Kennedy administration decided on a showdown with the Soviet Union by imposing a 'quarantine' on all vessels carrying missiles to Cuba, thereby compelling the Soviet government, much to the bitter disappointment of the Cuban leadership, to step back and remove the missiles.

Three distinct consequences flowed from this crisis. In the first place, United States hegemony in the western hemisphere was strikingly vindicated by the Soviet reaction. Secondly, some Latin American states, notably Brazil and Mexico, and to a lesser extent Bolivia, Ecuador and Chile, began,

[1] Formerly taken to signify Latin America and a few states in the Middle East, the term 'The Third World' now covers all parts of the world outside Europe, the Soviet Union, Anglo-Saxon North America and Anglo-Saxon Australasia.

somewhat belatedly, to canvass the idea of a nuclear-free zone in Latin America which, by its nature, carried neutralist overtones. Thirdly, Cuba's foreign policy had to undergo a reappraisal. The Cuban leadership had to decide whether it was more profitable in the long run to go on promoting guerrilla struggles in an all-out effort to set Latin America ablaze with social revolution, or whether to follow the course of diplomatic moderation now being counselled so insistently by the Soviet government in the hope of surviving the United States economic blockade with substantial economic aid from the Soviet Union. Either strategy would imply the abandonment of Cuba's hitherto painstaking neutrality in the Sino-Soviet dispute. For some time the Cubans remained undecided.

In 1964 Cuba's deteriorating economic position made Havana more amenable to advice from the Soviet Union. Favourable terms were obtained from Moscow for long-term deliveries of Cuban sugar, and the ambitious programme of industrial diversification was abandoned.

Unexpected diplomatic blows were suffered by Cuba when the Goulart administration in Brazil was overthrown by the military in April 1964, and when President Paz Estenssoro of Bolivia had to flee the country and make way for the military in October of the same year. The Castelo Branco administration which supplanted Goulart in Brazil returned to Brazil's pre-1959 policy of cooperation with the United States, and the military *junta* which ruled in La Paz similarly adopted a much less critical attitude towards the United States than its predecessor.

The question still left open by the Cuban 'missile' crisis was whether the United States would act in the event of a sudden collapse of an established Latin American government in chaotic circumstances or in the case of the gradual 'penetration' of an existing Latin American government by 'communists'. (The term 'communist' is never defined in United States diplomatic practice.)

This uncertainty was dramatically removed during the Dominican crisis of April 1965 when United States marines were sent in after an attempted coup there had half-collapsed. A significant minority of Latin American governments now virtually looked upon the United States as the aggressor. Among the most outraged governments were those of Chile, Peru, Ecuador, Venezuela, Mexico and initially even Argentina. Mexico and Uruguay in particular objected strongly to what they regarded as unilateral intervention on the part of the United States, and multilateral intervention on the part of a subsequently established Inter-American Force composed exclusively from contingents drawn from the closest allies of the United States, in the domestic affairs of a Latin American country. Mexico's determined stand conformed fully to the traditional defence she had always made of the principle of non-intervention; but Uruguay actually feared that if the case of the United States were conceded she would soon herself fall victim to unilateral intervention on the part of Brazil in the event of political disturbances breaking out in Uruguay.

Present Trends

The key to all Latin American foreign policies is provided by Brazil. Since the 1964 coup her foreign policy has been closely geared to that of the United States, but it does not necessarily follow that this will always be the case. New attitudes may also be expected to evolve in Argentina's foreign policy where the Dominican crisis has had a traumatic impact.

Mexico and Uruguay are the only survivors from what, in retrospect, must surely be regarded as the 'heroic' phase of Latin American foreign policies practised between 1960 and 1963, when half a dozen or more Latin American countries pursued identical policies in respect of Cuba. Mexico has since then been responsible for holding the neutralist ring in the matter of the nuclear-free zone, pending a diplomatic regrouping in Latin America.

The novel feature since the Cuban crisis has been the newly imparted vigour of Chile's foreign policy under President Eduardo Frei, which appears to have fallen heir to Argentina's habitual policy of fostering good relations with the countries of Western Europe in preference to the United States. Like Perón before him, President Frei is making clever diplomatic use of a trade union organisation, CLASC (Confederación latinoamericana de sindicatos cristianos), while maintaining that his ideological position 'resists the old concepts of capitalism and communism'.[1]

To inject real vitality into Latin America's foreign policies no less than a far-reaching harmonisation of diplomatic strategy is required between the two most independent-minded Latin American governments, those of Mexico and Chile. In 1966 Mexico's natural inclination was still to defend the principle of non-intervention against encroachments on it by the United States and its allies, and also to defuse Cold War issues affecting Latin America by working for the creation of a nuclear-free zone. Chile, on the other hand, appeared to be primarily interested in economic union. Its foreign policy stopped short of the reestablishment of diplomatic relations with Cuba, an issue likely to be made the measuring rod by Mexico with which to judge Chile's political sincerity.

Cuba, for its part, seemed predestined for some time to come to be fully exposed to the ups and downs of the Cold War, unable to take any real political initiative and forced to wait for leads from others. No short-term solutions of the diplomatic problems of Latin America are in sight, and the long-term prospects remain uncertain.

[1] *The Latin American Times*, New York, 26 August 1965.

BIBLIOGRAPHY

Box, P. H. *The Origins of the Paraguayan War*, Russell and Russell, New York, 1930.

Hill, L. F. *Diplomatic Relations between the United States and Brazil*, Duke Univ. Press, Durham, NC, 1932.

McGann, T. F. *Argentina, the United States and the Inter-American System, 1880–1914*, Harvard Univ. Press, Cambridge, Mass., 1958.

Quintanilla, Luis. 'Latin America', *Control of Foreign Relations in Modern Nations*, ed. P. W. Buck and M. B. Travis, W. W. Norton, New York, 1957.

Rippy, F. J. *Globe and Hemisphere*, Henry Regnery, Chicago, Ill., 1958.

THE UNITED STATES
AND LATIN AMERICA

WILLIAM D. ROGERS

THE PRE-MODERN ERA

SECRETARY of State John Quincy Adams warned from the beginning that there could be 'no community of interests or of principles between North and South America' (1820). But admiration for the *criollo* rebels and hatred for the Dons of Spain (along with fear of the Holy Alliance and suspicion of England's trade aspirations in Argentina) were all too strong. The United States was the first to recognise the new nations of Middle and South America as the Wars of Independence drew to a close (1822). President Monroe announced his doctrine—that any European attempt to recapture the lost Spanish colonies would be regarded as the 'manifestation of an un-friendly disposition towards the United States'—in 1823. Thus was tradition launched. The Americas were a community; the community would insulate itself from extraneous world issues; within the community the United States was possessed of special interests. (In 1824, half of the ten foreign diplomatic missions of the United States were in Spanish America; the other half in Europe.)

From the notion of paternal interest to the assertion of prerogative and power was but a step. Within a quarter-century the United States had annexed Texas and exacted half of Mexico's remaining territory as a humiliating prize in the war of 1848. This (with the exception of Puerto Rico fifty years later) exhausted North America's territorial ambitions in Latin America. A half-century of lull (1848–98) followed as the people of the United States directed their energies west, not south. Then came forty years of United States imperialism in the Caribbean (1895–1933), opening with the boast of Secretary of State Richard Olney that 'Today the United States is practically sovereign on this continent, and its fiat is law upon the subjects to which it confines its interposition.' (The opening of the world's first international organisation—now the Organization of American States (OAS)—in 1890 did not help matters much; the new body conferred only six times in the first thirty years of its existence.) The war of 1898 broke Spain's last hold in the New World in Cuba and Puerto Rico. Within the half-century before 1933, the United States moved troops into the Dominican Republic (1916–24), Haiti (1915–34), Nicaragua (1912–24), humiliated Mexico once more (1917), schemed to snatch Panama from Colombia for a transoceanic canal (1903), and intervened four times in Cuba under the Platt Amendment (1906, 1912, 1917 and 1933). All this was in the name, not of traditional empire (with such continuing responsibilities as empire has, on occasion, signified) but of right. For by then the United States had

425

become a Great Power; Latin America had failed the nation-building test of the 19th century. The period between the two Roosevelts added to the older concept of the self-contained community, a notion that the leadership of that community belonged to the United States and that the United States might enforce its mandate by force if necessary.

President Franklin Roosevelt initiated the era of the Good Neighbour with his Inaugural Address of 1933. His aim was not to dismantle the community, much less to renounce the paternal prerogatives of its most powerful member, but to demonstrate that the United States could stay its hand. The decade of the 1930s was a period of marked improvement in hemisphere relations. The United States formally renounced its right to intervene (1933) and the last Marines left Haiti (1934).

The second world war, however, forced the full attentions of the United States toward Europe and Asia. Latin America became a backwater to world events in the 1940s. The Marshall Plan gave Washington's slogans of hemispheric brotherhood a hollow sound. Latin America began to suspect that the community ranked low in the State Department's scale of priorities, and the suspicion was amply confirmed during the Eisenhower administration beginning in 1952.

Latin America began to feel isolated, forgotten—and threatened. Tender experiments in democracy were overrun by the military in Venezuela, Colombia and Peru (1948–52). Populations soared; farm output stagnated; peasants invaded the cities. And to add financial problems to social crisis, Latin American export earnings collapsed when the Korean War subsided. The United States, for all its paternal pretensions, was unconcerned, Secretary Dulles frankly bored, with Latin America. His foreign policy was largely an extension of a holy war on communism by other means. Latin America's problems were incomprehensible in such terms. Some State Department officials manfully tried to explain the rising demands for social and political change as communist-inspired. But the only fruit of this logic was an identification of US interests with such tyrants as Trujillo in the Dominican Republic and Pérez Jiménez in Venezuela. Latin American pleas for a community effort to meet the rising economic and social crisis (Brazilian President Kubitschek's Operation Pan America in 1958 was the most significant) met in Washington with either silence or Presbyterian moralising on the blessings of thrift. The United States missed one glorious opportunity after another to turn its leadership to constructive ends. The 1950s were the period of perilous lull.

Vice-President Nixon's trip in 1958—during which he was insulted, spat upon and threatened in life and limb—began to awaken some of the more perceptive of Dulles' lieutenants in Washington to the deterioration in US–Latin American relations. So it was that the Eisenhower administration in its closing months began, tentatively and grudgingly, to withhold its blocking veto on measures such as the Inter-American Development Bank (1959). But the modern era of inter-American relations began in earnest with President John F. Kennedy.

KENNEDY AND THE ALLIANCE FOR PROGRESS

Building on the notes of his 1960 campaign, the new president struck a full chord of United States policy for the hemisphere through the Alliance for Progress in March 1961: a 'vast new effort unparalleled in magnitude and nobility of purpose, to satisfy the basic needs of the American people for homes, work and land, health and schools—*techo, trabajo y tierra, salud y escuela.*' Yesterday's heresy would become today's orthodoxy; the United States would throw the full weight of its leadership behind the progressive democrats of Latin America. If the traditions of a century and a half proclaimed community, and if the United States had special obligations within that community, so be it. If Latin America would set itself resolutely to a process of profound economic, political and social change in education, agriculture, taxation and public administration, the United States would provide 'resources of a size and magnitude to make this bold plan a success.' The aim was an annual overall per capita increase in income of 2·5 per cent —'through the institution of representative democracy.'

Kennedy's initiative within the community followed shortly on Fidel Castro's announcement of his own plans for remaking the hemisphere. This was by no means accidental. Castro claimed that the United States, by its past misdeeds, had forfeited the prerogatives of future leadership. The United States was in alliance with the status quo. The status quo kept most Latin Americans in servitude. Hence revolution; the Andes must become the Sierra Maestra of Latin America, as Guevara told the ministerial meeting at Punta del Este in August of 1961. The fact that the ministers voted twenty to one in favour of the Charter of Punta del Este, and thus set the Alliance for Progress on its way, could not obscure the fact that 1961 was a year of glorious competing visions—Castro's and Kennedy's—of the future of Latin America.

The years since have disappointed the dreams of both. Castro has become a bad joke. It is no longer, as Costa Rican President Figueres warned, 'one minute to midnight' for democracy in Latin America. But Kennedy's own hope for a rapid 'revolution in freedom' has surrendered to the grim truth that political, social and economic development is, at best, the work of decades in Latin America.

The balance sheet of US-Latin American relations after half-a-dozen years of the Alliance for Progress nevertheless gives some cause for optimism. The United States still maintains its verbal and financial commitment to the ideals of the Alliance for Progress. And the accomplishments of the Alliance have been substantial. For several years overall per capita incomes have risen even faster than the 2·5 per cent per capita figure written into the Charter of Punta del Este. US aid, averaging over $1 billion per year, has helped build 28,000 new classrooms, irrigated a million acres of new land, constructed new dams and power plants, sparked housing projects in fifteen Latin American nations and financed potable water systems serving 20 million people. At the same time, domestic investment has increased; Latin American savings now account for nine-tenths of the new capital in the hemisphere. The Alliance for Progress has become more multilateral through the Inter-American Committee for the Alliance for Progress (CIAP). And perhaps most importantly, there is something of a new spirit abroad in the hemisphere. The Alliance has struck roots into the soil. By some curious chemistry, progressive democratic leaders, such as Presidents Frei and Belaúnde of Chile and Peru, have come to power, dedicated to the reform and development ideals of the Alliance.

FACTORS VITIATING US–LATIN AMERICAN RELATIONS

Yet, for all the treasure and first successes of the Alliance, US–Latin American relations are still troubled. The concept of community—inward-looking, exclusive—continues in all its glorious asymmetry. Other than the Marxists from their enclaves within the universities and intellectual communities, no substantial body of Latin American opinion would revoke the community arrangement, or contend that the United States should abdicate its special community responsibilities. The traditions of community allow too comforting a view of the world. Such is the legacy of Monroe and Olney, that Latin America may still delegate a fair share of its shortcomings to the United States. Thus the United States as a nation—and, by implication, its art, its life-style and its economy—is scarcely the object of widespread public devotion in the hemisphere today. Some commentators are even prepared to argue that contemporary US policy is only the imperialism of fifty years ago in modern disguise.

The United States, on occasion, snaps back. Since rural reform and educational development, the two critical domestic issues in every Latin American country, are in such pitiable state, Congress complains that its $1 billion annual aid is not matched by a record of self-help and reform. The US press writes daily obituaries for democracy in Brazil and Argentina. State Department officials are driven to a state of quiet exasperation by the apparent inability of some of their Latin colleagues to grasp the real significance of the Alliance for Progress. US investors regard Latin America (Mexico excepted) with scepticism.

These are surface evidences of the tedious conversations between North and Latin America today. There are several real issues beneath. All have a common thread. They are in each case an outcropping of the bedrock disparity of power and wealth within the community.

In matters economic, the crucial issues relate to foreign corporate investment in Latin America, and to trade. With respect to the first, though there has been a healthy ideological de-escalation in recent years, Latin Americans still tend to look on the US corporation with fear and suspicion. US investment in Latin America is significant. It now totals something over $10 billion. Latin Americans suspect that this mass of economic power can—as it has on occasion in the past—draw unto itself the great public policy decisions of resource allocation, foreign exchange practices, labour relations, budget and taxation so crucial to the development process.

In fact, there is nothing inevitable about the enslavement of peoples by foreign investment. The experience of the developed nations makes clear that by effective systems of incentive-cum-penalty taxation, by monopoly regulation of anti-competitive behaviour and by subtle use of credit and financial mechanisms, Latin American governments can induce private investment, preserve the essentials of a healthy market economy and yet maintain the public decision-making as the prerogative of the public. All that is wanting is the machinery of government—but that is no small thing in Latin America. For the moment, the practical accommodation of the public and the private is more dream than reality. Latin American policy making has not yet come to grips with the corporate phenomenon. The US corporation remains a critical problem in US–Latin American relations.

Closely related are the sensitivities generated in Latin America by the present workings of international trade. Mexican tourism aside, Latin America thus far has developed no major export industry not based on the growing of commodities or the extraction of minerals—oil from Venezuela, coffee from Brazil and Colombia, tin from Bolivia, copper from Chile. The Economic Commission for Latin America, struck by the fact that commodity prices have tended to fall while manufactured goods have become more costly in recent years, has concluded that the terms of trade inevitably run against sellers of raw materials. Some derive from this the notion that the developed countries consciously profit from Latin American poverty, and hence that the United States, in its own self-interest, will maintain the southern hemisphere in the penurious state of raw material producer.

Latin America's foreign exchange starvation troubles perceptive US policy-makers too. It is clear that the only serious long-term solution is for Latin American industry to compete effectively in world markets. Economic history since the second world war demonstrates that trade increases most rapidly among industrialised nations. The United States' best opportunities for mutually profitable exchange and investment now lie, not with Latin America, but with Europe, Japan and Canada. It is in the interests of the United States and of Latin America alike that the southern hemisphere increase its capacity to export manufactures.

To this end the United States has made substantial loans for relending to local industry, with high priority to the export sector. It has sought to educate entrepreneurs in the export business. And it has applauded and subsidised the Latin American Free Trade Area and the Central American Common Market, in spite of the potential short-term prejudice to the interests of US exporters, because the most promising experience for Latin American industry in the delicate art of export sales is to be gained in such protected markets. But much remains to be done. Latin America is slowly starving for foreign exchange. It has not yet developed any major enclaves of export manufactures like Hong Kong and the textile industry in India and Japan. Until it does, trade relations will continue to trouble the councils of the hemispheric community.

Foreign investment and trade issues are economic variants on the theme of power disparity within the community. When restated in security terms, the problem is even more unsettling. The point here, to many Latin Americans, is that the $25 billion which the United States now spends on Vietnam is roughly equal to the entire GNP of Brazil. Latin Americans are not greatly interested in Asia and Africa and so cannot share the US pre-occupation with military security in these distant areas of the world. They are able to understand, however, that the total US defence budget is fifty times its economic aid to what some State Department officials like to call 'our hemisphere.' Thus the notion that, for all the Alliance talk of develop-ment, the United States is really only interested in keeping Latin America quiet—that Eurocentrism, a preoccupation with world communism and Mr Monroe's sphere of influence syndrome are the realities of US policy in the hemisphere.

The Johnson–Kennedy Contrast

These Latin American misgivings have hardly been mollified by the difference in style between Kennedy and Johnson. Kennedy replaced Eisenhower. He was Catholic, masculine and intelligent (José Enrique Rodo's *Ariel* had taught three generations of Latin Americans that the United States was a paragon of graceless materialism). Kennedy tried to align the United States with democracy and reform. And he had even indulged in the flattering hyperbole that not Europe or Asia but Latin America was the 'most important area in the world' for the United States.

Lyndon B. Johnson tried to maintain the Kennedy momentum. Within days of Kennedy's death he recorded his determination that the Alliance for Progress be a 'living memorial to President Kennedy.' But though

Johnson embraced the Alliance slogans, he never quite succeeded in dulling the suspicion that here was a different breed of man—and so a different outlook. His dogged, sometimes brilliant, efforts to fight the Alliance appropriations through a sceptical Congress and his eloquent but sporadic calls for democratic reform were largely lost on Latin Americans, who took his style and his increasing preoccupation with Vietnam as a reversion to 19th-century great power politics.

And crisis seemed the proof of temperament. Kennedy blundered into the Bay of Pigs (1961) and admitted it. His handling of the Cuban Missile Crisis of October 1962 was a piece of masterful counterpoint, its sphere-of-influence overtones nicely muted by timely reference of the matter to the OAS. Johnson was not so fortunate or deft. His taste of hemisphere crisis came early in the Panama riots (1964). The result was a caricature of the power disparity in the community—the largest and the very smallest nations, face to face over ancient Canal rights. Few Latin Americans could comprehend Johnson's almost abrasive intransigence on the issue. A year later the United States intervened in the Dominican Republic. The early, cloaked manoeuvring of the US Marines to shore up the Dominican Army, the confused statements of US purpose, the afterthought resort to the OAS smacked more of the heavy-handed militancy of the earlier Roosevelt than the idealisms of the Kennedy administration.

What did not become clear was that US action in the Dominican Republic was not policy but the failure of policy—the bankruptcy of the earlier effort, which Latin America largely ignored but which the United States supported fairly lavishly, to build a viable, reformist state on the ruins of the Trujillo dictatorship through President Bosch. The heart of the Kennedy notion, not only in the Dominican Republic but throughout the hemisphere, was the use of the tradition and power of the community for effective internal economic, social and political development. He had come to understand that US national interest lay, not in the perpetuation of the inter-American status quo, but in tripping the springs of change and modernisation, even if the end result might be a more independent, less tractable community. The United States, he urged, must serve interests somewhat larger than its own security, even if it meant to serve its security interests as well.

'No Nation Can Save Another Nation'

It may be that such wisdom is the very least the community is entitled to expect from its one Great Power. The critical issue remains, nonetheless, the capacity of Latin Americans themselves to create viable, effective nations. And for this, paradoxically, the international processes of the community are of less relevance than the domestic politics of the members of the community. It may even be that the OAS system is largely anachronistic to the larger issues of contemporary US–Latin American relations, save to the extent that the community can provide a standard for internal reform efforts and help channel foreign assistance toward the more worthwhile of the Latin American reformers.

President Kennedy tried to turn the system of the community to the goal of development. But in taking on this large initiative to himself, he gave new force to the ancient tradition that the community should look to the United States for leadership, and to the custom that the community was sufficient unto itself. It may well be that in dramatising US leadership and the inward-looking character of hemisphere relations, he paradoxically strengthened

THE UNITED STATES AND LATIN AMERICA

two tendencies which can impede the very Alliance development objectives he strove for.

If so, then the most significant tasks in US–Latin American relations in the future should be two. The first is to blur the exclusive, inward-looking, bipolar character of the hemisphere community, in which the overwhelming power of the United States takes on such awesome meaning in time of crisis. The United States should become relatively less, not more, significant to Latin America. Europe, Japan and Canada have a rightful role to play in the process of internal modernisation. The Old World must come to redress the imbalance of the New.

The second task is kin to the first: to accept the fact that the United States cannot shape the destiny of the hemisphere, and that now, more than ever, when development has come to the top of the list of priorities, leadership is firmly the responsibility of Latin Americans themselves. The role of the United States is to stake change and progress, not to direct or command. As Teodoro Moscoso, the first US Coordinator for the Alliance for Progress, said, no nation can save another nation. Nations must in the end save themselves.

BIBLIOGRAPHY

Adams, Mildred (ed.) *Latin America: Evolution or Explosion?* (Part One: 'Latin America in the Western Hemisphere), Dodd, Mead, New York, 1963.

Adams, R. N. and others. *Social Change in Latin America Today: Its Implication for US Policy*, Oxford Univ. Press, London; Harper and Row, New York, 1960.

Connell-Smith, Gordon. *The Inter-American System*, Oxford Univ. Press for Royal Institute of International Affairs, London and New York, 1966.

Dreier, John C. *The Organization of American States and the Hemisphere Crisis*, Harper and Row for Council on Foreign Relations, New York, Evanston, Ill. and London, 1962.

Gordon, Lincoln. *A New Deal for Latin America. The Alliance for Progress*, Oxford Univ. Press, London; Harvard Univ. Press, Cambridge, Mass., 1963.

May, Stacy and Plaza, Galo. *The United Fruit Company in Latin America (United States Business Performance Abroad* series), National Planning Association, Washington, DC, 1958.

Mecham, John Lloyd. *The United States and Inter-American Security, 1889–1960*, Univ. of Texas Press, Austin, Texas, 1961.

Ronning, C. Neale. *Law and Politics in Inter-American Diplomacy*, John Wiley and Sons, New York and London, 1963.

Wood, Bryce. *The Making of the Good Neighbour Policy*, Columbia Univ. Press, New York and London, 1961.

van Wynen Thomas, Ann and Thomas, A. J., Jr. *The Organization of American States*, Southern Methodist Univ. Press, Dallas, Texas, 1963.

SPAIN AND LATIN AMERICA

STEPHEN CLISSOLD

SPAIN, as the ex-mother country of today's Spanish-speaking republics, retains towards them something of a special relationship which her government is now anxious to turn to political and economic account. Her image has changed greatly in the last century and a half. Now that her tyranny is no longer to be feared, many Latin Americans look to Spain with sentimental attachment, conscious of the common language, faith and cultural heritage composing the Hispanic element in their national make-up which sets them apart from the Anglo-Saxon ethos of the 'northern colossus'. It is significant that there are some 15,000 Latin American students today in Spain—more than the total to be found in all the universities of the rest of Europe, the United States and the Soviet bloc countries. Spanish priests still answer the call to continue their historic task of evangelisation in the new world. Spanish books are to be found in the bookshops of Latin America, and Latin American books in those of Spain. For the influence is now two-way. The ex-colonies have evolved a vigorous culture and a distinctive social and political structure of their own. They are able to influence, as well as be influenced by, their former metropolis.

THE CULT OF 'HISPANIDAD'

The loss of Spain's colonies did not mean that she lost all influence in the new world overnight. This was deplored by radicals like Lastarria, who branded Spanish rule as 'three hundred years of gloom' and her schools and universities as 'monuments of imbecility', and Echeverría who declared that 'the social emancipation of America can only be achieved by repudiating the heritage bequeathed by Spain.' Moderates like the great Venezuelan scholar Andrés Bello thought otherwise, and argued that the best elements in the Spanish past must be retained in the construction of Latin America's future. This school of thought in Spain and Latin America promoted the founding, in the 1890s, of the Ibero–American Union with the purpose of fostering relations between the Spanish-speaking peoples. The Hispanic tradition, with its Catholic and conservative overtones, was held up as the antithesis to that of the materialistic, aggressive United States which had just intervened against Spain in the Spanish–Cuban war and threatened to impose its will on all its weaker Latin American neighbours.

With the rise of the Falange in Spain and the outbreak of the second world war, the creed of *Hispanidad* was proclaimed in more militant tones. The Falange opened branches throughout Latin America, where it appealed to some extreme elements amongst the Spanish communities and right-wing Latin Americans. 'We have a will to Empire,' the Falangist press announced.

432

'We affirm that Spain's historical destiny is Empire. We stand for the unification of culture, power, and economic interests in the Latin-American countries. Spain maintains that her position as spiritual centre of the Spanish world is her claim to preeminence in world affairs.' After the defeat of the Axis powers, *Hispanidad* muted its pro-Fascist and anti-Yankee tones and it has concentrated on stressing the common cultural heritage of the Spanish-speaking peoples. It still proves useful to Spain politically in mitigating the international isolation of General Franco's regime and arousing sympathy for certain objectives of his foreign policy, such as Spain's claim for the recovery of Gibraltar.

THE REPUBLICAN REFUGEES

One result of the Spanish Civil War was to send a flood of refugees to Latin America—some 30,000 to Mexico, and another 40,000 to Brazil, Argentina, Peru, Venezuela and elsewhere. These immigrants, for the most part skilled and semi-skilled workers and members of the professional classes, have made valuable contributions to their adopted countries. Most have taken out naturalisation papers and have now become merged with the population; only some 200 of the original influx of refugees to Mexico still remain Spanish citizens. Mexico, conscious of its leftist and revolutionary traditions, was the one Latin American country to give effective help to the Republicans during the Civil War, and it still recognises a phantom Spanish Republican Government in Exile, though it keeps up a flourishing trade with General Franco's Spain and recognises one of his officials as commercial attaché. In this ambivalent attitude towards the present regime in Spain, Mexico does not stand alone. Cuba offers a still more remarkable example.

CUBAN–SPANISH RELATIONS

Cuba, which severed her ties with Spain only at the turn of the present century, possessed a large Spanish community numbering in its heyday more than half a million, or over 15 per cent of the island's population. Castro's expropriation of foreign-owned enterprises spelt the ruin of the community, and more than 15,000 of its members have since been repatriated to Spain. A dramatic incident occurred in 1960 when the Spanish ambassador rushed to the television studio to interrupt Castro in the midst of a broadcast which he deemed offensive to Spanish honour and was expelled from the country for his pains. Yet in spite of these events and of the facilities extended to the openly anti-Franco Spaniards in Cuba—and despite, too, the Caudillo's claim to have come to power at the head of an anti-communist crusade—political relations between the two countries remain tolerable and trade flourishes. Before the Cuban Revolution, Spanish–Cuban trade was running at less than 30 million dollars a year; in 1964 it had risen to 97 million dollars. Spain has purchased Cuban sugar at more than world prices, and considerable quantities of tobacco and preserved fruit, and has exported to Cuba agricultural equipment, food, wine, domestic goods, lorries and ships. Thanks to the latter, Cuba has rebuilt and expanded her merchant fleet.

Washington's pressure to join the policy of 'economic denial' to Cuba has been resisted by Madrid, and the sinking of a Havana-bound Spanish cargo-vessel by anti-Castro exiles in 1964, assumed to be acting with United States connivance, caused an outburst of indignation in Spain. Cuban defiance of the United States has also found an echo in Spain where, despite the advantages stemming from the economic and military agreements with Washington, anti-American feeling is not lacking either in nationalist or left-wing circles. Cuba and Spain, each in her own way, are conscious of their political isolation and feel drawn together by ties of interest, sentiment and kinship. There exists, as the Spanish newspaper *Ya* somewhat ruefully admitted, 'admiration in many social sectors in Spain for the regime of Fidel Castro. Spain's intransigent stand against communism almost seems to break down when it comes to Cuba. We can only explain it by the affection they have for a nation far removed in distance but very close in Spanish sentiment.'

SPAIN'S TRADE DRIVE IN LATIN AMERICA

If sentiment and economic interest have been enough to bring Spain and Cuba together despite their ideological differences, Madrid is confident that these factors can also be instrumental in leading to an all-round increase in her trade with the other Latin American countries. In November 1965, at a conference of the Organization of American States (OAS) at Rio de Janeiro, Spain made a spectacular offer of 1,000 million dollars worth of credit, to be extended to Latin America over a ten-year period. Though some scepticism was felt as to Spain's ability to undertake a programme of this magnitude, Spanish trade missions began to tour Latin America in an attempt to give substance to the offer through a series of bilateral agreements. Other channels for implementing the programme have been the Central American Bank for Economic Integration, the Inter-American Development Bank and the OAS. Spain's basic difficulty has been her unfavourable balance of trade with the area. Between 1961 and 1965 she imported from it about twice as much as she exported to it. In 1966, as a result of her new Latin American trade drive, the position improved, since not only was the total of trade greatly expanded but her volume of exports increased to more than two-thirds of her imports from that area. The following table shows this improved trend:

SPANISH–AMERICAN TRADE, 1960–6

($US million)

	1960	1961	1962	1963	1964	1965	1966
Imports from Latin America	67	110	139	188	203	259	326
Exports to Latin America	7	53	67	60	109	122	216
Balance in favour of Latin America	60	57	72	128	94	137	110

To many Latin American businessmen who distrust the agricultural policies of the EEC countries, Spain appears as an increasingly attractive market. Argentina, in particular, has been exporting more and more to Spain and accumulating a large favourable trade balance which Madrid has hopes of reducing by increased sales of ships and naval equipment. A new stimulus to Spanish–Argentine relations was given by the advent to power of General Onganía who lost little time in announcing that negotiations would begin with a view to increasing trade and in affirming his faith in the special ties which bound the two countries together. Colombia is another country with a large favourable trade balance which Spain hopes to reduce through the sale of ships and the construction, with joint Spanish and Colombian capital, of a sugar refinery for the processing of Colombian sugar for reexport to other European countries.

FUTURE TRENDS

Spain's relations with Europe and the United States will probably set the pace for her future development, but she is also likely to continue exploiting her links with the Latin American countries to the utmost. Her relationship with them is now conceived on less paternalistic and more cooperative lines. 'We Spaniards,' wrote the great Spanish thinker Unamuno, who died in 1936, 'must understand that in order to save Hispanic culture we must work with the Latin American peoples as equals. We must accept from them, and not content ourselves with merely giving to them'. In literature and the arts, Latin America is indeed now showing more creative vigour than Spain, and it is a Chilean, Pablo Neruda, who is generally accounted to be the greatest living poet in the Spanish-speaking world.

Nor may the reverse influence of the ex-colonies on their *madre patria* be confined to the purely cultural field. If the regime of General Franco is one day to give way to something different, there are three models in Latin America which may have some relevance to Spain's future development. One is the Cuban model—a Hispanic brand of communism, militantly hostile to the United States but resentful too of tutelage from Moscow or Peking, but probably too alien to Spain's deep-rooted Catholicism. Alternatively, there is the model of President Frei's brand of Christian Democracy, more radical than that of the Christian Democrat parties in Europe. Finally, there is the Mexican formula of the one-party power structure which—although its Indianist overtones clearly have no relevance for Spain—may not be without its attractions for a country where parliamentary democracy based on the two-party system has never taken root. At all events, it may well be that the future will see an increasingly active interchange not only of goods, but of trends and ideas as well, between Spain and the Spanish-speaking lands of Latin America.

BIBLIOGRAPHY

Artajo, Martín Alberto. *Hacia la comunidad hispánica de naciones (Discursos*, 1945–55), Ediciones Cultura Hispánica, Madrid, 1956.
Gibson, Charles. *Spain in America*, Harper and Row, New York, 1966.
Maeztu, Ramiro de. *Defensa de la Hispanidad*, Madrid, 4th ed. 1941.

FRANCE AND LATIN AMERICA

JEAN MEYRIAT

TRADITIONAL LINKS

WHEN the former Spanish colonies fought for their independence Napoleon's France was still a great empire, and more especially, revolutionary France lent her example to all peoples in process of emancipation. The influence of this bourgeois revolution and the vitality of the principles and ideals that inspired it made a deep impression on the Latin American nations and created a certain solidarity of political culture. While the political structure of France, successively imperial, monarchist, liberal, despotic and republican, was too unstable to provide an institutional model (the numerous constitutional experiments of the American republics were inspired by developments elsewhere), the desirability of choosing a progressive political ideal led the newly independent Latin American countries to join a group in which France for several decades provided leadership and inspiration. Soon afterwards she had to give up this role, but has kept some of the prestige derived from it.

The élite who governed 19th-century Latin America were precisely that section of the population which knew France best, becoming so closely attached to her as to consider her sometimes as a second fatherland. Thus after losing political and military hegemony in Europe, France attained success in other fields of action, and occupied an eminent position in the 19th-century world thanks to the quality of her intellectual achievements and to her financial prosperity. This was a time of considerable French capital investment in Latin America, and a flow of French emigrants, mainly businessmen and traders, formed strong-rooted enclaves that still remain, for example in Mexico, Chile (about 10,000), and Argentina (more than 80,000) where although they have assimilated themselves into their host country they constitute a link between the two cultures.

A closer attachment is created by the many Latin Americans who come to France either to study or on holiday. In this way the socio-political élite of the majority of the Latin American countries has imbibed French culture, going to the Sorbonne and other French universities, or frequenting literary and artistic circles. This tradition has been relatively long-lasting, and has only begun to weaken recently as the attraction exercised by the facilities available to Latin American students in the United States increases.

All this is not, of course, the same as actual political solidarity. On the diplomatic plane relations are usually courteous but remain somewhat distant in the absence of immediate common interests to defend. Friction occasionally arises on particular points, such as with Brazil over the respective privileges in certain zones of Brazilian and French fishermen. Sometimes French moves, like the decision to test atomic weapons in the Pacific, give rise to unease and discontent, e.g. in Chile. But these clashes, inevitable in relations between sovereign nations, never lead to real conflicts. Unwelcome episodes such as Napoleon III's imprudent expedition to Mexico lie forgotten.

TRADE RELATIONS

In contrast to the continuing cultural connection, trade links between France and the twenty Latin American countries are very weak. For these countries France has only a very secondary importance as a supplier and customer. As far as France herself is concerned, she purchases little in Latin America (4·1 per cent of total imports in 1962, 3·8 per cent in 1963), and sells still less (3·8 per cent of total exports in 1962, 3·2 per cent in 1963).

The small volume of these commercial transactions is a well established phenomenon, and the passage of time fails to reveal any signs of relative improvement. The reasons for this are varied and deep-rooted. The goods that Latin America could sell to France have to face competition from the produce of other closer regions, e.g. Africa, that benefit from traditional privileges. Moreover Latin American export policies towards Europe have not up to now been very systematic. As for selling, France has to face in the Americas both the very solid position of the United States and competition with other European countries like Britain, Germany and Italy. Finally, the desire for industrialisation, notably within the framework of the Latin American Free Trade Association, makes Latin America less willing to import manufactured goods, which are what France mainly has to offer.

This is not an encouraging situation for those Latin American republics attempting to diversify their foreign trade to avoid the emergence of a US near-monopoly, and seeking the widest possible markets for their raw materials. These countries have often complained of the obstacles allegedly created by French commercial policy that hinder the entry of their products. These complaints were most strongly voiced during the early years of the European Economic Community, which was accused of trade discrimination.

The French authorities have endeavoured to defend themselves against these accusations. For one thing, during the United Nations Conference on Trade and Development held at Geneva in the spring of 1964, in which Latin American countries were leading spokesmen for the developing nations, the French delegates came forward as the defenders of Latin American economic interests and tried to introduce new formulae 'both for raw materials and for manufactured and semi-processed goods from developing countries, especially those of Latin America' (Franco-Mexican joint communiqué of 18 March 1964). They upheld the thesis that free exchange rates were only a partial remedy, placing more emphasis on market organisation and—the essential point—guaranteed commodity prices. Again, France has gradually, throughout the 1960s, removed import restrictions from Latin American goods and lowered customs duties which for various reasons she had imposed. Finally, since 1962 the value of French imports from Latin America has been greater than that of her exports to it, a situation that provides a considerable source of foreign exchange for the latter.

In spite of all this, trade links between the two partners are still weak and would not be a substantial basis for common policies.

FRENCH INVESTMENT IN LATIN AMERICA

Until just before the second world war French investment in Latin America was second in importance only to that of the British. The war was to change the situation radically; the French authorities endeavoured to bring back as much overseas capital as possible to alleviate the exchange weakness at home while several Latin American states embarked on a policy of nationalisation of foreign interests.

After the war the flow of French investment did not continue. The authorities showed little interest and without actually restricting such investment did not encourage it. At most they gave permission for the large French banks to finance certain equipment projects. Doubtless French capital-holders retained bad memories of a past in which Latin American governments several times found it impossible to repay their foreign debts. Moreover French disposable capital had become scarce owing to the needs of the internal financial market. Capital for foreign investment was usually directed towards countries that had close geographical and historical ties with France, especially in the European Common Market or Africa. Latin America was less attractive: its regimes did not always offer guarantees of political stability or continuity in economic planning; furthermore, the French were ignorant of its real potential.

As a result of all this, during the seven years between 1957 and 1963 total new French investment in Latin America was only US$51·5 million, from which US$22·7 million should be subtracted to account for the liquidation of past investments, leaving a net total of only US$28·8 million. The overall amount of French capital invested in Latin America is very small. Brazil has the largest share, as much as US$300 million in 1962. But in Venezuela in 1964 the figure was less than US$15 million and in Chile less than US$10 million. The French share of foreign investment was less than 1 per cent in 1963 in these countries.

It is true that to capital investment from which the owners expect direct profit should be added the various forms of aid that since the 1950s have become essential components of international relations. However, if France is the country that sets aside the largest share of her national income for aid to the rest of the world, Latin America is very far from being the principal beneficiary. From 1960 to 1963 France contributed US$3,522 million of her public funds to developing countries. Of this total Latin America received only 0·8 per cent, i.e. US$30 million.

Like other European countries France has agreed to refinance the commercial debt owed by Argentina, Brazil and Chile. But though she allocates considerable resources to the sending abroad of technical experts, especially teachers, here again Latin America's share was a small one: in 1965 France kept 44,000 assistants abroad under bilateral aid programmes; amongst these only 563, of whom 418 were teachers, were serving in Latin American countries. Government loans were even more limited. The first France ever granted to a Latin American country, to Mexico in June 1963, was of a value of US$30 million, to which were added US$120 million in private credit and export guarantees. This last form of aid represents the highest sums. Between 1960 and 1964 the French government gave its guarantee to more than US$600 million in medium-term credit for covering exports to Latin America.

REDEPLOYMENT OF FRENCH POLICY

After the Algerian problem was solved in 1962 it seemed as if Gaullist France was in the process of embarking on more dynamic policies towards the rest of the world, including the Americas. At the end of 1963 de Gaulle broadcast a message in which he gave aid to developing countries priority as one of France's three main tasks for 1964. Latin America was given a more explicit place in the Jeanneney Report of July 1963. A committee under the chairmanship of former minister J. M. Jeanneney had been given the task of studying the 'policy of cooperation with developing countries'. Based on precise and objective analysis, this report showed the possibilities open to France in 'redeploying' her policy in the field of aid to *all* developing areas, not simply those African countries traditionally attached to France.

The report judged that the percentage of her income that France devoted to foreign aid could hardly be increased but should not decrease either. Consequently, the value of this aid should grow side by side with the growth of the national product, estimated at about 5 per cent per annum. That should make it possible to increase total resources devoted to bilateral aid in the public sector by two-thirds between 1961 and 1975. If during these fifteen years increased aid to countries in the present free trade zone were to be limited to 35 per cent, and the rest of the increase in aid devoted to the rest of the world, of which Latin America would be the most important part, French public funds granted to this area would be multiplied by eight. At the same time it would be possible for the French authorities to increase by even greater proportions, through the media of the international organisations, their country's share of multilateral aid—of which Latin America is the principal beneficiary. Private aid, which formed the largest part of total aid to countries outside the free trade zone at the beginning of the period, could be expected to keep pace with public aid.

Towards a New Policy

The brilliant diplomatic success of de Gaulle's 1964 tours of Mexico and South America posed the question of whether a new phase in Franco-Latin American relations was beginning.

On the economic plane a truly substantial strengthening of relations is still far off. France has not enough to offer. Her manufactured goods have many competitors. Her disposable capital is not large enough to satisfy enormous needs. She cannot absorb at short notice a considerably increased quantity of the goods and raw materials that the Latin American countries need to sell since she cannot sacrifice her other suppliers and radically change trade transactions that offer her numerous advantages; neither can she increase her consumption at will. As the prime minister told the National Assembly in 1964: 'France cannot shoulder the economic burden carried by the United States.' The Latin American heads of state know this too; just before the French president's tour they took care to give well-publicised audiences to the North American ambassadors, and during the tour they were prudent in their remarks.

At the end of the tour it was decided in principle that Paris would give favourable consideration to equipment projects in which one or other of the Latin American countries had asked for participation, but not much has come of these intentions. Two years after de Gaulle's return only one loan from public funds had been granted—a US$50 million loan to Chile.

In the field of cultural relations results have been more positive. It is here that France has most to offer. Cultural and technical cooperation agreements favouring both parties were signed in 1964 between France and most of the states visited by de Gaulle. French firms specialising in engineering have been offered important missions in Mexico. In French scientific and univer-

439

sity circles interest in Latin American problems, well established before de Gaulle's tours, is further increasing; study and research centres are being set up in Paris and the provinces, scholarships are being offered to Latin American students and university lecturers, and intellectual cooperation is being developed.

Nevertheless the French nation at large is indifferent towards far-off Latin America. It is not therefore surprising that government policy towards Latin America is not very different now from what it was five or ten years ago. A few statements voicing disapproval of US intervention in Santo Domingo did not inhibit the French government from maintaining a calm attitude in the ensuing crisis and taking care not to get involved in an affair which concerned it very little. Likewise French diplomacy played no part in the big debates which affected the evolution of inter-American relations in 1964 and 1965. At the most one event, important at any rate as a symbol, should be mentioned.

In 1964–5 Mexico and Chile took up an independent position that was certainly contrary to the wishes of the US State Department. At the consultative meeting of American Foreign Affairs Ministers held at Washington in July 1964 Mexico refused to break off diplomatic relations with Cuba when the latter was accused of anti-Americanism. At the 1965 Inter-American Conference at Rio Chile opposed proposals for creating an inter-American armed intervention force. Not only are these two countries amongst those visited by General de Gaulle, but, more importantly, their respective presidents had been officially received with much warmth in Paris in the months just preceding their taking up these positions. There may be more than coincidence in this. It is possible to see in it a sign of conscious solidarity between nations which have chosen of their own accord to be independent and not to align themselves unconditionally in the direction indicated by a guide or protector no matter how powerful.

It may well be that here lies the significance of the attitude adopted since 1963 by the French authorities towards Latin America. It is not yet a coherent policy but a beginning, which may gradually lead the way to such a policy.

BIBLIOGRAPHY

Chauvel, J. 'La France et l'Amérique latine', *Revue de défense nationale*, XX, 9, Paris, September 1964.

Fines, André. 'La France et l'Amérique, relations commerciales, concours techniques', *Revue juridique et politique*, XVIII, 3, Paris, September 1964.

Rostand, Olivier. 'L'Amérique latine et la France: les apports français au développement du continent', *Notes et études documentaires*, La Documentation française No. 3084, Paris, April 1964.

BRITAIN AND LATIN AMERICA

JAMES C. HUNT

For about a century, from the period of the emancipation, Britain was the most significant extra-continental power in Latin America. Her interests were commercial and strategic, not imperial. Even so the exercise of her naval power and her economic dominance gave rise at times to misgivings about her intentions. After the first world war Britain was overtaken by the United States in the economic field, having already in the latter part of the previous century effectively recognised the region—particularly the northern countries in and around the Caribbean—as falling within the United States' sphere of political influence. The decline in Britain's stake in Latin America dates from around 1930, with the shift in trading patterns that followed the depression. It was hastened by the second world war and has continued inexorably, if at reduced pace, since then. Yet there are signs that the trend could be and is being reversed, and in a fashion that responds to Latin American desires and objectives. Certainly it is the avowed aim of the British government that relationships should be reinvigorated.

BRITAIN AND THE EMANCIPATION OF LATIN AMERICA

Britain made a greater practical contribution than any other country to the emancipation of both Spanish and Portuguese America, but the interests of Britain and the revolutionaries were not in fact congruent during the struggle for independence.

Britain's primary objective was trade. Compelled by the pressures of war and her own industrial revolution, Britain seized the opportunities presented by the Napoleonic Wars to secure markets in an area where free access had been denied her for three centuries by Spain and Portugal, save only for limited treaty rights secured in the 18th century compounded by the bonuses from smuggling and piracy. Always more restrictionist than Portugal, Spain did not after the overthrow of Napoleon maintain the trading privileges granted Britain during hostilities, so that the British merchant interest sided against her resistance to the independence movements in America. More important, the Spanish American patriots themselves had become imbued with Adam Smith's doctrine equating free competition with natural liberty. The British invasions of the River Plate (1806–07), by briefly opening the channels of trade before Spain became an ally, had had this as one unwitting consequence.

Another was the nourishing of the ambitions of the creoles to take charge of their own affairs. They, however, were not prompted to rise until after Napoleon's usurpation of the Spanish throne. But the British in their turn diverted to Spain the expeditionary force assembled under Wellington to liberate Spanish America, a scheme influenced by Miranda who like many

441

other patriots at this time sojourned in London. Although for the rest of the struggle Britain remained neutral, many British volunteers and mercenaries enlisted in the patriot cause, and served with distinction out of proportion to their numbers. Generous tribute and homage were to be paid a century later at the Pan-American Centennial Congress of 1926 to the 5,000 strong British Legion, to Generals Miller and O'Leary and other officers who all fought under the Liberator, Simón Bolívar; and to such men as Admiral Lord Cochrane who served Chile and Brazil, and Admiral Brown, Argentina.

Official neutrality nevertheless did not signify disinterest. From the outbreak of the secessionist movements in 1810, the aims of Castlereagh and Canning as successive foreign secretaries were to mediate, and to deny Spain any help from other European powers. Supremacy of the seas ensured the latter on two occasions in particular: in 1817 when the issue in America hung in the balance, and in 1823 through the Polignac Memorandum—the French undertaking not to intervene—obtained by Canning shortly before the United States' proclamation of the Monroe Doctrine.

RELATIONS WITH INDEPENDENT LATIN AMERICA

Although Bolívar's vision of a Spanish American League under British guardianship was never more than that, Britain engaged actively in Latin American affairs during the 19th century, both to assure the conditions for sound commercial and financial relationships and also to maintain the connection with Europe generally, as against US aspirations of hemispheric exclusivism.

The stability of Latin American states has been of more concern to Britain than the types of regime that governed them. The delay in recognising the new nations, even after the United States had done so, reflected the principle that governments should first demonstrably exercise their authority. Thus the condition applied to Argentina, whose national integration took so long to achieve, was that Buenos Aires should speak for all the provinces. Again in the 1850s British diplomacy was conducive to the unity of Argentina after the downfall of the dictator Rosas. Over Brazil, Canning laboured successfully to underpin diplomatically a monarchical regime (1822–89) which eased the transition to independence and probably helped to avert the break-up of that huge country. Since then, whatever its preferences, British diplomacy has not sought to determine the types of Latin American governments to come to power, however achieved, whether by military coup as in Peru (1962) or Argentina (1966) or by revolution as in Cuba (1959). In this respect British policy has come closely to accord with the widely held Latin American view embodied in the Estrada Doctrine, enunciated in 1930 by the Mexican foreign minister Jenaro Estrada, that recognition of any new regime should be automatic.

In issues between Latin American states or between them and other powers, Britain more often than not remained a bystander. Her offers to mediate in the Mexican–Texan–US wars and the War of the Pacific, between Peru, Bolivia and Chile, were of no avail. In the thirty-year-long struggle between Argentina and Brazil, British policy was directed to the creation of Uruguay as a buffer state (1828) and the maintenance of its integrity subsequently. Though the United States saw in this an attempt to found a British colony, Britain declined the role of protectress preferred her. She did, however, agree to establish a protectorate (1844–60) along the Mosquito coast of Nicaragua but withdrew after protracted dispute with the United

States. The only cases of British territorial aggrandisement—in the Falkland Islands, British Honduras and British Guiana—all had their origins in the 18th century, but have been persistent sources of friction between Britain and her neighbours. In recent years considerable efforts have been made to find solutions to them.

Infringements of national sovereignty occurred for other reasons too. Brazil's failure to implement the 1830 agreement with Britain to halt the slave trade resulted for several years in sometimes drastic measures by the British navy to seize the ships involved. Like other powers, moreover, Britain asserted the right to enforce debt-servicing by governments which had flagrantly disregarded their commitments. This had unfortunate consequences following the intervention in Mexico (1860–1) when, by joining with France and Spain, Britain inadvertently opened the way for the ill-conceived Maximilian adventure of Napoleon III. The last debt-collection venture, the Anglo–German–Italian blocade of Venezuela (1902–03) had as its outcome the Roosevelt Corollary to the Monroe Doctrine. This was to mark Britain's effective acknowledgement of US primacy in the western hemisphere. In 1895 she had acquiesced in US pressures to submit to arbitration the Venezuelan–Guiana frontier dispute, and in 1901 Britain had agreed to abrogate a fifty-year-old treaty with the United States whereby both countries renounced rights to exclusive control over any canal built across the Central American isthmus.

These events were not to mark the end of Anglo–US rivalry, but with the advent of the Pan-American system it is not surprising that in neither of the world wars did any Latin American country cease neutrality until the United States had done so first. Yet, a pointer to Britain's continuing standing is furnished by the fact that she was invited to arbitrate in 1902 and again in 1966 between Chile and Argentina over a frontier dispute.

Economic Development

From the achievement of independence until the first world war, Britain was a major influence on Latin America's economic development, and made the chief external contribution to it through trade and investment. In the most dynamic period, the thirty-five years to 1914, British assets increased by over five times to a nominal value of about £1,000 million ($5,000 million), though the amount of capital that flowed in was probably a third less than that, and accounted for between over half and two-thirds of total foreign investment. Latin America in turn absorbed about a fifth of Britain's overseas stake; the proportion had been as high as a quarter during the first flush of interest in the area during the 1820s, but dropped to only a tenth in 1870. The direction and pattern also changed markedly. The share of the three largest countries—Argentina, Brazil and Mexico— increased sharply between 1880 and 1914 to two-thirds of the total at the expense of the Pacific coast countries. Argentina, moreover, replaced Brazil as Britain's main trading partner and destination of capital in Latin America. The uncertain attractions of mining gave way to constructing railways, which represented 46 per cent of British investment. These changes denoted a major shift to the temperate zones, especially around the River Plate basin where half the British interests came to be concentrated. Small wonder that Argentina in those days has been described as part of Britain's informal empire. Furthermore, in the countries where British involvement was not large it was often appreciable, e.g. in Chilean nitrates.

Inevitably these intimate relationships have been widely criticised: in Britain chiefly because the returns were not always as rewarding as was hoped, or consistently made in the case of government bonds; in Latin America on the grounds that local economies were developed in lopsided manner, in primary rather than manufacturing activities, and that economic interests interfered in domestic politics. Yet, whatever the validity of these points, if it is granted that the relationships were the product of their time, there is no gainsaying the powerful though irregular influence Latin America exerted on the British economy, nor conversely that the demands of the British market—which was taking a quarter of Latin American exports—coupled with British enterprise opened up large sectors of the region.

The period between the two world wars marked the watershed in Anglo–Latin American economic relations. Little fresh capital was to come from Britain for another forty-five years after its 1913 peak, though the value of investments did increase by about a fifth in nominal terms up to the 1930 depression. Commerce suffered correspondingly. For British exports the main obstacles in the 1920s were the overvaluation of sterling and an undue dependence on textiles. Latin American exports were sustained at a high level for longer, especially quantitatively. Britain reaped substantial benefit from her earlier investments, partly through direct returns, but mainly on account of relative price movements which were prejudicial to primary producers. With the depression, trade in both directions suffered more than with almost all other major Latin American trading partners. When the multilateral system of trade broke up, while Britain instituted the framework of Imperial Preferences, other European countries—notably Germany—concluded often tight bilateral agreements with Latin America. The nearest British parallel, the Roca–Runciman Agreement with Argentina, helped to moderate the downward trend, especially for British exports. Unfavourable to Argentina though the agreement has been sometimes regarded, it did not impose restrictions on currency surpluses which in an epoch of bilateralism was of decided advantage to Argentina.

The second world war resulted in the reduction of Britain's status to that of but one of several major economic partners with Latin America, all of them overshadowed by the United States. The withdrawal, however, was carried out with consummate skill by Britain and, by their collaboration, the Latin American governments rendered their chief contribution to the allied cause. By nothing more formal than arrangements between central banks, Argentina, Brazil, Peru, Uruguay, Bolivia, Chile and Paraguay agreed to accept blocked sterling, against a gold guarantee, to cover their trade surpluses with Britain during the war. Essential supplies were thereby maintained with a minimum burden on Britain's wartime economy. The build-up of the accounts—about £150 million for Argentina and £40 million for Brazil at their end-war maxima—also permitted the repatriation of most of these countries' outstanding official debt, while leaving surpluses for the purchase of the main British assets, the railways, whose concessions in Argentina expired in 1947. By such means Britain helped to finance the take-over of more than half of her former assets, a large proportion of which were no longer yielding any or much return. There were nonetheless instances, such as over the Mexican oilfields and the Buenos Aires tramways, which gave rise to such protracted dispute before their eventual settlement as to be damaging to mutual understanding.

In the past decade economic relations have apparently become stabilised, but they have at the same time tended to become more diversified. British exports have fluctuated without showing any tendency to grow beyond about 5 per cent of Latin America's total imports, and in 1966 were £162 million, an amount only a little above the average for the period. Of this, machinery and transport equipment account for over half, while textiles and other consumer goods are minor elements. British imports from Latin America, £283 million in 1966, have likewise not shown a secular growth. Primary produce is the overwhelming constituent, but Britain is a growing market for Latin American semi-manufactures and finished goods. The substantial overall trade deficit for Britain, a constant feature, is accounted for largely by Argentina and Venezuela, a trade surplus being enjoyed by Britain with Mexico and the Central American and Caribbean countries. Generally, nevertheless, Britain appears to run a balance of payments surplus with the region, sterling claims against it exceeding liabilities by as much as £82 million at the end of 1966, an exceptional year.

British investment in Latin America has revived since the late 1950s; in the years 1961–5 it was 7 per cent of total net direct overseas investment other than in the oil industry, and it was almost a quarter of the amount going to developing countries. The total value of British assets currently in Latin America is not easily calculated: official returns indicate direct investment at a total of £250 million in 1965, of which nearly a quarter was in Argentina and a fifth in Brazil. To this should be added the 40 per cent British share in the Shell stake of £375 million in Venezuela and the substantial assets of banking, insurance and portfolio holdings. Today these British interests in Latin America are second only to the United States', but are probably only a seventh as large.

Aid to Latin America has been a new feature: apart from the indirect contribution through the World Bank group, refinancing of commercial debt loans has been made to Argentina (£19 million in 1955 and £10 million in 1963–4), to Brazil (£7 million in 1961–4) and to Chile (£3·5 million in 1961 and 1963). Bilateral tied loans have been made to Colombia and Peru (each £2 million), Bolivia (£1 million) and Chile (£750,000). A contribution of £7 million has been made to the Inter-American Development Bank, partly through the first bond issue of its kind for many years on the London capital market (1964) and partly through a government grant. In addition British banking institutions have made revolving credits to Colombia (£5·5 million in 1963) and a consortium has taken an interest in a Colombian development corporation, to mention only the main operations both actual and pending. The rapid expansion in credit facilities, now covering about a quarter of British exports to Latin America, is a form of indirect aid. But the most significant development is the technical assistance programme which has grown rapidly since 1963. The provision of British technical and advisory schemes promises to have a multiplier effect on development out of proportion to the monetary outlays involved, which at over £500,000 a year are spread over most Latin American countries.

TOWARDS A LATIN AMERICAN POLICY

The coincidence of several factors in the 1960s has made for a revival of British interest in and towards Latin America, and provided the ingredients for a fresh policy. Harbingers of a change have been seen in the number of British ministers to visit Latin America since 1964, following an earlier round of royal visits, and reciprocally the state visit of President Frei of Chile in 1965, the first by a Latin American head of state.

The broad perspective was set by the rise of Castro and the formation of the Alliance for Progress. Attention has inevitably been focussed on the long-term issues of Latin America's place in the Western world and its adherence to social and democratic ideals instead of the doctrines of totalitarian revolution. Britain has faced something of a dilemma in responding at once to the desires of many Latin Americans to see a greater European— and hence also British—involvement in achieving the goals of the Charter of Punta del Este, as well as to her own desire to avoid substantial differences with the United States. In practice entanglements have been averted on account of Britain's inability to play a major role. Thus, on the aid front, Britain has kept her contribution distinct from, though coordinated with, the Alliance for Progress. In diplomatic affairs, without always agreeing with US methods, she has refrained from making political capital out of US difficulties, resisting the temptation to assume the role of critic without responsibility. In such crises as the Guatemalan, Cuban and Dominican, Britain has not fully concurred with US conceptions on the use of Inter-American peace-keeping machinery in preference to the UN's—a throwback from past divergences over the Monroe Doctrine. Trade policy has, however, given rise to several tensions, notably over the sale of arms to Latin American countries and over commercial intercourse with Cuba, whose government Britain recognises along with Mexico, alone amongst members of the Organization of American States (OAS). While Britain has applied the same embargo on military goods for Cuba as for Soviet countries, she has refused to restrict traffic, even on deals involving the extension of medium-term credit which, notably in the case of a £14 million fertiliser plant, the United States held to constitute aid. Venezuela too has objected keenly, blacklisting ships trading with Cuba, as does the United States.

In the context of the contemporary restructuring of the framework of international economic relations, Britain has shown a sensitive awareness of Latin American interests. These came to the fore over the 'third country' issue in the British negotiations (1961–3) to join the European Communities. Both during and after, the British government repeatedly urged joint European effort towards Latin America as a step on the road of common policies, which have in some measure been achieved through the Organisation for Economic Cooperation and Development. Also, Britain dropped her earlier discouragement of Latin American economic integration, and has pursued a positive approach towards commodity stabilisation schemes, being a major member of all those in existence. At the UN Conference on Trade and Development (1964), it was British intervention that resolved the differences between industrialised and developing countries, the Latin Americans being foremost amongst the latter. The first major step towards the realisation of the principles then agreed was the eventual conclusion of the GATT Kennedy Round (1967), in which Britain, taking a liberal view on tariff policy facilitated by the erosion of Imperial Preference and its prospective demise, sought to reconcile the trend towards economic regionalism with the demands of developing economies. Britain's further contributions in the economic field depend, however, on whether she is successful in joining the European Communities and on her policies for amplifying the functions of the IMF and World Bank through improved international credit facilities and the mitigation of foreign payments fluctuations in developing countries.

The loosening of bonds with the Commonwealth has, by relaxing British preoccupation with her responsibilities there, given more scope for attending to Latin American affairs. Welcome in principle as this may be in Latin America, some aspects may be less than healthy, such as the racialist undertones in the disillusion with the Commonwealth. A paradox too is to be seen in the way both extremes of left and right political opinion have looked unrealistically to much increased trade with Latin America as an alternative to membership of the European Communities. More constructively, Britain has looked favourably on the entry into the OAS of independent Commonwealth countries in the western hemisphere—Trinidad and Tobago has joined and Jamaica was on the verge of doing so in autumn 1967.

The sharpest departure from the past has come in the field of cultural relations. While the British Council has since the 1930s been active in Latin America, there has been no reverse relationship until lately beyond the cultural conventions with Brazil (1947) and Argentina (1961). The chief initiative has come with the institution of Latin American affairs as a proper area of academic study. Centres were set up at five universities following the report on Latin American studies in 1965 by a special committee established by the government. This was a natural development of the doubling of Spanish language teaching at schools over the previous decade. Hitherto, not only has the 'kith and kin' tie with Latin America been slight—in a century and a half gross British emigration has probably not exceeded 150,000—but the British communities there, chiefly in the River Plate area, have been more distinguished by their aloofness than by their adaptability. The recent developments should in time help give Anglo–Latin American relations a depth of understanding previously lacking and a more dependable quality than commercial considerations. But it may take a generation for the fruits to mature.

BIBLIOGRAPHY

'Britain and Latin America: a brief historical survey', Central Office of Information, London, 1961.

'Britain's Economic Links with Latin America and the Caribbean', Central Office of Information, London, 1964.

Ferns, H. S. *Britain and Argentina in the Nineteenth Century*, Oxford Univ. Press, London and New York, 1960.

Ford, A. G. *The Gold Standard, 1880–1914: Britain and Argentina*, Oxford Univ. Press, London and New York, 1962.

Humphreys, R. A. 'Anglo-American Rivalries and Spanish American Emancipation', *Transactions of the Royal Historical Society*, 5th Series, XVI, London, 1966. 'British Merchants and South American Independence', *Proceedings of the British Academy*, LI, London, 1966. *Liberation in South America, 1806–1827*, Univ. of London, Athlone Press, London, 1952.

Joslin, David. *A Century of Banking in Latin America: Bank of London and South America Limited*, 1862–1962, Oxford Univ. Press, London and New York, 1963.

Manchester, A. K. *British Pre-eminence in Brazil, its Rise and Decline*, Univ. of North Carolina Press, Chapel Hill, NC, 1933.

Mulhall, M. G. *The English in South America*, 'Standard' Office, Buenos Aires, 1878.

Platt, D. C. M. 'British Agricultural Colonization in Latin America', *Inter-American Economic Affairs*, XVIII, 3, 1964 and XIX, 1, 1965, Washington, DC.

Report of the Committee on Latin American Studies, HMSO, London, 1965.

Rippy, J. F. *British Investments in Latin America 1822–1949, A Case Study in the Operations of Private Enterprise in a Retarded Region*, Univ. of Minnesota Press, Minneapolis, Minn., 1959.

Webster, C. K. *Britain and the Independence of Latin America 1812–1830: Select Documents from the Foreign Office Archives*, 2 vols, Oxford Univ. Press, London and New York, 1938.

THE SOVIET UNION AND LATIN AMERICA

STEPHEN CLISSOLD

SOVIET interest in Latin America is of relatively recent growth. If we turn to the sixty-five volumes of the 'Great Soviet Encyclopaedia' (1927) we find that a mere 150 words are devoted to Bolívar, whilst one solitary article on a Latin American theme figures in the official list of all historical studies undertaken in the Soviet Union between 1917 and 1942. Yet the 1959 Library of Congress bibliography of post-second-world-war Soviet writing on Latin America lists 2,200 titles (fifty-one of them historical), and as many as 3,500 titles for the next five-year period (1959–64). How is this sudden Soviet interest in Latin America to be explained?

Some of the reasons are the same as those which have also prompted the West to take a new interest in Latin America: its potential wealth and growing importance as a market, its rapidly expanding population and its position as that part of the underdeveloped world probably nearest to economic take-off, its status along with Africa and Asia in the still uncommitted world, and its voting power in the United Nations. Furthermore, its social and economic stresses make it seem ripe for revolution. Above all, there is the explosive power of Latin American nationalism, which tends to vent itself against the 'Colossus of the North'. But if this trend clearly interests the Soviet Union in its confrontation with the United States, it is one which it will do well to encourage with circumspection. Washington remains immensely powerful in an area which it regards as vital to national security, and clumsy attempts to exploit United States vulnerability there—as the Cuban missile crisis of 1962 showed—will only backfire. Moreover, Latin American nationalism, though fiercely resentful of interference from Washington, is also liable to react sharply against interference from Moscow.

DIPLOMATIC RELATIONS

Soviet Russia is at present in full diplomatic relations with six Latin American countries: Mexico, Uruguay, Brazil, Argentina, Chile and Cuba. This does not necessarily imply, on the part of the Latin American countries concerned, any particular sympathy for the Soviet system, still less for the aims of their local Communist parties. President Frei of Chile reestablished relations, which had been broken off in 1947 following alleged Soviet attempts to stir up labour trouble and to subvert the country's Slav minority, after defeating the Communist-Socialist coalition in a fierce electoral contest. Marshal Castelo Branco of Brazil saw no reason to break with Moscow even after overthrowing the leftist regime of President Goulart which had restored the diplomatic links severed in 1947 as the result of Soviet press attacks on a

448

previous president, Marshal Dutra. In general, Latin American governments value relations with the Soviet Union as conducive to a more independent stance in foreign policy, though they have to accept the concomitant risks of Soviet involvement in domestic subversion or of pressure to adopt stiffer anti-American attitudes. The resulting fluctuations in their relations with the Soviet Union may be illustrated by the cases of Mexico and Uruguay.

Mexico entered into diplomatic relations with the Soviet government in 1924, only to break them off within six years as a result of the support the Mexican Communists were believed to be receiving from the Soviet embassy. They were renewed in 1942, when Russia's resistance to Nazi Germany greatly increased her popularity in Mexico, as in other Latin American countries. They came under fresh strain in 1959 when Mikoyan, who visited Mexico City to open an impressive exhibition of Soviet science and culture, went too far in trying to exploit Mexican resentment of the United States and in exaggerating the affinities between the Russian revolution and the Mexican revolution, of whose distinctive character and achievements Mexicans are justifiably proud.

Uruguay's national traditions and characteristics are very different. A vigorous democracy itself, the country takes pride in its social institutions and presents little in the way of a revolutionary situation to be exploited. But it does offer an excellent base for operations in neighbouring states. This perhaps explains the exorbitant size of the Soviet diplomatic mission which has caused the Uruguayan authorities some misgivings. In the early 1930s Montevideo was selected as the most suitable site for the Latin American headquarters of the Comintern. If, as occurred in 1931, the Argentine authorities closed the offices of a Soviet commercial firm suspected of serving as a cover for subversive activities, the office had only to transfer from Buenos Aires to Montevideo, where it was free to resume operations. But in 1935 Soviet abuse of diplomatic cover led Uruguay to break off relations. They were renewed during the war, but again jeopardised when the Soviet minister attempted to muzzle anti-Soviet comment in the Uruguayan press, and later when Moscow made a clumsy attempt to force Uruguay into protesting to the United States following the Bay of Pigs invasion fiasco in Cuba. Suspected Soviet encouragement of Uruguayan labour troubles and Soviet participation in the Havana Three Continents Conference of 1966 led to fresh Uruguayan protests and a Soviet disclaimer that the Soviet delegate to the Conference was speaking in an official capacity or that the Conference resolutions denoted any desire on the Soviet side to intervene in Latin American domestic affairs.

TRADE RELATIONS

There are a number of reasons why the Latin American countries might be attracted by the prospect of trade with the Soviet Union. It promises new markets for their exports, new sources of supply for their imports, and perhaps the possibility of loans and credits at favourable rates. Moreover, trade with the Soviet Union, like the establishment of diplomatic relations, appeals as a means of strengthening the independence of Latin American countries, or at least of strengthening their bargaining position vis-à-vis the United States. A country seen to be considering expanding its trade with the Soviet Union, or accepting an offer of Soviet aid, might expect competing offers from the United States on more attractive terms; but the game must be played carefully, for too serious a flirtation with the Soviet Union might well frighten off private investment and jeopardise the all-important economic connection between the country concerned and the United States.

The purely economic advantages which the Soviet Union expects to gain from trade with Latin America are more dubious. There are few of Latin America's basic exports for which it has a vital and permanent need, though it may be prepared to take them to suit temporary requirements, or even on a long-term basis if the political advantages are sufficiently great. The classic example of this is Cuba's sugar, which the Soviet Union could very well do without, but is willing to absorb in view of the political importance of keeping the Cuban economy afloat. How far it would be prepared to take on a similar commitment elsewhere in Latin America is doubtful, and it is sometimes argued that the Soviet Union could literally not 'afford' another Cuba. But temporary economic inducement remains a telling political argument. It has been asserted, for instance, that a Soviet offer of a trade pact with Uruguay, reportedly to the value of $30 million, helped to avert the danger of a rupture of diplomatic relations after the Havana Three Continents Conference, and to allay the uneasiness caused by the size of the Soviet diplomatic mission in Montevideo. Another economic gesture with obviously important political implications was Khrushchev's offer of a tin smelter to Bolivia (1960). But Moscow has been relatively sparing in her offers of aid. During the period 1954–65, Latin America's share (excluding Cuba) was only 5·4 per cent of the total offered by the Soviet bloc (half of it by the Soviet Union) to the developing countries, as compared with 18·1 per cent offered to Africa, 40·5 per cent to Asia, and 36 per cent to the Middle East. In the economic as in the political field Moscow's hands are tied by her conviction that Washington would use its immense influence to prevent any Latin American country from establishing too close a connection with the Soviet Union. The heart of the problem remains political; any substantial increase of trade or aid from the Soviet Union can only be expected from a country which (like Cuba) makes the political decision to follow a pro-Soviet course. The establishment of diplomatic relations is regarded as a valuable preliminary for this long-term aim, and Moscow has made it clear that it is reluctant to build up a substantial economic connection with any Latin American country which does not maintain political relations with the Soviet Union.

For all these reasons, the volume of trade between Latin America (apart from Cuba) and the Soviet Union has remained small. Over the period 1960–4, it did not amount to one per cent of the region's total trade, and was largely confined to Argentina, Brazil, Uruguay and Mexico. The volume of trade has, moreover, fluctuated a good deal from year to year, and it is difficult to discern any overall trend. It has also shown great instability in its commodity composition. One year a Latin American country may export a sizeable quantity of its chief commodity; the next year this may drop to next to nothing. Other features have been the tendency of the Latin American countries to export to, more than they import from, the Soviet Union, and for the latter to send them other raw materials rather than capital goods and equipment. The general picture, in short, does not suggest that there is any very solid basis for a major expansion of trade between these two areas, though a limited expansion, with political as much as economic motivation, may well take place. The signing of new trade agreements with Brazil (August 1966) and Chile (January 1967) are steps in the latter direction.

CULTURAL AND IDEOLOGICAL RELATIONS

The Soviet Union, like other great powers, attempts to project its image, create good will, influence public opinion, and generally further its policies, by utilising the standard media of propaganda and public relations. It encourages the flow of books and publications, promotes friendship societies and tours by musicians, artists, ballet dancers and scholars, and invites prominent Latin Americans to the Soviet Union. It broadcasts programmes in Spanish, Portuguese and Quechua—much of the latter crude incitements to revolt—that in 1965 totalled a weekly output of nearly one hundred hours. The Soviet Union also offers scholarships to young Latin Americans. In 1961 some 2,500 foreign students were believed to be studying in the Soviet Union, nearly one-eighth of them Latin Americans. In 1964 the total had risen to nearly 20,000, with a more than proportionate increase in the Latin American contingent. The bulk of the latter was made up of Cubans, the number of other Latin Americans amounting to something over 400. This seems a high figure when compared with the trickle of Latin American students to British universities, but still fairly modest in comparison with the 15,000 Latin Americans estimated to be studying in Spain. To what extent these students return to their own countries convinced and militant partisans of the Soviet Union it is impossible to say. But in countries where the educated class is small, their influence may well prove considerable.

The cultivation of relations in the ideological and cultural sphere has been accompanied by a Soviet reassessment of the great figures of Latin American history and the role that should be assigned to them in the Marxist revolutionary process. This has involved a rectification even of Marx's own view of Bolívar, whom he portrayed as 'striving to transform all South America into a federated republic, so that he could dominate it as a dictator.' From the mid-1950s a new note was sounded, and Soviet theoreticians explained that 'Marx did not have at his disposal a number of most important data', and that the truth was that 'the people loved and respected Bolívar as their guide and leader.' The new interpretation presented the wars of Latin American independence as the first stage in the process of national liberation—political emancipation from Spain—and an essential prelude to the second stage—the present struggle for economic emancipation from the United States. The other great figures in Latin American thought and action have been reshaped to support this thesis. Thus José Martí, the Cuban patriot who hated all forms of autocracy, censored Marx for fomenting hatred and violence, and lived for years in the United States which he warmly admired though he criticised its faults, is presented as an apostle of anti-Yankeeism, the forerunner of Cuba's communist regime, and John the Baptist to Castro's Messiah.

A notable part in this Marxist reassessment of Latin America has been played by the Latin American Institute, founded in Moscow in 1962. This body not only lays down the main lines of research, but works closely with other state organisations, keeps contact with Latin American scholars and institutions, and trains the new generation of the Soviet Union's Latin American experts. The close coordination between academic work and political objectives is illustrated by the fact that its first director was S. S. Mikhailov, formerly Soviet ambassador to Uruguay, who left the Institute to become Soviet ambassador to Brazil.

INTER-PARTY RELATIONS

During the 1920s Communist parties came into being in the main countries of Latin America. Some of these evolved, or split off, from earlier Socialist parties; others resulted from the fusion of extremist groups; others again from the direct action of the Comintern. The Soviet Union had not at first been in a position to pay much attention to developments in an area so remote from her more pressing interests. But in 1929, representatives of thirteen Latin American parties, together with their Comintern mentors, met in Buenos Aires for their first congress. This was the period of 'ultra-leftism', when Communist parties shunned any alliance with non-Communists in their zeal for violent revolution. Yet little serious attempt was made to analyse whether a revolutionary situation did in fact exist in the Latin American countries, and whether their efforts stood any chance of success. The one original analysis submitted to the 1929 congress was by the Peruvian José Carlos Mariátegui, who elaborated it in a celebrated book, *Siete ensayos de interpretación de la realidad peruana* (1928). In this he analysed his country's 'Indian problem', which he held to be basically social and economic and capable of solution only through an agrarian reform which would permit the Indians' collectivist instincts to lead them towards communism. This thesis was denounced in the Soviet Union by the then leading Latin Americanist Miroshevsky, who branded it as 'populism'.

During the 1930s two serious bids were made by the Latin American Communist parties to seize power. The first was in 1932, in El Salvador, where a peasant rising instigated by the Communists was suppressed with terrible bloodshed. The second was in 1935 in Brazil, when Luiz Carlos Prestes attempted to seize power by an army coup. As a young officer Prestes had previously won renown by heading a column which had moved through the Brazilian backlands, like the Chinese Communists in their 'long march', preaching a gospel of social justice. He had then gone to Moscow and been converted to communism. After the failure of the 1935 coup, Prestes gave up his belief in armed action as a short cut to power and led the Brazilian Communist Party along the new line, the attainment of power through the *vía pacífica*. 'Ultra-leftism' gave place everywhere to popular front tactics, which in Chile brought the Communists a share of power until, in 1947, they were ousted from the government and their party outlawed. In Cuba, too, the Communists were allowed a share of power by the dictator Batista until, after a break in relations with the Soviet Union (1952), they too were driven underground. It can be argued that by this time the Latin American Communist parties, though sometimes remaining organisationally strong, had lost their revolutionary dynamism to other Marxist parties such as the Chilean Socialists, whose extremism was nurtured by a radical nationalism untrammelled by any directives from Moscow, or the Trotskyist, and later pro-Chinese, splinter groups of the extreme left. The position is well illustrated by the story about the aging Latin American revolutionary who confided to his friends that he had decided to join his local Communist Party—so that he could spend his last years in peace.

Whatever the intrinsic revolutionary capacities of the Latin American Communist parties, and regardless of whether they sought to achieve power by the *vía pacífica* or the *vía armada*, the Soviet Union was caught in the dilemma that though her diplomats might genuinely work for good relations

---

[1] See 'The Indian Heritage', p. 577.

with non-communist governments, they often fell under suspicion—as has been noted above—of secretly encouraging the communist opponents of those governments. Thus the two instruments of Soviet influence, the regular instruments of diplomacy and the irregular instrument of communist-directed subversion, often impeded rather than reinforced each other. This dilemma has been sharpened, despite the great advantages reaped in other respects by the Soviet Union, by an event which Moscow neither planned nor foresaw; the advent of Fidel Castro's revolutionary regime in Cuba.

SOVIET–CUBAN RELATIONS

The Cuban Communists had given no support to Castro until the success of his movement appeared assured, and he himself had no Communist background.[1] Though he accepted Communists into his government, he did not establish relations with the Soviet Union until he had been in power for nearly a year and a half (May 1960). But Castro's deepening hostility to the United States and the extremism of his revolutionary policies accelerated his dependence—political, military, economic—on the Soviet Union. In December 1961 he declared himself to be a Marxist-Leninist, and in the following April *Pravda* acknowledged the Marxist-Leninist character of his regime and its place in the Soviet bloc. Moscow seems by then to have decided that Cuba was a windfall of which the fullest advantage should be taken. Though its economy, now sustained by the Soviet Union at increasing cost, was too shaky to present much of a communist show-window, Cuba exerted a strong propaganda appeal as an example of social revolution and nationalist defiance under the very nose of the United States, and served as a useful spring-board for action elsewhere in Latin America. Khrushchev indeed went further and sought to exploit his foothold there to tilt the world balance of forces in Moscow's favour, by establishing missile sites on the island (October 1962). Washington's vigorous response demonstrated the limitations imposed on Soviet strategy in an area where it was at so great a logistic disadvantage.

Though humiliated by the withdrawal of the Soviet missiles and his own marginal role in the crisis, Castro had no alternative but to continue his alliance with Moscow. China, which taunted the Russians with having let Cuba down, was in no position to replace them economically or militarily. Moscow, too, still needed Cuba in order to preserve her own image as a revolutionary power generally committed to the defence of revolutionary causes. It was thus decided to increase the already considerable Soviet stake in Cuba by the steady build-up of her armed forces, the provision of further technical and financial aid, and the conclusion of a five-year agreement (January 1964) by which the Soviet Union would buy the bulk of the annual Cuban sugar crop at a fixed price of six cents a pound. Castro's two visits to the Soviet Union (April 1963, and January 1964), but his failure to sign the Nuclear Test Ban Treaty and his reluctance to align himself openly with Moscow against Peking, marked the somewhat fluctuating course of Cuban-Soviet relations.

A meeting of the Latin American Communist parties at the end of 1964, however, seems to have reached agreement that Castro would as far as possible support the orthodox parties in preference to other extremist revolutionary groups in return for Soviet endorsement of the *vía armada* as

[1] See 'Cuba', p. 246.

the right tactics to be followed in at least some Latin American countries. That Cuban neutrality in the Sino-Soviet dispute[1] was really illusory was shown by Castro's polemics with the Chinese a year later, on the eve of the Three Continents Conference in Havana. The emergence from this conference of a 'Latin American Solidarity Organisation' indicated that Castro had lost nothing of his revolutionary fervour. The Soviet Union may well have acquiesced in the formation of this new 'guerrilla international' with some misgiving, to judge from the pains which it took to reassure those Latin American states which, individually and collectively, protested that the Conference proceedings violated the principle of non-intervention.

Though the Cuban alliance has gained a valuable foothold in Latin America for the Soviet Union, the latter should now realise that Castro's ambitions are less to serve as an obedient henchman than to assume for himself the leadership of the revolutionary movement throughout Latin America, much as Bolívar assumed it a century and a half ago. The Soviet Union does not share Castro's temperamental and ideological preference for the *vía armada;* nor do the orthodox Communist parties, some of whose leaders (e.g. the Venezuelans) Castro has publicly branded as mere theorists and revolutionary charlatans. The Russians fear that unsuccessful insurrections only compromise relations with governments with which they wish to remain, for the time being at least, on good terms. Moscow has, for instance, taken pains to cultivate close relations with President Frei's Christian Democrat government in Chile; Castro, however, has savagely attacked it and even launched scarcely veiled criticism against the Soviet government for supporting such a pseudo-revolutionary regime. There is also the long-term Soviet consideration of reaching some understanding with the United States, as well as reluctance to alienate the more moderate elements in the Third World who favour coexistence and relaxation of tension. Yet if they are not to lose ground to the more militant Chinese, the Russians dare not appear luke-warm in the revolutionary cause. A major country, such as Brazil or Venezuela, under a communist regime, would clearly be a rich prize, though a smaller, less viable republic like Haiti or Ecuador might well prove more of a liability even than Cuba.

Soviet policy towards Latin America thus appears ambivalent, cautious and uncertain. An upheaval with obviously revolutionary potentialities, such as the civil war that broke out in the Dominican Republic in April 1965, may evoke only a surprisingly mild response from Moscow. Though it is often proclaimed that Latin America is an area ripe for revolution, it is also one where the Soviet Union has learnt to tread warily.

[1] See Cuba, p. 250.

BIBLIOGRAPHY

Alexander, Robert J. *Communism in Latin America*, Rutgers Univ. Press, New Brunswick, NJ, 1957.

Allen, R. L. *Soviet Influence in Latin America: The Role of Economic Relations*, Public Affairs Press, Washington, DC, 1959.

Avarina, V. Ya. and Danilevich, M. V. (eds.) *Ekonomicheskiye problemy stran Latinskoy Ameriki* ('Economic Problems of the Countries of Latin America'), Institute of World Economy and International Relations, Academy of Science, Moscow, 1963.

García Trevino, Rodrigo. *La ingerencia rusa en México y Sudamérica*, Editorial America, Mexico, 1959.

Guber, A. A. *Borba za yediniy rabochiy i antiimperialistichesky front v stranakh Latinskoy Ameriki* ('The Struggle for a United Workers' Anti-imperialistic Front in the Countries of Latin America'), Academy of Social Sciences of the Central Committee of the CPSU, Moscow, 1963.

Halperin, Ernst. *Nationalism and Communism in Chile*, MIT Press, Cambridge, Mass., 1965.

Mariátegui, J. C. *Siete ensayos de interpretación de la realidad peruana*, Biblioteca Amauta, Lima, 1964.

Mikhailov, S. S. (ed.) *Osvoboditel'noye dvizheniye v Latinskoy Amerike* ('The Liberation Movement in Latin America'), Izdatel'stvo Nauka, Moscow, 1964.

Okinshevich, Leo A. and Gorokhoff, Cecila J. *Latin America in Soviet Writings, 1945–58; A Bibliography*, Library of Congress, Washington, DC, 1959.

Poppino, Rolle E. *International Communism in Latin America: A History of the Movement, 1917–63*, Collier–Macmillan, London; Macmillan, New York, 1964.

Ekonomika i vneshnyaya torgovlya stran Latinskoy Ameriki ('Economics and External Trade of the Countries of Latin America'), International Relations Publishing House, Moscow, 1966.

'Narody SSSR i Kuby naveki vmeste' ('The Peoples of the USSR and Cuba Will Always Stand Together—Documents'), *Pravda*, Moscow, 1963.

US Senate. *Soviet Bloc Latin American Activities and their Implications for US Foreign Policy*, US Government Printing Office, Washington, DC, 1960.

THE SINO-SOVIET DISPUTE AND REVOLUTIONARY MOVEMENTS

ALAIN JOXE

'Pro-Soviet' and 'Pro-Chinese' Positions

The Sino-Soviet ideological dispute, which became public in 1962, has an important bearing on the political strategy of revolutionary forces in Latin America. The area is characterised by urban economic development and the survival of feudal agrarian structures; both the Soviet and the Chinese models may, therefore, be relevant to any particular country. On the other hand, the geographical remoteness of the region from both the Soviet Union and China means that Soviet and Chinese military, cultural and political pressures are neither direct nor easily applicable. Moreover, the proximity of the United States makes a cautious approach advisable.

In physical terms the Chinese presence is very limited, despite the existence of colonies of overseas Chinese (Peru, Costa Rica, Mexico); for example, only three out of the ten correspondents of the New China News Agency in Latin America are Chinese. Between 1962 and 1965 China sent only 24 delegations to Latin American countries, and received 180 in return.

These factors might lead the observer to underestimate the relevance of the Sino-Soviet ideological dispute to the political realities of the area, except in the case of Cuba which is integrated into the economic system of the Eastern European bloc. However, the vocabulary and concepts used by both the Soviet Union and China are sufficiently general to be utilised in any political analysis. Though a position or strategy based on some of the concepts involved is not necessarily strictly 'pro-Soviet' or 'pro-Chinese', these terms will be used hereafter for convenience.

China and the Soviet Union agree that, in a number of Latin American countries, objective conditions exist favourable to an anti-imperialist revolution, and also that strategy must envisage large political fronts designed to include national bourgeoisie. They disagree on the following points: (1) whether to create 'subjective' revolutionary conditions by guerrilla warfare and armed struggle (the Castroist and pro-Chinese view) or to do so mainly by organisation and education of the masses in a framework of peaceful transition to socialism (one pro-Soviet view); (2) whether it is possible to create at once subjective conditions for a national democratic revolution under the leadership of the working class which, as the only real revolutionary class, could lead without interruption the socialist revolution after the national democratic one (the pro-Chinese view) or whether it is more realistic to aim first at a 'national-democratic' revolution eventually under the leadership of some representatives of the national bourgeoisie (one pro-Soviet view). These two strategical concepts are, in theory, absolutely incompatible; but in practice the divergences serve as an ideological undercurrent to local disputes and local sociological analysis and intermediary positions are in fact possible.

The fact that the dispute is confined to a small number of intellectuals and revolutionaries does not bring remoteness from socio-political realities. In fact the Sino-Soviet dispute in Latin America must be considered as a part of a larger set of arguments around two questions: (1) how the region can achieve economic development while avoiding the social injustice and/or upheavals which accompanied the same process in Europe; (2) how the peasant masses can be integrated into the economic and political life of their countries.

In 1966 most Latin American Communist parties were still pro-Soviet, i.e. traditionally linked to Soviet world policy and mainly representative of the urban workers' 'aristocracy' inclined towards reformism. Four (Bolivia, Brazil, Colombia and Peru) had split into two parallel organisations, while the Chilean and Argentine official parties complained of Chinese fractionalist activities. Of greater importance, however, is the fact that numerous guerrilla organisations, not directly connected with the local Communist parties when they began as nationalist and Castroist movements, have become increasingly inclined towards some form of Marxist ideology and have largely come under Chinese influence as regards the role of the people's war, but differ from the Chinese towards the roles of theory and of the Communist Party, which are considered less important than the guerrilla group for creating revolutionary spirit.

The debate, apart from its ideological implications, has taken place against the historical background of Latin American revolutionary activity in recent decades, which may be briefly summarised as follows:

(1) *Before, during and immediately after the second world war*
   Failure of the Chilean 'Socialist Republic' (1932)
   Failure of the Popular Front in Cuba (1943–4)
   Failure of the Radical alliance in Chile (1946–7)
(2) *From the death of Stalin to the public outbreak of the Sino–Soviet dispute*
   Failure of the Arbenz regime in Guatemala (1954)
   Success of the Cuban Revolution (1959), Bay of Pigs (1961) and missile crisis (1962)
   Failure of the first generation of guerrillas (1960–3)
(3) *Schism and reappraisal after 1962*
   Guerrilla activities in Colombia, Guatemala, Peru and Venezuela
   Tricontinental Conference, Havana, 1966 and new developments

This study will be confined to the events listed under (2) and (3) above.

FROM STALIN'S DEATH TO THE PUBLIC OUTBREAK OF THE SINO-SOVIET DISPUTE

Guatemala, 1954

President Arbenz was overthrown for two principal reasons: his political adversaries had full intelligence of his intended arms shipments from the Eastern bloc; and he hesitated to distribute the arms, fearing a clash with the regular army and civil war. The following conclusions were drawn from the failure of the Arbenz regime. The working class and not the bourgeoisie should lead a national revolution; commercial links with Eastern bloc countries should be developed, and not immediately take the form of a traffic in armaments; it was a mistaken step to undertake revolutionary

457

changes if the old army were left intact. The first and third of these theses became prominent in the Chinese ideological position, and the second in the Soviet one.

After 1956 the post-Stalin emphasis on the possibility of a peaceful transition to socialism gained favour in many Latin American Communist parties; it was allied to the thesis, which has traditionally gained popularity during periods of *détente* between the United States and the Soviet Union, that US liberals might conceivably make a contribution to the revolutionary process in Latin America. (This thesis, however, was never strong enough to overcome the equally traditional anti-Americanism of the Latin American left.)

The Cuban Revolution, 1959

Castro's success introduced a new element into the discussion. The traditional army of Cuba evaporated, and Castro found himself in the same position as Arbenz but without the obstacle that caused the latter's downfall. The 'rebel army' was entirely at his disposal, and when defections in it were noted, Castro formed an additional militia with Eastern bloc arms acquired by Raúl Castro in July 1960. At the time of the Bay of Pigs invasion Castro had at his disposal 45,000 soldiers and 200,000 militia.

In the Soviet view Castro was clearly embarking on a programme of reform with the full support of the Cuban proletariat after carrying out a violent 'national-bourgeois' revolution. This evolution of the Cuban Revolution towards socialism made some theorists interpret it as a 'peaceful transition to socialism' (e.g. Luis Carlos Prestes, secretary-general of the Brazilian Communist Party at a conference in Rio de Janeiro, 28 June 1962). This interpretation was categorically rejected by Castro himself in a speech a few months later, and the affair of veteran Party member Aníbal Escalante's expulsion from Cuba is significant in any theoretical analysis. In de-Stalinising the Cuban Party at the beginning of 1962 Castro was in point of fact de-Khrushchevising it. In other words, by doing away with the Old Guard Communists yet continuing to affirm that the new political formation (grouping the 26 July movement and other non-communist militants with the Communist Party) kept a full communist character, Castro was rejecting the argument according to which the transition to socialism in Cuba had been effected peacefully. The new party had an old history of fighting for socialism.

Castro's declared interpretation was that the transition to socialism began with the destruction of the machinery of the state and in particular of the traditional army, and that the subsequent dictatorship of the proletariat was assured by an armed militia. If the Cuban socialist revolution had not in fact been peaceful, then this fact diminished a favourite argument of those who advocated peaceful transition to socialism, i.e. the Soviet Communists. The background of the Escalante affair and the consequent loss of ideological prestige on the part of the Soviet Union played some role in the Soviet moves during the 1962 missile crisis.

The Cuban missile crisis, 1962

The installation of missiles in Cuba (whether prompted by the Soviet Union or Castro is ultimately irrelevant) had a precise significance in terms of the Sino-Soviet controversy. This step meant that, even if Cuba *had* achieved socialism by violent means, nevertheless the Soviet Union was prepared to take immense risks in her interests. As a means of demonstrating this point, the actual risks taken were at least partly justified, but the position could not be maintained at all costs. In the event, the Soviet-American agreement involving local supervision of nuclear disarmament in Cuba may even have strengthened the Soviet position. After the crisis it was possible to argue that the security of a socialist country depends on Soviet nuclear protection, and that subsequently such a country could be deprived of nuclear arms since it was in fact the world-wide strategic nuclear equilibrium between the United States and the Soviet Union which guaranteed this security. Every Communist Party, therefore, should realise that it was necessary to be sure of Soviet protection if it wanted to be certain of the survival of a socialist revolution (peaceful or otherwise).

The conflict with Castro therefore acquired great significance and aggravated the Sino-Soviet dispute. The argument turned on whether nuclear protection, and its withdrawal, deprived the state, the Party or the people of the attributes of sovereignty—this was particularly important in view of the nationalistic political basis of the Cuban regime (militia, popular support, etc.). It is difficult to assess the degree of support Castro found in the Chinese ideological position in resisting Soviet pressure in favour of inspection, but it probably played some part.

The early Castroist guerrillas

Between 1959 and 1962 the Cuban example encouraged numerous Castroist attempts at armed insurrection, despite revolutionary strategist 'Ché' Guevara's cautious attitude at that time towards the prospects of new, quick, successful guerrilla warfare. This first generation of guerrillas was rapidly destroyed. Their activities have little direct connection with the Sino-Soviet dispute, because Castro was not, at least at the beginning of the period, openly a Marxist and his imitators were not communists. Nevertheless, many people once connected with these guerrilla movements are today involved in the Sino-Soviet dispute, even though their movements are not Communist parties but guerrilla organisations with a Castroist and, in varying degrees, pro-Chinese orientation.

The following guerrilla movements were active in the period 1959–62:

GUERRILLA MOVEMENTS, 1959–62

Without Communist participation

Country	Movement	Date of origin
Argentina	Revolutionary Peronists	December 1959
Paraguay	Movimiento 14 de Mayo	November 1959
Dominican Republic	Movimiento 14 de Junio	Summer 1960
Colombia	MOEC	1961
Ecuador	Unión Revolucionaria de la Juventud Ecuatoriana	March 1962
Peru	Javier Heraud group (Castroist)	1962
Brazil	Paramilitary activities of Julião's peasant leagues	1962
Venezuela	First Venezuelan fronts	March 1962

With some Communist (including dissident) participation

Country	Movement	Date of origin
Paraguay	Frente Unido de Liberación Nacional (FULNA)	1962
Peru	FIR Trotskyist peasant syndicates	1962–3
Argentina	Guerrilleros del Pueblo	1964

During this period most Communist parties evolved a strategy based in fact on the conquest of power by peaceful means alone (the 'Soviet line'), e.g. those of Chile, Mexico, Bolivia, Brazil and Argentina; or in conjunction with armed struggle (Venezuela and Colombia). Generally, however, a left wing developed within the various parties, especially among youth, in opposition to the party bureaucracies still dominated by the older militants. This left wing was more sympathetic towards the guerrilla-warfare strategy.

<h2 style="text-align:center">Schism and Reappraisal after 1962</h2>

After 1962 the Sino-Soviet dispute became increasingly important in the history of the revolutionary left in Latin America. Both the Soviet Union and China launched an intensive propaganda drive to get support for their respective strategies; this had a catalytic effect on some Communist parties and led to overt dissensions and finally, in some cases, to splits. It was not, however, the only contributory factor: dissensions were already growing in connection with purely local matters. For example, in Colombia and Peru, where violent insurrection respectively in the shape of 'peasant republics' and Trotskyist activities had already taken place independently of the Communists, the discussion occurred before the Sino-Soviet dispute became public. In Brazil, the split was provoked by dissension over the strategy to be adopted towards the Goulart government.

Despite great internal dissension in the revolutionary movement, public schisms were avoided in Guatemala until January 1966, the conflict being then limited to the guerrilla organisation (FAR against MR 13) and in Venezuela until April 1967 (the Communist Party overtly for the pacific way, against Douglas Bravo and his guerrillas expelled from the Party). At the same time new efforts at coordination led by Guevara and a more flexible Soviet attitude towards Vietnamese developments may help re-unification or coordination between separate movements. A more detailed account of the situation in the four countries (Colombia, Guatemala, Peru and Venezuela) where guerrillas have been active for a number of years will illustrate these general observations.

Colombia

During the 'epoch of violence' (1948–53) 'zones of peasant self-defence' were created. Slowly penetrated by communist influence, the zones and the liberal guerrillas have only recently shown their truly defensive and peasant origin. When in May 1964 the Colombian army, US equipped and trained, attacked the zone of Marquetalia commanded by Manuel Marulanda—a member of the Central Committee of the Colombian Communist Party (PCC)—pro-Chinese elements recommended strengthening all the zones in order to force the Colombian army to disperse its forces. Though this advice was not immediately followed, in 1965 the PCC accepted the idea of a guerrilla tactical offensive.

On 18 February 1966 the presidents of Venezuela and Colombia issued a joint statement in which both governments agreed to 'establish a common front against the aggression and subversive activities directed from outside by those who are in the service of the totalitarian powers.' This ambitious attempt at large-scale guerrilla warfare on the model of Bolívar's campaigns contributed indirectly to inducing South American non-military governments to create a security system independent of the OAS, just when the

United States, after the Dominican crisis, was urging the creation of a permanent Panamerican force.

After the failure of the Castroist *maquis* launched in the north-east in January 1965 by the Ejército de Liberación Nacional (ELN), the PCC was favourably disposed to the formation, in April 1966, of the Revolutionary Armed Forces of Colombia (FARC), which unified all the zones of peasant self-defence of the 'southern bloc' and allowed the formation of a mobile force (effective from March 1967) independent of the peasant bases.

Although the Colombian population is two-thirds rural the PCC does not consider guerrilla warfare as the chief form of struggle at present; it knows the majority of the population is indifferent to it. But the PCC is exposed to increasing pressure from the government and has recently accepted the idea that as class conflict grows, armed struggle will become the principal form of revolutionary struggle on a national scale. Guevara in his communiqué of 16 April 1967 (if indeed he was the author),[1] Fabio Vasquez head of ELN, and Marulanda the communist head of FARC, have also expressed this way of thinking.

Guatemala

The nucleus of the guerrilla movement in Guatemala was the MR 13 led by Yon Sosa, which in 1961 attempted to overthrow President Ydgores Fuentes and to disrupt the military training by the CIA of anti-Castro volunteers who later took part in the Bay of Pigs invasion. Guerrilla operations were initiated in February 1962 in the mountains of Izabal and in the Sierra de las Minas, but collapsed through lack of mobility. In April 1962 negotiations with the Guatemalan Communist Party (Partido Guatemalteco del Trabajo—PGT) led to the creation of a new organisation, the FAR, led by Turcios Lima, a former lieutenant of Yon Sosa. The FAR has so far acted in fairly close cooperation with the PGT, whose line has been to keep open the possibility of negotiation between the guerrillas and the government with a view to ending the armed struggle and holding elections.

Differences grew in 1962–3 between the FAR and the MR 13, still led by Yon Sosa, who adopted a more radical ideological position. He insisted that the guerrilla must be the principal instrument of the revolution, and maintained that there was no 'national bourgeoisie' in Guatemala and therefore no possibility of a preliminary 'national-democratic' state, and that therefore the only road to socialism was the formation of a peasant-worker state, through propaganda and agitation leading to a seizure of power by these groups. The FAR denounced this thesis as Trotskyist (because of its exclusion of the bourgeoisie) and adventurist and unrealistic because the subjective conditions for a revolution of this nature did not exist in Guatemala. The FAR was supported publicly by Castro during the Tricontinental Conference at Havana in January 1966[2]; it is approximately Soviet in its ideological position, insisting on the importance of armed action in the cities and the need for an intermediate 'national-democratic state'. After Turcios Lima's death, Cesar Montes became leader of the FAR.

Peru

In Peru the ideological dispute and the discussion over revolutionary strategy are complicated by the proliferation of leftist organisations. In

[1] See 'Cuba', p. 249.
[2] See page 463.

1956 the Alianza Popular Revolucionaria Americana (APRA) was no longer very revolutionary, but it still had a large following, control of numerous trade unions, and a revolutionary tradition (pro-Indian, favourable to land reform, etc.). A left-wing faction, led by the lawyer Luis P. de la Puente Uceda, broke away from the APRA in 1959 and became the Movimiento de la Izquierda Revolucionaria (MIR). Between 1961 and 1964 various Trotskyist groups (e.g. the Partido Obrero Revolucionario or POR) and the Frente Izquierda Revolucionaria (FIR) with Hugo Blanco, tried to organise the peasants, training them to revolutionary land reform but without sufficient armaments.

At the time of the 1961 elections the Peruvian Communist Party (predominantly pro-Soviet) was illegal, and gave its support to the candidate of the legal Frente de Liberación Nacional (FLN); two other leftist groups also put forward candidates, but the left as a whole suffered a crushing defeat. The APRA gained a clear victory, but a military junta seized power shortly afterwards, and in the 1963 elections there was no leftist candidate at all. The PCP gave its support to Pedro Balaúnde Terry of the Acción Popular (AP); but the latter, once in power, was hampered by the opposition formed by the paradoxical combination of the APRA and the Unión Nacional Odriísta or UNO (led by the former dictator General Odría). The new government's comparative progress in the field of land reform and improvement of the standard of living of the Indians also proved an embarrassment to the Communists. In this difficult situation the PCP eventually split into two factions (each calling itself the Partido Communista Peruano), one of which was recognised by Moscow and the other by Peking. This schism further weakened the Communists.

The ineffectiveness of the other leftist organisations provoked the MIR into launching in 1965 a series of guerrilla offensives designed to create a new and militant mass movement of the extreme left. During that year there were five principal guerrilla groups in operation: the Tupac Amaru, commanded by Lobatón, operating around Santa Rosa; the Pachacutec, under the direct command of De la Puente, in the Convención Valley; the Manco Inca, also in the south, under Pablo Escobar; and in the north the Atahuallpa and César Vallejo groups.

The government reacted energetically to the guerrilla threat from July 1965 onwards, placing many leftist leaders in preventive detention and initiating a military campaign against the guerrillas. De la Puente and Escobar were killed in October 1965, and Lobatón in January 1966. The Ejército de Liberación Nacional (ELN) was created in November 1965 and operated in Agachuco Province, but a war ministry communiqué issued early in 1966 claimed that only the Tupac Amaru and Pachacutec groups were still in operation. By the beginning of 1967 guerrillas had in fact almost disappeared in Peru.

Venezuela

Here the armed struggle has been, since its inception, both urban and rural in scope. The guerrillas have operated in the countryside, but have always been commanded by intellectuals or soldiers from the cities, and have had great difficulty in gaining support amongst the rural population.

The Communist Party of Venezuela (PCV) and the MIR were banned in 1962, and divergences on strategy soon caused internal dissensions in both movements, the pro-Chinese elements advocating violent revolution and the pro-Soviet groups trying to establish contact with other leftist groups (notably the Democratic and Union Party (URD) led by Jóvito Villalba) and bring about a return to legality. The leaders of the Fuerzas Armadas de Liberación Nacional (FALN) have been ideologically pro-Chinese, and foresee a prolonged struggle for power based on guerrilla action in the countryside. At the same time they are aware of the importance of gaining support in the cities, particularly among the inhabitants of the *barrios* (shantytowns). This policy is dictated largely by the need for material support, often not forthcoming from the poor and scattered peasantry who, in general, continue to support either Acción Democrática, because of its land reform programme, or the Catholic party COPEI.

At the end of 1965 there were four guerrilla fronts in operation: Falcón, Trujillo, Lara-Portuguesa and Miranda. These were under the political command of Douglas Bravo and the military command of Major Ponte Rodríguez, and appeared to have been successful in frustrating military attempts to suppress them.

The clandestine PCV has preserved at least nominal unity on an ambiguous basis. A statement issued in early 1965 applauded the activities of the FALN, but also expressed a desire for a return of peace and, presumably, legality. In 1967 the PCV, under the influence of moderate leaders recently freed or fled from jail, accepted the 'pacific' line and ejected Douglas Bravo and his followers in the FALN from the Party.

THE TRICONTINENTAL CONFERENCE, HAVANA, JANUARY 1966 AND NEW DEVELOPMENTS

There had been conferences of this nature before, held under the auspices of the Afro-Asian Peoples' Solidarity Organisation (OSPAA), but the Havana Conference was the first to include Latin Americans as delegates. At the Fifth OSPAA Conference (Winneba, May 1965), the Soviet Union had slightly improved her position vis-à-vis China, owing to the intransigent and polemical attitude of the latter which alarmed many delegates. The decision to hold the next conference at Havana was a minor Soviet diplomatic success, in view of the rapprochement between Cuba and the Soviet Union. China, however, was consoled by the prospect of Castro adopting an ideological position close to hers, and of the inevitable presence at the Conference of representatives of the guerrilla movements who would constitute a pro-Chinese element. The Conference was, in fact, the scene of a Sino-Soviet conflict in which Cuba played the role of mediator, following the Soviet line as regards relations between powers, but maintaining an individual position with regard to revolutionary strategy.

The Conference led to the creation of two new organisations: the Tricontinental People's Solidarity Organisation with a secretariat in Havana, and the Latin American Solidarity Organisation. The latter, which included representatives from twenty-seven Latin American countries (including some colonial territories), established a secretariat with Brazil, British Guiana, Colombia, Cuba, Guatemala, Mexico, Peru, Uruguay and Venezuela. It will be observed that four of these countries are the scene of guerrilla activity and four are not; Cuba is in the position of mediator.

It would be unwise to expect the Latin American Solidarity Organisation (despite its similarity to a regional Comintern) to initiate any outbreak of violent guerrilla warfare inspired by 'Chinese' strategy. It is true that the Soviet delegate publicly expressed solidarity with the 'Venezuelan, Peruvian, Colombian and Guatemalan patriots in their struggle against the lackeys of imperialism'; but this was, perhaps, the price the Soviet Union was obliged to pay for its predominant position in the organisation. The debate on peaceful coexistence led to relative isolation of the pro-Chinese elements: a Cuban motion on the subject was adopted by 31 votes to 9, those voting against including the delegates of Peru, Guatemala and Venezuela. Neither Colombia nor the Dominican Republic followed the Chinese line on this issue.

Chinese ideological pressure in Latin America remains considerable, but effective support for revolutionary movements is channelled through the Latin American Solidarity Organisation, which is far from being a mere tool of Chinese policy. After the reverses suffered in Peru and Venezuela Chinese-inspired guerrilla activity appeared inopportune from the view-point of 1967. But Castroism and Guevarism continue to inspire ideologically new guerrilla movements like that which began in Bolivia in March 1967 and to systematise a special long-range revolutionary method different from the Chinese and the Soviet models, a method which insists on militarily autonomous guerrilla groups as nuclei for a new party aiming at the full political control of the whole revolutionary left. The August 1967 meeting of the Latin American Solidarity Organisation at Havana gave general acceptance to this approach, without offering very sophisticated national studies or concrete international planning. The death of Guevara and the collapse of the Bolivian guerrillas in October 1967 gave cause for a new assessment of guerrilla movements in Latin America.

BIBLIOGRAPHY

Castro, Fidel. *Étapes de la Révolution cubaine*, François Maspero, Paris.
Debray, Régis. *Révolution dans la révolution? Lutte armée et lutte politique en Amérique latine*, François Maspero, Paris, 1967.
Draper, Theodore. *Castroism. Theory and Practice*, Pall Mall Press, London; Frederick A. Praeger, New York, 1965.
Guevara, Ernesto Ché. *Guerrilla Warfare*, Monthly Review Press, New York, 1961.
Joxe, Alain. *Le conflit sino-soviétique et l'Amérique latine*, Montevideo, 1967.
Lieuwen, Edwin. *The United States and the Challenge to Security in Latin America (Mershon National Security Program No. 4)* (Part II: 'External Threats'), Ohio State Univ. Press, Columbus, Ohio, April 1966.

PART THREE

LATIN AMERICAN ECONOMIC AFFAIRS

THE BACKGROUND

LATIN AMERICA:
A SUMMARY OF ECONOMIC PROBLEMS

DAVID HUELIN

LATIN AMERICA may be seen as a vast region of great potential held back by its disparities. It contains one country that is too large to be governed effectively and several that are too small to be economically viable; in some areas the pressure of rapidly growing populations on inadequate land is causing problems of malnutrition, and in others there is not enough population to make large areas of land economically productive. The region suffers from excessive concentrations of activity separated by large areas of comparative inactivity.[1] The disparities of social and economic geography are matched by inequalities of income and living standards that pose political and economic problems for which many different solutions have been propounded, so far with only partial success. Latin America contains within itself many of the problems that currently divide the rich and the poor nations of the world, and these problems may even be seen within several individual republics.

URBANISATION AND THE NEGLECT OF AGRICULTURE

As historians have pointed out, the Conquistadores and the early Spanish settlers were essentially urban in outlook, a characteristic that has persisted to this day in many populations, and were more concerned to found cities and establish administrative and commercial organisation than to develop agricultural resources; typically the urban landowner's interest in his estates was purely as a source of income. Only in Argentina and Uruguay, and then only from the second half of the 19th century, has agriculture—as distinct from owning sugar plantations—been regarded as a serious occupation, mainly for export. The consequence of this was the early growth of urban middle- and upper-class society, financially based mainly on foreign trade, with a high level of consumption; the concentration of income in urban centres was established at an early stage in Latin America's history, and the preponderant element of foreign trade accounts for the fact that many of Latin America's major cities are on the coast.

The early concentration of income and consumption in the cities was centripetal and has progressively attracted human and financial resources away from rural areas and agrarian occupations. The rural sector has failed to keep pace with the urban; besides the complex question of land tenure it has been deprived of capital and of technical expertise and in many countries

[1] See 'The Geography of Latin America's Economic Development', p. 478.

468

is now frankly backward and inefficient.[1] Even in Argentina, the agricultural country *par excellence*, the introduction of technical improvements such as fertilisers and artificial pastures is perhaps thirty years behind the normal standard in the United States or Australia.

The consequences of technical and financial neglect have been compounded by progressive inadequacies of the rural infrastructure; the lack of proper storage and conservation methods, poor transport, and inefficient or corrupt and speculative marketing systems have all constituted barriers to prevent growing urban demand from being translated into increased production and higher rural incomes. Consequent shortages have tended to push urban consumer prices upwards—to the benefit of the middlemen rather than the producers—or governments have imposed price ceilings for political reasons.

This, as is pointed out elsewhere in this book,[2] is one of the causes of inflation in Latin America; the growing imbalance in the terms of trade between the urban and the rural sectors has limited agricultural production for urban consumption and has deprived industrial producers of effective rural markets. The countries in which rural incomes are less markedly below urban standards—notably Argentina and Uruguay—have proportionately smaller rural populations than, for instance, Brazil, Chile or Peru; the same problem exists in a slightly different form in both groups.

Many Latin American republics have adopted agrarian reform in principle, but few are engaged in carrying it out in all its aspects, including investment in the necessary infrastructure, social services and technical and financial assistance; only in Mexico, where it has been pursued for nearly half a century, can agrarian reform be said to have had a significant effect on food production and rural incomes, yet wide disparities still remain. Of the countries that have embarked more recently on this gigantic task, Chile and Venezuela have perhaps the most impressive evidence of success. Neither economists nor governments believe that higher agricultural prices provide the answer to the problem of the disparity between urban and rural incomes.[3] The Chilean thesis is that systematic modernisation of land tenure, irrigation, farming techniques, marketing mechanisms and all the allied aspects of an agrarian economy can—and in fact do—lead to reductions in cost and increases in volume and to appreciable improvements in money incomes, nutrition and general welfare in farming communities. It has been estimated, on the basis of results so far achieved, that Chile, which at present cannot feed its population of 9 million, could eventually feed a population of 20 million.

One of the consequences of the neglect of rural populations and the concentration of economic activity in the cities has been the constant, and in some countries growing, migration towards the cities; the influx of unemployed labour has been, and is, far in excess of the capacity of industry to absorb. All the major cities of Latin America are burdened with an unemployed, and virtually unemployable, population inhabiting shanty towns and creating serious problems in matters of health, education and all the social services. In theory a successful modernisation of agriculture and a raising of rural incomes should halt if not reverse this trend, and should allow an expansion of industrial activity sufficient to absorb most of the surplus labour force.

[1] See 'The Agrarian Problem', p. 487.
[2] See 'The Problem of Inflation', p. 502.
[3] See 'The Agrarian Problem', p. 499.

OBSTACLES TO ECONOMIC INTEGRATION

Disparities are also the cause of some of the obstacles that are preventing economic integration in Latin America as a whole. There is little doubt that the Latin American economies would be more viable, less wasteful, and less inflationary if there were an ideal division and mobility of human and financial resources. Enthusiasts for economic integration believe that none of the republics can fully develop its potential in isolation; the joint harnessing of natural resources, the pooling of production capacity and markets, and the formation of an economic bloc for the conduct of Latin America's foreign trade, are all legitimate objectives that may eventually be achieved.[1] The attraction exercised by the great economic centres, however, is as great among the smaller neighbour countries as in the rural areas of those countries where they occur. It is estimated, for example, that the adult population of Uruguay is actually declining in consequence of migration to Argentina and Brazil; there is a large community of able and ambitious Paraguayans in Buenos Aires, where there is far more scope for their talents than in Asunción. It may be assumed that capital movements follow the same pattern, since investment in the major centres is more profitable.

The Latin American Free Trade Association (LAFTA), which includes the ten Latin republics of South America and Mexico, is meeting obstacles to the expansion of trade within the region, also derived from disparities of many kinds. In its initial stages, which involved the liberalisation of existing trade between the member countries, progress was rapid; existing trade then consisted mainly of the primary commodities normally exchanged between tropical and temperate regions or between economies that are complementary in other respects. The difficulties arose when this stage was completed and consideration had to be given to products that were competitive, as many manufactures are. The problem is less intractable between the industrialised countries and the 'less developed' than where it involves the 'intermediate' economies with very small markets; that is to say, it is easy for Ecuador or Paraguay to make tariff concessions in favour of Argentine or Brazilian manufactures, since no real element of industrial competition is involved; it is much more difficult for Chile, Colombia, Peru or Uruguay to make such concessions since manufacturing costs in these smaller markets are higher than in the large countries, and liberalisation would put many of their industries out of business.

The pattern is made more complex by the diversity of tax structures, labour legislation, exchange regulations, credit policies, and many other factors affecting business operations. These differences reflect the diversity of economic conditions among the republics and the disparity of political and economic philosophies evolved in each country's national context. In general, however, it is observable that the inequalities of productivity and income that differentiate the major industrial centres from the agricultural communities in several individual republics are repeated in the economic relations of the three large advanced nations—Argentina, Brazil and Mexico—with their less developed neighbours. Such increases as there have been in trade among the LAFTA countries have mainly favoured the advanced economies which, as far as their neighbours are concerned, are beginning to replace Europe and the United States as sources of industrial products.

[1] See 'The Interamerican Development Bank' (p. 558).

The integration of the Latin American countries into a large common market or economic community—with all that this implies if it is taken in its European sense—is clearly rather distant. The visionary enthusiasm of men such as Raúl Prebisch, Filipe Herrera, Carlos Sanz de Santamaría and José Antonio Mayobre[1] has done much to show the urgent need to break down economic barriers and combine resources, but there are practical and political obstacles of some magnitude.

An indication of the manner in which integration may evolve is to be seen in the attempts to form sub-regional groups of countries with some geographical proximity, some problems in common, and an approximate parity of economic development. The Central American Common Market is the earliest of these attempts and, being confined to a small group of countries in a well defined area, has had more success in relation to its limited aims than the more ambitious LAFTA. The Andean republics—which in this context include Venezuela—reached an agreement in August 1966, entitled the Charter of Bogotá, whereby they will attempt a form of economic integration leading eventually to an Andean Common Market. The countries that include in their territories some part of the Paraná river system, known as the River Plate Basin, are studying the joint development of the region's resources, which could do much to promote economic expansion in hitherto slow-moving republics such as Paraguay. The concept of economic integration by regional stages seems more promising than the rather unrealistic idea of a common market embracing the whole of Latin America. The evolution of the individual economies is leading to greater disparities among them, rather than to conditions making naturally for integration, and it is evident that excessively ambitious aims that do not take enough account of economic realities are likely to be frustrated.

All these plans involve a great improvement in the countries' infrastructure[2]; each has developed its communications system on essentially national lines, and international connections are far from adequate. The geographical obstacles—responsible in some cases for existing political boundaries—are enormous; the Cordillera of the Andes and the Amazon basin are only the largest and most obvious of the many physical barriers to trade, communications and the development of the less advanced economies. The more imaginative planners, such as President Belaúnde of Peru, conceive the development of communications as a simultaneous opening-up of neglected areas within national territories and the connecting of neighbouring countries. Belaúnde's dream of a highway (Carretera Marginal) running north and south on the eastern side of the Cordillera would provide a central communications artery that would not only open up unpopulated areas of Peru, Bolivia, Ecuador, Colombia and Venezuela, but would link these areas to each other and, with tributary highways, would connect them with the Pacific coast and with Brazil, Paraguay, Chile and Argentina. These ideas presuppose the parallel development of other forms of infrastructure, though it is evident that transport is the first prerequisite for the promotion of economic activity in backward areas and the expansion of trade within the region. It may be assumed that where there is production and trade, other forms of improvement will follow.

[1] The 'Four Wise Men' who supported the common marketproject suggested by President Eduardo Frei of Chile. The same theme was repeated at the Conference of American Presidents in Punta del Este, April 1967.
[2] See 'The Latin American Free Trade Association', p. 547.

Visions of the large-scale development of the 'empty middle' of the South American continent immediately raise the question of how such projects are to be financed. The fiscal resources of even the richest of the republics are already strained to the limit with purely domestic calls; the cost of an agrarian reform plan alone, for example, is as much as most governments can contemplate. Latin America is receiving, and will continue to need, large sums in development financing from the International Bank for Reconstruction and Development, the Interamerican Development Bank and other foreign sources, especially the United States. If economic expansion is to be accelerated to a pace at which it can significantly overtake population growth and result in improved living standards for all Latin America's 250 million inhabitants, it is clear that the rich nations must somehow supplement Latin America's inadequate savings; moreover, this must be continued until products or incomes are raised enough to generate savings for future growth; whether this should be done by aid and loans or by reforms of the structure of international trade is discussed below.

It would be misleading to suggest that all the populations and governments of Latin America are inert, poverty-ridden and incapable of creative effort. Experience on a small scale in several countries, especially those with some indigenous and mestizo population, suggests that backward communities in remote districts are capable of remarkable feats of self-help once they are given professional guidance and the basic tools with which to work. The major obstacles have hitherto been ignorance and hopelessness, both basically the consequences of official neglect; the work of the government agency Cooperación Popular in Peru has shown that among indigenous communities the capacity for voluntary communal work in building, for example, schools and roads can be roused by the creation of incentives, the provision of some materials and the inspiration of a sound technical leadership. The deduction to be made from experiences of this kind is that social services and local communications can be improved in countless areas with a minimum of expenditure by governments; there is, in a sense, a greater need for organisation and technical expertise than for funds. It is also preferable that under-employed peasant communities should work, even unpaid, for tomorrow's improvements rather than that they should be left without incentives and unnoticed by their nominal governments.

THE PREBISCH EFFECT AND INDEBTEDNESS

Both the comparative slowness of the over-all growth rate of Latin America and the concentrations of economic activity in large centres are partly the consequence of the position of the republics in world trade as primary producers. The Prebisch Effect (how disadvantageous terms of trade tend to hold back the economic growth of countries on the 'periphery')[1] is, in fact, a world economic problem; it affects Latin America as acutely as it does India, for instance, and rather more acutely perhaps than it does countries that have not yet achieved high levels of urban consumption and are less disturbed by rising under-employed populations.

The thesis propounded by Prebisch shows that the free market mechanism by which virtually all primary commodities are traded renders primary producers especially vulnerable to the cyclical fluctuations in demand that occur in the industrial countries. In the high-income countries of the northern

[1] See also 'The Problem of Inflation', p. 503.

hemisphere an increase in purchasing power does not normally mean an increase in direct demand for primary commodities; it is rather reflected in greater demand for manufactures, which leads indirectly to a higher consumption of industrial raw materials. If this should cause a rise in the prices of raw materials, industrialists may seek economies in use or substitutes, so as to avoid any loss of competitive position through increased cost and prices. Conversely, when demand declines in the rich countries, industrialists will make every endeavour to reduce their expenditure on raw materials before they attempt to curtail dividends or wages. Thus the primary producers seldom or never reap the full benefit of the upward cyclical movement in the high-income countries and always bear the full brunt of the downward movement; the economic advantages of technical progress in the use of raw materials are not transferred to the producers and commodity prices remain inelastic in the upwards direction and unstable in the downwards.

Concurrently with this situation, the imports of primary producing countries consist largely of manufactured goods that are universally sold at administered prices reflecting the general level of wages in the high-income nations. This means, in other terms, that the primary producing countries are able to export only a small proportion of value added, at their domestic prices, but must import a large proportion of value added at high cost in the industrialised countries.

The various commodity agreements in force, whereby violent fluctuations in price are avoided by means of regulated export quotas, limitations on production and other devices, do no more than achieve a measure of stability in otherwise speculative markets organised by and for the benefit of users of commodities. These agreements obviously cannot, and are not intended to, overcome the difficulty caused by the tendency for the administered prices of the products of high-income countries to rise more steeply or more consistently than the prices of primary commodities. There is thus a long-term deterioration of the terms of trade of the primary producers, which include all the Latin American countries without exception; the gap between the rich and poorer nations is constantly widening.

This situation affects the pace of development of the republics very closely; export earnings are an important potential source of capital formation, and a country's export performance will naturally determine its import capacity. Moreover, foreign trade in both directions is traditionally one of the major sources of government revenue. It is partly because of the deterioration in the terms of trade that financial aid and development loans have become so important to the Latin Americans, but there is also a strong feeling that loans, which inevitably mean an accumulation of indebtedness, and are in many cases 'tied' to purchases of the lending country's goods, are an unsatisfactory substitute for export earnings.

In the private sector, especially in industry, the inadequacy of export income, and consequently of domestic capital as well as of foreign exchange, has led to an increasing reliance on suppliers' credits in the acquisition of capital goods. The extension of the suppliers' credit system—basically a mechanism evolved for financing trade in consumer goods and primary commodities—to include capital goods has meant that the exporters of such goods, or their bankers, have been financing the expansion of Latin America's industries by a method that is ill-suited to the purpose. The majority of suppliers' credits for capital goods are for terms ranging from three to seven years and are at interest rates appreciably higher than the discount rates of lending countries. In the inflationary countries where interest rates are extremely high, suppliers' credits are both cheaper and easier to obtain than local loans—hence their extensive use—but they are not an adequate substitute for capital investment and foreign exchange earnings.

Several of the Latin American countries have at various times been faced with an accumulation of commercial debt repayments that it was beyond their capacity to meet, and they have had to face the rather humiliating task of seeking postponements and official or private refinancing of commercial liabilities. It may of course be argued that these difficulties have arisen because of the unbalanced industrial expansion that has been allowed by official policy, and that the Latin Americans have no one to blame but themselves; this is true in part but does not invalidate the fact that the acceleration of population growth, and the consequent relative decline in domestic capital formation when an increase was most needed, has coincided with the post-war deterioration in Latin America's terms of trade.

DIFFICULTIES IN EXPORTING

There are two aspects to the problem of achieving a significant increase in export earnings, neither of which can be solved by the Latin Americans alone. One is the question of commodity prices; as already noted, demand and prices are not elastic; while commodities are sold on free markets producers cannot hope to achieve higher prices for a given volume, nor can they expect to increase the volume at the same price. Commodity agreements, as noted, help only to eliminate short-term fluctuations and cannot solve the basic problem. Although it is true that the trend of commodity prices is in general upward, the rise in the prices of industrial goods is more rapid, and the problem remains.

The second aspect of the problem of Latin America's export earnings is the difficulties that obstruct the export of manufactured goods. The high-income markets, where Latin American industrial products could in theory compete, are protected by tariff barriers that Latin American production costs are not, in general, low enough to overcome. For many manufactured products the high-income countries have a tariff structure in which the customs duty is higher in relation to the degree of processing to which a material has been subjected in the country of origin. If a raw material is imported duty-free but is dutiable on a rising scale according to the degree of processing or manufacture, the duty may be regarded as applying only to the value added by industry in the country of origin: this principle is criticised by economists who advocate a general expansion of trade, and is regarded by the Latin Americans as highly objectionable.

It does not seem likely that tariff reductions negotiated under the GATT will be substantial enough or rapid enough to satisfy Latin American export ambitions; greater expectations have been roused by the more dynamic approach of the UN Conference on Trade and Development (UNCTAD) which, with Raúl Prebisch as its secretary, cannot be accused of being a rich nations' club. Even so, the rich nations' governments, while apparently understanding and even expressing sympathy for the plight of the developing nations, are subject to pressure in the opposite direction from their own industrialists and labour unions, who are also electors.

The LAFTA includes among its aims the widening of markets within Latin America, as a step towards the formation of larger industries that may reduce costs by economies of scale. Progress in this direction is necessarily slow, since in the markets of relatively high purchasing power the products of a neighbouring country's industries must compete with established local industries, and in markets where such competition is slight or non-existent, purchasing power is low. Ideally a high degree of specialisation in each centre, and the reshaping of each industrial structure to avoid duplication and excessive competition, would in part overcome the difficulty of high costs, but the practical and even political obstacles to such a development are virtually insuperable. The economics of large-scale capital-intensive industries, as these are known, for instance, in the United States, are such that the decisions of their managements could have profound and not necessarily beneficial effects on any Latin American country's economic and monetary affairs.

Attitudes towards Foreign Capital and the United States

The Latin Americans, perhaps not without some justification, are suspicious of industrial giants, especially if they are foreign, and profoundly opposed to any activity savouring of monopoly. It is already noticeable in some of the highly sophisticated industries—especially motor-cars—not only that foreign capital has a controlling interest but that the interest changes hands as one foreign concern sells its shareholding to another, the tendency being towards the concentration of industries in fewer hands. There is at the same time a perceptible increase of foreign over domestic shareholdings, and a consequent loss of national influence in industries that influence a country's economy. In the motor-car industry especially, where competition among the international giants extends all over the world, the Latin Americans are finding themselves shouldered out as the big international companies manoeuvre for a larger share of the market.

In the Central American Common Market, where internal tariff eliminations and a common external tariff have made the establishment of regional industries a viable development—and where, indeed, there was otherwise little possibility of establishing any but the smallest and simplest of manufacturing plants—the opportunities for industrial operations to supply the whole area have attracted several foreign enterprises whose competitive superiority over small local concerns is causing apprehension and resentment.

The ambivalence in Latin American attitudes to foreign capital[1] is largely derived from the unpleasant consequences for small local manufacturers of the advent of large efficient foreign enterprises with vastly superior financial and technical resources. In Latin America, no less than in Europe, resentment at foreign domination runs concurrently with the desire for greater efficiency; in Latin America particularly the possibility of cost reductions that would make industrial exports competitive is a point in favour of large enterprises. Moreover the international giants can contribute significantly to industrial exports by arranging sales by a Latin American subsidiary to another elsewhere.

A point that causes some preoccupation is the growing tendency towards the setting up of capital-intensive industries in which the contribution to the employment problem is minimal, whereas the economic influence may be disruptive, at least in the early stages. To a certain extent this trend is a consequence of complex, and often costly, labour legislation, the bargaining strength of the trade unions, and similar factors that make the operations of labour-intensive industries uncertain if not actually unprofitable. Although

[1] See 'External Finance', p. 525.

it is obvious that the level of unemployment, and of wages, in any economy is directly responsible for much of its purchasing power, no individual entrepreneur is very willing to expose himself to risks if they can be avoided; several republics have a history of labour relations that may suggest caution to present-day foreign investors.

On the other side of the same question is the belief, widely held in Latin America, that all large United States enterprises are in some way connected with or acting in conjunction with the US government; this idea may seem less naïve when it is considered that Washington's official attitude towards private business is appreciably more friendly than is normal in Latin America. Washington's encouragement of private investment in Latin America, although it antedates the Alliance for Progress, is one of the paternalistic attitudes that suggest to Latin Americans that private US business is somehow furthering Washington's aims.

The reasons for the constant tension between many of the Latin American republics and the United States, particularly in connection with the Alliance for Progress, may also be traced to ambivalent Latin American attitudes. Latin America's economic and social stagnation, and therefore its manifestations of political instability, have been seen as the consequences of the ruling classes' long neglect of the agricultural sector, now exacerbated by the population growth.[1] The ambivalence lies in the enthusiastic response of many Latin American governments to offers of financial assistance and their simultaneous reluctance to accept, as conditions, the Alliance's conceptions of social, agrarian and administrative reforms. Moreover, since governments in Latin America do not represent informed opinion any more faithfully than they do elsewhere, Washington has been to some extent misled in assuming that a government's views represented those of its country.

In short, there is obviously no universally held 'Latin American' opinion, nor even a national opinion in any single country, on subjects as vital as social reform; it is inevitable that whatever Washington does or refrains from doing in the sensitive areas of the republics' domestic affairs will be profoundly wrong for one sector of opinion or another.

The Choice before the Rich Nations

The economic expansion, social progress, political continuity, and other desirable attainments, of Latin America depend not on aid or on foreign capital so much as on the removal of barriers; in virtually all the republics there are human and natural resources capable of productive organisation if internal obstacles were overcome and the disparities evened out. An adequate concentration of effort, rather than money, on organising the backward sectors would achieve integrated economies. Soundly balanced economies would find it easier to achieve integration with each other and thus reduce disparities between them.

Only then would Latin America as a bloc be able to participate in the remunerative foreign trade structure of the rich nations, unless the rich nations should first unexpectedly make an effort to remove the gross inequalities of terms that have for so long kept the republics at a disadvantage. Aid, loans, credits and other devices to enlarge the rich countries' sales to Latin America do little but create an accumulation of debts; the maintenance of trade barriers that virtually prevent Latin America from exporting the value added by industry to its native products can only perpetuate the impasse.

[1] See 'The Alliance for Progress', p. 566.

476

Latin America will continue to expand economically. It lies with the rich nations either to ignore the Latin Americans' problems and condemn them to uncertain intermittent progress punctuated by disturbances, or to assist them to develop their economies within the orbit of prosperity of the northern hemisphere.

BIBLIOGRAPHY

Baer, Werner. 'The Inflation Controversy in Latin America', *Latin American Research Review*, II, 2, Univ. of Texas, Austin, Texas, spring 1967.

Brandenburg, Frank. *The Development of Latin American Private Enterprise*, National Planning Association, Washington, DC, May 1964.

Hanson, Simon G. *Five Years of the Alliance for Progress*, Inter-American Affairs Press, Washington, DC, 1967.

Lauterbach, Albert. *Enterprise in Latin America. Business Attitudes in a Developing Economy*, Cornell Univ. Press, Ithaca, NY; Oxford Univ. Press, London, 1966.

Bank of London and South America. *BOLSA Review*, monthly, London.

Political and Economic Planning. *Trade Policies towards Developing Countries*, London.

United Nations. *The Process of Industrial Development in Latin America*.

See also the bibliography for 'The Problem of Inflation'.

THE GEOGRAPHY OF LATIN AMERICA'S ECONOMIC DEVELOPMENT

PETER R. ODELL

THE geographical concentration of economic activities in Latin America is one of the most outstanding features of the continent's economy; it is, however, one of the least studied and least understood aspects of its development.

The present pattern reflects, in part, the continuation of a phenomenon which can be traced back even to the pre-Columbian period. Significant geographical variations in the relative intensity of the use of land have been brought out in analyses that have been made of the distribution of population at the time of the Spanish Conquest. The Spanish were attracted, by and large, to those parts of the continent which offered precious metals and/or Indian labour for both mining and agricultural activities, and thus the colonial pattern of spatial economic development tended to emphasise the pre-existing situation with only limited use being made of the rest of the vast extent of the continent nominally under Spanish control. The Portuguese and other colonising powers, notably the British and the Dutch, had their main interests in areas largely devoid of an indigenous population but were able to make use of regions suitable for sugar cultivation by importing Negro slaves (and later indentured labourers from the far east) to work the plantations: but this led, in terms of land use, to little more than the development of a coastal strip of Brazil and of favourable areas in the Caribbean islands. Thus by the end of the colonial period only a very limited part of the continent had been effectively settled.

AGRICULTURAL LAND USE

For most of the independence period the main economic concern of the continent has been with agricultural activities. From the geographical viewpoint, four major changes must be noted. The most important has been the use of the temperate grasslands of Argentina and Uruguay for extensive agriculture. These hitherto unattractive, even repellent areas were, after the mid-19th century, to become the most important agricultural regions of the continent as geographical values changed under the impact of a rapidly growing world demand for meat, maize and wheat, etc.; of the development of rail and sea transport to get the products to the coast and thence to the foreign markets; of changes in agricultural techniques which made large-scale cultivation of the pampas possible; and of the availability of the labour required from large-scale European immigration.

The second major change, again arising from the growing demand for agricultural products in the industrialising nations of North America and

Western Europe, has been the great increase in the areas set aside for the production of tropical crops. For example, the acreage devoted to sugar cane cultivation was expanded in most tropical areas, particularly in the Caribbean region. Banana, coffee and other plantations were developed on lands which had previously been largely unused—as, for example, on the Caribbean coastlands of Honduras, Guatemala and Costa Rica. Such plantation development, however, did not necessarily lead to permanent use of the land—banana plantations are frequently abandoned as a result of land exhaustion or the onset of disease and so far few successful attempts appear to have been made to utilise the abandoned areas for other crops.

This feature of development in land use followed by a decline or even cessation of activities is the third aspect of change that should be noted. In contrast with the normal process of the progressive territorial expansion of economic activities outwards from a developed centre, expansion at the periphery has in certain cases been accompanied by a decline in the areas previously developed. This has been described as the phenomenon of the 'hollow frontier' and has been particularly important in the case of Brazil where the areas devoted to coffee production have progressively moved inland leaving behind abandoned or seriously under-used land. On the other hand, areas within Latin America that have experienced effective and ongoing rural expansion from nuclei to peripheries are relatively few in number. They do include, however, widening areas of effectively used land in the *meseta central* of Costa Rica; areas of recent European and Japanese immigration in southern Brazil; and newly opened-up territories of south-central Chile (the fourth change). But in many other parts of the continent where one might have expected such changes—under the impact of a growing rural population and the pressure of this population on the available land under cultivation—they have failed to materialise largely because of the structure of the land-ownership system, in which very large areas of unused or under-utilised land are alienated in very large, and very often absentee-owned, latifundia. It is only in Mexico, Bolivia and Cuba where there have been fundamental reforms of the agrarian structure with the redistribution of land to peasants that this system no longer acts as a major restraint on the effective use of the land.

Thus agricultural activities within Latin America remain geographically concentrated. This is only in part a function of the relationship between usable and non-usable land, for there are still large parts of the continent which are blessed with agricultural potential. These include, for example, the Pacific coastlands of Central America, large parts of the eastern provinces of Colombia, Ecuador and Peru, and the tropical valleys of north-east Bolivia. The failure of agricultural activities to expand to occupy the land that could be utilised is in much larger part a function of the economic and social systems of the countries of the continent. The role of the latifundistas in denying opportunities to many millions who would welcome an opportunity to cultivate land has already been mentioned. In addition, economic policies have been pursued by some governments whereby the incentives to keep land in effective production have been reduced. Such was the case, for example, in Argentina where the agricultural sector was obliged to subsidise the moves towards industrialisation through unfavourable exchange rates for agricultural exports, and where the state-owned railway system has been allowed so to decline in efficiency that it is unable to move all the products of the farms to the cities and the ports. In Venezuela, incentives to the agricultural sector have until recently had the lowest priority in programmes of government assistance with the result that the country has been largely dependent on imported foodstuffs.

EXTRACTIVE INDUSTRIES

Latin America's economic development is, however, becoming less and less a function of its agricultural sector. In terms of their contribution to GNP, non-agricultural activities are dominant in almost every country. Though this particular form of measurement does under-represent the role of agriculture in providing a livelihood for the population (because the productivity of labour in agriculture is, in general, much lower than in other activities), it does nevertheless clearly show that appropriate attention must be given to the location and distribution of extractive industries, manufacturing activities and services in an effective consideration of the geography of Latin America's economic development. Moreover, because it is the non-agricultural activities which provide the dynamics for the continent's expansion, the geographical distribution of these activities will, by and large, serve to pinpoint the main growth zones of the continent.

Extractive industries have, by definition, to be located with reference to the appropriate geological formations: but the distribution of such industries is not solely related to such geological considerations, for other factors such as the costs of extraction and the costs of transport together with political and social considerations are also important in determining their geographical pattern of development.

The search for mineral wealth led the Spanish to some of the more inaccessible parts of the continent in the high Andes of present-day Colombia, Peru and Bolivia and it also encouraged the Portuguese to strike into the interior of Brazil away from the plantations of the coast. The gold, silver, diamonds and other precious metals, etc. which were sought and obtained throughout the colonial period from these inaccessible inland areas still provide the basis of some development but their importance is now small and is still declining. Other metals occur in much the same broad geological regions as the precious metals but their development requires the creation of a much more complex infrastructure—particularly transport facilities. It appears that it has been the relative cost involved in developing this infrastructure which has differentiated between areas of potential growth both within Latin America and between Latin American opportunities and those elsewhere. An example of the second consideration at work is seen in the case of Bolivia's tin, whose importance on the world market has gradually fallen in the face of competition from more easily accessible supplies from countries such as Malaysia. The impact of the former consideration is perhaps seen in the inability of Peru to achieve the level of output of copper in Chile and of lead in Mexico. It has been possible to take the available resources in Chile and Mexico to a higher degree of development partly in light of the less difficult—and hence lower-cost—conditions for getting the metals to the points of overseas shipments. Thus even with high-value mineral wealth that is associated geologically with inland areas in Latin America one finds that exploitation is concentrated in the regions that are relatively most accessible.

But the extractive industries so far considered measure their annual output in no more than thousands of tons (in terms of weight of all these metals produced, Chile heads the list with about 500,000 tons per annum): there are other extractive industries concerned with millions of tons of annual output. Oil, iron ore and bauxite are the most important. In Latin America there are vast areas which are known to have the kinds of geological structure in which these minerals can occur—but to date the greater part of these areas have not been seriously explored. Exploration, in fact, has barely started in areas more than 200 miles from the coast so that today's limited production (limited, that is, in relation to the total potential) comes almost entirely from areas less than this distance from the coast. For example, the extraction of bauxite in the Guianas all takes place within 100 miles of tidewater. The most important iron ore producer, Venezuela, has developed resources only about 80 miles from the export points of the navigable river Orinoco. Most of Brazil's exports (second most important in the continent) are extracted less than 200 miles from the coast while production in Chile and Peru is located within a few miles of the exporting ports.

The most important extractive industry in the continent is oil—which also happens to be the most transportable commodity as it can be put through pipelines which can be built across-country, which would be impossible for roads and railways. In spite of this the search for and the production of petroleum has been almost entirely coastal. In 1965 over 95 per cent of Latin America's oil came from areas less than 100 miles from the coast, although these coastal areas contain only 5 per cent of the total area of Latin America from which oil is potentially available. Thus, contrasting with the small but intensively explored and developed Maracaibo basin in Venezuela (producing over 100 million tons of oil a year) is the very limited amount of development which has taken place in the Andean foreland of Colombia, Ecuador, Peru and Bolivia. Oil has been discovered there in significant quantities with relatively little effort but production is still less than one million tons per annum—almost entirely for local use. It is only since 1964 that studies to assess the economic feasibility of transporting oil from fields in eastern Bolivia, eastern Peru and southern Colombia have been initiated. Ultimately these areas could become of world significance as oil producers—but for the foreseeable future their potential will remain unexploited as a result of their unfavourable location.

SECONDARY AND TERTIARY INDUSTRIES

Manufacturing activities and services (or secondary and tertiary industries) in Latin America have a highly concentrated pattern of geographical development. Within each country the general rule appears to be the appearance of one main location for these activities. Few detailed studies have been made of this phenomenon, for little adequate statistical evidence is available on which examinations can be made but work that has been done on Mexico has shown that about 50 per cent of manufacturing industry is located in the Federal District—an administrative unit which forms less than 0·1 per cent of the land area of the country. An attempt to quantify the geographical pattern of industrial development in the continent is shown in Map 1. This is based on an examination of the location of electricity-generating capacity, which in Latin America is found in large degree in proximity to the demand centres, where the demand arises from the growth of secondary and tertiary activities and the concentration of population. In Table 1 these centres of activity have been ranked from 1 to 41. Three main points should be noted. First, the domination of Argentine, Brazilian and Mexican locations is very clear. This, of course, merely confirms the situation revealed in national figures of industrial output—these are Latin America's most industrial nations. Secondly, and more important from the

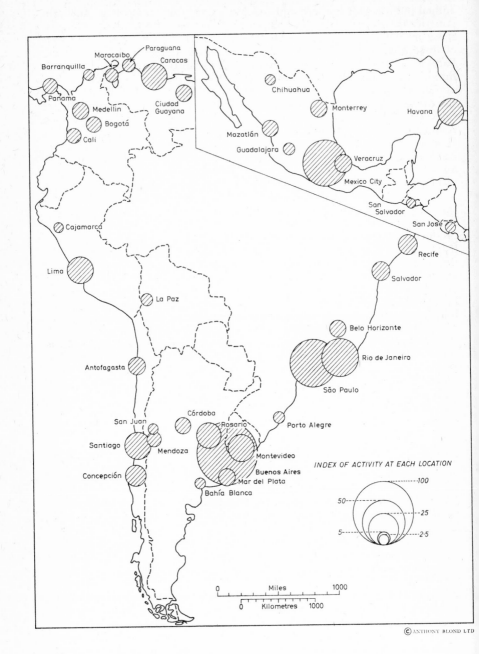

INDEX OF ACTIVITY AT EACH LOCATION

© ANTHONY BLOND LTD

1. MAJOR CENTRES OF ECONOMIC ACTIVITY IN LATIN AMERICA

RANKED CENTRES OF SECONDARY AND TERTIARY ACTIVITIES IN LATIN AMERICA

Rank	Centre	Country	Rank of centre within country	Index of activity (Buenos Aires = 100)
1	Buenos Aires [1]	Argentina	1	100
2	São Paulo	Brazil	1	63
3	Mexico, DF	Mexico	1	50
4	Rio de Janeiro	Brazil	2	34
5	Santiago	Chile	1	25
6	Havana	Cuba	1	18
7	Caracas	Venezuela	1	17
8	Lima	Peru	1	17
9	Rosario	Argentina	2	15
10	Montevideo	Uruguay	1	13
11	Antofagasta	Chile	2	9·1
12	Mar del Plata	Argentina	3	8·9
13	Belo Horizonte	Brazil	3	8·6
14	Maracaibo Oil Towns	Venezuela	2	8·4
15	Concepción	Chile	3	7·5
16	Veracruz	Mexico	2	7·0
17	Monterrey	Mexico	3	6·8
18	Medellín	Colombia	1	6·6
19	Ciudad Guayana	Venezuela	3	6·5
20	Mazatlán	Mexico	4	6·3
21	Córdoba	Argentina	4	5·8
22	Recife	Brazil	4	5·7
23	Bogotá	Colombia	2	5·7
24	Panama	Panama	1	5·3
25	Cali	Colombia	3	5·0
26	Mendoza	Argentina	5	4·8
27	Paraguana	Venezuela	4	4·7
28	Maracaibo	Venezuela	5	4·5
29	Salvador	Brazil	5	4·4
30	La Paz	Bolivia	1	3·8
31	Porto Alegre	Brazil	6	3·7
32	Guadalajara	Mexico	5	3·6
33	Tampico	Mexico	6	3·1
34	Barranquilla	Colombia	4	2·9
35	San José	Costa Rica	1	2·7
36	San Juan	Argentina	6	2·6
37	Chihuahua	Mexico	6	2·5
38	San Salvador	El Salvador	1	2·4
39	Santiago	Cuba	2	2·4
40	Cajamarca	Peru	2	2·4
41	Bahia Blanca	Argentina	7	2·3

[1] First entry from each country is italicised.

geographical viewpoint, is the evidence of the high degree of concentration of activities within limited parts of these countries coupled with a similar concentration in almost every other country of the continent. A more detailed analysis of the position in individual countries has revealed that up to 80 per cent of a country's total activity is located in and around the main centre—usually the capital city. The situation in Argentina, for example, is shown in Map 2a. It is only in Colombia that one finds a more dispersed pattern of activities shared between several centres, thus bringing out that country's unusual form of geographical development with industries

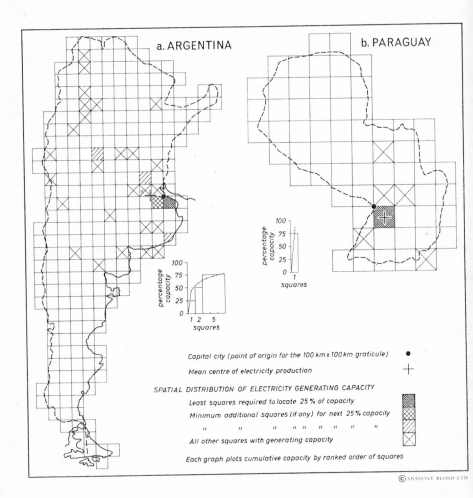

a. ARGENTINA   b. PARAGUAY

percentage capacity
100
75
50
25
0
1
squares

percentage capacity
100
75
50
25
0
1 2 5
squares

Capital city (point of origin for the 100 km x 100 km graticule)   ●

Mean centre of electricity production   +

SPATIAL DISTRIBUTION OF ELECTRICITY GENERATING CAPACITY

Least squares required to locate 25% of capacity

Minimum additional squares (if any) for next 25% capacity

"   "   "   "   "   "   "   "

All other squares with generating capacity

Each graph plots cumulative capacity by ranked order of squares

2. CONSIDERATION OF ELECTRICITY PRODUCTION IN ARGENTINA AND PARAGUAY

An indication of the degree of consideration of non-agricultural economic activities. There is a similar pattern in all other Latin American countries.

located in and around Bogotá, Medellín, Cali and Barranquilla. Thirdly, it will be noted from Map 1 that there are several countries—Paraguay, Ecuador, Honduras, Guatemala and Nicaragua—in which there appear to be no concentrations of secondary and tertiary activities. This, however, is mainly a scale problem for, in fact, each of these countries does have geographical concentration of activities, but in every case the total demand for generating capacity which is thereby created around the main centre (the capital city in every case except Ecuador, where Guayaquil is the single most important location) does not reach a total of 50 MW—the minimum shown on Map 1. Thus in Paraguay (see Map 2b) over 81 per cent of capacity is around Asunción with most of the rest of the country devoid of generating capacity and hence of secondary and tertiary economic activities. But the 81 per cent of capacity concentrated on Asunción represents an actual capacity of only 25 MW. Thus on a continental scale it would be inappropriate to designate it as a centre of secondary and tertiary activities; similar arguments apply to the remaining countries for which no values are recorded.

FUTURE PROSPECTS

The geography of Latin America's development is thus characterised by spatial concentration in each of the economic sectors. The possibilities for change are not great. In agriculture, major expansion in the areas of production seems unlikely—or perhaps even inappropriate in a situation in which the intensification of production from areas already exploited could be a more effective short-to-medium-term solution to problems of food supply and increased agricultural exports. The opening up of new areas for agriculture is a slow and often a capital-intensive process, such that investment in it will generally produce returns lower than those from an equivalent investment in part of the existing agricultural sector (assuming, of course, that the socio-political obstacles to development can be overcome).

For the extractive industries the possibilities of extending the search for resources over larger parts of the continent are to some degree restrained by political difficulties because foreign companies which are, in the main, responsible for such work are decreasingly welcome in most Latin American countries for these activities. Few countries will accept this kind of foreign interest to the same extent as, for example, Australia which strongly encourages the search for oil, gas, iron ore, sulphur and other commodities in its territory by international companies. If such companies have more favourable opportunities elsewhere in the world, then the interior of Latin America —where problems of transport and energy supplies, etc. make exploitation difficult in any case—seems unlikely to attract much attention in the foreseeable future.

As far as secondary and tertiary industry is concerned the present degree of concentration is by no means inevitable for there are many other locations which could be developed. Some countries have already made some efforts to secure a greater geographical dispersion of activities. Thus in Brazil the establishment of Brasilia as capital was in part an attempt to reduce the concentration of tertiary industries on Rio de Janeiro, whilst the significant financial incentives offered to manufacturing companies willing to locate in the north-east represented an effort to take jobs to the 20 million people in that part of the country who have totally inadequate economic opportunities, and to provide an alternative to the continuing migration of workers seeking jobs in the south-east. Chile has similarly attempted to persuade industrialists to choose locations other than in the Santiago/Valparaiso area by creating free-trade zones in the northern and southern parts of the country—at Arica and Punta Arenas respectively. In Argentina, the Córdoba area has been trying to attract new industries—particularly car plants—whilst the government has formally created incentives for industrial expansion in Patagonia and the north-west. In Mexico, infrastructure developments in transport and energy have been financed by the Federal Government for areas in which industrial development is necessary to provide alternatives to employment in largely subsistence agriculture. Almost all the efforts, however, have so far been too limited to offset the attractions of the existing industrial centres.

Only in the case of Venezuela can a different conclusion be reached. There the planned development of the major industrial complex of Ciudad Guayana on the lower Orinoco is well under way and by the end of the decade it should form an industrial growth point which will be an effective counter to the hitherto exclusive attractions of the Caracas Metropolitan Region. In Venezuela the growth potential in economic terms for Ciudad Guayana has been matched by the political acceptance of the need to diversify the country's spatial economy: elsewhere in the continent the need for change from the traditional pattern of concentration has not been unequivocally accepted. In such a situation it is particularly unfortunate that one of the brightest hopes for Latin America's economic development, the formation of a Latin American common market, has not been examined from the viewpoint of its likely effect on the geographical pattern of secondary and tertiary economic activities within individual countries. An integrated Latin America could become little more than a series of interconnected industrialised city-states (such as Buenos Aires, Santiago/Valparaiso, São Paulo/Santos, Mexico City/Veracruz) feeding on and having close relations with each other but largely divorced from any effective and mutually beneficial contact with the remainder of the national territory within which each one is situated. International integration might well turn out to be little more than a substitute for national spatial integration—and lead perhaps to an even greater concentration of economic development than Latin America suffers from today.

BIBLIOGRAPHY

Baer, W. *Industrialisation and Economic Development in Brazil*, Yale Univ. Economic Growth Centre Publications, New Haven, Conn., 1965.

Bird, R. 'The Economy of the Mexican Federal District', *Inter-American Economic Affairs*, XVII, 3, 1963.

Cole, J. P. *Latin America: An Economic and Social Geography*, Butterworth, London, 1965.

Di Tella, T. S. *La Teoría del Primer Impacto de Crecimiento Económico. Estudio de Regionalización Social de la Argentina*, Univ. of Buenos Aires (no date).

Friedmann, J. *Regional Economic Policy for Developing Areas: a Case Study of Venezuela*, MIT Press, Cambridge, Mass., 1966.

Furtado, Celso. *The Economic Growth of Brazil*, Univ. of California Press, Berkeley, 1963.

Jefferson, M. *Peopling the Argentine Pampa*, American Geographical Society, New York, 1926.

Odell, P. R. 'Latin American Economic Integration and the Location of Industrial Activities', *Papers of the International Geographical Union Regional Conference*, Mexico, DF, August 1966.

Yates, P. L. *El Desarrollo Regionel de Mexico*, Banco de Mexico, 1962.

Papers presented to the First Latin American Regional Science Conference: *Cuadernos de la Sociedad Venezolana de Planificación* (special issue), Caracas, September 1963. (Spanish and English versions available.)

THE AGRARIAN PROBLEM

SOLON BARRACLOUGH

SINCE the Cuban revolution the debate over agrarian policy has been sharply intensified in Latin America. Regional conferences of the Organization of American States and of various international agencies adopted strong resolutions calling for immediate agrarian reform doing away with '. . . unjust structures and systems of land tenure and use . . . so that . . . the land will become for the man who works it the basis of his economic stability, the foundation of his increasing welfare, and the guarantee of his freedom and dignity.' The majority of Latin American countries have adopted land reform laws, mostly ineffective. Agrarian reform was a principal issue in the 1964 Chilean and 1963 Peruvian presidential elections and it still strikes political sparks even in Mexico and Bolivia years after their land reforms have got under way.

The Inter-American Committee for Agricultural Development (CIDA) which is formed by the Food and Agriculture Organisation of the United Nations, the United Nations Economic Commission for Latin America, the Inter-American Development Bank, the Organization of American States and the latter's Institute of Agricultural Sciences have all made recent studies of land tenure and development in Latin America. The CIDA has completed analyses of the agrarian problem in seven countries (Argentina, Brazil, Chile, Colombia, Ecuador, Guatemala and Peru) which together include about two-thirds of the region's population and area. Agrarian problems in these countries can be considered fairly representative of Latin America except possibly for Mexico, Bolivia and Cuba where massive land tenure reforms have occurred. Most of the material here presented is based on these studies.

In synthesis, the agrarian problem is fundamentally a political one, based on a struggle for power, income and status. In traditional agrarian societies the ownership of land carries with it control of labour, wealth and prestige. The landowners' privileged position is legitimised by land tenure institutions which tend to be extremely rigid (the possession of great power implies being able to afford not to learn to adjust to new conditions). It is not surprising that the owners of large agricultural properties should become a focal point of attack by groups attempting to displace the old élite.

THE PROBLEM IN PERSPECTIVE

Sixteenth-century Europeans found a flourishing and highly sophisticated agriculture in what is now Latin America. Inca and Aztec farmers produced sufficient surpluses to support large urban populations and armies. Cotton, maize, tobacco, chocolate, potatoes, yams, manioc, quinoa, and many varieties of beans, squash and fruits, were only a few of the many crops selected and cultivated by indigenous breeders. The llama had been domesticated on the Andean Altiplano, providing a rather unsatisfactory basis for a real livestock economy but serving nonetheless as a beast of burden and a source of meat and wool. Irrigation and fertilisation techniques were highly developed. Even in large areas inhabited by semi-nomadic tribes, agriculture was well advanced. The organisation of agricultural production for the most part consisted of plots worked by family groups on communally-owned land with many tasks such as the construction of irrigation works being executed in common.

The conquerors superimposed new institutions upon this indigenous agriculture, quickly distributing the Indians and their lands among the more influential Spanish and Portuguese officers and civilians wherever the possibilities for commercial farming or mining made it profitable to do so. A few relatively small grants of land (*caballerías* and *peonías*) were made to lesser cavalry officers and common foot soldiers in the hope of encouraging farming to feed the new settlements. Most of the territory, however, was distributed in vast geographically-defined areas variously known as *encomiendas* (grants of Indians), *mercedes* or *donatarias*. The *encomenderos* in Spanish America and the *donatarios* in Brazil were given the right to use the labour of resident Indians but were also made responsible for their welfare and religious education. These grants of Indians and land eventually became converted into real property in land and formed the basis for the large estates that have dominated the organisation of Latin American agriculture ever since. On the basis of these grants two similar but in some ways distinct types of farm organisation soon began to develop—the plantation and the *hacienda*.

The plantation depended upon export markets and slave labour. It was first dominant in Santo Domingo, on the Caribbean coast near Veracruz and in the eastern Brazilian coastal region around Bahia, but it soon spread to other areas such as parts of coastal Peru, Valle in Colombia, and north-eastern Brazil where the cultivation of export crops such as sugar, cotton and indigo was profitable. There was a growing European demand for these products and many colonial fortunes were made on their export.

The plantation was a large centrally-directed estate with several hundred families living on it primarily producing an export crop. Capital investments were frequently high and the use of advanced technology profitable. Work was done by gangs of forced labourers under the close supervision of armed bosses. At first Indian labour was drafted, and when the Indians died, fled or were otherwise unavailable, African slaves were imported. The plantation labourers also often produced subsistence crops on family plots in much the same way as the natives had been farming since before the Conquest.

In the Andean region and much of Mexico, however, the Spaniards problem was initially not to export farm products but to feed their armies, animals and the natives drafted to work in the mines, at the sametime keeping the rest of the Indian population under control. As there was no profitable agricultural export market, there was little incentive to organise the *haciendas* primarily as commercial farms or to invest capital in improvements except where large mining operations resulted in regional urban markets. In these areas native social and economic institutions were largely maintained. Where profitable, grain and cattle farming was carried on by Indian labour directed by the *hacendado* and he often collected tribute in the form of crops and on occasion forced his Indians to cultivate commercial crops for him to sell.

The residual Indian communities in marginal or inaccessible areas formed the third major type of colonial agricultural organisation. These maintained their traditional farming methods and social institutions but were also frequently compelled to furnish labour and tribute to the conquerors.

The Latin American agrarian problem can best be understood in the context of the evolution of these three types of colonial farm organisation in response to shifting markets and growing urbanisation. With changing markets and improved transportation in the 19th century, commercial agricultural production became profitable in regions originally loosely organised in haciendas or left to the Indians. The tendency was to extend plantation-like production methods wherever new export markets developed and cheap labour was available, converting subsistence farming on family or communal plots into centrally directed large-scale commercial enterprises with subsistence plots for the labourers. Where large estates already existed this was simply a matter of evolution; where they did not it was a problem of usurping the land. This process is still going on. Extensively farmed haciendas producing cattle and a little grain and subsistence crops in coastal Ecuador and Guatemala are being converted to banana and cotton plantations, while smallholders in parts of Brazil and Peru suddenly find that their titles are not valid as it becomes profitable to incorporate them into neighbouring estates. Plantations and commercial enterprises on haciendas, on the other hand, have often disintegrated into loosely-organised subsistence operations when established markets have failed or soil resources become depleted. Many Brazilian plantations, for instance, that once exported cotton or **sugar,** are now producing mainly for local consumption and resemble traditional haciendas in organisation.

An excellent example of this process is an hacienda studied in coastal Ecuador. This property of nearly 30,000 acres is now owned by a Swedish company and is worked by more than 300 *peones*. It produces principally bananas, cocoa and coffee for export and has all the characteristics of a highly-capitalised modern plantation. Originally it was a typical hacienda belonging to a prominent Guayaquil family and producing cattle and subsistence crops. It became a highly profitable commercial plantation enterprise with the expanding cocoa market in the early years of this century. With the fall in cocoa prices in the late twenties it fell into the hands of a German company that practically abandoned it after purchase. During this period it disintegrated into a loosely-organised hacienda community of subsistence farmers paying rent in the form of labour and part of their production to the estate-owner. The present owners purchased it in the forties and it is now one of the most efficiently organised large commercial estates in the country, but nearly half the estates' residents have had to be expelled to achieve this.

Today's Agrarian Structure

Latin American agriculture is still largely organised in large estates worked by several families under the direction of a single owner, and in communities of smallholdings where each family performs both entrepreneurial and labour functions. The area in commercially operated estates has on balance increased at the expense of the smallholders and traditional haciendas, and the number of family-sized commercial farms and small commercial estates

TABLE I

DISTRIBUTION OF FARM FAMILIES ACCORDING TO SOCIO-ECONOMIC STATUS
(CIDA STUDY COUNTRIES)

	Argentina (1960)	Brazil (1950)	Chile (1950)	Colombia (1960)	Ecuador (1960)	Guatemala (1950)	Peru (1960)
Thousands of families in agriculture	768·6	5,404·2	344·9	1,368·8	440·0	417·4	1,124·5
				Per cent			
Status of families in agriculture							
Operators of large-sized[1] estates	0·4	1·8	3·0	1·1	·3	·3	·9
Operators of medium-sized[2] estates	4·8	12·8	6·5	3·9	2·1	1·5	2·1
Administrators of large and medium-sized estates	1·3	2·1	2·1	1·5	2·0	2·2	1·0
Operators of family-sized smallholdings	32·6	14·9	17·7	23·3	9·5	7·8	7·6
Operators of sub-family-sized smallholdings	25·9	8·6	23·1	47·0	53·6	63·6	61·7
Landless farm workers	35·0	59·8	47·6	23·2	32·5	24·6	26·7
TOTAL	100·0	100·0	100·0	100·0	100·0	100·0	100·0

Source: CIDA studies

[1] I.e. providing employment for over 12 people.
[2] I.e. providing employment for 4–12 people.

490

has also grown, but far less rapidly than colonial visionaries and liberal optimists had foreseen when they encouraged the handing out of *peonías* to disbanded soldiers and later when after independence from Spain and Portugal they abolished primogeniture and slavery. In the seven countries studied by the CIDA the owners of estates hold an average of over three-quarters of the agricultural land. Estates employing more than twelve workers include 82 per cent of all farmland in Peru, for example. Small-holders make up from 62 per cent (Brazil) to more than 96 per cent (Ecuador, Guatemala and Peru) of the number of farm units although they have very little of the land.

The agricultural population can be considered as being made up of four groups—estate-owners who may be entrepreneurs or merely rentiers, an intermediary group of estate administrators and supervisors, the landless workers on the estates, and the smallholders. The estate-owners comprise an agrarian aristocracy and with their families and estate-administrators make up from 4 to 16 per cent of the farm population in the countries studied. The peasants who work the land as smallholders or landless labourers comprise the rest (see Table 1).

A few of the smallholders with family-sized parcels and of the small-estate owners are in effect small commercial farmers in the European or North American sense. This is especially true of some immigrant groups such as the Japanese colonists near São Paulo, Italians near Mendoza in Argentina and many Germans in southern Chile. Apart from this group, the countryside is divided into two broad social and economic classes, the peasants who work the land with their hands and the estate-owners and administrators who do not. Composed originally of Indians and Negro slaves, with their numbers augmented later by miscegenation with the conquerors and the absorption of the least fortunate among immigrants and disbanded soldiers, the peasants have never enjoyed status or power.

About half of the agricultural population depends directly upon the estates for employment. As the landless labourers frequently receive small subsistence-sized parcels to cultivate in lieu of cash wages while many of the smallholders work part-time on the estates, the dividing line between these two peasant groups is not sharp. Slavery and forced labour having been legally abolished during the last century the estate-owner controls his labour-force largely by means of his monopoly of the land. With no alter-native employment or possibility of obtaining sufficient land of his own for subsistence the peasant is forced to work on the estate on the owner's terms. These arrangements, whereby the worker provides free or nearly free labour to the estate-owner in return for the use of land and pasture, are institutiona-lised in a variety of share-cropping and quasi-feudal share-labour agreements such as *huasipungaje* (Ecuador), *colonaje* (Peru and Guatemala) and *inquilinaje* (Chile). In view of the importance of these labour institutions, the holding idle of potentially productive land makes economic sense for the estate-owners.

On the estates the social hierarchy is rigid, consisting of the land-owning class, an intermediary group of managers, accountants, straw bosses and specialised workers and at the bottom those who actually till the soil. In the Latin American traditional scheme of values these class differences take on an almost caste-like appearance. The peasantry remains in large measure socially 'Indian' in Ecuador, Peru and Guatemala, for example, while elsewhere distinctive dress, manners and skin-shading usually set it apart from the estate-owners. Control on the estates is autocratic.

Estate-owners not only rule in their properties but also hold considerable power in the wider society. Most of the largest landowners are partially or fully absentee, maintaining residences, business and political interests in the provincial or national capital and occasionally abroad. Their children attend schools in the cities and their social life centres there, making them in many ways an urban class. Local social, political, educational and even religious institutions may depend upon the estate-owner for continued existence. Chilean priests who recently incurred the large farmers' displeasure by advocating land reform and better farm wages found the entry to several large estates barred, while Brazilian and Guatemalan ex-government officials and labour union organisers have been jailed for similar offences. The state's police power is generally at the estate owners' disposal to protect their property and this may be supplemented by private strong-arm forces such as the *capangos* in Brazil's north-east.

Irrigation projects, agricultural credit institutions and extension services generally operate for the estate-owner's benefit. Relatively large amounts of publicly subsidised credit are available for agriculture on liberal terms and the large owners get most of it. While in 1964 agricultural loans accounted for 35 per cent of all private and public institutional credit in Chile, it is estimated that smallholders got only about 7 per cent of this agricultural credit. Estate-owners have been almost the only beneficiaries of publicly financed irrigation projects, but they were required to repay less than 6 per cent of the costs of two large Chilean projects recently analysed. Land taxes are low in all the countries studied and effectively do not exist at all in Peru. A questionnaire of the officials working in the Ecuadorian agrarian reform agency revealed that about three-quarters of them came from the families of large landowners.

In contrast to the estates, the smallholding areas are characterised by only minor social differences within the community. Smallholding communities are generally bound together by kinship ties and a strong group solidarity against either outside pressures or the disruptive effects for the community of any single member acquiring a too disproportionate share of the land. While the estate-owners have direct contact with national political, social and economic institutions, the smallholders generally depend upon a small town-dwelling élite of merchants, government officials, ecclesiastics and landowners in their relationships with the broader society. In one Chilean smallholding community, for example, the government sent in agricultural agents to give supervised credit and organise a smallholders' cooperative. Local merchants and political bosses, who in some cases were also the larger landowners in the community, quickly took advantage of the credit and got control of the so-called cooperative. Most of the smallholders received no substantial benefits at all and remain suspicious of the programme.

Educational levels, housing and sanitary conditions are substantially poorer in most rural areas than in urban centres. Rural illiteracy ranges from about 23 per cent of the population over 14 years of age in Argentina to over 75 per cent in Guatemala. Housing and sanitation in wide areas of the countries studied compare with the worst in rural Asia, although the average is much better. In many areas nutrition is extremely unsatisfactory and in some such as Brazil's north-east there is frequently real hunger. Peasant annual incomes from all sources including the value of home consumption range from an equivalent of about US$200 per family of six or seven persons in the Andean highlands and north-east Brazil to about US$600 in central Chile and parts of Colombia and to nearly double that amount in parts of Argentina.

The Impending Crisis

According to historical trends there is no reason to expect the traditional pattern of large estates and smallholdings to disappear. On the contrary, a gradual commercialisation and modernization of the estates is to be expected while the peasantry remains in a distinctly inferior position with minimal political and social participation in the national society. When the vast reserve of partially employed rural labour has finally been absorbed into the cities, a bettering of the peasants' wages and position will become possible as a result of competitive bidding for their services, but not until then.

There are many reasons, however, for questioning whether a turning-point in past trends of agrarian organisation may not be imminent. Pressures are mounting to break up the traditional estate system and give more control of the land to peasant producers, the nation-state and other new institutions. In the first place, there are the examples of the recent peasant-supported revolutions in Mexico, Bolivia and Cuba. The pre-revolutionary agrarian structure in these countries was very similar to that described for the seven CIDA-studied countries. Something initiated a process of large-scale and accelerated change in the relationships between the various social groups controlling and working the land; there are many who expect to see this repeated in other countries.

Secondly, situations of overt conflict between peasant groups and estate owners are multiplying. Indian communities have invaded dozens of Peruvian haciendas during the past decade and a peasant strike forced the government to begin expropriating and distributing to the peasants the large estates in the Peruvian valley of La Convención. The federation of rural unions with the independent peasant unions and the Ligas Camponesas[1] in north-eastern Brazil were able to call a strike in 1962 in which some 230,000 peasants participated, demanding better wages and working conditions. The Brazilian military government—which evidently favours the landlords—has suppressed peasant union activity and many peasant leaders have been jailed, exiled or murdered, but the conditions creating agrarian unrest continue unabated. Rural Colombia has been torn by violence since 1949; although this has not yet assumed a primarily peasant versus estate-owner orientation, it has its roots in the country's traditional agrarian structure. In Guatemala return of estate lands to former owners after the Arbenz government had handed the lands to some 100,000 peasants did no more to alleviate Central American agrarian problems than did the massacre of some 18,000 peasants by the army of El Salvador in the 1930s. The CIDA study cited above has found several large Ecuadorian estates in disintegration with the peasants wresting more and more control from absentee owners as population increases both in the estates and in neighbouring smallholding communities.

The third pressure towards the break-up of the traditional estate system is the extremely rapid increase of population in Latin America, which exceeds the increase in agricultural production. Moreover, although rural population is growing more slowly than urban population because of migration to the cities, it is still increasing at an average of about one-and-a-half per cent annually. In rural areas such as central Guatemala, birth-rates are close to the biological maximum and death-rates rapidly decreasing due to the control of epidemics, while urban employment opportunities are minimal. The number of people in the smallholding community of San Juan de

[1] See 'Brazil', p. 51.

Ostuncalco in upland Guatemala, for instance, doubled between 1930 and 1960 although only marginal new areas could be brought into cultivation. The population explosion puts a double strain on the agrarian sector—that of accommodating more farmers and at the same time that of producing more per worker in order to feed the expanding cities.

While the colonisation of frontier areas can help to relieve population pressure, the difficulties are great and the costs high. Unsettled land that is not already held in large estates is frequently marginal for agricultural production and requires costly road construction, malaria control, drainage or irrigation works before it can be used. There is no possibility that colonisation can proceed rapidly enough to solve the agrarian problem in most old settled areas.

The fourth pressure is the acceleration of technological change. On the one hand, improved transport facilitates migration to city slum areas, and in spite of relatively slow industrial growth the continent is becoming increasingly urbanised. In the national society urban interests and urban values predominate more and more. On the other hand, technological progress in the rural areas is extremely uneven. A CIDA study of nine municipalities in Brazil found only about four per cent of the farms using fertilisers; there were only 464 tractors and 3,000 draft animals on 26,000 farms, the rest being worked entirely by hand. Estate-owners tend to introduce labour-saving machinery rather than more labour-intensive farming methods. Mechanisation reduces their dependence on a potentially unruly work-force and has greater prestige value but the net effect is often to increase peasant insecurity and unemployment. Also, changing technology requires redefining the traditional relations between peasants and management; a tractor-driver even if he is a bare-foot Indian has a different status from that he had when he drove only a yoke of oxen.

Whose Problem?

For the estate-owner the agrarian problem consists principally of maintaining his wealth, social position and political power in a changing world. Traditionally-minded landowners would prefer to do this with the least possible alteration of land tenure institutions. They vigorously oppose attempts to organise agricultural labour or to substitute cash wages for quasi-feudal obligations. Commercial producers, however, would generally support doing away with these cumbersome labour arrangements, substituting a free labour market, provided that their real power over the peasantry is not seriously undermined. Thus in Ecuador a group of more progressive large farmers is encouraging the military government to award *huasipungueros* small, less-than-subsistence-sized-plots of land with the knowledge that they will still have to depend upon the estates for employment, while in Chile liberal landowners accept the idea of creating workers' villages with garden-plots (*villorrios*) outside the boundaries of the estates.

Almost everywhere estate-owners see the immediate cause of the agrarian problem as subversive agitation, unfavourable price relationships and inadequate credit. They foresee economic and social disaster if the land is turned over to ignorant peasants. They see themselves as a bulwark against turning the continent back to the Indians.

The peasants' immediate aspirations are usually limited to greater security, better economic conditions and more opportunities for their children, Smallholders and tenants generally aspire to obtain title to the land they work, to have a little more, and if they are Indians they may dream of recovering some of the lands wrested from their forefathers. Workers on the estates, on the other hand, are more likely to be concerned with possible eviction, declining real wages, the personal treatment given to them by the management and the little favours that can be increased or withheld by the 'good' or 'bad' patron, such as the right to pasture more animals or to obtain a loan when needed.

A recent study in central Chile of the aspirations of the *inquilinos* on the large estates revealed that while most of them desire to be smallholders some day, the immediate problems of their everyday relations with the estate-owner and administrator and of providing a living for their families were of much more pressing importance. Temporary workers are often even more preoccupied with their economic conditions as labourers and they may see the smallholders' and permanent labourers' ambitions for land as a threat to their own job security. The peasants usually have no doubt, however, that they could cultivate the land better than the present estate-owners. They are, of course, the ones who do the actual work now, and most of them believe in their lifelong experience of the soil and husbandry.

Agrarian reform policies in Latin America are inspired less by the estate-owners' foresightedness or peasant pressure than by urban politicians and intellectuals. This can in part be explained by chronic shortages and rising food prices and by the problems created by a swelling stream of migrants from rural areas. Other factors may be of greater importance. One of these is the fear of property-owners that peasant unrest may trigger a Mexican or Cuban style revolution if something is not done soon—much of the half-hearted support for agrarian reform by the Alliance for Progress may be explained on this basis. Another is the ideological sympathy that organised labour has for reform and the hope of labour leaders that a victory over the estate-owners will weaken the position of employers everywhere. In the third place, politicians seeking populist support can appeal to most urban groups for agrarian reform without fear of losing votes, while the example of Cárdenas in Mexico and Luis Muñoz Marín in Puerto Rico leads them to hope that it might be possible to create a solid peasant-based political machine to carry their party to sustained national power.

The most influential single group pressing for agrarian reform, however, is to be found among the intellectuals. Moved by a moral commitment to social justice and national development, by an antipathy to the traditional élite common among intellectuals everywhere and by a strong desire to hold power and direct the national destiny, this group can be counted upon to maintain continuous pressure for building a new agrarian structure, although there is little consensus among them about what that new structure should be. Most would agree with Arnold Toynbee that 'in Latin America agrarian reform is the necessary starting point for political, economic and social change alike'.

THE DEVELOPER'S VIEWPOINT

Economists planning Latin America's development find the performance of the agrarian sector particularly frustrating. Production of meat, milk and most food crops lags while unmarketable surpluses of coffee clog warehouses and bananas rot in the fields. Idle land and farm manpower abound while the imports of agricultural products mount. Capital formation proceeds slowly even in years of bumper harvests and good export prices, while public investment in agricultural projects seems to fall into a bottomless pit. The lopsided distribution of farm income stimulates consumption of luxury goods from abroad while offering little opportunity for expanding the effective demand of light industries at home. Migrants arrive in the cities faster than jobs can be created or houses and schools constructed. As other agrarian development policies fail one by one, many planners are beginning to hope that reforms of the bi-polar agrarian structure of large estates and small-holdings might lessen many of these difficulties.

Agricultural production, while not stagnant, has been sluggish. The expansion of highly profitable export crops can occasionally be sensational, such as coffee in southern Brazil in the twenties, bananas in coastal Ecuador during the fifties and cotton and sugar in Colombia since 1960. Nonetheless, in 1965 both Argentina and Chile were forced to declare 'meatless days' because of lagging production while the consumption of meat per person has fallen drastically throughout the region. Chile imports one-quarter of its milk requirements in spite of highly suitable conditions for dairy production. The stores in upper-class districts in Ecuador and Peru stock their shelves with canned pineapples and other tropical fruits from the United States, Mexico and Japan. While total food production increased by some 10 per cent between 1958–59 and 1963–64, Latin America's population grew by about 14 per cent and per capita production fell (see Table 2).

Both agricultural land and labour are grossly underutilised even by the standards of the relatively primitive technologies that predominate in most areas. In Guatemala a 1964 farm management study of small upland holdings found only 1·1 hectares (2·5 acres) of cropland per farm, the culti-vation of which required at most only between one-tenth and one-fifth of the families' working hours. In Chile the CIDA analysis estimated between one-quarter and one-third of the available farm labour force to be unnecessary with existing technology, even making allowance for peak demands in certain seasons. Land, on the other hand, is on the average used only extensively. In the countries studied by CIDA only between one-third and one-tenth of the land in farms was found to be cultivated. While much of the uncultivated land would be marginal for intensive use, land classification studies show that in Chile, for instance, only about one-quarter of the arable land is under the plough and that in the fertile Central Valley one-third of the irrigated land is extensively used unimproved pasture.

Analysing production by size of farms reveals that in Colombia, Argentina and Ecuador more than one-half the total value of agricultural production comes from the smallholdings. In Chile the large and medium-sized estates with 92 per cent of the agricultural land account for about 80 per cent of total product, but if one separates the production of the share-croppers' and workers' plots on the estates, the conclusion is that they together with the independent smallholders produce 40 per cent of the total value of the country's crop and livestock on only 20 per cent of the *arable* land in farms. The CIDA data show that land in the large estates is used extensively with the value of production per acre averaging well less than half of what it is on the smallholdings. On the other hand, the value of production per man is greater on the estates, which is easily explained by the more favourable man-land ratio on the large holdings, making it possible for the work force to be more fully employed. Also labour-saving machinery is more frequently found on the estates. Underemployment is far more serious on the small-holdings, and in Chile it is more than three times as great as on the estates.

Classical economists argued that the concentration of land rentals in the

but also the problem of increasing effective demand for light consumer durables and other budding national industries, the planners find the distribution of agricultural income unsatisfactory on both counts. The formidable challenge of accelerating peasant investment and effective demand simultaneously can be met only by a combination of a highly dynamic agriculture with income redistribution. Experience in Mexico, Bolivia and Puerto Rico and in other parts of the world leaves hope that considerable investment can be made with no sacrifice in spending by means of the peasants dedicating part of their family labour supply to productive farm improvements.

Proposals to stimulate agricultural production, investment and better wages by improving the relationships between farm and industrial prices leave most planners unconvinced and many politicians and businessmen frankly hostile. Higher real food prices lead to urban unrest, strikes and increased manufacturing costs with the result that most planners prefer to resort to greater imports of surplus foods rather than permitting rapid price increases. Moreover, it is doubtful whether the desired economic benefits would actually result from higher food prices. During the Korean war, years which were favourable for agriculture, the agrarian problem persisted. Bigger incomes for estate-owners do not automatically lead to more productive investment or to higher wages for their labourers, although higher food prices are generally accompanied by a rapid rise in land values. The CIDA studies could find no consistent differences in wages paid to the peasants on inefficient properties with low returns, nor did farm wages rise in years of good prices to fall again in poor ones. To the extent that the peasant is a wage-earner and not producing on his own account to sell in the market, higher food prices may even depress his income.

Minimum wage regulations and social welfare legislation have been as ineffective in improving the peasants' incomes as has tax legislation in redistributing the estate owners', and for the same reasons—these measures are seldom enforced or designed to be effective. In Chile the 'regulated' agricultural wages decreased by 24 per cent in real terms between 1953 and 1964 while in Argentina they decreased by 30 per cent from 1956 to 1965. Meanwhile, the threat that the regulations might some day be enforced, if only haphazardly, or that labour unions might be organised, gives estate-owners additional reasons for attempting to reduce their labour force, thus increasing peasant insecurity.

Finally, the planners projecting maximum defensible rates of expansion of non-farm jobs conclude that urban centres could not possibly absorb immigration of peasants from rural areas much faster than they are now doing. In the countries studied by the CIDA 14 per cent of the rural population (more than one-half of the natural increase) emigrated to the cities between 1950 and 1960. The simple displacement of the agrarian problem to urban slums hardly seems a contribution to economic development. If this swelling stream of untrained and often illiterate immigrants is not somehow channelled and held in check, the best development plans may end in chaos.

Attempting to rationalise reality in terms of economic theory, the planners see the problem as one of agrarian structure. The estate-owners act rationally within the context of their society as they value their traditional privileges, power and way of life more than the additional monetary returns that could be obtained by changing farm organisation and methods or by dedicating more time and effort to being efficient farm managers. The peasants also act rationally. The traditional structure effectively bars them from obtaining land, or—if they are smallholders—more land, credit and other inputs needed for commercial expansion. They husband carefully the little they have and resist the change that experience has taught them to be fraught with insecurity. There is no incentive to make two blades of grass grow where one grew before if the absentee landowner or the smalltown trader is going to make off with both.

BIBLIOGRAPHY

Barraclough, Solon and Domike, Arthur L. *Evolution and Reform of Agrarian Structure in Latin America* (mimeograph), ICIRA, Santiago de Chile, 1964.

Carroll, Thomas F. 'The Land Reform Issue in Latin America', *Latin American Issues*, Albert O. Hirschman, Twentieth Century Fund, New York, 1961. 'Land Reform as an Explosive Force in Latin America', *Explosive Forces in Latin America*, ed. John J. Tepaske and Sydney N. Fisher, Ohio State Univ. Press, Columbus, Ohio, 1964.

Chonchol, Jacques. 'Land Tenure and Expansion in Latin America', *Obstacles to Change in Latin America*, ed. Claudio Veliz, Oxford Univ. Press, London and New York, 1965.

Feder, Ernest. 'The Rational Implementation of Land Reform in Colombia and its Significance for the Alliance for Progress', *America Latina*, VI, 1, Rio de Janeiro, 1963.

Flores, Edmundo. *Land Reform and the Alliance for Progress*, Princeton Univ. Press, NJ, 1963.

McBride, George. *Agrarian Indian Communities in Highland Bolivia*, American Geographical Society, New York, 1921. *The Land Systems of Mexico*, Research Series No. 12, American Geographical Society, New York, 1923.

Patch, Richard W. *The Peruvian Agrarian Reform Bill*, West Coast South America Series, XI, 3, American Universities Field Staff, New York, 1964.

Pearse, Andrew. 'Land Tenure, Social Structure and Development in Latin America', *America Latina*, VI, 3, Rio de Janeiro, 1963.

Wolfe, Marshall. *Rural Settlement Patterns and Social Change in Latin America: Notes for a Strategy of Rural Development*, ECLA, Santiago, 1954.

ECLA. *Agriculture in Latin America: Problems and Prospects* (UN, E/CN 12/686), New York, 1963.

FAO. *Agrarian Reform Policies*, Latin American Conference on Food and Agriculture, Doc. LARC/65/Conf/3, Viña del Mar, Chile, 1965.

Interamerican Committee for Agricultural Development (ICAD or CIDA). *Inventory Basic to the Planning of Agricultural Development in Latin America: Selected Bibliography*, Pan American Union, Washington, DC, 1964/5. *Land Tenure and Agricultural Development in Brazil*, Pan American Union, Washington, DC, 1966. *Land Tenure and Agricultural Development in Chile*, Pan American Union, 1966. There are further volumes in this series of studies, in Spanish, on Argentina, Colombia, Ecuador, Guatemala and Peru, and English translations are planned.

Land Tenure Center Library. *Bibliography: Agrarian Reform and Tenure*, Land Tenure Center, Wisconsin, 1964.

Latin American Center for Research in the Social Sciences. *Bibliography: Structure and Land Reform in Latin America*, Rio de Janeiro, 1962.

UN Department of Economic and Social Affairs. *Progress in Land Reform* (E/3603/rev. 1, ST/SOA/49), New York, 1962.

US Department of Agriculture. *Indices of Agricultural Production for the 20 Latin American Countries*, Washington, DC, 1963.

THE PROBLEM OF INFLATION

DAVID HUELIN

THE Latin American republics have in common virtually all the problems inherent in the need for social improvements and economic growth; but no republic is typical of all of them and each has its own approach to the matter. Inflationary forces are latent in the social and economic structures of virtually all the republics, but some of them have not yet embarked on programmes of economic expansion that would make such forces active, and in some there are special circumstances that have made development possible without serious inflation. The republics that afford examples of what has come to be regarded as endemic inflation are Argentina, Brazil and Chile; there are also inflationary problems in Colombia, Peru and Uruguay.

Probably none of Latin America's economic difficulties has been the subject of so much controversy as has inflation; it affects every economic activity and confuses the republics' foreign relations; it is a potent factor in domestic politics, and an element of instability in almost every aspect of the republics' affairs. There is the observed fact that economic growth has been accompanied by rapid inflation in Argentina and Brazil, but not in Mexico; from this stems a controversy between the 'structuralist' and the 'monetarist' views on the causes of inflation and the policies required to check it. Allied to this controversy is the debate on whether inflation is an inevitable accompaniment of economic growth; the example of Mexico suggests that it is not, but there are differing views on whether it is the reformed social and political structure of Mexico or the Mexican authorities' pursuit of cautious monetary policies that has prevented the appearance of inflation.

Before the relevance of these debates can be appreciated, it will be as well to examine the social and economic context in which inflation has occurred in Latin America, the course that it has taken, and the consequences of the measures used to check it. Inflation in Latin America does not differ from its manifestation elsewhere in the world in being the outcome of an excess of demand over supply and of consumption in relation to savings; it is in the structural reasons underlying these ordinary causes that Latin America has some particular characteristics. Not the least distinctive feature of the inflationary republics is the attitude of governments and business communities, who from long experience have learned to live with and to some extent protect themselves from inflation. They do not share the European or United States view that inflation is an intolerable evil.

THE STRUCTURAL SETTING

Domestic

The population of Latin America as a whole is growing at a rate of about three per cent a year, and the greater part of this growth is occurring in the lower social strata and particularly in depressed rural areas, in some of which the rate of increase exceeds four per cent a year. This means, statistically, that unless national incomes increase by more than five per cent annually there can be no perceptible rise in the average income per inhabitant. Average incomes are low; even the comparatively high per capita levels of Argentina and Uruguay are below one-half of the general level of northern Europe, and that of Brazil is barely one-third. Moreover, in most of the republics—Argentina and Uruguay being the main exceptions—the distribution of income is extremely unequal, with wide disparities between the upper and lower social classes and between the urban and rural communities.

This pattern reflects the social and agrarian structure inherited from the nineteenth century; in many countries including Chile and parts of Brazil, archaic systems of land tenure remain unreformed, with latifundia or plantation agriculture depriving peasant populations of land resources. Even where these conditions are not extreme, domestic agriculture is in general technically backward, under-capitalised, and low-yielding; its development has been impeded by poor communications and marketing mechanisms, taxes and price controls, and inadequate credit facilities. Moreover, the migration, mainly of young adults, towards the cities has been reducing the human potential in agriculture.

The growth of urban demand, and the failure of agricultural output to keep pace with it, has resulted in shortages and has been a primary cause of inflation. When demand has caused prices to rise, the effect has seldom penetrated through the distributive mechanisms to the producers; at various times governments have imposed price controls on essential food products so as to avoid rises in urban living costs. Rising demand has not been translated into increased production and increased rural incomes; accelerated economic activity in the cities has been accompanied by stagnant or even declining agricultural output, and the disparities between the two sectors have been accentuated. In Brazil and Chile, for example, the neglect of agriculture has led to these countries being no longer self-sufficient in food supplies, which Chile was until as recently as the mid-1950s, and their being obliged to spend foreign exchange on imports. Even in Argentina and Uruguay, agricultural countries *par excellence*, legislation has induced occasional shortages and has to some extent isolated agriculture from urban economic growth.

In the public sector there are other consequences. The depression of agriculture, in conjunction with the population growth and the rising tide of expectations, has attracted many thousands of rural workers to the cities, so that urban populations have been increasing at rates of some seven per cent or more annually. This has created an ever-rising demand for social services, housing, and public works, often exceeding governments' ordinary resources and giving rise to inflationary pressures.

The neglect and isolation of rural populations implies a waste of human and agrarian potential which is one of the major impediments to Latin America's balanced economic growth.

External

The Latin American nations have derived from the nineteenth century, and from international economic circumstances, a dependence on exports of primary commodities; many of the economies are geared to a single product, such as coffee or copper; few have highly diversified exports, and exports of manufactured goods, which began in a small way in the late 1950s and showed some promise in the early 1960s, are unlikely to reach a significant scale for some years to come.

Most of Latin America's exports are sold either on free world markets or through private commercial channels, and are subject to the price fluctuations generated by changes in the balance of supply and demand. The general trend of prices since the end of the Korean war boom has been downwards, with the result that the contribution of the export trade to economic growth has been declining, certainly relatively to the rate of growth itself, and in some cases absolutely. This has occurred precisely over the period when the social pressures for economic expansion have been greater than ever before.

Raúl Prebisch, doyen of Latin American economists, showed as long ago as 1950 how the mechanisms of free markets and international trade combine to transfer from the industrialised countries to the exporters of primary commodities through falls in prices all cyclical contractions in demand, but only a part of the rise in prices resulting from cyclical expansion, because of economies in the industrial use of primary materials or a greater use of substitutes. This means that the benefits of technical advances are not passed on to the developing countries. The process, which has come to be known as the 'Prebisch Effect', leads to the rich countries becoming richer while the expansion of the developing economies is delayed. The various expedients used in Latin America to overcome the worst effects have not proved to be adequate substitutes for export earnings; they have led to balance-of-payments difficulties and to inflationary pressures, as will be shown later.

An additional, and at times significant, cause of a shortage of both domestic capital and foreign exchange resources is the deeply rooted tradition among Latin American capital owners of depositing or investing funds abroad. Originally this was done as a safeguard against political instability—a sort of exile insurance—or simply to enable the rich to live in Europe; more recently it has been used as a hedge against inflation or for exchange speculation.

THE COURSE OF INFLATION

The private sector

In the more advanced republics where the growth of the urban middle classes dates from before the first world war, reflecting their thriving foreign trade and its allied developments, social pressures for economic expansion have been constantly at work. Two world wars and the intervening depression emphasised to the Latin Americans the dangers of relying on overseas suppliers for consumer goods, and on world markets for the export earnings to pay for such goods. This applied especially to Argentina and Brazil with their large Europe-oriented trade. Immediately after the second world war, in particular, domestic conditions were extremely propitious for industrial development aimed at the substitution of imports. Starved consumer markets were avid for manufactures, and demand was backed, especially in Argentina, by an exceptional increase in the money supply; this was the local currency counterpart of an accumulation of foreign exchange from exports maintained throughout the war and largely unrequited.

With a strong domestic demand and ample exchange reserves for imports of equipment, industrial growth was extremely rapid. As the former belligerents resumed their normal exports after the second world war, Latin American manufacturers were able easily to obtain from their governments protective barriers, behind which high costs—and high profits—were no impediment to expansion. There was an accompanying keen demand for industrial labour, and high wages were offered; this accelerated the drift of rural workers to the industrial centres which is still continuing; the rapid growth of the labour force—consisting largely of people earning hitherto unheard-of wages and neither acquainted with the idea of saving nor, in the absence of effective mechanisms for the purpose, being encouraged to save—added fresh impetus to consumer demand, especially for foods, with a consequent tendency for prices to rise.

Attempts by governments to limit price rises, because of their impact on living costs, created shortages and black markets, and belated price rises had repeatedly to be allowed. Cost-of-living indices in Latin America naturally give a heavier weighting to foods than they do in high-income countries; rising indices form the basis of wage claims. The governments of, for example, Perón in Argentina and Vargas in Brazil actively encouraged the formation of trade unions to strengthen labour's bargaining power, and frequently gave official support to wage claims, or even decreed general wage increases for the private sector no less than for the public. In Chile there was legislation that automatically ordered wage increases of the same percentage as the rise in the cost-of-living index in the previous year. In the highly protected climate in which industry has operated, manufacturers have been able, without fear of competition from imports, to pass increases in costs on to consumers, often in advance of impending cost rises. Thus classical price-wage-cost spirals have been generated.

The inflationary influence of industry has been accentuated by a lack of selectivity in official industrial promotion schemes; there has been excessive duplication among uneconomically small plants. These, being labour-intensive, have helped to improve employment statistics, but the technical shortcomings of their equipment have limited the productivity of the labour employed. On the other hand, the installation of modern capital-intensive plants has in some cases led to the creation of productive capacity far in excess of the market's potential, with consequently high operating costs. The pattern of duplication within each of the national economies is repeated in the regional context, as is mentioned below.

Import substituion gave considerable scope and impetus to manufacturing industries in the early stages, but it has been evident even in the comparatively large markets of Argentina and Brazil that the initial pace of expansion slowed down—in the absence of other outlets—as the process neared completion; since the late 1950s or so growth has been largely dependent on the ordinary expansion of domestic demand. Some further industrial development was achieved, especially in Argentina and Brazil, from about 1960 onwards in substituting imports of capital goods; but the limitations of the market and the large capital investments required have so far prevented any spectacular growth in this field.

The gradual slowing down of the pace of industrial expansion has not, in general, been accompanied by a parallel decline in the rate of increase in industrial wages. The tendency of wage costs to rise faster than ouput has had obviously inflationary effects.

In all the circumstances outlined, an important role has been played by the inflationary countries' banking systems. In the initial stages of industrialisation, when there was ample financial liquidity, large amounts of domestic capital were attracted by the high profits in industry; as the inflationary process advanced, the underlying inadequacy of savings in relation to consumption became increasingly manifest in the difficulty experienced by entrepreneurs in avoiding the erosion of their capital by rising costs. Even the extensive capitalisation of profits by the issue of new shares rather than cash dividends was not always enough to maintain a company's capital structure. Inflation itself has deterred savings and promoted consumption, especially of consumer durables, as a simple hedge, and has thus accentuated the imbalance.

Increasing difficulties in this respect have driven entrepreneurs to rely more and more on bank credit and loans, not only for working capital but even also for fixed capital. The banking systems have exercised their normal multiplying effect on the money supply, and this, in conjunction with high interest rates, has added further to inflation.

The public sector

Governments have felt the impact of rising prices, perhaps even more acutely than the private sector, because of their less flexible revenue. In most of the Latin American republics the reform of archaic tax structures has been slow and late, and collection has been far from efficient; only recently in a few countries (e.g. Chile and Brazil) has tax evasion ceased to be respectable and become an indictable offence; losses through evasion have been as high as forty per cent of nominal tax revenue. At best, many taxes are collected in arrears on values which in a highly inflationary economy are soon out-of-date.

In addition, great pressure has been put on fiscal resources by the social changes accompanying industrialisation and the migration of rural populations to the cities; industry itself has exercised an increasing demand for the investment of public funds in energy supplies, communications and similar services. Also there have been subsidies on certain essential consumer goods and on imports of vital supplies that have increased steeply with the growth of the cities. There has been, moreover, a great proliferation of bureaucracy with the creation of new agencies to deal with new social and economic phenomena; to this must be added the losses of state-owned public services, state-owned industries, and the financing by the state of agricultural crops, such as coffee.

The combination of sluggish revenue and rapidly rising costs has resulted in very large deficits in national accounts; on occasions in both Argentina and Brazil expenditure has been more than twice the amount of revenue. In an inflationary economy in which savings are inadequate and interest rates are very high, the ability of a government to finance its deficits by bond issues is very limited. Therefore only two methods of financing fiscal deficits have in effect been open to governments: borrowing from the commercial banking system by obliging the banks to take up special bond issues or to make compulsory deposits with the central bank, thus diverting resources from the private sector; and borrowing from the central bank itself. These additions to the money supply rapidly find their way into the private sector through government payments to contractors, employees and the recipients of subsidies; the commercial banking system exercises its normal multiplying effect, and further inflation ensues.

The structuralists maintain that increases in the money supply generated in the public sector are a reflection of inflationary pressures caused by structural defects in the economy, which would appear to be true. The monetarists contend that increases in the money supply without corresponding increases in production are a direct cause of inflation, which could not continue for long if monetary expansion were adequately regulated, which also seems undeniable.

The external sector

The Prebisch Effect in Latin America, as already noted, has prevented the rapidly developing republics from deriving from their export trade the domestic capital and the foreign exchange that they need to maintain adequate investments and imports. The double deficiency has been to some extent concealed, rather than overcome, by foreign assistance in various forms. Long-term loans to governments and official enterprises have contributed significantly to the economic infra-structure, but the private sector has had to rely mainly on private investments and on medium- and short-term credits.

Private investments by foreign industrialists in associated enterprises have made a substantial contribution to industrial development by their introduction of equipment and techniques. It has been argued, however, that some of these ventures, by establishing plants with excess capacity, by using local bank loans for installation expenses, and by adding their over-large demands for buildings and energy to already existing demand, have had indirect inflationary consequences.

In default of adequate domestic or foreign investment, industry has made extensive use of credits from foreign banks and suppliers of capital goods. Supplying countries have readily offered these credits as a means of promoting their exports, and Latin American governments have approved this means of enabling industrial expansion to continue without excessive immediate impact on the balance of payments.

The suppliers' credit system has been criticised as being an unsuitable method of financing industrial expansion; not only do such credits cost more to the borrower than investment capital, but they are short in relation to the borrower's needs. Both factors are an addition to the Latin American manufacturer's costs. It is probable that new equipment acquired in this way has enabled some industrialists to reduce costs, at least comparatively; but it is not certain that such reductions have compensated the additional costs implicit in the system.

The virtually unrestricted acceptance of these credits from the early 1950s onwards eventually led to accumulations of medium- and short-term foreign exchange liabilities that several countries' payments positions were unable to bear. In Chile and Brazil at the end of 1964 immediate commitments amounted to about fifty and forty per cent, respectively, of their probable export earnings in the same period, leaving a quite inadequate margin for necessary imports; Argentina and Colombia have been in a similar position. These four countries have at various times been obliged to negotiate fresh loans or the postponement of their obligations. The excessive use of the suppliers' credit system has accentuated existing distortions by being merely a transitory substitute for savings and concealing the real deficiency; it has led to additional exchange obligations without creating any export trade; and it has increased the Prebisch Effect by raising the actual cost of imports.

The protective barriers erected by all the industrialising countries have resulted in the excessive duplication of industries in Latin America as a whole, preventing exports of manufactured goods from one country to another, and thus making it impossible for industries to expand their activities beyond their national markets. The Latin American Free Trade Association is attempting to break down this structure, but it is clear that the extensive reorganisation of industries in each republic that will be required will take many years to achieve.

Latin American manufacturing industries have not yet achieved any significant volume of exports outside the region, which would be the most effective way of countering the Prebisch Effect. Their opportunities have been limited by their high production costs and the difficulty of obtaining effective export subsidies from impoverished governments, by the protective policies of the high-income countries, and perhaps by their own lack of experience.

REMEDIES FOR INFLATION

The structuralist-monetarist controversy and debates on the relative import-ance of demand and costs, and the implications of what Raúl Prebisch has called the 'false dilemma' of a choice between economic expansion and monetary stability, have all been heatedly argued when measures to restrain inflation have had to be devised and when the consequences of such measures have been felt. Anti-inflationary restrictions of differing intensity and effectiveness have been applied since the early 1950s; in no country has inflation been permanently and wholly arrested, though there have been several notable reductions of the pace. In other instances it is more doubtful whether governments have made very enthusiastic attempts, partly perhaps because of the difficult social and political consequences of recession—as for example in Argentina—and partly no doubt because of governments' unwillingness to curb their own expenditure, as in Brazil before 1964.

A very real dilemma has arisen on many occasions, notably in Argentina, Brazil, Chile and Colombia, when industrial expansion and inflation have combined to produce a crisis in the balance of payments. It is virtually essential for any Latin American republic in payments difficulties to apply to the International Monetary Fund for a credit; the necessity is dictated by the common practice among other creditors—government or private—of looking to the IMF for a lead and making their loans or credits conditional on IMF approval. The IMF correctly believes that inflation is an important factor in a country's balance of payments and wishes to ensure that inflation will be curbed so as to avoid the credit's becoming ineffectual through a further deterioration in the payments position, and the borrower's ultimate inability to repay drawings. It normally examines the borrowing country's monetary situation in detail, specifying the precise amount beyond which the money supply should not be allowed to expand, and requiring a letter of intent agreeing to these and other stipulations.

Latin Americans tend to regard these methods as an unwelcome interven-tion in their domestic affairs, and relations with the IMF have been on occasions strained. The structuralists are critical of the IMF because of its insistence only on monetary restraint rather than on structural reforms. Their case is strengthened by the observed consequences of monetary restrictions vigorously applied, which can be not only detrimental to econ-omic development but actually self-defeating.

IMF doctrine is based on restraint of the money supply, which is intended to curb demand. It does not affect costs, however, and a rigorous restriction of bank credit, on which businesses rely heavily in times of inflation, may cause a slowing down of industrial expansion or even an absolute contrac-tion, with perhaps a rise in unit production costs. It may also affect the distributive trades and lead to shortages of essential supplies. Perhaps its worst effect is the encouragement that it may give to 'parallel' money markets, where, as in Brazil for example, the cost of borrowing has in the past reached five per cent a month, and there is an increase in the velocity of circulation that partly neutralises quantitative restrictions of credit.

In Argentina in 1961 and 1962, despite an increase in the velocity of circulation, the restrictions were so effective that the private sector fell heavily into arrears with its tax payments; the government in turn was in arrears with its payments to contractors and employees, and within the private sector payments between businesses were excessively delayed; the consequence was a recession of unprecedented severity in 1962 and 1963, an unheard-of level of unemployment and considerable social hardship. These conditions led to a wave of bankruptcies, to disinvestments from enterprises that ceased to be profitable, and to a general crisis in confidence reflected in a massive flight of capital from the country. The theory that credit restraint will not only discourage the demand for imports but also persuade businesses to borrow working capital abroad and so give immediate relief to the payments position has here been proved not to be valid if confidence is weakened.

Even in less severe circumstances than those experienced in Argentina, a falling off of economic activity has reduced government revenues; as it has seldom been possible at short notice to curtail official expenditure to a significant extent without causing social hardship, the governments of the inflationary countries have had to meet their fiscal deficits with inflationary financing, even in times of severe credit restriction in the private sector. Argentina, Brazil, Chile and Colombia have all experienced the double evil of recession with continuing inflation.

The recent experience of Brazil suggests, however, that in rapid inflation there is a monetary element that can be brought under control without necessarily causing pronounced recession; the rise in the cost of living in Brazil was over eighty per cent in 1963, when discipline was lax; in the first quarter of 1964 the rise was at an annual rate of 140 per cent. After the change of government in April 1964 monetary discipline and financial and fiscal reforms were introduced, and confidence was greatly restored; the rise in the cost of living for the whole of 1964 was some ninety per cent, and in 1965, when the reforms had begun to be really effective, the rise was only about fifty per cent. The resumption of industrial expansion in 1965, after the contraction in 1964, showed continuing confidence in the government's policies. The achievement is notable and illustrates not only the importance of monetary discipline intelligently applied, but also the key role of confidence in a government's policies.

CONCLUSIONS

It seems possible to identify certain causes of primary inflationary pressure in Latin America that are undoubtedly structural and could be eliminated only by structural reforms. The economic and even social isolation of agriculture from urban prosperity has been a basic cause of shortages of essentials; in this context it matters little whether the isolation is caused by inherited patterns of land tenure, by poor communications, by lack of investment, or by deliberate policies. The inflationary forces latent in these situations became active when industrial expansion, in response to middle-class urban demand, attracted rural populations to the cities and added to the demand for both foods and manufactures.

Increased consumption was not accompanied by a parallel growth in savings and investment; capital formation has been inadequate both in agriculture and in industry, largely because of social attitudes and the absence of suitable institutions. The public sector has, largely for institutional reasons, failed to match expenditure with revenue, and for social and political reasons has intervened in the private sector with legislation that has tended to encourage consumption rather than to curb it in favour of savings. The various expedients used to overcome the deficiency of domestic capital formation in both sectors—amounting in effect to the creation of money in various ways—may be regarded as causes of a secondary stage of inflation, structural or political in its origins and monetary in its manifestations.

The experience of Mexico appears to confirm the structural hypothesis; the basic social and agrarian reforms were achieved before the appearance of the social pressures that have led to inflation in other republics. These reforms included the establishment of a strong and stable government and an efficient administration equipped with the power and the expertise required to eliminate structural inflationary pressures where they appeared and to apply wise monetary and fiscal policies. At the other end of the wide scale of development in Latin America are republics with small middle classes, small urban concentrations, low national incomes, little industrialisation, and no inflation.

PERCENTAGE CHANGES IN INDICATORS

Yearly Averages

	1953–55	1955–60	1961	1962	1963	1964	1965
Argentina							
Cost of living	+8·5	+66·9	+18·8	+31·7	+27·6	+18·1	+38·2
Money supply	+23·2	+41·0	+15·0	+6·9	+28·8	+39·9	+22·5[1]
Cost of US$1	+52·4	+21·7	+0·5	+61·2	−1·2	+13·9	+25·0
Brazil							
Cost of living	+22·8	+39·6	+43·0	+55·3	+80·6	+86·6	+50·8
Money supply	+23·7	+48·1	+50·6	+63·3	+64·0	+85·9	+50·7[2]
Cost of US$1	+87·4	+33·8	+80·0	+26·7	+30·5	+198·4	+20·0
Chile							
Cost of living	+123·8	+33·4	+9·7	+27·7	+45·4	+38·4	+25·9
Money supply	n.a.	+52·5	+13·2	+40·0	+28·7	+51·7	+35·6[2]
Cost of US$1	+129·5	+11·0	0·0	+127·9	+26·3	+7·3	+29·5
Uruguay							
Cost of living	+9·9	+34·1	+10·3	+11·2	+43·6	+35·4	+88·0
Money supply	+3·2	+38·2	+16·8	−5·5	+31·0	+38·2	+24·3[3]
Cost of US$1	+12·0	+33·5	−0·4	0·0	+58·9	+39·5	+183·4
Mexico							
Cost of living	+9·7	+4·8	−1·8	+1·8	0·0	+3·6	+2·6[2]
Money supply	+11·3	+10·1	+6·6	+13·2	+16·1	+17·6	−6·2[2]
Cost of US$1	+15·1[4]	0·0	0·0	0·0	0·0	0·0	0·0

[1] Provisional.

[2] September.

[3] March.

[4] The Mexican peso was devalued in April 1954 from 8·65 to 12·50 to US$1, where it has remained.

Argentina, Brazil and Chile have been evolving more balanced monetary policies and modernising their fiscal and financial administration, so that they are succeeding in checking what might be called a tertiary stage of super-inflation from purely monetary causes. The complete disappearance of inflation may have to await the execution of their plans for agrarian reform and agricultural modernisation and the emergence of a more stable political structure.

There is a need, finally, for reforms in the mechanisms of world trade to eliminate the Prebisch Effect and its inflationary pressures in Latin America and elsewhere, reforms calling for more enlightened policies than those at present followed by the high-income nations of the world.

BIBLIOGRAPHY

Eshag, Eprime and Thorp, Rosemary. *Economic and Social Consequences of Orthodox Economic Policies in Argentina in the Post-War Years*, Oxford Univ. Institute of Economics and Statistics, *Bulletin*, XXVII, 1, February 1965.

Gordon, Wendel C. *The Political Economy of Latin America*, Columbia Univ. Press, New York and London, 1965.

Hirschman, Albert O. *Journeys towards Progress* (chapter 3, 'Inflation in Chile'), Twentieth Century Fund, New York, 1963.

Hirschman, Albert O. (ed.) *Latin American Issues*, Twentieth Century Fund, New York, 1961. Contributions: David Felix, 'An Alternative View of the "Monetarist—Structuralist" Controversy'; Joseph Grunwald, 'The Structuralist School on Price Stabilization and Economic Development: The Chilean Case'; Roberto Oliveira Campos, 'Two Views on Inflation in Latin America'.

Macario, Santiago. *Protectionism and Industrialisation in Latin America*, UN Economic Commission for Latin America, *Bulletin for Latin America*, Santiago, IX, 1, March 1964.

Prebisch, Raúl. 'Economic Development or Monetary Stability: the False Dilemma', UN ECLA, *Bulletin for Latin America*, Santiago, VI, 1, March 1961. 'The Economic Development of Latin America and its Principal Problems', UN ECLA, *Bulletin for Latin America*, Santiago, VII, 1, February 1962.

Seers, Dudley. 'Inflation and Growth: A Summary of Experience in Latin America,' UN ECLA, *Bulletin for Latin America*, Santiago, VII, 1, February 1962.

CENTRAL BANKING

MIGUEL S. WIONCZEK

The Emergence of Central Banking in Latin America

The emergence of central banking in Latin America covers the span of four decades. Although the first central bank, the Banco Central de la Republica Oriental del Uruguay, was established in 1896, it took more than forty years to see the appearance of central monetary authorities in most of the area. But by the mid-1960s two governments (Haiti and Panama) still managed their monetary and financial affairs without a central banking authority, through arrangements with leading commercial banks endowing them with the exercise of rudimentary central banking functions.[1] In 1964 two new central banks emerged in the region—the Bank of Trinidad and Tobago (as a consequence of the progressive decolonisation of the West Indies), and the Banco Central da Republica do Brasil, a first serious attempt in that country to streamline and centralise a complicated mixture of uncoordinated monetary and credit control mechanisms and institutions.

Great variety exists in the political and socio-economic structure of Latin American countries. The great distance between the levels of economic development, inherited from the past, is clearly reflected in the monetary and financial systems of the twenty-two Latin American independent political units. In major countries such as Mexico, monetary and financial systems approach the level of sophistication of the developed countries of the northern hemisphere, while in the smaller republics of the Caribbean and South America, financial structures are still primitive and mainly directed towards foreign trade, and resemble those of many parts of post-colonial Asia and Africa.

The following are, however, important common features of Latin American economies closely relevant to the scope of action of central banks: 1) The presence of large non-monetised sectors, except in the three southernmost republics—Argentina, Chile and Uruguay. 2) The absence of diversified capital and money markets in practically all the area accompanied by strongly monopolistic or oligopolistic tendencies of the financial intermediary systems whenever they exist or are emerging. 3) The large degree of dependence of all economies, including three major fairly industrialised countries (Argentina, Brazil and Mexico) on primary commodity exports exposed to violent fluctuations of prices and of global external demand. 4) The extreme inadequacy of fiscal systems unable in most cases to provide necessary non-inflationary resources for the state current and developmental

---

[1] Panama represents a special and anomalous case. Although it is endowed with a sizable and diversified commercial banking system, mainly in foreign hands, the country has no currency of its own, using the US dollar as legal tender.

expenditure in spite of the heavy taxation burden in the southern part of the region.

Central banks have been operating in this environment since their appearance in Latin America and had to get adjusted to it gradually. This process was hindered by the fact that the majority of central banks were established between the 1920s and early 1950s under the direct influence of two advanced countries—the United States and Britain—whose financial control and monetary policy problems had both in the past and today little in common with those faced by the underdeveloped world.

Leaving aside the Central Bank of Uruguay, the first chapter in the history of central banks in Latin America opened shortly after the Brussels Conference in 1920. International financial experts gathered there under the auspices of the League of Nations for the purpose of restoring international monetary order based on the pre-1914 gold-standard agreed unanimously that 'in countries where there is no central bank, one should be established'. The main if not the only purpose of central banking at that time was to influence the national economies by pursuing the double goal of internal and external stability through regulation of supply of money. This definition of central banking was highly influenced by British pre-1914 experience and by the dominant theory of the working of the international gold standard. The arms at the disposal of a central banker at that time were few but allegedly powerful: monopoly of the issue of legal tender, the manipulation of the bank rate, open-market operations and the obligation to act as a lender of last resort to the private banking system.

The central banks established in Colombia, Chile, Ecuador, Bolivia and Peru between 1925 and 1931 followed the prevalent doctrine closely, although their charters also bear the imprint of the United States experience of the early stages of the Federal Reserve System. Three other central banks (in Guatemala, El Salvador and Argentina) were established in the inter-war period with direct British guidance. Only one central bank—the Banco de Mexico—was founded (in 1925) without any direct external influence; it was one of the first steps taken by Mexico to reestablish the institutional bases for the country's economic development after fifteen years of revolutionary strife.

Central banks established in the inter-war period under the influence of advanced countries shared—as was to be expected—all the main features characteristic of a sound central banking in the developed countries of the Anglo-Saxon world before the Great Depression. In addition to the monopoly of issue and acting as the government's banker, the first Latin American central banks considered their basic, if not exclusive, task to be the regulation of the supply of credit through the use of the discount mechanism. They were semi-public institutions, jointly owned by commercial banks and the public, with capital participation of the state in some cases, and run by boards of directors on which private banking and trade interests were fully represented. Their administrative independence from the treasuries was guaranteed by law. The right of currency issue was strictly linked to the level of gold and foreign exchange reserves and their respective statutes defined in detail conditions of rediscount operations for which only short-term commercial and agricultural paper was eligible. It was only in Mexico that the central bank was encharged with the pioneering function of promoting the establishment of new financial institutions in both public and private sectors. In all other cases Latin American central banks established between the mid-twenties and mid-thirties were expected to be neutral in this respect. It was assumed that after the revision of antiquated banking laws and under the supervision of newly created banking superintendencies (usually outside central banks) the private commercial banking systems would develop and adjust their operations autonomously and automatically to the needs of respective economies.

It was only after the onset of the Great Depression, on the occasion of the creation of the Banco Central de Argentina in 1935, that some novel features in Latin American central banking statutes appeared, clearly as a response to the break-up of the international gold standard, which left governments with the responsibility of thinking afresh and more or less continually about foreign-exchange policy and about financing government expenditures. The charter of the Argentine central bank, elaborated with British technical assistance by a group of young Argentine economists,[1] provided thus for the bank's intervention in the exchange market on behalf of the government and under supervision of the treasury, and for operations with government securities to cover temporary state budget needs. The central banks established in El Salvador, Costa Rica, Venezuela and Nicaragua between the mid-thirties and 1941 followed more or less traditional lines, the Banco Central de Costa Rica being, however, the first Latin American central bank fully owned by the government.

Thus by 1941 twelve out of the twenty Latin American republics had central banking authorities. Of the remaining eight only Brazil and Cuba carried considerable economic weight in the area. The Banco do Brasil, operating commercially since the beginning of the 19th century, has for some time carried on certain rudimentary central banking functions on behalf of the federal authorities in addition to its principal general banking business. Six other countries—Guatemala, Haiti, Honduras, Panama, Paraguay and the Dominican Republic—could be considered at that time as primitive export-orientated monoculture economies without indigenous banking systems and without any pretence at autonomous national monetary and financial policies.

Between the mid-forties and mid-fifties new central banks were established in Cuba, the Dominican Republic and Paraguay, with the assistance of the Federal Reserve System and United States Treasury officials. In Honduras, the International Monetary Fund gave a helping hand in the early fifties. In Brazil, the treasury created in 1945 the Super-intendencia da Moeda e do Credito (SUMOC) for the purpose of credit and exchange regulation and banking inspection. SUMOC became thus one of the four tiers of a very complicated system, consisting, in addition, of the treasury (in charge of currency issue)—an autonomous department of the Banco do Brasil—the Caixa de Redesconto (responsible for banking advances and rediscount operations) and the Banco do Brasil itself, dealing with foreign exchange and banking credit. In response to the decolonisation of the European possessions in the Caribbean three new banks emerged: in Surinam (1957), Jamaica (1961) and Trinidad and Tobago (1964). Finally, a general overhaul of the complicated banking structure in Brazil took place after the '1964 revolution' through the adoption of the Banking Reform Law which established a National Monetary Council and a central bank and also completely reorganised the Banco do Brasil. The new Banco Central da Republica do Brasil has taken over currency issue, rediscount and

[1] Dr Raul Prebisch, the present UNCTAD Secretary General and the foremost authority on Latin American economic development problems, was the Argentine central bank's first president.

foreign-exchange operations of the Banco do Brasil and all the functions of SUMOC, the only major central banking function left in the scope of its operations being that of banker and agent of the treasury.

REORGANISATION AND ADJUSTMENT OF LATIN AMERICAN CENTRAL BANKING: 1945–65

From the late forties onwards the central banks established in the inter-war period underwent reorganisation. In some cases the intention was to define in new terms their active participation in the elaboration not only of monetary and financial policies but also of overall economic policy. In others the relationship between the central bank and the government was at stake. In most instances, however, there was a need to redefine monetary and financial control instruments available to central banks under the old statutes and to introduce new ones, strengthening at the same time the central bank's position vis-à-vis private commercial banks and other financial intermediaries, which—as elsewhere—did their utmost to escape the restraining hand of the central bankers.

Broad generalisations can be misleading because 'central banks in Latin America are still undergoing processes of experimentation with techniques and policies, as well as of integration with the economic structure of various countries'.[1] It is clear that central banking does not develop in a vacuum, but must adapt itself to the specific socio-economic conditions of each country, which, as was mentioned earlier, differ widely. Some broad tendencies can be detected in this process of adaptation to post-war conditions and, especially, to the pressures for development.

First, a shift is clearly seen from the joint ownership of the central banks by state, private banking institutions and the public to exclusive government ownership. Only one central bank—that of Colombia—is still today fully privately-owned, whereas fourteen Latin American central banks, not including those in the newly independent Caribbean territories, are owned by the state. In the few remaining cases the participation of the private banks and the public in the central banks' capital has practically no influence upon their overall policy objectives and monetary and financial control measures. Concurrently, the independence of central banking authorities from the governments, and specifically from the treasury, largely disappeared, whatever some statutes may still say. The Banco Central de Argentina represents probably one of the few exceptions, at least in legal terms, in reaction to the complete surrender of that bank's autonomy under the Perón regime. The reform of the bank's charter undertaken in 1957 re-established some degree of its autonomy within the government. In Cuba, on the other hand, shortly after the Castro revolution the central bank was completely merged into the centralised state apparatus.

The overall control of the Latin American central banks by government is assured through various devices. Control may take the form of direct participation of the treasury or economic minister in the board of a central bank or in a higher body (monetary council or board) which takes decisions on major policy issues. The same control may also be exerted through designation of some central bank board members by the head of state or by the treasury, or—in still other cases—through the veto power wielded statutorily by the treasury on most of the central bank's decisions. Even in

---

[1] Frank Tamagna, *Central Banking in Latin America*, CEMLA, México, 1965, p. 68.

Colombia, where the central bank is wholly privately-owned, the treasury minister sits on its board of directors. In this respect, a situation described as ideal by a British central banker, Lord Cobbold—that through retaining much independence in its operations and its thinking the central bank should act in the closest harmony with government, but on the other hand 'treasury and central bank are not, and should not be, the same sort of animal', and the central bank should form its judgements from a market and economic point of view, independently of politics,[1]—has presently little practical application in Latin America.

Another post-war trend is the progressive withdrawal of the central banks from direct operations with the public, partly upon the prodding and insistence of the private banking interests. Here again the first example was given by Mexico's central bank which terminated its operations with the public as early as in 1931. At present only a few central banks in the region offer banking facilities to private enterprise and individuals. The list of those which still have some relations with the public would be longer, however, if foreign-exchange operations are included in countries practising exchange restrictions or applying advance deposits on imports, which although formally they do not fall under the exchange restrictions category have for all practical purposes a similar effect. In some countries the public may make this type of operation directly with the central bank.

The subordination of the policy-making functions and administration of central banks to the governments, which are unfortunately only rarely able to think in terms of long-term economic policy, brought about varied results. In certain cases, progressive restraints of the banks' autonomy in the determination of monetary policy, an autonomy which can hardly be defended for its own sake in the context of the need for economic development, had a dynamising effect upon central bankers, a very conservative breed by definition anywhere in the world, and forced them to search for new measures to substitute largely inoperative manipulation of the bank rate and largely non-existent open-market operations. Where, as in the case of Mexico, the institutional framework was conducive to the growth of the economy, proceeding in a relatively orderly way and at a fairly satisfactory rate, extremely useful monetary and financial control mechanisms have emerged under the prodding of the state.

Elsewhere, especially in the South American republics, in the absence of coherent national economic development policies, central banks have been largely transformed into financing agencies of government programmes which might or might not be related to real economic policy needs. Under these circumstances monetary policies, badly designed and badly executed, became often the only economic policies available. This led to unfortunate results in some cases, in spite of the proliferation of the development-oriented public and private financial intermediaries, because of the growing expansion of the public sector, whose lack of efficiency and pressures for low-cost financial resources fully matched at times similar propensities in the private sector.

Between these two extremes, one in which monetary and financial control and innovation functions of a central bank played a positive role in the development process, and another where they only compounded difficulties of internal and external origin, there lies a middle range of a limited number

---

[1] Lord Cobbold, *Some Thoughts on Central Banking* (The Stamp Memorial Lecture 1962), Athlone Press, London, 1962, pp. 6–8.

of cases in which central banks fought with some success battles with the governments on the one hand and with the private sectors on the other, trying to assure relatively rational distribution of available non-inflationary resources among conflicting needs. Among many instruments used, reserve requirements of quantitative and qualitative nature, direct credit controls, development of securities markets and intervention in foreign-exchange operations were of primary importance.

Instruments of Monetary and Financial Control

Within an inflationary context, characteristic of most of Latin America since the early forties, the use of reserve requirements became the main weapon of monetary control. Whereas until the outbreak of the second world war the obligation of commercial banks to hold a part of deposits with the central banking authority had as its purpose to assure their financial solvency, the growing use of the legal reserve requirements since the late forties has been aimed at controlling the total supply of money and credit. This is especially true when the latter is subject to wide and sudden fluctuations in response to changes in the foreign exchange flows because of the vagaries of external trade. Legal reserve requirements are applied both to the basic resources of the banking systems and to the margin and the ratios not only differ from country to country but are constantly adjusted to changing domestic conditions, their burden often falling heavily upon seasonal or fortuitous increases in the liabilities of private banks.

This mechanism gradually acquired complicated characteristics. First, for the purpose of enabling the banking business to earn something from its idle funds, a distinction was made between reserves held in non-interest-bearing accounts with the central bank and those which the private banking system was allowed to invest in the government and other longer-term securities offering yields far below current domestic interest rates. This practice was applied especially to marginal reserve requirements with a double aim: to provide the central bank with access to funds needed to finance public development expenditure and to offer some incentive to the private banking institutions for cutting down interest rates charged on remaining freely loanable funds. But while the first part of the proposition worked in a satisfactory way, the second objective has practically never been fulfilled, both because of the stickiness of interest rates toward downward adjustments under the prevailing oligopolistic conditions in the money markets and because of pressures upon freely available funds exerted by institutional and individual borrowers.

The wide use of legal reserve requirements was followed by measures aimed at directing loanable resources towards development, since the banking systems continued to show a strong preference for lending to commerce and real-estate speculation. Thus in a growing number of countries certain types of credit operations became exempt from reserve requirements or counted as their counterpart. Such practices merged quantitative and qualitative aspects of this credit control mechanism by influencing the liquidity base of the banking system and the composition of the individual bank's portfolios. Started originally in Mexico around 1950, the combination of reserve requirements and selective credit controls had spread throughout Latin America by the late fifties. This has had positive and negative side effects. As reserve requirements and selective controls were applied to the commercial banking institutions alone, a number of non-banking financial intermediaries—closely linked to the commercial banks but operating independently—were created for the specific purpose of avoiding central bank intervention. Thus the institutional diversification of the financial structure, a phenomenon healthy by itself, was more than offset by the growth of a sector able to escape the control of the central monetary authorities. The most outstanding case is that of Mexico, where during the fifties, resources of private finance companies, which borrowed short and lent long, and funds held by trust accounts in the commercial banks, grew much more rapidly that the total resources of the commercial banks themselves.

It took some time to bring these newly emerging financial intermediaries into the fold of the central banks' paternal control and in some countries the influence of central monetary authorities over a part of the growing financial sector is still as tenuous as their restraining effect upon the often extravagant financial behaviour of the public sector. In fast growing economies, however, the new intermediaries proved to be a very useful instrument for the mobilisation of private savings, which were not attracted by the low interest rates paid by the commercial banks on time-deposits or by savings institutions. These developments led, in turn, to the relative decline of non-organised money markets over which no central banks can have any control and whose extremely profitable operations escape also the mechanism of faulty fiscal systems.

In two fields central banks in Latin America have been somewhat un-successful, mainly for reasons not of their own making. Very few instances are known, for example, of a successful application of 'moral suasion', which plays such an important role in Britain and other advanced countries. A Latin American private banker is not too prone to be persuaded through informal guidelines. He will respond only to concrete financial sanctions such as, for example, penalty interest on default in legal reserve requirements.

Most of the attempts to control or bring down interest rates have also been unsuccessful. Many Latin American central banking statutes contain clauses empowering monetary authorities to fix minimum rates on deposits and/or differential maximum rates on various types of credit operations. For obvious reasons, although the first part of these powers was accepted by financial intermediaries, the implementation of maximum rates on credit operations remains largely inoperative. In cases where central banks tried to do something about this, private banks displayed a high degree of in-genuity in escaping such regulations by means of hidden service commissions, increasing the size of the deposits to be held by the borrower against the total credit operation, discounting interest payments from the loan before its maturity, and so on. Attempts to link the interest rate charged by the lender to the eligibility of paper for the rediscount at the central bank also failed, partly because of the intrinsic difficulty of manipulating bank rates in developing and inflationary economies and also because of the relatively small spread existing between the cost of funds freely mobilised by the commercial banks and the price charged to the final credit user.

The general scarcity of private savings is only one of the reasons behind the failure of the attempts to control interest rates in Latin America. The unrealistic level of official rates is another. With the onset of inflationary pressures in the forties, relatively low statutory rates on loans, fixed by central banks, turned often into negative real interest rates. But their official periodical upward adjustment was made impossible by, among other things, increasing holdings of government paper by the banking systems under legal reserve requirements. Such increases would have affected the cost of the management of the public internal debt, a proposition unacceptable to both treasuries and monetary authorities.

Thus the relative tightness of credit in the private sectors as compared with its availability for state budget support and the high concentration of loanable funds in few hands resulted in a growing spread between 'official' rates and market rates, even if no account is taken of the practices of the unorganised money markets to which medium and small borrowers largely turned, particularly in agriculture. Although few studies are available about the magnitude of non-institutional financial intermediaries in Latin America, it is common knowledge that a very large volume of credit operations, ranging from very short to medium terms, is transacted on abusive terms outside the control of the monetary authorities, even in countries where diversified financial markets had appeared by the end of the fifties.[1]

To cope with the problem the central banks founded state-owned institutions for the direct financing of economic activities which otherwise would not find ready and equitable access to private banking credit facilities. By now, practically all Latin American countries have one or more development banks provided with working capital mainly by central monetary authorities. These resources may originate in private banking assets held under legal reserve requirements, in foreign aid funds and, in some instances, in autonomous and obviously inflationary new currency issues. Some of these development institutions specialise in financing a particular sector of the economy, while others cater to various sectors at the same time. In this last case, their lending priorities may change abruptly in response to development patterns and government policy objectives. As a rule, these institutions operate from the capital of a country in close cooperation with the central bank, but in Argentina, Mexico and Venezuela the development banks have organised a network of local agencies to act as intermediaries between the central office and final users of credit facilities in the interior. Brazil evolved a mixed system, composed of the national development bank with headquarters in Rio de Janeiro and half-a-dozen regional multi-purpose development banks enjoying a considerable degree of autonomy.

No uniform pattern can be detected in the area with respect to the relationship between these relatively new financial intermediaries and the central banking authorities, on the one hand, and the credit users on the other. The charters of most development banks allow a large degree of autonomy in credit operations and administrative procedures, but in most cases both the treasury minister and the top official of the central bank are *ex-officio* members of their governing boards. In practically all instances, development banks rely heavily on central banks for provision of new financial resources and for assistance in raising funds in domestic markets and abroad. In some countries, as Mexico, the principal development bank (Nacional Financiera), one of the oldest institutions of the type in Latin America, acts as a major intermediary between international financial institutions and foreign private capital markets and both public and private sectors.

In spite of largely ideologically motivated prodding from outside Latin America in favour of the private ownership of development banks, practical results have been disappointing for the obvious reason that the strictly commercial bank offers very considerable pecuniary rewards with much

---

[1] See U Tun Wai, *Tasas de interés en los países subdesarrollados*, CEMLA, Mexico, 1964.

smaller risks. This does not mean, however, that—especially in the larger countries—private banking activities were left unchanged under the triple impact of industrialisation, the appearance of state-owned development banks and the central banks' credit control measures. Progress in this field, however, has been very uneven and has not resulted in unmixed blessings to the countries concerned.

In many instances the process of diversification which started from commercial and mortgage banks and extended to insurance business and finance companies resulted in the effective control by a few financial groups of an impressive array of industrial and commercial enterprises with easy access to capital resources and credit facilities at the expense of independent firms. The absence of effective anti-monopoly legislation and the fact that the legislation providing for the divorce of banking from other activities is a dead letter in most of Latin America encourages the monopolistic concentration of property and makes it extremely unlikely that any attempts to improve income distribution will succeed. As, in addition, widespread industrial cartel practices are present together with constant pressure exerted upon central banks by the state for financing public sector deficits, all major ingredients for inflationary pressures exist in the large majority of Latin American economies. Only very orthodox thinkers and economic policy practitioners can, under these conditions, believe that monetary measures alone are sufficient to guarantee economic growth with relative stability. The failure of all the economic stabilisation programmes—except in Bolivia and Paraguay—undertaken during the past ten years under the auspieces of the IMF, heavily biased toward the use of monetary control measures as a basic weapon to bring about external and internal equilibrium, suggests that the origins of inflationary pressures in the developing countries go far beyond those suggested by the 'monetarist' school. In brief, Latin American experience demonstrates that central banking efforts and monetary control measures are not a substitute for coherent national economic policies in production, fiscal and anti-monopoly fields.

CONTRIBUTION OF CENTRAL BANKS TO ECONOMIC EDUCATION AND THEIR PARTICIPATION IN REGIONAL INTEGRATION EFFORTS

The limitations imposed by overall underdevelopment on central banking efforts to influence the course of Latin American economies must be weighted against the important contribution of monetary authorities in the area as agents of economic education, advisers to governments and participants in regional integration efforts. In spite of the rapid decline in their relative autonomy the central banks have increasing ability to advise the state in many matters which go beyond the monetary and financial field. This advice is at times influential, especially when central banks are in charge of national external financial relations, and in view of the relatively high turnover of finance ministers in many republics.

Most central banking institutions have built up fairly competent economic research departments in charge of gathering basic economic statistics, interpreting periodical demographic and production censuses, elaborating national accounts and analysing developments in the external sector and the world economy. Annual reports of the various central banks, appearing since the thirties, represent probably the most important single source of information about the behaviour of the Latin American economy during the past three decades. A quarter of a century ago, when the first generation of

Latin American economists returned from universities overseas, the central banks were often the only national institutions able to offer them the possibility of a professional career and facilities for independent economic research. This tradition has been carefully sustained, if only because the monetary authorities could not rely on economic information coming from elsewhere.

The positive contribution of Latin American central banks to the development of economic knowledge in the region may be fully appreciated when one considers the role of many former central bank economists in the formative period of the UN Economic Commission for Latin America (ECLA), whose decisive contribution to the elaboration of the regional economic development idea is widely recognised today. It may well be that the ECLA's open distrust of the effectiveness of monetary and financial policies in the developing countries is partly attributable to the opportunities its staff has had of seeing these policies in action at close range.

The active participation of central banks in the efforts towards economic integration dates from the mid-fifties and precedes by a few years the signature of the treaties of Montevideo and Managua which set up the Latin American Free Trade Association and the Central American Common Market respectively. If on the continental scale and in the case of LAFTA very little progress can be reported until now, the responsibility is certainly not that of the central banks. Monetary and financial cooperation is difficult enough under conditions of strong inflation in some countries and relative price stability in others, but in this case it was made even more difficult by outside interference.

In contrast, monetary and financial cooperation among the five Central American central banks keeps pace with the rapid progress of the Central American Common Market. Some 80 per cent of the payments for intrazonal trade and service transactions passes through the regional clearing house; the closest contacts exist between national monetary authorities and the Banco Centroamericano de Integración Económica, and a Central American Monetary Council was established in 1964 with the longer-term objective of preparing the monetary union of member countries. The monetary stability in the area obviously helps all these measures, but they would not have been possible without strong political support at the highest level in each country. In more than one sense, the successful cooperation among Central American central banks opens possibilities largely unexplored by the monetary authorities in the rest of Latin America.

BIBLIOGRAPHY

Desmukh, C. D. *Per Jacobbson Foundation Lectures*, Basle, October 1965 (general statement on the nature of central banking tasks in the developing world).

Dorrance, Graeme S. 'The Instruments of Monetary Policy in Countries without Highly Developed Capital Markets', *IMF Staff Papers*, XII, 2, Washington, DC, July 1965.

Gomez, Rodrigo. *Per Jacobbson Lectures*, Basle, October 1964 (general statement on the nature of central banking tasks in the developing world).

Gonzalez del Valle, Jorge. 'The Intra-Central American Payments System and Trade', *Economic Integration in Latin America—Experiences and Prospects*, ed. Miguel S. Wionczek, Frederick A. Praeger, New York, 1966.

Hirschman, Albert O. (ed.) *Latin American Issues—Essays and Comments*, Twentieth Century Fund, New York, 1961.

Wionczek, Miguel S. 'Los bancos centrales y los acuerdos de integración en America Latina', *Problemas de pagos en America Latina*, CEMLA, Mexico City, 1964.

CEMLA. *Coordinación de la banca central en America Latina*, Mexico City, 1965.

Tamagna, Frank. *Central Banking in Latin America*, CEMLA, Mexico City, 1965.

EXTERNAL FINANCE

HUGH HOLLEY

Among the developing areas of the world, Latin America is in a relatively advantageous position; not only are most of the republics well endowed with natural resources in relation to the size of their population, but incomes per head—and hence the capacity to save and invest—are substantially higher than in most of Africa and Asia. In the years since the war Latin America has financed over 90 per cent of its investments from its own resources.

Foreign capital has nevertheless played, and must for the foreseeable future continue to play a much more significant role than this figure might suggest. Although by far the greater part of Latin American investments are financed out of domestic savings, the proportion financed externally has risen substantially since the war, and the foreign contribution has been of decisive importance for development in many of the key sectors. Investment from abroad is also valuable as a means of acquiring the advanced industrial techniques generally associated with such investments, and, perhaps most important of all, the inflow of capital helps to overcome the obstacles to growth imposed by the shortage of foreign exchange. Even if they were able to provide all their capital requirements themselves, the republics would not be able to pay, out of their earnings of foreign currency, for all the imported goods and services needed for development; indeed, by the late 1950s this shortage of foreign exchange had become critical for a number of the republics, and a source of concern for most of the others.

FOREIGN INVESTMENT BEFORE 1939

Latin America's external finance now presents a much more complex pattern than that prevailing before the second world war, when virtually all the capital entering the area was private capital. This took two main forms: direct investment—principally in transport, electricity supply and other utilities, and in the production and processing of commodities for export; and portfolio investment in the bond issues floated by Latin American governments, national, provincial and municipal, on the capital markets of Europe and the United States.

Up to 1914, Britain played the dominant role. The preceding fifty years saw a massive inflow of British capital—above all into Argentina—that reached its peak in the decade immediately before the first world war, by which time Latin America accounted for at least one-fifth of all British investment abroad. Britain's example was followed, on a smaller but still substantial scale, by France, Germany and other European countries, and at the turn of the century, after the Spanish-American War, United States investors became increasingly interested in the republics to the south.

521

After the first world war, the United States supplanted Britain as the main source of external capital for Latin America; new investment from Britain continued, though at a much lower level, and there was little net increase in the total of British or other European capital invested. US investments, on the other hand, continued to grow both during and after the war: direct investments, hitherto concentrated in the nearer republics, spread throughout South America, and the republics enjoyed an easy access—far too easy, as it was to prove—to the New York capital market. By 1930, more than one-third of all US investment abroad was in Latin America, and in absolute amount it had reached a figure that was not to be regained until as late as 1950.

The depression of the 1930s brought to an end a period of some seventy years during which foreign capital, with little restriction on the part of either the capital-exporting countries or of the Latin American republics themselves, had been a major agent of development, financing, either directly or indirectly, port works, railways, power supplies and other basic services and giving to the economies of Latin America their characteristic orientation towards the export markets of Europe and North America. Caught in a world economic crisis, and themselves powerless to influence events, the Latin American republics suffered a catastrophic fall in the prices of their exports and in their foreign currency earnings. With access to new capital cut off simultaneously, every Latin American country except Argentina defaulted on its external debt, and even in Argentina payments were suspended on some provincial and municipal bond issues.

The experiences of the depression years were traumatic for Latin America. The republics were thrown back on their own resources, and it became an axiom of economic policy that through industrialisation they should lessen their dependence on the outside world. In the event, and despite the enormous growth of Latin American industrial production for the home market, this goal still seems far from achievement, even by the most developed countries of the region. But in the 1930s foreign capital seemed more of a burden than an agent of growth, and these were years of rising economic nationalism. Popular resentment was especially focused on foreign-owned enterprises engaged in transport and other public services, many of which, because of restrictions on their freedom to fix charges, became unprofitable and ultimately incapable of providing adequate services. In Mexico foreign-owned petroleum companies were expropriated and foreign as well as domestically-owned estates were affected by land reform.

In the first few years after 1945 it seemed that Latin America's position vis-à-vis the outside world had changed for the better. The republics were physically unscathed by the second world war, demand for their exports was high in the period of post-war reconstruction and many of them had accumulated reserves of foreign currency through unrequited exports to the belligerent countries. Though US private investment had been resumed, the immediate post-war years were a period of net disinvestment in Latin America. Reserves of foreign currency were used to repatriate investments in public services, of which the most important were the British- and French-owned railways and US telephone and telegraph companies in Argentina, British railways in Brazil, and railways, tramways and waterworks in Uruguay. By the end of the war a large part of the external bonded debt of the Latin American countries had also been repatriated through open market purchases and normal amortisation, as well as by scaling down the nominal value of bonds, notably those of Brazil and Mexico, under debt renegotiation agreements. The European investment stake in Latin America was thus reduced to a small fraction of its former size. Some US investments had also been liquidated, but new investment by that country was already taking place, while European investment in Latin America was not to be resumed on any important scale for a decade.

DIRECT INVESTMENT SINCE 1945

Despite the growing importance of official development aid, export credits and other new forms of financing, private direct investment was to remain the largest single source of external capital for Latin America until the end of the 1950s.

During the years 1950–60 well over half of the total inflow of long-term capital came in this form, and the value of US direct investments alone rose by over 80 per cent from US \$4,400 million to US \$8,400 million. In the 1960s the pattern has changed, both because of a decline in the amount of private capital invested and an increase in lending to Latin America by the international agencies and under bilateral aid programmes.

The salient feature of post-war direct investment has been its very uneven distribution between countries and economic sectors. Transport and utilities, formerly so important as a field for investment, have been effectively closed in an increasing number of the republics. There has been some growth of old investments in both tropical and temperate agriculture, and investors formerly engaged in plantation agriculture in Africa and Asia have turned their attention to Latin America, but agriculture has accounted for only a very small part of post-war foreign investment in the area. Construction, trading, banking and other services have continued to attract foreign capital, but the really significant investments have been those in petroleum, mining, and manufacturing industry for the local market.

Investment in the extractive industries in Latin America, while dependent on the terms on which the republics have been prepared to accept foreign capital in these fields, has been closely related to the world commodity situation. The shortage of many minerals at the time of the Korean war raised prices and stimulated large investments in developing new sources of supply. Major investments in Latin America in the 1950s included those in copper mining in Peru and to a lesser extent in Chile, and in iron ore in Venezuela, which was also the main focus for investment in petroleum. When in 1957 the Venezuelan government offered new concessions for auction, the annual flow of US direct investment capital into Latin America reached a peak of US \$1,400 million. Thereafter, and largely as a result of declining investment in mining and petroleum, and even of some withdrawal of capital from those sectors, the growth of US investments in Latin America slackened progressively until 1962, when it was only US \$236 million. From this low point, US private direct investment recovered to show a net increase of US \$375 million in 1964.

Post-war US investment in manufacturing industry has been far more consistent than that in the extractive industries, though there have been considerable fluctuations in the flow of capital into individual countries. An annual average of about US \$200 million of US capital was being invested in Latin American manufacturing in the late 1950s and early 1960s. The three countries that offer the largest internal markets—Brazil, Argentina and Mexico—have attracted the bulk of foreign investment in this field, and much has naturally depended on conditions in these republics.

Lesser amounts have been invested in Colombia, Venezuela, Peru, Chile and, more recently, in Central America under the stimulus of the formation of the regional market in the isthmus. Political and economic stability in the years since the war have encouraged a fairly steady inflow of investments into manufacturing industry in Mexico. The picture has been rather different in Argentina and Brazil. The Perón regime (1946–55) in Argentina was initially hostile to foreign capital, and a belated attempt, in the face of mounting economic difficulties, to reverse its policies in this respect met with little response from abroad. The abolition of exchange controls, and the re-establishment of constitutional government in 1958, were followed by a substantial inflow of foreign investment capital in 1959–62, a movement that was brought to an end by renewed political uncertainty following the downfall of the Frondizi government, economic recession and the reimposition of restrictions on the remittance of profits and dividends.

The pattern of post-war investment in Brazil has also been closely related to changes in government policy and to the pace of the country's economic expansion. In the mid-1950s the establishment of a free foreign exchange market and provision of special facilities for the import of capital goods by foreign investors paved the way for a substantial inflow of direct investment, which made an important contribution to the rapid industrial expansion of the Kubitschek era and especially to the growth of the motor-vehicle industry. The deteriorating political climate in the early 1960s, slackening economic growth, rising inflation and balance of payments difficulties progressively discouraged the inflow of private capital, which virtually ceased after the passage of the Foreign Capital Law in 1962, to be resumed again, on a more moderate scale, after the change of regime in 1964.

European[1] Investment

European countries, preoccupied with the needs of reconstruction at home, made little new investment in Latin America before 1955. Apart from petroleum in Venezuela (where the Shell group is one of the major operators) and to a lesser extent in other countries, post-war European investment has been heavily concentrated in manufacturing and in the southern republics where trading and other links remain strongest. Perhaps half of new investment in Brazil in 1955–62 was of European origin and about one-third of that in Argentina in 1959–62. But the proportion has certainly been much less in other countries; even in Mexico European interest was surprisingly slow to develop, and in the early 1960s probably about 80 per cent of new investment in that country was still North American in origin. A number of factors have tended to inhibit the growth of European investment in Latin America. The EEC provided a focus for investors both inside and outside the Community. In certain countries, especially Britain, both the inclination of investors and the pattern of exchange controls favoured investment in associated territories overseas. Most European countries had liberalised direct investment abroad by the early 1960s, but Britain still maintained controls with varying degrees of severity, depending on the balance-of-payments situation, on investment in countries outside the sterling area. Furthermore, the liquidation of much of the former European investment in Latin America, which had involved investors in substantial losses, provided an unfavourable psychological background. Germany, though it had suffered

[1] Here denoting the non-Communist countries of Europe.

the loss of overseas assets in two world wars, tended to be less inhibited by attitudes derived from the past, and was foremost among European countries in taking advantage of the opportunities offered in the 1950s in Brazil, where more German capital has been invested than in any other country except Switzerland. About one-fifth of all German direct investments abroad since the war have been made in Latin America.

Investments from countries other than the United States and Europe have been relatively small. Significant Japanese investments have been made in shipbuilding and other industries in Brazil and on the west coast, and there have been some Canadian investments of importance. Mexican, Venezuelan, Argentine and other Latin American firms have invested in other countries of the region, but except for Argentine investments in Uruguay these do not bulk large in the total inflow into any of the republics.

LATIN AMERICAN ATTITUDES

Direct investment, unlike other forms of external financing, involves foreign ownership or control, and it is not only in Latin America that attitudes towards this kind of investment tend to be ambivalent. Apprehensions about the extent of foreign ownership of important sectors of the economy have been expressed in quite forceful terms in both Canada and Australia. While the events of the 1930s produced a strong reaction in Latin America against foreign capital, attitudes tended to become gradually more favourable after the war, and in the 1950s many of the republics took legislative measures to attract investment generally or in the establishment or expansion of specific industries. Foreign companies for their part have shown an increasing awareness of Latin American susceptibilities and of the need to identify themselves more closely with the countries in which they operate by admitting greater local participation in management and even ownership.

With the obvious exception of Cuba, no Latin American government has ever sought to exclude foreign investment altogether; even a nationalist regime such as that of Perón kept its hostility to foreign capital within limits and was prepared to modify it in the interests of expediency. Policies as regards foreign investment in the mid-1960s are not on the whole doctrinaire, though clearly there is a considerable difference between a country such as Peru, where liberal attitudes are deeply rooted in both government and business circles, and Mexico, where there are important reservations about the place of foreign investment in the economy and restrictions on the employment of foreign capital are extensive. Nationalisation and disputes affecting foreign investment have in most countries been confined to two sensitive fields—public services and the extractive industries.

The nationalisation of many foreign-owned railways and utilities in the immediate post-war years was followed by the gradual extension of public ownership over this field. In Mexico the 'Mexicanisation' of the remaining foreign-owned electric power companies was carried out in 1960, and Argentina and Chile have moved in the same direction, though in Peru both rail transport and public electricity supply remain largely under foreign management. The extractive industries and especially petroleum tend to excite nationalist feeling, because they involve the depletion of an irreplaceable asset, and often, as with petroleum in Venezuela and copper in Chile, occupy a key position in the economy. In Mexico, Brazil and Chile, the state has a monopoly of petroleum exploration and development (though not necessarily of refining and distribution) and Venezuela has decided to offer no more concessions for either petroleum or iron mining. In Argentina the decision by President Frondizi to admit foreign petroleum companies—under service contracts that avoided infringement of the state monopoly—made an important contribution towards reducing the country's dependence on imported oil, but was nevertheless repudiated by the next constitutional government. In Chile the status of the large foreign-owned copper companies has been a major issue of public policy in the 1960s.

Other fields of investment in which certain Latin American governments maintain restrictions or prohibitions on the employment of foreign capital include banking and insurance, publishing and broadcasting, but these are of minor significance in the general picture. Over the wide range of trading and manufacturing industry the field is remarkably open. The pattern of controls is most complex in Mexico, where successive governments have sought the benefits of foreign capital and techniques in the development of industry, while ensuring that key sectors do not fall under foreign domination. It is significant that Mexico, where the role of foreign capital is seen as a frankly subordinate one, is the Latin American country that has attracted the most consistent inflow of direct investment capital since the war; whatever the difficulties or conditions attached to entry, they have been offset by the prospects of profitable investment in a stable and expanding economy.

DEVELOPMENT LOANS AND EXPORT CREDITS

The capital markets of the United States and Europe were closed to Latin America for a generation after the defaults of the 1930s and for most Latin American governments they remain still closed. Although servicing of the old bonded debt was resumed under agreements negotiated in the 1940s and early 1950s, the memory of past losses and the general reputation of instability attributed to Latin American countries made it impossible for governments to raise new finance by the issue of external bonds. Mexico was the first Latin American country to re-establish its credit standing in capital markets abroad: substantial placements of securities in the United States by Nacional Financiera were followed in the early 1960s by Federal government bond issues in New York—the first for more than forty years. Argentine bonds were issued in rather special circumstances in Europe in 1961 and Venezuelan government external bonds placed on the New York market in 1965, but it seems at present unlikely that the sale of government securities can become for most of the republics an important, or even a possible means of raising long-term funds abroad.

The place formerly held in Latin American development finance by external bond issues has to some extent been taken by loans from the international agencies. All the republics, except Cuba which withdrew in 1960, are members of the World Bank. Between 1948 and 1965 the World Bank made loans totalling well over US $2,000 million in Latin America—about one-quarter of its total lending. By far the greater part—over 90 per cent—of these loans has been for economic infrastructure projects, especially for electric power and transport; relatively little has been lent for industrial development. Of the institutions affiliated to the World Bank, the International Development Association, which makes 'soft' loans in the form of interest-free 50-year credits, has operated chiefly in India and Pakistan, and only about one-tenth of the total credits authorised has been granted to Latin American borrowers; on the other hand, Latin America has provided the main field of operations of the International Finance Corporation, whose chief activity has been to provide and coordinate financing of industrial development in the private sector, either directly or through the intermediary of local development banks.

Important though the contribution of the World Bank has been in financing such major developments as the Furnas and Guri hydro-electric schemes in Brazil and Venezuela, the Bank and its associated institutions could meet only a part of Latin American needs. In addition to finance for large-scale projects in the economic infrastructure, Latin American borrowers have had to obtain credit abroad to finance many smaller but still important developments in both the public and private sectors requiring imported machinery and equipment, for which neither was appropriate credit available locally, nor could the necessary foreign exchange have been provided by the monetary authorities. In these circumstances the Latin American republics made increasing use of credit extended by the exporting countries. For exports from the United States the principal channel through which credit was provided was the Export-Import Bank of Washington: European countries have financed their corresponding exports of capital goods to Latin America through the mechanism of suppliers' credits. In these cases the finance is generally provided, directly or indirectly, by the banking systems of the countries concerned. The cost of this form of finance tends to be higher and length of credit shorter than that of loans from international agencies. For many goods such long-credit terms would in any case be inappropriate, but limits have also been set by the capacity of the banks to provide long-term finance and by the policies of the official export-credit insurance organisations. These at first attempted to keep the upper limit for such credits to five years in order to prevent a 'credit race' from developing, though in practice, under pressure from Latin American importers on the one hand and of competition between suppliers on the other, credit terms have gradually lengthened. The need to repay these credits was an important element in the growing debt problem of a number of Latin American countries in the late 1950s and early 1960s. Excessive use of suppliers' credits has been frequently criticised by the international organisations, but it must be acknowledged that they have provided the means whereby much necessary capital equipment has been imported that could not otherwise have been financed.

TRADE AND PAYMENTS PROBLEMS

Industrialisation has altered the nature rather than the degree of the republics' dependence on the outside world. They now produce much of the manufactured consumer goods that were formerly imported, but they remain to varying degrees dependent on imports for capital equipment, for industrial materials and components, and even in some cases for fuels and foodstuffs. As Latin America has made very little progress in exporting manufactured goods, imports—unless financed from abroad—still have to be paid for out of the proceeds of exports of primary products, and most countries still export the same narrow range of these commodities as before the war.

By the mid-1950s all Latin America's major exports were facing increasingly difficult marketing conditions. The price of many commodities fell sharply and continued to drift downwards, while the prices that Latin America had to pay for its imports tended to move upwards. The terms of trade, i.e. the ratio of export to import prices, moved against Latin America until

1962, and though there has subsequently been a reversal of the trend, this has not restored Latin America's former position. According to the United Nations Economic Commission for Latin America, the region as a whole suffered in 1955–60, as a result of the deterioration in the terms of trade since 1950–4, a loss in income of US $7,300 million—a figure approximately equal to the net inflow of capital, US $7,000 million, in the same period. There is clearly an element of artificiality in such calculations, but most countries undoubtedly suffered, as a result of the fall in commodity prices, a considerable loss of income that they were unable to offset by increasing the volume of exports.

Stagnation or slow growth of exports and recourse to short- and medium-term borrowing of various kinds put an increasing strain on the balance of payments of many of the republics. Colombia was unable to meet its commitments in respect of import payments after the fall in coffee prices in 1954/55, and Argentina had to seek a consolidation of its commercial indebtedness after the fall of Perón in 1955. These were among the first of a series of balance-of-payments crises resulting in the accumulation of backlogs of unpaid commercial and other debts or requests for emergency assistance in the form of refinancing credits from the supplying countries. Such requests were usually accompanied by application for credits from the International Monetary Fund. The loans or postponements offered by the creditor countries thus tended to become part of a 'package deal' and to depend on agreement first having been reached with the IMF; this in turn involved the adoption of a 'stabilisation' programme agreed by the IMF and the government concerned. These programmes, drawn up on orthodox lines of monetary policy, which had worked fairly successfully in correcting the inflationary and associated balance-of-payments problems of Peru and Paraguay, failed in the more complex situations of Argentina and Chile. Brazil managed to avoid entering into this kind of commitment, and made no serious attempt at stabilisation until after the change of political regime in 1964.

LATIN AMERICA AND THE UNITED STATES

Latin American countries' concern at their deteriorating trade position and the threat that this posed to development was plainly expressed at the Economic Conference of the Organisation of American States which was held in Buenos Aires in 1957. If, as the United States took for granted, there was a special relationship between the two Americas, it seemed to Latin Americans that the United States should be prepared to give the sister republics a special place in its economic assistance programmes. They contrasted the aid given to Latin America with the large amounts made available to Europe under the post-war economic recovery programme and subsequently to other and less reliable allies of the United States in areas deemed of strategic importance in the cold war. Though Latin American pleas for special consideration fell on unreceptive ears, much was to happen in the next three years to bring about a change in United States attitudes— the mounting evidence that the United States had suffered a serious loss of prestige in Latin America, the fear that potentially dangerous political forces might gain the ascendancy if the economic situation continued to deteriorate, and above all events in Cuba.

The first concrete result of the reappraisal by the United States of its economic policies towards Latin America—which was to culminate in the announcement of the Alliance for Progress—was the withdrawal of its opposition to the formation of a specific Latin American development institution. This, the Inter-American Development Bank (IDB), began active operations in 1961 and in its first five years pursued an energetic policy, the total of its loans amounting to over US $1,500 million. All the Latin American republics except Cuba are members together with the United States, which has naturally been the largest subscriber to its capital as well as providing additional amounts to be administered by the Bank through the 'Social Progress Trust Fund'. The IDB has increased its resources by floating bond issues and by obtaining contributions from non-member countries, and seems likely to grow in importance as a channel for multilateral aid funds for Latin America. Loans by the IDB have been granted, like those of the World Bank, for major infrastructure projects and also for industrial enterprises in both the public and private sectors; loans on 'soft' terms are made for agricultural development and land settlement, and for such social projects as low-cost housing, water supply and sanitation, and higher education.

The operations of the IDB and a higher rate of lending by the World Bank substantially increased official capital flows into Latin America from 1960 onwards. In addition, the United States has at its disposal, through the Export-Import Bank and the Agency for International Development, a wide range of instruments for channelling aid to Latin America under the Alliance for Progress—loans both for specific projects and for general import needs, shipments of surplus foodstuffs and housing and technical aid. However, an increased flow of official aid funds has not provided the means to solve all the external financing problems of the Latin American republics.

These have been most critical in Argentina, Brazil, Chile and Uruguay, which have all at one time or another in the present decade had to hold up payments abroad because of lack of foreign exchange and to seek emergency financial assistance, while some other countries, notably Colombia, have had to maintain very severe import restrictions to keep their external payments in balance. It is clearly no coincidence that the most serious balance-of-payments problems have been associated with rapid internal inflation (which tends to discourage exports and to encourage imports and the flight of capital); the remedy for these associated problems has, however, been the subject of much controversy. After the failure of the attempts at stabilisation in Chile and Argentina, which resulted in major recessions in those countries without achieving their primary objective, there has been a more general recognition of the complexity of causes of inflation in Latin America, and more scepticism about the validity of orthodox monetary measures, based on the experience of advanced economies, to halt inflation and correct deficits in the balance of payments.

Two of the republics where these problems have been most intractable—Argentina and Brazil—are among the most developed countries of the area. Yet Mexico, which shares with Argentina and Brazil the lead in industrialisation and has incurred a comparable external indebtedness, has never since the war failed to meet its external commitments or had to ask for emergency refinancing of its debts. Mexico has one advantage in that it enjoys a large income from tourism that helps to offset its deficit on visible trade, but equally important have been the advantages derived from its record of economic and political stability—the confidence of both private and official leaders and investors.

Conclusions

Despite their dependence on trade and capital inflows, in respect to both of which the initiative and advantage seems to lie with the advanced industrial countries, the Latin American republics can themselves take positive action to improve their external payments position. Though world trading conditions have not been favourable for the primary producers, Latin America as a whole has done less well since the war than other developing areas in maintaining its share of world exports, and this cannot convincingly be attributed to the advantages enjoyed by colonies or ex-colonies in the metropolitan markets of Europe. Peru avoided the discrimination against exports so long practised by countries such as Argentina, consistently encouraged the entry of foreign capital and through the development of its fishery and mineral resources was able to double its export earnings between 1957 and 1964. Peru may appear to be an exceptional case, but there are other examples: the success of Mexico and of the Central American republics in expanding exports of cotton contrasts sharply with the results achieved with the same crop by Brazil, and Chile could improve its balance of payments by producing at home much of the food that is now imported.

Greater stability would help both to attract a larger volume of private foreign investment and lessen the incentive for Latin Americans themselves to place their savings abroad for greater security. How large this flight of capital has been is not known with any precision and some of the very large estimates that have been quoted in the press of the amount of private Latin American capital in securities or bank deposits in Switzerland and the United States are greatly exaggerated. Nevertheless it seems clear that there has been a much larger outflow of local capital from Latin America than from other developing areas, and at times of political or economic crisis the flight of capital has in a number of countries reached serious proportions. Latin America has been deprived of much capital that could be usefully employed at home if its owners had confidence in their own countries and currencies, and if local capital markets offered adequate outlets for their savings.

While there is thus scope for the Latin American republics themselves to effect some improvement in their external payments position (and there are signs that export promotion is now being taken more seriously), it would be unrealistic to look for any reduction in Latin America's total needs for external financing, especially if there is to be an acceleration in rates of economic growth. Even a country like Venezuela, which is in a relatively strong position because of its revenue in foreign currency from the oil industry, needs to have recourse to external borrowing for economic and social projects that require very long-term finance.

The effectiveness of the external contribution to Latin American development depends not only on its quantity, but also on the manner in which it is adapted to Latin American needs. The Inter-American Development Bank has been particularly imaginative in its approach, and as well as providing finance directly for a wide range of economic and social projects, has sought other means whereby it can fill the gaps in the local financial structure. It has, for example, made lines of credit available to government banks in the more industrially advanced republics for financing exports of capital goods to other countries in the region on terms comparable with those offered by exporters in the United States and Europe, and has made substantial loans to local Latin American development banks for re-lending to small industrialists

US DIRECT INVESTMENTS IN LATIN AMERICA
($US million, end of period)

	1950	1955	1960	1964[1]
Argentina	356	447	472	883
Brazil	644	1,115	953	994
Chile	540	639	738	788
Colombia	193	274	424	520
Cuba	642	736	956	—
Dominican Republic	106	[2]	105	[2]
Guatemala	106	[2]	131	[2]
Honduras	62	[2]	100	[2]
Mexico	415	607	795	1,035
Panama	58	[2]	405	663
Peru	145	305	446	460
Uruguay	55	[2]	47	[2]
Venezuela	993	1,428	2,569	2,808
Others	131	1,057	247	780
Total Latin America	4,445	6,608	8,387	8,932
Total world	11,788	19,313	32,778	44,343

[1] Provisional.
[2] Included under 'Others'.

Source: US Department of Commerce,
Survey of Current Business

UK DIRECT INVESTMENTS IN LATIN AMERICA[1]
(£ million, end 1962)

Argentina	39·7
Brazil	38·4
Chile	3·9
Colombia	1·7
Mexico	25·5
Peru	3·3
Uruguay	2·2
Venezuela	9·9
Others	39·8
Total Latin America	164·4
Total world	3,375·0

[1] Excluding oil, insurance and banking.
Source: Board of Trade

GERMAN DIRECT INVESTMENTS IN LATIN AMERICA
(DM million, end 1964)

Argentina	289·9
Brazil	823·9
Colombia	74·8
Mexico	95·2
Panama	39·0
Others	191·7
Total Latin America	1,514·5
Total world	7,205·1

Source: Deutsche Bundesbank

Note: The figures given in these tables are not strictly comparable with each other, because of differences in coverage and definition. The figures for the UK in particular are considerably understated, because they do not include the important investments in petroleum, and, to a lesser extent, because of other omissions.

and farmers who would otherwise have difficulty in obtaining credit for purchases of equipment abroad. A significant and relatively new type of contribution by private capital has taken the form of participations by foreign financial institutions and industrial companies in the capital of local development banks. Such banks, which have been established in Colombia and elsewhere, can perform an important function in developing local capital markets and in bringing together finance from different sources, both internal and external. Operating on a larger scale than the national private development banks is the ADELA investment company, established in 1964 with a nominal capital of US $40 million, of which the greater part was subscribed by private financial institutions, industrial companies and trading firms in Europe, North America and Japan, and which provides capital and technical knowledge for private sector developments in Latin America and aims to mobilise additional funds, both local and foreign, for this purpose.

As far as official development finance in Latin America is concerned, the main contribution has come and must for the foreseeable future continue to come from the United States. European assistance has for the most part taken the form of guaranteed export credits and refinancing operations, together with an indirect contribution through the international agencies. Germany, France, Britain and other countries have made some additional loans in Latin America, but compared with either those from the United States or with European aid to other parts of the world, they have been relatively small. By the mid-1960s there were clear signs of increasing European political interest in Latin America, but this has been reflected in hardly more than a token increase in financial and technical assistance. Greater European aid for Latin American development could only come about through a rise in total foreign aid or through a reallocation in favour of Latin America. The first seems unlikely for budgetary reasons, the second possibility is limited by existing commitments in other continents. In 1965 nearly 85 per cent of Britain's official aid went to Commonwealth countries, and France in particular also has extensive obligations to associated territories overseas. For the more distant future there may well be a shift of emphasis towards the Western hemisphere; how quickly this happens will perhaps depend as much on events in other continents as in Latin America itself.

BIBLIOGRAPHY

Rippy, J. Fred. *British Investments in Latin America 1822–1949*, Archon Books, Hamden, Conn., revised ed. 1966.

Urquidi, Victor L. *The Challenge of Development in Latin America*, Frederick A. Praeger, New York; Pall Mall Press, London, 1964. 'Some Implications of Foreign Investment in Latin America', *Obstacles to Change in Latin America*, ed. Claudio Véliz, Oxford Univ. Press for Royal Institute of International Affairs, London and New York, 1965.

IBRD and affiliates. Annual Reports, Washington, DC.

Inter-American Development Bank (including Social Progress Trust Fund). Annual Reports, New York.

UN Department of Economic and Social Affairs. *Foreign Capital in Latin America*, New York, 1955. *The Economic Development of Latin America in the Post-War Period*, New York, 1964. *External Financing in the Economic Development of Latin America* (Document E/CN 12/649/Rev. 1). *Economic Survey of Latin America* (annual), New York.

AID TO LATIN AMERICA

TERESA HAYTER

THERE is no generally accepted definition of aid. It is sometimes taken to include all transfers of resources from developed to developing countries, both by governments and from private sources, but it is more usual to include in figures on 'aid' only transfers of resources and skills which are financed by the governments of developed countries, and it is with this kind of 'aid' that this chapter is concerned. Even thus defined, the concept is not clear. The most widely used and internationally comparable figures are compiled by the Development Assistance Committee (DAC) of OECD. But the DAC does not commit itself to a definition of aid; it describes its statistics as 'the flow of long-term financial resources to less-developed countries', recording official and private flows separately. Its method, as far as the public flows are concerned, is to add up all disbursements of public grants and loans to developing countries in particular years at their face value, plus public expenditures on technical assistance, including research, the sending of personnel to developing countries, and scholarships for students from developing countries. Its figures are net of repayments. They exclude loans repayable in less than five years, and government expenditure for certain purposes clearly unconnected with the economic development of recipient countries, for instance expenditure on diplomatic representation and all forms of military expenditure, including assistance to the national armies of developing countries.

According to the DAC net official aid from its member countries and multilateral agencies to all developing countries in 1964 amounted to $6,257 million. The DAC's member countries are Austria, Belgium, Britain, Canada, Denmark, France, Germany, Italy, Japan, the Netherlands, Norway, Portugal and the United States; together, these account for over 90 per cent of aid from all countries; the other 10 per cent is provided by the communist countries, Australia, New Zealand, Israel, and a few very small donors. Of the $6,257 million of DAC net official aid disbursed in 1964 Latin America received $1,018 million or 16 per cent. Brazil was the biggest recipient in Latin America, followed by Chile and Colombia.

AID FROM THE UNITED STATES

The United States provides more than three-quarters of all aid to Latin America. In August 1961, under the Alliance for Progress, the United States government undertook to provide $1,100 million annually in aid to Latin America. Since 1961 Latin America has received altogether $4·6 billion under the various United States official aid programmes. It has also been specifically exempted from many of the restrictions placed by Congress on the use of aid. Of total United States aid commited for 1965 for all countries, amounting to $4,895 million, 26 per cent, or $1,282 million, was for Latin America.

Two acts of Congress provide the legal authority for most present United States aid. They are the Foreign Assistance Act of 1961, covering most financial and technical aid, and the Agricultural Trade Development and Assistance Act of 1954 (usually known as Food for Peace or PL 480) covering aid in the form of surplus agricultural commodities. In addition, official financial aid is provided through the Eximbank, and some technical assistance by Peace Corps volunteers. The United States subscribes to the Inter-American Development Bank (IADB), and has established a Social Progress Trust Fund which is administered on its behalf by the IADB. The Agency for International Development (AID), which is an autonomous agency within the United States State Department, is responsible for the direction, planning and coordination of all aid activities; it has direct administrative responsibility for all programmes under the Foreign Assistance Act, and shares the administration of PL 480 with the Department of Agriculture. AID maintains large autonomous missions in major Latin American countries; elsewhere aid is managed by officials attached to embassies.

Of the total commitment of $1,282 million for Latin America for 1965, $258 million were commitments from the Eximbank. Official United States aid to Latin America began on a significant scale in the late 1930s. The Eximbank, set up in 1934, became the major channel for loans during the second world war. The Bank is a public institution; its capital is provided from public funds, and it is empowered to borrow from the United States Treasury. It makes long-term loans to cover the export of United States goods and services; repayment periods are generally between 10 and 20 years; interest rates vary, but are usually around $5\frac{1}{2}$ per cent. Loans from the Eximbank to Latin America reached a peak of $450 million committed for 1961, but have since declined in relation to other forms of United States aid.

Latin America has also received official grants and loans financed from the Federal Budget, under the Marshall Plan (1949–52), the Mutual Security Act (1953–61) and the Foreign Assistance Act (from 1962). These are now administered by the AID. They have increased from $19·5 million in commitments over the four years of the Marshall Plan to $532·2 million for 1965; between 1960 and 1962 the amount thus committed more than quadrupled. Rather more than two-thirds of the sums committed for 1965 were loans, with 40-year repayment periods and interest rates of $2\frac{1}{2}$ per cent (1 per cent during the grace period). The rest were grants mainly for technical assistance. A small part of this aid is 'supporting assistance'; this may consist of either grants or loans, and is provided for countries with budgetary or balance of payments difficulties and generally with what the United States regards as vital security problems; the Dominican Republic is now the main recipient of this form of aid. The bulk of AID aid to Latin America consists of 'development loans'. These are tied to the procurement of goods and services in the United States, and are not available for local costs. Most of these loans are also tied to specified projects, agreed with the government concerned. Some have been provided as 'program loans', whose use is not specified apart from the fact that they must be spent in the United States; these are generally provided in support of particular development policies, for instance the policies of stabilisation or reform in Brazil, Colombia and Chile.

In addition to the above the United States committed $250 million for the IADB for 1965, and $101 million for the Social Progress Trust Fund administered by the IADB. The United States had contributed more than half of the IADB's capital resources since the Bank was set up in 1959. It set up the Social Progress Trust Fund in 1961 in order to provide aid in the social and educational fields, and is the sole contributor to this fund.

The other major form of aid provided by the United States is surplus commodities under PL 480. For 1965 the commitment for these was $107 million; it has been considerably higher in previous years. The bulk of the commodities are sold for local currencies (counterpart funds). The United States retains roughly 20 per cent of these funds for its own uses in the country concerned; the rest are granted or loaned back to the recipient for

UNITED STATES AID: NET OBLIGATIONS AND LOAN AUTHORISATIONS
(fiscal year 1965; $million)

	AID programmes			Food for Peace (PL 480)	Exim-bank	Social Progress Trust Fund	Sub-scription to IADB	Peace Corps, etc.
	Loans	Grants	Total					
Argentina	17·8	1·5	16·3	—	22·7	3·5		—
Bolivia	6·0	8·4	2·4	4·6	—	3·3		2·2
Brazil	218·4	12·4	230·7	23·6	6·0	6·7		4·6
British Guiana	5·5	6·3	11·8	0·4	—	—		—
British Honduras	—	negl.	negl.	0·1	—	—		0·3
Chile	96·6	2·5	99·0	12·9	8·2	5·8		2·7
Colombia	negl.	3·7	3·6	11·4	6·8	10·5		3·5
Costa Rica	6·4	1·7	8·1	1·7	—	4·9		0·8
Dominican Rep.	15·5	37·4	52·9	16·4	12·7	3·8		1·1
Ecuador	7·8	3·3	11·1	6·9	8·0	0·3		2·1
El Salvador	1·2	4·3	5·5	1·9	—	10·4		0·5
Guatemala	5·0	2·0	7·0	1·1	—	3·0		1·8
Haiti	—	1·4	1·4	0·7	—	—		—
Honduras	0·5	1·7	2·2	0·4	0·4	0·4		0·8
Jamaica	3·8	0·6	4·4	1·8	—	—		0·6
Mexico	24·5	0·4	24·9	7·2	163·2	4·8		—
Nicaragua	14·2	2·0	16·2	0·9	—	5·2		0·9
Panama	9·2	1·7	10·9	0·5	3·5	2·5		6·2
Paraguay	—	2·3	2·3	2·5	—	4·9		—
Peru	1·5	4·8	6·3	6·5	14·2	6·0		3·2
Surinam	1·0	negl.	1·0	0·1	—	—		—
Trinidad and Tobago	—	2·8	2·8	0·1	—	—		—
Uruguay	2·4	0·9	1·5	0·7	—	—		0·3
Venezuela	—	1·6	1·6	4·2	12·5	20·0		2·2
Other West Indies	—	—	—	0·2	—	—		0·2
ROCAP (Central America)	39·5	3·3	42·8	—	—	—		—
Regional	25·0	26·0	1·1	0·1	—	5·0	250·0	—
Total Latin America	399·4	132·8	532·2	106·7	258·2	101·1	250·0	33·7

Source: *Proposed Economic Assistance Programs FY 1967*, AID

use on development projects or programmes; in this way the United States maintains some control over their use. Part of the surplus commodities are available as grants for famine relief, school-lunch programmes, etc., or for use as part-payment of wages in kind for community development projects and labour-intensive public works. A small part is sold for dollars on long-term credit.

Most of the remaining $34 million of the United States commitment for 1965 ($1,282 million) was spent on providing Peace Corps volunteers on two-year technical assistance assignments.

United States policy is now to concentrate its aid on a few countries where it appears to be capable of achieving results, or where foreign policy problems are greatest. 92 per cent of all United States aid in 1967 was to be concentrated on twenty countries, of which six were Latin American countries (Bolivia, Brazil, Chile, Colombia, the Dominican Republic and Peru); 84 per cent of 'development loans' was to be spent in eight countries, including Brazil and Chile; the Dominican Republic was one of the five countries receiving 93 per cent of 'supporting assistance'. Within Latin America, 90 per cent of United States aid committed for 1967 was for the same six countries listed above, plus the five countries of the Central American Common Market. The other countries received mainly technical assistance, and relatively few development loans (*cf.* the table above for 1965).

US aid is increasingly regarded not merely as a transfer of resources, but, as a means of persuading recipient countries to make changes in their overall economic and social policies, and of inducing what are commonly described as 'self-help' measures. The AID, which has permanent missions in Latin America, is concerned to promote the efficient use of the whole of a country's resources, not merely of those provided by the United States in the form of aid; it hopes to achieve this through a dialogue with officials of the country concerned, reinforcing the position of those who have similar views to the United States on the correct methods of achieving economic development. The Alliance for Progress was originally intended to institutionalise this process, and to involve Latin Americans more closely in its objectives.

AID FROM MULTILATERAL INSTITUTIONS

The Inter-American Development Bank was set up in 1959 in order to provide funds on a multilateral basis for Latin American development. Its members are the United States and nineteen Latin American Republics (Cuba is not a member) and the newly independent state of Trinidad and Tobago. The Bank derives its capital from the subscriptions of its member countries, from raising funds in American and European capital markets, from the Social Progress Trust Fund endowed by the United States in 1961, and, more recently, from separate contributions from non-member countries including Canada, Spain, Germany, Italy, the Netherlands and Britain. In 1965 the Bank's total new loan authorisations amounted to $373 million; disbursements on these loans in 1965 amounted to $182 million. The Bank provides some technical assistance in the pre-investment field; one of its objectives is to encourage regional integration. The Bank varies its terms according to the nature of the projects financed.

Latin America has also benefited from an early stage from the operations of the main international lending agencies: the World Bank (IBRD), the International Development Agency (IDA) and the International Finance Corporation (IFC). The IBRD makes loans on fairly hard terms (interest rates of 6 per cent and repayment periods of 7 to 25 years) for projects mainly in the economic infrastructure. Latin America has been one of the main areas for IBRD operations; the IBRD made its first loan there in 1948. The IFC makes investments on commercial terms in the private sector; it made its first investment in Latin America in 1957, the year after it was set up. The IDA makes loans on much softer terms (zero interest rates, a service charge of 0·75 per cent and 50-year repayment periods) for IBRD-type projects; it made its first loan in Latin America in 1961, the year after it was set up. In 1965 the IBRD contributed $212 million for Latin America, the IFC $10 million, and the IDA $18 million. Total contributions from the three institutions, from the beginning of their operations in Latin America to 1965, have been respectively $2,208 million, $68 million and $100 million.

Latin America also receives contributions from United Nations technical assistance agencies; in 1965 these amounted to $48 million.

AID FROM FRANCE

France's aid has been overwhelmingly concentrated on its ex-colonies in Africa. Efforts are now being made to redeploy French aid, and one of the areas in which the French would particularly like to expand their aid activities is Latin America.

Before 1960 France provided no official financial aid to any developing country which had not been under French rule. In August 1960 a Finance Amendment Act enabled the French government to make loans to countries outside the Franc Area. Interest rates on these loans are 3 to 4 per cent, and repayment periods 20 to 25 years. Chile was the first 'traditionally foreign' country to receive such a loan; a commitment of 20 million francs (about $4 million) was made in 1961. A commitment for Mexico of 150 million francs (about $30 million) was made in 1963. By September 1964 nearly 18 million francs of the Chile loan had been disbursed (nearly 4 million francs in 1964); disbursements had not begun on the Mexico loan. The 1960 act also enabled the French government to guarantee private export credits to non-Franc Area counties of more than 5 and up to 13 years' maturity. The official loans have been committed as part of a general agreement involving a much larger commitment for officially guaranteed private export credits; in Mexico's case the total agreement was for $150 million. In a sense, the loans merely amount to a further softening of the terms of private export credits. In addition, France has provided official refinancing credits for Brazil and Argentina; disbursements on these amounted to $18 million in 1964.

France has been providing technical assistance to non-Franc Area countries for much longer. Special administrative arrangements for dealing with this were made in 1956, in a way which ensured that the dominant concern was with the position of the French language. In 1964 France spent $8 million on technical assistance in Latin America, which was about a quarter of all French technical assistance to non-Franc Area countries (including the three ex-French countries in South-East Asia). The amounts spent by France on technical assistance in Latin America have been increasing steadily over the last few years.

AID FROM GERMANY

Germany has no particular reason for concentrating its aid in a geographical area, although a high proportion of German aid has in fact been provided under the India and Pakistan consortia. Latin America has in recent years generally received about 10 per cent of official German aid; but in 1964 the net level of aid to Latin America was much lower than in previous years because of a high rate of loan repayment. In 1964 net disbursements of German official aid to Latin America amounted to $6 million. Loan repayments ($51 million) exceeded disbursements on new loans ($50 million); in addition, Germany spent $7 million on technical assistance. New commitments for German aid to Latin America in 1964 were $10 million for technical assistance and $17 million for loans. Loan terms vary (from interest rates around $5\frac{1}{2}$ per cent and repayment periods of up to 15 years to interest rates of $3-3\frac{1}{2}$ per cent and repayment periods of 20–25 years) according to the nature of the project financed. Germany considers that the most suitable channel for capital transfers to Latin America is private investment; net private direct investment by Germany in Latin America amounted to $11 million in 1964.

AID FROM BRITAIN

Like France, Britain has concentrated its aid in its ex-colonies. The government has also stated its intention, in a 1964 White Paper, of increasing its aid to Latin America.

British aid to Latin America (excluding the Commonwealth West Indies) until recently amounted only to a £19 million refinancing credit for Argentina in 1955 and a similar credit of £2·5 million to Brazil in 1961 and 1962, plus very small isolated loans to Bolivia and Chile in connection with British-owned transport facilities. In 1964 total British gross disbursements of aid to Latin America were £3·4 million (roughly $9·5 million), of which £3 million were loans to Argentina, Brazil, Chile and Bolivia. Expenditure on technical assistance was minimal (£179,000), and was distributed among most Latin American countries; a few very small grants were made to one or two countries. In 1965 the total was under £3 million and the distribution much the same; £2 million were loans to Brazil and Chile. The loans have been official export credits on near-commercial terms (roughly 6 per cent interest rates and 10 or 16 year repayment periods), administered by the Export Credit Guarantee Department.

Britain made in addition a commitment of over £7 million ($20 million) for the IADB in 1964. Of this £3 million were to be raised by floating a bond issue on the London market. The British government agreed in April 1966 to disburse the remaining £4 million as official loans, to be administered by the Bank and used for the purchase of British goods and services. The manner in which this agreement was announced gave the impression that the British government was more concerned with its relations with the United States than with economic development in Latin America.

CONCLUSION

Latin America receives significant aid only from the United States and, to a lesser extent, from the various international institutions which function in the area. Aid from other countries has little more than symbolic value: it mitigates the exclusiveness of Latin America's relationship with the United States, it probably has some useful effects on certain sectors of development, but its effects on the general development of Latin America are marginal.

BIBLIOGRAPHY

Hayter, Teresa. *French Aid*, Overseas Development Institute, London, 1966.
Little, I. M. D. and Clifford, J. M. *International Aid*, George Allen and Unwin, London; Aldine, Chicago, Ill., 1965.
Mason, Edward S. *Foreign Aid and Foreign Policy*, Harper and Row, New York for Council on Foreign Relations, 1964.
White, John. *German Aid*, Overseas Development Institute, London, 1965.
Agency for International Development. *Proposed Economic Assistance Programmes*, summary presentation to Congress, 1967. Available from Superintendent of Documents, US Government Printing Office, Washington, DC. *US Economic Assistance Programmes*, administered by the Agency for Economic Development and predecessor agencies, Statistics and Reports Division, Washington, 3 April 1948 to 30 June 1964.
ECLA. *External Financing in Latin America*, UN, New York, 1965.
Inter-American Development Bank. *European Participation in the Financing of Development in Latin America*, Washington, DC, 1966.
OECD. *The Flow of Financial Resources to Less Developed Countries, 1956–1963*, Paris, 1964.
Overseas Development Institute. *British Aid, 1–6*, London. *ODI Review—British Development Policies 1966*, London.
British Aid, Overseas Development Ministry Statistics, HMSO, London, 1966.
La Politique de coopération avec les pays en voie de développement (The Jeanneney Report), La Documentation Française, Paris, 1964.
Overseas Development: The Work of the New Ministry, HMSO (Cmnd. 2736), London, 1965.

Reports

Development Assistance Efforts and Policies, annual reports, OECD, Paris.
Operations Report, annual, Agency for International Development, Washington, DC.
Inter-American Development Bank, annual reports, Washington, DC.
International Bank for Reconstruction and Development (IBRD) and International Development Association (IDA), annual reports.
International Finance Corporation (IFC), annual reports.
International Monetary Fund (IMF), annual reports.
Social Progress Trust Fund, annual reports, Inter-American Development Bank, Washington, DC.

ORGANISATIONS

THE LATIN AMERICAN FREE TRADE ASSOCIATION

CHRISTOPHER ECKENSTEIN

OWING to their common Iberian culture and history and the similarity of their economic, social and political problems, the Latin American countries —more than those of any other continental region in the underdeveloped part of the world—present an image of unity. In fact, however, from an economic point of view Latin America is split up into a plurality of national compartments with very little intercommunication. By the establishment, on the basis of the Montevideo Treaty of 18 February 1960, of the Latin American Free Trade Association (LAFTA), a process has been set in motion that is aimed at breaking down this mutual isolation, and leading progressively to a region-wide market. The eleven countries that were members of LAFTA in mid-1967 (Argentina, Bolivia, Brazil, Chile, Colombia, Ecuador, Mexico, Paraguay, Peru, Uruguay, Venezuela) account for nearly 90 per cent of Latin America's total population. The countries of the Central American isthmus and the Caribbean islands remain outside LAFTA.

THE ORIGINS OF LAFTA

LAFTA was set up as a result of the convergence of two different initiatives. On the one hand, the secretariat of the United Nations Economic Commission for Latin America (ECLA), headed by Raúl Prebisch, was concerned at the stagnation of the traditional exports of primary goods from the Latin American countries which made it impossible for them to import from the industrialised countries the equipment and intermediate goods which were needed in ever-increasing amounts. To take up the production of these goods in Latin America was thus essential for the acceleration of development; but to reap the important economies of scale that are characteristic of these industries, the national markets of most countries were too small. ECLA's case for an integrated market of all countries of the Latin American region was also borne out by the duplication of identical investments in neighbouring countries and the overcapacity of many existing productive facilities and by the resulting unnecessarily high cost of industrialisation and waste of scarce investment resources. A plan was accordingly elaborated for a common market to be implemented in two stages, the first consisting in a substantial reduction, but not complete elimination, of tariffs and other trade barriers over a period of ten years.

Simultaneously with this perception of the long-term needs of Latin America's development, a second initiative was taken by four Latin American countries (Argentina, Brazil, Chile and Uruguay) in response to a pressing

542

problem—the sharp decline of their mutual trade, which constituted the major part of intra-Latin American trade. With a view to bringing their monetary and trade policies into line with the requirements of international organisations like the International Monetary Fund, these countries had indeed moved away from the bilateral compensation agreements on the basis of which they had long given advantages to each other's trade. In order to reach again the previous levels of trade, they considered—also with ECLA assistance—extending among themselves tariff preferences on a multilateral basis that would at least formally correspond to the free trade area concept provided for in the GATT. By showing their determination to go ahead with their own less ambitious project and by taking over some features of ECLA's more elaborate and apparently less easily negotiable common market programme, the four countries induced first Peru, Paraguay and Mexico and, shortly after the Treaty's signature, also Ecuador and Colombia to join them. Montevideo was chosen as the headquarters of the permanent executive committee and the secretariat of LAFTA.

TRADE LIBERALISATION COMMITMENTS

Though the Montevideo Treaty sets the long range objective of forming a Latin American common market, its contents are mainly concerned with the methods and special modalities for eliminating trade barriers to the members' mutual trade. The parallel application of two methods is provided for. First, annual negotiations take place in the course of which each country has to grant reduction of duties on imports from partner countries amounting to 'not less than 8 per cent of the weighted average applicable to third countries'. While the individual countries' concessions that form the *national schedules* differ, they benefit all other partner countries; they can, however, be withdrawn in return for adequate compensation. Secondly, the member countries are committed to negotiate every three years a *common schedule* consisting of products for which all trade barriers must irrevocably be abolished by all members by 1973 at the latest. To reach this aim the items placed on the common list have to correspond, at the end of each of four consecutive three-year periods, to an additional 25 per cent of the value of the trade carried out within LAFTA. Thus in contrast to the European Economic Community and the European Free Trade Association, the Montevideo Treaty does not establish an automatic and linear trade liberalisation scheme, but relies on the partners' willingness to find in item-by-item negotiations sufficient products to fulfil the Treaty's targets.

After the first five annual rounds of negotiations, 9,054 concessions of widely different magnitude had been included in the national lists, 7,593 having been granted in the first two and 1,461 in the last three rounds. One-fifth of the concessions involved the total freeing of the imports concerned within the area. Only about 25 per cent of the concessions, and a much smaller proportion of the negotiated trade volume, concern manufactures. Member countries have indeed been generally unwilling to grant reductions of trade barriers whenever the item concerned is domestically produced, or whenever it is hoped to do so in the more or less distant future. Moreover, where such concessions have been granted, it takes time for the manufacturers to take advantage of the new market opportunities and to establish the necessary trade channels. Furthermore the methods of calculation for the targets of liberalisation as established in the Treaty do not provide any incentive for including in the schedules items that have not been traded in the past; it is possible to fulfil these minimum targets by concentrating concessions only on those products that compose the existing trade among LAFTA countries. More than 60 per cent of this intra-trade consists of agricultural products, approaching 75 per cent if forestry and fishery products are included. It was thus inevitable that the 175 products of the first negotiated segment of the common schedule consisted to a large extent of agricultural products, manufactured products being very few, though their inclusion in the common schedule would have particular importance in ensuring investors access to the whole regional market. Agreement became possible only once it had been established that member countries would be able to invoke with regard to agricultural imports an escape clause even after the end of the transitional period.

COMPLEMENTARITY AGREEMENTS

For the purpose of including new products into the reciprocal trade pattern and expediting the liberalisation process on specific products, the Treaty made it possible for some or all member countries to conclude complementarity agreements on the basis of which producers could distribute the manufacture of components and parts throughout the area or organise specialisation within a larger sector. Harmonisation of the treatment accorded to basic materials and components used in the manufacture of particular finished products may be provided for in such complementarity agreements. Until now member governments have largely left it to the private sector to take the initiative in reaching these agreements, which are subsequently formally concluded by the governments. To date only two agreements (concerning data-processing machines and electronic valves) have entered into force; both involve foreign-owned firms. The producers' interest in negotiating such agreements has considerably increased since it was established that LAFTA countries which choose not to subscribe to a particular agreement can no longer unconditionally take advantage of the tariff concessions granted under it; concessions are now extended only to members that offer adequate compensation. With a view to promoting cooperation among producers themselves, LAFTA has in recent years also been organising meetings of entrepreneurs in numerous branches of industry; these have resulted in joint proposals to governments for including products in the national schedules.

THE LESS ADVANCED AND THE SMALL COUNTRIES

The concern for a fair distribution of the benefits of market enlargement is also apparent in the special status provided for the relatively less advanced member countries (Paraguay, Ecuador, Bolivia). These countries have first to grant only partial reciprocity for the concessions they obtain. Moreover, they may receive preferential concessions that are not extended to the other LAFTA countries. Nearly 7,000 concessions of this unique type had been granted by the spring of 1966. Investments with a view to exporting to other LAFTA countries on the basis of such concessions have, however, been extremely few, so that efforts have been made to identify industries that could be located in these two countries and, if need be, internationally financed. Further refining its approach, LAFTA has also come to recognise an intermediate group of countries (Chile, Colombia, Peru, Uruguay, Venezuela). Their common characteristic is to possess domestic markets of insufficient size and to be thus at a disadvantage with respect to the 'Big Three' (Argentina, Brazil and Mexico) which have been able to attract larger industrial investment. But it has not yet been possible to agree which specific measures would be justified for compensating these countries' handicap.

THE AIMS OF HARMONISATION AND COORDINATION

With every year of LAFTA's existence more emphasis has been placed on the aim of the common market enunciated in the Treaty. It has been generally regretted that LAFTA in its first years made progress only in trade liberalisation, but did not tackle the fulfilment of the other requirements of a common market. Thus various countries argued that the trade liberalisation process could not go much further if the tariffs on the basic materials and the margins of preference granted to finished goods were not brought closer together; the establishment of a common external tariff became therefore the subject of extensive study.

The distorting effects of diverging monetary policies upon competition were also recognised, and a coordination of these policies was proclaimed to be necessary. A first step in the direction of monetary cooperation was taken when the central banks established in 1965 a system of reciprocal credits and of multilateral clearing every two months with the purpose of reducing the inhibiting effects of the dollar shortage on the trade among them. Member countries have, moreover, recognised the necessity of coordinating their national development policies if wasteful duplication of investment and the emergence of new obstacles to the achievement of a region-wide market are to be avoided and if new investment is to be distributed between countries in an equitable manner. Since the need for some measure of planning is increasingly admitted at the national level, few are willing to rely merely on the play of market forces in the wider regional framework. It has been agreed that harmonisation of policies regarding foreign investments is necessary because countries that have adopted special protective measures for domestic enterprise or specific national interests fear their being undermined by imports from partner countries. The desire to harmonise national policies has also motivated studies in the field of agriculture, transport and recently fiscal and social policies. In almost all the fields where harmonisation and coordination have been envisaged, however, agreement upon obligations as to coordination and the content of harmonised policies has not yet been reached; study, the establishment of committees and the adoption of general principles are all that has been achieved.

ACHIEVEMENTS OF LAFTA

The main achievements of the Montevideo Treaty are to date still to be found in the field of trade expansion. Trade among member countries, after declining to a level of 6 per cent of their total trade in 1961, recovered to constitute more than 11 per cent of total trade in 1965, thus exceeding the levels attained in the period of the bilateral trade and payments agreements. Exports among LAFTA countries increased from $299 million in 1961 to $635 million in 1965, the average yearly increase being larger than in EEC or in EFTA; with respect to a series of items previously imported both from LAFTA countries and from third countries, the share of LAFTA increased substantially. A uniform tariff nomenclature for negotiations and better statistical tools have also been established. Above all, the frequent confrontations of producers, traders and officials from member countries in negotiations, study groups and private associations contribute to the overcoming of traditional mutual ignorance and to discovery of market opportunities and sources of supply existing in their own continent. LAFTA has become the focal point for the creation of a collective consciousness in Latin America with regard to integration, and this has in turn enabled Latin Americans to act with a greater degree of unity in their dealings with developed countries.

On the other hand, LAFTA's effect on economic growth in the member countries has been almost nil, though both in the preamble of the Montevideo Treaty and in the launching of the Alliance for Progress integration has solemnly been declared a prerequisite for the acceleration of the continent's economic development. Awakened but unfulfilled hopes built up a growing sentiment of frustration that led in the course of 1965 to a series of initiatives with the purpose of revitalising LAFTA.

Revitalisation of LAFTA

At the request of Eduardo Frei, president of Chile, four leading Latin Americans in charge of economic institutions concerned with Latin America (Raúl Prebisch—the pioneer of Latin American integration, Felipe Herrera, José Antonio Mayobre and Carlos Sanz de Santa Maria) launched at the beginning of 1965 a blueprint for a common market. They proposed that tariffs within the region be reduced automatically over ten years to a ceiling of 20 per cent, that a common tariff be set up, that investments be planned regionally within sectoral agreements, and that a payments union be set up; and the establishment of a ministerial council with some measure of majority voting, and of an independent executive commission inspired by the example of EEC, was suggested.

The need to give LAFTA a new political impulse had also been felt by the member governments themselves so that in November 1965 the first ministerial conference since the signature of the Treaty could take place. Its resolutions called, among other things, for an annual meeting of ministers, for the setting up of a 'technical commission' composed of four independent personalities whose task it would be to submit proposals for the speeding up of the integration process, for the establishment of a Latin American parliament to familiarise public opinion with the problems of integration, for the study of the modalities of an automatic scheme for the abolition of trade barriers and for the setting up of a system of settlement of disputes based on majority voting. Before this institutional strengthening, LAFTA had not recognised any exceptions to the principle of unanimity, and all its decision-making bodies were composed of officials. Simultaneously, the Inter-American institutions also began to give greater support to LAFTA. The Inter-American Development Bank, which had defined itself as the 'bank of integration', set up a fund for financing pre-investment studies of a multi-national character, and it also supports the exploration of the possibilities of arriving at sectoral common markets carried out in Santiago under ECLA's inspiration. The Inter-American Committee of the Alliance for Progress (CIAP), too, promised to focus attention on the investment and financial aspects of the integration movement. All these developments were facilitated by the warm endorsement of the idea of integration by the United States government which originally, at the time of the negotiation of LAFTA, had adopted a rather cool attitude. The culmination of this process was the conference of the American heads of state which assembled in April 1967 in Punta del Este (Uruguay). At this conference, the Latin American presidents finally undertook to create progressively, from 1970 onwards, a Latin American common market to be substantially achieved before 1985. The United States simultaneously promised financial support for solving some of the problems of integration.

Obstacles to Progress

Nevertheless it is by no means certain that the integration of Latin America will move ahead quickly. Integration would for a variety of reasons appear to be more difficult in Latin America than it has been in Europe. The many industries that already exist in Latin America have generally been completely sheltered against competitive imports and stiffly resist any reduction of trade barriers; the governments in their turn are unwilling to override the latter because of widespread unemployment. The concern for the balance of payments furthermore makes member governments reluctant to reduce trade barriers unless they are absolutely certain that equivalent advantages can be gained on the export side. In the case of new industries member governments are unwilling to abandon the possibility of granting—even against regional partner countries—the protection that is a decisive means of attracting new investment providing employment. As compared to Europe, which began integration with mature industries used to some degree of competition, with full employment and mostly with important currency reserves, the starting position is far less favourable in Latin America.

Progress is further complicated by the vast discrepancies in the degrees of industrial development of the various countries, which motivates the fear that a multinational free market would lead to further polarisation, the more advanced becoming richer and the less advanced poorer. Yet it is politically difficult for the more advanced countries to adopt programmes to benefit their less advanced partners since they often possess within their own borders large areas at a similarly backward stage. At enterprise level, differences in productivity within the same branch are particularly vast, and since foreign enterprises tend to lead in this respect, the suspicion exists that domestic entrepreneurs would hardly be the main beneficiaries of integration, thus adding another obstacle to the assumption of commitments. Lastly the present transport and tele-communications network of the continent does not permit any large expansion of mutual trade since it is geared to Latin America's relations with the northern hemisphere with which 90 per cent of its foreign trade takes place. More than 90 per cent of Latin America's present internal trade is effected by sea because railway, road and fluvial communications between the countries are often limited to a single line—whereas in Europe and the United States non-maritime transport facilities carry the bulk of trade. The low volume of traffic and the generally poor condition of ports contribute moreover to the very high cost of maritime transport so that it tends to be more expensive to ship goods from one Latin American country to another than between Europe or North America and Latin America. The very establishment of a regional infrastructure is thus an enormous task which is now being tackled with the support of international institutions.

Such reasons explain why Latin American promoters of integration regard a free trade area as much too narrow and inadequate a concept and aim at a continental common market or economic community. Yet every one of the requirements of such a common market stands in drastic contradiction to present Latin American realities: the differences between the tariff levels and trade policy instruments of the various countries are incomparably greater than they were among the European countries before integration. The resulting much greater difficulties of harmonisation are further enhanced by the fact that the imports from third countries to which the eventually harmonised tariffs would have to apply constitute a much larger share of total imports than was the case in Europe, where intra-trade was substantial. A particularly great effort would have to be made in the field of monetary policies since Latin American countries have experienced everything from periods of stability to runaway inflation. Since the rate of exchange often does not follow the internal price fluctuations, commercial transactions lack a stable basis and reciprocal over- or under-valuation distorts the conditions of competition. As regards harmonisation of legislation toward foreign capital, it is difficult to see what its basis would be in view of the wide differences between countries' political options in this respect.

As to investment planning for the area as a whole, studies have revealed that billions of dollars of investment resources could be saved and prices substantially reduced if for strategic sectors like iron and steel, petrochemicals, aluminium, fertilisers, pulp and paper a pattern of industries could be established that would cater for the demand of the whole of Latin America rather than of single countries only. However, action in this field will be very difficult; at present the elaboration of national plans takes place in mutual isolation, with attention being paid to regional perspectives only in extremely rare cases. Equally, agreement among a plurality of countries on investment programmes, for instance, for particular industrial sectors, will not be easy to achieve. Lastly, plan implementation which is already far from satisfactory at national level will be even more difficult within the wider region, all the more so because in the essentially private-enterprise economies of Latin America investment does not necessarily go to the locations agreed upon.

Avenues for Future Advances

In order to overcome all these difficulties, the conviction of the necessity of integration will have to spread well beyond the international secretariats and be reflected not only in the political resolutions of inter-governmental meetings, but also at the operative levels of the national governments. A habit of inter-governmental cooperation on concrete matters and a spirit of mutual confidence will have to be formed—as was the case in the OEEC— if the far-reaching intentions proclaimed at Punta del Este are not only to be embodied in treaty but also applied by the governments concerned. It would also appear to be necessary that special attention be given to the formulation of intermediate targets that would stop short of the common market ideal, but would still represent a progress over the present method of 'micro-negotiations' on each and every item. Along this line of thinking, it has been proposed that the Latin American countries start by undertaking a very few rounds of across-the-board reductions, thus establishing first a preferential zone and demonstrating to governments and industries that a move away from item-by-item negotiations has no dramatic consequences.

It has also been suggested that countries agree on a ceiling for protection against each other's imports. The average tariff level in Latin America has recently been estimated to be more than 100 per cent, while individual tariffs of 600 per cent and more can also be found, not to speak of even more stringent non-tariff barriers. If the Latin American countries could at least for their mutual trade think in terms not of complete abolition of trade barriers but of establishing reasonable protection levels, some trade currents could take place without complicated harmonisations being indispensable. In this respect it is promising that the need for submitting existing industries to some doses of outside competition is being increasingly recognised by Latin American economists and international organisations.

The desirability of giving due consideration to more modest aims would appear to apply also to the geographical scope of future commitments. Harmonisation and coordination become indeed more difficult the more partner countries are to be involved in negotiations. Smaller groups of countries, particularly if they have approximately the same development level, are likely to find the necessary common denominator more easily, as the example of the Central American Common Market would appear to indicate. The Andean group of countries (Colombia, Venezuela, Ecuador, Chile, Peru and Bolivia) is beginning to think along similar lines. If progress remains slow in LAFTA, there is a real possibility that these small and medium-sized countries may exploit the potentialities of more rapidly reducing trade barriers and generally cooperating among themselves; they would thus strengthen their bargaining power toward the big countries which have domestic markets of a size permitting a substantial degree of industrialisation and for which integration has therefore less urgency.

Moreover, the solution of many particularly difficult problems of Latin American integration is conditional upon or would be facilitated by the availability of important financial resources. Thus the establishment of a regional infrastructure of transport and telecommunications, the modernisation of inefficient existing industries, the identification and establishment of enterprises in the less advanced partner countries, the preparation of sufficient multinational projects to enable all countries to share in the benefits of trade liberalisation, the strengthening of domestic versus foreign enterprise and the constitution of a revolving fund for a regional payments scheme have been repeatedly singled out by Latin Americans as instances where outside aid would be indispensable if integration is to move ahead. At Punta del Este the US government promised to channel funds to the fulfilment of some of these purposes. But the more diversified the sources of this aid are, the more will Latin Americans feel that the autonomy of the integration process is likely to be respected. Latin America looks therefore also to Europe for support of its self-help efforts. For the same reason protagonists of Latin American integration do not by and large want to combine the setting up of a Latin American common market with that of a western-hemisphere preferential trading system that would include the United States and link North and South America even more closely; for them integration is becoming indeed more and more an expression of Latin America's aspirations for greater self-determination and less dependence on its powerful northern neighbour. The process started by LAFTA on a modest commercial basis is becoming therefore the embodiment of political hopes. But if these are to be more than pious wishes, Latin American governments will have to tackle the problem of regional cooperation and integration with the same determination that would be needed for effecting the overdue economic and social changes within their own countries.

BIBLIOGRAPHY

Dell, Sidney. *A Latin American Common Market?*, Oxford Univ. Press, London and New York, 1966.

Urquidi, Victor L. *Free Trade and Economic Integration in Latin America*, Univ. of California Press, Berkeley, Calif., 1962.

Wionczek, Miguel S. *Latin American Free Trade Association*, Taplinger, New York for Carnegie Endowment of International Peace, 1965.

ECLA. *The Latin American Common Market*, UN Sales No. 59, II G.4, UN, New York, 1959. *Multilateral Economic Co-operation in Latin America*, UN Sales No. 62, G.3, UN, New York, 1962. *Towards a Dynamic Development Policy for Latin America*, UN Sales No. 64, II, G.4, UN, New York, 1963.

THE CENTRAL AMERICAN
COMMON MARKET

ALBERTO FUENTES MOHR

HISTORICAL BACKGROUND

WHEN Central America became independent from Spain in 1821 it was organised as a federal republic composed of five states: Guatemala, El Salvador, Honduras, Nicaragua and Costa Rica. The lack of communications and of an effective central government, however, led in 1839 to the dissolution of the federation; each state became a separate republic and developed an export economy which linked it more to the outside world than to its neighbours. Many efforts were subsequently made to reestablish political and economic unity, but such attempts—generally pervaded by party politics—failed one after another.

By 1950 the five Central American countries—with a total area of 441,000 square kilometres and a little over eight million inhabitants—could be counted among the least developed in Latin America. The total GNP was US$1,586 million—that is, a per-capita of $198—and primary forms of production predominated while industrial development was very limited. As is the case in most underdeveloped countries, sustained economic growth was impeded by lack of savings and capital, backward technologies and the instability of foreign markets. But apart from these factors, the size of each local market, compounded by an uneven distribution of income, gave each country little capacity to develop even the consumer-goods industries which mushroomed in other Latin American republics. Unable to develop internally, the Central American countries continued to depend almost exclusively on a few export commodities, mainly coffee and bananas, and to a lesser extent cotton and cocoa. This made for acute economic instability and seriously limited the possibilities of providing employment for a rapidly growing population.

Against this background, in 1951 the five Central American governments requested assistance from the United Nations Economic Commission for Latin America (ECLA) to undertake a programme 'to develop agricultural and industrial production and the transportation systems of their respective countries in such a manner as to promote the integration of their economies and the creation of larger markets through the exchange of their products, the coordination of their development plans and the establishment of enterprises in which all the countries, or some of them, might be interested'. Later, at a meeting in August 1952, an Economic Cooperation Committee, composed of the economics ministers of the five countries, was set up under the ECLA's auspices and thereafter a series of studies was undertaken by technical bodies which began to outline the future development of the integration programme. It should be noted that in contrast with the legalistic Latin American tradition, and in contrast also with the European Common Market, the Central American programme was not derived from a fully comprehensive and logically consistent framework. It was, on the contrary, the result of a series of ad hoc decisions superimposed on one another.

The Treaties Creating the Common Market

An instance of the pragmatic approach mentioned above was the fact that the Central American countries, while engaged in a multilateral integration programme, went on developing a network of bilateral free trade treaties. Even before 1951 one such treaty existed between El Salvador and Honduras, and from 1951 to 1959 several agreements came into force establishing six free trade areas: between Guatemala and El Salvador, El Salvador and Honduras, Guatemala and Honduras, El Salvador and Nicaragua, Guatemala and Costa Rica, and El Salvador and Costa Rica. All these treaties listed a number of locally produced goods which were to be traded free of duties between the two countries concerned.

At the multilateral level, meanwhile, a treaty was signed by the five countries in June 1958 which sought the establishment of a Central American free trade area over a period of ten years, and the development thereafter of a customs union. In practice, however, the treaty abolished duties for only a limited number of goods and further inclusions to the original list were subject to new agreements. In other words, there was no automatic procedure gradually to widen the scope of free trade. Apart from this circumstance, Costa Rica's ratification of the treaty was not assured, so that the multilateral integration programme appeared in danger of stagnation at its very outset.

Faced with this situation, in February 1960 the three countries whose trade based on bilateral treaties was the largest—Guatemala, El Salvador and Honduras—concerted a Tripartite Treaty of Economic Association which introduced a revolutionary element into the multilateral programme. Instead of listing the duty-free goods as the previous treaties had done, the Tripartite Treaty established free trade for all goods produced by any of the three countries except for a limited list for which preferential tariffs or restrictive quotas were established for a five-year transition period.

Although the Tripartite Treaty evoked misgivings in Nicaragua and Costa Rica, it soon proved its effectiveness as a dynamic factor in the integration programme. The same year in which it was signed and put into effect, a General Treaty of Central American Integration was agreed upon by Guatemala, El Salvador, Honduras and Nicaragua, which came into force in 1961 and was signed and ratified by Costa Rica in 1962. The General Treaty was really a geographical extension of the Tripartite Treaty. It provided for free trade for most goods produced in all the Central American countries, the only exceptions being some agricultural products, petrol, liquors and tobacco, which were subject to special interim regimes to be automatically liberalised over a five-year period ending in June 1966.

With the free movement of goods produced in the area assured by the General Treaty, the adoption of a uniform tariff towards the outside world was secured by means of an agreement on the equalisation of import duties signed by the five countries in 1959 and by a series of subsequent protocols which widened the scope of the original agreement. By 1967 uniform import duties had been agreed for about 98 per cent of all items covered by a common tariff nomenclature. Moreover, a Central American Customs Law had also been adopted. Thus the basis has been set for the establishment of the customs union which the several free trade treaties set as a goal.

THE DEVELOPMENT OF TRADE WITHIN THE COMMON MARKET

Before the establishment of the Common Market, intra-Central American trade was negligible. By 1960 the several bilateral treaties then in force had raised intra-regional trade figures to $32·7 million—6·3 per cent of total Central American imports. But the more substantial increase came after the signing of the General Treaty. In 1962 the value of commercial transactions among the five states reached $50·8 million, and since then trade within the Common Market has experienced a spectacular rise to $176·2 million in 1965, which amounts to 20 per cent of total imports.

In 1965 the country with the largest share of regional trade was El Salvador, which accounted for 30 per cent of imports within the Common Market and for 33 per cent of exports. It was followed by Guatemala, with 19 and 23 per cent; Honduras, with 20 and 12 per cent; Costa Rica, with 13 per cent of imports and 15 per cent of exports; and Nicaragua, with 13 and 7 per cent. Exports from El Salvador, Guatemala and Costa Rica were mainly of manufactured goods; those from Nicaragua were evenly balanced between manufactured and agricultural products; and those from Honduras were predominantly agricultural.

The Common Market has made it possible for Central America to substitute imports of certain light manufactured goods which came formerly from outside the area. This import substitution, however, has not gone against an expansion of trade with the outside world. From 1962 to 1966, Central American imports—intra-regional trade excluded—rose from US$500 million to 677 million, and exports from 463 million to 673 million. The import substitution furthered by the Common Market is reflected in the changing composition of regional trade. By 1960 manufactured goods amounted to only 40 per cent of the total, chiefly textiles, garments, leather and rubber goods, and oils and fats. Trade in grains, livestock and raw materials was still quite important. By 1966, however, manufactured goods accounted for nearly 70 per cent of regional trade, including items such as canned products, paints, plastics, detergents and other consumer goods.

The question which faced the Common Market in 1966 was how far trade expansion within it would continue with the same dynamism as before. A very serious limiting factor is the extremely defective income distribution in the member countries, except for Costa Rica. Out of a total population of thirteen million inhabitants, probably a little over half may be classed as effective consumers. It must also be taken into account that idle capacity in industry has been considerably reduced, so that expanded production and trade will require new investments. The possibilities of sustained commercial growth within the Common Market in the next few years, therefore, may depend largely on a change in the pattern of industrialisation.

INDUSTRIAL INTEGRATION WITHIN THE COMMON MARKET

From the outset of the integration programme in 1952 to 1965, the participation of industry in the total GNP of the Central American countries rose from 12 per cent to nearly 16 per cent. Investment in industry has been centred round the production of light consumer goods, which account for

82 per cent of industrial output. The integration programme, however, aims to further the development of new types of industry, such as pulp and paper, fertilisers, chemicals, tires and glass.

The promotion of these new industries, however, has presented several problems. The relatively large investments to be made required a guarantee that the size of the market might not be reduced through the establishment of duplicate plants which, apart from entailing cut-throat competition with high social costs, could lead to the final predominance of large foreign firms to the detriment of Central American investors. There was also a need to secure a balanced industrial development among the five countries, since no one of them was ready to assume the role of the Italian Mezzogiorno. An attempt was made to solve these problems through a treaty signed in 1958, the 'Agreement on the Regime for Integration Industries'. This Agreement established the conditions under which a given plant would acquire the category of an 'integration industry', which meant basically exclusiveness of free trade for its products for a ten-year period, fiscal prerogatives and the undertaking to submit itself to price and quality controls.

Although the Agreement on Integration Industries was duly ratified, it became a controversial instrument insofar as some sectors saw in it an attempt to establish state-backed monopolies or to open the way for state intervention in industry. This, in fact, was the view of the United States government, which presented a formal note to each of the five Central American Governments pointing out that the Agreement might result in discrimination against foreign investment and that funds of US origin would not be available to finance any industry established under the Agreement. This, among other reasons, explains why so far only three plants have been granted the category of integration industries. The fact is, however, that the new industries are not being established rapidly enough either within the framework of the Agreement on Integration Industries or by just availing themselves of the Common Market. In this connection, it must be pointed out that according to a protocol to the Agreement, once a factory has been established and has enjoyed free trade for its products under the provisions of the General Treaty, no integration industry of the same type may be established which would enjoy exclusiveness of free trade. Thus it cannot be argued that the prospect of applying the Agreement in the future might dampen investment possibilities. It should also be noted that in the absence of any discrimination towards foreign investment, outside capital is tending rather to purchase the established industries which have grown under the Common Market instead of developing new fields.

Altogether, it can be said that industrial development within the Common Market has been somewhat anarchic. The governments have attempted to channel it by means of a uniform law on fiscal incentives, but it appears that this must be complemented by a regional system of programming and promotion which will ensure balanced industrial development among the states of the Common Market.

OTHER FIELDS OF ECONOMIC INTEGRATION

Apart from its success in creating the Common Market and its less rewarding efforts to promote a new type of industrial development, the integration programme has encompassed other fields which call for common action on the part of the Central American Republics. In the field of agriculture, although little has been done to solve the problem of a rather stagnant production of maize, rice and beans—the staples in the Central American diet—it has been possible nevertheless to ensure free trade of these products within the Common Market by means of a coordinated price stabilisation scheme. Regarding public works, a road network has been jointly programmed, to be completed by 1969. Plans have also been drawn for the interconnection of hydroelectric power systems. Finally, a project is under consideration for the establishment of a telecommunications network linking the five countries.

THE INSTITUTIONS OF THE COMMON MARKET

The political body in charge of directing the integration programme at the highest level is the Central American Economic Council, formed by the economics ministers of the five countries. Under them, an Executive Council formed by undersecretaries oversees the technical studies and discussions of several working groups. Both Economic and Executive Councils are served by the General Secretariat for Economic Integration (SIECA).

One of the most important institutions of the Central American Common Market is the Bank for Economic Integration (BCIE), specially created to finance projects, both private and public, which may directly further economic integration. Its capital is made up of contributions from the five governments and its board of governors consists of the economics ministers and the presidents of the five central banks.

The other regional institutions created within the framework of the Common Market are the Monetary Union, established under the auspices of the central banks with a view to unifying monetary policies and to creating eventually a common currency; the Central American Technological Institute for Industry (ICAITI); and the Central American Institute for Public Administration.

OUTLOOK FOR THE FUTURE

The Central American Programme for Economic Integration has been highly successful in the establishment of a Common Market which allows its member countries to achieve a faster rate of development than they might otherwise be able to attain. Although the free movement of people and capital within the area remains to be fully secured, the development of free trade might easily lead to the establishment of a full-fledged customs union in the near future. The advantages which Central America may obtain out of the Common Market, however, depend largely on realistic planning. This is necessary in order to achieve an adequate infrastructure, a new type of industrial development, a higher productivity in agriculture, and larger and more diversified exports.

It must also be emphasised that the Central American Common Market needs to plan an aggressive export drive towards the rest of the world. Commercial agreements with other countries or groups of countries will have to be furthered, and while Central America cannot lose its identity as an integrated unit, it may well be that in the future it will participate in a wider scheme for Latin American integration. In such a case, the experience acquired in creating and developing its own Common Market may prove useful not only to itself but also to the whole Latin American community.

THE CENTRAL AMERICAN COMMON MARKET: BASIC DATA

TABLE 1

AREA AND POPULATION

	Area (sq. km.)	Population (1965)	Population density (per sq. km.)
Guatemala	108,889	4,554,200	41·8
El Salvador	21,393	3,010,900	140·7
Honduras	112,088	2,333,000	20·8
Nicaragua	148,000	1,682,100	11·4
Costa Rica	50,700	1,557,700	30·7
TOTAL	441,070	13,137,900	29·8

TABLE 2

GNP IN 1965 (US$ MILLION—1962 MARKET PRICES)

	Gross	Per capita
Guatemala . .	1,365·5	299·8
El Salvador . .	774·1	257·1
Honduras . .	485·9	208·3
Nicaragua . .	491·2	292·0
Costa Rica . .	585·9	376·1
TOTAL . .	3,702·6	281·4

TABLE 3

FOREIGN TRADE IN 1965 (US$ MILLION)

	Imports (goods)	Exports (goods)
Guatemala . .	240·6	184·1
El Salvador . .	201·8	188·6
Honduras . .	121·8	123·8
Nicaragua . .	158·1	143·0
Costa Rica . .	157·9	114·2
TOTAL . .	880·2	753·7

TABLE 4

DEVELOPMENT OF TRADE WITHIN THE COMMON MARKET (US$ MILLION)

Year	Total	% increase over previous year
1952 . . .	10·8	5·9
1953 . . .	11·9	10·2
1954 . . .	14·0	17·5
1955 . . .	13·1	−6·4
1956 . . .	13·7	4·6
1957 . . .	16·9	23·4
1958 . . .	21·1	24·9
1959 . . .	28·7	36·0
1960 . . .	32·7	13·9
1961 . . .	36·8	12·5
1962 . . .	50·8	38·0
1963 . . .	72·1	41·9
1964 . . .	106·4	47·6
1965 . . .	135·4	27·8
1966 . . .	176·2	30·2

BIBLIOGRAPHY

'A Common Market that Works', *Statist*, CXC, 4593, London, 18 March 1966.

Castillo, C. M. *Growth and Integration in Central America*, Pall Mall Press, London; Frederick A. Praeger, New York, 1967.

'Central America—Towards Monetary Union,' *Bank of London and South America Ltd Fortnightly Review*, V, 3, London, July 1965.

'Fast Growing Market in the Isthmus', *Statist*, CXC, 4604, London, 3 June 1966.

La integración económica latinoamericana (Part IX: 'Integración centroamericana'), Banco Nacional de Comercio Exterior, Mexico City, 1963.

Wionczek, Miguel S. (ed.) *Latin American Integration: Experiences and Prospects* (Part Three: 'Central American Integration Program'), Frederick A. Praeger, New York, Washington, DC, London, 1966.

THE INTER-AMERICAN DEVELOPMENT BANK

FELIPE HERRERA

SINCE the Inter-American Development Bank was officially created in December 1959 by nineteen Latin American countries and the United States, it has become one of the prime factors in promoting Latin American economic and social development. In addition to the high level of financial and technical assistance which it provides to its Latin American member countries, the Bank's scope of action is expanding year by year as its member countries place additional responsibilities on it. Thus the Bank is the principal source of public international financing for Latin America today. In addition, it is a prime mover in the growing movement towards Latin American integration. Its broad impact on the Latin American economic and social scene can be measured by the names which have been applied to it. The Bank has been referred to as the 'Bank for Latin American Integration,' the 'Bank of the Alliance for Progress,' and the 'Bank of the Latin American University,' all titles reflecting just a few of the Bank's major concerns.

The fundamental purpose of the Bank is to promote the development of its member countries, individually and collectively. In fulfilling this purpose the Bank had, up to the end of June 1967, authorised loans totalling $2·1 billion to help finance economic and social development projects and programmes in Latin America costing a total of $5·5 billion. This loan volume, of which nearly 40 per cent has been disbursed, provides an index of the rising significance of the Bank in the process of capital formation and development in Latin America. The Bank's financial contribution to the economic and social progress of its member countries has been made possible thanks in large measure to the growth of its resources derived from contributions of the member countries themselves and from borrowings in the capital markets of the United States and capital-exporting countries in Europe. The diversity of its resources has permitted the Bank to finance a wide range of development projects, with special emphasis on the agricultural and industrial sectors. More than half of the Bank's financing operations have been of a 'soft' loan nature, in keeping with a policy of improving the terms and conditions for repayment of loans by its member countries.

Side by side with its loan operations, the Bank has supplied its member countries with a considerable volume of technical assistance, often in cooperation with other regional and international agencies. This technical assistance has been devoted to the preparation and execution of programmes and projects, to the establishment and reorganisation of development institutions and to the training of specialised personnel. Development planning has also received considerable support from the Bank.

Through its loan and technical assistance operations the Bank has helped to strengthen the process of Latin American economic integration. In this connection it is financing the export of capital goods among its Latin American member countries; it has established an Institute for Latin American Integration in Buenos Aires to study and analyse the integration process and has established a Preinvestment Fund for Latin American Integration.

THE BANK'S FINANCIAL STRUCTURE

The Bank was established with two completely separate sources of funds: its ordinary capital resources and its Fund for Special Operations. Under an agreement signed in 1961 with the United States government, the Bank also administers the Social Progress Trust Fund, created to finance social development projects in Latin America under the Alliance for Progress programme.

The ordinary capital resources are used to finance development projects on conventional terms. The resources of the Fund for Special Operations, on the other hand, are lent on conditions more favourable than those from the ordinary capital resources. This is done in order to cope with special circumstances arising in certain countries or in connection with certain projects. Since 1965 the Fund for Special Operations has also been devoted to financing sectors previously covered by the Social Progress Trust Fund; namely, housing for low-income families, improved land use, water supply and sanitation facilities, and advanced education and training. This change stemmed from a decision to channel new funds for social development into the Fund for Special Operations in the future rather than to the Social Progress Trust Fund.

The ordinary capital resources are currently authorised at a total of $2·15 billion, of which $475 million is paid-in and $1,675 million is callable capital. The $475 million in paid-in capital includes $381,580,000 subscribed by the twenty member countries and $93,420,000 available for subscription partly by current member countries and partly by countries which might join the Bank in the future. Fifty per cent of the subscribed capital has been paid in United States dollars and 50 per cent in the currencies of the respective member countries.

The $1,675 million in callable capital includes $1,388,240,000 subscribed by the member countries and $286,760,000 which is available for subscription by current or future members. The subscribed callable capital constitutes, in effect, a guarantee for the Bank's obligations and enables the Bank to borrow funds on the world's capital markets. So far the Bank has sold eight bond issues and obtained one direct loan. These total $374 million and have been added to the ordinary capital resources available for lending. Three of the bond issues totalling $225 million were sold in the United States; two totalling $48 million in Italy; one for $15 million in Germany; one for $8·4 million in Great Britain; and the last, a short-term issue amounting to $65 million, was sold primarily in Latin America, although Spain and Israel also purchased part of it. The direct loan, amounting to $12·5 million, was obtained from Spain.

In addition to these operations the Bank has sold participations in its ordinary capital loans to private banks in the United States, Europe and Canada. As of 30 April 1966 such sales totalled $27,066,889. The contributions of the member countries to the Fund for Special Operations currently total $820,391,500. Another $299,082,500 is scheduled to be provided by the member countries by 31 December 1966 for a total of $1,119,474,000.

The total resources which the United States placed under the administration of the Bank in the Social Progress Trust Fund amounted to $525 million. These resources have been virtually exhausted in initial loan commitments and, as indicated, projects previously financed by the Social Progress Trust Fund are now handled by the Fund for Special Operations.

In addition to the above-mentioned resources, which have been supplied by the member countries, the Bank administers or helps to channel other resources from non-member countries to assist in the development of Latin America. These resources include: 40 million Canadian dollars provided by the Canadian government for loans extended at terms of up to 50 years and at little or no interest; 15 million Canadian dollars from the Export Credits Insurance Corporation for use in extending standard commercial loans in cooperation with the Bank on a parallel or an independent financing basis; the equivalent of $10 million supplied by the Netherlands government to finance projects in Latin America and defray technical assistance costs also under parallel financing arrangements or on an independent basis; the equivalent of $11·6 million made available to the Bank by Great Britain to finance economic assistance projects in the region. In April 1966 Sweden also pledged to create a Development Fund for Latin America in an amount of $5 million. These resources will be made available to the Bank for financing economic development projects such as those financed with the Bank's ordinary capital resources.

OPERATIONS AND POLICIES

Since the Bank made its first loan in February 1961 its operations have risen steadily. Up to June 1967 these had reached 415 loans totalling $2,104·5 million. In 1966 the Bank's loan commitments reached their highest yearly level, amounting to $396·1 million. This volume represented an increase of 29·5 per cent over the annual average figure of $300 million registered in the 1961–5 period. The magnitude of the Bank's contribution to the development of the region may be better appreciated if it is borne in mind that the volume of public international financing channelled into Latin America rose from an annual average of $427 million during the 1957–60 period to an average of $987 million in the 1961–4 period.

Loans authorised by the Bank up to the close of June 1967 from its different sources of funds may be summarised as follows:

Ordinary capital resources: 144 loans totalling $831·1 million.

Fund for Special Operations: 145 loans totalling $755·6 million.

Social Progress Trust Fund: 117 loans totalling $501·2 million.

Other resources: nine loans totalling $15·6 million extended from the Canadian funds administered by the Bank.

The important role being played by the Bank in helping to mobilise development resources in its member countries can be judged by the fact that the Bank's loans of $2,104·5 million are helping to finance investments totalling about $5·5 billion. Thus Latin American member countries are contributing nearly two-thirds of the total investment. The funds disbursed by the Bank under its authorised loans amounted to $907 million as of the end of June 1967, or approximately 43 per cent of the total value of all its authorised loans.

In this regard it might be pointed out that the purchases made from the proceeds of the Bank's ordinary capital resources are untied to any particular area or country. Thus up to 31 December 1966 approximately 42 per cent of the purchases proceeding from the ordinary capital resources were made in Latin America (the overwhelming part in the country where the project was being carried out); 22·9 per cent was spent in Europe; 22·5 per cent was spent in the United States; and the remainder was spent in other countries.

In its operating policies the Bank has sought to give preferential attention to financing development projects and programmes in the relatively least developed member countries. It has also sought to assure balanced development in both economic and social sectors in member countries. Cumulative figures for the loans authorised by the Bank from the beginning of its lending operations to December 1966 show that 44·5 per cent of those loans have gone to directly reproductive sectors, chiefly agriculture, industry and mining; 17 per cent have gone to economic infrastructure, primarily electric power and transportation; 33·6 per cent to social development projects, including water and sewage systems and housing; and the remaining 4·9 per cent has gone into higher education, preinvestment studies and export financing. Both public and private sectors in Latin America have benefited from the Bank's loan operations. Excluding the operations of the Social Progress Trust Fund, out of a total of $1,404·1 million in loans authorised by the Bank up to December 1966, 62 per cent helped finance public projects and 38 per cent helped finance projects in the private sector. Because of the social character of the projects financed with the Trust Fund, the majority of loans made from it have been extended to agencies in the public sector.

Seeking to meet additional development needs in its member countries, the Board of Executive Directors of the Bank in 1965, in connection with a $900 million increase in the Fund for Special Operations which was put into effect by the Bank's member countries early in 1965, reviewed its lending policies from the Fund and decided to broaden its fields of action to include: financing of agricultural and rural development on an integral basis through coordinated programmes related to such economic infrastructure facilities as electric power, roads and irrigation, to such social development aspects as housing, public health and education, and to the extension of credit and other facilities to improve the farm sector; financing urban development programmes on a similar basis of coordinated attention to housing, water and sewage systems, community facilities, and other services; broadening financial assistance for higher education and extending such assistance to technical and vocational education fields; intensifying aid to member countries in the preinvestment field through programmes designed to identify investment projects and then prepare feasibility studies for them.

The conditions on which the Bank's loans are granted depend on the source of the funds used. Loans granted from the ordinary capital resources are made on so-called 'hard terms'; those from the Fund for Special Operations and the Social Progress Trust Fund are extended on more flexible conditions, including the possibility of repayment in the currency of the borrower.

More than 80 per cent of the loans granted by the Bank have been extended at terms of 10 to 30 years, including grace periods. The interest rate on loans from the ordinary capital resources takes into account the cost to the Bank of obtaining funds on the world's capital markets. The rate is currently 6 per cent per annum. However, loans granted with funds obtained by the Bank in Western Europe through bond sales carry service commissions of between 1 and 2 per cent, in order to compensate the Bank for the higher cost of obtaining funds in the European capital markets. On loans granted from the Fund for Special Operations, the Bank has charged interest rates ranging from $2\frac{1}{4}$ per cent to $5\frac{3}{4}$ per cent, depending on the type of project financed, although the vast majority of such loans have fallen below 4 per cent. The interest rate on loans from the Social Progress Trust Fund has ranged from $1\frac{1}{4}$ to $2\frac{3}{4}$ per cent per annum, plus a service charge of $\frac{3}{4}$ per cent which is charged on principal amounts outstanding.

Loans granted from the ordinary capital resources are repayable in the currencies lent. Those from the Fund for Special Operations may be repaid either in part or totally in the currency of the borrowing country. Loans from the Social Progress Trust Fund may also be repaid partially or totally in the currency of the borrower country. In practice most repayments have been made in such currency.

Technical assistance extended by the Bank in the 1960–6 period amounted to $82·1 million, of which $66·6 million was reimbursable and $15·5 was nonreimbursable.

The Financing of National Development Plans

One of the principal policy objectives of the Bank has been to promote the preparation of national economic and social development plans by its member countries. To work towards this objective, the Bank has collaborated with its member countries in the establishment and strengthening of national planning agencies and in the preparation and execution of such development plans. This work has been done in cooperation with other regional organisations, particularly through the Tripartite Committee established by the Bank, the Organisation of American States and the United Nations Economic Commission for Latin America.

Coordination of the external financing for the development plans of its member countries is another field to which the Bank has devoted preferential attention. The Bank has participated in the meetings sponsored since 1964 by the Inter-American Committee on the Alliance for Progress (CIAP) which examine the financial needs, both external and internal, of its member countries and the progress made in their development plans and programmes. The Bank has also helped obtain global financing for the national development plans of some of its member countries. In this connection it acts as financial agent in seeking the external financing required to implement Ecuador's national development plan and is studying the possibility of acting in such a capacity for other member countries.

Since it is not easy for small- and medium-scale entrepreneurs in Latin America to obtain foreign credit, the Bank has sought to channel resources into that important sector of the economy by granting loans to national development institutions. Under this policy, during the first six years of its operations the Bank extended a total of $393 million, or 28 per cent of the total value of its authorised loans, to such institutions. These development loans are frequently accompanied by technical assistance which helps improve the organisation, policies and procedures of such development institutions.

New Fields of Activity

From the beginning of its activities in 1960, the Bank has sought continuously to review its policies and procedures and its fields of activity in order to meet changing circumstances in its member countries. During 1966, for example, it recognised the need to expand its activities in the preinvestment field and in such social and economic fields as education, urban development and rural community development.

In the preinvestment field the Bank has decided to expand its aid to member countries in promoting the identification and preparation of high-priority projects and has begun making global preinvestment loans to development agencies in its member countries. To the extent possible, the Bank endeavours to foster the establishment of revolving preinvestment funds whose resources may be recovered as the resultant projects are put into operation.

In regard to education, the Bank views this sector as one of the corner-stones of development and has extended financial assistance for the execution of many education projects. Up to the end of June 1967 the Bank had loaned some $75 million in eighteen member countries for projects in this field. Such loans in the past were devoted to strengthening advanced education, but the Bank is now devoting attention also to technical and vocational education.

Since the beginning of its operations the Bank has actively financed housing, potable water and sewage projects and has effectively contributed to the solution of social problems in its member countries. However, owing to the great magnitude of urban problems, the Bank also proposes to increase its activities in this field through integrated development programmes. Such integral development programmes will also be applied to rural communities.

Support for Economic Integration

The Bank attaches great importance to the economic integration of Latin America as one of the principal means of intensifying the region's industrialisation, broadening and diversifying its foreign trade and accelerating the economic development of its member countries. In doing so, the Bank fulfils one of the principal functions assigned to it in the Agreement Establishing the Bank; namely, to 'cooperate with the member countries to orient their development policies toward a better utilisation of their resources, in a manner consistent with the objectives of making their economies more complementary and of fostering the orderly growth of their foreign trade.'

One of the ways in which the Bank has sought to implement this policy has been to make economic integration an important criterion in evaluating loan applications. The Bank has authorised several loans which have directly contributed to the integration process, including five totalling $32 million to the Central American Bank for Economic Integration to finance projects that will benefit the area as a whole and another of $3 million to the national universities of Central America, also channelled through the Central American Bank, to finance a general programme for the development of instruction in the basic sciences. The Bank has also financed highway projects of regional significance in Honduras, Uruguay and Brazil. Another activity of the Bank in support of regional integration is its programme to finance exports of capital goods among its Latin American member countries. Under a programme launched in 1964, the Bank has authorised lines of credit totalling $28 million for such purposes. The basic aim of this programme is to spur the development of basic industry in Latin America through the expansion of intra-regional trade.

In 1963 the Bank also started a special programme of technical assistance to promote studies relating to integration. This programme is largely based on formulas of cooperation with other agencies for the purpose of making better use of the human and financial resources available to the region. In order to acquire the basic information needed to orient the programme towards the most immediate possibilities and needs, in early 1963 the Bank held a meeting of representatives of various agencies interested in Latin American integration. This meeting considered many initiatives which were later implemented. Noteworthy among these was a study of some basic sectors of the Latin American economy undertaken in collaboration with several agencies and regional organisations; the study of the possibilities for the integrated development of the Colombian-Venezuelan frontier zone, carried out in 1964 in cooperation with the Latin American Institute for Economic and Social Planning; and another similar study on the possibilities for the integrated development of the Colombian-Ecuadorian frontier zone, presented to those two governments in 1965. Some of the projects envisaged in the first study are already in process of execution with financial assistance from the Bank. In 1965 also, the Bank authorised a technical assistance grant of $100,000 to the Latin American Free Trade Association (LAFTA) to finance three programmes designed to accelerate the integration process. Two of these are for the performance of integration studies in the industrial and agricultural fields, and the other is for the identification of specific branches of production that might be encouraged in LAFTA's comparatively less-developed members.

Among the most significant accomplishments of the Bank in support of regional integration is the establishment of the Institute for Latin American Integration, which operates as a unit of the Bank and has its headquarters in the city of Buenos Aires. The Institute engages in the systematic study of the regional integration process in its several aspects and seeks the best means of facilitating that process. In the pursuit of its objectives, the Institute engages in research, training, advisory services and publication activities.

In April 1966, during the Seventh Annual Meeting of the Board of Governors of the Bank in Mexico City, the member countries approved a recommendation to establish a special fund to finance preinvestment studies for the execution of multinational development projects. The Board of Executive Directors of the Bank was directed by the Board of Governors to determine the resources of this fund and to write its regulations. The preinvestment fund, now set up, is permitting the Bank to make yet fuller contribution to the economic integration of its Latin American member countries, an increasingly indispensable requirement for the solid and harmonious development of the region.

BIBLIOGRAPHY

'Development Banking in Latin America', *Quarterly Review*, V, 3, Bank of London and South America, London, 1965.

Herrera, Felipe. 'The Inter-American Bank: Catalyst for Latin American Development', *The World Today*, XX, 11, Royal Institute of International Affairs, London, November 1964.

'The Inter-American Development Bank', *Latin American Business Highlights*, XII, 1, Chase Manhattan Bank, New York, 1962.

Publications by the IDB (Washington, DC)

Herrera, Felipe. *The Inter-American Bank—Instrument for Latin American Development*, August 1962. Mende, Tibor. *The Inter-American Development Bank: A Forerunner among Financial Institutions*, December 1964. IDB pamphlets and annual reports.

THE ALLIANCE FOR PROGRESS

PETER NEHEMKIS

LATIN AMERICA is the graveyard for United States foreign policies and the Alliance for Progress is the most recent policy to be entombed. As a United States Senator John F. Kennedy did not show any special interest in Latin America, but his presidential campaign speeches were sharply critical of the sterility of United States diplomacy during the Eisenhower years, and in Latin America they aroused hopeful expectations that at long last Latin America would receive the attention it deserved.

Kennedy's enunciation of the Alliance for Progress (the slogan was coined at Harvard University in December 1960, at a meeting of businessmen and distinguished academics) gave many Latin Americans a genuine sense of participation in its political creation. Though it can scarcely be claimed that much progress has been made under *la alianza para el progreso*, its mere existence is enough to have made Kennedy a legendary figure in Latin America.

THE ORIGINS OF THE ALLIANCE

Though it bears the imprint of the United States, the underlying philosophy of the Alliance is Latin American. Juscelino Kubitschek, former president of Brazil, first propounded the design for an Inter-American partnership in 1958. Kubitschek's plan, *Operacão Pan Americana*, was in turn influenced by the studies of the Inter-American Economic and Social Council and the United Nations Economic Commission for Latin America. All these plans and programmes embodied certain common hopes and aspirations which had been articulated for years by Latin American statesmen.

The foundation for the Alliance was laid in 1960 at a hemispheric conference at Bogotá, Colombia, where President Eisenhower's Under-Secretary of State, Douglas Dillon, offered to make $500 million of 'social capital' available initially, with a commitment of large additional sums in the years ahead. A coherent philosophy for Latin America's social problems was incorporated in the Act of Bogotá. At Punta del Este, Uruguay, in August 1961, at a meeting of the finance ministers of the Western hemisphere, the 'constitution' of the Alliance for Progress was hammered out in two basic documents: The Declaration to the Peoples of America and the Charter of Punta del Este.

In its original conception the Alliance for Progress was not intended to be another conventional American foreign aid programme. What President Kennedy originally proposed was unprecedented in the Western world. It was an offer by the United States to underwrite a social revolution in Latin America. The reforms were to cover the spectrum of social change. The actual text of the Declaration approved at the Uruguayan resort of Punta del Este in August 1961 committed the signatories to

'accelerate economic and social development, to encourage programmes of comprehensive agrarian reform . . . with a view to replacing latifundia and dwarf holdings by an equitable system of property . . . , to assure fair wages and satisfactory working conditions, to wipe out illiteracy, to reform tax laws, demanding more from those who have most, to punish tax evasion severely, and to redistribute the national income to benefit those who are most in need, to maintain monetary and fiscal policies which, while avoiding the disastrous effects of inflation or deflation, will protect the purchasing power of the many, to stimulate private enterprise, to accelerate the integration of Latin America.'

All this was to be achieved 'through the institution of representative democracy'. On its part, the United States agreed to make available 'a major part of the minimum of twenty billion dollars' needed to make all this possible, but these funds would be available only to those governments which effectively fulfilled the conditions laid down at Punta del Este, principally the one about implementing this programme democratically. Because the Washington of John F. Kennedy understood little of Latin America, the Alliance was expected, in the late Adlai Stevenson's words, to 'take the bold, brave, difficult steps' to achieve peaceably and democratically reforms which had been accomplished elsewhere through violent revolution.

These great hopes, however, were not realised. For about a year and a half following the promulgation of the Alliance, inactivity in Latin America and bureaucratic entanglement in the United States reduced the new idea and the bold programme to homogenised blandness.

President Kennedy signalled for an Alliance, which is commonly understood to mean joint responsibilities, mutual involvement—in short, a partnership. The organisational response from the Washington establishment was the conventional wisdom of foreign aid—'Another structure competing with aid for Asia, Africa and the Middle East!' The Alliance soon lapsed into a United States cheque-writing agency which spent almost half its capital on emergency transfusions to meet balance-of-payment crises. To this day, despite efforts at 'Latinisation', the Alliance remains largely a United States foreign aid programme with its focus on governments and technicians— the mandarinate of the capital cities. Its programme and projects are those which have been employed on all the continents where United States foreign aid has flourished or withered. What the United States bureaucracy has been unable to perceive is that Latin America's problem is primarily political and only secondarily economic. The Washington establishment, however, persists in putting the cart before the horse. It insists on long-range development plans when the political environment necessary to accommodate the results of such plans is not present. The economic superstructure is therefore erected on political quicksand.

During the first years after its birth, the Alliance was greeted with scepticism in the influential Latin American intellectual circles of the Marxist left. For many, there was the unanswered question: does the Alliance for Progress represent a commitment of the heart? For others, it had the smell of another cold-war gambit—Washington's answer to Castro and his Cuban revolution. To the Marxist-Leninist left, the Alliance was—and is—merely a clever invention of Yankee imperialism, a financial device by which to keep Latin America tied to Washington.

MISCONCEPTIONS AND FALSE ASSUMPTIONS OF THE ALLIANCE

From their experience with the Marshall Plan in Europe, the New Frontiers-men unwittingly assumed that Latin America was a continental community in the way that Europe was a community of shared interests, possessed of a common heritage and a collective sense of responsibility. Latin America is a collection of fragmented, frustrated, and disoriented societies, all remarkably different, some scarcely able to govern themselves, lacking the characteristics of modern nations, unified only by their deep suspicion of the colossus of the north.

There is a profound difference between the motivation for reconstruction (Europe's problem in the late 1940s) and the motivation for reform (Latin America's problem in the early 1960s). Europe had the political leadership that was able to furnish the necessary drive—Ernest Bevin, Paul-Henri Spaak, Robert Schuman, and Jean Monnet to provide the conceptual framework—for a unified, continental response to General Marshall's offer of aid. They were assisted powerfully by the Paul Hoffman-Averell Harriman axis.

At the launching of the Alliance the political infrastructure was not in place; nor were the political technicians at hand. (The enthronement of the economist as the high priest of development puts the emphasis on the wrong kind of technician. Unless he happens to be in a position of political decision-making—as was Roberto Campos as Minister of Planning in Brazil—the economist functions in a vacuum.)

Washington's policymakers had assumed that the big countries—Mexico, Brazil, Chile and Argentina—would carry the torch for the Alliance. Mexico, however, is wrapped in a mystical cocoon of non-intervention. Mexicans believe that their country, as the senior revolutionary country in the hemisphere—her revolution of 1910 antedated the Russian revolution—has nothing to learn from other revolutionaries, and the idea of being taught by the élite of the New Frontier was greeted by scorn. Indeed, reference to the Alliance is conspicuously absent from official Mexican pronouncements. Only in 1965, in his message to Congress, did President Díaz Ordaz see fit to depart from precedent by saying a kind word for the Alliance. Following Jânio Quadros' flight from the presidency, Brazil for a period of four months was for all practical purposes without a functioning government. Under the regime of the left-leaning João Goulart, Brazil's diplomatic relations with the United States grew frigid. Brazil turned her back on the Alliance until Goulart was deposed by a military coup in 1964. Chile, at the inauguration of the Alliance, was stagnating under former President Alessandri. Under President Eduardo Frei—since 1964—Chile has assumed the mantle worn by Argentina in the 1930s and is challenging United States hegemony in every domain from the Alliance for Progress to intervention in the Dominican Republic and the restructuring of the Organization of American States. The military seizure of power in Argentina after the fall of Perón plunged that country into an economic and political wasteland. The bankruptcy begun by Perón was completed as the military engaged each other in bloody conflict. Argentina staggered from one crisis to another and was unable to provide leadership for herself, let alone for her neighbours.

DIPLOMATIC AMATEURISM OF THE NEW FRONTIER

In its eagerness to find acceptance for the Alliance, the New Frontier forgot Talleyrand's celebrated advice to a young diplomat: *et surtout pas trop de zèle.*

First, Argentina was wooed. When Frondizi was hustled off to prison Washington gave its embrace to Brazil. Goulart sent his finance minister, San Tiago Dantas, to conclude an agreement with David Bell, administrator of the Agency for International Development (AID), whereby in return for United States financial assistance Brazil agreed to carry out a series of stabilisation measures for the control of inflation. Upon his return to Rio Dantas was denounced as a traitor by Goulart's demagogic brother-in-law, Leonel Brizola. Goulart promptly fired Dantas. So ended any attempt by Goulart to deal with a ravaging inflation that consumed Brazil's economy. This was, too, the beginning of the end of the United States infatuation with Goulart. When Brazil's military rose against him, Washington sent congratulatory cables to the new 'constitutional' government even before Goulart fled the country.

It was Colombia's turn. Colombia was singled out by President Kennedy on his South American tour. Ciudad Kennedy—the largest housing project in Latin America financed with Alliance funds—was inaugurated during his visit. Colombia was to be a showplace for the Alliance for Progress. As from an endless cornucopia, loans were lavished on her totalling $500 million. (If the commitments of the international lending agencies are included total foreign aid to Colombia is close to $1,000 million.)

Colombia soon demonstrated the chronic Latin American inability to govern and manage her economy. Frente Nacional, a coalition formed in 1957 by the Liberals and Conservatives to end their internecine warfare that resulted in the slaughter of some 300,000 inhabitants, fell apart. Congress was immobilised. In a large area south of Bogotá, there was no effective control by the central government over at least five long-entrenched bandit zones that became virtually 'independent republics', organised on communist lines. An incipient Castro insurrectionary movement made itself felt with sporadic bombings, kidnappings, killings and gunfire. Beset by the typical frustrations of the Latin American chief of state—to which his own political ineptness contributed—Colombia's poet-president, Guillermo León Valencia, described his predicament thus: 'The political groups, the pressure groups, and the conspiracies have not let me govern.'

American enthusiasm towards Colombia cooled and financial support was abruptly discontinued in 1964. At the November 1965 Rio conference of Latin American foreign ministers, it was Colombia that drove the shaft into the United States by openly criticising American intervention in Santo Domingo.

Ecuador's military junta next became a favourite. Officialdom was jubilant over the 'Four Horsemen of the Apocalypse'—the popular name for the military leaders who overthrew President Arosemena in July 1963. Teodoro Moscoso, former administrator of the Alliance for Progress, in hailing the military junta said: 'This government is getting on with the reforms outlined in the Charter of Punta del Este.' Two and a half years later, amidst growing tension and rioting, the junta dismissed its air-force member. A few months later, in March 1966, the remaining three military members of the junta were forced to seek refuge in Brazil, unable to control popular discontent. A civilian—Clemente Yerovi Indaburu—was nominated provisional president and entrusted with the tasks of solving the serious economic crisis and of bringing about a restoration of democratic, civilian rule. It is not unreasonable to conclude that the fate of the junta is a fair indication of the real effectiveness of military governments as instruments for progress in Latin America.

The Illusion of the Democratic Left

Washington incorrectly assumed that resistance to reform by the traditional conservative centres of power could be overcome by the non-communist parties of the democratic left. Muñoz Marín of Puerto Rico, Betancourt of Venezuela and Figueres of Costa Rica—all are today out of power—were regarded as prototypes of Latin America's democratic left.

Puerto Rico is the showpiece of the Caribbean—its hotels rival those of Miami Beach, Florida and the record $900 per capita income is the highest in Latin America. But Puerto Rico's political stability and economic progress are due to the island's special relations with the United States—it is associated by a commonwealth arrangement—and to the peculiar ability of the statesman Luis Muñoz Marín. The Puerto Rican experience, however, is not an article for export to the rest of Latin America. Indeed, many believe that the real relationship between Puerto Rico and the United States is one of colonial dependence.

To be sure, Costa Rica provides a beacon of political maturity in Central America and the country's most distinguished political figure, former President José Figueres, is an acknowledged Caribbean statesman. Though its spokesmen at hemispheric gatherings are respected, Costa Rica has no weight in the continental balance of power. Indeed, many feel that more often than not Costa Rica is the tail to the Venezuelan kite, that her oft-repeated opposition to the overthrow of 'constitutional' governments is doctrinaire and unrealistic.

That Rómulo Betancourt was the first Venezuelan president to complete his term of office does not cover his shortcomings as a political leader. Despite the hold of Betancourt's party on the trade unions, the civil service and city workers on the government's payroll, an informed public in Caracas repudiated Acción Democrática. After five years in office, Betancourt failed to integrate the youth of Venezuela into the national community. Instead, the radicalism of the university students was converted into outright warfare against society. Terrorism, arson and gunfire will continue in Venezuela— as it will in Panama and the Dominican Republic—because many of the young people have repudiated democracy as a method of attaining a genuine social revolution.

The political management of social and economic reform in Latin America is as difficult and delicate a problem in the complex art of government as exists. It requires a high order of political skill, flexibility and realism in order to preserve a balance between the accelerating demands for reform from the people on the one hand, and the resistance to change from the traditional centres of power on the other. It necessitates political dexterity which can take the wind out of the sails of the extremist left by implementing reforms and, at the same time, avoid antagonising the right by moving too fast too soon.

The real question that needs to be asked is whether there is in fact a political democratic left in Latin America. In Argentina the Peronistas constitute 35 per cent of the voting population. Though divided into warring factions, they do not give their allegiance to the traditional democratic parties. Without the integration of this bloc into the traditional parties of the centre, Argentina remains a frustrated and fragmented society in search of a national identity. Uruguay's Colorado party continues its historic dedication to democratic government and social reform, but it is out of power. Social reform has reached a dead end in Uruguay—the welfare state is paralysed, the country is bankrupt and tensions are close to flashpoint.

Brazil's military regime has abolished the thirteen parties that composed her heterogeneous political groupings. They were not 'parties' as they are known in Britain or the United States but rather *ad hoc*, opportunistic coalitions that represented only the ambitions of their leaders. What has in fact emerged is a 'party of the revolution' and a 'tolerated opposition.' Brazil is desperately groping for the right political formula by which to govern the world's fifth largest country as an open society. This prescription will be Brazilian rather than a carbon copy of the United States system. Bolivia is ruled by an 'elected' air force general, whose military is immobilised by a handful of Castro-inspired guerrillas.

On the southern continent only Chile's Christian Democratic party is an effective political party of the democratic left. Its brilliant performance in electoral organisation and ability to communicate a reform programme to all sectors of Chilean life is without parallel in Latin America. Its leader, Eduardo Frei, is a professional politician with a deep sense of public responsibility. He is flexible, moderate, and has a rare instinct for compromise. The agreements concluded in December 1964 between the United States copper companies in Chile and President Frei mark a watershed in the historic relationships between foreign companies which previously dominated the economic life of Chile and the nationalist aspirations of an underdeveloped country. Production, marketing, finance, labour and administration, among other managerial decisions, are now within the purview of the Chilean government by virtue of its stock ownership and representation on the directorate of formerly wholly American-owned companies. 'Chileanisation' of the copper industry shows that confiscation of foreign-owned industries through the crude device of expropriation is passé.

Frei's statesmanship enables Chile to enjoy the best of two worlds—to render unto nationalism the things that are nationalism's, and to continue to be the beneficiary of United States foreign aid and corporate technology and management. But a crisis in Frei's government is likely to arise from the pressures of extremists within his own party, accenting 'revolution' to the neglect of 'liberty' in the party slogan 'Revolution in Liberty'. Americans and Europeans who see in Chile's Christian Democratic regime a pattern for the rest of Latin America are deluding themselves. There is no other country with a political sophistication comparable to that of Chile; the Christian Democratic party of Eduardo Frei is a flower that may be able to blossom in Chile, but it cannot be transplanted to other climates.

In Peru, though President Belaúnde is himself a dedicated reform democrat, the quantity of reform measures by his government has been negligible. On the northern rim of South America a democratic party of the left exists only in Venezuela, and the effectiveness of Acción Democrática is arguable.

In Central America, only Costa Rica's National Liberation party—engaged in a bitter struggle for survival—can boast of being a party of the democratic left. Mexico's Institutional Revolutionary party is the cornerstone of a unique one-party system that merges the regional political machines, labour unions, peasant leagues, professional and business organisations and the military establishment under the leadership of the president of the republic who is selected by the hierarchy of the party and whose 'election' is a foregone conclusion. The presidential election of June 1966 in the Dominican Republic repudiated Juan Bosch, an archetypal demagogue of the Caribbean democratic left.

Of the nineteen Latin American countries that constituted the Inter-American system in the summer of 1966 six were military regimes, two were still in the classical Latin American tradition of one-man dictatorships ('controlled' elections being permitted), and another was ruled by a voodoo-practising medical doctor known as 'Papa Doc'; one Caribbean country was a quasi-American protectorate occupied by foreign troops; in three countries the government was virtually paralysed and scarcely able to function. Putting Mexico to one side because it is *sui generis*, in only three countries out of nineteen were democratic parties of the left in power.

Such is the melancholy tale of the democratic left. Nonetheless, from its inception the Alliance for Progress took it for granted that the pressure for reform would come from the left-of-centre parties. Another of the delusions of the Alliance was its belief that the parties of the democratic left, controlled by the aging lions and tired oxen of democracy, are capable of communicating the need for social reform in an idiom that appeals to Latin American youth, the professional and managerial class, and junior military officers. The barrenness of the appeal of the democratic left is nowhere more apparent than in the lack of response of Latin American youth. Among the young people, who constitute almost half the population, the concept of democracy is suspect. Indeed, the word 'democracy' has been so debased by dictators that it has lost its value. Latin America's young people have little faith in democracy as a process for attaining peaceable reform; for them, social justice and revolutionary authoritarianism are almost synonymous.

The Great Illusion—A Latin American Middle Class

The great illusion of the New Frontier was its belief that the democratic left possessed a broad base of middle-class support. Acción Democrática and Alianza Popular Revolucionaria Americana (APRA) have been unable to attract the support of the urban groups described as 'middle-class' in Caracas and Lima. The parties of the democratic left find their strength in the rural areas, not in the cities. Left-wing strength is diminishing among urban dwellers but increasing among the peasants. Salvador Allende, the leader of the Chilean Marxist coalition FRAP, increased his vote in the rural areas from 1958 to 1964 by 58 per cent. In the 1964 Chilean presidential elections, Allende's strength in the rural areas was not great enough to overcome a combination of circumstances: the traditional opposition from the land-owners; the heavy financial support from the Chilean right, which was willing to spearhead anti-communism as the major issue in the campaign; Frei's promise of agrarian reform; the massive support for Frei by Chilean women, strongly influenced by Frei's Catholicism and Allende's Marxism; the superb campaign organisation run by the Christian Democrats; and finally, the reformist mood of the country which responded overwhelmingly to Frei, an extraordinarily gifted professional politician.

Latin America's middle-income groups are not hellbent for reform. They are essentially conformist and emotionally identified with the institutional *status quo*. Dr Claudio Véliz has correctly pointed to a fallacy in the assumption prevalent in the United States regarding the existence of a great surging middle class in Latin America. Dr Véliz writes:

'The fundamental error in the US approach, however, has to do with its definition of the middle class. US scholars, politicians, and journalists have gleefully discovered a Latin American middle class and, without pausing to find out what kind of middle class it really is, they have proceeded to credit it with all sorts of qualities it does not possess. In fact, the only claim which the Latin American urban middle groups have to the description 'middle class' is based on the fact that they are in the middle, between the traditional aristocracy and the peasants and workers.'[1]

This view is supported by Professor F. B. Pike:

'Chile's urban middle sectors have traditionally demonstrated colossal indifference to the social problems and have dedicated themselves to defending the value-judgements of the upper classes . . . the readily observable traits of the middle class have led to the introduction into the Chilean vocabulary of the *siútico*. A *siútico* is a middle class individual who emulates the aristocracy and its usages and hopes to be taken for one of its members. It is generally agreed that Chile's middle class abounds in *siúticos*.'[2]

Much the same can be said of Brazil's middle classes. Indeed, perhaps the only true middle class in Latin America is to be found in Argentina and it is composed of immigrants from Italy, Spain, Germany, France, Switzerland, Britain and Austria. Though Argentina's middle class has dominated the 'radical' parties (in Latin American nomenclature 'liberals' are conservative and 'radicals' are liberal but never radical) it has been unable—even when holding power—to provide Argentina with democratic government of the British or United States variety.

THE FAILURE OF THE ALLIANCE

Four years after the Alliance for Progress set out to help 200 million Latin Americans make progress, half-a-dozen countries still teetered on the brink of political and economic chaos. According to the sombre 1965 report of the Food and Agriculture Organisation of the United Nations, Latin America had lost the capacity to feed itself. The projected per capita food production for 1965–6 was 11 per cent less than the pre-war average. Two-thirds of Latin America's population (some 140 million people) were not—and are not—in the mainstream of the 20th century. This is the invisible Latin America that seethes with the accumulated frustrations, bitterness and social unrest of more than three centuries of neglect and indifference on the part of its ruling classes.

While in Latin America there is blithe talk, encouraged by the United States, of a decade of development, the hard reality is that the area is squeezed between the vice-jaws of uncontrolled population growth and unproductive agriculture. Agriculture does not receive the attention that it demands because, first, it involves hard political decisions, and secondly, industry has more prestige and glamour. Political leaders in the main— Frei of Chile and Belaúnde of Peru are notable exceptions—are indifferent to birth control for the underlying population. With few courageous except-ions—a scattering of padres who brave the wrath of their bishops—the Roman Catholic Church evades the issue. United States assistance in family planning and contraception is timid, at home and abroad. Latin America is sliding rapidly towards a Malthusian catastrophe; its current rate of popu-lation multiplication is certainly beyond the capacity of the Alliance for Progress as it is now constituted. If Latin America is to be spared from sinking into a Western hemisphere version of pre-Communist China, it will require an emergency mobilisation of the resources and organisational abilities of the West on an agricultural-population programme dwarfing the Marshall Plan.

[1] 'Obstacles to Reform in Latin America,' *The World Today*, London, January 1963.
[2] *Chile and the United States 1880–1962*, Notre Dame, Indiana, 1963, pp. 284–5.

If the accomplishments of Latin America are measured by the crude bench-marks fixed by the Charter of Punta del Este, the results are dismal. The target of a general 2·5 per cent annual per capita growth rate is nowhere in sight. In Brazil and Argentina—containing about one half of the population of the region—per capita growth rates were actually negative for 1961–5. Chile and Colombia barely sustained any growth during this period. Colombia is sinking into a slough of stagnation. Mexico's momentum cannot be attributed to the Alliance for Progress. Venezuela's economic progress is a bounty of nature—the country floats on oil. The high growth rates of Peru, El Salvador and Nicaragua were due to favourable export demand—the prolonged industrial boom in the United States and Western Europe—rather than adherence to policies and programme of the Alliance.

With the exception of Mexico, Brazil and Chile, Latin American countries have not seriously applied their political processes and decision-making, such as they are, to the problems of development. Indeed, development plans read more like academic exercises than plans for action. Planning organisations exist and operate in a vacuum. Rarely is there awareness of the need for releasing the energies of the private sector. Planning bodies evade the implications of a 'Malthusian swamp of humanity', avoid coming to grips with inadequate and obsolete educational systems, downgrade the priority which agriculture demands, and concentrate on flashy industrial projects. Though seven countries have undertaken reforms in their tax systems, in no country is the tax system adequate to the needs for revenue, equitable or effectively enforced. (Brazil's director of internal revenue reported that in 1964 only 5,000 persons paid individual income taxes exceeding 2 million cruzeiros—about $1,000.) Though fourteen countries have land reform legislation on the statute books, and in some land reform has been taking place for decades (e.g. Mexico and Colombia), the surface has hardly been scratched. Venezuela is the only country in which land distribution has been extensive, and here it has taken place under initiatives unrelated to the Alliance for Progress. In Brazil, Peru and Chile, where the need for land reform is critical, there is as yet no perceptible sign of progress.

National budgets are archaic in Latin America—nowhere are they employed as a tool for the control of investment and fiscal policy. Little progress is discernible in the elimination of waste, inefficiency and corruption in the management of public resources. Where rampaging inflation has been checked, as in Brazil, the penalty is the unpopularity of the military regime. Latin American presidents, who have followed the classical remedies of austerity preached by the International Monetary Fund, have paid with their political careers—Frondizi in Argentina and Reid Cabral in the Dominican Republic are examples. The few countries that enjoy satisfactory fiscal conditions—Mexico, Peru and Paraguay, for example—do so for reasons other than policies induced by the Alliance for Progress.

THE JOHNSON ADMINISTRATION AND THE ALLIANCE

The difference between the attitude towards Latin America of Kennedy's New Frontier and that of the Great Society of Lyndon B. Johnson, who has extended the Alliance for Progress beyond the time period envisaged in the Charter of Punta del Este and pledged continued United States aid, is the difference between passionate honeymoon and humdrum marriage. After the ardent Kennedy courtship Latin Americans feel 'let down' in the prosaic relations with Johnson.

An oft-repeated charge by Latin Americans and doctrinaire American liberals is that Johnson's Washington is enamoured of military juntas. In reality the Johnson administration is neither pro-military nor anti-military: it has merely recognised a Latin American fact of life—in a continent wracked by revolutionary ferment, Latin America's armed forces are the only centres of stability. In the majority of the countries of the region they form the dominant power structure. With few exceptions, the military is for all practical purposes *the* government and its influence is determinative. This fact of life is the real reason for a United States military presence in Latin America. By supporting Latin America's military establishments with the comparatively small sum of $55 million annually, Washington buys a kind of insurance policy against a repetition of Cuban-style revolution. Where the local military is unable to prevent a communist attempt at seizure of power in an area within the American defence perimeter, United States policy is to intervene with its own armed forces, as it did in Santo Domingo in April 1965.

If there is any lesson to be learned from the diplomatic innocence of the Kennedy administration, it is that the withholding of diplomatic recognition of a military junta will not cause its demise. The Latin American military is utterly indifferent to whether Washington grants or withholds recognition. For Latin America's military understands thoroughly—and recent experience in Argentina, Peru, Guatemala, Ecuador, Honduras, Bolivia, the Dominican Republic and Brazil serves only to underscore this assurance—that the United States has no alternative but to grant diplomatic recognition to a military junta whether it operates behind the thin gauze of a civilian regime (as it did in Argentina) or holds the levers of governmental power directly (as it did in Peru, Ecuador and Guatemala and currently does in Brazil, Argentina, Bolivia and Honduras).

An annual investment in Latin America by the United States of $1,000 million of public funds—the amount pledged under the Alliance for Progress —represents only one-seventh of one per cent of the United States GNP. This is a small price for a great and affluent power to pay for a foreign aid programme designed to help poor countries to lift themselves out of the misery of backwardness, a programme that may mean the difference between economic chaos and some semblance of order. Though the United States business presence is disliked, the firm underpinning which it provides to the economy of the region cannot be ignored. The wages and salaries to almost one million local employees, expenditures on supplies and materials and taxes paid—United States companies pay about one-fifth of all taxes in Latin America—contribute around $6,100 million annually to Latin America's economy.

What the Alliance for Progress cannot supply is a missing ingredient in the Latin American character—an instinct for organisation and a capacity for management. The Alliance cannot supplant political dilettantes by political professionals. Nor can it supply an indigenous political leadership that possesses realism, skill, flexibility, a deep sense of public responsibility, impeccable honesty, and respect for other people's ideas. It cannot convert demagogues into democratic statesmen.

The Alliance dramatises the enormous psychological distance between the United States in the north of the continent and the disunited states in the south. The constellation of reforms embodied in the Alliance might have made sense in a political environment in which social cohesion prevailed and continental solidarity existed, where there were well-tested rules for carrying out social change, literate constituencies and disciplined political parties, led by sophisticated political leaders responsive to an informed electorate. This situation is, however, a fantasy in Latin America, which is an active theatre in subversive warfare aggravated by the bitter Sino-Soviet conflict, a region gripped by virulent nationalism and revolutionary violence, where accession to power is usually illegitimate and its transfer occurs by insurrection.

In Latin America the United States is confronted by the modern dilemma of a great power in the age of revolution. It cannot lead because it is saddled with the millstone of the past; it cannot lead in any event because Latin Americans will not follow. The United States is unable to withdraw from Latin America without leaving a power vacuum to be exploited by the disciples of Moscow, Peking and Havana.

BIBLIOGRAPHY

Drier, John C. (ed.) *Alliance for Progress: Problems and Perspectives*, Johns Hopkins Press, Baltimore; Oxford Univ. Press, London, 1962.

Gil, Federico G. 'Latin America: Social Revolution and United States Foreign Policy', *World Pressures on American Foreign Policy*, ed. Marian D. Irish, Prentice-Hall, Englewood Cliffs, NJ, 1964.

Gordon, Lincoln. *A New Deal for Latin America: The Alliance for Progress*, Harvard Univ. Press, Cambridge, Mass.; Oxford Univ. Press, London, 1963.

Nehemkis, Peter. *Latin America: Myth and Reality*, Alfred A. Knopf, New York, 1964; revised ed. (paperback) New American Library, New York, 1966.

Raushenbush, Hilman Stephen. *The Challenge to the Alliance for Progress*, Public Affairs Institute, Washington, DC, 1962.

Seegers, Kathleen. *Alliance for Progress: The Challenge of the Western Hemisphere*, Coward-McCann, New York, 1964.

Stevenson, Adlai Ewing. *The Alliance for Progress—A Road Map to New Achievements*, US Department of State, Washington, 1961.

THE ECONOMIC COMMISSION FOR LATIN AMERICA

PETER CALVO

The Foundation of ECLA

The idea of an Economic Commission for Latin America was originally put forward on 1 August 1947 by Hernán Santa Cruz, the prominent Chilean representative to the United Nations Economic and Social Council (ECOSOC). The proposal was at first cold-shouldered by the Western powers who, throughout the ECOSOC debates on the subject, maintained an attitude of negative reserve. However, Santa Cruz, largely through his own personal diplomacy, managed to secure Asian support for the establishment of ECLA in return for Latin American support for an Economic Commission for Asia and the Far East.

The Latin Americans argued that they had a different set of problems with a different degree of urgency from those of the war-devastated countries of Europe or Asia whose main problem was that of immediate organisation of reconstruction programmes through their regional economic commissions. The Latin American feeling was that they were indirectly but severely affected by the economic consequences of the war and that only concerted action organised on a regional basis could have tackled their difficulties. However, the real intention was to use ECLA as a research institute for the study of development problems, and the Latin American insistence on problems arising out of the war was largely a cover to justify an economic commission for Latin America.

The opposition of the United States was motivated by several factors. First, being the most economically powerful nation the United States looked upon regional economic arrangements with suspicion, regarding them as potentially prejudicial to free movement of products, i.e. American products. Furthermore, the United States, considering Latin America as its own sphere of influence, suspected the creation of a UN body exclusively concerned with that region. In American eyes, the Pan-American Union (PAU) constituted the only proper organisation through which Latin American problems could be solved. However, the Inter-American Economic and Social Council passed a resolution in January 1948 supporting the creation of an economic commission for Latin America and this removed the US objection that there might be a sizeable Latin American opposition that could come to its own in the more imposing atmosphere of the PAU.

The Soviet Union also opposed the Chilean proposal although for different reasons. This opposition was motivated by fear that the Commission would be used as a tool of further US expansion in Latin America, especially in view of the fact that the chances of the Soviet Union's inclusion in the membership of the Commission were very slight. Unlike the case of the other two commissions, the Soviet Union would have no voice in influencing the activities of the new commission. In fact when in the final debate and under great pressure from Latin American and Asian countries the Soviet Union did agree to the establishment of ECLA, its delegate hopelessly insisted on Soviet membership in the new body 'on the same grounds' as those governing US membership.

At last ECLA was established in February 1948 by ECOSOC's Resolution 106 (VI) by thirteen votes to none with four abstaining, Canada's vote being one of them. The membership of the Commission included the twenty Latin American countries (Mexico, Guatemala, El Salvador, Honduras, Cuba, Nicaragua, Costa Rica, Panama, Haiti, Dominican Republic, Ecuador, Colombia, Venezuela, Peru, Brazil, Chile, Bolivia, Paraguay, Uruguay, Argentina), the United States and the three European countries with colonial responsibility in the area—France, the Netherlands, and Britain; Canada decided to join in 1962. In the same year and with the coming of independence Jamaica and Trinidad and Tobago became members of the UN and automatically acquired full membership of ECLA. Newly independent Guyana joined the United Nations in September of that year. British Honduras is an associate member. It is significant to note that ECLA and its sister Commissions in Europe and Asia were created as an experiment. It was by no means certain that they would necessarily become permanent organs of the UN. Their permanent status was only confirmed by ECOSOC in 1951, after a detailed appraisal of all three Commissions. In theory however ECLA's existence could be terminated at any time by ECOSOC.

From the beginning there were a number of factors at work which provided a favourable atmosphere for ECLA. First, the lack of interest in turning ECLA into an instrument of a recovery programme created a valuable sense of independence which proved of great significance for the pioneering work of the Commission. In addition, there were two more decisive factors in favour of ECLA: that in the context of the PAU Latin America had developed habits of co-operation through international institutions; secondly, that the peace-keeping machinery of the inter-American system to which all inter-state disputes could be submitted left ECLA out of such possible conflicts, enabling it to devote all its attention to problems of economic development. Finally, ECLA from the start was asked 'to initiate measures', that is, to take independent action, for economic co-operation and development in the region. In the case of the earlier Commissions, there was no mention of such an initiative in their terms of reference. They were specifically set up to deal with the reconstruction problems of war-devastated areas; it was only later that their scope of activity was extended to include the function of 'initiation of measures' for economic development.

ECLA in Practice

The broad outline of ECLA's economic thought was laid out in 1949 by Dr Raúl Prebisch, later Executive Secretary of ECLA[1], in a brochure

[1] The Executive Secretaries of ECLA have been Gustavo Martínez Cabañas of Mexico (1948–50), Raúl Prebisch of Argentina (1950–63), José Antonio Mayobre of Venezuela (1963–6) and Carlos Quintana of Mexico (from 1967).

The Economic Development of Latin America and its Principal Problems (UN, 1950). This amounted to a powerful criticism of the international market economy and advocacy of the extension of the principles of welfare state to international economic relations. The central thesis of this ECLA manifesto was the existence of the 'asymmetry' in international economic relations which was not accounted for by the traditional international trade theory. The overall pattern of international economic relations was predominantly one of trade between a few industrially developed countries and the rest of the world producing mainly food and raw materials for the great industrial centres. The justification for this system of economic relations was based on the traditional notion of international trade theory that as a consequence of the international division of labour all countries would benefit equally from trade and that the advantages of technical progress anywhere would be shared everywhere by all participants in the world economy.

In Latin America, however, Prebisch maintained, the consequences of international trade led to a totally different economic landscape than the one required by the traditional theory. The benefits of technical progress were not shared equally by the centre and the periphery. The Prebisch thesis demonstrated that the most important dynamic element in the international economy has been the systematic displacement of industry and trade of the periphery mainly due to the effect of technical progress and capital accumulation. In these circumstances industrialisation is the only means of fulfilling the social objective of raising the standard of living. From this conclusion flowed a whole series of policy recommendations such as trade protection, import controls, manipulation of the balance of payments, the speeding up of the process of import substitution, the creation of larger economic units, the need for foreign capital and the necessity for long-range planning.

Thus, to the question where lies the responsibility for the Latin American lag, in Latin America or in the exploiting outside world, ECLA's answer clearly pointed at the biased nature of international trade mechanism which benefited the strong and penalised the weak. To the question how can Latin America make progress, by imitating others or by fashioning her way, ECLA's formula consisted of both elements; imitation in terms of objectives and required technology for their achievement but adaptation and organisation of these processes in the light of the Latin American experience.

Although Prebisch's brochure was primarily concerned with Latin America, its general propositions have acquired universal acceptance in under-developed countries. The influence of the 'Prebisch thesis' in the reshaping of international economic relations was evident in the *Report of the UN Conference on Trade and Development* (Geneva, 1964). The report amounted practically to an elaboration of Prebisch's original ideas in the early days of ECLA's existence. The unanimous support of the Conference showed the extent to which these ideas have become institutionalised. Also the fact that Dr Prebisch was made a member of President Kennedy's economic brains trust, 'the nine wise men', had a symbolic significance. It directly foreshadowed some policy changes in the direction of quickening the pace of Latin American economic and social development by means of increased foreign aid, one of ECLA's most important policy recommendations; the tangible outcome of this was the opening of the Inter-American Development Bank (IDB) in 1960 and the launching of the Alliance for Progress at Punta del Este in 1961.

PLANNING

Having set a mood of militancy and defined the economic problems of the region in broad terms, it now became necessary for ECLA to demonstrate in practice the advantages and feasibility of overall planning in individual Latin American countries. ECLA's basic principles of 'global programming' were expounded in a pamphlet *An Introduction to the Technique of Programming* (UN, 1953).

The technique is concerned with drawing up long-term economic development plans on the basis of a close analysis of empirical data available. The problem involved here consists in determining the possible targets of development in a given economy. This can be resolved only by a prior review of past events and present possibilities. In this process the way in which a country has evolved in latter years and the dynamic factors which have played a part in its growth have to be examined. The technique, in other words, starts out by determining a capital–output ratio. On this basis, ECLA maintained, it should be possible to assess the economy's growth potentialities and the degree of effort required to attain various rates of growth. The next step is to establish projects for individual sectors of the economy with more detailed estimates of capital required by each, so that the general projections of investment can be subsequently amended. The process is then one of passing from the general to the particular, only to return once more to the aggregate projections, introducing necessary adjustments there.

ECLA has applied its techniques of programming to a number of countries: Ecuador (1952), Brazil (1955), Colombia (1957), Argentina (1958), Peru (1959), El Salvador (1959), Honduras (1960) and Nicaragua (1965). In 1959 ECLA established its advisory groups programme to assist Latin American governments in the preparation of overall development programmes; advisory groups have been provided for Colombia, Cuba and Bolivia as well as small nuclei for Chile and Venezuela. In 1961 ECLA decided to consolidate its training and advisory activities through the establishment of a Latin American Institute for Economic and Social Planning to be financed by the UN Special Fund and the IDB.

However, the serious question which arises in relation to ECLA's planning techniques is to what extent would it be possible in practice to maintain a regular and systematic growth year by year, even assuming full co-operation on the part of the authorities responsible for the programme? ECLA's answer to this is that there must be elements of flexibility in each programme which will keep pace with the constantly changing circumstances without losing sight of the fundamental objectives. But it does not show how the flexibility can be achieved in practice; nor has there been any study of the way in which such 'flexibility' is likely to affect ECLA's conclusions as to the necessary rate of economic growth for the region. Further, the technique is far too dependent on the use of capital–output ratios which are theoretically difficult to interpret and practically hard to measure.

Closely related to these problems is that of structural maladjustment in Latin American economic and social systems: land tenure arrangements, fiscal systems, institutional rigidities, patterns of government expenditure, the structure of political power and popular participation, the organisation of pressure groups and their effectiveness; all these are structural components of the development process. In this context, the problem of inflation and its relation to growth have been brought up for discussion. The various views held on this subject were polarised some years ago at the height of the great debate into two schools of thought: the 'structuralists' and the 'monetarists'. The structuralist school, whose theories were developed in various ECLA studies, states that inflation is the expression of fundamental maladjustment in the economic structure and that a purely anti-inflationary policy would only paralyse growth. The monetarists (especially the IMF) argue that inflation must be stopped before development can take place, and that inflation must be controlled by monetary restrictions. This view ignores the fact that an effective stabilisation policy can be formulated only within a long-term development programme designed to achieve structural changes which are needed. However, indiscriminate policies of financial restraint, as recommended by the IMF, would seriously impair economic growth. The emergence of structuralist theories has not only made an original contribution to the field of economic growth, but is also the first indigenous school of economics in an underdeveloped region.

Economic Integration

The drive for economic integration was already implied in Raúl Prebisch's brochure in 1950. In June 1951 ECLA passed a resolution asking its secretariat to undertake a number of studies and determine possibilities of achieving full economic integration in Central America. ECLA also set up a Central American Economic Committee composed of the ministers of economy of the Central American countries.

Later ECLA recommended two agreements, the Multilateral Treaty on Free Trade and Central American Integration, and the Agreement on the Regime for Central American Integration Industries, which were signed in June 1958. Then in April 1960 the ECLA secretariat prepared a draft for a Central American agreement on 'accelerated economic integration' which eventually led to the signing, in December 1960, of the General Treaty of Central American Economic Integration. The Treaty stipulated a five-year limit for the creation of a common market.

On the broader Latin American plane, ECLA began in 1948 by considering the possibility of a payments union for the region and requested a report on the subject from the IMF. The IMF opposed the idea mainly on the grounds that intra-Latin American trade formed only a tiny segment of Latin American trade, amounting to no more than one-tenth of the total, and that it would not be worthwhile setting up an elaborate scheme to deal with such a small proportion; this argument ignored the fundamental point that the new arrangement was not needed to finance trade that already existed but to support a much larger increase which ECLA was trying to bring about. In spite of this the ECLA secretariat continued its research on multilateral solutions between Latin American countries and on intra-regional trade and payments; in 1955 it set up a Trade Committee to find formulae for co-operation in these fields.

At this stage the establishment of the European Common Market began to exert a powerful influence in Latin America both as an example and because of its possible adverse effects on Latin American exports of their raw materials; the Trade Committee set up a group of experts in 1958 to study the possibility of Latin American regional markets. Meanwhile during the post-war period, a system of bilateral payments was developed which linked together the countries of South America. Argentina's attempts at economic integration of the southern-zone countries of Latin America were, however, frustrated mainly because of mistrust of Perón's political motives by neighbouring countries; nor was the Quito agreement of 1948 for a customs union among Colombia, Ecuador, Panama and Venezuela ever ratified. Political antagonism and economic nationalism proved too powerful to allow the realisation of economic integration goals. Now, because of the approaching termination of bilateral payments agreements, the four southern-zone countries, Argentina, Brazil, Chile and Uruguay, were anxious to reach a multilateral arrangement which would also liberalise their reciprocal trade and help to settle balances arising out of monetary agreements. ECLA, on the other hand, set out to prepare a blueprint for the economic integration of the region within the context of a common market which was a far more radical posture than the southern-zone intention to merely liberalise trade. Hence the incompatibility of the two positions.

In the meantime the southern countries met in 1958 and decided on a free trade area which would also have the tactical advantage of solving their urgent payments problems. At the ECLA meeting of May 1959 at Panama City ECLA ignored the report of the southern-zone countries and in fact adopted a resolution which endorsed the report of its own working group for a common market. But it soon became clear that the only possible agreement would be on the lines of a free trade area. There is evidence of some waning of ECLA influence in the subsequent meetings of the southern-zone countries. Finally, the four southern-zone countries together with Bolivia, Paraguay and Peru met in September 1959 to finalise the proposal for a free trade area and in February 1960, with the incorporation of Mexico, the Latin American Free Trade Association was created. The result in 1960 was a far less radical arrangement than the ECLA project but it at least was more in keeping with Latin American economic and political possibilities.

COOPERATION IN OTHER FIELDS

Apart from these broader operational activities, ECLA has completed a large number of studies, usually in conjunction with other international agencies, and convened an increasing number of working groups and seminars to deal with a wide range of special topics. It would be impossible here to summarise the multifarious activities of ECLA. A synoptic view of its work in these fields, however, may be useful in consideration of its future potentialities.

Traditionally, ECLA has given a great deal of attention to problems of industrial development. Its earlier studies on iron and steel industry led in 1959 to the establishment of the Latin American Iron and Steel Institute. Similar ECLA/FAO studies on pulp and paper industry resulted in the setting up, in 1955, of the ECLA/FAO/BTAO Pulp and Paper Advisory Group. Initial studies have been followed by further research and discussions on railway equipment, the chemical industry, machine tools and metal-transforming industries. ECLA/ILO studies on problems of productivity in 1962 and 1963 paved the way for an ECLA/Institute/IDB Joint Programme for the Integration of Industrial Development in 1964. Finally, two major ECLA studies on industrialisation in Latin America formed the basis of discussion at the Latin American Symposium on Industrial Development convened by ECLA and the UN Center for Industrial

Development in March 1966 as part of a series of regional meetings in preparation for an international conference in 1967.

ECLA has carried out extensive research on natural resources and energy problems in Latin America. An ECLA/BTAO/RTEB Electric Power Seminar was organised in 1961 and a number of water resources missions were undertaken with BTAO, WMO and WHO between 1958 and 1965. There have been many joint ECLA/FAO studies on agricultural aspects of economic development. Recently ECLA participated with FAO, IDB, OAS and the Inter-American Committee for Agricultural Sciences in the formation of the Inter-American Committee for Agricultural Development, which has conducted research on problems of land reform as well as agricultural extension services. In the field of transport ECLA has been active since 1951 when it began the study of the subject in the Central American countries. Since 1962 research on transport has been conducted jointly with OAS; a comprehensive study on maritime, railway and air transport problems in Latin America was published in 1965. This is a unique document as it contains the first analytical account of the subject on a region-wide basis.

After a late start ECLA has made substantial progress in the study of the social aspects of economic development including those arising in the process of adaptation of the Latin American societies to the new functions required by economic development. An outline of these problems was drawn up in 1955. Seminars, working groups and advisory services have been organised on such policy areas as community development, social services and, more recently, on housing, as well as co-operation in setting up research and training centres. Subjects of such meetings and seminars organised or co-sponsored by ECLA in recent years include financing of housing (1955 and 1957 with BSA and OAS), urbanisation problems (1959, with BSA, UNESCO, ILO and FAO), population census data (1959, with BSA and UNESCO), education and economic and social development (1962, with the UN Statistical Office, BSA, IASI and ECE), community development (1964, with BSA), children and youth in national development (1964, with UNICEF and the Institute). A second conference on education was co-sponsored by ECLA and UNESCO in June 1966, designed to bring together ministers of education and officials responsible for development planning. Demographic studies, too, occupy an important place in ECLA's activities, especially in view of the close co-operation with the Latin American Demographic Centre (CELADE). Population data is published regularly and ECLA encourages Latin American authorities to exchange views on population problems and provides them with some of the necessary background material. Also housing questions have been explored for many years in relation to the Central American Integration Programme; in 1964 research started on overall problems of housing policy in Latin America. This work was further developed during a course on housing planning given by ECLA, the Institute and BTAO in May-July 1966.

As a result of these activities there is now a clearer understanding of the magnitude and complexity of Latin America's social problems; they have also contributed to the formulation of techniques and methods of planning for the various social sectors. The task ahead lies in deeper studies of such broad questions as social structures of Latin America and relevance of 'popular participation' in the formulation and execution of policies and plans, 'regionalisation' of social programmes, and problems of communication between policy-makers, social scientists and the public.

An Assessment

Over the past eighteen years ECLA has played a vital role in the Latin American economy by providing descriptions of current economic events and pointing out the main areas to which economic development should be directed. By emphasising the nature of asymmetry in international economic relations it has given expression to feelings of discontent among intellectual circles in Latin America; and by showing the way to an economic renaissance of the region it has, to some extent, diverted national emotions to constructive channels.

ECLA's methodology is based on a priori reasoning; starting from general propositions which have become almost an ideology[1] ECLA's use of empirical data tends to be selective and used for the promotion of ECLA's global position. This method has its own advantages but it has also meant very little work in the way of detailed presentations of the basic framework of analysis underlying ECLA's work. That has been presented more by way of general criticism of 'traditional' economics than a coherent body of theory. Though the basic assumptions of orthodox economics have been attacked, little attempt has been made to develop a new body of consistent theory that will change the assumptions under attack.

Although ECLA's economic thought does not amount to a well-rounded body of ideas, it will probably serve as a core for a Latin American economic development theory. With its emphasis on the fundamental points that Latin America is unable to develop as long as it relies on foreign trade exclusively, that the vicious circle of poverty cannot be broken in a hurry by forced saving and domestic capital accumulation alone, that industrialisation is the only means to a much higher standard of living, and that the periphery does not benefit from the classical notion of international division of labour, ECLA has largely diagnosed the economic disease of Latin America. It has also provided part of the cure, i.e. planning, a larger import of foreign capital and economic integration. But ECLA's economic thesis, if it is to provide an all-round theory of development, needs further broadening to include even a larger number of cultural, sociological and political elements such as the political influence of land-owning classes and the army, persistence of anti-work attitudes, the reforming potentialities of 'populism' following examples of Perón and Castro, and other socio-economic factors. It is within a broad and inclusive framework of this kind that it may be possible to find a solution to the most important problem facing Latin America in the 1960s: the failure of industrialisation to lead to significant structural change in society as a whole.

[1] See bibliography: Hirschman and Massad.

BIBLIOGRAPHY

Dell, Sidney. *A Latin American Common Market?*, Oxford Univ. Press, London and New York, 1966.

Hirschman, Albert O. 'Ideologies of Economic Development in Latin America', *Latin American Issues: Essays and Comments*, ed. Albert O. Hirschman, Twentieth Century Fund, New York, 1961.

Lincoln, Gordon. 'Economic Regionalism Reconsidered', *World Politics*, XIII, 2, Princeton, NJ, 1961.

Massad, Carlos. 'Economic Research in Latin America', *Social Science Research on Latin America*, ed. Charles Wagley, Colombia Univ. Press, New York, 1964.

Mikesell, Raymond F. 'The Movement Toward Regional Trading Groups in Latin America', *Latin American Issues: Essays and Comments*, ed. Albert O. Hirschman, Twentieth Century Fund, New York, 1961.

Seers, Dudley. 'A Theory of Inflation and Growth in Underdeveloped Economies Based on the Experience of Latin America', *Oxford Economic Papers; 14*, No. 2, Oxford Univ. Press, London and New York, 1962.

Urquidi, Victor L. *Free Trade and Economic Integration in Latin America*, Univ. of California Press, Berkeley, Calif., 1962. 'The Common Market as a Tool of Economic Development', *Latin American Issues: Essays and Comments*, ed. Albert O. Hirschman, Twentieth Century Fund, New York, 1961.

ECLA. *Theoretical and Practical Problems of Economic Growth* (UN, E/CN 12/221), New York, 1951. *The Influence of the Common Market on the Economic Development of Latin America* (UN, E/CN 12/C.1/13), New York, 1959. *Consultations on Trade Policy* (report of the third series of meetings between Colombia, Ecuador and Venezuela (UN, E/CN 12/555), New York, 1961. *International Co-operation in a Latin American Development Policy*, UN, New York, 1954. *Economic Survey of Latin America 1948–1966*, UN, New York, 1966. *Economic Bulletin for Latin America 1956–1965*, UN, New York, 1965.

CASE STUDIES

THE INDUSTRIALISATION OF MEXICO

EDWARD J. WYGARD

Economic take-off has perhaps been achieved in Mexico. If the country can sustain its economy on this basis and succeed in narrowing or bridging the gap which separates the poor countries from the rich, then it will be a living proof that deliberately accelerated development is possible and may become a pattern for other poor countries to follow. To an observer in 1967 it certainly looked as though the Mexican experiment might succeed; and because Mexican policy has strongly stressed industrialisation (an emphasis it shares with the policies advocated by the United Nations Economic Commission for Latin America), it is now widely accepted in other countries in the region that industrial development is an essential part of the process of accelerated economic growth. Certainly Mexico's performance has been spectacular.

Since 1940, GNP has averaged an annual increase of 6·3 per cent, and has consistently exceeded the increase in population, estimated at just over 3 per cent. In 1964 real income per head reached $460 and GNP climbed an unprecedented 10 per cent over the previous year. Manufacturing industry accounted for over 25 per cent of GNP. The broad industrial sector—including in addition to manufacturing: mining, the petroleum industry, power-generation and the construction industry—accounted for 35 per cent of GNP (see Table 1), with agriculture dropping to under 18 per cent (yet it was probably the growth of agricultural exports, notably

TABLE I

COMPOSITION OF GNP OF MEXICO (*per cent*)

Sector	1940	1945	1950	1955	1960	1904
Agriculture	24·2	19·8	22·5	22·0	18·8	17·7
Broad industrial sector	31·3	31·0	30·2	30·7	33·1	35·5
Mining	5·9	4·2	3·0	2·6	2·2	1·8
Petroleum	3·0	2·5	2·7	2·8	3·2	3·3
Manufactures	17·9	18·8	20·5	21·0	23·0	25·1
Construction	3·6	4·7	3·1	3·2	3·5	3·8
Electric power	0·9	0·8	0·9	1·1	1·2	1·5
Transport	4·5	4·6	4·8	5·2	4·9	4·3
Commerce	24·0	25·6	26·2	25·7	25·8	26·2
Government	3·1	3·3	3·2	2·9	2·7	2·8
Other activities	13·0	13·7	13·1	13·5	14·7	13·5
Total	100·0	100·0	100·0	100·0	100·0	100·0

Source: *Bank of Mexico*

cotton, coffee and sugar, that prevented an even greater gain for the broad industrial sector). Within the sector, manufacturing grew in the period 1940–64 at an annual rate of 7·7 per cent, exceeded only by power generation which grew at 7·9 per cent; these were the highest increases in any sector of the Mexican economy. In 1964 the Mexican power system produced 16,000 million kwh; a million cars, lorries and buses covered 30,000 miles of roads; the steel mills turned out 2·3 million tons of billet; the chemical industry produced 440,000 tons of su'phuric acid and 95,000 tons of caustic soda. The Mexicans listened to 6 million radios and watched 1 million television sets. Mexico City, capital of a nation of 44 million people, is a metropolis of 6 million inhabitants and at least two other cities, Guadalajara and Monterrey, are approaching or have passed the million mark.

THE GROWTH OF INDUSTRY

The period between 1920 and 1940 marks the creation of the legal and institutional instruments which laid the groundwork for the economic development of the country. The Central Bank, the government development bank, Nacional Financiera, and the Federal Electricity Commission were created before 1940 and have since become important factors in industrial development. Land reform, an article of faith in the constitution, was initiated and while its immediate economic impact may be in doubt, its social effects in terms of national self-confidence and mobility, and its consequences in terms of breaking the political power of the large landowners (many of whom moved to the towns and became industrial entrepreneurs), can now be clearly appreciated. In the longer run, it led to a somewhat better distribution of income and, because of strong government commitment, to badly needed investments in roads and irrigation, which in turn increased both agricultural production and the market for manufactured goods. It was also during this period that the expropriation of the petroleum industry took place, having as its most important immediate effect a strengthening of national self-confidence; Mexico has not only managed to run the industry but has more than quadrupled refinery capacity. Moreover, compensation to the expropriated firms has been punctually and fully paid. Perhaps more important than any other single element during this period of institutional development was the political stability which continues to the present day and which is a rare thing in Latin America.

In 1940, clearly as a result of the outbreak of the second world war, industrial production began to acquire momentum. Imported goods became scarce and for the first time in its history, Mexican industry found itself working at full capacity. Between 1940 and 1945, industrial production grew at a rate of 9·4 per cent a year. Exports of raw materials brought prosperity to many sectors of the economy and some manufactured products were even exported. By the end of the war existing equipment was worn out, and as new equipment became available large sectors of industry began to replace their plant. In 1947 industrial investment was almost five times that of 1937 and represented 30 per cent of total investment in the country. Nevertheless, by the time the new plant came into operation, competition from more efficient producers abroad reappeared; external markets no longer bought Mexican industrial products and the rate of industrial production dropped to 2·3 per cent a year. Two successive devaluations (which stimulated exports and internal demand) and the strengthening of the protective tariff barrier gave a new impetus to industry and during 1950 a record growth of 14 per cent was achieved. This was also a time of increased public investment, roads, electrification and education.

The decade 1950–60 has been called the period of 'extensive industrialisation' because of the establishment of a large number of plants in new fields of industrial activity—factories making household appliances, simple machinery such as pumps and compressors, fabricated metal products, wireless and television sets, etc. In fact, a well diversified consumer durables industry made its appearance. Plants making a variety of chemicals from detergents to fertilisers sprang up around the major towns. This multiplication of industries coincided with and may have been caused by a revolution in distribution: the profusion of small grocers' shops began to yield to supermarkets; the few old-fashioned department stores, reminiscent of the Paris Printemps of the thirties, gave way to modern stores and methods; the colourful but unhygienic public markets were replaced (at least in the bigger towns) by clean modern buildings; and towards the end of the decade, the giant 'discount store' and the suburban shopping centre began to attract crowds of middle-class shoppers.

Since 1960 the emphasis has been on 'integration', by which is meant the local manufacture of the greatest possible amount of parts and components, which were before imported for assembly. The automobile industry, the chief though by no means the only target of 'integration', had achieved almost 70-per-cent integration by 1966. It is not obvious, however, that the benefits of integration in terms of employment and use of other resources outweigh the sacrifice made by the community in paying higher prices for highly protected products. Anyone visiting Mexico City, Monterrey, Guadalajara, Puebla or any one of a dozen smaller industrial centres can confirm for himself the picture of accelerated industrialisation outlined above. But a journey between these centres through the countryside and especially off the main road will reveal that poverty and underdevelopment still prevail.

As in other developing countries, Mexican manufacturing industry grew mostly by substitution of imports behind powerful protective barriers. At first, products were manufactured which required simple technology and little capital; this meant chiefly non-durable consumer goods such as food, textiles and beverages. With more experience and growing markets increasingly complex technologies were introduced, to substitute consumer durables such as domestic appliances and refrigerators, and certain intermediate products such as steel, cement and basic chemicals. Finally, with markets and capital (both national and international) available, Mexican industry ventured into the field of capital goods such as agricultural machinery, cranes, diesel engines, certain kinds of chemical plant, etc., and also into more sophisticated chemicals.

By the mid-sixties the substitution of consumer goods had reached its limit—some 90 per cent of consumption. In capital goods a substitution of perhaps 60 per cent and in some intermediate goods of some 40 per cent has been achieved and cannot go much further: on the one hand, many of the more complicated capital and intermediate goods need scales of production far in excess of the capacity of the Mexican market; on the other, it is in the nature of industrialisation that it creates a demand for ever more complex plant and new raw materials, some of which have to be imported. In any case, substitution may be a necessary stage in industrial development, but it is certainly not the high road to an affluent society.

TABLE 2

THE BROAD INDUSTRIAL SECTOR IN MEXICO (1960)

	Total	Extractive and manufacturing industry (private)[2]	Extractive and manufacturing industry, except petroleum (government controlled)	Construction industry (private)	Electric power industry (public)[3]	Petroleum industry (public)
Number of establishments[1]	102,578	101,212	56	888	333	89
Value of production[1]	5,310	4,270	198	260	162	444
Invested capital[1]	6,770	3,970	430	310	894	1,190
Fixed capital[1]	4,101	2,000	250	104	770	981
Working capital[1]	2,608	1,970	176	204	124	207
Total employees	1,174,367	971,609	31,673	90,924	34,070	46,091

[1] US$ million.
[2] 'Extractive industry' consists of fishing and mining.
[3] By 1966 almost all power generation was in public hands.

Source: *1960 Industrial Census*, Mexico

TABLE 3

MANUFACTURING INDUSTRY IN MEXICO[1] (1960)

	Number of establishments	Total labour force[2]	Total investment[3]	Value of production[3]	Wages and salaries[3]	Raw material consumed[3]	Electric power consumed (M KWH)	Fuel and lubricants consumed[3]
Manufacturing industry	100,335	791,440	3,750	3,930	611	2,100	4,227,886	86
Up to five employees	88,774	73,913	135	234	26	111	177,672	8
Six or more employees	11,561	717,837	3,615	3,700	585	1,986	4,050,214	78

[1] Excluding government enterprises; including artisan workshops.
[2] Excluding non-remunerated personnel.
[3] US$ million.

Source: *Seventh Industrial Census*, Ministry of Industry and Commerce, Mexico, 1961

The Structure of Industry

Incidence of state-controlled industry

Industry in Mexico is predominantly private. Of over 100,000 enterprises, less than 500 are government-owned or -controlled. These account for only 14 per cent of production and employ about 10 per cent of the total industrial working force.

On the other hand, the public industrial sector, which includes principally the petroleum and electrical industries, accounts for 36 per cent of industrial investment (see Table 2). Thus the exploration, production, refining and distribution of petroleum products are a state monopoly. In addition, Petróleos Mexicanos (PEMEX), the government agency in charge of the oil industry, reserves the right to manufacture 'basic' petroleum chemicals, leaving intermediate and final chemical products to private industry. These basic petrochemicals are defined, somewhat loosely, as compounds whose immediate raw material is a petroleum product. In fact, PEMEX produces such chemicals as ammonia, ethylene and benzene, but also has exclusive rights to the manufacture of styrene and polyethylene, which might be considered intermediate or final products. In practice, negotiations with PEMEX determine in each case the dividing line between basic and non-basic petrochemicals.

Since 1960, the government has acquired by purchase most of the private electric power enterprises in the country. All production is coordinated by the Federal Electricity Commission. At the end of 1964, installed capacity was over 5 million kw, a 70-per-cent increase over 1960.

Public investment in the manufacturing industry, mostly controlled through Nacional Financiera (see above), is concentrated in a few enterprises. These include the largest iron and steel complex in the country, the manufacture of railway equipment, two large paper mills, a plant manufacturing electrical equipment, etc. In the total picture, however, public investment in manufacturing is hardly significant.

Geographical concentration of industry

Over half industrial output is produced in the area surrounding the capital (which includes the Federal District and the State of Mexico) where one-fifth of the country's population lives. Another 20 per cent of output is produced in three smaller industrial areas concentrated around the cities of Veracruz, Monterrey and Guadalajara.

This centralisation of industry brings with it great differences in standards of living between the few industrial and the many agricultural areas. Considerable efforts are being made by the government to decentralise industry. While these efforts cannot be said to have been highly successful, because industries tend to cluster around each other and prefer to be close to financial and government services, there has been a clearly discernible movement out of the Federal District to nearby towns such as Puebla, Toluca and Querétaro. But the fact remains that the high concentration of industrial activities is a serious problem for Mexico. With increased in-dustrial development, the inequalities in income between industrial and agricultural areas will increase dramatically unless drastic steps are taken to decentralise industry through regional planning and incentives.

Size of enterprise

If we consider the number of establishments, Mexican industry consists preponderantly of artisan workshops employing five or less workers. Almost

90 per cent of all establishments fall into this class (see Tables 3 and 4); these are virtually those enterprises whose invested capital is below half a million pesos, or £14,000. It is the remaining 10 per cent of establishments that constitutes the manufacturing industry proper, giving employment to 90 per cent of the industrial labour force and producing 95 per cent of industrial output.

TABLE 4

SIZE DISTRIBUTION OF MANUFACTURING INDUSTRY IN MEXICO

Capital investment[1]	No. of establishments	No. of workers employed	No. of establishments
Up to 0·5	95,000	1–5	89,000
0·5–20	5,500	6–100	10,500
20 –100	400	101–500	1,300
Over 100	53	Over 500	200
Total	101,000	790,000	101,000

[1] 1 million pesos = £28,500 sterling.

Source: *Seventh Industrial Census* Mexico, 1961

There is also an important segment of medium-sized enterprises (i.e. with an invested capital of up to 5 million pesos or £140,000) inside the manufacturing sector proper, which accounts for over half of the total value of manufacture and where much of the future growth of industry may occur. This group suffers chronically from deficient industrial management and lack of adequate financing, and is therefore unable to use its existing capacity effectively; this despite the fact that the government, through Nacional Financiera, provides special credit facilities for small and medium-sized industries. Nevertheless, if properly assisted, medium-sized industry could represent an important potential for a rapid increase in industrial production. It has been estimated that a 30-per-cent increase could be achieved in this segment over two to three years, by suitable financing and technical assistance, almost without additional investment.

Branches of industry

Mexican industry is extremely diversified (see Table 5). It is also open to new ideas. In almost all branches of industry, plants with up-to-date technology press ever more successfully upon the old-fashioned, protection-minded manufacturer.

It is significant that the most dynamic branches of industry are those with the fastest changing and most complex technologies. Between 1950 and 1960 manufacture of machinery and transport equipment (groups 17 to 19 in Table 5) showed a growth rate of over 16 per cent a year; the chemical industry and the basic metal industry grew by 14 per cent a year. The growth in the electrical appliance industry has been remarkable. Between 1963 and 1964 alone the output of TV sets grew by 63 per cent, radio sets by 42 per cent, refrigerators by 39 per cent, and washing machines (in a country where one can still get a good maid for £15 a month) by 18 per cent.

The manufacture of motor cars and lorries reached 95,000 units in 1964, a 28-per-cent increase over 1963 with, significantly, only a 6-per-cent increase

TABLE 5

BRANCHES OF MANUFACTURING INDUSTRY IN MEXICO (1960)[1]

		Number of establish- ments	Total personnel employed[2]	Total investment[3]	Value of production[3]
1.	Food manufacturing industries, except beverage industries	37,661	138,465	674	878
2.	Beverage industries	2,272	44,495	288	299
3.	Tobacco manufacture	74	6,850	67	72
4.	Textiles manufacture	2,932	137,289	545	470
5.	Manufacture of footwear, other wearing apparel and made-up textile goods	14,601	49,224	82·5	120
6.	Manufacture of wood and cork, except furniture	4,137	19,731	53·2	48·4
7.	Manufacture of furniture and fixtures	2,745	18,976	42	49·5
8.	Manufacture of paper and paper products	373	21,187	172	156
9.	Printing, publishing and allied industries	2,681	30,630	95·4	113
10.	Manufacture of leather and leather-and-fur products, except footwear and other wearing apparel	1,219	6,247	16·3	29·4
11.	Manufacture of rubber products	1,415	10,214	70·6	85
12.	Manufacture of chemicals and chemical products	1,991	72,061	436	491
13.	Manufacture of products of petroleum and coal	73	3,231	26·2	27·5
14.	Manufacture of non-metallic mineral products, except products of petroleum and coal	3,673	43,981	231	169
15.	Basic metal industries	142	31,537	374	286
16.	Manufacture of metal products, except machinery and transport equipment	5,685	47,477	151	159
17.	Manufacture of machinery, except electrical machinery	2,191	12,731	50	45·2
18.	Manufacture of electrical machinery, apparatus, appliances and supplies	4,521	32,994	138	163
19.	Manufacture of transport equipment	7,901	32,575	123	202
20.	Miscellaneous manufacturing industries	3,976	21,504	102	63
	Total	100,263	781,399	3,736·9	3,925·6

[1] Including artisan workshops.
[2] Excluding non-remunerated personnel.
[3] US$ million.

Source: *Seventh Industrial Census*, Mexico, 1961

TABLE 6

OUTPUT OF MAJOR INDUSTRIAL PRODUCTS IN MEXICO (1964)

BASIC METALS[1]		GLASS	
Pig iron	926,263	Containers[3]	881,413
Steel billet	2,326,496	Ampoules[3]	186,105
Electrolytic copper	34,867	Flat glass[5]	11,462
CHEMICALS[1]		CEMENT[1]	
Sulphuric acid	439,728	Grey cement	4,339,000
Caustic soda	94,886		
Anhydrous ammonia	175,950	VEHICLES[3]	
Artificial fibres	33,009	Cars	62,757
Coal tar derivatives	35,659	Lorries and buses	32,322
Hydrogen peroxide	2,883		
Ethyl alcohol	42,824	FOOD AND DRINK	
FERTILISERS[1]		Beer[4]	965,702
Nitrogen (N)	114,209	Sugar[1]	1,789,000
Phosphate (P_2O_5)	42,567		
		CONSUMER DURABLES[3]	
RUBBER[2]		Wireless sets	956,428
Tyres	1,797	TV sets	188,639
Inner tubes	1,130	Refrigerators	96,054
		Washing machines	48,607
PULP AND PAPER[1]		Kitchen ranges	235,461
Pulp	327,531	Electric irons	785,926
Paper and carton	557,664	Liquefiers	160,000

[1] Metric tons.
[2] Thousands of units.
[3] Units.
[4] Thousands of litres.
[5] Square metres.

Source: Nacional Financiera, *Annual Report*, Mexico, 1964

in imported parts. The iron and steel industry now fully supplies the country's needs with the exception of special steels. Production of steel ingot rose from 600,000 tons in 1954 to 2·3 million tons in 1964. Steel-making capacity is expected to reach 2·9 million tons by 1967. The chemical industry has been growing not only by expanding production of existing chemicals but also by continuing additions of plants to manufacture new chemical intermediates whose production becomes economically feasible as industry grows. During recent years the greatest advances, however, have been made in ammonia, nitrogen fertilisers, ethyl alcohol and artificial fibres (which include rayon, acetate, nylon and polyester). The production of sulphuric acid, which amounted to 440,000 tons in 1964, has been expanding continuously, also reflecting increased use of fertilisers.

The relative advancement of Mexican industry can be measured roughly by the share of industrial production contributed by the traditional industries —food (including beverages and tobacco), textiles and apparel. The less developed the industry of a country, the higher the participation of these traditional industries. In Mexico the food, textile and apparel industries accounted for 62 per cent of industrial production in 1950; this share dropped to 48 per cent in 1960. By comparison, in the less developed countries of Latin America the proportion represented by the traditional industries is

593

75 per cent, while in the United States in 1962 it was 17 per cent. In Mexico the metal and chemical industries are gaining in importance against the traditional activities; their combined share increased from 20 per cent of total industrial production in 1950 to 35 per cent in 1960.

MAINSPRINGS OF DEVELOPMENT

Promotion of industry

Successive Mexican governments have made industrial development a keystone of their policies. Mexico has an industrial incentive law which grants tax exemptions to new and 'necessary' industries, graduated according to the importance of the activity. Necessary industries are defined as those whose products are already made in the country but whose volume of production or quality is inadequate for the needs of the country. It is difficult to assess, even in retrospect, how effective this law has been in stimulating industrial investment. There is a suspicion that many of the investments would have been made even without the law's incentives and that its benefits were simply an additional premium given to industrial initiative.

Probably more effective in stimulating industrial investment has been the consistent policy of protecting local industry against foreign competition. This was done at first by imposing relatively high import duties; then increasingly by control of imports through import permits. After Diaz Ordaz became president in 1964, there began a salutary tendency to keep down prices of locally manufactured goods by maintaining protection at reasonable levels. The new general criterion is that the price of products should not exceed their price in the United States by more than 15 to 20 per cent.

The work of Nacional Financiera in promoting some of the large-scale industrial enterprises, and in providing financing especially tailored to the needs of industry, also contributed to the growth of industry. But the most powerful instrument of industrial promotion in Mexico was neither legal nor institutional: it was the deliberately pragmatic attitude of the authorities in granting benefits, giving assistance and attracting industrial investment. Such a flexible manner of promoting industry has many advantages and some dangers. In the early stages the system lent itself to many errors and abuses; in time the officials administering the industrial programme acquired greater competence, the unwritten but well known criteria governing official policy were clarified and the effectiveness of the programme increased.

Climate of investment

The deliberate promotion and stimulation of industrial development in Mexico, however intensive, cannot by itself explain the growth of the country's industry. Political stability has played its important part: Mexico is one of the few countries in Latin America (or for that matter in the whole 'third world') that can boast a thirty-year record of undisturbed continuity without dictatorial compulsion. The social mobility created by the revolution has also been an important factor. The Mexican revolution of 1910, the first great social upheaval of the present century, freed the country from the rigid neo-feudal structure which still prevails in many other Latin American countries. From the revolutionary chaos and suffering emerged a new society in ferment, able and willing to be moulded into new patterns propitious to development. A third important factor has been the government's monetary policy, which by 1966 had maintained the exchange rate stable for well over a decade and had kept annual inflation in an expanding economy to some 5 per cent. This stability was recognised in 1965 by the International Monetary Fund when it listed the Mexican peso among the 'hard' currencies.

Outside influences

In addition to the internal factors mentioned, the influence of Mexico's geographical situation on its economic development should be recognised. The closeness of the United States has had a dual effect: the impact of a lively economic and social interchange combined with the response to the challenge of a nearby industrial civilisation. The United States is Mexico's most important customer, and in turn Mexico is not only the largest Latin American buyer of United States products, but also receives the largest share of United States investment in Central and South America. There is a constant northward stream of Mexican businessmen, matched by a south-ward flow of United States businessmen travelling to Mexico. As the former learn about American industrial organisation, the latter begin to understand how to adapt it to Mexican conditions. For many years there have also been annual migrations of Mexican agricultural workers to American farms, although by the mid-sixties the pressure of organised labour in the United States had diminished this flow.

And then there is the bonanza of tourism which yearly flips the Mexican balance of trade from red into black. The tourists, who in 1964 left $240 million in Mexico, not only provide a vast market for products and services; they also demand high standards of quality of merchandise and service and they carry with them an economic and social 'demonstration effect'. The Mexicans' response to the challenge of an expansive industrial economy on their doorstep has been a Toynbeean one which runs the gamut from imitation through intransigence to open opposition—but almost always provides an incentive to change and development.

The list of factors creating a climate favourable to industrial development in Mexico could be extended further: the emergence of a consuming middle class; the increase, slight in relative terms but important in the aggregate, of agricultural income; the public investments in power-generation, roads and irrigation; the spectacular increase in educational levels (23 per cent of the 1966 budget was devoted to education, against 10 per cent for the armed forces); all these have played their part in bringing Mexico to the stage of economic take-off.

PROBLEMS AND SOLUTIONS

In the mid-sixties considerable difficulties face Mexico in its further industrial (and general economic) development. The chief of these is the narrowness of the market for manufactured products. No longer is it possible for a local manufacturer to take over a ready-made consumer goods market by sub-stituting imports. Everything worthwhile in the consumer field has been substituted. In the fields of intermediate and capital goods further substitution requires scales of production for which the Mexican market is too small. Furthermore, at the present level of income and with the present pattern of income distribution, the internal market for many products is saturated. As a result, most Mexican manufacturing plants work far below capacity.

It is true that there is a great purchasing potential, chiefly in the now underfed, underclothed and underhoused rural population, provided it can be made to produce more by better services, more roads, additional credit facilities, more education and so forth. A great deal can also be accomplished by better methods of distribution, both of agricultural products to the cities and of manufactured products to the countryside. It is estimated that of the 20 million *campesinos* only some 4 million buy manufactured goods. Thus the strengthening of the internal Mexican market is an essential and continuing task of the government.

One rarely mentioned aspect of the limitations of the internal market is the high price, especially in real terms, of locally manufactured products. Protected industries are rarely efficient; but as costs rise and profits shrink, there is a growing incentive to increase productivity. In a great variety of consumer products lower prices resulting from higher efficiency might encounter a greatly expanded demand.

Mexico's interest in the Latin American Free Trade Association, apart from its political meaning, stems from the need to find new markets for its manufactured products; but LAFTA markets have limitations similar to those of Mexico and while growth in this direction will occur, it is not likely to solve the immediate problem of Mexican industry. The only answer which might produce results in the short run is for Mexico to take the plunge into industrial maturity and start to export manufactured goods to the markets of industrialised countries. These countries are increasingly importing manufactured products which it is no longer economical for them to produce. There is no reason why Mexico, with a determined effort, should not become a supplier of such products, especially to the United States. A successful policy of stimulating export industries may have an ancillary but highly welcome result: the increased efficiency of industries which must compete in international markets may enable them to lower their domestic prices and expand their internal markets far beyond the mechanical projections based on increase of per capita product.

These are not mere speculations. In the mid-sixties ministerial speeches, seminars organised by industrial associations, government measures to stimulate exports, all point to a gathering climate of opinion which may soon result in action. The awareness that exports of manufactured goods show the greatest promise for industrial expansion is rapidly spreading among businessmen and government officials. Mexico may yet emerge, in the words of *The Economist*, as a new Japan on the American continent.

BIBLIOGRAPHY

Navarrete, R. Alfredo. 'El desarrollo industrial de México; situación y perspectivas', *El Trimestre Económico*, Fondo de Cultura Económica, Mexico, XXX (4), 120, October–December 1963.

Ortiz Mena, Raul; Urquidi, Victor L.; Waterston, Albert; Haralz, Jonas H. *El desarrollo económico de México y su capacidad para absorber capital del exterior*, Nacional Financiera, Mexico, 1953.

Vernon, Raymond. *The Dilemma of Mexico's Development*, Harvard Univ. Press, Cambridge, Mass., 1963.

Vernon, Raymond (ed.) *Public Policy and Private Enterprise in Mexico*, Harvard Univ. Press, 1964.

Banco Nacional de Comercio Exterior, Mexico. *Mexico, 1963, Facts, Figures, Trends*, 1963.

Bank of Mexico. Annual Reports.

Law School of Harvard University, Cambridge, Mass. *Tax Incentives for Industry in Mexico*, 1959.

Little, Arthur D., Inc. *Survey of the Institutional and Financial Requirements of Medium and Small Industry in Mexico*, Centro Industrial de Productividad, Mexico, 1963. *Opportunities and Developments in Mexican Industry*, Cambridge, Mass., 1965.

Nacional Financiera, Mexico. Annual Reports.

THE INDUSTRIALISATION OF ARGENTINA

JORGE KATZ and EZEQUIEL GALLO

ARGENTINE industrialisation is frequently associated with the name of General Perón and with the supply constraints imposed on the country by the second world war. This is, however, a misleading conception. In 1940 the manufacturing sector, which in 1900 had contributed only 14 per cent to GDP, had already increased its share to 28 per cent; in 1965 its share was 36 per cent. At the same time it is true that after the second world war, and particularly since the middle 1950s, growth has been especially evident in most consumer durables and in very many capital-intensive industries in which a modern and sophisticated technology was introduced, such as motor cars, petrochemicals, chemicals, metals, agricultural equipment, machinery and electrical equipment, cement and steel.

In spite of the fact that manufacturing has significantly increased its share of GDP and that many new industries have been started since the end of the war, Argentine industrialists have continued to be noticeably weak at an institutional and political level; they have failed to gather sufficient strength to influence the authorities to implement a sound all-round industrialisation policy, as distinct from simple tariff protection whose long-run benefits are far from clear.

THE BEGINNINGS OF MANUFACTURING INDUSTRY (1870–1930)

The appearance of manufacturing industry in Argentina is closely associated with the rapid economic expansion which took place during the years 1870–1914. The opportunity to import machinery and equipment as a result of heavy exports of agriculture and livestock products, the opening up of a network of railways which facilitated a rapid expansion of the domestic market, the rapid increase in manpower and capital as a result of European immigration and capital inflow were among the major factors which made possible the beginnings of industrialisation in Argentina (see Table 1).

TABLE I

POPULATION, RAILWAYS, AND MAJOR EXPORTS, 1890–1914

Years	Population (000)	Railways (000 km.)	Cereals	Exports of Wool (000 m. tons)	Meats
1890–4	3,612	12·7	1,038	139	27
1910–4	7,203	31·1	5,294	137	376

Source: G. Di Tella and M. Zimelman, *La etapas del desarrollo económico argentino*, EUDEBA, Buenos Aires, 1965, p. 25

Between 1900 and 1914 the manufacturing sector as a whole grew at an average rate of 5.2 per cent per annum, and sectors such as chemicals, metals, leather, textiles and foodstuffs exhibited annual rates of expansion above the overall average for the industrial sector. While the Second National Census reported the existence in 1895 of 22,204 industrial firms employing 175,000 men, the Third National Census taken in 1914 reported the existence of 48,779 firms and 410,000 industrial workers. Thus manufacturing employment grew during these years at a rate of about 4 per cent per annum, leaving room for an annual rate of growth of labour productivity of around 1·2 per cent.

In spite of the atmosphere of success and expansion which surrounded the early achievements of the industrial sector, Argentine industrialists stayed basically isolated from the institutional and political life of the country. Their social and political marginality largely explains the lack of correlation between the role of the industrial sector in the economic life of the country and its remarkably low ability to obtain from the authorities long-term policies favourable to its expansion. Perhaps the chief reasons for this divergence between the economic and the socio-political status of the entrepreneurial classes during the formative years of Argentine manufacturing are, firstly, that manufacturing industry came into being to a large extent intimately connected with and as an appendix to the agricultural and pastoral sector, and, secondly, that the country lacked a political structure capable of integrating the massive number of immigrants.

The Census of 1895 clearly indicates that the largest and most capital-intensive industries were those that processed raw materials from the agricultural and stock-breeding sectors. It has been shown[1] that in 1895 under 2,000 enterprises possessed total capital of more than 60 per cent of that possessed by over 22,000 enterprises; the first group, enjoying the benefits of scale and capital-intensive technology, had an average capital of about 100,000 pesos per enterprise, and the second, formed mostly by small, labour-intensive artisan workshops, averaged about 10,000 pesos per enterprise. The great majority of the plants processing domestic raw materials were in the hands of the native ruling classes whereas approximately 85 per cent of the remaining industrial entrepreneurs and about 65 per cent of the labourers employed were foreigners of recent immigration.

Dependent to a large extent on the traditional agricultural sector in its more efficient branches, and highly fragmented and in the hands of isolated, less efficient and institutionally marginal immigrants in the remaining sectors, Argentine industry was from the first politically and socially isolated. Furthermore, at a time of rapid socio-economic expansion—per capita GDP grew at an annual rate of around 2·5 per cent between 1900 and 1914, and social mobility was very high—Argentine industrialists found it difficult to challenge the free-trade ideology of the ruling classes, an ideology not specifically conducive to the growth of the manufacturing sector.

In the early 1920s and in the 1930s the political weakness of industrialists was shown by their incapacity to obtain from the government favourable policies regarding tariffs, taxes, bank credits, etc. The case of tariff duties after the first world war is representative. The efforts industrialists made to get from the government tariffs that would maintain the natural protection

[1] Roberto Cortes Conde, 'Problemas del crecimiento industrial en la Argentina (1870–1914)', *Desarrollo Económico*, April 1963.

they enjoyed during the war were a complete failure. Despite minor changes the position of industrialists has continued to be basically weak up to the present time. It is no longer a problem of protectionism, since two world wars and the great depression of the 1930s led to a considerable degree of protection. The way the recurrent balance of payments difficulties have been handled over the last decades—by repeated devaluation of the peso and by deflating the economy at short intervals (1956, 1959, 1962–3 and 1966)— once again reveals the continuing weak position of Argentine industrialists and the lack of a coherent ideology of industrialisation among the ruling classes.

Manufacturing Growth in the Post-War Period (1946–65)

Between 1946 and 1965 real manufacturing output in Argentina grew at an average annual rate of nearly 4 per cent. The rate of growth of output and the sources of manufacturing expansion underwent a considerable change during the 1950s. The twenty-year period can be divided into two remarkably different sub-periods, the first 1946–54 and the second 1955–65.

In 1952–3 important changes occurred in both domestic and international affairs which had long-term repercussions on the pattern and rate of expansion of Argentine industry. On the domestic side, there was a radical change in the government's foreign investment policy and a gradual change in labour policy. These policy changes brought about an increasing use of capital-intensive techniques of production which affected most industries in the late 1950s and early 1960s. Fast technical progress, hardly at all a determinant of growth during the previous years in which the country remained relatively isolated from the international sources of technical progress, became a basic factor of growth after 1955.

In 1953 the administration passed the Law 14222 with the specific intention of attracting foreign private capital into Argentina's industrial sector. This law represented a major policy decision which was not reversed by subsequent governments. The principle was henceforth held that foreign private capital and technology were necessary for Argentina's industrial growth, and for the first time in the country's history deliberate policies were designed in this belief, such as a more generous foreign investment law in 1957 (Law 14780) and a law of industrial promotion in 1958.

During the period 1948–53, as well as during the war, the flow of foreign private capital into Argentina had almost disappeared. Foreign capital had been rejected by the administration on political grounds, and the nationalisations of 1947–50 discouraged foreign enterprises from investing in the local market. The change in domestic policy on foreign private investment produced the desired fruits in the late 1950s and early 1960s, as shown in Table 2.

Table 2 also shows the dramatic difference between the effects of the four successive foreign investment laws passed by Argentine governments during the period 1953–61. The simultaneous issue of a law of industrial promotion in 1958 has recently been considered as the probable reason for the great success of Law 14780. Both pieces of legislation favoured the reception of foreign private capital in industries such as vehicles, petrochemicals, machinery and electrical equipment, metals and chemicals. These industries were greatly affected both in their capital intensity and in their technology by the effects of the new legislation.

A second major change in government policy at the beginning of the 1950s

TABLE 2

FLOW OF FOREIGN PRIVATE CAPITAL IN ARGENTINE MANUFACTURING SECTOR DURING PERIOD OF FOREIGN INVESTMENT LAWS, 1954–61

(*ooo pesos*)

Years	*Law* 14222	*Circular* 2324	*Circular* 2881	*Law* 14780	*Total*
1954	2,174				2,174
1955	10,026				10,026
1956		19,986			19,986
1957		14,727	2,805		17,532
1958		4,128	987	7,835	12,950
1959				298,299	298,299
1960				26,569	26,569
1961				83,834	83,834

Source: O. Altimir, J. Sourouille and H. Santamarina, 'Las inversiones extranjeras y la acumulación de capital en la industria', forthcoming in *Revista de Desarrollo Económico*, Buenos Aires

was in the field of labour. After the severe depression of 1951–2, strongly alarmed by the mounting inflationary pressure, the government took a stand for restraint in wage increases. Wages were frozen for a minimum period of two years between 1952 and 1954. Trade unions reacted strongly against the government and open clashes became frequent in most industries. A long and painful process of power redistribution between trade unions and central government started and continued at an increasing pace in the late 1950s and early 1960s. This brought about increasing difficulties in the labour market, constituting a second and independent source of pressure for capital-labour substitution.

A third important change occurred at this stage, this time in the international scene. In April 1953 the US Department of Commerce stated in a public report that the opportunity for new investment of foreign private capital in Argentina seemed 'to lie in the introduction of specialised products, of technologically advanced processes developed for the more highly industrialised economies'.[1] The attitude towards Argentina of the international business community, and particularly the attitude of American entrepreneurs, clearly went about an important change in the middle and late 1950s.

Thus at the same time as a new and more capital-intensive technology was being introduced into the industrial sector, making the substitution of capital for labour easier, the growing difficulties in the labour market and the increasing wage-rental ratio made such substitution more desirable from the point of view of entrepreneurs.

The forces described above were under operation from 1954 or thereabouts, gradually modifying the basic sources of growth of Argentine industry. Technological progress and increasing returns to scale became important forces of growth in many sectors acting alongside the accumulation of capital. We may now consider the basic patterns of growth which obtained in the periods 1946–54 and 1955–65.

[1] A. Whitaker, *The US and Argentina*, Cambridge, Mass., 1955.

Patterns of growth: 1946–54

During this period, disregarding the depression of 1952, the industrial sector grew under conditions of full employment. The physical volume of output increased by 35 per cent, or at an approximate rate of 3·5 per cent per annum. Employment, on the other hand, grew at the rate of nearly 2·5 per cent per annum leaving room for an annual increase in labour productivity of around 1 per cent. However, such an aggregate figure for labour productivity growth can be highly misleading.

Several industries, such as petrochemicals, chemicals, paper, foodstuffs, and some branches of the metallurgical industry, produced remarkably good all-round performances, but their success was totally neutralised by a dramatic failure in other industries, notably textiles, vehicles (formed mainly by garages of repair and maintenance), wood and leather manufacturing.

The first group of industries, the dynamic ones, had good records of capital formation, mostly financed by domestic savings. By increasing the capital equipment per operative the productivity of labour went up in spite of the fact that the techniques 'embodied' in the new capital goods (increasingly of a domestic origin), failed to be 'best practice' techniques according to international standards. In the second group of industries, the stagnant ones, the situation was by no means so promising. Given the heavy flow of rural population into the main urban areas, and given also that most of such industries required small amounts of initial capital plus only limited skills which were already available in the country, those sectors suffered an over-expansion of employment in plants of very small size, with consequent depressive impact on labour productivity.

Interestingly enough, such uneven performance among industries with regard to increases in labour productivity failed altogether to be reflected in relative price changes. Had relative prices been flexible with respect to changes in productivity then they would have tended to move over the long run more or less inversely with changes in labour productivity. In other words, had relative prices been flexible, those industries in which labour productivity increased more would have increased their money prices less than the increases in money prices in those other industries in which labour productivity gains were less spectacular. This, however, did not happen. Since the 1930s relative prices in the Argentine industrial sector have become increasingly rigid, and have increasingly failed to reflect uneven changes in productivity among industries.

In fact, during the period 1946–54 the benefits of differential increases in labour productivity went into higher profit margins in the successful industries. The causal mechanism was the following. The period 1946–54 was one of pronounced government intervention in the economy. Collective bargaining lost part of its significance and wages were geared to circumstances other than productivity changes. The overall wage policy managed by the government accorded all trades fairly similar treatment disregarding the fact that some industries were more successful than others in terms of their gains in labour productivity. Given that those industries were not induced by the pressure of competition to reduce their relative prices, above-average increases in productivity permitted them to raise their profit margins also above average. From the point of view of the long-run pattern of growth the fact that productivity increases were passed into increased profit margins had a disturbing effect. Too much investment was attracted to consumer goods industries where such profits could be easily obtained, while insufficient investment was attracted to capital goods industries where risks were greater, the pay-off period of investment longer, etc.

The process of import substitution was carried almost to the limit of complete self-sufficiency in the late 1940s and early 1950s in industries such as foodstuffs, tobacco, etc. Immediately after this, interest centred on relatively easy durable commodities whose imports were gradually replaced. Important among these industries were textiles and many light consumer durables (cookers, refrigerators, washing machines, etc.); these new commodities were not, however, produced on integrated lines of production. In most cases new plants started by simply assembling imported parts, and they gradually made progress by substituting some of the imported parts by national imitations of them.

This pattern of expansion had some important repercussions which were evident in the middle 1950s: 1. The manufacture of light consumer durables developed fast in Argentina in a period in which a revolutionary change in productive techniques for these commodities was well under way in the industrial countries. Within a lapse of a few years the technological lag between the techniques used in Argentina and those of the more efficient countries was quite marked. Such disadvantage forced the administration to protect domestic industries by imposing increasingly heavy import duties. 2. The substitution of imports of consumer durables had a negative net effect on the balance of payments. The domestic production of consumer durables brought about a rapidly increasing demand for basic raw materials, fuel and heavy capital equipment.

Patterns of growth: 1955–65

Labour productivity went up by 3 per cent per annum during these years (output increased by over 4 per cent and employment by 1 per cent per annum). Labour productivity was increased in most industries, particularly in vehicles, machinery and electrical equipment, petrochemicals, chemicals, printing and publishing. In these industries the volume of output also went up faster than average, increasing their share of total manufacturing output.

During the late 1950s and early 1960s capital-intensive techniques were introduced in several industries, and this gradually transformed the basic forces underlying the expansion of manufacturing. The new capital equipment embodied a technology superior to the existing one, and also favoured the development of new skills in the labour force needed to operate it. The new equipment permitted several industries to benefit from increasing returns to scale that were enjoyed as output expanded.

In recent years it has become clear that the more the system moves towards a greater capital-intensity in the dynamic industries, the greater the difficulties faced by the economy in absorbing the increasing urban population. The falling unit labour requirements of new techniques of production, together with a relatively slow expansion of output due to the limitations of the domestic market, has seriously affected the rate of growth of the industrial labour force. As a consequence of this structural failure employment in the service industries and in the civil service has gradually and uneconomically over-expanded.

That foreign investment alone should be credited for the developments of the late 1950s and early 1960s is far from clear. It is certainly true that foreign investment played an important part in the settlement in Argentina of several modern and sophisticated new industries such as extraction and refining of petroleum, manufacturing of heavy capital equipment (railway equipment, electrical generators), vehicles, basic chemicals (sulphuric acid, synthetic rubber, etc.), and that those industries induced the expansion of productive capacity in less sophisticated sectors closer to the final stages of production; but it is also true that domestic capitalists followed suit in the process of modernisation and that a considerable amount of indigenous resources are today employed in association with a modern technology.

There is, however, an element of failure in this otherwise very impressive process of change, and it is related to the way in which the process has been financed. Capital formation and technical progress have been financed by short-term credits of suppliers in an increasing proportion. Over 50 per cent of the finance obtained by firms from sources other than internal accumulation of profits derived during these years from credits of suppliers. This has heavily endangered the prospects of the Argentine balance of payments for the late 1960s and clearly points out the need of an overall policy of industrialisation compatible with a healthy long-term balance of payments.

CONCLUSIONS

It is now clear that the manufacturing sector of Argentina has been transformed in recent decades by the introduction of foreign technology in most branches. It is also clear that since the 1930s, and especially since the end of the war, it has become the more dynamic part of the Argentine economy, and that part on which a great deal of the future growth potentialities of the country are concentrated. Yet although the major basis for a further transformation of Argentina into an industrialised society has been set up in the last decades, many obstacles remain in the way of a more rapid rate of industrial growth.

Some of the problems are well known and have received much attention from social scientists, namely the need for reducing and stabilising the rate of inflation, the need for an appropriate policy regarding the foreign exchange rate, the need for some sort of incomes policy that would plan an appropriate rate of increase of money wages and profits, compatible with the achievement of the required rate of capital formation and also with some long-term equilibrium in labour relations, etc.

There are grounds for believing that the utilisation of capital-intensive techniques is likely to continue in Argentina on an increasing scale. Under these circumstances the possibility of recurrent waves of technological unemployment, subsequent to successive rounds of capital investment with a higher degree of mechanisation, appears likely. It is of course a matter of government policy to maintain near-full employment. Such a policy opens, at the same time, the possibility of widening the industrial structure, expanding the substitution of imports in areas in which labour-intensive techniques might be employed.

Several industries in the Argentine manufacturing sector (see above) seem to be working under conditions of increasing returns to scale, and their expansion is therefore worth subsidising. Given the limited size of the domestic market the expansion of output in the relevant cases entails expanding their exports. Further grounds can be given in favour of a policy that would subsidise the exports of manufactures: such a policy might be thought of as an alternative to subsidising import-substitution through tariff protection. Government action in this context might vary along a wide range of choices, from simply favouring institutional arrangements for product specialisation (in and outside the LAFTA area) to assisting the exports of manufacturing through subsidies, export credit guarantees, exchange policy, etc.

However, in a country without a tradition of manufacture exports, and in which influential sections of the population are still ideologically committed to the need of complete agricultural specialisation, scepticism must remain regarding the political viability of a sound all-round industrialisation policy that would contemplate the possibility of major movements into the international industrial markets. Nonetheless, it is also extremely difficult to see Argentina as a strong industrial producer without a considerable enlargement of her present markets.

BIBLIOGRAPHY

Chilcote, R. 'Integrated Iron and Steel Industry for Argentina', *Inter-American Economic Affairs*, XVI, 4, Washington, DC, Spring 1963.

Cochran, T. and Reina, R. *Entrepreneurship in Argentina Culture: Torcuato di Tella and SIAM*, Univ. of Pennsylvania, Philadelphia, Pa., 1962.

Cortes Conde, R. 'Problemas del crecimiento industrial de la Argentina (1870–1914)', *Desarrollo Economico*, III, 1 and 2, Buenos Aires, April and September 1963.

Diaz Alejandro, C. F. *Exchange Rate Devaluation in a Semi-Industrialized Country: The Experience of Argentina, 1955–1961*, MIT Press, Cambridge, Mass., 1965.

Eshag, E. and Thorp, R. 'Economic and Social Consequences of Orthodox Economic Policies in Argentina in the Post War Years', *Bulletin of the Oxford University Institute of Economics and Statistics*, XXVII, 1, Oxford, February 1965.

Ferrer, A. *La Economia Argentina. Las etapas de su desarrollo y problemas actuales*, Fondo de Cultura Economica, Buenos Aires, 1963.

Fillol, R. *Social Factors in Economic Development: The Argentine Case*, MIT Press, Cambridge, Mass., 1961.

Imaz, J. L. *Los que mandan*, EUDEBA, Buenos Aires, 1964.

Sigaut, Lorenzo. *Desarrollo agropecuario y el proceso de industrialización*, OECEI, Buenos Aires, 1964.

di Tella, G. and Zymmelman, M. 'Etapas del desarrollo economico argentino', *Revista de Economia Latinoamericana*, Caracas, September 1961.

Whitaker, A. *The United States and Argentina*, Oxford Univ. Press, London; Harvard Univ. Press, Cambridge, Mass., 1955.

United Nations. *El desarrollo industrial de la Argentina*, Economic and Social Council, Santiago, Chile, 1966.

Journals
The Review of the River Plate, Buenos Aires.
Panorama de la Economia Argentina, Buenos Aires.

THE INDUSTRIALISATION OF BRAZIL

CELSO FURTADO

ONLY after 1930 did manufacturing make a significant contribution to the Brazilian economy and investment in the industrial sector begin to break away from its dependence on the external factors which had traditionally conditioned the behaviour of overall demand.

The industrialisation process that began in the 1930s may be divided into three phases of development. The first phase (1930–45) proceeded under conditions of profound depression in the external sector and was orientated towards the substitution of non-durable consumer goods, whose imports had been abruptly curtailed. In the second phase (1945–60) relative recovery in import capacity, coupled with a higher rate of investment, permitted an acceleration in the pace of industrialisation, which was directed chiefly towards the substitution of previously imported durable goods and certain intermediate products. The third phase (from 1960) is characterised by a declining rate of growth in the manufacturing sector under the effect of complex factors, among them chronic insufficiency in import capacity and narrowness of markets. The prospects for future industrialisation in Brazil depend essentially on the country's ability to overcome these obstacles.

INDUSTRIALISATION BEFORE 1930

Throughout its first century of political independence, Brazil retained its colonial character in the economic sphere. The vast extent of the territory and the diversity of its climatic conditions made it possible for the decline of one export product to be offset by expansion of another product favoured by prevailing world market conditions. Thus the coffee crisis of the first decade of this century was relieved by the boost in rubber production, which permitted recovery of international credit and the financing of coffee stocks. In the north-east, the effects of the decline of sugar were counterbalanced by the expansion of cotton and cacao.

The political decentralisation created by the Republican regime established in 1889 strengthened the agricultural ruling class at a stage when the urban population was beginning to have some say in politics. Ideas on the possible role of industrialisation in the modernisation of the country were offered from time to time by intellectuals exposed to foreign influence. However, short-term problems created by the permanent instability of the exchange rate, a consequence of the instability of prices of primary products in world markets, completely absorbed the attention of government. Thus some important attempts at industrialisation failed principally for lack of government support. For instance, Irineu Evangelista de Sousa, Viscount Mauá, who founded numerous industries including shipping yards during the second half of the 19th century, finished ruined after having failed to obtain the support of the ruling groups for his projects. Delmiro Gouveia met with a similar fate; at the beginning of this century he initiated some impressive projects, including one for utilising the hydroelectric potential of Paulo Alfonso in the north-east, but again without success for lack of the minimum support indispensable during the preliminary phase of installation.

The 1920 industrial census indicated the existence of only 240 manufacturing establishments in the country founded before 1880. The few figures available indicate that at the beginning of the Republican period (1889) the number of workers employed in manufacturing was 54,000. In 1907, when the first partial industrial census was carried out, this number had been approximately trebled (151,000). However, these industries were still essentially of a craft character. Nine-tenths of the 'manufacturing units' employed only two or three people, and it was impossible to distinguish them from the traditional craft industries. Nevertheless, there were a certain number of textile factories, established on the industrial pattern of the time. These factories were scattered about a number of different regions, often in rural areas, protected by the high costs of inland transport and favoured by the local production of cotton.

The dispersion of factories throughout the country, and their location in rural areas where a patriarchal outlook prevailed, prevented this first phase of manufacturing development from assuming the form of true industrialisation. In effect, it led neither to the formation of a working class nucleus, with the sociological features which this class had exhibited in Europe, nor to the emergence of an industrial mentality able to exert any significant influence within the ruling class.

The first world war provides a significant landmark in Brazilian industrial development. The blocking off of normal trade channels created conditions similar to those of unlimited protection. Consequently, manufacturing activity expanded rapidly, particularly in the regions where the standard of living had been raised during the preceding half-century of coffee expansion; these were also the most urbanised regions. The presence of a large contingent of recent European immigrants in cities in these regions was doubtless a decisive factor in the increase of manufacturing activity, given the lack of any industrial experience among the country's traditional population groups. The 1920 industrial census indicates the existence, in the previous year, of 275,000 people engaged in the manufacturing industries, distributed among 13,336 establishments. However, 87 per cent of these establishments employed only four workers or less, which indicates the prevalence of a craft manufacturing character. The development of the textile industry had been considerable. In 1919 its output accounted for approximately 29 per cent of the value of total production and employed over 88,000 workers. Industrial production is calculated to have increased by 110 per cent between 1914 and 1919. In the latter year 13 per cent of the economically active population was already engaged in manufacturing.

Two observations must be made as regards this first phase of industrial development, which arose out of the impetus given by the world war. The first relates to the rapid development of the southern region, particularly São Paulo. The second concerns the emergence of a nucleus of capital goods industries, which was to have important consequences in the subsequent phase. According to the 1920 census, there were in 1919 approximately 650 establishments, including 150 foundries, 13 rolling mills and wire-drawing works, and 230 workshops for constructing and assembling transport equipment. This industry, largely concentrated in the state of São Paulo, was based on relatively small establishments, each employing an average of 25 workers.

In the 1920s the accidental nature of the industrial growth promoted by the war years was revealed. Given the impetus provided by the profits yielded and accumulated, imports of plant and equipment continued. Thus imports of textile machinery increased rapidly in the first phase of this period, rising from an annual 2,800 tons for 1918-9 to an average of 12,000 tons in 1924-6. This enormous drive to reequip and modernise the textile industry was not, however, justified by a similar expansion of the market. Average production for 1924-6 was 10 per cent lower than the level of production for 1920. This declining trend continued in the second half of the decade; production in 1929 was one-fifth less than that in 1920. As regards total industrial output, the 1920s were not as unfavourable as in the case of the textile industry. During the decade 1919-29 industrial production rose by nearly 30 per cent, while for the same period the import quantum was more than doubled. The process of substituting imports with locally manufactured goods which had taken place during the war period was now in a state of rapid regression. The margin of idle capacity in certain industries, particularly in the textile industry, began to create serious problems. However, although from 1925 to 1929 the country was importing an annual average of more than 7,000 tons of cotton piece goods, representing approximately 6 per cent of the value of the import total, the solution sought for this crisis was much nearer a ban on imports of textile equipment than restriction of textile imports.

The fact that the prosperity of the export sector in the 1920s allowed the traditional ruling class to reestablish the pre-war liberal policy, creating serious problems for the nascent industries, did not prevent certain industrial sectors from continuing to consolidate their positions. This is a sure indication that the first nucleus of a genuine industrial class had been formed, particularly in regions such as São Paulo, where recent European immigrants exerted a powerful influence. In effect, the level of imports of industrial equipment, excluding the textile industry, was maintained at an average of 80,000 tons annually for the period 1925-9. On the other hand iron and steel production, using charcoal for smelting, was begun in 1925 with an output of 8,000 tons of steel and had risen by 1929 to 27,000 tons, representing 6 per cent of domestic requirements, i.e. half a million tons. Cement production began in 1926 and in that year amounted to 13,000 tons, reaching 96,000 tons by 1929, or 15 per cent of domestic consumption, which was 631,000 tons. Thus the small industrial nucleus which had expanded abruptly during the war had managed to put down roots and to begin its process of diversification, supported by the availability of local raw materials. The failure to grasp the problem on the political plane is explained by the fact that the country continued to be ruled basically by the same class of large landowners which had emerged in the colonial period. Nevertheless, despite the lack of any political outlook reflecting consciousness of the problem, conditions had at last arisen for the small industrial nucleus in the country to consolidate its expansion.

REPERCUSSIONS OF THE 1929 WORLD ECONOMIC CRISIS

To understand the full impact of the 1929 crisis on Brazil, it should be remembered that coffee accounted for more than 70 per cent of total export values in 1925-9, and that in this period there was already a considerable imbalance between world supply and demand. High prices were maintained by holding back large stocks in Brazil, financed by the government through loans obtained abroad. Relatively high prices and a guaranteed market (the government bought up surplus production) encouraged expansion of coffee planting, which meant that production continued to increase at the beginning of the 1930s as the new plantations began to yield, the period required for trees to reach bearing age being three to five years. Thus after 1929 Brazil found herself facing the dual crisis of collapse of external demand and overproduction whose effects combined to aggravate the situation in some respects and to cancel each other out in others. The main effect was the export crisis, which manifested itself in the dramatic decline of capacity to meet external liabilities. But another important effect was the inflationary expansion of money income. Service of the foreign debt had to be suspended and imports had to be drastically curtailed. The terms of trade declined by more than half, if we compare the average index for the 1930s with that for the 1925-9 period. During the period 1930-4 the import quantum was halved, as against the average for the preceding five-year period. During the second half of the 1930s there was still a 30-per-cent reduction in the volume of imports over the 1925-9 period.

Repercussions of the 1929 crisis on the industrial sector were various. The abrupt and prolonged decline of import capacity led to a sharp rise in prices of imported manufactured goods, which created a protectionist barrier for locally produced goods. This protection arose under conditions of reduced aggregate demand caused by the decline of the export sector. On the other hand, the need to avert a greater collapse of the coffee-growing sector led the government to continue its policy of buying up surplus coffee. This unmarketable surplus was largely destroyed in order to save the costs entailed in storage. Once foreign credit reserves had been used up, the government was compelled to resort to expansion of the means of payment in order to finance the purchase of surplus coffee. This expansionist monetary policy, coupled with unproductive investment, had important indirect consequences. It not only averted the multiplying effects of imported depression; it also encouraged compensatory domestic expansion. Finally, the rise in the relative prices of imported equipment had to be taken into account, a factor which inevitably had adverse repercussions on industrial investment. Nevertheless, it must be pointed out that during this period there were possibilities of acquiring second-hand equipment at low prices, in view of the world-wide trade depression. Some of the largest factories installed in Brazil during the 1930s made use of second-hand equipment which had been dismantled in other countries.

The ultimate result of the operation of these various factors was undoubtedly positive for the industrial sector. The crisis did not lead to a decline of manufacturing production, which remained stationary between 1929 and 1933 and began to rise in 1934. By 1939 it had already surpassed the 1929 level by 54 per cent. From the point of view of the industrial sector, therefore, the decade had been much more favourable than the preceding one.

Expansion of industrial production in the 1930s was made possible largely by the existence of a margin of idle capacity in important sectors such as that of textiles. Production in this sector increased by 100 per cent between 1929 and 1937. From the phase when available industrial capacity was underemployed, a system of working double shifts began to operate. Conditions were thus created, through a substantial rise in the rate of profit, for an acceleration in the pace of investment in the industrial sector. On the other hand, the existence of a nucleus of industries producing capital goods became an influential factor in the new conditions. Steel production rose from 27,000 tons in 1929 to 114,000 tons in 1939, contributing 26 per cent of domestic market requirements, which showed a lower level of demand than in the previous decade. Cement production rose from 96,000 tons to 698,000 tons, almost meeting local needs at a higher level of demand than that of the previous decade.

Between 1929 and 1939 the industrial nucleus succeeded in becoming the dynamic centre in the country's economy. Having hitherto been entirely dependent on external impulses to stimulate expansion of its activities, the Brazilian economy now entered a phase in which industrial investments linked to the domestic market were beginning to play an important role. It is in this sense that industrial development may be said to have begun seriously in this period.

The industrial census of 1940 indicates the existence, in 1939, of 40,860 industrial establishments as against the 13,336 establishments that existed in the country in 1919. The textile industry accounted for a smaller percentage of total production by value than in the previous census: approximately 23 per cent as compared to its former 29 per cent. The metallurgical and mechanical industries had increased their share of total production from 11 per cent to 19 per cent, and the chemical industry from 6 per cent to 10 per cent.

THE MOST RECENT PHASES OF INDUSTRIALISATION

After the second world war, certain sectors of Brazilian society became aware that industrialisation, supported by the public authorities, was essential to the development of the country. However, those fully cognizant of this need were only occasionally given the opportunity to exert any effective influence on the country's general policy. In this way, measures designed to foster industrialisation did not reflect conscious decisions based on consistent criteria, although they sometimes had far-reaching effects. Towards the end of the 1930s, for example, a plan for a national and modern steel industry had been conceived under the auspices of the government. It was thanks to the fact that this plan was carried out that industrialisation was able to proceed in the immediate post-war period on a much more ample basis than would otherwise have been possible. In this period the government prepared a plan for investment in infrastructure (the Salte Plan) which, although modest and only partially carried out, contributed to an increase in investment in the public sector. Nevertheless it was again owing to purely circumstantial factors that Brazilian industrialisation was able once more to go ahead at a rapid pace in the immediate post-war period.

The new conditions that arose in the world market for coffee, with the decline of Brazilian production after fifteen years of semi-neglect and the growth of demand for coffee created by economic reconstruction or reconversion in the great consuming countries, led to the recovery of the Brazilian export sector, which brought some relief to the import situation in the 1947–52 period. However, the changes that had occurred in the structure of the Brazilian economy, with the substantial increase of the industrial sector and the significant decline of the external sector, prevented a repetition of the experience of the 1920s. Although exchange and fiscal policies reverted to the liberal character of two decades previously, the difficulties encountered in maintaining a stable balance of payments were of another order. These difficulties led the government to introduce an exchange policy which had a number of consequences. By external overvaluation of the cruzeiro this policy, in its first phase, created difficulties for the industrial sector, which had inadequate tariff protection. However, as the demand for imports grew more rapidly than import capacity, the need arose to exercise quantitative and selective control of imports, since the exchange rate of the cruzeiro was to be maintained (largely to protect world coffee prices). Industry benefited considerably from this second phase since, in rationing the available foreign exchange, priority was given to imports of raw materials and equipment. Finally, in a third phase, the effective rate of exchange was raised and the liberal system reestablished, which, while it removed the differential advantages which had benefited the industrial sector, nevertheless established a relatively high level of protection.

Industrialisation in the post-war period was a complex process based essentially on import-substitution. Rise in total demand occurred at different times and to a different degree from the combined action of three factors: the increased income of the export sector; the relative increase in the public sector's share of GDP and the increase in investment in the public sector; and finally, the increase of the industrial share in total private investment. Both public and private sectors benefited at times from foreign investment. Whatever the origin of the impulse given to growth, this tended to spread to the industrial sector, where investment expanded following the line of least resistance offered by import-substitution. In this way the Brazilian economy managed to grow more rapidly than its import capacity, whose expansion encountered a series of obstacles, principally of an external nature. Thus the share of imports in the total supply of goods and services, which had been in the region of 10 per cent in 1948–9, had been reduced to approximately 7 per cent by 1961.

Growth of industrial output in the post-war period up to 1961 was extremely rapid. From 1947 to 1956 the average annual rate of growth was nearly 9 per cent. From 1957 to 1961 production was accelerated and rate of growth increased to nearly 13 per cent. At prices obtaining in 1947, the industrial sector's contribution to GDP rose from 21 per cent in that year to 34 per cent in 1961. In the same period the contribution of the agricultural sector dropped from 27 per cent to 22 per cent of GDP. However, since relative prices had changed in favour of the agricultural sector, the industrial sector's contribution effectively amounted to 27 per cent in 1961, or the same as the contribution of the agricultural sector.

The census figures for 1950 and 1960 indicate some of the more important structural changes that took place in Brazilian industry during this period. Thus in 1959 the capital goods industries already accounted for 35·5 per cent by value of total industrial production as compared with 22·5 per cent in 1949. The metallurgical industry had caught up with the textile industry, whose share by value of total production had been reduced to 12 per cent. The share of the mechanical and electrical goods industries had increased from approximately 6 per cent to 15 per cent, and that of the chemical industry from 5 per cent to 9 per cent.

The process of import-substitution, which from 1930 to the end of the second world war had already made a significant advance in the sectors producing non-durable consumer goods, in the phase 1945–60 made great progress in the intermediate products, durable consumer goods and capital goods sectors. Thus between 1949 and 1961 the contribution of imports to total supply dropped as follows: for metallurgical products from 22 to 12 per cent; machinery 64 to 46 per cent; electrical products 45 to 17 per cent; transport equipment 57 to 19 per cent; chemical and pharmaceutical products 29 to 17 per cent. Total manufactured goods imported dropped from 16 to 10 per cent. The table below gives some figures for the physical volume of production in the basic sectors of Brazilian industry covering the period 1950–62.

GROWTH IN BASIC INDUSTRIES 1950–62

	1950	1957	1958	1959	1960	1961	1962
			Million barrels				
Petroleum:							
Production	0·3	10·1	18·9	23·6	29·6	34·8	33·4
Refining	—	—	48·4	53·6	63·7	77·5	101·0
			Thousand metric tons				
Iron ore	1,987	4,977	5,185	8,908	9,345	10,220	10,778
Manganese ore	196	918	882	1,033	999	1,016	1,171
Coal	1,959	2,073	2,240	2,330	2,330	2,390	2,508
Steel ingots	789	1,470	1,659	1,866	2,282	2,493	2,625
Cement	1,386	3,376	3,790	3,841	4,474	4,711	5,038
			Thousand kilowatts				
Electric power:							
Installed capacity	1,883	3,444	3,993	4,115	4,800	5,205	5,783
			Million kilowatt-hours				
Production	7,000	16,963	19,766	21,108	22,865	24,405	26,895
			Units produced				
Automobiles	—	30,700	61,129	96,243	133,078	145,674	191,194
Tractors	—	—	—	—	—	4,056	7,586

Source: C. Furtado, *Diagnosis of the Brazilian Crisis*, Univ. of California Press, Berkeley, 1965

In the 1960s growth rate slowed markedly. GDP, which in 1955–60 had been growing at an average annual rate of approximately 6 per cent, showed a rate of below 4 per cent in 1960–4. In 1962–4 the average growth rate was 1·4 per cent, less than half that of the rate of population increase. Even more significant was the fact that the average rate of growth of industrial production for this two-year period was only 1 per cent, and hence lower than the corresponding rate for total production. These figures obviously reflect, in the first place, a short-term situation characterised by serious upsets in the government and administration of the country. Nevertheless, there are further causes of this loss of dynamic impulse.

The rapid development of Brazilian industrial production in the post-war period, while a complex process, was nevertheless basically directed towards import-substitution. It was a dynamic process in the sense that targets were continually shifting through the workings of a feedback mechanism. From investment made in order to meet a demand previously satisfied by imports, overall demand continued to expand, and with it the need to keep importing old products as well as new. This process faced growing obstacles, since it was only natural that substitution should have started with the 'easier' sectors, both from the point of view of the size of the market and from that of the resources, industrial technique and knowhow available. In view of the prevailing concentration of income, the demand that tended to grow most rapidly was that in the durable consumer goods sector. However, this sector, which absorbed substantial investment, remained relatively small. In the current consumer goods sector, which was relatively free from problems of scale of production, demand grew slowly. A reduction in the rate of increase of production could therefore be expected as a result of the declining efficiency of investment destined for the substitution of imports. This slowing down does not, of course, signify that industrialisation is coming to a standstill. However, everything seems to indicate that it will be difficult to repeat the great expansion of the 1950s unless new factors intervene.

OBSTACLES TO PROGRESS

One important new factor may be Latin American economic integration. Since Brazil needs to increase its imports from countries outside the Latin American area in order to benefit from the technological advances made in the great industrial centres, it must diversify its exports to traditional markets. A partial solution to the problem of the present narrowness of markets might be found in the interchange brought about by Latin American regional integration.

Latin American integration, however, can only be expected to proceed at a very slow rate. It is also unlikely, within the foreseeable future, to benefit the non-durable consumer goods industries, which are precisely those in which stagnation has longest been noticeable. These industries are already considerably developed in the principal regions of the country and nearly everywhere show margins of idle capacity.

The basic cause of Brazil's industrial stagnation would seem to be excessive concentration of income in the hands of a small minority, due to the traditional way of life of a society with an agrarian and semi-feudal base. For industrialisation to proceed in earnest, modernisation of the country's social and institutional structure is indisputably necessary to break up this concentration of income, which is responsible for the present structure of demand, making it difficult for the industries producing for the mass market to expand.

The restrictive effects of the traditional pattern of income distribution are aggravated by industrialisation of the import-substitution type. During the phase when industrialisation created employment on a considerable scale, even a stationary level of wages in the industrial sector could influence the standard of living of the masses, since industrial wages were much higher than those offered in rural areas and the craft industries. Today, when the absorption of manpower by the manufacturing sector has less effect on the spending power of the masses, expansion of the market for current consumer goods is faced with serious obstacles.

Narrowness of import capacity calls for a strong effort to be made to diversify imports. Such diversification should, however, be progressively supported by the industrial sector itself, i.e. it presupposes the existence of a dynamic industrial sector. A prosperous and developing industrial sector is a prerequisite if Brazil is to expand its external sector to include its industrial products, which in turn would make it easier for the industrial sector itself to gain greater dynamism.

In the course of the last three decades Brazil's industrialisation has made remarkable progress, and the industrial sector is today an important dynamic centre which, under certain conditions, could provide an impetus for the development of the country's economy. However, unless a new external impulse revitalises import-substitution, the industrial sector would not seem to be in a condition to generate the impulse that would give dynamism of an autonomous nature to the country's economy as a whole. An important phase awaits completion if Brazil is to become a fully industrialised nation, a phase likely to have characteristics different from those of the previous phase, which in many respects remained a reflection of the traditional foreign-market-based economy. In this phase, if and when it comes, industrialisation will take its place in a wider process involving modernisation of Brazil's social structure.

BIBLIOGRAPHY

Baer, Werner. *Industrialization and Economic Development in Brazil*, Economic Growth Centre, Yale Univ., New Haven, Conn., 1965.

Furtado, Celso. *The Economic Growth of Brazil: A Survey from Colonial to Modern Times*, Univ. of California Press, Berkeley, Calif., 1963. *Diagnosis of the Brazilian Crisis*, Univ. of California Press, Berkeley, Calif., 1965.

Loeb, G. F. *Industrialization and Balanced Growth: With Special Reference to Brazil*, Groningen, Netherlands, 1957.

Stein, Stanley J. *The Brazilian Cotton Manufacture: Textile Enterprise in an Underdeveloped Area, 1850–1950*, Harvard Univ. Press, Cambridge, Mass., 1957.

ECLA. *Economic Survey of Latin America 1949*, UN, New York, 1951. *Analysis and Projections of Economic Development*, II: 'The Economic Development of Brazil', UN, New York, 1956. *Economic Bulletin for Latin America*, IX, 1, UN, New York, March 1964. *Economic Survey of Latin America 1964* (mimeographed), Mexico City, May 1965.

THE INDUSTRIALISATION OF CHILE

HÉCTOR SOZA

The Industrial Structure of Chile

CHILE is a country of about nine million inhabitants, with an annual income per head of about US$450 a year. It is predominantly urban with only about 30 per cent of the population living in rural areas. However, in contrast to the case in the most developed countries of Europe, in the United States and in some of the more industrialised countries of Latin America, urban development in Chile has not been accompanied by intensive industrialisation. In fact, manufacturing industry provides less than 25 per cent of GNP in Chile, compared to a level of 30–40 per cent achieved in the developed countries.

If it is accepted that economic development is coterminous with industrialisation, then the relatively slight importance of the Chilean manufacturing sector is a reflection of the underdevelopment of the country and its low level of income. In addition, the economic structure of Chile shows a serious distortion in the exaggerated importance of the trade/services sector, which represents almost 60 per cent of GNP. This can perhaps be interpreted as a reflection of a lack of dynamism in the productive sectors, especially industry and agriculture.

The product of the self-employed artisan class, which has not been absorbed into larger industrial units, represents about 30 per cent of manufacturing output. The self-employed artisans are concentrated mainly in the clothing and footwear industries (50 per cent), food, woodworking and furniture (about 25 per cent) and the metal-working trades (again about 25 per cent). The development of manufactures has reached an intermediate stage of industrialisation. Rather more than 50 per cent of output is of traditional products—typically, non-durable consumer goods—some 35 per cent is of semi-finished products, and only about 15 per cent is of products of the metal-using and engineering industries (see Table 1).

This structure contrasts sharply with those of more industrialised countries, where the metallurgical and engineering group is of greater importance. In countries where the annual income per head is US$500–1,000 a year and industry provides about 30 per cent of GNP a greater balance exists, with the metal-using and engineering group producing up to 30 per cent of the industrial product. Where there is an annual income per head of US$1,000–1,500, and industry produces about 40 per cent of GNP, industrial production is divided more or less equally between the three industrial groups set out in Table 1.

The contrast shown between the three industrial groups in Table 1 is a reflection of the underdevelopment of Chile, and particularly of the low

614

TABLE I

OUTPUT STRUCTURE OF CHILEAN MANUFACTURING INDUSTRY IN 1964[1]

Industrial activity (according to UN uniform industrial classification)	Percentage of total value
Traditional industries (consumer goods, especially non-durable)	*50·3*
Food	18·1
Drink	2·8
Tobacco	1·1
Textiles	14·4
Clothing and footwear	8·0
Furniture and fittings	1·4
Leather and products	0·9
Printing	3·6
Intermediate industries (semi-finished products)	*35·2*
Cellulose, paper and products	3·4
Rubber products	2·1
Chemicals	6·6
Petroleum products	4·8
Non-metallic mineral products	6·6
Basic metal products	11·7
Metal-using and engineering industries (capital and durable consumer goods)	*14·6*
Finished metal products ⎫	
Machinery ⎪	
Electrical goods ⎬	13·3
Transport equipment ⎭	
Various	1·3
	100·0

[1] Manufacturing industry is here defined as including all establishments employing five or more workers.

> Source: Based on data from the Chilean Industrial Census of 1957, adjusted to 1964 on the basis of the industrial production index of the Dirección de Estadística y Censos, Santiago.

degree of industrialisation. However, the structure of Chilean industry can be compared favourably with that of most Latin American countries; only Argentina, Brazil and Mexico show more advanced structures.

The type of structure found in Chile results in a considerable dependence on imports for supplies of semi-finished goods and particularly of machinery and equipment. Chile imports about one-fifth of the raw and semi-finished materials, and by far the greater part of the machinery and equipment, used by the industrial sector. This situation produces a certain vulnerability to external influences, to which Chile is particularly sensitive because of the structure of its foreign trade. Chile is an exporter of primary products to the extent of 90 per cent of exports by value (one product alone, copper, accounts for 65 per cent) so that its import capacity is subject to the price fluctuations and unfavourable trading conditions affecting all export trade in primary products. On the other hand imports, which are mainly of manufactures (about 80 per cent), are made up to the extent of almost 70 per cent of semi-finished goods, raw materials and capital goods (see Table 2). This means that the import structure is extremely rigid, in that the adjustments often rendered necessary by the unfavourable terms of trade for primary products are difficult to make without affecting the basis of the economy, and particularly of industry. Furthermore, a significant proportion of imports (about a quarter) consists of farm products, mainly essential foodstuffs, so that the backwardness of Chilean agriculture, which could itself produce a large part of those imports, renders the import structure even more rigid and increases the difficulties of industrial operation and development.

TABLE 2

COMMODITY EXPORTS AND IMPORTS: ANNUAL AVERAGE, 1960–4

	US $ million
Exports (f.o.b.)	496
Primary products:	
Minerals	424
Farm products	39
Manufactures	33
Imports (c.i.f.)	598
Primary products	135
Manufactures	463
Of which:	
Capital goods	215
Raw materials and semi-finished goods	191
Consumer goods	192

Source: Superintendencia de Aduanas
and Banco Central de Chile.

The low degree of industrial integration in Chile becomes even more apparent if the composition of each industry's output is examined. For example, most of the chemical industry's production is of consumer goods; the opposite is the case in the more-developed countries, where the production of basic materials for processing is more important. Similarly, in the metal-using and engineering industries, the most important sectors in Chile are repair workshops, the manufacture of domestic equipment, and assembly work, whereas the making of machinery, capital equipment and motor vehicles is of much more importance in the industrialised countries.

These considerations do not imply that a country with a small internal market should seek to achieve industrial self-sufficiency; on the contrary, self-sufficiency is actually socially undesirable in view of the economies of scale and specialisation resulting from modern technology in many metal-using and capital goods industries. Together with the unfavourable export structure, these points lead to the opinion that Chile should undertake the export of manufactures, with the aim of continuing its industrial growth, diversifying into other capital goods and metal-using industries, and strengthening its terms of trade. A similar process has been the economic salvation of many of the smaller European countries, and Chile has been attempting to dovetail its economy with that of the rest of Latin America so as to alleviate market stringencies and diversify its foreign trade, and also to profit from the advantages resulting from more competitive conditions.

The fact that Chile has not arrived at the same level of industrialisation and production structure as countries with a higher income level or larger internal markets, or both, does not however mean that its industrial achievements have been insignificant.

It should first be stressed that Chilean industry satisfies virtually the entire national market for non-durable consumer goods. Only marginal quantities of these goods are imported, except for a considerable amount of foodstuffs (US$54 million in 1964); this last is a result of the backwardness of Chilean agriculture and its inability to produce the necessary raw materials. The country produces most of its requirements of durable consumer goods, though with a considerable content of imported components. The motor-vehicle industry consists essentially of assembly plants, where some Chilean-made parts are incorporated into the finished product; complete vehicles are no longer imported except in special cases. Further, certain semi-finished goods industries have achieved significant success, which has under-lined the importance of this sector (see Table 1).

TABLE 3

PRODUCTION OF IMPORTANT MANUFACTURES
IN 1964[1]

Sugar	(*'000 tons*)	245[2]
Spaghetti and pastas		55
Paper		129
Rayon fibre and yarn		5
Cement		1,267
Cast iron (liquid weight)		437
Steel ingots		544
Tinplate		30[3]
Beer	(*million litres*)	107
Cigarettes	(*million units*)	6,438
Cloth (cotton, wool and silk)	(*million metres*)	44[4]
Tyres and inner tubes	(*'000 units*)	827
Paraffin oil (kerosene)	(*'000 cubic metres*)	301
Liquefied gas		229[3]
Motor spirit (including aviation fuel)		1,013
Diesel oil		465
Fuel oil		572
Glass plate	(*'000 square metres*)	834

[1] Products for which official information is published regularly.

[2] About 63 per cent (1963) is refined from imported cane sugar; the remainder is sugar from beets produced in Chile.

[3] 1963.

[4] Rough estimate.

Sources: Dirección de Estadística y Censos,
Cía de Acero del Pacifico, and
Empresa Nacional de Petróleos,
Santiago

V

The paper and cellulose industry, which is organised for large-scale production, not only supplies the Chilean market almost entirely, but also exports large quantities of newsprint and cellulose in highly competitive conditions. An important branch of rubber industry, which also supplies most of the local market, is the manufacture of tyres and inner tubes for motor vehicles, though it is necessary still to import certain special types at a cost of US$3 million a year. The chemical industry is one of the most advanced in Latin America; about 50 per cent of its output is of semi-finished goods (against 37 per cent in the seven most advanced Latin American countries taken together, and 63 per cent in the United States). However, the value of the chemical industry's output (the equivalent of about US$80 million a year) is no more than the value of imports in that sector; this suggests considerable scope for the development of the Chilean industry.

Chile's oil refineries satisfy local demand except for heavy products, particularly diesel oil. The composition of Chilean deposits is such that the country is forced to import part of its crude petroleum requirements (about US$12 million a year in value) to bring the production of refined products into line with the pattern of demand. In the non-metallic minerals industry (besides the china, crockery and glass industries and similar activities which are well developed) the production of cement, glass, sanitary equipment and other building materials easily satisfies local demand. The most important of the base metal industries is that of steel, which in 1964 produced 580,000 tons of rolled steel products from the mill at Huachipato, and already supplies more than 80 per cent of national requirements; Chilean annual consumption per head is now some 75 kg., one of the highest figures in Latin America. However, development of the industry has not been sufficiently rapid, as is proved by the decline of the quantity available for export from 152,000 tons in 1957 to 20,000 in 1964; domestic demand has increased at a higher rate than productive capacity.

The relative degree of development of the metal-using and engineering sector is considerably less than that of the traditional and semi-finished goods industries. This is reflected not only in its lowly position vis-à-vis total industrial production (see Table 1), but also in the extent of imports. During the period 1960–4 the annual average value of imports of metal goods, machinery and 'various' items was US$300 million or 65 per cent of total imports of manufactures and 50 per cent of the total of all purchases abroad. The greater part of these imports (US$215 million) consisted of machinery, transport equipment and other capital goods, which have not yet been greatly affected by the import-substitution process.

The Process of Industrialisation

Chile has seen industrial development since the beginning of its independent history—pronounced until the middle of the 19th century, but arrested when free trade became general throughout the world. The tide turned again later, but the process gained real momentum only after the world crisis of 1930. Until that crisis, the export of primary products, especially of minerals, was the main dynamic element in the Chilean economy as a result of external demand (i.e. 'development outwards'). This stage ended with the world crisis, which afflicted Chile perhaps more violently than any other country in the world.

The peak of 'development outwards' was achieved in 1925–9; during this period the value of exports reached 23 per cent of GDP; at present this figure is only 10 per cent. The tendencies of primary goods exports became unfavourable (in relation to quantity and terms of trade) to the extent that Chile's capacity per head to import was in 1960–4 only just over one-third of the 1925–9 level.

In consequence of the world crisis and the diverging trends between falling demand for primary goods exports on the one hand and the growing need for imports of manufactures on the other, the country was forced to impose strict controls on purchases from abroad. These controls have introduced protection—not always deliberately–for the import-substitution process; local manufacturers, freed from the competition of the much more experienced and efficient foreign suppliers, were given favourable conditions for expansion.

This protectionism brought its rewards, as it had previously done in the United States and other countries that are now developed, which are also favoured by the large size of their internal markets. However, though import-substitution has produced certain benefits, as a dynamic factor in the economy and as a means of saving foreign exchange, the external attrition of the Chilean economy continues, because the primary products structure of exports persists, bringing almost invariably unfavourable terms of trade. In addition, the backwardness of the country's agrarian sector has resulted in a growing need to import farm products, of which domestic supplies are becoming increasingly inadequate. Finally, in the absence of a systematic, continuous and selective policy of industrialisation import-substitution has been concentrated on consumer goods, the production of which is relatively simple and the demand direct and apparent, with little thought for the growing need created by industrialisation for semi-finished and capital goods.

The most systematic efforts towards industrial development in Chile were made in the 1940s, through the action of the Corporación de Fomento de la Producción (CORFO), a state agency established in 1939. An electrification plan, oil and steel industries, a sugar programme and other initiatives of the state were due to CORFO, which also fostered tyre, wood-processing, and paper and cellulose industries as well as various activities in the fields of metal-processing, electrical goods and chemicals, and fishing.

Apart from the direct participation of the state in the process of industrialisation, both as entrepreneur and as promoter, a further powerful incentive was provided by the shortage in the early 1940s, due to the second world war, of various imported manufactured goods. Chilean industrialisation entered upon a period of rapid expansion, which affected not only consumer goods but also included semi-finished products and some capital goods. During the first half of the 1940s the rate of industrial growth was about 10 per cent a year (see Table 4); in the decade 1945–55 this rate declined to 4 per cent as a result of the greater availability of imports and the exhaustion of the most obvious possibilities for import-substitution. At this time, however, most of the basic industries founded by CORFO reached a stage of consolidation, and several metal-using and engineering plants began operation near the steel mill at Huachipato.

From 1955 the annual rate of industrial expansion weakened to 3·5 per cent, with a period of virtual stagnation between 1958 and 1961; in fact industrialisation actually stopped during the decade 1955–65, in that the industrial growth rate, at 3·5 per cent, was lower than the total growth rate, at 4·2 per cent. This decline coincided with a lesser degree of activity on the

TABLE 4

POPULATION, INDUSTRIAL AND TOTAL GROWTH

(*average rates of cumulative annual growth, per cent*)

Period	Population	GDP Total	GDP Industrial	GNP per head
1940–45	1·8	3·1 ·	9·5	1·3
1945–55	2·0	3·6	4·1	1·6
1955–65	2·8	4·2	3·5	1·4
1940–65	2·3	3·7	4·9	1·4

Source: *CORFO; Cuentas Nacionales de Chile 1940–54*, Editorial del Pacífico Santiago, 1957; *Cuentas Nacionales, de Chile 1958–63*, Santiago, June 1964. For 1965, estimates on the basis of the industrial production index of the Dirección de Estadística y Censos, Santiago

part of CORFO, which is now responsible for very few new initiatives in the industrial field; the entrepreneurial role of the state in industry has been almost nullified, and even the Huachipato steelworks have been transferred to private enterprise. Moreover, the decade 1955–65 saw the introduction of orthodox anti-inflation policies, with strong emphasis on the reduction of demand and the relaxation of foreign trade controls. As a result, commodity imports increased substantially: the annual average rose from US$340 million in 1950–4 to US$420 million in 1955–9 and US$600 million in 1960–5. This increase in imports was largely financed out of foreign loans and credits, which reached the gross total of nearly US$370 million a year in 1961–5.

Chilean industrialisation, as has been indicated above, has been closely linked to the vicissitudes of foreign trade and to state initiative. Private enterprise, which controls much the greater part of the industrial sector, has made praiseworthy efforts and achieved significant successes, but in many basic industries the role of private enterprise is seriously limited by the extent of the investments necessary, the technical and administrative complexities and the risks involved.

The process of industrialisation over the last twenty-five years has developed in a period of slow general economic growth (see Table 4) and of great instability, and without significantly affecting the main structural problems of the Chilean economy; these are the primary-product composition of exports, the inequitable distribution of income, the backward agrarian sector, and the lack of a competitive atmosphere for the development of industry itself.

It may be stated without hesitation that the accumulation of these factors has had a negative effect on industrialisation in Chile. The slowness of economic growth implies a low rate of expansion in the demand for manufactures, which is the principal stimulus and determining factor for industrialisation. Inflation has stimulated speculative investments rather than the accumulation of fixed capital in industry. The reliance on exports of primary products, the tendencies of which are unfavourable and fluctuating, is one of the main causes of Chile's economic instability. The uneven distribution of income restricts the market for popular manufactured consumer goods and hinders the growth of positive social attitudes and individual initiative. The backwardness of the agrarian sector is another source of instability and leads to the expenditure of foreign exchange on products that could be grown in Chile, to the multiplication of foreign trade problems, and to the exclusion of some three million rural workers and their families from the market for manufactures. The lack of a competitive atmosphere—thanks to tariff protection and the fact that the internal market is, for many industries, not large enough to support a competitive structure of companies of sufficient size—has resulted in a lack of interest in efficiency, costs and quality; nor do present conditions encourage any improvement in utilisation of productive capacity.

Chile's industrialisation must be assessed in the light of the main problems of the Chilean economy: the serious employment problem should be added to those already considered. Though these problems are not entirely the responsibility of industry, it is perhaps true that industry has not been a very positive factor in their resolution, except as regards the success of import-substitution. As for the employment problem, industry has not contributed much: it is estimated that manufacturing, the high-productivity category, gives employment to only 250,000 people and that self-employed artisans number about 200,000. However, it can be plainly stated that although industrialisation has not reached high intensity and indeed virtually ceased in the decade 1955–65, there would have been no development at all without the part played by the state and the more dynamic business circles in fostering industry.

For Chilean industry to become the power-house of the economy requires a new industrial phase of boldness in establishing capital and semi-finished goods industries and aggressiveness in exporting. The export trade, as has been stated above, might provide an escape from the stranglehold of the foreign trade situation and the restrictions imposed by the internal market, to new industrial fields in which the scales of production are higher and specialisation and technical complexities have more importance. In this respect expectations are being aroused in Chile by the idea of economic integration with other countries of Latin America, especially with the other members of the Latin American Free Trade Association.

BIBLIOGRAPHY

Nolff, Max. 'Industria manufacturera'. *Geografía Económica de Chile*, Corporación de Fomento de la Producción–Fundación Pedro Aguirre Cerda, Santiago, Chile, 1962 and 1965.

Pinto, Anibal. *Chile, un caso de desarrollo frustrado*, Editorial Universitaria, Santiago, Chile, 1959.

Soza, Hector. 'Comercio Exterior', *Geografía Económica de Chile*, Santiago, Chile, 1962 and 1965.

Corporación de Fomento de la Producción (CORFO). *Programa nacional de desarrollo económico 1961–1970*, Santiago, Chile.

Instituto de Economía (Universidad de Chile). *Desarrollo económico de Chile, 1940–1956*, Editorial Universitaria, Santiago, Chile, 1956. *Formación de capital en las empresas industriales* (with English summary: IE No. 33), Santiago, Chile, 1963. *Utilización de la capacidad instalada en 42 empresas industriales* (IE No. 56), Santiago, Chile, 1963.

Instituto Latinoamericano del Fierro y el Acero (ILAFA). *Economía siderurgica latinoamericana. Monografías nacionales. Chile*, Editorial Universitaria, Santiago, Chile, 1963.

United Nations Economic Commission for Latin America. *The Process of Industrial Development in Latin America*, E/CN12/716/Add.1, New York, 1966.

THE ECONOMICS OF THE CUBAN REVOLUTION

ROBIN BLACKBURN

THE greatest achievement of the Cuban revolution in the economic field is that Cubans can now make their own mistakes. Before the revolution there was, in a sense, no such entity as a 'Cuban' economy. Neither the economic successes nor the economic failures of the island owed very much to the policy of Cuban governments or to the exertions of Cuban entrepreneurs. Pre-revolutionary Cuba's arrested development and her combination of wealth and poverty were the consequence of international market forces, the trade policy of the United States government and the responses of foreign investors. Emancipation from the economic embrace of the United States has not reduced Cuba's ultimate external dependence but it has decisively enlarged the government's ability to conduct its domestic economic and social policy. Together with an economy of her own Cuba has acquired a host of problems which her novice planners and economists have often aggravated. Those who dislike revolutions would be unwise to count on any lasting comfort from this entirely natural process—making their own mistakes the Cubans are at least more likely to learn from them.

UNDERDEVELOPMENT AND OVEREXPLOITATION

When Fidel Castro overthrew Batista's military regime in January 1959 Cuba was one of the richest underdeveloped countries in the world. With GNP per capita in the mid-1950s at $360 (a conservative estimate) Cuba was comfortably above the world average figure ($200 per capita) and well ahead of Japan ($254 per capita) and Spain ($240 per capita), while most of the population inhabited a world entirely different from that of the miserable peasant masses of India ($72 per capita: an average figure which, like all the others, conceals great inequalities of distribution). Despite this Cuba was essentially *underdeveloped*. Even with a heavy public works programme, unemployment in the *tiempo muerto* ('idle season') of August to October 1956 ran at 20 per cent of the labour force. During the sugar harvest of February to April 1957 registered unemployment was still 9 per cent. About a quarter of Cuba's farm land was kept as a reserve in case high sugar prices warranted a sudden increase in production: in 1956 the sugar companies who owned or controlled 188,000 *caballerías*[1] of land cut only 74,000 *caballerías* of cane. Many owned land primarily for prestige reasons. One consequence of this was cattle densities on Cuban soil no greater than

[1] One caballería is equal to approximately 33 acres.

those on the dusty plains of Texas. Neglect of the country's natural resources occurred particularly where they could be developed only for the home market. The island's feeble agriculture and fishing industry coexisted with imports of food, drink and tobacco which averaged $168 million in 1955-7, between one-quarter and one-third of the total import bill. Cuba's mineral resources include the world's largest known deposits of nickel, a steel alloy which has enjoyed high prices and rising demand since the beginning of the second world war, yet nickel contributed only 2 per cent to the total value of exports. The United States government which controlled the nickel deposits preferred to hoard them as strategic reserves. Taking into account both unemployed labour and under-utilised resources there is little doubt that Cuba's development potential exceeded that of many countries in the underdeveloped world.

Cuba's comparatively high GNP per capita in the 1950s was a legacy of a prodigious expansion of the sugar industry that had already reached its peak in the mid-1920s. Income per capita in 1922-5 averaged $200 in current prices (perhaps $400 per capita using the prices of the mid-1950s). The intervening period of stagnation was a consequence of the fact that Cuban sugar exports had reached the saturation point of a market which was attracting rival producers. Of course the large economic surplus generated by sugar should have been used to develop other lines of production as well as to improve the productivity of the sugar industry itself. Neither of these things happened. Not only was the size of the sugar crop similar in the 1950s to what it had been thirty years earlier but so were the methods used to produce it. In the words of the 1950 *Report on Cuba* prepared by the IBRD, the Cuban sugar industry 'displayed a conspicuous lack of technical progress'.

The island's population doubled between the 1920s and the 1950s so that only a rise in sugar prices and an expansion of non-sugar production prevented a rapid fall in living standards. Thus between 1945 and 1958 income per capita declined at an average annual rate of 0·3 per cent. However, in this period the economy was probably faring better than it had from 1925 to 1945. Whereas population rose by 41 per cent between 1925-9 and 1945-9, consumption of rice was estimated to have risen by 22 per cent, of potatoes by 5 per cent, of electricity by 12 per cent and of cement by 5 per cent. Moreover, these long-period comparisons conceal the fact that Cuba's extreme dependence on sugar (consistently 80 per cent of exports) meant that the country's entire economy was at the mercy of the fluctuations of the sugar market. Bad years, like those of the late 1920s and most of the 1930s, were very bad indeed. The statistical information available on many aspects of the Cuban economy is open to question but the near-unanimity of the longer-period figures reliably indicates that increases in consumption rarely exceeded population growth and more usually fell below it.

The immediate explanation of Cuba's prolonged stagnation lay in the failure of those who received the economic surplus to reinvest it in the right places and in sufficient amounts. New capital formation averaged only just over 10 per cent of GNP, one of the lowest rates in the world. Cuba's sharply unequal income distribution, and extremely lenient tax system, would only have been justified in an economic sense if the Cuban rich had ploughed their money back into productive investments. Most of them preferred to spend it in luxury consumption so that more money was spent by Cuban tourists in the United States than was earned by Cuba's own tourist industry and more was spent importing fashionable foreign drinks than was earned by the export of Cuban rum. The fact that a large proportion of the

Cuban economy was foreign-owned also contributed greatly to the loss of investable resources. In 1955 US companies owned 40 per cent of raw sugar capacity, 90 per cent of the telephone and electric services and 50 per cent of the public service railways. Direct remittances of profits and interest to the United States totalled $378 million between 1950 and 1958. This drain of capital was indirectly increased by the practice of foreign companies establishing subsidiaries in the island to whom they then sold intermediate products at above market prices. Indeed it was an attempt by the Castro government to end a situation like this in the field of oil-refining which led to the break with the United States.

The lack of enterprise demonstrated by businessmen operating in Cuba must be explained mainly in terms of the economic structure they confronted. The Cuban domestic market was small but a sizeable middle class could, under other circumstances, have provided a spring board for economic development. It was the extreme vulnerability of this market rather than its smallness which deterred the Cuban investor: vulnerability, that is, both to the fluctuations of the sugar market and, even more important, to over-whelming competition from United States manufacturers. The trade treaties by which the United States established a sugar quota for Cuba also gave products from the United States preferential entry to the Cuban market. No Cuban businessman could hope to compete with the giant US corporations and these corporations were given little incentive to establish subsidiary plants on a wide scale in a market which they could penetrate without appreciable transport or tariff costs. A report on investment in Cuba published by a US Government Department in 1955 pointed out:

> A high percentage of US investments in manufacturing in Latin America have resulted from tariff or import restrictions which have made local manufacture or assembly practically unavoidable. Cuba has, with exceptions, followed a tariff policy which permits a considerable freedom of choice between local production and importation. It has also largely avoided non-tariff controls, such as import licensing, quota restrictions, and exchange measures.

The foreign subsidiaries which were established were concentrated in the service sector or closely linked to it (telephones, railways, petrol, tyres, soft drinks).

Under the circumstances it is not surprising that Cuban investment capital was squandered, exported or left idle. Between 1950 and 1958 some $300 million seems to have been invested by Cubans abroad. The corruption of which government officials were guilty leads one to suspect that this figure understates the true position—in 1955 for example the category 'errors and omissions' in the balance of payments accounts was baldly listed as minus $58 million. The island's financial system was invariably highly liquid with banks holding one-third to a half of their assets in cash. The only sector of the economy to experience an investment boom was construction, both public and private. Eighty per cent of this building took place in Havana where casinos, hotels and luxury apartment blocks did little to add to the country's productive resources or to raise the living standards of the mass of the population. A feature of an economy like Cuba's at this period, so intimately linked by trade and investment to that of another country, is that progress in one sector may easily fail to spill over into other sectors. The notional character of 'the Cuban economy' was revealed by the weakness of inter-sectoral integration—the multiplier effects of new public or private activity usually led to a rise in imports, not to complementary domestic production.

In summary, the features which so drastically retarded the Cuban economy before the revolution formed an intricate system, mutually reinforcing one another. The richness of the country in no way mitigated this system—indeed it was battened on by it. For example public revenue was large enough to finance a scheme of industrial development but such a scheme inevitably foundered on the hopeless corruption of all concerned—politicians, administrators, businessmen. In an economic sense this corruption could have been justified if the personal fortunes it created had been invested in the island. Corruption, as such, does not necessarily stifle economic growth, as the case of Mexico demonstrates, but it will help to do so where there is little incentive for private investment. The Cuban economy was overexploited because the chances of making money out of it greatly exceeded the attractions of reinvesting that money. Monoculture was the consequence rather than the cause of this situation. If in pre-revolutionary Cuba the government and business community had collectively decided to change the state of affairs which they maintained and profited from singly, then perhaps some development could have been achieved. After all, economies initially founded on primary production with a high incidence of foreign investment and dominated by a single market have still been able to reach take-off point (e.g. Australia). Indeed, in some ways Cuba enjoyed a more favoured position than do most other underdeveloped countries today. In particular the sugar agreement with the United States came to protect Cuba to some extent from the fluctuation and deterioration of world market prices to which most primary products have been subject. Nevertheless the ability to use this advantage to develop the island's economy as a whole was quite beyond the Cuban élite. This group was mortally infected by the fatalism which history and geography naturally created in the island. Cuba's political and business leaders had never succeeded in assuming responsibility for the country's economic fortunes and even as late as 1958 there seemed to be no pressing reason why they should wish to do so.

The Creation of a Cuban Economy

Fidel Castro's immediate economic programme after the revolution combined income expansion, income redistribution and structural change. The existence of unused and underused resources meant that in *economic* terms this programme could be remarkably effective. However, it involved very considerable *political* problems which were in the end to halt economic success.

The first policies of the revolutionary government redistributed income from rich to poor and, as part of this, from the cities to the countryside. Castro's Rebel Army had been sustained in its struggle by the small peasantry of the Sierra Maestra so that it is not surprising that the first major act of the revolutionary regime was the Agrarian Reform promulgated in May 1959. This first reform expropriated all private estates above a certain size (in most cases 30 caballerías). Where the land had formerly been worked by small peasants on a tenancy or share-cropping basis it was distributed to them in the areas of large-scale cultivation; where estates had been run as a single unit, cooperatives and state farms were formed. The reform involved the abolition of rural rents which had previously run at $74 million a year, and it gave land to over a hundred thousand peasants. In the towns the Rent Reduction Act of March 1959 lowered rents by a minimum of 30 per cent and a maximum of 50 per cent; urban rents had previously amounted to

$99 million a year. In both 1959 and 1960 rises in agricultural and industrial wages also added to the expansion of purchasing power. Government expenditure on social services (health, education and housing in particular) raised public expenditure from $390 million in 1959 to $1,321 million in 1961, greatly contributing to the expansion and redistribution of income.

Felipe Pazos, president of the National Bank in 1959 before he emigrated, has estimated that the sum effect of the various measures sponsored by the revolutionary regime in its first two years was to transfer about 15 per cent of the national income from property-owners to wage workers and small peasants. Moreover, in the words of the UN *Economic Survey of Latin America*, 1963; 'Under the stimulus of the marked expansion of internal demand, economic activity increased at a rapid rate in 1959 and 1960'. The unemployed who had numbered 627,000 in the summer of 1956 had been reduced to 376,000 by the summer of 1960. In the agricultural sector rice production rose from 167,000 tons in 1957 to 306,000 tons in 1960, and tomato production from 44,000 tons to 116,000 tons in the same period.

The counterpart to previously idle land in agriculture was surplus capacity in industry. The UN survey quoted above further reports that: 'In 1959 the proportion of utilised capacity was estimated at not more—and often less—than 60 per cent in the following branches of industry: metallurgy and metal transforming, certain chemical products, rubber, textiles, foods and beverages, and certain mining products'. In pre-revolutionary Cuba's narrow domestic market restrictive and monopolistic practices had flourished among both employers and unions. The great expansion of employment and demand in the first year or so of the revolution removed the economic rationale for these practices even where they were not directly abolished by the government. In the summer of 1960, before the break with the United States, the revolutionary government had already 'intervened'[1] an estimated $200 million of assets for various reasons, including the island's largest textile mill, the ten firms which comprised the so-called 'Match Trust', the Telephone Company, the Matanzas Bus Company, four frozen fish companies and Havana's twenty-four leather supply companies. Some of these assets were taken over by the government on the grounds that their owners had acquired them corruptly. On other occasions companies were taken over because it was felt that the owners were unsympathetic to the aims of the revolution. Increasing government control of the economy, and the threat of greater control, ensured that industrial production was allowed to meet rising demand up to the limits of installed capacity. The production of cotton fabrics rose from 3,000 tons in 1957 to 11,000 tons in 1960. During the same period production of cement rose from 651,000 tons to 813,000 tons.

The danger of the government's expansionary policy was that it might stimulate imports rather than domestic production. To forestall this, import quotas and tariffs were imposed on a wide range of consumer goods. In April 1960 the revolutionary government announced a trade agreement with the Soviet Union under which Cuba was to purchase Soviet oil at an estimated annual saving of $20 million. The international oil companies refused to allow their Cuban subsidiaries to refine this oil and, as a result, the refineries were 'intervened' by the revolutionary government. In response the United States government cut Cuba's sugar quota for 1960 by the outstanding amount. In the ensuing clash the Cuban government nationalised all foreign property in Cuba, including US owned assets worth over $1,000 million,

---

[1] 'Intervention' is a Cuban legal formula by which the state assumes control, though not ownership, of property.

as well as large-scale private property owned by Cubans. The United States imposed a complete embargo on trade with Cuba and later persuaded many other countries to follow suit.

THE TIME OF TROUBLES

The sugar harvest in 1961 was the second highest in Cuban history—this was to be the revolution's last unequivocal economic success for some time. In the space of a few months Cuba had transformed the structure of ownership and management in all sectors of the economy. Simultaneously it had totally changed both its sources of supply and its export market. Moreover, these upheavals coincided with the loss of many thousands of managers and technicians. At more or less the same time the distinct threat of invasion involved the diversion of national resources to defence. Thus the typical, newly appointed Cuban manager found himself running a newly created enterprise whose machinery came from a country with which Cuba could no longer trade. The new suppliers and customers were many thousands of miles away and employed completely different trading practices. Under the circumstances it is not surprising that the boom of 1959 and 1960 was checked despite the continuing pressure of domestic demand.

The advantages of the new industrial and agricultural structure were only likely to appear in the long run. Indeed, in the short run the new control which Cuba's leaders exercised over the economy led to mistakes which worsened the economy's problems. In this period the economic policy of the government was informed by a diagnosis of the economy which corresponded closely to that which can be found in almost every major study of Cuba before the revolution. Such reports invariably concluded that vigorous government action was needed to diversify agriculture and to foster industrialisation on the basis of import-substitution. As implemented in the years 1960–3 this policy led to a number of unfortunate results. Diversification of agriculture led to a severe drop in the sugar harvest just at a time when beet failures in Europe produced high international sugar prices. The expansion of non-sugar agriculture in 1959–61 had, it was thought, brought into production all the previously idle land or, at any rate, those lands which could conveniently be cultivated given existing transport facilities. As a consequence, in the course of 1962–3 about one-third of the area planted to cane was transferred to other uses. The execution of this switch seems to have been carried through with insufficient technical advice so that it was not always the least productive cane lands that were ploughed up nor those most suitable for other crops. Moreover, the expansion of non-sugar agriculture created an acute shortage of labour at the peak of the sugar harvest.

The policy of import-substitution seems to have deserved more limited application than was realised at the time. The production of light consumer products, with high domestic inputs, was certainly wise—for example, the expansion of cigarette production. Indeed one of the remarkable features of the economy during the revolution has been its ability to maintain and even increase the supply of basic goods to the population. Unfortunately even success during this early period was liable to have negative aspects—it tended to breed subjectivism and over-optimism. Available resources were spread over too many new projects with wasteful lengthening of the period of time necessary for completion. Hasty project evaluation led to the purchase of factories requiring too high a proportion of imported raw materials: about sixty complete industrial plants were purchased abroad in

1961 and 1962 alone. Failure to reach absurdly high targets (based on an excess of optimism and a paucity of reliable statistics) threw real planning out of gear.

The visiting French agronomist René Dumont in a series of critical but sympathetic studies of Cuba's economic policy expressed alarm at the 'dangerous generosity' of the government, especially to the rural workers. He found the state farms far too big for effective management and feared that overcentralisation of the economy was leading to 'bureaucratic anarchy'.[1] Clearly political as well as economic considerations accounted for some of these features of the Cuban economy. The newly established revolution was committed to pursue a 'generous' policy towards previously neglected sections of the population. Centralised control was unavoidable in a revolution which had, to a large extent, come from 'above'. However, the difficulties and setbacks of 1962-3 were serious enough to prompt a reorientation of policy and a more realistic assessment of the island's resources. In late 1963 the policy of diversifying at the expense of sugar was replaced by a plan which envisaged the sugar crop rising to some 10 million tons a year by 1970. In March 1964 the Soviet Union agreed to buy, at the very fair price of 6 cents a pound, 2·1 tons of sugar in 1965 rising to 5 million tons by 1970. The Cubans hoped that by the late 1960s the foreign exchange earned from sugar sales could then be used for a genuine diversification of the economy. Until that time the tempo of industrialisation would slow down and resources would be concentrated in those sectors which promised a quick return— fishing, cattle-raising and nickel. A second Agrarian Reform in October 1963 brought the remaining middle-sized estates into the public sector, reducing the private (small peasant) sector of agriculture to some 40 per cent of total cultivated area. Since 1963-4 there has been a partial recovery of the economy though most foods are still rationed. By June 1965 the London Economist Intelligence Unit in its *Quarterly Report* on Cuba pointed to a recovery of sugar production:

> The beginnings of mechanisation coupled with a strenuous national effort by volunteers from the Premier down, overcame the chronic labour shortage in the cane fields so that production is now at the pre-revolutionary level. This has been an impressive performance given the fact that regular employment in the sugar fields is far below the level of the years before 1959, and that American-made mill equipment has been without spare parts from the United States for five years so that improvisation has been the rule.

In the industrial sector the 1965 position was summarised by the *Report* as follows: 'Despite the difficulties and the retrenchment, industrial production under the present government is considerably higher than it was under capitalism.' Employment in the non-agricultural sector has risen rapidly— more rapidly than the rise in production. By 1963 employment in industry and construction already accounted for a labour force of 420,000 compared with 290,000 in 1956-7.

Taking the revolutionary period as a whole, the most consistently successful aspect of its policies has been the provision of social services. For a large number of Cubans, especially those in rural areas, the government's efforts in this field offset the shortages of those consumer goods and foodstuffs which were formerly imported.

[1] See René Dumont, *'Cuba et le socialisme'*, Paris, 1964.

The number of hospital beds in Cuba in 1958 was 22,000: by 1963 the figure had risen to 42,000. Public expenditure on education and culture was $11 per capita in 1958: by 1962 it had risen to $38 per capita. The phenomenal expansion of education included a campaign which, it was claimed, reduced illiteracy to insignificant proportions and at the same time brought the urban volunteer teachers face to face with conditions in the countryside. Technical instruction on a large scale was made available for the first time. The transformation of social and economic priorities led also to a switch from urban to rural construction. A road system was begun in the Sierra Maestra, while the building industry concentrated on factories, schools, clinics and low-cost housing rather than casinos and hotels. Formerly exclusive housing in Havana vacated by the émigrés is now used to house scholarship-holders from the countryside.

The Resilience of the Cuban Economy

What is most puzzling about the performance of the Cuban economy in the post-revolutionary period is that despite Cuban incompetence, and despite the US blockade, it has kept going, nowhere failing to provide a minimun flow of goods and services and increasing this flow in some sectors.[1] Though domestic production has not quite filled the vacuum previously occupied by imported consumer goods it seems as if it might be able to do so in the near future. Aid from the Soviet Union and other communist countries partly explains this. It has been estimated that up to the end of 1964 the Soviet Union alone had extended economic aid worth $300 million to Cuba and had given trade credits worth an equivalent sum. Moreover, the Soviet Union was able to provide goods on a scale and of a type which Cuba could not have obtained elsewhere.

The resilience of the Cuban economy is also to be partially explained in terms of the suppressed productivity of the pre-revolutionary economy. A continuing theme of the post-revolutionary economy has been the mobilisation of national resources for the previously neglected internal market. Whereas the 'internal market' was almost confined to Havana before the revolution, it now embraces even the most remote mountain settlement. An especially critical feature of the new economy is suggested by Martin Bronfenbrenner.[2] His central contention is that the public 'confiscation' of privately owned productive resources in underdeveloped countries would make possible 'economic development without sacrifice to the scale of living of the mass of the people . . . by shifting income to developmental investment from capitalists' consumption, from transfer abroad, and from unproductive "investment" like luxury housing'. As we have seen, property income was largely eliminated in Cuba by confiscation.[3] Whereas new capital formation averaged just over 10 per cent of GNP before the revolution it subsequently rose to about 18 per cent in 1961–3. This 'Bronfenbrenner effect' will continue to operate in the future when the path of Cuba's development is compared with that of any country where those who receive the national economic surplus do not reinvest it in the national economy.

[1] Visiting experts from both West and East are continually surprised, even perhaps shocked, to discover that Cuban mistakes do not seem to bring upon them proportionate failures.

[2] See the bibliography at the end of this chapter.

[3] Where compensation was paid, valuation was usually based on tax declarations in which the owners had invariably attempted to evade taxation by grossly understating the value of their property.

As Bronfenbrenner takes pains to demonstrate, even quite large-scale government incompetence is unlikely to dissipate the positive advantages of confiscation. In the case of Cuba it can be seen that the effect of expropriation goes beyond a switch of resources towards developmental investment. It forces the economic decision-makers to start formulating, as a matter of urgency, a strategy of development for the economy as a whole. Moreover, they now possess a formidable ability to mobilise the resources of the economy to this end. A revolution tends to make the whole population intensely concerned with economic affairs. At first fatalism is likely to be replaced by voluntarism, but at least the underdevelopment of the economy is henceforth experienced as a challenge rather than as a destiny. For this reason it is not surprising that vigorous debate took place in Cuba in 1963–5 concerning the nature of the new economic order. The experience of 1961–3 had led to the abandonment of over-hasty diversification, to a slower pace of industrialisation and to a concentration on directly productive investment. The debate which followed did not focus so much on specific policies of this sort as on the criteria to be used for deciding between rival policies and on the means for implementing them.

In the debate one school of thought, represented mainly by Alberto Mora, the then minister of foreign trade, advocated the use of a market mechanism for pricing policy and project evaluation. Material incentives and a measure of decentralised autonomy were to be used to raise the productivity of the existing labour force. The other tendency, represented primarily by Ernesto Che Guevara, then minister of industry, emphasised the primacy of non-market criteria for an underdeveloped country aiming at a socialist form of society. The economy should be run as if it were one great enterprise with firm central budgetary control. Guevara also believed that 'moral' or social incentives could play a large part in a post-revolutionary society where identification with the aims of the revolution was widespread. He feared that the use of material incentives would corrode revolutionary consciousness by reawakening the competitive and possessive individualism of a market society. The French economist Charles Bettelheim also intervened in the dispute with the publication of an article in *Cuba socialista*. Though sympathetic to Guevara's proposals he suggested that Cuba did not have the resources (administrators, technicians, statisticians, etc.) to implement effectively the central control which he envisaged. Until Cuba had reached a more advanced stage of development Guevara's ideas would tend to encourage the proliferation of bureaucracy as the absence of real administrative control was illusorily corrected by multiplying regulatory measures. At the Trade Union Congress of August 1966 Fidel Castro came out in favour of Che Guevara's ideas and since then they have informed government policy. At the same time a vigorous campaign against 'bureaucracy' has been launched: not only have the ministries and other central organs been severely reduced in size but they have also been stripped of their special powers and privileges. Castro himself constantly tours the countryside with a team of economists and technicians tackling problems at the grass roots level. For the moment this style of leadership helps to minimise the dangers pointed out by Bettelheim though in the long run it may produce problems of its own as it inhibits the development of long-range planning. The full consequences of the economic debate have yet to be worked out but it is already evident that, unlike discussions in the past, this one is being directly related to policy implementation.

Conclusions

In the future Cuba will be facing many of the same problems as all small developing countries. The prospects for sugar are if anything worse than for other primary products. A small internal market provides too narrow a base for industrial exports. Moreover, Cuba will probably have the continued disadvantage of geographical isolation.

In January 1967 the Economist Intelligence Unit arrived at the following balance sheet: 'On the credit side of the ledger are the facts that the average Cuban today is better fed, better housed and better educated than he ever was before. On the debit side are the mistakes and misguided experiments that led to an overambitious industrialisation plan which had to be scrapped at the cost of millions of dollars of scarce foreign exchange used to buy plant and equipment that now lie idle.'

Living standards should rise with investments in fishing and cattle-raising. The expansion of nickel mining should earn valuable foreign exchange. Mechanisation should greatly increase the productivity of the sugar industry and the new flow of technicians will raise standards throughout the economy. The scarcity of managerial and administrative skills is likely to remain a more difficult bottleneck to remove. Lastly, the level of future Soviet aid and trade will condition many of the possibilities of the Cuban economy. While it would seem that Cuba's sub-tropical agriculture complements Soviet needs, there will always be the possibility of cheaper alternative suppliers on the world market. Though many of Cuba's economic problems cannot be solved in isolation from those which afflict the developing world as a whole, her new economic system has at least already shown itself to be much more dynamic, and more egalitarian, than that which it replaced.

BIBLIOGRAPHY

De Santis, Sergio. 'The Debate in Cuba', *International Socialist Journal*, II, 10, Rome, August 1965.

Dumont, René. *Cuba et le socialisme*, Editions du Seuil, Paris, 1964.

Huberman, Leo and Sweezy, Paul. *Anatomy of a Revolution*, Monthly Review Press, New York, 1963.

Le Riverend, Julio. *Historia económica de Cuba*, Editorial Universitaria, Havana, 1964.

MacGaffey, Wyatt and Barnett, Clifford. *Twentieth Century Cuba*, Doubleday-Anchor, New York, revised ed. 1965.

O'Connor, James. 'Industrial Organisation in the Old and the New Cubas', *Science and Society*, XXX, 2, New York, spring 1966.

Seers, Dudley (ed.) *Cuba: The Economic and Social Revolution*, Oxford Univ. Press, London and New York, 1964.

Walters, Robert S. 'Soviet Economic Aid to Cuba', *International Affairs*, XL, 1, London, January 1966.

International Bank for Reconstruction and Development. *Report on Cuba*, Johns Hopkins Press, Baltimore, Md, 1951.

UN. *Economic Survey of Latin America 1963*, New York, 1965.

US Bureau of Foreign and Domestic Commerce. *Investment in Cuba*, Washington, DC, 1956.

THE ROLE OF COFFEE IN THE BRAZILIAN ECONOMY

JOHN C. G. BROOKS

HISTORY

Though for a century coffee has dominated the Brazilian economy, this was not always so. The plant was introduced into northern Brazil from French Guiana about 1730, but during the following fifty years attracted little attention because Brazil was still in its 'sugar and gold' phase. By 1780 planting of coffee in the vicinity of Rio de Janeiro had begun on a large scale, and when the attraction of sugar-planting had been diminished by West Indian competition and, later, by Napoleon's addiction to beet, coffee was ready to take its place as a boom crop. Plantings spread up the River Paraíba into São Paulo and Minas Gerais, and in 1818 the first substantial exports were made.

During the 19th century, though coffee-planting spread to almost all parts of Brazil, the State of São Paulo remained much the most important producing area—a position it maintained up to 1960 when it was finally overtaken by Paraná, to the south. Brazil in this period was gradually establishing its place as the world's chief source of coffee; by 1870 production stood at nearly 4 million bags, or somewhat over half of world output; by 1900 at over 11 million bags, or nearly 80 per cent of world production.

In the imperial period (1822–89) Brazil was uniquely favoured as a producer of coffee. The government appreciated the benefits coffee brought to the economy and pursued policies helpful to its development. The *terra roxa* of south-central Brazil was particularly suitable soil for the crop, and the existence until 1888 of a large slave-labour force was an important factor. Lastly, transport facilities between coast and interior were at that time superior to those of most of Brazil's competitors, and were developed specifically with export of coffee in mind.

The period immediately after the end of the Empire in 1889 was a serious one for coffee. Until the great wave of European immigration began in the 1890s there was a considerable shortage of labour due to the emancipation of the slaves (1888), and as the coffee boom was still in full spate there had been very heavy new plantings prior to 1888 which came into full production in the 1890s. The crisis came in 1906, when the Brazilian harvest alone was estimated at 20 million bags, compared with world demand at 14 million bags. The solution to this desperate situation was the introduction by the State of São Paulo of the first of the 'valorisation' schemes, by which Brazil has sought to hold surplus coffee off the market until it can be sold later to compensate for a low crop. The 1906 scheme was successful in rescuing prices, and was succeeded by another in 1917 and by a Federal scheme in

632

1923, which operated with more or less success until the world depression of 1930.

The idea of 'valorisation' has two serious faults from the trading point of view, which Brazil is only now attempting to remedy. The first is that with an artificial reduction in the amount of Brazilian coffee available and an artificial rise in its price, the way has been clear for the intensification of competition, and the importance of other producing countries, both in Latin America and later in Africa, has steadily grown. The second is that it has been very difficult to restrain growers from increasing plantings, in view of the favourable prices they have received as a result of valorisation. To these points should be added the consideration that very large financial resources, which in a country as poor as Brazil would be better used for development purposes, are required to buy and stock the surplus coffee.

After the collapse of the 1923 scheme more drastic methods became necessary. The artificially maintained high prices during the 1920s had caused heavy extra planting, and by 1931 it became apparent that crops were expanding far beyond what demand in a depression-racked world could ever reach. Stocks would have risen to astronomical figures, so it was decided to burn part of the crop. Burnings, which continued until 1943 and accounted for 78 million bags (equal to four years' crops at that time) played their part in maintaining prices, but again left the door open to competition, especially, this time, from the cheaper robusta coffee produced by the African countries.

Brazilian production was low during the war years, partly because the current low prices had not encouraged harvesting and partly because the adverse conditions of the 1930s had discouraged new planting. The average crop for the five years ending 1933-4 was 24-25 million bags; this figure declined to an average of 14-15 million bags for the five years ending 1945-6.

The Brazilian coffee industry was ill-prepared to meet the resurgence of demand after the 1939-45 war, which reached an acute stage in 1950 after all existing stocks had been sold. (In the absence of stocks the trade could not react quickly to changes in demand, because the coffee tree does not produce at all until four years after planting and does not enter into full production for ten years; the problem is compounded by the wide variation in the size of crops from year to year.) The result was a vertiginous rise in prices (which had averaged 20 US cents a pound of Santos 4 beans in the 1920s, about half that in the 1930s, and was fixed at approximately 13 cents from 1941 to 1945) from approximately 26 cents in 1947-8 to 50 cents in 1950, when extensive new planting was begun as a result in the State of Paraná. The shortage continued until 1956 when the new plantings began to take effect and the customary surplus began to reappear; from an average of 79 cents a pound in 1954 (caused by speculation following the severe frost of 1953) the price declined to 48 cents in 1958 and as low as 34 cents in 1962; it has since recovered as a result of the International Coffee Agreement.

The following tables demonstrate the evolution of Brazilian coffee production and exports, in comparison with world figures, in recent years. The decline in the relative importance of Brazilian coffee, both in relation to the world coffee industry and to other Brazilian production, is clearly shown.

The series of gradually expanding coffee stabilisation agreements to which Brazil has been a partner (from the 1957 Mexico City agreement of seven Latin American countries to the 1958 agreement of fifteen, and the subsequent world-wide agreements of 1959 and 1962) have succeeded in bringing a degree of stability to exports and therefore to world market prices,

TABLE 1

BRAZILIAN TOTAL AND EXPORTABLE COFFEE PRODUCTION IN RELATION TO WORLD PRODUCTION, 1953-4 to 1965-6

Season	Total production (million bags of 60 kg.)	% of world production	Exportable production (million bags of 60 kg.)
1953-4	19·7	45	14·3
1954-5	18·1	43	14·2
1955-6	23·5	47	21·3
1956-7	18·0	39	11·7
1957-8	26·0	45	20·8
1958-9	31·0	50	26·0
1959-60	43·8	56	37·0
1960-1	29·0	44	22·0
1961-2	35·0	49	28·0
1962-3	27·0	40	20·0
1963-4	28·2	40	21·2
1964-5	10·3	19	3·0
1965-6	37·0	46	29·8
1966-7 (estimates)	21·0	32	14·0

Source: United States Department of Agriculture.

TABLE 2

BRAZILIAN COFFEE EXPORTS IN RELATION TO WORLD COFFEE AND BRAZILIAN TOTAL EXPORTS, 1954-65

Year	Volume of Brazilian exports (million bags)	% of volume of world coffee exports	Value of Brazilian exports (US$ million)	% by value of total Brazilian exports	Santos 4 New York price, per lb. (US cents)
1954	10·9	34	948	61	78·7
1955	13·7	40	844	59	57·1
1956	16·8	44	1,030	70	58·1
1957	14·3	40	846	61	56·9
1958	12·9	35	688	55	48·4
1959	17·4	42	733	57	37·3
1960	16·8	39	713	56	36·7
1961	17·0	39	710	51	36·3
1962	16·4	35	643	53	34·0
1963	19·5	40	748	53	34·1
1964	14·9	33	760	53	47·5
1965	13·5	n.a.	707	44	44·7

Source: Pan-American Coffee Bureau and
Bank of London and South America Ltd.

but unfortunately not to production. The reduced prices of the last ten years have still been sufficiently remunerative to growers to induce them to continue new plantings, and it was not until 1962 that steps were finally taken to finance the uprooting of uneconomic trees and their replacement mainly by other crops but partly by new, high-yielding coffee plants.

THE IMPACT AND THE PROBLEM

The importance of the coffee industry to the Brazilian economy, as expressed in terms of GNP and total exports, is suggested by the following table.

TABLE 3

THE COFFEE SECTOR IN THE BRAZILIAN ECONOMY

Average for period	% of GNP (at current prices)	% of exports by value (US$)	Exports as % of GNP (at current prices)
1947–9	5·1	42·2	5·0
1950–5	7·1	61·1	5·7
1956–9	4·9	54·1	3·0
1960–2	4·5	48·2	2·2

Source: Unpublished estimate of Centro de Estudos Agrícolas, Getúlio Vargas Foundation.

Expressed as a function of agricultural output only, the importance of the coffee sector is shown as follows: when in 1964 coffee production fell by 37 per cent from the 1963 level, the rise in the index of agricultural production for that year was increased, if coffee is excluded from consideration, from 4·7 to 8 per cent. Similarly, when in 1965 production of coffee rose by 90 per cent from the 1964 level, the agricultural production index showed a rise of 10·4 per cent with coffee included, and only 5·5 per cent without coffee. It would appear from these figures that the value of the coffee sector is about one-tenth of the value of all agricultural and livestock production in Brazil.

The four main coffee-producing states of Brazil, in present order of size of crop, are Paraná, São Paulo, Minas Gerais and Espírito Santo. Production in other states, such as Rio de Janeiro, Bahia and Goiás, is comparatively unimportant, amounting in aggregate to less than 2 million bags a year.

The differences between the four main producing states go far to explain some of the contradictions of Brazilian coffee policy. The production of Paraná, the newest coffee area, which is subject to frost damage and therefore fluctuates more widely than that of other states, was less than half of São Paulo's as late as the 1957–8 season but surpassed it in 1959–60. This was because of very extensive planting following the boom in the early 1950s; Paraná now normally produces half of the Brazilian crop. São Paulo, the traditional area, produces Brazil's highest quality coffee (Mogiana), but many of the trees are on the verge of becoming uneconomic and several areas have been turned over to the production of cotton and citrus. The standard of husbandry is higher than in Paraná and the soils are basically more suitable for coffee; São Paulo still produces about one-third of Brazil's total crop. Minas Gerais and Espírito Santo, which together produce on average about one-sixth of the total crop, are regarded as declining areas; they produce mainly coffee of the lower grades, and produce it much more expensively than is the case in Paraná.

This very wide variation between the low production costs of Paraná and western São Paulo on the one hand, and the older areas of São Paulo, Minas Gerais and Espírito Santo on the other, is the key to Brazil's price and market policy: whereas Paraná is one of the world's lowest-cost producing areas, able to compete easily with the African countries which now provide the most formidable competition in world markets for lower-grade coffees, the older coffee regions are now high-cost areas. It is impossible for Brazil to permit an entirely free market to operate even within the country, because it is not feasible for social reasons to allow the coffee industry in the old areas to perish until financing is available for uprooting the coffee trees and planting other crops; this problem explains Brazil's concern to keep coffee prices high instead of relying on the action of the free market.

In the post-war period, the need for the artificial maintenance of prices became apparent in 1957, when world supplies of coffee surpassed world demand for the first time since 1945, and stocks began to accumulate. It is estimated that stocks in July 1957 amounted to about 8 million bags, and rose to about 54 million bags in four years. In 1963 and 1964, following the serious drought, frost and fires in Paraná in 1963, stocks were reduced, but were estimated to have reached about 50 million bags again by July 1965, with the likelihood of a rise to 65 million bags by July 1966. These stocks, which are controlled by the Brazilian Coffee Institute acting as agent of the government, are financed by a contribution quota which amounts to about 55 per cent of the equivalent in cruzeiros of the total of foreign exchange earned by each bag of coffee exported. This contribution is not always enough; in 1965 the Coffee Defence Fund was exhausted and the government had to provide extra financing amounting to the equivalent of almost £10 million. The coffee interests greatly resent paying this 'exchange confiscation', as it is called, but while the surplus remains it is only fair that the planters, who are unwilling to envisage close control of new plantings and production, and are insistent on maintaining high prices, should finance the means of export control.

Meanwhile, Brazil has a pressing need to maximise receipts of foreign exchange from exports. During the early 1950s when export receipts were high, a comprehensive industrialisation programme was begun, and could not be left unfinished when export receipts later fell. The difference was made up by heavy foreign investment inflows (which dried up in 1962 when restrictive foreign capital legislation was introduced and only began to recover in 1965 after the partial repeal of that legislation) and by short-term borrowing from abroad, to the extent that in 1963 debt service claimed 43 per cent of Brazil's total foreign exchange earnings, as against the 15 per cent which the World Bank considers the maximum advisable upper limit for a developing country. Rationalisation of the coffee industry, to ensure that Brazil can in future sell its whole output without the necessity of financing heavy surplus stocks, is therefore increasingly necessary.

THE SOLUTION

Clearly it is not in Brazil's interest that the course of the next fifty years should mirror that of the last fifty, with Brazil's part of the world market declining continuously and its efforts to maintain prices simply increasing opportunities for its competitors. Fortunately, there have been several factors, appearing together in the course of the last few years, which render this unlikely.

The first of these is the International Coffee Agreement, renewed annually since 1959 and placed on a five-year basis in 1962, which no producing country considers perfect but which none wishes to abolish. This agreement limits Brazil to a basic export quota of about 18 million bags (40 per cent of the world total), which may be raised or lowered according to price trends. This quota is little more than half Brazil's total production in a good year, but until coffee consumption increases it is unlikely to be raised. (The only possibility of raising exports under the International Agreement lies in increasing shipments to 'new' consumer countries, such as the Soviet Union and Japan, which are small importers but considered likely to expand consumption.) In fact Brazil has on occasion failed to supply even this quota; in the coffee year ending in September 1965 exports within the agreement amounted to under 13 million bags against a quota of 17 million. This was attributed to the Coffee Institute's decision to fix its export prices high, and to the fact that, owing to unfavourable weather, the quality of the beans was lower than usual.

Secondly, a systematic eradication scheme has appeared in Brazil. The Executive Group for the Rationalisation of Coffee-Growing (GERCA) was established in 1962 to finance the uprooting of uneconomic plants and the substitution of new ones; under its programme 207 million trees were destroyed in 1962 and 381 million in 1963. The number of trees destroyed fell to 98 million in 1964 because the compensation figure had been fixed in 1962 without provision for the depreciation of the cruzeiro and because the recovery in coffee prices had again rendered marginal plants economic. In 1965 the government set up a top-level cabinet committee to review the eradication policy; in view of the fact that there are probably about 4,000 million coffee trees in Brazil, rather more than half of which are either uneconomic or produce very low-grade coffee, a definitive solution of the Brazilian coffee problem awaits the inception of an effective scheme.

A third factor is the speculative element. The Coffee Institute's price maintenance policies have induced coffee-planting in several areas unsuited to it—especially the highlands in the Paraná Nova and Paraná Novíssima areas, where frosts are not uncommon and the sandy soils are not appropriate —and much planting has been done speculatively by industrialists, bankers and businessmen with little concern for the long-term interests of the coffee sector or for the maintenance of soil fertility and the quality of the product. However, the catastrophic weather in Paraná in 1963—drought, frost and fires in quick succession—resulted in heavy losses in the areas least suited to coffee, which are now reported to have been largely turned over to other crops and to pasture.

A fourth factor is the growth in the use of soluble coffee which favours the consumption of strong-flavoured beans such as Brazil's and the African robustas, against the mild arabicas of Colombia and Central America. Brazil has already begun to manufacture soluble coffee for export, and it is more profitable to export soluble coffee, because of its higher labour content, than raw coffee. Furthermore, with the application of the accelerated freeze-drying process to soluble coffee, its market should widen to cover some consumers who previously objected to the flavour of the soluble product.

In conclusion, it may be pointed out that if a judicious policy is followed of eradication and substitution of uneconomic plants, and possibly the destruction of some of its surplus stocks, Brazil should in future be able to take advantage of the low production costs of its most favourable areas, and look its competitors firmly in the face. The coffee interests have in the past been so powerful that they have been able to force the government to follow high-cost policies in the short-term interests of the growers, but these same policies have been deleterious to the industry in the long-term, because they have encouraged the maintenance of uneconomic plantations and the spread of coffee into areas not really suitable for it. Competition is now too strong to allow the continuance of these outmoded habits; Brazil is essentially a low-cost producer, and once the industry is properly rationalised it will be able to compete on equal terms with any other coffee industry in the world.

BIBLIOGRAPHY

Rowe, J. W. F. *The World's Coffee*, HMSO, London, 1963.

Uribe, Andrés C. *Brown Gold: The Amazing Story of Coffee*, Random House, New York, 1954.

Bank of London and South America Ltd. *Fortnightly Review* and *Quarterly Review*, London.

FAO. *The World Coffee Economy* (FAO Commodity Bulletin Series, No. 33), 1961. Obtainable through HMSO, London. *Monthly Bulletin of Agricultural Economics and Statistics*. Obtainable through HMSO, London.

Instituto Brasileiro de Geografia e Estatística. *Anuário Estadístico do Brasil*, Rio de Janeiro.

Pan-American Coffee Bureau. *Coffee Statistics*, New York (annual).

US Department of Agriculture. *Foreign Agricultural Circulars*, Washington, DC.

THE ROLE OF COPPER IN THE CHILEAN ECONOMY

GREGORIO AMUNÁTEGUI

MODERN electrical and thermal technology has brought copper, the next best conductor after silver, to the fore among non-ferrous metals. Yet this essential metal is in relatively short supply. It has been estimated that copper represents only 0·01 per cent of the earth's crust. There are large parts of the world where it is virtually non-existent; conversely, in other areas inordinate concentrations are found, with a density warranting development of the deposits on a commercial scale. Among these privileged regions is Chile. The deserts of the Norte Grande, the arid Norte Chico and the fertile Valle Central contain what is perhaps the richest concentration of copper in the world.

THE DEVELOPMENT OF COPPER PRODUCTION IN CHILE

Centuries ago the country's indigenous inhabitants mined copper and substituted it for iron in the making of weapons and carpentry tools, and it was much in demand for pins to fasten clothing. With the Conquest came widespread exploitation of the deposits. Between 1601 and 1810 the country's output of copper amounted to 81,550 tons, which were exported to Spain and Peru, mainly for casting pieces for ordnance and making brass. After 1810 the history of copper production falls into two distinct periods.

The period to 1955

During the first of these, which extended up to 1955, the government treated the industry with an odd mixture of interest and indifference. Between 1851 and 1880 Chile was the world's leading producer, accounting for one-third of total output. Its importance then dwindled until on the eve of the first world war it was contributing no more than 4 per cent of the world total. Then after the opening up of three very large deposits its share in world production climbed to over 20 per cent in 1934, only to fall to 11 per cent by 1954.

During this period the Chilean copper mines produced approximately 13 million tons. Yet this huge volume was shipped abroad without the state's having an adequate grasp of production and marketing, or of official evaluation and control of the activities of producer enterprises. A comment by an ex-member of the British Colonial Office staff that appeared in *The Times* long ago is of relevance here: 'But minerals are a different matter. Once they are mined they are mined, and the country from which they are extracted is that much the poorer. The only right objective is to get the maximum amount of return from each ton extracted, not to get the maximum amount of extraction during some given period.'

The period from 1955

Hence the second phase in the history of Chilean copper production, which began in 1955, was attended at its start by two distinctly unfavourable economic circumstances. In the first place, the preceding period's immense output had been exported without specialised official knowledge and, therefore, in conditions completely at variance with the pragmatical spirit of the remark by the British civil servant quoted. Secondly, Chile's importance as a world supplier of refined copper had declined.

A law passed on 5 May 1955 was designed to remedy this situation. First it offered the investor reasonable tax and exchange incentives with a view to securing an expansion of installed capacity for the production of refined copper. Secondly it established an agency called the Copper Department (Departamento del Cobre), later known as the Chilean Copper Corporation (Corporación del Cobre de Chile), to be responsible for the study of all matters concerning the copper industry, particularly costing and marketing.

The repercussions of the new legislation, and especially of the activities of the Copper Department, are clearly reflected in statistics. Production of primary copper, which in 1954 had amounted to 355,365 metric tons, reached 633,343 tons by 1964. The year 1954 had also witnessed a very low output of refined copper, totalling only 190,000 tons. In the ensuing decade this figure was raised to 256,000 tons. Moreover, during the period under review two major projects were launched, which were to exert a decisive influence on the development of copper mining in Chile: the Electrolytic Refinery of the Andes Copper Mining Co. which went into operation in January 1965, and the Las Ventanas Smelter and Electrolytic Refinery owned by the Empresa Nacional de Minería.

The Copper Department also extended its activities to promotion of the uses of copper; accordingly, Latin America's first centre of this kind was set up in Chile in 1962 and has been working since then in close association with the corresponding centres in Europe and the United States. During this period, too, the Copper Department concerned itself with copper marketing problems, and while the volume exported by Chile steadily increased, more and more care was taken to see that every ton was sold at the best possible price obtainable on the market.

STRUCTURE OF THE CHILEAN COPPER INDUSTRY; ITS PLACE IN WORLD PRODUCTION

Of the 633,300 metric tons of copper produced by Chile in 1964, 527,800 represented the output of the so-called Gran Minería ('large mining companies') and 105,500 that of the Mediana y Pequeña Minerías ('medium-scale and small enterprises'). The Gran Minería, which accounts for 83 per cent of copper production in Chile, comprises, at the time of writing, three agencies of United States companies: the Braden Copper Company, a subsidiary of the Kennecott Copper Corporation (New York) and owner of El Teniente, one of the largest underground mines in existence; the Chile Exploration Company, a subsidiary of the Anaconda Company (New York), which owns Chuquicamata, the biggest open-cut copper deposit in the world; and the Andes Copper Mining Company, which is also a subsidiary

TABLE 1

COPPER PRODUCTION, 1954–66

(thousands of tons)

Year	Gran Minería	%	Mediana y Pequeña Minerías	%	Total
1954	323·2	(88·9)	40·5	(11·1)	363·7
1955	391·7	(90·4)	41·8	(9·6)	433·5
1956	443·7	(90·7)	45·5	(9·3)	489·2
1957	434·9	(90·6)	45·3	(9·4)	480·2
1958	418·6	(90·0)	46·3	(10·0)	464·9
1959	497·1	(91·2)	47·7	(8·8)	544·8
1960	479·2	(90·0)	53·3	(10·0)	532·5
1961	481·1	(87·8)	66·6	(12·2)	547·7
1962	510·2	(87·1)	75·7	(12·9)	585·9
1963	507·4	(84·4)	93·7	(15·6)	601·1
1964	527·8	(84·9)	94·0	(15·1)	621·8
1965	479·2	(81·9)	106·1	(18·1)	585·3
1966	540·9	(81·7)	120·9	(18·3)	661·8

TABLE 2

EXPORTS, 1954–66

(millions of dollars)

Year	Copper	Iron, saltpetre and iodine	Industrial and agricultural production	Total
1954	221·5	93·4	68·5	383·4
1955	327·4	87·8	74·2	489·4
1956	333·7	98·0	66·2	497·9
1957	246·0	84·6	66·2	396·8
1958	195·1	84·4	74·5	354·0
1959	279·3	91·6	86·9	457·8
1960	322·1	77·0	62·6	461·7
1961	304·7	80·1	69·7	454·5
1962	332·3	95·6	62·5	490·4
1963	335·9	95·6	62·9	494·4
1964	374·8	106·3	109·3	590·4
1965	428·5	126·7	123·7	678·9
1966	575·7	132·6	136·1	844·4

Source: Chilean Copper Corporation

of the Anaconda Company, and to which belongs the El Salvador mine. The Mediana y Pequeña Minerías consist of a group of holdings developed by private individuals or enterprises controlled by Chilean, French, Canadian, Japanese and United States capital.

In 1964, as in the immediately preceding years, Chile's total volume of production placed it second among world producers, following the United States and ahead of Zambia and the Soviet Union. Its importance in the copper industry, however, stems not only from its position as one of the world's leading suppliers, but above all from the size of its reserves, which appear to amount to something approaching 50 million tons. The United States comes next, with 35 million tons, and then Zambia with 24 million, the Republic of the Congo with 20 million, the Soviet Union with 16 million, and Peru with 12 million, out of a world total of 188 million tons.

The Impact of Copper on the Chilean Economy

In 1964 the Chilean GDP stood at 15,072 million escudos, in which the share of the Gran Minería was 656·4 million, or 4·36 per cent. With respect to visible and invisible earnings—in other words Chile's international means of payment—which in 1964 represented the equivalent of 470·1 million escudos, the contribution of the Gran Minería was 223·9 million or 47·6 per cent, and that of the Mediana y Pequeña Minerías 62·7 million or 13·3 per cent. Consequently 61 per cent of Chile's total foreign exchange earnings was attributable to copper. The incidence of copper production on tax receipts is also highly significant. Since tax revenue in 1964 totalled 1,716·7 million escudos, and taxation on the Gran Minería amounted to 278·1 million, it can be seen that this sector of the copper industry accounted for 16·2 per cent of total tax revenue. If income tax alone is considered, of the 639·8 million escudos collected in 1964 the Gran Minería was responsible for 278·1 million, i.e. 43·5 per cent.

Three other factors help to determine the vital importance of the copper industry in Chile. First it is a principal source of employment in the mining industry, for out of a total number of 64,960 persons employed in mining in Chile, 17,500 find work in the Gran Minería and 15,000 in the Mediana y Pequeña Minerías. In the former sector wages and salaries are high in comparison with those received by the rest of the Chilean labour force, and the purchasing power thus generated is of major importance for development and trade in three large provinces. The second factor consists in the growing volume of local products bought by the Gran Minería companies, whose purchases in Chile increased from $26 million in 1956 to $49·7 million in 1965. Within the same period the proportion of these companies' total domestic and foreign purchases represented by the local products in question rose from 28·3 to 53·7 per cent. Lastly, the Gran Minería is also the means whereby the most advanced technical knowledge is introduced into the country.

Chile is faced with the urgent necessity of diversifying and expanding its exports in order to increase its foreign exchange earnings. Diversification is a long-term goal linked to economic and financial measures whose effects are slow to make themselves felt. Expansion of exports, on the other hand, is much more feasible as a short-term proposition. Thus the pressing need for economic development would seem to entail a correspondingly rapid expansion of the Chilean copper industry. Fortunately, this expansion of production is not only possible but can hardly be deferred. It is called for, in the first place, by the predicted increase in world copper consumption. Secondly, Chile's copper reserves are obviously rich enough to make it commercially worth while to develop them. Thirdly, no other Chilean export commodity shows a greater difference between industrial production costs and world sales prices than the copper produced by the Gran Minería. Hence it is obvious that the expansion of the Chilean copper industry is a matter of urgency linked with the necessity of expediting the country's economic development.

FUTURE PROSPECTS

Shortly after President Frei assumed office, a Commission made up by the executive vice-presidents of the Chilean Copper Corporation, Javier Lagarrigue, and of the Development Corporation (Corporación de Fomento), Raul Sáez, concluded an agreement with the companies forming the Gran Minería and with the Cerro Corporation, the implementation of which was authorised by Congress under the terms of Law No. 16,425 passed on 25 January 1966.

According to the provisions of the agreement the Braden Copper Company is committed to increase its present capacity by 90,000 tons within a period of five years, so as to reach a total annual production capacity of 252,000 metric tons. The Anaconda Group (Chile Exploration Company and Andes Copper Mining Company) which, as previously stated, mines the Chuquicamata and El Salvador deposits in Chile, envisages the addition of a further 90,000 tons to its capacity in the same period, which will bring its total annual production capacity up to 447,000 tons. This volume will be augmented by the output of the new Exótica mine—adjacent to Chuquicamata —which by 1971, according to estimates, should show an annual production capacity of approximately 100,000 tons. Thus the Group is expected to enlarge its annual production capacity by 190,000 metric tons, or 46·5 per cent, while the Exótica mine will be the fourth deposit belonging to the Gran Minería to be incorporated in the national economy. The agreement also covers the exploitation of the Río Blanco mine, owned by the Cerro Corporation. Its development will contribute an estimated 60,000 metric tons per annum to the expansion of Chile's production capacity.

These programmes deriving from the agreement—the expansion of current operations at El Teniente, Chuquicamata and El Salvador, the beginning of production at the Río Blanco mine and the incorporation of the new Exótica deposit—will mean that by the end of 1971 annual production capacity in this sector will have reached 970,000 tons; to which volume must be added the probable increase in the production capacity of the Mediana y Pequeña Minerías, estimated at approximately 120,000 tons by the close of 1970. Thus, at the end of 1971 Chile should be in a position to produce 1,100,000 metric tons of primary copper annually. On the basis of projects already executed and others stemming from the agreement, the proportion of Chile's total exports represented by refined copper may be expected to rise from 33 to 55 per cent between 1964 and the end of 1971.

All these developments will have a decisive influence on Chile's economic growth. For instance, the undertakings described will signify capital formation to the extent of $566 million in five years. This amount is equivalent to the public sector's total annual investment and not only implies an increase of at least 25 per cent in Chile's net capital formation to 1970 but by its direct effect alone will help to raise the country's annual growth rate 1 per cent above any attainable under ordinary development and investment programmes.

At the same time, the projects will mean a real increase in annual foreign exchange earnings which, from a minimum of $237 million, might rise to as much as $276 million. If this latter increment were achieved, by 1971 Chile's real foreign exchange income from exports of goods (taking 1964 as the basic year) would have expanded by an estimated 83·5 per cent. These figures are computed on the assumption that the price of copper will be 29 dollar cents per pound, so that they would be higher still if sales prices were to rise in 1970. (The Gran Minería was selling its copper at 36 cents per pound in 1965 and in 1966 obtained 62 cents.) Government officials estimate that on the basis of the 29-cent price level, income from taxation and royalties would increase by $54 million, and every additional cent per pound would mean an income increment of roughly $14 million.

In the field of employment the new agreement will result in an increase in the number of permanent jobs available on the production side by 15,500, and in supplier industries, services, etc. by a further 46,000, which in turn will give rise to a chain of additional employment opportunities. In all, an extra 61,000 permanent jobs should be provided as the direct or indirect outcome of the agreement. During the execution of the expansion projects there will be opportunities of temporary employment for about 10,000 workers on the sites, and approximately twice as many in supplier industries and services.

The agreement is also of great importance inasmuch as it will enable Chilean technicians and professionals to acquaint themselves more closely and thoroughly with the wide variety of complex tasks involved in the production and marketing of copper on a world scale. This will be facilitated in the following ways:

(1) The Braden Copper Company (a subsidiary of the Kennecott Copper Corporation and owner of El Teniente) is to become the Compañía Minera El Teniente SA, in which the government of Chile will hold 51 per cent of the stock and Kennecott 49 per cent.

(2) The new Exótica deposit is to be developed by a Chilean corporation, in which Anaconda will hold 75 per cent of the stock and the government of Chile 25 per cent.

(3) For the development of the Rio Blanco deposit, owned by the Cerro Corporation, another national joint stock company is to be established, the Compañía Minera Andina SA, in which the government of Chile will hold 25 per cent of the stock and the Cerro Corporation the remainder.

(4) Anaconda (51 per cent) and the Copper Corporation (49 per cent) are to form a corporation which will decide, on the basis of the studies it carries out, whether or not a given deposit is suitable for development. Its initial research will relate to a number of holdings placed at its disposal by the Anaconda Group. In the event of its determining that a particular deposit (whether of copper or not) is worth exploiting, a joint company will be formed to develop it.

(5) Any innovation or change in sales policy with respect to the copper produced in Chile by Anaconda will be determined jointly by the Copper Corporation and Anaconda. To this end the Copper Corporation will have full access to the meetings and records of the Anaconda Sales Committee (New York), which is the Group's executive sales agency.

The copper production expansion programmes are bound to exert a dynamic influence on Chilean industry as a whole through the increase in the mining companies' local purchases. Further, the studies which will be carried out in connection with this huge expansion may result in greater efficiency in the recovery of a number of mineral by-products of the copper industry. Among those already being obtained are gold, silver and molybdenum. New by-products which it may prove economically worthwhile to recover in the future include selenium, tellurium, platinum (and the platinum metals palladium, iridium, osmium, rhodium and ruthenium), nickel, bismuth and antimony.

BIBLIOGRAPHY

Amunátegui, Gregorio. 'La política chilena del cobre', *Revista finis terrae*, No. 49, Universidad Católica de Chile, May–June 1965.

Lagarrigue, Javier. 'Chile: the Importance of Copper', *Metal Bulletin Special Issue*, London, May 1965.

Saez, Raúl. *Chile y el cobre*, Departamento del Cobre, Santiago, 1965.

Vera, Mario. *La política económica del cobre en Chile*, Univ. of Chile Press, Santiago, 1962.

Vicuña Mackenna, Benjamin. *El libro del Cobre*, Cervantes, Santiago, 1883.

Vera, Mario. *La política económica del cobre en Chile*, Univ. of Chile Press, Santiago, 1962.

Corporación del Cobre de Chile. *Estadísticas anuales*, Departamento de Estudio de Mercados, Comercial, Auditoría de Costos y Control de Importaciones, Santiago.

THE FISHING INDUSTRY OF PERU

GERALD ELLIOT

ALONG the coast of Peru there run the cold waters of the Humboldt current. These give the country its rainless coastal desert, and in recompense provide one of the richest areas of marine life in the world. For many years the main value to Peru from her seas was constituted by the guano deposits laid down on offshore islands over thousands of years by the huge bird population, which lives on the anchoveta shoals. Now the fish forms the direct raw material for a fish meal industry which stretches from Chimbote in the north to Ilo on the Chilean border.

The anchoveta is a small fish, reaching a maximum size of about 17 cm., which is found near the surface and close to the coast in large shoals all the year round. It is captured by the simple technique of the purse seine. The fishing boat finds a shoal and moves round it, letting down a vertical curtain of net. When the circle is complete the bottom of the net is drawn together and the shoal is caught in the bag, to be taken on board by pumping or by a small scooping net. In this way 150 tons or more—enough to fill the boat—can be caught in one cast. At the port the fish is sucked out, again by pump, and delivered to a fish meal plant.

Fish meal factories perform the processes of cooking the fish, squeezing out the free liquors for recovery of the oil which it contains, drying the 'presscake' in long rotating driers usually heated by direct flame, and finally grinding and sacking the meal. The liquors are passed through high-speed centrifugal separators which take out the oil, and the liquors themselves may then be concentrated in evaporators and fed back into the meal.

The resultant basic products are meal and oil. Fish meal is a feeding stuff of high protein content which is exported to the United States and Europe and is an important component of feeding compounds for chickens and pigs. Fish oil is purified and hardened for margarine and cooking fats.

DEVELOPMENT OF THE INDUSTRY

The peoples of Peru have been fishermen for many centuries, as is shown from the frequent fish motifs on the pots of the pre-Incan coastal civilisations. But it was only after the second world war that the first steps were taken to catch anchoveta in the large quantities necessary to support a fish meal industry. To begin with the Peruvian government was reluctant to encourage development. There was a fear that if large-scale fishing was started the guano bird population would disappear and the guano industry would be killed. But the economic potential of the industry was enough to push aside this consideration and from 1956 onwards it started to expand very fast. In 1956 there were twenty-seven factories which produced 31,000 tons of meal. Six years later the number of factories had grown to 110, with a production of 1,120,000 tons. Peru's total catch of nearly 9 million tons of fish in 1964 has put her in front of Japan as the world's leading fishing nation.

The first factories were put up in Callao, the seaport of Lima, and at Chimbote in the north. As these two places showed excellent fishing results new factories were added there. Then, in the belief, not always justified, that the anchoveta could be found in a solid ribbon right down the coast, plants were started in every place where shelter for boats, fresh water and labour were available and sometimes in spots where none of these were to be found. Many factories were built in the central zone between Callao and Chimbote, with concentrations in Supé, Carquin and Chancay, and there was a smaller expansion in the south at Ilo and Mollendo.

The industry in the early years was a remarkable success story of capitalist enterprise, which perhaps only Peru of South American countries could have produced. Plants could be financed by low subscriptions of local capital, supporting a heavy structure of bank loans and credits from the suppliers of equipment. Boats were often bought by individuals, making use of the same sort of credit facilities, and were operated to supply fish on contract to the plants. Business and professional people of all types put up money and if they were lucky saw it show a substantial return. Fish was abundant and close at hand, so that a boat could sometimes fill up and discharge twice a day and more. The simplest type of processing seemed to be adequate, and the price of meal was good.

THE 1960s

In the early 1960s conditions became more difficult. The price of both meal and oil dropped, as demand had not kept pace with the increase in production. Fish became harder to get, partly because the initial surplus available when a virgin stock is first fished had gone, and partly because there were very many more boats competing for the same fish. When these setbacks occurred the weaker companies suffered, particularly those in ports which turned out to be in poor natural fishing areas. Boats started to break down in the more rigorous fishing conditions, and could not be repaired. Good fishing crews became more difficult to get. The fish, now smaller and brought in after a longer voyage, was harder to process, and the old machinery bought cheap from abroad could not cope with it. The requirements of plant workers and fishermen for better wages squeezed the gap between costs and profits, and many who had no regular control of their costs suffered. As there were no financial reserves to provide for trouble the small equity capital soon disappeared, leaving companies in the hands of their creditors. These either closed down the company, or if they were more heavily committed carried miserably on with operations in the hope of recovering something eventually in salvage.

These troubles were still with the industry in 1967 to an acute degree. In 1964 and 1965 the prices of meal and oil rose very steeply but in the following year there was a sharp reaction. Demand dropped while world production continued to increase. By the middle of 1967 prices had fallen to a level at which only the most efficient producers could cover their operating costs. This would be a disastrous situation if it continued for any long period. But the chances are that present stocks will be quickly cleared at the low price level and that prices will then recover. A removal of all export taxes would give some relief, although the government, faced by budgetary troubles, is not keen to do this. There must sooner or later be a devaluation of the Peruvian sol to a more realistic level which will compensate for the recent steep cost increases through inflation. Peru is still basically a low-cost producer and there seems no cause for concern for the industry in the long term.

CONTRIBUTION OF THE INDUSTRY TO THE NATIONAL ECONOMY

Fish meal has made an enormous difference to Peru's economy. It is now the biggest earner of foreign currency, having outstripped the two main traditional exports, copper and cotton, and may well remain the keystone of Peru's trade balance. Without the fish meal industry, indeed, it is inconceivable that President Belaúnde's government could have embarked on its ambitious development programme without major financial troubles. As it is, Peru has managed to keep the same foreign exchange rate since 1960, a considerable feat for a South American country. Her stability has given her a high reputation among both foreign companies and international development organisations, and capital has poured in from abroad. All this rests principally on fish meal.

On the domestic stage the industry plays its part in providing employment for some of the thousands who migrate each year down from the sierra in search of a livelihood and swell the populations of the coastal towns. Many of these migrants find work as fishermen on the boats, or as operators in the plants, or (the women) mending nets. Men from the sierra, who have never seen the sea before, become excellent fishermen, tough and hard-working. They find it, as might be expected, more difficult to settle into the jobs of a processing factory, since these involve not only the mastery of complicated machinery but also the acceptance of a discipline of industrial work which is quite foreign to them. But this is mainly a matter of time and training.

Besides the direct employment it provides, fish meal production has brought into existence a number of ancillary industries. Processing machinery is made by several firms, and there is a big boat-building industry. In the early days all boats were made of wood. During the boom hulls could be seen under construction parked in any available open space in Callao. More recently the demand has been for steel boats of much more sophisticated design. The backyard builders have fallen out, and building is concentrated in half-a-dozen shipyards. New industries of this sort are sheltered by a high tariff on imports. This creates a burden for the operator, whose costs are increased so that the infant national industries can survive. But the hope is that as they develop sufficiently to stand on their own feet the government will drop the tariff protection and force them to become as efficient as their foreign competitors.

OVER-FISHING AND OVER-PRODUCTION

In recent years the question of possible over-fishing of the anchoveta stock has been of increasing concern. The 1964 catch rose to a record level of 8,800,000 tons of anchoveta, a figure far beyond anything dreamed of ten years before. In 1965 fish was much scarcer. Only 7 million tons were taken, and the fish, which had previously been present throughout the year, disappeared entirely during three months of the winter. Much of this drop seems to have been due to the influence of 'el niño', the warm current which every eight years or so disturbs the normal temperatures of the Humboldt, brings rain to parts of the Peruvian coast and either kills the anchoveta or drives it away. But there were also signs that the exploitation of the anchoveta stocks had reached a point at which it might affect stock level in the future and eventually lead to the anchoveta's being fished out.

The Food and Agriculture Organisation of the United Nations, already doing valuable work through the Instituto del Mar of Peru, was called in to make a report. The conclusion of its experts was that there was no danger of the stock's being exhausted, though the maximum catch was now being taken. The government, acting on the advice of the Instituto, fixed a close season for 1966 and a catch limit of 8 million tons for 1965–6. More recently the biologists have been inclined to the view that considerable natural fluctuations in fish stocks must be expected and that catch can be left to vary each year accordingly. Thus in the 1966–7 season when fish was relatively abundant the Instituto did not oppose the government decision to allow a catch of over 9 million tons. More research is needed to find out the right principles for conservation.

The enormous production of Peru, currently about 40 per cent of total world production, gives her an overriding importance in fish meal markets. In 1959 and 1960 the large increases in supplies from Peru outstripped the capacity of world demand to absorb them. Prices collapsed, and the fall was accentuated by the weakness of a myriad of small companies who had to sell quickly to get cash. To cope with this situation the Peruvian producers under the leadership of Luis Banchero, then as now the dominant figure in the industry, formed a joint marketing organisation, the Consorcio Pesquero del Peru, with the aim of raising the price of meal by stronger selling and by developing new markets. During the period in which the Consorcio has operated there has been a substantial increase both in price and consumption. In 1960 world consumption was 2 million tons with a market price of $90 per ton; in 1964 it was 3,600,000 tons, but the price had risen to $135 per ton. Though the expanding feeding stuffs industry has provided favourable conditions, there seems no doubt that the Consorcio's firm and vigorous marketing policy has paid off. The Consorcio has at times controlled as much as 80 per cent of the production of Peru. With its initial goal achieved its influence has now waned somewhat, but it still sells 50 per cent of current production.

The government of Peru has on the whole worked closely with the fish meal industry and appreciated its vital importance to the economy. In 1964 when the industry was passing through one of its regular 'crises' some relief was given by the suspension of the export tax. Otherwise the government has concerned itself only with overall control. This has included restriction of licences for new factories, at first in certain zones, but now over the whole coast; control on emission of fumes, rarely effective, since economics tends to take precedence over amenity; supervision of the activities of the Instituto, which is financed by the industry; and the controls on fishing already discussed. It also acts as arbitrator between the rival claims of the industry and the state-owned Guano Corporation, both exploiting the same resource. The Corporation is naturally alarmed that with intensive fishing there may not be enough anchoveta available to sustain its army of producers. But it is very doubtful whether the fluctuations which take place in the bird population have anything to do with the fishing activity. In any case it is difficult to find any economic or social grounds to restrict the fishing industry simply in order to maintain supplies of guano. A bird is a much less efficient processor of raw fish than a fish meal plant, and the employment provided by guano is, in comparison to fish meal, unpleasant and poorly paid.

FUTURE DEVELOPMENTS

The next few years are likely to see considerable changes in the industry. The small wooden or steel boat of 100-ton capacity which provided most of the catch in the early 1960s is being gradually superseded by much larger boats ranging from 150 to over 250 tons in capacity. These bigger boats can go after fish much farther from the factory, operate in worse weather conditions, and handle a bigger net. They have power-operated blocks to bring in the net, and pumps to bring the fish on board, as standard equipment. Some of them now have sonar, horizontal fish-detectors which have revolutionised purse-seining in the North Sea; these too will become standard in time. To man these boats properly new skills will have to be acquired. Skippers will have to learn to navigate as well as fish, and engineers to keep their motors running for two or three days at sea instead of a few hours. All these developments reflect the change from abundant fishing close inshore to sparser shoals which must be searched for up to twenty hours away from the plant. The small boatowner, unable to meet these financial and technical requirements, will be squeezed out. Companies owning plants will tend to replace independent boats, supplying fish under contract, with their own boats, which they can control more closely. But there will always be a place for strong fleets of independent boats managed by skilled fishermen, which can produce results as good as the best company fleets.

On the shore side fish meal producers are beginning to appreciate the importance of getting good machinery and making it work properly. With a relatively high cost of fish and limited supplies a manufacturer who needs 7 tons of fish for each ton of meal he produces will have to close down when his neighbour with a $4\frac{1}{2}$: 1 yield is still making profits. In the future not only yield but quality of meal will be important. As the feeding stuffs industry becomes more scientific it will demand a meal which is more consistent in quality and has higher protein and feeding value. Manufacturers will have to adapt their plant and methods to meet this. In time fish meal may be further upgraded for human consumption, though the economic prospects here are not encouraging.

In these conditions, with greater capital requirements, many companies who cannot operate their plants properly, control their use of labour, and generally check their costs will find it difficult to survive. There will be an increasing tendency to amalgamate into units of two, three or four factories, placed in different ports so that fishing risks are spread, and so that part of the fleet can be moved from port to port as the fishing changes. These amalgamations will also be able to support a higher grade of management and technical staff.

Such adjustments, which are the natural response of a 'gold rush' industry to the economic pressures which sooner or later must appear, should be welcomed as they will help to put it on a healthy basis for the future. Another asset is the stabilising influence that has been provided by the recent arrival of a number of foreign companies, often with previous experience in fish meal manufacturing. It is distasteful to many Peruvians that any part of the industry which they have created should pass into the hands of foreigners, but the finance and technical knowledge which they are contributing are certainly of great value to the country.

This analysis suggests that the troubles of the industry lie not, as widely suggested, in shortage of capital or in scarcity of fish. Money is not scarce for good enterprises, and Peru still has the world's best fishing grounds. The real deficiency lies in management and technical skill. There is a chronic shortage of managers in Peru and it is particularly acute in the fish meal industry, where sudden expansion has given no time to train new people. On the technical side there are virtually no trained fish meal engineers, and the chain of ignorance stretches down to shift foremen and plant operators. The vacuum at the top shows up only too clearly in the way plants and boats are run. New machinery breaks down after a few months' running through lack of maintenance. There is little sense of the importance of regular control of production at each stage by chemical analysis. Boats spend half their time in port with minor troubles because no-one sees that they get to sea again. There is a big gap between appearance and reality. The organisation chart hangs on the wall of the manager's office, and the technical publications of the Instituto lie on the engineer's table, but what happens outside belongs to another world. The failure to convert intellectual knowledge into effective action is, here as elsewhere, a basic problem.

These troubles will be reduced over time as experience is gained, though it will take more than a few years for Peru to acquire the general industrial background which in Europe and the United States is taken for granted. Progress can be helped if government and industry set as first priority a thorough training programme to teach the basic techniques of fishing and processing. Such courses are now starting, but they still lack support from the industry, and will only be successful if they have the services of foreign experts. In this sphere FAO and the developed countries could make their greatest contribution.

Fresh Fishing

This survey has so far concentrated on the fish meal industry to the neglect of fishing for the fresh market. This reflects the present balance in Peru, where 97 per cent of the tonnage of fish caught goes to fish meal. But the waters of the coast are rich in other types of fish very suitable for human consumption including bonito, merluza (hake) and tollo (dogfish). These resources should be able to contribute much more to the feeding of Peru. The problem lies in the distribution side. Local markets are badly organised, with high margins to middlemen. Wider distribution is hampered by the long distances between centres and by poor roads. To provide fresh fish to the sierra transport on ice or in refrigerated trucks is needed and this puts prices out of reach of most of the population. The market for salt or dried fish, perhaps a better long-term prospect, is still relatively underdeveloped. But recently a new impetus has been given to fresh fishing in two ways. The government has interested itself in the distribution side and has agreed a levy on the fish meal producers to finance this; and the producers themselves, faced with a three-month period of idleness for their boats, are vigorously looking for alternative fishing employment. This should accelerate progress in fresh fishing.

Peru has been blessed with a great natural resource off her coast. She is still learning how to use it properly. Once she has done so it will be her strongest economic support and contribute enormously to her development.

BIBLIOGRAPHY

Francis, Pamela. 'Fishmeal Freeze Up', *Statist*, CXCI, 4619, London, 16 September 1966.
Kennett, Audrey. 'Peru's Anchovy See-saw', *The Geographical Magazine*, XXXIX, 8, London, December 1966.

OIL AND POLITICS IN LATIN AMERICA

PETER R. ODELL

MOST Latin Americans think of oil as one of the commanding heights of their economy. A continually increasing supply of petroleum fuels is in fact a prerequisite for economic development in a situation in which alternative fossil fuels are important in only very limited areas and in which severe limitations to the supply of capital restrict the expansion of hydro-electric and nuclear power capacity. It is unlikely that the contribution of petroleum fuels to the total provision of energy within the continent will fall much below its present level of about 75 per cent in the foreseeable future (see the map on page 659 for details of oil production, refining and consumption in each country).

This situation in itself provides adequate reason for the involvement of the oil industry in the politics of the countries of Latin America, in the same way that most Western European nations have sought and obtained direct or indirect controls over basic sectors of their economies. But in addition, another factor has made oil in Latin America increasingly liable to political involvement—the role of foreign companies, mainly American, in the development of the continent's oil industry. These companies have been concerned with Latin American oil from the earliest days of the industry and over this long time have achieved the reputation of being one of the main agents of economic imperialism—although the industry contributes some $2,000 million a year to national revenues! Nationalistic reaction against foreign control of a major sector of the economy makes the politics of oil much more an issue of foreign policy in Latin American countries than of domestic policy. Throughout most of the continent there is broad agreement between parties and groups deeply divided on other issues that oil should be brought under effective national control; the disagreements arise over means rather than ends. Contrasts in the means employed to bring the 'international petroleum cartel', in which terms the international oil industry is still generally thought of in Latin America, under control provide one way in which to examine oil and politics in the continent.

MEXICO

The single most important event in the process of the containment of the power of the international oil companies in Latin America was the nationalisation of the Mexican oil industry in 1938. This action was by no means, however, the first step in the process. In 1927 both Argentina and Chile took steps to restrict certain aspects of oil industry development to national entities. Even tiny Costa Rica maintained a system of state monopoly over the importation and marketing of gasoline throughout the 1920s and 1930s.

These earlier attempts at control were, however, less than comprehensive, in that elements of private foreign ownership and interest were permitted to continue, and were also made at a time and in situations in which oil was of much less significance. Their impact was, therefore, of little more than local interest at the time. It was the attitude of the oil companies to the Mexican revolutionary situation culminating in the 1938 expropriation which marks the beginning of the deep involvement of oil in the politics of the continent. The inability of the companies to accept the implications of the revolution and their unwillingness to renegotiate their concessionary arrangements and their largely extra-territorial and statutory positions (so extreme that some of the companies had what amounted to private armies for protecting 'their' lands) made nationalisation inevitable.

In more senses than one, Mexico's attitude to the oil industry since 1938 has provided an example for the rest of Latin America. Politically, it showed that the power of the 'international petroleum cartel' could be contained by resolute action in which, in the final analysis, the companies would have to acquiesce. Technically, it demonstrated that a state oil enterprise, responsible for all aspects of oil operations from exploration to sales, could successfully run an industry. And economically, it indicated how a nationally owned oil company could be organised and controlled by state forces to meet the required national objectives of an increasing supply of energy at low prices to the consumer. The success story of Petróleos Mexicanos (PEMEX) is well publicised in Latin America, but much less well read are the warning signs of difficulties that lie in the path of state involvement in oil.

PEMEX's status as an enterprise worthy of support by foreign financiers is often highlighted, for it shows how a state company with responsibilities for a capital-intensive industry can, in a country short of capital, secure its investment requirements. But what other would-be state oil monopolies ought also to note is the length of time which PEMEX has taken to achieve 'financial respectability'. Before 1961 it was able to borrow only on a maximum three-year basis and at rates of interest which were not particularly attractive. Its 'A1' credit rating and its ability to negotiate for long-term loans at favourable rates of interest is a feature of the last few years. This success, moreover, has been achieved partly as a result of PEMEX's belated victory in gaining the right to charge reasonable prices for its products— that is, the right to act much more as a commercial enterprise rather than as an instrument of state forced to allocate its products at less than average, let alone marginal, costs. Thus the growing ability of PEMEX to obtain outside credits has gone hand-in-hand with its ability to generate investment funds out of sales income. Other state companies—and governments—still pursuing low-prices-at-all-costs policies might do well to take note of PEMEX's example, as well they might of PEMEX's recent decision to bring in foreign oil companies as 'partners' in order to assist both with capital availability and with technical know-how in the development of production and other activities. A further drawback to running oil-development as a national enterprise and an organ of state is that the pursuit of certain other politico-economic objectives is denied where they might otherwise be achieved. Thus PEMEX operates successfully only within an autarkic system in which it is protected absolutely against competition from foreign sources of energy. It is possible even in Mexico, with its relatively low-cost petroleum production, that some regions of the country or, perhaps, some sectors of industry would have benefited from the opportunity to seek their energy requirements abroad. Other countries in Latin America, less well endowed with petroleum resources, might, in following the example of Mexico, add significantly to manufacturing and transport costs and thus create a situation in which economic progress is made more difficult. Yet another drawback to national control over oil resources may be seen in the inability of PEMEX to seek customers wherever they might be found. PEMEX is, in general, forbidden to export crude oil on the grounds that this crude can be converted into refined products which are then 'worth' several times as much. This doctrine of 'inherent worth' ignores the reality of the world trading pattern in oil, a pattern which creates a broad market for crude oil but a limited one for refined products, as importing countries with their own refining capacity mainly seek the former rather than the latter. In that PEMEX has built up a reserves ratio (i.e. total proved reserves divided by present annual consumption) position of 32 years—well exceeding its statutory requirement of 25 years—and in that it has an estimated shut-in productive capacity (i.e. potential additional production given the existing physical facilities such as wells and pipe-lines), of some 2·5 million tons per year, it could clearly have embarked on a modest crude export campaign with a good chance of success. Mexico may well consider that it can afford to forgo some £10 million per year in foreign exchange earnings by refusing its national oil company the right to export crude oil, in line with some pseudo-economic argument, but few other Latin American countries which might look to Mexico as an example could afford to do the same.

It is, however, the generally effective role of PEMEX in aiding Mexico's national economic development that has encouraged other countries in Latin America in their dealings with foreign oil companies and there is little evidence that they are concerned with the potential difficulties of state ownership. In fact, elsewhere in Latin America the less powerful state oil enterprises have often been used by governments for ends other than the technico-economic tasks of producing and/or marketing oil for which they were formed. The 'failure' of these enterprises to do the tasks expected of them arises time and time again from political intervention in their activities.

No other country in Latin America has yet taken such extreme political action against the foreign oil companies as did Mexico in 1938, although it is worth noting that in 1937 Bolivia expelled Standard Oil of New Jersey from its concessions in south Bolivia because of the company's alleged complicity with Paraguay during the Chaco War. The newly formed Bolivian state oil entity, Yacimientos Petrolíferos Fiscales Bolivianos (YPFB), to which Standard Oil's interests were handed over, remained poor, however, and lacked the resources needed for the expansion which would have enabled it to make a contribution to the country's economic development. In 1956 the country was again opened up to foreign companies, and YPFB remained with only partial control over the country's oil industry.

URUGUAY AND CHILE

Of the other countries of Latin America, Uruguay and Chile have approached most closely to total state control over oil. In Uruguay the oil refining industry is a state monopoly—part of the ANCAP enterprise (Administración Nacional de Combustibles, Alcohol y Portland). All petroleum requirements are imported in the form of crude oil (there being no local production) with half the imports purchased by the state company and the remainder brought in for processing at the state refinery by the private foreign companies having marketing interests. These companies market under a system of state supervision and of price control over most products and thus have only a very limited degree of freedom in their activities. Today even their right to bring in crude supplies in line with their share of the Uruguayan market is under discussion, and it is possible that the state will take sole responsibility for imports by 1967—to which the companies may well react by withdrawing from the marketing function. Uruguay thus seems to be moving inevitably towards the final establishment of an entirely state-owned and -managed oil sector.

Chile too has almost achieved this position. Here the continued presence of Shell and Esso depends upon their willingness to work within a situation which guarantees them profits only within a very rigidly circumscribed framework of operations under the overall control of the Empresa Nacional del Petróleo (ENAP), the state oil company established in 1950 when promising oil fields were discovered in Tierra del Fuego by contractors working for the national development agency Corporación de Fomento de la Producción (CORFO). State control, however, goes back to 1927 when the first monopoly law restricting oil industry development to the state was passed; since then the idea of state ownership has not been seriously challenged and even under the 'businessman's' government of Alessandri a proposal to break the monopoly by opening up Chile's northernmost provinces to exploitation by foreign private companies attracted less than one-third of the votes in the Congress.

Today there seems to be no question in Chile of the government monopoly over exploration, production and refining being changed, and as ENAP is legally prevented from entering into any form of partnership with private enterprise the possibilities of extra-legislative action to achieve cooperation are also remote. Part of the remaining interests of the private companies—providing part of ENAP's crude oil requirement and selling imported products directly to the mining companies of the north and to other designated large consumers—will gradually decline as Chilean oil production increases and hence eliminates the need for imported supplies. Shell and Esso will then be left with an interest only in distributing and marketing oil within the country under a system of quotas and price control administered by ENAP. To all intents and purposes, Chile's oil economy will then differ little from the Mexican model.

ARGENTINA AND BRAZIL

In both Argentina and Brazil, thirty years and more of conflict and competition between foreign private oil interests and advocates of national state control have to date been insufficient to resolve the issues once and for all. In general there has been a gradual attrition of the former's interests, though not without swings of the pendulum in the opposite direction.

Such a succession of swings has occurred in Argentina over the last few years. The overthrow of Perón in 1957 was due in part to rumours that he was negotiating with American oil companies with a view to granting them concessions to develop Argentine oil. Following his overthrow, the provisional government re-emphasised the long-standing and intensely nationalistic attitude towards the oil industry, an attitude which had the strong support of Frondizi, one of the contenders for the presidency. In 1959, however, Frondizi—now president and recognising the economic handicap which

655

Argentina suffered by having to spend almost 25 per cent of its available foreign exchange on importing petroleum whilst having large enough reserves within the country to satisfy national demand if they could only be got out of the ground—made contractual arrangements with foreign oil companies whereby they were given the right to develop Argentina's oil resources. In 1960, therefore, for the first time for over thirty years, the pendulum swung strongly back in favour of the foreign private development of Argentine oil. This was a swing which certainly produced the petroleum required (output of oil increased over three times between 1960 and 1963 and the country became virtually self-sufficient, producing almost as much oil as Mexico), but it also produced a violent political reaction and may be considered one of the most important factors behind the deposition of Frondizi. In 1963 all Frondizi's contracts with the companies were revoked in an action which re-established the paramountcy of state interests in the oil industry. The private foreign companies had to leave Argentina not because they failed to deliver the goods on the terms agreed (terms which, although too favourable to the companies could, nevertheless, have been renegotiated within the same framework of contractual arrangements to the mutual satisfaction of both parties) but because their very presence offended national pride and aspirations.

In Brazil early public interest in oil arose from the lack of interest by the international companies in exploration. In 1938 petroleum was declared a public utility and was placed under the direction of a National Petroleum Council which, however, took little effective action to develop the country's oil industry. By the late 1940s the international companies were expressing a keener interest in Brazilian possibilities under the stimulus of rapidly expanding markets for oil products. A bill to permit foreign participation in the search for crude was introduced but never passed and the issue became one of those which helped to bring Vargas back to power in 1950. Vargas, who had campaigned under the slogan 'O Petróleo e Nosso', then put through a comprehensive piece of oil legislation. This greatly widened the powers of the National Petroleum Council which together with the newly-formed Petróleo Brasileiro (Petrobras) was given monopoly rights for exploration, exploitation and all new refining development. Existing privately owned refineries were permitted to continue and the private companies retained their marketing functions.

In spite of its failure to find and to produce oil in the quantity required and in spite of a series of financial scandals that have affected the organisation, Petrobras has more than maintained its position, gradually being empowered with additional responsibilities. Under President João Goulart steps were taken to endow it with monopoly rights. Although these measures were revoked by the present military government, even this right-wing administration has left Petrobras largely untouched—confirming the view held by some that it is essentially part of the intensely nationalistic military establishment. If this is so, then there can be little doubt that Petrobras will continue whatever the vicissitudes of Brazilian politics.

VENEZUELA

In one way, of course, the attitudes of countries such as Brazil, Argentina and Chile towards the oil industry are of minor importance to the international petroleum companies for they constitute but a tiny part of their total world-wide operations. Thus actions against the companies in these countries produce limited reactions. The reaction which followed nationalisation in Mexico has not been repeated in spite of all the measures which Latin American nations have taken since then to curb the activities of the foreign private companies. An angry reaction, reflecting serious harm to invested capital and resources, has been kept in reserve in case of need, perhaps the main fear of the oil companies being that the example of country after country in Latin America in bringing oil under national control would eventually persuade Venezuela to follow suit. Such action on the part of Venezuela, to which the international companies turned for their main activities in the western hemisphere (outside the United States) following their expulsion from Mexico, would produce the need to bring the angry reaction out of reserve.

The fears of the oil companies seemed likely to have an early realisation when, in the late 1940s, Venezuela came under the control of Acción Democrática (AD), a left-wing party long pledged to the nationalisation of oil. AD, however, concentrated on increasing the nation's share of the profits from oil operations in the country. This was a development against which the companies could fight effectively—in the short term, by cutting back on their rate of growth in Venezuela as it became more profitable to produce the additional oil from other parts of the world; and in the medium term, by taking whatever action seemed appropriate to secure the overthrow of the government. The latter was achieved in 1950 and the companies then enjoyed almost a decade of a highly acceptable politico-economic environment in which they lifted annual output from 75 million to 150 million tons. New concessions in extenso were auctioned to enthusiastic bidders and the country under the dictator Marcos Perez Jiménez became an island of freedom for the foreign oil companies in a continent in which the reins were gradually being drawn more tightly. The overthrow of Perez Jiménez in 1957 and the election in 1959 of another Acción Democrática government under President Rómulo Betancourt gave the companies much concern. Their automatic reaction was to prepare for the worst and they quickly cut back their exploration and development efforts, fearful of expropriation. The worst, however, did not happen and the companies were persuaded to live with the new government by the United States, which, in the light of the deteriorating situation in Cuba, regarded Venezuela as the key to stability in the whole of the Caribbean area and did not wish to see the companies engaging in activities designed to bring down the government—whose fall, it was feared, might lead to an extreme left-wing takeover.

The oil companies were persuaded to go along with this policy whilst reserving the right to switch anticipated production increases elsewhere in light of the reduced profitability of their operations in Venezuela owing to increased labour costs and changes in the taxation and royalty arrangements which increased the government's share of the industry's gross profits from some 55 per cent to about 70 per cent[1]. The Acción Democrática government of Betancourt for its part, however, was in no position to initiate a revolutionary change in the structure of the oil industry. Internally, it remained in power by courtesy of the military establishment which might well have reacted against any such display of extremism. Externally, it was not unaware that its acceptance by the United States rested on the expectation that it would not resort to extreme measures. It also knew that this situation could

---

[1] The government's share of the gross profits of the petroleum industry has exceeded $1,000 million a year since 1958. Oil revenues still account for almost two-thirds of total government revenue.

w*

change overnight and be followed by action which could lead to its over-throw. But aside from these political considerations, the government was also faced with the knowledge that Venezuelan oil had a rapidly declining comparative advantage in most markets of the world as a result of rapidly increasing supplies of low-cost Middle Eastern oil. If the major companies operating in the country, responsible for over 90 per cent of total exports, were taken over by the state, there was little likelihood that exports could be maintained. Thus both the government and the companies have had a real interest in preventing a confrontation.

In the period since 1959 both government and companies have taken positive steps to re-evaluate both their own and the other side's positions. Out of this has emerged an understanding in government-company relation-ships based on an appreciation of certain areas of immediate mutual interest. There now seems likely to be a long period of relative quiescence in which the government will merely try to achieve a somewhat greater degree of direct participation in the industry by gradually expanding the activities of the Corporación Venezolana del Petróleo (CVP), the state oil enterprise which has been launched by the AD government. Such expansion, in its early stages, will be in the relatively unimportant domestic refining and marketing sector of the oil economy over whose loss the major companies will shed few tears as it represents a minor part of their total activities in Venezuela and is, moreover, barely profitable because of government control over retail prices. CVP will also be given responsibilities for operating in the petro-chemical industry and may also become involved in the ownership of ocean tankers available for charter by the companies exporting Venezuelan oil.

More important than any of these developments in altering the basic structure of the Venezuelan oil industry will be the arrangements that are eventually made for expanding the industry's producing activities into new areas of the country. The government has set its face firmly against new concessions to the private companies. Neither is there any point in CVP's doing the work, for the organisation is already unable to sell abroad the oil it produces from its wells in Lake Maracaibo, being prevented from offering its oil at realistic prices by the government policy of maintaining posted price levels that it believes to be fair and reasonable. Thus the only solution is the development of contractual arrangements between CVP and the oil companies whereby the companies would participate in the work for a fee and in return guarantee to find outlets for the oil within the framework of their associated overseas marketing companies. The willingness of the companies to accept this type of arrangement will essentially depend upon factors external to Venezuela, for most of the companies concerned have a choice as to how they shall meet their future international crude oil require-ments; they will only be willing to accept contractual arrangements with CVP if these offer better prospects for profitable investment than are avail-able elsewhere in the world.

In a situation in which the world-wide availability of oil seems likely to remain in excess of demand, the prospects of further significant expansion of the Venezuelan oil industry are small, and the government's policy to make the country less dependent on oil is in part recognition that the oil industry cannot grow given the politico-economic environment created by the AD. Paradoxically, the gradual curtailment of the importance of the foreign oil companies in the political and economic life of the country may well turn out to be the best possible insurance against revolutionary change.

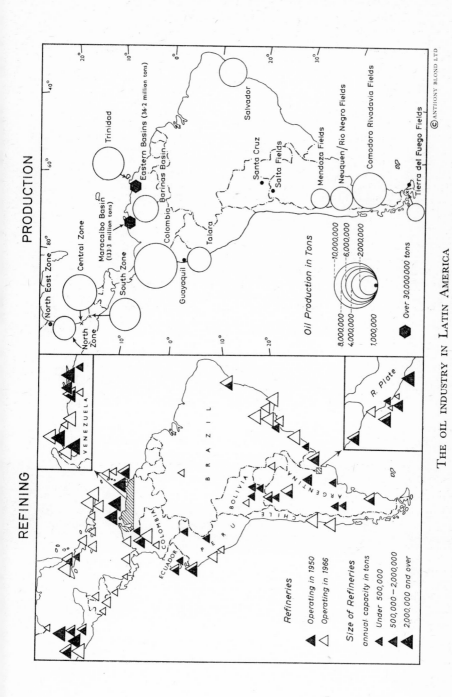

PRODUCTION

REFINING

North East Zone

Central Zone

North Zone

South Zone

Maracaibo Basin
(133.3 million tons)

Guayaquil

Talara

Colombia–Barinas Basin

Trinidad

Eastern Basins (36.2 million tons)

Salvador

Santa Cruz

Salta Fields

Mendoza Fields

Neuquen/Rio Negro Fields

Comodoro Rivadavia Fields

Tierra del Fuego Fields

Oil Production in Tons

10,000,000
8,000,000
6,000,000
4,000,000
2,000,000
1,000,000

Over 30,000,000 tons

VENEZUELA

COLOMBIA

ECUADOR

PERU

BRAZIL

BOLIVIA

CHILE

ARGENTINA

R. Plate

Refineries

Operating in 1950

Operating in 1966

Size of Refineries
annual capacity in tons

Under 500,000

500,000–2,000,000

2,000,000 and over

© ANTHONY BLOND LTD

THE OIL INDUSTRY IN LATIN AMERICA

TABLE 1

OIL PRODUCTION IN LATIN AMERICA 1950–65
(*Millions of metric tons*)

Country	1950	1955	1960	1965
Venezuela	74·9	107·8	142·3	172·5
Mexico	10·3	12·6	14·1	16·4
Colombia	4·8	5·8	7·9	9·1
Trinidad	2·8	3·5	6·1	7·1
Argentina	3·5	4·5	9·1	14·4
Peru	2·0	2·3	2·6	3·2
Chile	—	0·3	0·9	2·0
Brazil	—	0·3	3·9	4·7
Bolivia	—	0·4	0·4	0·6
Total (all Latin America)	98·8	137·9	187·7	230·0

TABLE 2

MAJOR PRIVATE-ENTERPRISE
OIL OPERATIONS IN LATIN AMERICA

Company	Natio-nality	Production in Latin America (million tons)	Main areas of production	Refining capacity (million tons)	Main refining locations
Standard Oil of NJ (Esso)	US	64·5	Venezuela 96%, Peru and Argentina	61·5	Venezuela 44% Netherlands West Indies 40%
Shell	Anglo-Dutch	50·3	Venezuela 96%, Colombia, Trinidad and Argentina	41·6	Venezuela 42% NWI 36%
Gulf	US	24·0	Venezuela 100%	9·6	Venezuela 75%
Texaco	US	12·7	Venezuela 66%, Colombia and Trinidad	17·6	Trinidad 95%
Sun	US	10·6	Venezuela 100%	—	—
Mobil	US	7·2	Venezuela 100%	4·0	Venezuela 100%
Phillips	US	3·7	Venezuela 100%	—	—
Sinclair	US	3·3	Venezuela 75%, Colombia 25%	2·0	Venezuela 100%
Cities Service	US	3·2	Argentina 70%, Colombia 30%	—	—
Chevron	US	2·8	Venezuela 100%	2·6	Venezuela 90%
British Petroleum	British	2·1	Trinidad 65%, Colombia 35%	—	—
Richmond	US	1·6	Colombia 100%	—	—
Pan American	US	1·4	Argentina 100%	—	—
Common-wealth	US	—	—	5·7	Puerto Rico 100%
Ref. Panama	Anglo-American	—	—	2·6	Panama 100%

TABLE 3

STATE OIL COMPANIES IN LATIN AMERICA

Country	Name of company	Abbreviation	Date of formation	Activities			Percentage	
				Production	Refining	Marketing	State co.'s share of national production	Total national refining
Argentina	Yacimientos Petrolíferos Fiscales	YPF	1922	*[1]	*	*	68	60
Bolivia	Yacimientos Petrolíferos Fiscales Bolivanos	YPFB	1936	*	*		100	100
Brazil	Petróleo Brasileiro	Petróbras	1953	*	*	*	100	82
Colombia	Empresa Colombiana de Petróleos	Ecopétrol	1948	*	*	*	17	45
Chile	Empresa Nacional del Petróleo	ENAP	1950	*	*		100	100
Cuba	Instituto Cubano del Petróleo	ICP	1959	*	*		100	100
Mexico	Petróleos Mexicanos	PEMEX	1938	*	*	*	100	100
Peru	Empresa Petrolera Fiscal	EPF	1934	*	*	*	12	2
Uruguay	Administración Nacional de Combustibles, Alcohol y Portland	ANCAP	1931		*		—	100
Venezuela	Corporación Venezolana del Petróleo	CVP	1960	*	*	*	0·2	0·2

1 Indicates activities undertaken by the state.

IMPLICATIONS OF ECONOMIC INTEGRATION

The problems created by the clash of nationalistic governments with the international oil companies remain over most of the continent, and are now being supplemented by others arising from the moves towards economic integration. In view of the dominating position of oil in the continent's energy economy, and in the light of the complementarity of the industry's operations in different countries and regions of Latin America, any effective programme of economic integration must inevitably involve the industry. Ultimately, it seems possible to think in terms of a Latin American Petroleum Authority—on lines similar to the Coal and Steel Community in Western Europe—the formation of which the international companies will almost certainly view with misgivings. At best, such an Authority would have the effect of taking their Latin American business out of their globally planned operations and of putting it into a regional straitjacket with a consequent adverse effect on their profitability: at worst, it would assume control and direction over intra-Latin American trade in crude oil and petroleum products and take over responsibility for determining the patterns of production and refining in the region, a responsibility which implies a high degree of control over investment decisions. The fact that the first moves in this direction have now been taken by the association of Latin American state oil enterprises (Asistencia Recíproca Petrolera Estatal Latinoamericana or ARPEL, founded in 1965), gives the oil companies some justification for fearing that the recurring political battles they have had to fight against 'statism' at the national level will now have an added dimension—a continent-wide struggle against statism within an economically unifying Latin America.

BIBLIOGRAPHY

Bermudez, Antonio J. *The Mexican National Petroleum Industry: A Case Study in Nationalisation*, Stanford Univ. Press, Stanford, Calif., 1963.
Betancourt, Rómulo. *Venezuela: política y petróleo*, Fondo de Cultura Económica, Mexico, 1956.
Frondizi, Arturo. *Petróleo y política*, Raigal, Buenos Aires, 2nd ed. 1955. *Petróleo y nación*, Transición, Buenos Aires, 1963.
Klein, H. S. 'American Oil Companies in Latin America: The Bolivian Experience', *Inter-American Economic Affairs*, XVIII, 2, Washington, DC, autumn 1964.
Lieuwen, E. *Petroleum in Venezuela: A History*, Univ. of California Publications in History, XLVI, Berkeley, Calif., 1954. *Venezuela*, Oxford Univ. Press, London and New York, 2nd ed. 1965.
Malave Mata, H. *Petróleo y desarrollo económico de Venezuela*, Pensamiento Vivo, Caracas, 1962.
O'Connor, Harvey. *The Empire of Oil*, Monthly Review Press, New York, 1955. *World Crisis in Oil*, Monthly Review Press, New York, 1962.
Odell, P. R. 'Oil and State in Latin America', *International Affairs*, London, October 1964. 'The Oil Industry in Latin America', *Bank of London and South America Quarterly Review*, London, January 1965. 'Petroleos Mexicanos: An Example for Latin America?', *Statist Review of Mexico*, London, January 1965.
Reyes Heroles, J. 'Statement on the Occasion of the 25th Anniversary of Petroleum Nationalisation', *El trimestre económico*, XXXII (3), 127, Mexico, 1965.

There are official annual publications by the appropriate ministry in several countries of Latin America. These are often supplemented by monthly or even more frequent bulletins. The various state oil companies all publish annual (or more frequent) accounts of their activities as well as specially commissioned reports, etc. The UN Economic Commission for Latin America is now studying the oil industry in more detail and is expected to report on the situation from time to time. The newly-formed Association of State Oil Companies in Latin America (ARPEL) will also be publishing information on its activities. The international oil companies active in Latin America tend not to publish material concerned with the continent as a whole but have available information on their activities in different countries and will respond to requests for such material.

PART FOUR

THE LATIN AMERICAN SOCIAL BACKGROUND

THE PEOPLE

THE POPULATION OF LATIN AMERICA

CARMEN A. MIRÓ

The Fastest Growing Region in the World

The twenty countries of Latin America, with an estimated population of nearly 244 million at mid-1966 (around 60 million at the turn of the century) constitute the fastest growing region of the world today. Rosenblat[1] has estimated that there were in 1492 a little over 12 million Indians in the territories known today as Latin America. Their decimation brought about by warfare, forced labour, exposure to new imported diseases and general disruption of their way of living is evident if the figure given by Carr-Saunders for the population of the region more than 250 years afterwards, when the area had received many immigrants from Europe and Africa, is considered valid—11 million in 1750. After the middle of the 18th century, according to Carr-Saunders, the Latin American populations grew slowly, the average annual rate of growth to 1900 being 1·2 per cent.

The staggering acceleration of population growth in the present century may be seen from Table 1 in which the years quoted mark periods adding 50 million to the population.

TABLE 1

GROWTH RATE OF POPULATION IN LATIN AMERICA, 1750–1968

Date	Estimated population (million)	Approximate number of years needed to add 50 million	Approximate average annual rate of growth in the period (%)
1750 . . .	11	—	—
1900 . . .	61	150	1·2
1934 . . .	111	34	1·8
1951 . . .	161	17	2·2
1961 . . .	211	10	2·7
1968 . . .	261	7	3·1

A comparison of the rates given in Table 1 with those estimated for other areas of the world for 1950–60 shows Latin America's leading rate of population growth today.

The Dynamics of Growth

How has this unprecedented growth come about? Carr-Saunders has estimated that immigrants to Latin American countries in the period

[1] See bibliography for references.

1821–1932 numbered almost 13 million. As a significant proportion of them are presumed to have returned to their places of origin, as immigration decreased considerably after 1930, and as the number of immigrants was small compared to the receiving population, one may conclude that the acceleration of population increase is mainly the result of excess of births over deaths.

TABLE 2

GROWTH IN WORLD POPULATION, 1950–60

	Average annual growth rate (%)
Total world	1·7
More developed areas	1·3
Europe	0·8
Soviet Union	1·7
North America	1·8
Oceania	2·1
Less developed areas	1·9
East Asia	1·5
South Asia	2·1
Africa	2·1

Source: Estimated on basis of *Provisional Report on World Population Prospects as Assessed in 1963*, UN, New York, 1964, Table 5.1, page 38

In the more developed areas of the world these two demographic variables, fertility and mortality, have been closely associated with changes in the socio-economic structures of the societies concerned. Decline in mortality and increase in length of life occurred gradually as epidemic infectious diseases were reduced or eliminated, improved medical treatment was made available, public health and sanitation measures and better housing conditions were introduced—in short, as standards of living rose, usually with accompanying industrialisation and rural emigration. Fertility, on the other hand, having social, cultural and ethical determinants, responded more slowly to the new demographic conditions created, following mortality in its downward trend after some time-lag, which was dependent on the pace at which other social changes were introduced. In England and Wales, for example, decline in mortality began as early as the middle of the 18th century while birth rates show a distinct downward trend only around 1880.

In the case of Latin America, mortality has declined faster and population increase has been in general much more spectacular. Lack of reliable statistics makes it impossible to establish exactly when the downward trend in mortality actually started, but as has been pointed out by Stolnitz, 'most of the survival records that can be found for Latin America–Africa–Asia through the 1920s were below the Western averages of the 1840s.' In addition, Latin American mortality, as measured by the crude death rate, continued to decrease at a pace not experienced by the developed countries. The figures given in Table 3, pertaining to eight Latin American countries which can be taken as representative of the trend experienced in others, indicate a striking decrease in mortality. In a period of about 20 years the crude death rates of these countries were reduced by percentages ranging between 22 (Guatemala) and 51 (Costa Rica).

TABLE 3

DECLINING MORTALITY IN LATIN AMERICAN COUNTRIES, 1935-58

Country	Crude death rate per 1,000 population		Percentage change
	1935-9	1955-8	
Costa Rica	20·0	9·8	−51·0
El Salvador	21·1	13·5	−36·0
Guatemala	26·5	20·6	−22·3
Mexico	23·3	12·9	−44·6
Argentina	11·6	8·4	−27·6
Chile	23·3	12·5	−46·4
Uruguay	10·0	7·4	−26·0
Venezuela	17·8	9·9	−44·4

Source: *United Nations Population Bulletin No. 6—1962*, New York, 1963, Table III.12, page 34

COUNTRIES FROM REGIONS OTHER THAN LATIN AMERICA

Country	Crude death rate per 1,000 population		Percentage change
	1935-9	1955-9	
United Arab Republic	26·9	17·2	−36·1
United States	11·0	9·4	−14·6
Ceylon	24·5	9·9	−59·6
Japan	17·4	7·8	−55·2
Thailand	16·4	9·7	−40·9
Belgium	13·2	11·9	−9·8
Czechoslovakia	13·2	9·7	−26·5
France	15·7	11·8	−24·8
Sweden	11·7	9·6	−18·0
United Kingdom	12·2	11·6	−4·9

Source: *United Nations Demographic Yearbook*, 1957 and 1961

While comparisons based on the crude death rate are open to objection on the basis of the limitations of this index in measuring variations in the pattern of mortality of populations with different age structures, percentage changes in crude death rate can accurately point to differences in trends. The twenty-year period in which the death rate of England and Wales declined most was 1905–25. Percentage decline was 22—the percentage indicated in Table 3 by which mortality was least reduced in a Latin American country in 1935/9–55/8. In halving her death rate Costa Rica accomplished in 20 years what took England and Wales 150.

While the rate of decline in mortality seems to have slackened during the 1960 decade, there exists room for substantial improvement in the rate of decline for a considerable portion of the Latin American population. A further reduction of the overall average crude death rate—estimated in 1959–61 to be 12–14 per thousand per year—is therefore to be expected.

It should be emphasised that the enormous reduction in mortality in Latin America has not been matched by an increase in the standard of living for the majority of the population. Mortality trends seem to have behaved to a considerable degree independently of the course followed by economic and social developments. New medical techniques, particularly modern disease-control methods, have benefited people who have at the same time remained illiterate, undernourished and underemployed.

The other variable, fertility, has remained very much at its premodern level. With very few exceptions (which will be discussed later) Latin American fertility seems to have stabilised at rather high values. The United Nations Economic Commission for Latin America estimated the average crude birth rate for the region around 1960 to be of the order of 40–42 per thousand per year. There are strong indications to suggest, in spite of the deficiencies of statistical data, that the birth rate for most Latin American countries must have been over 40 per thousand per year ever since the beginning of the present century. Contrary to the case of mortality, a distribution of the twenty Latin American countries according to their birth rates in the period 1945–50 as compared with that of 1959–61 shows very little change (see Table 4).

TABLE 4

DISTRIBUTION OF COUNTRIES ACCORDING TO BIRTH RATE

| | Number of countries within each group | | | |
| | Latin America | | Ten selected countries from other regions | |
Annual birth rate (per thousand)	1945–50	1959–61	1945–49	1959–61
50 and over	2	0	0	0
45–49	12	10	0	0
40–44	2	6	1	1
35–39	1	1	1	1
30–34	1	1	1	1
Under 30	2	2	7	7

TEN SELECTED COUNTRIES FROM REGIONS OTHER THAN LATIN AMERICA

| Country | Annual birth rate (per thousand) | |
	1945–49	1959–61
United Arab Republic	42·4	43·3
United States	23·4	23·7
Ceylon	38·2	36·5
Japan	30·2	17·2
Thailand	24·4	34·0
Belgium	17·3	17·2
Czechoslovakia	22·4	15·9
France	20·3	18·1
United Kingdom	18·3	17·4
Sweden	19·0	13·9

Source: *Statistical Bulletin for Latin America*, ECLA, II, 2 and *United Nations Demographic Year-book*, 1965

It should be noted that the figures in Table 4 are only approximations of the true birth rate, and the conclusion that there has been a reduction of fertility in the 16 countries which show rates above 40 per thousand in the two periods under examination must be tentative.

A closer examination of the pattern of fertility by age may disclose that there have not been any significant decreases in the over-all reproductive rate. In fact, increases appear to have occurred in fertility as a result of increasing average length of life. Even granting that there has been a reduction in fertility it must be admitted to have been very small, and there are only four countries in Latin America which seem to have clearly entered the demographic phase characterised by declining mortality *and* fertility.

It is easy to understand why fertility should not yet have responded to the new conditions created in Latin America by declining mortality. First, the latter trend, while proceeding at a very rapid pace, is a comparatively new phenomenon. Secondly, it is now well known that as prerequisites for a downward trend in fertility to gather momentum certain fundamental changes have to occur in the societies concerned, such as the attainment of higher educational levels, increasing urbanisation, and with the latter a shift in attitudes concerning the advantages of large families traditionally associated with subsistence farming. The changing role of women in society, increased social aspirations, the modification of rigid social structures inhibiting upward mobilisation are some of the symptoms that precede declining fertility. There are signs that modifications of social norms, especially in connection with reproductive behaviour, have begun in several countries of Latin America. These developments are examined below. The process, though, is slow, and in the meantime the rapid decline in mortality has brought about an unprecedented rate of demographic growth.

REJUVENATION

The unusual combination of declining mortality with high and stabilised fertility, besides producing high and accelerating rates of growth, also generates age structures characterised by a large proportion of children and young adults and a small percentage of persons of 60 years and over (between 4 and 6 per cent of the total population). While this structure is mainly due to sustained high fertility, declining mortality is also a contributory factor since most additions to expectation of life at birth are the result of reductions in the risk of death among the young rather than the old. This is particularly true in those countries which started with the highest mortality rates.

According to population censuses taken around 1960, in six of the 14 countries for which information is available the proportion of persons under 15 years of age was 40 per cent and over. In five countries it was 45 per cent or more. The trend is for the population to become younger with the passing of time. Table 5 shows the variation 1950/60 in the proportion of persons under 15 years in 13 countries.

TABLE 5

LATIN AMERICAN POPULATION AGED UNDER 15, 1950–60

	Number of countries in each category	
Percentage of persons aged under 15	*Census in or around 1950*	*Census in or around 1960*
45 and over	0	5
40 to 45	11	6
Less than 40	2	2
Total . . .	13	13

It is evident that in a situation where the fertility pattern remains more or less unchanged through time while the proportion of those entering the reproductive ages increases in relation to the total population and where the mortality rate is declining fast, the population has a high growth potential. This is precisely the case of most of Latin America.

REGIONAL DIFFERENCES

The countries of Latin America may be grouped into four demographic types as follows.

Type 1. Fertility and mortality have reached rather low levels with a corresponding low rate of natural increase (around 1·5 per cent per year). This is the case of two countries in temperate South America, Argentina and Uruguay, representing 10 per cent of the total estimated population of the region in 1966. They received in the past significant numbers of European immigrants and have high levels of literacy and urbanisation.

Type 2. Mortality has declined significantly and continues its downward trend; fertility seems to be responding in equal manner. Chile and Cuba are the cases in point, with a population accounting for 7 per cent of the region's total and a rate of growth that can be called moderate (close to 2·5 per cent per year). Their literacy and urbanisation are also high.

Type 3. The mortality rate has declined only moderately and is still relatively high, which combined with high and unchanging fertility gives rise, as in the case of Type 2, to moderate rates of growth (less than 2·5 per cent per year). This type differs from Type 2 in that growth rate is accelerating as mortality decline develops momentum. The countries belonging to this group are Bolivia and Haiti, containing only 4 per cent of Latin America's population. Among other features, these countries have some of the highest levels of illiteracy in the region and the lowest of urbanisation.

Type 4. This is the typical Latin American situation: fast declining mortality which has reached moderate and low levels, with a high and stable fertility, produce a high and accelerating rate of growth (around 3 per cent per year and in at least two countries exceeding 3·5). This group includes 14 countries with 79 per cent of the region's total population.

As is to be expected, differences in fertility rates give rise to age structures clearly differentiated as to the proportion of children and young adults as well as to that of older ages. In Argentina and Uruguay persons under 15 years of age represent 31 and 28 per cent of the population respectively, while the corresponding percentages for those over 60 years are 9 and 12. Chile, Cuba, Bolivia and Haiti have less than 40 per cent of their populations in the under-15 group and between 6 to 7 per cent in the older group. In the other countries the under-15 group represents over 40 per cent of total population. Associated with these demographic differences are other socio-economic indices such as degree of urbanisation, level of literacy, proportion of the male labour force engaged in primary activities and per capita income. Table 6 shows the relationship of these to the demographic situation of each country under the typology used above.

OTHER FEATURES OF THE LATIN AMERICAN POPULATION

Paradoxically, in the face of rapid urbanisation (defined as increasing concentration of people in cities) Latin America continues to be, in general, a rural continent with its population sparsely distributed in large areas with every now and then a big metropolis. The United Nations has estimated

TABLE 6

LATIN AMERICAN POPULATION AND OTHER DEMOGRAPHIC FEATURES COMPARED WITH SOME SOCIO-ECONOMIC INDICES, 1966

Country	Total population in 1966 (thousands)[1]	Rates (per thousand) 1959–61[2]			Percentage under 15 years[3]	Percentage urbanised (1960)[8]	Percentage of illiteracy (15 years and over)[3]	Percentage of males engaged in primary activities (1960)[3]	Real per capita income (US$, 1961)[12]
		Birth	Death	Natural Increase					
Type 1									
Argentina	22,691	23–24	8–9	14–15	28.9[4]	57.5	8.6[10]	23.6	799.0
Uruguay	2,677	22–23	8–9	13–15	27.8	61.3[9]	9.7	25.0	560.9
Type 2									
Chile	9,007	35–36	12–13	22–24	39.6	54.7	16.4	39.2	452.9
Cuba	7,675	30–34	8–9	22–25	36.4[5]	45.3	22.1[5]	47.4[5]	516.0
Type 3									
Haiti	4,751	45–50	20–25	22–25	42.3	5.1[6]	89.3[6]	86.6[6]	149.2
Bolivia	4,234	43–45	21–23	21–23	45.9[6]	19.6	67.9[6]	74.3[6]	122.3
Type 4									
Brazil	83,670	40–43	11–13	29–31	42.7	28.1	51[13]	65.8[6]	374.6
Mexico	44,172	46–47	12–13	33–35	44.3	29.6	34.6	60.3	415.4
Colombia	18,298	43–46	14–17	28–31	44.1[2]	29.2	37.7[7]	65.2[7]	373.4
Peru	12,012	43–45	14–15	28–30	43.3	28.3	39.5[11]	57.4	268.5
Venezuela	9,030	47–50	9–12	35–38	45.3	45.9	33.5	40.3	644.5
Ecuador	5,199	46–50	15–18	30–33	45.0	25.4	32.7	63.9	222.7
Guatemala	4,475	48–50	18–20	28–30	42.3[6]	14.3	70.6[6]	76.2[6]	257.7
Dom. Rep.	3,715	48–50	15–17	32–35	47.2	18.7	35.5	65.1	313.2
El Salvador	3,008	48–50	14–16	32–34	44.8	17.2	51.0	71.4	267.5
Honduras	2,396	47–50	15–17	32–34	47.8	11.2	55.0	76.3	251.7
Paraguay	2,061	42–45	14–17	26–29	45.0	16.7	25.7	63.0[6]	193.2
Nicaragua	1,815	46–50	14–16	33–35	48.4	21.1	50.2	71.8	288.4
Costa Rica	1,524	48–50	9–11	38–40	47.6	23.4	15.7	57.7	361.6
Panama	1,229	40–41	10–12	28–29	43.4	33.1	23.3	57.1	371.0
Total	243,639								

[1] *Statistical Bulletin for Latin America*, ECLA, III, 1, February 1966. [2] *Ibid.*, II, 2, August 1965. [3] *UN Demographic Yearbook*, 1964.
[4] Under 14 years. [5] 1953. [6] 1950. [7] 1951. [8] Percentage living in centres of 20,000 or more. [9] 1963. [10] 14 years and over.
[11] 17 years and over. [12] ECLA, *El Desarrollo Económico de América Latina en la Postguerra*, E/CN, 12/672, United Nations, New York, November 1963.
[13] 1950, 10 years and over.

672

that around 1960, 68 per cent of the region's population lived in centres of under 20,000 inhabitants. Of the remaining 32 per cent, almost one-third crowded in four big cities (Buenos Aires, Mexico, Rio de Janeiro and São Paulo) comprising more than 22 million inhabitants.

As a consequence of the dynamics described above, the economically active population of Latin America grows at a particularly fast pace, faster than the rest of the population. Like the total population it rejuvenates through time. The economically active population was estimated by ECLA and CELADE to be of the order of 68 million in 1960. By 1980 it will have increased to 122 million, which represents an average rate of growth of 2·9 per cent per year. Of the estimated 3·3 million entering the labour force in 1966 approximately 95 per cent were under 20 years of age. The average number of annual entrants to the labour force around 1980 is expected to be over 5 million, of whom a percentage similar to that already mentioned may be under 20 years.

THE FUTURE

No plausible projection of the Latin American population can be made assuming the continuation of the trends of fertility and mortality already described. For this would imply accepting the possibility of the continued decline of mortality irrespective of the prevailing socio-economic conditions, or alternatively improvement of the standard of living in the face of a persistently high fertility, both assumptions being logically and historically unwarranted. While there is evidence that mortality decline has already slowed down in some countries, e.g. Chile, it may be expected that before this trend becomes more general and hopefully long before the downward movement of mortality starts reversing, the Latin American populations will have introduced significant changes in their reproductive behaviour. There are clear signs that such changes have already started and that birth control is becoming increasingly applied. Several Latin American governments have recently sanctioned the use of national health systems to diffuse information and advice and to render family planning services.

The future size of the Latin American population will, of course, depend on the ultimate behaviour of the two variables discussed above. Assuming rapid decline of fertility and a continued decline of mortality, one arrives at what the United Nations has termed 'low growth', which estimates the total population of the region for the year 2,000 at around 505 million. A less rapid decline of fertility with a continued decline of mortality gives the 'medium growth' assumption, which places the total population at the end of the present century at 612 million. Within these two limits will lie the most probable size of the Latin American population.

BIBLIOGRAPHY

Carr-Saunders, A. M. *World Population. Past Growth and Present Trends*, Frank Cass, London; Barnes and Noble, New York, 1964.

Notestein, F. W. 'The Economics of Population and Food Supplies', *Proceedings of the Eighth International Conference of Agricultural Economists*, Oxford Univ. Press, London and New York, 1953.

Rosenblat, Angel. *La Población indígena y el mestizaje en América*. I: *La población indígena, 1492–1950*, Editorial Nova, Buenos Aires, 1954.

Somoza, J. and Tacla, O. *La mortalidad en Chile según las tablas de vida de 1920, 1930, 1940, 1952 y 1960*, CELADE, Series A/17.

ECLA. *Statistical Bulletin for Latin America*, II, 2, UN, New York, August 1965.

Political and Economic Planning (PEP). *World Population and Resources*, London, 1959.

UN. *Provisional Report on World Population Prospects as Assessed in 1963*, New York, 1964.

THE URBAN WORKING CLASS

DANIEL PÉCAUT

The Political Integration of Latin American Labour

At the turn of the century it seemed probable that Latin American labour movements would be formed on the model of those in existence in Europe. In the most industrialised Latin American countries, at least, anarcho-syndicalist and communist influences and the presence of many European immigrants resulted in forms of action and ideology fairly similar to those to be observed in Europe. Strikes and violent revolts, recourse to the general strike, refusal to accept the existing social system were all manifestations of an opposition syndicalism which expressed simultaneously the social isolation and the weakness of a working class in the making. This is to be seen in the history of the FORA in Argentina and the general strike it organised in 1910; in the 1919 strikes in Brazil, notably at Recife; and in the 1907 strike at Iquique, Chile.

Subsequently, however, these movements took a very different direction. Their history merges largely with that of populist rather than true labour movements: Getulism, Peronism and, in a slightly different way, the Chilean Popular Front led by Pedro Aguirre Cerda manifest this new orientation. The basic situation is no longer isolated nuclei of workers excluded from participation in national political life; the labour movement becomes institutionalised and thus to some extent politically integrated. Abundant social legislation and the increasing role of ministers of labour, paralleled by a sharp increase in the number of trade unionists, are evidence of this change. Through the movements which Gino Germani has called 'national-popular' the urban working class gained indirect participation in power.

This phenomenon is fundamental to an understanding of the condition of the Latin American urban working class. It is not simply a historical accident, as is amply proved by the continuing importance of Peronism and Getulism. It must therefore be explained both how such developments were possible and why they still affect the evolution of the Latin American labour movement. In this connection one must begin with the conditions in which Latin American industrialisation occurred. The speed with which waves of rural immigrants submerged the former workers' nuclei, the sensitivity of Latin American economies to fluctuations in the world market, state intervention in economic life, are all factors which have had a profound influence on the orientation of the Latin American labour movement. From the very beginnings of industrialisation the workers obtained access to certain political and social rights which European workers were to wait long to enjoy. They thus obtained considerable powers of influence, but at the same time these were not so much won by autonomous labour movements as conceded by governments seeking support from the masses while controlling them. This experience and its effects lead us to the analysis of a double tradition: on the one hand participation and influence; on the other, heteronomy—a strength which is also a weakness.

URBANISATION AND INDUSTRIALISATION

Latin American working-class attitudes could not be analysed without first recalling some features of the urban environment in which they are founded. This environment was formed extremely rapidly. Argentina has a 68 per cent urban population, Chile 66 per cent, Colombia 48 per cent. All the large towns therefore have a large percentage of recent migrants. In 1960 nearly 42 per cent of the population of a town such as Belo Horizonte in Brazil had arrived during the ten previous years. Moreover, the migrations concentrated on a few metropolises: thus the Buenos Aires agglomeration alone comprises 30 per cent of the population of Argentina, that of Santiago 26 per cent of the population of Chile.

The fact that industrialisation has lagged far behind the rhythm of urbanisation would seem even more important. In 1960 only 29 per cent of the gainfully employed population of Argentina worked in the industrial sector; in Brazil the figure was under 17 per cent. These figures would obviously be much lower still if the workers employed in firms of 10 persons and over were alone taken into account. In many cases they would then scarcely exceed 10 per cent. These figures appear lower still if compared with those of individuals employed in the services sector: 44 per cent in Argentina, 21 per cent in Brazil. This means that the worker, and especially the factory worker, is comparatively isolated within a population, a large part of which lives off marginal activities.

But this urban environment assumes the character of a privileged environment when compared with the rural zones from which most migrants come. In Brazil, for example, average income in the State of Guanabara is ten times higher than in the State of Piaui. In Mexico 65 per cent of the gainfully employed rural population had in 1961 a monthly income of less than 300 pesos, as against 21 per cent of the gainfully employed urban population.

The Latin American urban working class can therefore be defined as simultaneously belonging to a minority within the city, involved in a process of rapid change and participating in the comparatively privileged world formed by the urban environment.

ADJUSTMENT TO THE CITY AND ADJUSTMENT TO INDUSTRIAL LABOUR

It is understandable that in these circumstances the new worker as a rule adjusts easily to both the urban and the industrial environment. The transition from rural norms, often involving a high degree of social control, to urban norms which in contrast mean a comparative disintegration of this social control, may produce an adjustment problem for the migrant; but this problem is reduced both by the nature of the urban environment and by the actual circumstances of individual mobility, which indeed has a place within a collective movement giving it meaning. In fact we are concerned not so much with individual migration and problems of individual adjustment as with participation in collective migration and social changes brought about by a mass of migrants. The migrant enters an unformed environment which he plays a part in forming. The most varied values coexist in it, some introduced by the waves of migrants, others inherent in urban environments. This mixture facilitates the newcomer's adjustment, though it can in other respects slow down the process of change in his attitudes. Thus the migrant may retain some connection with his original values, a connection encouraged by frequently encountered phenomena such as the strengthening of family ties or regrouping with other migrants of the same origin, or yet again the resurgence of traditional values in syncretic forms; in the last respect the significance of the Brazilian messianic cults is well known. In short, the possible tensions entailed by entry into an urban environment are reduced by the variety of sub-cultures coexisting with an urban culture distinguished by orientation towards such values as education, consumption, etc.

The meaning the migrant gives the urban environment must also be considered: most often driven by the necessity of finding work or of giving his children an education, he sees in the town a privileged socio-economic environment, the symbol of a *higher* standard of living, but above all of a *different* manner of living. The expectation of change allows him more easily to overcome the obstacles to his integration into the new environment. The same would seem true of entry into the industrial world, expectation of change there too enabling the migrant to overcome ordinary adjustment problems. Factory work appears to him as the road necessary for achieving the manner of urban living, rather than the manifestation of a 'worker condition'. Here too the reverse side of the facility for adjustment is the maintenance of pre-industrial attitudes: one need only mention how often migrants retain the desire to leave industry to set up in business on their own. Such a desire reveals that little meaning is attached to the labour experience; almost its only meaning is an economic one for the individual desiring social ascent.

It must be added that adjustment to work may be accelerated by the subsistence of 'traditional' norms, as in the case of the city. The maintenance of a strong paternalism in many Latin American firms cannot be explained solely by the employer's desire to control labour; it also reveals passive acceptance of norms to which migrants were accustomed in their relations with landowners.

In these circumstances, the labour experience will scarcely give rise to a highly organised working-class consciousness; urban themes will often take on more importance than labour themes, challenging the establishment of an autonomous labour movement.

ADJUSTMENT AND POLITICAL BEHAVIOUR

The foregoing allows a glimpse of both potential and limits of organised labour action. The potential is certainly great, owing to the ease with which new workers can adjust and hence share, at least partly, urban and industrial values, their situation no longer being marginal. Moreover, the experience of new urban workers always gives rise to some discontent: entering an urban environment means contact with the problems of precarious living accommodation, lack of facilities in new quarters, and above all the sometimes fierce rise in the cost of living. Entering industry also means entering a hierarchy and becoming vividly aware of social distance. Entering metropolises also involves confrontation with state bureaucracy and politicians' canvassing. All these are possible sources of discontent which receive mention in trades union declarations. This discontent may result in some radicalisation of the urban working class; thus it has been shown that in Venezuela, Chile and Brazil radicalism increased in the transition from small towns to large metropolises.

However, the limits of this radicalisation must be emphasised. There is a great difference between discontent and the organisation of autonomous action. Very often this discontent is expressed only by appeals to the state, or, in the case of industry, to the employer. Trade union leaders themselves very often expect pay improvements from the employer rather than from trade union action, even when they profess a radical ideology. Discontent may therefore go hand in hand with heteronomy. Rather than being the source of an autonomous labour movement, it can produce a broad disposition towards the 'national-popular' type of movement and leader.

In order to explain the origin of this heteronomy we must return to the forms of urban adjustment. As we have seen, they express the multiplicity of urban cultural patterns as well as the nature of the migrants' expectation of change in a new environment. The former means that the individual, without renouncing 'traditional' norms, enters a world of different consumption norms. Understandably he may be tempted by the canvassing of leaders promising him access to these new norms. This multiplicity may find direct expression in the contradictions of electoral behaviour. In Brazil it has been noted that the working class may vote for conservative candidates at legislative elections in which they are subject to a traditional type of propaganda, and for the populist candidate at presidential elections in which they respond to canvassing by urban mass media. The migrants' expectations of change can only emphasise this flexibility, to the extent that ideals of social betterment find more opportunity for satisfaction by allegiance to charismatic leaders; the discrepancy between the migrants' desires and their satisfaction is thus reduced by the appeal to personalities who appear to embody social change.

The urban environment itself tends to encourage such an appeal; it gives rise to a vision of society in terms of social levels rather than in terms of social classes; the prime distinction appears the one between rich and poor, between powerful and weak. The appeal to the *descamisados* or to the *clases humildes* in these conditions is obvious: it is easy to win over the barely organised discontent of these new urban masses. Moreover, the worker belongs to a minority within an urban population, a large part of which lives on marginal occupations. He is therefore urged to share the only means of action at the disposal of this urban population, i.e. appeals for governmental action to transform a situation against which the latter can protest, but can act only with difficulty. Nevertheless, while the worker participates in this form of demand, reflecting the fundamental dependence of masses living in precarious conditions, he remains comparatively privileged: in many cases, therefore, his discontent expresses the wish to defend this privilege against the threats implied by inflation, etc. This contradiction increases the flexibility of his attitudes.

It seems, therefore, that the urban experience as a rule goes against the formation of a working class consciousness. The labour experience therefore requires a minimum of stabilisation to resist other more prestigious urban appeals, a stabilisation often lacking, so that flexibility of worker attitudes recurs within the industrial framework. The trade union may appear simply as a distributor of social services, and the worker may even have relations with the trade union leader scarcely different from his relations with the employer. The content of demands is often limited to the concession of increased social benefits; greater control by workers over their work or over the management of some departments of the firm is rarely demanded; in fact, trade union action often appears simply action to set in motion the intervention of official arbitration by the minister of labour or his representatives. In short, trade union action sometimes takes place in a profound ideological vacuum, and its militant base is rarely relieved by political action; it is even rare for it to involve real questioning of employers' power. Wage claims seem detached from political action.

The labour experience does not therefore seem, as a rule, to provide a source of class action. It also seems subordinate to the experience of collective mobility, which appears the essential source of change. Migrants are readily heteronomous, since they are seeking above all to become integrated into society and they appeal to charismatic leaders in order to extend and institutionalise their social participation. For this reason Latin American labour movements or trade unions are often defined as *instruments of socialisation* rather than as *instruments of dispute*. For example, some studies have shown that radicalism may diminish—with trade union or political participation—even in the Communist Party, that labour organisations are often merely a means of integrating a recently mobilised mass, and that radicalism is the expression of a still marginal adjustment, decreasing with the institutional participation won by the trade unions.

TRADE UNION ACTION AND POPULAR MOVEMENTS

The meaning of national-popular movements is therefore clear: they are a manifestation of the privilege enjoyed in the urban experience and the experience of collective mobility as compared with the labour experience. They are also the manifestation of an increased desire for social participation which conflicts with institutional obstacles. Nevertheless, the continuing importance of these movements and the differences they have caused in the history of labour organisation in Latin American countries, depending on whether they triumphed or failed—e.g. Peronism in Argentina and Gaitanism in Colombia—would be misunderstood if they were considered merely as a desire for integration. What was actually established through these movements was the link between a high degree of collective mobilisation and such values for change as nationalism or economic development. It is no accident that the themes of the *descamisados* and of nationalism have been so frequently associated. In short, these movements are important because they combined a wish for social participation with an early assumption of society values which are not identical with class values only.

The mobilisation of the working class masses has indeed most often been accomplished round three complementary poles, as A. Touraine has shown: class, nationalism and economic development. This plurality of values reflects the conditions in which the urban proletariat was formed: it entered industrial labour at the same time as it entered mass consumption and became conscious of the dependent position apparent in its link with underdevelopment. It is understandable that in these conditions the working class problem was complicated by these other factors and that class action might often have appeared subordinate to the action of popular movements.

The assumption of these multiple values also reflects the forms of Latin American industrialisation. The Latin American industrialist has very often seemed more like a politician or a speculator than an innovator: market instability encourages him too to appeal to state protection or to speculate on the short-term state of the market. The firm therefore has difficulty in forming a framework for containing trade union action, since it is not an autonomous decision-making centre but part of a complex network of pressure groups aiming at winning state support. Thus trade union action is itself inevitably induced to appeal to 'the top' where decisions are actually taken; it is no accident that in most Latin American countries demands are in fact discussed at the ministry of labour much more than within the firm.

The ambiguity in which trade union action is placed is therefore obvious. On the one hand it expresses the discontent of workers of rural origin who conflict with obstacles in their wish to attain a new way of life. On the other hand it is itself involved as a pressure group at state level and therefore in accepting to a great extent its place within the framework of the existing social system. Finally, on account of pressure from the new urban population, it is driven to challenge the existing social system by invoking the requirements of development or the preservation of national autonomy.

This ambiguity constitutes a fundamental obstacle to the birth of real workers' movements in Latin America. Moreover, it often recurs even within each trade union: on the one hand trade union machinery can be involved in state decision-making mechanisms to the extent that they become mere bureaucratised pressure groups; while on the other hand the militant base, sensitive to the themes of urban discontent, challenges these same decision-making mechanisms and puts more trust in popular leaders than in workers' leaders. The problem for Latin American trade unionism lies between these two forms of heteronomy: the machinery trapped in power participation, and the base tempted by popular-demagogic movements.

It is true that trade union action could sometimes be better organised. Thus in the case of a powerful industry trade union action is apt to be more autonomous. In strategic sectors such as oil, copper, tin, and generally in industries dominating the country's economy, more organised forms of trade union action occur and class ideology seems more important. This is because the various values we have mentioned combine at industrial level. A direct link is established between wage demands and action in the name of the country's development or independence. Moreover, the temptation to appeal to 'the top' is weaker, to the extent that the economic importance of these industries gives them a broad independence. In short, the strategic role of such industries means that trade union action can develop more easily and independently and consequently can sooner create a strong class consciousness. Even here, however, the limits of such action should be pointed out. In many circumstances class ideology can in fact conceal the defence of privileges enjoyed by workers in these sectors, and trade union action may do no more than simply create the practice of collective bargaining. Class ideology is then only an expression of a trade union's position of strength. This is proved by the resistance these same trade unions are apt to show to a progressive government which tries to close the gap between the privileged and non-privileged sectors. Therefore even in this case trade union action is not entirely free of ambiguity.

In non-strategic industries labour conflicts are even more insufficient to cause a truly organised trade union action; action is here often limited to setting state arbitration in motion. The experience of conflict in Latin American industry is therefore generally not strong enough to counterbalance the attractions to labour we have mentioned.

The strength of the Latin American labour organisations is also their weakness. They have a good deal of access to power and often a large number of affiliates, who however often see their labour organisations merely as social services. The organisations' access to power largely expresses the importance of the urban themes which arouse discontent; this discontent can often be more easily channelled by the national-popular type of movement than used by real labour movements. The labour experience can itself emphasise this heteronomy by inciting appeals to the state, to the extent that it is at state level rather than at industrial that the true field of action is situated.

This explains the frequent weakness of labour organisations and the scarcity of labour movements in Latin America. We do not find a working class confronting the power of the employers, nor an absence of worker political participation. We find a working class in the making, confronting simultaneously the problems of underdevelopment, social inequality and national dependence. The working class, therefore, encounters the problem of bringing about social change while being involved at the same time in national systems of decision-making.

BIBLIOGRAPHY

Alexander, R. J. *Labor Relations in Argentine, Brazil and Chile*, McGraw–Hill, New York and London, 1962.

Bonilla, F. 'The Urban Worker', *Continuity and Change in Latin America*, ed. John J. Johnson, Stanford Univ. Press, Stanford, Calif., 1964.

Casanova, P. G. 'L'évolution du système des classes au Mexique', *Cahiers Internationaux de Sociologie*, XXXIX, Paris, 1965.

Germani, G. *Política y sociedad en una epocha de transición: de la sociedad traditional a la sociedad de masas*, Editorial Paidos, Buenos Aires, 1965.

Hauser, P. (ed.) *L'urbanisation en Amérique Latine*, UNESCO, Paris, 1962.

Kahl, J. A. (ed.) *La industrialización en America Latina*, Fondo de Cultura Económica, Mexico, 1965.

Landsberger, H. A., Barrera, M. and Toro, A. 'The Chilean Labor Union Leader: A Preliminary Report on his background and Attitudes', *Industrial and Labor Review*, XVII, 3.

Pereira, L. *Trabalho e desenvolvimento no Brasil*, Difusão Europeia do Livro, São Paulo, 1965.

di Tella, T., Brams, L., Reynaud, J. D. and Touraine, A. *Huachipato et Lota: étude sur la conscience ouvrière dans deux entreprises chiliennes*, Centre National de la Recherche Scientifique, Paris, 1964.

Touraine, A. 'Mobilité sociale, rapports de classe et nationalisme en Amérique Latine', *Sociologie du Travail*, 4, Paris, 1965.

Touraine, A. (ed.) 'Ouvriers et syndicats d'Amérique Latine', *Sociologie du Travail*, special number, 4, Paris, 1961.

Weffort, F. C. 'Estado y masas en el Brasil', *Revista Latino-Americana de Sociologia*, 1, Buenos Aires, 1965.

THE AGRARIAN WORKING CLASS

DAVID LEHMANN

Origin of the 'Latifundio'

THE Spanish colonies generated a social structure in which labourers and large landholders were entirely separate groups with no mobility between them. The *encomienda* system, whereby the Indian's tribute to the Spanish crown, ceded as a reward to the Conquistadors, was almost always collected in the form of labour, resulted in a situation which did not take long to develop into a market relationship in which the Indians were exploited in a manner which made them little different from slaves. This was made possible by land grants, theoretically separate from encomiendas, which gave a small class of landowners a monopoly over most of the land in the colonies. Efforts by the Spanish crown to protect Indians, to allow them to pay their tribute in cash or kind, to limit their obligations by statute, to halt their masters' worst excesses, were little more than unenforceable moral exhortations. Once this institutional structure had been established, the landlords had no incentive to perform what could be considered their 'feudal' duties. Hardly capitalist in the Weberian sense—neither efficient nor impersonal nor ascetic—they evolved methods which resulted in market relationships between strong landowners and weak labourers based on a monopolistic situation which is a salient characteristic of Latin American agrarian history down to the present day.

At first the landowners used violence; but this was self-defeating since the Indians died, collapsed, fell ill or fled. In Brazil the Portuguese imported them to the littoral by force, and were eventually compelled to have recourse to African slaves. In Chile there was always a chronic shortage of labour, especially since the Indians resisted the Spaniards in an intermittent war lasting from 1536 until the 19th century. This shortage hastened the decline of the encomienda in the 17th century and poor Spaniards, landless because there simply was not enough land to be granted, took the Indians' place, first as 'borrowers' of land, then as tenants, and finally as tenant-labourers. This structured paternalism, originating in a friendly favour but evolving into dependency and exploitation, with the personal relationship as the common factor, is also to be found in the Loja province of Ecuador where tenant-labourers are not Indian and are called by a Spanish name— *arrimados* (the Indian equivalent is *huasipungueros*). Today the structure remains without the paternalism, and in other cases paternalism, where it exists, is and was only a means of lessening the impact of, and thereby facilitating, the employment of cheap labour. Brazilian paternalism developed on the plantations worked by slave labour where domination was tempered by free sexual unions between masters and female slaves. Today paternalist protection is becoming more and more of a myth.

681

The function of the encomienda was to destroy the social system of the tribe and its nexus with communal land, and to integrate the Indian, illiterate and powerless, into the *latifundio* (large estate). True, Indians continued to have their own communities, living in them and working on the large estates, and there was a constant territorial conflict between community and estate. But with the advent of liberal economic doctrines in the 19th century the community lands all but disappeared under the pressure of the estates. The labourer had little or no land of his own and had no choice but to submit to the landowners' monopoly or to starve.

The latifundio has been until recently, and sometimes still is, isolated and self-sufficient. The *latifundista* creates about him an aura of grandeur and omnipotence, riding on a horse and followed by a retainer, building a splendid residence and, nowadays, in many cases absenting himself most of the time. It is rare for him to own land primarily in order to make an efficient enterprise of his farm. Land-ownership is a symbol of prestige, a hedge against inflation, a qualification to be a member of the aristocracy. Above all, it is a way of preserving power and a way of life, since it effectively blocks the labourers' upward mobility. The landlord's aura is but an attempt to sanctify his position in order to make the labourer accept it. That he must make the effort reflects the fragility of the system. The labourer accepts his own position as long as he knows of no alternative, and as long as he can earn enough to subsist. Two factors are likely to modify his attitude: contact with the outside world, and increase in population density to the point where he begins to demand more rights—in the form of land or of wages. A wage-increase or its equivalent might lead to higher productivity, and on the vast majority of estates it could easily be absorbed in existing profits or by bringing unused land under cultivation, but such a demand implicitly threatens the landlord's prerogative to dictate all that occurs on his property. He knows that to give in now would lead to a never-ending succession of demands; a show of weakness would be fatal, and consequently his response is invariably to suppress demands by economic or sometimes even violent means.

The Evolution of 'Minifundismo'

There was one other mode of evolution for the land grants: sub-division through inheritance. Even a large estate may soon grow into a group of very small plots if all sons of each successive generation take a share, and daughters take one for their dowry. Today, 400 years after the Conquest, we find areas of extreme sub-division, with holdings of microscopic size. Many owners may own more than one plot, or farm, if it is large enough to deserve that name, but their holdings will not be adjacent. In one area in Chile, admittedly the most highly sub-divided in the country, over 96 per cent of landholders own land under 5 hectares in extent; over 8 per cent own less than 0·1 hectare; over 66 per cent less than 1 hectare. Clearly many are unable to live on the income from their holdings. They produce partly for subsistence, partly for the market, and they work each other's fragmented holdings as sharecroppers or tenants. Some have as many as four or five jobs. By means of the most intricate arrangements these smallholders manage to cultivate their lands and preserve themselves from utter chaos. Survival, rather than profit, is their goal, and they develop a community spirit which would appear quite impossible in the circumstances. They have a detailed system for distributing irrigation, and communal pastures in the nearby foothills. That cultivation in such an area is grossly uneconomic is but an illustration of the peasant's attachment to landownership; nor does sub-division necessarily create conflicts, for peasants living at subsistence level are unlikely to be anarchic individualists or seekers of power and status.

THE MARKET SITUATION OF LABOUR; LAND TENURE

A peasant is never part of a complex division of labour; he always produces an entire product, he ploughs, sows and harvests a crop, he cares for a tree and picks its fruit. He does his best never to conceive of himself as a wage-earner. If he works on someone else's land it is in order to gain access to the produce of that land and not just to be paid in cash; he is even prepared to pay in kind or in labour for that access. In this light it is not difficult to see that in Latin America, where landownership is so highly concentrated, the peasant exposes himself to all kinds of exploitation. Very often he becomes, to the observer, no more than a wage-earner, but the reason is precisely that he conceives of himself as an independent operator.

Of course the industrial worker is also involved in a market relationship with his employer, but the relationship is conditioned only by the labour supply, and above all the interdependence in an industrial work-situation makes for cohesive collective action by a large number of workers. The peasant, on the other hand, although partly depending on the supply of labour, also exposes himself in a weak position as debtor, buyer and seller, and is not as a rule part of an integrated group of members of his class. His rights to a piece of land are usually based on verbal agreement, so that he is all but powerless if the landlord cares to expel him. Peasant unions which are forming now in Latin America are demanding written contracts for holders or land for the landless rather than wage-increases. In Chile legislation allows their formation only within the estate, and by peasants resident on the estate, thus preventing effective group action by the peasants as a class. At present the forms of tenure everywhere reflect the vulnerability of the peasant in a monopolistic situation.

THE 'COLONO' SYSTEM

This is a generic term for tenant-labourers, who exist in almost every Latin American country. In each one they have acquired a local, often Indian, name: in Chile *inquilinos*, in Ecuador *huasipungueros*, in Peru *yanaconas*. Some of these terms are applied to poor Spaniards, but in the northern Andean countries the tenant-labourers are almost all Indians, and it is clear that this form of tenancy is a fairly simple method of tying workers to a farm. In return for working a specified number of days per week on the farm, the labourer is given a house, certain grazing rights, food, wood and a plot of land to cultivate for subsistence. Very often other members of his family also work on the farm as more or less permanent wage-earners and live in his house, thus guaranteeing the landlord an added supply of labour. Within this framework variations are numerous.

On one large Chilean estate, bordering on the sub-divided area mentioned above, the inquilinos are allowed liberal grazing rights on the farm's pastures and not just on their own plot, and thereby are able to build up savings. They are also given more land to cultivate for themselves if they are prepared to supply more labour. For this purpose they hire others to work the owner's land and devote themselves to cultivating their own land. Thus they are really tenants who pay rent in the form of the wages of the man they hire. Their ambition is to save enough to buy a plot in the adjacent sub-divided area: then they will attain the status of landowners.

In other situations the *colono* is not so well treated. Since the minimum wage was instituted in Latin American countries the peasant has hardly benefited at all. In Brazil it is no secret that the minimum wage legislation is never applied in the countryside. In general, where before the peasant received his house and meal on the fields during the day and other benefits, they are now deducted from the minimum wage. René Dumont (see bibliography) calculated that the plot, the house and the grazing rights of a Chilean inquilino, in other words his rent, in the Central Valley came to 45 per cent of his income when deducted from his wage. Although the practice is dying out, at least in Chile, it was for a long time common for these workers to be paid in coupons, or even coins made for a particular estate, which could be spent only at a shop on that estate; prices were extortionate and in effect the landlord got back whatever wages he might have paid out. The effect of this kind of procedure is to make it impossible for the worker to save and acquire some land of his own. The impossibility of saving is one of the salient characteristics of the Latin American rural working-class.

The colono system, then, is not invariable, but a framework within which the peasant's ability to save depends on the good will of the landlord. Sometimes the landlord is willing to allow the colono a degree of freedom so long as he provides labour, and is prepared to operate on a piece-work basis allowing him the status of an independent operator, and the peasant can save. But elsewhere the landlord assumes that the colono is an appendage to his farm and acts in such a way as to perpetuate that condition by, for example, prescribing what crops are to be grown or insisting that they be sold to him, or allowing his cattle to stray and wreck the colono's crops.

Conflict and Change: The Threat to the 'Latifundio'

The declining market position of the peasant who operates independently or semi-independently has driven many off the large estates. Some go to the cities, others become hired labourers. These hired labourers are disliked both by the landlords, for whom they create trouble and expense, and by resident labourers who see in them a threat to their traditional position. Nevertheless these workers, often seasonal and nomadic, are bringing new values to the countryside, especially if they have come from the towns; their greater militancy is at least a small threat to the status quo.

But the latifundio is also being threatened internally. The kind of situation described above will survive for so long as the peasants continue to recognise the legitimacy of land-ownership, whatever use it is put to. The causes of non-recognition—contact with the outside world and over-population—have already been mentioned. An example of how the situation can develop subsequently is found in Ecuador.

Apart from the colono system, Ecuador also possesses a system which derives both from the colono system and from minifundismo: that of the *yanaperos*. These are owners of small plots bordering on the large estates of the Sierra. They have to pay for the right to use roads across the estates, and if their cattle stray from the roads the penalty may vary from 20 days of unpaid labour to the shooting of the animal.

This severe treatment arises from circumstances already fraught with tension. On one estate studied by CIDA (see bibliography) the yanaperos had once been tenant-labourers, but were dismissed when the owner abandoned sheep-farming, whereupon they settled on the outskirts; as their numbers grew, they exerted increasing pressure on the estate's land. The estate ceded to a certain extent and sold some land to them; but it still demanded payment in work for use of its roads, mill, water and so on. Furthermore the twelve tenant-labourers resident on the estate itself were limited to one hectare of land; if they failed to appear for work for any reason their wage was withheld, and if they appeared late they were sent away; if their animals strayed on to the estate's farmland and harmed the seeds, they were attacked, as were even the peasants themselves on occasion. This estate, run by a manager, possessed a social structure perpetuated only by coercion. The minifundio areas around estates such as this exhibit a further characteristic which seems to be universal in all developing countries: the gross inadequacy of credit and resulting usurious practices.

CREDIT

Here we come upon the middleman, who is in some cases a very small businessman indeed; but the local priest may also fulfil the same function.

In many Latin American countries the state has an agricultural credit scheme of its own; it is also very often trying to combat inflation. It is therefore not prepared to lend money unless it has very good security, and demands hard terms (though if there is an inflation of 40 per cent per annum even a 20 per cent interest rate will still allow the borrower to make a profit). A glaring example of this occurs in Chile, where what happens in effect is that the rich farmers obtain credit to finance their day-to-day operations, thus freeing their profits for other activities, in particular a house in town, a trip to Europe, etc. Intermediate landowners have less chance of being given as much as they ask for, the rich obtain two-thirds of the credit though they constitute only 1 per cent or 2 per cent of agricultural workers. They also do not use their credit for long-term improvements. The small farmers, who are the most economic users of land, obtain less credit than their economic performance would demand, for non-economic reasons.

Not only is this credit system wasteful of resources, it drives the small-holder to the usurer since he cannot possibly plant a crop without borrowing money unless he is making a good profit. The lender often asks for a portion of the crop as interest or repayment and the borrower has little choice but to agree, thereby probably being obliged to sell at below market prices. It is not rare for interest to be 50 per cent of the annual crop if the borrower is unable to pay off the debt at harvest time, and this practice perpetuates that inability.

These petty capitalists function as intermediaries between town and country. They travel about the country buying up crops from smallholders at well below market prices or lending money in return for a portion of the following year's crop. In Ecuador a case has even been recorded by CIDA in which they waylaid peasants on their way to market and used violence to force them to sell them their produce (see bibliography). By taking advantage of the peasants and maintaining high prices in the market these middlemen may be one of the sources of Latin American inflation.

The middleman is not the only person responsible for debt slavery. The rubber companies in the Amazon river basin employ similar methods; although they have no legal right to the rubber the planter collects he is still entirely dependent on them as suppliers and buyers and his debt is perpetual.

It is in Brazil that credit and land tenure coincide in the most striking fashion. Here the old order is more threatened than anywhere else, and coercion, economic and physical, is common. Many landowners have a private police force and are tightening and reinforcing their hold on the land. Not only are they buying more and more land, they are excluding peasants from access to its produce. This trend is probably a consequence of the rise of rural syndicates, known as *ligas camponesas*.

The Ligas originated in the north-east during the 1940s. After a decline of sugar production during which plantation land had been leased to peasants, an improvement in world market prices put these plantations back into operation, even more highly mechanised than before, and many peasants found themselves landless or severely limited in their tenure rights. It was the convergence of the impact of a factory type of farm and the peasants' attachment to land-ownership which gave birth to the Ligas. The share-croppers and smallholders who feel threatened have been the more moderate and stable members of the Ligas, whereas the extremist socialist wing led by Francisco Julião has met with relative failure. Although only a tiny fraction of the peasants have joined, the influence of the Ligas has been out of proportion to their membership, encouraging peasants in their demands and hardening land-owners' resistance. One reason for the low membership is simply the unwillingness or refusal of landowners to employ members.

The reaction of landowners to the rise of militancy has been uncom-promising. Many mechanise production or convert to livestock to reduce their employment requirements. Taking advantage of the abundance of labour they impose debt slavery on sharecroppers and tenants, insisting that the cropper's share or tenant's produce be sold to them; for this purpose they give credit to be repaid in kind at below market prices, thereby involving themselves in no outlay whatsoever and losing nothing by inflation. The Central Bank requires a guarantor for loans, and the landlord may refuse to do this, in which case the cropper will be forced to borrow from him; at times the owner will relend at higher rates money which he himself has borrowed from the Central Bank at favourable rates. The practice of paying rent in kind is common in all countries of Latin America in communities producing for subsistence, and where the money economy has not fully penetrated. It reduces the integration of the producer into the wider market economy, lessens his capacity to save, and prevents him from having to make the kind of calculations conducive to his own economic success and that of agriculture in general.

THE SHARECROPPER

Fundamentally the sharecropper is a landless peasant who pays for access to the produce of a piece of land with part of that produce. The owner may or may not provide tools, and the degree to which he shares investments determines the cropper's incentive to make them. Ideally, he should pay a proportion of the investments equal to the proportion of crop he receives (usually 50 per cent). Thus, more perhaps than any other type of worker, the cropper depends on credit, whether it comes in the form of the landlord's contribution, or from a usurer, or from an institution. In Latin America innumerable forms of sharing are found, from the Ecuadorian middleman who even takes from the crop the equivalent of the seed he has contributed, to the relatively enlightened Brazilian landowner in an onion-growing area who provides land, money, water and 50 per cent of the seed and buys the cropper's share at current market prices.

Sharecropper and tenant-labourer overlap in Brazil, since the cropper finds himself very often forced to provide labour to discharge his debt, or simply at the landlord's insistence. One of the targets of the Ligas has been the *cambão*—one day a week of unremunerated labour given to the landlord for no apparent reason except as recognition of his superior status; it may be declining in this explicit form, but the bargaining power of the peasant is so small that if unpaid work is demanded he may have to give it.

This evolution, which is really a regression, towards payment in kind or in labour, may be bound up with the inflationary process. However this may be, its effects on the status of the cropper and the tenant-labourer impose heavy strains. The cropper, unable to sell his crop independently, becomes a wage-earner, if that. Credit is an instrument for effectively preventing the cropper from saving. It is hardly even a wage, in cases where interest rates are high and debt is permanent. The tenant-labourer's position is becoming less and less stable as he finds that the landowner may take back his land at any moment without warning or compensation for improvements. If he goes to court the tenant may well win his case but he is unlikely to be awarded his full due: the court will opt for a compromise. The peasant is beginning to perceive that his self-image as an independent operator, however unreal it may have been in the past, is now in outright contradiction with reality.

In Brazil the fragile balance which supported the latifundio is on the verge of collapse and the status quo is only maintained by economic and physical coercion. This situation exemplifies the comparative lack of control over the power of large landowners in Latin America generally.

In face of this kind of situation the peasant has three alternatives. He can take a number of jobs at the same time; he can become a day-labourer, living in a town and working in the countryside; or he can make for the city. This 'polyvalency' of rural employment has been noted in Chile but is certainly a widespread phenomenon on the continent.

The day-labourer who lives in a small town occupies the lowest status in the intricate peasant hierarchy. One might expect him to be the most militant type of peasant, but he has renounced his pretensions to land-ownership and no longer considers himself entirely a peasant. It appears that peasants are more militant when demanding land than when seeking higher wages. Nor can the day-labourer consider himself entirely a town-dweller; unsure where to seek his future, he does not channel his full energies either into peasant militancy or into urban agitation—if he is militant at all. On the level of simply earning his living the pattern is the same; he is not motivated by the peasant's access to the produce of the land or by his aspiration to land-ownership, and hence he has no prospect of advancement from his low status and low income. He has renounced the land but is still bound to it, and the only way to resolve the contradiction is to work as well as to live in the city, and that means the capital city.

URBANISATION

This is, in fact, what innumerable Latin American peasants are now doing. The process is occurring at a moment when there is over-abundance of labour both in the countryside and in the towns, with the result that in

Brazil, to take one example, little more than 14 per cent of the urban labour force is engaged in manufacturing and mining (Kahil, see bibliography). What is most striking about this phenomenon is that the peasant's life changes so little when he reaches the city. Shanty-towns have existed for a long time in Buenos Aires, Santiago, Lima, Rio de Janeiro, Mexico City and Caracas. They do not house as large a proportion of the urban population as is often imagined, but they soften the impact of arrival in the town; they are almost exclusively inhabited by peasants whose kinship groups and communities are as tightly knit as they were in the country, and which protect them from the shock of the big city.

One consequence of rural-urban migration has been the appearance of stages of urbanisation; in the first stage an aggregate of individuals, hardly a group, lives along a roadside eking out a living from marginal occupations; a second stage is the small town which has failed to develop a function of its own and has become only a centre for middlemen and a staging-post for peasants on their way to the capital city.

URBAN AND RURAL POPULATION TRENDS IN CIDA STUDY COUNTRIES, 1950–70[1]

				Thousands			Percentage	
				Urban	Rural	Total	Urban	Rural
Argentina								
1950	.	.	.	11,199·1	5,893·9	17,093·0	65·5	34·5
1960	.	.	.	15,001·9	5,664·1	20,666·0	72·6	27·4
1970	.	.	.	18,200·8	6,260·2	24,461·0	74·4	25·6
Brazil								
1950	.	.	.	18,783·0	33,161·0	51,944·0	36·2	63·8
1960	.	.	.	31,991·0	38,976·0	70,967·0	45·1	54·9
1970	.	.	.	51,000·0	44,300·0	95,300·0	53·5	46·5
Chile								
1950	.	.	.	3,389·7	2,364·2	5,753·9	58·9	41·1
1960	.	.	.	5,028·0	2,346·0	7,374·0	68·2	31·8
1970	.	.	.	6,925·0	2,467·0	9,392·0	73·7	26·3
Colombia[2]								
1950	.	.	.	3,160·7	8,107·5	11,268·2	28·0	72·0
1960	.	.	.	5,353·0	8,961·0	14,314·0	37·4	62·6
1970	.	.	.	8,394·0	9,897·0	18,291·0	45·9	54·1
Ecuador								
1950	.	.	.	914·0	2,289·0	3,203·0	28·5	71·5
1960	.	.	.	1,422·0	2,787·0	4,209·0	33·8	66·2
1970	.	.	.	2,235·0	3,395·0	5,630·0	39·7	60·3
Guatemala								
1950	.	.	.	701·0	2,101·0	2,802·0	25·0	74·9
1960	.	.	.	963·0	2,579·0	3,542·0	27·2	72·8
1970	.	.	.	1,353·0	3,172·0	4,525·0	29·9	70·1
Peru								
1950	.	.	.	3,058·6	4,773·4	7,832·0	39·0	61·0
1960	.	.	.	4,607·0	5,542·0	10,149·0	45·4	54·6
1970	.	.	.	7,229·0	6,433·0	13,662·0	52·9	47·1

[1] These figures are based on rates of population increase rather than on past rates or projections of rural-urban migration.
[2] Meta, Chocó, Comisarías and Intendencias are not included.

The above picture is unfair to the exceptions, to those countries—Mexico, Cuba and Bolivia—which have had land reforms, and to those few land-owners who, however paternalistically, are trying to improve the peasant's situation. The writer has, however, attempted to portray one of the most characteristically Latin American situations with all its paradoxes, and to identify the forces making for change in that situation. These are partly economic, partly demographic, but their root lies in the landowners' realisation that their position is untenable since it has been seen to be maintained solely in order that they may preserve their power and their status. This strain, far from provoking their retreat, has forced them to use coercive measures based on their monopolistic position, which are causing the peasants to question that very monopoly. However, it appears that the resulting movements rarely build up momentum, and that the situation of the peasantry is such that they remain fragmentary and intermittent.

BIBLIOGRAPHY

Baraona, R., Aranda, Q., Santana, R. *Valle de Putaendo: Estudio de estructura agraria*, Editorial Universitaria, Santiago de Chile, 1960.

Dumont, R. *Lands Alive*, Merlin, London; Monthly Review Press, New York, 1965.

Fals Borda, O. *Peasant Society in the Colombian Andes*, Univ. of Florida Press, Gainesville, Fla., 1955.

Feder, E. 'Feudalism and Agricultural Development: The Role of Controlled Credit in Chile's Agriculture', *Land Economics*, XXXVI, Madison, Wis., February 1960.

Freyre, G. *The Masters and the Slaves*, Alfred A. Knopf, New York, 1956.

Góngora, M. *Origen de los Inquilinos de Chile Central*, Universidad de Chile, Santiago, 1960.

Griffin, K. 'Reflections on Latin American Development', *Oxford Economic Papers*, XVIII, 1, March 1966.

Kahil, R. 'The Absorption of Manpower by the Urban and Rural Sectors of Brazil', *Bulletin of the Oxford Institute of Economics and Statistics*, XXVII, 1, February 1965.

Hauser, P. M. (ed.) *Urbanization in Latin America*, UNESCO, Paris, 1961.

McBride, G. M. *Chile: Land and Society*, American Geographical Society, New York, 1936.

ECLA. 'Rural Settlement Patterns and Social Change in Latin America: Notes for a Strategy of Rural Development', *Economic Bulletin for Latin America*, X, 1, UN, New York, March 1965.

Interamerican Committee for Agricultural Development (ICAD or CIDA). *Los rasgos fundamentales de los sistemas de tenencia de la tierra en el Ecuador*, Pan American Union, Washington, DC, 1966. *Brazil: Land Tenure and the Socio-economic Development of the Agricultural Sector*, Pan American Union, Washington, DC, 1966. *Chile: tenencia de la tierra y desarrollo socio-económico del sector agrícola*, Santiago, 1966.

THE INDIANS OF THE ANDES

ANDREW PEARSE

'INDIAN' AS SOCIAL GROUP

USE of the word 'Indian' in South America varies greatly from one country to another and within each country; it may acquire meaning both from the context in which it is used and from the status of the user. Some years ago a circular was sent out to all military units in Colombia forbidding the use of the word 'Indian' in addressing recruits and privates. The word had ceased to refer to specific social groups which composed the earlier population, and had become a term of abuse, to imply all the despised qualities of the countryman as seen by the town-dweller. 'Indian' may also be used to refer to physical features which approximate to some generally held stereotype of the pre-Hispanic inhabitants of the Americas.

In each of the Andean highlands of Ecuador, Bolivia and Peru the word refers to people who think of themselves as a distinct social group. The remainder of society recognises and treats them as such, so that there is little ambiguity of identity. Nevertheless there is much variety in the characteristics of local so-called Indian social groups, and hence a tendency to drop the classification 'Indian' from national censuses. The Ecuadorean census, for example, includes indicators such as language, footwear, type of dwelling, and sleeping arrangements, but draws no conclusions as to the total number of Indians.

Angel Rosenblat gave the following figures for 1930 and 1940:

INDIAN POPULATION OF ECUADOR, PERU AND BOLIVIA

	1930		1940	
	No. of Indians	% of total population	No. of Indians	% of total population
Ecuador	960,000	48·0	1,000,000	40·0
Peru	3,200,000	52·0	3,247,196	46·2
Bolivia	1,635,000	54·5	1,650,000	50·0

We may now examine the factors which determine membership of these social groups, distinct in behaviour and appearance from the rest of society. Biologically the Indians result from the mixing of European with native stock, with the native predominating. But the same description might be given of the biological character of many other non-Indian populations in these countries. The various subcultures themselves are syncretic; a form of colonial catholicism has been practised for three hundred years. Peculiarities of dress probably owe more to earlier provincial Spanish styles than to those of pre-colonial times. In agriculture, art, crafts, food and medicine, belief and practice show native habits side by side with those acquired during colonial times and since.

Forms of social organisation have been those imposed successively by the various colonial and republican regimes as a means of subjection and exploitation. Thus it is not surprising that many common features of behaviour and personality of the enclave cultures owe more to common resorts in the art of self-preservation than to racial character.

The real significance of the Indians lies not in their race or culture, but in their status and social function. The word 'Indian' denotes members of social groups to which society apportions special treatment implying a restriction of rights, a limited field of cultural expectations and contractual inferiority to the citizens and institutions of the national societies. To these groups is ascribed the function of productive rural labour and therefore they are roughly coterminous with the highland peasantry. One is born into the group but neither birth nor physical appearance is a condition of membership, rather learned culture and 'co-livelihood', and the individual may withdraw from the group if he can fit himself for an alternative livelihood.

The ethnic denomination of a subject peasantry expresses a widespread view that the three countries in question suffer from an 'Indian problem', that is to say that their relative backwardness is attributable to the continued presence of an unredeemed mass of Indians who are resistant, both culturally and personally, to civilisation and progress. The problem is rather why, after four hundred years of functional interdependence in economic and social life, the highland peasantry should still be culturally separate from the rest of the society and subject to it. The question is one of problem societies, not of problem races or problem cultures.

ETHNIC DISPERSION IN LATIN AMERICA

The survival of ethnically and biologically different social groups within each of the three countries here under consideration can be explained historically. But it will be convenient first to consider the Latin American region as a whole.

In northern Mexico, Uruguay and large parts of Argentina the Conquistadors encountered hunters who had accumulated neither the wealth nor the numbers necessary to form an organised labour force, and who fled from areas of settlement and were progressively wiped out. The societies which then developed in these zones were fed by European migration, and ethnic difference has little importance in their social structure.

In the lowlands of South America the Spaniards encountered 'slash-and-burn' horticulturalists who were occasional hunters or fishers living in small makeshift villages. The low density of population, primitive productive techniques achieving little beyond subsistence, and the ease of escape from capitivity into a friendly hinterland akin to the already accustomed habitat, afforded few possibilities of large-scale exploitation of labour. Nevertheless, natives could be absorbed into the colonisers' cattle-raising and agricultural enterprises on a smaller scale, and in many places where this happened a mixing of the conquerors with the native populations took place, and cultures embodying elements from both sides evolved. The anthropologist Elman Service refers to these and similar areas as *Mestizo America*, as distinct from *Euro-America* indicated above and from *Indo-America*. In Mestizo America (that is, Paraguay, Costa Rica, central Chile and parts of the interior of Brazil) the society which emerged from cultural and biological mixing at an early stage has not perpetuated an enclave social group called Indian.

That part of Indo-America lying in South America coincides fairly closely with the populations of the highlands of Ecuador, Bolivia and Peru. Indo-America is a vestigial heartland of what was once the domain of the Inca, which occupied the Andean Altiplanos, mountain slopes, valleys and some of the Pacific coastal areas, in a long strip from northern Chile to southern Colombia, a distance of more than 2,000 miles. The peoples of the Inca empire were profoundly different from the tribes at a lower level of organisation and development encountered by the Spaniards. Intensive agriculture was practised, the valley slopes were terraced at great cost in labour, and irrigation was used where necessary. On the firm base of a surplus-producing agricultural economy the whole superstructure of a great state was mounted, with a hierarchical form of social organisation involving a professional bureaucracy, a complex taxation system, the use of large-scale labour organisation, a developed town life and a generally high population density.

THE ESTATE SYSTEM

The Conquistadors, by their organisation of the labour of the conquered masses to extract wealth from the soil, founded a new society based on the institutions governing the exploitation of labour and the distribution of land. Until the end of the 16th century massive Indian labour was employed by means of two institutions, the *encomienda* and the *mita*. The encomienda was a tract of land which with the native inhabitants on it was allotted to a Spaniard who either wielded influence or had distinguished himself in the Conquest. Each *encomendero* was responsible for the maintenance of order within his encomienda, for levying tribute, and for ensuring the instruction of the natives in the Roman Catholic faith. He was in return permitted to appropriate the services of the people of his territory for his own use. However, the encomendero frequently abused this system by the illegal extension of his territory at the expense of the Indians' subsistence lands and by the practice of slavery. The *mita* was a system of forced labour by which the Spanish authorities requisitioned between a quarter and a fifth of the native working population, whether or not settled within the encomiendas, for work in the mines, in construction, transport, field labour and manufacture. Both these systems resulted in population depletion, and reform came at the end of the 16th century. The encomendero was given the opportunity to become legal proprietor of that part of his encomienda to which he had valid rights. Lands were also allotted as reservations (*resguardos*) for the dwelling and subsistence of the Indians. These reservations were governed internally according to special regulations and administered directly by Spanish officials and Indian hereditary leaders called *curagas*. They were obliged not only to pay taxes to the crown but also to pay labour service to both individuals and the government.

During the greater part of the 17th and 18th centuries the labour needs of the Spaniards were met by the various forms of labour service imposed upon the Indians of the reservations and an ever-growing nucleus of working families bound to the encomiendas and resident upon them. But towards the end of the 18th century this supply was found insufficient, and the reservations were 'squeezed' by the expedient of auctioning those where population density was less. The families rendered homeless sought refuge in the remaining reservations or joined a floating landless population. Thus a new labour surplus was created for the estates and other productive enterprises.

The colonial society of the Andean highlands, which lasted nearly three centuries, was a society regulated by laws based on the view that men are not born equal. The system of 'estates', i.e. legally ascribed status at birth, conferred rights and duties relating to such things as permitted trades and occupations, land rights, holding of public office, payment of taxes and tribute and contribution of labour in both public and private service. The system of estates regulated questions of subordination in relations between individuals and groups, and in particular it regulated dress, ornament and overt behaviour so that the different estates could be recognised and identified easily in public and the appropriate relationships observed.

In the earlier colonial period the number of legally defined strata multiplied rapidly with the growing complexity of society and the genetic mixing of European, African and native stock. The larger distinctions as regards the ascription of functional social roles were probably those between persons born in Spain, persons born in the colony of Spanish origin, free persons of mixed descent, persons of the conquered race bound to perform labour-service, and slaves.

The estate system is not to be confused with that of castes, in spite of the use of racial origin as a criterion. A person of native or mixed stock who had wealth and influence could obtain a legal certificate of 'whiteness'. Though most slaves were of African stock, anyone could be a slave, and the slave-born could become legally free. Persons bound to perform labour-service were those whose birth and sojourn placed them in institutions, communities and social systems established to extract wealth from the conquered native population, and therefore they were mainly of native stock, and known as Indians, even when of mixed native and European origin. And those of native stock who by chance or design slipped through the interstices of these land-labour institutions could cease to be Indians.

The Neo-Estate Society

With the collapse of the Spanish colonial system liberal constitutions embodied universalistic citizens' rights and withdrew the legal basis of the estate society. But the new rulers, whose economic power lay in land-ownership and commerce, refused to undertake reforms curtailing their enjoyment of cheap captive labour. The republican period, from 1820 onwards to the present, has witnessed the gradual liquidation of many feudal or colonial arrangements such as the legal maintenance of class divisions, entail, slavery, mortmain lands, the common lands of towns (*ejidos*) and Indian community lands (*comunidades*). Both land and labour became commodities of freer negotiability. In these conditions the *hacienda* or landed estate came to dominate the agrarian structure, its owners taking over traditional subsistence lands of rural populations by purchase, encroachment, violence and fraud. The rural families thereby excluded from access to subsistence lands met the labour-needs of the proprietors. More than 80 per cent of the highlands and temperate valleys had become incorporated in estates in the Andean republics by 1950 (Ecuador 70 per cent, Peru 80 per cent and Bolivia 90 per cent).

One of the characteristics of the hacienda is its economic duality. Apart from its political and prestige advantages, the proprietor looks forward to monetary rewards from the sale of his goods on the national or even the international market. But within the hacienda, relations still exhibit some feudal features. The owner's labour force consists mainly of service-tenants, who in return are allowed access to a plot of land on the hacienda for their own subsistence, a labour force producing for the market while not itself a market consumer. Much land of the hacienda is unused or under-used; in the land-monopoly system of social domination these idle lands deprive the peasantry of any major alternatives to bare subsistence and to dependence on the estates. Thus a tame labour force is ensured. Additional hands when needed are drawn from the surrounding peasant communities, usually by demanding labour in payment for some utility, such as water, right of way, firewood, etc., or else from migrant labour forced out of the poorer communities by hunger.

The majority of the peasantry lives under ever-increasing population pressure on the remains of land left over by the haciendas. Studies made by the present writer in Ecuador of an extensive zone of 62 smallholders' communities showed that of these 24 averaged 0·5–2·5 acres per family, 18 averaged 2·5–5 acres, and 20 more than 5 acres. Individual holdings were furthermore subdivided to excess: one case studied showed that a three-quarter acre holding was made up of 18 separate lots.

Just as the tenant must deliver his daily labour to the hacienda in return for a subsistence plot, and thus be excluded from market relations with the greater society, so the peasant of a smallholders' community is forced into marginality. This is not merely the marginality of the subsistence sector driven out to sell occasional labour for survival, but also a condition of the independent smallholder, whose relation to society is mediated by the small town. Shopkeepers, merchants, petty officials, priests, petty proprietors and money-lenders living in the small towns are accustomed to making their livings out of Indian peasants by renting land, selling bad liquor and extravagant paraphernalia for *fiestas*, collecting tithes and first-fruits, charging interest, exploiting 'voluntary' labour-service for church and town, 'buying green', short weighting, exacting fines, providing quack legal advice, and other ingenious methods of exacting from the peasant any surplus in produce, cash or labour. Thus the peasant is barred from a possible improvement of his lot through reinvestment of occasional surpluses in his agriculture.

Republican society, in accord with its own interests, continued the colonial system of simple dichotomy between 'Indians' and other citizens. But the universality of its constitution and its codes of law created an institutional ambivalence. Administration of the law, keeping of order, use of public services, the market, the labour contract, the service-tenancy, the municipal taxation system, the church and the church tithes, and even weights and measures all have one set of rules or values for the Indian and another set for the rest. Thus the service-tenant may be legally 'fareworthy' but if he decides to leave the hacienda, a word from the proprietor will ensure his forced return by the police. The tithe contractor who buys the priest's rights for cash is permitted to enter the harvest fields of the Indians with his men and take by force what he deems to be his share. The burden of legal impositions, obligations and restrictions of the colonial Indian has been replaced by systematic localised abuses sanctioned by custom in republican society. Maintaining a system of this kind has required that Indians must be immediately recognisable (by clothes, etc.), so that the appropriate face of the Janus-like institutions may be turned to them. They are physically separated as neighbourhood groups whenever possible.

BEGINNING OF THE END OF THE NEO-ESTATE SOCIETY

The neo-estate society in the Andean highlands, with its division into two culturally different orders based on performance of different economic functions not founded on law as in estate society but on consensus among the members of the one order to maintain the other's subjection *in spite of* the law, has recently shown signs of breaking down. In Bolivia the Indians broke out of their cultural isolation in the 1952 revolution and in many parts of the country themselves enforced the 1953 Land Reform Law abolishing the hacienda. In Peru the last few years have witnessed the formation of peasant syndicates to improve conditions on the haciendas, and the extensive invasion by Indian communities of unused hacienda lands; there has also been some participation by Indians in the armed struggle against the government organised by urban-based middle-class leaders. In both these countries new urban groups aspiring to power are not only uninterested in the survival of the neo-estate system but are also anxious to mobilise the Indians as a new popular political base. The neo-estate institutions of the hacienda and the Indian community appear to have a low potential contribution to development. More intense intercourse with and migration to the towns offers cultural alternatives which confuse the boundaries between Indians, ex-Indians and non-Indians. Finally, the new politicians, mass communications and urban influence are leading Indians to broaden their self-identification. From membership of a purely local segregated social group suspicious of sibling groups, they are moving towards class consciousness, and aspiring to values hitherto considered out of their reach.

Thus as modernising influences begin to replace the neo-estate system by the open-class society, the word 'Indian' is in prospect of losing its reference to a clearly distinguishable social group, but will probably survive as a way of qualifying the rural and the traditional. There are also signs that it may be given a more positive value, and that popular political and nationalist movements will become 'Indianist', seeking solidarity in the use of symbols drawn from the Incaic period or from its cultural survivals, or from Quechua names associated with the insurgent movements during the colonial period.

BIBLIOGRAPHY

Bennett, Wendell C. and Bird, Junius B. *Andean Culture History*, Doubleday, New York, 1964; Robert Hale, London, 1965.

Clissold, Stephen. 'The Indian Problem in Latin America. Changing Attitudes in the Andean Republics', *Race*, VII, 1, London, July 1965.

Collier, John. *The Indians of the Americas*, W. W. Norton, New York, 1947.

Huxley, Matthew and Capa, Cornell. *Farewell to Eden* (story of the Amahuaca Indians of the Peruvian Montaña), Chatto and Windus, London, 1965; Harper and Row, New York.

Osborne, Harold. *Indians of the Andes: Aymarás and Quechuas*, Routledge and Kegan Paul, London, 1952.

THE INDIANS OF CENTRAL AMERICA

RICHARD N. ADAMS

General Classifications

THE term *indio* or *indígena* over the entire area of Central America (Guatemala, El Salvador, Honduras, Nicaragua, Costa Rica and Panama) is primarily social and cultural and only secondarily racial in content. This is particularly true in the region which we will define shortly as *Meso-America*, and somewhat less true in the remaining portions of the region. An Indian is an individual who is recognised, and who recognises himself, as belonging to a community of individuals that are in turn called Indian. Such communities are characterised by certain formal cultural features which set them aside from the rest of the national population. It is difficult to specify what these formal features are since they vary from one area to another. For instance, there are highly acculturated Indian communities—i.e. communities which have acquired the dominant culture in place of their own—in Costa Rica, Nicaragua, Honduras, El Salvador and Guatemala—with few or no obvious cultural differences from the rest of the population. Nevertheless, the people in question refer to themselves as Indians, and prefer to differentiate themselves from the rest of the national population. With a few specific exceptions such as the area around Quezaltenango in Guatemala, the Indian population composes one part of the large rural and small-town-dwelling lower sector or lower class of the general Central American population.

It is useful to distinguish two major indigenous cultural traditions in Central America: the Meso-American and the South American. The Meso-American cultural tradition comprises the Indian populations derived from the old high cultures of Mexico and Guatemala. These people had reached a level of state development and in the case of the Maya and various Mexican groups were developing into imperial organisations at the time of the arrival of the Spanish. The South American tradition consisted of a large number of tribal and sub-tribal groups which occupied what is now the greater part of Honduras, Nicaragua, Costa Rica and Panama; the evolutionary stage of the state had been reached in certain of these, but had not become strongly consolidated. The relative level of evolution of these two traditions is significant because in the Meso-American tradition the Spaniards encountered highly organised agrarian-based communities which enabled them to establish hegemony once they had achieved military conquest. Among the tribes of South American tradition, since the level of organisation was considerably lower, the establishment of the Spanish empire resulted in the rapid decimation and decline of the Indian population, and in some places its complete elimination. This was the situation in much of eastern Guatemala, Honduras, Nicaragua and Costa Rica, as well as the isthmian area of Panama.

During the colonial period the Spaniards ruled Central America from Guatemala City. The area produced little wealth as did Mexico or Peru, and attracted relatively few Spanish immigrants. Only Panama existed outside this realm, belonging instead to Neuva Granada. The colonial period saw an intense effort to undertake mining activities and it was this particularly that led to heavy destruction of Indians in Honduras. The Pacific coastal population of Nicaragua was famous for its ready adjustment to the demands of Spanish culture and society and the term *ladino* was early applied to these Indians. In that period this term referred to an Indian who had taken over the religion and cultural trappings of the Spaniards. Today this term has come to refer to any non-Indian in Guatemala, Honduras and El Salvador, although it is frequently used with a depreciatory connotation. The areas of north central Guatemala became known as the Verapaz, due to the conquest of the region by Bartolomé de las Casas. In this area there was no military conquest and hence its name, 'the area of the true peace'.

The independence of Central America took place in 1821 but brought little change to the Indian population. It continued to be, as it still is in great part today, a basically poor sector of an exploited population made up of peasants and labourers.

Today the Indians of Central America form a continuous population from the Chiapas highlands of Mexico as far east as Guatemala City, and down into the south-western Piedmont. This block extends north into the Peten region, where currently it is expanding due to population growth in the Verapaz. From Guatemala City to the east and south, Indians are to be found in enclaves. The largest of these are the Chorti and Pocomam Indians of eastern Guatemala and neighbouring Honduras, and the Lenca Indians of Honduras. Further to the south and east there are Indian communities which still maintain overt and visible differences such as the Xinca of Chiquimulilla, and Guazacapan in Guatemala, Izalco and Pachimalco in El Salvador, Subtiaba and Monimbó in Nicaragua, and Matambú in the Guanacaste peninsula of Costa Rica. The last named set of communities are in many respects indistinguishable from neighbouring ladino or mestizo populations, except in that they are, or were until recently, systematically distinguished in terms of social relationships. There are no very distinctive formal cultural differences and it may be anticipated that within a generation or two they will no longer be regarded as Indian at all.

Almost all the Indians in the surviving South American enclaves are highly acculturated. This is especially true in Honduras, Nicaragua and Costa Rica; only the San Blas Cuna and Chocó in Panama have retained highly distinctive cultures. Many of the Talamancan Indians of Costa Rica and the San Blas Cuna of Panama, as well as the Guaymí at Panama, are protected to some degree by a reservation system granted by the national government. The long-term effectiveness of this kind of status, with its many problems for national integration of the Indian population, is unclear.

El Salvador has tended to take the opposite position with respect to its surviving Indian population, and not only provides no special protection, but in terms of all government activities simply regards them as part of the general rural population. Honduras makes official recognition of the Indian groups and has set in motion occasional programmes for their welfare, but in general they survive with little direct aid from the government.

Central American mestizos and ladinos often remark that the Indians, particularly of Guatemala, provide a serious obstacle to development. But on any rational view, it is clear that the Indians are not so much the problem as is the general power structure of the country, which inhibits any development within the Indian community areas. Indians have often shown little enthusiasm for the formal attributes of ladino and national life, since these have usually been beyond their grasp economically or politically. Following an Indian revolt (1932) in south-western El Salvador, the government reprisal caused such a loss of life that the surviving Indians of the area gave up much of their overtly distinguishing Indian culture traits in order to avoid being identified and thereby continuing to be the targets of an incensed government. Aside from this kind of incident the Indian has generally taken a somewhat defensive stance and protected and perpetuated many distinguishing traits in order to set himself apart from the ladino.

It is difficult to distinguish the degree to which the maintenance of the Indian's values and culture traits is due to a defensive posture against the repression, and to what degree it is due to the fact that many ladino culture traits are unavailable to him. The educational system works only in Spanish and the monolingual Indians have almost no access to the national scene.

The governments of the 1944–54 revolution in Guatemala made severe efforts to integrate the Indian into the national political scene. This is continuing today but with less concentrated efforts of the government, and an increased participation of independent political parties and welfare organisations.

Mayan and Nahuatl Speaking Indians of Guatemala, El Salvador and Western Honduras

The most important Indian population of Central America, both in terms of surviving culture and numbers, are the Mayan speaking Indians of Guatemala, neighbouring Mexico and Honduras. Closely related culturally to these groups are the Mexican speaking populations found in El Salvador and, until recently at least, in the south-eastern coastal area of Guatemala.

At the time of the conquest the Mayan Indians of this area were organised into states roughly approximating separate linguistic groupings, each with a capital city or ceremonial centre. The states were in various stages of warfare with one another at the time of the arrival of Don Pedro de Alvarado, the conquistador whom Cortez sent south to occupy this area. As with Cortez in Mexico, Alvarado succeeded in using one Indian group against another, and thereby dominating the region within a very brief period. The Indians have since been subjected to, and have taken over, a basic series of Catholic traits as well as colonial organisational features. They have maintained, however, a very strong portion of indigenous beliefs as well as a basically aboriginal environmental adjustment. During the 19th century the Indians essentially crystallised a synthetic religion.

In the 1870s the introduction of coffee farming forced attendant heavy migrations on the Indians and initiated a major cultural reorientation. At first peonage and vagrancy laws provided Indian labour for the developing coffee farms in the Pacific piedmont and the Verapaz. Since that time seasonal labour migration has increased with the expansion of the coffee farms and with the natural increase of the Indian population. The Indian increase has made it impossible to survive on the lands available to them in their own communities, and the dependence on seasonal migration has become crucial. It is estimated today that as many as half a million Guatemalan Indians alone migrate annually to coffee harvests and in recent years also to cotton, and occasionally to sugar cane harvests. Indians are also moving north into the unoccupied area of the Peten, and neighbouring Izabal. This is a basically agrarian migration and is unrelated to any special crop developments.

Until recent years the Indians of the western highlands have maintained a fairly rigid religious-political organisation within each village, wherein a man would begin taking communal and ecclesiastical responsibilities at a young age, stepping from one post to another as he got older and could afford a greater contribution of his time and income. Those who proved themselves incapable, or financially unable to continue, would drop out of the running. The remainder would continue until only a few would reach the exalted status of elder of the community. Communities were strongly controlled by the elders and occasionally a shaman-like individual who was able to cure and divine.

Beginning particularly with the revolutionary government of 1944–54 and the concomitant introduction of political parties, labour unions, agrarian leagues and agrarian committees to handle agrarian reform, the old Indian structure tended to crumble. Young men began to dominate the positions previously held by elders of the villages. Labour unions upset the former dominance of the large landowners over their own resident labour and migrant labour. While these new forms of organisation were brought to a temporary end in 1954 the memory of them continued and the Indians are gradually becoming increasingly politicised. The rate of this change should not be overestimated since a great proportion of the Guatemalan Indians today are still monolingual and devices for direct communication between them and the government and other ladinos are still very limited. Nevertheless, programmes are beginning to appear on the radio spoken in the more important Indian languages.

The basic economy of most Indian highlanders is a corn-based peasant agriculture. Land is either owned or rented in small plots, and supplementary income is gained through specialised crop production or handicrafts, and/or through seasonal migration to the piedmont and lowlands for labour or for the rental of additional agricultural lands. Agricultural work is still essentially a hand process with the hoe, machete and digging stick being the primary tools. The Spanish wooden plough has been relatively unimportant among the Indian groups of Guatemala, and the *burro* as a beast of burden has never been taken over. Only very wealthy Indians have horses or mules as beasts of burden. Traditionally the human being has been the cargo animal, but today Indians depend heavily on bus and truck transport.

The western Indian area is dominated by regional markets such as Chichicastenango, Chimaltenango, Sololá, Momostenango, etc. These are attended both by local vendors, regular itinerant vendors from towns specialising in such marketing practices and buyers from the entire immediate region. Annual and other periodic fiestas in most of the Indian towns are marked by costume representational dances, usually concerning legends or historical events such as the battle between the Moors and the Christians, between the Spaniards and Indians, and so on.

Relationships between the Indians and ladinos vary from region to region. In the western highlands Indians dominate the rural population and ladinos are primarily townsmen and businessmen. While much of the land is owned by ladinos, either in middle size or large holdings, a great deal of this land is rented out to Indians. Some land is held in what is known as *fincas de mozos*, that is, large farms in which the Indians are allowed to cultivate the land in return for which they are obliged to work on the land-owners' coastal farms during the coffee-picking season. In towns of the heavily Indian populated areas, it has been traditional for the Indian to be represented in the local municipal government. While this is not recognised in the official municipal code of the country, it is practised through either an informal parallel Indian government which is responsible to the ladino government, or through the overt recognition within the municipal government of certain positions which traditionally must be held by Indians. Ladinos have traditionally dominated in political and profit-making economic activities; nevertheless, in certain areas, such as Quezaltenango, the Indians have succeeded in dominating the local commerce. A consciousness of 'Indianism' is developing in this region so that serious attempts have been made, although as yet with little success, for the Indians collectively to take an increasingly political role. This is the only part of the country where this particular development has been observed.

In general the Indian continues to suffer the fate of the small landholder in areas of expanding population and expanding economy. Increased population forces the small-holder continually to subdivide his land (*minifundio*), thereby pressing him into circumstances where he must eventually sell to others who are trying to consolidate bigger holdings. This situation has forced increasing numbers of Indians to look for income elsewhere. The major alternatives have been to go to Guatemala City which has grown rapidly in recent years owing to this influx, or to go to the lowlands in search either of labour or new land. Since most land in this southern part of the country is already owned, the only available land for new cultivation is in the north. Attempts at colonisation in the north have still been on a fairly small scale, although large-scale plans are in preparation.

The Guatemalan government recently established a development corporation in the unoccupied area of the Peten to promote both immigration and development of that region. Thus far most of the migration, however, has not been under the patronage of this organisation, but rather has been casual and voluntary on the part of the Indians, and therefore essentially uncontrolled and undirected.

The surviving Mexican language groups of El Salvador, principally in the communities of Izalco and Panchimalco, have received very little study. The latter was reported on by Alejandro Dagoberto Marroquín in 1959. In general terms both communities are highly acculturated and are thereby similar to the modified and semi-ladinoised Indian communities of Guatemala.

THE LENCA INDIANS OF WESTERN HONDURAS

The largest single non-Mayan speaking group in Central America today are the so-called Lenca Indians of south-western Honduras. Together with surviving Indian populations in Santa Barbara, known locally as the Illama group, they are the largest single Indian population in Honduras, but have received relatively little study. Most of our information comes from work done by Doris Stone and a few surveys by others.

The Lenca are agriculturally based town and village dwellers. They resemble the neighbouring Mayan and Mexican speaking groups in their economy and the imprint of colonial social organisation. The greatest number of inhabitants are in the Department of Intibucá, and somewhat fewer are to be found in neighbouring La Paz and Lempira. The present writer estimated the population to be approximately 78,000 in 1950, an increase of almost one-and-a-half per cent over the 1935 census figures for the same group. As Doris Stone has noted, 'The Lenca have always been a loosely knit group bound together more by agreement ceremonies called *Guancasco*, than even by their own tongue which has been described as "confused" at least since the early XVIII century. It is significant that very few Lenca communities still talk their language, and in these few it is generally spoken by the older people.' The Guancasco is an inter-village visiting ceremony whereby on certain saints' days, saints from one village visit the saints of another, and this is reciprocated on a later occasion. This has been interpreted, probably correctly, as a device established to maintain amicable relations between communities. A similar pattern is still to be found in parts of El Salvador and Guatemala, but not under the same name. The Lenca differ in many respects from the other Honduran groups and by the same token are more similar to Mayan and Mexican speaking groups. They use the tortilla, build adobe houses, do not make bark cloth and have had cotton cloth traditionally since before the Spanish conquest.

ATLANTIC LOWLAND INDIANS OF HONDURAS AND NICARAGUA

Very little consistent and intensive ethnographic work has been carried on among these populations. The major groups are the so-called Miskito, a racially negroid group that maintains a predominantly Indian culture and occupies the lower reaches of the rivers of both Nicaragua and eastern Honduras; the Sumu, who occupy upper reaches of the same rivers; the Paya of the Departments of Olanchito and Colón, Honduras; the Rama, a remanent occupying the Rama Cay of Bluefields, Nicaragua; and the Guatuso, a collection of refugee groups in north Costa Rica, reported to have been reduced to about 150 people.

It was reported in 1958 that there were about 740 Sumu in Nicaragua and 50 in Honduras; 20,723 Miskito in Nicaragua and 5,000 in Honduras. There were reported to be about 250 Payas at that time.

Most of our contemporary information concerning these groups comes from short-term visitors and reports by Edward Conzemius and Doris Stone (see the bibliography at the end of this chapter). The only Atlantic Lowland group in Honduras to have received intensive study (by Anne Chapman) over recent years are the so-called Torupan Jicaque, a group located in a north central Honduran highland region where a reservation of 1,875 acres was set aside in 1929.

All these Indians tend to be marked more by poverty and deculturation than strongly surviving traits. Chapman reports the presence of a dual organisation reminiscent of that found in the Amazonian lowlands. Lack of intensive work among other groups makes it impossible to know the degree to which dual organisation may be present elsewhere. All are agriculturally based, although the riverine groups do depend to some degree on river food and the Miskito and Sumu specifically take jobs in the mines of the Atlantic coastal area of Nicaragua. A number of medical surveys have been done in that region.

Although linguists tend now to relate the Jicaque language to the Hokan group, much of the general culture of these and the other Atlantic coastal groups is strongly reminiscent of South America. Tubers and fruits predominate among foodstuffs and corn plays a secondary role. The basic tortilla of Meso-America is all but absent.

THE CUNA CHOCÓ AND GUAYMI OF PANAMA

Reina Corres de Arauz reported in 1962 that there were approximately 22,300 Cuna Indians—20,000 inhabiting the San Blas Archipelago on the north-east coast of Panama, and the remainder occupying inland regions that have been granted to them by the government. The Chocó, numbering approximately 4,000, occupied scattered homesteads on rivers of the Department of Chocó and neighbouring Colombia.

The archipelago-dwelling San Blas Cuna are not highly organised politically and have maintained a defensive stance with respect to the Panamanian state and population. The Cuna women occupy an important place in the society and curing specialists and ceremonial singers are granted considerable prestige. The political chiefs perpetuate the historical traditions of the society. The inland Cuna are subjected to much stronger Panamanian cultural influences owing to the increasing contact with mestizos. As the Darien area is increasingly opened, many Indians are taking to day labour. There is also an increasing infiltration of Negroes from the Colombian Chocó into both the Panamanian Chocó and the area occupied by the Cuna.

The Chocó mix little with the Negroes who are gradually moving into the area, but maintain fairly amicable relations with them. They have essentially no political organisation or tribal unity. Although all the Indians in Panama constitute refugee groups from the colonial and early republican periods, the Chocó seem to have suffered the most extreme deculturation (i.e. loss of native culture).

Both the Chocó and inland Cuna are agricultural as are the island Cuna. The island Cuna, however, have their lands on the mainland and commute to carry on the cultivation.

The most numerous of Panama's Indians are the Guaymi. They occupy adjacent portions of the departments of Bocas del Toro, Chiriqui and Veraguas. According to the 1960 census, the Indians of these three departments numbered almost 36,000. Today the Guaymi are composed of what must be remnants of various refugee groups derived from the colonial and earlier republican periods. There are believed to be two major dialect groups, an eastern and western. The best known set of Guaymi is probably the Bogata, one of the eastern group; they have been studied by Nordenskiold and more recently by students from the University of Panama. The Guaymi are generally very poor, and retention of traits such as the bow and arrow is due as much to poverty as to anything else. They are an agricultural people, as are the Chocó and Cuna, but the women play a much more important role in cultivation than they do in the latter groups. The Guaymi are particularly well known for a game called *balseria*, apparently a large social gathering in which members of two groups will throw sticks at each other. It is evidently related to the planting of crops, as well as being a matter of intergroup adjustment.

THE BLACK CARIB

In addition to the indigenous population of Central America another population, known as the Black Carib, should be noted here. These peoples have occupied the littoral from Belize down to the east coast of Nicaragua. They are descendants of a group originally transported to the Honduran

THE INDIANS OF CENTRAL AMERICA

Bay Islands in the latter part of the 18th century from the Lesser Antilles. At that time they consisted of a population which had racially been dominated by African Negroes, but culturally was still basically an Antillian Indian way of life. Today they occupy small villages and towns scattered along this area. It has been pointed out that many traits of this population can still be identified as having had their origin among the Indians of the Lesser Antilles. However, it has also been made clear that most of the basic culture that these people manifest today is similar in general aspects to the Antillian Negroes of the various parts of the Caribbean. Today they plant coastal crops and the men migrate in groups for extended periods as labourers.

BIBLIOGRAPHY

Adams, Richard N. *Culture Surveys of Panama–Nicaragua–Guatemala–El Salvador–Honduras* (Scientific Publication No. 33), Pan American Sanitary Bureau, Washington, DC, 1957.

Adams, Richard N. (compiler). *Political Changes in Guatemalan Indian Communities*, Middle American Research Institute, Tulane University, New Orleans, 1957.

Conzemius, Eduard. *Ethnographical Survey of the Miskito and Sumu Indians of Honduras and Nicaragua* (Smithsonian Institution, Bulletin 106), United States Government Printing Office for Bureau of American Ethnology, Washington, DC, 1932.

Marroquín, Alejandro D. *Panchimalco; Investigación sociológica*, Editorial Universitaria San Salvador, El Salvador, 1959.

Stone, Doris. *The Talamancan Tribes of Costa Rica*, Peabody Museum (Harvard University) Papers, Vol. XLIII, No. 2, Cambridge, Mass., 1962. *The Borucas of Costa Rica*, Peabody Museum (Harvard University) Papers, Vol. XXVI, No. 2, Cambridge, Mass., 1949.

Stout, D. B. *San Blas Cuna Acculturation: An Introduction*, Viking Fund Publications in Anthropology, No. 9, New York, 1947.

Tax, Sol (ed.). *Heritage of Conquest*, The Free Press of Glencoe, Illinois, 1952.

Wagley, Charles. *The Economics of a Guatemalan Village*, American Anthropological Association Memoir No. 58, Washington, DC, 1941. *The Social and Religious Life of a Guatemalan Community*, American Anthropological Association Memoir No. 71, 1949. *Santiago Chimaltenango*, Seminario de Integración Social Guatemalteca, Guatemala, 1957.

Wauchope, Robert (general editor). *Handbook of Middle American Indians*, Vols. I–XI, Univ. of Texas Press, Austin, for Middle American Research Institute, Tulane University, New Orleans, 1964 and following.

THE INDIANS OF MEXICO

PETER COY

OUT of a total population of more than 29 million persons over the age of five years at the census of 1960, monolingual and bilingual speakers of indigenous Indian languages in Mexico numbered more than 3 million. Although this is already a substantial indication of the distinctiveness of the Mexican nation, it disguises the influence of a largely autochthonous culture upon those Mexicans who are Indian in everything but speech. The use of the language spoken as a criterion of a Mexican's ethnic affiliation has been reinforced, in recent censuses, by a summary of his domestic habits: whether he wears sandals instead of shoes; whether he eats maize-cakes in preference to bread, and so on. These criteria, although more realistic, are not altogether satisfactory because they do not exclude the many members of other ethnic groups who have assumed the stigmata of Indian civilisation without having had an early grounding in its philosophy. Nor do these cultural criteria uncover the many indigenous Mexicans whose rural, Indian upbringing is now clothed in urban and industrial trappings. Such Mexicans help to swell the fiction that Mexican society is an outcrop of Western European society. No-one who penetrates beneath the professional, governmental and higher business strata of Mexican society, or even merely moves off the main central streets of Mexico City, can fail to recognise that Mexico is the home of a largely Amerindian nation. Today's trends towards an industrialised, better integrated nation may diminish the purely Indian content of its way of life; an understanding of the average Mexican adult of the present generation, however, still depends upon a knowledge of the nature of his autochthonous civilisation.

PHYSICAL AND CULTURAL CHARACTERISTICS OF THE INDIAN

As is well known, the indigenes of the Americas were called 'Indians' by their European discoverers because the latter thought they had encountered the inhabitants of southern Asia. Some justification is afforded to this epithet by the fact that, generally speaking, the colouring of the hair, eyes and skin of Mexican Indians is dark. Body-hair and facial hair, however, are normally extremely sparse whilst hair on the head is straight and black. Skin colour varies according to tribal grouping between olive and ruddy. Although grouped most frequently with the Asiatic, among human types, the Mexican Indian does not uniformly display the characteristic eye-fold. Nor is it possible to indicate a typical height of stature, although the extremes to be found, say, in Africa, do not exist in Mexico.

As befits the site of one of the world's grain-based higher civilisations, almost all Mexico's linguistic groups have long abandoned hunting and gathering for agriculture. The staple crop is universally maize, which is to be found wherever Mexicans and water coincide with a patch of soil. Collectivism, too, is a characteristic of the original Indian communities which historical influences have made more durable: the lack of regular rainfall combined with population increases probably led to the introduction of irrigation, for which collective labour and control were inevitable; the introduction of cattle in colonial times on to the best land in the highland valleys of Central Mexico drove some Indian groups into the isolation and introspection of mountain residence. Subsequently political loyalty to the aims of the social revolution in Mexico early in the 20th century, with its nostalgia for communal ownership of the land, has made of collective action an institution into which the rural Mexican can sink his individuality. Finally all linguistic groups in Mexico are strongly influenced by their religions and by associated beliefs concerning the causes of natural phenomena, such as disease, crop failure and death, as well as the methods to be employed in ascertaining and perhaps overcoming such causes.

The Mexican Environment

Physically, Mexico resembles a funnel with a curled spout: in prehistoric times groups of Indians poured into its arid mouth from the plains of North America and were pressed together; some were held back in the semicircle of volcanoes at the southern end of the central plateau; some were enmeshed in the fissured mountains where the 'funnel' narrows; and some passed through the 'spout' on to the limestone platform of Yucatán, which juts out between the Gulf and the Caribbean Sea. Where the environment favoured a surplus of production over current needs, as in the Valley of Mexico, trade and an economy based on conquest and tribute helped to develop the specialised activities and artistic skills of a high civilisation.

The Total Hard-core Indian Population

The Indian peoples of Mexico comprise more than fifty identifiable groups speaking variations of thirty languages. A comparison between the changing numbers of speakers of Indian languages during the last thirty years provides the bases for reasonable working hypotheses as to the development of hard-core Indian populations.

Census year	Speakers of Indian languages and dialects alone
1930	1,185,162
1950	795,069
1960	1,104,955

As can be seen, during the twenty years which elapsed between 1930 and 1950, the numbers of monolingual speakers diminished by a quarter. In so far as language is a yardstick to indicate acculturation, i.e. acquisition of the dominant culture in place of the native Indian, then one can say that the drop in monolingual speakers may represent a movement away from Indian culture. When one takes into consideration the more or less constant national birth rate during the period (around 4·5 per cent) and the sharp decline in the general mortality rate (from 2·66 in 1930 to 1·62 per cent in 1950) it becomes evident that this movement may have been greater than the crude figures suggest. The trend away from Indian languages was, however, reversed during the ten-year period between 1950 and 1960. With a further decline in the general mortality rate, the national population growth rate climbed to over 3 per cent. Since this increase is reflected in the total of monolingual speakers of Indian languages for 1960, one may reasonably assume that the Indians of Mexico are now obtaining an equal share of the national resources as well as hanging tenaciously on to their indigenous languages and culture. 'The national resources' can be taken to mean 'enough land upon which to grow an adequate supply of food to maintain a reasonable level of nutrition, and protection by inoculation against infanticidal diseases.' In the thirty years which elapsed between 1930 and 1960 the number of speakers of Indian languages who also spoke Spanish increased from 1,066,000 to 1,925,000. This rise in the bilingual total demonstrates that the 'deculturation' process, i.e. loss of specifically Indian culture, was not so marked among the bilingual speakers as it had once been among the monolingual ones: although the historical evidence points to a gradual seepage of bilingual speakers into the great mass of the Mexican nation which speaks only Spanish, the bilingual stratum appears to be holding a large number of its speakers.

The Aztec-speaking peoples

The most significant Indian language group in Mexico is the Uto-Aztecan. Not only was it the group containing the largest number of monolingual speakers in 1950, but it also embraces nations and tribes ranging from small groups with simple economies living on the Sonoran border with the United States to the survivors of the high civilisation of the Nahuatl-speakers living in modernised villages in the highland Valley of Mexico. The 1,500-mile distribution of Aztecan languages down the Pacific coast of northern Mexico has pointed to the probable migration route of their speakers, and the extension of Nahuatl across the isthmus has indicated the extent of the occupied portion of the Aztec empire. This neck of land south of and including the central plateau, where the capital cities of the empire were situated, remains the heartland of the Nahua tribes. They are to be found today in the States of Guerrero, Morelos, México, Hildalgo, San Luis Potosí, Tlaxcala, Puebla and Vera Cruz. There were over 200,000 monolingual speakers of Nahuatl in 1950. Interspersed among these are the descendants of the unrelated Otomí tribes which probably preceded the Nahua into the Valley of Mexico; speakers of Otomí numbered 58,000 in 1950. Also pressed into the western mountains of the State of Mexico by the Nahua tide were 16,000 Mazahua.

The remaining Aztecan language speakers are to be found in the escarpment, deeply fissured by canyons, and set back from the coast of northwestern Mexico, known as the Sierra Madre Occidental. These include the Mayo, Huichol, Cora and Yaqui in small numbers. The largest and most interesting of these minor groups is that of the Tarahumara (8,000 speakers) in southern Chihuahua. This people has developed a mixed nomadic economy suited to its unfavourable environment. Its members raise their staple crops of maize, beans, squash, wheat and barley, and graze their cattle, sheep and goats on the upper slopes of the Tarahumara mountains of Chihuahua State in the summer; in the winter they take their flocks to the tropical canyons in the foothills, exchanging a temperature of minus 16 degrees centigrade for one of 40 degrees above zero. This way of life is thought to have had great influence on several aspects of the Tarahumara's culture: its nomadic aspect gives him a strong physique, making him Mexico's regular entry for the Olympic marathon race; the need for mobility and the mountain cold call for a simple breechclout surmounted by a shirt and woven jacket; its chronic impermanence and the isolated residence of family groups may account for his fatalism and for the slightness of his material culture.

The Maya-speaking peoples

The Mayan group of languages constitutes the next most important one in Mexico: there were over 160,000 monolingual speakers in 1950. Mexico shares this group with Guatemala in that the first manifestations of Mayan civilisation occurred in the Petén region of Guatemala; soon afterwards religious centres surrounded by agricultural settlements grew up on the peninsula of Yucatán, which thrusts northwards between the Caribbean and the Gulf. During the 8th century, however, the principal sacred city of the Yucatán Mayas was conquered by the Itza, a Nahua tribe from the west; the second flowering of Mayan civilisation which ensued incorporated the best of the sculpture and architecture of the two greatest civilisations of Middle America. The spread of Maya-speakers along the Gulf coast of Mexico shows less cohesion than that of the Aztec-speakers on the Pacific coast: the Mayas themselves inhabit the whole peninsula of Yucatán, including the State of Campeche and the Territory of Quintana Roo; their linguistic relatives the Tzotzil (44,000), Tzendal (32,000), Choles and Chontal all live close by in the State of Tabasco or in the mountains of the border State of Chiapas. The Huaxtecs, on the other hand, are only to be found at the northern end of the State of Vera Cruz and in the State of San Luis Potosí, separated from the rest of the Maya family by groups of Zoque- and Popoloca-speakers living in the States of Vera Cruz, Puebla, northern Oaxaca and western Chiapas; these include Totonacs (54,000), Mixe (21,000), Mazatecs (47,000), Zoque and Popoloca. All these groups engage in small-scale agriculture, the Mayas and the Totonacs producing the *henequén* fibre and growing cocoa and fruits suited to the tropical lowlands upon which they are situated, and the remainder depending upon maize for subsistence in the mountains and precipitous ravines of northern Oaxaca and Chiapas.

Tarascans, Zapotecs and Mixtecs

The 10,000 monolingual speakers of Tarascan in the State of Michoacán conserve a language which is as difficult to relate to its neighbours as is Basque in Europe; this may be due to its mountain isolation to the west of Lake Pátzcuaro. Like the Nahua of Tlaxcala, the Tarascans never submitted to the Aztec empire. The 61,000 Zapotecs and their relatives the 8,000 Chatinos of central Oaxaca represented in 1950 the hard-core of a civilisation which, although overrun in the west by the similarly gifted Mixtecs, has maintained its artistic skills and separate language. The 77,000 Mixtec- and the 6,000 Amusgo-speakers of western Oaxaca were the descendants of a civilisation which not only surpassed the Zapotecs in fine craftmanship, especially in jewellery, but is credited with having carried codex-painting to the Nahua communities of the Valley of Mexico.

The linguistic settlement pattern of the Indians of Mexico permits us to postulate a situation which is the result of successive waves of invaders. Large groups such as the Otomí are thought to have preceded the more aggressive civilisations into southern Mexico and were probably fragmented by them. Smaller groups such as the ancestors of the 16,000 Chinantecs of northern Oaxaca and the 12,000 Tlapanecs of eastern Guerrero were pressed into an environment in which they had less opportunity to expand. Minimal groups like the fishing and gathering Seris of the Gulf of California and the Kikapoo of Coahuila State are positively restricted by the severity of their environment. There thus developed four great cultural complexes which have retained their territorial integrity and a considerable influence upon the social institutions of Mexico: the Nahua peoples of the Sierra Madre Occidental and the central plateau; the Maya of the Guatemalan border; the Mixtec/Zapotecs of Oaxaca and the Tarascans of Michoacán.

Indian Institutions

Many customs remain in Mexican rural life which either have direct reference to Indian antecedents or are adaptations of Spanish usages; many of these institutions remain strongly in evidence even in communities whose members no longer speak an Indian language and are therefore no longer considered to be Indians. Institutions which are Spanish in form may be found to have an Indian content.

The more obvious aspects of Indian life concern those products of the material culture which are put to a domestic use: the conventions regarding clothing; indigenous or introduced methods of cooking and of using farming implements; the use of baths and ovens for utilitarian or ceremonial purposes. Except for extreme cases, like that of the Tarahumara already described, clothing for Indian men comprises a cotton jacket and trousers and *huarache* sandals. In central Mexico the wide-brimmed conical hat has long been abandoned for a light-weight Stetson-style one. A compromise garment between the European dress and the pre-Columbian *huipil* and skirt is worn by most Indian women, with embroidered decorations a common feature. The foundation for most meals is ground maize, which may be cooked in a number of ways. Charcoal ovens are used and, in some regions, earth ovens. Steam baths are widely used, not only for the sake of hygiene but for curative and ceremonial purposes. Home industries are characteristic of many Indian villages, with pottery, basketware and textile products prominent. Each village engaged in these industries often produces only a single type and takes it to a central market, for exchange with the products of other villages or for cash; such concentration upon a single product is both the artistic strength and the economic weakness of the Indian way of life.

Indian influences are to be found not only in these tangible artifacts but also in the visible indigenous spirit to be observed in such displays as regional dances. Whilst some dances are fusions of European and American models, others have purely autochthonous antecedents even if their modern names are in Spanish. These externalised manifestations of an Indian culture are there for all to see who walk through an Indian village or attend an Indian festival. Not so obvious but perhaps more important are those half-obscured vestiges of an Indian past which may also persist where not a word of an Indian language is now spoken. Shamans, for example, who are found from Chihuahua to the Yucatán, are specialists in divining the cause of communal and individual ills and in curing them. Their divinatory and curative skills are also practised in the acculturated villages of the Valley of Mexico. In rural Mexico not everything can be taken at its face value, least of all the religious beliefs of the Indians, in whom there persists a strong feeling of dependence upon their patron saints. Whilst the Indian is a sincere adherent of the church and a devoted worshipper, his sponsorship of feasts in honour of his favourite patron saint has become an opportunity to validate his, the sponsor's prestige. 'Participation' is a keynote of the celebration of Christian feast-days by the Indian; whilst reenacting the Stations of the Cross can be related to existing, universal, Catholic practices, the visitation of burial grounds on All Saints' and All Souls' Days and the belief in the return of infant and adult spirits to their former homes are Indian customs. An institution which at first sight appears to be borrowed from Europe is the *compadrazgo;* this system of 'co-parenthood', which in Europe is intended merely to reinforce existing personal relationships, in rural Mexico is found to be a method of extending the web of mutual obligation between parents and god-parents to as many people as possible. Mexican Indians are devout Christians but they have welcomed and developed those religious practices which seem to them to answer their needs most usefully.

The most striking perhaps of all Indian institutions is that of cooperative labour. In its private form among the Tarahumara it is the occasion for a corn-beer feast; in its public form it provides the labour for tasks of communal usefulness: building a school or washhouses; repairing roads or irrigation channels. Among the Nahua unpaid public labouring is called the *cuatequitl, tequio* or *fáina;* among the Zapotecs it is *tsunlex;* and among the Maya it is the *fagina.* Whether for private or for public ends cooperative labouring is a characteristic manifestation of the inclination of the Mexican Indian to merge his individual personality into that of the group.

BIBLIOGRAPHY

Beals, Ralph. *Cherán: A Sierra Tarascan Village*, Smithsonian Institution, Washington, DC, 1946.
Bennett, W. C. and Zingg, R. M. *The Tarahumara*, Univ. of Chicago Press, Chicago, Ill., 1935.
Covarrubias, Miguel. *Mexico South: The Isthmus of Tehuantepec*, Alfred A. Knopf, New York, 1946.
Furer-Haimendorf, Christof von. 'Mexico's Racial Mixture', *New Society*, London, 1 October 1964.
Garibay, Angel María. 'The Mexican Indian', *Month*, 33, London, February 1965.
Lewis, Oscar. *Life in a Mexican Village*, Univ. of Illinois Press, Urbana, Ill., 1963.
Madsen, William. *The Virgin's Children*, Univ. of Texas Press, Austin, Tex., 1960.
Miller, Frank. 'Tzotzil Domestic Groups', *Journal of the Royal Anthropological Institute*, 94, London, July-December 1964.
Parsons, E. C. *Mitla, Town of Souls*, Univ. of Chicago Press, Chicago, Ill., 1936.
Redfield, R. and Villa Rojas, A. *Chan Kom: A Maya Village*, Phoenix Books, Chicago and London, 1962.
Toor, Frances. *A Treasury of Mexican Folkways*, Crown Publishers, New York, 9th ed. 1962.

INSTITUTIONS

EDUCATION

ASHER TROPP

LATIN America has shared to the full the growing emphasis throughout the world on education as a source of development. A series of inter-American seminars and meetings of ministers of education, courses and seminars on educational planning, a gigantic 'Conference on Education and Economic and Social Development' in Santiago in March 1962 (culminating in a 'Declaration of Santiago') and an OAS Special Commission (Task Force) for the Programming and Development of Education, Science and Culture in Latin America have been signs of the new interest in education as a 'mainspring' of development. The OAS Task Force in its Final Report of 1963 declared that:

> Economic and social development is only possible in those countries that provide their citizens with a suitable education; underdevelopment, with all its consequences, is mainly the result of an illiterate and uninformed population . . . It is only through educational systems wholeheartedly animated by democratic ideas that the most noble and historic objective of the Charter and the Alliance can be strengthened in the hearts and minds of the peoples of Latin America . . . Education is the very backbone of the Alliance for Progress.

ENROLMENT, LITERACY AND WASTAGE

Education thus appears to have become the great panacea for all evils. The broad statements on the need for universal literacy and for technological education have been readily accepted. From what position then is Latin America to commence its educational advance? What has been achieved in the first burst of educational enthusiasm? What are the major obstacles to educational progress?

It may be seen from Table 1 below that there are considerable differences between the twenty republics in all educational indicators. Judged against other countries Argentina, Chile and Uruguay rank with Italy and Spain in literacy and proportion of persons enrolled in higher education. The richer the country the 'better' the educational indicators, but Latin American countries show relatively low levels of school enrolments in relation to certain Asian and European countries with similar per capita incomes.

But enrolment figures can be misleading and literacy figures notoriously overestimate the true rate of functional literacy. According to a UNESCO survey the duration of the average primary school education received in Latin America is only 2·2 years. The problem is firstly one of lack of provision of schools, teachers and educational facilities. Secondly, there is a 'misuse' of what facilities do exist. In Latin America as a whole only some 20 per cent of students complete their primary education and of every hundred enrolled

TABLE 1

INDICATORS OF LEVEL OF EDUCATION IN LATIN AMERICA, 1950

	Proportion of total population illiterate at 15 and over	Enrolled proportion of those aged		Higher Education per 100,000 persons
		5–14 in primary schools	15–19 in secondary schools	
Argentina	14	66	21	480
Bolivia	68	24	7	166
Brazil	51	26	10	98
Chile	20	66	18	290
Colombia	43	28	7	94
Costa Rica	21	49	7	192
Cuba	22	49	.	.
Dominican Republic	57	40	7	106
Ecuador	44	41	9	127
El Salvador	61	31	4	65
Guatemala	71	22	7	84
Haiti	89	15	.	28
Honduras	65	22	3	57
Mexico	43	39	4	111
Nicaragua	62	23	3	81
Panama	30	54	24	190
Paraguay	34	51	9	121
Peru	58	44	.	193
Uruguay	15	62	17	484
Venezuela	48	40	6	137

Source: *The Economic Development of Latin America in the Post-War Period,* UN, New York, 1964, p. 60

in the first year of intermediate schools only twenty-two complete their studies. It has been stated that 70 per cent of first-year university students do not get promoted and that large numbers everywhere take the first year over and over again (see bibliography, Acton). There is thus an enormous degree of wastage at all levels.

The Latin American Demographic Centre has analysed the situation for the four primary-school generations of 1950–3 in Brazil.

TABLE 2

COMPLETE EDUCATIONAL HISTORY OF PRIMARY-SCHOOL PUPILS IN BRAZIL

Cohort of 1950–3 (average percentage)

	Grade				Completing course
	I	II	III	IV	
Initial number	100	30	17	10	7
Dropping out during year	−15	−5	−2	−1	
Failures in examinations	−46	−8	−4	−2	
Dropping out between years	−9	−1	−1	—	
Survivors	30	17	10	7	

Source: Latin American Demographic Centre, *A Demographic Analysis of the Educational Situation in Latin America,* Santiago, 1962 (UNESCO/ED/CEDES/8), p. 139

TABLE 3

RELATIVE VALUES OF ENROLMENT IN EACH GRADE IN RELATION
TO THAT OF FIRST GRADE OF PRIMARY SCHOOL, 1960

	Argentina	Brazil	Colombia	Chile	Haiti	Mexico	Panama	Peru	Uruguay	Venezuela	Latin America
Primary 1	1,000	1,000	1,000	1,000	1,000	1,000	1,000	1,000	1,000	1,000	1,000
Primary 5	493	169[1]	124	305	40	189	401	342	488	214	136
Intermediate 1	520	81	123	195	38	72	288	210	272	175	128
Intermediate 5	73	30	22	67	9	7	75	61	144	15	30
Higher 1	57	7	10	26	4	16	34	44	111	24	17
Higher 4	16	2	4	11	0·2	5	12	11	29	5	5
Higher 6	7	0·3	1	2	.	1	3	3	7	0·6	1

[1] Primary 4.

Source: Organization of American States, *Development of Education in Latin America. Prospects for the Future. Final Report*, 1963, p. 193

The educational history in Table 2 clearly shows the great wastage during the first year. Some of these children will re-enter the school at a later date and try again.

A further analysis has been carried out by the OAS Task Force which allows some comparison of the rate of erosion in various Latin American countries (see Table 3 above). Unlike the figures in Table 2, those in Table 3 are a picture of the situation in a given year rather than the experience of a 'generation' of primary-school children.

The 1950s showed a pronounced increase in enrolments in every country in Latin America; enrolment outstripped population growth. Similarly the percentage of aggregate national budget devoted to education rose from 11 per cent in 1957 to 23 per cent in 1962.

TABLE 4

ANNUAL INCREASE IN EDUCATIONAL ENROLMENTS (%)

	Primary	Secondary	Higher
1950–5	4·5	7·9	11·5
1955–60	7·0	11·75	5·2

Source: Organization of American States, *loc. cit.*

However, in spite of this hopeful growth in overall enrolment and expenditure the problems of retardation and wastage remained as serious as ever. The 1962 Santiago Conference had a report before it to the effect that 'while in quantitative terms the situation has evolved favourably since 1950 . . . nevertheless, the rise in the average educational level attained by the population must have been barely perceptible, since the decrease in school wastage rates has been very light at all educational levels, and particularly in the primary schools from the second grade upwards. The number of children receiving primary education has increased, but there has been no parallel improvement in the length of time they stay at school.' Children still enter primary school late, are frequently absent, fail their examinations and tend to leave school for good after one or two years desultory attendance. As in advanced industrial societies, but with much greater effect, economic and social factors are at work.

The average age at which children enter school and their success at school are closely related to the social and economic status of their parents. The lower the latter the higher the average age of entry and the higher the percentage of drop-outs and examination failures. In Santiago, Chile in 1950 out of every hundred children entering primary school from the 'upper' class 73 passed into secondary schools. Out of every hundred from the middle class the number entering secondary school was 32 and from the lower class 14. Similar results are appearing in surveys from other countries. In the continent as a whole girls tend to be less successful than boys and the situation in rural areas is worse than in urban areas.

The figures in Table 4 show a remarkable increase in secondary enrolment. This seems, at first sight, to be one of the most encouraging features. However, it is due in very large part to the unplanned increase in private general secondary education. In the aggregate almost half of the secondary pupils enrolled in Latin America are taught in private schools. It is the pressure from the urban middle classes for general secondary education for their children and for 'certificates' which will provide an entry into the university or to immediate white-collar employment that has been mainly responsible for the increase in secondary enrolment. At the primary school level also the private school is becoming increasingly important.

The majority of intermediate schools are of a general secondary or commercial type. In 1960 only 1 per cent of the secondary enrolment was in agricultural courses and 9 per cent in industrial courses. Marshall Wolfe reports that in one extreme case, in Brazil, a network of post-primary agricultural schools organised by the Federal government had a capacity of 20,000 students in 1958, but only 5,000 students enrolled. In agricultural schools as a whole the overwhelming majority of the students come from the urban middle classes and seek urban jobs after graduation.

Teachers and Teaching Methods

The teaching profession in Latin America is not only under-strength but a large proportion is untrained and uncertificated. After an exhaustive analysis of the position in Colombian public schools, the National Administrative Department of Statistics of Colombia concluded that 'only 23·2 per cent of the entire teaching personnel in Colombia are equipped to pursue their high calling in a scientific and responsible way.' While academically qualified members of the profession have been increasing in relative strength there has been a tendency in the majority of countries for the pupil-teacher ratio to increase. But the average number of pupils actually attending school per teacher is often quite low. Teachers are poorly paid and lack security of tenure or prospects of advancement. The school year is short, regulations are irregularly applied and teachers all too often take full advantage of opportunities to be absent due to 'sickness'. Many use their training as a stepping stone to white-collar employment or minor business activities.

Teaching methods tend to be oral and expository and encourage memorising and repetition. The curriculum is traditional and overburdened and the secondary curriculum is not related to that of the primary school. For the rural child, in particular, syllabuses have no attractions or incentives to offer. The OAS Task Force summarised the defects of secondary education in Latin America as 'verbalism, learning by rote, absence of student-orientation and guidance services, predominance of rigid, undifferentiated, uncorrelated and encyclopaedic curricula, defective science teaching, little personal use of the scientific method, and virtual nonexistence of laboratory work, use of unsuitable systems for measuring academic performance, lack of communication between teachers and lack of means for exchanging experience and documentation. In addition, there is the inadequacy of premises and lack of supplies and equipment for facilitating teaching. Textbooks are also defective and out of date.'

At university level there is increasing pressure from students working with syllabuses often traditional in content and under an ill prepared and often part-time faculty in a situation of administrative chaos. Failure rates are high and examinations often rely on memorising and ritual repetition of texts.

Distribution of Education

While the situation is slowly improving the recent United Nations report *The Economic Development of Latin America in the Post-War Period* (1964) has rightly summarised the situation in its statement that 'the education provided in Latin America, in addition to involving an enormous waste because of high rate of desertion, does not fulfil its function as a means of social transformation, that is, as a means of selection and social ascent, nor as an instrument of technical progress.'

The growing volume of research on the economics of education, manpower forecasting and educational planning aims to provide clear and rigorous guide lines to governments on the correct amounts and forms of educational provision they need if they are to develop their economies. But so far the experts have had little to say on the question of who is to enjoy the improved educational provisions. All governments are faced with the perennial dilemma of whether to spread the provision of education as evenly as possible over the different strata and regions and to emphasise all stages of the educational process or alternatively to emphasise the provision of a highly educated élite group by concentrating on those 'most likely to benefit.' Professor C. Arnold Anderson has argued forcibly that, as in the development of education in Western Europe, governments should concentrate educational provision in the first instance in the urban areas and among the middle classes. They should support private schools, charge fees and finance higher education through student loans. The mediocre education provided to the majority of the peasant and urban lower class population of Latin America seems to do little except offer them a fleeting acquaintance with literacy and to be useless in economic terms. There are growing pressures either to hold fire on the rural population (where it is often extremely difficult to provide adequate facilities owing both to the reluctance of teachers to stay in the backlands and also to the dispersed nature of much of the Latin American rural population) or else to provide rural children with a minimum education slanted towards life in the countryside.

There are two arguments that can be used against this facile view. The first is that it has been estimated that between a third and a half of the children born and raised in the countryside will move to the towns and seek urban employment. Throughout Latin America the towns are suffering from a shortage of skilled workers and a growing surplus of completely unskilled rural migrants. Education would best therefore train the rural child both for continued life in the countryside and also for the new tasks of urban-industrial employment.

Of equal importance is the political and social argument. The major function of education in Western Europe and North America has been the civic integration of the developing nation-states. Only recently has economic efficiency emerged as a dominant purpose of educational systems. It is true that the developing nations face the immediate needs of creating a skilled labour force and of accumulating capital under far less auspicious conditions than in the corresponding period of Western industrialisation. It is equally true that most of the Latin American republics are torn by cleavages of many kinds—class, regional, rural-urban and ethnic—and that the process of economic development itself creates new cleavages as fast as it abolishes old ones. Education can serve as a countervailing influence to the divisive factors inherited from the past and created by the present. It does this both by providing a common core of values and a common sense of nationality and also by providing both the appearance and the reality of opportunity to rise in the social scale by acquiring an education above the average. Policy choices in regard to educational planning must therefore take into account both the strictly economic and manpower needs and also the vaguer, but no less important demands of the individual for opportunity and the needs of the society for a minimum degree of integration and moral consensus. It is too much to hope that the educational plan which would maximise economic efficiency would always be compatible with maximum equality of opportunity or social integration. Balances have to be struck and they are struck not by a disengaged and priest-like class of economists and technologists but by administrators coping with the harsh realities of the population and urban explosions, with existing educational structures, ideologies and vested interests and with pressures from powerful groups in the population for preferential treatment for their own children.

CONTENT OF EDUCATION

Latin American countries cannot start from scratch as they all have educational systems and ideologies dating back to the Conquest. The system is essentially dual, with one branch confined *de facto* to the middle and upper classes ranging from the private school through the academic secondary school to the university and the other branch intended for the lower classes and limited to the public primary school and a few vocational schools, with scant chance of access to secondary or higher education. Jacques Lambert has written that 'a ruling class deriving its resources from landed property looks to education for a means not of increasing its income but rather of cultivating the mind. The whole public education system [in Latin America] has been organised as a preparation for higher education and more particularly for the type of education provided in the faculties of law, which give instruction not only in the law, but also in political and social science, for a class of political leaders . . . All too often . . . it is imagined that it is enough to give all children access to an aristocratic education in order to make it democratic.'

The distinguished Brazilian educator Anisio Teixeira has written that 'instead of the merger which transformed the two systems in the developed countries, education development in Brazil primarily followed the academic type, or what was considered as such . . . The school systems we aimed at imitating have been changed into a combination of academic scientific and technological studies, access to which is based solely on ability or merit. We, on the other hand, are expanding what in European education was the result of anachronism and erroneous psychological theories. Our school systems are thus in the unbelievably incongruous position of being converted into a vast collection of schools dedicated to the cult of leisure at a time when work and output are the chief characteristics of civilisation . . . In Brazil . . . we boasted the most antiquated and moribund aspect of the educational systems we were endeavouring to imitate . . . Education was thus transformed into an empty rite, a series of formalities, as if it were a mere matter of convention that could be acquired legally by going through the prescribed motions.'

What Anisio Teixeira says of Brazil is true to a greater or lesser extent of all the republics. Rural education is a wasteful and pathetically ineffective imitation of urban education and 'popular' urban education in turn imitates the academic education meant to prepare a leisured administrative élite. As the middle classes and the emerging 'aristocracy of labour' press for more education for their children their pressure moves into academic and élitist grooves already formed by past generations.

INDIVISIBILITY OF REFORM

The picture painted so far is extremely sombre. It takes no account of the differences between countries and between different regions of the same country. Still less does it pay the tribute due to the dedicated educational administrators and teachers at all levels and in all countries who are striving to improve and extend their educational systems. One cannot but be impressed by the effort that is being made to improve conditions in Latin American educational institutions. This effort is particularly notable in higher education; new universities are being founded, old universities modernised, new subjects introduced, research institutes and regional centres set up and students and faculties sent abroad for higher training. Great efforts are being made to make literacy universal and to improve rural and technical education. It should never be forgotten, however, that educational reform is either an accompaniment of economic, political and social reform or it is nothing. In the countryside, for example, literacy campaigns are of little effect unless they go hand in hand with land reform and general agricultural improvement. Increasing educational opportunities in a static and rigid society may only create new rigidities and new obstacles to change. The educational reforms in Mexico and Cuba went together with substantial reforms in all areas of life. To hope for too much from education in itself and for itself is to be misled as to the true sources of backwardness in Latin America. Equally, to plan economic, social and political development without a massive effort both to enlarge and to modernise the educational system is to miss one of the major springs of progress in the modern world.

BIBLIOGRAPHY

Acton, R. P. The Latin American University', *Die Deutsche Universitätszeitung*, 17 February 1962.

Benjamin, H. R. W. *Higher Education in the American Republics*, New York, 1965.

Havighurst, R. J. and Moreira, J. R. *Society and Education in Brazil*, Univ. of Pittsburgh Press, Pittsburgh, 1965.

Ruiz, R. E. *Mexico. The Challenge of Poverty and Illiteracy*, Huntington Library, San Marino, 1963.

Social and Economic Studies, XIV, 1, Univ. of West Indies, Jamaica, March 1965.

United Nations. *Economic Bulletin for Latin America*, VII, 2, New York, October 1962: 'Conference on Education and Economic and Social Development in Latin America' and 'Economic Development and Education in Latin America'. *La Situación Educativa en America Latina*, UNESCO, Paris, 1960. *Social Aspects of Economic Development in Latin America*, I, UNESCO, Paris, 1963.

THE UNIVERSITIES OF LATIN AMERICA

J. A. LAUWERYS

HISTORY

WITHIN a hundred years of the discovery of the New World five universities had been founded in America: Santo Tomás de Aquino, Santo Domingo (1538); Mexico (1551); San Marcos de Lima (1551); the Jesuit Santiago de la Paz (1558); Santa Fé de Bogotá (1563). In Brazil students were being prepared for Coimbra at the Jesuit College of Bahia by 1575. Seven more universities were started, mainly by Jesuits or Dominicans, in the 17th century and five in the 18th. The aim everywhere was to train men who would help to administer the new territories, who would spread the faith and heal the sick. The supply of monks and clerics was sufficient to staff the faculties of law, arts and theology but it proved exceedingly difficult to maintain schools of medicine. The model followed was that of Salamanca: for example, the faculty of arts was organised to teach the seven liberal arts. A bachelor's degree was awarded after three years in philosophy, after four in theology and laws. The licentiate and Doctorate were granted later, after public defence of a thesis. In brief, the score or so universities of Latin America at the beginning of the 19th century were largely medieval in outlook and organisation, almost untouched by the Enlightenment, uninterested in science, technology or research. The quality of work done was, in general, low. The professors were mainly priests.

No universities were founded in Brazil, though the Jesuit Colleges of Bahia and Rio prepared about a dozen students a year who then proceeded to Coimbra. When Prince João moved to Rio in 1808, he encouraged studies in medicine, surgery, agriculture, pharmacy and economics. He created academies and established the Botanical Garden, the Library and the Royal Press. Later, faculties of laws and medicine, as well as polytechnical, engineering and mining schools were established. But the first full universities came later. They were Rio (1920), Minas Gerais (1927) and São Paulo (1934).

Many of the leaders of the wars of liberation and the groups who held power after the separation from Spain belonged to the Freemasonry and were therefore strongly anti-clerical. Influenced by the ideas of French revolutionaries and of the Physiocrats, they favoured science and its application. They realised that the future of their countries depended upon securing an ample supply of well-trained professional men. They had a deep respect for academic freedom but favoured the extension of state-supported education at all levels. The reforms undertaken by the new regimes reflect all these attitudes: establishment of state-supported, mainly secular universities; appointment of those entrusted with power, such as rectors and deans, by open elections; security of tenure and academic freedom for the teachers;

professionalism and vocational training rather than general education and research. The last 150 years have witnessed the working out of these trends and have exposed their insufficiencies and drawbacks. The decay of the progressive notions of the revolutionary period has left a deposit of hidebound traditions which are *contraproducente*, irrelevant to the needs of modern societies, opposing economic and social advance.

KINDS OF UNIVERSITIES

More than 150 institutions in Latin America are concerned with higher education. The Union of Latin American Universities has 132 members, of which nearly half were founded after 1945. There is thus about one university for one-and-three-quarter million inhabitants, a not unsatisfactory proportion. But their geographical distribution is as haphazard as is their size or their quality or, for that matter, their name. They may be called colleges, faculties, universities, institutes, centres or academies. Some units cater for a score of students and have a staff of four or five part-time teachers; at the other extreme are internationally famous universities with 50,000 or more students, well equipped with laboratories, libraries and research centres. The number of full-time students varies greatly from country to country and a substantial number earn their living, usually in full-time posts. Of 571,000 students enrolled in 1962, 283,000 (50 per cent) studied in ten central universities.

TABLE I

STUDENTS ENROLLED AT CENTRAL UNIVERSITIES, 1962

Country	Population (million)	Number of universities	Number of students	Population/ students
Argentina	22	12	133,000	1,650
Bolivia	4·5	5	7,000	640
Brazil	75	19	53,000	1,400
Colombia	14	21	30,000	465
Chile	8·5	8	31,000	274
Ecuador	4·7	6	12,000	392
Mexico	45	30	173,000	260
Peru	11	10	31,000	355
Uruguay	2·5	1	37,000	68
Venezuela	8	6	34,000	235

With very few exceptions Latin American institutions of higher education are not universities in the European or North American sense. They are not principally devoted to research or to the advancement of learning. They are not communities of scholars but collections of professional schools preparing professional men—doctors, lawyers, engineers, teachers, architects and so on. They are, in fact, technical colleges with a rather narrow curriculum; purely utilitarian, with no time for classical languages, literature, humanities, etc., except as these may perhaps be needed to do a job, e.g. to teach.

The 132 universities can be classified into four chief groups:

(1) The federal or national universities are usually the largest and oldest, financed by the state and enjoying special privileges. They tend to set norms and to control higher education.

(2) State or provincial public universities, while distinct from the first group, may enjoy the same privileges. Many are owned by local authorities

or were started as joint local government and community ventures. Most are recent foundations and some are organised on modern lines. They draw funds from the state, from private donors, etc.

(3) Many Catholic universities are long-established, conservative and traditional, others recent and modern in outlook. They usually include faculties of theology, laws, education, engineering and social sciences. They are often subsidised both by the state and the church.

TABLE 2

SOME DATA ON UNIVERSITIES

Date of foundation	Number of universities	%
Before 1810	12	9
1810–1940	58	44
1940–66	62	47

Number of students	Number of universities	%
Less than 1,000	40	30
1,000–3,000	49	37
3,000–5,000	22	17
5,000–8,000	8	6
8,000–20,000	6	5
More than 20,000	7	5

(4) Private non-denominational universities number about a dozen which are among the most modern on the continent. They have been created by communal effort, usually with the assistance of industry and commerce. They enjoy a high degree of autonomy, limited only by their relations with the national university or, occasionally, by legal regulations. They draw funds from the state, the municipalities, private donors, etc.

ADMINISTRATION

There are, of course, differences between countries and between universities in the same country. But the descriptions given below are of typical cases and would apply to most universities both in Spanish and Portuguese speaking countries.

The bodies responsible for prescribing the courses to be followed, for maintaining discipline and for awarding diplomas were in the past—and usually are now—the faculties. Formerly members of faculties were appointed by the university council or by the government, usually on the nomination of the council. They were often distinguished men but not necessarily university teachers. After the faculties acquired professional status and autonomy (between 1850 and 1925) together with the right of self-government, it became the custom to appoint to the faculty only serving teachers: the first step towards the transformation of the faculty board into a board of professors, concerned with their own special interests. Gradually the university, in consequence, became merely a loose collection of independent faculties. This meant the loss of interdisciplinary contacts and an impoverishment of human relations. The situation was worsened when the growth of higher education led to the physical scattering of the schools to distant parts of great cities.

Schools (or departments) for the teaching of related subjects originally came under one faculty. But the centrifugal example of the faculties themselves, the conflicting interests of different chairs, and the inferior status of some have often tempted the latter to establish their own separate faculties, thereby accentuating the fragmentation of the universities.

The head of each faculty—the dean—has considerable administrative and financial power and responsibility. He is elected by the members for a period of two or three years only. Occasionally he is not eligible for reelection. It goes without saying that it is not always the most distinguished or energetic member who is chosen, while the need to gratify the wishes of his constituents as well as the shortness of his term of office makes it hard for even the most devoted dean successfully to carry through a consistent plan of development and reform.

The supreme authority is the university council. Usually, it consists of the deans (or representatives of the faculties), representatives of the political authorities, and *ex officio* members designated by law. In many cases, students and ex-students are also represented in varying proportions. Such student representation spread particularly after the 1918 student rebellion in Córdoba (Argentina) and the subsequent reforms.[1] There are now universities where the student representatives have a majority on the Council and dominate it. While it may be conceded that such representation is from one point of view democratic yet it is frequently an element of weakness and disorder because students may use it to pursue narrow political ends. The council has teaching, administrative, disciplinary and financial functions, limited in practice by the powers of the faculties.

A note must be added regarding the *institutos*. The nearest English equivalent would be 'department' but the range of activities is different and the instituto may have a good deal of autonomy. An instituto is an institutionalised chair. Examples may clarify: in the faculty of philosophy and letters of the University of Buenos Aires there are institutos of anthropology, didactics, philosophy, philology, geography, history, literature, library science. All these are chairs (*cátedras*) which have evolved into institutos. In La Paz there are three faculties divided into three institutos and thirteen schools; thus the faculty of biological sciences consists of an instituto of biological sciences, a school of medicine and surgery, a school of dentistry, a school of pharmacy and biochemistry and a school of natural sciences. The other faculties are social sciences and exact sciences, the latter consisting of an instituto of exact sciences and schools of civil engineering, architecture, industrial engineering, mines and petroleum, agronomy, and mathematical physics.

The executive authority of the university, as well as its legal representation, is vested in the rector, who is elected by the university council or by the full assembly of all the professors. Sometimes he may be appointed by the government. There are cases where all three of these may have to ratify the decision of one of them. The rector's term of office varies from one to four years—a very short term. The drawbacks of electing in open assembly an officer charged with heavy administrative and financial power and responsibility are obvious. They help to explain the difficulty of achieving drastic and fundamental reform and modernisation since it is hard to

---

[1] See 'Students in Politics', p. 380.

pursue for any length of time a policy which is bound to hurt vested interests. Examples could be quoted of cases where valuable and much needed changes have been stopped because the rector lost an election at the wrong moment. In any event, the rector's authority is checked by that of the faculties and by the laws of the country. Hence he has only a limited power to initiate change or make university life more dynamic.

TABLE 3

EXAMPLES OF UNIVERSITY ORGANISATION

University	Number of faculties	Number of escuelas	Number of institutos
Brazil	8	6	6
São Paulo	5	4	1
Bogotá	6	2	6
Costa Rica	10	—	—
Chile	10	Many	Many
Quito	4	13	3
El Salvador	6	—	—
Guatemala	7	—	—
Haiti	5	4	1
Honduras	5	—	—
Nicaragua	—	7	—
Panama	6	1	1
San Marcos	10	Many	Many

In the words of Rector Gonzalez of the University of Concepción in Chile: 'The administrative organisation of Latin American universities has remained substantially the same for a hundred years. There has been a traditional hostility to controls and to the adoption of a business type of administrative and financial organisation, which is considered to be incompatible with the intellectual and educational character of universities. The haphazard growth and expansion, the dispersion and autonomy of the faculties and other bodies, the relative weakness of the central administration and the grafting of modern elements on to their antiquated structure have led to an anarchic form of organisation, overlapping and inefficient administration.'

PROFESSORS

The teaching unit is the chair, occupied by a professor, normally appointed for life, who sometimes thinks of it as a personal and inalienable title to a source of revenue. In colonial times, he was required to lecture on particular texts and to follow a prescribed course. Later he was allowed to teach as he saw fit—or indeed not to teach at all. There is now a general tendency to oblige professors to lecture in accordance with a programme of studies.

For the most part, professors work only part-time in the university: usually they have a separate profession and draw most of their income from it. University salaries are usually very low—sometimes nominal—and it is only the distinction, social and professional, which accrues to the professor that tempts the holder of a chair. It will be clear that, in consequence of all this, relations with students are weak or non-existent, that very little research is done and hardly any is organised. Frequently the professor takes a taxi from his office to the university, delivers the lecture he has often given before and hurries home.

TABLE 4

FULL-TIME PROFESSORS

% full-time professors	Number of universities	% of universities
0	12	11
0–10	49	45
10–20	15	14
20–40	13	12
40–70	11	10
More than 70	9	8

All this fits the previously mentioned professionalism of the Latin American university. If the aim is simply to turn out competent professional men there is little reason why the students should not be taught or lectured to by competent professional men. It is a system which turns out good lawyers but few jurists, adequate pharmacists but few discoverers of new drugs, satisfactory agronomists but few agricultural scientists. And the system is crystallised and structured by the existence of faculties which are most often only professional—laws, engineering, medicine, etc. It is rare to find a faculty of arts or of science. As a result, in many universities it is impossible, for example, to study English language and literature except by registering in the faculty of education and taking a full course of preparation to become a teacher, or to study biology except by registering as an intending pharmacist (when the biology will be chiefly botany) or an intending medical man (when it will be mainly anatomy and physiology) or an intending agronomist.

COURSES

As a rule students register in a particular professional faculty which has its own standards and requirements—sometimes it may carry its independence to the point of deciding when to end and when to begin the academic year. Thus students belong to the university only in a very loose general sense—they may see little of their fellows specialising in other fields except at meetings or demonstrations.

Requirements in terms of lecture courses are laid down fairly rigidly. Instruction stresses verbalisation and memorising—students may sometimes be seen learning by heart a text written by a professor. Examinations are held regularly and those who fail at the end of the year have to repeat the course—often the whole course and not only that part of it in which they failed. Failure in one subject may thus involve the loss of a whole year.

Within the faculties options exist: thus in engineering there are specialisms such as electrical, petroleum, mechanical, chemical, industrial, aeronautical, mining, etc.; in agriculture—animal husbandry, veterinary medicine, forestry and so on. Many universities have, since 1950, created new centres, schools or even faculties in subjects like social work, journalism, business, accounting, nursing and domestic science. Length of courses varies. In agriculture, from two to six years; in the physical and natural sciences, from three to six or even seven years. A chemical technician must study seven years in Argentina, six in Peru, at least four in Mexico and Brazil, four in Chile, three in the Dominican Republic and Colombia. In education, length of courses varies between two and six years; in nursing, from one-and-a-half years to five; in dentistry, from three to six.

Little work of a general, cultural or humanistic kind is done: in principle all the courses are professionalised. Only in the faculties of law and education are there opportunities of learning about, say, Greek philosophy or mathematical logic. Very few universities award degrees in science, literature or other disciplines of a general nature and even fewer provide for postgraduate studies. It should be added that in several cases (e.g. Concepción, Lima) attempts are being made to introduce a preliminary or propaedeutic year of a general kind. This is partly to correct the deficiencies of secondary education and partly to allow a wiser and sounder allocation of the students among the faculties.

Normally, successful completion of courses is marked by the award of a professional certificate, *título*; for example, *Professor de Estado* or, say, a Diploma in Agronomy and not a degree (*grado*). Very few universities confer a master's degree or a doctorate. Academic dress is not worn.

STUDENTS

In principle, all students should have completed their secondary education and hold the school leaving certificate (*bachillerato*). In some countries (e.g. Peru) they will thus be at least 17 years of age, elsewhere 18. Frequently the *bachillerato* gives the legal right to enter a university, though not any particular faculty.

Contrary to what is often thought, university students do not belong exclusively to the wealthy classes: a rapidly increasing proportion come from modest homes, even from manual workers. Since there are only limited opportunities of getting any kind of maintenance grants, this means that more and more students study only part-time, much of their energy being spent on earning a living. Tuition fees are, however, either very low or non-existent. While all this is satisfying evidence of a broadening equality of educational opportunity, it helps still further to strengthen professionalism, as most students attend in order to master the technique of a profession which will bring in money and raise social status. They expect to be taught and make little effort to learn by themselves. They are interested in 'facts' not 'ideas', and by facts they mean only those directly related to their future profession. As mentioned earlier, students take an examination at the end of each year and failure in one subject normally means that the whole year has to be repeated. It is quite usual for 50 per cent to repeat the first year.

Most 'careers' impose a five-year course, which with 'repetition' may stretch to seven or eight. On the average, far fewer than half complete their courses and are awarded a diploma. And of these, a half take more than the minimum time. The 50 to 60 per cent who drop out receive no certificate of any kind.

If a student changes from one faculty to another, he receives no credit for courses taken, even if relevant. The total result of the excessive length of courses, padded out as they are with obsolete and unnecessary stuff, together with the high wastage rate, is that university training is very costly to the state. In spite of the meagre salaries paid to staff and the poor facilities offered to students it costs more to produce one medical doctor or one engineer in many of the republics than it does in London, Paris or Zurich.

Very few universities provide hostels for students: most live at home or in lodgings. There is an increasing number of canteens or refectories where the meals may be subsidised from general funds. The importance of student welfare services (medical, dental, psychiatric, loan service, athletics, etc.)

is seldom recognised. Student societies are active and organise meetings, week-end discussions, etc., usually of a political or quasi-political kind. Strikes of students are frequent, involving waste of time and of public money, though often they have little or nothing to do with educational or university problems. They are simply a symptom of unrest and illustrate the fact that the university is frequently a centre of political disaffection and of opposition to the government.

CRITICISMS

Since about 1950 there has been a growing volume of criticism of the structure and organisation of higher education in Latin America as well as of the ways in which the universities discharge their functions. The great American foundations have been active and so have international agencies like UNESCO and the UN Technical Aid Agencies. The Council for Higher Education in the American Republics (CHEAR), the education section of the Pan-American Union and other governmental and voluntary agencies have all helped to create and maintain a climate which favours drastic change.

The criticisms put forward may be summarised as follows.

—Too little research, especially in the sciences, is being done. Not only does this harm teaching, which may often be far behind the advancing front of knowledge, but as a further result new professors are not being trained adequately.

—Laboratory and library resources are very inadequate and badly organised.

—There is little or no post-graduate work.

—There are too many part-time professors who expend most of their time and energy outside the university. Salaries paid are miserably low. Hence the teaching and lecturing suffer.

—There are too many part-time students who expend too little energy on their studies. Discipline among them is poor. There are too many strikes.

—The teaching is verbal and dogmatic. Memorisation takes the place of understanding.

—The number of years needed to obtain a professional qualification is too great. There is an urgent need for the establishment of shorter courses (2 or 3 years) leading to intermediate qualifications, and a ladder of degrees, such as exists elsewhere.

—Far too many students 'drop out' before completing their course. This increases the cost of training personnel and wastes talent.

—There is no well planned and organised system for selecting students and allocating them to faculties where they would be prepared for a profession useful to society. It should be possible for really gifted students to obtain scholarships or grants to enable them to concentrate on their studies.

—Many countries are too small and too poor to be able to maintain departments specialising in fields such as nuclear physics, astrophysics, meteorology or archaeology. There is evident need for close international cooperation among the twenty republics. This is true also regarding the production of textbooks, many of which are badly produced and obsolete.

REFORM

The growing demand for reform is being nourished by three main forces:
(1) First and very powerful is the example and the influence of the

universities of the United States, many of which have close and formal links with institutions in Latin America. The great prestige traditionally enjoyed by European universities has declined of late and North American universities now appear to many as exemplary; progressive, dynamic, wealthy, organised on modern lines with laboratories, libraries and full-time professors, devoted to active education, interested in the sciences, engaged in research.

(2) Latin Americans are increasingly aware of the fact of their own technological backwardness and are beginning to blame their educational systems for their poverty and underdevelopment. They think that the sciences which their universities have failed to pursue, the technology which their schools have somewhat despised, the research on the exploitation of natural resources which they themselves have not been able to carry out, are the secrets behind the progress of industrialised countries. Latin Americans have woken to the fact that education is a most effective instrument for achieving economic advancement and that investment in education is always highly profitable. They have become convinced, too, that concentration on professional preparation to the exclusion of 'pure' science is a mistake because the latter alone can fertilise the former.

(3) The 'explosion' of would-be students, nourished by a population explosion and the rising expectations and aspirations of the masses, makes it absolutely necessary to adapt structure and offerings of the universities.

Since about 1955 at least a dozen universities have initiated drastic reforms, among them Concepción (Chile), Puerto Rico, San Marcos (Peru) and Costa Rica. Other newer foundations like Los Andes and Oriente (Venezuela) are proceeding along modern lines. New universities, like that of Brasília, have been founded and given an administrative structure which will ensure that they will be able to serve national needs.

The reforms have in common certain major features:

—The provision of an organisational and administrative structure which will ensure continuity in policy, i.e. diminish the upsets and changes of direction caused by the short tenure of office of rectors and deans and by their election in open meeting.

—Attempts to integrate the faculties more closely into the university, thereby diminishing academic anarchy.

—The building of more laboratories in which students can do individual work, and of adequate libraries.

—The appointment of full-time professors (*dedicación exclusiva*) with duties of promotion and planning of research.

—The introduction of a one-year or two-year compulsory general course for all students, dealing both with the sciences and the humanities, leading to selection of students for professional faculties.

—The development of courses in pure science (e.g. biology, physics and chemistry) and in the humanities (e.g. modern languages and classics) in central institutes not dependent upon professional faculties. The establishment of a ladder of degrees (bachelor's, master's, doctor's) in the 'pure' subjects.

—The introduction of 'short career' (2- or 3-year) courses leading to intermediate qualifications.

—Modernisation of teaching: introduction of tutorial and seminar methods, use of modern aids to learning, etc.

—Validation of courses by a system of points and grades, somewhat on the lines adopted in North American universities.

—Provision of housing for students (hostels) and attempts to gather new buildings on to a central campus (e.g. Buenos Aires, Brasília).

—Strengthening of student welfare services. Promotion of the idea that the students themselves should organise their own athletic and recreational activities.

The reforms now in hand (1966) are meeting with much greater success than the boldest optimists would have dared to hope ten years ago. It should be realised that to attempt the transformation of a great and highly honoured university—say that of Chile—with tens of thousands of students, dozens of separate teaching units, a long tradition and a splendid record of achievement is exceedingly hazardous and difficult. Nevertheless, there is so much good will and courage that it seems certain that within the next twenty years the Latin American academic scene will have changed totally, that the universities will have modernised themselves and taken their place beside their sisters in Europe and North America, that they will at last be in a position—which they are not now—to help the Latin American peoples to utilise the rich natural resources of their continent for the satisfaction of human needs.

BIBLIOGRAPHY

Benjamin, Harold R. W. and Carnelli, Delia J. *History and Aims of Higher Education in the Latin American Republics*, Council on Higher Education in the American Republics, Washington, DC, 1961.

Benton, William. *The Voice of Latin America*, Harper and Row, New York, 1961; Weidenfeld and Nicolson, London, 1962.

Bowles, F. *Access to Higher Education*, I and II, Columbia Univ. Press for UNESCO, New York, 1965.

Havighurst, Robert J. 'Latin American and North American Higher Education', *Comparative Education Review*, 4, February 1961.

Larrea, Julio. 'Changing Aims and Objectives of the Universities in Latin America', *World Year Book of Education*, Evans Brothers, London, 1959.

Lourenco-Filho, M. B. 'Professional Studies in the Universities of Brazil', *World Year Book of Education*, Evans Brothers, London, 1959.

Mantovani, Juan. 'Freedom in the Argentine Universities before and after the Perón Régime', *Year Book of Education*, Evans Brothers, London; Teachers College, Colombia University, NY, 1959.

UNESCO. 'Higher Education', *World Survey of Education*, IV, International Publication Service, New York, 1966. *Higher Education and Development in Latin America* (Report of a meeting of experts held in Costa Rica, 1966), Paris, 1966.

Further information, including addresses, can be obtained from the Secretariat of the Unión de Universidades de América Latina, Lavalle 465 PB, Buenos Aires, Argentina.

THE ROMAN CATHOLIC CHURCH

Rev. RENATO POBLETE BARTH, SJ

THE COLONIAL ERA

THE Roman Catholic Church is one of the basic institutions of Latin America; almost one-third of the Roman Catholic population of the world—over 200 million people—live on this continent while Latin American bishops were the most numerous single group at the Second Vatican Council. The work of the Church began with Columbus' second arrival in 1493, with the group of Dominican priests who accompanied him. Since that time missionaries preached not only to the Spaniards but also to the conquered Indians in the New World. During this period christianisation was carried out according to the old missionary norms, like those of Pope Gregory the Great, who instructed the bishops of England not to destroy the pagan temples but rather to make them serve the Christian cause.

The missionaries tried to understand the Indians' primitive religion and the transition from paganism to Christianity was not too difficult. The Incas as well as the Aztecs readily accepted the idea of a supreme power; monotheism along with the idea of a life after death and the veneration of 'saints' was quite common. Hence the religious conquest was accomplished without excessive struggle. It is difficult to say how deep the Indians' conversion was. Institutions like those of the *fiscal*, *alferez* and *doctrinero* placed laymen in charge of communities of Indians and mestizos. These laymen would lead the people in prayer every Sunday and in some cases baptise infants. Despite these methods, mass baptism was not accompanied by previous religious instruction. In 1531 the first bishop of Mexico, Zumárraga, reported that the Franciscans alone had baptised more than a million Indians. It is obvious that these mass conversions left many syncretisms which would remain for many centuries.

During the early colonial period the Roman Catholic Church played a vital role in pacifying the Indians and at the same time insisting upon a more respectful treatment of them as human beings. Among the most famous priests of this period we find Antonio de Montesinos and Bartolomé de las Casas who in their preaching severely condemned the abuses of the Spaniards. Las Casas put these problems to the king of Spain. He obtained better legislation for the natives and tried especially to change the system of the *encomiendas*, allotting the Indians, not to individual colonists, but to a sacred trust in each village under the supervision of a friar. The work of Las Casas was not always successful. The struggle against Spanish officials was difficult; injustice was quite common, but the Church had the merit of being alone in appealing to the king for the protection of the Indians.

Another outstanding experiment of the Roman Catholic Church in Latin America was the work of the missions. The mission village was a sort of settlement for the Indians which protected them against the slave-hunting colonists, instructed them in the Catholic faith, and trained them for skilled work. The most famous were the *reducciones* in the area of the River Plate, covering much of Paraguay. The *reducciones* were utopian communities which had a strong impact upon the Indians. They were attacked by civil authorities and actually raided by the Brazilian colonists from São Paulo who were trying to engage the Indians as slaves.

The 100,000 Indians who lived in the missions had the benefit of the Church's protection but the system was undoubtedly paternalistic. Nevertheless, the missions prospered, the Indians were content and were probably enjoying better conditions that their fellow North American Indians. This experiment came to an end in 1767 with the expulsion of the Jesuits from the whole of the Spanish Empire. The Jesuits had been the guardians of the intellectual life of the colonies; they identified the action of the Church with progress. They opened canals for irrigation, brought new trees from Europe, introduced fine cattle for better breeding, and their skill in farming was celebrated. They also organised manufacturing industries, making textiles, rope, pottery, etc. The Jesuits maintained a monopoly in education. Schools and universities, good libraries all over Latin America were run by them. In Mexico in 1767 300 Jesuits were conducting 22 colleges, 19 schools and 10 seminaries. This work provoked the jealousy and friction with civilian authorities in Spain which led to their expulsion from all the Spanish and Portuguese colonies. The Society was restored in 1814 and its missionaries returned to many Latin American countries during the following three decades.

In the colonial era the Church flourished especially in the larger cities of Latin America, building magnificent cathedrals and churches like those in Mexico, Quito and Lima. This epoch also enriched the Catholic Church in Latin America with some of its notable members like Santa Rosa de Lima, Santo Toribio de Mogrovejo, San Martín de Porres in Peru, San Pedro Claver in Colombia, Anchieta and Nobrega in Brazil.

INDEPENDENCE AND THE CHURCH

The Catholic Church reacted in different ways to the wars of independence. Some bishops had republican inclinations, like the bishop of Quito, while the bishop of Santiago, in Chile, was a staunch royalist. The native clergy in Mexico and Argentina fought actively for independence. In Mexico over 100 priests led battalions, while in Argentina 17 priests were present at the first independent assembly of May 1810. However, the revolution had its negative effects from the religious point of view: the separation from Spain stopped the continuous flow of clergy from Spain and Portugal while the war brought about a disorganisation of the seminaries and many dioceses found themselves without bishops for several years.

Relations with the pope remained uncertain for a long time because the new governments tried to retain the privilege of 'patronage', whereby the king of Spain had the right to appoint bishops. Rome was unwilling to extend this right to the new republics due to its deep-seated suspicion of liberal governments. The prolonged and complex negotiations had an adverse effect upon religious life leaving the organisation of the Catholic Church in a very poor state. At the same time there raged an ideological struggle between the Church and the liberal movements. In some places it was bitter and led some governments to take over the property of the Church and expel the clergy from their dioceses. In most Latin American countries foreign religious priests were forbidden to practise their ministry.

By 1829 there was not a single bishop left in Mexico. Some of the anti-clerical measures of O'Higgins in Chile and Rivadavia in Argentina also produced tension. In Brazil during the turbulent period of the Regency, Diego Freijo, a liberal priest who served as regent, proposed a project to nationalise the Church and establish a married clergy. In Venezuela the hierarchy became the victim of the personalism of Antonio Guzmán Blanco. The same happened in Paraguay with the dictator Gaspar Rodríguez de Francia.

DEMOGRAPHIC AND SOCIAL FACTORS

Latin America is now a predominantly urban society. In 1945 only 39 per cent of the population was considered urban; today well over 50 per cent are living in cities. This process runs parallel to the building of a technical, industrial civilisation which is—among other things—changing society fundamentally. However, the benefits of this technical civilisation are felt by only a small minority and this in turn results in grave social and political problems. The Catholic Church is facing these problems in very unfavourable conditions. The number of dioceses, parishes and priests to look after the spiritual welfare of Catholics is now smaller, in proportion, than what the Church had in the 18th century.

Today there is about one priest in Latin America for every 5,700 persons, with a range varying from 3–4,000 in Chile and Colombia to 11,000 in Guatemala and 16,000 in Honduras. There is great socio-economic and cultural diversity among the different Latin American countries and the same is true of Latin American Catholicism; the total number of priests and the proportion of inhabitants per priest is given in the following table.

	Total number of priests	Inhabitants per priest
Argentina	4,922	4,064
Bolivia	581	5,958
Brazil	9,116	7,766
Chile	2,357	3,114
Colombia	3,841	3,679
Costa Rica	235	4,983
Cuba	730	9,310
Dominican Republic	246	12,252
Ecuador	1,170	3,690
Guatemala	335	11,239
Haiti	463	7,570
Honduras	119	15,899
Mexico	6,512	5,373
Nicaragua	190	7,773
Paraguay	426	4,150
Panama	141	7,482
Peru	1,496	7,257
Puerto Rico	400	5,902
Salvador	310	8,067
Uruguay	688	4,109
Venezuela	1,249	5,371

In spite of the considerable effort to increase the number of priests, the demographic explosion makes illusory any hopes of maintaining the above proportions. In the last fifteen years Latin America has had an increase of 12,000 priests but the population has increased by 50 millions.

The traditional pastoral structure of the parish is unwieldy and no longer applicable to the religious needs of today. The area of the parishes fluctuates between 100 and 600 square miles and the average parochial population varies between 10,000 in Paraguay and Ecuador to 25,000 in Honduras (in Cuba probably 32,000); some cities have an average of over 50,000 inhabitants per parish.

Another difficulty facing the Church is the transmission of religious ideas. In the past this was easily accomplished since it was diffused in a culture. There were many institutions, such as the family, school and parish, that corroborated the doctrine preached by the priest. Also social control and authority helped not only the transmission of these ideas but also the maintenance of a certain stability in patterns of social and personal behaviour. Today pluralistic societies are to be found everywhere in Latin America. There is not just one set of norms, values, attitudes and opinions, but different values and norms emanating from secularism, communism and laicism. The intermediate groups, such as the school, family, communal groups and parish, do not reinforce the same doctrines but are often in competition, opposing the ideas that are communicated to them by the Church. Furthermore, social pressure is not as strong today as in the past. A more personal commitment is needed; traditional methods of religious instruction are no longer sufficient.

STRENGTH OF THE CHURCH

The national census is the least reliable sign of religious affiliation; in 1966 it showed, throughout Latin America, a percentage of nominal Catholics varying from 65 per cent in Uruguay to 98 per cent in Colombia and Peru. It is this fact that accounts for the classification of Latin America as a Catholic continent.

Mass attendance implies a sense of belonging and participation stronger than the mere response to the national census. There is to be found a statistical number that varies widely from rural to urban practice and from one socio-economic group to another. In some worker areas in big cities from 1 to 3 per cent of the adult population attends Mass. In some of the middle- and upper-class parishes attendance at Sunday Mass varies 30 to 50 per cent. This index of religious affiliation does not have the same meaning that it has in the Anglo-Saxon countries since lack of priests, long distances and poverty make Mass attendance difficult in Latin America. Furthermore people migrating from the country to cities are often not in the habit of seeing a priest more than once or twice a year. Such people traditionally show their religious sentiments and sense of belonging to the Church in other ways.

CHANGE

In June 1958 CELAM ('Consejo Episcopal Latinoamericano'—Bishops' Council of Latin America) was created. With its general secretariat in Bogotá CELAM is the representative organ of the different Bishops' Councils of each nation, serving as an organ of contact and collaboration for Latin American bishops. Many activities such as education, social action, catechesis and liturgy have been coordinated. CELAM works in close contact with a special committee created by the Vatican in Rome, CAL (Commission for Latin America).

CELAM has fostered a series of institutions to bring about the hoped-for renewal of the Church. A Latin American Institute for Catechetical Studies is preparing large groups of priests, sisters and laymen for the teaching of the Christian doctrine. For some years the Pastoral Institute of Latin America has also been very active. The institute is composed of a team of priests who go from one city to another organising weeks of study for priests and laymen. The same type of work is being carried out in different countries organised on a national basis. Probably the greatest change is evident in the organisation of laymen. Catholic Action in its multiple forms has become a significant force. Movements such as the Young Christian Workers, the Catholic Movement of University Students and the Christian Family Movement are active.

SOCIAL INFLUENCE OF THE CHURCH

Private education is traditionally conducted in large part by the Church. Every country has its Catholic university, and many of them have an outstanding level of scholarship with several thousand students enrolled. Those at Santiago, São Paulo, Lima, Caracas, Río de Janeiro, Mexico City and Bogotá are among the most notable. In Colombia the Church is responsible for over half of all secondary school students. In Argentina, Paraguay and Nicaragua the proportion of students in Catholic schools is over 35 per cent of the total. In Chile almost one-half of the Catholic schools are free. Another field of education in which the Church has been a pioneer is basic education for adults and young people. The radiophonic schools in Sutatenza (Colombia), in Honduras, Peru and Brazil probably reach millions of illiterate people, teaching them not only how to read and write but also how to achieve material improvement. In almost all Latin American countries the Church is conducting such schools in addition to those for farmers and workers.

The contribution of the Church to society may also be seen in the inspiration and promotion of social movements. The Christian-social doctrine has been the inspiration of important trade union groups started by priests in Colombia, Chile and Brazil. The CLASC (Confederation of Latin American Christian Trade Unions) has been active in all countries attempting social justice. It may be said that the Christian Democratic parties have also been inspired by the principles of the Church.

A principal task of the Church is to teach and to inspire and in recent years this role has been fulfilled through a series of pastoral letters and other documents reminding the faithful of their duties. They are a positive proof of the Church's interest in helping to change the unjust social order in which the Latin American countries live. The pastoral letter of the Chilean bishops *Social and Political Duties* as well as the Brazilian bishops' statement *Basic Reforms for a Just Social Order* are classic documents translated and distributed throughout Latin America. Former Senator Humphreys asked the consent of the US Senate to print in the Congressional Record the pastoral letter of the Chilean bishops. Both letters touched current problems such as rural and tax reforms, the immorality of evasion and the need for fuller participation of workers in the profits of industries.

The Church's increased effect comes in great part from the far-sighted social and economic philosophy of Pope John's encyclicals *Mater et Magister*

734

and *Pacem in Terris*. With the recent encyclical *Progressio Populorum* the Church in Latin America has yet another blueprint for social action. In certain countries it is very much aware of the socio-economic repercussions of demographic growth. Although the execution of the Church's policy as regards this problem differs from country to country, there is a tendency toward non-interference in government plans for responsible parenthood, leaving the last decision to the personal conscience.

The Church is frequently active itself in social reform. Bishops in Chile and other countries, for example, have divided their lands amongst the needy. With the help of German bishops an institute for the study and evaluation of social projects called DESAL (Desarrollo Económico y Social para Américan Latina) is helping this development all over the continent.

The Catholic Church's efforts in Latin America were as at June 1967 in the hands of 11 cardinals, 601 bishops and 38,347 priests (of whom 19,770 were religious priests) and 102,149 religious women. The growing importance of Christian laymen in this apostolate has been one of the most encouraging developments in the past half century, restoring to the Church its universal missionary character.

BIBLIOGRAPHY

D'Antonio, William V. and Pike, Fredrick B. (eds) *Religion, Revolution and Reform. New Forces for Change in Latin America*, Burns and Oates, London; Frederick A. Praeger, New York, 1964.

Bonino, José. 'Catholics and Protestants in Latin America' *Frontier*, II, 8, London, summer 1965.

Houtart, François and Pin, Emile. *The Church and the Latin American Revolution*, Sheed and Ward, New York, 1965.

Mecham, John Lloyd. *Church and State in Latin America. A History of Politico-Ecclesiastica Relations*, Univ. of North Carolina Press, Chapel Hill, NC, revised ed. 1966.

THE TRADE UNION MOVEMENT

JORGE BARRIA

HISTORY

THE Latin American trade union movement has its origins in the *mutualista* tradition of mutual help and friendly societies formed in the 19th century. This 'friendly society' mentality still dominates many trade unions to the present day, especially in countries like the Central American countries and Ecuador where the impact of industrialisation has not substantially modified the social structure.

The trade union movement began to acquire importance towards the end of the last century and its growth was encouraged by the activities of immigrant workers of anarchist or socialist affiliations. Meetings to celebrate May Day began to be held in Argentina as early as 1896, and in Chile two years later. Fully-fledged trade unions made their appearance at that time in Argentina, Uruguay and Mexico, and there is evidence that in other Latin American countries there were small anarchist or socialist groups with more limited influence. In Mexico, the Casa del Obrero Mundial (International Workers' Home) played an important part in the Revolution which began in 1910, while the Argentine workers were the first to organise a national congress in 1890. The struggle between socialists and anarchists contributed to the internal difficulties of the early unions, and in addition their formation was hampered by the intransigence of employers, government hostility, and the small number and low educational level of the urban workers.

Between the wars communism became a political force and made a bid for the leadership of the trade unions then in existence. In 1929 the Communist Party established another labour organisation. About this time unions were grouped in national confederations in several countries, notably Argentina, Chile, Uruguay, Mexico, Ecuador, Colombia and Peru. These bodies were in turn federated, in 1938, in the Confederación de Trabajadores de América Latina (Workers' Confederation of Latin America); this movement consolidated its strength during the war.

Since 1945 the trade union movement has expanded more slowly. The activities of the trade unions have been greatly affected by political developments. As the wave of democratic governments after the war was followed by various military regimes, trade union activities were curtailed and at present there are several regimes that severely restrict political and trade union activities.

The migration of rural workers to the cities, the absence of a tradition of organised labour and the prevailing social structure, all constitute tremendous obstacles both to unionisation and to the continuity of labour organisations.

In addition, the process of industrialisation has sometimes resulted in the formation of a proletariat which has subsequently disappeared when the industries have declined. The existence of a large number of small and medium-sized businesses is yet another obstacle to the development of a strong trade union movement, both because of the small numbers of the workers concerned and the paternalistic system of employee-management relations.

General Characteristics of Latin American Unionism

Paternalism is a pronounced characteristic of the system of employer–worker relations in Latin America and is deeply ingrained in the social structure, owing to historical causes and the limited degree of social evolution. However, the state plays an important role in labour relations. All countries have labour codes, and several of the written constitutions specifically recognise the rights of labour. The Mexican constitution of 1917 was the first to recognise social rights, other countries following suit. As to labour codes, the first and most comprehensive of such bodies is the Chilean one of 1924. Then followed those of Mexico (1931), Cuba (1933), Ecuador (1938), Bolivia (1939) and Brazil (1934). States have passed laws to regulate minimum wages, working conditions, procedures for the solution of industrial conflicts, trade union organisation and social security. In general, trade union organisation is subject to the various labour codes, and governments exercise a degree of administrative control that varies with the prevailing political situation. The exercise of collective bargaining is limited by the fact that most labour legislation makes provision, at least theoretically, for the majority of the objectives that unions would seek to attain. This legalistic background to industrial relations is the result of the action of politicians, who have introduced these measures to gain electoral support; it is also the result of pressure from the unions themselves, which have preferred to achieve these ends through legislation.

The trade union movement in Latin America has about twelve million members. In general, the entire active population capable of being organised belongs to groups based on particular industries, although there is a tendency to form national labour confederations. The nucleus of trade union organisation is the union of workers employed by a single company, which results in a large number of small organisations with limited financial resources, inadequately trained leadership and little strength to support their claims. The Latin American labour movement is not integrated into society as a whole and is isolated from other social groups. Only in Mexico and Cuba is it fully associated with the government.

Although the ideology of the trade union movement is reformist, and some would add leftist and nationalist, at the local and industrial level the over-riding preoccupation is that of wages and conditions. The labour movement tries to play a role in society as a whole, and does not attempt to become a working-class movement in the European sense; on the contrary, it constitutes an instrument of social mobility and a means of integrating the worker into the newly forming industrial society of Latin America. The labour movement is to a certain extent independent of political parties, especially in those countries where it enjoys relative freedom; nowhere—with the exceptions of Mexico and Cuba—do trade unions either form or give formal support to a political party, even though there may be among its leaders overwhelming support for such a party. This situation is reflected in the fact that the members of trade unions enjoy higher wages than other urban workers and, of course, than the peasants. This contrast is even more pronounced in those sectors of the economy with high productivity and based on foreign capital.

The Latin American trade union movement owes its influence chiefly to its strategic position in the key sectors of the national economies: petroleum, copper, meat-packing, plantations, railways, etc. Strikes therefore inevitably have repercussions on the economic life of the country in addition to their effect on the political and industrial sectors directly concerned.

On the other hand, political parties have a strong influence on the labour movement. The various important political movements of the continent—national-revolutionary, socialist, communist, Christian Democrat and right-wing—are engaged in a struggle for the leadership of the organised workers. This results in a diminution of the normal activities of the unions, especially in those countries where they are weakest owing to internecine party-political quarrels. The political character of the labour movement, reflected in its activity within a country, is closely connected with the fact that political freedom on the one hand, and economic development under the government's direction on the other, have a considerable influence on the development of the labour movement.

These general observations with regard to the Latin American labour movement must be modified in accordance with the peculiar factors that have affected its development in each of the Latin American republics.

TRADE UNIONS IN SOUTH AMERICA

Argentina. This country now has one of the best organised and most active labour movements. It is organised under the denomination of Confederación General del Trabajo (General Confederation of Labour), which was founded in 1930 by Socialist and independent forces. This Confederation fell under the control of Juan D. Perón, as minister of labour, in 1943. Peronism decreed obligatory incorporation of workers into trade unions on 20 July 1943, and also industrial legislation (the National Institute of Social Security is a result of this): his most fervent political supporters at the present time are to be found among the rank and file of trade unionists. The General Confederation of Labour, with two and a half million workers organised in industrial federations, covers all sectors of the economy. The metallurgical, textile, clothing, transport, municipal and salaried workers unions are the strongest. The Confederation has been a party to collective agreements drawn up for each industry and service, and these affect over 90 per cent of the working population of the country. Augusto Vandor, José Alonso and Armando March are among the outstanding leaders of the General Confederation of Labour.

Brazil. Here the labour movement is still in the early stages of development. It derives from the New State of the late President Getulio Vargas, and retains the semi-corporativist administrative structure established during his rule. A trade union law was passed in 1937, whereby workers were organised into four national confederations covering industry, land transport, maritime transport and commerce. Moreover, this law ruled out the establishment of a general confederation of labour. At present these four organisations have a joint membership of two and a half million. The Labour Code contemplates a system of arbitration tribunal to investigate and resolve industrial conflicts.

The workers are obliged to pay contributions, and union funds are administered by the state.

Bolivia. The rise to power of the National Revolutionary Movement in 1952 provided a great opportunity for the labour movement which supported it. The Confederación Obrera Boliviana (Bolivian Workers' Confederation) was formed in the same year, based on the miners' union; it was expanded to include the peasants, and succeeded in enrolling 200,000 members all told. Dissensions within the governing party contributed to the disintegration of the Confederation, and this situation facilitated the seizure of power in October 1964 by the armed forces, which have established strict control over the unions.

Colombia. The traditional political division of the country, where two parties have shared power for the past twelve years, has also affected the labour movement. As a result, there is a Confederación de Trabajadores de Colombia (Workers' Confederation of Colombia), having a membership of 320,000, which is aligned with the Liberal Party, and the Unión de Trabajadores de Colombia (Workers' Union of Colombia), established in 1946, with 150,000 members and connections with the Catholic Church and the Conservative Party. The leaders of the CTC are Víctor J. Silva and José Mercado. The Union of Colombian Workers is led by Antonio Díaz and Justiniano Espinoza. There is a Communist minority group, the Confederación Sindical de Colombia (Trade Unions Confederation of Colombia), with a membership of 10,000.

Chile. The 400,000 trade unionists are distributed among several organisations. The most representative of them is the Central Unica de Trabajadores (United Workers' Confederation), which was founded in 1953 and has a membership of 300,000. Its leaders are mostly Socialists and Communists and prominent among them are Luis Figueroa and Oscar Núñez. The Confederación de Empleados Particulares de Chile (Confederation of Salaried Employees of Chile) dates back from 1948; its present membership amounts to 30,000 and its leader is Ernesto Lennon. There is also the Confederación Cristiana de Trabajadores (Christian Workers' Confederation), with a membership of 2,000. It should be noted that Christian workers make up a strong minority in the United Workers' Confederation, apart from this Confederation. The strength of the trade union movement is based on the 'closed shop' system, and there is considerable governmental control over the administration of union affairs and in the field of collective bargaining.

Ecuador. The labour movement is weak, with about 75,000 members. The unions are grouped in various federations, of which the most important is the Confederación de Trabajadores del Ecuador (Workers' Confederation of Ecuador), founded in 1944 under Socialist and Communist leadership and affiliated to the WFTU. The present interim government has given assurances that it will respect trade union freedom.

Paraguay. The military government has sponsored a Confederación Paraguaya de Trabajadores (Paraguayan Workers' Confederation) which claims to represent the country's 20,000 unionists.

Peru. The present democratic government has given full freedom to trade unions: the vast majority of trade unions are affiliated to the Confederación de Trabajadores del Perú (Workers' Confederation of Peru), founded in 1944 and reorganised in 1956, with over 500,000 members among the urban workers and a strong peasant sector. Its most important leaders are Julio

Cruzado, Francisco Taboada and Félix Loli, who, like most trade union leaders, are of Aprista affiliation.

Uruguay. In this country the workers have not succeeded in establishing a united front, and are divided among several federations, among which are the Confederación Sindical del Uruguay (Trade Unions Confederation of Uruguay) founded in 1954, the Central de Trabajadores del Uruguay (Workers' Confederation of Uruguay) and various unaffiliated unions. Total membership is 170,000. In 1964 the Convención Nacional del Trabajo (National Labour Convention) was established, with the support of almost all the unions, and this organisation has since been very active under the leadership of José D'Elía and Héctor Rodríguez.

Venezuela. The political situation has permitted the establishment of a powerful labour movement, supported by about 200,000 urban workers—oil workers being outstanding—and nearly one million peasants in various unions. These are all affiliated to the Confederación de Trabajadores de Venezuela (Workers' Confederation of Venezuela), which was reorganised in 1959 and whose leaders are José González Navarro, Augusto Malavé and Luis Tovar, all connected with the ruling Acción Democrática party. There is also a Communist minority group, the Central Unitaria de Trabajadores de Venezuela (Unitarian Confederation of Venezuelan Workers).

TRADE UNIONS IN CENTRAL AMERICA AND THE CARIBBEAN

The situation in this area is basically determined by the agrarian structure of the economy, the absence of political democracy, the strongly entrenched position of military dictatorships and the lack of coherent political forces. The movement is weak, and the few labour organisations lead a precarious existence owing to the disturbed political situation. Such is the case in Guatemala, Honduras, El Salvador and Panama; none of these countries has over 25,000 organised workers, the banana workers' union in Honduras being the most important. In Costa Rica there is a free trade union movement, affiliated to the Confederación Costarricense de Trabajadores (Costa Rican Confederation of Workers), which is supported by 16,000 of the country's 20,000 trade unionists.

Mexico. In this country there is a labour movement supported by 2 million urban workers and peasants; most unions are affiliated to the Confederación de Trabajadores de México (Workers' Confederation of Mexico), founded in 1936. The latter is closely connected with the Institutional Revolutionary Party, which has been in power since 1946. The leaders are Fidel Velásquez, Alfonso Sánchez, Jesús Jurén and Salvador Carrillo.

Cuba. The labour movement, which had reached an advanced stage of development before the 1959 Revolution, has been consolidated along the lines of those in communist countries. Over 1,400,000 workers, organised in national federations, are affiliated to the Confederación de Trabajadores de Cuba Revolucionaria (Confederation of Workers of Revolutionary Cuba).

In Haiti, the lack of democratic government has prevented the development of a labour movement. Likewise, in the Dominican Republic, the transition to democratic government after thirty years of dictatorship has not resulted in the political stability needed for the consolidation of the recently formed labour movement. In Puerto Rico there is a labour movement with over 100,000 members, which is closely connected with the American Federation of Labour–Congress of Industrial Organisations (AFL–CIO).

TRADE UNION MEMBERSHIP PER COUNTRY

Argentina	2,600,000
Brazil	2,670,000
Bolivia	200,000
Colombia	670,000
Chile	400,000
Ecuador	75,000
Paraguay	20,000
Peru	500,000
Uruguay	270,000
Venezuela	1,200,000
Guatemala	15,000
Honduras	24,000
El Salvador	25,000
Panama	15,000
Costa Rica	24,000
Mexico	1,500,000
Cuba	1,400,000
Haiti	3,500
Dominican Republic	20,000
Puerto Rico	150,000
Total	11,781,500

CONTINENTAL ORGANISATIONS

Ever since the labour movement began, there have been attempts to create an organisation that would cover the whole of Latin America. The first step was taken by the American Federation of Labour and the Mexican Workers' Confederation, which together established in 1918 the Federación Panamericana de Trabajadores (Panamerican Workers' Federation). This organisation lasted for twelve years but, apart from the two groups sponsoring it, managed to establish close links only with the *mutualista* unions in Central America.

The anarchists in 1929 held a congress in Buenos Aires and established a continental centre. This, however, had only a short life, in spite of the fact that the Congress was attended by delegations from Argentina, Uruguay, Brazil, Chile, Peru and Bolivia. In that same year, and for the same purpose, the Red International of Trade Unions held a congress in Montevideo, attended by a number of communist delegates; these set up the Confederación Sindicalista Latinoamericana (Latin American Trade Unions Confederation). This organisation was more effective as an instrument of propaganda than as a step towards labour unity; its most important affiliated body, the Chilean Workers' Federation, was dissolved in 1936, and its members joined the CETAL.

The most successful attempt to achieve a united front representing the workers of the whole continent was the establishment in 1938 of the Confederación de Trabajadores de América Latina (Workers' Confederation of Latin America or CETAL), which played an important part during the period of ten years during which it maintained more than nominal unity. It encouraged the growth of trade unionism in several countries, helped to achieve unity (eventually twelve labour confederations were affiliated to the CETAL), conducted an energetic campaign against Fascism, aligned the workers of the continent solidly behind the Allied cause, collaborated with governments and negotiated with military dictatorships. The aspirations towards unity felt by the workers, the Popular Front movement and the war were the factors that contributed to the coexistence and cooperation within the CETAL of socialist, national-revolutionary, communist and liberal-democratic factions. The development of the CETAL followed that of world trade unionism. The CETAL played a part in the foundation of the World Federation of Trade Unions, and remained affiliated to that body even after the schism that took place in 1948, which resulted in the establishment of a rival organisation, the International Confederation of Free Trade Unions. Moreover, in the same year various labour federations that had broken with the CETAL—among them those of Mexico, Cuba and Peru—resolved to build up a new continent-wide labour organisation that would include the workers of the United States and Canada. In January 1948 the Interamerican Confederation of Labour was founded, and two years later it became the Organización Regional Interamericana de Trabajadores (Inter-Regional Organization of Workers or ORIT), affiliated to the International Confederation of Free Trade Unions (ICFTU). This body has remained in existence up to the present day, and recently held its Sixth Continental Congress. Supported and financed largely by the AFL-CIO, its main member, it has succeeded in retaining the affiliation of the major confederations of Mexico, Venezuela and Peru, the two Colombian organisations, and the most important federations of Central America and the Caribbean. It has laid great stress on the training of union leaders.

The International Federation of Christian Trade Unions established in 1954 the Latin American Confederation of Christian Trade Unions (CLASC), which has already held four congresses. As its name indicates, it represents individual trade unionists, and it has devoted particular attention to the task of training union leaders and securing representation of labour in international organisations. The growth of Christian Democracy as a political movement may encourage the development of trade unions of this type; in certain countries such as Venezuela, Costa Rica and Chile they already constitute sizeable groups within existing labour organisations.

On the initiative of the labour confederations of Chile, Cuba and Bolivia, and certain Brazilian unions, and with the support of the WFTU, a congress was held in 1964 in Brasilia which became the 'permanent congress of labour unity of the Latin American workers'. This body has had little success, owing to the unsettled political situation and the absence from its ranks of representative labour organisations. On this occasion, however, the CETAL was formally dissolved.

BIBLIOGRAPHY

Alba, Víctor. *Historia del movimiento obrero en América Latina*, Libreros Mexicanos Unidos, Mexico, DF, 1964.

Alexander, Robert J. *Labour Relations in Argentina, Brazil and Chile*, McGraw-Hill, New York, 1962.

Snow, Sinclair. *The Pan-American Federation of Labour*, Duke Univ. Press, Durham, NC, 1965.

Touraine, Alain (ed.) *Ouvriers et syndicats d'Amerique latine (Sociologie du Travail*, Special No. 4/61), Editions du Seuil, Paris, 1961.

Troncoso, Moisés Poblete and Burnett, Ben G. *The Rise of the Latin American Labor Movement*, College and Univ. Press, New Haven, Conn., 1960.

FOOTBALL

ERNEST HECHT

On 16 July 1950, in Rio's Maracana stadium, Uruguay beat Brazil 2–1
thus to become the winners of the fourth World Cup Competition. Unexpected as was this result in view of the Brazilians' excellence and previous
form in the competition, for the 200,000 crowd present and to the millions of
Brazilians following the match on radio, the event was considered nothing
less than a national tragedy. Almost a hundred people fainted from shock, a
large part of the stadium's attendance and all the players openly wept; a
number of people both in Uruguay and Brazil died from heart attacks
induced by the excitement and disappointment. 16 July became a day of
national mourning in Rio, whilst in Montevideo fervent celebrations in the
streets went on all night. When in 1958 Brazilian national honour was
restored by their team winning the Sixth World Cup in Sweden and thus
becoming the first South American nation to win the trophy in Europe,
and when in 1962 they went on to complete a unique double by becoming
World Champions again in Chile, crowds in their hundreds of thousands
turned out to hold a carnival of celebration in Rio, Sao Paulo and other
main cities, though the games had been played in far distant lands.

Whilst Uruguay and Brazil as the old and new leaders of Latin American
soccer might be expected to react in this way, the little republic of Chile
which staged the World Cup Competition of 1962 was not to be left behind.
When the national side defeated Russia in a quarter-final held in distant
Arica, the streets of Santiago were packed for days afterwards with cries of
Viva Chile, singing and dancing continuing into the early hours of the morning.

Sport as a factor of patriotic pride is not a uniquely Latin American
institution, but nowhere else perhaps is it so intensively identified by the
people with their personal and national honour. And though all sports have
their adherents, it is soccer that is king. Only in Mexico, where bull fights
and cock fights vie for attention and in Venezuela where baseball is popular,
does soccer have a rival as the main spectator and participant sport.

FOOTBALL AS A SOCIAL FACTOR

Without question football is one of the principal factors bridging the social
and cultural distance between the white and coloured races. Professor
Gilberto Freyre, the distinguished Brazilian sociologist, has written[1] 'Subli-
mating all that is most primitive, young and elemental in our culture, it was
natural that football in Brazil should be elevated into a national institution,
elevating also the Negro and his descendants, the mulatto, the cafuso, the

---

[1] In a foreword to Mario Filho, *O negro no futbol Brazileiro*, Rio de Janeiro.

mestizo. Amongst the means by which the social ascendancy of the Negro, mulatto and cafuso was accomplished during the last twenty years, there is none which surpasses soccer in importance . . . ' Whilst Brazil is not typical in all respects of other Latin American countries, most of the factors that apply there in making soccer one of the keys of the national social scene are relevant also to the other nations of the continent.

First and foremost is the link between poverty and football. Sport has often been the means by which under-privileged sections of the population seek to better their status, both financially and prestige-wise. The number of Negro and Jewish world boxing champions coming out of the United States, or the fact that the current cricket world champions are the West Indies, are other examples that spring to mind. In Latin America, where poverty exists on a vast scale, football is a means by which a member of the poorest classes, to whom opportunities of education may frequently be denied, can rise not only to riches but to status in a society that might otherwise shun him. There can hardly be a child in Latin America who does not know the rags to riches saga of Edson Arantes do Nascimento, otherwise known as Pele, the world's greatest footballer who, from being so poor that he had to play football with a ball made of old socks, has now become a multi-millionaire, owning apartment houses, Cadillacs and being received as an honoured guest by heads of state. Whilst a Pele comes once in a lifetime, players who reach professional standards, whether at country, state or club level, all are able to reach an affluence well beyond that which they could otherwise attain. In many countries the leading clubs are backed by rich employers so that opportunities for capitalising on footballing skill exist even beyond the game. Even at the lowest level football offers a young man a better chance of earning a good income than do other and slower opportunities. Whilst there are obviously wide variations between countries and even areas, a professional footballer even at the lowest rung can bring in about five times the salary available to an ordinary worker.

Whilst the number of players who might thus rise is obviously numerically limited, there is no boundary for the identification that millions of the poor can make with their soccer heroes, the largest proportion of whom come from their ranks. As they watch the stars, they know that there but for the grace of God they might be, and for all his millions Pele is still one of them. His success and magic belong to them as inexorably as it is produced by his wonderful feet.

Football is thus a sport that belongs to the numerically largest section of society in Latin America. Watching it is frequently not cheap for spectators in terms of typical wage rates, but it is a high spot of the weekly life, to be savoured in person if possible, or vicariously through radio and television. Games are covered by dozens of radio stations and hundreds of commentators; thousand listen to transistors and watch at the same time. Football and the cinema vie with each other as entertainment in Latin America, and where wages do not allow the regular sampling of both, it is football that has the ability of best enhancing the pleasures of daily life, for it is always possible to savour it from personal experience.

No-one who has witnessed a Latin American crowd's involvement can be in any doubt of the importance of football as a means of expression of joy. Equally a Latin American player is at his happiest when he has a ball at his feet, seemingly tied to his bootlaces, when he can caress it, and the vocabulary in Portuguese, for instance, in dealing with football is full of phrases that suggest joy and love. One 'caresses a football', one 'has to be good to her', the ball being feminine, and many of the terms used to describe football events have an amatory or even sexual connotation.

In countries where there are wide disparities between rich and poor football also acts as a leveller between the classes, for in a football argument the street sweeper's opinion is as good as the factory boss's and neither will pull rank on the other. The degree to which the upper classes are involved in football varies from country to country, ranging from its almost total involvement in Brazil to a minute stratum in some Central American states.

THE POLITICAL ASPECT

The contrasts of poverty and riches are violent all through South America, and the sig' of some of the most superb stadiums in the world costing millions to erect, standing side by side, sometimes literally so, with shantytown dwellings, poses an immediate question in the mind of any European visitor. The charge has frequently been levelled at South American governments that they tend to utilise the great popularity of football to divert popular attention from social problems, to anaesthetise them from the painful facts of daily life. Sport has undoubtedly been opportunistically used by politicians throughout South America, especially at local or state level—to be photographed by the side of a popular player is frequently worth many votes—but in South America it could well be said that the usage of sport is almost a will of the people, which would certainly not be true of some political activities in other spheres.

Very often because of the population's involvement in football, the politicos' overt action in some footballing matter is but an extension of their voters' feelings, arrived at either through personal involvement or as a response through the efficient working of the antenna developed by any successful public figure. Thus when in 1962, whilst listening to the commentary of the Chile-Brazil World Cup semi-final, the Brazilian government was dumbfounded by the news that their star Garrincha had been sent off the field after considerable provocation, the then prime minister, Tancredo Neves, immediately cabled Sir Stanley Rous, the president of FIFA (the organising body): 'Brazilian Government expects FIFA authorities overlook any misunderstandings, and allow full team play Final specially that extraordinary athlete Garrincha whose discipline is renowned throughout the world.' In so doing, he was not only expressing the spontaneous reaction of his football-involved government but putting into words the feelings of virtually every voter in Brazil. This gesture would possibly become more important than any plank of his party's future political platform. Equally when in 1962 the Chilean government decided after the considerable economic damage caused by earthquakes to allocate three million pounds towards the staging of the World Cup there, it was a decision welcomed by a population in spite of the hardship involved, who saw in this a means of showing that their small country was worthy of the responsibility, and as a way of demonstrating their equality with some of their larger neighbours of the continent.

LINKS WITH EUROPE

Football in South America as elsewhere in the world was a British invention, and here this fact is still greatly remembered and honoured. British referees have made a considerable contribution to Latin American football, their conduct helping to raise the stature and standards of their local equivalents.

British football and Britain as its traditional home continue to be an important factor in the goodwill that face any British visitor.

Latin America now repays the compliment by exporting to Europe not only many of its stars, the Argentinians Di Stefano, Sivori, the Uruguayans Santa Maria, Schiaffino, the Brazilians Dino, Mazzola, Amerildo, the Chilean Toro, to name but a few recent examples, but also its coaches and above all its footballing ideas, ranging from important tactical innovations to new styles of football equipment.

Tactically the Latin Americans, at international level at least, are now superior in technique to European nations (despite their defeat in the 1966 World Cup). Whilst they have already shown (in 1958) that they could become World Champions whilst playing in Europe, the possibility of a European nation winning a Championship in South America is for the moment almost unthinkable. Whereas the basic game was British and European, the South American player has over the years evolved his own style, showing a flexibility, individual skill and panache that make football as played in South America more exciting and quite different a spectacle from its original model.

The National Scene

Latin American football is dominated by three giants, Brazil, Uruguay and Argentina.

Brazil

This is the country synonomous in European minds with the exceptional grace and style of South American football, and as winners of the 1958 and 1962 World Championships, without doubt the land of football par excellence. Players like Pele, Didi, Garrincha would qualify for any selection of the world's best of all time. These and some of the other players who made up the two Championship sides have become household names wherever football is played, but it is on its remarkable strength on the ground with thousands of clubs organised into playing competitions that Brazilian football is nurtured and looks likely to continue to dominate the world scene. Rio alone has 11,000 clubs registered, its Flamengo Beach district has over 1,000 clubs playing, and the same story is true of its other leading centres such as Sao Paulo, Minas Gerais, Bahia, Belo Horizonte. There is no Brazilian championship for club sides in view of the vastness of the country. There are leagues in most states, and the national title is fought for in a cup competition between chosen state sides. Brazil not only pioneered tactical systems such as 4–2–4, now 4–3–3, but also brought to Europe ideas for floodlight competitions, a new lightweight boot, and some magnificent concepts in the building of football stadia. The giant Maracana Stadium in Rio can hold 200,000 people, of whom 120,000 can sit, and within its confines includes even a hotel that can house a visiting team. A new stadium in Belo Horizonte modelled on it and the stadia in Sao Paulo continue to be far ahead of their equivalents in Europe. Wembley, which after preparation for the 1966 World Cup has covered accommodation throughout, can seat only 45,000 of its maximum total of 100,000 spectators.

Uruguay

These are the giants of the past, who dominated Latin American soccer in the 1920s and 1930s in a similar way to Brazil of today. Coming unheralded to Europe in 1924, they carried off the Olympic title, and repeated their triumph again in 1928. As a result of this unique double, FIFA staged the first World Championship in 1930 in Montevideo and here again Uruguay became Champions, though unlike later tournaments only a limited number of nations had entered. No such reservation could be made about their next win in 1950 when defeating Brazil in Rio on that 16 July to which reference has already been made. In recent years the national side has suffered from the emigration of many of its leading players to Argentina and Europe where earnings are higher for them than in their own country of $2\frac{1}{2}$ million people. Santa Maria, a great centre-half, of Real Madrid and Schiaffino of Milan are names that most readily come to mind in Europe. Nevertheless the leading club side, Peñarol, frequently wins the Latin American Club Championships.

Argentina

Perhaps their own worst enemies, the Argentinian footballers have never been able to transfer their frequent lead of the Latin American football scene into a triumph on a world scale. Winners of the South American Championships ten times, runners-up seven times, winners in 1964 of the 'Little World Cup' in Brazil, whom they manage to beat with monotonous regularity in ordinary matches, Argentina has nevertheless yet to make a major impact in a World Cup competition. Marvellously organised, with fifteen major soccer grounds in Buenos Aires alone, and with vast memberships of the leading clubs which are also social centres, Argentina produces footballers who on an individual level can compete with the world's greatest. If Pele had a rival for this title, it can only have been an Argentinian, Alfredo Di Stefano, whose genius transformed the Real Madrid Club of Spain into the greatest club side of the post-war period. Omar Sivori, who plays in Italy, and Rattin of their national side remain as individuals almost without peer. Regrettably the familiar story of friction when it comes to World Championships has continued with the preparation of the 1966 side during which both the coaches resigned and the players at one stage went on strike, and during play itself when, in the match against England, the remainder of the team had to be coaxed back onto the field after Rattin had been sent off.

Other countries

Perhaps the most currently enterprising of the other Latin American countries is Chile which, as a result of the impetus given to its football by being chosen as the stage for the 1962 World Cup, produced a team which, backed by the vociferous support of the local population, reached the semifinals of the competition, and deservedly so on their footballing merit. Emigration of their stars to more prosperous clubs, and their team manager for a spell to Europe, have held them back somewhat but they again qualified for the 1966 Championships. Mexico had in 1966 almost 80,000 registered footballers, and has produced individual players like veteran goalkeeper Antonio Carvajal who would not be disgraced in major company. Paraguay though having a population of only one million has frequently produced a team of surprising quality; Colombia was for a time able to attract many foreign stars by the amount of financial backing available for its leading club sides; Peru has staged some notable matches at its Lima stadium, and has provided in recent years some of the best of the native South American referees. Ecuador and Bolivia, though having small populations to draw on, have had their local hours of glory and increasing financial backing looks like becoming available in both.

747

BIBLIOGRAPHY

Fabian, A. H. and Green, Geoffrey (eds.) *Association Football*, 4 vols, Caxton Publishing Co., London, 1962.

Mario Filho. *O negro no futbol brazileiro*, Civilizacao Brazileira, Rio de Janeiro.

Meisl, Willy. *Soccer Revolution*, Phoenix Books, London, 1955.

Smith, Stratton (ed.) *Brazil Book of Football*, Souvenir Press, London, 1963. *International Football Book*, Souvenir Press, London, annual.

Smith, Stratton; Becker, Friedebert; and Jeffrey, Gordon (eds.) *World Cup*, Souvenir Press, London, 1962.

PART FIVE

CONTEMPORARY ARTS OF LATIN AMERICA AND THE CARIBBEAN

THE CULTURAL BACKGROUND

THE INDIAN HERITAGE

STEPHEN CLISSOLD

How 'Latin' is Latin America? Anyone who has stood in the market-place of a Guatemalan or Bolivian village, or gazed on an ancient Mexican carving or the ruins of Machu Picchu will know how inadequate is the usual designation for this vast and varied area. Bolívar described it as 'mankind in microcosm, neither Indian nor European, but something intermediate'. If the European impress is generally dominant in its language and literature, its science and its institutions, the Indian heritage nevertheless lives on with surprising vigour. Sometimes one can discern an Indian infrastructure beneath what seems modern and familiar, like the Incaic masonry on which the Spaniards raised their churches and palaces at Cuzco. Sometimes a remarkable degree of cultural synthesis seems to have occurred, as in Paraguay, where Guaraní ranks with Spanish as the medium for conversation or literature. Elsewhere, as in Peru, two disparate worlds coexist, still separate or living more in symbiosis than synthesis.

THE PRE-COLUMBIAN CULTURES

The Indian heritage is made up of many strands. One of the most remarkable, the Maya civilisation, was already in decline by the time the Spaniards reached America. Its vestiges are not only the famous temple-pyramids and a sophisticated calendar (by which the Indians of Guatemala still regulate their farming processes) but a remarkable book, preserved for posterity by a Spanish priest, in which the myths and legendary origins of the race are vividly enshrined. The *Popol Vuh*, or Book of the People, tells the Mayas' story of creation: how the gods sought to fashion human beings, first from mud, then from wood, and finally by kneading them from the maize flour which is the staple food of Central America, and how the first human beings joined with birds, beasts and insects in the incessant game, for which the stakes were life or death, of trying to placate or outwit the gods. Despite the intrusion of contemporary political and social pressures, the Indians' world is today still shaped by myth and magic. In such novels as *Hombres de Maíz* (1949) by the Guatemalan writer, anthropologist, and politician Migel Angel Asturias, we recognise that it remains essentially the world of the *Popol Vuh*.

Our vision of ancient Mexico is coloured by the lurid hues of the human-sacrifice cult which the Aztecs made the chief rite of their religion and an obsessive feature of their military and civic life. Yet we find, too, in baffling juxtaposition, admirable qualities of civilised living, morality and artistic refinement. Poetry in the Nahuatl language, now rendered more accessible through the labours of scholars such as Angel María Garibay, reveals an unexpected nobility of thought and delicacy of feeling. In verse where the accents of Omar Khayyam blend with those of the *Waste Land*, the poet-king Nezahualcoyotl laments the transitoriness and futility of life, from which the gods seem to have turned away their faces; 'the jade is shattered, the quetzal-plume rent'. The fate of this city-state, at first reluctantly allied to the Aztecs and then swallowed up by them, may perhaps offer a clue to the Mexican enigma. Starting as a primitive warrior tribe, the Aztecs imposed their rule on the higher Toltec culture, based probably on Teotihuacán, whose imposing ruins stand some thirty miles from Mexico City, in part assimilating it and in part perverting it to serve their own power politics. They enthroned their war-god Huiztilopochtli by the side of the beneficent plumed serpent Quetzalcoátl and the other gods of the Toltec pantheon. Holding that it was only by the constant offering up of human hearts that disaster could be averted and the sun sustained in the heavens, the Aztecs claimed for themselves the mission of providing the divine nourishment through a ceaseless toll of captives. This horrific vision of the world eclipsed, if it never entirely extinguished, the more civilised values of an earlier age.

The Incas, like the Aztecs, were a race of warriors and sun-worshippers. They too had risen to power on the ruins of older civilisations whose matchless textiles and pottery testify to the degree of culture they had attained. The Incas' genius was primarily for social organisation. Under their ordered but rigid government, sometimes inaccurately described as 'socialist', each man contributed and received his allotted share. Their empire was bound together by an admirable network of roads, the mnemonic device of *quipus* or knotted strings for purposes of record and communication, and by the use of Quechua as a *lingua franca*. This language was an expressive medium for poetry, much of which—including moving invocations to Viracocha, the Supreme Being— has come down to us. It is probable that some form of drama was also cultivated. One example, though only in an 18th-century version which seems to bear traces of Spanish influence, is the drama *Ollontay*. This is the story of an Indian warrior who falls in love with an Inca princess, raises a rebellion, is defeated and finally pardoned by the magnanimous Inca. The romantic tale is diversified by humorous passages, by verses of a rare lyrical quality, and by exotic touches such as a scene in the Temple of the Virgins and a love message sent by *quipu*.

INDIANS AND SPANIARDS

Another Quechuan drama, written not long after the Spanish conquest, recently came to light in Bolivia. The *Death of Atahualpa*, though lacking the literary qualities of *Ollontay*, is interesting for the light it throws on the Indians' attitude to their conquerors. It ends by showing Pizarro, the murderer of the Inca, at the court of the king of Spain, where he falls dead at his master's rebuke. Wretched as was their lot after the Conquista, the Indians could at least look to protection to two institutions, the church and the crown. The latter, to the chagrin of the more rapacious conquistadores, ruled at the outset that the natives were to be treated as subjects rather than slaves, and the great body of legislation known as the Laws of the Indies is evidence of the crown's earnest desire to protect them from injustice and exploitation. The Indians, despite the abuses suffered at the hands of their masters, were aware of this. One of the most remarkable works to reach us from the early colonial period is an account written by a full-blooded Indian, Huamán Poma de Ayala, describing the traditional way of life of his people

753

and their sufferings under Spanish misgovernment. His *Nueva Coronica y Buen Gobierno* is composed in semi-literate Spanish interlarded with Quechua and is illustrated by naive but vivid sketches. The author tells us that it took thirty years to write, and that when it was finished he journeyed to Lima and presented it to the royal officials with the request that it be sent to the king.

The church was the other institution which offered the Indian protection and status, albeit that of ward rather than adult, in the alien order introduced by the Spaniards. The Indians' tragedy was that they had not only lost their rulers, the Incas, by the Conquista; their very gods had failed them. But the church stepped in with a new faith. Bartolomé de las Casas is but one of the many friars who spent their lives heroically teaching, evangelising, and defending the natives. If the sacred books were often consigned to the flames as manifestations of witchcraft, there were also enlightened priests like Bernardino de Sahagún whose monumental *Historia General de las Cosas de Nueva España*, written in the 16th century, is an incomparable source for our knowledge of Mexican antiquity and the cornerstone of ethnological studies. As time went on, the church became increasingly identified with the interests of the landowning class, but it had done much, in its first missionary impetus, to bridge the gap between conquerors and conquered. Though the Spaniards might hold the Aztec gods as no more than devils to be destroyed, and their abhorrent rites to be rooted out, in Peru the confrontation of the two faiths did not appear so irreconcilable. There the worship of Viracocha seemed almost to foreshadow that of the true God. The churches which were built on the site of Incaic temples were beautified by native craftsmen, and the old songs could be heard in them sung to new Christian words. The Indians took part in the plays and pageants staged for the inculcation of Christian dogma, and some of these were even composed in Quechua or Aymara by mestizo authors.

The fusion of Indian and Spanish achieves its fullest literary expression in the Inca writer Garcilaso de la Vega's *Comentarios Reales*, written towards the end of the 16th century. 'Feeling myself under obligation to two races, since I am the son of a Spanish father and an Indian mother', relates the author, he composed his work 'not only for the honour and renown of the Spanish nation which has accomplished such great things in the New World, but no less for that of the Indians...for they too appear worthy of the same praise'. His books give a fascinating account of 'the origins of the Inca kings, their ancient customs, their idolatry and conquest, their laws and order of government both in peace and war'. Mellowed by time and distance, Garcilaso's scenes are evoked with poetic melancholy, and his Indians idealised into the prototype of what a later generation was to hail as the noble savage. Yet his account was a sufficiently authentic expression of the Indian genius to cause the authorities to ban its reading, together with performances of the Quechuan drama *Ollontay*, as likely to promote national-ist feeling amongst the natives, after the latter had risen in revolt towards the end of the 18th century.

In the wars of independence against Spain which followed a few decades later, the Indians failed to take up any united stand. Some served with the insurgents, others in the royalist ranks. They had little hope that 'indepen-dence' would improve their lot or restore their ancient glories. Some creole leaders paid occasional lip-service to such ideals—Miranda even placed before Pitt an exotic scheme for a South American parliament under a constitutional Inca monarchy—and the idealists who framed the constitutions of the new republics thought justice could be done to the Indians by simply decreeing the legal equality of all citizens. But these expectations proved illusory. The native peon remained as subordinate as ever to his *patrón* or master, who found himself freer to increase his lands at the expense of the Indian *comunidad* now that the protective status previously accorded the latter had been abolished as discriminatory. The Indian himself showed disappointingly little wish or capacity to 'better himself'. He seemed to remain, as described by the Bolivian poet Tamayo, 'a soul turned in upon himself'. The belief gained ground that, though individual Indians might be redeemed by simply ceasing to be Indians, the race itself did not deserve to survive. 'The Indian is useless', declared Gabriel René Moreno, a representative of this extreme view, in the 19th century, 'but by some monstrous deformity he is indeed a living force in Bolivia—a passive, inert mass, a stone blocking the viscera of the social organism. Let the Indian and the mestizo vanish as soon as possible; let them be stamped out by European immigration'.

THE MEXICAN REVOLUTION

But the Indian did not vanish. Only in Argentina was the scanty native population virtually wiped out and replaced by European immigration. Elsewhere, the Indians continued to demonstrate their tenacious capacity for survival if not for 'progress'. But they had to wait for a century after the winning of independence from Spain before a serious attempt was made to make good the watchword of the present Mexican Indian Institute that 'to redeem the Indian is to integrate the nation'. At its outset, the Mexican revolution had not been inspired by any particular concern for Indian rights. But as the tide of revolution rose, the peasants, Indian or near-Indian for the most part, succeeded in occupying the great estates belonging to their white or mestizo masters. The triumph of the revolution, which began in 1910, was hailed as the end of four centuries of alien domination. The rejection of the colonial past, and also of much of the ensuing century of oligarchic rule and foreign influence, led to a corresponding exaltation of Mexico's pre-Columbian heritage. It found spectacular expression in the work of the great muralists headed by Rivera, Orozco and Siqueiros, whose glorification of the Indian past is proclaimed from the walls of so many of Mexico's public buildings. Not Cortés the Conquistador, but Cuauhtémoc, his victim and the last of the Aztec princes, became the symbol of the nation. No country in the world has built a more splendid monument to its past glories than the great National Museum of Anthropology in which the history, life and art of the ancient inhabitants of Mexico are superbly commemorated.

Yet despite such tribute to the Indian heritage, the practical rehabilitation of the Mexican Indian remains incomplete. A great drive for educational advance and national integration was made in the early years of the revolution, but there are still today Indian communities living in poverty and isolation. The legacy of exploitation on the one side, and of distrust on the other, cannot be easily overcome.

THE INDIANIST NOVEL

Even before this refurbishing of the Amerindian image by the Mexican revolution, a certain current of thought, mainly literary and romantic, had called in question the assumption of white superiority. Garcilaso's idealised picture of the Incas, and the cult of the noble savage made fashionable by

Rousseau, Marmontel, Bernardin de Saint Pierre and Chateaubriand stimulated novels extolling the Indian past and idealising the Indians of today. The authors showed little concern with models they might have found living under their noses. One of the most famous of these tales, Manuel Galván's *Enriquillo* (1878) was written on the island of Santo Domingo, where the Indians had long been extinct. Brazilian writers, as in José de Alencar's popular *O Guarani* (1857), a tale of romantic love between an Indian brave and a white maiden, gave a similarly idealised picture, though the Indians had little ethnic or cultural importance in Brazil. But these romantic novels sometimes contained a note of social protest which in time swelled to a chorus that has both typified and influenced much Latin American thinking about the Indians. Three outstanding examples of such novels may be briefly considered here.

The Indians depicted in *Raza de Bronce* (1919) by the Bolivian historian and man of letters Alcides Arguedas are no noble savages dreaming of the glories of the Incas. They are ignorant peons toiling on a great estate under conditions of such brutality that they are at last driven to revolt. Two characters in the book discuss whether education offers the native race any hope of salvation. 'The day when the Indian gets a schoolmaster', asserts the *patrón*, 'life will become impossible for us. Woe the day when these two million Indians learn to read, handle the law-books, edit newspapers. They will do away with our estates and become the masters'. The Indians too discuss the matter, and their innate distrust of their white masters leads one of them to observe: 'There must be some foul poison about letters, for whenever one of us learns to read, he turns against his own flesh and blood and uses his knowledge to exploit us too'. The Indians here acknowledge the old thesis that they can win a decent place in society only at the cost of ceasing to be Indians, and indeed of ranging themselves against their own kith and kin. A more favourable, if perhaps somewhat idealised, picture of the Indians is given in the Peruvian Ciro Alegría's novel *El Mundo es Ancho y Ajeno* (1941). This relates the destruction of an Indian community at the hands of a grasping landowner and a crafty lawyer. Some Indians, in desperation, turn bandits, others perish as rubber-gatherers in the jungle. When the remainder attempt to rebuild what is left of their community elsewhere, they are hounded to their death by the rapacious and vengeful landowner. Their only memorial is the example of their fortitude, dignity and humanity, which the author believes must hold the ultimate salvation of their race. In *Huasipungo* (1934), the Ecuadorean Jorge Icaza also describes the destruction of an Indian community. Here the landlord sells his land to a foreign company who wish to set up a timber mill. The Indians are first made to build a road, then, no longer needed, are driven from the land and destroyed. The villains of this dark story are the landowner, the political boss, the priest and the foreign capitalist. If they seem to belong to a world of crude political propaganda rather than of literature, we need only turn to the columns of the newspapers to find similar cases of Indian misery and violence from real life.

Towards an Indian resurgence?

Whilst these attempts were being made to explore and interpret South America's Indian heritage in terms of literature, political writers and organisers were beginning to consider what practical implications might follow. We have noted that it was generally assumed that the Indian could find salvation only through assimilation. But from the beginning of the present century a new and sometimes more militant note has made itself heard. 'The condition of the Indian can be improved in two ways', wrote the Peruvian Manuel González Prada in 1900: 'Either the heart of the oppressor is softened to the point of recognising the rights of the oppressed, or else the oppressed should become stout-hearted enough to turn against the oppressors'. Since history has shown few signs of the former phenomenon, he deduced that 'the Indian should not be exhorted to humility, but rather to pride and rebellion'.

González Prada was a prophet rather than a political organiser. It was left to his compatriot, José Carlos Mariátegui, to work out the implications of his revolutionary exhortations. Mariátegui is one of the few Latin American writers ever to have attempted an original analysis of his country's problems in Marxist terms. He died young in 1930, after founding a group which became the Peruvian Communist Party. His writings were branded for a time by the party pundits as Populist, and though his literary reputation now stands so high that more than one revolutionary group eagerly claims to inherit his ideas, there is much in the latter which today commands fairly general assent. In his *Siete Ensayos* (1928) he described Peru as 'a country where natives and conquistadores still go on living cheek by jowl, without intermingling, without understanding each other'. He analysed the power structure which bolstered the landowning oligarchy; the judiciary, the legislature, the police and the army. Education too, since it was controlled by the *patrón*, he thought unlikely ever to become a means for the Indians' regeneration.

Mariátegui argued that the only solution for the Indians was to cut at the basis of the oligarchy's power—the ownership of land. He advocated an agrarian reform based on the native *ayllus*, the surviving native communities where 'there still persist robust and tenacious habits of cooperation and solidarity which are the empirical expression of a Communist spirit'. Quoting examples of Indian communities which had successfully adopted new techniques and so given the lie to allegations of their congenital inferiority, he concluded that the *ayllus* should become the cornerstone for radical social change 'not on abstract principles of justice nor for sentimental traditional reasons, but on sound practical and economic grounds'.

There has in fact been growing recognition that the state needs somehow to take more account of the Indians' instinct for communal action. Haya de la Torre, founder of Peru's powerful Apra movement, expressed views originally similar to those of Mariátegui and attempted to give currency to the term 'Indo-America' as an alternative to 'Latin America'. Fernando Belaúnde, before being elected president of the Republic, developed his ideas in a book significantly entitled *The Conquest of Peru by the Peruvians*. His thesis was that the country must look for inspiration to its pre-Columbian past, rediscovering and applying in a modern context the Incas' genius for planning and their concern with communications, and the Indians' tradition of voluntary work for such local projects as irrigation schemes and the building of hospitals and clinics. This view has found a response amongst the students and young people of the towns who, by voluntarily cooperating in such projects, have begun to learn for themselves how the Indians live and think.

But it has been in Bolivia, not Peru, that the Indians of South America have shown the most promising signs of entering at last into their political inheritance. The Chaco War had uprooted tens of thousands of Bolivian Indians and given them a common baptism of suffering and a new awareness of their solidarity as citizens. When in 1952 the miners and radical intelligentsia of the towns rose in the resolve to put an end to the old social order, the Indians began their revolution too. They invaded and took over the large estates, sometimes peacefully, sometimes with the sort of violence described by Arguedas in his *Raza de Bronce*. The government, deeming it prudent to control and legalise this process, made the land over to the Indians by enacting an Agrarian Reform Law, and also recognised their full status as citizens by giving the Indians the vote. Since then, the country's whole political and social structure has been gradually transformed. The process has not been uniform nor its outcome invariably successful; there are areas where the Indians still seem sunk in apathy and backwardness, but others where they have made notable progress. 'Bolivia is at present in the process of becoming an Indian nation, or a modern nation that is predominantly Indian in culture', wrote the American anthropologist John F. Goins in 1960, giving impressive instances of the Indian's capacity to absorb new ideas while preserving his own.

How far is this re-emphasis of Indian values in Bolivia, and the awakening of interest in Indian affairs in Peru, leading towards what some enthusiasts already describe as a Quechua renaissance? Certainly the Quechuan language seems to be held in honour as never before—though some Indians prefer their children to be taught Spanish at school and look upon instruction in Quechua as a device to perpetuate their inferior status—and its written form is being enriched both by original compositions, mostly in the form of poems and short stories, and by translations of classics (e.g. Garcilaso's *Comentarios Reales*) into Quechua. Important political results might in time conceivably follow this stirring of what could almost be called 'pan-Quechuan' sentiment. But the Andean Indian has always been inscrutable, and if he cherishes any secret aspirations, he is unlikely to divulge them to the non-Indian.

BIBLIOGRAPHY

Alegría, Ciro. *Broad and Alien is the World*, Farrar and Rinehart, New York, 1941; Nicholson and Watson, London, 1942.

Baudin, Louis. *Daily Life in Peru under the Last Incas*, Allen and Unwin, London, 1961; Macmillan, New York, 1962.

Clissold, Stephen. *Latin America. A Cultural Outline*, Hutchinson, London, 1965.

Gann, Thomas W. F., and Thompson, J. E. *The History of the Maya*, Scribner, New York and London, 1931.

Garcilaso de la Vega, el Inca. *The Incas. The Royal Commentaries*, Orion Press, New York, 1961; Cassell, London, 1963.

Icaza, Jorge. *Huasipungo*, Dobson, London, 1962.

León Portilla, Miguel. *Aztec Thought and Culture*, Univ. of Oklahoma Press, Norman, Okla., 1963.

López y Fuentes, Gregorio. *El Indio*, Bobbs Merrill, Indianapolis, 1937; issued in England as *They That Reap*, Harrap, London, 1937.

Mason, J. Alden. *The Ancient Civilisations of Peru*, Penguin, Harmondsworth, 1957.

Nicholson, Irene. *Firefly in the Night. A Study of Ancient Mexican Poetry and Symbolism*, Faber and Faber, London; Grove Press, New York, 1959.

Popol Vuh. The Sacred Book of the Ancient Quiché Maya, Univ. of Oklahoma Press, Norman Okla., 1950; Hodge, London, 1951.

Séjourné, Laurette. *Burning Water. Thought and Religion in Ancient Mexico*, Thames and Hudson, London, 1957.

THE IBEROAMERICAN HERITAGE

RAÚL SILVA CASTRO

IT IS a semantic phenomenon not without importance that outside the
southern part of the American continent the term *Latin America* is applied to
the group of nations stretching from Mexico in the north to Argentina and
Chile in the south. This term is not, however, universally accepted in these
countries. The terms *Iberoamerica* or *Hispanic America* are preferred, because
the word *Latin* is vague and misleading. In this essay the term Iberoamerica
will be used for what is known in Europe and elsewhere as Latin America.

THE LINGUISTIC FOUNDATIONS

Two European languages are spoken in this part of the world, Spanish and
Portuguese, and to these French might be added; the latter, however, is
less widespread, being spoken only in Haiti. French has nevertheless made a
great contribution by serving for many years as a cultural lingua franca
used in translations, so that influential books written in German, English,
Russian and other languages had to be translated into French before being
accepted by the most discriminating readers. This combination of Spanish
or Portuguese with French is still fundamental to the cultural life of Iberoamerica, into which, it may be said in passing, English has only recently
begun to penetrate.

It may be said that Spanish and Portuguese are languages alien to the
most profound demographic strata of the New World countries, since the
real native languages are the Amerindian. But this assertion is really only
true in a relative sense, since several countries of the New World contain
only tiny remnants of the ancient aboriginal peoples. In Chile, for instance,
although Spanish is the common language of nearly eight million people,
the aboriginal language (Araucanian or Mapuche) is known and used by
barely half a million. It would be illogical to propose that the language of
this minority should be imposed by force on the majority, merely because in
a particular period in history, that is to say before the invasion by Pedro de
Valdivia and his followers, the Indians were the only inhabitants of Chile.
We must accept the fact that the great cultural invasion that took place after
the discovery of America produced certain effects which continued to be
felt during the succeeding centuries and were amplified and extended in
every imaginable way, and that this phenomenon has determined the use of
the Spanish and Portuguese languages as irrevocably as if they had been
created on the American side of the Atlantic.

A language is not merely a system of phonetic articulations, but forms the
basis of an entire cultural world. The cultures that exist today and make
their influence felt in the Iberoamerican countries of the New World were

originally inevitably a continuation of Spanish and Portuguese culture, just as in the United States the pattern was England. Yet if we consider the present situation, we shall soon see that this is no longer true. It is true that Spanish is still spoken in Mexico City, Santiago, Lima and Buenos Aires, and Portuguese is spoken in Rio de Janeiro; but the cultural pattern of the new countries no longer reflects that which one finds in the capitals of the old empires. What has happened? We do not know.

SPAIN AND PORTUGAL AND THE NEW WORLD

A working hypothesis might be constructed on an analogy: children draw apart from their parents, renounce them, refuse their assistance, misunderstand them and disparage them. Not all children, it is true, but certainly a considerable number of them, to such an extent that to the psychologist antipathy between two contiguous generations appears normal. From this it might be concluded that the countries of the New World, when they left the tutelage of the old metropolitan countries, adopted the fundamental behaviour-pattern of the child: to oppose its father and mother even when it owes much to them. Spain was accused of errors, malicious destruction, lack of understanding, iniquities, atrocities, in history books and many other places, and attempts were made to deny her influence in all the spheres where she was still preeminent—in literature, for instance, where she did not need to make any effort at penetration because this had already been achieved. Now it is worth noting that these diatribes filled with hatred and abuse, in which outstanding minds competed, were conceived, written and published in—the Spanish language.

After the independence movements early in the 19th century, the American nations of Spanish and Portuguese origin tried to develop their lives while keeping their backs turned on their former mother-countries. With this end in view, and since they were incapable of inventing anything themselves, they resolved to copy what seemed best to them. State education was generally modelled on French lines, to such an extent that in many areas the term *liceo* is universally used to designate the type of school known in Spain as an *instituto*, simply and solely because such schools were and are called *lycées* in France. If the model chosen had been Germany, they would have been called *gimnasios*. Military organisation, at first imitated from French models, was later copied exactly from Germany, principally because Germany was the power that defeated France in the war of 1870. Physics and biology, and the techniques of agriculture and the professions and trades, were usually studied in French textbooks. From this source, among others, stems the agrarian ideal of the smallholding, which may be useful and advantageous in France for a multitude of reasons, but in the countries of the New World faces overwhelming obstacles, not the least of which are the size of the territory involved and the consequent lack of roads.

Wherever one looks, one sees that in the New World everything is copied, reproduced, imitated; and to such an extent that an irreverent and caustic Spanish writer, Pío Baroja, went so far as to describe Iberoamericans as 'ape-like'. Possibly imitation—which is anyway an inevitable principle of civilisation—is particularly evident in America because it is concentrated into a few centuries and in so clearly defined a geographical area.

IBEROAMERICAN CULTURE

The earliest writers in the Iberoamerican countries were of Spanish nationality, and some of them lived in America only for a short time. An outstanding example is Alonso de Ercilla (1533–96), the author of *La Araucana*, an epic description of the struggle between the Spaniards and the Chilean Indians, who resisted invasion with such success that more than once the armies of Spain were forced to admit defeat. Ercilla spent only a few years in Chile and Peru and then returned to Spain, where he published his only important work after devoting no less than thirty years of his life to its conception, development, publication and revision.

It might be supposed that the transition to a more American literature, at least in the sense that it is the product of American minds, has been smooth and almost imperceptible. This is true, but if we consider the literature of the different countries of Iberoamerica throughout their development, it is easy to observe the process of differentiation; so pronounced is this that it would now be very difficult to confuse an Iberoamerican writer using the Spanish language with a writer of Spanish nationality. This is not merely a question of geographical nomenclature (Mexico, Peru, Buenos Aires, etc.), but also of more profound and substantial factors. In short, it can be said that a new mentality is being formed, and with it an Iberoamerican sensibility that strives for literary self-expression that must inevitably change the mother-language. Since the coming of independence to most of the subcontinent in the first third of the 19th century there have been two sharply differentiated worlds on the shores of the Atlantic, two worlds which have developed along parallel lines and can never again be confused, just as the embryo enclosed in the mother's womb cannot be divided again into the two elements that gave it life.

In the fields of science and the arts something new is every day added to the stock of specifically Hispanic American cultural manifestations, the creators of which have made a conscious effort to emancipate themselves from European models. Iberoamericans are still copying, as Baroja said, but they are also, little by little, becoming different. One of the possibilities open to them is that of creating autocthonous traditions among cultural groups that still lack them. Artists from the Iberoamerican countries go to Europe to study their respective fields of interest, and in recent years they have also been going to the United States, where they find an atmosphere that is stimulating, agreeable and full of opportunities. There may come a day when they have no further need to make these journeys, when they find in their own countries the cultural nourishment needed for their development.

It has sometimes been thought that tradition must necessarily be found among the traces of Iberoamerica's aboriginal past, and certain outstanding artists have followed this path. But the artist is still copying or imitating unless he is himself the descendant of the old Indian tribes or clans, which in some nations of the New World have been completely exterminated. And here it is worth pointing out that such extermination does not always take the form of complete physical annihilation, for there remain numerically considerable masses of people of aboriginal American descent. It is rather a question of the Indians' loss of confidence in their own survival as an ethnic entity, of faith in an ideal that was suppressed when the first Europeans set foot on the continent, and which it was later impossible to restore or recuperate. In such circumstances, where there is no inherent capacity for development, 'copying' is inevitable.

LANGUAGE AND RELIGION

If it is asked what in particular the Iberoamerican cultural world owes to Spain and Portugal the reply is: its language and its religion. Andrés Bello affirmed that the Spanish language, spoken in common by the Hispanic American countries, was a heaven-sent means of intercommunication and, in consequence, must not be destroyed by fragmentation. To prevent this happening, he compiled an entire grammar of the language, a work that still occupies a distinguished place among the products of the Iberoamerican intellect. Moreover, the language is now being enriched by Iberoamerican contributions as well as by Spanish; it grows and flourishes as the number of cultured people who use it to express themselves increases. The possibility of disintegration or fragmentation, which undoubtedly existed in Bello's time, is now remote. The network of communications covering the world, fostered by the thirst for knowledge that characterises the masses of the present day, who have the cinema, the radio and television at their disposal, has now made impossible any fragmentation of the kind that was once feared. The development of a local language—be it Argentine, Mexican, Chilean or Peruvian—even though based on Spanish, would bring about the immediate isolation of the country where the linguistic fragmentation had taken place.

In the years following the discovery and conquest, any alternative to the absolute hegemony of the Catholic Church over the nations of the New World was inconceivable. Nowadays there are Protestant churches, catering for a small number of denominations, and also synagogues and places of worship for other confessions. There is religious tolerance and there is atheism. But religion in general, and Roman Catholicism in particular, continues to influence the conduct of all Iberoamericans.

In religion, in contrast to what happened in the case of language, no modification has taken place. Faith is more uniform than speech. Adopting Pío Baroja's terminology we may say that, if the Iberoamerican is guilty of 'ape-like' behaviour, he shows this more than anywhere else in his religion, in which he meticulously follows directives from the headquarters of his particular faith, be it Rome, the synagogue or the mosque.

Nowadays it is evident that it is not only the Iberoamericans who have been 'ape-like', for all peoples have copied something from somebody, at some stage in their historical existence. It is also obvious that imitation to a limited degree is a fundamental biological principle, without which the entire structure of human relationships collapses. How foolish if, simply in order not to repeat the actions of those who invented and used the wheel, the wheel were jettisoned and an alternative sought.

BIBLIOGRAPHY

Haring, Clarence Henry. *The Spanish Empire in America*, Oxford Univ. Press, London and New York, revised ed. 1952.

Kirkpatrick, F. A. *The Spanish Conquistadores*, A. and C. Black, 2nd ed. 1963.

de Madariaga, Salvador. *The Rise of the Spanish Empire*, Hollis and Carter, London, 1947. *The Fall of the Spanish Empire*, Hollis and Carter, London, 1947. *Latin America Between the Eagle and the Bear*, Hollis and Carter, London, 1962.

CONTEMPORARY ARTS

THE SPANISH AMERICAN NOVEL

JEAN FRANCO

THE Spanish American novel began to attract international attention in the 1920s with the emergence of a number of regionalist novelists such as the Argentine Ricardo Güiraldes (1886–1927) and the Venezuelan Rómulo Gallegos (b. 1889) who charted unrecorded aspects of American experience, being especially interested in man's struggle against nature. Following in their tracks came a vast number of realistic novels in the 1930s and 1940s, novels which often had a strong social message and usually registered protest against prevailing injustices. The writer became the voice of the mute illiterate masses. The Peruvian Ciro Alegría (1909–67) in *El mundo es ancho y ajeno*, 1941 (*Broad and Alien is the World*),[1] and the Ecuadorean Jorge Icaza (b. 1906) in *Huasipungo*, 1934 wrote powerful novels of protest against the exploitation of the Andean Indians. Realistic novels on social themes predominated in Mexico where Mariano Azuela (1873–1952) had initiated the 'novel of the Revolution' as early as 1916 with his *Los de abajo* (*The Underdogs*), in Chile with the novels of Juan Marín (b. 1900), in Uruguay with those of Enrique Amorim (1900–60), and especially in Ecuador where a group of realistic writers from Guayaquil—among them Demetrio Aguilera Malta (b. 1909) and Alfredo Pareja Diez Canseco (b. 1908) wrote about the coastal regions of their country.

In the 1940s a number of novels made a significant break with realism and explored a variety of new techniques. The pioneers in this were the Argentine Leopoldo Marechal (b. 1898) whose *Adán Buenosayres*, 1948 presented a *Ulysses*-like vision of Buenos Aires; José Revueltas (b. 1914) whose *El luto humano*, 1943 used the stream of consciousness technique in order to tell the story of a group of Mexican peasants trapped by floods; and Miguel Angel Asturias (b. 1899), a Guatemalan writer whose *El Señor Presidente*, 1945 (*The President*), drew a savage picture of dictatorship using an expressionistic technique which revealed the effects of oppression on the personality. Since these novels were written, the exploration of new techniques has been carried much further in a vast number of works which fuse the social concern of previous generations with an aesthetic interest in the chosen form.

The abandonment of social realism opened a poetic world of myth and fantasy. Asturias, for instance, followed his *El Señor Presidente* with *Hombres de maíz*, 1949 which combined a social theme—the exploitation of the Indian over a long historical period—with a myth-like presentation of his material. The rules of ordinary life are suspended in this novel in which an Indian chief becomes a legendary phantom, in which a postman changes into a coyote. But these myths are also significant comments on the national

[1] English titles are those of published translations.

situation. Thus when the woman María Tecún runs away from her blind Indian husband, she becomes the symbol of the loss and separation suffered by the Guatemalan Indian communities after the conquest. Many of Asturias's subsequent novels such as the 'banana plantation' trilogy—*Viente fuerte*, 1950 (*The Cyclone*), *El Papa verde*, and *Weekend en Guatemala*, 1955 continue to use this technique of myth (or 'magic realism' as the author calls it) while having a strong element of social protest.

The poetic quality of Asturias's writing is a feature of many other contemporary novelists. As in poetry, their work is built on a series of metaphors. The Paraguayan novelist Augusto Roa Bastos (b. 1917) presents in his *Hijo de hombre*, 1959 (*Son of Man*) a vast canvas of Paraguayan history from the 19th century to the present. The unity is provided by the image of a crucified Christ which overlooks the village where the action is set and which symbolises the spirit of revolt of succeeding generations of Paraguayans. A novel like *Hijo de hombre* is perhaps nearer to epic than to the 19th-century bourgeois novel. This is also true of two novels by the Peruvian José María Arguedas (b. 1911), *Todas las sangres*, 1954 and *Los ríos profundos*, 1958. The author, though of Spanish descent, was brought up in Indian villages in the mountain regions of Peru. He draws on Indian myth, folk-lore and song in his novels not as mere illustration but as the core of his main theme—the authenticity of the Indian culture in Peru compared with the artificiality of white civilisation.

From these few examples it will be appreciated that the contemporary Spanish American novelist works on an ambitious scale, often aiming at nothing less than interpretation of national reality. At the same time he wants to address himself to an audience wider than the merely national. Hence he must present his material so that it can be universally understood; this means finding an 'objective correlative' for national problems. In the following paragraphs an attempt has been made to show how the structures and character relationships of contemporary novels reflect writers' national preoccupations.

The Novel and History

For many contemporary novelists the key to the present lies in understanding the past and many novels written over the last decades are either set in a significant historical period or, if set in the present, take the reader back into the past through a series of flashbacks. The Venezuelan novelist Miguel Otero Silva (b. 1908), for instance, described the death of an old colonial town in *Casas muertas*, 1955 and the rise of a brash new oil city in *Oficina número 1*, 1961, thus encompassing the two main stages in the growth of modern Venezuela. In *Al filo del agua*, 1947 (*The Edge of the Storm*) the Mexican Agustín Yañez conveyed the parched anguish of a church-dominated Mexican town on the eve of the Revolution. He has since written a series of novels covering aspects of Mexican society both before and after the Revolution.

One of the most talented writers to have turned to historical themes is Alejo Carpentier (b. 1904) who began his artistic career as a musician in Cuba, and who now writes in baroque style which, he claims, is the appropriate style for a novelist of the tropics. His first major novel was *El reine de este mundo*, 1949 (*The Kingdom of this World*), a violent, nightmarish work about uprisings of Haitian slaves, closely allied in technique to the novels of Roa Bastos and Miguel Angel Asturias. This was followed by *Los pasos perdidos*, 1953 (*The Lost Steps*) which recorded a journey up the Orinoco.

Though set in the present, the journey is also a retracing of the 'lost steps' leading to the origin of American civilisation.

In *El siglo de las luces* (*Explosion in a Cathedral*) Carpentier plunges deeply into a significant period of Caribbean history. The central character, Victor Hugues, an idealist revolutionary who becomes a cynical dictator in Guiana, is based on a historical character whose career typifies the early history of all the newly independent Spanish American republics and their speedy fall from idealism to authoritarian government.

The choice of a central character who is also symbolic of a historical period or of a national type is a common recourse of contemporary Latin American writing. Two Mexican novels of the last decade, for instance, *Pedro Páramo* by Juan Rulfo (b. 1918) and *La muerte de Artemio Cruz* by Carlos Fuentes (b. 1929) have eponymous protagonists who symbolise significant aspects of Mexican experience. The very name Pedro Páramo is symbolic, for *páramo* means 'wasteland' and refers both to the barren region in which the novel is set and also to the sterility of the pre-revolutionary period of landlords and latifundia. Pedro Páramo, a vigorous, lusty and cruel landowner, had lorded over an entire region. His story is narrated by a young man, one of his sons, who returns to the village in order to seek the man who had fathered him. When he arrives, the narrator finds that Páramo and all the other villagers are dead and all that remains of them are dreams, memories and legend in the form of the conversations of the dead which linger in the air. Few contemporary novels have shown with greater subtlety man's relationship with the past. The narrator, like the whole of Mexico, is an offspring of a cacique-dominated past which ended with the Revolution; the dreams and memories that he evokes revive this past but in a softened form so that the harsh contours of reality are blurred.

Carlos Fuentes' *La muerte de Artemio Cruz* chronicles the death-bed thoughts of a man who has fought in the Mexican Revolution, and who has prospered because of his betrayal of his revolutionary ideals. But Artemio Cruz is not only the symbol of the post-revolutionary epoch but also embodies that weakness of the Mexican character, that need to exploit or 'rape' in order to avoid being exploited that has been commented on by many thinkers from Samuel Ramos (1897–1959) to Octavio Paz. Carlos Fuentes thus not only shows us a historical period in Artemio Cruz but through him also criticises its failures. An earlier novel by Fuentes, *Las buenas conciencias*, 1959 (*Clear Consciences*) gives a direct vision of the past through the growth to manhood (and corruption) of the central character in the period just before and after the Mexican Revolution. His first novel, *La región más transparente*, 1958 (*Where the Air is Clearer*), though set in the present, presents the past of a vast spectrum of Mexico City characters and the moment when their adult corruption and betrayal begins.

THE CLASH OF GENERATIONS

In many recent Spanish American novels the writer looks back on the past with loathing rather than affection. A symbol of this loathing is the father figure who is either ritually killed or threatened with death; an example is Alejandra's murder of her father in *Sobre héroes y tumbas* by Ernesto Sábato (b. 1911) and her suicide in the purifying flames of the fire which burns her house; Alejandra is the youngest member of a once heroic and now decadent Argentinian family, and her father is mad and corrupt. Many novels set in the present day attack the corruption of their country through a clash of generations in which the young are usually pure and honest whilst the old are corrupt, dogmatic or life-denying. In *Gracias por el fuego* Mario Benedetti describes a man's revolt against the dominating influence of his father, a millionaire who is both ruthless in his private life and who also represents the national corruption which is stifling the country. The son is caught between the sheer dishonesty and hyprocrisy of the older generation and the dogmatic rebellion of his own left-wing son. His attempt to kill his father and hence to liberate himself and his country fails and he kills himself instead. In *La muerte de Artemio Cruz*, Artemio's corruption is contrasted to the integrity of his son who dies fighting in the Spanish Civil War. In *El paredón* by the Uruguayan Carlos Martínez Moreno (b. 1917) the father-and-son relationship is friendly but they find mutual communication difficult. The two generations are inseparably divided in outlook and beliefs. The father is a product of a generation which has put its faith in liberal democracy and, despite disillusionments, still clings to a liberal outlook. The son, who inhabits an ideological wilderness, finds in Cuba the energy and purpose which are lacking in his own country.

The most sensitive and original treatment of the theme of the clash of generations is in a Chilean novel, *El peso de la noche* by Jorge Edwards (b. 1931). Three generations of an old Santiago upper-class family live side by side yet inhabit different worlds cut off from one another by age and time. Señora Cristina, whose illness and death overshadow the novel, represents the dying generation with its rigid structures and traditional faith. Joaquín, one of her sons, has broken away from the traditional structure without being able to find a satisfactory alternative; unable to form any real relationship, he is slowly destroying himself by drink. When Cristina dies, Joaquín makes an attempt (probably only partly successful) to re-enter the world of order and convention. Meanwhile a new generation of rebels represented by his adolescent nephew, Francisco, has emerged—a generation which, it is suggested, will make a more authentic and definitive revolt. Without having recourse to the obvious symbolism of many contemporary Spanish American novels, Edwards has achieved a penetrating study of the relationship between the individual and the group.

THE NOVEL AS MICROCOSM

Many contemporary writers have created their own imaginary communities as micro-models of the American tragedy. The Colombian Gabriel García Márquez, for instance, sets all his novels and short stories in the hot and isolated village of Macondo. The Uruguayan Juan Carlos Onetti has created the port-town of Santa María. Frequently in Latin American contemporary novels the setting is a community cut off from the outside world. The closed world they describe may be an isolated village, a boarding school, the building site of *Los albañiles* by the Mexican Vicente Leñero (b. 1933), the ship of Julio Cortázar's *Los premios* or a family circle like that in José Donoso's *Coronación*. In all these novels, the central relationship is that of a community and its special rules and conventions with the outside world. The historical novel uses the clash of different generations to expose the mistakes of the past. In the closed communities of these novels of insulation, the rigid inhuman code of a group within society is exposed through a conflict with human values.

This conflict takes the form, in two Colombian novels, of a just man's unsuccessful attempts to assert human values in the cold war of hate that grips a village community. In *El Cristo de espaldas* by Eduardo Caballero Calderón (b. 1910), the just man is a priest who tries to prevent the summary execution of a suspected murderer who, because he belongs to a defeated political party, is not given the right of a fair trial. In *El coronel no tiene quien le escriba* by Gabriel García Márquez (b. 1928) the just man is an army colonel who, after fighting loyally and honestly for his country, waits twenty years for a pension to arrive. The village where he lives is controlled by the political enemies who have killed his son; starving to death, without money or hope, he withstands all temptation to compromise his principles. The symbol of his pride is a fighting cock which he refuses to sell even though the money would ease his last days. The striking characteristic of both these novels is the way in which hate and violence almost take over the village— a microcosm of Colombia—and hope, if any, is expected only from outside.

The same claustrophobic effect is conveyed by two Peruvian novels set in boarding schools. *La ciudad y los perros* by Mario Vargas Llosa (b. 1936) is set in a military academy where the sons of the Peruvian middle class are sent to be disciplined. The 'dogs' of the title are the cadets, a group of whom form themselves into a circle to resist the bullying of older pupils. The leader of the circle, the 'Jaguar', is himself a born bully who leads his gang in tormenting the 'slave', a cadet who hates fighting. When one of the Jaguar's associates steals the questions to an examination paper, the slave denounces him and is shortly afterwards shot by the Jaguar when they are out on manoeuvres. The officers insist on treating the incident as an accident although the truth is betrayed to them by one of the slave's friends.

The world of the 'dogs' is a sordid world of homosexuality and perversion, of betrayal and torture. The 'city' represents an escape into a more relaxed and feminine world of mothers and girl-friends. But ultimately it is for this world that the college trains the boys and the rot is not only in the military school but in a whole society in which 'being a man' and being loyal to a closed circle is more important than anything else. The two characters of the novel who deny this code assert human values against the 'establishment' code.

In *La ciudad y los perros* (*The Time of the Heroes*) the outer world of the city invades the closed community. In another novel by Vargas Llosa, *La casa verde*, 1967 (*The Green House*) there are two contrasting types of closed community—a convent in the jungle region of Marañón and a brothel in the parched town of Piura. The asceticism of the one struggles against the luxury of the jungle whilst the sensuousness of the other defies the surrounding desert. Between these two extremes Vargas Llosa draws the threads of many lives and journeys, giving his story the mythic quality which is a feature of so much contemporary Spanish American writing. Yet another 'closed community' type of novel is José Donoso's *Coronación*, 1957 (*Coronation*) set in an aristocratic Chilean family for long members of a closed élite. But the family is in decline and the 'coronation' of the dying matriarch at the end of the novel by her servants is the mocking ritual which marks the death of their power.

The Rules of the Game

It is remarkable in how many recent novels there is the element of a game or play. The 'circle' of *La ciudad y los perros*, the 'coronation' of José Donoso's novel in which the old lady is crowned by her drunken maids, even the game-cock of *El coronel no tiene quien le escriba* all raise the game to a serious if not sinister level. The detective story with its strict form provides an ideal method of challenging accepted attitudes, enabling the writer to demonstrate the inadequacy of conventions and hence of facts, rules and artificial structures. Following the example of the Argentine short-story writer Jorge Luis Borges, who often used the detective story to show how facts could be falsified, other writers have also modelled their plots on detective fiction—notably the Mexican Vicente Leñere (b. 1933) and the Argentine Marco Denevi (b. 1922) in *Rosaura a las diez*, 1955.

No-one has gone further in this particular direction than the brilliant Argentinian novelist, Julio Cortázar. In *Los premios* (*The Prizes*) and *Rayuela* (*Hopscotch*), he has constructed vast fictional games which appear in some ways rather like life and the theories we weave about life. In *Los premios* a group of people from Buenos Aires, from all walks of life, receive the lottery prize of a free cruise. They embark and are at once asked to obey a set of rules. They are not allowed to go onto the bridge, nor are they expected to be very curious about their destination. Otherwise they are free to enjoy themselves. Very quickly, the passengers divide into two groups—those who accept the rules and are content to abide by them and those who question the rules and try by every means in their power to get onto the bridge. One of the 'rule-breakers' is killed; the voyage comes to an abrupt end with both groups returning to Buenos Aires where they are absorbed into the city as if nothing has happened. In a witty postscript, Cortázar discourages us from symbol-hunting and claims that the novel is 'a happening' and nothing more. The reader may make his own interpretation of the happening but this will be no more valid than the next man's completely different interpretation. Despite Cortázar's disarming warning, the novel is clearly an analogue of human existence in which man lives with certain limitations. There are those who accept the terms of existence without questioning and those who challenge—but ultimately, it comes to the same thing.

In *Rayuela* (a word which refers to a kind of hopscotch), Cortázar takes his game imagery even further. Here the protagonist, a student called Oliveira, insists on making his own rules in the game of life and refuses to accept the game as played by others; all his actions are therefore spontaneous and arise out of inner necessity. Oliveira and his girl-friend prefer to meet by chance because people who make dates 'are those who need lined paper to write on and who squeeze the toothpaste tube from the bottom'. Oliveira and his friends are continually inventing their own games. Sometimes they concentrate on dragging up from the depths of memory the most insignificant details; at other times they play games with words, and invent systems of communication and meaning. These games stand for the private order which Oliveira and his friends impose in defiance of socially accepted order or the empty formulae and conventions by which most people live. Any game invented on the spur of the moment, the novel implies, is closer to our personal truth than the patterns we derive from established modes and attitudes.

Such a view amounts to the assertion of anarchy and, indeed, many of Cortázar's characters are outsiders from society, bohemian drifters, students, tramps, circus employees, lunatic asylum inmates. The average man or the respectable citizen, if he appears, appears as a target of attack or is parodied. Cortázar's characters, therefore, tend to fall into two groups—those who refuse to live according to convention and are therefore outside society, and those who accept the conventions. The characters of the first type assert personal anarchy in a world whose order appears absurd to them, and this assertion has striking similarities to the attitudes found in some contemporary North American novels. Saul Bellow, for instance, makes a character exclaim 'Society is what beats me. Alone I can be pretty good'; we can be sure that these sentiments would be echoed by many of the characters of *Rayuela*.

THE CITY AND ALIENATION

Of all the forms of social organisation described in the contemporary Spanish American novel, the city offers the most ambiguities. Far from the social censure of village and countryside, the novelist's city characters slip freely from one stratum of society to another, and adventure into dockland, night-time cafés and distant suburbs as if they were no-man's land. Cortázar's characters, for instance, live in the city like vagabonds in the steppe. For the city, paradoxically, offers the greatest freedom as well as the greatest restraint.

Sometimes the tension between the freedom and rootlessness of city-dwellers and the restraining forces of law and order explodes into violence. The Chilean Manuel Rojas (b. 1896) shows this process in *Hijo de Ladrón*, set largely in the port of Valparaíso. The narrator, a young vagabond whose father is in jail and who has wandered across Argentina and Chile, finds himself caught in street-rioting in which the strange fauna of the slums suddenly emerges and bears down with destructive violence on the city centre, wilfully smashing shops and street-cars.

Other writers prefer their city-dwellers in moods of quiet desperation. The truncated and poverty-stricken life, the routine of family and office has been captured by Mario Benedetti. The stories of *Montevideanos* are deliberately low-key, deliberately centred on the 'ordinary' Uruguayan and his minor tragedies. Benedetti shows that the drama of the city is essentially the drama of the rootless; his characters, if they are office-workers, seem to have no families, or if they have families, no relations or neighbours. Each unit seems separate and apart.

In cities like Buenos Aires and Santiago there is a special drama of rootlessness which is the drama of the immigrant. The anguish of the immigrant, and of all city-dwellers, is described by Eduardo Mallea (b. 1903) in *La ciudad junto al río inmóvil* and by the Uruguayan Juan Carlos Onetti (b. 1909) who lived in Buenos Aires for some years. No contemporary Spanish American has captured the fragmented life of the big city better than Onetti in his *Tierra de nadie*. In this novel, as well as in some of his short stories, his themes are moral as much as social, for they concern the nature of the self and the process of alienation. Precisely because the city offers extreme flexibility of relationships, Onetti shows that there are correspondingly greater opportunities for betrayal.

THE NOVEL AND THE PUBLIC

Onetti, Benedetti and many of the other novelists mentioned in this chapter deal with themes familiar to all of us, and their attraction for the European reader has certainly nothing to do with exoticism. Despite this universality, there has never been a generation of writers more firmly rooted in Spanish American experience. Their technique may be non-realistic but there is always great concreteness of detail. The streets of Buenos Aires, of Mexico City, of Santiago are painstakingly named. Vargas Llosa even appends a map to *La ciudad y los perros*. The slang and racy colloquialisms of Argentina and Mexico are faithfully recorded; Cortázar and Vicente Leñero, in particular, have a wonderful ear for the speech rhythms of their countrymen. The contemporary novelist's concern for authenticity has, therefore, borne fruit in the emergence of an unprecedented number of good and perhaps even great novels, which speak directly both to a national and an international public.

Perhaps it is no coincidence that this flowering should have occurred at a period that has also seen the emergence of a novel-reading public in Spanish America. No longer can the writer complain, as Amado Nervo once did, that he writes for other writers. Nowadays, there is an increasing middle class of state employees, intellectuals and technicians who are eager to read novels that reflect their own experience, their concrete situation. More than anything else, it is the presence of this reading public which makes possible the existence of professional writers and hence of novels of today's high standard.

BIBLIOGRAPHY

Alegría, Ciro. *Broad and Alien is the World (El mundo es ancho y ajeno)*, Merlin Press, London, 1962; Signet Classics, New York, 1963 (paperback).
Alegría, Fernando. *Breve historia de la novela hispanoamericana*, Ediciones de Andrea, 2nd ed. 1966. *Novelistas contemporáneos hispanoamericanos*, Heath, Boston, Mass., 1964.
Asturias, Miguel Angel. *The President (El Señor Presidente)*, Gollancz, London, 1963. *The Cyclone (Viento fuerte)*, Peter Owen, London, 1967.
Azuela, Mariano. *The Underdogs (Los de abajo)*, Signet Classics, New York, 1963 (paperback).
Carpentier, Alejo. *The Lost Steps (Los pasos perdidos)*, Gollancz, London, 1956; Alfred A. Knopf, New York, 1965. *Explosion in a Cathedral (El siglo de las luces)*, Compañía General de Ediciones, Mexico, 1962; Gollancz, London, 1963. *The Kingdom of this World (El reino de este mundo)*, Alfred A. Knopf, New York, 1957.
Cohen, J. M. *Writing Today in Latin America*, Penguin, London, 1967.
Cortázar, Julio. *The Winners (Los premios)*, Souvenir Press, London; Pantheon, New York, 1965; *Hopscotch (Rayuela)*, Pantheon, New York, 1966; Collins, London, 1967.
Donoso, José. *Coronation (Coronación)*, Nascimento, Santiago, Chile, 1957; Bodley Head, London; Alfred A. Knopf, New York, 1965.
Fuentes, Carlos. *The Good Consciences (Las buenas conciencias)*, Obolensky, New York, 1961. *Where the Air is Clear (La región más transparente)*, Obolensky, New York, 1960. *The Death of Artemio Cruz (La muerte de Artemio Cruz)*, Collins, London; Farrar, Straus, New York, 1964.
Icaza, Jorge. *Huasipungo (Huasipungo)*, Dobson, London, 1962.
Roa Bastos, Augusto. *Son of Man (Hijo de hombre)*, Gollancz, London, 1965.
Rodríguez Monegal, Emir. *Narradores de esta América*, Alfa, Montevideo. 'The New Novelists', *Encounter*, London, September 1965.
Rojas, Manuel. *Born Guilty (Hijo de ladrón)*, Gollancz, London; Library Publishers, New York, 1955.
Vargas Llosa, Mario. *The Time of the Heroes (La ciudad y los perros)*, Grove Press, New York, 1966; Jonathan Cape, London, 1967. *The Green House (La casa verde)*, Harper and Row, New York, 1967.
Yañez, Agustín. *The Edge of the Storm (Al filo del agua)*, Univ. of Texas Press, Austin, Texas, 1963.

SPANISH AMERICAN POETRY

J. M. COHEN

FORMATION OF THE LATIN AMERICAN STYLE

THE last twenty-five years have seen the final emergence of Latin American poetry from colonial status and its achievement of complete independence. Till the 19th century all that was written in the New World followed—and often exaggerated—the styles of the Iberian homelands. With the coming of Romanticism, French influence with Byronic overtones replaced Spanish and Portuguese. Even the revolutionary *modernismo* of the Nicaraguan Rubén Darío (1867–1916) at the turn of the century was little more than last year's Paris fashions cut in new Spanish cloth. The most remarkable effect of his Parnassian and Symbolist confections was that they started the poetry of Spanish America, and indeed of Spain itself, into new life. Influence flowed for the first time from the New World to the Old. Yet Darío's effect was not altogether good; he left a pattern of high-sounding rhetoric into which the lesser poets of Spanish America still fall almost naturally.

The movement of true independence, which began only in the late 'thirties of this century, was essentially an *antirubendarismo*: an attempt to discard rhetoric, thus 'wringing the neck of the swan of deceptive plumage', as Darío's Mexican contemporary Enrique González Martínez (1871–1940) had recommended in his famous sonnet, 'Tuércele el cuello al cisne de engañoso plumaje'. But the swan died hard. Sometimes, as in the case of the Chilean Vicente Huidobro (1893–1948), it exchanged its old Verlainean plumage for a new one borrowed from Apollinaire and Max Jacob. Although Paris remained the poetic capital some specifically Latin American qualities had by now begun to appear. Already in some of Darío's poems on Latin American subjects and in the much over-praised work of the Chilean Nobel Prize winner Gabriela Mistral (1889–1957) there appears a certain directness of language, which Mistral called *rusticidad*, and which was her principal strength.

The three poets who acted as liberators in the poetic field all practised a form of this *rusticidad*. The Peruvian César Vallejo, the Chilean Pablo Neruda and the Mexican Octavio Paz are all non-European in a way that Huidobro was not. All speak with the accents of their own countries, writing Spanish as a Latin American language. All draw their imagery from their own lands rather than from the common and now largely alien European heritage. Thanks to their examples, the work of younger writers is even more strongly Latin American, and increasing differences of style, imagery and subject have come to distinguish the nascent national sub-traditions of Argentina, Chile, Peru, Mexico, Brazil and Cuba.

PERU

Perhaps the most profoundly Latin American of the three, whose work still has the impact of novelty thirty years after his death, is César Vallejo (1895–1938). Born in a small town in the Andes, he began by writing *modernista* poetry strongly local in colour and with violent imagery which expressed his essential attitude. Half-Spanish, half-Indian, Vallejo became a bitter rebel after an unjust imprisonment following a popular uprising. Exiling himself to Paris, he encountered the same current poetical fashions as Huidobro but was more cautious in adapting them to his uses. The poems of his Paris collection *Trilce* (1922) are harshly nostalgic. Vallejo strikes the attitude of a 'man of suffering', yet without egoistic display. For him 'Je est un autre'. Ignoring the sequence of time, he relates the unhappy events of his life to a single pattern of fatality. Childhood, imprisonment; himself, a fellow-prisoner; the living, his dead parents and brothers are juxtaposed in a single static time in which he, the prototype of oppressed man, suffers 'blows as from God's hatred' ('golpes como del odio de Dios'). He is the exemplary victim, personal and political, the bearer of an existential human cross, religious in his anti-religion, and more deeply Peruvian for his exile.

Vallejo wrote very little poetry between *Trilce* and the autumn of 1937, eighteen months before his death, when he was starving and already mortally ill. In the interval he had written a novel and much journalism and worked for the Communist party. Then under the impact of his own plight and that of the Spanish republic, with which he had identified himself, he began to write poetry of even harsher and more direct imagery than before. *Poemas humanos* (1939) is still deeply Peruvian; though Vallejo here makes a European humanist's protest against death, at the same time he welcomes it with Indian fatalism:

> Considerando en frío, imparcialmente,
> que el hombre es triste, tose y, sin embargo,
> se complace en su pecho colorado;
> que lo único que hace es componerse
> de días;
> que es lóbrego mamífero y se peina . . .
> Considerando
> que el hombre procede suavemente del trabajo
> y repercute jefe, suena subordinado . . .[1]

Vallejo sums up man's urban condition in flat urban language, interspersed with harshly simple metaphor. He sees death as the moment when the shoes are there but not the man. Yet especially in the poems of *España, aparta de mí éste cáliz* ('Spain, let this cup pass from me'), written in his last year, he allows himself a dim, non-religious hope. In the poem 'Masa' ('The Masses'), at the end of the battle the living surround the dead man, begging him to return to life: 'Twenty, a hundred, a thousand, five hundred thousand, shouting "So much love and to be powerless against death!" '

> Entonces todos los hombres de la tierra
> le rodearon; les vío el cadáver triste, emocionado;
> incorporóse lentamente
> abrazó al primer hombre; echóse a andar . . .[2]

[1] Considering coldly and impartially/that man is sad and coughs, yet all the same/delights in his scarlet breast;/that the one thing he does is to compose himself/of days;/that he is a gloomy mammal and combs his hair . . ./Considering/that man comes mildly from his job,/ reverberating like a boss, but sounding like a subordinate . . .

[2] Then all the men on earth surrounded him;/the sad corpse looked at them, touched,/ slowly got up,/embraced the first man and began to walk . . .

Almost without readers in his own day, Vallejo impressed himself from the mid-fifties on his successors in Latin America and, like Darío, in Spain also. The first to discard 'poetic' language, he was the first also to use truly Latin American Spanish, as North American poets have lately used their versions of English.

Poetry in Peru has only latterly transcended the influence of surrealism to make fresh links with Vallejo's revolutionary realism. The new poetry, while owing much to Vallejo, has also been much affected by recent translations of the pre-Conquest Quechua hymns and love-songs, which have the importance for a unified Peruvian culture that Father Garibay's translations from the Náhua had for the Mexican generation of Octavio Paz (see page 775). Among the later writers, Carlos Germán Belli (b. 1927) and Alejandro Romualdo (b. 1926) combine Vallejo's concentration and social passion with a density of image which may still owe something to surrealism but is recognisably Peruvian. Other poets, such as Francisco Bendezú (b. 1928) have lyrical force but are more hermetic.

CHILE

Pablo Neruda (b. 1904), beginning with a certain *rusticidad* in *Veinte poemas de amor y una canción desesperada* ('Twenty love poems and a song of despair', 1924) which told a love-story with carnal directness, on leaving Chile for first Asia and then Europe, adopted surrealist techniques for the three series of *Residencias en la tierra* ('Residences on earth'), written between 1925 and the Spanish Civil War, which made him a communist. The *Residencias*, still considered by many his best books, are too solid to be really surrealist. Far from indulging in chance dream associations, Neruda identifies himself with material objects, inventing a mysticism of things. For him timber has the secret beauties of a rose: 'Dulce materia, o rosa de alas secas' ('Sweet matter, rose with dry wings'). But war, first in Spain and then in Europe, invented its own surreal landscapes; and the Andes, when Neruda returned to Chile, provided similar dream-emptinesses. The finest poems in Neruda's masterpiece *Canto general* ('Song of the continent' is an approximate rendering of the title), written in 1950, portray his own continent before the coming of man, in the days of the Incas and of the Conquistadores; bare rock, rain, rivers incarnate Neruda's concern with *things*. The Inca fortress of Macchu Picchu is the past and also, in the labour of the thousands of anonymous tribesmen who built it, the Latin American present:

> Aquí los pies del hombre descansaron de noche
> junto a los pies del águila, en las altas guaridas
> carniceras, y en la aurora
> pisaron con los pies del trueno la niebla enrarecida,
> y tocaron las tierras y las piedras
> hasta reconocerlas en la noche o la muerte[1]

In other parts of *Canto general*, Neruda writes of revolt and oppression and of the ultimate triumph of Juan, the common man, after whom the land will be named: 'La tierra se llama Juan'. His three series of *Odas elementales* (1954-7) celebrate a variety of natural objects in short lines which suggest a kind of pointillisme, the medium perhaps in which Juan himself may learn to write when he is master of the land. Neruda's later books are discursive

[1] Here men's feet rested at night/beside the eagle's claws, in high carnivorous/lairs, and at dawn/trod the scattering mist with the feet of thunder/touching the fields and stones/until they could recognise them in night or death

and occasional; the best poems in them are those that refer most directly to the poet's native landscape.

Younger Chilean poets have been quick to revolt against Neruda. His immediate successors returned to formal measures and lyrical subjects. The 'anti-poetry' of Nicanor Parra (b. 1914), on the other hand, while loudly proclaiming its anti-Nerudism, returned to and further exploited the flat language of the *Odas*. His *Poemas y antipoemas* (1954) alternate between two moods: a sentimental lyricism derived from Lorca and an ironical prosaic statement, very flat in language and brutally simple in its imagery. Huidobro described himself as 'anti-poet and mage'; Parra is 'anti-mage' as well. In 'Soliloquio del individuo', he speaks for the individual disillusioned by society who turns back like primitive man to carve the rock-face, though without any belief in the value of communication or even of life itself:

> Mejor es tal vez que vuelva a ese valle,
> A esa roca que me sirvió de hogar,
> Y empiece a grabar de nuevo,
> De atrás para adelante grabar
> El mundo al revés.
> Pero no: la vida no tiene sentido.[1]

In 'La víbora' ('The viper'), 'Los vicios del mundo moderno' ('The vices of the modern world') and 'La trampa' ('The trap'), Parra narrates his depressing experience of women and of the urban scene. His later poetry however has become increasingly occasional. But his influence as anti-poet, reinforced by that of the more apocalyptic San Francisco 'Beats', has had a profound effect on younger poets, particularly in Argentina.

The outstanding Chilean poet of the younger generation, Enrique Lihn (b. 1929), has returned to magic, even to hermeticism, though on the basis of a flatly anti-poetical style. The individual who soliloquises in *La pieza oscura* ('The dark room', 1963) is a child who has strayed into the world of adults, a Jonah bearing an uncertain prophecy of doom and equally uncertain in whose name he speaks. Several of Lihn's poems dwell on early intimations of immortality, and on the theme of bewilderment; others on the recurrences of history. He contrasts the personal timeless world with the blind alleys of objective existence, yet always with some vestigial political hope for the redemption of those imprisoned in 'the dark room'. His latest volume, *Poesía de paso, la derrota y otras poemas* ('Casual poetry, the rout and other poems'), won the Casa de las Américas prize in Havana, 1966, open to all poets writing in Spanish.

MEXICO

Vallejo was born into a world ignorant of its pre-Columbian tradition; the Mexican Octavio Paz (b. 1914) by contrast came to poetic maturity at a moment when his country's poetic past was being rediscovered. The religious poetry of the Aztecs was being translated and interpreted by the scholar-priest Ángel María Garibay (*Poesía indígena*, 1940). Though his beginnings were surrealist and though he too was devoted to the cause of the Spanish republic, Paz was even more vitally concerned to define his *mexicanidad*: the double inheritance that made him both Spanish and American. The tradition of modern poetry was already strong in Mexico. Ramón López Velarde (1888–1921) had interpreted the sensual nostalgia and religiosity of the Mexican provinces; Carlos Pellicer (b. 1899) had portrayed the tropical

---

[1] Perhaps it would be better for me to return to that valley,/To that rock that served me as a home,/And begin to carve again,/From back to front carve/The world inside out./But no, life has no meaning.

south in a bold 'cubist' style of great virtuosity; and José Gorostiza (b. 1901) had written his only considerable poem 'Muerte sin fin' (1939), an abstract and almost transparent hymn to the human intelligence, seen as a perpetual appetite for form, and to poetry, seen as the endeavour to express the incommunicable.

Paz has affinities with all his three precursors; metaphysics, the tropics and the Mexican provinces are all constituents of his poetry, which is primarily concerned with the contrast and reconciliation of the inner and outer life. The best of his early poems are preoccupied with the nature of creation, the dream sources of poetry, which he later identified with the unconscious culture of the pre-Columbians. To advance, man must first go back and renew contact with his forgotten roots:

> hay que soñar hacia atrás, hacia la fuente, hay que remar siglos arriba,
> más allá de la infancia, más allá del comienzo, más allá de las aguas del bautismo,
> echar abajo las paredes entre el hombre y el hombre, juntar de nuevo lo que fue separado,
> vida y muerte no son mundos contrarios, somos un solo tallo con dos flores gemelas,
> hay que desenterrar la palabra perdida, soñar hacia adentro y también hacia afuera[1]

Paz used the sonata form of T. S. Eliot for his longer poems, but with less contrast between his movements. The finest, 'Piedra de sol' ('Sun stone'), is cyclical and ends with a repetition of its opening. Its symbol is the great sun-stone on which the Aztec calendar is inscribed, its subject the repetition of history within an eternity of two aspects, represented by the morning and evening appearances of the planet Venus. The inset movements reflect moments in the poet's life and the contemporary world. After his group of extended poems collected with his earlier work in the complete *Libertad bajo palabra* (lit. 'Liberty on my word', 1960), Paz achieved a fresh concentration in the small and densely lyrical volume *Salamandra* ('Salamander', 1962). Since his appointment as Mexican ambassador in New Delhi, he has returned to the themes of metaphysical reality and poetic creation, expressing them in terms derived from Indian thought and imagery drawn from the Indian scene. Indian thought, which was never alien to him even when he stood close to surrealism, is most strongly influential in his long reflection on the eternal present, 'Viento entero' ('The whole wind').

Mexican poetry since the second world war has followed the paths opened up by Paz, with considerable independence but with no formal rejection of his influence. Alí Chumacero (b. 1918), a poet of great concentration and small production, explores themes of nihilism and frustration; his scene is Mexico city, his medium the monologue of some more desperate Prufrock, lost in metaphysical abysses. Jaime Sabines (b. 1925), closer stylistically to Vallejo and López Velarde than to Paz, speaks for the Indian lost in the poverty and mercilessness of city life, yet dominating it by his sensuality and the force of his legends. Rosario Castellanos (b. 1925) also writes from the Indian standpoint. For her as for Paz, the instinctive world of the native Indian is the source of poetry. But in at least two of her finest poems, 'Lamentación de Dido' and 'La extranjera', she identifies it also with the life of woman, the 'stranger' with no possessions but her numinous power.

[1] We have to dream backward, toward the source, to row up the stream of the centuries,/ beyond infancy, beyond the beginning, beyond the baptismal waters,/to tear down the walls between man and man, to join together anew that which was put asunder,/life and death are not worlds in opposition, we are one single stalk with twin flowers/we have to dig up the lost word, to dream inward and as well to dream outward. (Trans. Muriel Rukeyser.)

Among the younger generation Marco Antonio Montes de Oca (b. 1932) stands out for his great resources of imagery, which only occasionally crystallise into a perfect poem. Montes de Oca is concerned like Paz with the nature of poetry; his best poems generally reflect on the creative act itself. Like Dylan Thomas, he often masks intellectual fumbling with the brilliance of his language.

ARGENTINA

The poetic development of Argentina has been slower than that of the other major countries of Spanish America. Leopoldo Lugones (1874–1938), the chief Argentinian *modernista*, wrote in a variety of styles, varying from that of Jules Laforgue in *Lunario sentimental* (lit. 'Love poems to the moon', 1909) to the *gaucho* mannerism of *Romances del río seco* ('Ballads of the dry river', 1938) but failed to inaugurate anything markedly Argentinian. The poets of the Martín Fierro group of the 'twenties were more European than their contemporaries in Mexico or Chile. J. L. Borges (b. 1899) in *Fervor de Buenos Aires* (1924) invented a mythology for the capital. But although he was one of the founders of *ultraísmo*—a movement relying on violence of metaphor—his poetry lacks the originality of his short stories.

The finest poet of his generation, Ricardo Molinari (b. 1898), portrays the empty vastness of the Argentinian *pampa* in a number of odes in his large collection *Mundos de la madrugada* ('Worlds of the dawn', 1943) and its successors. For him isolation and emptiness of spirit are the psychological counterparts of the landscape. Though he has only once been to Europe, Molinari sees himself as an exile from a lost heaven that is at once geographical and spiritual. In all his collections he alternates his odes in vers libre with sonnets and songs of greater compression which echo the Spanish baroque and even the Arabic *qasida*. He also uses themes from his country's history in a manner recalling Lugones, in a vain attempt to create an Argentinian myth. In contrast to Neruda and Vallejo, he lacks sensual contact with the objective world. His poetry is pure, but not universal.

The next generation of Argentinian poets was equally provincial, and even more closely dependent on European models. In the 'forties surrealist influence predominated, to be followed by *invencionismo*, which derived from France also by way of Huidobro's example. The outstanding Argentinian surrealist is Enrique Molina (b. 1910), but the best poet of the time is the independent and hermetic Alberto Girri (b. 1919). Girri, a European poet in everything but domicile, uses 'sub-conscious' imagery with great compression. His poetry, which sometimes follows Italian models, is that of a solitary pursuer of essences, melancholy and sensitive to the magic of place and reverie.

The anti-aesthetic break in Argentinian development comes with the Poesía Buenos Aires group, among whom Mario Trejo (b. 1926) sustains the influence of Vallejo and turns from dream to political reality. After the formal compression of Rudolfo Alonso (b. 1934) and Francisco Urondo (b. 1930), the less revolutionary members of the group, follows the concentrated violence of Juan Gelman (b. 1930) and of the more radical poets who contribute to the magazine *El escarabajo de oro* ('The golden scarab', Buenos Aires). Here anti-poetry assumes political tones, and linguistic resources are expanded to include the slang of streets and dockside. Gelman and the even more colloquial Victor García Robles (b. 1933) inaugurate a truly Argentinian poetry, urban, angry and immensely allusive. The latter's *Oíd mortales* ('Listen, mortals', which won the Casa de las Américas prize for 1965) contains long poems, as by some modern counterpart of Laforgue, a constant influence in Argentina, which sometimes fall into vulgarity without ever losing impact. Another member of the group, Noé Jitrik (b. 1928), owes something to Parra but is more smoothly ironic.

CUBA

Only after Fidel Castro's revolution did Cuban poetry free itself from outside domination. Earlier poetry moves from 'pure' lyricism after the Spanish model of Juan Ramón Jiménez to the Negro rhythms of Nicolás Guillén (b. 1902). Emilio Ballagas (1908–1954) practised both. Guillén's *Sóngoro cosongo* (Songs in folk rythms, 1931) moves from the folkloric to the political, but the medium soon became merely picturesque, an Antillan counterpart of Lorca's *Romancero gitano*. The hermetic movement that followed was remarkable for the tightly written literary poetry of José Lezama Lima (b. 1912), which despite its influences from Valéry, Rilke and the Spanish baroque is still creole in its imagery.

Lezama's followers in the Orígenes group yielded to the generation of the revolution whose work underwent fresh European and North American influences in their years abroad. Roberto Fernández Retamar (b. 1930) and Fayad Jamis (b. 1930) reflect the exile's view of an alien but beguiling culture. Heberto Padilla (b. 1932) in his sequence on the childhood of William Blake, brings together 18th-century England and the Cuba of the Batista dictatorship. Most of these poets lapsed into sentimental over-simplicity when writing on patriotic subjects, but have since regained balance. Retamar's *Historia antigua* (1964) and some uncollected poems of Jamis celebrate the rebirth of personal values in the present years of stress and shortage. The fourth outstanding poet of this generation is Pablo Armando Fernández (b. 1930), whose earlier work was diffuse, but who has succeeded in *Libro de los héroes* (1964) in creating a mythology of the revolution, placing those heroes who were killed in the Sierra Madre or in Batista's prisons in the spirit world of Afro-Cuban legend. Fernández writes of his dead friends without sentimentality, placing them in the recession of history and portraying them briefly in the decisive moments of their lives. Two other Cuban poets, Rolando Rigali (b. 1941) and Domingo Alfonso (b. 1925) continue his concentrated manner.

The revolution has opened Cuba to the influence of Vallejo and anti-poetry. At the same time younger poets of other countries have become less hermetic and more political by identifying themselves with the cause of Cuba, which represents for them what the Spanish republic did for European poets of the 'thirties. They have shown their sympathy by visiting Cuba, by contributing to Cuban magazines and by competing for Cuban literary prizes. In this way a Spanish American literary international has come into being, even though national styles remain distinct and are perhaps becoming more so.

BIBLIOGRAPHY

Cohen, J. M. (ed.). *Penguin New Writing in Latin America* (anthology), Penguin, London, 1966.
   Cuba Sí (anthology of contemporary writing in Cuba), Penguin, London, 1967.
Cohen, J. M. *Poetry of This Age*, Hutchinson, London, 2nd ed. 1966.
Neruda, Pablo. *Heights of Macchu Picchu and Other Poems*, trans. Nathaniel Tarn, Cape/Penguin, London, 1967.
Paz, Octavio. *Selected Poems*, trans. Muriel Rukeyser, Indiana Univ. Press, Bloomington, 1963.
   Sun Stone, trans. Muriel Rukeyser, New Directions, New York, 1959.
Vallejo, César. *Poems from Trilce*, trans. Charles Tomlinson, Oxford Univ. Press, London, 1967.

BRAZILIAN LITERATURE

FERNANDO SABINO

BRAZIL differs from the rest of Latin America not only in its size and language but also in its Portuguese cultural inheritance. Contemporary Brazilian literature is characterised by growing nationalism and a preoccupation with social problems. These characteristics it shares with the literature of other Latin American countries, but the way in which they are manifested in Brazil is distinctive.

It was through a movement for political independence from Portugal that Brazilian literature began to affirm itself. It was through a movement for cultural independence from Europe that it affirmed its Brazilian character. The present striving of Brazil after economic independence may give its literature the universality it has not yet achieved. Up to 1822 Brazilian literature, with rare exceptions, was no more than a by-product of the Portuguese. The colonial period produced a few works of historical rather than literary merit, yoked to Portuguese canons. Nativist feeling as a source of literary inspiration arose out of the struggles to defend the territory against foreign invasions, such as those of the Dutch and the French, and reached its peak with the poets of the Minas Conspiracy, conspirators who placed their poetic talents at the service of a heroic cause doomed to tragic failure. After independence in 1822 Brazilian writers deliberately sought another source of inspiration, and despite the insistence on national themes they found it in the romanticism imported from Europe.

However, nothing had foreshadowed the appearance of the first outstandingly important writer: Machado de Assis (1839–1908). Whereas other writers of the period were content with the superficial expression of nationalist feeling, Machado de Assis, a self-taught mulatto of humble origins with a profoundly humanistic outlook, probed deeply into the Brazilian soul in search of a universally significant human condition. His work has become the great heritage of Brazilian literature. Novels such as *Memórias póstumas de Brás Cubas* (*The Posthumous Memoirs of Bras Cubas*)[1], *Dom Casmurro*, *Quincas Borba*, *Esaú e Jacó* (*Esau and Jacob*) have been translated into several languages.

BIRTH OF THE MODERN MOVEMENT

From 1922 onwards, writers launched an attack on the precious and recherché literary language hitherto used. The moment for a second movement for independence had arrived. This time it was no longer simply a question of independence from Portugal, but from the European influence all-pervasive in the country's culture. Paradoxically the movement sought

---

[1] English titles given are those of published translations.

its inspiration in dadaism, futurism, surrealism and all the other 'isms' that assailed Europe after the first world war. The 'Modern Art Week' held in 1922 by a group of young artists gave birth to the independence movement that was to give Brazilian literature its present character. Mário de Andrade (1893–1945), essayist, novelist, short-story writer, musicologist and art critic, was at the head of this movement. He preached a genuine literary nationalism. Language was finally freed from its bondage to Portuguese syntax, and writers sought to use a fresh, spontaneous turn of phrase based on authentic national usage. This use of the spoken language in literature was elevated to a principle by another of the modernists, Oswald de Andrade (1890–1954), with all the irreverence of the iconoclast in his *Gramatiquinha da língua brasileira* (*A Little Grammar of the Brazilian Language*). With his 'joke' poems, at first written under the influence of Marinetti and other futurists then in vogue, and later with genuine nationalist inspiration, Oswald de Andrade laid the foundations for a new literary concept which he called 'anthropophagic', but he did not succeed in creating a school. In his prose works, particularly in *Memórias de João Miramar*, and in his avant-garde plays, he was a precursor of pop art. Later, in his panoramic novel *Marco Zero*, he portrayed the cosmopolitan life of São Paulo.

POETRY

Since 1922 writers have increasingly attempted to find a distinctive form for national themes which have excited their imagination. Seated at his desk in São Paulo, Mário de Andrade was transported, as he tells us in one of his poems, to the world of the Amazonian rubber-gatherer, trying to conjure up his actions at that very moment, to visualise his movements, lost in the vast forest like one of its wild animals. The poem concludes dramatically with the statement: 'That man is Brazilian, as Brazilian as I am.' With the lyricism of Manuel Bandeira (b. 1886), the doyen of Brazil's modern poets, the demands of traditional metrics were sharply rejected: 'I'm sick of all this temperate lyricism, of this well-behaved lyricism, this public servant lyricism, with its signing-in book, its office hours, its routine, and its expressions of esteem for the head of the department.' He called for a poetry 'made up of all rhythms, above all, the rhythms that can't be measured.' Carlos Drummond de Andrade (b. 1902) became the Brazilian interpreter of what could be called the 'feeling of the world', the title of one of his books, *Sentimento do mundo*. This 'feeling' involves awareness of a world full of social problems and contradictions which profoundly affect the Brazilian situation. His poetry is terse, contained, dry, as hard as stone. Indeed, a stone became one of his themes, in a poem that became famous as an example of modernist writing *pour épater les bourgeois*. He threw a stone at the academic verse-writers, the poem consisting of a repetition, with variations, of the line: 'There was a stone in the middle of the road', only two lines being different: 'Never shall I forget this event/In the life of my tired-out retinae.'

The great problems of our time are seen in Carlos Drummond de Andrade's poetry through his subdued poetic material: humble elements of everyday life such as a dress hanging on a door, the scraps of food left on a plate, the nocturnal sound of water dripping into a tank. It is the poetry of fear, solitude and death. But it is also, as in the *Canto do homen do povo a Charlie Chaplin* (*Song of a Man of the People to Charlie Chaplin*), the poetry of human solidarity, the outstretched hand, the revolt against social injustice.

After Carlos Drummond de Andrade, Vinicius de Moraes (b. 1913) brought sensual melody to Brazilian poetry. He is a minstrel who sings of love and the physical perfection of women, who for him are 'the adorable constant of eternal poetry.' Seeking themes ever closer to the people, whose feelings he attempted to identify, he became the driving force behind the renewal of popular music: he revolutionised the Brazilian samba with the introduction of the bossa nova, with its new rhythmic patterns in both words and music. His compositions, in which he collaborated with other Brazilian composers—such as *The Girl from Ipanema*—are sung throughout the world. The versatility of his talent led him to the theatre, and he used the theme of one of his plays as the basis for his screen-play for *Black Orpheus*.

Of the modern poets, it was perhaps Cecília Meireles (1901–64) who remained most faithful to the Portuguese origins of Brazilian lyric poetry. Her sensitivity to nature, however, always assumed a universal character. Augusto Frederico Schmidt (1906–64) brought back into poetry the great eternal themes deliberately rejected by the modernists. His sonnets, written in blank verse, have a Biblical tone. Unlike Cassiano Ricardo (b. 1895) who emerged from modernism to consolidate his poetry through the use of everyday elements from contemporary urban life, Murilo Mendes (b.1901) is another poet who embarked on a mystic adventure through his poetry. His surrealistic world verges 'on the apocalyptic and is inhabited by falling stars and luminous comets, demons wearing brassières and angels riding bicycles (*Poesia em pânico, Fronteiras da eternidade*). Jorge de Lima (1895–1953) sought in God the beginning and end of his inspiration. In his last book, written shortly before his death, Jorge de Lima returned to the origins of Brazilian poetry, drawing his inspiration from Camoens to conceive a Brazilian Lusiad, *A invenção de Orfeu* (*The Invention of Orpheus*).

In João Cabral de Melo Neto (b. 1920) we see the most extraordinary poetic revelation since Carlos Drummond de Andrade. His lines are short and dry, as cutting as the knife-blade tone he uses for vivisecting the elements of his poetry. His poetic material is the life that throbs inside an egg, the organic debris carried by a river after a flood—leather, wood, glass, water; mud, bones, flesh, hair, Man. His poetic sensibility penetrates beyond the secret web of composition, on the lines of Valéry, and reaches extremes of phenomenological perception. The way in which this poet stripped bare the verbal forms of expression cleared the way for the 'concretist' experiments of his successors. Some lost themselves in the esotericism of poetic diagrams, or in sterile aesthetic experiments outside the frontiers of traditional literature. Others attempted to free themselves from hermeticism by reducing poetry to popular themes and extolling the need for social reforms.

THE NOVEL

This preoccupation with social reality can be more genuinely extended to the Brazilian novel. Using his experience of the north-east as the material for his novels, José Lins do Rego (1901–57) revealed the social conditions prevailing in a large part of Brazil in the novels which make up the *Ciclo da cana de açucar* (*Sugar Cane Cycle*), including *Fogo morto* (*Dead Fire*), perhaps the most expressive. His work denounces the violent economic contrast between the powerful sugar-mill owners and the poor rural population. The banditry resulting from this situation, which has given birth to the legendary figure of the *cangaceiro* (outlaw), such as the famous Lampeão, is the source of some of José Lins do Rego's finest characters. José Lins do Rego and the other novelists of the north-east are inspired by the land, denouncing the dramatic condition of misery and poverty in which millions of Brazilians exist. The struggle against a hostile natural environment is allied to the violence of social injustice in the short masterpiece by Graciliano Ramos (1892–1953), *Vidas sêcas (Barren Lives)*. His style is unornamented and incisive. His book *São Bernardo* is a study of jealousy set in the poverty-stricken Brazilian backlands. His most important work, *Memórias do cárcere (Memoirs of Prison)*, narrates the terrible experiences he lived through as a political prisoner under Vargas.

Jorge Amado (b. 1912) sought material for his novels in the drama of the miserable population of the Cacao region (*Terras do Sem Fim—The Violent Land*) and in the lives of the fishermen of the Bahian coast (*Mar morto—Sea of the Dead*). He has both undeniable talent as a novelist and an ideological awareness of the class struggle that has attracted left-wing readers throughout the world, and his novels have been translated into dozens of languages, particularly in the Communist countries. In his later novels the tragic has given way to the picturesque, as in *Gabriela, cravo e canela (Gabriela, Clove and Cinnamon)*. Another contemporary novelist of international repute is Érico Veríssimo (b. 1905). His later work, in which he seeks to portray the political and social evolution of Rio Grande do Sul as the basis of Brazil's history in this century, makes up a romanesque frieze: *O tempo e o vento (Time and the Wind)*, unfolding in *O continente (The Continent)*, *O retrato (The Portrait)* and *Arquipélago*. These novels chronicle the lives of successive generations of gauchos.

Several novelists have led Brazilian fiction into the deep terrain of the psychological world. Some, like Lúcio Cardoso (b. 1913) in *Crônica da casa assassinada (Chronicle of the Murdered House)* and Rosário Fusco (b. 1910) in *Dia de juizo (Day of Judgment)* have obstinately sought the redemption of man in the desperate battle between good and evil. Among these belongs Octavio de Faria (b. 1908) whose *Tragédia burguesa (Bourgeois Tragedy)* consists of seventeen volumes and is still in progress. Although his grandeur assures him of a devoted following, particularly in Catholic circles, the sheer size of his novels and the heaviness of his style prevent his work from becoming more popularly known. Others, such as Cornélio Pena (1896–1958), attempt to pinpoint the contradictions of the human soul through a daring literary analysis of the subconscious world. None, however, is as well-equipped for this kind of adventure as Clarice Lispector (b. 1923). Gifted with amazing verbal resources and employing images and metaphors of poetic novelty, Virginia Woolf-like she manages to achieve through language, in novels such as *A maçã no escuro (The Apple in the Dark)* and *A paixão secundo G.H.* (*The Passion according to G.H.*), the miracle of saying the unsayable, the felt but not the thought.

Cyro dos Anjos (b. 1906) in *Amanuense Belmiro (Belmiro the Clerk)* takes up the thread of irony and wry humour that follows the classic example of Machado de Assis. Adonias Filho (b. 1915) attempts to employ psychological analysis for the themes of the north-eastern backlands in *Corpo vivo (Living Body)*, or turns to old legends as in *O forte (The Stronghold)*. Antônio Calado (b. 1917), Carlos Heitor Cony, Autran Dourado (b. 1924) and Assis Brasil are others who have emerged since 1950. Some of the most notable of short-story writers are Machado de Assis, Mario de Andrade, Clarice Lispector, Dalton Trevisan (b. 1924), Otto Lara Resende (b. 1922), Alcântara Machado (1901–44), Anibal Machado (1894–1963), João Alphonsus (1901–44) and Marques Rebelo (b. 1907). The children's stories of Monteiro Lobato (1882–1948) have enchanted for two generations. Rubem Braga (b. 1913) has created a new literary genre by giving art form to his newspaper articles.

No modern writer can be compared in importance to João Guimarães Rosa (b. 1908). Guimarães Rosa was a humble backwoods doctor when he decided on a diplomatic career and made a relatively late appearance as a writer. His first book, *Saragana*, consists of tales written in regional idiom, an outlandish vocabulary piling up picturesque and colloquial expressions. This was followed by a collection of longer novellas, *Corpo de baile (Dance Ensemble)*, in which the linguistic density for the first time goes to the heart of the psychology of the backwoodsman. At the same time he produced a literary monument, *Grande Sertão—Veredas (The Devil to Pay in the Backlands)*, a work of such magnitude that it at last gave to Brazilian literature an epic dimension. It presents a panorama of the doings and customs of the *bandoleiros* of Minas Gerais in a period similar to the American Wild West. Its episodes recall the romances of medieval chivalry in which it seems the author found his inspiration. The narrative is in the stylised language of an ex-bandit who has made a pact with the Devil, but the characters are creatures of flesh and blood of great psychological complexity. The work is the quintessence of baroque style conceived in literary terms; in addition to neologisms, periphrases and other feats of verbal virtuosity, his capture of the spoken word makes this book a living storehouse of Portuguese etymology.

Guimarães Rosa seems to mark the end of an era in the literary interpretation of Brazil. Nevertheless, after him Mário Palmério (b. 1916) and José Cândido de Carvalho in *O coronel e o lobisomem (The Colonel and the Werewolf)* have opened up new horizons in the backwoods epic. In Cândido de Carvalho's book the tragic and the picturesque once more blend in a synthesis of the Brazilian soul the like of which only Machado de Assis had hitherto formulated in literary terms.

BIBLIOGRAPHY

Amado, Jorge. *Gabriela, Clove and Cinnamon (Gabriela, cravo e canela)*, Alfred A. Knopf, New York, 1962; Chatto and Windus, London, 1963. *Home is the Sailor (Os velhos marinheiros)*, Chatto and Windus, London; Alfred A. Knopf, New York, 1964. *The Violent Land (Terras do Sem Fim)*, Alfred A. Knopf, New York, 1965.

Andrade, Carlos Drummond de. *In the Middle of the Road*, selected poems ed. John Nist, Univ. of Arizona Press, Tucson, Ariz., 1965.

Assis, Joaquim Maria Machado de. *Dom Casmurro*, Noonday Press, New York, 1953. *Epitaph for a Small Winner (Posthumous Memoirs of Braz Cubas)*, Noonday Press, New York, 1952; W. H. Allen, London, 1953. *Esau and Jacob*, Univ. of California Press, Berkeley, Calif., 1965; Peter Owen, London, 1966. *The Heritage of Quincas Borba*, W. H. Allen, London, 1954.

Azevedo, Aluizio de. *A Brazilian Tenement (O cortiço)*, Robert M. McBride, New York, 1926.

Azevedo, Fernando de. *Brazilian Culture*, Macmillan, New York, 1950.

Lima, Jorge de. *Poems*, R. Monteiro, Rio de Janeiro, 1952.

Ramos, José Lins do. *Pureza*, Hutchinson, London and New York, 1948.

Rosa, João Guimarães. *The Devil to Pay in the Backlands (Grande Sertão: Veredas)*, José Olympio, Rio de Janeiro; Alfred A. Knopf, New York, 1963.

Veríssimo, Érico. *Night*, Macmillan, New York, 1956. *Time and the Wind (O tempo e o vento)*, Macmillan, New York, 1951. *Brazilian Literature: An Outline*, Macmillan, New York, 1945.

LITERATURE OF THE
ENGLISH-SPEAKING CARIBBEAN

COLIN RICKARDS

UNTIL the early 1950s there were only a handful of writers from the English-speaking Caribbean and of them only one or two were known outside the West Indies. C. L. R. James, the distinguished Trinidadian novelist, historical writer, pamphleteer and cricket specialist, was probably the best known and his writing spans the period from the old school of West Indian writers to the new school. W. Adolphe Roberts of Jamaica, novelist, political writer and historian, was also fairly widely known but other writers had only a small following in their home territories.

In 1941 Edgar Mittelholzer published *Corentyne Thunder* in London. He was still living in British Guiana and though the book received a certain amount of critical attention it never had a wide reading public because a bomb dropped on to the warehouse. It was not until 1950 that Mittelholzer, by now living in England, published a second novel, *A Morning at the Office*, which won him a reputation and established him as a novelist. It was the first West Indian novel to be published by Penguin. Before his death in 1965 Mittelholzer had published upwards of twenty novels, a travel book and a work of autobiography.

In his wake and encouraged by his success came a number of talented young writers like George Lamming of Barbados, Samuel Selvon of Trinidad, Roger Mais and Vic Reid of Jamaica and V. S. Naipaul of Trinidad. The new school had really begun and since then almost every year there has been at least one novel from a new West Indian writer, as well as more works from the established writers. The best-known writers who have proved themselves over more than one novel include Andrew Salkey and H. Orlando Patterson of Jamaica, Jan Carew, Wilson Harris, Denis Williams and O. R. Dathorne of Guyana, Geoffrey Drayton of Barbados and Michael Anthony and Earle Lovelace of Trinidad.

Authors from the English-speaking Caribbean have never been seriously interested in writing the type of anti-slavery novel which came from Cuba at the end of the last century, nor in the *négritude* concept of Aimé Césaire and the writers of the French-speaking Caribbean. They have ranged widely over the social conditions and class/colour stratifications of the complex society from which they have come, and they have written of life in the West Indian territories, or about West Indians in Britain, Canada, the United States and even Africa. Humour is an underlying factor even in the most serious of books by English-language West Indian writers and when they have turned to writing works of humour some little classics have been created.

The poets, on the other hand, have taken the land, the sea and the people as their main themes. Derek Walcott of St Lucia is the best-known poet from the region and his two volumes of poetry so far published in Britain have both been award-winners. A. L. Hendriks of Jamaica has also been published in book form and Professor John Figueroa of the University of the West Indies has edited two anthologies of poetry which give a good idea of the variety of content and style of these poets, whose age range is spread over many years.

The English-speaking Caribbean does not give much scope to playwrights and those who are known outside the area have usually worked in Britain either for the stage or for television. Jan Carew and his Jamaican wife Sylvia Wynter (both of them also novelists) have written radio plays as well as television scripts, while Evan Jones from Jamaica (a poet too) has created a number of highly successful filmscripts. Errol John of Trinidad has had his plays performed on the West End stage, as has Barry Record of Jamaica.

BIBLIOGRAPHY

This bibliography is far from exhaustive; it is intended merely as a list of preliminary suggestions

Prose (mostly fiction)

Anthony, Michael. *The Games Were Coming*, Deutsch, London, 1963.

Bennett, Alvin. *God the Stone-Breaker*, Heinemann, London, 1964.

Braithwaite, Edward R. *To Sir, With Love*, Bodley Head, London, 1959; Prentice–Hall, Englewood Cliffs, NJ, 1960.

Clarke, Austin C. *Survivors of the Crossing*, Heinemann, London, 1964. *Amongst Thistles and Thorns*, Heinemann, London, 1965.

Dathorne, O. R. *Scholarman*, Cassell, London, 1964.

Dawes, Neville. *The Last Enchantment*, Macgibbon and Kee, London, 1960.

Fraser, Fitzroy. *Wounds in the Flesh*, New Authors, London, 1962.

Harris, Wilson. *Heartland*, Faber and Faber, London, 1964.

Hearne, John. *Land of the Living*, Faber and Faber, London, 1961; Harper and Row, New York, 1962.

Hercules, Frank. *I want a Black Doll*, Collins, London; Harcourt, Brace, New York, 1967.

Lamming, George. *Season of Adventures*, Michael Joseph, London, 1960.

Lauchmonen (Peter Kempadoo). *Old Thom's Harvest*, Eyre and Spottiswoode, London, 1965.

Mais, Roger. *The Three Novels of Roger Mais*, Jonathan Cape, London, 1966.

Mittelholzer, Edgar. *A Morning at the Office*, Hogarth Press, London, 1950.

Naipaul, V. S. *A House for Mr Biswas*, Deutsch, London, 1961; McGraw–Hill, New York, 1962. *The Mystic Masseur*, Deutsch, London, 1957; Vanguard, New York, 1959. *Mr Stone and the Knight's Companion*, Deutsch, London; Macmillan, New York, 1963. *The Mimic Man*, Deutsch, London, 1967.

Patterson, H. Orlando. *Children of Sysyphus*, New Authors, London, 1964. *An Absence of Ruins*, Hutchinson, London, 1967.

Reid, Victor. *Sixty-five*, Longmans, London, 1961.

Salkey, Andrew. *Escape to an Autumn Pavement*, Hutchinson, London, 1960. *Hurricane* (first in a series of children's stories), Oxford Univ. Press, London and New York, 1964. *A Quality of Violence*, Hutchinson, London, 1959.

Salkey, Andrew (ed.) *West Indian Stories*, Faber and Faber, London, 1960. *Stories from the Caribbean*, Elek, London, 1965.

Selvon, Samuel. *The Housing Lark*, MacGibbon and Kee, London, 1965.

Williams, Denis. *Other Leopards*, New Authors, London, 1963.

Wynter, Sylvia. *The Hills of Hebron*, Jonathan Cape, London; Simon and Schuster, New York, 1962.

Poetry

Braithwaite, Edward R. *Rights of Passage*, Oxford Univ. Press, London and New York, 1967.

Figueroa, John (ed.) *Caribbean Voices I*, Evans Brothers, London, 1966.

Hendriks, A. C. *On This Mountain*, Deutsch, London, 1965.

Salkey, Andrew (ed.) *Commonwealth Poets*, Heinemann, London, 1965.

Walcott, Derek. *In A Green Night*, Jonathan Cape, London, 1962. *The Castaway*, Jonathan Cape, London, 1965.

AA*

LITERATURE OF THE FRENCH CARIBBEAN

MARYSE CONDÉ

> My negritude is not a stone, its deafness
> hurled against the clamour of the day
> My negritude is not a speck of dead water
> on the dead eye of the earth
> My negritude is neither a tower nor a
> cathedral.
>
> AIMÉ CÉSAIRE

THE French Antilles, a few tiny islands of no world significance, have produced a literature that is internationally known and whose impact on French-speaking African literature and African literature as a whole is not to be disregarded.

For years the French West Indian writer was a French writer; he gazed at the landscapes of his islands but paid no attention to the inhabitants. If he happened to be concerned with them, he used the clichés invented by Europe, which likes to see in the islands of the tropics and their population a new version of the lost Paradise. The literature of the French Antilles was only born when the West Indians realised that if history had brought them under French rule, this did not mean they should be mere copies of the French people; when they started to question this rule and look for their real identity as men and women of African descent. French West Indian literature was born with the rise of nationalism.

As far as literature is concerned, Guadeloupe and Martinique can be regarded as one world. Their literature is dominated by Aimé Césaire (b. 1913, Martinique). After attending secondary school in Fort-de-France, he studied at the École Normale Supérieure in Paris, where he met Léopold Sédar Senghor. At first seeming doomed to become a brilliant illustration of the French *assimilé*, he became with Senghor the soul of a group who denounced first the cultural then the political and economic oppression of colonialism. Césaire coined the word *négritude*, the concept around which the literature of the whole Black World revolves. White civilisation seemed to him to be over-mechanised, over-sophisticated, dehumanising, and aroused in him the conviction that Africa before colonialism possessed civilisations of great splendour and deep human value. Césaire wrote: *Les armes miraculeuses*, 1946; *Cahiers d'un retour au pays natal*, 1947; *Soleil coupé*, 1946; *Discours sur le colonialisme*, 1955; *Les chiens se taisaient*, 1956; *Ferrements*, 1960; *Toussaint Louverture*, 1960; *Cadastre*, 1961; *La tragédie du roi Christophe*, 1963; *Une saison au Congo*, 1966. Throughout his poems, plays and essays Césaire's main themes are the cultural alienation of the West Indian people (which is but one consequence of colonialist exploitation), the negation of Western values and discovery of Africa, Old Mother Africa. His style is immensely powerful, full of surrealist images and metaphors.

Guy Tirolien (b. 1918, Guadeloupe) wrote *Balles d'or*, 1958. His poetry, although nationalist and highly political like Césaire's, possesses a languid grace of its own. Tirolien refuses to be blinded by the 'splendours of the islands of the Caribbean', but at the same time sings them with moving tenderness.

Edouard Glissant (b. 1930, Martinique) stands half way between poetry and novel. *La lézarde*, 1959, *Le quatrième siècle*, 1962, are novels, but their style is poetical, almost obscure, and their heroes, although engaged in revolutions, seem to belong to a dream-universe. The novel *La lézarde* received the Prix Goncourt. Mention should also be made of Joseph Zobel (b. 1918, Martinique) for his novel *La rue Case-Nègres*, 1950.

The Martiniquan Frantz Fanon (1930–52) has won a permanent place in French Caribbean literature and thought. A doctor, he looked at the cultural alienation of the West Indian people as a form of mental disease to be clinically studied. He later broadened his views and came to see the whole colonised world as an underworld suffering from identical diseases to be cured only by political liberation. (He died in Algeria during the war of liberation.) He wrote: *Peaux noires, masques blancs*, 1952; *Les damnés de la terre*, 1960 (*The Wretched of the Earth*); *L'an V de la Révolution Algérienne*, 1961. His essay *Les damnés de la terre* is a classic; his analyses of the behaviour and reactions of a colonised man as well as his insight into the dangers following independence in a new society seem beyond criticism.

The same 'wind of change' blew on the literature of French Guiana in the second quarter of the present century as on the French Antilles. The most prominent figure in poetry is Léon Gontran Damas (b. 1915). The alienation of the West Indian people, the rejection of Western values and the urge for a spiritual return to the African motherland—these are the themes of all contemporary Negro writing in the Caribbean: the only difference lies in the methods with which each writer treats them. Damas chooses bitter irony and dark humour. His main works are *Pigments*, 1957 and *Black Label*, 1959. In the field of the novel mention must be made of Bertène Juminer (b. 1928) who wrote *Les bâtards*, 1962.

Haiti has been an independent country since 1804, but for a very long time the Haitian writer was satisfied with copying his former French models and masters. Invaluable to the literature of the country are the numerous essays of Dr Jean Price Mars, which awakened intense national feeling. He denounced the racial prejudices of the Haitian élite and encouraged the study of the African heritage and civilisations for the light they can throw on Haitian civilisation. His most important essay is *Ainsi parla l'oncle*, 1928.

The first great Haitian novelist is Jacques Roumain (1907–44). His masterpiece is *Gouverneurs de la rosée*, 1939 (*Masters of the Dew*), where he describes with tenderness and illuminating faith in the future the life of peasants in a small village. He proclaims the brotherhood in suffering and the revolt of the Negroes of the world. His mysticism culminates in the work of Jacques-Stéphen Alexis (b. 1929), the author of two very powerful novels, *Compère Général Soleil*, 1955 and *Les arbres musiciens*, 1957. The first is an epic, the epic of an urban people who day after day face unemployment, hunger, violence and finally exile in the near and better off Dominican Republic; the second expresses a philosophy based on voodoo spirituality. Mention should be made, too, of Edris Saint Amand (b. 1925) who wrote *Bon Dieu rit*, 1955.

As far as Haitian poetry is concerned, the most prominent figure is René Depestre (b. 1930). In exile since 1950, he has published *Minerai noir*, 1956 and *Traduit du grand large*, 1958, where he joins in the denunciations of the white world, the nostalgia for Africa and the belief in human brotherhood.

BIBLIOGRAPHY

Alexis, Jacques-Stéphen. *Compère Général Soleil*, Gallimard, Paris, 1955. *Les arbres musiciens*, Gallimard, Paris, 1957.

Césaire, Aimé. *Cahiers d'un retours au pays natal*, Bordas, Paris, 1947. *La tragédie du roi Christophe*, Présence Africaine, Paris, 1963.

Coulthard, G. R. *Race and Colour in Caribbean Literature*, Oxford Univ. Press, London and New York, 1962.

Fanon, Frantz. *The Wretched of the Earth (Les damnés de la terre)*, 1966.

Roumain, Jacques. *Masters of the Dew (Gouverneurs de la rosée)*, Regnal and Hitchcock, New York, 1964.

Sartre, Jean-Jacques. *Orphée noir*, Présence Africaine, Paris, 1948.

Zobel, Joseph. *La rue Case-Nègres*, Jean Froissart, Paris, 1950.

THE LATIN AMERICAN THEATRE

FRANK DAUSTER

Few Latin American nations have more than one extended metropolitan area, and activity outside these centres has been largely neglected. Recently, however, there has been considerable success with substantial programmes composed of professional and university theatre tours, training programmes and drama competitions. The roots of today's movement are in the experimental groups of the late 1920s; in several nations the support of governmental cultural agencies and university drama groups, who consistently do some of the best work, has been decisive. The most important dramatists are deeply committed to their own time, to an awareness of world problems and a search for the meaning of their existence and the place of Latin America in the 20th century.

MEXICO

The Mexican movement dates from the foundation in 1928 of Teatro Ulises, an experimental group whose members are important as the teachers of the present generation and as dramatists in their own right, such as Xavier Villaurrutia (1903–50), Salvador Novo (b. 1904) and Celestino Gorostiza (b. 1904). Not directly affiliated with this group was Rodolfo Usigli (b. 1905), whose sardonic and indignant probing of the Mexican character in many works, notably *Corona de sombra* (*Crown of Shadows*[1], 1947) and *El gesticulador* (*The Gesticulator*, 1947) has led many to consider him Latin America's foremost dramatist. The new generation which appeared after the second world war has been stimulated by the foundation of the Department of Theatre of the National Institute of Fine Arts, the School of Dramatic Arts and the National Theatre Festivals. From the latter comes Pablo Salinas, whose *A caza de amor* was voted best play of 1965 by drama critics. Probably most important of established playwrights is the gifted and restless Emilio Carballido (b. 1925), who ranges from *Rosalba y los Llaveros* (*Rosalba and the Llavero Family*, 1950), a witty and skilful work which awakened Mexican audiences to the possibilities of comic treatment of serious problems, to *Medusa*, 1965, a complex vision of man's spiritual death in the modern world. Although the recipient of an award for best unproduced Mexican play and a special prize in the UNESCO Latin American theatre contest, *Medusa's* only production has been in English at Cornell University. Carballido's *Yo también hablo de la rosa*, 1966, showed once more his assimilation of varying techniques to his highly personal style and his deep sense of human compassion.

---

[1] English titles are those of productions in English.

Other important members of this group include Luisa Josefina Hernández (b. 1928), Sergio Magaña (b. 1924), Elena Garro (b. 1918) and Carlos Solórzano (b. 1922). Hernández has evolved from realistic treatment of the frustration of provincial life and woman's role in Mexican society, to a Brechtian technique with a marked social content; Magaña writes little, but like other members of his generation has achieved considerable success with his restless experiments in form. Garro is closely related to the theatre of the absurd, while Solórzano, influenced by Camus and Ghelderode, has progressed toward a concept of total theatre which he uses to present his vision of man's eternal struggle against repression, both human and cosmic. The recent appearance of a new group of directors and dramatists attests to the vitality of Mexico's theatre; in spite of sporadic censorship and economic problems created by low fixed prices, the Mexican drama is flourishing.

ARGENTINA AND URUGUAY

Linked by a common culture, these two nations must be treated as one. Uruguay has depended heavily on Argentine productions, while many of Argentina's most important dramatists are Uruguayan. The death of the masters of the naturalistic movement of the early part of the century left a vacuum which has been filled primarily by the independent, or experimental, movement, reacting against a frivolous commercial stage. Begun about 1930 in socialist workers' clubs, by 1949 it was a powerful force in the theatre, coinciding with and in part causing an influx of new ideas in the commercial theatre. Doyen of Argentine dramatists is Samuel Eichelbaum (b. 1894), whose work focuses on psychological problems and questions of conscience, but it is the younger group which provides the interest today. Carlos Gorostiza (b. 1920) produced a revelation in 1949 with *El puente*, whose technical finesse and social commitment led to simultaneous productions by independent and commercial companies. His later work has been less well received, due at least in part to his concentration on more universal themes of human commitment and isolation. Agustín Cuzzani (b. 1924) is highly imaginative and anti-realistic, but obsessively social. *Para que se cumplan las escrituras*, 1966 retains the theatricality and avoids some of the trickery of his earlier work. Best of this generation is Osvaldo Dragún (b. 1929), whose *Historias para ser contadas*, 1957 is a staple of university groups in Spain and Spanish America. *Y nos dijeron que éramos inmortales* (*And They Told Us We Were Immortal*, 1965) is typical of the best new Latin American drama in its synthesis of Brechtian and music-hall techniques to interpret the moral questions facing a disenchanted Argentine youth. *Heroica de Buenos Aires*, 1966 received the Cuban Casa de las Américas prize, making Dragún the only dramatist so honoured twice. The disillusionment visible in his work appears in much recent drama, from *Santa Juana de América*, 1960, an effort at epic theatre by Andrés Lizárraga (b. 1919), to the hit of 1964, *Nuestro fin de semana* by Roberto Cossa (b. 1934). The previously little-known Cossa struck a responsive chord in Argentine audiences, dismayed by years of dictatorship and a rapidly degenerating economic system, with his inexorable stripping away of superficial comfort to reveal the abrasive realities of middle-class life.

The break in diplomatic relations between Argentina and Uruguay in 1945 found the latter almost totally dependent for theatre on the sister capital, Buenos Aires. The development of a strong independent movement and the work of the National Theatre have alleviated the situation to the point where many critics are alarmed at the deterioration of artistic levels and the economic rivalries caused by intense competition among proliferating independent groups. No clearly defined group of authors has yet appeared, but several have done interesting work, notably Mario Benedetti (b. 1920) in *Ida y vuelta*, 1958 and Mauricio Rosencof (b. 1928), whose plays are promising but stridently social. Carlos Maggi (b. 1922) may be the best of his generation if he continues to develop the scintillating satire of such works as *La biblioteca*, 1959. Uruguayan theatre is still at a hesitant moment, and its future depends largely on the nation's ability to solve its economic and social problems.

CHILE

Chile is an example of the cooperation between public and private theatre interests. The drama schools of the State University of Chile, founded in 1941, and the private Catholic University, established two years later, have produced most practising dramatists; their professional approach and financial dedication, assisted by government-sponsored contests and awards, have created greater activity than at any time previously. Chilean works are frequently staged abroad, notably *El prestamista*, 1956 by Fernando Josseau (b. 1924), a tour de force monodrama which played throughout Latin America for many years and has won a variety of international prizes. The most important playwrights are youngish and visibly experimental. Luis Alberto Heireman (1928–64) excelled in psychological dramas and wrote the book for the first Chilean musical comedy hit, *Esta señorita Trini*, but his most important work is his experimentation with the popular tradition, notably in *Versos de ciego*, 1960. His effort to infuse the Nativity play with new symbolic content caused major distress for the conservative sector of the theatre public, which was obviously unaware of some of the more piquant aspects of the medieval models. Egon Wolff (b. 1928) has evolved from realistic analysis of middle-class indifference and social climbing to an apparent realism which underlines the basically unreal elements he finds in modern society. Alejandro Sieveking (b. 1934) is a versatile playwright at his best in psychological realism such as the striking tensions of *La madre de los conejos*, 1961. Sergio Vodánovic (b. 1927) has achieved great success, notably with his *Deja que los perros ladren*, while alternating between high comedy and attacks on social and political corruption.

Chilean theatre has a strong realistic tradition, and even its most avant-garde established dramatists have done considerable work in this vein, but the most recent playwrights are perhaps more staunchly anti-realistic than in any other Latin American nation. Enrique Molleto Labarca (b. 1923) constructs sinister and menacing worlds whose meaning eludes us like quicksilver, and Jorge Díaz Gutiérrez (b. 1930) is violently vanguardist. His French antecedents are perhaps too obvious, but his undisciplined imagination and strong social theme have attracted much attention. With an established group still barely forty and younger playwrights of the calibre of Molleto and Díaz, the Chilean theatre promises much for the future.

BRAZIL

Despite the distinct linguistic, cultural and ethnic patterns of Brazil, its drama shows essentially the same patterns as that of the rest of Latin America.

The commercial theatre was jarred in 1943 by *Vestido de noiva* (*Bridal Gown*) of Nelson Rodrigues (b. 1912); its criticism of accepted social standards and introduction of what were, for Brazil, revolutionary staging techniques and Freudian emphasis, had broad impact. Soon there appeared a serious experimental movement in São Paulo and by 1950 it had spread to a number of provincial cities. The theatre now appears to be concentrating itself in Rio de Janeiro, but São Paulo continues to be an important centre.

Although still in a critical period, Brazilian drama has produced several dramatists of real significance, some of whom have achieved considerable international reputation. Ariano Suassuna (b. 1927) reflects the same spirit of revolt and anticlericalism visible in the novels of his native north-east; *Auto da compadecida* (*The Rogue's Trial*, 1957) uses the medieval religious allegory as a framework for social protest. Jorge Andrade (b. 1922) has interpreted his nation's past in a series of experimental works, notably *A moratória* (*Moratorium*, 1956), influenced by Arthur Miller in style and staging. One of Brazil's most polemical dramatists is Pedro Bloch (b. 1914), internationally famous for *As maos de Eurídice*, 1950; his theatre of passion is based on tour de force acting. Much more intellectual is Guilherme Figueiredo (b. 1915), in the cosmopolitan tradition of the theatre of ideas. His best known play, *A rapôsa e as uvas*, 1953, has been staged in over thirty nations.

Other South American Nations

The other nations of South America are still in an early stage of the developmental process, owing to acute social underdevelopment and a severe lack of public and private economic support. In Bolivia and Ecuador the drama consists of small amateur groups, usually affiliated with a university and often harassed by bureaucratic obstructionism. In Paraguay there have been unfruitful sporadic attempts, while the smaller nations have no theatre movement.

Colombia, Venezuela and Peru are in more advanced stages of progress. The former has had a tenuous dramatic tradition of long standing, but new currents have found expression primarily through the Experimental Theatre of Cali, headed by Enrique Buenaventura (b. 1925), himself a disciple of Brecht's epic theatre. The success of the ETC has led to a number of similar groups and the gradual appearance of young playwrights. Fanny Buitrago (b. 1944) received the 1964 National Theatre Prize for her strangely moving *Hombre de paja*, a parable of man's guilt for his world, which indicates the remarkable progress in Colombian theatre. Venezuela too has advanced rapidly since the foundation of several experimental groups in 1950. Several dramatists have achieved considerable reputation due more to their championing of left-wing causes at a time of severe political unrest than to real calibre. Best of young playwrights is Isaac Chocrón (b. 1932), who avoids the emphatic note common to others and focuses on man's solitude and failure.

Peru's situation is much the same; theatre people publicly lament the public indifference and lack of subsidisation which hamstring their efforts. A fundamental conservatism within drama circles has perpetuated interest in the indigenous past, which frequently expresses itself in awards to works which are more pageants of the Incas than vital modern dramas. Enrique Solari Swayne (b. 1915) achieved startling commercial and critical success in several countries with his only performed work, *Collacocha*, 1956, and has inspired younger playwrights who previously felt it useless to try for production. The death at the height of his career of Sebastián Salazar Bondy (1924–64) deprived Peru of its finest dramatist, who bitterly criticised what he considered the spiritual desolation of his country. The harsh criticism directed at him for alleged negativism and imported existentialism reflect the basic conservatism of the Peruvian drama establishment.

CENTRAL AMERICA

Few of the Central American countries have developed more than sporadic manifestations, although recently there has been interesting experimental work in several. Guatemala is the most advanced, although it is as yet impossible to determine whether anything important may result. The high degree of poverty and illiteracy in several nations makes theatre an impossibility. Most provocative of practising dramatists are Walter Beneke (b. 1928) of El Salvador and José de Jesús Martínez (b. 1929) of Panama. Both are alert to contemporary ideas, but at this writing neither is residing in his native country.

THE CARIBBEAN

By their very size and because of cultural and economic underdevelopment, most of the Caribbean islands have little or no theatre. Two major exceptions are Cuba and Puerto Rico. The Puerto Rican movement dates from 1938, and annual drama festivals, initiated in 1958, have become an important feature. The stress on the island's anomalous political status and severe economic problems led to a crushing naturalism in the early years, but this has given way to a much broader concept of drama, and even those writers such as Manuel Méndez Ballester (b. 1909), who led the naturalistic movement, have evolved towards a more symbolic approach. René Marqués (b. 1919) scored his first success with *La carreta* (*The Ox-Cart*, 1954), a plea for a return to a traditional way of life, but his later works are complex symbolic visions of a Puerto Rico trapped in a cultural impasse, with a Spanish tradition slowly being eroded by American materialism. In his best work, *Los soles truncos*, 1958, and *Un niño azul para esa sombra*, 1960, he developed moving dramatic metaphors of a people driven by their own guilt.

Francisco Arriví (b. 1915) is preoccupied with his island's mixed African and European ethnic and cultural heritage. In his best work, *Vejigantes*, 1958, named after an African folk ritual still practised in the island, and *Bolero y Plena*, 1956, one-act plays named after two types of popular music, he studies the need to accept this heritage or face a spiritual mutilation which would destroy his people. Arriví is a skilful technician and is largely responsible for the establishment of a fine physical plant in San Juan's Tapia Theatre, as well as the continued success of the annual theatre festivals. Together with the work done by the University Theatre Group, these facilities have aided the development of a younger group who are greatly influenced by Marqués.

Post-war pre-revolutionary Cuban drama was only occasionally productive in spite of a number of talented dramatists. Interested chiefly in a symbolic psychological theatre, they were frustrated by disinterest and lack of support, and their works were seldom produced. Although the majority of this group are no longer writing for the theatre, the succeeding generation has found encouragement under the present government; socially oriented, they are in the main not writing propagandistic theatre, although there is a considerable amount of overt propaganda by lesser writers. Abelardo Estorino (b. 1925) and Manuel Reguera Saumell (b. 1928) have both done outstanding realistic work, although both have experimented with other forms. Estorino's *El robo del cochino*, 1961, is a brilliant analysis of the disintegrating family structure in rural pre-revolutionary Cuba. This theme also fascinates Reguera Saumell, and in *Recuerdos de Tulipa*, 1962, he brilliantly fused musical comedy and realistic techniques. Antón Arrufat (b. 1935) and José Triana (b. 1935) are far more vanguardist. Arrufat is particularly interested in the possibilities of the popular musical farce which dominated Cuban theatre in much of the 19th and 20th centuries, and its relationship to contemporary forms, while Triana excels in the use of popular types on a multiple symbolic level, as in *La muerte del Ñeque*, 1963, or the inexorable evil of personal relationships in *La noche de los asesinos*, 1965, in which three adolescents play out their festering hatreds in shifting roles reminiscent of Genet. An important contribution of Cuba to the rapidly expanding Latin American theatre has been the series of annual theatre festivals and contests at Havana which have brought international attention and recognition to dramatists from a number of nations.

BIBLIOGRAPHY

GENERAL

Arrufat, Antón, *et al.* 'An interview on the Theater in Cuba and in Latin America', *Odyssey Review*, II, 4 December 1962.
Dauster, Frank. *Historia del teatro hispanoamericano. Siglos XIX y XX*, Historia literaria de Hispanoamérica, IV, Edics. de Andrea, Mexico, 1966.
Del Saz, Agustín. *Teatro hispanoamericano*, 2 vols., Vergara, Barcelona, 1963.
Guerrero Zamora, Juan. 'The Spanish-Speaking Drama Astride Two Continents', *World Theatre*, XI, 4, Brussels, winter 1962–3.
Solórzano, Carlos. *Teatro latinoamericano en el siglo XX*, Pormaca, Mexico, 1964. 'The Contemporary Latin American Theatre', *Prairie Schooner*, XXXIX, 2, Lincoln, Nebraska, summer 1965.

CUBA

Dauster, Frank. 'Cuban Drama Today', *Modern Drama*, September 1966.
González Freire, Natividad. *Teatro cubano 1928–1961*, Ministerio de Relaciones Exteriores, Havana, 1961.

CHILE

Durán Cerda, Julio. 'Actuales tendencias del teatro chileno', *Interamerican Review of Bibliography*, Washington, D.C., XIII, 1963.

MEXICO

Magaña Esquivel, Antonio. *Medio siglo de teatro mexicano, 1900–1961*, Instituto Nacional de Bellas Artes, Mexico, 1964. 'El teatro mexicano contemporáneo', *Interamerican Review of Bibliography*, XIII, 1963.

PUERTO RICO

Arriví, Francisco. *Entrada por las raíces*, Serie La Entraña, San Juan, 1964.
Dauster, Frank. 'Drama and Theater in Puerto Rico', *Modern Drama*, September 1963.

ARGENTINA AND URUGUAY

Marial, José. *El teatro independiente*, Alpe, Buenos Aires, 1955.
Ordaz, Luis. *El teatro en el Río de la Plata*, Leviatán, Buenos Aires, 2nd ed. 1957.

LATIN AMERICAN PAINTING AND SCULPTURE

LEOPOLDO CASTEDO

French Influence

LATIN American art today has a unity of expression and at the same time national individualities which reflect the essential character of the subcontinent. During the whole of the 19th and much of the present century, official 'academic' art followed the European classic–romantic dualism. French academic canons completely dominated the taste of the upper class, purely Latin American themes being pursued for the most part by itinerant artists such as the German Juan Mauricio Rugendas (1802–58). A few indigenous, 'cultivated' painters, however, put Latin American man and landscape onto canvas. The Mexican José María Velasco (1840–1912) transcended academic and impressionistic fashions in his powerful paintings of landscapes, ruins and historical episodes. Prilidiano Pueyrredón (1823–70) portrayed both sophisticated society and simple people of Buenos Aires and the Argentine pampa. In his small-sized canvases Juan Manuel Blanes (1830–1901) chronicled the history of Uruguay and gaucho customs.

French influence culminated in a local impressionism of little value. The Uruguayan Pedro Figari (1861–1938) is an outstanding exception; he progressed from the 'plein air' style to achieve a combination of free strokes and vibrant colours in his depictions of the popular life of Montevideo and particularly the *candombé* Negro dances. The traditions of popular life were also preserved in commissioned cartoons and etchings, lithographs on naive religious themes and hieratic portraits. The Peruvian Pancho Fierro (1803–79) satirised Lima society in his water-colours; the Mexican José Guadalupe Posada (1852–1913) produced political satire, and love-tales, crime and fantasy with skeletal protagonists directed at an illiterate public.

Mexican Muralism

The first movement of native artistic expression in Latin America coincided with the Mexican Revolution of 1910. While Posada reflected popular tastes and concerns, José Vasconcelos, philosopher and minister of education under President Obregón, organised the official support which made possible the development of Mexican muralism, the origins of which are to be found in the movement begun by the utopian anarchist Dr Atl (Gerardo Murillo, 1875–1963), who as an anti-Hispanic gesture changed his name to 'Atl' which means *water* in the Nahuatl language. Together with José Orozco, Dr Atl organised the first exhibition to dissociate itself from the Mexican Academy in 1910 immediately before the outbreak of the Revolution. Mexican muralism found full expression in the work of José Orozco,

795

David Alfaro Siqueiros and Diego Rivera. Its doctrine was voiced in Siqueiros' *Declaración social, política y estética* addressed 'to the indigenous races suppressed down the ages; to the soldiers made murderers by their commanding officers; to the workers and peasants chained by the rich; and to the intellectuals who have not sung the praises of the bourgeoisie.' The movement repudiated all art produced by the traditional upper-class intelligentsia.

José Clemente Orozco (1883-1949) first dedicated himself to social caricature. In his 1916 exhibition he portrayed a sick society of dwarfs, cripples and prostitutes, a society in need of transformation by the work of the heroes of the Revolution. In 1923 he painted his great mural with the archetypal trinity of peasant, worker and soldier. Unlike Rivera, Orozco distorted reality to achieve greater dramatic impact. All his work is defined by pain and animated by a plastic conception independent of narrative interest and revolutionary subject-matter. From 1927 to 1934 he worked in the United States: at Pomona College, Claremont (California) he painted a Prometheus in despair, in New York *La Mesa de la fraternidad universal* ('The Table of Universal Fraternity') with a Negro presiding, in Hanover, New Hampshire an historical allegory of the American continent in which 'Christ destroys his cross'. After he returned to Mexico in 1934 his castigation of society increased in violence. In *La Katharsis* (Academy of Fine Arts) an avalanche of men and arms provokes the laughter of cynical prostitutes.

David Alfaro Siqueiros (b. 1896) is the foremost innovator in contemporary Latin American mural painting. Among his most notable works are *Retrato de la burguesía* (Headquarters of the Electricians Union, Mexico City) and *Por una seguridad completa y para todos los mexicanos* (in the Social Security Hospital, Mexico City). His constant experimentation with ideas as well as techniques has meant the loss of many of his murals, the best known of which was probably *América tropical* (Plaza Art Center, Los Angeles). His canvases have a greater freedom, e.g. *Madre proletaria, Nuestra imagen actual* and the recent *Abstracciones*.

Diego Rivera (1886-1957) studied and absorbed all the 'isms' of the century in Paris. After his encounter with Siqueiros in 1920 he adopted socialist realism as a permanent style, depicting Mexican history with mastery of line and colour, in a photographic idiom expressing primordial truth. His masterpiece, the murals in the National Palace of Mexico, was begun in 1929 and left unfinished in 1952. Rivera's output is copious; his canvases range from impressionism to surrealism through all intermediary stages, and he produced mosaics and stone reliefs for Mexico University City. He was the first Latin American painter to receive world recognition.

Mexican muralism exercised a definite influence on the course of modern Latin American art. The success of Rivera, Orozco and Siqueiros engendered an indigenous mannerism that threatened for a time to sterilise creative capacities throughout the continent. There grew up in reaction a series of simultaneous movements characterised on the one hand by their determination to liberate Latin American art from local and historical interests, to universalise it, and on the other by their attempt to give a newly acquired idiom Ibero-American identity.

THE MODERN MOVEMENT ELSEWHERE

In Brazil the desire for change was voiced in the São Paulo *Semana da Arte*, founded in 1922, and in the *Manifiesto regionalista de Recife*, launched by the sociologist Gilberto Freyre in 1926 with the aim of shaping the ideas that should guide modernisation and national expression in art. The violence of the theories of the sculptor Víctor Brecheret, the painters Oswaldo Goeldi, Anita Malfati and Emiliano di Cavalcanti and others including the composer Heitor Villa-Lobos culminated in the Antropófago and Pau Brasil movements which explored the primitive pre-Portuguese world of Brazil.

In Cuba the rebellion against the traditionalist San Alejandro Academy, directed by the artist-intellectual Víctor Manuel, was based on the attempt to rediscover the popular culture of the past and on unbounded admiration for Rivera. The *Revista de Avance* was founded by Jorge Mañach and other writers to support new art. An aspiring architecture thrived in Venezuela some years later on the new wealth brought to the country by the petroleum boom; its moving spirit was Carlos Raúl Villanueva, in his capacities as town-planner, architect and educator. His University City in Caracas is one of the most distinguished attempts in the modern world to integrate the decorative with the spacial in architecture.

In Uruguay too a modern movement was launched by Joaquín Torres García on his return from Europe, hallowed for his active contribution to avant-garde painting in Paris. In Buenos Aires the modern movement received its impetus from Petoruti, Spilimbergo and Raquel Forner and later the Voluntad y Acción group of architects.

From the beginning of the 1930s the integration of painting and sculpture with architecture became an obsession in Latin America. Le Corbusier's visit to Brazil, Uruguay and Argentina in 1929; the formation of architectural schools after Mies van der Rohe, Gropius and the SOM group (Skidmore, Owings and Merrill); the teachings of Henry Moore; Picasso's support of a number of young painters—all this contributed towards the realisation of the new ideals starting with the Mexican revolutionary movement of 1910.

Post-muralism split into two opposed streams in Mexico, one continuing the work of the 'three greats', the other—'subjective realism'—seeking an escape from folk-lorism. Juan O'Gorman (b. 1905), a follower of Rivera, of enormous mural output, represents the first of these streams. His best known work is the pictography covering the entire external surface of the windowless Mexico University library building, a mosaic of natural stones mingling symbols of Western culture with Mexican pre-Columbian motifs. In the second stream, Rodríguez Lozano (b. 1895) attempted to give Mexican colour to images of desolation, Carlos Orozco Romero (b. 1898) created discordant ape-like figures, and José Luis Cuevas (b. 1933) renovated and exaggerated the monstrous aspects of José Clemente Orozco.

In Brazil, Emiliano Di Cavalcanti (b. 1897) expressed the violence of tropical colour and the sensuality of the mulatto, while Cándido Portinari (1903–62) established a Brazilian counterpart to Mexican muralism, depicting not exotic, carnivalesque themes but national history with workers and men of action as heroes. Portinari's tile and fresco murals are integrated with the new architecture. His best tile murals are those in the Ministry of Education building in Rio and in Niemeyer's church at Pampulha, Minas Gerais; his best frescos and canvases are to be found in the Library of Congress in Washington and the United Nations building in New York.

The Argentinian Raquel Forner (b. 1902) and the Cuban Fidelio Ponce (b. 1895) both worked out their conceptions of pain, nightmare and war in terms of subjective realism. In Colombia, Enrique Grau (b. 1920) ridiculed contemporary society and Fernando Botero (b. 1932) portrayed bishops in undignified positions, being shipwrecked, rolling up into balls or merely standing gaping.

Other experiments were made concurrently with subjective realism in the 1920s and 30s. The Argentinian Emilio Pettoruti (b. 1892) preserved the essentials of cubism, enhanced by harmonious delineation of flat planes of colour. The Cuban Amelia Peláez (b. 1897) created a personal style with acquired techniques and imparted chromatic tropical vibrancy to her flat, aggressive colours, an element of the baroque—always present in the Ibero-American spirit—enriching her complex curves and arabesques. Wilfredo Lam (b. 1902), another Cuban, adopted after 1939 a personal idiom in the school of Picasso. The Argentinian Antonio Berni (b. 1905) built up caricatures in collage suggestive of flesh-and-blood people. The Ecuadorian Osvaldo Guayasamín (b. 1918) applied Picassoesque formulae to his Indian subjects.

In joining the abstract movements modern Latin American painting definitely acquired an international character. An abstract style of complete formal freedom came to be employed principally by Latin Americans resident in New York and Paris. A number of Japanese painters identified with Latin America contributed to this school, the foremost of whom is Manabu Mabe (b. 1924). Alejandro Obregón (b. 1920), in his condors, iguanas and tropical plants, combines a figurative, idealistic painting with abstract elements.

Among the abstract schools, the 'geometric' or 'optical' style has gained currency in Latin America through the work of the Brazilian Alfredo Volpi (b. 1896) and the Guatemalan Carlos Mérida (b. 1891), who is assimilated to Mexican painting and revives the values of Mayan art in his triangular semi-figures, and through the influence of Uruguayan constructivism. The Venezuelan Rafael Otero (b. 1921) ultimately found a style similar to Kandinsky's improvisation. Dispensing with colour, subject-matter and form as related plastic values he invented 'colour-rhythms', parallel planes of straight fine lines.

Roberto Burle Marx (b. 1909) exemplifies in his polyfaceted personality (he is a musician, painter, sculptor, architect and town-planner) the integration of the arts that is characteristic of contemporary Brazil. He earned his present reputation largely as a landscape gardener. His studies of tropical flora and his plastic sense would seem to have assisted him in finding an original abstract drawing style approaching three-dimensional concepts.

García, Tamayo and Matta

Within or attached to the schools above-mentioned three figures are paramount in contemporary Latin American painting: Torres García, Rufino Tamayo and Roberto Matta. The Uruguayan Joaquin Torres García (1874–1949) founded the review *Cercle et carré* with Seuphor in Paris before his return to Montevideo in 1932, and organised an exhibition of abstract art with Kandinsky, Mondrian, Arp, Léger, Le Corbusier and others. He arrived at constructivism through his discovery of the figurative and symbolic geometrism of pre-Columbian art. In a thousand-page book entitled *Universalismo Constructivo, contribución a la unificación del arte y de la cultura en América* he expounded the theory underlying his art. He later published *La tradición del hombre abstracto*, in which he revitalised Cézanne's geometric conception of nature. Torres García's historical importance in Latin America lies not least in his having put an end to surrealism. His painting is defined by right angles and perfect balance; each of his units exists independently, but the whole is indivisible.

The work of Rufino Tamayo (b. 1899) may be divided to date into six periods. In the first he abandoned the muralists' historical and archaeological bias and adopted an international style without losing his Mexican qualities, marked by daring experimentation with colour. The human figures of his second period are saturated with ancient Monte Albán theogony (he is a Zapotec Indian). In his *Amantes contemplando la luna, Hombre contemplando el firmamento* and his well known *Músicas dormidas* Tamayo is the painter of anxiety. In contrast with Rivera's photographic socialist realism, Tamayo seeks a subjective representation of the Mexican soul; the still-lives of his third period tend increasingly towards abstract form. In his fourth and fifth periods Tamayo returns to figurative painting and human subjects, with progressively purer use of colour; in his sixth and latest his mass and colour return by abstract means to Mexican roots.

The Chilean painter Roberto Matta (b. 1912) defines himself as a 'southern realist' rather than a 'surrealist'. His subject-matter includes anticipations of 'cosmic-age' landscapes. His paintings achieve a definite raison d'être concerned with space, and displace themselves in their own orbit. Matta imparts infinite transparency to opaque objects which partake, often indistinctly, of cosmic grandeur and the simplicity of embryonic life. His major achievement lies in his capacity to render dimensional values. His objects, suspended in space, lose their point of reference, becoming worlds in themselves or parts of a world that science is only beginning to discover.

SCULPTURE

Sculpture, far from being the poor relation of painting and sculpture, is a category *per se* in Latin America, not only in its integration with architecture but also in an abundance of individual work. Since its emergence from a stage parallel to academic and 'indigenist' painting, its definite characteristic has consisted in its constant search for American roots, a search expressed in a predilection for geometric and architectonic concepts. Hence totemic form, which is directly linked with the pre-Columbian past, has an important place in present-day Latin American sculpture.

The Mexicans Ignacio Asúnsolo (b. 1890), Francisco Zúñiga (born in Costa Rica, 1913), Arenas Betancourt (born in Colombia, 1919) and German Cueto (b. 1893) have attempted to give modern expression to the pre-Columbian past in stone, metal and terra-cotta. Mathias Goeritz (born in Danzig, 1915) has contributed to the internationalisation of Mexican sculpture in his work from 1949 onwards.

In Colombia Francisco Narváez (b. 1908) led the movement away from the figurative, and the visit of the English sculptor Kenneth Armitage to the country in 1959 gave a further stimulus to new techniques. Like Roberto Matta, Torres García and Rufino Tamayo, the Colombian Edgar Negret (b. 1920) has found a recognisable style. Preoccupied with his search for subject-matter symbolising the contemporary world, Negret probes the informal aesthetic of mechanical artefacts. The use of nuts, screws, crowbars and steel plates is no novelty in sculpture, but Negret's originality lies in his capacity to render the inhuman nature of mechanical objects while at the same time endowing them with a mysterious significance.

The Peruvian Joaquín Roca Rey (b. 1923) has followed Henry Moore's

experiments with volume, space and dynamism. His mature style is characterised by a 'choreographic' feeling, particularly notable in his prize-winning
work *Monumento al prisionero político desconocido* (Panama). Roca Rey has
moved from figurative sculpture to abstract experimentation in metal.

Many women have made a significant contribution to contemporary
Latin American sculpture. The Chilean Marta Colvin (b. 1915), like a
number of other Latin American artists, has done most of her work in Paris,
there discovering the formal values of her own artistic tradition and expressing them in totemic structures sometimes reminiscent of monuments
like the Puerta del Sol at Tiahuanaco. She won the International Prize at
the Eighth Biennial Exhibition at São Paulo in September 1965. Lily
Garáfulic (b. 1915), also a Chilean, whose early work is obsessed with the
idea of monumentality, has developed an energetic abstract style in which the
natural properties of her material are incorporated in an overall plastic idea.

The Argentine Alicia Peñalba (b. 1918) arrived at totemism before her
Chilean contemporaries; her flowers and leaves lose their formal significance
and become architectonic abstractions. For many a Buenos Aires playground
Peñalba has sculpted mysterious hollows and gulleys that delight children,
involving them in tactile confrontation with the sculpture.

Brazilian sculpture has largely taken the form of architectural integration.
Victor Brecheret (1894–1955) belonged to the school of Mestrovich, while
the work of Bruno Giorgi (b. 1908) and Alfredo Ceschiatti (b. 1912) is
figurative with composition predominant. Among Giorgi's contributions to
architectural integration are his *Monumento a la Juventud* (Ministry of Educa-
tion, Rio de Janeiro) and *Os guerreiros* (Praza dos Tres Poderes, Brasilia).
Ceschiatti contributed the *Bronze* at the main entrance of the Palacio da
Alvorada, Brasilia and the conventional reliefs in the church designed by
Niemeyer at Pampulha. The conventional military figures of his *War
Memorial* at Rio de Janeiro are juxtaposed with an airy metal bird by
Julio Catelli Filho. María Martins (b. 1906) also contributed a bronze to
the Palacio da Alvorada (rear door). Of Brazilian artists Martins has most
richly expressed the baroque, sensual exuberance of tropical vegetation.
Marío Cravo (b. 1923), another former pupil of Mestrovich, foresook
figurative sculpture around 1955 after completing his tortuous, agonised
Cristo bahiano. His monumental wood sculpture incorporates the contours of the
material in the sculptural idea. His main interest since 1960 has been in metal
work. Like Negret, Cravo is concerned with the plastic implications of metal
tube and sheet, differing from the Colombian in his attempts to give soldered
masses of nuts, hoops and metal sheets allusions to animal and vegetable life.

The sculptor who embodies the most typical Latin American qualities is
the Bolivian Marina Núñez del Prado (b. 1910). To understand her work
it is necessary to think of the Andean Altiplano: the pristine luminosity of
the atmosphere at a height of over 4,000 metres; man's integration with the
mineral world in which he participates as an inanimate object; the hieratic
petrifaction—Henry Moore's dictum 'the mountain is sculptural energy'
applied to the great flat-topped mountain range, the Bolivian 'roof of the
world'. Del Prado's early work was oriented towards total realism (*Mi
madre, onix*), which she perfected through study of the dancing and penta-
tonic music of the Altiplano; products of this period are *Guacatocoris* and
Cóndores. Her most prolific period was concerned with the depiction of
society (*Los mineros*), after which her forms became progressively less figurative and more quintessential; she gives petrified, abstract form to clouds in
an apparently atmosphere-less sky.

BIBLIOGRAPHY

Acha, V. and Juan, W. *Art in Latin America Today. Peru*, Pan American Union, Washington, DC.

Cardoza y Aragón, Luis. *Mexico: Active Painting*, Ediciones Era, Mexico, 1961.

Castedo, Leopoldo. *The Baroque Prevalence in Brazilian Art*, Charles Frank, New York, 1964.

Damaz, Paul F. *Art in Latin American Architecture*, Reinhold, New York, 1963.

Diament de Sujo, Clara. *Art in Latin America Today. Venezuela*, Pan American Union, Washington, DC, 1962.

Joaquín Torres, Garcia (texts by Jean Cassou and Guillermo de Torre), Instituto Torcuato Di Tella, Buenos Aires, 1964.

Mujica Láines, Manuel. *Art in Latin America Today, Argentina*, Pan American Union, Washington, DC, 1961.

Romero, Antonio R. *Art in Latin America Today. Chile*, Pan American Union, Washington, DC, 1963.

Tibol, Raquel. *Historia general del Arte mexicano. Epoca moderna y contemporanea*, Ediciones Hermes, Mexico, 1964.

Villarroel Claure, Rigoberto. *Art in Latin America Today. Bolivia*, Pan American Union, Washington, DC, 1963.

LATIN AMERICAN ARCHITECTURE

JAIME BELLALTA
MARCOS WINOGRAD
GLADSON DA ROCHA
CARLOS ALBERTO

ALEC BRIGHT
RON HOUGHTON
ALBERTO GONZÁLEZ
DIRK BORNHORST

INTRODUCTION

At the time of the discovery of America in 1492, about two-thirds of the population of the southern continent—10 million people—lived in an area stretching from 24 degrees north to 20 degrees south and 75 degrees west. Here the Mexican, Maya and Andean peoples lived in cities built following a carefully planned layout, the expression of a society that could afford to have craftsmen to build the great temples and fortresses and to fashion the works of art that were later to be incorporated into the traditions of the new nations.

The American colonies of Spain started at the Antilles and along the coastlines of the Caribbean Sea, but quickly expanded over the rest of the southern continent. From 1520 to 1550 the main cities of the region were founded: Mexico (1521), Quito (1534), Lima (1535), Buenos Aires (1536), Asunción (1537), Bogotá (1538), Santiago (1541), La Paz (1548) and Rio de Janeiro (1565). Sometimes these cities overlapped, expanded or replaced the urban centres of pre-Columbian America. The concepts ruling the layout of these urban centres went beyond mere statements about such things as street organisation; they also took account of social and economic considerations to such an extent that the Conquistadors were able to keep much of what was already there without coming into conflict with the directives comprehensively legislated for in the foundation of cities in the Leyes de Indias, that extraordinary set of rules which shaped almost all urban architectural expression in Latin America with the exception of Brazil.

For obvious reasons of defence, communications and accessibility the majority of the new settlements were near the sea. The extremely difficult geographical and sometimes climatic conditions hindered the possibility of physical or cultural links between cities. But this did not prevent layouts in Mexico, Chile or Argentina looking very similar. By contrast we find that the new Portuguese cities in Brazil tended to repeat aspects of a medieval approach to city living, and their development was more free and spontaneous. This characteristic of early colonial times has influenced the distinctive flavour of contemporary Brazilian architecture.

For more than two-and-a-half centuries these cities developed at normal colonial pace, receiving their main inspiration in physical and cultural organisation from Spain and Portugal exclusively, and interpreting it with a more or less 'folkloric' approach depending on the extent of pre-Columbian traditions of craftsmanship in the areas in question. With independence the new countries turned freely to the influence of other nations: England, the United States, but particularly France. The civic architecture of practically all these nations took its inspiration mainly from French neo-classicism and from contemporary European city design. We find, for example, certain neighbourhoods in Buenos Aires that look very much like a sector of Paris. Mexico City also has large sections dating from the 19th and early 20th centuries which look very French—as French as Algiers—as do parts of Santiago, Rio or Montevideo, whereas Valparaiso is more British-looking in its commercial and business area, and the high-income suburbia of Buenos Aires is also British-looking. Further, certain areas of southern Brazil and southern Chile show a distinct German influence.

Until the present century, and in some countries not until as late as the 1930s, the task of shaping both urban and rural environment was traditionally that of the engineer, and so it is only comparatively recently that architecture has become an independent activity in Latin America. Contemporary Latin American architects have drawn their original inspiration mainly from the international movements as represented by their greatest exponents: Le Corbusier, Gropius and the Bauhaus, Van der Rohe and Frank Lloyd Wright. In trying to become faithful disciples of these movements and keeping to the principles to which they had been rapidly converted, Latin American architects became aware that authentic forms of expression must be found which relate to the socio-economic as well as to the physical conditions of the areas in which they work. Latin American architects had previously tended to emphasise visions of a better environment with enormous zeal and idealism, but also, more often than not, disregarding the pressing problems of the developing society to which they belonged. Under the influence of the great international movements they have developed an instinct by which architecture is understood as 'manifestation in space of a full human situation.'

Now cities are exploding, and although this is a world-wide phenomenon it is especially intense in Latin America where the schism between town and country planted by the Spanish and Portuguese has been critically exposed, showing that the individual who leaves the country is not at all prepared for life in a town and that the town is not really prepared to receive him. These are not just housing problems, but 'total environment' problems. This is the main challenge to Latin American architects, and their natural approach to architecture primarily as an art is being put to the test. Regional and climatic differences have already been put to architectural effect. Latin American architects are now turning to other aspects of the problems that face them. The ingenuity required to tackle these problems without sacrifice of ideals and artistic fulfilment could give a truly original stamp to Latin American architecture.

J.B.

Argentina

Almost half the national territory is covered by a density of only 5 persons per sq. km., while 30 per cent of the total population of 21 million lives in the ever-increasing conurbation of Buenos Aires. There is a housing shortage of 2 million dwellings. As elsewhere in Latin America, Argentina's territorial density and urban development results from long economic backwardness. The last two decades, however, have seen the acceleration of light industry development, and this is reflected in the growth of some inland towns (Córdoba, Mendoza, Rosario).

Civil building (housing, offices, shops) is at present almost entirely within the free market economy, the only control being a maximum height for buildings. There are no regional plans, and there are very few towns with a master plan. Even those which have one cannot get past the proposal stage, and any action is impeded by political difficulties and lack of adequate legislative and financial support. There are a few exceptions to this situation such as the development plans for the north-east province of Misiones, partially put into effect between 1956 and 1960, within whose framework some good architecture was executed. Another exception is the important research work and proposals of the Buenos Aires Master Plan Office. The architectural department of the National Post Office has helped to raise architectural standards in the interior of the country by the construction of many branch offices. The most important low-cost housing development for a decade was recently executed by the municipality of Buenos Aires—the South Catalinas estate. There has been no other state activity whatever in the field of civil building or planning.

The 3,000 architects practising today in Argentina received their training at one of the six national and one regional schools of architecture. Of these the largest and most important is the Architecture and Town Planning School of the University of Buenos Aires; with more than 5,000 students it is one of the biggest in the world. The chief shortcoming of architectural graduates, who may have creative ability and architectural culture, is a lack of solid knowledge of the material and cultural problems of Argentine society. Hence their work tends to be aesthetically somewhat à la page and bear little relation to environmental reality. The avant-garde looks forward to a hypothetical future instead of actively participating in the present. However, a change of approach is noticeable in some schools, where accepted theories are being reinterpreted in terms of the real needs of the country and research is being started into concrete problems. Institutes for the study of technology and housing are also being founded.

The speculative character of much modern urban building, together with the tradition, inherited from the colonial period, of the division of urban land into small plots, tends to make for a townscape of visual chaos, the progressive disappearance of green spaces, the concentration of activity at a few urban points and the desertion of others. In this situation a certain amount of good work has nevertheless been achieved by some architects.

Recently there have appeared on the scene buildings and housing schemes promoted by cooperative institutions or trade unions. They undoubtedly tackle the problem of economic housing, but are architecturally hampered by the urban conditions already described. An example is the 'Hogar Obrero' (workers' home) building by Fermin Beretervide, W. de Acosta and A. Felici. Also of recent vintage are the prestige head-office buildings of important firms; these have established a new style of commercial architecture, more cultured, more 'modern'—for example the offices of the Bank of London and South America by S. Sánchez Elía, F. Peralta Ramos, A. Agostini and Clorindo Testa. The latter building, situated on a characterless corner site in Buenos Aires, is built entirely in reinforced concrete with expensive shuttering. It is rigid in its spatial organisation and 'futurist'. A few years ago it was fantastic to think that a building like this could be built in Buenos Aires.

An outstanding characteristic of Argentine architecture today is the contradiction between built and 'drawn' work. 'Drawn' architecture is usually the result of competitions promoted by official institutions. Though

ARCHITECTURE

their themes and programmes match the real needs of the country, it seems as though the architects approach them in the knowledge that the winning designs are rarely built. They remain blueprints. There is a long list of important projects that remain indefinitely on the shelf.

Modern Argentine architecture has an eclecticism born of assimilating avant-garde ideas without first testing them in practice. The work of Le Corbusier, Mies van der Rohe, Wright and Aalto shaped their development, and the ideas of Team 10, Tange and Kahn influence their buildings, but creative authenticity is missing. It is of course only from the social, structural and spatial evidence provided by buildings built and occupied that a real measure of the achievement of Argentine architecture can be obtained. But it is precisely this evidence which is missing because so much that is designed is never built. To remedy this situation involves the creation of the right political and social background. This is the task, no less architectural than that of creating 'images', which Argentine architects are beginning to face.

M.W.

BRAZIL

In 1922 a 'Week of Modern Art' was organised in São Paulo by a group of writers, poets, painters and sculptors, with lectures, discussions and exhibitions suggesting a new direction for Brazilian art and the need to use national themes. Three years later the architects joined issue, but it took a decade more for the modern movement to materialise in Brazilian architecture. Gregori Warchavchik produced the first recognisably contemporary house in 1928, and Le Corbusier gave two lectures in Brazil in 1929, but the 1930 revolution interrupted practical developments, though it gave material and moral support to the idealists who were seeking to establish the basic principles of modern architecture in Brazil. Without the Federal government's support the modern movement would never have had such a brilliant beginning.

In 1935 a government competition for the design of the new Ministry of Education building for Rio de Janeiro was won by a conventional academic design. The enlightened minister Gustavo Capanema, however, while stipulating that the cash prizes be paid, invited the architect Lucio Costa to undertake a new study for the building and, at his suggestion, extended the invitation to include a number of other young architects, including Oscar Niemeyer Soares Filho. Le Corbusier was invited to Rio de Janeiro and for three months the team was in daily contact with him. Fired with enthusiasm by the ideas expressed in his two sketches for the Ministry building, the Brazilian team produced a final project in January 1937, which differed in height and layout from Le Corbusier's but was much influenced by his ideas. The building, now the Palace of Culture, was completed in 1939. Here for the first time architect, structural engineer, painter, sculptor and landscape designer had worked together as a team and, with unsurpassed brilliance, set the seal on the methods and procedure to be followed for the development of an informed Brazilian architecture, of recognisably Brazilian character and perfectly adapted to its physical surroundings. It also revealed the extraordinary talent of Oscar Niemeyer, who has since taken his place among the great architects of our time.

At the invitation of Benedito Valadares, governor of the State of Minas Gerais (an invitation subsequently confirmed by the new governor and future president Juscelino Kubitschek de Oliveira) Oscar Niemeyer designed, in 1942, a highly original group of buildings around the artificial lake at Pampulha. The Church of St Francis of Pampulha, a magnificent example of total a-verticality, created a new form of architectural space, and contributed —with the collaboration of the structural engineer, Joaquim Cardoso—to the evolution of reinforced concrete design technique. Reinforced concrete was now the material chosen for the creation of new forms.

In 1956 President Kubitschek obtained Congress approval for a new capital city, and in a competition for its master plan, first prize was awarded to Lucio Costa. In his design for Brasilia (seat of the Federal government since 1960), architecture expresses the different aspects of zoning by use and function. In the more compact urban area it generally conforms to a pattern in which the unity of the whole is the prevailing concept, but special treatment is permitted for isolated volumes. The universally acclaimed architecture of Oscar Niemeyer at Brasilia expresses a concept of beauty that embraces the consideration of all the factors involved in the creation of an architectural work. The columns of the Presidential Palace, and the buildings which house the Executive and Judicial Powers, have a sculptural form which in no way detracts from their structural function, and their curve is a message of optimism and faith in the ability of future generations.

The best example of good modern architecture in low-cost housing is the Pedregulho residential development near Rio de Janeiro, designed by Afonso Reidy for the municipality in 1950. In the field of landscape architecture Roberto Burle Marx's work has become world famous. The high reputation of their work in Brazil has brought Brazilian architects a number of important commissions in other countries: Roberto Burle Marx has designed parks and gardens in Venezuela; the Roberto brothers have designed a bathing resort in Italy; Lucio Costa has planned a new city for Texas; and Oscar Niemeyer has received commissions in the United States, Germany, Venezuela, Israel and Ghana, and in 1965 was invited to hold an exhibition of his work in the Louvre in Paris, the museum's first one-man architectural exhibition. Interest in research and the use of new building techniques with a view to industrialising architecture, and the new generation's contribution in this field (particularly the work of Paulo Magalhaes), promises continuity in the evolution of modern Brazilian architecture.

G. da R.

CHILE

Chile, 2,800 miles from north to south and averaging 110 miles from east to west, is divided into three distinct zones: hot arid wasteland in the north, fertile valleys with a Mediterranean climate in the centre, and broken coastline, fjords and rainy forests in the south. Development has consequently been mainly in the centre since the time of the Conquest.

Organised architecture and urban planning have existed for many centuries in Latin America (a heritage from both Indians and Spaniards), and Chile has always been architecturally conscious. There are three main university schools of architecture with a total student population of about 400. There are about 1,500 practising architects[1] (out of a population of nearly 8 million), all compulsory members of the College of Architects which decrees that all building plans must be signed by an architect.

The post-war development of social legislation has increased the amount

[1] In Britain there were in 1967 about 20,000 practising architects out of a population of 54 million.

of building controlled by government agencies, particularly in the field of housing (CORVI, the Corporación de la Vivienda) and more than 50 per cent of the architects now work with or for them. These agencies coordinate and direct all programmes sponsored either by the state, or by employees and workers through their building societies, or by private cooperatives and individuals. The housing shortage being acute (as throughout the continent) the problem facing architects was at first a purely quantitative one, and on occasion improved shanty towns were built. Recently, however, various housing schemes have been completed in which the economic limitations have been successfully transformed into the generating force for the whole spatial expression.

Architects have also had to learn about buildings under earth movement. (Three major earthquakes in Chile—1906, 1939 and 1960—caused immense damage.) Hitherto, height and massiveness of structure have been limited by bye-laws. But a new structural approach to larger buildings has begun to produce a distinct architectural character.

Two dissimilar housing schemes by Bresciani, Castillo, Valdés and García Huidobro serve to illustrate the standards attainable, the variety of problems to be met and the impossibility of specialisation. First there is the large Portales mixed development for 10,000 people in a park in Santiago. The architects succeeded in avoiding monumentality by piercing the large blocks at intervals to lighten their effect and maintain a human scale. There being no money for lifts, access to the flats was considered horizontally. Advantage was taken of the sloping site—a 'street', beginning at the upper end, develops single-storey houses beneath it as the slope falls, and finishes by cutting through the length of the blocks of flats at second storey level, giving easy access by foot to the upper storeys, and adding greatly to the richness of its form. Inside the flats an added sense of space is gained by double height in living-rooms, and cross-ventilation is provided everywhere to cope with summer heat. The use of up-to-date construction and material keeps down costs; and the use in new contexts of traditional materials and patterns, or heavy walls reminiscent of adobe, helps the occupants to feel at home.

The Chinchorro housing scheme in Arica, in the sub-tropical arid north, presented quite a different problem—that of grouping identical houses in a non-monotonous way. The climate made patio houses desirable, the central 'room' not only serving many purposes but also visually extending each of the surrounding rooms. Projecting bricks on the blank outer walls provide an interesting display of light and shade.

In all their work, these architects succeed in demonstrating that low budgets need not prevent the creation of an architecture commensurate with international standards.

C.A.

COLOMBIA

Colombia—as large as Spain, France and Portugal combined and presenting environmental contrasts ranging from equatorial rain-forest to desert, and temperature variations from tropical heat to perpetual snow—had no historic civilisations with stone architecture, as had Mexico, Guatemala or Peru, and contemporary architecture therefore lacks the allusions to a past which can be seen, for example, in Mexico University City. The Conquest imposed an advanced town planning code and an architecture of sober beauty using local materials. The building style now called *estilo colonial* spread over the land and skilfully adapted to the different climates. With independence in 1810, this architectural tradition was rejected and styles were imported, first from France and later from England.

Reacting against these styles around 1936, young Colombian architects began the movement which has resulted in today's architecture. The architecture faculty of the National University was founded at this time (there are now nine architectural schools in Colombia). A notable teacher of this period was Bruno Violi, who is largely responsible for the reinforced concrete tradition in Colombia.

Many architects combine design, construction and quantity surveying in one office, a practice forbidden in Britain but which has led to excellent results in Colombia, perhaps because of the high sense of professional ethics of the architects, and because the *interventor*, a sort of clerk of the works but of higher standing, ensures that the architect's specifications are complied with. Other architects prefer to prepare plans and details and supervise construction, choosing a building contractor who may well also be an architect, or for smaller jobs a *maestro de obra* (master-builder). Serious problems between architect and builder are rare.

The principal contribution of contemporary Colombian architects has been the good-class, expensive, urban house for a single family. In less costly housing the Banco Central Hipotecario has given a lead in design, first under the direction of the architect Carlos Arbelaez and then of Samuel Vieco. The late Hans Drews with Arturo Robledo and Dickens Castro designed for the Bank a two-storey house, expandable to three, which was relatively cheap and embodied plan variations and additions which many owners have now carried out without destroying the unity of design of the house or neighbourhood. The Bank also built several blocks of flats in the Barrio Polo Club, where the architects, Rogelio Salmona and Guillermo Bermúdez, used fair-faced brickwork. But Carlos Uribe is the only architect to have produced a well-designed system for prefabricated houses and schools. The Instituto de Crédito Territorial is grappling with the low-cost housing problem common to all urbanising countries, and finding it hard to achieve architectural quality.

Another typical Colombian contribution is the design of the office block, which in the last thirty years has been developed to a remarkable degree in Bogotá, Cali, Medellín and Barranquilla. Here the larger firms, doing their own building and sometimes producing their own prefabricated components, dominate the field. Size has not lowered quality.

Contemporary Colombian architecture reflects on the one hand the immense energy of the people, and on the other a lack of urban planning. Outstanding individual works exist in a chaotic urban framework. The unity of the colonial towns has also been lost while technical progress has been made; this world-wide phenomenon is particularly striking in Colombia because of the country's cultural diversity.

A.B.

CUBA

Under the Spaniards Havana, because of its excellent natural harbour and its situation at the entrance to the Gulf of Mexico, was the defence centre of the Spanish Empire in the New World and the most populous port in America. The indigenous Indian population of the island, and its culture, was eliminated entirely. During this epoch a great wall was built around the city and a series of forts were built. The convent of San Francisco and the

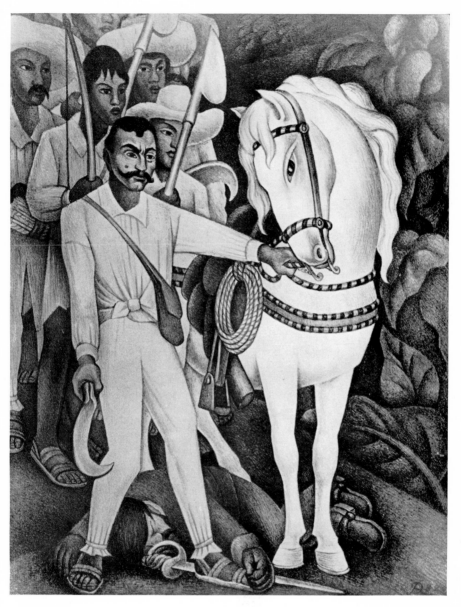

PLATE 1
Diego Rivera (1886–1957) *Zapata*: fresco at Cuernavaca, Mexico

PLATE 2

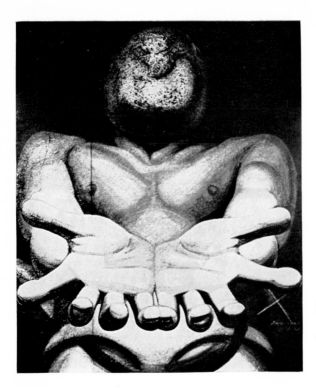

David Alfaro Siqueiros (b. 1896) *Nuestra imagen actual:* oil on masonite

Rufino Tamayo (b. 1899) *Hombre a la puerta:* oil on canvas

Above: Antonio Berni (b. 1905) *La mujer del sweater rojo:* oil on canvas

Left: Emilio Pettoruti (b. 1892) *Autorretrato:* oil on hardboard

PLATE 3

Fernando Botero (b. 1932) *El hombre de las barbas:* oil on canvas

PLATE 4   *Above:* Cándido Portinari (1903–62): Fresco on the reredos wall of the Church of St Francis, Pampulha (Belo Horizonte) depicting Christ as friend of the poor, sick and erring. *Below:* Osvaldo Guayasamín (b. 1918) *Cansancio* (detail)

PLATE 5

Right: Wilfredo Lam (b. 1902) *Figura:* oil on canvas. *Below:* Joaquín Torres García (1874–1949) *Uruguay:* oil on canvas

PLATE 6   *Above:* Alejandro Obregón (b. 1920) *Toro y condor:* oil on canvas. *Below:* Roberto Matta (b. 1912) *Le même si:* oil on canvas

PLATE 7

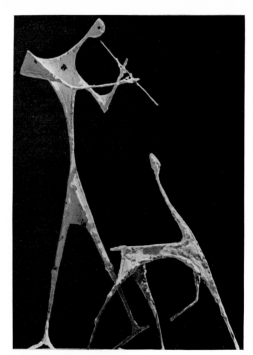

Bruno Giorgi (b. 1908): Bronze

Lily Garáfulic (b. 1915) *Signo I:* bronze

PLATE 8

Above: Edgar Negret (b. 1920) *Aparato mágico:* painted aluminium

Right: Alicia Peñalba (b. 1918) *Absente:* bronze

PLATE 9   Bank of London and South America, local head office,
Buenos Aires: exterior and interior (Sánchez Elía,
Peralta Ramos, Agostini, Clorindo Testa, 1966)

PLATE 10

Above: Parliament buildings, Brasília (Oscar Niemeyer)

Right: Ministry of Education building, Rio de Janeiro (Lucio Costa and Oscar Niemeyer, 1937–42)

PLATE 11   Church of St Francis, Pampulha, near Belo Horizonte
(Oscar Niemeyer, 1943). *Above:* rear view. *Below:*
front view

PLATE 12 *Above:* Portales housing scheme, Santiago (Bresciani, Valdés, Cástillo, García Huidobro, 1961). *Below:* Chinchorro housing scheme, Arica (Bresciani, Valdés, Cástillo, García Huidobro)

PLATE 13 *Above:* Schools of Art, Havana (Porro, Garatti, Gottardi, 1964–6). *Below:* School of Plastic Arts, Havana (Porro)

PLATE 14

Left: Office block, Paseo de la Reforma, Mexico DF (Augusto H. Alvarez, 1965). *Bottom:* Restaurant at Xochimilco (Felix Candela, 1960). *Below:* Monterrey office building, Mexico DF (Enrique de la Mora y Palomar, 1962)

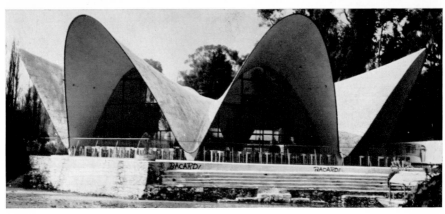

PLATE 15

University City Library, Mexico City (O'Gorman)

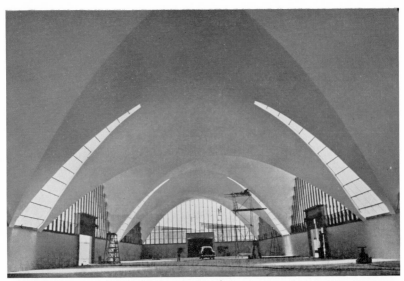

PLATE 16

Top: Bacardi bottling plant, Mexico DF (Felix Candela, 1958). *Centre:* Rector's building, University of Caracas (Carlos Villanueva). *Bottom:* 'Helicoid' commercial centre, Caracas (Romero Gutiérrez, Neuberger and Bornhorst)

baroque cathedral were built by the powerful Church. Some wealthy merchants built baroque-influenced Renaissance-style palaces. In the 19th century the prevailing style was neo-classical. In the countryside the typical form of dwelling was the *bohío*, a primitive hut with earth floor and a palm-leaf thatched roof. Considerable US investment followed US intervention in 1898 after the wars against Spanish rule, and Cuban architecture became greatly influenced by North American fashions.

After the second world war neo-classical and academic styles were abandoned, and large department stores, blocks of flats, luxury hotels and private houses were built making full use of the possibilities of reinforced concrete, the most recent of these being the Havana Hilton (now the Habana Libre) hotel. Many of the designs for these buildings came from outside Cuba, but Cuban architects were already developing the typical Latin American structural flamboyance. Following the revolution of 1959 there was a new emphasis on social building, and a number of school and public housing programmes were launched. A new organisation, Viviendas Campesinas, was responsible for the construction of a series of villages in conventional and prefabricated systems. The quality of these dwellings was high, in spite of the speed with which they were built. Eventually the organisation was incorporated into the Ministry of Building, which now controls all building in Cuba. In this period, too, a new suburb of Havana, Habana del Este, was built. This is a remarkable neighbourhood unit, built with great enthusiasm (and without much regard to cost) in the first days of the revolution; it was the first real group of urban buildings ever built as a whole in Cuba. Here also the formal dexterity of the Cuban architect is seen.

The new buildings after the revolution did not at first form part of any town plan, but now a physical plan (related to the national economic plan) for the island has been worked out, and the emphasis is on economic buildings related to production. In the countryside this means that villages are sited far more carefully and related to the farm units where the inhabitants work. The majority of house construction is now rural, as Cuba is a country with a basically agrarian economy. New urban housing is confined to demands arising from new industries. For example, a textile factory in a small town near Havana (Alquizar) is being built, and on a neighbouring site 400 flats with a school and shopping centre are being built for new employees.

Whilst the architects of the Vice-Ministry of Housing and the Ministry of Industry are dealing with the problems of maintaining high environmental and architectural quality, and at the same time using standardised buildings and components and working to very tight budgets, there are other buildings —one-offs—where the restraints are less severe. Among these are the new buildings for the University of Santiago, the Havana Art Schools and the University of Havana School of Technology.

Perhaps the most remarkable of these is the group of buildings which form the five Schools of Art. This complex was conceived as a centre not only for Cuban but for Latin American students. The Schools of Art and Modern Dance were designed by a Cuban architect, Ricardo Porro. Those of Ballet and Music were designed by a young Italian architect, Vittorio Garatti, and the School of Drama by another Italian, Roberto Gottardi. The buildings are dispersed about a large park on the outskirts of Havana. The architects agreed a series of principles which each was to follow, and then each went his own way. They had one common limitation: to avoid use of steel in a period of steel shortage. For this reason all the buildings make much use of the 'Catalan vault'.

The school of Plastic Arts has a frankly sexual design, one of Porro's tenets being that the African and sensual part of Cuban culture (brought by Negro slaves imported by the Spaniards to replace the wiped-out native labour) is its richest and most important component. The vaulted corridors curl and wrap themselves sinuously around the circular studios, which have a central roof lantern allowing light to fall on the subject from above. Students sit all round, receiving reflected working light from a series of low openings. The studio is in the form of a tiled dome, resting directly on the ground. Washing facilities and the entrance are behind a curving wall of brick. The corridors are in the form of a continuous barrel vault of the same brick-red tiles as the studios, resting on brick piers. Pavings are also brick or tile. Each studio is separated from its neighbour and barely attached to the wall-less corridor, so that there is a constant sensation of lightness and respiration (breeze is all-important in the Cuban climate), and also an obvious reference to the African village.

The unfinished School of Music by Garatti can already be seen to belong with more commitment to the 20th century. A range of rehearsal and practice rooms wind down a hillslope, but behind them is a near-plug-in piazza connecting them to the domed auditorium. The rehearsal rooms are like control rooms or computer consoles, and due to be equipped with elaborate sound insulation, tape recorders and air conditioning. The passage that joins them together, although also in brick and tile, has more in common with the 'finger' of an airport than the screen of the kraal. Garatti's Opera and Ballet School is, strictly speaking, fantastic. Walls here curve and spin, perform pirouettes under roofs which are delicate traceries, under saucer domes where the great half-cartwheel fanlights are enlarged versions of the traditional Cuban fanlight.

The School of Technology of the University of Havana (together with its hostel) is already in use and houses the School of Architecture. The teaching buildings are well designed and were built in the lift-slab technique. The hostels form a very long building, a sort of street with only one side, and have a precast ladder-frame structure, clad after erection with precast floor and wall panels.

Cuban architecture is still passing through a crisis. Trained to produce startling designs for luxury buildings, Cuban architects have not easily adapted to new needs. They are only beginning to consider questions which have preoccupied European architects for decades, and their structural virtuosity is of limited value in mass housing programmes. However, they are working with dedication and enthusiasm to meet the new demands, and make up for some inexperience with a great deal of inspired improvisation.

R.H.

Mexico

Around the year 1929 the young architect Juán O'Gorman built in pure Le Corbusier style a studio-house for the painter Diego Rivera, and introduced modern architecture into Mexico. Years later other architects joined the battle for functionalism. But there was no appropriate technology to support them. Their only clients, the post-revolution bourgeoisie of the 1930s, who were of predominantly rural and provincial extraction, brought remnants of an indigenous and colonial past even into their growing nationalism. Functionalism had to survive as best it could while the building industry made technical progress. From 1945 onwards, architecture can best be understood in terms of the economic and political structure of the country: a regime combining private enterprise and state control. Most of the work carried out by the state was entrusted to private architects, and it is here that pure functionalism is found, though it is not always recognisable under the vast decorative murals with which revolutionary and nationalist fervour cloaked it.

In low-cost housing different tendencies are to be seen, as in the capital's huge Nonoalco-Tlaltelolco high-rise scheme (1964) by Mario Pani and Associates for 70,000 people, and the suburban low-rise San Juán de Aragón (1964) by Hector Velázquez for 40,000 people. In the former, many of Le Corbusier's theories were adopted, though diluted through being in a central area that contains pre-Columbian and colonial remains. On the other hand, San Juán de Aragón is an obvious concession to the cultural requirements of an urban proletariat of recent rural extraction.

Of vital interest to the future was the work done between 1958 and 1964 by architect Pedro Ramírez Vázquez for the Federal School Programme Committee. His prototype rural school, made mainly of prefabricated components, resulted in one whole school per hour coming off the assembly line.

Mexico University City (1953) involved the whole architectural community during its erection. Many of the buildings, such as the Science Faculty by Raul Cacho, Eugenio Peschard and Felix Sánchez, are extravagantly functionalist; others, like O'Gorman's Central Library, clad their purism in nationalist murals. The romantic touch is present too, as in the Olympic Stadium of Augusto Pérez Palacios, Raul Salinas and Jorge Bravo, the sloping stone walls and geometric forms harmonising well with the lava rock setting.

Recently the functionalism/nationalism contradiction has begun to be resolved, as can be seen in buildings like the National Anthropological Museum (1964) in Mexico City by Pedro Ramírez Vázquez, Rafael Mijares and Jorge Campuzano. Quite apart from its masterly conception, it succeeds in expressing in contemporary terms a series of architectural concepts from Mexico's past.

Although there has been a great deal of private enterprise building, only a small proportion of it has been architect-designed. Nevertheless, it is here that the biggest variety of styles is found, great efforts having been made, especially in the realm of speculative commercial and residential buildings, to produce something unusual. The office towers recently built for finance or insurance companies are good examples, such as the Monterrey building (1962) by Enrique de la Mora. The Monterrey building is constructionally of great interest: the main body of six floors of offices is suspended by metal tension cables from a superstructure of steel beams which in turn rest on a concrete beam whose only two supports carry the whole load of the building down to the foundations.

Another category of building which has opened up new possibilities is that of industrial architecture. Economic and spatial requirements have led to the development of wide-span, light structures, and especially to the single and double curvature concrete shells designed by the engineer Felix Candela, as in his Bacardi (1958) factory at Puebla. These shells allow for such an inexhaustible stream of new forms that they have also been used for church architecture, giving a new direction to Mexican architecture. The churches of Nuestra Señora de la Soledad (1957) in Mexico City and of San Vicente de Paul (1959) in Coyoacan DF, both by Enrique de la Mora and Felix Candela, mark successive advances in the use of shell concrete.

Finally, there is the vast field of private houses. Here all styles are to be found, but all rely on a relationship between an asymmetrical arrangement of plain and patterned volumes, the texture of simple traditional materials, and the luminosity of the sky.

A.G.

Venezuela

During the colonial period rules were laid down in the 'Leyes de Indias' (Laws of Indias) to give a layout and an order to the new cities, worthy of the name; all the elements were rationally zoned around the main 'plazas' and were condensed in a clearly expressed mixed development on the perimeter. Houses, grouped harmoniously round churches, formed with these the basic unit: the parish. Poverty, and the lack of specialised craftsmen and rich materials, permitted only a humble domestic architecture, but it triumphed because of its simplicity, its structural clarity and the infinite grace of its proportions and forms. The town house, enclosed within thick walls, opened inwards onto patios which were the spiritual core of the compound. The same plan used for rural residences developed long and spacious halls oriented towards carefully selected vistas.

These words of Carlos Raúl Villanueva and Carlos Celis express the principles of Venezuelan colonial architecture which together with 'decadent' imitation of 19th and early 20th century French architecture formed the starting-point of modern architecture in Venezuela. Around 1925 a handful of architect-engineers emerged from the larger group of civil engineers predominant at that time in the country. Among them Villanueva was the architect who most strongly influenced the evolution of modern architecture in Venezuela. A graduate of the École des Beaux Arts of Paris, he attempted at first to renew the traditions of the colonial style, but soon became acquainted with the new architectural ideas and followed them passionately. His mastery of large-scale composition enabled him to carry out the huge building programmes resulting from the country's rapid development. His spontaneity and dynamic approach to design problems are best reflected in the way he handled his favourite building material, exposed concrete. His active collaboration with painters and sculptors is best expressed in his most important work, the University City in Caracas. His influence is evident in the architectural quality of the large building programmes of the Banco Obrero, whose main objective is the building of low-cost housing.

After the war a group of young architects, most of them graduates of universities in the United States, returned to Venezuela, bringing with them the influence of the modern movement. In 1948 the first class of eleven graduated from the new School of Architecture at the Central University, Caracas (UC). An immense field of activity awaited them.

Caracas is expanding rapidly; it had about 360,000 inhabitants in 1941 and more than 1,300,000 in 1962. Other cities like Maracaibo, Valencia, Maracay and Barquisimeto also show rapid increases in population. The Comisión Nacional de Urbanismo is trying to impose master plans on various cities. The Centro Simón Bolivar, a monumental avenue dominated by two symmetrical skyscrapers and cutting through the heart of the old city of Caracas, has to be absorbed. Around 1960 the Oficina de Planeamiento Urbano, directed by the architect Antonio Cruz Fernández, took over the task and is in charge of the master plan for Caracas.

The few architects practising in the country up to 1958 were overloaded with work; new ideas were accepted without much hesitation and often materialised. The result was a period of dynamic and refreshing architecture, even if somewhat eclectic and incoherent as a whole. Oscar Niemeyer (Brazil) designed a museum for Caracas conceived as an inverted pyramid, Rino Levi (Brazil) a parabola-shaped office building, Richard Neutra (United States) a compact city centre for Caracas. None of these designs was built, but they served as an inspiring apprenticeship for collaborating young Venezuelan architects. One of the best known 'visionary' projects of this period is the Helicoid, a gigantic commercial centre formed by four kilometres of interlocking shopping roads spiralling round a hill close to the centre of Caracas. This complex, designed by Jorge Romero Gutiérrez with Pedro Neuberger and the present writer, is an attempt to elevate the road to the level of architecture and to blend it into the landscape. Though its concrete structure was completed, work was interrupted by the crisis in the building industry around 1958, caused by the turbulent political situation after the fall of Perez Jiménez.

The 1958 crisis marked the end of the 'pioneer period' in which a few architects with little experience but great professional enthusiasm tackled the task of establishing architecture as a profession in a country where hitherto only the engineer was recognised, and started the first School of Architecture and Town Planning, established the Venezuelan Society of Architects (SVA), and published architectural magazines like *Integral* and *Revista SVA*. The crisis equally marked the beginning of a period known as the 'New Regionalism', in which a larger number of young architects (today there are some 500 registered architects, and about 1,300 students in three universities) contribute rather sober, pure and rational designs to solve the multiple building problems of the exploding population. Exposed concrete is often contrasted with red brick or plain white surfaces or the texture of ventilating blocks, the play of light and shadow created by sun screening devices adding rhythm and plasticity to this straightforward architecture, which has many traces of the so-called 'brutalism'.

D.B.

BIBLIOGRAPHY

Balcombe, George. 'Brasilia', *Architectural Design*, London, May 1964.
Bellalta, Jaime and Ling, Arthur. 'Architecture in Chile', *Architectural Design*, London, April 1964.
Bullrich, Francisco. *Arquitectura Argentina Contemporanea*, Ediciones Nueva Visión, Buenos Aires; George Wittenborn, New York, 1964.
Cetto, Max L. *Modern Architecture in Mexico*, Alec Tiranti, London, 1961.
Damaz, Paul F. *Art in Latin American Architecture*, Reinhold, New York and London, 1963.
Faber, Colin. *Candela: The Shell Builder*, Architectural Press, London; Reinhold, New York, 1963.
Hitchcock, Henry-Russell. *Latin American Architecture since 1945*, Museum of Modern Art, New York, 1955.
Kidder Smith, G. E. *Brazil Builds*, Architectural Press, London.
Martínez, C. and Burbano, E. *Arquitectura en Colombia*, Ediciones Proa, Bogotá, 1962.
'Mexico', special number, *Architectural Design*, London, September 1963.
Moholy-Nagy, Sibil. *Carlos Raul Villanueva and the Architecture of Venezuela*, Reinhold, New York, 1964.
Rowntree, Diana, 'Architecture of Castro's Cuba', *Architectural Forum*, New York, April 1964.

Magazines
Argentina (Buenos Aires): *Nueva Visión; Obrador; Summa*. Brazil: *Acropole*, São Paulo; *Modulo*, Rio; *Arquitetura*, Rio. Chile: *Arquitectura, urbanismo, construcción, arte*, Santiago. Colombia (Bogotá): *Proa; Escala*. Cuba: *Arquitectura Cuba*, Havana. Mexico (Mexico City): *Arquitectura; Arquitectos de Mexico; Calli*. Venezuela (Caracas): *Integral; Revista SVA*.

The nationalism of Carlos Chávez is very different: it may be said to be of a social character, born of the Mexican revolution. Chávez disapproves of the use of folk elements in composition, but he does not hesitate to quote revolutionary songs in his scores and, in conformity with the philosophy of the revolution, tries to emphasise the Indian contribution, which in his country is of the utmost importance in the field of visual arts but rather modest, because almost entirely lost, in the field of music.

NATIONALISM AGAIN

The desire to write music of a national character was not completely lost by the composers of the generations following Villa-Lobos. Some, like the Brazilian Camargo Guarnieri (b. 1907), the Mexicans Daniel Ayala (b. 1908), Blas Galindo (b. 1911), Salvador Contreras (b. 1912) and Pablo Moncayo (b. 1912) and the Argentine Alberto Ginastera (b. 1916), have remained more or less attached to this type of music.

Camargo Guarnieri has been the most intransigent advocate of musical nationalism in Latin America. In polemics with Hans Joachim Koellreutter in 1950 he proclaimed that dodecaphony was 'a kind of formalism that could bring the national character of our music to degeneration'. The statement was prompted by aesthetic rather than political considerations, but it happened that the idea expressed seemed particularly designed to please politically minded groups of young musicians, since the previous year, in a manifesto issued by the Prague Congress of Composers and Music Critics under the inspiration of André Jadanov's doctrines, 'formalism' had been inexorably condemned. The influence of Camargo Guarnieri has been considerable; many of today's younger Brazilian composers have been his pupils.

Ayala, Galindo, Contreras and Moncada, who formed in 1935 the so-called Grupo de los Cuatro, do not have the importance of their great Mexican predecessors—Chávez, their teacher, and Silvestre Revueltas (1899–1940), composer of many scores conceived in the most genuine Mexican national tradition and taste. They do not have so much to say.

Alberto Ginastera is considered by many to be the foremost composer active in Latin America today. Starting with works that employ folk melodies or invented melodies in the folk tradition, he has evolved a musical idiom in which the most recent techniques are not neglected. The spirit of his music remains at the same time American, if not typically Argentine.

As we have seen, the first attempt to combat 'nationalism' in Latin American music was the introduction by some composers in the 1930s of counterpoint and classical structures. Villa-Lobos's *Bachianas Brasileiras*, in which an attempt is made to combine the polyphonic writing of J. S. Bach with the spirit of Brazilian music, represented the starting-point of this movement, whose most fervent exponents are to be found in Chile and Cuba. In these two countries, however, 18th-century Spanish music provided the models, and not the baroque polyphony of J. S. Bach or Viennese classicism. Thus Chilean and Cuban 'neo-classic' composers once more affirm their fidelity to national traditions, as contributed by the strong cultural roots of their European past. In the works of composers such as the Chilean Juan Orrego Salas (b. 1919), José Ardevol (born in Spain in 1911 but living in Cuba since 1930) and the Cuban Julián Orbón (born in 1925 in Spain where he spent his infancy) we find vocal scores with poetical texts from the Spanish classics (the Marquis of Santillana, Juan del Encina, Gil Vicente,

Fray Luis de León, San Juan de la Cruz, Luis de Góngora, Lope de Vega, José de Valdivieso) or illustrating a dramatic action conceived in the Spanish tradition; even the titles sometimes suggest the archaic Spanish atmosphere cherished by these composers (*Escenas de Cortes y Pastores* by Orrego Salas, *Homenaje a la tonadilla* by Julián Orbón).

This neo-classicism is by no means always opposed to strong national feeling in which Indian and Negro elements are present. Many of the symphonies, concertos, divertimentos, quartets and sonatas of Latin American composers, though conceived in the neo-classic vein, far from rejecting melodic characteristics and rhythmical patterns of national tradition, treat them as constituent elements of sonata form. The work of Guarnieri, for example, supplies many examples of such music, which has been called by Cuban purists (of the Grupo de Renovación Musical) *música de idiosincrasia fiel al ser nacional* ('music of idiosyncrasy loyal to the national character').

SPANISH AMERICA: THE PRESENT SITUATION

Before 1940 musical supremacy in Latin America indisputably belonged to two countries—Brazil and Mexico. In recent years, however, new talents have appeared in many countries of the continent, even in small ones like Panama which in the past had little or no creative musical life. The contribution of some of these countries to Latin American music today is more important than that of the mother countries of Villa-Lobos and Chávez.

Argentina occupies a leading position in the musical life of the continent, not only because Buenos Aires is one of the world's most important musical centres, and because an Argentine, Alberto Ginastera, is the most acclaimed Latin American composer living, but also by virtue of the number and quality of its young composers and the work achieved by the Latin American Centre for Advanced Musical Studies of the Institute Torcuato di Tella, created and energetically directed by Ginastera himself. The most gifted young composers of Latin America are given fellowships to work there with him and with well known European composers invited to lecture and give practical instruction.

Argentine composers have been numerous and well trained since the beginning of the century, and include one of the pioneers of today's avant-garde music—Juan Carlos Paz (b. 1897). Today Roberto Caamaño (b. 1923), Mauricio Kágel (b. 1931), Antonio Tauriello (b. 1931), Mario Davidovsky (b. 1934) and Armando Krieger (b. 1940) are the outstanding new talents. Caamaño, an excellent pianist, represents with Tauriello the best traditions inherited from the great 20th-century masters who have rejected atonalism and serialism. With the scores of Mauricio Kágel we reach the utmost degree of experimentation in music; the composer employs the most advanced techniques in his attempt to create new sounds. After studying under Juan Carlos Paz, Kágel settled in 1957 in Cologne where he worked at the electronic studio of the Westdeutscher Rundfunk. Davidovsky and Krieger, both pupils of Ginastera, have ventured too into the field of electronic music.

Juan Carlos Paz was not the only pioneer of the 20th-century musical revolution in Latin America. The Mexican Julián Carrillo (1875–1965) became interested in the problem of microtone in 1894 and created the 'thirteenth sound' theory. He not only composed quarter-tone music, but used intervals of eighths and sixteenths of tones and had instruments specially manufactured for the performance of his music.

Hector Tosar (b. 1923), living in Puerto Rico, is the most gifted Uruguayan composer. In Chile Gustavo Becerra (b. 1924) produces lively music employing new techniques, while Roberto Falabella (1923–1958) and José Vicent Asuar (b. 1933), founders of the group 'Agrupación Tonus' devoted to twelve-tone composition, have enriched the high standards that the Institute of Musical Arts and Sciences and the Institute of Musical Extension, both created by Domingo Santa-Cruz, secured for all aspects of Chilean musical life. Enrique Iturriaga (b. 1918), Celso Garrido Lecca (b. 1926) and Charlotte Pozzi Escot (b. 1931), the first two traditionalist and the last an energetic innovator, are the most representative composers of Peru, and Roberto Pineda Duque (b. 1910), Luis Antonio Escobar (b. 1925) and Fabio González-Zuleta (b. 1926) of Colombia, Escobar being traditionalist and affecting neo-classicism, and the other two being exponents of twelve-tone composition. The Panamanian Roque Cordero (b. 1917) is one of the most popular living composers of Latin America. His music, personal and powerful, is free from the dogmatic ties with schools and groups that prevail with so many of his colleagues.

In Cuba the Spaniard José Ardévol has been the guide and mentor of the new generation of composers that succeeded the nationally minded Amadeo Roldán (b. 1900–39) and Alejandro Garcia Caturla (1906–40). The most gifted of these composers is the individualist Julián Orbón, who has moved to Mexico. Edgardo Martin (b. 1915) and Harold Gramatges (b. 1918), who with Orbón were original members of the Grupo de Renovación Musical founded in 1942 by Ardévol, are extremely active in the cultural life of revolutionary Cuba. Aurelio de la Vega (b. 1925) is unconnected with the Ardévol Group; educated in Austria and the United States, where he lives and teaches, he is considered, by virtue of his musical compositions and his writings, one of the most distinguished representatives of modern Latin American music.

BRAZIL

After Guarnieri the most deservedly famous Brazilian composer is Claudio Santoro (b. 1919) who evolved from his instinctive atonalism (carefully cultivated by his teacher Koellreutter) to 'progressive nationalism' of political inspiration, and from there to a more balanced position with creative freedom paramount. Santoro's music is eloquent, tender and warm. He is a true musician and in all phases of his evolution the works he has produced preserve the freshness and strong inventiveness that make them so attractive to both critics and public. Other talented composers are Osvaldo Lacerda (b. 1927), a pupil of Guarnieri and imbued with his conception of musical nationalism, Edino Krieger (b. 1928), like Santoro a former student of Koellreutter, and Marlos Nobre (b. 1939), who worked with Ginastera at the Latin American Institute for Advanced Musical Studies, Buenos Aires. In São Paulo an active experimental group of young musicians closely associated with avant-garde poets is to be noted: Willy Correia de Oliveira, Rogério Duprat and Gilberto Mendes.

BIBLIOGRAPHY

Aylor March, Barbara. 'Latin American Music Today', *Inter-American Music Bulletin*, 21, Washington, DC, January 1961.

Chase, Gilbert. 'Current Musical Trends in South American Lands', *Musical America*, New York, February 1957. 'Alberto Ginastera', *Musical Quarterly*, New York, October 1957. 'Alberto Ginastera—Portrait of an Argentine Composer', *Tempo*, 44, London, 1957. 'Creative Trends in Latin American Music', *Tempo*, 48 and 50, London, 1958 and 1959. *Introducción a la Música Americana Contemporánea*, Editorial Nova, Buenos Aires, 1958.

Corrêa de Azevedo, Luiz Heitor. 'Music', *Brazil*, ed. Lawrence E. Hill, Univ. of California Press, Berkeley, Calif., 1947.

Espinosa, Guillermo. 'Colombian Music and Musicians in Contemporary Culture', *Inter-American Music Bulletin*, 27, Washington, DC, January 1962.

Jong, Gerrit de. 'Music in Brazil', *Inter-American Music Bulletin*, 31, Washington, DC, September 1962.

Hume, Paul. 'Alberto Ginastera', *Inter-American Music Bulletin*, 48, Washington, DC, July 1965.

Mariz, Vasco. *Heitor Villa-Lobos—Brazilian Composer*, Univ. of Florida Press, Gainesville, Fla. 1963.

Orrego Salas, Juan. 'The Young Generation of Latin American Composers—Backgrounds and Perspectives', *Inter-American Music Bulletin*, 38, Washington, DC, November 1963.

Queiroga, Daniel. 'The Present State of Music in Chile', *Inter-American Music Bulletin*, 9 and 10, Washington, DC, January and March 1959.

Vega, Aurelio de la. 'New World Composers', *Inter-American Music Bulletin*, 43, Washington, DC, September 1964.

Vincent, John. 'New Opera in Buenos Aires', *Inter-American Music Bulletin*, 44, Washington, DC, November 1964.

THE LATIN AMERICAN CINEMA

HOMERO ALSINA THEVENET

ONLY four Latin American countries have an established film industry: Argentina, Brazil, Cuba and Mexico. None of the others has gone beyond the newsreel, the documentary and an occasional feature film as the public is uneconomic. The four film-producing countries, furthermore, are in competition with each other: they protect their own products by means of import and export quotas and taxes, and subsidise the making and showing of local films, to the detriment of the Latin American cinema as a whole. Cuba is a special case, since her film production and distribution abroad is governed by political considerations both in Cuba and in the receiving countries. But the film industries of the other countries pay no heed to the fact that they would benefit if they pooled their markets and thus doubled their potential public. Without foreign markets they cannot hope to survive on any but a modest scale.

MEXICO

Since Salvador Toscano Barragán produced his newsreels at the end of the 19th century the Mexican film industry has been blighted by isolation from the national culture and from foreign trends, by censorship and by official protection enabling a handful of businessmen to enrich themselves. The result has been a stultifying reliance on melodrama, cheap folk-lore and primitive humour. A constant feature of the film industry in Mexico has been the 'closed-shop' attitude of trade unions, which have prevented the discovery of new talent—directors, screen-writers, actors and technicans—and nipped in the bud any 'new wave' such as France, England, Italy, Poland and even Hollywood and the Soviet Union have seen in recent years. Credit facilities are made available to film-makers through the Banco Nacional Cinematográfico (set up by President Alemán in 1951), but this money is handled almost exclusively by the large companies. Independent producers can exist only if they dispose of sufficient capital to finance their films by themselves, or if they can manage to entice competent directors and actors away from the large companies. The cinema in Mexico is thus fossilised and modernisation with new faces, new stories and new styles constitutes an extremely difficult task.

In the years 1945–50 the most highly rated Mexican director was Emilio Fernández (*La perla, Enamorada, Rio escondido, Pueblerina*). His films, usually dramas in a rural setting, though greatly enhanced by the virtuosity of his cameraman Gabriel Figueroa, were marred by over-literary dialogue, an over-elaborate story-line and a languid rhythm, a complacent lingering on a beautifully photographed image. When they were first shown, however, his films impressed by combining a passion for the cinema with a perceptive view of rural life in Mexico. Later Fernández fell from grace and had to resign himself to being an actor in the films of others, so that he is, as a director, a figure of the past. Yet his name remains first and foremost in a list of craftsmen of the last twenty years which includes Roberto Gavaldón (*Macario*), Ismael Rodríguez (*La Cucaracha*) and Benito Alazraki (*Raíces*). All of them, and some forty other directors, have over and over again been forced to compromise with the commercial cinema, and have had to churn out 'vehicles' for the greater glory of Maria Felix, Jorge Negrete, Pedro Infante, Catinflas, Sara García, Tin Tan and other names exploited or created by the industry. Occasionally individual talent makes its mark, as in the case of Fernández, Armendáriz, Dolores del Rio or the cameramen Figueroa and Alex Phillips, but the average product of the Mexican cinema suffers from poor scripts, excessive dialogue and the lack of anything to say.

There are two exceptions, however. Since he joined the Mexican cinema in 1946, the Spaniard Luis Buñuel has directed a dozen straightforward melodramas, which no doubt he secretly derides, but he has also made some major films, including *Los olvidados* (1950), *Ensayo de un crimen* (1955), *Nazarin* (1958), *El angel exterminador* (1963), the short film *Simeon en el desierto* (1965) and *Viridiana*, shot on location in Spain. These films bear witness to their author's creative temper: they are often cruel and morbid, always anti-religious and full of the surrealists' yearning for pure and direct feeling, uncontaminated by social convention or mere logic.

The other exception is Manuel Babachano Ponce, who produced *Raíces* (1953, directed by Alazraki), a film which showed in four powerful episodes the life of the Mexican peasant. When Alazraki thereafter abandoned all artistic pretensions and devoted himself whole-heartedly to the commercial cinema, the influence of Barbachano in this first film became apparent. Three years later Barbachano produced and Manuel Velo directed a strange documentary, *Torero*—a day in the life of the bull-fighter, Luis Procuna, which delved deeply into the psychological mechanism of a man risking his life in the ring. *Sonatas*, based on the works of Valle Inclán, was another of Barbachano's ventures (directed by the young Spaniard Juan Antonio Bardem); it was panned by the critics and not widely distributed.

At present the worst feature of the Mexican cinema is its failure to understand the modern cinematographic idiom, centred on the image rather than on the spoken word. Films like *Tiburoneros* (by Luis Alcoriza) suffer from inflated dialogue far more involved than the subject demands. Even such 'avant-garde' efforts as *Los bienamados* (by Juan José Gurrola and Juan Ibañez) are so literary that they seem out of place on the screen.

CUBA

Only a few weeks after Castro's rise to power on 1 January 1959 a new Law (Nr. 169) beginning with the words 'Inasmuch as the cinema is an art . . .' established the Instituto Cubano del Arte e Industria Cinematográficos (ICAIC), and laid down the rules that were henceforth to govern production, distribution, studios and credits. The ICAIC has been run from the start by Alfredo Guevara, who launched *Cine Cubano*, a magazine dealing with all aspects and problems of the film industry and providing a considerable amount of information regarding local production. At the same time the ICAIC provides both specialised training for students and more general and popular educational programmes.

When the tension between Cuba and the United States came to a head in 1961, the revolutionary government completed the seizure of foreign firms, cinemas and film material. This has led to a paradoxical situation, in which films from Hollywood (and other countries) do not enter Cuba, and yet the ICAIC possesses an enviable film-library as a result of the confiscation. This stock has been a valuable educational aid in the effort to popularise the cinema. Another boost has been the interest shown in the Cuban cinema by visitors from abroad (Gérard Philipe, Cesare Zavattini, Joris Ivens, Chris Marker, Agnes Varda), who have helped to tighten the links between Cuba and Europe.

Coproductions have given added scope to the Cuban film industry, such as *Pasa quién baila la Habana* by Vladimir Cech (with Czechoslovakia), *Preludio 11* by Kurt Maetzig (with East Germany), and *Soy Cuba* by Mikhail Kalatozov (with the Soviet Union). Exchange programmes have taken Cuban film people to the Communist countries of Europe for further training, and brought Czech and Russian teachers to the Cuban film school set up by the ICAIC. In this connection Guevara has taken pains to point out that Cuba makes her own decisions in artistic matters and that exchanges and collaboration should not be taken to mean subordination.

Naturally the Cuban cinema has from the outset been ideological, with many short films, most of them documentaries, on social and political subjects. These short films, a number of cartoon films and an educational series called *Enciclopedia popular* have reared a growing group of directors, script-writers, cameramen, technicians and actors. By 1961 more government funds were set aside for the cinema and laboratories installed, so that more, and more ambitious, feature films could be produced. In 1959 no more than four short films were made, revealing the talent of Julio García Espinosa and Tomás Gutierrez Alea. In 1964 the yield included as many as seven feature films. Among the best films of these years were *Historias de la Revolución* (Gutierrez Alea), *Cuba baila* (García Espinosa), *El joven rebelde* (García Espinosa), *Las doce sillas* (Gutierrez Alea), *Año Nuevo* (Jorge Fraga), *El otro Cristóbal* (Armand Gatti, with a mixed French-Cuban team), *Crónica Cubana* (made by the Uruguayan director Ugo Ulive), *Cumbito* (Gutierrez Alea), *La decisión* (José Massip), *Tránsito* (Eduardo Manet), *En días como éstos* (Jorge Fraga). With the exception of *Giselle* (a ballet film directed by Enrique Pineda Barnet starring the dancer Alicia Alonso) all these films are markedly political. The subject is invariably bound up with matters of national interest: the life of the peasants, the agrarian reform, the drama of the Revolution, the threat of a foreign invasion. The films suffer from the typical defects of propaganda—over-simplification and wooden and sententious dialogues, though humour and music provide occasional leaven.

The Cuban cinema is practically unknown in the other countries of Latin America. The Cubans blame the United States, whom they accuse of putting indirect pressure on distributors and exhibitors; the Americans deny this and state that there is simply no demand for Cuban films on the sub-continent. In France and in the Communist countries of Europe Cuban films have been more successful and have even obtained prizes and recognition in the Festivals of Moscow, Sestri, Levante, Oberhausen, Leipzig, Karlovy-Vary, London and Cracow.

BRAZIL

Brazil is extraordinarily rich in dramatic, musical and human resources, and thus a happy hunting-ground for foreign producers in search of exotic settings for their films. Spectacular examples of this were *Orfeo negro* (Marcel Camus) and *The Man from Rio* (Philippe de Broca). At the same time, vast regions of Brazilian territory are culturally backward, so that the scope for development of a film industry having to rely for various reasons (principally that of the language) on its home market has of necessity been slight. There have been several attempts, on the part of producers and artists, to overcome these limitations. In the years 1949–54 such endeavours culminated in the founding of the Vera-Cruz production company under the auspices of the dynamic producer-director Alberto de Cavalcanti, a globe-trotting and cosmopolitan Brazilian who tried for a few years to infuse new life into the film-industry of his mother-country. This period produced some worth-while films with a markedly national flavour: *Terra e sempre terra* (Tom Payne), *Caicara* (Adolfo Celi), *O canto do mar* (Cavalcanti), *Sinha Moca* (Payne) and above all *O Cangaceiro* (Lima Barreto), prizewinner of the Cannes Film Festival, which made the world aware, not only of the Brazilian cinema's potential, but of its proven ability to create a valid style of its own, both with regard to subject matter and the visual conception of its photography and editing.

When a production crisis hit the industry in 1945 it was saved from annihilation by the initiative of a few independent producers. In 1955 Nelson Pereira dos Santos made *Rio 40°*, showing a cross-section of the capital's inhabitants and their life and drawing on the music and poetry of the city's poor. This film launched what was later known as the New Cinema. Pereira himself went on to make *Rio Zona Norte* (1957), *Mandacaru Vermelho* (1961), *Boca de curo* (1962) and *Vidas secas* (1963), which owe much to neo-realism but show considerable individual maturity. At the same time, with *Na garganta do diabo* (1959), Walter Hugo Khoury—a young director influenced by Bergman, Lang and von Sternberg—revealed an artistic refinement far superior to the melodramatic material he used as a base. Another young director, Roberto Farías, made *Cidade Ameacada* (1960), in the tradition of the Hollywood thriller, and has earned praise for his sensitive handling of the medium.

Apart from these individual efforts, the Brazilian film industry survived commercially by pandering to the demand for popular musical comedies, *chanchadas*, which were crudely made and exploited the pop-songs of the moment. These films were mass-produced for the home market and did nothing for the prestige of the Brazilian cinema abroad. A group of young film-makers rebelled against this state of affairs and 1962, with its 19 feature films, became the first year of the 'New Brazilian Cinema'. Five 1962 films won prizes at festivals and were bought for distribution abroad: *Os Cafajestas* (Ruy Guerra), *O pagador de promessas* (Anselmo Duarte), *O assalto ao trem pagador* (Roberto Farías), *Tres cabras de Lampiao* (Aurelio Teixeira) and *Mandacaru Vermelho* (Pereira dos Santos). This was the beginning of the Brazilian equivalent of the French Nouvelle Vague. Further films by Khoury, Pereira, Glauber Rocha, Ruy Guerra and Paulo César Saraceni induced the French critic Louis Marcorelles to speak of 'a young cinema, a creature of chance and audacity rather than the result of a clear-cut political and economic situation.' The same French critic points out that 'in Brazil they want to create a new cinema that is neither demagogical like neo-realism in its decline' nor gratuitous like the Nouvelle Vague at cocktail-time.

The problems tackled by these low-budget productions, made outside the studios and often with a hand-held camera, are the problems that afflict Brazil, and it is no coincidence that several have come up against the moral and political censorship. On the one hand they dramatise the hardships of rural life, with its hunger and violence (*Vidas secas*); on the other hand, like the films of Fellini and Antonioni, they dissect the uncertainties and moral dilemmas which beset the city-dwellers, as in Saraceni's *O desafio* (1965), which was favourably received at the Rio de Janeiro Festival. True individualists, the young Brazilian directors consider style as important as content. They are keen on camera-effects, of which the swift and circular panoramic shots around a naked woman in *Os Cafajestas* are a good example.

For the time being, the New Cinema has not managed to achieve international distribution. Few of its films are widely known in Europe or even in Latin America, since they are not usually shown outside festivals and small art cinemas.

ARGENTINA

The Argentine film industry dates back to the introduction of sound, and of the two companies founded almost simultaneously in 1933, Argentina Sono Film and Lumiton, the former still exists. The industry established itself rapidly, relying on the popular appeal of its stars. Some films of the first few years showed quality, such as *Viento Norte* (Mario Soffici, 1937) *Prisioneros de la tierra* (Soffici, 1939), *La Guerra Gaucha* (Lucas Demare, 1942), drawing on the history and countryside of Argentina. Other directors of the period (Manuel Romero, José A. Ferreyra, Leopoldo Torres Rios) brought to the screen another equally important facet of Argentine life in their comedies with an urban setting.

The Perón regime imposed guide-lines on the cinema and controlled vital aspects of production (such as the distribution of raw-stock); the film industry, in turn, went out of its way to gain the approval of politicians. In the resulting confusion Mexico forged ahead in the capture of Latin American markets and a number of Argentine stars were driven into voluntary exile. At a time when Italy was just coming to the end of its so-called 'era of the white telephone' and was giving birth to neo-realism, Argentina drew back from a cinema with authentically popular roots, and launched a trend of conventional and culturally pretentious film adaptations of the works of Tolstoy, Flaubert, Andreyev, Dostoyevsky and Pirandello or screen biographies.

The overthrow of the Perón regime in September 1955 opened a new chapter in the history of the Argentine cinema. The Instituto Nacional de Cinematografía, founded in April 1957, offered a different kind of official protection and made it possible for independent film production to develop side by side with the commercial cinema. The succeeding chairmen and officials of the Institute, none of them specialists of the cinema, imposed a tax on the sale of tickets, classified Argentine films according to merit, made their exhibition throughout the country obligatory, selected the films they considered suitable for the various international film festivals and —above all—established a credit scheme (an advance on production costs) and distributed annual prizes. The open protectionism of these measures have earned the Institute a great deal of criticism and by now, after numerous conflicts with producers and distributors, corruption has crept into the mechanism of credit and prize awards. Bribery is not unknown and the major companies have been allowed to hinder the efforts of the young film-makers to improve the Argentine cinema. Oddly enough, in spite of all the official protectionism little has been done to promote Argentine films on foreign markets.

In spite of all difficulties and thanks to the talent, the inspiration and the high vision of individual directors, an independent cinema has branched out. The most distinguished member of this school is Leopoldo Torre Nilsson (son of Torres Ríos), who has digested the influence of Buñuel, Bergman, Bresson and other European directors and developed a personal style in his highly visual films that show, at times, an inclination towards morbid detail. With *La casa del ángel* (1957) and subsequent films (*El secuestrador, La caída, Fin de fiesta, La mano en la trampa, La terraza*), he is an example to his young compatriots and colleagues and has established contact with other countries. Not only have his films been shown at festivals; he himself has travelled far and wide to promote them abroad and succeeded in selling them for distribution on the foreign market. Moreover, he has been a pioneer of coproductions with France, Brazil and the United States.

Along with Torre Nilsson, his friend Fernando Ayala has since 1956 (*Ayer fue primavera, Los tallos amargos*) been promoting a style and a type of cinema that bear witness to the national character and the problems that beset his country. This attitude led to the making of *El jefe* (Aries) in 1959. Ayala persisted with further attempts at social criticism, of which the best example is *Paula cautiva*, but a string of commercial failures obliged him in 1966 to come out with a merely competent farce, *Hotel alojamiento*, whose box-office success has compensated for serious financial losses.

Other young directors have distinguished themselves with a smaller number of films each: they are David José Kohon (*Prisioneros de la tierra, Tres veces Ana*), Rodolfo Kuhn (*Los jóvenes viejos, Pajarito Gómez*), Lautaro Murúa (*Shunko, Alias Gardelito*), Fernando Birri (*Los inundados*), José Martinez Suárez (*Dar la cara*), Ricardo Alventosa (*La herencia*) and Leonardo Favio (*Crónica de un niño solo, Romance del Aniceto*). All of them, and the makers of short films and documentaries too, have been faced with enormous difficulties in the production and distribution of their films in competition with a powerful industry. The fact that neither Birri nor Murúa has obtained any of the fifteen annual awards, though their films have won prizes at international festivals, is but a symptom of this conflict. Another is the practice of giving credits to those films which are likely to make most money, regardless of the need to protect films of greater quality. It is not surprising, therefore, that several young directors have abandoned the cinema or left the country, leaving others to continue the struggle against the prevailing system. Meanwhile, the opinion is shared by many that the only way the situation will be improved is by a change of regime.

BIBLIOGRAPHY

García Riera, Emilio. *El cine mexicano*, Era, Mexico, 1963.
Nubila, Domingo di. *Historia del cine argentino*, Buenos Aires, 1959.
Cine Cubano, ICAIC, Havana (journal).

THE LATIN AMERICAN PRESS

SERGIO DE SANTIS

ALTHOUGH nearly a thousand daily papers are published throughout Latin America with an overall circulation of more than 15 million copies, the effectiveness of the Latin American press as a mass medium is limited. Of 240-50 million Latin Americans approximately 50 per cent are country-dwellers whose rate of illiteracy in certain areas is as high as 70 per cent. Thus a large section of the population remains cut off from the printed word. This situation is beginning to change with the growing assimilation of the peasant masses into the towns, but there is little evidence that a parallel cultural integration is taking place, since the incoming flow of people finds its way mainly to the backward shanty-town communities, mushrooming at an alarming rate around the big cities. Rio has its *favelas*, Buenos Aires the *villas miseria*, Santiago de Chile the *poblaciones callampa*, Caracas its *ranchitos*, and so on.

In 1965 155 copies of daily newspapers were printed for every 1,000 inhabitants in Argentina (as compared with 357 copies in the United States). However, Argentina is an exception, for she not only boasts one of the lowest rates of illiteracy in the whole of Latin America, but has one of the largest urban populations, a solid middle class and one of the most effective unionised working classes in the continent. In Brazil, which is undergoing rapid economic development, only 54 copies of newspapers are printed for every 1,000 inhabitants, which means that the reading of daily papers is still largely the prerogative of an elite. Newspaper readership is still lower in most of the Central American and Caribbean republics, and in the developing countries of the south such as Bolivia and Paraguay.

In spite of its limited readership the Latin American press still has great significance both for its potential as a news source from the continent and for the degree of its political influence. Only the Latin American press has it in its power to remedy the present dearth of day-to-day information on the countries of the continent in most parts of the world, a situation in which prejudices and misconceptions readily accepted about Latin America are due to the absence of first-hand news and to an excessive reliance on the established news agency reports. The accurate reporting of news is jeopardised by non-Latin American information sources, particularly those based in the United States, like the Associated Press (AP) and the United Press International (UPI).

DAILIES

The level of news-reporting in the majority of the thousand dailies that appear in the twenty republics, however, is discouragingly low. Many of them are in fact afternoon tabloids full of crime items, sensational stories and 'scandal' scoops; many also are provincial papers of exclusively local interest—not to mention those papers which openly indulge in blackmail. Alongside this mass of newspapers there exists a handful of big dailies with a fine tradition and a high degree of professionalism—*La Prensa* and *La Nación* in Buenos Aires, *El Tiempo* in Bogotá, *El Mercurio* and *El Diario Ilustrado* in Santiago de Chile, *El Nacional* in Caracas, *El Comercio* in Lima, *Excelsior* in Mexico City, *O Estado de São Paulo* in São Paulo, *O Correio de Manha* in Rio de Janeiro, and a few others. Nevertheless interest even in these papers is usually wholly national-centred. They provide a far higher element of information on the political and public life of their own countries than do European newspapers (parliamentary debates are frequently reproduced verbatim, while more important pieces of legislation are printed in full).

The big dailies reflect the lack of communications between the countries of Latin America and are marred by the absence of first-hand news from their neighbours. A newspaper of the calibre and wide reputation of *Excelsior* can have not a single correspondent based outside Mexico! The present state of affairs is due in great part to the heavy reliance of the Latin American press upon AP reports. This agency has in fact few full-time correspondents in Latin America and bases its reports on freelance articles. UPI despatches are quite often combined with those of the Agence France Presse (AFP), but it is generally true that 'Latin American' news reports concocted by the big local dailies are no more and no less reliable than those put together by the editorial staff on any European paper. One recent welcome development has been the foundation of an independent news agency, the Inter Press Service (IPS), having a network of correspondents throughout Latin America. Its aim is to provide a channel of communication both between Latin America and Europe and between Latin American countries. The activities of the IPS are, however, as yet limited.

PERIODICALS

The lack of a truly 'continental' news coverage hitherto has also limited the quality of the weekly press. There are indeed few magazines published in Latin America, and it is significant that *Vision-Visão*, which has the biggest circulation, should be financed and largely controlled by United States businessmen with interests in Latin America. *Vision-Visão* is published in two languages (Spanish and Portuguese) and in three editions (Argentine, Mexican and Brazilian). It is well-informed and often supplied with reliable revelations, yet remains essentially identified with the interests of the United States. It is nonetheless worthy of mention for its good coverage of the main threads of the continent's affairs as well as its frequent surveys of problems and events of overall continental interest (such as the Alliance for Progress, the Latin American steel industry, the role of the military and so on). Another weekly, *O Cruzeiro*, published in Rio de Janeiro on a *Life* formula, is attractive for its layout and for the excellence of its photographs, but disappointingly poor in content. *Marcha*, a Uruguayan left-wing weekly, is quite different. While devoting much space to national news it presents systematic reports on continental affairs, though tending usually to confine its attention to some of the major countries such as Brazil, Argentina, Bolivia, Chile, Peru and Colombia. It prefers to ignore the Caribbean and Central American areas except when such newsworthy items as the Dominican question or the Guatemalan insurrection occur. In spite of this limitation *Marcha* is probably the only Latin American magazine to cultivate a truly continental outlook, through its thorough coverage of 'the Latin American reawakening' and its comprehensive network of internationally known contributors (Adolfo Gilly, Rogelio Garcia Lupo, and many others).

The higher-level periodicals are in a healthier state, particularly in Mexico which boasts one of the major publishing houses in Latin America, the Fondo de Cultura Económica. It produces *El Trimestre Económico*, the most serious review of economic studies in Latin America. Another periodical connected with the Fondo is *Cuadernos Americanos* (published six times a year), under its versatile editor Jésus Silva Hertzog who brings together articles of the highest level on politics, history, literature and archeology. *Panoramas*, another Mexican review (which ceased publication in 1966), was edited for three years by Victor Alba for the Congress for Cultural Freedom. It became to some extent the ideological mouthpiece of Latin American social-democracy when four-year-old *Combate* (produced by the Costa Rican Institute of Political Education) ceased publication in 1963. *América Latina*, a Spanish-Portuguese quarterly published in Rio de Janeiro under the auspices of UNESCO by the Latin American Centre for Social Science Studies, is another review with a truly continental standpoint.

On the literary side, *Sur*, an Argentine review edited by Victoria Ocampo, stands out for its continental reputation as a cosmopolitan journal. Another interesting cultural review is *Atenea*, published by the University of Concepción in Chile. There is a wealth of publications devoted to national topics. Brazil's many academic reviews include *La Revista Brasiliense* (São Paulo), organ of the Vargas Economic Foundation. In Venezuela the most aggressive and progressive publication is the fortnightly *Que Pasa en Venezuela;* another important Venezuelan review is *Política* (published eight times a year) connected with the left wing of the Acción Democrática party; *Política*, edited by Luis Beltran, was founded some years ago as a 'continental review' but has progressively narrowed its scope to purely national politics.

Another periodical called *Política* is published in Mexico. This is an anti-regime left-wing fortnightly which sometimes offers very good first-hand reports. During the recent presidential campaign it gathered together all the speeches made by the candidate of the official party Gustavo Díaz Ordaz (now President). Also in Mexico the Bank for Overseas Trade publishes a first-class monthly, *Comercio Exterior*, with contributions from leading Mexican economists. While in theory intended to cover only overseas trade and relations with LAFTA, in practice it follows all aspects of the Mexican economy. In the rest of Latin America there are a great many news weeklies and fortnightlies such as *Ercilla* in Chile, *La Nueva Prensa* in Colombia, *Caretas* and *El Mundo* in Peru, *Primera Plana*, *Todo* and *Confirmado* in Argentina, *La Calle* in Ecuador, *Ahora* in the Dominican Republic. Humorous papers are few in Latin America. Two alone are worthy of mention, *Topaze* in Chile and *Tia Vicenta* in Argentina, both specialising in political satire.

Marxist and Catholic Publishing Blocs

The Marxist and Catholic publishing blocs occupy an important place in Latin American journalism. Both Catholic and Marxist periodicals have a network covering almost the whole of Latin America; with their ideological standpoints they make serious attempts to get at the root of national and continental questions in a way not commonly found in Latin American journalism. (The word 'Marxist' is here used instead of 'Communist' because the periodicals edited by the 'orthodox' Communist parties are only a sector of this publishing bloc.) The most important ideological publications of Latin American Communist parties are *Nueva Era* (Argentina), *Principios* (Chile), *Estudios* (Uruguay), *Novos Rumos* (Brazil, now banned), *Nueva Epoca* (Mexico) and *Principios* (Venezuela). There are in addition other outlets: in Chile, for instance, there is the communist daily *El Siglo*, while in Argentina the party publishes the periodicals *Propositos*, *Nuestra Palabra*, and *Cuadernos de Cultura* (part ideological, part literary).

The Marxist wing also comprises other groups—from various shades of Trotskyites to socialists, pro-Castroists and National Liberation Fronts (FLN). Most of these groups have their own press outlets: *Izquierda* (Venezuelan MIR), *Arauco* (Chilean Socialist party), *Voz Rebelde* (Peruvian MIR), *Batalla* (Colombian pro-Castroists), *Revolución Peru* (Peruvian FLN), *Sucesos* (Mexican pro-Castroist), *Punto Final* (independent left-wing, Chilean), *Plan* (pro-communist, Chilean) and so on. Argentina probably has the highest proportion of these left-wing periodicals since both the Communist and Socialist parties in Argentina have provoked a number of splinter groups. To these may be added the various Peronist groups, the whole resulting in such reviews as *Voz Proletaria*, *Palabra Obrera*, *Frente Argentino*, *El Obrero*, *Marcha hacia la Revolución Socialista*, *Política Obrera*, *Socialismo de Vanguardia*, *La Pala* and *Revista de la Liberación*. All too frequently their interest is diminished by their descent to personal and factional polemics. But one of them, *Pasado y Presente* (published eight times a year), is worthy of mention for the high level of its articles and essays. It is edited by Jose Arico and published in Córdoba.

The two principal Cuban dailies, published in Havana, *Revolución* (once spokesman for the M-26/7) and *Hoy* (once mouthpiece for the PSP and Communist Party) were recently amalgamated under the name *Granma*. This paper is now of some importance as an 'official' information source on Cuba, but its treatment of events in the rest of the continent, apart from the subject of guerrilla warfare, is summary. The periodical press, however, which is mainly ideological and/or technical, has proved more rewarding. For six years the regime's principal exponent of theory *Cuba Socialista* (now suspended) often presented comprehensive analyses of the most significant aspects of the Cuban scene (the formation of party cadres, agrarian reform, socialist education, etc.). The weekly *Panorama Económico Latino-americano* (*PEL*), another review worthy of reference, specialises in technical articles on Cuban and Latin American economic problems. *Nuestra Industria Económica*, *Comercio Exterior* and *Política Internacional* are published respectively by the Industrial, Export and Foreign Ministries. The speeches of government leaders are printed verbatim in ad hoc publications (for some years *Obra Revolucionaria* and now *El Orientador Revolucionario*).

The Catholic ideological bloc embraces both party and religious publications. Many of these, frequently of the highest standard, appear in Chile which has the strongest, most progressive Christian Democrat party in Latin America. The most important of all is *Política y Espíritu*, founded nineteen years ago by Eduardo Frei and published in Santiago. There are several lesser party publications such as *Dece* and *Noticias de Chile*. Also worth noting are *Mensaje* (published eight times a year), a doctrinaire periodical edited by a Jesuit, Roger Vekemans (propounder of the 'Christian Revolution' theory), the Curia weekly *La Voz* (which only recently ceased publication), and *Bidi*, voice of the International Catholic Student Movement. Among notable publications in the rest of the continent are *El Voto*

Nacional (Colombia), *Nuevo Orden* and *Nueva Generación* (Venezuela), *Comunidad Democristiana, IEI, Siglo Cero* (Argentina), and a host of newssheets. Another interesting venture has been *Cuadernos de Economía Humana*, published in Uruguay through the agencies of the Centro Latinoamericano de Economía Humana, and inspired by the solidarity theories of Father Lebret.

FREEDOM OF THE PRESS

How far is the Latin American press a free press? Every constitution in Latin America guarantees freedom of speech, and most of them actually condemn press censorship. In fact active censorship applies only in countries under such iron dictatorships as those in Haiti, Paraguay and Nicaragua. Nevertheless, in countries where no official censorship exists, the government in office keeps a close eye on the opposition press. Indirect control may be exercised by means of the massive regulations governing the licensing of publications, the correct professional registration of journalists, the allotment of newsprint quotas, and so on. Newspapers may often be compelled to print lengthy government statements and may even be banned if their anti-government attacks become too vehement.

The Vargas regime in Brazil and that of Perón in Argentina immediately spring to mind in connection with government pressure on the press. Vargas reduced the *Estado* of São Paulo to passive acquiescence, while Perón took over *La Prensa*. Government pressure is more widespread than might be supposed. In Venezuela, for instance, in 1961–2, the Betancourt regime systematically persecuted not only such left-wing papers as the communist *Tribuna Popular* and the MIR *Izquierda*, but even a number of moderate opposition papers like the radical *La Hora, URD* and *El Pueblo*—which were actually suppressed. In Mexico the government controls the allotment of newsprint through an ad hoc body (PIPSA), while newspapers must undertake, on pain of closure, to abide by a 'code of ethics' laid down by a special committee.

Financial backing is yet another controlling factor, since most newspapers are invariably owned by major economic pressure groups in their respective countries. There are a great many examples: in Chile, for instance, the Edwards group owns *El Mercurio, La Segunda, Las Ultimas Noticias* and *La Estrella* of Valparaiso, while a mixed group of capitalists controls Zig Zag, publisher of the weeklies *Ercilla, Vea* and *Zig Zag*. In Panama the Arias group runs *El Panamá America, La Critica* and *La Hora*. In Ecuador the three main newspapers, *El Comercio* of Quito, *El Universo* and *El Telégrafo* of Guayaquil are owned respectively by the Mantilla, Perez Castro and Castillo families.

All this may explain why the major newspapers, and especially the dailies, are almost invariably conservative and even initiate denunciation of anti-government activity. The case of Carlos Lacerda, whose *Tribuna da Imprensa* of Rio played a decisive role in pushing Vargas to suicide and in bringing down two presidents suspected of left-wing sympathies (Janio Quadros and Joas Goulart), is symptomatic. It cannot be said to be exceptional. There does exist a Sociedad Interamericana de Prensa (SIP, or IAPA as it is known in the United States), which is on the whole a formal body, and raises its voice against only the most flagrant violations of freedom of the press. Moreover the SIP is unequivocally pro-American and anti-communist, and is consequently willing to turn a blind eye when unethical action against free speech is cloaked under the expedient of keeping the continent free of so-called 'communist infiltration'.

Country	Number of newspapers	Total daily printing	Copies per 1,000 inhabitants
Argentina . . .	233	3,186,000	155
Bolivia . . .	6	116,000	34
Brazil	291	3,837,000	54
Colombia . . .	44	788,000	56
Costa Rica . . .	6	115,000	94
Chile . . .	47	1,047,000	134
Dominican Republic .	5	82,000	27
Ecuador . . .	24	251,150	58
El Salvador . .	14	117,000	45
Guatemala . . .	6	88,300	23
Haiti	6	38,000	11
Honduras . . .	6	46,000	25
Mexico . . .	189	2,992,000	83
Nicaragua . . .	8	94,000	66
Panama . . .	10	106,000	97
Paraguay . . .	5	64,000	37
Peru	49	492,000	45
Uruguay . . .	26	754,000	260
Venezuela . . .	29	646,000	96
United States . .	1,763	59,211,464	326

Sources: SIP Report for 1965. The Cuban figures have been omitted, as the SIP maintains that there is no true press in Cuba.

BIBLIOGRAPHY

Chilcote, Ronald H. 'The Press in Latin America, Spain and Portugal', *Hispanic American Report*, special issue, Stanford, Calif., 1963.
Hopper, Rex and Harris, Janice. 'Cultura de masas en America Latina', *Rivista Venezuelana Politica*, 18, Caracas, October–December 1961.
Lambert, Jacques. *Amérique latine; structures sociales et institutions politiques*, Presses Universitaires de France, Paris, 1963.
Needler, Martin. *Latin American Politics in Perspective*, Van Nostrand, Princeton, NJ, 1963.

NOTES ON CONTRIBUTORS

ADAMS, RICHARD NEWBOLT. Scientist, World Health Organisation, Central America, 1952–6; Professor of Sociology and Anthropology, Michigan State University, 1956–62. Currently Professor of Anthropology, University of Texas, where he is chairman of the Department of Anthropology and Assistant Director of the Institute of Latin American Studies. Has done field research in social anthropology in Costa Rica, El Salvador, Guatemala, Honduras, Nicaragua, Panama, Bolivia, Chile and Peru. President of the Society for Applied Anthropology, 1962–3.

ALBERTO, CARLOS. Practising architect and Professor in the Faculty of Architecture and Fine Arts in the Catholic University of Chile, Santiago.

AMUNÁTEGUI, GREGORIO. Independent barrister, 1950–8; appointed Legal Adviser to the Chilean Ministry of Mining Affairs, 1958; Deputy Executive Vice-President and Chief Legal Adviser of the Departamento del Cobre de Chile, 1959–62. Adviser to the Corporación del Cobre de Chile since 1965. Has travelled extensively in North, Central and South America, Europe and Africa both privately and in official capacities.

ANGELL, ALAN. Research Fellow in Latin American Politics, St Antony's College, Oxford and the Royal Institute of International Affairs, London. Previously lectured in Comparative Politics, University of Keele; worked for UNESCO at the School of Public Administration in Colombia; lectured for the British Council at the University of the Andes, Bogotá.

BARRACLOUGH, SOLON. Currently on leave from Cornell University, where he is a Professor in the Department of Agricultural Economics, as FAO Project Manager of the Land Reform Research Institute (ICIRA), Santiago, Chile.

BARRÍA, JORGE. Professor of History, Geography and Law at the University of Chile; an authority on trade union history and organisation. Author of *Trayectoria y estructura del movimiento sindical chileno* (1962).

BELLALTA, JAIME. Technical Director of the Corporation for Urban Renewal (government agency), Santiago, Chile. Professor of Architecture at the Catholic University of Chile, 1952–7; studied and practised in London, 1958–67.

BLACKBURN, ROBIN. Assistant Lecturer in Sociology at the London School of Economics. Member of editorial board of *New Left Review*, London. Co-edited with Perry Anderson *Towards Socialism* (1965) and with Alexander Cockburn *The Incompatibles: Trade Union Militancy and the Consensus* (1967).

BORNHORST, DIRK. Architect. Work realised includes the Customs Building, Maracaibo, the Centro Profesional del Este and the Helicoid, Caracas. Currently Professor at the School of Architecture and Town Planning, Central University, Caracas. Co-editor of the magazines *Integral* (1953–8) and *Revista CAV* (since 1962). President of the Associación Cultural Humboldt, Caracas; founder member of the Sociedad Bolivariana de Arquitectos.

832

BRIGHT, ALEC STENNING. Architect. Taught at the University of the Andes, Bogotá, 1953–6; Interamerican Housing Centre, Bogotá, 1956–60; teaching post at the University of the Andes and private practice in Bogotá since 1961.

BROOKS, JOHN C. G. On the staff of the Economic Intelligence Department of the Bank of London and South America Ltd. Previously the Department's representative in Brazil, and *Financial Times* correspondent in Rio de Janeiro, 1962–4. Has lectured and contributed to periodicals extensively on Brazilian subjects.

CALVO, PETER. Currently preparing Ph.D. thesis on Latin America and international economic relations at London University.

CASTEDO, LEOPOLDO. Expatriated from Spain, 1939; now a Chilean citizen. Formerly Titular Professor at the University of Chile; has been visiting professor to many universities in the United States and Latin America. Has written extensively on Latin American history and art.

CLISSOLD, STEPHEN. Lived in Chile for some years. Author of several books on Latin American history and culture.

COCKS, KENNETH P. Joined the Research Department of the Bank of London and South America Ltd in 1949. Head of the Bank's Research Department in Buenos Aires, 1960–1; travelled in Argentina, Brazil, Paraguay, and Uruguay. Now executive officer, Economic Intelligence Department.

COHEN, J. M. Writer, translator, broadcaster, etc. Has been interested in modern Spanish-language poetry for more than twenty years and is personally acquainted with many poets. Member of jury of annual poetry prize given by the Casa de las Américas, Havana, 1965. Translations include *Don Quixote* (1950), *The Penguin Book of Spanish Verse* (1956), *The Life of Saint Teresa* (1957) and Bernal Diaz, *The Conquest of New Spain* (1963).

CONDÉ, MARYSE. Lecturer in English and French literature in Conakry, Guinea, 1960–4; head of the French Department of the Ghana Institute of Languages, Accra, 1964–6. Joined the BBC in 1967 (African Magazine, French Section).

CONNELL-SMITH, GORDON. Senior Lecturer in History, University of Hull. Fellow of the Royal Historical Society. Awarded the Julian Corbett Prize for Modern Naval History at the Institute of Historical Research, 1949. Publications include *Forerunners of Drake* (1954), *Pattern of the Post-war World* (1957), *The Inter-American System* (1966) and numerous articles on inter-American relations.

CORRÊA DE AZEVEDO, LUIZ HEITOR. Has lectured at the Sorbonne Institute of Latin American Advanced Studies since its creation in 1954. Formerly on staff of the National Institute of Music, Rio de Janeiro: editor of its review *Revista Brasileira de Música* and Professor of National Folk-lore. Music Specialist at UNESCO, Paris, 1937–65. Publications include *Música e músicos do Brasil* (1950), *Bibliografía musical brasileira* (1952) and *150 anos de música no Brasil* (1956).

COY, PETER. Lecturer in the Department of Anthropology and Sociology, Monash University, Melbourne. Elected to the first Philip Bagby Studentship in Social Anthropology at Oxford University, he undertook a study of the Nahuatl-speaking peoples of Mexico, and subsequently studied (in Mexico) Mexican systems of land tenure and the social organisation of the Mexican village.

DAUSTER, FRANK. Professor of Romance Languages at Rutgers State University. Author of *Breve historia del teatro hispanicoamericano: Siglos XIX y XX* (1966), etc.

ECKENSTEIN, CHRISTOPHER. Member of the Geneva bar, 1952; legal practice in New York and Geneva; journalist in Asia and Latin America, 1954 and 1962; Division of Commerce of Swiss government dealing with OEEC, EFTA and EEC affairs, 1956–62; advisor to East African governments for relations with EEC, 1963; trade policy consultant for ECLA, Santiago, Chile, 1963–4; special adviser on policy matters to the secretary-general of the United Nations Conference on Trade and Development, Geneva.

ELLIOT, GERALD. Has worked since 1948 with the whaling, fishing and shipping company Chr. Salvesen & Co. Ltd of Leith, Scotland, and is now a managing director. Salvesen operate fish meal plants in Peru with Peruvian partners.

FANGER, ULRICH. Coordinator of a socio-pedagogical research project at the Instituto Centroamericano de Extensión de la Cultura, San José, Costa Rica. Formerly Research Assistant, Latin American Department of the Arnold Bergstraesser Institute of Social Sciences, Freiburg.

FERGUSON, JOHN HALCRO. Latin American correspondent for *The Observer*. On staff of the British Embassy in Buenos Aires, 1941–5; in Bogotá, 1946; joined *The Observer* in 1948. Has visited all Latin American countries (Cuba four times). Author of *Latin America: The Balance of Power Redressed* (1960), *The Revolutions of Latin America* (1963), *The River Plate Republics: Argentina, Uruguay, Paraguay* (1964); *Nationalism in Latin America* in preparation.

FRANCO, JEAN. Reader in Latin American Literature at King's College, London. Has published translations and numerous articles, edited two editions of Spanish American short stories, and is writing a book on art and social conscience in Latin America.

FUENTES MOHR, ALBERTO. Worked with the United Nations Trusteeship Department, 1956–7 and the Economic Commission for Latin America, 1957–8; head of the office in charge of Central American integration at the Guatemalan Ministry of Economy, 1958–61; Deputy Secretary General, Central American Secretariat for Economic Integration, 1962. Since 1963 head of the Joint Planning Mission for Central America and Council member of the Latin American Institute for Economic and Social Planning.

FURTADO, CELSO. Professeur Associé in the Faculty of Law and Economic Science of the Sorbonne; Associate Professor of the Institute of International Studies, University of Chile. Formerly ECLA economist; Director of the Development Bank of Brazil; Executive Head of the Superintendency for the Development of the North-East of Brazil; Minister for Planning in the Goulart government. Publications available in English (all published by the Univ. of California Press): *The Economic Growth of Brazil* (1963), *Development and Underdevelopment* (1964), *Diagnosis of the Brazilian Crisis* (1966).

GALLO, EZEQUIEL. Historian. Lecturer at the Universidad Nacional del Litoral, Santa Fé, 1961–5; member of the editorial board of *Desarrollo Económico*, Buenos Aires, 1964–5; researched at the Centro de Sociología Comparada, Instituto Torcuato di Tella, Buenos Aires, 1964–6. Currently reading for a post-graduate degree at Oxford University.

GONZÁLEZ, ALBERTO. Architect practising in Mexico City.

HAYTER, TERESA. On staff of the Overseas Development Institute, London. Published a book on French aid in 1966.

HECHT, ERNEST. Chairman and Managing Director, Souvenir Press Ltd and associated companies. Has visited Latin America several times. Publishes *International Football Annual;* has also published *Brazil Book of Football, The Real Madrid Book of Football* and the autobiography of Matt Busby.

HENFREY, COLIN V. F. Born in Kenya; educated in England. In British Guiana as community development worker, 1959–60; Harkness Fellow, United States, in Anthropology and Latin American Studies at Cornell University, 1964–5. Currently planning research in Latin American social history. Author of *The Gentle People: A Journey amongst the Indian Tribes of Guiana* (1964).

HENFREY, JUNE M. (née GOLLOP). Born in Barbados. Currently a Research Fellow at St Anne's College, Oxford, where she is preparing a thesis on Aimé Césaire.

HENNESSY, ALISTAIR. Reader in History at Warwick University and Research Fellow, St Antony's College, Oxford. Formerly Lecturer in History at Exeter University. Author of *The Federal Republic in Spain* (1962).

HENRIQUES, FERNANDO. Professorial Fellow and Director of the Research Unit for the Study of Multi-Racial Societies, University of Sussex. Formerly Lecturer in Social Anthropology, University of Leeds, 1948–64.

HERRERA, FELIPE. President of the Inter-American Development Bank since 1960. Professor of Political Economy, University of Chile, 1947–58; Chilean Minister of Finance, 1953; on board of International Bank for Reconstruction and Development and International Monetary Fund, 1953–8; Executive Director, IMF, 1958–60.

HOETINK, HARRY. Director of the Centre of Latin American Research and Documentation, University of Amsterdam and Professor of Sociology at Rotterdam University. Lived for twelve years in the Caribbean area, of which seven years in Curaçao. An English edition of his book under the title *The Two Caribbean Variants* is in preparation.

HOLLEY, HUGH ANTONY. Senior Research Officer, Bank of London and South America Ltd. Member of international working group set up by the Inter-American Development Bank to study Europe's participation in the financing of Latin American development, 1964–5. Author, with the late Professor Frederic Benham, of *A Short Introduction to the Economy of Latin America* (1960).

HOUGHTON, RONALD. Architect. Has worked in London, Paris and Cuba. Currently on staff of the Greater London Council Architects' Department.

HOWARTH, DAVID A. Writer. Author of *The Golden Isthmus* (1966), etc.

HUELIN, DAVID. Formerly on staff of the Buenos Aires Great Southern and Western Railways; Assistant Editor, *Review of the River Plate*, Buenos Aires, 1943–50. Joined the Bank of London and South America Ltd in 1952; currently Manager, Economic Intelligence Dept.

HUNT, JAMES C. Latin American specialist with the Economist Intelligence Unit Ltd, 1953–8; Executive Secretary, Britain in Europe, London, 1958–61; Assistant Director General and Education Director, the Hispanic and Luso-Brazilian Councils, London, 1962–6; Director, International Economic Development Group Ltd, 1966–7. Founder member and Hon. Treasurer,

Society for Latin American Studies, London. Freelance journalist and broadcaster.

JOXE, ALAIN. Historian. On staff of the Centre d'Études de Politique Étrangère, Paris, where he has organised a study-group on Latin American problems and is preparing a thesis on the 1962 Cuban crisis and the world system; also on staff of the École Pratique des Hautes Études. Currently Visiting Professor at the Institute of International Studies, University of Chile. Author of *Le conflit sino-soviétique et l'Amérique latine* (1967).

DE KADT, EMANUEL. Lecturer in Sociology at the London School of Economics and Research Specialist in Latin American Affairs at the Royal Institute of International Affairs, London. Has spent a year in Brazil (1965/6) doing research on the involvement of Catholic groups in social reform.

KATZ, JORGE. Economist. Member of research staff of the Federal Council of Investment, Buenos Aires, 1960–3; member of the Dirección Nacional de Promoción Industrial, Buenos Aires, 1963–4. Currently preparing a thesis on post-war manufacturing growth in Argentina at Oxford University.

LAUWERYS, JOSEPH A. Professor of Comparative Education at the University of London Institute of Education. Has visited most Latin American countries. Consultant to the University of Chile, 1962; UNESCO Expert in the Universities of Concepción, 1964/5 and Bahia, 1966. President of the Comparative Education Society in Europe and Chairman of the International New Education Fellowship.

LEHMANN, DAVID. Currently preparing for a research degree in Sociology at Oxford University.

LYONETTE, KEVIN J. Harkness Fellow in the United States (Universities of California and Harvard), 1962–4 in Latin American Studies. Has visited various Latin American countries, including Colombia, on research projects.

MARROQUÍN, ALEJANDRO D. On staff of the University of El Salvador since 1944; currently teaching Central American Sociology; Director, Department of Social Sciences. Has also taught at Mexico, Honduras and Illinois universities. Vice-President of the Latin American Association of Sociology; founder and President of the El Salvador Association of Sociology. Author of books on sociology, economics and theory of history.

MEYRIAT, JEAN. Professor (Directeur d'Études) at the École Pratique des Hautes Études, Sorbonne (Section des sciences économiques et sociales); Professor at the Institut d'Études Politiques and at the Institut des Hautes Études d'Amerique Latine, University of Paris. Founded in 1952 the Centre d'Étude des Relations Internationales, a research department of the Fondation Nationale des Sciences Politiques, and is co-director. Author of various books on political and economic subjects.

MIRÓ, CARMEN A. Director of the United Nations Latin American Demographic Centre. Formerly Director of Statistics and Census of the Republic of Panama; Vice-President of the International Union for the Scientific Study of Population and of the Inter-American Statistical Institute. Currently Fellow of the American Statistical Association. Her studies on the population of Latin America, on Latin American fertility and on training and research in demography have appeared in several books and journals.

MORÓN, GUILLERMO. Professor of the History of Venezuelan Literature at the Andres Bello University, Caracas. Studied at several European universities. Professor of Spanish American Culture at the University of Hamburg,

1956–8; Member of the National Academy of History of Venezuela; editor of Shell of Venezuela's *Revista Shell;* Coordinator of Shell Foundation's Cultural and Educational Programmes.

NEHEMKIS, PETER. Lawyer. Consultant on Latin American affairs; Guest Lecturer at the US Department of State Foreign Service Institute; a Trustee of the Pan American Development Foundation. Participated in preparation of the report *Alliance for Progress* for President Kennedy, December 1960; in 1962 appointed by the OAS to the Inter-American Commission to monitor the first free Dominican elections and subsequently invited by the Dominican government to prepare a plan for holding elections; has served on the Committee for the Alliance for Progress of the US Department of Commerce. Author of *Latin America: Myth and Reality* (1964).

ODELL, PETER R. Senior Lecturer in Geography at the London School of Economics. Specialist in economic geography with special reference to regional economic development in developing countries (mainly Latin America) and the economic geography of energy. Economist with a major international oil company, 1958–61 (responsible for Latin America); joined staff of the London School of Economics, 1961. Author of *An Economic Geography of Oil* (1963), *Oil: the New Commanding Height* (1965); contributed to E. Penrose (ed.), *The Large International Firm in Developing Countries,* 1967 ('The International Oil Industry in Latin America').

PARKER, FRANKLIN D. Professor of History, University of North Carolina, Greensboro. Has lived in Central America, and held Fulbright lectureships at the Universities of Peru (1961) and Colombia (1964). Author of *José Cecilio del Valle and the Establishment of the Central American Confederation* (1954) and *The Central American Republics* (1964).

PARKINSON, FRED. Assistant Director, London Institute of World Affairs. Formerly lectured in the Department of International Law and Relations, University College, London and edited the *Year Book of World Affairs.*

PEARSE, ANDREW. Head of Department of Rural Sociology at the Land Reform Research Institute (ICIRA), Santiago, Chile. In 1956 undertook sociological research in education with UNESCO in Brazil; subsequently worked in Colombia, Ecuador, Venezuela and Bolivia. President of Round Table on Sociology of Education at the Sixth Congress of Sociology, 1966; Named Appointed Research Fellow at St Antony's College, Oxford, 1968–9; currently preparing a book on the agrarian situation in Latin America.

PÉCAUT, DANIEL. On staff of the Laboratoire de Sociologie Industrielle, Paris.

PENDLE, GEORGE. Has visited Latin America frequently since 1930. British Council Representative in Paraguay, 1942–4; General Manager for Latin America of the Book Export Scheme, 1945; BBC special correspondent to Brazil and Argentina, 1955. Author of a number of books on Latin America, including *South America: A Visual Geography* (1958), *Uruguay* (3rd ed. 1963), *Argentina* (3rd ed. 1965), *Paraguay: A Riverside Nation* (3rd ed. 1967) and *A History of Latin America* (3rd ed. 1967).

PIKE, FREDRICK B. Professor of Latin American History, University of Pennsylvania. Formerly a member of the history faculty of the University of Notre Dame, Indiana. Conducted research in Chile, 1959–60, and in Peru, 1963–4. Author of an award-winning study of US–Chilean relations and of a history of Peru, and numerous articles on Latin America.

POBLETE BARTH, REV. RENATO, SJ. Professor of Sociology of Religion at the Catholic University of Chile, Santiago; a Director of the Religious Sociology Bureau of the Chilean Bishops and of the Socio-Religious Centre (FERES) in Chile; Director of the Centre of Socio-Religious Research, Centro Bellarmino, Chile. Conducts research for the Pastoral Letters of the Bishops of Chile. Member of the Catholic Interamerican Co-operation Program (CICOP) Committee.

PRESTON, DAVID A. Lecturer in Geography in the University of Leeds. Did doctoral research at the London School of Economics on an Ecuadorian Andean Negro area.

VAN RENSELAAR, HERMAN C. Research Fellow at the Royal Institute for the Tropics, Department of Anthropology, Amsterdam. Lived in Surinam, 1958–61 and visited the country again in 1966.

RETTIE, JOHN. Freelance journalist and commentator. On staff of Reuters news agency, 1952–7; Deputy Foreign News Editor and Commonwealth Correspondent, *News Chronicle*, 1959–60; correspondent in Mexico, Central America and the Greater Antilles for the BBC, *The Economist* and *The Daily Telegraph*, 1961–4.

RICKARDS, COLIN. Freelance journalist specialising in the Caribbean and Central America. Has worked as a correspondent for every major Caribbean newspaper and also covered special assignments for *The Daily Express*, *The Daily Telegraph* and *The Washington Post*. Frequent contributor to BBC Overseas Services; author of *Caribbean Power* (1963) and other books.

DA ROCHA, GLADSON. Architect practising in Rio de Janeiro.

ROGERS, WILLIAM D. Entered private legal practice, 1953. Appointed Special Counsel to US Coordinator for the Alliance for Progress Teodoro Moscoso, AID, Dept of State, 1962; Chief of Delegation to Annual Meetings of Inter-American Economic and Social Council (IAESC) at Expert Level, 1963 and 1964; appointed US Coordinator for the Alliance for Progress and Deputy Assistant Administrator, AID, 1963; Permanent Alternative Representative to IAESC, 1964–5; AID Distinguished Service Award, 1965; resigned 1965 to return to private practice. President, Center for Inter-American Relations, New York City, etc.

SABINO, FERNANDO. Writer and journalist. His published fiction includes *A vida real* ('Real Life'), *A mulher do vizinho* ('The Neighbour's Wife'), *O homem nu* ('The Naked Man') and *O encontro marca* ('A Time to Meet'; translated into German, Spanish and Dutch). Head of cultural affairs at the Brazilian Embassy, London, 1964–6.

SANGER, CLYDE. Journalist. On staff of *The Guardian* since 1959; now based at the United Nations and also covering Latin America and the Caribbean.

DE SANTIS, SERGIO. Editor of *Telegiornale* (RAI-TV, Rome); also responsible for Latin American section of the *International Socialist Journal*, Rome and contributor to other intellectual and political reviews. Has lived in and visited many Latin American countries. Translated and edited Italian edition of Jacques Lambert, *Amérique latine: Structures économiques et institutions politiques*.

SEGOVIA, RAFAEL. Professor, El Colegio de México. Director, Foro Internacional, 1962–6. Currently preparing a study of the politicisation of Mexican children.

SILVA CASTRO, RAÚL. Journalist and writer. Member of editorial board of *El Mercurio*, Santiago since 1924. Head of the Chilean section of the Biblioteca Nacional since 1931. OAS adviser in Chile for *Revista interamericana de bibliografía* and *Diccionario de literatura latinoamericana*. Author of numerous books on literature and cultural subjects, including *Panorama literario de Chile* (1961), *Pablo Neruda* (1964), *El modernismo y otros ensayos literarios* (1965), *Antología crítica del modernismo hispanoamericano* (1963).

SOUTHERN, RICHARD. Lecturer in Spanish at the University of Leeds. Formerly employed in the overseas marketing companies of the Royal Dutch/Shell Group; Sales Manager of Shell in the Dominican Republic from June 1960 to September 1961.

SOZA, HÉCTOR. Civil engineer. On staff of the Chilean government Dirección de Planeamiento de Obras Públicas, 1952–6; Planificador General (Chilean Ten-Year Economic Development Plan) in the Corporación de Fomento de la Producción, 1957–9; UN Adviser to the Colombian government on industrial planning, 1959–61; head of Industrial Planning Unit, UN Latin American Institute of Economic and Social Planning since 1962.

DI TELLA, TORCUATO S. Professor of Sociology, University of Buenos Aires. Specialist in political sociology and the study of social change. Publications include *El sistema político argentino y la clase obrera* (1964), *Socialismo en la Argentina?* (1965), *La teoría del primer impacto del crecimiento económico* (1965) and (co-edited with G. Germani and J. Graciarena) *Argentina, sociedad de masas* (1965).

THEVENET, HOMERO ALSINA. Film critic of *Marcha* magazine, Montevideo, 1945–52; founder of *Film* (1952); columnist of *El País*, 1954–65; frequent jury-member at Latin American film festivals, and jury-member at Karlovy–Vary festival, 1964. Writes for *Adán* magazine, Buenos Aires. Co-author (with E. Rodríguez Monegal) of *Ingmar Bergman: un dramaturgo cinematográfico* (1964).

TROPP, ASHER. Professor of Sociology at the University of Surrey. On staff of the Department of Sociology, London School of Economics, 1948–67 (resigned as Reader). Has travelled widely in Latin America in recent years. Author of *The School Teachers* (1957).

VÉLIZ, CLAUDIO. Director, Institute of International Studies, University of Chile, Santiago (founded 1966). Formerly Professor of Economic History and Research Fellow of the Institute of Economics of the University of Chile; Senior Research Fellow, Royal Institute of International Affairs (RIIA), London, where he organised a seminar on contemporary problems of Latin America (still active) and a conference on 'Obstacles to Change in Latin America' (February 1965). Author of a history of the Chilean merchant marine; editor of *Obstacles to Change in Latin America* (1965) and *The Politics of Conformity in Latin America* (1967) published by the RIIA.

WINOGRAD, MARCOS. Chairman of the Teaching and Research Department of the Habitat Center Studies, Buenos Aires. Formerly Professor of Architecture at the Universities of Buenos Aires and La Plata.

WIONCZEK, MIGUEL S. Adviser, Center for Latin American Monetary Studies (Mexico City) and Research Fellow, Center for International Affairs, Harvard University. Editor of *Latin American Economic Integration—Experiences and Prospects* (1966) and co-author of *Planning Economic Development*

64), *Public Policy and Private Enterprise in Mexico* (1965) and *How Latin merica Looks at the US Private Investor* (1966).

VYGARD, EDWARD J. Trained as chemical engineer. Joined the UN as industrial economist of the Central American Integration Programme, 1953; later UN adviser on industrial development to the governments of Peru and Ecuador. Currently an industrial consultant; has worked in many Latin American countries. Past chairman of the British Chamber of Commerce in Mexico.

ACKNOWLEDGEMENTS

ILLUSTRATIONS

Grateful acknowledgement is made to the following for their kind permission to reproduce copyright photographs: Courtauld Institute of Art, London (Rivera); Museo de Arte Moderno, Mexico City (Siqueiros); Instituto Torcuato di Tella, BA (Pettoruti, Torres García); *La Nación*, BA (Berni); Brazilian Embassy (London), Commercial and Information Service (Portinari); Casa de la Cultura Ecuatoriana, Quito (Guayasamín); Guillermo Angulo (Intercol photo), Bogotá (Obregón); Courtauld Institute of Art and Gimpel Fils, London (Matta); Rebeca Yañez (Garáfulic); M. Chilo (Peñalba); Sánchez Elía, Peralta Ramos, Agostini, Clorindo Testa, architects (Bank of London and South America, interior and exterior); Jun Miki, Tokyo (Parliament buildings, Brasília); Radio Times Hulton Picture Library, London (Min. of Education, Rio de Janeiro); Marcel Gautherot, Rio de Janeiro (Church of St Francis, Pampulha, front and rear); C. Bresciani B., H. Valdes Ph., F. Cástillo V., C. G. Huidobro G., architects (Portales and Chinchorro housing schemes); Ronald Houghton (Schools of Art, Havana; School of Plastic Art); Guillermo Zamora, Mexico DF (office block, Paseo de la Reforma; Monterrey building); Félix Candela (restaurant at Xochimilco; Bacardi bottling plant); Mexican National Tourist Council (University City Library); Centro Audiovisual, Caracas (Rector's building, Univ. of Caracas); Studios Jacky, Caracas (Helicoid). Acknowledgement is also made to Richard N. Adams for his kind permission to draw upon a map published by him ('Cultural Components of Central America', *American Anthropologist*, LVIII, October 1956) in the preparation of the map on page 24 of this book.

BASIC INFORMATION (*see* PART ONE)

Data are derived from national and international sources too numerous to list here. However, special mention must be made of the wealth of information published by the UN Statistical Office, the UN Economic Commission for Latin America, the UN Food and Agriculture Organisation, the World Bank, the International Monetary Fund and the Pan American Union. The use of differing sources accounts for some statistical discrepancies between the data given here and that given elsewhere in this book. These differences arise principally because of different methods of classification or definition.